D0461471

INTERPERSONAL
BEHAVIOR
IN SMALL GROUPS

INTERPERSONAL
BEHAVIOR
IN SMALL GROUPS

Edited by

RICHARD J. OFSHE

University of California at Berkeley

PRENTICE-HALL, INC.   *Englewood Cliffs, New Jersey*

© 1973 by Prentice-Hall, Inc.
Englewood Cliffs, New Jersey

All rights reserved. No part of this book may be
reproduced in any form or by any means without
permission in writing from the publisher.

Library of Congress Catalog Card Number: 72-9905

ISBN: 0-13-475020-9

Printed in the United States of America

10 9 8 7 6 5 4 3 2

Prentice-Hall International, Inc., *London*
Prentice-Hall of Australia, Pty. Ltd., *Sydney*
Prentice-Hall of Canada, Ltd., *Toronto*
Prentice-Hall of India Private Limited, *New Delhi*
Prentice-Hall of Japan, Inc., *Tokyo*

301.18
I 61   197736

When an author chooses to dedicate a book, it is usually to some individual or group of individuals believed to have been important to his personal development or to the ultimate creation of the book. A dedication to one's parents is an example of a dedication for the first of these two reasons. There are at least two causes for dedications of the second type. Sometimes, individuals, such as a former teacher or a colleague whom the writer believes were important for reasons of intellectual stimulation, are the persons named in dedications. Most frequently, it seems to me, the person or persons named in the dedication are selected for reasons that are not related to the writer's intellectual development but are nevertheless related to the actual creation of the book. Since authors are more likely to be males than females, the dedications usually consist of thanks to a man's wife for tolerating his avoidance of family chores during the six years he toiled on the book, for cooking cordon bleu quality meals during this period, for attending to his clothing, for keeping the house clean, and for generally providing him with those services that are so necessary to survival that had they not been performed the book would certainly never have been completed. It strikes me that failing to publicly acknowledge receipt of these services would be a breach of etiquette of the worst sort. I would therefore like to thank the following individuals and organizations for providing those services upon which the production of books seems to depend.

> Bob of Bob's House Cleaning Service
> The owner and staff of the Claremont Laundry
> The chef and staff of King Tsien Restaurant
> The chef and staff of Casa de Eva Restaurant
> The cook and staff of Kip's (upstairs) Restaurant
> John of Tony and John's Foreign Car Service
> and many others too numerous to mention at this time

MILLS COLLEGE
LIBRARY

A life without a cause is a life without effect.

—Jason Peacock

CONTENTS

9

Group Control of Deviance, 425

IV

LEADERSHIP AND GROUP DECISION MAKING

10

Leadership, 460

11

Group Decision Making, 495

The Classic Experiments, 557

V

THE ASCH EXPERIMENT

VI

COMMUNICATION NETWORK EXPERIMENTS

midterm

VII

GAMING EXPERIMENTS

12

The Prisoner's Dilemma, 630

13

A Two-Person Bargaining Game, 673

VIII

COALITION FORMATION EXPERIMENTS

PREFACE

The preface of a book is usually the point at which the author thanks the people who have helped him at every significant stage of his intellectual life, up to and including the securing of an envelope large enough to hold the finished manuscript. Most of the people who know me would probably predict that I am incapable of thanking anyone. Although this is almost true and great outpourings of gratitude and thanks in the preface of a reader seem out of place, I'm going to thank some people anyway. My reasons are that I have actually learned some things from some individuals, that I have been helped in different ways in connection with the development of this book, and that I feel this reader is somewhat different in purpose and organization from typical collections.

I have attempted to build this volume around my understanding of what this field is substantively concerned with and how the subject develops. My understanding was acquired during my years at Stanford, mostly through interaction with some of my fellow graduate students, as we worked on the problems of acquiring the intellectual standards of the our instructors and helping them to understand where they had gone wrong in their research activities. This, of course, is the usual result of good graduate education —as soon as a student learns something he wants to apply it. The most convenient and pleasant thing to apply his new knowledge to is the work of those who are both actually engaged in research activity and who have power over him. I learned quite a bit from Joe Berger, Buzz Zelditch and Bernie Cohen. I also learned quite a bit and became practiced in applying ideas by going through graduate school with Lynne Roberts, Hamit Fisek, Paul Crosbie Murray Webster, and Lee Freese.

Three successive Prentice-Hall sociology editors oversaw the putting together of this book: Jim Clarke, Al Lesure, and Ed Stanford. While four years is a long time to wait for a reader, I think that those four years were well spent in revising and re-editing and reordering. The final version reflects all the work these gentlemen and I put into it.

INTRODUCTION

In preparing this volume I have attempted to assemble a set of articles which reflect two major aspects of research on interpersonal behavior in small groups. This volume is therefore organized into two sections. The first segment, Interpersonal Processes in Small Groups, is composed of a collection of papers which report substantive research on a series of topics that I regard as core problems, problems towards which work in the field has been directed in the past and/or on which there is currently substantial research activity. The second section of the book, The Classic Experiments, is organized around those relatively standardized experimental settings in which a great deal of research has been conducted on one or more substantive problems. The papers grouped in this section are in no sense papers on methodology. Each has its own importance and either fits with the other papers in its subsection in similarity of focus or fits with papers on similar research topics appearing in the first segment of the book.

I feel that this division fairly reflects the continuity of methodological and substantive development which characterizes activities in the field. On the one hand, there are a series of problems that have received considerable attention over a period of years and have been investigated in a variety of settings to produce a growing body of knowledge. There is a continuing refinement of these research problems as the task of explanation moves from relatively gross points to relatively fine points. The field is also characterized by the development of a number of laboratory situations which were initially developed for the study of some particular problem and which have subsequently been refined both for work on this problem and for research on other entirely different issues.

The use of standardized experimental situations for research on interpersonal behavior has two important advantages. The first is that the results of different investigations may be readily compared and interpreted. The second advantage such situations have over the creation of entirely new experimental settings for each piece of research is that as procedures become widely known and utilized by different research teams, it becomes easier to distinguish between behavior produced either by demand characteristics built into the procedures themselves or by unanticipated experimenter effects and behavior that is a function of the independent variables under study.

In addition to organizing the book along lines that reflect aspects of the field I believe students should see, I have tried to accomplish one other goal through the overall organization of the volume and the selection of papers. All of the readings books I have ever examined seem to me to be structurally modeled after basic texts. That is, the purpose of a basic text is usually to cover in some (typically minimal) degree of depth the entire range of problems considered to constitute a field. Something must therefore be said about each topic. Most basic textbooks can be thought of as rather thin lines running from one end of a field to the other. If the editor of a reader attempts to accomplish the same objective, he is faced with the probem of severe limitations in the number of articles he can accommodate. Therefore, rather than being able to create a line from one end of the field to the other, he ends up selecting a number of points which, if connected, would form the desired line. He probably also chooses to try to make the points equidistant from one another in order to minimize the size of the gaps in the line.

It appears to me that this strategy is the reason that when I look at a table of contents of a reader, even in fields I know well, I can't imagine how students can end up with any impression other than that the field is populated by raving pedants, that all research is trivial, and that different pieces of research have no real relation to one another. I don't believe that readers and textbooks should serve or have the same purpose or that it is very likely that a satisfactory reader can be built on the textbook design.

Articles published in professional journals are fundamentally different in their organization from chapters in texts. They are connected to other papers in a vertical rather than in a horizontal fashion. To appreciate the significance of a journal article a reader must know something of the history of past research on the problem and something of how this paper settles questions left unanswered in previous work or how it amplifies important points raised elsewhere. The typical brevity of introductory summaries of previous works on the same problem makes sense only if one is writing for an audience that has read these papers and just needs to be reminded of the point at which the present investigation picks up. Without the necessary background, however, readers will view papers published in most issues of professional journals as the outpourings of pedants who live in great fear of the devouring publish-or-perish monster.

In selecting articles for this book I have tried to provide the type of vertical integration that will give a student what I believe to be a more correct impression of what research in all about and of how a field is developed through research activities. I have tried to accomplish this in three ways. In some cases I have selected papers that provide fairly detailed summaries of the work leading up to the current investigation and which make clear to the reader precisely how this research fits into the progression. In other cases, I have chosen papers that report a series of experiments which build upon one another. In these instances, either the development of the problem is demonstrated within a single paper, or the article is the clarification of a number of points relating to the same problem that is the focus. The third manner in which I have attempted to produce vertical integration is by selecting a series of papers that build upon one another in the traditional fashion. In these instances students should find themselves in a position similar to that of a professional who is keeping up with work on a certain topic. He or she can really make sense of the summary provided by the author and can evaluate the relationship of the new work to past research.

I have, of course, tried to accomplish all of the above and still provide a good coverage of the important substantive problems that define the field. Whether I have succeeded on any of these counts will be decided by the users of this volume.

INTERPERSONAL
BEHAVIOR
IN SMALL GROUPS

INTERPERSONAL PROCESSES IN SMALL GROUPS

I

ATTRACTION, MEMBERSHIP, AND CONSENSUS FORMATION

1

Attraction to Groups

THE EFFECT
OF SEVERITY OF INITIATION
ON LIKING FOR A GROUP*

Elliot Aronson and Judson Mills

It is a frequent observation that persons who go through a great deal of trouble or pain to attain something tend to value it more highly than persons who attain the same thing with a minimum of effort. For example, one would expect persons who travel a great distance to see a motion picture to be more impressed with it than those who see the same picture at a neighborhood theater. By the same token, individuals who go through a severe initiation to gain admission to a club or organization should tend to think more highly of that organization than those

who do not go through the severe initiation to gain admission.

Two questions are relevant here: 1. Is this "common observation" valid, that is, does it hold true when tested under cotrolled conditions? 2. If the observation is valid, how can it be accounted for? The relationship might be simply a result of differences in initial motivation. To take the case of initiations, persons who initially have a strong desire to join a particular club should be more willing to undergo unpleasantness to gain admission to it than persons who are low in initial interest. Therefore, a club that requires a severe initiation for admission should be joined only by those people with a strong desire to become members. On the other hand, a club that does not require a severe initiation should be joined by some individuals who like it very much, and

* Elliot Aronson and Judson Mills, "The Effect of Severity of Initiation on Liking for a Group," *Journal of Abnormal and Social Psychology*, 59 (1959), 177–81. Copyright 1959 by the American Psychological Association, and reproduced by permission.

by others who are relatively uninterested. Because of this self-selection, one would expect persons who are members of clubs with severe initiations to think more highly of their club, on the average, than members of clubs without severe initiations.

But is there something in the initiation itself that might account for this relationship? Is severity of initiation positively related to group preference when motivation for admission is held constant? Such a relationship is strongly implied by Festinger's (1957) theory of cognitive dissonance. The theory of cognitive dissonance predicts this relationshp in the following manner. No matter how attractive a group is to a person it is rarely completely positive, i.e., usually there are some aspects of the group that the individual does not like. If he has undergone an unpleasant initiation to gain admission to the group, his cognition that he has gone through an unpleasant experience for the sake of membership is dissonant with his cognition that there are things about the group that he does not like. He can reduce this dissonance in two ways. He can convince himself that the initiation was not very unpleasant, or he can exaggerate the positive characteristics of the group and minimize its negative aspects. With increasing severity of initiation it becomes more and more difficult to believe that the initiation was not very bad. Thus, a person who has gone through a painful initiation to become a member of a group should tend to reduce his dissonance by overestimating the attractiveness of the group. The specific hypothesis tested in the present study is that individuals who undergo an unpleasant initiation to become members of a group increase their liking for the group; that

is, they find the group more attractive than do persons who become members without going through a severe initiation.

METHOD

In designing the experiment it was necessary to have people join groups that were similar in every respect except for the severity of the initiation required for admission—and then to measure each individual's evaluation of the group. It was also necessary to randomize the initial motivation of subjects (Ss) to gain admission to the various groups in order to eliminate systematic effects of differences in motivation. These requirements were met in the following manner: Volunteers were obtained to participate in group discussions. They were assigned randomly to one of three experimental conditions: A *Severe* initiation condition, a *Mild* initiation condition, and a *Control* condition. In the Severe condition, Ss were required to read some embarrassing material before joining the group; in the Mild condition the material they read in order to join the group was not very embarrassing; in the Control condition, Ss were not required to read any material before becoming group members. Each S listened to the same tape recording which was ostensibly an ongoing discussion by the members of the group that he had just joined. Ss then evaluated the discussion.

The Ss were 63 college women. Thirty-three of them volunteered to participate in a series of group discussions on the psychology of sex. The remaining 30, tested at a somewhat later date, were "captive volunteers" from a psychology course who elected to participate in the group discussions on the psychology of sex in preference to several other experiments. Since the results obtained from these two samples were very similar, they were combined in the analysis presented here.

Each S was individually scheduled to "meet with a group." When she arrived at the experimental room, she was told by the experimenter (E) that he was conducting several group discussions on the psychology of sex. E informed her that she was joining a group that had been meeting for several weeks and that she was taking the place of a girl who had to leave the group because of scheduling difficulties. E stated that the discussion had just begun and that she would join the other members of the group after he had explained the nature of the experiment to her. The purpose of the foregoing instructions was to confront S with an ongoing group and thus make plausible the recorded discussion to which she was to be exposed.

E then "explained" the purpose of the experiment. He said that he was interested in investigating the "dynamics of the group discussion process." Sex was chosen as the topic for the groups to discuss in order to provide interesting subject matter so that volunteers for the discussion groups could be obtained without much difficulty. E continued as follows:

But the fact that the discussions are concerned with sex has one major drawback. Although most people are interested in sex, they tend to be a little shy when it comes to discussing it. This is very bad from the point of view of the experiment; if one or two people in a group do not participate as much as they usually do in group discussions because they are embarrassed about sex, the picture we get of the group discussion process is distorted. Therefore, it is extremely important to arrange things so that the members of the discussion group can talk as freely and frankly as possible. We found that the major inhibiting factor in the discussions was the presence of the other people in the room. Somehow, it's easier to talk about embarrassing things if other people aren't staring at you. To get around this, we hit upon an idea which has proved very successful. Each member of the group is placed in a separate room, and the participants communicate through an intercom system using headphones and a microphone. In this way, we've helped

people relax, and have succeeded in bringing about an increase in individual participation.

The foregoing explanation set the stage for the tape recording, which could now be presented to the S as a live discussion conducted by three people in separate rooms.

E then mentioned that, in spite of this precaution, occasionally some persons were still too embarrassed to engage in the discussions and had to be asked to withdraw from the discussion group. S was asked if she thought she could discuss sex freely. She invariably answered affirmatively. In the Control condition S was told, at this point, that she would be a member of the group.

In the other two conditions, E went on to say that it was difficult for him to ask people to leave the group once they had become members. Therefore, he had recently decided to screen new people before admitting them to the discussion groups. The screening device was described as an "embarrassment test" which consists of reading aloud some sexually oriented material in the presence of E. S was told that E would make a clinical judgment of her degree of embarrassment, based upon hesitation, blushing, etc. and would determine whether or not she would be capable of participating in the discussion group. He stressed that she was not obligated to take this test, but that she could not become a member unless she did. Only one S declined to take the test. She was excluded from the experiment. It was also emphasized, at this point, that the "embarrassment test" was a recent innovation and that the other members had joined the group before it was required for admission. These instructions were included in order to counteract any tendency to identify more strongly with the group as a result of feelings of having shared a common unpleasant experience. Such a process could conceivably bring about a greater preference for the discussion group on the part of Ss in the Severe condition, introducing ambiguity in the interpretation of the results.

In the Severe condition, the "embarrassment test" consisted of having *S*s read aloud, from 3 × 5 cards, 12 obscene words, e.g., fuck, cock, and screw. *S*s also read aloud two vivid descriptions of sexual activity from contemporary novels. In the Mild condition, *S*s read aloud five words that were related to sex but not obscene, e.g., prostitute, virgin, and petting. In both the Severe and the Mild conditions, after each *S* finished reading the material, she was told that she had performed satisfactorily and was, therefore, a member of the group and could join the meeting that was now in progress.

It was of the utmost importance to prevent the *S* from attempting to participate in the discussion, for if she did, she would soon find that no one was responding to her statements and she would probably infer that the discussion was recorded. To insure their silence, all *S*s were told that, in preparation for each meeting, the group reads an assignment which serves as the focal point of the discussion; for this meeting, the group read parts of the book, *Sexual Behavior in Animals*. After the *S* had indicated that she had never read this book, *E* told her that she would be at a disadvantage and would, consequently, not be able to participate as fully in this discussion as she would had she done the reading. He continued, "Because the presence of a participant who isn't contributing optimally would result in an inaccurate picture of the dynamics of the group discussion process, it would be best if you wouldn't participate at all today, so that we may get an undistorted picture of the dynamics of the other three members of this group. Meanwhile, you can simply listen to the discussion, and get an idea of how the group operates. For the next meeting, you can do the reading and join in the discussion." *S*s were invariably more than willing to comply with this suggestion. The above instructions not only prevented *S* from attempt to participate in the discussion but also served to orient her toward the actual content of discussion.

Under the guise of connecting the *S*'s head-phones and microphone, *E* went into the next room and turned on the tape recorder. He then returned to the experimental room, put on the headphones, picked up the microphone, and pretended to break into the discussion which supposedly was in progress. After holding a brief conversation with the "members of the group," he introduced the *S* to them. Then he handed the headphones to her. The tape was timed so that at the precise moment that *S* donned her headphones, the "group members" introduced themselves and then continued their discussion.

The use of a tape recording presented all *S*s with an identical group experience. The recording was a discussion by three female undergraduates. It was deliberately designed to be as dull and banal as possible in order to maximize the dissonance of the *S*s in the Severe condition. The participants spoke dryly and haltingly on secondary sex behavior in the lower animals, "inadvertently" contradicted themselves and one another, mumbled several *non sequiturs*, started sentences that they never finished, hemmed, hawed, and in general conducted one of the most worthless and uninteresting discussions imaginable.

At the conclusion of the recording, *E* returned and explained that after each meeting every member of the group fills out a questionnaire expressing her reactions to the discussion. The questionnaire asked the *S* to rate the discussion and the group members of 14 different evaluative scales, e.g., dull-interesting, intelligent-unintelligent, by circling a number from 0 to 15. After completing the questionnaire, *S* made three additional ratings, orally, in response to questions from *E*. Nine of the scales concerned the *S*'s reactions to the discussion, while the other eight concerned her reactions to the participants.

At the close of the experiment, *E* engaged each *S* in conversation to determine whether or not she was suspicious of the procedure. Only one *S* entertained definite suspicions; her results were discarded.

Finally, the true nature of the experiment was explained in detail. None of the *S*s expressed any resentment or annoyance at having been misled. In fact, the majority were intrigued by the experiment and several returned at the end of the academic quarter to ascertain the results.

RESULTS AND DISCUSSION

The sum of the ratings for the 17 different scales provides an index of each S's liking for the discussion group. The means and SDs for the three experimental conditions for this measure are presented in Table 1. Means and SDs are also presented in Table 1 separately for the eight scales which tapped the Ss' attitudes toward the discussion and the seven scales which tapped their attitudes toward the participants. The significance of the differences between the means for the different conditions were determined by t tests. The t values and significance levels are presented in Table 2.

Examination of Table 1 shows that Ss in the Severe condition rated both the discussion and the participants higher than

Table 1

MEANS OF THE SUM OF RATINGS FOR THE DIFFERENT EXPERIMENTAL CONDITIONS

Rating Scales	Experimental Conditions		
	Control ($N=21$)	Mild ($N=21$)	Severe ($N=21$)
Discussion [9]			
M	80.2	81.8	97.6
SD	13.2	21.0	16.6
Participants [8]			
M	89.9	89.3	92.7
SD	10.9	14.1	13.2
Total [17]			
M	166.7	171.1	195.3
SD	21.6	34.0	31.9

Table 2

SIGNIFICANCE LEVELS OF THE DIFFERENCES BETWEEN EXPERIMENTAL CONDITIONS

Rating Scales	Differences Between Conditions		
	Control-Severe	Mild-Severe	Control-Mild
Discussion	$t=3.66$	$t=2.62$	$t=.29$
[9]	$P<.001$*	$P<.02$	N.S.
Participants	$t=2.03$	$t=1.97$	$t=.15$
[8]	$P<.05$	$P<.10$	N.S.
Total [17]	$t=3.32$	$t=2.33$	$t=.49$
	$P<.01$	$P<.05$	N.S.

* The P values given are based on both tails of the t distribution.

did those in the Control and Mild conditions. The over-all difference between the ratings by Ss in the Severe condition and Ss in the Control condition reaches the .01% level of significance. The over-all difference between the ratings by Ss in the Severe initiation condition and Ss in the Mild initiation condition reaches the .05 level.

These differences cannot be explained by differences in initial motivation to become members of the group, since Ss (with varying degrees of motivation) were randomly assigned to the three experimental conditions. The differences in liking for the group must be considered a consequence of the unpleasant experience. The results clearly substantiate the hypothesis: persons who undergo a severe initiation to attain membership in a group increase their liking for the group. This hypothesis follows directly from Festinger's theory of cognitive dissonance. According to the theory, Ss in the Severe initiation condition held the cognition that they had undergone a painful experience to become members of the discussion group. Then they listened to a dull, banal discussion. Negative cognitions about the discussion which they formed from listening to it were dissonant with the cognition that they had undergone a painful experience to gain membership in this group. The presence of dissonance leads to pressures to reduce it. *S*s in this condition could reduce their dissonance either by denying the severity of the initiation or by distorting their cognitions concerning the group discussion in a positive direction. The initiation of the *S*s in the Severe condition was apparently too painful for them to deny—hence, they reduced their dissonance by overestimating the attractiveness of the group.

There was no appreciable difference between the ratings made by *S*s in the Control condition and those made by *S*s in the Mild condition. It would seem that the Mild condition was so devoid of unpleasantness as to constitute little investment in the group. Hence, little dissonance was created. If any dissonance did occur in this situation it would be more realistic for the *S* to reduce it by minimizing the pain of the initiation, than by distorting her cognitions concerning the discussion. Thus, it is not an initiation per se that leads to increase in liking for a group. The initiation must be severe enough to constitute a genuine investment and to render it difficult to reduce dissonance by playing down the extent of the pain involved.

An examination of Table 1 shows that the rating scales concerning the discussion show greater differences between the conditions than the scales dealing with the evaluations of the participants in the discussion. There are at least two possible explanations for this result: (*a*) It may

be easier for people to express negative criticism about an impersonal discussion than about the people involved. Thus, *S*s in the Control and Mild conditions may have inflated their ratings of the participants to avoid making negative statements about fellow college students. (*b*) It is possible that *S*s in the Severe condition had less need to distort their perception of the participants than of the discussion itself. The dissonance of the *S*s in the Severe condition resulted from the actual discussion: they experienced dissonance between going through an unpleasant experience and taking part in worthless, uninteresting discussions. The most direct way for them to reduce this dissonance would be to change their perceptions of the discussion in a positive direction. The participants in the discussion were peripheral to the cause of dissonance. If *S*s in the Severe condition had less need to distort their perceptions of the participants than their perception of the discussion, their evaluations of the participants could be expected to be closer to the evaluations of the participants made by *S*s in the Control and Mild conditions.

SUMMARY AND CONCLUSIONS

An experiment was conducted to test the hypothesis that persons who undergo an unpleasant initiation to become members of a group increase their liking for the group; that is, they find the group more attractive than do persons who become members without going through a severe initiation. This hypothesis was derived from Festinger's theory of cognitive dissonance.

College women who volunteered to participate in discussion groups were randomly assigned to one of three experimental conditions: A *Severe* initiation condition, a *Mild* initiation condition, and a *Control* condition. In the Severe condition, subjects were required to read some embarrassing material before joining the group; in the Mild condition the material they read in order to join the group was not very embarrassing; in the Control condition, subjects were not required to read any material before becoming group members. Each subject listened to a recording that appeared to be an ongoing discussion being conducted by the group which she had just joined. Afterwards, subjects filled out a questionnaire evaluating the discussion and the participants. The results clearly verified the hypothesis. Subjects who underwent a severe initiation perceived the group as being significantly more attractive than did those who underwent a mild initiation or no initiation. There was no appreciable difference between ratings by subjects who underwent a Mild initiation and those by subjects who underwent no initiation.

REFERENCE

FESTINGER, L. A. *Theory of Cognitive Dissonance.* Evanston: Row, Peterson, 1957.

THE EFFECTS
OF SEVERITY OF INITIATION
ON LIKING FOR A GROUP:
A REPLICATION*

Harold B. Gerard and Grover C. Mathewson

The experiment by Aronson and Mills (1959), in which a positive relationship was found between the severity of initiation into a group and subsequent liking for that group, is open to a variety of

* Harold B. Gerard and Grover C. Mathewson, "The Effects of Severity of Initiation on Liking for a Group: A Replication," *Journal of Experimental Social Psychology*, 2 (1966), 278–87. Reprinted by permission of Academic Press, Inc.

interpretations other than the one the authors give. The purpose of the experiment to be reported here was an attempt to rule out some of the more cogent of these alternative interpretations.

The observation that people often tend to value highly things for which they have suffered or expended a great deal of effort can be interpreted as having been due to dissonance reduction. The hypothesized process involved assumes that knowledge held by the person that he had suffered or expended a great deal of effort for a desired goal is inconsistent with knowledge that the goal or certain aspects of it are worthless. Such inconsistencies produce psychological dissonance which is unpleasant, and the individual will attempt to reduce this unpleasantness by cognitive work. In this case he can either distort his beliefs about the amount of suffering or effort he expended by coming to believe that it was less than he had previously thought, or he can distort his belief about the worthlessness of aspects of the goal by coming to believe that these aspects were really not worthless. In their study, Aronson and Mills attempted to create a laboratory situation in which the latter hypothesized process could be examined. Let us review that experiment in some detail so that we may then point up the basis for the other interpretations of the data.

The subjects were college coeds who were willing to volunteer for a series of group discussions on the psychology of sex. The ostensible purpose of the study was presented to the subject as having to do with the investigation of group dynamics. Before any prospective member could join one of the discussion groups she was given a "screening test" to determine her suitability for the group. The severity of this screening test (or initiation) was varied; in the "severe" treatment the subject read obscene literature and a list of dirty words out loud to the experimenter (who was a male), whereas in the "mild" condition the subject read sexual material of an innocuous sort. The subject was told that the screening test had been necessary in order to weed out people who were too shy to discuss topics related to sex. After the initiation, each experimental subject was informed that she had passed the test and was therefore eligible for membership in the group. She was led to believe that the group she was to join had been formed several weeks ago and that she was to take the place of a girl who had to drop out. Her "participation" in her first meeting with the group was limited to "overhearing" via headphones what was presented to her as an ongoing discussion by the group on aspects of sexual behavior in animals. The reason she was given for not being able to participate actively in the discussion was that the other three girls had prepared for the discussion by reading a book on the sexual behavior of animals. It was also suggested to her that overhearing the discussion without participating in it would give her an opportunity to get acquainted with how the group operates. What she heard was not an ongoing discussion but was instead a standardized recorded discussion on the sexual behavior of animals that was extremely boring and banal. The discussion was contrived to be worthless in order to maximize the dissonance of the subject in the "severe" initiation group, since the knowledge that she had suffered to get into the group would be dissonant with finding out that the discussion was worthless.

After hearing the taped recording, the subject was asked to evaluate the discussion and the participants on a number of semantic differential–type scales. A control group was also run in which the subjects evaluated the discussion without having received any initiation whatsoever. The findings of the experiment supported the derivation from dissonance theory, namely that the subjects in the "severe" treatment evaluated the discussion more favorably than did the "mild" or control subjects. A dissonance theory interpretation conceives of the "severe" initiation as confronting the subject with the "problem" of having suffered for something that was later found to be worthless and the prediction is based upon how that problem is "solved." One of the reasons why the results are important and provocative is that they are exactly opposite to what a strict application of secondary reinforcement theory would predict in which it would be expected that the unpleasantness of the initiation would "rub off" and generalize to the discussion.

While the results are consistent with dissonance theory, they lend themselves to a variety of other, quite plausible interpretations. For example, there is an entire *family* of interpretations that derives from the fact that the content of the initiation and the content of the discussion are so closely related, both having to do with sex. One could argue that the initiation aroused the girls sexually to a greater extent in the "severe" as compared with the "mild" treatment and they were therefore more anxious to get into the group in order to pursue the discussion of sex. Along similar lines, one could also argue that the girls in the "severe" treatment did not know the meaning of some of the dirty four-letter words and believed that they could find out their meaning by joining the discussion group. This is a variation of the uncertainty–affiliation hypothesis. Still another possibility is that the subjects in the "severe" treatment were intrigued by the obscene material and the dirty words and may have believed that, if not now, sometime in the future these things would be discussed by the group. One could continue to list related interpretations based upon the assumed arousal of one or another motive in the "severe" treatment that might be satisfied by joining the discussion group (thus making the group more attractive).

Another possible interpretation, a "relief" hypothesis, is that the reading of the obscene material built up anxiety which was subsequently reduced by the banal, innocuous material of the group discussion. Since the discussion was responsible for reducing the anxiety, it took on positive value for the subject in the "severe" treatment.

Schopler and Bateson (1962) find partial support for a "dependency" interpretation of the Aronson and Mills findings. Following Thibaut and Kelley (1959), Schopler and Bateson suggest that, as contrasted with the "mild" initiation, the "severe" initiation induced in the subject dependence upon the experimenter. This, according to them, occurred because the experimenter had "moved" the subject in the "severe" treatment through a "wide range of outcomes," consisting of the unpleasant shock and the pleasantness associated with the pride experienced by the "severe" subject upon learning that she had passed the test. Subjects in the "mild" condition had not experienced this range of pleasantness of outcome and hence were less dependent. Also, their argument continues, somehow the subject assumed that the experimenter expected her to like the discussion. Due to the assumed differential dependency induced by the initiation treatments, the subject in the "severe" treatment was more concerned with pleasing the experimenter than was the subject in the "mild" treatment and hence attempted to a greater extent to meet his expectations by indicating to him that she liked the discussion.

Chapanis and Chapanis (1964) suggest an "afterglow" hypothesis to explain the data. All subjects in the experiment were told that they had passed the embarrass-ment test. Presumably, subjects in the "severe" treatment perceived the test as being more difficult than did subjects in the "mild" treatment and, according to Chapanis and Chapanis, they therefore may have had a greater sense of accom-plishment. This self-satisfaction somehow "rubbed off" onto other aspects of the task situation, including, presumably, the the group discussion. This might then account for the "severe" subjects' more positive disposition toward the discussion.

Still another, even more plausible inter-pretation of quite a different sort, is that any experience following the "severe" initiation, which we assume was unplea-sant, would by contrast seem more pleasant than it would following the "mild" initi-ation. It is important that this rather simple "contrast" hypothesis, which is a compelling explanation of the Aronson and Mills data, be ruled out, if possible.

A problem in the experiment related to the first set of interpretations concerns the nature of the initiation itself. Was the "severe" initiation really more unpleasant than the "mild" one? The authors do not report any check of the success of the experimental manipulation in producing differences in unpleasantness. Without the assurance that this all-important require-ment was met, certain other interpreta-tions of the data are quite plausible. It is not unlikely that many of the subjects in the "severe" treatment found the ex-perience pleasant and exciting.

METHOD

An Overview of the Design

Two basic treatments were compared, one in which the subject received electrical shocks as part of an initiation procedure and one in which she received shocks as part of a psy-chological experiment, the "noninitiate" treat-ment. Within each of these treatments, half of the subjects received strong shocks and half received weak shocks. Half of the "severe" and half of the "mild" initiates were told that they had passed the screening whereas the other half of each were not told whether they had passed. After the shocks, all subjects heard and then evaluated a boring and worth-less group discussion about cheating in col-lege. The "initiates" believed that this was a recording of a previous meeting of the group that they were slated to join, whereas the "noninitiates" evaluated the discussion as just one of a series of stimuli to which they were being exposed.

Procedure

The subjects were 48 female undergraduate volunteers contacted at random from the stu-dent body of the University of California at Riverside. All subjects were first contacted by telephone. During the telephone contact a subject selected to be an "initiate" was asked whether or not she would like to volunteer for a discussion club that was to discuss the prob-lem of morals on university campuses. The "noninitiates" were asked, during the tele-phone contact, whether they would like to volunteer to be a subject in a psychological experiment. Thus, half of the subjects reported to the laboratory believing that they were going to be members of a discussion club whereas the other half believed that they were participating in a psychological experiment. The procedure followed during the experi-mental session was essentially the same for both "initiates" and "noninitiates." The "non-initiate" condition was introduced in an at-tempt to rule out the "contrast" and "relief" hypotheses. If the unpleasant experience rep-resented by the initiation was not seen as in-strumental to joining the discussion club and the same effect was found as in the Aronson and Mills experiment, both alternative explanations would receive support. If, however, the "initiates" showed the effect and the "noninitiates" did not, both the "contrast" and "relief" hypotheses would have been effectively ruled out. We might expect a secondary reinforcement effect in the "noninitiate" condition which would manifest as a negative relationship between the unpleasantness of the shocks and the evaluation of the discussion, the assumption being that the effect produced by the shocks would generalize to the discussion.

When the "initiate" arrived in the laboratory she was seated in an isolation booth and was told:

> "In the past we have had considerable difficulty with some of the girls who have joined these discussion clubs. The problem is that some people cannot maintain an attitude of objectivity during the discussion. When this happens, naturally the discussion tends to deteriorate and emotions run very high. In order to avoid this difficulty in the future we have just instituted a screening test to weed out those girls who would tend to let their emotions run away with them during a discussion. You are the first person to whom we will be administering the test which is a very good one that has been used by psychologists for many years. It consists of determining your physiological reaction to a series of stimuli. We do this by hooking you up to these electrodes [the experimenter shows the subject a pair of dummy GSR electrodes] that detect changes in your skin resistance during the test which is done with the aid of this recorder [the experimenter shows the subject a small strip chart recorder]. By your response on this chart we can tell how objective you are likely to be under conditions represented by the morals discussion."

The subject was told that she was the first one to take the test in order to eliminate the possibility that she would want to be in the group in order to compare her reactions to the test with those of the girls already in the discussion group.

The "noninitiate" was told when she arrived at the laboratory.

> "You are going to be a subject in a psychological experiment which involves your being exposed to a variety of different kinds of stimuli. We are going to determine your reaction to these stimuli with the aid of these electrodes [the experimenter shows the subject the GSR electrodes] which are hooked up to this instrument [the experimenter shows the subject the strip chart recorder]."

All subjects were hooked up to the electrodes and received exactly the same sequence of stimuli which was designed to be a credible screening test for the "initiate." The sequence consisted of a spray of perfume from an atomizer placed in the ceiling of the subject's booth, a series of slides of paintings projected on the wall in front of the subject's booth [the paintings were: Roualt, *The Apprentice*; Picasso, *Madame Picasso, Portrait of A. Vollard, Figure by the Sea*; La Tour, *Self Portrait*; Matisse, *Landscape*; and Klee, *Girl Possessed*]. Each painting was presented for 15 seconds with a 15-second pause between presentations. After all of the paintings were shown, the subject was fitted with headphones and heard the shooting sequence in Copland's ballet, *Billy the Kid*. Finally, the subject received the critical stimuli which were a series of three shocks delivered 15 seconds apart by a Lafayette inductorium. In the "severe" treatment the shocks were quite strong whereas in the "mild" treatment they were barely supraliminal. This method of varying suffering would be more likely, on the face of it at least, to produce greater uniformity of psychological state within each of the two suffering levels than the method used by Aronson and Mills. Using electric shock to produce suffering effectively separates the content of the initiation from the content of the discussion. If the Aronson and Mills effect were to be found by using shock this would rule out the family of interpretations that are all based upon the similarity of content of the two phases of the experiment.

Aronson and Mills informed all of their subjects that they had passed the screening test. The subject, thus, had acquired that for which she had suffered. It was inappropriate in the present experiment to inform the "noninitiates" as to how they had done in responding to the sequence of stimuli since they had not been told that they were taking a test. In order to control for this difficulty, half of the "initiates" were told, after receiving the shocks, that they had passed the screening test, whereas the other half were treated like the "noninitiates" by not receiving any feedback concerning their performance on the screening test. This "told" vs. "not-told" factor was counterbalanced across the "severe" and "mild" initiates. More importantly, this treatment also enables us to test the Chapanis and Chapanis "afterglow" hypothesis, the plausibility of which is based on the assumption that the pleasure experienced in passing the severe initiation generalized to the group discussion. If those subjects who were told that they had passed showed the Aronson and Mills effect and those who were not given this information did not show the effect, the "afterglow" explanation would be supported. The Schopler and Bateson "dependence" hypothesis would also be supported if the Aronson and Mills replicated in the "told" but not in the "not-told" treatment, since the assumed broader range of outcomes experienced by the "severe" subject depends on the pleasure experienced by the subject upon learning that she had passed the test.

All subjects then listened to a five-minute tape recording of three girls having a discussion of cheating in college. This discussion was absolutely worthless, consisting mostly of hemming, hawing, clearing of throats, and pauses. The "initiate" was told that this was a recording of a previous discussion of the group that she was slated to join. The "noninitiate" was merely asked to listen to the discussion as one of the sequence of stimuli. Aronson and Mills presented the recording as an ongoing discussion. This difference in procedure in our "initiate" treatment did not seem to us to be critical.

In the final phase of the experiment, all subjects evaluated the discussion using semantic differential-type scales similar to those used by Aronson and Mills. Eight scales dealt with the qualities of the participants and eight with qualities of the discussion itself. Each scale was numbered from 0 to 15, the polarity of the scales being alternated in order to counteract any response bias. After this evaluation sheet was filled out, the subject was administered a post-experimental questionnaire which asked her to rate the pleasantness or unpleasantness of the various stimuli. The subject's evaluation of the shocks on this questionnaire was, of course, the check on the manipulation of suffering.

Results

The two shock levels clearly induced different degrees of pleasantness. The post-questionnaire contained a 7-point scale on which the subject rated the pleasantness of the shocks. The difference between the

Table 1

The Effects of Severity of Shock, Initiation, and Feedback on Evaluation of the Group Discussion

	Initiate				Noninitiate	
	Mild shock		Severe shock		Mild shock	Severe shock
	Told	Not told	Told	Not told		
Participant rating	11.5	26.1	31.1	41.0	19.8	13.2
Discussion rating	11.0	15.6	27.0	28.2	9.1	5.8

a The larger the number, the more favorable the evaluation.

two shock conditions was extremely large ($p < .001$ by chi-square[1]) with the majority of subjects in the "severe" condition indicating that the shocks were "extremely unpleasant." No subjects in the "mild" treatment found the shocks more than only "mildly unpleasant."

The discussion evaluation data are shown in Table 1. The figures in the table represent the means of the pleasantness ratings for both the participant and the discussion evaluation, summed over the eight scales used for each. Tables 2 and 3 present the analysis of variance for each

---

[1] Chi-square was used as a test of significance because the distribution in the "severe" treatment was skewed.

of the two evaluations. We see a clear main effect of the initiation factor. When the subject anticipated joining the group whose discussion she had heard, she tended to evaluate both the discussion and the participants more highly than she did when there was no such expectation. This shows a general "effort effect" in line with dissonance theory. There was also a main effect of severity that is accounted for by the "initiates." The crucial degree of freedom that concerns us here is the interaction between initiation and severity which also yields a significant F-ratio. A t test applied within the "initiates" and within the "noninitiates" shows that both trends, which are opposite, are significant, the trend in the "initiate" treatment being

Table 2

ANALYSIS OF VARIANCE OF THE PARTICIPANT EVALUATION

Source	SS	df	MS	F[b]
Initiation (I)	1276	1	1276	8.28
Severity (S)	1045	1	1045	6.78
I × S	1504	1	1504	9.77
Told (T)	1201	1	1201	7.80
S (I) × T[a]	45	1	45	
Error	6471	42	159	

[a] Interation of feedback (Told vs. Not-told within the initiate condition).
[b] F .05 = 4.07, F .01 = 7.27.

Table 3

ANALYSIS OF VARIANCE OF THE DISCUSSION EVALUATION

Source	SS	df	MS	F
Initiation (I)	1811	1	1811	13.22
Severity (S)	850	1	850	6.20
I × S	835	1	835	6.09
Told (T)	69	1	69	
S (I) × T	23	1	23	
Error	5774	42	137	

stronger ($p < .01$) than the trend in the "noninitiate" treatment ($p < .05$). Whether or not the "initiate" received feedback about her performance on the screening test (the "told" vs. "not-told" variations) appears not to have interacted with severity of the shock. We do see, however, that for the participant evaluation there does seem to be a main effect of feedback. Informing the subject that she had passed the test appears to have reduced the evaluation of the participants.

Since there was some variation in both the "severe" and "mild" shock conditions in the perception of unpleasantness by the subject, we were in a position to do an internal analysis of the data by examining the correlation between *perceived* severity of the shock and liking for the group discussion. On the basis of dissonance theory we would expect a positive relationship only within the "initiate" condition. The overall correlation with the "initiate" treatment is .52 for the participant rating and .45 for the discussion rating ($p < .01$ for both correlation coefficients). The corresponding correlations in the "noninitiate" treatment are .03 and .07.

DISCUSSION

The data from the experiment strongly support the "suffering-leading-to-liking" hypothesis and effectively rule out a number of other interpretations of the original experiment by Aronson and Mills. Our data for the "initiate" treatment are much stronger than those in the first experiment. This is probably attributable to the shock manipulation which undoubtedly produced more uniform within-treatment levels of suffering. The fact that the con-

tent of our suffering manipulation was divorced from the content of the group discussion eliminates the family of interpretations of the Aronson and Mills data that invoke some motive for wanting to affiliate that would be assumed to be greater in the "severe" than in the "mild" initiation treatment. The fact that there was an interaction between the initiate and severity factors eliminates the "contrast" and "relief" hypotheses. Both hypotheses predict the same difference under the "initiate" and the "noninitiate" treatments. We see instead an effect within the "noninitiate" treatment that supports a secondary reinforcement interpretation; the more severe the shock the *less* did the subject like the discussion. The internal correlational analysis adds further support for the "suffering-leading-to-liking" hypothesis and further weakens the "contrast" and "relief" hypotheses, since within the "initiate" treatment the greater was the perceived suffering the greater did the subject like the group discussion, whereas no such relationship was found within the "noninitiate" treatment.

Both the Chapanis and Chapanis "afterglow" and the Schopler and Bateson "dependence" hypotheses depend upon the subject having had a success experience after learning that she had passed the screening test. This success experience is presumed to have been greater in the "severe" than in the "mild" initiation treatment. Greater liking for the discussion under the "severe" initiation should therefore, according to both hypotheses, occur under the "told" but not under the "not-told" treatment. The lack of such an interaction effectively rules out both hypotheses.

Feedback did have a main effect on the evaluation of the participants. The high evaluation of the participants in the "not-told" as compared with the "told" condition may reflect a desire to be in the group. When informed that she had passed the screening test and would be in the group, the subject reduced her evaluation. Objects that a person is not sure he can have may appear more attractive to him under certain circumstances than similar objects that he already possesses. Having suffered or expended effort in order to acquire the object may be just such a circumstance. This effect was not predicted and our interpretation, therefore, must be considered as highly speculative.

REFERENCES

ARONSON, E., and MILLS, J. "The Effect of Severity of Initiation on Liking for a Group," *Journal of Abnormal and Social Psychology*, 1959, 59, 177–181.

CHAPANIS, N. P., and CHAPANIS, A. "Cognitive Dissonance: Five Years Later." *Psychological Bulletin*, 1964, 61, 1–22.

SCHOPLER, J., and BATESON, N. "A Dependence Interpretation of the Effects of a Severe Initiation." *Journal of Personality*, 1962, 30, 633–649.

THIBAUT, J., and KELLEY, H. H. *The Social Psychology of Groups*. New York: Wiley, 1959.

EFFECTS OF WAITING
WITH OTHERS
ON CHANGES IN LEVEL
OF FELT ANXIETY*

Lawrence S. Wrightsman, Jr.

An old familiar saying has it that "misery loves company." This having been verified empirically by Schachter (1959),

* Lawrence S. Wrightsman, Jr., "Effects of Waiting with Others on Changes in Level of Felt Anxiety," *Journal of Abnormal and Social Psychology*, 61 (1960), 216–22. Copyright 1960 by the American Psychological Association, and reproduced by permission.

a next question might simply be "Why?" Why is it that most people, ordinarily content to be left alone, become seekers of others when they become upset, moody, or threatened? Why does an increase in a person's level of anxiety cause him to be more likely to want to be with others?

Several possible reasons for the relationship between anxiety and the affiliative tendency come easily to mind, including the expectation of irrelevant and diverting conversation with others and the idea of "safety in numbers." But a series of analytic experiments by Schachter rule out some of these as valid explanations. Schachter concludes that an anxious subject's desire to be with others is determined by (*a*) needs for direct reduction of anxiety, and/or (*b*) needs for evaluation of one's emotional state. The present study examines some of the implications of the relationship between anxiety and affiliation.

The first explanation implies that people want to be with others when anxious because they expect from others sympathy and reassurance that is directly anxiety-reducing. ("Anxiety" refers here to a feeling of uneasiness or concern about participating in an impending unpleasant event; unlike generalized anxiety or manifest anxiety it is conceived as linked to a specific situation.) According to the first hypothesis of the study, then, if persons are anxious about an impending event, being with others is more effective in reducing their anxiety than is being alone.

Despite the widely held belief in the effectiveness of the presence of other people in moderating one's extreme fears, there is no direct evidence that other people's statements facilitate the reduction of anxiety about a specific situation. Indirect evidence, however, comes from Schachter's study (1959). His subjects were given a description of the "electric shock experiment" in which they were to participate. By varying description of the anxiety-producing features of the "experiment" and the alternatives involved in a short waiting period before anticipated participation in it, Schachter found that *S*s who expected a very painful experi-

ment more frequently chose to wait with others than did their counterparts who were led to believe that the experiment would be painless. Further evidence is afforded by the study of Davitz & Mason (1955), who found that the presence of one rat tended to reduce the strength of a fear response in another rat.

The second hypothesized explanation for the link between anxiety and affiliation implies that the presence of others gives a person a chance to evaluate his own level of emotion by comparing it with that of others. Perhaps the situation is so novel or ambiguous that a person is unclear about the appropriate emotional response. In such a case the responses of others may serve to indicate the proper level of concern.

This interpretation would seem to follow from an extension to the evaluation of emotions of the scheme developed by Festinger (1954) for explaining how certain processes of social comparison operate in the evaluation of an ability or an opinion. (The theory has been verified empirically by Dreyer, 1954; Gerard, 1953.) Festinger hypothesizes that there is a drive to evaluate one's own abilities and opinions, and when no objective method of evaluation is possible, the person uses social reality—the statements and behaviors of others—to aid in his self evaluation. For social comparison to be most informative, the person's comparison objects should be other persons whose levels of ability or opinion are similar to his own. The process of social comparison thus gives rise to pressures toward uniformity, by which the levels of others are brought closer to the person's own level.

According to Festinger, these pressures toward uniformity result in three maneuvers: (*a*) change in the person's own ability or opinion so as to bring it closer to that of the comparison persons, (*b*) the attempt to move others toward one's own level, and (*c*) cessation of comparison of one's own position with those of persons whose abilities or opinions differ widely from one's own.

One of the purposes of this study is to determine whether the emotion of anxiety is similar to abilities and opinions in being evaluated in ways subject to influence by the responses of others. If the same social comparison processes obtain, the same maneuvers should be found in a group of people placed in a sudden anxiety-producing situation that emerge in people seeking to evaluate their opinions. The second hypothesis of this study is, then, that pressures toward uniformity in level of anxiety, namely influence processes and rejection tendencies, develop when groups of persons are placed in an ambiguous emotional situation.

But is it correct to assume that felt emotions are, in part, cognitively determined, and that there is a conceptual similarity between the determinants of emotions and the determinants of opinions? The tenor of much thinking about the emotions seems to suggest that both physiological and cognitive processes determine experienced emotions. Ruckmick (1936), for example, states that "there is a tendency ... to admit that purely bodily expression without the cognitive or 'intellectual' factor does not qualify as an equation for the experienced real emotion," (p. 343) and that "What the child ... feels depends more on what he cognizes or, in short, on the accumulations of his perceptual and ideational experiences," (p. 448). Young (1943) has a similar

point of view. To the extent that cognitive factors do determine emotional states, emotions, like opinions, may be expected to be susceptible to social influence.

METHOD

Subjects

The subjects (*S*s) were 204 students, 120 females and 84 males, enrolled in undergraduate psychology classes. By participating the students earned bonus points applied to their examination scores.

Experimental Session

Four *S*s of the same sex were used in each experimental session. When each *S* arrived, *E* or his nurse assistant[1] placed him in a separate room in which *S* found a tray containing hypodermic needles, syringes, cotton, alcohol, and other injection equipment. After completing a few biographical questions, including several dealing with his physical health, each *S* heard over the intercommunication system a tape recording describing the experiment in which he was to participate. The experiment was described as one dealing with glucose level and mental activity. *S* was told that his glucose level was to be drastically changed by a series of injections of either a depressant drug or a glucose additive. Because these substances had to be injected directly into the bloodstream, it was likely that they would be more painful than routine injections. *S* was then warned that the injection of the depressant drug might make him feel drowsy and lacking in energy but that he should be able to respond. If he was given the additive, it would raise his glucose level to an absolute

---

[1] The author wishes to think Bernice P. Flynn, who served authentically as the nurse assistant.

maximum amount near the point which brings on glucose-shock, fainting, and similar symptoms of hyperglycemia or diabetes. A quick blood test to determine glucose level would be given by pricking a finger. All the above operations were to occur in private.

Immediately after hearing this, each *S* was asked to indicate on a formsheet how at-ease or ill-at-ease he felt about participating in the described experiment by writing a number from 0 (completely at-ease) to 100 (completely ill-at-ease).

At this point the procedure was varied for the three conditions of the experiment. Two Together conditions were used, along with an Alone condition. Verbal communication was forbidden in one Together condition, but allowed to run its course in the other, to permit measuring the possible effects of verbal communication on reduction of anxiety. All four *S*s in a particular experimental session were in the same condition, the particular condition being determined at random.

If the *S*s were in the Together-Talk (T-T) condition, they were brought to a large waiting room and told:

> You are supposed to wait here until we are ready to use you. You can read or smoke or study if you like. If you want to talk, that's okay. You can talk about the experiment or anything you like. There will be only a short wait.

If the *S*s were to be in the Together-No-Talk (T-N-T) condition, they were brought to the same room and told:

> You are supposed to wait here until we are ready to use you. You can read or smoke or study if you like. However, please do *not* talk. Part of the experiment is of a verbal nature and we want only your own ideas to be given. Therefore, it is important that you not talk about the experiment or anything else. There will be only a short wait.

If the four *S*s were in the Alone condition,

Table 1

MEAN RESPONSES AND CHANGES IN MEASURES OF ANXIETY
(Data for 17 groups in each condition, 68 *S*s in all)

Condition	Pre-waiting-Period Measure	Post-waiting-Period Measure	Change from Pre- to Post-waiting-Period Measure
Together-Talk	43.7	37.3	–6.4
Together-No-Talk	42.8	36.6	–6.2
Alone	41.3	37.2	–4.1

each was left in his separate room and told:

> You are supposed to wait here until we are ready to use you. You may read or smoke or study if you like. There will be only a short wait.

Immediately after this announcement, *E* and his assistant left the room for 5 min. *S*s in the Together conditions were observed through a one-way screen. All *S*s in the T-N-T condition followed the restriction against talking. After 5 min. the assistant returned and told the *S*(s), "We are about ready for you but before we begin I need to get some more information from you." She then gave each *S* a set of questions which consisted of a repetition of the prewaiting-period measure and other questions dealing with *S*'s concern about the experiment.

When they completed these, *S*s were brought together if they had been separated and a "catharsis" session was held, in which the true purpose of the experiment and the need for deception were explained. *S*s' questions were answered, and they agreed to keep the true nature of the experiment secret. Each *S* then completed a questionnaire dealing with his experimental background, his suspicions about the described experiment, and the extent of his friendship with the other *S*s at that session.

Results

Effect of Being with Others on Reduction of Anxiety

If the first hypothesis is correct, *S*s waiting together should show greater reduction of anxiety than do *S*s waiting alone. Table 1 presents the mean responses for the pre- and postwaiting-period measures for *S*s in the three conditions. Means for the three conditions are quite similar on all measures. None of the differences between conditions is statistically significant, nor are differences between Alone condition *S*s and all Together condition *S*s pooled together. In each condition the average change was in a downward direction, from four to six points. When all conditions are combined, the

mean level of anxiety of 37.0 on the postwaiting-period measure was significantly less ($p < .001$) than the mean of 42.5 on the same measure before the waiting period.

The number of *S*s wishing to withdraw from the experiment without receiving experimental credit was also similar in each condition. That 26 of the 203 *S*s responding to this question wished to withdraw, gives some indication of the effectiveness of the described experiment in creating anxiety.

The nonsignificant differences pertaining to the first hypothesis give no support for the belief that being with others directly reduces anxiety. But Schachter (1959) found that the relationship between anxiety and the desire to be with others was almost entirely restricted to those *S*s who were first or only children. Accordingly, such *S*s might be affected more strongly than others by the social situation. Table

Table 2

Mean Responses on Anxiety According to Birth Order of *S*

Condition (First-born and only-child *S*s)	N	Prewaiting-Period Measure	Postwaiting-Period Measure	Net Change, Pre- to Postwaiting Period	Gross Change, Pre- to Postwaiting Period
T-T[a]	32	39.8	31.8	−8.0[b]	10.8[c]
T-N-T[d]	33	43.2	33.9	−9.3[b]	9.9[b]
Alone[a]	41	42.1	38.6	−3.5	4.2
(Later-children *S*s)					
T-T[a]	35	47.8	42.9	−4.9	6.6
T-N-T[d]	35	42.4	39.1	−3.3	4.2
Alone[a]	26	39.9	35.4	−4.5	6.0

[a] Birth order of one *S* in T-T (Together-Talk) condition and one *S* in Alone condition were not recorded.

[b] Significantly different from comparable Alone condition mean at .05 level, using Mann-Whitney *U* test.

[c] Significantly different from comparable Alone condition mean at .01 level, using Mann-Whitney *U* test.

[d] Together-No-Talk.

2 presents the results of an analysis by birth order.

First-born Ss in each of the Together conditions showed a greater net change than did first-born Ss in the Alone condition. In both the Together-vs.-Alone comparisons, differences are significant at the .05 level, using a two-tailed Mann-Whitney U test because of the heterogeneity of variances. Thus, it appears that for Ss *who are first children or only children,* being with others is indeed effective in reducing anxiety over an impending unpleasant event.

In the case of the Ss in Table 2 who were later children, however, the mean net change does not differ from one condition to another. No mean differences are statistically significant. For these Ss being with others appears not to have reduced anxiety.

Table 2 introduces a new measure, that of "gross change," or the absolute magnitude of change disregarding direction. For this measure the same tendency is found. First-born Ss waiting together show significantly greater gross change than first-born Ss waiting alone; again in the case of later-children Ss there are no differences. There is a notable difference between the first children in the T-T and T-N-T conditions: those in the T-T condition show greater gross change but less net change than do first-children Ss in the T-N-T condition. A comparison of first borns and later children *within* the T-T condition indicates that they differ significantly in gross change but not in net change. On the other hand, in the T-N-T condition first-born Ss show significantly greater change, both gross and net, than do later-children Ss. It thus appears that verbal communication may actually lead to an increase in anxiety.

On the remaining postwaiting-period measures of anxiety, the between-condition differences in birth order were similar to those already presented.

Effect of Being with Others on Self-Evaluation

If others are used as objects of social comparison in a group situation, changes in a person's self-ascribed level of anxiety and influence on that of others should occur. According to the second hypothesis of this study, then, interindividual variability in level of anxiety should be reduced during the waiting period for groups of four people waiting *together*. Such homogenization should not occur in sets of four Ss each waiting alone. The four Ss at each session were treated as a unit, and the ratio of the range after the waiting period divided by the range before the waiting period was used as a measure of homogenization. The second hypothesis then holds that lower average range ratios should occur in the Together conditions than in the Alone condition.

The results confirm the expectation. The mean homogenization ratios in both of the Together conditions are significantly less ($p < .05$) than the mean ratio for the Alone condition (T-T, 17 sets, .83; T-N-T, .84; Alone, .98). The Alone condition shows a level of homogenization that does not differ significantly from the expected ratio of 1.0, while in the Together conditions the ratios are significantly smaller than 1.0 at the .02 level or better.

Since the mean initial ranges for the three conditions were quite similar, the differences between conditions cannot be attributed to regression effects. But in the two Together conditions other possible artifactual causes of homogenization should be considered, particularly those related to the general tendency toward reduction of anxiety and to "floor" effects associated with the zero point of the scale. This kind of artifact should have the effect that groups in which anxiety was substantially reduced should also show a high degree of homogenization; there should be a sizable correlation between the amount of reduction in anxiety and the measure of homogenization. In the T-T condition this correlation is +.31 and nonsignificant, indicating that any such artifact has a minimal effect. But in the T-N-T condition it is +.57, which is significant at the .02 level. Part of the homogenization of levels of anxiety in the T-N-T condition thus appears to be attributable to the general reduction in anxiety and the floor set by the zero point of the scale.

To the extent that interindividual variability in anxiety is nonartifactually reduced, indirect evidence is provided for the first two of Festinger's hypothesized maneuvers to reduce discrepancies—change in the person's own responses and the attempt to change the responses of others. If Ss employ processes of social comparison to facilitate self-evaluation of their emotional states, evidence should be present in the T-T condition for Festinger's third hypothesized maneuver—cessation of comparison with those who differ widely from the person's own position. In the T-T condition, this effect should emerge more often in groups in which the initial range in levels of anxiety is great. In such groups, from the perspective of a given member, other group members should often appear so deviant and so resistant to change that they are not within the limits necessary for social comparison. There should thus be less homogenization of levels of anxiety in such groups than in the groups with moderate initial range.

Few pressures toward uniformity should

be expected in T-T groups with a narrow initial range because the members are already quite uniform in level of anxiety; less homogenization of levels of anxiety may therefore be expected in such groups than in those with a moderate initial range. In groups under the Alone condition, on the other hand, homogenization should be unrelated to initial range since there is no opportunity for social comparison to occur. The T-N-T condition is more difficult to predict but should resemble the T-T-condition results to some degree if processes of social comparison are operating.

Figure 1 indicates that the data are in agreement with these predictions. (Because the initial range for most groups was a multiple of five, ranges have been grouped together in Fig. 1. From one to five groups are represented by each point.) The three T-T groups with initial ranges of 90 points or greater and the

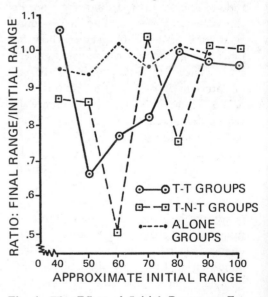

Fig. 1. The Effect of Initial Range on Extent of Homogenization. (T-T refers to the Together-Talk condition; T-N-T to Together-No-Talk.)

two groups with an initial range of 40 points or less showed less homogenization than did the 12 groups with moderate initial ranges. (Of the latter groups, five had a range of approximately 50 points, one 60 points, five about 70 points, and one of 80 points.) No such pattern is evident for the sets in the Alone condition, where homogenization is unrelated to initial range. The results for the T-N-T condition were more erratic, but their resemblance to those for the T-T condition tentatively suggests that comparison processes may be active in the absence of verbal communication.

A possible artifactual cause for the differences in homogenization between wide-range and moderate-range groups might lie in a tendency for those *S*s whose initial reaction was extreme (either less than 25 or greater than 75) to be more resistive to change, but a further analysis of the data gives no support to this possibility.

DISCUSSION

Effect of Being with Others on Reduction of Anxiety

The differences according to birth order in the anxiety-reducing effect of being with others fit in neatly with Schachter's finding (1959) that first-born *S*s have a greater desire to be with others when anxious. It now appears that their reason for this greater desire can be attributed to the fact that being with others directly reduces their anxiety. Later-children *S*s, for whom being with others does not have this effect, therefore have no particular desire to be with others when anxious.

The results for the T-N-T condition are consistent with another of Schachter's findings, that first-born *S*s desire to be with others when anxious even when verbal communication is not permitted. The present study finds, correspondingly, that when such *S*s *are* placed in a situation without verbal communication, where only the sheer physical presence of others is available, they respond with a greater reduction in anxiety than occurs in similar *S*s who remain alone.

But why this birth-order effect? The cause is certainly not a contemporary one; it must be traced to childhood experiences. There are indications in the literature that first and later children differ in various ways in their early environment. Studies of the parental treatment of different siblings (Gesell & Ilg, 1942; Sears, Maccoby, & Levin, 1957) indicate that the first child receives more attention and nurturance from his parents than do his later siblings. Sibling rivalry, with the displacement of hostilty upon the younger child (Baldwin, 1955), appears to occur frequently. On the basis of present knowledge, however, there is no compelling reason for preferring any one of several possible explanations, which invite further research.

Effect of Being with Others on Self-Evaluation

The strong support given to the second hypothesis indicates that Festinger's scheme for explaining self-evaluation through a social comparison process is useful for the emotion of anxiety as well as for opinions and abilities. Can it then be concluded that because cognitive factors have some effect in determining this particular emotional state that the emotions in general are also susceptible to social influence? Some evidence for an affirmative answer is found in a study which demonstrates that another emotion —the state of boredom or satiation—can be influenced by processes of social comparison (Horwitz, Exline, Goldman, & Lee, 1953). In this investigation of the effects of different group characteristics on task satiation, it was found that in the one condition where verbal communication was present, the variability among the members' levels of satiation was much less than the variability within the no-communication conditions.

SUMMARY

Two determinants for the relationship between anxiety and the affiliative tendency have been proposed. These are the need for direct reduction of anxiety and the need for self-evaluation of level of anxiety. The purpose of this study was to examine some of the implications of these two explanations. It was hypothesized that (*a*) being with others would be more effective in reducing anxiety than would being alone, and (*b*) pressures toward uniformity in level of anxiety would be elicited in groups of persons placed in an ambiguous emotional situation, as a consequence of requirements for self-evaluation of level of anxiety.

The first hypothesis was not confirmed, but an alternative hypothesis—that for first-born *S*s, being with others is more effective in reducing anxiety than is being alone—received strong support.

The second hypothesis received strong support. Pressures toward uniformity in regard to level of anxiety emerged in *S*s waiting together. It was concluded that a person does evaluate his level of anxiety through the process of social comparison and that level of anxiety shares with opinion the feature of being partially determined by cognitive processes.

REFERENCES

BALDWIN, A. L. *Behavior and Development in Childhood.* New York: Dryden, 1955.

DAVITZ, J. R., and MASON, D. J. "Socially Facilitated Reduction of a Fear Response in Rats. "*J. comp. physiol. Psychol.*, 1955, 48, 149–151.

DREYER, A. S. "Aspiration Behavior as Influenced by Expectation and Group Comparison." *Hum. Relat.*, 1954, 7, 175–190.

FESTINGER, L. "A Theory of Social Comparison Processes." *Hum. Relat.*, 1954, 7, 117–140.

GERARD, H. B. "The Effects of Different Dimensions of Disagreement in the Communication Process in Small Groups." *Hum. Relat.*, 1953, 6, 249–272.

GESELL, A., and ILG, FRANCES, L. *Infant and Child in the Culture Today: The Guidance and Development in Home and Nursery School.* New York: Harper, 1942.

HORWITZ, M., EXLINE, R. V., GOLDMAN, M., & LEE, E. J. "Motivational Effects of Alternative Decision Making Processes in Groups. *ONR tech. Rep.*, 1953. (Contract N6ori-07144, Group Psychol. Branch)

RUCKMICK, C. A. *The Psychology of Feeling and Emotion.* New York: McGraw-Hill, 1936.

SCHACHTER, S. *The Psychology of Affiliation.* Stanford, Calif.: Stanford Univer. Press, 1959.

SEARS, R. R., MACCOBY, ELEANOR, & LEVIN, H. *Patterns of Child Rearing.* Evanston, Ill.: Row, Peterson, 1957.

YOUNG, P. T. *Emotion in Man and Animal.* New York: Wiley, 1943.

ANXIETY, FEAR,
AND SOCIAL AFFILIATION*

Irving Sarnoff and Philip G. Zimbardo

In his ... monograph, Schachter (1959) reports that anticipated exposure to a painful external stimulus determines the degree to which persons wish to affiliate with each other: the greater the anticipated pain, the stronger the desire to await the onset of that pain in the company of others in the same predicament. In attempting to account theoretically for this finding, Schachter mentions such motivational forces as the subjects' needs for reassurance, distraction, escape, and information. However, among the various possible explanations, Schachter appears to favor one derived from Festinger's (1954) theory of social comparison processes. Adapting that theory to the phenomena under investigation, Schachter postulates that the arousal of any strong emotion evokes a need for comparison. Emotions are assumed to be quite unspecific states of affect. Hence, persons can only evaluate the quality, intensity, and appropriateness of their emotions properly by comparing their own reactions with those of others. Moreover, novel emotion producing stimuli should induce a greater tendency to affiliate than familiar stimuli. By definition, a novel stimulus is one that is more difficult to fit into a person's established frame of reference for emotive states. Accordingly, the individual is more obliged to seek out others in order to define the emotional effects of novel stimuli.

The explication of Schachter's (1959) results in terms of the theory of social comparison processes is appealingly parsimonious. However, it requires the assumption that all emotive states have the same effect on affiliative behavior. Thus, Schachter, like many contemporary psychologists, does not deal with the possible conceptual distinctions between fear and anxiety. Yet, it seems to us that by adopting an alternative assumption about the psychological properties of emotions, to be presented briefly below, it is possible to formulate predictions concerning affiliative responses that could not have been derived from the theory of social comparison processes. Indeed, by employing Freud's (1949a, 1949b) conceptual distinctions between fear and anxiety, we are led to predict a tendency toward social isolation—rather than affiliation—as a consequence of certain conditions of emotional arousal.

The present experiment was, thus,

* Irving Sarnoff and Philip G. Zimbardo, "Anxiety, Fear, and Social Affiliation," *Journal of Abnormal and Social Psychology*, 62 (1961), 356–63. Copyright 1961 by the American Psychological Association, and reproduced by permission.

undertaken with two objectives: to assess the empirical validity of conceptual differentiation between fear and anxiety, and to evaluate the extent to which the theory of social comparison processes may be applied to the relationship between all emotions and affiliative behavior. In order to implement these objectives, we have conducted an experimental investigation of the differential effects of fear and anxiety upon social affiliation.

Functional Relationship between Emotions and Motives

The guiding assumption of our experiment holds that all emotions are consciously experienced epiphenomena of motives.[1] When our motives are aroused, we experience subjective reactions to which we learn, over time, to attach commonly agreed upon labels that signify the various emotions.

Motive, on the other hand, is defined as a tension-producing stimulus that provokes behavior designed to reduce the tension. Each of our motives (innate or learned) requires the performance of a *different* response for the maximal reduction of its tension.

Fear and Anxiety Viewed as Motives

The motive of fear (which Freud called objective anxiety) is aroused whenever persons are confronted by an external object or event that is inherently dangerous and likely to produce pain. Only one type of overt[2] response can maximally

reduce our fear: separation from the threatening aspects of the feared object, accomplished by flight from the object, at one extreme, and conquest, at the other. In the case of fear, then, one's energies are mobilized toward dealing with the external stimulus; to eliminate, through some mode of escape or attack, the threat that is clearly and objectively present in the stimulus.

If we examine the consequences of anxiety (which Freud termed neurotic anxiety), we see no such correspondence between the internal disturbance of the person and an objectively harmful environmental stimulus. Instead, anxiety is typically aroused by stimuli which, objectively considered, are *innocuous*.[3] For example, in the case of the classical phobias, harmless objects possess a special motivational significance for certain people. These objects activate some motive other than fear, and this other motive, in turn, arouses the consciously perceived motive of anxiety. Hence, the emotional reaction of the anxious person is inappropriate to the

---

[1] The concept of motivation which we have chosen to employ has been elaborated elsewhere (Sarnoff, 1960a).

[2] Space limitations do not permit a consideration of the two types of covert (ego defensive) responses, denial and identification with the aggressor, which persons may employ in their efforts to cope with external threat. A full discussion of these ego defenses is presented by Sarnoff (1960a).

[3] In fact, since anxiety-arousing stimuli are often related to unconscious libidinal motives, they may be regarded by most people as intrinsically pleasurable, rather than in any way painful. For example, owing to the manner in which their heterosexual motives have been socialized, some men may tend severely to repress their sexual cravings for women. Hence, when such men are shown photographs of voluptuous nudes, stimuli which might be quite evocative of pleasurable fantasies among most of their fellows, they are likely to experience anxiety (Sarnoff & Corwin, 1959).

inherent characteristics of the external stimulus.

Regardless of their content, the motives whose arousal evokes anxiety share a common property: they are all *repressed*. These repressed motives continue unconsciously to press for the reduction of their tensions; and anxiety signals the threat of possible expression of these repressed motives. Consequently, the person develops a number of additional ego defenses that function to safeguard the initial effects of repression. If the ego defenses do their work effectively, the motives are kept under repression, the inner danger passes and the individual's anxiety is reduced.

Implications of the Motives of Anxiety and Fear for Affiliative Behavior

It follows from the foregoing discussion that, when their anxieties are aroused, people are more inclined to become preoccupied with the reassertion of inner self-control than with modes of dealing with the anxiety evoking external object. Because the anxious person tends to be aware of the element of *inappropriateness* in his feelings, he is loath to communicate his anxieties to others. To avoid being ridiculed or censured, he conceals anxiety aroused by stimuli which he guesses do not have a similar effect upon others, and which, he feels, ought not so to upset him. Thus, when anxiety is aroused, a person should tend to seek isolation from others. On the other hand, when fear is aroused and he is unable to flee from the threatening object, he welcomes the opportunity to affiliate. Since the usual responses to fear, flight and fight, are restricted in the experimental situation, the subject seeks other fear reducing responses. Therefore, the probability of affiliation increases be-

cause it mediates fear reduction through the potentiality for catharsis and distraction as well as the emotional comparison offered by interpersonal contact.

We are led, therefore, to the hypothesis that the motives of fear and anxiety should influence social affiliation behavior differently: the greater the fear aroused, the more the subjects should choose to be together with others while they await actual contact with the fear arousing object. Conversely, the greater the anxiety elicited, the more the subjects should choose to be alone while they await contact with the anxiety arousing object.

METHOD

The experiment was presented to the subjects as a physiological investigation of the cutaneous sensitivity of various parts of the body. A 2 × 2 design was used in which two levels of fear and of anxiety were experimentally aroused. The dependent variable of social affiliation was measured by having the subjects state whether they preferred to spend an anticipated waiting period alone or in the company of others.

Subjects

The subjects were 72 unpaid, male undergraduate volunteers from six introductory psychology classes in Yale University. An additional 36 subjects were used to pretest the manipulations and measuring devices, and an additional 13 subjects were excluded from the analyses because they did not qualify as acceptable subjects, i.e., were friends, misunderstood the instructions, did not believe the rationale.

Procedure

Background information was collected by an accomplice alleged to be from the counseling program of the Student Health Department. A questionnaire was designed to obtain background information on the subjects and also their preferred mode of defense mechanism. The latter data were in response to four Blacky cards. As in an ... experiment by Sarnoff (1960b), each card was accompanied by three alternatives that were to be rank ordered according to the subjects' reaction to the theme of the card (sibling rivalry, achievement, and two of sucking). The alternatives reflected predominantly an acceptance of the motive, projection of the motive upon others, or a reaction formation against the motive.

About one month later, the experimenter was introduced to the psychology classes as a physiological psychologist studying physiological responses to sensory stimuli. The subjects were subsequently recruited individually, and randomly assigned to the four experimental treatments. The specious purpose of the experiment and of the conditions of waiting were further established by marking the experimental room "Sensory Physiology Laboratory" and two nearby rooms "Waiting Room A" and "Waiting Room T." Because of absentees, the size of the groups tested varied from three to five, and was usually composed of four subjects. In order to avoid the development of superficial friendships during the experiment, and eliminate the possibility that the subjects might react to cues from each other or from the experimenter, the subjects were isolated in adjacent cubicles, no communication was allowed, and the tape-recorded instructions were presented through earphones.

The experimental conditions and instructions common to all subjects will be presented first. After rolling up their sleeves, removing their watches from their wrists, and gum or cigarettes from their mouths ("They interfere with the recording electrodes"), the subjects were told:

Our experiment falls in the general area of physiological psychology. As you may know, one branch of physiological psychology is concerned with the reactions of the sense organs to various kinds of stimulation. Our present experiment deals with the skin [or mouth] as an organ of sensation. We are interested in studying individual differences in response to particular stimuli applied to it.

There has been a good deal of controversy about the relative sensitivity of the fingertips [lips] as compared to the palms [tongue], and upper surface of the hand [palate]. Our experiment will help to provide data upon which we may be able ultimately to draw a detailed map of the cutaneous sensitivity of the human hand [mouth].

In order to measure your physiological reactions, we are now going to attach some instruments to your arm and finger [corner of your mouth]. These instruments are electrodes which are connected to a machine which records exactly the strength of your response to each stimulus. ... Electrode jelly will be applied first to the area to insure that we get a good electrical contact. (The electrodes were then attached by a female laboratory assistant of middle age.)

In order to provide a reasonable basis for asking the subjects to wait in other rooms (and, thus, for making the choice of affiliation or isolation), the subjects were told that it was necessary to assess their basal rates of responding prior to the application of the actual stimuli. They were led to believe that their individual sensitivities were being recorded while they viewed a series of slides of a typical subject who had participated in the experiment. They anticipated that a waiting period would come after the slides, and then in the second—and purportedly major—part of the experiment their direct reactions to the actual stimuli would be measured. Accordingly, they were told:

Now that your basal rates have been recorded on our polygraph recorder, it will take us about 10 minutes while we tally the data and reset our measuring instruments so that they will be geared to your individual basal rates as you are run one at a time through the rest of the experiment. While we are doing these things, we are going to ask you to wait in other rooms which are available to us. We will come to get you when it is your turn to go through with the experiment. Incidentally, we have found that some of our subjects prefer to do their waiting alone, while others prefer to wait together with other subjects. Therefore, we are going to give you your choice of waiting alone or with others. In either case, you will be ushered to a comfortable room furnished with adequate reading material.

After indicating their preference of waiting alone or together with others, the subjects also indicated the intensity of this preference on an "open-ended" scale in which 0 represented a very weak preference and 100 a very strong preference. On this relatively unstructured scale there was as much as 175 points of difference between subjects (from "75-alone" to "100-together").

Presentation of the slides during the experiment served two purposes in addition to the one previously mentioned. The content of the slides (appropriate to each experimental treatment) served to reinforce the subjects' differential expectations of the nature and severity of the stimulus situation. Furthermore, the subject seen in the slides became a focal point for measuring the effectiveness of the experimental manipulations. It was assumed that a direct attempt (by means of a scaled question) to appraise the level of the subjects' fear or anxiety would be likely to: sensitize them to the true purpose of the experiment; yield unreliable results since the subjects might neither be consciously aware of, nor able to verbalize, their anxiety reaction; and evoke resistance since some subjects might not want to admit to being anxious or fearful, calling their masculinity into question.

Therefore, it was necessary to use an indirect, disguised measure to evaluate whether the experimental inductions had actually aroused two levels of both fear and anxiety. Immediately after the slides had been shown (but before the affiliation choices had been made), the subjects were told:

As you may know, an individual shows his physiological reaction in a variety of behavioral forms. We are interested in seeing whether it is possible to estimate how ill-at-ease or upset individuals are at the prospect of receiving the stimulation in this experiment. Recalling the subject whom you just saw in the slides, how upset or ill-at-ease did he seem to you? Please assign a number anywhere from zero to 100 to indicate your feeling. (Zero = unconcerned, at ease; 100 = extremely concerned and ill-at-ease.)

Since the subject in the slides was a posed model instructed to remain poker faced throughout, it was assumed that there was no objective difference in his expression. Thus, any systematic difference in ratings between groups should reflect a projection of the subjects' own motives upon this screen.

However, because the content of the slides was not identical for every group but rather "tailored" to each specific treatment, it was possible that the model may have actually looked more fearful in the slides shown to the subjects in the High Fear than in the Low Fear condition. As a control check on this possibility, four additional introductory psychology classes ($N = 108$) served as judges. They were told that the slides were of a typical subject in a recently completed experiment, and their task was to estimate how ill-at-ease and concerned he appeared (on the same scale used by the experimental subjects). Two of the classes saw only the face of the model (the rest of the slide was blacked out) and were told only that he was a subject in a physiological experiment in which stimuli were applied and responses measured. The other two classes saw the entire stimulus field of the slides and were given the same complete description that the experimental subjects received. Since each class of judges rated the slides for all four experimental treatments, the order of presentation was counterbalanced.

After the projective measure of motive arousal and the measure of affiliation, the electrodes were removed and a measure taken of the subjects' reasons for choosing to affiliate or be isolated. This was done with the rationale that a social psychologist had become interested in the fact that some of our subjects preferred to be together while others preferred to be alone, and he had asked us to get some information for him about the reasons underlying this preference.

The questionnaire, designed by Gerard and Rabbie (1960), contained both open-ended and structured questions asking for reasons for the affiliation choice. Finally, the subjects noted whether or not they wished to continue in the experiment. Only one subject (in the High Fear condition) refused to remain for the "stimulation" part of the experiment.

The true purpose, hypothesis, design, and reasons for the various deceptions (and, at a later time, the results) were explained fully to each subject.

High Fear

A high level of fear was induced by leading the subjects to anticipate a series of painful electrical shocks. Although they expected to endure each of the shocks for 2 minutes, the subjects were assured that the shocks would not cause damage or injury.

The female assistant (dressed in a white lab coat, as was the experimenter) then attached electrodes to each subject's arm and fingertip and strapped his arm onto a cotton-padded board. The leads from the electrodes appeared to go to a polygraph recorder, which also was seen in the series of slides of the typical subjects. Another slide showed an enormous electrical stimulator, and the implication was that it was behind a curtain in the experimental room. It was called to the subjects' attention that:

> The four dials shown in the upper right-hand corner of the stimulator enable us to regulate automatically the frequency, duration, delay, and intensity of the shock you will get.

The other slides portrayed the subject with earphones and electrodes attached (like the subjects themselves), "listening to the instruc-tions", and then "about to receive his first painful shock," administered by the experimenter, who could be seen in the background manipulating the dials on the stimulator. A final situational factor that may have enhanced the effectiveness of the High Fear manipulation was that the experimental room housed electrical generators which made a continuous buzzing sound, a cue interpreted by the High Fear subjects as the electrical stimulator "warming up," but unnoticed or quickly adapted to by the other subjects. An unobtrusively posted sign reading "Danger/High Voltage," present only for the High Fear subjects, gave further credence to this notion.

Low Fear

In the Low Fear condition the word "shock" was never used, and all cues in the situation associated with shock, fear, or pain were removed; i.e., no white lab coats, arms not strapped to boards, etc. The expectations of these subjects were guided by instructions stating that our methodology was to apply a 10-second stimulus of very low intensity that would be just sufficient to elicit a measurable physiological response.

In the series of slides viewed by these subjects, the imposing electrical stimulator was replaced by a small innocuous looking apparatus (actually a voltmeter), and the experimenter was seen not in the active role as an agent of pain, but in the passive role of recording data from the polygraph recorder.

High Anxiety

Anxiety was manipulated by arousing a motive that was assumed to have been repressed by most of the subjects. In Freudian terminology, the motive might be called "oral libido," a desire to obtain pleasurable gratification by sucking on objects that are clearly related to infantile nursing experiences. The female breast is, of course, the prototype of such objects, but others include nipples, baby bottles, and pacifiers. Thus, to arouse this oral motive and, hence, the anxiety that should follow its arousal, subjects in the High Anxiety condition were led to believe that they would have to suck on a number of objects commonly associated with infantile oral behavior. They were told that their task would be to suck on these objects for 2 minutes while we recorded their physiological responses from the skin surfaces stimulated by the objects. In clear view in front of the subjects were the following items: numerous baby bottles, oversized nipples, pacifiers, breast shields (nipples women often wear over their breasts while nursing), and lollipops.

The same variety of stimulus objects was shown arrayed in front of the subject in the slides. He could be seen, tongue hanging out, lips puckered, about to suck his thumb (as one of the objects of stimulation) or one of the other objects. Subjects were told that the contact taped to the mouth recorded the direct reaction to the oral stimulation, while the arm contact recorded peripheral reactions.

Low Anxiety

The instructions to the Low Anxiety subjects did not mention "suck," nor any stimulation that they would receive from putting the objects in their mouths. Moreover, they were led to believe that they would keep each object in their mouths for only 10 seconds. The stimulus objects were not in immediate proximity to the subjects while their electrodes were being attached. The stimulus objects which they anticipated putting in their mouths were shown in the slides: whistles, balloons, "kazoos," and pipes. Since these objects do not require sucking (but rather, in general, blowing), the model's tongue was not seen as he prepared to use the stimuli in the slides.

Results

Evidence of the Effectiveness of the Experimental Manipulations

In using the subjects' estimates of the degree to which the model seen in the slides was upset by the prospect of receiving the stimulation in the experiment, it

Table 1

MEAN PROJECTION SCORES FOR EACH EXPERIMENTAL TREATMENT

Motive	Level of Arousal		p value
	Low	High	
Fear	24	42	$<.01$ ($t=3.05$)
Anxiety	14	31[a]	$<.01$ ($t=2.95$)
	ns	*ns*	

Note.—The larger the score, the greater the degree of projection.

[a] Variance greater than in High Fear group, $p<.10$; *SD* for High Anxiety$=24$, for High Fear$=16$.

was assumed that the subjects would tend to project their induced level of fear and anxiety. Table 1, which presents the mean projection scores for each experimental treatment, offers evidence that this assumption was valid and the manipulations effective. The High Arousal subjects perceived the model to be significantly[4] more upset, concerned, and ill-at-ease than did the Low Arousal subjects.

Our theoretical distinction between fear and anxiety, and the way these concepts were operationally defined in this experiment, lead to the prediction that, assuming similarity of past experience, persons facing the same clearly, objectively present threat should react in a relatively homogeneous fashion. This close correspondence between stimulus and response is not assumed to hold for anxiety. We have already noted that a stimulus that produces anxiety for some persons is not an anxiety producing cue for many others. Since the significance of the stimulus depends upon its symbolic and generally

---

[4] All p values reported throughout the paper are based on two-tailed tests of significance.

idiosyncratic associations, one would expect that a stimulus which elicited anxiety for persons with relevant predispositions (repressed motives) would have less effect on those who had more adequately resolved the conflict over the expression of the same motives. Thus, one way of determining whether our experimental manipulations produced two different motives, fear and anxiety (rather than only two levels of one motive), is to compare the variability in response between treatments.

The heterogeneity of response in the High Anxiety group is, as predicted, greater than in the High Fear and the Low Arousal conditions. The same difference in response variability between the High Anxiety group and all other groups is manifested as well in the dependent variable of social affiliation. The questionnaire data to be presented in a later section offer further support to the distinction between fear and anxiety.

Before presenting the major results, it is necessary to account for two possible sources of artifact in the just-reported data on projection. They are: by chance sampling, the High Arousal groups could have contained more subjects who characteristically used projection as a mechanism of defense than the Low Arousal groups; and the subject seen in the High Fear and High Anxiety slides was objectively more upset and concerned than he was in the Low Fear and Low Anxiety slides. If either of these alternatives were true, then the projection measure would not be a reflection of differences due to the experimental arousal of levels of fear and anxiety.

The pretest data of the subjects' mode of defense preference on the Black Projection test show no initial significant difference between any of the groups in their tendency to use projection.

Among the groups of neutral judges who evaluated all the slides shown in the study, from 68%–98% reported perceiving either no difference in the degree to which the model appeared upset, or a difference opposite to that reported in Table 1. This result holds for both fear and anxiety, and regardless of the order of presentation or amount of the stimulus field seen (model's face only or entire slide). Thus, it appears that the projection measure can be used as an index of the efficacy of the experimental conditions and manipulations.

Effects of Fear and Anxiety on Social Affiliation

The results bearing upon the hypothesis of the study are presented in Table 2, where for each condition the mean intensity of desire to affiliate, as well as the

Table 2

RELATIONSHIP OF MOTIVE TO SOCIAL AFFILIATION

| | Mean Affiliation Strength[a] | Number of Subjects Choosing | |
		Together	Alone or "0-Together"
Fear			
Low	34.0	12	3
High	51.0	19	1
Anxiety			
Low	27.0	11	4
High	8.0	11	12

Interaction: (Motive × Level) $p < .05$, $t = 2.30$, $df = 68$.

[a] The larger the score, the greater the affiliation tendency; isolation intensity score subtracted from affiliation intensity score.

number of subjects choosing to affiliate and to be alone, are presented. It is evident that there is a strong positive relationship between fear and the index of affiliative tendency, but a strong negative relationship between anxiety and affiliation, so that as fear increases affiliation also increases, while an increase in anxiety results in a decrease in affiliation. Thus, our prediction of an interaction between kind of motive and level of arousal is clearly supported by the data. While some 95% of the High Fear subjects chose the "together" alternative (with more than 0 intensity), only 46% of the High Anxiety subjects chose to wait together. The marked mean difference between these groups in intensity of choice (51.0–8.0) is significant well beyond the .01 level ($t = 3.63$). The large mean difference in affiliative tendency between the High and Low Fear groups ($p < .07$, $t = 1.96$) represents a replication of Schachter's (1959, p. 18) results. While the mean difference between High and Low Anxiety was even larger than that between the Fear conditions, it only approached significance ($p = .16$, $t = 1.46$) due to the marked heterogeneity of variance of the High Anxiety group.

Reasons Given for Affiliation Choice

The final measure taken was a questionnaire that explored the reasons the subjects gave for choosing to wait together with others or to wait alone. The 11 structured items on the questionnaire each presented a possible motive for affiliation; and each was accompanied by a 70-point scale on which the subject indicated how important he thought the motive was in determining his choice. The highly significant interaction between experimental treatment and questions ($p < .001$, $F = 3.74$, $df = 30.570$) on a repeated-measurement analysis of variance justified a search for those questions (motives for affiliation) that differentiated the groups.

Since there were too few subjects choosing the alone condition, the analysis is limited to those wanting to affiliate. The motives for affiliation that were most important for the High Fear subjects and most distinguished them from the Low Fear subjects were (the lower the mean, the greater the importance; 10 = extremely important):

1. I am not sure whether I am reacting in the same way as the others to the prospect of getting shocked and would like to compare my reactions to theirs. [Emotional comparison] High Fear $\bar{x} = 38$, Low Fear $\bar{x} = 54$, $p < .001$.

2. I feel worried about getting shocked and would like to know to what extent the others are worried too. [Extent of comparison] High Fear $\bar{x} = 40$, Low Fear $\bar{x} = 61$, $p < .001$.

3. I want to be distracted in order to take my mind off the prospect of getting shocked. [Distraction] High Fear $\bar{x} = 44$, Low Fear $\bar{x} = 59$, $p < .01$.

4. I am worried about the prospect of getting shocked and felt that talking with someone about it would get it off my chest. [Catharsis] High Fear $\bar{x} = 50$, Low Fear $\bar{x} = 59$, $p < .05$.

The reasons for affiliation given spontaneously to a single open-ended question also reflect the importance of these same considerations. Among High Anxiety subjects choosing to be alone, the major reason given spontaneously and supported by the scaled questions is the desire "to be alone to think about personal affairs and school work."

Curiosity as to "what the others were

MILLS COLLEGE
LIBRARY

like" was important, but equally so across all conditions. Of least importance among all subjects are the following motives for affiliation ("oral stimulation" substituted for "shock" for Anxiety groups):

> "It would be clearer in my own mind as to how I feel about getting shocked if I could express my reactions to someone else." "I anticipated that the others would offer reassuring comments." "I want to be with others to reassure myself that I am not the only one who was singled out to be shocked." "I feel that perhaps together we could somehow figure out a way to avoid getting shocked."

There are several large differences between the High Fear and High Anxiety groups; with the former finding the following motives as significantly more important: emotional comparison, extent of comparison, distraction, catharsis, and the physical presence of others ($p < .05$ in each instance). Similarly, an internal analysis of the High Fear group reveals these same motives (especially catharsis and emotional comparison) to be more important for those subjects who chose to affiliate most strongly than for those below the group median in affiliation strength.

Ordinal Position and Its Relation to Affiliation

While the reasoning used in the planning of the present study did not include predictions of the effects of ordinal position upon affiliation, data relevant to this question was nevertheless obtained, to check on Schachter's (1959) finding that affiliation tendencies increased with emotional arousal only among first- and only-born children. This finding is duplicated in the present study. First-born children want to affiliate significantly more than later-borns under conditions of high fear, but not when the level of fear is low. While the mean affiliation intensity for the first-born High Fear subjects was 62, it was only 23 for the later-born High Fear subjects ($p = .05$, $t = 2.10$). This same general finding holds for the High Anxiety group, but again the within-group variability does not permit the large mean difference obtained (16 for first-borns and -3 for later-borns) to be statistically significant.

DISCUSSION

Since our basic hypothesis has been supported, our results lend credence to the previously drawn conceptual distinction between fear and anxiety. In view of the fact that our anxiety arousing stimulus was specifically designed to tap only one kind of repressed motive, it of course remains an empirical question whether or not the evocation of other types of presumably repressed motives also leads to social isolation.

In order to predict the consequences of the arousal of a motive, therefore, it is necessary to know which responses are required to reduce its tension. The probability of the social comparison response is, thus, a function of: the kind of motive aroused, the intensity of the motive, the degree of novelty of the emotional experience, the response hierarchy associated with the specific motive, and certain attributes of those with whom the person is to affiliate.

We do not question the assumption that the need for some kind of cognitive-emotional clarity and structure is a basic human motive. However, we feel that the need for self-evaluation is not the *most* salient motive aroused in the experimental situations that Schachter (1959) and we employed. We do not view the cognitive need to structure a vague emotional state as the primary motive in these experiments; we see social comparison not as an end in itself but merely as one of the several responses that are *instrumental* in reducing the tension associated with the situationally more salient motives of fear and anxiety.

Strict application of the theory of emotional comparison processes to the present experimental situation should lead one to predict greater affiliation tendencies for the High Anxiety subjects than the High Fear subjects, since the Anxiety situation was more unusual than that of Fear, and the emotion aroused was probably more novel and vague. The opposite prediction, supported by the results, demands an approach, such as the one followed here, that specifies the probability of the response alternatives evoked by the dominant motives aroused.

As the emotional experience becomes very novel and unusual, the need for comparison of one's reactions with others should increase, and, hence, intensify affiliation tendencies. The induction of esoteric states of consciousness by "anxiety producing drugs" (being studied presently by Schachter) may be the kind of situation in which emotional comparison theory offers the best explanations and predictions. Under such circumstances, it may be possible to create emotional states that are epiphenomena of motives whose neurophysiological bases had never previously been set into motion. A more natural counterpart of this novel emotional experiences occurs the first time a person experiences the emotions associated with the death of a loved one.

The predictive importance of knowing the specific responses appropriate to the motive aroused is clearly illustrated by the following examples. If a person's guilt is aroused, his response to feelings of guilt should be to seek out others only if they could be expected to punish him and, thus, to expiate his guilt, but not to affiliate with individuals perceived as unable to fill this role. Similarly, if repressed homosexual anxieties are aroused, isolation should generally be preferred to affiliation, as with oral anxiety in the present study. However, affiliation tendencies should increase if the subject is allowed to wait with females, but not if he can wait only in the company of males.

While our questionnaire data offer support for the importance of emotional comparison, they also point up the role of other motives such as need for catharsis and distraction. The marked difference in the importance of the reasons given for affiliation between the High Fear and High Anxiety groups is perhaps the most substantial evidence that the experimental manipulations have indeed led to the arousal of two quite different motives.

A final point of interest concerns the data about ordinal position. The finding that firstborn children show greater affiliation tendencies than later-born children when either fear or anxiety are aroused supports Schachter's (1959) results. Theoretical and experimental attempts to uncover the dynamics underlying this "static" variable should prove interesting and fruitful.

SUMMARY

This experiment tests the utility of the psychoanalytic distinction between fear

and anxiety for making differential predictions about social affiliation. It also
assesses the breadth of generalization of
Schachter's (1959) empirical finding of
a positive relation between emotional
arousal and affiliation. Seventy-two subjects were randomly assigned to four experimental treatments in which low and
high levels of fear and anxiety were
manipulated. The success of these inductions was established by a projective device
and questionnaire data. The dependent
variable of social affiliation was measured
by having the subjects choose to await
the anticipated exposure to the stimulus
situation either alone or together with
others.

The results show that, while the desire
to affiliate increases as fear increases (a
replication of Schachter's, 1959, results),
the opposite is true for anxiety; as anxiety
increases the desire to affiliate decreases.
Thus, as predicted, our findings lend empirical support to the theoretical distinction between fear and anxiety. At the
same time, our results suggest that the
theory of social comparison processes may
not be adequate to account for the general
relationship between emotions and affiliative tendencies.

REFERENCES

FESTINGER, L. "A Theory of Social Comparison Processes." *Hum. Relat.*, 1954, 7,
117–140.

FREUD, S. *Inhibitions, Symptoms, and Anxiety*. (Originally published 1936) London:
Hogarth, 1949. (a)

FREUD, S. *New Introductory Lectures on
Psychoanalysis*. (Originally published 1933)
London: Hogarth, 1949. (b)

GERARD, H. B., and RABBIE, J. M. "Fear and
Social Comparison." Unpublished manuscript, Bell Telephone Research Laboratories, 1960.

SARNOFF, I. "Psychoanalytic Theory and Social Attitudes." *Publ. opin. Quart.*, 1960,
24, 251–279. (a)

SARNOFF, I. "Reaction Formation and Cyni-
cism." *J. Pers.*, 1960, 28, 129–143. (b)

SARNOFF, I., and CORWIN, S. M. "Castration
Anxiety and the Fear of Death." *J. Pers.*,
1959, 27, 374–385.

SCHACHTER, S. *The Psychology of Affiliation*.
Stanford: Stanford Univer. Press, 1959.

2

The Effects
of Group Membership

SOME EFFECTS
OF SHARED THREAT AND PREJUDICE IN
RACIALLY MIXED GROUPS*

Eugene Burnstein and Adie V. McRae

When members of a social system are threatened, marked changes seem to occur in social relationships (Jacobson & Schachter, 1954; Schachter, Nuttin, de Monchaux, Maucorps, Osmer, Duijker, Rommetveit, & Israel, 1954). Where the consequences of the threat and the responsibilities for coping with it are shared, an increase in group cohesion and a reduction in disruptive antagonisms may occur (French, 1941; Leighton, 1945; Pepitone & Kleiner, 1957; Sherif & Sherif, 1953;

Wright, 1943)[1]. The application of this general finding to the study of particular social problems can have important con-

---

[1] A shared threat has also been observed to increase hostility among group members. In Nazi concentration camps, inmates went so far as to identify themselves with the source of the threat (Bettelheim, 1943; Cohen, 1953). At present it is not completely clear what are the necessary and sufficient conditions for a shared threat to reduce intermember hostility. However, a review of the literature suggests the important determinants are (*a*) the overwhelming nature of the threat, (*b*) the degree to which group action can ameliorate the threat, and (*c*) the degree to which members equally share the consequences of the threat and the responsibilities for coping with it. In the concentration camp the threat was quite over-

---

* Eugene Burnstein and Adie V. McRae, "Some Effects of Shared Threat and Prejudice in Racially Mixed Groups," *Journal of Abnormal and Social Psychology*, 64 (1962), 257–63. Copyright 1962 by the American Psychological Association, and reproduced by permission.

sequences. If the social system in question is a society, community, or group containing distinct religious or racial subgroups, concern about a shared threat may lead to a decrease in the amount of hostility expressed toward these minorities.

In the first explicit attempt to test the hypothesis that shared threat reduced social prejudice, Feshbach and Singer (1957) presented a set of questions to individuals designed to provoke concern about dangers which confront the community as a whole, e.g., floods, hurricanes, atomic attack. Immediately afterward a social prejudice questionnaire was administered. Responses on the final questionnaire were compared to those the person made a month earlier. The authors reasoned as follows:

> Under the impact of a common threat ...one's reference group may become the population that is subjected to the danger. If this reference group now includes both Negro and white, whereas under ordinary stimulus conditions the reference group has been primarily the white population, then the social distance between white and Negro should decrease, with a corresponding decrement in social prejudice (p. 412).

The results gave only weak support to the hypothesis. However, there are considerations which suggest the shared threat induced by this method may have been relatively weak.

Requiring people to think about a community-wide disaster does not insure that they view it as one in which the suffering and responsibilities are equally distributed

among all community members. In a pilot study conducted by the senior author, 47 male students in the elementary psychology course at the University of Texas were administered the first four of the five "Flood and Hurricane Threat questions" from Feshbach and Singer (1957). In addition they were asked if such a disaster struck Austin, Texas, would all or nearly all socioeconomic levels, ethnic groups, or neighborhoods be equally affected. Only 27% thought this to be likely. Over 30% thought that there would be large differences among various groups in the degree to which they suffered from such disasters. Similar differences occurred in regard to the distribution of the burden for coping with the disaster. Therefore, given this method of induction, the extent to which the subjects perceived the threat to be shared is ambiguous.

Furthermore, in a highly complex social system such as a community, multiple group membership is the rule. During a disaster, the person may experience severe role conflicts. In spite of the perception that the threat is shared equally by all community members, the role of a father, neighbor, or plant manager may be more salient than that of community citizen. This phenomenon is vividly documented by Killian (1952) in his study of the Texas City explosion and of three tornado-torn towns in Oklahoma. Thus, even when a shared threat is perceived to exist in a community setting, it is uncertain whether the community as a whole or some subsystem will become the salient reference group. In the latter case, minorities within the community remain outgroups in terms of the social relations which are salient for the person at that time. Under such conditions, social prejudice may be unaffected.

In order to test the hypotheses that

---

whelming. Group action provided little amelioration; in fact, for many inmates a reduction in threat was only possible by dissociating themselves from the group. Treatment varied with the category of the inmate, and little role differentiation occurred other than imposed by the camp administration.

shared threat reduces the expression of hostility toward minorities either one of two general procedures can be used to minimize these processes which vitiate the threat induction: some method may be introduced to assure that the person faced by a community-wide threat takes the community as the salient reference group, or the threat may be induced in a simpler social system in which the number of group memberships available to the person is sharply reduced. Both procedures attempt to decrease the likelihood that roles or reference groups external to the threatened social system become salient. The present experiment utilizes the second method. Members of racially mixed groups cooperate to solve a logical problem. In these groups, failure is clearly shared by all members. At the same time all members have a role in coping with the status loss that results from failure (Deutsch, 1953). The social system, furthermore, is simple enough so that under the threat of status loss few, if any, alternative roles are likely to become salient other than membership in the particular problem solving group.

Another source of variation in the expression of hostility toward an individual Negro that should be controlled is the attitude of the other members toward this racial group as a whole. The stronger the person's anti-Negro attitudes, the more likely is he to be hostile toward a Negro member of his problem solving group. Thus, in the present study anti-Negro attitudes as well as shared threat will be examined.

If the expression of hostility toward a Negro group member varies directly with the strength of anti-Negro attitudes and inversely with the degree of shared threat, then the following predictions can be made: (*a*) high prejudiced individuals under nonthreatening conditions will express the greatest amount of hostility toward the Negro member; (*b*) low prejudiced individuals under shared threat will express the least amount of hostility toward the Negro member; (*c*) high prejudiced individuals under shared threat and low prejudiced individuals under nonthreatening conditions will display an intermediate amount of hostility toward the minority group member. In the situation under study, hostility may be manifested in direct evaluations made of the Negro, in the frequency with which the Negro is rejected from the group, and in the avoidance of communication with him during the problem solving interaction.

METHOD

Subjects and Confederate

Forty-eight male students in the elementary psychology course at the University of Texas were used as subjects. Participation fulfilled a course requirement. Several weeks before the experiment they were assessed as to their level of anti-Negro prejudice by means of Holtzman's D scale (Kelly, Ferson, & Holtzman, 1958), in the form of a "Student Attitude and Opinion Questionnaire." This was administered by the instructors in a number of the sections of the course. The distribution of prejudice scores was split at the median; subjects falling above the median were considered high in prejudice, those below the median, low in prejudice. In order to minimize the possibility of prior acquaintanceship, the four subjects used in each experimental group were drawn from separate sections.

A Negro confederate was paid to serve as a member in all experimental groups. The four other members were, in one half of the groups, all high prejudiced subjects, in the other half, all low prejudiced subjects. The confederate participated in several pilot groups to attain maximum familiarity and skill with the type of problem to be used in the experiment. It was necessary to tell him about all phases of the experiment and its objectives. The only information that was withheld from him was the extent of prejudice of the subjects with whom he was to work.

Procedure

Six groups were run with low prejudiced subjects and six with high prejudiced subjects. Within each of these two conditions of prejudice, shared threat was induced in half of the group, while a nonthreatening or successful state of affairs was induced in the other half. The design, therefore, consisted of three groups of four subjects, plus the confederate, under each of the following conditions: High Prejudice, Nonthreat (HPNT); Low Prejudice, Nonthreat (LPNT); High Prejudice, Threat (HPT); and Low Prejudice, Threat (LPT).

Communication among the subjects occurred around a table similar to that used by Leavitt (1951). The subjects were seated so that each was separated from the next by a vertical partition extending from a post in the center of the table. The center post had slots allowing subjects to push written messages to other members. Direct communication was permitted among all members. Messages were written on colored cards corresponding to the color of the cubicle from which each subject operated.

As each subject arrived he was given a seat in front of his cubicle. When all subjects had taken their places, they were asked to stand and see who the other members were but not to engage in any conversation. A copy of the instructions was given to each member and they were asked to follow as the experimenter read them aloud. In summary form, the instructions were as follows:

> The purpose of this procedure is to evaluate how groups work together in solving problems when communication is limited to written messages. It has been found that a procedure such as this can be used to single out groups with different levels of skillfulness, efficiency, and creativity. The university recently has become quite interested in estimating how productively undergraduates can work together in groups. They have suggested that the Psychology Department initiate this program of evaluating groups of students with respect to these qualities. Thus, a record will be kept for the university administration of the performance of the group participating in this preliminary testing. Skillful, efficient, and creative group problem solving will be reflected in the time that it takes the group to solve the problem, i.e., how long after starting before every member has the correct answer. Each member will receive a grade that is based on how well his group performs in solving these problems. This means, of course, that everybody in the group gets the same grade. The grade a group receives will depend on how its performance compares to that of a large number of other groups of college students in Texas who have worked on the same type of problem in the same type of situation.

During the reading of the instructions the subjects were standing facing each other.

All groups were given four successive problems to solve—Leavitt's (1951) "common symbol" problem. They were instructed that each member had been given a different set of symbols and that their task, as a group, was to discover the symbol that was common to all members. When a member knew what this symbol was, he was to put it on a white slip and place it on top of his section of the center post. The group was considered to have completed the problem when all members had placed their white slip on the center post.

At the conclusion of Task 2, subjects were told to stand, stretch their legs, but not to converse. They were seated and given an evaluation of their performance. Half of the high prejudiced groups and half of the low prejudiced groups (HPNT and LPNT) were told that their performance was well above average. The remaining high prejudiced and low prejudiced groups (HPT and LPT) were informed that they had performed poorly compared to the average performance of similar groups. The experimenter reinforced these evaluations by making two or three positive or negative statements about the group's performance during or immediately after both Task 3 and 4. At the end of Task 4, the experimenter similarly evaluated the groups with respect to their overall performance. While the final evaluation was made subjects were standing in front of their cubicle facing each other.

Immediately following the final evaluation a postquestionnaire was administered. On six-point scales, subjects rated the experimenter in terms of his "competence as a psychologist" and in terms of their "liking" for him. Similarly, the test situation was rated for its "fairness," its "worthwhileness," and its "interest." To partially assess the success of the threat induction, subjects were asked to rate how "depressed" they felt at the results of the test. Three items allowed subjects to evaluate the other four members. Two of these items involved ranking members in terms of their contribution to the solutions and in terms of who the subjects liked best. The third item required subjects to rate other members for their estimated "communication and problem solving skill in everyday life." At the end of the questionnaire subjects were given a sheet which asked if they wished to replace one of the present members with a new one from the subject pool at the next testing session. If they did desire to do so, they were to indicate the rejected member by encircling one of the four listed colors which corresponded to the color of his cubicle.

After completing the questionnaires, subjects were given a full explanation of the nature of the experiments.

RESULTS

An analysis of variance of the mean times required for task completion by the four experimental groups indicates that completion time decreases significantly over trials ($F = 8.06$, $p < .001$). This is in accord with Leavitt's (1951) findings regarding improvement in performances over successive tasks.

To assess the success of the threat induction, two t tests were made, one on the self-ratings of depression as a result of the test, another on the subjects' ratings of themselves and other white members for their communication and problem solving skills in everyday life. The tests indicated that threatened subjects felt more depressed than nonthreatened subjects ($t = 2.82$, $p < .01$). Similarly, threatened subjects graded themselves and other white members significantly lower in everyday communication skills than nonthreatened subjects ($t = 3.67$, $p < .001$). There were no reliable differences as a function of threat in regard to the subjects' evaluations of the experimenter and of the test situation.

To determine differences in hostile expression resulting from shared threat and prejudiced attitude, t tests were run on the postquestionnaire items in which the subjects ranked the confederate in terms of contribution to task solutions, liking for him, and in which they estimated his everyday communication and problem solving skill. It was predicted that maximum hostility would be expressed in HPNT conditions; the least in the LPT conditions; while HPT and LPNT subjects would express an intermediate amount. In Table 1 the mean rank for contribution to the solutions given to the Negro confederate are presented. A rank of 1 indicates the greatest contribution, a rank of 5, the least contribution. The order of these mean ranks corresponds exactly to the predicted order. However,

Table 1

EVALUATION OF NEGRO CONFEDERATE

	Mean task contribution rank		Mean likability rank		Mean skill ratio	
	Shared threat		Shared threat		Shared threat	
	Present	Absent	Present	Absent	Present	Absent
Prejudice						
High	2.58	4.33	2.60	3.25	1.02	1.37
Low	2.42	3.25	2.58	2.83	.91	1.17
Difference tested	t		t		t	
HPNT vs. HPT	3.12****		2.57***		2.50***	
HPNT vs. LPT	3.42****		2.16**		2.52***	
HPNT vs. LPNT	1.85*		1.02[a]		—	
LPT vs. LPNT	1.28[a]		—		1.33[a]	
LPT vs. HPT	—		—		—	

[a] Not significant.
* Significant at .10 level.
** Significant at .05 level.
*** Significant at .02 level.
**** Significant at .005 level.

only the differences between HPNT and HPT and between HPNT and LPT are statistically reliable. The difference between HPNT and LPNT approaches, but does not reach an acceptable level of significance ($p < .10$). For the mean rank given to the Negro confederate in regard to "liking," a score of 1 indicates the greatest relative liking for the confederate, 4 indicates the least liking. The Negro would be expected to be ranked lowest in the HPNT condition, highest in the LPT condition, and intermediate in the LPNT and HPT conditions. The results show the order of mean ranks once again conforms to what was hypothesized. Only the differences between HPNT and HPT and between HPNT and LPT are significant. On the third item, subjects were required to estimate their fellow members' every-

day communication and problem solving skill. In the context of this item, hostility may be expressed toward the Negro by rating him lower than the other group members. Ratings of group members, however, were shown to be biased by the presence or absence of threat. This is corrected by using a ratio of the rating given to the Negro by each subject over the mean rating given by the subject to all other members. A high degree of similarity between the Negro's rating and the mean rating is indicated as the ratio approaches 1. A ratio greater than 1 means that the confederate is considered less skillful than the average group member, less than 1 indicates he is considered more skillful than the average. Once again the obtained order fits the prediction exactly. However, only the differences between HPNT and

HPT and between HPNT and LPT are significant.

With respect to the more general hypothesis that shared threat reduces the expression of hostility toward the confederate, responses to the above three items were analyzed by *t* tests for subjects exposed to shared threat and those not exposed, regardless of prejudice. The mean ranks given to the confederate on the first two items and the mean ratio given on the last item by threatened individuals were 2.50, 2.54, and 0.96, respectively. The same means for nonthreatened subjects were 3.70, 3.04, and 1.27, respectively. The difference between threatened and nonthreatened subjects on the first item was significant at the .005 level; the difference on the second item was significant at the .05 level; and the difference between the ratios was significant at the .01 level.

If they wished, subjects were given the opportunity to vote privately on rejecting a member from the group. In the HPNT condition 9 of the 12 subjects decided to reject a member. Of these 9 rejections, 6 were of the Negro confederate. With 9 subjects making use of their privilege to reject 1 of the 4 members in their group, it is highly improbable that as large or a larger number of these rejections would be directed toward one member by chance ($p < .01$). In the LPNT condition, 8 subjects wished to reject another member. The confederate received 3 of these rejections. Both in the HPT and LPT conditions 9 subjects decided to reject another member; and in each of these conditions 2 rejections were directed toward the confederate. In none of the latter three conditions did the frequency of rejecting the confederate depart significantly from what would be expected by chance alone. Thus,

only under the HPNT condition, where the strongest expression of hostility toward the confederate was expected to occur, is the Negro rejected more frequently than chance.

Another significant source of information concerning the orientation of the members toward the Negro is the proportion of the task messages sent to him during the course of the problem solving interaction. Earlier studies have shown that interpersonal dislike can be coordinated to an increase in the barriers to communication (Festinger, Cartwright, Barber, Fleischl, Gottsdanker, Keysen, & Leavitt, 1948; Festinger, Schachter, & Back, 1950; Potashin, 1946). Thus, it is reasonable to expect that the amount of task communication with the Negro would vary inversely with the degree of hostility felt toward him. The total number of messages each subject sent to all other subjects was counted. The percentage of this total which the subject sent to the confederate was then computed. This was done only for those tasks following the initial induction of shared threat, i.e., tasks 3 and 4. The analysis of variance of these percentages indicates that only the *F* ratio (4.64) for prejudice is significant ($p < .05$). The differences between threat conditions and between tasks did not approach significance. Figure 1 shows that the low prejudiced subjects, both threatened and nonthreatened sent a greater proportion of their messages on Tasks 3 and 4 to the confederate than subjects in either high prejudiced condition.

Discussion

It appears that the expression of hostility toward a Negro group member varies directly with the strength of anti-Negro attitudes, and inversely with the degree of shared threat. Moreover, prejudice against Negroes as a group may be expressed through a reduction in communication to an individual Negro. This is similar to Schachter's (1960) observations regarding communication to a persistent deviant. Of course, since there could be no question of the Negro changing his "deviant" position, i.e., his status as a Negro, there was no initial rise in communication to the confederate as was found by Schachter during the early phases of interaction. Moreover, it is interesting to note that avoidance of communication with the Negro by high prejudiced subjects occurred in a situation where messages were of an impersonal, task oriented nature and where the Negro member possessed information of value to other members in solving the problem.

The prediction that shared threat would inhibit tendencies to avoid communication with the Negro was not confirmed. No difference in communication to the confederate appeared as a function of shared threat. There are a number of possible explanations as to why shared threat reduced the expression of hostility toward the Negro in terms of direct evaluation on the postquestionnaire, but had no effect on the tendency to avoid communication with him. The first bears on the procedure used to induce the threatening and nonthreatening conditions. It will be recalled that the evaluations of the group's performance by the experimenter, which was the means whereby threat was induced, was not made until after the second task. This was relatively late in the problem solving process. The reorganization of the person's initial attitude toward the Negro may take some time. Thus, attitude change may not have occurred in time to appreciably affect task communication. This explanation loses some of its force when one notes in Figure 1 that the differences in communication to the Negro as a function of prejudice occur more markedly in the second two tasks than on the first two. An ongoing attitude change process should at least prevent such a difference from becoming more pronounced. Nevertheless, it might still be argued that with partitioned cubicles, a relatively long period of time is required before subjects become impressed with the fact that one member is a Negro; and still later, more time is needed for failure and status loss to sink in. Thus, the experiment may have obtained a sample of behavior when the subjects had fully noted the presence of the Negro but before the shared threat had an appreciable effect on communication. On this basis it would be predicted that if more than four

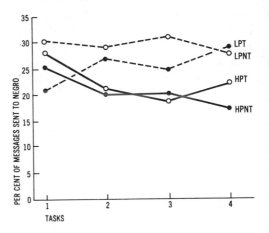

Fig 1. Percentage of Messages Sent to Negro Confederate by Low Prejudiced, Nonthreatened (LPNT) Groups, High Prejudiced, Nonthreatened (HPNT) Groups, Low Prejudiced, Threatened (LPT) Groups, and High Prejudiced, Threatened (HPT) Groups over the Four Tasks.

tasks were given, subjects in the HPT condition would eventually begin to increase communication with the confederate.

A second line of reasoning assumes that avoidance of communication is a less direct form of hostile expression than rating the person as poor with respect to certain valued attributes. It also focuses on what is being affected by the induction of shared threat. Are prejudiced attitudes being remolded, or are the expressions of hostility stemming from such attitudes being inhibited without any underlying attitude change? If attitude change had occurred under shared threat, less overall hostility, direct and indirect, should be expressed toward the confederate. This did not occur. If, however, shared threat served to inhibit direct aggression without modifying prejudiced attitudes, our expectation would be quite different. In this case, it would be anticipated that high prejudiced individuals confronted by a common threat would express a smaller amount of direct hostility toward a minority group member than equally prejudiced but unthreatened individuals. Both groups, nevertheless, would be expected to express a similar amount of indirect hostility (avoidance of communication with the Negro) which would be greater than that manifested by less prejudiced individuals.

Finally, discriminatory behavior based on cultural norms and the affective orientation toward Negroes may under certain conditions be uncorrelated. One can follow the discriminatory practices of one's group without necessarily entertaining feelings of hostility. This suggests a third possible interpretation. Since about 75% of the items on the prejudice scale used in this study concern appropriate behavior toward Negroes, a high anti-Negro prejudice score may indicate that the person has strongly internalized the discriminatory behavior patterns of Texas culture. The strength of these norms regarding behavior may not be appreciably modified by a momentary event in a temporary group. Thus, the shared threat induced may have produced a positive change in the affective orientation toward the Negro group member while having no influence on conformity to cultural patterns which stress avoidance of equal status interaction.

SUMMARY

The purpose of this experiment was to test the relationship between shared threat and the expression of prejudice hypothesized by Feshbach and Singer (1957). Forty-eight subjects, varying with respect to anti-Negro prejudice, were placed under conditions of shared threat or nonthreat, in task oriented, cooperative work groups. A Negro confederate was a member in each group.

It was found, as hypothesized, that under conditions of shared threat a reduction in the expression of prejudice occurs in terms of direct evaluation of the Negro by other group members on a posttask questionnaire. No significant differences in the amount of communication to the confederate occurred as a result of the threat induction. However, significantly fewer messages were addressed to the Negro by the high prejudiced subjects, regardless of the presence or absence of shared threat.

REFERENCES

BETTELHEIM, B. "Individual and Mass Behavior in Extreme Situations." *J. abnorm. soc. Psychol.*, 1943, 38, 417–452.

COHEN, E. A. *Human Behavior in the Concentration Camp*. New York: Norton, 1953.

DEUTSCH, M. "The Effects of Cooperation and Competition upon Group Processes." In D. Cartwright & A. Zander (Eds.), *Group Dynamics Research and Theory*. Evanston, Ill.: Row, Peterson, 1953, Pp. 319–353.

FESHBACH, S., and SINGER, R. "The Effects of Personal and Shared Threat upon Social Prejudice." *J. abnorm. soc. Psychol.*, 1957, 54, 411–416.

FESTINGER, L., CARTWRIGHT, D., BARBER, KATHLEEN, FLEISCHL, JULIET, GOTTSDANKER, JOSEPHINE, KEYSEN, ANNETTE, and LEAVITT, GLORIA. "A Study of a Rumor: Its Origin and Spread." *Hum. Relat.*, 1948, 1, 464–486.

FESTINGER, L., SCHACHTER, S., and BACK, K. *Social Pressures in Informal Groups: A Study of a Housing Community*. New York: Harper, 1950.

FRENCH, J. R. P., JR. "The Disruption and Cohesion of Groups." *J. Psychol.*, 1941, 36, 361–377.

JACOBSON, E., and SCHACHTER, S. (Eds.) "Cross-National Research: A Case Study." *J. soc. Issues*, 1954, 10(4), 5–68.

KELLEY, J. G., FERSON, J. E., and HOLTZMAN, W. H. "The Measurement of Attitudes Toward the Negro in the South." *J. soc. Psychol.*, 1958, 48, 305–317.

KILLIAN, L. M. "The Significance of Multiple-Group Membership in Disaster." *Amer. J. Social.*, 1952, 57, 309–314.

LEAVITT, H. J. "Some Effects of Certain Communication Patterns on Group Performance." *J. abnorm. soc. Psychol.*, 1951, 46, 38–50.

LEIGHTON, A. *The Governing of Men*. Princeton: Princeton Univer. Press, 1945.

PEPITONE, A., and KLEINER, R. "The Effects of Threat and Frustration on Group Cohesiveness." *J. abnorm. soc. Psychol.*, 1957, 54, 192–199.

POTASHIN, R. "A Sociometric Study of Children's Friendships." *Sociometry*, 1946, 9, 48–70.

SCHACHTER, S. "Deviation, Rejection, and Communication." In D. Cartwright and A. Zander (Eds.), *Group Dynamics Research and Theory*. Evanston, Ill.: Row, Peterson, 1960. Pp. 223–248.

SCHACHTER, S., NUTTIN, J., DEMONCHAUX, CECILY, MAUCORPS, P. H., OSMER, D., DUIJKER, H., ROMMETVEIT, R., and ISRAEL, J. "Cross-cultural Experiments on Threat and Rejection." *Hum. Relat.*, 1954, 7, 403–440.

SHERIF, M., and SHERIF, C. *Groups in Harmony and Tension*. New York: Harpers, 1943.

WRIGHT, M. E. "The Influence of Frustration on the Social Relations of Children." *Charact. Pers.*, 1943, 12, 111–122.

PRENEGOTIATION EXPERIENCE AND DYADIC CONFLICT RESOLUTION IN A BARGAINING SITUATION*

Daniel Druckman

Several conditions of prenegotiation experience were compared for their efficacy in facilitating conflict resolution between opposing team representatives. Participants played roles of union or company representatives in a simulation of the collective bargaining process. Prenegotiation experience that involved unstructured discussion, from a unilateral perspective, among teammates, or bilateral study with an opposing representative, irrespective of whether he was to be a bargaining opponent, facilitated resolution. Team consultation that included spelling out strategies and rationale produced resistance to resolution, but bargainers in this condition were no more resistant than those in a control condition consisting of essentially no prenegotiation experience. Other effects of formal strategy preparation before bargaining included more consensus, among teammates, on the ranked importance of the issues, more perceived commitment to the team positions, and a consideration of the debate as more of a "win-lose" competition than the other conditions. Also, the results indicate that the perception of the debate as a "win-lose" contest or as a "problem-solving" collaboration may be an intervening variable, linking prenegotiation experience with negotiation behavior.

Several investigators in the area of intergroup conflict resolution have highlighted the role of group commitment or group loyalty as an important source of constraint on the resolution of conflicts between groups (e.g., Blake and Mouton, 1962; Sherif and Sherif, 1965; Withey and Katz, 1965). However, Druckman (1967) claimed that a number of experiments on intergroup conflict resolution confounded group representation with team postion-planning before intergroup confrontation (e.g., Bass and Dunteman, 1963; Blake and Mouton, 1962; Sherif, Harvey, White, Hood, and Sherif, 1961). It was hypothesized[1] that this experience before confrontation, rather than group loyalty per se, was responsible for the ob-

---

* Daniel Druckman, "Prenegotiation Experience and Dyadic Conflict Resolution in a Bargaining Situation," *Journal of Experimental Social Psychology*, 4 (1968), 367–83. Reprinted by permission of Academic Press, Inc.

---

[1] Blake and Mouton (1962) observed adult representatives negotiating over which group produced the best product while Sherif *et al.* (1961) manipulated competition between children's camp groups. In the former study, deadlock was the invariable result. This finding has been replicated by others, notably by Bass and Dunteman (1963).

served resistant behavior.[1] In that experiment prenegotiation experience was separated from group representation in a complex bargaining situation. It was found that when opposing teams or individuals planned positions or strategies apart from one another before bargaining (unilateral strategy) they were more resistant to compromise than when opponents discussed the issues together before bargaining (bilateral study). However, group representatives were no more resistant to resolving the conflict than were individuals who represented themselves. In fact, the prenegotiation experience main effect was large and consistent for all of the measures of conflict resolution while the group-representation–self-representation main effect accounted for a negligible portion of the variance on each measure. This large prenegotiation effect merits further investigation.

Teams (or individuals) in the unilateral-strategy condition created in Druckman (1967) were: (a) separated before bargaining, (b) focusing on their own positions, and (e) preparing rationale or strategies for bargaining. In the contrasting bilateral-study condition teams (or individuals) were: (a) together before bargaining, (b) focusing on both positions, and (c) not preparing strategies or rationale for their own positions. Thus the two conditions differed in terms of the structural arrangement of the competing teams (apart versus together) as well as the type of activity engaged in during the session (plan strategies versus study and discuss). Since these factors were not separated, their relative contribution to the resulting differences in bargaining behavior could not be determined. The activity of strategy formation may not have provided any

additional constraint on resolution attempts beyond that imposed by team separation and unilateral focus. That is, it remains to be determined whether unilateral focus versus bilateral focus contributed most of the variance between the conditions or whether the addition of strategy preparation to unilateral focus accounted for the large differences obtained.

The constraints on position change as a function of team separation and constraints due to strategy preparation (or the effort that goes into such preparation) are both documented in the literature. With reference to the Blake and Mouton (1962) experiments, Ferguson and Kelley (1964) claimed that as a result of unilateral discussion of a team product a person sees more of its positive features than one who has not had the same experience. The tendency to focus on the ingroup position prevents opponents from delineating the "region of validity" in the other's stand or position (Hammond, Todd, Wilkins, and Mitchell, 1966; Rapoport, 1961). Rapoport (1961) suggested a conflict-resolving technique that involves; (a) restating accurately the other person's position, (b) exploring areas of agreement in the opponent's stand, and (c) inducing assumptions of similarity. None of these activities is likely to be engaged in when bargaining opponents remain reticent. Bilateral discussion, before bargainers have a chance to focus on their own position, may be a necessary precondition for applying the "region of validity" technique.

However, there is some evidence that indicates that unilateral focus without formal position-planning may not provide any more restraint on resolution attempts than does bilateral focus. Hammond *et al.* (1966) reported no differences in overt compromise or cognitive change between subjects in unilateral and bilateral focus (using the "region of validity" technique) conditions. However, in a similar experimental-task situation, when pairs of subjects were told to adopt a problem-solving, system-building orientation toward the problem (or were given a set to be analytical) they developed more initial conflict and had less of a tendency to compromise during the conflict session than subjects who were told to adopt a "hunch-playing" or intuitive orientation for dealing with the problem during training (Rappoport, 1965). Thus it appears that when unilateral focus is augmented with the preparation of rationale or strategies before debate, bargaining opponents are more resistant to reaching an agreement.

Discussions of international negotiations among career diplomats have noted the cognitive constraint produced by position formation. For example, Rusk (1955) commented that "if negotiations between representatives were to occur before a fixed position was taken, the possibility of reaching an acceptable solution might be increased" (see also Blake, 1959, and Pearson, 1959). Implications for this problem may also be drawn from experimentation, stimulated by the dissonance-theory formulation, on the effects of effort on subsequent attitudes and behavior. Lewis (1965), in a review of work in this area, concluded that "the data on the effect of the expenditure of effort on the value of a stimulus event associated with effort indicates that value can be enhanced by effort" (see Aronson, 1961, and Festinger and Aronson, 1969). A hypothesized concomitant of high evaluation is commitment. The more committed one is to a position, the more dissonant it is to give

in to an opposing position. Thus the successful use of techniques for inducing commitment should produce resistance to yielding.

The intention of this study was to investigate the effects of several prenegotiation-experience conditions on the resistance to or facilitation of resolution in a conflict-of-interest situation. The investigator sought to determine whether team consultation about an impending negotiation produces rigidity because positions are usually taken during these sessions, or simply because of the experience of meeting with a team. Two prenegotiation sessions that involved team separation were compared to a session in which team members studied the issues with a member of the opposing team before debate. In the latter condition team members consulted with a member of the opposing team who was not to be a future bargaining opponent. Thus the activity of bilateral study was not confused with communication with a future bargaining opponent. Also, in order to determine the effects of previous interaction per se, a condition was created in which bargainers had essentially no prenegotiation experience. A description of the prenegotiation conditions created for this study is followed by the task procedure.

METHOD

Prenegotiation Conditions

The task was a simulation of the collective bargaining process. In three of the conditions a prenegotiation session, which lasted for approximately 40 minutes, preceded the bargaining. Four types of prenegotiation sessions were designed for this study. In two conditions teams were separated before bargaining. The instructions for one of these conditions were specific with regard to the way in which positions were to be prepared, while in the other condition the instructions emphasized more informality and less effort in preparing for the debate.[2] The instructions for the *unilateral position-formation* condition were as follows:

> The next 40 minutes will be spent with your own team. You are to use this time to plan your bargaining strategy. First gain an understanding of the issues. Then you are to plan a formal position for entering into bargaining. You are to write down, as a team, and so that each person has a copy, a list of points defining the rationale or arguments for your team's position on each issue. This strategy should be prepared so as to guide the bargainers through the negotiations. You may decide on items that you think each man representing you should remain firm on. It may also in-

clude potential concessions, anticipations for trading, setting goals, and the like.

After the bargaining session, the experimenter examined the written rationale to make sure that both teams complied with the instructions.

A *unilateral-discussion* condition was created in order to separate unilateral experience from formal position preparation. The instructions were as follows:

> The next 40 minutes will be spent with your own team. We want you to use this time to gain an understanding of your situation and the issues. You are to discuss the issues among yourselves. While you may do some strategy, you are not to plan a formal position to enter into bargaining with. In other words, it is not necessary to write anything down or to formulate a list of points defining the rationale or arguments for a team position. Just discuss the issues informally among yourselves. The purpose of this session is to give you a "frame of reference," gained through familiarity with the issues, with which to enter the negotiations. In order to do this we feel that the most effective procedure is through informal discussion with one's own team.

Through observation of these sessions it appeared that participants were concentrating on supportive arguments for their team's assigned positions, but formal position formation did not take place.

In the *bilateral-study* condition, the bargainers were divided into three study pairs made up of a member from each team. The study pairs were separated into three corners of the laboratory. The composition of the dyads was determined randomly, with the restriction that the opposing representatives could not compete against each other in the bargaining session. (In the former study, bilateral study was not separated from communication with a future bargaining opponent. It is conceivable that this latter factor, apart from the activity of study, may have facilitated resolution.) The emphasis in this

---

[2] The latter instructions represented an attempt to separate unilateral experience from unilateral formal position-formation. The *unilateral-strategy* condition, created in Druckman (1967), was perhaps ambiguous with regard to the specific means to be used in strategy preparation. The nature of the activity of team members during the unilateral strategy session was not homogeneous across all sessions. It appeared that while some teams were putting in a great deal of effort in preparing formal positions for debate, other teams spent most of the allotted time discussing the issues from a unilateral perspective without preparing formal positions. Each of these activities is perhaps represented in the two unilateral conditions created in this study. Team members in the unilateral position-formation condition were to prepare formal positions, while informal discussion characterized those in the unilateral-discussion condition. Thus, it might be expected that the former condition would produce more rigidity while the latter condition would result in less rigidity than the unilateral-strategy condition.

condition was on bilateral focus and mutual understanding. The instructions were as follows:

> The next 40 minutes will be spent in bilateral study. You are to use this time for learning as much as possible about Company and Union perspectives. We feel that the best way to achieve this is to split the teams up into study pairs made up of a member of each team. The pairs were randomly chosen before this session. Study the issues in order to gain understanding of both points of view as well as areas of greater or lesser agreement between proponents of either. Do not formulate or plan strategies for bargaining from either position. Do not take a position and argue its merits.
>
> The discussion should not break down into an inter-term competition. If it does the experimenter will stop it and remind participants of the goal. You should try to act bipartisan with respect to the issues during this session. There is no need to use any form of propaganda in order to obtain later gains. Openly discuss the issues. The emphasis is on informality and there is no one observing you or recording data. Understanding is the goal!

While the experimenter did not actively interfere with any study dyad, he maintained some degree of surveillance to make sure that the participants were "studying" and not bargaining or competing.

A fourth condition was created in which bargainers had essentially no prenegotiation experience. All participants were given 10 minutes before the bargaining session to familiarize themselves, individually, with the issues and background information. No intra- or inter-team experience took place before bargaining. The purpose of this condition was to assess whether certain prenegotiation conditions *facilitated* resolution or whether other conditions produced a *restraint* on resolution attempts. This is referred to below as a *control* condition.

Data from the *unilateral-strategy* condition and from the *bilateral-study* condition, reported in Druckman (1967), will be referred to. Bargaining outcomes from the two unilateral conditions created in this study were compared to the outcomes resulting from the unilateral-strategy condition in the former study. Also, bilateral study apart from a future bargaining opponent was compared to bilateral study with a future bargaining opponent, a condition created in the earlier study.

Selection of Participants

In order to increase identification with the assigned positions, participants were chosen on the basis of their attitudes toward labor unions and management. Another selection criterion consisted of scores on a modification of the Dogmatism Scale. Items from the Labor-Management Scale and the Modified Dogmatism Scale were administered together to a large sample of Northwestern University undergraduate psychology students. Respondents were informed that we were interested in recruiting people with similar attitudes for participation in an interesting experiment. As soon as both scales were scored, eligible respondents (upper and lower quartiles on both scales) were recruited by phone and session times were arranged.[3]

Since dogmatic attitudes (or attitudes toward resistance to compromise) were found to relate to resolution behavior (Druckman, 1967), an equal number of high- and low-dogmatic sessions were conducted in each condition. Also, an equal number of sessions with male and female participants were included in each condition. Each run of the simulation was homogeneous by attitude-disposition and by sex. There were twelve bargaining dyads per condition, three in each combination of sex and dogmatic attitudes. Since three dyads were included in each

---

[3] The correlation between the scales was .01. There was thus no trouble in recruiting pro-labor and pro-company respondents who scored at both ends of the Modified Dogmatism Scale.

group session, there were two sessions with male participants, two sessions with female participants, two high-dogmatic sessions, and two low-dogmatic sessions, for each of the four prenegotiation conditions.[4] Across the four conditions, 96 subjects or 48 dyads participated. The mean score on the Labor-Management Attitudes Scale for the company representatives was 90.31 $(V = .098)$, while the mean for the union representatives was 63.79 $(V = .087)$.[5]

Procedure

One intention of this investigation was to determine which factor was responsible for the large prenegotiation-experience effect found in the previous study. Thus it was necessary to maintain comparability by employing the same task, setting, subject population, and selection criteria. The following is a brief synopsis of the task, which is described in more detail in Druckman (1967).

The prenegotiation conditions used in this study necessitated the use of laboratory

---

[4] Crowne (1966) presented data showing a relationship between family orientation and competitive choices in a prisoner's dilemma game. In an attempt to determine whether this relationship held for a complex bargaining situation, dyads were also homogeneous with regard to family orientation. An equal number of "entrepreneurial" and "bureaucratic" pairs were placed in each condition and for each sex (i.e., this variable was not confounded with condition or sex). No relationship was found between this variable and any measure of resolution behavior.

[5] V is the coefficient of variability $(V = s/\bar{x})$. These means are almost identical to those of the previous study $(\bar{x} = 80.47$ and $\bar{x} = 62.73)$. Also, the means for the high-dogmatic and low-dogmatic participants were very similar to those reported in the earlier study (145.13 versus 143.70 and 113.31 versus 112.96).

group representatives rather than individuals who represented themselves. Since the group-representation–self-representation variable accounted for a negligible portion of the variance on any measure of conflict resolution, it is assumed that these findings have implications for bargainers representing themselves as well as for group representatives. The task was a non-zero-sum simulation of the collective bargaining process. Participants were assigned to a three-man union or company team of the hypothetical Acme Steel Corporation. They were told that this assignment was based on their attitudes as expressed on a questionnaire filled out some weeks earlier. Members assigned to the same team had similar attitudes. Each team received four issues, each arranged on a 17-step continuum with the starting positions of each side at either end. Between the starting positions were possible compromises that might have been considered. The issues were *wages, off-the-job training, hospital plan*, and *paid vacation*. Below each position on the issue scale the estimated cost to the company for the duration of the contract was listed. In order to give bargainers a common perspective, a page of background information was provided. This contained a brief statement of union and company rationale for each of their demands, and "going rates" at four other similar hypothetical companies in the industry. However, the amount of information supplied was limited in an attempt to insure that the teams would be given sufficient latitude to be flexible in deciding on a mutually agreeable position.

The first phase consisted of the prenegotiation manipulation. Following this, members from both teams were brought together to rank, independently, the issues in terms of importance. Then the representatives from both teams were randomly divided into three bargaining dyads. In order to insure independence, the pairs were separated into three corners of the room and screens were placed around each table. Any given dyad was kept virtually unaware of the progress, situation, or completion of any other pair of bargainers. To make sure that team identification was maintained, the representatives were told that the results of all bargaining dyads would be combined to yield team totals. Thus each subject was bargaining for his team and, perhaps, expected to be measured against how well his two colleagues fared. This competitive set was pitted against the advantages of a quick settlement. The latter pressure was created by informing the bargainers that each five minutes of debate time would result in a loss of $5,000 to each side in lost wages or profits due to the prolongation of the strike. Five minutes simulated one day of negotiation. The experimenter served as a "referee" and announced each five minutes of debate time.

There was a 30-minute (or six-"day") time limit on debate. If all issues were not settled in this period of time, deadlock ensued. Bargainers were provided with contracts. They were told to circle the position of settlement on any settled issue and to initial their contract beside the issue. If an issue was not settled at the deadline, they were asked to indicate, independently, how far they were willing to go in order to get an agreement on the issue. At the conclusion of bargaining all participants filled out postnegotiation questionnaires while the "simulation manager" combined the results across the dyads in order to provide feedback on team totals.

RESULTS

Conflict Resolution

The means and standard deviations for six conditions of prenegotiation experience for each of three dyadic measures of conflict resolution are presented in Table 1. The effect of the manipulated conditions was assessed across the two bargainers as well as across the four issues.

The behavior of one bargainer was not independent of his opponent and the independence of the four issues during debate was questionable.

Speed of resolution. The harmonic mean time to complete the contract (the reciprocal of the mean of the reciprocals of the original values) was used as a measure of speed of resolution. A reciprocal transformation was performed on time to complete the contract in order to insure stability in the variances (Edwards, 1960) and so that deadlocks could be taken into consideration. Deadlocks were assumed to be settled in an infinite amount of time. Since the reciprocal of infinity is zero, deadlocks could be treated as zero values and included in a distribution with the reciprocals of all the other obtained values. The harmonic mean times (see Table 1) are inflated due to deadlocks.

The differences in speed of resolution between the four conditions of this study are significant ($F = 3.14$, 3 and 44 *df*, $p < .05$). Unilateral position-formation resulted in slower resolution than did unilateral discussion ($t = 2.19$, 22 *df*, $p < .05$)[6] or bilateral study apart from a future bargaining opponent ($t = 2.58$, 22 *df*, $p < .02$). The difference in speed of resolution between unilateral discussion and bilateral study apart from a bargaining opponent is small and nonsignificant. Dyads in the control condition were slower to resolve the conflict than those in both the unilateral-discussion ($t = 1.86$, 22 *df*, $.50 < p < .10$) and bilateral-study conditions ($t = 2.13$, 22 *df*, $p < .05$). However,

---

[6] All of the reported probability levels are for two-tailed tests.

Table 1

Means and Standard Deviations for Six Conditions of Prenegotiation Experience on Three Measures of Conflict Resolution

Condition	Speed of resolution (minutes)		Average distance apart		Average yielding	
	Mean	S.D.	Mean	S.D.	Mean	S.D.
Unilateral position-formation	101.85	.018	2.021	2.018	7.365	.909
Control	78.74	.019	1.521	1.646	7.323	.716
Unilateral strategy[a]	49.93	.022	1.592	2.249	7.292	.982
Unilateral discussion	31.56	.030	.458	.714	7.771	.357
Bilateral study apart from future bargaining opponent	33.92	.019	.396	.808	7.844	.366
Bilateral study with future bargaining opponent[a]	23.55	.042	.458	.833	7.771	.416

[a] These data are from Druckman (1967) and are based on 30 dyads in each condition.

the difference between the controls and the unilateral position-formation condition is nonsignificant. The hypothesized effect of the two unilateral conditions in producing both more (in the case of unilateral position-formation) and less (in the case of unilateral discussion) resistance to resolution than the unilateral-strategy condition, reported in Druckman (1967), is supported. The harmonic mean for the latter condition fell between the means for the two conditions created in this study. The difference between the unilateral position-formation ($N = 12$ dyads) and unilateral-strategy conditions ($N = 30$ dyads) approached significance ($t = 1.77$, 40 df, $0.5 < p < .10$). Also, bilateral study with a future opponent resulted in slightly faster resolution than bilateral study apart from a future opponent, but the difference is nonsignificant ($t = 1.01$).

Average distance apart and average yielding. These measures are represented in Table 1 as dyadic means taken across all four issues. Distance apart refers to the number of steps on an issue scale (each issue was arranged on a 17-step scale) separating the bargainers' final positions at the conclusion of bargaining, while yielding refers to the average number of steps on the scale that a bargaining dyad moved from their respective starting positions. The differences between the four conditions of this study, on average distance apart, are significant ($F = 3.89$, 3 and 44 df, $p < .05$). Bargainers were further apart after unilateral position-formation than after either unilateral discussion ($t = 2.53$, 22 df, $p < .02$) or bilateral study apart from a future bargaining opponent ($t = 2.59$, 22 df, $p < .02$). Also, the control dyads were further apart than those in both the unilateral-discussion ($t = 2.05$, 22 df, $.05 < p < .10$) and bilateral-study conditions ($t = 2.13$, 22 df, $p < .05$), but the difference between the controls and unilateral position-formation was nonsignificant ($t = .67$, $p > .10$). As with the speed-of-resolution measure, the average distance apart for the unilateral-strategy condition, reported in Druckman (1967), fell between the means for the two unilateral conditions created in this experiment. The difference between unilateral strategy ($N = 30$ dyads) and unilateral discussion ($N = 12$ dyads) approached significance ($t = 1.70$, 40 *df*, $.05 < p < .10$). The mean differences between unilateral discussion, bilateral study apart from a bargaining opponent, and bilateral study with a bargaining opponent are small and nonsignificant.

A similar pattern of findings was obtained for the average-yielding measure. The control dyads were more resistant than the unilateral-discussion ($t = 1.94$, 22 *df*, $p < .10$) and bilateral-study conditions ($t = 2.24$, 22 *df*, $p < .05$), but did not differ from the unilateral position-formation dyads. While the unilateral position-formation dyads were more resistant to yielding than dyads in the unilateral-discussion and bilateral-study conditions, the differences did not quite reach significance. Also, unilateral discussion did not differ from bilateral study in average yielding.

Number of unresolved issues. Table 2 shows the number of contracts or dyads with 0, 1, 2, 3, or 4 unsettled issues for each condition. A Kruskel-Wallis one-way analysis of variance (see Siegel, 1956) showed the differences between the conditions to be highly significant ($H = 13.60$, 3 *df*, $p < .01$). The results of Mann-Whitney U tests, corrected for ties, indicate that unilateral position-formation led to a higher rate of unsettled issues per contract than did unilateral discussion ($U = 42$, $p < .10$) or bilateral study apart from a bargaining opponent ($U = 31$, $p < .02$). The control dyads had a higher rate of unresolved issues than did bilateral study ($U = 40.5$, $p < .10$), but did not differ significantly from unilateral position-formation or unilateral discussion. As with the other measures, the difference between unilateral discussion and bilateral study apart from a bargaining opponent was small and nonsignificant.

Differential Effectiveness of Manipulations in Producing Perceived Commitment

The amount of perceived commitment to the assigned positions and the extent to which the debate is perceived as a "win-lose" competition rather than as a "problem-solving" venture may be inter-

Table 2

NUMBER OF DAYS WITH 0, 1, 2, 3, OR 4 UNRESOLVED ISSUES FOR FOUR CONDITIONS OF PRENEGOTIATION EXPERIENCE

Condition	Number of unresolved issues					
	0	1	2	3	4	*N*
Unilateral position-formation	3	2	2	1	4	12
Control	4	2	3	2	1	12
Unilateral discussion	7	2	1	1	1	12
Bilateral study apart from future bargaining opponent	9	1	1	1	0	12
Total	23	7	7	5	6	48

vening variables accounting for the bargaining outcomes (e.g., see Gladstone, 1962) or concomitant effects of the "win-lose" syndrome (e.g., see Blake and Mouton, 1962) produced in differing degrees by the manipulations. The results of two postnegotiation questions are presented as evidence for these perceptual counterparts of the observed bargaining behavior. Representatives were asked to indicate, on a five-step scale, "how committed you felt to the positions that you or your team took?" The scale ranged from "extremely committed" (1) to "quite noncommitted" (5). Bargainers from the unilateral position-formation condition felt more committed ($\bar{x} = 2.09$) than bargainers from both the unilateral-discussion condition ($\bar{x} = 2.42$) and the bilateral-study condition ($\bar{x} = 2.71$). The mean for the control conditions ($\bar{x} = 2.46$) was about the same as that for the unilateral-discussion condition. The difference between the means for unilateral position-formation and unilateral discussion approached significance ($t = 1.83$, 45 df, $p < .10$), as did the difference between the former condition and the controls ($t = 1.73$, 45 df, $p < .10$). A highly significant difference was obtained between unilateral position-formation and bilateral study ($t = 2.99$, 45 df, $p < .001$). The mean differences between the controls, unilateral discussion, and bilateral study were nonsignificant.

Representatives were also asked to indicate, on a six-step scale, "the extent to which you perceived the situation as a win-lose debate with both sides committed to a position or as a problem-solving venture in which both teams collaborated in order to reach a compromise or settlement." The scale ranged from "win-lose" (1) to "collaboration" (6).

The order of the conditions in terms of the perception of a "win-lose" contest is: unilateral position-formation ($x = 3.70$), controls ($x = 4.04$), unilateral discussion ($x = 4.46$), and bilateral study ($x = 4.83$). The difference between the means for unilateral position-formation and unilateral discussion approached significance ($t = 1.90$, 45 df, $p < .10$), while the difference between the former condition and bilateral study was highly significant ($t = 3.08$, 45 df, $p < .001$). Also the controls differed significantly from bilateral study ($t = 2.28$, 46 df, $p < .05$). Thus, as a result of strategy planning before bargaining, bargainers felt more committed to the assigned positions and considered the debate to be more of a "win-lose" contest than did representatives in the other conditions. The next step is to determine the relationship between these variables and bargaining behavior.

Correlations were computed between the two postnegotiation questions, and between the average response to each question by both members of a bargaining dyad and the measures of dyadic conflict resolution. Position commitment and the perception of a "win-lose" debate were strongly related ($r = .54$, $p < .01$). The correlations between perceived commitment and each measure of conflict resolution are as follows: speed ($r = .19$, $p > .05$), distance apart ($r = -.33$, $p < .05$), yielding ($r = .20$, $p > .05$), and number of unresolved issues ($rho = -.35$, $p < .05$). The extent to which the debate was considered as a "win-lose" contest was related to each measures as follows: speed ($r = .34$, $p < .05$), distance apart ($r = -.60$, $p < .01$), yielding ($r = .50$, $p < .01$), and number of unresolved issues ($rho = -.43$, $p <$

.01). It appears that the tendency to consider the bargaining task as a "win-lose" contest with both sides committed to positions was strongly related to resolution behavior, and was also characteristic of bargainers in the position-formation condition and, to a lesser extent, of those in the control condition. Perceived commitment to the assigned positions was also related to resolution behavior but the correlations were not so large.

Consensus among Teammates on the Ranked Importance of the Issues

Another hypothesized effect of formal position-formation is that it produces team solidarity, as reflected in agreement among members with regard to stands on issues and the relative importance of issues. An index of the extent to which consensus is produced among team members as a result of prenegotiation experience is agreement on the ranked importance of the issues. After the prenegotiation session, members from both teams were brought together to rank, independently, the issues in terms of importance. Position-formation may be expected to produce more consensus on ranked importance than unilateral discussion. If, as a result of unilateral discussion, team members "focus on the ingroup positions," they should be more consensual on the ranking of the issues than teams from the bilateral-study or control conditions, where there was no ingroup experience prior to bargaining. That is, team experience per se may be expected to produce some degree of consensus with regard to the issues. Thus unilateral position-formation should have resulted in more agreement among team members

than unilateral discussion and bilateral study in that order. The controls would not be expected to differ from bilateral study.

The method for determining the extent of agreement among three members of a team (there were eight teams per condition) was to take the absolute differences between the ranks assigned each issue by each member and to sum the differences. The "agreement scores" were ranked, and Mann-Whitney U tests were performed (see Siegel, 1956). The hypothesis was confirmed. Unilateral position-formation before bargaining resulted in significantly more agreement among team members on the ranked importance of the issues than did unilateral discussion ($U = 16.5$, $p < .052$), bilateral study apart from a future bargaining opponent ($U = 5.5$, $p < .002$), and the control condition ($U = 1$, $p < .001$). Unilateral discussion resulted in more agreement among team members than bilateral study ($U = 17.5$, $p < .065$) and the control condition ($U = 12$, $p < .02$). The controls did not differ from bilateral study ($U = 26.5$, $p > .10$). Thus, as predicted, the order of the conditions is as follows: UPF > UD > C = BS. Also, unilateral position-formation resulted in more agreement among team members that the unilateral condition reported in Druckman (1967) ($U = 24$, $N_1 = S$, $N_2 = 20$, $p < .01$). Perhaps it is even more interesting to note that there was perfect agreement among the three members of almost every team in the unilateral position-formation condition. Clearly, this condition produced dramatic effects on team consensus as reflected in private and independent ratings.

Amount of consensus was not unrelated to other characteristics of the "win-lose" syndrome. Amount of perceived commitment to positions and the extent to which the debate was considered to be a "win-lose" contest were averaged over the three members of each team and correlations[7] were computed between these variables and amount of consensus. The average perceived commitment to the positions by team members was strongly related to the amount of consensus on the issue ranking ($rho = .61$, $p < .01$). The amount of team consensus was also related to the extent to which the debate was considered as a "win-lose" contest ($rho = .37$, $p < .10$).

DISCUSSION

The immediately apparent contrast suggested by these findings is that between the unilateral position-formation and control conditions on the one hand and the unilateral-discussion and bilateral-study conditions on the other. When teams prepared strategies and attempted to justify their assigned positions before debate, their representatives found it difficult to achieve agreements. Nine out of twelve bargaining dyads ended in deadlock and four of these could not agree on any of the four issues. However, this high rate of resistant behavior did not differ significantly from the resolution behavior of bargaining dyads in the control condition. Representatives who bargained without a prenegotiation session were also highly resistant to conflict resolution. Eight out of the twelve bargaining dyads in this condition ended in deadlock.

The provision of certain types of

---

[7] Since "amount of consensus" was considered to be an ordinal variable, Spearman rank-correlation coefficients (rho) were computed.

prenegotiation experience apparently *facilitated* the achievement of resolution. Opponents who bargained after consultation or informal discussion with members of their own team or with members of the opposing team had little trouble in reaching agreements and were more cooperative than the control dyads. A very interesting and, perhaps, unexpected finding was that bargaining dyads, after informal discussion with teammates, were only slightly (and nonsignificantly) more rigid than those dyads whose prenegotiation experience involved consultation with a member of the opposing team using a bilateral-focus technique.

An implication of these results is that informal discussion before debate that is concentrated on the issues is a technique for inducing cooperation. Whether the informal discussion consists of unilateral focus with teammates or bilateral focus with opponents seems to make little difference in bargaining outcomes. (This finding is attributable to the greater amount of cooperation in the unilateral-discussion condition, rather than to the lesser amount of cooperation in the bilateral-study conditions.) These results do not, however, imply that the activity of generating supportive arguments and bargaining strategies predisposes bargainers to be more competitive. It is interesting to note the parallel between this pattern of result and that obtained by Harrison and McClintock (1965) in a study which employed a prisoner's dilemma game. These investigators explored the relationship between reward for previous cooperative behavior between members of a dyad and cooperative choices on the prisoner's dilemma task. They also manipulated the time period (immediate versus delayed) between the previous dyadic interaction and the game. Significantly more cooperative responses were made in the re-ward-immediate, reward-delay, and the nonreward-delay conditions than in the nonreward-immediate condition. However, the nonreward-immediate condition did not differ from a control group where members had no previous interaction experience. Thus, the nonreward-immediate condition did not increase competition but the former conditions served to induce cooperation. The unanticipated high level of cooperation demonstrated by dyads in the nonreward-delay condition of the Harrison and McClintock (1965) study parallels the obtained, and unanticipated, high level of cooperation by dyads in the unilateral-discussion condition of this investigation.

Rapoport's (1961) notion of bilateral focus as a conflict-resolving mechanism is only partially supported. The bilateral-study conditions did produce more cooperation than the control and position-formation conditions. However, it appears that a Rapoport-type debate is not much better than unstructured discussion among teammates. As mentioned earlier, Hammond *et al.* (1966), investigating noncompetitive conflict, also failed to obtain a difference between an "Own Focus" and a "Region of Validity" condition. While there was clearly no difference between these conditions in this study that approached significance, on any measure of conflict resolution, there was a slight tendency for bargainers in the unilateral-discussion condition to be somewhat more resistant to compromise. Perhaps if a "technique" for *unilateral focus* were more clearly spelled out in instructions for the unilateral-discussion condition, bargaining outcomes for dyads in this condition may have more closely resembled those obtained in the control condition. It is conceivable that the lack of difference

between unilateral discussion and bilateral study reflected the tendency of the simulated representatives, in both conditions, to engage in similar activity.

There is evidence which indicates that the structural arrangement of groups (viz., unilateral versus bilateral) per se, apart from unilateral or bilateral focus, makes little difference in resolution outcomes. Bass (1966), in a recent study that employed a similar labor-management bargaining task, found no difference in speed of resolution between unilateral-study and bilateral-study conditions. Bargainers in both unilateral and bilateral arrangements were instructed to focus on and gain understanding of both positions. Thus it appears that unilateral focus among teammates without formal position-preparation facilitates resolution as much as unilateral or bilateral study. It is also interesting to note that in the Bass (1966) study, bargainers from a unilateral-strategy condition, similar to the one created in Druckman (1967), were slower in resolving the conflict than those in three types of group-study conditions—with participants representing the same position, with members representing opposing positions, and bilateral-study groups including bargaining opponents. In this investigation a similar pattern obtained, with bargainers from the unilateral-strategy condition being somewhat slower in resolving the conflict than those in the unilateral-discussion and bilateral-study conditions.[8]

---

[8] In the Bass (1966) study the type of activity was the same for both unilateral and bilateral arrangements, while the unilateral-discussion conditions of this study emphasized own-position focus. The bilateral-study conditions in Bass (1966) consisted of eight-man study groups, while direct confrontation between a union and a company representative

A question may also be raised concerning the generalizability of these results to groups with a history of unilateral interaction (e.g., see Sherif *et al.*, 1961). Perhaps, in more cohesive groups, simple group experience (with or without explicit unilateral focus) may be enough to produce loyalty to assigned group positions as reflected in resistance to conflict resolution. At the current stage of empirical development it is difficult to assess the relevance of findings from simulated groups for groups with their own developmental history. Several new unilateral-discussion conditions may be established and compared to the prenegotiation conditions created in this design. For example, members of the same relatively permanent preexperimental group (e.g., members of the same fraternity, athletic teams, bunkmates, campus organizations, etc.), varying in terms of degree of familiarity among themselves, may be assigned to the same laboratory team. Another possibility is that of establishing laboratory groups that consist of members who have worked together for several laboratory sessions on a number of tasks unrelated to the bargaining situation. It would be interesting to determine whether these additional manipulations increase resistance to resolution more than does the unilateral-discussion condition created in this study.

While the position-formation condition produced more perceived commitment to the assigned positions than did the control condition, bargainers in the former condition were only slightly more resistant to

---

in study dyads was the procedure used in both study conditions of this investigation. Laboratory teams were not created in the former investigation.

compromise. Perhaps the lack of difference in resolution behavior between these conditions may have been, to some extent, a function of the imposed 30-minute deadline. Conceivably, dyads in both conditions may have reached close to an upper limit of resistance within the confines of a time limit. The results of the postnegotiation question on perceived commitment perhaps indicated that the position-formation dyads had more "potential" for rigidity. (Also, four dyads in this condition did not settle any issue at the deadline as compared to only one control dyad.) Differences between these conditions may have emerged if there were no deadline. This might be explored.

A prebargaining atmosphere which leads to a consideration of the debate as a collaborative, problem-solving venture in which neither side is committed to unilateral positions appears to facilitate conflict resolution. Prenegotiation conditions which consist of open discussion of the issues before representatives have a chance to develop a rationale or a cognitive context for their own positions appear to constitute such an atmosphere. However, as indicated in the research of Blake and Mouton (1962), bilateral study or focus which occurs after position-taking is not effective in reducing rigidity. Also, it seems to make little difference whether this activity is carried out with a future bargaining opponent, opposing representatives who are not bargaining opponents, or teammates. (While communication with one's opponent before bargaining resulted in somewhat faster resolution of the conflict than bilateral study apart from a future opponent, the difference between these conditions was not strong enough to be significant on any measure.)

REFERENCES

ARONSON, E. "The Effect of Effort on the Attractiveness of Rewarded and Unrewarded Stimuli." *Journal of Abnormal and Social Psychology*, 1961, 63, 375–380.

BASS, B. M. "Effects on the Subsequent Performance of Negotiators of Studying Issues or Planning Strategies Alone or in Groups." *Psychological Monographs*, Whole No. 614, 1966.

BASS, B. M., and DONTEMAN, G. "Biases in the Evaluation of One's Own Group, Its Allies and Opponents." *Journal of Conflict Resolution*, 1963, 7, 16–20.

BLAKE, R. R. "Psychology and the Crisis of Statesmanship." *American Psychologist*, 1959, 14, 87–94.

BLAKE, R. R., and MOUTON, JANE S. "The Intergroup Dynamics of Win-Lose Conflict and Problem-Solving Collaboration in Union-Management Relations." In M. Sherif (Ed.), *Intergroup Relations and Leadership*. New York: Wiley, 1962. Pp. 91–140.

CROWNE, D. P. "Family Orientation, Level of Aspiration, and Interpersonal Bargaining." *Journal of Personality and Social Psychology*, 1966, 3, 641–645.

DRUCKMAN, D. "Dogmatism, Prenegotiation Experience and Simulated Group Representation as Determinants of Dyadic Behavior in a Bargaining Situation." *Journal of Personality and Social Psychology*, 1967, 6, 279–290.

EDWARDS, A. L. *Experimental Design in Psychological Research*. New York: Holt, 1960.

FERGUSON, C. K., and KELLEY, H. H. "Significant Factors in Overevaluation of Own-Group's Product." *Journal of Abnormal and Social Psychology*, 1964, 69, 223–228.

FESTINGER, L., and ARONSON, E. "The Arousal and Reduction of Dissonance in Social Contexts." In D. Cartwright and A. Zander (Eds.), *Group Dynamics*. (2nd ed.) New York: Harper & Row, 1960. Pp. 214–231.

GLADSTONE, A. I. "Relationship Orientation and Processes Leading Toward War." *Background*, 1962, 6, 13–25.

HAMMOND, K. R., TODD, F. J., WILKINS, MARILYN, and MITCHELL, T. O. "Cognitive Conflict Between Persons: Application of the "Lens Model" Paradigm." *Journal of Experimental Social Psychology*, 1966, 2, 343–360.

HARRISON, H. A., and McCLINTOCK, C. G. "Previous Experience Within the Dyad and Cooperative Game Behavior." *Journal of Personality and Social Psychology*, 1965, 1, 671–675.

LEWIS, M. "Psychological Effect of Effort." *Psychological Bulletin*, 1965, 64, 183–190.

PEARSON, L. B. *Diplomacy in the Nuclear Age*. Cambridge, Massachusetts: Harvard Univ. Press, 1959.

RAPOPORT, A. *Fights, Games, and Debates*. Ann Arbor, Michigan: Univ. of Michigan Press, 1961.

RAPPOPORT, L. H. "Interpersonal Conflict in Cooperative and Uncertain Situations." *Journal of Experimental Social Psychology*, 1965, 1, 323–333.

RUSK, D. "Parliamentary Diplomacy—Debate Versus Negotiation." *World Affairs Interpreter*, 1955, 26, 121–138.

SHERIF, M., HARVEY, O. J., WHITE, B. J., HOOD, W. R., and SHERIF, CAROLYN W. *Intergroup Conflict and Cooperation: The Robbers Cave Experiment*. Norman, Oklahoma: University Book Exchange, 1961.

SHERIF, M., and SHERIF, CAROLYN W. "Research on Intergroup Relations." In O. Klineberg and R. Christie (Eds.), *Perspectives in Social Psychology*. New York: Holt, 1965. Pp. 153–177.

SIEGEL, S. *Nonparametric Statistics for the Behavioral Sciences*. New York: McGraw-Hill, 1956.

WITHEY, S., and KATZ, D. "The Social Psychology of Human Conflict." In E. B. McNeil (Ed.), *The Nature of Human Con-* *flict*. Englewood Cliffs, New Jersey: Prentice-Hall, 1965. Pp. 64–90.

BYSTANDER INTERVENTION
IN EMERGENCIES:
DIFFUSION OF RESPONSIBILITY*

John M. Darley and Bibb Latané

Several years ago, a young woman was stabbed to death in the middle of a street in a residential section of New York City. Although such murders are not entirely routine, the incident received little public attention until several weeks later when the New York Times disclosed another side to the case: at least 38 witnesses had observed the attack—and none had even attempted to intervene. Although the attacker took more than half an hour to kill Kitty Genovese, not one of the 38 people who watched from the safety of their own apartments came out to assist her. Not one even lifted the telephone to call the police (Rosenthal, 1964).

Preachers, professors, and news commentators sought the reasons for such apparently conscienceless and inhumane lack of intervention. Their conclusions ranged from "moral decay," to "dehumanization produced by the urban environment," to "alienation," "anomie," and "existential despair." An analysis of the situation, however, suggests that factors other than apathy and indifference were involved.

A person witnessing an emergency situation, particularly such a frightening and dangerous one as a stabbing, is in conflict. There are obvious humanitarian norms about helping the victim, but there are also rational and irrational fears about what might happen to a person who does intervene (Milgram & Hollander, 1964). "I didn't want to get involved," is a familiar comment, and behind it lies fear of physical harm, public embarrassment, involvement with police procedures, lost work days and jobs, and other unknown dangers.

In certain circumstances, the norms favoring intervention may be weakened, leading bystanders to resolve the conflict in the direction of nonintervention. One of these circumstances may be the presence

* John M. Darley and Bibb Latané, "Bystander Intervention in Emergencies: Diffusion of Responsibility," *Journal of Personality and Social Psychology*, 8 (1968), 377–83. Copyright 1968 by the American Psychological Association, and reproduced by permission.

of other onlookers. For example, in the case above, each observer, by seeing lights and figures in other apartment house windows, knew that others were also watching. However, there was no way to tell how the other observers were reacting. These two facts provide several reasons why any individual may have delayed or failed to help. The responsibility for helping was diffused among the observers; there was also diffusion of any potential blame for not taking action; and finally, it was possible that somebody, unperceived, had already initiated helping action.

When only one bystander is present in an emergency, if help is to come, it must come from him. Although he may choose to ignore it (out of concern for his personal safety, or desires "not to get involved"), any pressure to intervene focuses uniquely on him. When there are several observers present, however, the pressures to intervene do not focus on any one of the observers; instead the responsibility for intervention is shared among all the onlookers and is not unique to any one. As a result, no one helps.

A second possibility is that potential blame may be diffused. However much we may wish to think that an individual's moral behavior is divorced from considerations of personal punishment or reward, there is both theory and evidence to the contrary (Aronfreed, 1964; Miller & Dollard, 1941, Whiting & Child, 1953). It is perfectly reasonable to assume that, under circumstances of group responsibility for a punishable act, the punishment or blame that accrues to any one individual is often slight or nonexistent.

Finally, if others are known to be present, but their behavior cannot be closely observed, any one bystander can assume that one of the other observers is already taking action to end the emergency. Therefore, his own intervention would be only redundant—perhaps harmfully or confusingly so. Thus, given the presence of other onlookers whose behavior cannot be observed, any given bystander can rationalize his own inaction by convincing himself that "somebody else must be doing something."

These considerations lead to the hypothesis that the more bystanders to an emergency, the less likely, or the more slowly, any one bystander will intervene to provide aid. To test this proposition it would be necessary to create a situation in which a realistic "emergency" could plausibly occur. Each subject should also be blocked from communicating with others to prevent his getting information about their behavior during the emergency. Finally, the experimental situation should allow for the assessment of the speed and frequency of the subjects' reaction to the emergency. The experiment reported below attempted to fulfill these conditions.

Procedure

Overview. A college student arrived in the laboratory and was ushered into an individual room from which a communication system would enable him to talk to the other participants. It was explained to him that he was to take part in a discussion about personal problems associated with college life and that the discussion would be held over the intercom system, rather than face-to-face, in order to avoid embarrassment by preserving the anonymity of the subjects. During the course of the discussion, one of the other subjects underwent what appeared to be a very serious nervous seizure similar to epilepsy. During the fit it was impossible for the subject to talk to the other discussants or to find out what, if anything, they were doing about the emergency. The dependent variable was the speed with which the subjects reported the emergency to the experimenter. The major independent variable was the number of people the subject thought to be in the discussion group.

Subjects. Fifty-nine female and thirteen male students in introductory psychology courses at New York University were contacted to take part in an unspecified experiment as part of a class requirement.

Method. Upon arriving for the experiment, the subject found himself in a long corridor with doors opening off it to several small rooms. An experimental assistant met him, took him to one of the rooms, and seated him at a table. After filling out a background information form, the subject was given a pair of headphones with an attached microphone and was told to listen for instructions.

Over the intercom, the experimenter explained that he was interested in learning about the kinds of personal problems faced by normal college students in a high pressure, urban environment. He said that to avoid possible embarrassment about discussing personal problems with strangers several precautions had been taken. First, subjects would remain anonymous, which was why they had been placed in individual rooms rather than face-to-face. (The actual reason for this was to allow tape recorder simulation of the other subjects and the emergency.) Second, since the discussion might be inhibited by the presence of outside listeners, the experimenter would not listen to the initial discussion, but would get the subject's reactions later, by questionnaire. (The real purpose of this was to remove the obviously responsible experimenter from the scene of the emergency.)

The subjects were told that since the experimenter was not present, it was necessary to impose some organization. Each person would talk in turn, presenting his problems to the group. Next, each person in turn would

comment on what the others had said, and finally, there would be a free discussion. A mechanical switching device would regulate this discussion sequence and each subject's microphone would be on for about 2 minutes. While any microphone was on, all other microphones would be off. Only one subject, therefore, could be heard over the network at any given time. The subjects were thus led to realize when they later heard the seizure that only the victim's microphone was on and that there was no way of determining what any of the other witnesses were doing, nor of discussing the event and its possible solution with the others. When these instructions had been given, the discussion began.

In the discussion, the future victim spoke first, saying that he found it difficult to get adjusted to New York City and to his studies. Very hesitantly, and with obvious embarrassment, he mentioned that he was prone to seizures, particularly when studying hard or taking exams. The other people, including the real subject, took their turns and discussed similar problems (minus, of course, the proneness to seizures). The naive subject talked last in the series, after the last prerecorded voice was played.[1]

When it was again the victim's turn to talk, he made a few relatively calm comments, and then, growing increasingly louder and incoherent, he continued:

> I-er-um-I think I-I need-er-if-if could-er-er-somebody er-er-er-er-er-er-er give me a little-er-give me a little help here because-er-I-er-I'm-er-er-h-h-having a-a-a real problem-er-right now and I-er-if somebody could help me out it would-it would-er-er-s-s-sure   be-sure   be   good . . . because-er-

---

[1] To test whether the order in which the subjects spoke in the first discussion round significantly affected the subjects' speed of report, the order in which the subjects spoke was varied (in the six-person group). This had no significant or noticeable effect on the speed of the subjects' reports.

there-er-er-a cause I-er-I-uh-I've got a-a one of the-er-sei—er-er-things coming on and-and-and I could really-er-use some help so if somebody would-er-give me a little h-help-uh-er-er-er-er-er c-could somebody-er-er-help-er-uh-uh-uh (choking sounds).... I'm gonna die-er-er-I'm ... gonna die-er-help-er-er-seizure-er-[chokes, then quiet].

The experimenter began timing the speed of the real subject's response at the beginning of the victim's speech. Informed judges listening to the tape have estimated that the victim's increasingly louder and more disconnected ramblings clearly represented a breakdown about 70 seconds after the signal for the victim's second speech. The victim's speech was abruptly cut off 125 seconds after this signal, which could be interpreted by the subject as indicating that the time allotted for that speaker had elapsed and the switching circuits had switched away from him. Times reported in the results are measured from the start of the fit.

Group Size Variable. The major independent variable of the study was the number of other people that the subject believed also heard the fit. By the assistant's comments before the experiment, and also by the number of voices heard to speak in the first round of the group discussion, the subject was led to believe that the discussion group was one of three sizes: either a two-person group (consisting of a person who would later have a fit and the real subject), a three-person group (consisting of the victim, the real subject, and one confederate voice), or a six-person group (consisting of the victim, the real subject, and four confederate voices). All the confederates' voices were tape-recorded.

Variations in Group Composition. Varying the kind as well as the number of bystanders present at an emergency should also vary the amount of responsibility felt by any single bystander. To test this, several variations of the three-person group were run. In one three-person condition, the taped bystander voice was that of a female, in another a male, and in the third a male who said that he was a premedical student who occasionally worked in the emergency wards at Bellevue hospital.

In the above conditions, the subjects were female college students. In a final condition males drawn from the same introductory psychology subject pool were tested in a three-person female-bystander condition.

Time to Help. The major dependent variable was the time elapsed from the start of the victim's fit until the subject left her experimental cubicle. When the subject left her room, she saw the experimental assistant seated at the end of the hall, and invariably went to the assistant. If 6 minutes elapsed without the subject having emerged from her room, the experiment was terminated.

As soon as the subject reported the emergency, or after 6 minutes had elapsed, the experimental assistant disclosed the true nature of the experiment, and dealt with any emotions aroused in the subject. Finally the subject filled out a questionnaire concerning her thoughts and feelings during the emergency, and completed scales of Machiavellianism, anomie, and authoritarianism (Christie, 1964), a social desirability scale (Crowne & Marlowe, 1964), a social responsibility scale (Daniels & Berkowitz, 1964), and reported vital statistics and socioeconomic data.

RESULTS

Plausibility of Manipulation

Judging by the subjects' nervousness when they reported the fit to the experimenter, by their surprise when they discovered that the fit was simulated, and by comments they made during the fit (when they thought their microphones were off), one can conclude that almost all of the subjects perceived the fit as real. There were two exceptions in different experimental conditions, and the data for these subjects were dropped from the analysis.

Effect of Group Size on Helping

The number of bystanders that the subject perceived to be present had a major effect on the likelihood with which she would report the emergency (Table 1). Eighty-five percent of the subjects who thought they alone knew of the victim's plight reported the seizure before the victim was cut off; only 31% of those who thought four other bystanders were present did so.

Every one of the subjects in the two-person groups, but only 62% of the subjects in the six-person groups, ever reported the emergency. The cumulative distributions of response times for groups of different perceived size (Figure 1) indicates that, by any point in time, more subjects from the two-person groups had responded than from the three-person groups, and more from the three-person groups than from the six-person groups.

Ninety-five percent of all the subjects who ever responded did so within the first half of the time available to them. No

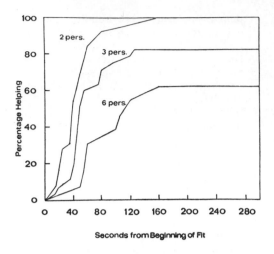

Fig. 1. Cumulative Distributions of Helping Responses.

subject who had not reported within 3 minutes after the fit ever did so. The shape of these distributions suggests that had the experiment been allowed to run for a considerably longer time, few additional subjects would have responded.

Speed of Response

To achieve a more detailed analysis of the results, each subject's time score was transformed into a "speed" score by taking the reciprocal of the response time in seconds and multiplying by 100. The effect of this transformation was to deemphasize differences between longer time scores, thus reducing the contribution to the results of the arbitrary 6-minute limit on scores. A high speed score indicates a fast response.

An analysis of variance indicates that the effect of group size is highly significant ($p < .01$). Duncan multiple-range tests indicate that all but the two- and three-person groups differ significantly from one another ($p < .05$).

Table 1

EFFECTS OF GROUPS SIZE ON LIKELIHOOD AND SPEED OF RESPONSE

Group size	N	% responding by end of fit	Time in sec.	Speed score
2 (S & victim)	13	85	52	.87
3 (S, victim, & 1 other)	26	62	93	.72
6 (S, victim, & 4 others)	13	31	166	.51

Note.—p value of differences: $x^2 = 7.91$, $p < .02$; $F = 8.09$, $p < .01$, for speed scores.

Victim's Likelihood of Being Helped

An individual subject is less likely to respond if he thinks that others are present. But what of the victim? Is the inhibition of the response of each individual strong enough to counteract the fact that with five onlookers there are five times as many people available to help? From the data of this experiment, it is possible mathematically to create hypothetical groups with one, two, or five observers.[2] The calculations indicate that the victim is about equally likely to get help from one bystander as from two. The victim is considerably more likely to have gotten help from one or two observers than from five during the first minute of the fit. For instance, by 45 seconds after the start of the fit, the victim's chances of having been helped by the single bystanders were about 50%, compared to none in the five observer condition. After the first minute, the likelihood of getting help from at least one person is high in all three conditions.

Effect of Group Composition on Helping the Victim

Several variations of the three-person group were run. In one pair of variations, the female subject thought the other bystander was either male or female; in another, she thought the other bystander was a premedical student who worked in an emergency ward at Bellevue hospital. As Table 2 shows, the variations in sex and medical competence of the other

---

[2] The formula for the probability that at least one person will help by a given time is $1-(1-P)^n$ where n is the number of observers and P is the probability of a single individual (who thinks he is one of n observers) helping by that time.

Table 2

EFFECTS OF GROUP COMPOSITION ON LIKELIHOOD AND SPEED OF RESPONSE[a]

Group composition	N	% responding by end of fit	Time in sec.	Speed score
Female S, male other	13	62	94	74
Female S, female other	13	62	92	71
Female S, male medic other	5	100	60	77
Male S, female other	13	69	110	68

[a] Three-person group, male victim.

bystander had no important or detectable effect on speed of response. Subjects responded equally frequently and fast whether the other bystander was female, male, or medically experienced.

Sex of the Subject and Speed of Response

Coping with emergencies is often thought to be the duty of males, especially when females are present, but there was no evidence that this was the case in this study. Male subjects responded to the emergency with almost exactly the same speed as did females (Table 2).

Reasons for Intervention or Nonintervention

After the debriefing at the end of the experiment each subject was given a 15-item checklist and asked to check those thoughts which had "crossed your mind when you heard Subject 1 calling for help." Whatever the condition, each subject checked very few thoughts, and there were no significant differences in number or kind of thoughts in the different, experimental groups. The only thoughts checked by more than a few subjects were "I didn't know what to do" (18 out of 65 subjects), "I thought it must be some sort of fake" (20 out of 65), and "I didn't know exactly what was happening" (26 out of 65).

It is possible that subjects were ashamed to report socially undesirable rationalizations, or, since the subjects checked the list *after* the true nature of the experiment had been explained to them, their memories might have been blurred. It is our impression, however, that most subjects checked few reasons because they had few coherent thoughts during the fit.

We asked all subjects whether the presence or absence of other bystanders had entered their minds during the time that they were hearing the fit. Subjects in the three- and six-person groups reported that they were aware that other people were present, but they felt that this made no difference to their own behavior.

Individual Difference Correlates of Speed of Report

The correlations between speed of report and various individual differences on the personality and background measures were obtained by normalizing the distribution of report speeds within each experimental condition and pooling these scores across all conditions ($n = 62$–65). Personality measures showed no important or significant correlations with speed of reporting the emergency. In fact, only one of the 16 individual difference measures, the size of the community in which the subject grew up, correlated ($r = -.26$, $p < .05$) with the speed of helping.

DISCUSSION

Subjects, whether or not they intervened, believed the fit to be genuine and serious. "My God, he's having a fit," many subjects said to themselves (and were overheard via their microphones) at the onset of the fit. Others gasped or simply said "Oh." Several of the male subjects swore. One subject said to herself, "It's just my kind of luck, something has to happen to me!" Several subjects spoke aloud of their confusion about what course of action to take, "Oh God, what should I do?"

When those subjects who intervened stepped out of their rooms, they found the experimental assistant down the hall. With some uncertainty, but without panic, they reported the situation. "Hey, I think Number 1 is very sick. He's having a fit or something." After ostensibly checking on the situation, the experimenter returned to report that "everything is under control." The subjects accepted these assurances with obvious relief.

Subjects who failed to report the emergency showed few signs of the apathy and indifference thought to characterize "unresponsive bystanders." When the experimenter entered her room to terminate the situation, the subject often asked if the victim was "all right." "Is he being taken care of?" "He's all right isn't he?" Many of these subjects showed physical signs of nervousness; they often had trembling hands and sweating palms. If anything, they seemed more emotionally aroused than did the subjects who reported the emergency.

Why, then, didn't they respond? It is our impression that nonintervening subjects had not decided *not* to respond. Rather they were still in a state of indecision and conflict concerning whether to respond or not. The emotional behavior of these nonresponding subjects was a sign of their continuing conflict, a conflict that other subjects resolved by responding.

The fit created a conflict situation of the avoidance-avoidance type. On the one hand, subjects worried about the guilt and shame they would feel if they did not help the person in distress. On the other hand, they were concerned not to make fools of themselves by overreacting, not to ruin the ongoing experiment by leaving their intercom, and not to destroy the anonymous nature of the situation which the experimenter had earlier stressed as important. For subjects in the two-person condition, the obvious distress of the victim and his need for help were so important that their conflict was easily resolved. For the subjects who knew there were other bystanders present, the cost of not helping was reduced and the conflict they were in more acute. Caught between the two negative alternatives of letting the victim continue to suffer or the costs of rushing in to help, the nonresponding bystanders vacillated between them rather than choosing not to respond. This distinction may be academic for the victim, since he got no help in either case, but it is an extremely important one for arriving at an understanding of the causes of bystanders' failures to help.

Although the subjects experienced stress and conflict during the experiment, their general reactions to it were highly positive. On a questionnaire administered after the experimenter had discussed the nature and purpose of the experiment, every single subject found the experiment either "interesting" or "very interesting" and was willing to participate in similar experiments in the future. All subjects felt they understood what the experiment was about and indicated that they thought the deceptions were necessary and justified. All but one felt they were better informed about the nature of psychological research in general.

Male subjects reported the emergency no faster than did females. These results (or lack of them) seem to conflict with the Berkowitz, Klanderman, and Harris (1964) finding that males tend to assume more responsibility and take more initiative than females in giving help to dependent others. Also, females reacted equally fast when the other bystander was another female, a male, or even a person practiced in dealing with medical emergencies. The ineffectiveness of these manipulations of group composition cannot be explained by general insensitivity of the speed measure, since the group-size variable had a marked effect on report speed.

It might be helpful in understanding this lack of difference to distinguish two general classes of intervention in emergency situations: direct and reportorial. Direct intervention (breaking up a fight, extinguishing a fire, swimming out to save a drowner) often requires skill, knowledge, or physical power. It may involve danger. American cultural norms and Berkowitz's results seem to suggest that males are more responsible than females for this kind of direct intervention.

A second way of dealing with an emergency is to report it to someone qualified to handle it, such as the police. For this kind of intervention, there seem to be no norms requiring male action. In the present study, subjects clearly intended to report the emergency rather than take direct action. For such indirect intervention, sex or medical competence does not appear to affect one's qualifications or responsibilities. Anybody, male or female, medically trained or not, can find the experimenter.

In this study, no subject was able to tell how the other subjects reacted to the fit. (Indeed, there were no other subjects actually present.) The effects of group size on speed of helping, therefore, are due simply to the perceived presence of others rather than to the influence of their actions. This means that the experimental situation is unlike emergencies, such as a fire, in which bystanders interact with each other. It is, however, similar to emergencies, such as the Genovese murder, in which spectators knew others were also watching but were prevented by walls between them from communication that might have counteracted the diffusion of responsibility.

The present results create serious difficulties for one class of commonly given explanations for the failure of bystanders to intervene in actual emergencies, those involving apathy or indifference. These explanations generally assert that people who fail to intervene are somehow different in kind from the rest of us, that they are "alienated by industrialization," "dehumanized by urbanization," "depersonalized by living in the cold society," or "psychopaths." These explanations serve a dual function for people who adopt them. First, they explain (if only in a nominal way) the puzzling and frightening problem of why people watch others die. Second, they give individuals reason to deny that they too might fail to help in a similar situation.

The results of this experiment seem to indicate that such personality variables may not be as important as these explanations suggest. Alienation, Machiavellianism, acceptance of social responsibility, need for approval, and authoritarianism are often cited in these explanations. Yet they did not predict the speed or likelihood of help. In sharp contrast, the perceived number of bystanders did. The explanation of bystander "apathy" may lie more in the bystander's response to other observers than in presumed personality deficiencies of "apathetic" individuals. Although this realization may force us to face the guilt-provoking possibility that we too might fail to intervene, it also suggests that individuals are not, of necessity, "noninterveners" because of their personalities. If people understand the situational forces that can make them hesitate to intervene, they may better overcome them.

REFERENCES

ARONFREED, J. "The Origin of Self-Criticism." *Psychological Review*, 1964, 71, 193–219.

BERKOWITZ, L., KLANDERMAN, S., and HARRIS, R. "Effects of Experimenter Awareness and Sex of Subject on Reactions to Dependency Relationships." *Sociometry*, 1964, 27, 327–329.

CHRISTIE, R. "The Prevalence of Machiavellian Orientations." Paper presented at the meeting of the American Psychological Association, Los Angeles, 1964.

CROWNE, D., and MARLOWE, D. *The Approval Motive*. New York: Wiley, 1964.

DANIELS, L., and BERKOWITZ, L. "Liking and Response to Dependency Relationships." *Human Relations*, 1963, 16, 141–148.

MILGRAM, S., and HOLLANDER, P. "Murder They Heard." *Nation*, 1964, 198, 602–604.

MILLER, N., and DOLLARD, J. *Social Learning and Imitation*. New Haven: Yale University Press, 1941.

ROSENTHAL, A. M. *Thirty-Eight Witnesses*. New York: McGraw-Hill, 1964.

WHITING, J. W., and CHILD, I. *Child Training and Personality*. New Haven: Yale University Press, 1953.

GROUP INHIBITION
OF BYSTANDER INTERVENTION
IN EMERGENCIES*

Bibb Latané and John M. Darley

Emergencies, fortunately, are uncommon events. Although the average person may read about them in newspapers or watch fictionalized versions on television, he probably will encounter fewer than half a dozen in his lifetime. Unfortunately, when he does encounter one, he will have had little direct personal experience in dealing with it. And he must deal with it under conditions of urgency, uncertainty, stress, and fear. About all the individual has to guide him is the secondhand wisdom of the late movie, which is often as useful as "Be brave" or as applicable as "Quick, get lots of hot water and towels!"

Under the circumstances, it may seem surprising that anybody ever intervenes in an emergency in which he is not directly involved. Yet there is a strongly held cultural norm that individuals should act to relieve the distress of others. As the Old Parson puts it, "In this life of froth and bubble, two things stand like stone—kindness in another's trouble, courage in your

own." Given the conflict between the norm to act and an individual's fears and uncertainties about getting involved, what factors will determine whether a bystander to an emergency will intervene?

We have found (Darley & Latané, 1968) that the mere perception that other people are also witnessing the event will markedly decrease the lieklihood that an individual will intervene in an emergency. Individuals heard a person undergoing a severe epileptic-like fit in another room. In one experimental condition, the subject thought that he was the only person who heard the emergency; in another condition, he thought four other persons were also aware of the seizure. Subjects alone with the victim were much more likely to intervene on his behalf, and, on the average, reacted in less than one-third the time required by subjects who thought there were other bystanders present.

"Diffusion of responsibility" seems the most likely explanation for this result. If an individual is alone when he notices an emergency, he is solely responsible for coping with it. If he believes others are also present, he may feel that his own responsibility for taking action is lessened, making him less likely to help.

To demonstrate that responsibility diffu-

* Bibb Latané and John M. Darley, "Group Inhibition of Bystander Intervention in Emergencies," *Journal of Personality and Social Psychology*, 10 (1968), 215–21. Copyright 1968 by the American Psychological Association, and reproduced by permission.

sion rather than any of a variety of social influence processes caused this result, the experiment was designed so that the onlookers to the seizure were isolated one from another and could not discuss how to deal with the emergency effectively. They knew the others could not see what they did, nor could they see whether somebody else had already started to help. Although this state of affairs is characteristic of many actual emergencies (such as the Kitty Genovese murder in which 38 people witnessed a killing from their individual apartments without acting), in many other emergencies several bystanders are in contact with and can influence each other. In these situations, processes other than responsibility diffusion will also operate.

Given the opportunity to interact, a group can talk over the situation and divide up the helping action in an efficient way. Also, since responding to emergencies is a socially prescribed norm, individuals might be expected to adhere to it more when in the presence of other people. These reasons suggest that interacting groups should be better at coping with emergencies than single individuals. We suspect, however, that the opposite is true. Even when allowed to communicate, groups may still be worse than individuals.

Most emergencies are, or at least begin as, ambiguous events. A quarrel in the street may erupt into violence, but it may be simply a family argument. A man staggering about may be suffering a coronary or an onset of diabetes; he may be simply drunk. Smoke pouring from a building may signal a fire; on the other hand, it may be simply steam or air-conditioning vapor. Before a bystander is likely to take action in such ambiguous situations, he must first define the event

as an emergency and decide that intervention is the proper course of action.

In the course of making these decisions, it is likely that an individual bystander will be considerably influenced by the decisions he perceives other bystanders to be taking. If everyone else in a group of onlookers seems to regard an event as nonserious and the proper course of action as nonintervention, this consensus may strongly affect the perceptions of any single individual and inhibit his potential intervention.

The definitions that other people hold may be discovered by discussing the situation with them, but they may also be inferred from their facial expressions or their behavior. A whistling man with his hands in his pockets obviously does not believe he is in the midst of a crisis. A bystander who does not respond to smoke obviously does not attribute it to fire. An individual, seeing the inaction of others, will judge the situation as less serious than he would if he were alone.

In the present experiment, this line of thought will be tested by presenting an emergency situation to individuals either alone or in the presence of two passive others, confederates of the experimenter who have been instructed to notice the emergency but remain indifferent to it. It is our expectation that this passive behavior will signal the individual that the other bystanders do not consider the situation to be dangerous. We predict that an individual faced with the passive reactions of other people will be influenced by them, and will thus be less likely to take action than if he were alone.

This, however, is a prediction about individuals; it says nothing about the original question of the behavior of freely interacting groups. Most groups do not have preinstructed confederates among their members, and the kind of social influence process described above would, by itself, only lead to a convergence of attitudes within a group. Even if each member of the group is entirely guided by the reactions of others, then the group should still respond with a likelihood equal to the average of the individuals.

An additional factor is involved, however. Each member of a group may watch the others, but he is also aware that the others are watching him. They are an audience to his own reactions. Among American males it is considered desirable to appear poised and collected in times of stress. Being exposed to public view may constrain an individual's actions as he attempts to avoid possible ridicule and embarrassment.

The constraints involved with being in public might in themselves tend to inhibit action by individuals in a group, but in conjunction with the social influence process described above, they may be expected to have even more powerful effects. If each member of a group is, at the same time, trying to appear calm and also looking around at the other members to gauge their reactions, all members may be led (or misled) by each other to define the situation as less critical than they would if alone. Until someone acts, each person only sees other nonresponding bystanders, and, as with the passive confederates, is likely to be influenced not to act himself.

This leads to a second prediction. Compared to the performance of individuals, if we expose groups of naive subjects to an emergency, the constraints on behavior in public coupled with the social influence process will lessen the likelihood that the members of the group will act to cope with the emergency.

It has often been recognized (Brown, 1954, 1965) that a crowd can cause contagion of panic, leading each person in the crowd to overreact to an emergency to the detriment of everyone's welfare. What is implied here is that a crowd can also force inaction on its members. It can suggest, implicitly but strongly, by its passive behavior, that an event is not to be reacted to as an emergency, and it can make any individual uncomfortably aware of what a fool he will look for behaving as if it is.

METHOD

The subject, seated in a small waiting room, faced an ambiguous but potentially dangerous situation as a stream of smoke began to puff into the room through a wall vent. His response to this situation was observed through a one-way glass. The length of time the subject remained in the room before leaving to report the smoke was the main dependent variable of the study.

Recruitment of subjects. Male Columbia students living in campus residences were invited to an interview to discuss "some of the problems involved in life at an urban university." The subject sample included graduate and professional students as well as undergraduates. Individuals were contacted by telephone and most willingly volunteered and actually showed up for the interview. At this point, they were directed either by signs or by the secretary to a "waiting room" where a sign asked them to fill out a preliminary questionnaire.

Experimental manipulation. Some subjects filled out the questionnaire and were exposed to the potentially critical situation while alone. Others were part of three-person groups consisting of one subject and two confederates acting the part of naive subjects. The confederates attempted to avoid conversation as much as possible. Once the smoke had been introduced, they stared at it briefly, made no comment, but simply shrugged their shoulders, returned to the questionnaires and continued to fill them out, occasionally waving away the smoke to do so. If addressed, they attempted to be as uncommunicative as possible and to show apparent indifference to the smoke. "I dunno," they said, and no subject persisted in talking.

In a final condition, three naive subjects were tested together. In general, these subjects did not know each other, although in two groups, subjects reported a nodding acquaintanceship with another subject. Since subjects arrived at slightly different times and since they each had individual questionnaires to work on, they did not introduce themselves to each other, or attempt anything but the most rudimentary conversation.

Critical situation. As soon as the subjects had completed two pages of their questionnaires, the experimenter began to introduce the smoke through a small vent in the wall. The "smoke" was finely divided titanium dioxide produced in a stoppered bottle and delivered under slight air pressure through the vent.[1] It formed a moderately fine-textured but clearly visible stream of whitish smoke. For the entire experimental period, the smoke continued to jet into the room in irregular puffs. By the end of the experimental period, vision was obscured by the amount of smoke present.

All behavior and conversation was observed and coded from behind a one-way window (largely disguised on the subject's side by a large sign giving preliminary instructions). If the subject left the experimental room and reported the smoke, he was told that the situation "would be taken care of." If the subject had not reported the presence of smoke by 6 minutes from the time he first noticed it, the experiment was terminated.

---

[1] Smoke was produced by passing moisturized air, under pressure, through a container of titanium tetrachloride, which, in reaction with the water vapor, creates a suspension of tantium dioxide in air.

RESULTS

Alone Condition

The typical subject, when tested alone, behaved very reasonably. Usually, shortly after the smoke appeared, he would glance up from his questionnaire, notice the smoke, show a slight but distinct startle reaction, and then undergo a brief period of indecision, perhaps returning briefly to his questionnaire before again staring at the smoke. Soon, most subjects would get up from their chairs, walk over to the vent, and investigate it closely, sniffing the smoke, waving their hands in it, feeling its temperature, etc. The usual alone subject would hesitate again, but finally walk out of the room, look around outside, and, finding somebody there, calmly report the presence of the smoke. No subject showed any sign of panic; most simply said, "There's something strange going on in there, there seems to be some sort of smoke coming through the wall. . . ."

The median subject in the alone condition had reported the smoke within 2 minutes of first noticing it. Three-quarters of the 24 people who were run in this condition reported the smoke before the experimental period was terminated.

Two Passive Confederates Condition

The behavior of subjects run with two passive confederates was dramatically different; of 10 people run in this condition, only 1 reported the smoke. The other 9 stayed in the waiting room as it filled up with smoke, doggedly working on their questionnaire and waving the funes away from their faces. They coughed, rubbed their eyes, and opened the window—but they did not report the smoke. The difference between the response rate of 75% in the alone condition and 10% in the two passive confederates condition is highly significant ($p < .002$ by Fisher's exact test, two-tailed).

Three Naive Bystanders

Because there are three subjects present and available to report the smoke in the three naive bystander condition as compared to only one subject at a time in the alone condition, a simple comparison between the two conditions is not appropriate. On the one hand, we cannot compare speeds in the alone condition with the average speed of the three subjects in a group, since, once one subject in a group had reported the smoke, the pressures on the other two disappeared. They legitimately could (and did) feel that the emergency had been handled, and any action on their part would be redundant and potentially confusing. Therefore the speed of the *first* subject in a group to report the smoke was used as the dependent variable. However, since there were three times as many people available to respond in this condition as in the alone condition, we would expect an increased likelihood that *at least* one person would report the smoke even if the subjects had no influence whatsoever on each other. Therefore we mathematically created "groups" of three scores from the alone condition to serve as a base line.[2]

In contrast to the complexity of this precedure, the results were quite simple. Subjects in the three naive bystander condition were markedly inhibited from

reporting the smoke. Since 75% of the alone subjects reported the smoke, we would expect over 98% of the three-person groups to contain at least one reporter. In fact, in only 38% of the eight groups in this condition did even 1 subject report ($p < .01$). Of the 24 people run in these eight groups, only 1 person reported the smoke within the first 4 minutes before the room got noticeably unpleasant. Only 3 people reported the smoke within the entire experimental period.

Cumulative Distribution of Report Times

Figure 1 presents the cumulative frequency distributions of report times for all three conditions. The figure shows the proportion of subjects in each condition who had reported the smoke by any point in the time following the introduction of the smoke. For example, 55% of the subjects in the alone condition had reported the smoke within 2 minutes, but the smoke had been reported in only 12% of the three-person groups by that time. After 4 minutes, 75% of the subjects in the alone condition had reported the smoke; no additional subjects in the group condition had done so. The curve in Figure 1 labeled "Hypothetical Three-Person Groups" is based upon the mathematical combination of scores obtained from subjects in the alone condition. It is the expected report times for groups in the three-person condition if the members of the groups had no influence upon each other.

It can be seen in Figure 1 that for every point in time following the introduction of the smoke, a considerably higher proportion of subjects in the alone condition had reported the smoke than had subjects in either the two passive con-

---

[2] The formula for calculating the expected proportion of groups in which at least one person will have acted by a given time is $1-(1-p)^n$ where p is the proportion of single individuals who act by that time and n is the number of persons in the group.

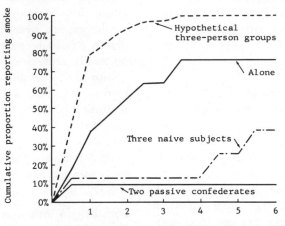

Fig. 1. Cumulative Proportion of Subjects Reporting the Smoke over Time.

federates condition or in the three naive subjects condition. The curve for the latter condition, although considerably below the alone curve, is even more substantially inhibited with respect to its proper comparison, the curve of hypothetical three-person sets. Social inhibition of response was so great that the time elapsing before the smoke was reported was greater when there were more people available to report it (alone versus group $p < .05$ by Mann-Whitney U test).

Superficially, it appears that there is a somewhat higher likelihood of response from groups of three naive subjects than from subjects in the passive confederates condition. Again this comparison is not justified; there are three people free to act in one condition instead of just one. If we mathematically combine scores for subjects in the two passive confederates condition in a similar manner to that described above for the alone condition, we would obtain an expected likelihood of response of .27 as the hypothetical base

line. This is not significantly different from the .37 obtained in the actual three-subject groups.

Noticing the Smoke

In observing the subject's reaction to the introduction of smoke, careful note was taken of the exact moment when he first saw the smoke (all report latencies were computed from this time). This was a relatively easy observation to make, for the subjects invariably showed a distinct, if slight, startle reaction. Unexpectedly, the presence of other persons delayed, slightly but very significantly, noticing the smoke. Sixty-three percent of subjects in the alone condition and only 26% of subjects in the combined together conditions noticed the smoke within the first 5 seconds after its introduction ($p < .01$ by chi-square). The median latency of noticing the smoke was under 5 seconds in the alone condition; the median time at which the first (or only) subject in each of the combined together conditions noticed the smoke was 20 seconds (this difference does not account for group-induced inhibition of reporting since the report latencies were computed from the time the smoke was first noticed).

This interesting finding can probably be explained in terms of the constraints which people feel in public places (Goffman, 1963). Unlike solitary subjects, who often glanced idly about the room while filling out their questionnaries, subjects in groups usually kept their eyes closely on their work, probably to avoid appearing rudely inquisitive.

Postexperimental Interview

After 6 minutes, whether or not the subjects had reported the smoke, the interviewer stuck his head in the waiting room and asked the subject to come with him to the interview. After seating the subject in his office, the interviewer made some general apologies about keeping the subject waiting for so long, hoped the subject hadn't become too bored and asked if he "had experienced any difficulty while filling out the questionnaire." By this point most subjects mentioned the smoke. The interviewer expressed mild surprise and asked the subject to tell him what had happened. Thus each subject gave an account of what had gone through his mind during the smoke infusion.

Subjects who had reported the smoke were relatively consistent in later describing their reactions to it. They thought the smoke looked somewhat "strange," they were not sure exactly what it was or whether it was dangerous, but they felt it was unusual enough to justify some examination. "I wasn't sure whether it was

a fire but it looked like something was wrong." "I thought it might be steam, but it seemed like a good idea to check it out."

Subjects who had not reported the smoke also were unsure about exactly what it was, but they unifomly said that they had rejected the idea that it was a fire. Instead, they hit upon an astonishing variety of alternative explanations, all sharing the common characteristic of interpreting the smoke as a nondangerous event. Many thought the smoke was either steam or air-conditioning vapors, several thought it was smog, purposely introduced to simulate an urban environment, and two (from different groups) actually suggested that the smoke was a "truth gas" filtered into the room to induce them to answer the questionnaire accurately. (Surprisingly, they were not disturbed by this conviction.) Predictably, some decided that "it must be some sort of experiment" and stoicly endured the discomfort of the room rather than overreact.

Despite the obvious and powerful report-inhibiting effect of other bystanders, subjects almost invariably claimed that they had paid little or no attention to the reactions of the other people in the room. Although the presence of other people actually had a strong and pervasive effect on the subjects' reactions, they were either unaware of this or unwilling to admit it.

DISCUSSION

Before an individual can decide to intervene in an emergency, he must, implicitly or explicitly, take several preliminary steps. If he is to intervene, he must first *notice* the event, he must then *interpret* it as an emergency, and he must decide that it is his personal *responsibility* to act. At each of these preliminary steps, the bystander to an emergency can remove himself from the decision process and thus fail to help. He can fail to notice the event, he can fail to interpret it as an emergency, or he can fail to assume the responsibility to take action.

In the present experiment we are primarily interested in the second step of this decision process, interpreting an ambiguous event. When faced with such an event, we suggest, the individual bystander is likely to look at the reactions of people around him and be powerfully influenced by them. It was predicted that the sight of other, nonresponsive bystanders would lead the individual to interpret the emergency as not serious, and consequently lead him not to act. Further, it was predicted that the dynamics of the interaction process would lead each of a group of naive onlookers to be misled by the apparent inaction of the others into adopting a nonemergency interpretation of the event and a passive role.

The results of this study clearly support our predictions. Individuals exposed to a room filling with smoke in the presence of passive others themselves remained passive, and groups of three naive subjects were less likely to report the smoke than solitary bystanders. Our predictions were confirmed—but this does not necessarily mean that our explanation for these results is the correct one. As a matter of fact, several alternatives are available.

Two of these alternative explanations stem from the fact that the smoke represented a possible danger to the subject himself as well as to others in the building. Subjects' behavior might have reflected their fear of fire, with subjects in groups feeling less threatened by the fire than single subjects and thus being less concerned to act. It has been demonstrated in studies with humans (Schachter, 1959) and with rats (Latané, 1968; Latané & Glass, 1968) that togetherness reduces fear, even in situations where it does not reduce danger. In addition, subjects may have felt that the presence of others increased their ability to cope with fire. For both of these reasons, subjects in groups may have been less afraid of fire and thus less likely to report the smoke than solitary subjects.

A similar explanation might emphasize not fearfulness, but the desire to hide fear. To the extent that bravery or stoicism in the face of danger or discomfort is a socially desirable trait (as it appears to be for American male undergraduates), one might expect individuals to attempt to appear more brave or more stoic when others are watching than when they are alone. It is possible that subjects in the group condition saw themselves as engaged in a game of "Chicken," and thus did not react.

Although both of these explanations are plausible, we do not think that they provide an accurate account of subjects' thinking. In the postexperimental interviews, subjects claimed, *not* that they were unworried by the fire or that they were unwilling to endure the danger; but rather that they decided that there was no fire at all and the smoke was caused by something else. They failed to act because they thought there was no reason to act. Their "apathetic" behavior was reasonable—given their interpretation of the circumstances.

The fact that smoke signals potential danger to the subject himself weakens another alternative explanation, "diffusion of responsibility." Regardless of social influence processes, an individual may feel less personal responsibility for helping if he shares the responsibility with others (Darley & Latané, 1968). But this diffusion explanation does not fit the present situation. It is hard to see how an individual's responsibility for saving himself is diffused by the presence of other people. The diffusion explanation does not account for the pattern of interpretations reported by the subjects or for their variety of nonemergency explanations.

On the other hand, the social influence processes which we believe account for the results of our present study obviously do not explain our previous experiment in which subjects could not see or be seen by each other. Taken together, these two studies suggest that the presence of bystanders may affect an individual in several ways; including both "social influence" and "diffusion of responsibility."

Both studies, however, find, for two quite different kinds of emergencies and under two quite different conditions of social contact, that individuals are less likely to engage in socially responsible action if they think other bystanders are present. This presents us with the paradoxical conclusion that a victim may be more likely to get help, or an emergency may be more likely to be reported, the fewer people there are available to take action. It also may help us begin to under-

stand a number of frightening incidents where crowds have listened to but not answered a call for help. Newspapers have tagged these incidents with the label "apathy." We have become indifferent, they say, callous to the fate of suffering others. The results of our studies lead to a different conclusion. The failure to intervene may be better understood by knowing the relationship among bystanders rather than that between a bystander and the victim.

REFERENCES

BROWN, R. W. "Mass Phenomena." In G. Lindzey (Ed.), *Handbook of Social Psychology.* Vol. 2. Cambridge: Addison-Wesley, 1954.

BROWN, R. *Social Psychology.* New York: Free Press of Glencoe, 1965.

DARLEY, J. M., and LATANÉ, B. "Bystander Intervention in Emergencies: Diffusion of Responsibility." *Journal of Personality and Social Psychology,* 1968, 8, 377–383.

GOFFMAN, E. *Behavior in Public Places.* New York: Free Press of Glencoe, 1963.

LATANÉ, B. "Gregariousness and Fear in Laboratory Rats." *Journal of Experimental Social Psychology,* 1968.

LATANÉ, B., and GLASS, D. C. "Social and Nonsocial Attraction in Rats." *Journal of Personality and Social Psychology,* 1968, 9, 142–146.

SCHACHTER, S. *The Psychology of Affiliation.* Stanford: Stanford University Press, 1959.

3

The Development of Consensus

STABILITIES
UNDERLYING CHANGES
IN INTERPERSONAL ATTRACTION*

Theodore M. Newcomb

It is a safe prediction that individuals who are initially strangers to one another will, under conditions assuring that they will become well acquainted, experience many changes in the degree of their attraction toward one another. Such changes, like any others that scientists investigate, presumably occur in orderly ways, and the principles governing both change and nonchange correspond to constancies. Lewin (1947), paraphrasing Cassirer (1923), notes that "throughout the history of mathematics and physics problems of constancy of relations rather

* Theodore M. Newcomb, "Stabilities Underlying Changes in Interpersonal Attraction," *Journal of Abnormal and Social Psychology*, 66 (1963), 376–86. Copyright 1963 by the American Psychological Association, and reproduced by permission.

than of constancy of elements have gained importance and have gradually changed the picture of what is essential" (p. 5). The present report points to a few such constancies of relations that have been observed on the part of two populations of initial strangers over a 4-month period, while their attitudes (elements involved in the relations) toward one another were characterized by a good deal of inconstancy.

As reported more fully elsewhere (Newcomb, 1961), two sets of 17 male students served in two successive years as subjects in an investigation of the phenomena of getting acquainted. They had been successfully selected as total strangers to one another, and lived and took their meals together in a house reserved for them. During each of 16 weeks they responded to a selected set of questionnaires, attitude scales, or other instruments, many of which were repeated from time to time. In particular, they rated or ranked each other as to favorability of interpersonal attitudes (henceforth referred to as *attraction*) during almost every week. In addition, they frequently estimated one anothers' attitudes of various kinds. The present paper partially summarizes and also supplements findings reported in the original monograph, for the specific purpose of noting constancies that underlie inconstancies.[1]

The theoretical considerations from which the investigation stemmed were direct descendants from Beider's (1958) theory of "balanced states." For the purposes of this study, the elements among which a balanced relationship may exist for an individual are: his degree of attraction, positive or negative, toward another individual; his attitude, favorable or unfavorable, toward some object (in the inclusive sense, referring to persons, issues, and abstractions like general values); and the second individual's attitude, as perceived by the first individual, toward the same object. A balanced state exists among these elements insofar as attraction is positive and the individual perceives that his own and the others' attitudes are similar. Perceived dissimilarity together with positive attraction represents an inbalanced state; negative attraction (with which this paper does not specifically deal) together with perceived similarity of attitudes may be either imbalanced or merely nonbalanced (a matter of indifference); together with

perceived dissimilarity, negative attraction may be either balanced or merely nonbalanced.[2] These rules of balanced relationships include the specification of certain conditions, most important of which are that the attitude objects be of relatively high importance and be considered to have common impact upon self and others in similar ways.[3]

The significant feature, for present purposes, of balanced and imbalanced states is, in Heider's (1958) words, that "if a balanced state does not exist, then forces toward this state will arise. If a change is not possible, the state of imbalance will produce tension" (p. 201). Thus balanced states tend to be stable and imbalanced ones unstable. In either case we are dealing with relations, in Lewin's terms, and not merely with elements attitudes.

INDIVIDUALS' ATTITUDES

It is to be expected that individuals' attraction to the remaining group members will at first be unstable, because initial attraction responses (made on the third

---

[1] There were, of course, individual instances of nonchange, but as population variables most of the attitudes here considered were highly inconstant.

[2] This description of balance as associated with negative attraction differs from Heider's position, according to which negative attraction together with dissimilarity is balanced and imbalanced together with perceived similarity. Theoretical considerations suggest that the former combination need not be rewarding nor the latter distressing; and empirical findings from the investigation here reported indicate that the former combination often does not have the stability that is characteristic of balanced relationships, while the latter does not necessarily have the instability characteristic of imbalanced relationships.

[3] For a fuller statement concerning this theoretical approach, see Newcomb (1953, 1959).

day) are necessarily based upon first impressions only; and that week-to-week changes should be in the direction of increased stability—that is, that the rate of change will be a declining one, because in successive weeks the amount of "new" information that individuals receive about one another will decline. The kinds of information about another person that are relevant to attraction toward him are, in general, those that result in the attribution to him of properties that are regarded as rewarding. These are not necessarily persistent or "inherent" personal properties; they may equally well include properties that are elicited only in interaction with specific other persons and they may, of course, be idiosyncratically attributed. Changes in attraction result not only from new discoveries of what characteristics another person already has, but also from observing qualities that, whether one knows it or not, has oneself helped to elicit in him.[4]

Table 1 presents means of week-to-week "reliability coefficients"; each subject's rank ordering of the other 16 subjects in attraction at each week was correlated with his rank ordering for the following week. Table 2 shows similar coefficients, computed over longer intervals. The two tables together provide strong support for both predictions: initial responses have little predictive value even for so short a period as 5 weeks, whereas Week 5 responses predict almost as well to Week 15 as to Week 10 ($p < .001$ in either case). Change continues throughout the entire period, but the rate of change declines hardly at all after the first 5 or

---

[4] Certain distinguishable sources of interpersonal reward, and thus of attraction, have been elsewhere described by Newcomb (1960).

Table 1

MEANS OF 17 INDIVIDUAL CORRELATIONS (rho's) FOR PAIRS OF ADJACENT WEEKS

Weekly interval[a]	Year I	Year II
0–1	.51	.65
1–2 through 4–5[b]	.82	.84
5–6 through 9–10[b]	.86	.91
10–11 through 14–15[b]	.88	.90

Note.—In rank ordering attraction toward other 16 subjects.

[a] Week numbers refer to the number of preceding weeks of acquaintance.

[b] Variations within these sets of adjacent weeks are so slight that values for the pairs of weeks have been averaged, rather than presenting each one.

Table 2

MEANS OF 17 INDIVIDUAL CORRELATIONS (rho's) OVER VARYING INTERVALS OF TIME

Weekly interval	Year I	Year II
0–15	.29	.31
0–10	.32	.35
0–5	.38	.43
5–15	.66	.70
5–10	.82	.84
10–15	.83	.85

Note.—In rank ordering attraction toward other 16 subjects.

6 weeks. Except for very unpopular subjects, whose high attraction choices are not reciprocated and continue to be relatively erratic, attraction choices show comparatively little change after the first 6 weeks.

Such changes should occur, hypothetically, in spite of the individual's tendency to maintain a constant relationship between degree of perceived agreement and attraction to others concerning objects of importance to himself. If it may be assumed that the self is such an object, and in general a positively valued one, then it is to be expected that high attraction toward others will be associated with the perception of reciprocation of high attraction toward oneself. Table 3 supports this prediction for Year I, and results for Year II are almost identical. All estimates of reciprocation by Rank 1 choices are at all times in the upper half of the distribution, and most of them in the upper eighth. There is a very strong tendency (not necessarily warranted) to assume that one's highest ranked associates return the compliment.

It is to be expected, on similar grounds, that attraction to other individuals will be paralleled by perceived agreement with them as to the relative attractiveness of the remaining House members. As shown in Table 4, which summarizes relationships between level of attraction to others and degree of perceived agree-

Table 3

RELATIONSHIP BETWEEN GIVING HIGH ATTRACTION AND PERCEPTION OF RECEIVING HIGH ATTRACTION FROM SAME PERSONS
(Year I)

Estimated rank of reciprocated attraction	Number of subjects estimating reciprocation from their Rank 1 choices at level indicated		
	Week 1	Week 5	Week 15
1–2 (very high)	14	14	12
3–4 (high)	3	2	2
5–8 (second quarter)	0	1	3
9–16 (lower half)	0	0	0
Total	17	17	17

Table 4

SUMMARY OF RELATIONSHIPS FOUND BETWEEN LEVEL OF ATTRACTION TO OTHER SUBJECTS AND PERCEIVED AGREEMENT WITH THEM ABOUT ATTRACTIVENESS OF REMAINING SUBJECTS

Time of response	χ^2	df
Year I, Week 1	55.81***	2
Year I, Week 5	31.13***	2
Year I, Week 14	38.94***	2
Year II, Week 2[a]	17.54***	1
Year II, Week 5[a]	6.73*	1
Year II, Week 12[a]	9.95**	1

[a] In Year II only 5% of all possible estimates, based on a randomly drawn sample, were made. The somewhat lower significance levels in Year II result, in part at least, from the smaller Ns in that year.
 * $p<.01$.
 ** $p<.005$.
 *** $p<.001$.

ment with them about the relative attractiveness of other House members, there is in both populations, at all stages of acquaintance, a significant relationship between these two variables.

A special instance of this tendency is to be found in the almost universal tendency to assume that one's two most preferred sociometric choices are highly attracted toward each other. (In view of the fact that reciprocated attraction from Rank 1 and Rank 2 choices is also perceived as very high, this set of phenomena may be labeled "the perception of perfect triads.") According to the Year I data, which for this purpose are more complete than in Year II but which are well supported by the latter, the relationships shown in Table 5 are typical of all stages of acquaintance. It

Table 5

SUMMARY OF SIGNIFICANCE LEVELS AT
WHICH TWO HIGHEST RANKING
CHOICES BY ALL SUBJECTS ARE
JUDGED TO BE HIGHLY
ATTRACTED TO EACH OTHER
(Year I, Week 5)

Category of esti-mated attraction	Number of estimates		χ^2	df
	Ob-tained	Ex-pected		
Highest quarter	22	8.5	26.51*	1
Upper half	33	17.0	28.30*	1
"Favorable"	34	23.6	13.68*	1

* $p < .001$.

seemed to be almost unthinkable to these subjects that their two most preferred choices should be hostile to each other, and almost so that they should be merely "neutral." Early estimates to this effect were in several cases quite inaccurate; lack of information invites autistic judgments. Later ones were highly accurate; as earlier perceptions of perfect triads were discovered to be erroneous, preferences shifted in such manner as to justify the perception of perfect triads.

Balance inducing forces should also result, at all times, in the perception of closest agreement with most attractive others with respect to objects other than the self and House members. The data most suitable for testing this prediction are subjects' rankings of the six Spranger values in Year II, to together with their estimates of how each other subject would rank them. Both at Week 2 and at Week 14 the relationship between attraction toward other subjects and estimates of agreement with them were

highly significant; x^2 values are 17.19 and 11.63, respectively, corresponding p values being $< .001$ and $< .005$, $df = 2$. The slight decline in this relation, from Week 2 to Week 14, is also found in other tests of the same prediction; it reflects in past the countereffects of greater accuracy with increasing acquaintance.

Thus the data show a continuing increase, though at a rapidly declining rate, in the stability of attraction toward others. They also show that at all times, to about the same degree, attraction toward others is related to perceived agreement with them concerning a variety of things.

DYAD RELATIONSHIPS: MUTUAL ATTRACTION AND ACTUAL AGREEMENT

Insofar as subjects were alert to increments of information about one another with continued interaction among them, it is predictable that estimates of others' attitudes will become increasingly accurate with continued acquaintance; and that actual relationships between mutual attraction and agreement will increasingly approach the perceived relationships. The latter prediction presumes that, with increasing accuracy, subjects will discover that some of their assumptions about agreement with attractive others are not justified, and will tend either to modify their own attitudes or to shift their attraction preferences to individuals with whom they are in fact more closely in agreement.

With respect to the self as an object, the data do not support the first prediction: estimates of others' attraction toward oneself do not become more accurate with increasing acquaintance, and this is true at all levels of expressed attraction. Frequencies and magnitudes of inaccuracies are quite constant, although they are at all times predominantly in the direction of overestimating the true level of reciprocated attraction. Estimates are in general fairly accurate, especially at the extremes of expressed attraction. Most subjects, apparently, are rather sensitive to others' indications of attraction toward themselves, at all times, and at all times there is a constant tendency to exaggerate the degree to which one's own attraction toward another person is reciprocated at about the same level.

The accuracy with which subjects estimate each others' attraction preferences toward other House members does increase. During the early period (Weeks 0–5) this increase is significant only for the estimator's highest attraction ranks, representing individuals with whom he is likely to have associated frequently enough after 5 weeks to estimate their preferences reasonably well. By Week 15 the trend is unmistakable at all attraction ranks: in Year I (the population in which these data are most nearly complete) 15 of 17 subjects were more accurate than at Week 1—the binomial probability of which is beyond .001.

Subjects' accuracy in estimating others' rank ordering of Spranger values increases at a high level of significance, as shown in Table 6, in which the indices of accuracy represent rank-order correlations between each subject's estimated rank ordering of each other subject's responses and the latter responses as actually made. The mean accuracy of 272 estimates, according to this index, is .25 at Week 2 and .49 at Week 14.

Table 6

RELATIVE ACCURACY OF ESTIMATING OTHERS' RANK ORDERING OF SPRANGER VALUES, EARLY AND LATE

Accuracy level[a]	Number of estimates at indicated levels of accuracy		
	Week 2	Week 14	Total
$\geq$.60	66	110	176
<.60, >.14	103	95	198
<.14	103	67	170
Total	272	272	544

Note.—$\chi^2 = 17.92$, $p = .001$, $df = 2$.
[a] Rho between each estimated rank with actual rank.

Turning now to actual dyadic relationships, it is to be expected that sensitivity to others' responses to oneself will increasingly result in similar levels of attraction on the part of dyad members, whatever that level may be. Insofar as forces toward balance with regard to the self are tempered with considerations of reality, dyad members should come to assign about the same degree of attraction to one another. Table 7 shows that this is indeed the case. A large proportion of the dyads whose members accord very different levels of attraction to each other include a very popular or a very unpopular individual, or both. Apart from this consideration, the tendency toward increasing reciprocation of attraction by dyad members at closely similar levels is almost universal. This fact about objective dyadic relationships, combined with the unchanging tendency to perceive favorably reciprocated attraction, reflects shifts in actual attraction preferences: changes are such that increasingly accurate judgments of

Table 7

Ns of Dyads Whose Members' Attractions to Each Other Differ by 3 (of 16) Ranks or Less

Time of response	Ob-tained	Ex-pected	χ^2	df
Year I, Week 0	51	50	.00	1
Year II, Week 0	59	53	.61	1
Year I, Week 15	77	53	10.61**	1
Year II, Week 15	72	53	6.46*	1

* $p < .02$.
** $p < .002$.

others' attraction toward oneself result in increasingly close reciprocation.

With respect to Spranger values, also, the effects of increased accuracy in judging others, together with constant forces toward balance, are that actual agreement is increasingly associated with high mutual attraction. At Week 2, when these responses were first obtained, there was no relationship between pair agreement and mutual pair attraction ($\chi^2 = 1.17$, $p < .50$, $df = 1$). At Week 14, however (when responses were last obtained), the relationship had become highly significant, as shown in Table 8. The χ^2 value of this distribution, with both variables equally dichotomized, is 9.52, $df = 1$, and $p < .001$ by a one-tailed test.

It happened that there were almost no changes in subjects' ranking of the six Spranger values between early and late acquaintance; it was therefore possible to predict later dyad attraction from initial agreement nearly as well from early as from late agreement; early agreement did not, however, predict to early attraction. Similar results were obtained with two other sets of attitude items, each quite wide-ranging in content, from which indices of dyad agreement were computed; first responses to these items were made on the third day of acquaintance in Year I, and by mail one month before subjects arrived at the university in Year II. As shown in Table 9, in neither case did preacquaintance agreement bear any relationship to early scores of mutual at-

Table 8

Relationship between Degree of Agreement about Spranger Values and Mutual Pair Attraction
(Week 14, Year II)

	Number of dyads at attraction level indicated				
Level of agreement	Highest quarter[a]	Second quarter[a]	Third quarter[a]	Lowest quarter[a]	Total
Highest quarter	12	6	9	6	33
Second quarter	10	16	6	4	36
Third quarter	9	4	8	11	32
Lowest quater	7	4	10	14	35
Total	38	30	33	35	136

[a] For reasons described in the full report, dyad scores are routinely categorized according to proportions of *expected*, not obtained, frequencies, which typically show slight differences.

Table 9

PREDICTIVE VALUE OF HIGH ATTITUDINAL AGREEMENT AT EARLY
PERIODS FOR HIGH MUTUAL ATTRACTION AT EARLY AND
LATE PERIODS

Nature of attitudes	Year	Week of attitude response	Week of attraction response	χ^2	df
Miscellaneous	I	0	0	.46	1
Miscellaneous	II	−4	0	.00	1
Spranger values	II	2	2	1.17	1
Miscellaneous	I	0	13	8.78*	1
Miscellaneous	II	−4	13	11.68**	1
Spranger values	II	2	14	9.52**	1

* $p<.005$.
** $p<.001$.

traction, but high preacquaintance agreement in each year predicted significantly to high mutual attraction 4 or 5 months later.

In view of the general increase in accuracy of estimating others' attitudes and in view of the constant tendency to prefer balanced to unbalanced states, it follows that with increasing acquaintance there should be an increasing tendency toward relationships that are balanced not merely phenomenologically but also in fact. This means that, except in the case of attitudes that show little or no change, change in mutual attraction between dyad members should be accompanied by change in their actual agreement. This prediction is best tested with respect to agreement about the relative attractiveness of House members. As shown in Table 10, the early relationship between mutual dyad attraction and agreement about House members approached zero in both populations, and increased to a significant level in the later weeks. Typically, there was a good deal

of shifting about during the earlier weeks, both with respect to mutual attraction and to preferences among other House members, with the result that the relationship between attraction and actual agreement becomes a highly significant one. It can also be shown, by more detailed analysis, that among dyads at a high level of mutual attraction in early weeks there is significantly higher agreement 3 months later

Table 10

SUMMARY OF MEAN CORRELATIONS
BETWEEN MUTUAL ATTRACTION AND
ACTUAL AGREEMENT ABOUT OTHER
HOUSE MEMBERS ON THE PART OF
136 DYADS

Week	Year I	Year II
0–1	.15	.18
2–5	.45	.37
6–9	.52	.40
10–13	.50	.43
14–15	.46	.58

on the part of dyads whose mutual attraction remains at the same high level than on the part of dyads whose mutual attraction has decreased. Change or nonchange in these two respects proceeds together and interdependently.

HIGH ATTRACTION STRUCTURING WITHIN POPULATIONS

Both a rationale and supporting evidence have been presented for the expectation that with increasing acquaintance subjects will shift their attraction preferences in such manner as to satisfy constant preferences for balance (that is, agreement with attractive others about objects of importance), and to take into account considerations of reality, with continuing increments of information about one another. With specific reference to dyad members' agreement about the attractiveness of other House members, this expectation leads to the prediction of increasing numbers of high attraction triads and larger subgroups, for the following reasons. Dyad members will tend to find one or more other individuals toward whom each of them is strongly attracted; dyads in which this does not occur will tend to be unstable. It is likely, as has been shown, that this high attraction will be reciprocated in kind by a third individual; if so, a high attraction triad has been formed, composed of the three mutually attracted pairs; if not, in the case of some particular person, it is likely to occur with a different one. Once a high attraction triad has been formed, similar processes tend toward further accretion, with the attendant formation of high attraction tetrads and larger subgroups.

With respect to triads, such processes did occur, in both populations. Since our principal interest lies in stable triads we took, as a criterion of stability, triads all three of whose component dyadic relationships maintained a high level of mutual attraction for 3 consecutive weeks. During the first 3 weeks of acquaintance only 2 of 17 possible triads remained stable by this criterion in Year I and 3 of 13 in Year II. During the last 3 weeks, however, 7 of 13 in Year I and 14 of 19 in Year II remained stable; the respective p values, by exact test, based on Ns of early and late triads that were stable and that were unstable, were .036 and .017. Numbers of stable triads do increase with acquaintance; there were too few high attraction tetrads and pentads at any time to be studied.

The attraction structuring of the total populations can be described in various ways, which might include numbers of high attraction subgroups of various sizes, the attraction relationships among them, and the number of isolates (individuals who have no mutually high attraction relationships at all). The two population structures did not differ in important ways at first, but interesting differences later appeared, as suggested by the sociograms presented in Figure 1, which show all subgroups of two or more whose members' levels of mutual attraction reached a rather high criterion. The visual appearance of these two sociograms, together with certain other evidence not here reported, suggests differences along a dimension that might be called centrality versus divisiveness—a difference not predicted on the basis of any theoretical considerations. A rather simple index of divisiveness confirmed the appearance, and a post hoc hypothesis was formulated concerning

Year I, Week 15   Year II, Week 15

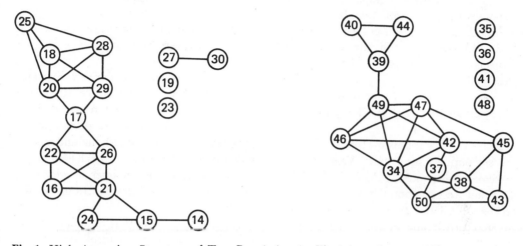

Fig 1. High Attraction Structure of Two Populations on Final Acquaintance. (Circles represent individuals; connecting lines represent mutual attraction at high levels.)

the sources of this difference. This hypothesis rests upon the contribution of two variables to centrality: the degree of interconnectedness among high, mutual attraction dyads on the part of the individuals having the highest attraction power ("popularity"), and the amount of attraction power concentrated in these individuals. It was found that among the most popular six individuals in each population, who together accounted for somewhat more than half of the attraction power in each population, 20% of all such dyads met the criterion of interconnectedness in Year I as compared with 53% in Year II. Moreover, there was more attraction power concentrated in the six most popular individuals in Year II than in Year I. Thus each variable contributes to the greater centrality in Year II. It is, in fact, an artifactual necessity that whichever of two populations of the same size has these characteristics will be

the more centrally structured: greater interconnectedness at high levels of mutual attraction among individuals having most attraction power; and greater attraction power on the part of the same number of popular individuals. These are not necessarily the only variables that contribute to centrality, but they do necessarily contribute to it, for the following reasons. Popular individuals who are multiply connected by high mutual attraction constitute a triad or larger subgroup that serves as a core substructure, each of whose members brings with him several "hangers-on" who are thus added onto the core structure. And the more "hangers-on" thus added, the larger the substructure becomes.

Our post hoc hypothesis as to why so few popular subjects were multiply interconnected in Year I and so many in Year II is simply that there was more agreement among the six popular individuals in the latter than in the former year; the evidence abundantly supports it.

1. The most nearly comparable attitude responses made by both populations were to miscellaneous batteries of items; in Year I the 15 dyads among the six popular subjects agree with each other no more closely than did all other pairs, whereas in Year II their agreement was significantly closer than that of other pairs ($p <$ .05).

2. In authoritarianism (F score), five of the six popular subjects in Year II were extremely low, ranking 1, 2, 3, 4, and 5 in a low scoring population; in Year I, on the other hand, the six popular subjects covered nearly the entire range, from 2 to 17.

3. Although no comparable data are available for Year I, five of the six popular subjects in Year II were in extraordinarily close agreement in Spranger values —and they knew it: the mean of their 10 intercorrelations in actual response was .72, and the mean of their estimated agreements with each other was .75. (The sixth, who disagreed with all of the others both in F score and in Spranger values, was Number 39, the only one of the six not having high mutual attraction with more than one of the others.) Thus the central proposition concerning balance accounts for the close interconnectedness of six popular subjects in one year and for the absence of it in the other year, and thus accounts for the different attraction structurings in the two populations. It does not, of course, account for the fact that in Year II but not in Year I popularity was pretty much concentrated among a set of five closely agreeing individuals. Our general theory has nothing to say about the characteristics which led to popularity in these populations, and

we can only say that our random methods of selecting subjects had this consequence.

INDIVIDUAL CHARACTERISTICS OF SUBJECTS

Several theoretically derived expectations have been shown to be supported by empirical findings. Our tests, however, have been statistical ones, pertaining to populations or subpopulations and not to individuals. There are two relevant questions concerning the manner in which individuals' characteristics contribute to the findings.

First, it is possible that a comparatively few individuals contribute all or most of the variances that account for the statistically significant findings; if so, the generalizability of the findings is severely limited. The findings depend rather heavily on assumptions concerning two kinds of individual tendencies: to prefer balanced to imbalanced relationships; and at the same time to take account of "reality" in the form of accretions of information that may disturb existing states of balance. Individual indices of both of these tendencies (sensitivity to balance, and accuracy in judging others) were therefore constructed. Results of intensive analyses of all 34 subjects may be summarized as follows:

1. Individual differences are clearly apparent, with respect to both balance and accuracy.

2. In estimating others' attitudes toward varying kinds of objects there are in each population typically one or two individuals who show little or no sensitivity to balance, or no greater than chance accuracy in making estimates.

3. The subjects who are deviant in these

ways with respect to one attitude object at a particular stage of acquaintance are not necessarily deviant with respect to other attitude objects, or at other times.

In sum, the tendencies to be sensitive to balanced relationships and to judge others' attitudes more accurately with increasing acquaintance, which underlie our theoretically derived predictions, appear to be present, at least in some degree, in all of our subjects.

As to measured individual characteristics, authoritarianism (as measured by the F Scale) seemed most likely to be relevant to the problems of this investigation. Our expectations concerning authoritarianism stem from several studies suggesting that F Scale scores (Adorno, Frenkel-Brunswik, Levinson, & Sanford, 1950) are related to "perceptiveness of others" (Christie & Cook, 1958, in a review of the relevant evidence on this point, pp. 180–183). Such evidence leads to the expectation that low F scorers should be relatively accurate in estimating others' attitudes. With one exception (estimates of others' ordering of attraction toward House members in Year I), the prediction is supported with respect to various attitude objects, and according to different indices of accuracy, in both populations. The data that best lend themselves to detailed analysis of accuracy consist of estimates of others' rank ordering of Spranger values, made in identical manner at Weeks 2 and 14 of Year II. These data show that on the rather difficult task of ranking other subjects according to agreement with the estimator, the nonauthoritarians excel the authoritarians in accuracy on late but not on early acquaintance; the correlation of .56 between F score and accuracy at the later time is significant at $< .01$.

Inaccurate estimates of others' attitudes may represent distortions either in the balance promoting direction or in the opposite direction; the former may be considered autistic, and if we assume that imbalanced relationships represent a form of ambiguity, of which authoritarians are relatively intolerant (cf. Adorno et al., 1950), then it is to be expected that high F scorers' inaccuracies will be in the autistic direction, relative to low F scorers. No difference in this respect appears at Week 2, when autistic errors are relatively frequent at all F score levels; but the prediction is well supported at Week 14: comparisons of autistic, accurate, and contra-autistic estimates for low, intermediate, and high F scorers yield a χ^2 of 13.02 in the predicted direction, significant at $< .01, \ df = 4$, by a one-tailed test.[5]

These and other findings are consistent with the following interpretation. The greater sensitivity of the very low F scorers enables them to select as most attractive those with whom they are in fact most closely in agreement about a rather wide range of values. The nonauthoritarians' characteristic solution to imbalance is nonautistic: they tend to achieve balance not by exaggerating actual agreement with those to whom they are attracted (on other grounds), but by judging rather accurately who is in agreement with them and letting their highest attractions be determined accordingly. The characteristic solution of the more authoritarian subjects tends to be just the reverse: instead of letting their personal preferences be

---

[5] If the "accurate" estimates are ignored, in order to compare autistic and contra-autistic responses only, the inverse relationship between autism and authoritarianism is still significant at the .05 level.

determined by accurate perceptions of agreement, they tend to perceive more agreement than actually exists with those toward whom they are already attracted.

NATURE OF CONSTANT RELATIONS

Three kinds of elements, in Lewin's (1947) sense, have been considered: an individual's attraction toward another person; his attitude toward some object other than that person; and that person's attitude, as he perceives it, toward the same object. Under the conditions of the investigation here reported, the stability curves of these three kinds of elements were quite different: attitudes toward nonperson objects (especially toward general values) showed little change from first to last acquaintance; attraction toward other House members, on the part of most subjects, became relatively stable by the end of the first 6 weeks or so; and estimates of others' attitudes were relatively slow in stabilizing, though with individual differences. If the study had been concerned only with subjects' own attitudes and attractions, it might well have been terminated after 6 rather than 16 weeks. But in view of the crucial place, in the present formulation, of perceptions of others' attitudes, and in view of the relatively slow and continuing changes in estimates of others' attitudes, it might be argued that the study should have been continued for another several weeks.

What does remain relativly constant, in spite of these differential rates of stability and change, is the second-order relationship between the relationship of two of them (own and other's perceived attitude) and attraction. With regard to such diverse attitude objects as the individual subject

himself, other group members, and a range of nonperson objects, such a relationship, described as a balanced one, is found at all stages of acquaintance. This constant relationship is maintained despite the fact that all of the related elements are changing, or some of them are changing while others are not. Eventually, the single elements tend to become stable, but the level at which they do so is governed by the same constancy of relationships that prevailed throughout the earlier periods of change.

The psychological processes by which intrapersonal states of balance are maintained may be described as follows. As group members interact with one another, each of them selects and processes information—about objects of common interest, about one another as sources of attitudes toward those objects, and about one another as objects of attraction—in such ways that the inconsistencies and conflicts involved in imbalanced relationships tend to be avoided. Both autistic processes ("balance at all costs") and realistic ones ("the truth, whatever it costs") are involved, their respective weightings being determined both by individual differences and by the strength of the attitudes involved. When interaction begins with total strangership, increments of information are inevitable; attitude change results from the necessity to adapt simultaneously to increments of information and to constant preferences for balanced relationships.

Interacting members of dyads and larger groups necessarily make such adaptations to one another simultaneously. Insofar as they do so realistically, the consequence of reciprocal adaptation is a mutual relationship that is in fact maximally satisfying to both or all of them—that is, maximally within the limits of what is possible. Realism tends to increase with acquaintance and, combined with constant tendencies toward balance, the inevitable trend is toward mutuality of attraction. Stable relationships tend to persist, and relationships that are in fact balanced tend to be stable because they are mutually rewarding and not likely to be disturbed by increments of information with continued interaction.

Viewed intrapersonally, the generalizable constancies underlying changes in interpersonal attraction that apply to all individuals—regardless of their differences in preferring some personal properties to others and regardless of the personal traits that others present are preferences for balanced relationships, and tendencies to adapt to information regarded as valid. Viewed interpersonally, the generalizable constancies are the necessities (which may become internalized as preferences) confronting each of a set of interacting persons to make successive adaptations to one another, simultaneously and reciprocally, in the direction of establishing relationships that are both realistic and balance promoting for each. It is relationships that are simultaneously rewarding to each and realistically apprehended by each that tend to be stable. Such relationships are both psychologically (intrapersonally) balanced and objectively (interpersonally) balanced.

Attitude changes that are governed by these constancies stem from a triple confrontation that is characteristic of *la condition humaine*. Each of us must somehow come to terms, simultaneously, with the other individuals and groups of which our interpersonal environment is constituted; with the world that we have in common with those persons and groups; and with our own, intrapersonal demands, including the preference for balanced states.

Insofar as the individual's confrontation is characterized by changing input of information, the elements that correspond to his attitudes are subject to inconstancy, but the lawfulness with which they change corresponds to certain constancies in relationships among the elements. It is such constancies that make possible viable adaptations, simultaneously, to multiple confrontations.

REFERENCES

ADORNO, T. W., FRENKEL-BRUNSWIK, ELSE, LEVINSON, D. J., and SANFORD, R. N. *The Authoritarian Personality.* New York: Harper, 1950.

CASSIRER, E. *Substance and Function.* Chicago: Open Court, 1923.

CHRISTIE, R., and COOK, PEG. "A Guide to Published Literature Relating to the Authoritarian Personality Through 1956." *J. Psychol.*, 1958, 45, 171–199.

HELDER, F. *The Psychology of Interpersonal Relations.* New York: Wiley, 1958.

LEWIN, K. "Frontiers in Group Dynamics: Concept, Method and Reality in Social Science; Social Equilibria and Social Change." *Hum. Relat.*, 1947, 1, 5–41.

NEWCOMB, T. M. "An Approach to the Study of Communicative Acts." *Psychol. Rev.*, 1953, 60, 393–404.

NEWCOMB, T. M. "Individual Systems of Orientation." In S. Koch (Ed.), *Psychology: A Study of a Science.* Vol. 3. New York: McGraw-Hill, 1959. Pp. 384–422.

NEWCOMB, T. M. "Varieties of Interpersonal Attraction." In D. Cartwright and A. Zander (Eds.), *Group Dynamics: Research and Theory.* (2nd ed.) Evanston, Ill.: Row, Peterson, 1960. Pp. 104–119.

NEWCOMB, T. M. *The Acquaintance Process.* New York: Holt, Rinehart, and Winston, 1961.

COGNITIVE CONSISTENCY
AND
LANGUAGE BEHAVIOR*

Richard Ofshe

Theories which incorporate the idea of cognitive consistency occupy a position of considerable importance in current social psychology.[1] It has even been argued that they constitute the field's 'first truly general . . . and compelling theoretical system' (Brown, 1962). Consistency theories have already been constructed for perceptual phenomena (Heider, 1946, 1958), belief-action events (Festinger, 1957), consensus formation (Newcomb, 1953, 1959) and attitude change (Abelson & Rosenberg, 1958). Applications of consistency formulations have been made to phenomena as widely ranging as group structure (Flament, 1963), spread of status value in organizations (Zelditch et al, 1966), wage inequities (Adams, 1963)

and the dynamics of status systems (Zelditch & Anderson, 1966). While the preceding enumeration of the varieties of, and uses to which, consistency theories have been put is by no means exhaustive, it does serve to illustrate the fact that these formulations are proving to be powerful tools in the analyses of numerous phenomena.[2]

At present there are two major problems to which research on consistency theories is being addressed. The first entails further specification and testing of the basic axioms of the theories and development of formulations treating complex structures and continuous variables (c.f. Price et al, 1966; Davis, 1967, and Zajonc & Bernstein, 1965). The second problem concerns identification of the scope limitations of the theories. That is, clarification of the question, to which phenomena may consistency theories reasonably be applied and under what conditions do their predictions fail (c.f. Oeser & Harary, 1962, 1964, and Brem & Cohen,

---

* Richard Ofshe, "Cognitive Consistency and Language Behavior," *Human Relations*, 23, No. 2 (April 1970), 139–51. Reprinted by permission of Plenum Publishing Company Ltd.

[1] The various consistency formulations are treated here as a set of models. Since, as Brown (1965) notes, each of these formulations is directed to a slightly different aspect of behavior no attempt will be made to rank or differentiate the models on any criterion other than that of their point of focus. We do not wish to bring religious beliefs into the discussion.

---

[2] Several excellent reviews of consistency theory and research are available in the literature (see Brown, 1962, 1965; Feldman, 1966; Osgood, 1960, and Zajonc, 1960).

1962)? This aspect of the research has a dual payoff. The initial result is that it provides information relevant to the development of a more general and better understood theory of cognitive consistency. In addition, it yields information of direct substantive import since investigations are carried out in the context of a particular research area (i.e. status systems, group structure) and new data are usually generated in order to test the theory's power.

The purpose of this paper is to report the test of an extension of a consistency formulation which attempts to conceptualize and explain the process through which signs (language symbols) come to take on similar psychological meanings for actors who engage in extended periods of mutual interaction. In order to specify more clearly the aspect of language behavior to which this research is addressed, it is necessary to distinguish between two types of meaning conveyed by a sign. For any user, a sign shall be assumed to possess both a formal, denotative meaning as well as a psychological or connotative meaning. For example, the sign 'mother' has an accepted denotative meaning of female parent. For a particular actor, it might have connotatve meanings such as 'kind', 'warm', 'loving' and 'generous' or possibly 'cold', 'hard', 'stern' and 'stingy'. Sets of connotative meanings may, of course, be more complex such that for a given actor the sign 'mother' connotes 'loving', 'stern' and 'generous'.

Once a distinction is made between the two meaning components of signs, it becomes obvious that in human communication a receiver's correct understanding of a message depends upon his accurately identifying both the denotative and connotative meanings the sender encoded through his choice of signs. Although

members of two sub-cultures who nominally speak the same language may assign different denotative meanings to a given sign and denotative meanings may actually come to be changed through time, they are like to be relatively more uniform and stable throughout a population than the connotative meanings associated with the same sign. For any actor, the connotative meaning of a sign is determined by both his objective and social experiences with its significate (significate refers to the object or action the sign identifies). Hence, it would be expected that a set of actors would show considerable variability in their assignments of connotative meanings to a given sign and a particular actor would alter the connotative meanings he associates with a sign as a function of both his own experiences with its significate and the connotative meanings it has for actors with whom he regularly interacts and communicates.

Given the assumption that the assignment of connotative meanings to signs is a dynamic process, the problem is to specify precisely how it operates. In order to begin conceptualization, it shall be assumed that the process can generally be treated as an instance of consensus formation and that a consistency formulation of the development of consensus will be applicable.

The most widely known consistency type formulation which deals with consensus formation is Newcomb's (1953, 1959) A-B-X model. As Newcomb formulated the model, it was designed to account for development of symmetric orientations towards an object (X) on the part of actors (A and B) who engage in interaction and exchange communications concerning X. Orientations towards X are defined as having both cathectic and cognitive components. Cathectic orientations concern the sign and intensity of A or B's attitude towards X. Cognitive orientation encompasses an actor's beliefs and structuring of cognitions relating to X. The first paper on the A-B-X model (Newcomb, 1953) did not clearly explicate the 'cognitive structuring' aspects of orientation. In a later paper, however, the term was clarified and the cognitive aspect of orientation was defined as referring to the structuring of attributes of objects 'only in respect to the relative salience of specified attributes' (Newcomb, 1959 p. 391).

Although Newcomb's formulation was clearly not intended to encompass the development of symmetry in connotative meaning, the reasoning which led to postulating the basic structure of the model is appropriate for the process considered here. Newcomb (1953) argued that since increasing the degree of symmetry in A and B's cognitive orientations towards an X results in: '(1) each actor being more easily able to predict the other's behavior and (2) a reduction in the necessity for either one of them to "translate X" in terms of the other's orientations' (p. 395), a strain towards attainment of a high degree of symmetry will be induced in the A-B-X system. Note that 'strain' is not introduced solely in response to the discovery that 'P dislikes an object that O likes' as in Heider's (1946) consistency theory. In Newcomb's formulation it is sufficient that a discrepancy impede communication in order for it to give rise to tendencies to change the status quo. Achievement of consensus with regard to cognitive orientations need not be conceptualized as following from a sudden discovery of difference, but rather can be thought of as the end result

of a gradual elimination of blocks to efficient communication between actors. It is precisely for the reason that it is a consistency formulation which rests upon assumptions about communication processes in general that the A-B-X model is expected to be an appropriate conceptualization of the dynamics of change in the assignment of connotative meanings to signs.

The most general postulate of the A-B-X model asserts the following: The stronger the forces toward A's co-orientation in respect to B and X, (a) the greater A's strain toward symmetry with B in respect to X; and (b) the greater the likelihood of increased symmetry as a consequence of one or more communicative acts. (Newcomb, 1953 p. 395).

Given that A and B differ with regard to the connotations they assign to some X (a sign) the theory identifies three possible consequences which affect communication process. Strain reduction can be accomplished by either or both actors changing the connotations they associate with the sign in a manner such that the discrepancy between actors is reduced. This response reduces the degree to which communications from one actor to the other need to be 'translated' to compensate for the discrepancy in meaning. A second strain reducing response entails distorting one's beliefs about the connotations the other assigns to the sign. That is, to assume that the other's meaning is similar to one's own when it is not. This strategy results in a false ease in communication in which the receiver incorrectly believes that he 'understands' the sender. The third possible result is simply to tolerate the strain. In terms of the communication process this response indicates that the individual recognizes that the sign has a different meaning for the other and continually takes account of the discrepancy when decoding messages.

The conditions under which actors tend to exhibit one or the other strain reducing response have nowhere been formulated. Therefore, in any empirical application of the A-B-X model one would expect to find evidence of both consensus formation and distortion. One goal of this extension of the model is to identify one set of antecedent conditions which produces a particular type of response to discrepancies in connotative meaning.

An important prediction of the A-B-X model concerns the effect of object relevance on strain reducing responses. It is assumed in the general postulate that if forces toward co-orientation are increased, the magnitude of strain generated will be increased. Since forces toward co-orientation are assumed to be directly related to the relevance of X to A and B, it follows that the greater the object-relevance the greater the strain reducing response. The obvious prediction of the model is that for X's of great relevance there will be greater development of consensus and greater distortion in the direction of consensus.

For the extension of the model, the following hypotheses relating the magnitude of object-relevance to reactions to strain shall be proposed. In keeping with the model's original formulation it is predicted that the greater the objective-relevance of an X to A and B the greater the development of consensus with regard to the connotative meaning of the sign of X.

The new predictions to be advanced concern the conditions under which actors will tend to tolerate strain *not reduced through the development of consensus* or further reduce strain through the mech-

anism of distortion of perception. That is, when will strain result in consensus formation and distortion, and under what conditions will it produce only consensus formation? These two different responses to strain are believed to be related to the magnitude of object-relevance of an X. It is predicted that for signs of objects of great relevance to A and B's interaction, the tendency through time will be for actors to *reduce* the degree of distortion in their perceptions of the other's connotative meaning. For signs of objects of low relevance to A and B it is predicted that there will be a tendency for actors to *increase* the magnitude of distortion through time.

The predictions advanced above result from an attempt to formulate the conditions which lead actors to react to imbalance by 'agreeing to disagree'. It has often been observed that one reaction to imbalance is to tolerate the tension of strain generated by imbalance rather than actually to change or distort perception of a relation (Heider, 1958; Newcomb, 1953). It is here suggested that this result obtains only when an X is of great importance to A and B (or P and O). There is wide recognition that in so far as an X is a focus of interaction for two actors, agreement about X facilitates their interaction. Given any degree of true agreement about X, it would seem likely that when X is important to A and B's interaction, any distortion of perception of the other's position will be difficult to maintain. Inappropriate behaviors resulting from incorrect conclusions about the meaning of the other's communication are more likely to be noticed and reacted to when both actors are concerned about the subject of the communication. On the other hand, when an X is of little relevance to A and B's interaction it would seem to be possible to maintain a distorted perception of the other's position since errors are less likely to be discovered. Under conditions of minimum object-relevance, gross distortion of perception therefore becomes a viable strategy for strain reduction.

Method

The research to be reported below was designed to test the applicability of a consistency model to one aspect of language behavior. In order to accomplish this end, it was necessary to discover whether or not individuals who interact for long periods of time come to assign similar connotative meanings to language symbols and if the degree of relevance of an object affects the rate of development of consensus and the type of reaction to strain as predicted by the model.

Subjects

A total of ninety individuals, forty-five subject pairs, participated in the research. All subjects were either senior undergraduate or graduate students attending a metropolitan university, or the college-educated spouses of these students. Fifteen subject pairs were composed of one male and one female who had never met each other prior to the research. The remaining thirty pairs were comprised of individuals who were either engaged or married to one another. These thirty pairs were divided into two fifteen-pair groups on the basis of the length of time the pair members had been in interaction.

This division resulted in three subject groups with considerably varying length of prior interaction. Group 1, the fifteen pairs of strangers, provided a sample with no prior interaction. This group was used as a baseline against which to measure the effects of varying lengths of interaction. Groups 2 and

Table 1

Mean Number of Months in Interaction

Group	Type of Subject Pairs	X Months in Interaction	S.D.
1	Strangers	0	0
2	Engaged and Married	21	10.19
3	Engaged and Married	62	21.84

3 were each composed of both married and engaged pairs and had substantially different mean periods of interaction (See *Table 1*).

Procedures

The procedures employed to obtain the data necessary to test the applicability of the model were designed around the use of the semantic differential. As pointed out by Osgood and his associates (1957, pp. 1–31 and pp. 318–331) the techniques of semantic differentiation provides a method for measurement of the psychological, connotative meaning of signs.

Subject pairs participating in the study met separately with the researcher. All subjects were first required to differentiate identical sets of twelve signs by scoring each one on ten, seven-point bi-polar adjectival scales. The scales were frequently varied between signs so that for the total of 120 differentiations made by a subject, 85 different scales were used. An illustration follows of the task which confronted subjects. For the sign 'house', ratings were required on the scales: complete-incomplete, unfriendly-friendly, congenial-quarrelsome, vulgar-refined, comfortable-uncomfortable, constrained-free, masculine-feminine, cool-warm, orderly-disorderly and simple-complex.

For the first series of differentiations subjects were provided with a written set of standard instructions for use of the semantic differential (see Osgood et al, 1957, p. 82). When this part of the research was completed the subjects' booklets were collected and certain background information was obtained. A second set of booklets was then distributed and each subject was requested to attempt to score the signs as they thought their partners had on the first differentiation. The sole difference between the booklets used in the first and second segments of the research was that the signs were presented in a different order in the second booklet. Both the scales used and the orders in which they appeared for each sign were identical to the first booklet.

Two measures were constructed by varying the sets of differentiations which were compared. The first measure called for a direct comparison between pair members' initial differentiations of the signs. Numerical scores for discrepancy in meaning on each sign were calculated by taking the sum of the square of the absolute number of scale steps separating ratings on each of the ten scales. The resulting score varied directly with the magnitude of discrepancy in the connotative meaning of a sign for a pair of subjects. A mean discrepancy score was generated for each pair by taking the average of the discrepancy scores for all signs.

The second measure was based on a comparison of each subject's first and second differentiations of signs. Since for the second differentiation subjects were required to score the signs as they thought their partners had on the first rating, the difference between a subject's first and second differentiations could be taken as a measure of the discrepancy he assumed to exist between his partner and himself. The procedure for calculation of this assumed discrepancy score was identical to that used for the first measure.

Two types of stimuli were selected in order to vary the object-relevance of signs. One set of stimuli consisted of signs whose significates were judged to be highly salient to the activities of individuals who were either planning or operating a family of procreation. The signs in the high-relevance set were: birth, family, hospital, house, in-laws and marriage.

The second set of stimuli was composed of signs which were judged to be more general in nature and not as salient in the interaction of engaged and married pairs. The signs were: beef, bit, hope, party, sin and symphony.

RESULTS

The first prediction to be tested concerns the development of consensus about the connotative meaning of signs. *Table 2* presents the mean scores for discrepancy in connotative meaning for the three subject groups. Scores for high and low-relevance stimulus signs are presented separately. Note that since scores reflect differences in the connotative meaning of signs for pairs of subjects, the lower the score the greater the degree of consensus between pair members on the meaning of the signs.

The mean scores for the three groups are as predicted by the model. Observe that there is a continual reduction in the difference in connotative meaning with length of interaction. The predicted effect is evident for the aggregated data as well as for the high and low-relevant stimuli considered as separate samples.

Table 2

MEAN SCORES FOR DISCREPANCY IN CONNOTATIVE MEANING*

Stimulus Set	Subject Group		
	1	2	3
All signs (N=12)	54.75	43.65	38.03
High-Relevance Signs (N=6)	59.36	46.19	39.42
Low-Relevance Signs (N=6)	50.13	41.12	36.63

* The lower the score the higher the degree of consensus.

The statistical significance of the differences between groups was tested by application of the Jonckheere test (1954). This is a k-sample non-parametric test which tests the null hypothesis that three (or more) samples were drawn from the same population against the alternative that they were drawn from three (or more) different populations which are stochastically ordered in a specified fashion. In the present application the alternative hypothesis is that group 3 pairs have attained a greater degree of consensus in connotative meaning than group 2, which in turn have attained a greater degree of consensus than pairs of subjects in group 1. The test was applied to all three sets of data with the result that the order hypothesis was confirmed in every case (all signs $p < .01$, high-relevance sub-set $p < .01$, low-relevance sub-set $p < .02$).

As additional tests of the model's prediction that length of time in interaction is related to the development of consensus on the meaning of signs, it is possible to examine the correlation between the length of time a given pair of subjects have been in interaction and the degree of consensus they have attained (this applies only to groups 2 and 3 since the strangers had no previous history of interaction). Further, the data on the engaged and married couples can be examined separately in order to determine whether or not the consensus phenomenon postulated by the model operates in both interaction settings. Spearman rank correlations between length of interaction and consensus are presented in *Table 3*.

It is clear that there is a significant positive relationship between the length of time a pair of subjects have been in interaction and the degree of consensus they exhibit. As indicated by the correlations for the engaged and married couples, treated as separate samples, the consensus formation process manifests itself in both interaction contexts. These results strongly support a developmental conceptualization of the phenomenon.

The second of the model's predictions to be evaluated is that the strain towards symmetry induced for signs of objects of high-relevance will be greater than that introduced for signs of objects of low-relevance and therefore, there will be a greater movement towards consensus on high-relevant signs. *Table 4* presents the data on magnitude of change towards consensus for the two types of signs.

The entries in *Table 4* were constructed as follows. The first entry, $+13.17$, was arrived at by subtracting the mean consensus score for group 2 (46.19) from the score for group 1 (59.36). The resulting value is equal to the amount of change in consensus from group 1 to group 2. The sign of the value indicates the direction of the change. If the result is positive, the net change was towards greater consensus. If the result was negative, the change was away from consensus. The same set of calculations was carried out for changes on low-relevance signs between groups 1 and 2 and yielded a result of $+9.01$. The difference in amount of change for the

Table 3

SPEARMAN RANK CORRELATIONS
BETWEEN LENGTH OF TIME IN
INTERACTION AND DEGREE
OF CONSENSUS

Subject Pairs	N	r_s	P
Engaged and Married	30	.39	$<.05$
Engaged	15	.81	$<.01$
Married	15	.65	$<.01$

two sets of signs was then calculated by subtracting the change on the low-relevance signs from the change on the high-relevance signs. A positive result in these cases indicates that there was greater change on high-relevant signs.

The observed magnitude of change towards consensus is clearly greater for signs in the high-relevance set. For each of the three possible comparisons of differences in mean consensus scores there is a substantially greater change for signs of high-relevance to A and B. For the comparison between groups 1 and 2, the movement towards consensus is 46 percent greater for high-relevance signs. For the comparison between groups 2 and 3, the magnitude of difference is 51 percent greater for this stimulus set. In the extreme comparison, groups 1 and 3, the change towards consensus for the high-relevance signs exceeds the change on low-relevance signs by a margin of 48 percent.

Since the research design was cross-sectional rather than longitudinal, the differences reported in *Table 4* are for group means rather than for differences for the same pair of subjects at two points in time. The nature of the data is therefore

such that there is no currently available statistical model which can reasonably be employed to evaluate the statistical significance of the differences. In sight of this inability, the only conclusions to be drawn from the results presented in *Table 4* are that the data offer no negative evidence for the theory in that they reveal no inconsistencies with the model's predictions.

The final two predictions to be tested concern the relationship between the relevance of a sign and the type of response to strain. The first of the two predictions is that for signs of X's of high relevance to A and B, interaction results in a tendency to reduce distortion of perception. That is, the longer the period of interaction, the less the degree of distortion of perception in the direction of consensus. The second prediction is that for signs of objects of low-relevance to A and B, the longer the period of interaction the greater the degree of distortion in the direction of consensus.

Both of these effects are predicted to operate independently of the actual degree of consensus attained by A and B. The dynamics of the interaction system which is being considered are assumed to

Table 4

CHANGE TOWARDS CONSENSUS AND DIFFERENCE IN MAGNITUDE OF CHANGE FOR SIGNS OF HIGH AND LOW-RELEVANT X's

Stimulus Set	Change Between Groups*		
	1 and 2	2 and 3	1 and 3
High-Relevance	+13.17*	+6.77	+19.94
Low-Relevance	+ 9.01	+4.49	+13.50
Difference (High − Low)	+ 4.16*	+2.28	+ 6.44

* A + indicates either that the group with the longer period of interaction, or the high-relevant signs showed the greater magnitude of change (i.e. +13.17 signifies that group 2's mean score was 13.17 points closer to consensus than group 1's and +4.16 signifies that the change towards consensus between groups 1 and 2 was 4.16 points greater for the high-relevance signs).

be such that at least three variables are operating simultaneously. It has already been established that as the length of time that a pair is in interaction increases, the degree of consensus the pair members attain increases. Further, the available evidence on the question of the rate at which consensus develops supports the model's prediction that there will be greater development of consensus for signs of objects of high-relevance. The final two predictions assert that at the same time consensus is developing there will be a *reduction* in the degree of perceptual distortion towards consensus for high-relevant signs and an *increase* in perceptual distortion towards concensus for lower-relevant signs. The prediction that for high-relevant signs there will be a reduction in the degree of distortion towards consensus is equivalent to the prediction that for signs of this type the only viable strain reducing strategy is a development of true consensus. The prediction that for low-relevant signs there will be an increase in the degree of distortion towards consensus is, in effect, a prediction that in addition to reduction of strain through development of consensus, for objects of this type, it is possible for actors to achieve further strain reduction through misperception.

In order to test these two predictions it was necessary to obtain a measure of distortion which was comparable for the three subject groups. Since subjects in the three groups were known to be significantly different in the degree of consensus they had attained at the time of the research, the measure had to be one which controlled for the actual degree of consensus existing between a pair of subjects. A simple estimate of the magnitude of distortion in perception would have been insufficient. The measure of distortion which

was used controlled for the level of consensus between pair members by calculating distortion in terms of the proportion of the distance actually separating pair members which was reduced through misperception.[3]

In addition to the obviously necessary controls for magnitude of object-relevance and length of time in interaction, a third variable, sex of subject, was controlled for in the analysis of data on distortion. Since the predictions dealing with the relationship between object-relevance and distortion should apply equally to both actors in the A-B-X system, controlling for sex permitted an additional consistency check to be made on the model's predictions. The data on proportional distortion towards consensus on the connotative meaning of signs is presented in *Table 5*.

The general trends in the data are in agreement with the model's predictions. For the high-relevance signs, the expectation is for there to be a *decrease* in the proportional distortion towards consensus with an increasing length of time in interaction. For the low-relevance signs, the expected trend is an *increase* in the proportional distortion of perception with longer periods of interaction. The model's predictions for reactions to the two sets of signs call for completely opposing behaviors. Consider the data reactions to magnitude of relevance for all subjects (sex not controlled). Note that for the extreme comparisons (groups 1 and 3),

---

[3] The formula for the calculation of an actor's proportional distortion towards consensus on each sign was P.D. $= 1-(A/C)$. Where A equalled difference the actor assumed to exist between his connotative meaning for the sign and the other's meaning and, C equalled the actual difference between actors.

Table 5

MEAN PROPORTIONAL DISTORTION
TOWARDS CONSENSUS IN BELIEFS
ABOUT OTHER'S CONNOTATIVE
MEANING OF SIGNS

		Group		
Relevance	Subjects	1	2	3
High	All	.27	.18	.14
	Male	.27	.21	.21
	Female	.26	·14	.06
Low	All	.15	.19	.29
	Male	.15	.20	.33
	Female	.15	.17	.24

the average change in proportional distortion on high relevance signs is a .13 *decrease*. For the same comparison on the low-relevance signs, the data reveal an average *increase* in distortion of .14. When the same type of comparisons are made for male and female subjects separately the resulting changes are −.06 and +.20 for males and +.20 for males and −.20 and +.09 for females.

The statistical significance of the group differences within each of the four sets of data in which both relevance and sex were controlled were analyzed through application of the Jonckheere test (1954). *Table 6* summarizes the predictions and results of the four analyses.

The Jonckheere test analyses reveal that only two of the four sequences of data attain statistical significance. The model's predictions are sustained for female subjects on high-relevance signs and male subjects on low-relevance signs. Although in the remaining two sets of data the trend is in the predicted direction, the probability levels are far from significant. There appears to be an unanticipated interaction effect between the sex of the subject and the relevance of the sign. The effect operates to inhibit the extent to which male subjects reduce distortion on high-relevance signs and female subjects increase distortion on low-relevance signs.[4]

SUMMARY AND CONCLUSIONS

In attempting a summary and conclusion about the research reported above, it should be kept in mind that the work

Table 6

PREDICTED ORDERINGS OF GROUPS AND
JONCKHEERE TEST PROBABILITY VALUES

Relevance	Sex of Subject	Predicted Ordering of Groups	P
High	Male	1>2>3	=.37
	Female	1>2>3	=.05
Low	Male	1<2<3	=.05
	Female	1<2<3	=.37

---

[4] One possible explanation of the results reported in *Tables 5* and *6* is that because of differences in their social roles, the signs within each of the simulus sets (high and low-relevance) were reacted to differently by males and females. That is, we suspect that the females treated both the high and low-relevance signs as being more important than did not males. This reaction could be explained as being due to a greater importance placed on the interaction system by the females. Therefore, relative to the males, the females would be expected to *more* markedly decrease distortion on high-relevance signs. Further, since females are more concerned than males, even for signs of absolutely less importance, they would be expected to distort relatively *less* on low-relevance signs. This response pattern is precisely what the data reveal.

was designed to provide information on which it would be possible to base a preliminary decision as to whether or not a consistency model could be formulated and usefully applied in the study of a specific aspect of language behavior. As a first step in research on the problem it was necessary to clearly demonstrate that actors engaged in interaction in 'natural settings' develop consensus on the meaning of signs. Although for theoretical reasons it was expected that development of consensus would come about, it might well have been that in a 'natural setting' the variables considered by the theory had only a trivial effect on behavior. In choosing to conduct the research with subjects who had a history of meaningful interaction the question of whether or not the phenomenon occurs in the 'real world' could be settled immediately. The costs of conducting a study rather than an experiment were a certain reduction in the degree of control which could be attained, some extra difficulty in testing causal explanations and an unavoidable reliance on natural variation (i.e., subjects were divided into groups on the basis of the length of time they had been in interaction prior to the research). The major gain from the decision was in terms of an increase in confidence that the phenomenon under study was one that manifested itself in naturally occurring communication situations.

In order to compensate for the relative looseness of the design, the strategy in the analysis of the data was to examine the overall patterning of results and check on the consistency with which the model was able to accurately predict behavior. The complex set of findings which emerge from the data must be viewed as supporting the predictions of the theory. Strong support for the model is given by the fact

that there is a continual increase in consensus with length of time in interaction and that the relationship holds equally well for engaged and married couples. In addition, the data on relative magnitude of change towards consensus is also predicted by the model (there is a greater increase in consensus on high-relevant signs than on low-relevant signs).

Finally, on the question of the relation of high and low states of object-relevance to reactions to strain, there are two issues to consider. First, the model predicts certain interaction-dependent trends in behavior and its predictions are clearly sustained by two of four tests. Note, however, that in the cases in which the predictions are not unambiguously supported, the data do not reveal any effects which are directly contradictory to theoretical expectations. The effects are simply diminished. The second point hinges on the fact that the predictions for reactions to high and low-relevance signs call for directly opposing behaviors. A simple inspection of *Table 5* reveals that reactions to high-relevance signs are quite different from reactions to low-relevance signs. As noted previously, the gross effects of the relevance variable are to produce decreasing distortion for high relevance signs and increasing distortion for low-relevance signs. This result is theoretically quite important since it identifies a point at which to begin better controlled, experimental investigations of the causation of differential reactions to imbalanced cognitive structures.

The research has opened up a new area of investigation through the application of consistency theory. The theory led to the expectation that a certain important phenomenon should be occurring in interpersonal communication and the research demonstrated that: 1) it does occur and,

2) the phenomenon behaves as the theory predicts it should. The discovery of a process of consensus formation on the connotative meaning of signs is particularly important in that it raises numerous researchable questions about the relationships between efficiency and accuracy of communication and the stability of interpersonal relations.

REFERENCES

ABELSON, R. P., and ROSENBURG, M. J. (1958). "Symbolic Psychologic: A Model of Attitudinal Cognition." *Behav. Sci.* 3, 1–13.

ADAMS, J. S. (1963). "Towards an Understanding of Inequity." *J. abnorm. soc. psychol.* 67, 422–36.

BREM, J. W., and COHEN, A. R. (1962). *Explorations in Cognitive Dissonance*, New York: Wiley.

BROWN, R. (1965). *Social Psychology*, New York: Free Press.

BROWN, R. (1962). "Models of Attitude Change," in Brown, Roger, Galanter, Eugene, Hess, Eckard, H. and Mandler, George, *New Directions in Psychology*. New York: Holt, Rinehart & Winston.

DAVIS, J. A. (1967). "Clustering and Structural Balance in Graphs." *Hum. Relat.* 20, 181–188.

FELDMAN, S. (ed.) (1966). *Cognitive Consistency: Motivational Antecedents and Behavioral Consequences*. New York: Academic Press.

FESTINGER, L. (1957). *A Theory of Cognitive Dissonance*, New York: Row, Peterson.

FLAMENT, C. (1963). *Applications of Graph Theory to Group Structure*, Englewood Cliffs: Prentice-Hall.

HEIDER, F. (1946). "Attitudes and Cognitive Organization." *J. Psychol.* 21, 107–12.

HEIDER, F. (1958). *The Psychology of Interpersonal Relations*, New York: Wiley.

JONCKHEERE, A. R. (1954). "A Distribution-Free k-Sample Test Against Ordered Alternatives." *Biometrika* 41, 133–45.

NEWCOMB, T. M. (1953). "An Approach to the Study of Communicative Acts." *Psychol. Rev.* 60, 393–404.

NEWCOMB, T. M. (1959). "Individual Systems of Orientation," in S. Koch (ed.). *Psychology: A Study of a Science*, New York: McGraw-Hill.

OESER, O. A. and HARARY, F. (1962). "A Mathematical Model Structural Role Theory," I. *Hum. Relat.* 15, 80–109.

OESER, O. A. and HARARY, F. (1964). "A Mathematical Model for Structural Role Theory," II. *Hum. Relat.* 17, 3–17.

OSGOOD, C. E. (1960). "Cognitive Dynamics in the Conduct of Human Affairs." *Public Opinion Quarterly* 24, 341–65.

OSGOOD, C. E., SUCI, G. and TANNENBAUM, P. H. (1957). *The Measurement of Meaning*, Urbana: University of Illinois Press.

PRICE, K. O., HARBUG, E. and NEWCOMB, T. M. (1966). "Psychological Balance in Situations of Negative Interpersonal Attitudes." *J. Pers. Soc. Psych.* 3, 265–70.

ZAJONC, R. (1960). "The Concepts of Balance, Congruity and Dissonance." *Public Opinion Quarterly* 24, 280–96.

ZAJONC, R. and BERNSTEIN, F. (1965). "Structural Balance, Reciprocity, and Positivity as Sources of Cognitive Bias." *J. Pers.* 33, 570–83.

ZELDITCH, M. JR. and ANDERSON, B. (1966). "On the Balance of a Set of Ranks," in J. Berger, M. Zelditch Jr. and B. Anderson (eds.), *Sociological Theories in Progress*, Boston: Houghton Mifflin.

OPTIMUM CONFORMITY
AS AN
INGRATIATION TACTIC*

Robert G. Jones and Edward E. Jones

The present investigation concerns the manner in which a person resolves a particular dilemma in making himself attractive to another. It is one of a series of studies investigating the use of restricted communication opportunities for ingratiating self-presentations. If a person is concerned with presenting an attractive "face" to another and has been apprized of the other's opinions, a convenient and common way to accomplish this is to express opinions which are highly similar to those of the other, to agree with him or at least to minimize the degree of disagreement. A number of studies have shown that Ss do reduce the discrepancy between their private opinions and the stated opinions of another when motivated to be approved or accepted by his (Deutsch & Gerard, 1955; Thibaut & Strickland, 1956; Jones, Gergen, & Jones, 1963). But the resulting opinion conformity is rarely if ever complete, and even if the "conformer" is especially concerned with making himself attractive, he will most likely

express a few minor disagreements in a setting of general agreement. This will be true for two reasons: (*a*) the potential ingratiator in our culture is unwilling to acknowledge to himself that he is willing to change his views markedly to gain attraction, and (*b*) for strategic reasons he will wish to avoid arousing suspicions in the target person that his agreement has been managed for its manipulative effects. He is most likely to arouse such suspicions if his opinions are monotonously close to the target person's in a setting where he is obviously dependent on the target person for favors, approval, or more generally, attraction.

A study by Jones, Jones, and Gergen (1963) showed that slavish agreement in such a setting does indeed give rise to the impression that the person agreeing is self-promoting, lacking in candor, and generally disliked. In that study, bystanders were exposed to a tape-recorded opinion exchange allegedly between two students like themselves. Following instructions given on the recording, one of these students always expressed his opinions after hearing the opinions of the other. It was so arranged that the degree of agreement was always very close in one treatment and moderately close or variable in

* Robert G. Jones and Edward E. Jones, "Optimum Conformity as an Ingratiation Tactic," *Journal of Personality*, 32 (1964), 436–58. Reprinted by permission of Duke University Press.

another treatment. A cross-cutting variation presented the opinion interchange in two different contexts: approximately half the Ss heard the interchange described on the recording as a preliminary to a lucrative and attractive experiment —*if* the students ended up attracted to each other; the remaining Ss heard the interchange presented as a first impression session in which candor and accurate self-revelation were crucial. The major dependent variable was the rated impression of the student forced to go second in the recorded interchange. As predicted, Ss disliked and deprecated this student when the context raised the importance of attraction and he responded with slavish opinion agreement.

But, one might ask, what would the implications be if this high degree of agreement were genuine and coincidental? Would not the second speaker, then, be unfairly judged in the eyes of others if he spoke his true opinions? If the second speaker did hold the same opinions as the first, he would be victimized by the situation and forced into a dilemma of self-presentation: whether to be true to his opinions in the face of agreement with another, and quite possibly have his intention misunderstood, or whether to vary his opinions in an effort to avoid the imputation of manipulative intentions. The present investigation sought to determine whether such a combination of events would be perceived as a dilemma and whether the implied threat of being labeled a self-promoting conformist would lead Ss to adopt mild nonconformity as a tactic of ingratiation.

In spite of the many technical problems involved in proceeding to explore these questions, the possibility of demonstrating that we sometimes modify our opinions in order to make them seem autonomously determined, seemed worth the experimental effort. In the experiment to be described, each S was involved in an exchange of opinions with another person who always came first in expressing his views on each issue. For approximately half the Ss, it was arranged so that the initiator always expressed the opinions which had been endorsed in an earlier session by the S; i.e., the initiator pre-empted the S's opinions (Same condition). The remaining Ss were exposed to opinions from the initiator which varied systematically from their own earlier recorded ones (Discrepant condition). As in the "bystander" experiment, the interchange was set in one of two distinct contexts. Ss were either motivated to make themselves attractive (High-Dependence condition) or to be accurate (Low-Dependence condition). The major dependent variable was the extent to which the S agreed with the initiator in the experimental situation, though confidence and attraction ratings were also gathered to shed further light on the dilemma and its resolution.

The major hypothesis of the present study rests on two important conditions: (1) reasonable opinion stability over time; (2) realization by the S that a person dislikes someone who agrees with him only for ulterior reasons. Stability of the particular opinions involved is a precondition for subjective victimization, for if the S's opinions at the time of the experiment cannot be predicted from his opinions at an earlier date, there is no effective way to arrange for the initiator to pre-empt them. The hypothesis also assumes that the S has some appreciation for the cognitive dynamics of the initiator —the uses to which he is likely to put combined information about the setting and the S's behavior—or no true dilemma will exist for him. If these conditions hold, then the following prediction seems a straight-forward derivation from the theoretical argument developed above: When there is a high discrepancy between A's incoming opinions and B's previously recorded opinions, B will agree more closely with A in the High-Dependence than in the Low-Dependence condition. When A pre-empts B's previously recorded opinions on every issue, B will agree more closely with A in the Low-Dependence than in the High-Dependence condition. Statistically, the hypothesis predicts an interaction between opinion discrepancy and dependence in the production of initiator-subject agreement.

METHOD

Subjects

Sixty male volunteers from the Duke introductory psychology course participated in the experiment in groups of five. Eleven Ss, scattered across the various conditions, indicated suspicion of the experimental procedure. Data from these Ss were not included in the data analysis, though the results would not have been altered by their inclusion. The results were based on the remaining 49 Ss: 10 in the High-Same, 11 in the Low-Same, 15 in the High-Discrepant and 13 in the Low-Discrepant groups.[1] In addition, two control groups were also run. In one (consisting of nine Ss) high dependence instructions were given but the Ss initiated rather than re-

---

[1] Since internal analysis of the Discrepant conditions was anticipated, slightly more Ss were run in these cells. Also, on occasions when only four Ss showed up, a paid assistant sat through the instruction as S.

sponded to each message. In the other, 20 randomly selected students from the same introductory class filled out the opinion-rating form at the beginning and end of the semester in a classroom setting. In neither control group could the S be directly affected by an incoming opinion message and any conceivable effects of the setting itself on the expression of opinions could be studied by comparing the two.

Experimental Instructions: High and Low Dependence

The crucial opinion exchange was set in one of two contexts which differed in the extent to which the S was dependent on the opinion imitation for the attainment of a desired goal. Dependence is herein used, then in the sense specified by Thibaut and Kelley (1959), as the reciprocal of power rather than a regressive emotional condition. The supervisor has more power than the judge in the present experiment, because he can provide both more positive and more negative outcomes for the S. It may help the reader to consider that the normal or usual conditions of self-presentation, where dependence is neither high nor low, give rise to a joint concern with being attractive (congenial, acceptable, etc.) and with being faithful to one's private feelings. The High-Dependence condition was designed to make the former concern of greater importance than the latter, while the Low-Dependence condition was designed to reverse this differential concern. Neither, then, is necessarily more normal or neutral than the other.

High Dependence. The experiment began with five Ss and the E seated around a large conference desk. Prominently displayed on the desk were five place cards reading "Supervisor," "Production Manager," "Copy Writer," "Copy Writer," and "Worker." On a nearby table was arrayed a stack of magazines, colored paper, scissors, a glue bottle, and similar art supplies. After introducing himself, the *E* informed the *S*s he was studying productivity in groups with two different kinds of organizational structure. One arrangement had the person most attractive to the leader immediately under him in the chain of command, the other arrangement placed that person at the bottom of the chain of command. The *E* then said the present group would be organized along the former lines to produce advertising copy—as he nodded to the supply of materials on the table. Next he enumerated the jobs in the work group and deliberately moved the place cards around the desk indicating where the job holders would subsequently be located. The supervisor, he continued, would be selected at random by a roll of a die and the other positions would be determined by how attractive he judged each of the others to be on the basis of an exchange of opinions. The *E* then stated that for the present group the person judged most attractive by the supervisor would be the production manager and the one judged least attractive would be the worker; the other two would be the copy writers. After relative attraction to the supervisor had been determined on the basis of an opinion exchange in another room, he continued, the group would return to the office, each would assume his assigned position around the desk, and together they would work for 30 minutes on advertising copy. The clear implication was that everyone would know how everyone else had been rated by the supervisor and it was expected that *S*s would get emotionally involved in such a popularity contest.

Low-Dependence Variation. *S*s in the Low-Dependence conditions were instructed in the same setting except the place cards, magazines, etc., had been removed. The *E* explained that he was interested in what sorts of persons are "highly sensitive and accurate in their appraisals of other people." He indicated that earlier studies were open to question because they involved one person judging only one other and chance accuracy could never be ruled out. His innovation in this research was to have a judge who would make appraisals of four persons. In this way he could more carefully select accurate judges and compare their personalities with inaccurate judges. The test of a judge's accuracy, it was explained, was carefully controlled by only allowing him to have information about the others which he could gather from an opinion exchange. After stating that the judge for that session would be determined by a roll of a die, the *E* emphasized that the other *S*s had a delicate task too, because they would have to present themselves as honestly as possible in the opinion exchange if their judge was to have a fair chance of being accurate in his subsequent appraisals of them. Then the *E* asked each *S* to fill out a slip naming the two persons on campus who could give the best evaluations of him; these persons were to be contracted by the *E* within the week. Rating made by the two friends would be pooled with the *S*'s own rating of himself to determine the standard by which to compare the judge's accuracy. The *E* concluded this part of the instructions by commenting that he hoped the judge from that group would prove to be highly accurate.

Cross-cutting Variation: Same and Discrepant Messages

When the *E* had concluded the instructions pertaining to the dependence variable, he went on to explain that attractiveness (in the High-Dependence condition) or accuracy (in the Low-Dependence condition) would be determined by a message exchange to be held in another room where there were a number of small booths. Each *S*, he continued, would enter a separate booth after which the supervisor/judge would be randomly selected. The supervisor/judge (hereafter called Target Person or Target) would then begin sending messages to the others. They were to answer each as it was received and send it back—the *E* serving as messenger. The anonymity provided by the booths, it was suggested, would rule out the possibility of bias based on prior acquaintance (though Ss were not allowed to participate in the experiment with friends), physical appearance, and the like. In the High-Dependence condition the E also commented that keeping the precise identity of each correspondent from the supervisor would put them all on an equal footing at the beginning. The E concluded by asking if there were any questions, briefly answered any which arose, and then led the Ss to the other room where they were arbitrarily assigned to separate booths.

In planning the experimental design, it was assumed that a victimization effect would result from a combination of High Dependence and the receipt of opinions identical to the S's. That is, the S would run the risk of appearing opportunistic if he expressed his true opinions. Opinions from the Target in this, the Same condition, and its counterpart, the Discrepancy condition, were prepared on the basis of each S's responses to a "Campus Opinion Questionnaire." This questionnaire was administered to all male students in the introductory course early in the semester. It was composed of 50 opinion items, each accompanied by a 12-point scale running from "Agree Completely" to "Disagree Completely." Ss were asked to check their agreement or disagreement with each statement.

The "Campus Opinion Questionnaire" also asked the Ss to check those statements they found unusually important. It was suggested that this could be determined by "whether it would make any difference in how much you liked a new acquaintance if he held a very different opinion from yours on the item." Thirty items were selected for the opinion exchange portion of the experiment: the 10 checked important by all Ss most frequently, the 10 checked least frequently, and the 10 in the middle range of frequency. While no specific hypotheses were formulated concerning this variation in item importance, it seemed quite possible that Ss would respond differently to important and unimportant items in resolving the victimization dilemma.

Each S in the experiment received the messages in a different random order with the following restrictions: five middle important items began the exchange, and five concluded it. The high and low items were randomly presented between with five high and five low in messages 6–15 and 16–25.

The opinion items themselves ranged over a wide variety of topical issues and pertained to academic, social, political, and personal matters. Two low important items were: (a) It will only be a matter of years before the horse becomes as extinct as the buffalo, and (b) Some way should be found to restrict any influence the alumni have over university policies and programs. Two middle important items were: (a) Television programs have become so bad that we should seriously consider federally sponsored programming during certain hours of the day, and (b) College student government associations are generally useless and don't deserve the support of the students. Two high important items were: (a) Negroes should be more severely punished for crimes against whites than for crimes against other Negroes, and (b) A belief in God is necessary in order to give a stable base to ethical standards in society.

Once in the booths, Ss in the Same condition were exposed to opinion ratings from the Target which were identical to their own pre-experimental ratings. Ss in the Discrepant condition received Target opinions which were four points removed from the S's pre-ratings either in the direction of greater agreement or disagreement. It was possible to maintain the deception that these opinions were actually coming from a naïve supervisor or judge because, of course, each S was isolated and prearranged messages tailored to the S's own opinions could be delivered by the E.

A number of steps were taken to facilitate the deception involved and to reinforce the experimental inductions. After the S had entered his booth, he was visited by the E who reiterated the significance of the messages. In the High-Dependence conditions, the

E emphasized that the attractiveness rating would be based entirely on the *S*'s replies to incoming messages. Low-Dependence *S*s were reminded to express their true opinions and to avoid trying to impress the judge. The *S* was then given a copy of the rating form which would allegedly be used by the supervisor or judge in assessing the *S*. These rating forms had been carefully constructed to reflect the clearly evaluative emphasis of the assessment in the High-Dependence conditions and the clearly nonevaluative emphasis in the Low-Dependence conditions. *S*s in the latter conditions, for example, saw that the judge always had to choose among positive or among negative attributes and never between the two types.

As the interchange began, the *S* received two introductory messages which were designed to convey the Target Person's clear understanding of the Dependence instructions (high or low). These were followed by a series of 30 messages, allegedly coming from, and after a few minutes picked up for delivery to, the Target Person. On each of these messages the opinion statement, worded identically to one on the earlier Campus Opinion Questionnaire, was printed twice with a 12-point scale of agree-disagree under each printing. The Target had presumably circled a number reflecting his opinion on the upper scale, and the *S* was to respond by circling a number on the lower scale. In addition, the *S* was asked to express, on a five-point scale, the degree of confidence he had in the correctness of his position on each issue.

The Postexperimental Questionnaire

When the message exchange was completed the *E* gave to each *S* a final questionnaire, commenting that it would take the supervisor/judge a while to make his rating and indicating his interest in some additional information. The questionnaire included seven questions. The first asked the *S* to rate the supervisor/judge on four dimensions: attractiveness, soundness, intelligence, and candor.

The second question asked separately how much of an effort has *S* had made to gain the (*a*) approval and (*b*) respect of the person sending the messages. The *S* was to check in each case one of five pertinent statements placed in descending order of concern with approval and respect. The intention here was to establish the effect of the dependence instructions. As a check on perceived influence, question three inquired whether or not the *S* had been influenced either to agree or disagree with the other person's opinions. The fourth question was directed toward the same interest and asked the *S*s to indicate the number of items in which they had felt pressure to agree, disagree or had felt no pressure at all. The fifth question asked how similar the *S*s' initial private opinions were to the other person's. The final two questions asked to what extent the *S*s felt they were agreeing too much, or disagreeing too much.

When the questionnaires were completed, the *S*s returned to the office where the experimenter declared the experiment was over, disclosed all deceptions and discussed with the *S*s the scientific purpose of the study. They were then asked not to discuss the experiment with others.

RESULTS

Validation of Experimental Inductions

Before examining the data relevant to the major hypothesis, it is necessary to establish whether the specific objectives of the experimental inductions were achieved, and whether the opinion ratings had sufficient temporal stability to permit a true pre-empting of opinion in the same conditions.

Dependence variation. Instructions in the High-Dependence condition made it clear to the *S* that he was in an attractiveness or popularity contest the results of which would be brought to the attention of his fellow Ss. The instructions themselves gave no hints concerning the components of attractiveness, but a copy of the supervisor's evaluation sheet was made available to the High-Dependence Ss and from this it was clear that they would be eventually judged on attributes relating both to affection and respect. If the dependence variation was effective, there should be evidence in the post-experimental questionnaire that High-Dependence Ss were more concerned with being liked and respected than Low-Dependence Ss. This was indeed the case; on separate questions the Highs expressed more concern with being liked $(F = 23.01, \ p < .001)$ and with being respected $(F = 19.79, \ p < .001)$ by the supervisor.

Discrepancy variation. Evidence concerning the differential perception of same and discrepant messages was also provided by the postexperimental questionnaire. Here Ss were asked to indicate the similarity between the supervisor's opinions and their own. As expected, Ss in the Same conditions perceived less discrepancy than did Ss in the Discrepant conditions $(F = 69.96, \ p < .001)$. Ss in the Same conditions also found the Target more likeable $(F = 12.88, \ p < .001)$, more sound $(F = 57.94, \ p < .001)$, more brilliant $(F = 15.96, \ p < .001)$, and more candid $(F = 13.43, \ p < .001)$.

Opinion stability. Questions concerning the extent to which unreliability of opinion rating was a factor in the experiment are difficult to answer except by circumstantial evidence. Rating changes by the experimental subjects were presumably a mixture in unknown proportions of unsystematic pre-post variation and systematic changes effected by the ex-

perimental variables. Evidence from two control groups, however, suggests that the amount of unsystematic opinion change was considerable. A first control group (C_1) was exposed to the High-Dependence instructions in the experimental situation but in the opinion exchange these Ss always preceded rather than followed the prospective supervisor. A second control group (C_2) consisted of 20 randomly chosen students who twice filled out the opinion questionnaire —once toward the beginning and once at the end of the semester. The average scale change per opinion item (direction disregarded) was 2.13 for C_1 and 2.09 for C_2 respectively. Since we may assume that these values estimate the amount of unsystematic change occurring in the experimental conditions as well, preconditions for a true "victimization dilemma" were probably not achieved. Ss in the Same conditions viewed the opinions received as considerably closer to their own than those in the Discrepancy conditions, but there is serious doubt that the average S in the former conditions felt his precise opinions were pre-empted. As we shall see, therefore, the phenomenal situation of the Ss in the High-Dependence-Same condition was rather different from that specified as a precondition for the main hypothesis.

Perception of influence and victimization. In spite of the undoubted pre-experimental changes in opinion characterizing all Ss, there still is some evidence from the final questionnaire that Ss in the Same conditions were more aware of influence pressures than those in the Discrepant conditions. (The dependence variation did not seem to affect this kind of awareness one way or the other.) Same condition *S*s generally denied that they felt any influence to agree or disagree with the incoming statement, but they still acknowledged more influence than did *S*s in the Discrepant conditions (*F* = 6.02, *p* < .05). Similarly, when asked if they felt they had "agreed too much," all *S*s tended to deny this as a problem. Nevertheless, the Same condition *S*s once again were less vigorous in their denial (*F* = 9.90, *p* < .01). It would seem, then, that being exposed to a sequence of opinions agreeing closely with one's own created at least some detectable

conflict, regardless of the social context in which this exposure occurred. The probable nature of this conflict will be discussed below.

Opinion Conformity: Accommodation to Target's Opinions

The main hypothesis of the present investigation predicted an interaction among the two independent variables in affecting the final discrepancy between the Target's and the *S*'s opinions. A smaller discrepancy was predicted in the

Table 1

DISCREPANCY FROM TARGET AND FROM BEFORE SCORES
(COMPARISON OF EXPERIMENTAL AND CONTROL *S*s).

		Experimental *S*s			
		Discrepancy from Target[a]		Discrepancy from Before Scores[b]	
		High Dep.	Low Dep.	High Dep.	Low Dep.
Same	$\overline{X}$	1.47	1.67	1.47	1.67
	SD	.67	.37	.67	.37
	N	10	11	10	11
Discrepant	$\overline{X}$	2.68	3.45	2.13	1.98
	SD	.46	3.4	3.8	4.3
	N	15	13	15	13
		Control *S*s			
				Laboratory (C$_1$)	Classroom (C$_2$)
	$\overline{X}$			2.15	2.09
	SD			.56	.55
	N			9	20

[a] These values represent the average difference per item between the *S*'s and the Target's opinion ratings. Thus, the lower the discrepancy score, the greater the agreement with the Target. Comparisons: Same vs. Discrepant, *p* < .001; High vs. Low, *p* < .01; interaction, *p* < .05.

[b] Since the Target's ratings are identical to the *S*'s ratings in the Same condition, the means are the same in the first row of the table. In the third and fourth columns, the lower the score, the less the change (direction disregarded) from before to after rating. Comparisons between experimental and control *S*s: Control (C$_1$+C$_2$) vs. High Same, *p* < .02; vs. Low Same, *p* < .06; vs. High Discrepant, n.s.; vs. Low Discrepant, n.s.

Low Dependence Same condition than in High Dependence Same; a larger discrepancy was predicted in Low Dependence Discrepant than in High Dependence Discrepant. As Table 1 shows, the predicted interaction was indeed significant (along with both main effects), but the reversal of differences specified in the prediction did not occur. When there is a fairly sizable discrepancy between two persons' opinions and the importance of attraction is made salient, the individual responding second attempts to reduce this discrepancy beyond that expected in a comparison condition where the initial discrepancy is as great but attraction is minimized. This portion of the predicted interaction was confirmed to a highly significant extent ($t = 5.03$, $p < .001$). When the initial discrepancy is minimal, however, the results do not show a reversal of this effect: instead, there is no reliable difference in resulting discrepancy as a function of the salience of attraction (i.e., the dependence variable), and the mean difference is in the same direction as that in the Discrepant conditions. As the significant main effect for Dependence implies, pressures to be attractive produce change in the direction of conformity regardless of the degree of initial discrepancy, though the interaction tells us that this change is much greater when the discrepancy is substantial. Only in a relative sense, then, is the main hypothesis confirmed and the discrepancy results may be accounted for without reference to any effects of victimization. For one thing, Ss in the Discrepant conditions have more room for movement in the Target's direction than those in the Same conditions. It might also be noted that item importance did not greatly affect the observed variations in opinion discrepancy, though the High-Same Ss should show slightly more conformity on important than on unimportant items (cf. Jones, Gergen, Gumpert, & Thibaut, in press). Finally, there were no systematic effects as a function of item sequence or position.

Signs of a Self-Presentation Dilemma

The present study was mainly concerned with the potential dilemma facing Ss in the High-Dependence-Same condition, with the remaining conditions serving as points of comparison. As originally described, the dilemma was to emerge out of competing pressures to be true to one's own opinions while avoiding the appearance of slavish and manipulative conformity. In view of the instability of Ss' opinion ratings, and the resulting fact that their opinion during the experimental session could not be accurately pre-empted by a repetition of their previously recorded ratings, there is serious question that such a dilemma was in fact created. The question remains serious in view of the failure of Ss in the Same conditions to confirm the hypothesis on the discrepancy or conformity data. But there are interesting data from other resources which argue that a kind of dilemma *was* created in the High-Same Ss. For these Ss the problem was not, as initially proposed, one of remaining true to their own opinions while avoiding the appearance of conformity. Instead, however, the Ss faced a more benign dilemma: how to gain attraction and respect by conforming without appearing to conform and without having to acknowledge their conformity to themselves. The remainder of this section will concern itself with the evidence bearing on this dilemma and its resolution.

Perhaps the first thing to note is the fact of high variability in the High-Same cell. Ss in this cell vary from each other in discrepancy score more than Ss in the Low-Same cell ($F_{9,10} = 3.28$; $p < .05$). A reasonable interpretation of this difference would suggest greater conformity conflict in the High-Same Ss. Relative to the Low-Same cell, some High-Same Ss showed more agreement with the Target and some showed less, suggesting that the position of the Target was more of a factor in determining their position. The Target's opinions were either more attractive or more repelling, but not apt to be ignored by the High-Same Ss. That the tendency to conform or to resist influence represented a general (if implicit) decision is suggested by the lack of any differences in variability across items. Thus, relative to Ss in other conditions there was no greater tendency for Ss in the High-Same condition to conform more on some items than others.

The conflict hypothesis becomes more plausible when some of the correlates of conformity in the High-Same cell are examined. As Table 2 shows, this is the only condition in which there is a significant positive correlation between attraction to the Target (as measured by a postexperimental questionnaire item) and conformity. In fact, in spite of the small samples involved, this correlation is significantly greater ($p < .01$) than the nonsignificant negative correlation in the Low-Same cell. Interpreting the psychological meaning of such a correlation involves the consideration of three major alternatives. It may be that Ss who happen to find themselves in closer agreement with the Target therefore

like him better, or it may be that those who start out feeling positively toward the Target therefore agree with him more. While both of these alternatives are plausible, there does not seem to be any reason why either should characterize the High-Same group and not lead to similar correlations in the other cells. A third alternative is that those who tend to conform in a situation where too much agreement might be suspect attempt to justify this conformity to themselves by increasing their liking for the Target. In other words, the high correlations in the High-Same cell may reflect the operation of dissonance reduction processes (cf. Festinger, 1957): dissonance is produced when the cognition that one is honest and consistent coexists with the cognition that one yields solely to win favor. By convincing himself that the Target person is likeable, the S thus reduces the dissonance created by conformity. Since the conditions for dissonance are not present to the same degree in the other cells, the correlations there are negligible.

Table 2 also presents evidence of a relationship between expressed desire to be respected on the one hand, and conformity in the High-Same and High-Discrepant cells. In the High-Same cell, the relationship between these variables appeared to be curvilinear by inspection. Therefore, each discrepancy score was subtracted from the cell median (ignoring sign) to produce a derived "optimum conformity" score. Thus, the optimum conformity score is a measure of the degree to which the S in question overconformed or underconformed relative to the median S. The only correlation which approaches significance is that in the High-Same cell where the coefficient of .461 suggests that the

Table 2

RELATIONSHIPS BETWEEN:
(a) OPINION CONFORMITY AND LIKING THE TARGET,
(b) OPINION CONFORMITY AND DESIRE TO BE RESPECTED, AND
(c) OPTIMUM CONFORMITY INDEX AND DESIRE TO BE RESPECTED

(Product moment correlations)

(a) Opinion conformity and liking the target		
	Dependence	
	High	Low
Same	.774**	−.321
Discrepant	.276**	.102

(b) Opinion conformity and desire to be respected		
	Dependence	
	High	Low
Same	−.095	−.387
Discrepant	.563**	.189

(c) Optimum conformity index[a] and desire to be respected		
	Dependence	
	High	Low
Same	.461	−.051
Discrepant	.064	.163

[a] Derived by taking the absolute value of the discrepancy between the cell median score and the S's score.
** $p < .01$.

desire to be respected relates to moderate conformity. It would be dangerous to make too much of this *ad hoc* result obtained with a derived score, but the fact that a curvilinear relationship exists does make good psychological sense. When a premium is placed on "being attractive to a Target and the Target is aware of this," those Ss most concerned with obtaining this goal adopt an optimum strategy of moderate conformity. A loss of respect is risked either if they conform too obviously or if they hold opinions too much at variance with those of the Target.

When attraction is still salient but there is no danger of being judged a manipulative conformist, one would expect this curvilinear relationship to change into a linear one with desire for respect being related positively to degree of agreement with the Target person. That this is indeed the case is clearly suggested by the significant correlation between raw discrepancy score and desire to be respected in the High-Discrepant cell. Ss in this cell had no need to fear being perceived as conforming for manipulative reasons. Their problem was rather to show enough agreement with the supervisor to avoid being judged ridiculous in his eyes and thus unworthy of his respect.

It is hardly surprising that the desire to be respected is positively correlated with the desire to be liked (coefficients ranging from .605 to .803). If in Table 2 ratings indicating the desire to be liked are substituted for ratings of desire to be respected, the correlations are similar but slightly lower in magnitude. But there is theoretically relevant evidence that *S*s do make a distinction between being liked and respected in their efforts to be ingratiating, and that this distinction bears a logical relationship to conformity in their mind. The means in Table 3 strongly suggest that *S*s respond to the dilemma created in receiving the Target's opinions by modifying their goals or aspirations in

Table 3

CONCERN WITH BEING LIKED AND WITH BEING RESPECTED

A. Mean and standard deviation for each group on both items[a]

		Concern for being liked[b]				Concern for being respected[b]	
		Dependence				Dependence	
		High	Low			High	Low
Same	$\bar{X}$	3.1	1.8	Same	$\bar{X}$	2.7	1.6
	SD	.57	.92		SD	.95	.70
Discrepant	$\bar{X}$	2.6	1.4	Discrepant	$\bar{X}$	3.3	1.7
	SD	.97	.70		SD	.95	.95

B. Summary of analysis of variance

Source	DF	MS	F
Between *S*s	39	17.94	33.90***
B: Dependence (H-L)	1	33.80	
C: Discrepancy (S-D)	1	.05	
B × C	1	.20	
Error (*b*)	36	.997	
Within *S*s	40	20.00	
A: Like-respect	1	.20	
A × B	1	.05	
A × C	1	3.20	7.16*
A × B × C	1	.45	
Error (w)	36	.447	
Total	79		

[a] *N* for all groups is 10. Nine *S*s were randomly discarded to equate cell frequencies for this analysis.

[b] Higher scores signify greater concern with the given attribute.

*$p < .05$.

***$p < .001$.

the situation. When "concern for being liked" and "concern for being respected" are scored separately and placed in a mixed factorial design, two significant results emerge from the resulting analysis of variance. As indicated previously, Ss in the High-Dependence condition are more concerned both with being liked and with being respected than Ss in the Low-Dependence condition. In addition, the significant interaction reflects the fact that Ss in the Same conditions express more interest in being liked, while Ss in the Discrepant conditions express more interest in being respected. Putting together the relevant evidence, we may conclude that Ss are swept along by the discrepancy variation into a resulting position of rather close agreement (in the Same condition) or rather great disagreement (Discrepant condition). Their respective goals or "desires" are then, apparently, changed to accommodate their perceived accomplishments: Ss who are swept into agreement tend to relinquish the goal of being respected; Ss who are in disagreement tend to relinquish the goal of being liked.

Confidence Ratings and Ingratiation

In addition to recording their opinions on each message form received, the Ss indicated their confidence on a scale from 1 (much confidence) to 5 (little confidence). These confidence scores may be examined in a number of different ways. The analyses attempted were those which seemed to give promise of relating the expression of confidence to ingratiation pressures. This becomes particularly pertinent following our realization that conformity itself (in the Same conditions at least) was not put to clear use as an instrument of ingratiation. Perhaps, then, variations in confidence might serve as a

more subtle and less risky tactic in making oneself attractive.

By averaging each S's confidence scores across the 30 opinion items, it is possible to obtain an over-all confidence measure. As Table 4 shows, Ss in the crucial High-Same cell are almost significantly more confident than Ss in the Low-Same cell ($p < .10$) and are significantly more confident than all other Ss combined ($p < .05$). It is tempting to conclude that Ss facing the dilemma of wanting to be attractive without running the risks of slavish conformity, attempt to further their aim by a combination of moderately high conformity and high self-confidence in their opinions. A breakdown of items into those of high, intermediate, and low importance (as in Table 4) shows that this difference in confidence scores appears only for items of intermediate and especially of high importance. It is relevant to point out that the High-Same Ss show greater conformity in the important than the unimportant items while the Low-Same Ss conform more on the unimportant items. However, since this "interaction" is far from significant, the confidence of High-Same Ss on important items cannot be completely accounted for by their increased agreement with the Target. The pattern of confidence ratings across levels of importance is at least consistent with the hypothesis that important issues are likely to be more salient in the process of gaining and awarding approval, so it is with respect to such issues that the tactical use of confidence ratings is apparent.

Turning to individual differences in the tendency to express confidence in one's opinions, there is a strong relationship between confidence and conformity which appears only in the High-Same cell. As Table 5 shows, those Ss who show the most conformity in this cell also express

Table 4

CONFIDENCE RATINGS BY CONDITIONS AS A FUNCTION OF ITEM IMPORTANCE

Condition		High	Importance[a] Intermediate		Low	Total
High same	$\bar{X}$	1.65	1.89		2.20	1.91
	SD	.39	.40		.48	.39
Low same	$\bar{X}$	1.96	2.20		2.28	2.15
	SD	.27	.28		.21	.20
p_{diff}		.05	.06		n.s.	.10
High discrepant	$\bar{X}$	1.95	2.13		2.35	2.15
	SD	.37	.47		.49	.39
Low discrepant	$\bar{X}$	1.97	2.32		2.35	2.21
	SD	.45	.36		.34	.29
p_{diff}		n.s.	n.s.		n.s.	n.s.
Column totals		1.88	2.14		2.30	
p_{diff}			$p < .01$	$p < .06$		

[a] Low scores = High confidence.

the greatest confidence in their opinions. It should be noted that this is a correlation between conformity and confidence across all items, and does not necessarily imply that confidence is highest in the High-Same group on those items where the resulting discrepancy is lowest. In fact, correlations of confidence and conformity taking individual items into account (and thus computing a correlation for each S) are uniformly low and do not vary significantly by conditions. We are thus left with the more general conclusion that, only in the High-Same cell, Ss who present themselves as confident (on the average) also express opinions which are similar to the Target's. A reasonable interpretation of the high correlation is that those Ss who employ the risky tactic of conformity in the High-Same cell emphasize their confidence in the attempt to signify their autonomy and their resistance to social influence. This strategy would present the Target with a pattern of congenial opinions independently developed. Those Ss who do not tend to agree as much, on the other hand, reduce their "disagreeableness" by expressing less confidence in their opinions.

Table 5

RELATIONS BETWEEN OPINION CONFORMITY AND CONFIDENCE

	High Dep.	Low Dep.
Same	.671*	−.213
Discrepant	.076	−.149

*$p < .05$.

DISCUSSION

Stated in its most general form, the main hypothesis of the present investigation was that a person who is obviously motivated to win the approval of another must avoid the Scylla of overconformity and the Charybdis of errant disagreement. The avoidance of conformity should be demonstrable if the person finds that his own opinions have been pre-empted by the very person he wants to impress. Under the circumstances, he can only be true to himself at the expense of being judged a self-seeking conformist. Therefore, attraction pressures should induce mild disagreement. Obversely, the avoidance of extreme disagreement should be demonstrable if the person finds that his own opinions differ markedly from those of the person he is trying to impress. He can only be true to himself at the expense of offering offense to the other. Attraction pressures should thus reduce the discrepancy between the opinion expressed first and the reply. The results of the experiment clearly confirmed the disagreement-avoidance part of the hypothesis, but the evidence with respect to conformity-avoidance turned out to be equivocal and complex.

The conformity-avoidance part of the hypothesis was tested by comparing two conditions in which the opinion initiator presented opinions identical to those previously endorsed by the S. In one condition, attraction was the induced goal of the interchange, so that the S was dependent on the other person for approval (presumably some combination of liking and respect). In the comparison condition, dependence was minimized by instructions emphasizing accuracy and valid self-disclosure. Contrary to the hypothesized conformity-avoidance effect, Ss in the High-Dependence-Same condition showed slightly more conformity than those in the Low-Same condition. In our judgment, the hypothesis was probably not confirmed because of the basic in-

stability of the S's opinion ratings. Thus, Ss in both "pre-empt" conditions could show general agreement without slavish conformity and still be convinced that they were expressing their true opinions.

While there is no evidence of conformity-avoidance in the discrepancy data, the High-Same Ss showed in a number of ways an implicit awareness of the dilemma posed by a setting in which too much conformity would negate their attraction strivings. In each of the following respects, unique findings were obtained in the High-Same cell:

1. While the cell mean showed slightly less opinion discrepancy than the Low-Same cell, High-Same Ss were significantly more variable than Low-Same Ss.

2. Those Ss who conformed more also liked the Target more. This relationship between conformity and postexperimental ratings of liking appeared only in the High-Same cell.

3. Conforming Ss tended to express greater confidence in their opinions throughout the message exchange. This relationship was again found only in the High-Same cell.

4. Ss in the High-Same cell were more confident in general than the other Ss and this is especially true when only the most important issues are considered.

5. The High-Dependence instructions are associated with a relationship between "desire for respect" and degree of conformity. However, this relationship was positive and linear for the Discrepant condition Ss and curvilinear for the Same condition Ss. In the latter group, desire for respect (and to a lesser degree desire to be liked) was highest in those Ss showing intermediate conformity.

Putting together these ways in which the High-Same Ss differed from those in other cells makes it possible to salvage a complicated but still meaningful picture of the subtleties of self-presentation in the service of attractiveness. Faced with the dilemma of impressing someone who expresses opinions very close to their own, Ss show evidence of conflict and search for ways to (a) convince the other person of their sincere similarity of views and (b) convince themselves that agreement with the other is not merely manipulative in intent. It may be plausibly argued that the former goal was mediated by expressing much confidence when agreement was high and little confidence when agreement was low. In the first case, the S attempts to convince the other that he happens to agree but is independent and autonomous. In the second case, the S softens the impact of his disagreement by his lack of self-confidence, implying that ultimately closer agreement could be reached. The goal of self-justification was mediated by a general denial of being influenced and a tendency to see the Target as more likeable when he had an influence on the Ss' opinions. In addition, there was evidence that High-Dependence Ss rationalized their interpretation of attraction to accord with their ultimate discrepancy from the Target, Same Ss claiming a greater interest in being liked than respected and the reverse being claimed by Discrepant Ss.

In view of the technical difficulties encountered in the present study, it is not clear whether an effective pre-empting of opinions could be arranged. Any attempt to increase the reliability of opinion statements by using only well-crystallized issues or reducing the number of scale points also increases the expectancy of close opinion agreement and thus takes the sting from the dilemma. In any event, while it cannot be said that the present High-Same Ss were truly victimized by the experimental arrangements, they did use their limited communication resources to reach for approval in the subtle ways recounted above. We may conclude, then, that these Ss showed some awareness of the likely cognitive dynamics of the Target and shaped their behavior to take account of these dynamics.

SUMMARY

The present study was primarily concerned with variations in opinion expression as a function of two cross-cutting experimental treatments. Ss engaged in an exchange of opinions with a target person, and in all cases the target person expressed his opinions first. In one treatment variation the target person expressed opinions identical to those the S had expressed on a prior questionnaire, or he expressed quite different opinions (Same versus Discrepant variation). The exchange took place in one of two contexts: the S was either led to believe that he was dependent on the other for an evaluation of his attractiveness as a person, or that his task was to present himself as accurately as possible (High- versus Low-Dependence variation). Since it was expected that Ss in the High-Dependence treatment would wish to avoid being perceived as agreeing for devious or manipulative reasons, the prediction was that Ss in the High-Dependence-Same condition would show less resultant conformity than those in the Low-Same condition, whereas those in the High-Discrepant condition would show more conformity than those in the Low-Discrepant condition. Only the second part of this hypothesis was confirmed. While Ss in the High-Same condition did not show less conformity than those in the Low-Same condition, those who were most concerned with attraction in this cell showed moderate ("optimum") conformity and avoided consistent agreement or disagreement. In addition, the greater the opinion agreement in the High-Same condition, the greater the expressed confidence, and the greater the rated attraction for the target person. The results were interpreted as reflecting the existence of a "self-presentation dilemma" in the High-Same Ss and as showing how these Ss employed alternative ways to deal with the dilemma by the use of subtle variations in the communication resources available.

REFERENCES

DEUTSCH, M., and GERARD, H. B. "A Study of Normative and Informational Social Influence Upon Individual Judgment." *J. Abnorm. Soc. Psychol.*, 1955, 51, 629–636.

FESTINGER, L. *A Theory of Cognitive Dissonance.* Evanston, Ill.: Row, Peterson, 1957.

JONES, E. E., GERGEN, K. J., GUMPERT, P., and THIBAUT, J. W. "Some Conditions Affecting the Use of Ingratiation to Influence Performance Evaluation." *J. Abnorm. Soc. Psychol.*, in press.

JONES, E. E., GERGEN, K. J., and JONES, R. G. "Tactics of Ingratiation among Leaders and Subordinates in a Status Hierarchy." *Psychol. Monogr.*, 1963, 77, 3 (Whole No. 566).

JONES, E. E., JONES, R. G., and GERGEN, K. J. "Some Conditions Affecting the Evaluation of a Conformist." *J. Pers.*, 1963, 31, 270–288.

THIBAUT, J. W., and KELLEY, H. H. *The Social Psychology of Groups.* New York: Wiley, 1959.

THIBAUT, J. W., and STRICKLAND, L. S. "Psychological Set and Social Conformity." *J. Pers.*, 1956, 25, 115–129.

II

STATUS AND
ORGANIZATIONAL PROCESSES
IN SMALL GROUPS

4

The Evolution of Power
and Prestige Orders

THE PROCESS OF STATUS EVOLUTION*

M. Hamit Fisek and Richard Ofshe

The development of status or social-dominance orders in face-to-face interactive situations is a topic that has received considerable attention in the past and continues to be one of the dominant issues in social-psychological research on interpersonal behavior (cf. Bales *et al.*, 1951; Bales, 1953; Slater, 1955; Horvath, 1965; Leik, 1965; Kadane and Lewis, 1969). Since it is likely that when a comprehensive theory of the process of status evolution is formulated and verified it will include propositions that participate in explanations of phenomena such as leadership, stability and change in group structure, intra-group conflict and conformity to group pressure, the topic can reasonably

be regarded as one of the key areas in the development of social-psychological theory. Recognition of its importance as an area for research is apparent in the classic work of Bales and his associates (Bales, 1950; Heinecke and Bales, 1953; Parsons and Bales, 1955) and is evident in the current research on the problem (cf. Burke, 1968; Kadane and Lewis, 1969; Kadane *et al.*, 1969).

In this paper we will present an analysis of temporal changes in the behaviors of members of small, freely interactive task-oriented groups in units of time and action that are sufficiently small to permit a precise description of the process of status evolution. Although it has been well documented that status orders are in evidence in these groups at the end of periods of interaction of as little as forty-five minutes duration (Bales *et al.*, 1951; Kadane *et al.*, 1969), the manner in which individuals in

 * M. Hamit Fisek and Richard Ofshe, "The Process of Status Evolution," *Sociometry*, 33, No. 3 (September 1970), 327–46.

such groups become differentiated with respect to status has never been made clear.[1] That is, there are no reports which provide a detailed description and analysis of changes in the behaviors of group members as they move from a condition of undifferentiated status equals to a condition in which members are ordered with respect to status within the group, i.e., their degrees of control over the activities of the group and their recognized importance and prestige within the group.[2]

The fact that such an analysis is nowhere available is especially surprising since their seems to be widespread acceptance of a conceptualization of the process of status evolution which postulates that if individuals are apparent equals in terms of their visible, general (diffuse) status characteristics (age, sex, race, social class, etc.), they will be undifferentiated in their initial behaviors in the group situation and the status order that is observed at the end of the period will emege as a product of the group members' interactions (Bales

et al., 1951; Heinecke and Bales, 1953; Berger ct al., 1966).[3]

Our analysis of the literature on which this conceptualization is based has failed to discover any substantial body of data that supports this process formulation in its entirety. The final result, that of the display of status orders at the end of single discussion sessions, is rather well established since it is reported by a number of investigators who base their conclusions on substantial bodies of data (Bales *et al.*, 1951; Stephan and Mishler, 1952; Kadane *et al.*, 1969). The crucial and insufficiently researched part of the argument is that group members begin the discussion session in a state of behavioral equality and evolve during their interaction into a group in which the members display the behavior differences that are taken to indicate the existence of a status order. The contention that there is an *initial state of equality between members* that *changes* into an *ordered set of relations* is based primarily on observations and impressions reported by Bales (Bales *et al.*, 1951; Parsons *et al.*, 1953; Parsons and Bales, 1955) and interpretations of Bales' *findings* of the following sort: "groups tend to become quickly differentiated internally in the exercise of authority" (Parsons *et al.*, 1953, p. 249). There is a lack of empirical support for the contention that the differentiated state is preceded by one of non-differentiation.

Obviously, since definitive relevant evidence is lacking for the contention of

---

[1] The characteristics of a group that are taken to indicate a status order are that, "marked inequalities develop over time in the rate at which members are observed to initiate interaction," and, "those who initiate action most frequently tend to be ranked highest on the criteria of 'best ideas' and 'guidance' and tend to receive actions from others at the highest rate" (Bales *et al.*, 1951). By a status order within such groups is meant an ordering of individuals with respect to the extent to which they initiate action, are evaluated as contributing the "best ideas" and greatest "guidance" to the group and have the communications of the other members directed toward them.

[2] The process of status differentiation has been studied in highly controlled experimental situations (cf. Berger *et al.*, 1969) but not in freely interactive settings.

[3] In situations in which group members differ with regard to general status characteristics such as age, sex, race, and social class, these variables determine the status order within the group (cf. Strodtbeck *et al.*, 1957; Strodtbeck and Mann, 1956; Moore, 1968, 1969).

status evolution, there can exist no strong support for the opposite assertion: that status orders are in evidence from the start of the interaction. There is, however, some evidence that this may be the case. For example, in an attempt to evaluate a proposed model for participation in Bales-type discussion groups based on the assumption of a developing status structure, Lewis (1970) reported that the model's fit to data for the first segment of the discussion session was poor. The model and the data were in disagreement on the question of the equality with which group members were participating early in the session. The data showed considerably greater early differentiation among group members than was expected by the model.

The research reported below is intended to provide data to clarify the question of the manner in which status structures originate in task-oriented groups.

Method

The subjects for this research were all male, first-year undergraduate students at Stanford University. Subjects were assigned to three-person discussion groups which were composed of individuals who had no prior acquaintance with one another and did not differ in any obvious manner with regard to age, social class, or race. A total of 59 such three-person discussion groups comprise the sample used for this study.

When subjects arrived for the study they were taken to an observation room equipped with a one-way mirror and sound recording equipment. Participants in the research were informed that they were taking part in a study of group problem solving and that their discussion would be observed from another room. They were then presented with the

problem that was to be discussed. The task on which the subjects were to work was one of creating a problem to be used as the subject for a group decision making study. The task was further defined such that the problem had to be one on which group members in the population to be studied would find the subject interesting, were unlikely to have special knowledge about the problem, and were unlikely to hold strong value positions concerning the subject of their discussion.

The data reported in the remainder of this paper are from the time period that began from the start of the discussion and ended forty minutes later. The final five minutes of the forty-five minute discussion period have been dropped from the analysis since some groups concluded their work on the task prior to the end of the session. Since the problem addressed in this study is the distribution of member participation and social organization during task activity, it was necessary to control for the point at which the task discussion ended by dropping the final five minutes of the discussion session from the analysis.[4]

Results

In presenting the analysis of the data generated by the discussion groups we will proceed in the following manner. The first task will be to establish that the groups participating in this research display the characteristic status structures reported in previous investigations. We will then proceed to analyze the manner in which the groups arrive at this state of differentiated individual performance and social organization. We will explore the questions of whether the group members start from a

---

[4] The raw data on which all computations are based are reported in Fisek (1968).

state of behavioral equality or whether the status structure is in any sense imposed on the group from the start of the members' interactions. The final task will be to provide a detailed picture of the temporal dimension of the interaction between participants in the discussion.

The unit of data on which analysis will be carried out is that of a participation. A participation is defined as a complete speech by an individual uninterrupted by an extended pause. Obviously, participations can vary greatly in terms of the member of "acts" they contain under the Bales Interaction Process Analysis (1950) definition of an act. Whether a speaker interjects only a single word and then yields the floor or speaks for several minutes, his contribution is coded as a single participation. It was decided to code only participations rather than attempt traditional Interaction Process Analysis since it has recently been shown that when used for coding act-to-act sequences the method produces insufficiently reliable results (Waxler and Mishler, 1965).[5]

The first point to consider is whether or not the groups in this study display a status structure by the close of the session. The data from the last twelve minutes of the interaction period were aggregated for each group and organized as follows. Treating the data for every group as a separate case and using only the final twelve minutes of the session, the pro-

portion of the total number of participations made by each of the three group members was calculated. The members of each of the fifty-nine groups could then be ordered with respect to the relative proportion of their group's activity that they contributed. The mean proportion of contributions made by group members of high, medium, and low activity levels are reported in Table 1. The summary data reported in Table 1 reveal substantial mean differences in performance levels for the three members of the groups. The most active man contributes approximately 60% more does the least active man. The mean participation levels reported in Table 1 reflect the typical behavior differences displayed by members of groups with established status orders.

Two checks were made in order to establish that the proportions reported in Table 1 indicated the existence of status structures rather than simply chance deviations from situations of equal participation by group members. The first check consisted of a chi-square test of the observed distribution of participation against the distribution that would be expected if all members participated equally. Since the fifty-nine groups in the sample represent fifty-nine independent cases, it was possible to take advantage of the additive property of the chi-square statistic (Cochran, 1952) and calculate the chi-

---

[5] Waxler and Mishler (1966) report the results of a number of reliability tests of the Interaction Process Analysis method and conclude: "We have found in our experience with the category system that it is impossible to raise the act-by-act reliability level through training much beyond 60%."

Table 1

MEAN PARTICIPATION LEVELS FOR THE FINAL TWELVE MINUTES

Level	Proportion of Total Participations
High	.42
Medium	.36
Low	.24

square statistic for each group separately and then to sum these values to arrive at a single statistic for the entire sample. That is, chi-square values are calculated for each group, using expected frequencies based on the no-differentiation hypothesis. The separate chi-square values are then summed, the number of degrees of freedom adjusted and the resulting chi-square value evaluated. This procedure resulted in a chi-square of 496.37, which has a probability of being obtained by chance of less than .001 (d.f. = 118).

The three individuals in each group have been ordered with respect to their average activity levels during the final twelve minutes of the interaction period and it has been shown that the differences in the average participation levels of high, medium, and low active members are highly unlikely to have occurred by chance. Although we have established that there are definite differences in proportional participation among members by the end of the session it is still necessary

to demonstrate a second point; that members of these groups display the characteristic evaluations of one another that are elements of the definition of a status structure. At the end of the session each participant was asked to provide data on his evaluation of the relative positions of all group members with respect to three variables: contribution of best ideas, contribution of guidance, and ability at the task. It is generally agreed that these three variables define characteristics of status structures in task group situations and should be positively related to activity level if the groups in the study are to be classified as having developed status structures. The relationship between an individual's rank on each of the three evaluation variables and his participation level is reported in Table 2. In each case, there is an obvious association between average participation level (in the final twelve-minute period) and rank on each of the evaluation variables. Based on the data reported above it seems reasonable to con-

Table 2

PARTICIPATION LEVEL AND RANK ON THREE EVALUATION VARIABLES

Participation Level	Rank on Best Ideas*			Rank on Guidance**			Rank on Ability***		
	1	2	3	1	2	3	1	2	3
High	70	55	48[1]	64	56	54	70	55	48
Medium	48	73	52	55	67	52	56	64	53
Low	58	43	72	59	48	67	54	50	69

* These data were collected in paired comparison form and converted into ranks. Rankings could not be obtained from data provided by participants who produced intransitive orders and hence their judgments are not reported in the table. The data for 4 subjects have been excluded from the cross-tabulation of Participation Level and Best Ideas.

** The data for 3 subjects have been dropped from this cross-tabulation.

*** The data for 4 subjects have been dropped from this cross-tabulation.

[1] The entries in these tables are not independent since each participant judged all of the members of his group. For this reason, none of the currently available statistical models are appropriate for these data and therefore it is not possible to evaluate the statistical significance of the associations reported in the tables.

clude that status orders are in evidence by the close of the discussion session.

In the following section we will consider certain temporal aspects of behavior in the discussion situation. In order to follow this analysis it should be remembered that the identification of an individual as a high, medium, or low activity participant was based on his rank within his three-man group during the final twelve minutes of the interaction period and consequently no data from the first twenty-eight minutes of the discussion session were used in determining an individual's participation level. Figure 1 reports the mean probabilities of partici-

pations in blocks of time spanning the entire discussion period for individuals who were identified as high, medium or low contributors on the basis of their performance in the final twelve minutes of the session.

The data from the final twelve minutes of the interaction period are reported in Figure 1 as the final four three-minute time blocks. Note that the mean participation probabilities of individuals with high, medium, and low average activity rates during this period are perfectly ordered for each of the four time blocks that comprise the twelve minute period. It is clear from the data reported in Figure 1

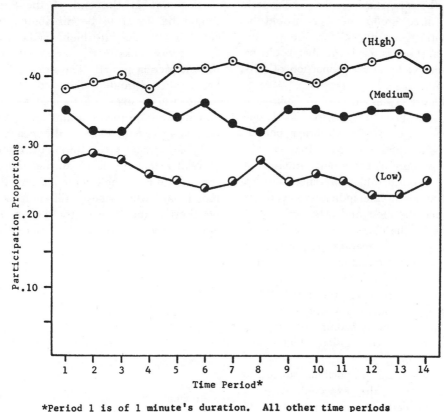

*Period 1 is of 1 minute's duration. All other time periods are of 3 minutes' duration.

Fig. 1. Participation Proportions Through Time.

that selecting high, medium and low contributors on the basis of performance during the final twelve minutes of the session permits the prediction of mean participation levels for all previous time blocks. Using the final segment estimates of participation level it is possible to predict perfectly the ordering of participation levels of group members for all preceding time blocks.

The data reported in Figure 1 are directly contradictory to the argument that the development of status orders is solely the result of interaction among group members since if a group's status structure is developed only during the interaction period it would be expected that in the early stages of the session each of the three group members would be contributing equally to the group's interaction. That is, each member could be characterized by a .33 proportion of participation.

In Figure 1, as in all the following figures, the first time period is of one minute's duration and all other periods are three minutes long. Note that even in the first minute of the group's interaction there is a considerable difference between the behaviors of the individuals who are to become the most and least active participants by the close of the session. The difference in the average proportions of their initiating interactions is .10 (high = .38 and low = .28). There is also some differentiation between the average behaviors of the individuals who are to become the high and medium participants by the close of the session (high = .38, medium = .35).

Although these proportions suggest a departure from the expected state of equality as early as the first minute of the interaction period, they do not provide a sufficiently precise description of the

distribution of behavior within each group to permit any conclusion to be reached. A more appropriate manner through which to evaluate whether or not there exists a state of behavioral equality during the early part of the discussion period can be arrived at by the following reasoning. If the status structures that are in evidence at the close of the session are solely the product of the interaction among group members, then it should be the case that no relationship exists between an individual's relative activity level at the close of the session and his relative activity level during the initial segment of the interaction among members of his group. That is, individuals who are high level participators at the end of the session should be found to be distributed with equal frequencies into high, medium and low activity ranks in the early segment of the interaction period. The same relation between final and initial activity rank would also be expected to hold for individuals who are medium and low activity participants at the close of the session.

Table 3 reports the initial distribution of relative activity levels during the first seven minutes of the interaction period for individuals who occupy different status positions at the close of the session. It is obvious from inspection of Table 3 that

Table 3

END OF SESSION ACTIVITY LEVEL AND INITIAL ACTIVITY LEVEL

End Level	Initial Level Frequency*		
	High	Medium	Low
High	30	17	12
Medium	16	31	12
Low	13	11	35

* $\gamma = .352$ (p<.01)

the observed distribution is different from the distribution that would be expected given an hypothesis of no association between final and initial rank. A test of association (gamma) between initial and final status position reveals that a significant relationship exists between an individual's status positions at the start and close of the session ($\gamma = .352$, $p < .01$). The data reported in Table 3 reveal the probability to be .51 that a high participator at the beginning of the session will be the dominant participator at the close of the discussion. The probabilities are .53 and .59 that those individuals who are the medium and low participators early in the session will occupy the same relative positions at the close of the discussion period.

The data reported in Table 3 lead to a definite rejection of the argument that members of all of the groups begin the interaction session in a state of behavioral equality. This does not, of course, permit acceptance of the opposite conclusion: that status structures are in evidence in all groups from the start of the interaction between members. When taken as 59 separate cases, inspection of the data on proportional participation by group members indicates that during the first segment of the session there is bi-modality in the participation characteristics of members of different groups. The members of a substantial number of groups begin the discussion period by contributing similar proportions of the total activity while in the remainder of the groups members show quite marked inequalities. The following procedure was used to differentiate between groups that could be reasonably classified as beginning the interaction period with no dominance order in evidence from those groups for which a dominance order was clearly present. A chi-square was calculated between the observed distribution of participation during the first seven minutes of the interaction period and the distribution that would be expected given an initial state of equality. The distribution of chi-square values was examined and bi-modality with a natural breaking point corresponding to a .20 probability value was observed. All groups that produced a chi-square which had a probability value greater than .20 were classified as being initially differentiated in terms of dominance and those groups producing chi-squares with probability values of less than .20 were classified as initially undifferentiated.[6]

The procedure outlined above produced two nearly equal size subsets of the original sample. The subset of groups that showed

---

[6] Attempts to determine whether or not the sample was composed of two or more distinct types of groups and to identify the most reasonable partitions among groups were made using techniques other than the one reported above. We used procedures that are typically employed to discriminate between alternative models for the same data (c.f. Atkinson *et al.*, 1965; Holland, 1965) and obtained essentially the same results as obtained with the procedure reported above.

The partition of the 59 group sample into initially differentiated and initially undifferentiated subsets probably mis-classifies a few groups in one direction or the other. The important point is not that approximately half of the groups we observed started in each state since even if our classification procedures were perfect this would represent only a single sample with a relatively small N and given any reasonable expectation for sampling error it could easily turn out to be the case that repeated samplings might show the true population distribution to be two-thirds of one type and one-third of the other. The important point is that there are two distinct types of groups and the available evidence indicates that there are likely to be substantial numbers of each type in any sample.

initial dominance differentiation contained 30 groups and the initially undifferentiated subset contained 29 groups. Treating these subsets of the original sample separately, a second check was made on the association between an individual's activity level during the final twelve minutes of the session and his activity level during the first seven minutes of his group's interaction. The distribution of initial participation level given final participation level for members of both types of groups are reported in Table 4. The association between initial and final participation level is not statistically significant ($\gamma = .141$) for the subset of groups that were identified as initially undifferentiated. For the subset classified as initially differentiated in terms of proportions of participation, the association is significant ($\gamma = .450$, p < .01). The data reported in Table 4 support the contention that there are two types of groups represented in the sample.

Given that it has been shown that within the original sample there are two subsets of groups which differ with regard to the display of an initial participation order, the next point to consider is whether or not there are any other variables that distinguish between the two types of groups. In the following sections we will consider the questions of differences between initially differentiated and initially undifferentiated groups in terms of the behaviors of group members through time, the perceptions of the status structures of their groups by members of the two subsets of groups, and possible qualitative differences in the behaviors of the members of the different types of groups.

The graphs reported in Figures 2 and 3 were produced by using the identifications of high, medium, and low activity level participants that were established on the basis of performance during the final twelve minutes of the discussion and a reorganization of the data in accord with the decomposition of the original sample into two subsets. Figure 2 reports the mean proportions of participations across time blocks for different activity level participants for groups that displayed initial differentiation. Figure 3 reports the same data for the initially undifferentiated groups.

The process data for the initially differentiated groups (Figure 2) demonstrate that as early as the first minute of the group members' interaction there exist marked inequalities in participation probabilities which are nearly as strong as the inequalities observed during the final

Table 4

INITIAL ACTIVITY LEVEL BY GROUP TYPE AND END ACTIVITY LEVEL

Initially Differentiated Groups (N=30)			
	Initial Level Frequency*		
End Level	High	Medium	Low
High	18	7	5
Medium	7	19	4
Low	5	4	21

* $\gamma = 4.59$ (p<.01)

Initially Undifferentiated Groups (N=29)			
	Initial Level Frequency**		
End Level	High	Medium	Low
High	12	10	7
Medium	9	12	8
Low	8	7	14

** $\gamma = .141$ (n.s.)

ticipation level is not statistically significant ($\gamma = .141$) for the subset of groups that were identified as initially undifferentiated. For the subset classified as initially differentiated in terms of proportions of participation, the association is significant

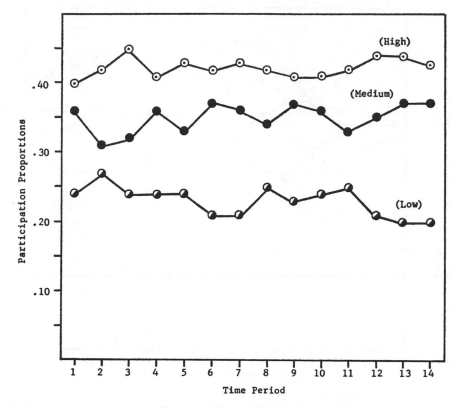

Fig. 2. Participation Proportions Through Time—Differentiated Subset.

segment of the session. What appears to be happening in these groups over the period of the discussion is that the dominant individual controls an approximately fixed proportion of the available opportunities to speak at all times and fluctuations in the participation rates of the second and third ranked individuals can be viewed as exchanges between occupants of these positions.

It can be seen from the data reported in Figure 2 that symmetric variations in the curves for participation probabilities of the second and third ranked men are quite pronounced. Although the second individual's participation level is close to that of the dominant individual's through-

out the session, there is no evidence which indicates any sort of status struggle between them. Increases in the second man's activity level are not at the expense of the dominant individual but rather at the expense of the least active member of the group. The second and third ranked individuals appears to vary their relative shares of those opportunities to participate that are not taken by the dominant group member.

The graphs in Figure 3 report the participation probabilities for high, medium, and low activity level members for groups that display an initial state of behavioral equality and subsequently develop a status structure. Variations in

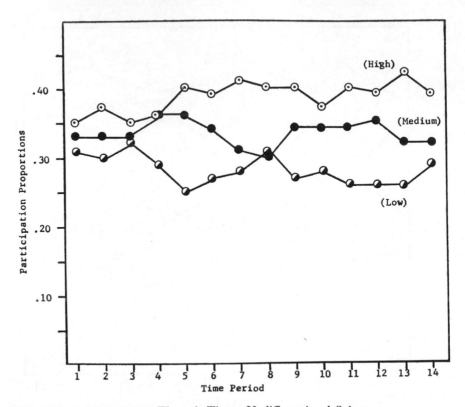

Fig. 3. Participation Proportions Through Time—Undifferentiated Subset.

activity levels among group members in the initially undifferentiated groups do not appear to follow the same pattern as did the exchanges between members of the initially differentiated groups. It can be seen from the data reported in Figure 3 that changes in one member's activity level during a time block can substantially affect any other member's activity level during the same time period. For example, the high participator's activity increase at block five is at the expense of the third ranked group member while the third ranked individual's increase at block eight is accompanied by a decrease in the second ranked member's activity during this period.

The data presented in Table 5 report the change in participation proportions

from the first seven minutes of the discussion session to the final twelve minutes for different activity level participants in the two groups. This data, together with the data reported in Figures 2 and 3, indicate that the characteristic ordering of group members' participation probabilities are in evidence in both types of groups. In terms of the magnitudes of the differentiations among group members, the initially undifferentiated groups display a less well developed status order at the close of the discussion session than do the initially differentiated groups.

The extent to which members of the initially differentiated and initially undifferentiated groups display the cognitions associated with fully developed status structures is reported in Table 6. The

Table 5

PARTICIPATION PROPORTIONS DURING INITIAL AND FINAL SEGMENTS
OF THE DISCUSSION

Type of Group	Activity Level	Initial Segment	Final Segment	Change
Differentiated	High	.43	.43	0
	Medium	.32	.36	+.04
	Low	.25	.22	−.03
Undifferentiated	High	.36	.40	+.04
	Medium	.33	.33	0
	Low	.31	.27	−.04

Table 6

PARTICIPATION LEVEL AND RANK ON EVALUATION VARIABLES BY GROUP TYPE

	Initially Differentiated*								
Participation Level	Rank on Best Ideas			Rank on Guidance			Rank on Ability		
	1	2	3	1	2	3	1	2	3
High	41	25	23[1]	36	28	25	41	26	19
Medium	28	43	19	29	40	20	25	38	23
Low	22	19	48	28	17	44	24	20	42

	Initially Undifferentiated**								
Participation Level	Rank on Best Ideas			Rank on Guidance			Rank on Ability		
	1	2	3	1	2	3	1	2	3
High	29	30	25	28	28	29	29	29	29
Medium	20	30	34	26	27	32	31	26	30
Low	36	24	24	31	30	23	30	30	27

* Due to failures of transitivity, data for 1 subject were dropped in the cross-tabulation on the Best Ideas variable, for 1 subject on the Guidance variable, and for 4 subjects on the Ability variable.

** Due to failures of transitivity, data for 3 subjects were dropped in the cross-tabulation on the Best Ideas variable, and for 2 subjects on the Guidance variable.

[1] Since entries in these tables are not independent, there is no available statistical model that allows us to evaluate the significance of the association between participation level and rank on any of the evaluation variables.

groups in the subset classified as initially differentiated clearly display the characteristic association between a member's participation rank and his rank on each of the three evaluation variables. The situation is different for the groups in the

Table 7

PROPORTIONAL DISTRIBUTION OF ACTS BY TYPE OF GROUP AND PARTICIPATION RANK*

Subject	Initially Undifferentiated			Initially Undifferentiated		
	Participation Rank			Participation Rank		
	High	Medium	Low	High	Medium	Low
Evaluations	.02	.02	.02	.02	.01	.02
Organization	.04	.05	.10	.05	.09	.08
Task	.95	.93	.89	.94	.90	.89

* Six groups were eliminated from the analysis of qualitative aspects of the data due to the impossibility of coding their audio tapes.

initially undifferentiated subset. The associations between participation level and rank on the evaluation variables are not in evidence. Although by the close of the session the members of the groups in this subset have become differentiated with regard to participation level, the members have not yet developed the cognitions typically associated with differentiated participation.

In an attempt to identify qualitative differences between the behaviors of members of the initially differentiated and initially undifferentiated groups during the first segment of the discussion session, the first twenty participations made in each group were divided into acts (using the Interaction Process Analysis [Bales, 1950] definition of an act) which were then coded into one of three categories on the basis of their subject. The categories were: evaluation of other individuals, the internal social organization of the group, and the task set by the researchers.

Table 7 reports the results of this coding. The distribution of verbal activity is similar in both types of groups. Between each type of group individuals of different activity levels show generally similar behaviors. It is evident from Table 7 that while all groups' members place major stress on task directed activities there is a slight tendency for an individual's participation level to be positively related to emphasis on task activity and negatively related to questions of the internal social organization of the group.[7]

The mean number of acts per participation were calculated for the first twenty participations in each group. The result, reported in Table 8, is the only other characteristic we were able to identify that distinguished between groups. Members of the initially differentiated groups were ordered in mean participation lengths in the same manner as they were ordered in mean participation probabilities. That is, on the average, the individual who is most likely to speak presents the greatest number of acts per speech; the second most likely speaker incorporates the second greatest number of acts per speech and the least active participant contributes the fewest number of acts per speech. The

---

[7] Traditional I.P.A. coding (from tape recordings) was carried out on this data and revealed no additional obvious differences between members of different types of groups or among different activity level participants.

Table 8

PARTICIPATION LEVEL AND MEAN NUMBER
OF ACTS PER SPEECH

Type of Group	Participation Level		
	High	Medium	Low
Differentiated	2.4*	1.8	1.4
Undifferentiated	2.1	1.7	1.7

* Mann-Whitney U Tests, between sets of data from adjacent cells within each row produce the following pattern of results: Differentiated—High>Medium (p<.05), Medium>Low (p<.05) and Undifferentiated — High — Medium (n.s.), Medium—Low (n.s.).

situation in the initially undifferentiated groups is quite different. There are no statistically significant differences between the mean length of participations of group members. The individual who is to become the dominant member by the end of the session does, however, contribute a somewhat greater number of acts per participation than either of the other group members.

CONCLUSIONS

In this paper we have shown that there are two different paths to status positions in task-oriented groups composed of individuals who are apparent equals in terms of their general status characteristics. Approximately half of the groups that participated in the study reported here displayed marked differentiation in member participation as early as the first minute of their group's session. The remaining groups in the study displayed near equality in initial particpation and appeared to evolve dominance structures during the course of the members' interactions.

It appears that for a substantial number of the discussion groups it is not possible to account for the emergence of the end-of-session status order through the analysis of the group's interaction. Obviously, if status orders precede interaction in time, the dynamics of the group members' interactions can hardly serve as causal variables in explanations of the initial emergence of the status order. For at least this subset of the discussion groups it must be the case that attributes of the participants themselves are the variables that determine the groups' status structures. That is, in the same manner that general status characteristics determine status orders in task group in which members differ with regard to these variables (cf. Strodtbeck *et al.*, 1957; Strodtbeck and Mann, 1956), there must exist a set of variables which cause differences in the behaviors of individuals who are apparent status equals. Probably in the status equal case these variables are socialization differences which result in different conceptions of self on the part of individuals, and in different behavior styles which in turn serve as cues in interaction.

For the remainder of the groups that participated in the study it is reasonable to regard the members as beginning the session in a state of behavioral equality which is transformed during the discussion session into a situation in which the group members are clearly differentiated with regard to their proportional participation in the group activity. The typical structure of beliefs about how abilities and contributions to the task are distributed among group members is not in evidence by the close of the session. It appears that for these groups it was possible during the period of the discussion session to evolve structured relations with regard to participation in the group's activities, but not to develop differentiated conceptions of members' competencies that are correlated with participation rank.

There is a crucial point about the sequence of events that task groups move through during the process of developing status structures which can be clarified by the data reported in this paper. The question is the following: In the course of the interaction among group members, do individuals first develop differentiated beliefs about each other's abilities and then adjust their behaviors such that those individuals who are believed to be more competent receive deference and thereby are moved into positions of leadership, or is the sequence of events one in which differentiated structural positions are evolved first with the recognition (or perception) of differential competence developing after individuals begin performing leadership roles? Obviously, both of these sequences result in the typically observed final correlation between participation level and beliefs about competence.

The data presented here make it possible to differentiate between the two possible sequences and strongly support the second conceptualization of the process. In the case of the groups that display initial differentiation in participation it is obvious that the group members participate differentially in the group's activity as early as the first minute of the discussion session. It is also clear that perceptions of differential competence among group members are in evidence by the close of the session and that participation rank is positively related to perceived competence. We have therefore observed a situation in which there was both initial behavioral differentiation and systematically related cognitive differentiation by the close of the session. In the case

of the groups that display initial behavioral equality, it is clear that by the close of the session the group members have become differentiated with respect to participation but do not display cognitive structures in which participation rank is associated with conceptions of each other's competence. In this case, we have observed a situation in which behavioral differentiation has recently occurred and there is no correlated cognitive differentiation.

If the cognition → deference → status order description of the process of status development is correct, it would be necessary to assume that participants in the initially differentiated groups developed cognitions about member's relative competencies in less than one minute's time. While this is possible, it does seem to strain the argument. The cognition → deference → status order description is decidedly weakened by the data provided by the initially undifferentiated groups. These data are completely contradictory to the postulated sequence. Consider that if this description were correct and group interaction were terminated before status orders developed fully there could be two and only two permissible states of affairs. It would be consistent with the description if it were observed that the group members displayed cognitive structures that revealed no differentiation among members in terms of competence and the group members were also undifferentiated in terms of participation, or if group members displayed differentiated cognitive structures but were still undifferentiated in participation. The condition that was observed for these groups at the close of the discussion session was, however, that the members were differentiated in terms of participation but that ranks on the participation variable were not associated with cognitions about competence.

The description that postulates status order to evolve through the sequence: differential participation → differential cognition, is consistent with the data provided by both the initially differentiated and the initially undifferentiated groups. The crucial observation is that by the end of the session the members of the initially undifferentiated groups display differences in proportional participation but do not hold cognitions about competence that are correlated with participation rank. It should be noted that one empirical point is lacking in the available data. It is that the members of these groups would develop cognitions about competence that were correlated with participation rank if the groups were permitted to interact for a longer period of time. Although this evidence is not necessary in order to reject the argument that cognition causes differentiated participation, it is necessary to prove unequivocally that the alternative is the correct description.

REFERENCES

ATKINSON, R., G. BOWER and E. CROTHERS, *An Introduction to Mathematical Learning Theory.* New York: Wiley, 1965.

BALES, R., *Interaction Process Analysis.* Reading, Massachusetts: Addison-Wesley, 1950.

———, "The Equilibrium Problem in Small Groups." Pp. 111–161 in T. Parsons et al. (eds.), *Working Papers in the Theory of Action.* Glencoe, Illinois: The Free Press, 1953.

BALES, R., F. STRODTBECK, T. MILLS and M. ROSEBOROUGH, "The Channels of Communication in Small Groups." *American Sociological Review* 16 (August 1951), 461–468.

BERGER, J., B. COHEN and M. ZELDITCH, "Status Characteristics and Expectation States." Pp. 29–46 in J. Berger et al. (eds.), *Sociological Theories in Progress,* Vol. I. Boston: Houghton Mifflin, 1966.

BERGER, J., T. CONNER, and W. McKEOWN, "Evaluations and the Formation and Maintenance of Performance Expectations." *Human Relations* 22 (December 1969), 481–502.

BURKE, P., "Role Differentiation and the Legitimation of Task Activity." *Sociometry* 31 (December 1968), 404–411.

COCHRAN, W., "The X^2 Test of Goodness of Fit." *Annals of Mathematical Statistics* 23 (1952), 315–334.

FISEK, M. H., *The Evolution of Status Structures and Interaction in Task Oriented Discussion Groups.* Unpublished Ph.D. dissertation, Department of Sociology, Stanford University, 1968.

HEINECKE, C., and R. BALES, "Developmental Trends in the Structure of Small Groups." *Sociometry* 16 (February 1953), 7–38.

HOLLAND, P., *Minimum Chi-Square Procedures.* Unpublished Ph.D. Dissertation, Department of Statistics, Stanford University, 1965.

HORVATH, W., "A Mathematical Model of Participation in Small Group Discussions." *Behavioral Science* 10 (April 1965), 164–166.

KADANE, J., and G. LEWIS, "The Distribution of Participation in Group Discussions: An Empirical and Theoretical Reappraisal." *American Sociological Review* 34 (October 1969), 710–723.

KADANE, J., G. LEWIS, and J. RAMAGE, "Horvath's Theory of Participation in Group Discussions." *Sociometry* 32 (September 1969), 348–361.

LEIK, R., "Type of Group and the Probability of Initiating Acts." *Sociometry* 28 (March 1965), 57–65.

LEWIS, G., "Bales Monte-Carlo of Small Group Discussions." *Sociometry* 33 (March 1970).

MOORE, J., "Social Status and Social Influence: Process Considerations." *Sociometry* 32 (June 1969), 145–158.

———, "Status and Influence in Small Group Interactions." *Sociometry* 31 (March 1968), 47–63.

PARSONS, T., and R. BALES, *Family, Socialization and Interaction Process.* Glencoe, Illinois: The Free Press, 1955.

SLATER, P., "Role Differentiation in Small Groups." *American Sociological Review* 20 (June 1955), 300–310.

STEPHAN, F., and E. MISHLER, "The Distribution of Participation in Small Groups: An Exponential Approximation." *American Sociological Review* 17 (October 1956), 598–608.

STRODTBECK, F., R. JAMES, and C. HAWKINS, "Social Status in Jury Deliberations." *American Sociological Review* 22 (October 1957), 713–719.

STRODTBECK, F., and R. MANN, "Sex Role Differentiation in Jury Deliberations." *Sociometry* 19 (January 1956), 3–11.

WAXLER, N., and E. MISHLER, "Scoring and Reliability in Interaction Process Analysis: A Methodological Note." *Sociometry* 29 (March 1966), 28–40.

COMPETENCE AND CONFORMITY
IN THE ACCEPTANCE OF INFLUENCE*

E. P. Hollander

When one member influences others in his group it is often because he is competent in a focal group activity. A member may show such competence by individual actions that further the attainment of group goals (cf. Carter, 1954); more specific situational demands may variously favor the ascent of the

*E. P. Hollander, "Competence and Conformity in the Acceptance of Influence," *Journal of Abnormal and Social Psychology*, 61 (1960), 365–69. Copyright 1960 by the American Psychological Association, and reproduced by permission.

expediter, advocate, or what Bales and Slater (1955) have termed the task specialist. An additional condition for the acceptance of influence involves the member's perceived adherence to the normative behaviors and attitudes of his group. His record of conformity to these expectancies serves to sustain eligibilty of the sort Brown (1936) calls "membership character."

A person who exhibits both competence and conformity should eventually reach a threshold at which it becomes appropriate in the eyes of others for him to assert influence; and insofar as these assertions are accepted he emerges as a leader. But it is still necessary to account for the "nonconformity" that leaders display as they innovate and alter group norms. Certain shifts must therefore occur in the expectancies applicable to an individual as he proceeds from gaining status to maintaining it.

This process has been considered recently in a theoretical model of status emergence (Hollander, 1958). It features the prospect that behavior perceived to be nonconformity for one member may not be so perceived for another. Such differentiations are seen to be made as a function of status, conceived as an accumulation of positively disposed impressions termed "idiosyncrasy credits." A person gains credits, i.e., rises in status, by showing competence and by conforming to the expectancies applicable to him at the time. Eventually his credits allow him to nonconform with greater impunity.[1] Moreover, he is then subject to a new set of expectancies which direct the assertion of influence. Thus, whether for lack of motivation or misperception, his failure to take innovative action may cause him to lose status.[2]

It is readily predictable that in task oriented groups a member giving evidence of competence on the group task should with time gain in influence. If he simply nonconforms to the procedures agreed upon, the opposite effect should be ob-

served. But the sequential relationship of nonconformity to competence is especially critical.

From the model, it should follow that, with a relatively constant level of manifest competence, the influence of a person who nonconforms *early* in the course of group interaction should be more drastically curtailed than in the case of a person who nonconforms *later*. Indeed, a reversal of effect would be predicted in the latter instance. Once a member has accumulated credits, his nonconformity to general procedure should serve as a confirming or signalizing feature of his status, thereby enhancing his influence. Accordingly, it may be hypothesized that given equivalent degrees of task competence, a member should achieve greater acceptance of his influence when he has conformed in the past and is now nonconforming than he should when nonconformity precedes conformity.

METHOD

Design

Twelve groups, each composed of four male subjects, were engaged in a task involving a sequence of 15 trials. A group choice was required for each trial from among the row alternatives in a 7×7 payoff matrix (see Table 1). In every group, a fifth member was a confederate whose prearranged response was contrived to be correct on all but four trials, i.e., 2, 3, 6, and 12, thus reflecting considerable competence on the task. All interactions among participants took place through a system of microphones and headsets from partitioned booths. Subjects were assigned numbers from 1 to 5 for communicating with one another. The central manipulation was the confederate's nonconformity to procedures

---

[1] This is a newer formulation of an observation long since made regarding the latitude provided leaders (e.g., Homans, 1950, p. 416). It is further elaborated in Hollander (1959).

[2] This proposition is consistent with various findings suggestive of the greater social perceptiveness of leaders (e.g., Chowdhry & Newcomb, 1952).

Table 1

MATRIX USED IN GROUP TASK

	Green	Red	Blue	Yellow	Brown	Orange	Black
Able	−1	−12	+5	−1	−2	+15	−4
Baker	+10	−1	−2	−7	+4	−3	−1
Charlie	−5	+5	−3	+3	−11	−1	+12
Dog	+5	−7	+10	−2	−5	+1	−2
Easy	−4	−1	−1	+1	+13	−10	+2
Fox	−6	+15	−5	−1	−3	−1	+1
George	−1	−1	−2	+10	+4	−2	−8

agreed upon by each group in a pretrial discussion. In terms of a division of the 15 trials into three zones—early, middle, and late—of 5 trials each, six treatments were applied: nonconformity throughout, nonconformity for the first two zones, for the first zone alone, for the last two zones, for the last zone alone, and a control with no nonconformity. In one set of treatments the confederate was designated number 5, and in the other number 4, to test possible position effects. Acceptance of the confederate's influence was measured by the number of trials by zone in which his recommended response was accepted as the group's. This was supplemented by post-interaction assessments.

Subjects

The 48 subjects were all juniors in the College of Engineering and Science at the Carnegie Institute of Technology. All had volunteered from introductory psychology sections after being told only that they would be taking part in a study of problem solving in groups. Care was taken in composing the 12 groups so as to avoid either placing acquaintances together or having membership known in advance. Thus, no two subjects from the same class section were used in the same group, and subjects reported at staggered times to different rooms. By the time a subject reached the laboratory room where the experiment was actually conducted, he had

been kept apart from the others and was not aware of their identity. The subjects never saw one another during the entire procedure, nor were their names ever used among them.

Instructions and Set

Once seated and assigned a number, every subject was given a sheet of instructions and the matrix used for the task. These instructions fell into two parts, both of which were reviewed aloud with each subject individually, and then with the entire group over the communication network. The first part cautioned the subjects to always identify themselves by number (e.g., "This is Station 3 . . .") before speaking and not to use names or other self-identifying references. The second part acquainted them with the procedures to be used, emphasized the aspect of competition against a "system," and established the basis for evident procedural norms. It read as follows:

1. You will be working with others on a problem involving a matrix of plus and minus values. Everyone has the same matrix before him. The goal is to amass as many plus units as possible, and to avoid minus units. Units are worth 1 cent each to the group; the group begins with a credit of 200 units. You cannot lose your own money, therefore. There will be fifteen trials in all.

2. In any one trial, the task involved is for the group to agree on just *one* row—identified by Able, Baker, Charlie, etc.—

which seems to have strategic value. Once the group has determined a row, the experimenter will announce the column color which comes up on that trial. The intersecting cells indicate the payoff. Following this announcement, there will be thirty seconds of silence during which group members can think individually about the best strategy for the next trial, in terms of their notion about the system; note please that there are several approximations to the system, although the equation underlying it is quite complex. But work at it.

3. At the beginning of each trial the group members must report, one at a time, in some order, as to what they think would be the best row choice on the upcoming trial. Members may "pass" until the third time around, but must announce a choice then. Following this, groups will have three minutes on each trial to discuss choices and reach some agreement; this can be a simple majority, or unanimous decision; it is up to the group to decide. If a decision is not reached in three minutes, the group loses 5 units.

4. Before beginning the trials, the group will have five minutes to discuss these points: (*a*) The order of reporting; (*b*) How to determine the group choice for a given trial; (*c*) How to divide up the money at the end. These decisions are always subject to change, if the group has time and can agree. After the 15th trial, group members may have as much as five minutes to settle any outstanding decisions. Then headsets are to be removed, but group members remain seated for further instructions and the individual payment of funds.

Instruments and Procedure

The matrix was specially constructed for this study to present an ambiguous but plausible task in which alternatives were only marginally discrete from one another.[3] The

number of columns and rows was selected to enlarge the range of possibilities beyond the number of group members, while still retaining comprehensibility. The fact that the rows are unequal in algebraic sum appears to be less important as a feature in choice than the number and magnitude of positive and negative values in each; there is moreover the complicating feature of processing the outcome of the last trials in evaluating the choice for the next. All considered, the matrix was admirably suited to the requirements for ambiguity, challenge, conflict, immediate reinforcement, and ready manipulation by the experimenter.

The confederate, operating as either 4 or 5 in the groups, suggested a choice that differed trial by trial from those offered by other members; this was prearranged but subject to modification as required. Since subjects rather typically perceived alternatives differently, his behavior was not unusual, especially during the early trials. For the 11 trials in which the confederate's row choice was "correct," the color that "came up" was contrived to yield a high plus value without at the same time providing a similar value for intersection with another person's row choice. Had his recommendation been followed by the group on these trials, high payoffs would have accrued.

The device of a 5-minute pretrial discussion had special utility for establishing common group expectancies, in the form of procedures, from which the confederate could deviate when called for in the design. Predictable decisions on these matters were reached unfailingly. But their importance lay in having a public *affirmation* of member intent. Thus, on order of reporting, it was quickly agreed to follow the order of the numbers assigned members. Each group, despite minor variants suggested, decided on simple majority rule. Regarding division of funds, equal sharing prevailed, sometimes with the proviso that the issue be taken up again at the end.

In the zones calling for nonconformity, the confederate violated these procedures by speaking out of prescribed turn, by question-

---

[3] The matrix is an adaptation, at least in spirit, of a smaller one used with success by Moore and Berkowitz (1956).

ing the utility of majority rule, and by un-supported—but not harsh—challenges to the recommendations made by others. He manifested such behaviors on an approximate frequency of at least one of these per trial with a mean of two per trial considered optimum. Thus, he would break in with his choice immediately after an earlier respondent had spoken and before the next in sequence could do so; when there were periods of silence during a trial he would observe aloud that maybe majority rule did not work so well; and he would show a lack of enthusiasm for the choice offered by various others on the matter of basis. Lest he lose credibility and become a caricature, in all instances he chose his moments with care and retained an evident spontaneity of expression.[4]

RESULTS AND DISCUSSION

The task gave quite satisfactory signs of engrossing the subjects. There was much talk about the "system" and a good deal of delving into its basis, possibly made the more so by the subjects' academic background; the returned matrices were littered with diagrams, notations, and calculations. Though quite meaningless in fact, the confederate's tentative accounts of his "reasoning" were evidently treated with seriousness, perhaps as much because of the contrived time constraint, which prevented probing, as of his jargon regarding "rotations" and "block shifts." In any case, the confederate at no time claimed to have the system completely in hand. He delayed his response from the sixth trial onward to suggest calculation of an optimum choice in the face of conflicting alternatives; and the four trials on which

he was "wrong" were spaced to signify progressive improvement, but not total perfection.

Most pertinent, however, is the fact that there were no manifestations of suspicion concerning the confederate's authenticity. The others seemed to believe that he was one of them and that he was "cracking" the system; the post-interaction data were in full agreement.

Since all of the interactions were available on tape, it was possible to derive a number of indices of acceptance of influence. The most broadly revealing of these appeared to be the frequency of trials on which the confederate's recommended solution was followed.

In Table 2 this index is employed to discern the effects of three major variables. The analysis is arranged by zones (Z) of trials, and in terms of the confederate's nonconformity (NC) in the *current* zone and immediate *past* zone.[5] The means given in each cell indicate the number of trials, out of five per zone, on which the confederate's choice was also the group's. In a chi square test, the effect of position upon this measure was found to be nonsignificant, and is therefore omitted as a distinction in the analysis of variance.

The significant *F* secured from Zones is in accord with prediction. It reveals the ongoing effect of task competence in increasing the acceptance of the confederate's choice, to be seen in the rising means across zones. While current nonconformity

---

[4] The same person, H. E. Titus, was the confederate throughout.

[5] For Zone I, the "past zone" refers to the discussion period. If he was to nonconform there, the confederate would question majority rule and suggest that the division of funds be left until the end rather than agree then on equal shares.

Table 2

MEAN NUMBER OF TRIALS ON WHICH A GROUP ACCEPTS
CONFEDERATE'S RECOMMENDED SOLUTION

Confederate's Previous Conformity	Zone I (Trials 1–5)		Zone II (Trials 6–10)		Zone III (Trials 11–15)	
	Noncon-forming[a]	Con-forming	Noncon-forming	Con-forming	Noncon-forming	Con-forming
With	1.67	—	3.25	3.00	4.00	5.00
Procedural nonconformity in immediate *past* zone	6[b]		4	2	4	2
Without	—	2.00	5.00	3.75	5.00	4.75
Procedural nonconformity in immediate *past* zone		6	2	4	2	4

ANALYSIS OF VARIANCE

Source	SS	df	MS	F
Current Nonconformity	.20	1	.200	—
Zones	47.05	2	23.525	35.01**
Past Nonconformity	3.36	1	3.360	5.00*
Int: Current NC×Z	1.22	2	.610	—
Int: Current NC×Past NC	13.52	1	13.520	20.12**
Int: Z×Past NC	.72	2	.360	—
Int: Current NC×Z×Past NC	4.11	2	2.055	3.06
Residual	16.12	24	.672	
Total	86.30	35		

[a] Confederate showed procedural nonconformity on the trials in this zone.
[b] Indicates number of groups upon which cell is based.
* $p < .05$.
** $p < .001$.

does not yield a significant effect, past nonconformity does. Viewing the table horizontally, one finds that the means for "without" *past* NC exceed the means for "with" *past* NC in all instances but one. Regarding the significant interaction of *current* and *past* NC, the combination "without-without" has a sequence (2.00, 3.75, 4.75) of persistently higher value than has "with-with" (1.67, 3.25, 4.00); this, too, is in line with prediction. Finally, the maximum value of 5.00 in Zone II

for the combination "without" *past* NC but "with" *current* NC confirms the key prediction from the model, at least within the context of the relative magnitudes there; the same value is also seen in Zone III for the identical combination; still another reading of 5.00 holds there, however, for the inverse combination, but in a tight range of values quite beyond separation of effects for interpretation.

Considerable consistency was found too in the post-interaction data. On the item "overall contribution to the group activity," 44 of the 48 subjects ranked the confederate first; on the item "influence over the group's decisions," 45 of the 48 ranked him first. Two things bear emphasis in this regard: subjects had to individually write in the numbers of group members next to rank, hence demanding recall; and their polarity of response cut across all six treatments, despite significant differences among these in the actual *acceptance of influence*. That the confederate therefore made an impact is clear; but that it had selective consequences depending upon the timing of his nonconformity is equally clear.

In detail, then, the findings are in keeping with the predictions made from the model. The operational variable for measuring acceptance of influence was confined to the task itself but nontask elements are touched as well. In that respect, the findings corroborate the subtle development of differential impressions as a function of even limited interpersonal behavior.

Some unquantified but clearly suggestive data are worth mentioning in this regard. Where, for example, the confederate began nonconforming *after* the first zone, his behavior was accepted with minimal challenge; by the third zone, his suggestion that majority rule was faulty yielded a rubber stamping of his choice. Again, if he had already accrued credit, his pattern of interrupting people out of turn not only went unhindered but was taken up by some others. Quite different effects were elicited if the confederate exhibited nonconformity from *the outset*, notably such comments of censure as "That's not the way we agreed to do it, five."

The findings are especially indicative of the stochastic element of social interaction and its consequence for changing perception. Especially interesting is the fact that these effects are produced even in a relatively brief span of time.

SUMMARY

A study was conducted to test the relationship between competence on a group task and conformity or nonconformity to procedural norms in determining a person's ability to influence other group members. Data were gathered from 12 groups engaged in a problem solving task under controlled conditions. Each was made up of five members one of whom was a confederate who evidenced a high degree of competence during the 15 trials. His nonconformity to the procedural norms agreed upon by the group was introduced at various times, early, middle, or late, in the sequence of trials. Influence was measured by the number of trials (per segment of the entire sequence) in which the confederate's recommended solution was accepted as the group's choice. As a broad effect, it was found that a significant increase in his influence occurred as the trials progressed, presumably as a function of the successive evidences of competence. Past conformity by the confederate was also found to be positively and significantly related to the acceptance of his influence; finally, there was a statistically significant interaction between past and current nonconformity reflected in high influence in the groups in which the confederate had conformed earlier in the sequence of trials but was presently nonconforming. These results were all thoroughly consistent with predictions made from the "idiosyncrasy credit" model of conformity and status.

REFERENCES

BALES, R. F., and SLATER, P. E. "Role Differentiation in Small Decision-Making Groups." In T. Parsons, R. F. Bales, et al. (Eds.), *Family, Socialization, and Interaction Process.* Glencoe, Ill.: Free Press, 1955.

BROWN, J. F. *Psychology and the Social Order.* New York: McGraw-Hill, 1936.

CARTER, L. F. "Recording and Evaluating the Performance of Individuals as Members of Small Groups." *Personnel Psychol.*, 1954, 7, 477–484.

CHOWDHRY, KAMLA, and NEWCOMB, T. M. "The Relative Abilities of Leaders and Non-Leaders to Estimate Opinions of Their Own Groups." *J. Abnorm. Soc. Psychol.*, 1952, 47, 51–57.

HOLLANDER, E. P. "Conformity, Status, and Idiosyncrasy Credit." *Psychol. Rev.*, 1958, 65, 117–127.

HOLLANDER, E. P. "Some Points of Reinterpretation Regarding Social Conformity." *Soc. Rev.*, 1959, 7, 159–168.

HOMANS, G. C. *The Human Group.* New York: Harcourt, Brace, 1950.

MOORE, O. K., and BERKOWITZ, M. I. "Problem Solving and Social Interaction. *ONR Tech. Rep.*, 1956, No. 1. (Contract Nonr-609(16), Yale University Department of Sociology).

EXPERIMENTS ON THE ALTERATION
OF GROUP STRUCTURE*

Alex Bavelas, Albert H. Hastorf, Alan E. Gross,
and W. Richard Kite

A fundamental problem in social psychology is the relationship between an individual's behavior and how that behavior is perceived and evaluated by others. For

* Alex Bavelas, Albert H. Hastorf, Alan E. Gross, and W. Richard Kite, "Experiments on the Alteration of Group Structure," *Journal of Experimental Social Psychology*, 1 (1965), 55–70. Reprinted by permission of Academic Press, Inc.

example, there has been persistent interest in the process which generates a status hierarchy in small face-to-face groups such that some members are perceived as "leaders" and others not. Most of the research on this question has attempted to chart the course of a naturally emerging structure, sociometrically define the leader, and then attempt to define those aspects of his behavior that led to his being perceived as the leader. However, the behavior of the leader is normally so complex that it has been exceedingly difficult to isolate the behaviors that significantly influence the perceptions of the other group members. Bales (1950) has explored this approach most thoroughly, with one of the most persistent findings being that the people seen as leaders talk a great deal.

This report will describe a series of studies in which an attempt is made to alter experimentally the verbal behavior of an individual in a group discussion by the use of an operant conditioning procedure. Our primary concern was to develop a workable procedure for increasing one group member's verbal output, to define some of the variables which appear crucial to this procedure, and to explore the other group members' perceptions of this change in behavior on such dimensions as quality of ideas and leadership.

Previous research with operant conditioning techniques in group situations has most commonly made use of confederates. Pepinsky, Hemphill, and Shevitz (1958) demonstrated that "accepting" or "rejecting" reactions on the part of confederates influenced the number of leadership attempts made by a naive subject. By making a straightforward application of a standard verbal conditioning procedure to a group situation, Bachrach, Candland, and Gibson (1961) have shown that the verbal output of a naive group member can be increased by the headnods, "umm humms," and agreements of two confederates. It should be noted that in both of these studies, the "group" aspects of the experimental situations were severely attenuated by the use of confederates. In such an experimental set-up it is impossible to obtain data on other group members' perceptions of the "target" subject whose behavior was being altered.

Oakes, Droge, and August (1960) demonstrated that verbal behavior can be either increased or decreased by the use of lights as reinforcers or punishers. Aiken (1964) has described a similar procedure in which lights as reinforcers or punishers were used for subjects in a group situation where each subject is provided with private feedback on his performance. This procedure has the significant advantage of bringing about a change in the verbal behavior of a subject in the presence of other subjects who are unaware of the exact nature of the reinforcements given the "target" person.

The studies reported below are directed toward answering the following questions. When lights are used as signals or reinforcers in a group situation, how much change in verbal behavior can be obtained? Must the reinforcing lights be directly contingent on talking or will a random pattern of lights also increase verbal output in a group discussion atmosphere? If an increase in the verbal output of a group member is obtained, will that person maintain his new verbal level in a following session where no lights are expected? Finally, how do the other group members evaluate the contributions of the "target" person? Do they increase his status on such dimensions as quality of ideas and leadership?

EXPERIMENT I

Method

Subjects. Seventy-two male students from industrial psychology and industrial engineering classes at Stanford University were recruited "to participate in group discussions of case problems." The Ss were divided into eighteen four-man groups, half of which were assigned to the Experimental condition and half to the Control condition. Group members were not well acquainted with each other prior to the experimental session.

Apparatus. Each of four positions at a discussion table was equipped with a reflector box which contained two small lights, one green and one red. These boxes were flared toward each participant so that only he could see the lights facing his position. The lights were controlled from an observation room which was separated from the discussion room by one-way glass. Clocks and counters were used to record talking time and frequency for each *S*. Whenever an *S* talked, or whenever a red or green light was turned on, an Esterline-Angus pen recorder was activated, thereby providing a sequential event record.

Procedure. The *S*s were told that the discussions would be observed and recorded from behind the one-way glass. The *E* explained that he was interested in the study of group discussion techniques from an educational viewpoint. It was further explained that several different human relations problems would be discussed so that the dynamics of the group discussion process could be analyzed. Following these brief and purposely vague introductory remarks, the four *S*s read the first case problem and were instructed to begin a 10-minute discussion period during which they "should discuss the pertinent facts which will affect a decision."

This initial discussion was intended to provide an operant level or baseline measurement of verbal activity. An observer operated the clocks and counters, which provided, respectively, a record of cumulative talking time and a record of the total number of times each *S* talked. This recording procedure was also followed in the two subsequent discussions.

At the end of each discussion period, *E* reentered the discussion room and administered a short sociometric questionnaire. The *S*s were required to rank all group members, including themselves, on four key items: amount of participation, quality of ideas, effectiveness in

guiding the discussion, and general leadership ability.

After reading the second case problem, the groups were given further oral instructions. The *E* stated that in contrast to the usual non-feedback procedure, group discussions might be more effective "if the participants are given an occasional sign that they are doing the kinds of things that will help the group arrive at intelligent solutions while at the same time yielding the maximum educational benefit to the group." The *S*s were then told that some discussion groups work on their own and some groups "are provided with feedback information as to how they are doing as the discussion proceeds." At this point the experimental groups were told that they would be receiving feedback. The *E* directed attention to the small red and green lights which had previously been dismissed as extraneous equipment that "we won't be using now," and told the group that these lights would serve as the source of the feedback information. Control groups were told that they would receive no feedback.

Both Experimental and Control groups received vague descriptions of the criteria that were to be used in evaluating the discussion:

Many psychologists have studied group discussion of problems such as this one. Most of these investigators have found that maximum benefit is gained from such discussions when the group proceeds in an orderly way through various stages of development. For instance, one psychologist has cautioned against proceeding into the problem-solving stage of discussion too rapidly before there has been enough orientation. Other research has given us clues as to the value of cooperation, suggestion, conciliation, and other forms of group behavior during certain stages of the discussion process.

The case you have just read has been thoroughly analyzed in terms of how it can be discussed most effectively. Although, of course, there is no single correct solution to the problem, we have developed a definite set of principles, such as those I have just mentioned, which enable us to know whether or not you are following the best course; that is, using the best techniques in contributing to the discussion for the benefit of the group. Note that although this will be a group discussion, it will be your individual contributions to the discussion that will be judged.

At this point the Control groups were reminded that they would not receive any feedback as to how were being evaluated. However, the Experimental groups were told that they would receive feedback which would be contingent upon the vaguely defined quality of their contributions:

> Thus, whenever you make a contribution to the discussion which is helpful or functional in facilitating the group process, your green light will go on like this (green lights turned on). Are all your green lights on? Fine. Whenever you behave in a way which will eventually hamper or hinder the group process, your red light will go on like this (red lights turned on). Are all your red lights on? Good. It is conceivable that even remaining silent when you might have been clarifying a point that had been made earlier is a dysfunctional or hindering type of behavior. This would rate a red light indicating you should have said something at that point. On the other hand, silence might be good when talking would serve to confuse a good point that had already been made.
>
> Since it is often impossible for us to determine the effect that a single statement or thought will have on the group discussion, a feedback light might be referring to the cumulative effect of two or three successive contributions to the discussion. Of course much of the time neither of your lights will be on, indicating that your behavior has been neither helping nor hindering the group, or that we simply can't validly analyze what has been going on in the group at that time.
>
> Note that the discussion table is constructed so that each participant can see only the lights directly in front of him. During the discussion the fact that your lights are either on or off should not be

mentioned. This would, of course, tend to disrupt the natural discussion atmosphere.

Group members in both conditions were told the discussion would last for 20 minutes and that they should "try to bring in the various possible facts that can be considered relevant to the problem in the case."

At the end of the first discussion period, the Ss were rank-ordered on the basis of objective behavior measured by the clocks and counters and on the basis of the perceptions of the group members measured by the responses to the four sociometric items. There was usually a close correspondence between amount of talking and average ranking on the four sociometric items. In the few cases in which these measures were inconsistent or contradicted each other, the ranking adopted was made on the basis of total talking times.

The third or fourth ranked man in this hierarchy was designated as the target person (TP). One of the less talkative men was selected so that here would be "room" to effect a relatively large change in verbal behavior. An exceedingly quiet man was not selected as the TP because it was felt that if he had been extremely quiet it would be difficult to alter his behavior. The man who was ranked first was designated $M-1$; the other two men were labeled $M-2$ and $M-3$, respectively.

The experimental manipulation consisted of flashing TP's green light whenever he made declarative statements or stated an opinion, and flashing the others' red lights if they ($M-1$, $M-2$, $M-3$) engaged in these same behaviors. Occasionally, TP received a red light for remaining silent, and other group members received green lights for interacting with TP, especially for agreeing with him.

No definite criteria or set of rules were followed for administering lights or for controlling the number of lights distributed. The light operator's task was to increase the TP's verbal output during the second discussion and to decrease or inhibit talking by the other group members. The operator was to select for reinforcement those statements by the TP

which would intuitively appear to result in increased sociometric status.

After the second discussion, the Ss again completed the sociometry questionnaire and then read the third case problem. The Experimental groups were told the lights would "not be operating—just as in the first case discussion; so don't pay any attention to the equipment." At the end of this final 10-minute discussion, the last sociometric questionnaire was administered, followed by a postsession questionnaire. Each S was asked to rank the three case problems from most to least liked and to indicate whether he felt that he had talked more, less, or about the same as usual during each of three discussions.

Experimental Ss responded to items which asked how much attention was paid to the lights and whether the lights were perceived as helping or hindering the discussion.

After this questionnaire was completed, the purpose and design of the experiment was fully explained to the Ss, and questions were answered.

Results

The experimental procedure is clearly effective in altering both the distribution of verbal outputs and the sociometric structure of the group. In all nine Experi-

Table 1[a]

SOCIOMETRIC RANK AND VERBAL OUTPUT OF TARGET PERSON

Experiment	Mean rankings received by TP from other group members (1 to 4)			Time talked by TP expressed as a percentage of total group talking time		
	Discussion period			Discussion period		
	1	2	3	1	2	3
Control (N=9 groups)	3.05	2.81	2.80	17.3	20.2	19.5
Exp. I (N=9 groups)	3.23 1 vs. 2 & 3, $p<.01$ 2 vs. 3, $p<.05$	1.70	2.30	15.7 1 vs. 2 & 3. $p<.01$ 2 vs. 3, $p<.01$	37.0	26.9
Exp. II (N=7 groups)	3.18 1 vs. 2 & 3, $p<.02$	2.13	2.36	17.4 1 vs. 2, $p<.05$ 1 vs. 3, $p=.02$	31.1	29.0
Exp. III (N=7 groups)	3.12	2.80	2.75	19.8	20.4	20.9
Exp. IV (N=7 groups)	3.24	2.95	3.11	20.9	22.2	18.6
Exp. V (N=7 groups)	3.08	2.66	2.82	19.3	24.3	22.2

[a] Only p values of less than 0.10 are indicated. All p values are two-tailed. Differences for experimental groups between first and second discussions were compared with corresponding differences for control groups by the Mann-Whitney Test. Significance levels for differences between the second and third discussions and first and third discussions were computed by the sign test.

Table 2

MEAN SELF-RANKINGS OF TARGET PERSON

Experiment	Discussion period		
	1	2	3
Control	2.67	2.31	2.30
I	2.91	1.36	2.05
	1 vs. 2, $p < .02$		
	2 vs. 3, $p < .05$		
II	2.79	1.64	1.64
	1 vs. 3, $p < .05$		
III	2.93	2.64	2.79
IV	3.04	2.14	2.50
V	2.68	2.07	2.39

mental groups, TP's talking time and frequency of talking increased during the second discussion when lights were being used. Furthermore, this change was strongly reflected in the sociometric votes of the other group members: all nine Experimental TPs received higher average rankings after the second discussion than after the first discussion (Table 1). Frequency of talking data, which are correlated with total talking time ($r = .91$) are omitted from Table 1. Since the rankings for guidance, best ideas, participation, and leadership turned out to be highly correlated, the sociometric data is reported as the mean ranking of these four items. The TPs' self-rankings are excluded from these averages.

In eight of nine cases TPs' ratings drop somewhat following the discussion of the third case, but in only one group do the ratings the TP receives drop back below the baseline level of the first period.

Increased sociometric ratings and length of talking time in the second period for Experimental TPs are significantly greater than the slight increase shown for Control group TPs. The drop-off from the second to third discussions is significant for the objective talking measures and the sociometric data. Despite the drop-off, TPs' level of output and sociometric ratings remain significantly higher than they were after the first discussion.

The TPs' perception of their own behavior as reflected in their self-ratings followed a similar pattern. Their self-ratings also rose after the second period and then dropped off somewhat when the lights were not used in the third period. The TPs' self-ratings are presented in Table 2. Although mean self-ratings for each discussion period are slightly higher than ratings received from others, the magnitude of change between discussions is very similar to changes in ratings made by others.

Data from the postsession questionnaire are presented in Table 3. These data indicate: (1) a strong liking for the second case problem among Experimental TPs, while no such consistent preference exists for any one case among the other group members; (2) TPs were aware that they talked a great deal during the second discussion: 6 of 9 felt that they talked

Table 3

POSTSESSION QUESTIONNAIRE DATA

Experiment		N	Case preference (1=most liked, 3=least liked)			Estimate of talking (1=more, 0=same, −1=less)			Influence of lights (Frequencies)		
			Case 1	Case 2	Case 3	Period 1	Period 2	Period 3	Help	No diff.	Hinder
Control	TP	9	2.56	1.56	1.89	−0.22	+0.33	−0.11	—[a]	—[a]	—[a]
	Others	27	2.30	1.81	1.89	−0.04	+0.07	−0.04	—[a]	—[a]	—[a]
I	TP	9	2.56	1.00	2.44	−0.33	+0.67	+0.22	8	0	1
	Others	27	2.15	2.07	1.78	+0.04	−0.37	+0.07	8	9	10
II	TP	7	2.43	1.86	1.71	−0.43	+0.43	+0.57	4	3	0
	Others	21	1.86	2.67	1.48	+0.19	−0.48	+0.05	7	4	10
III	TP	7	2.29	2.14	1.57	−0.29	−0.29	+0.29	1	4	2
	Others	21	2.14	2.05	1.81	−0.04	+0.07	−0.04	3	12	6
IV	TP	7	2.17	1.50	2.33	−0.50	+0.33	.00	4[b]	2	0
	Others	21	2.17	2.17	1.67	−0.22	−0.05	−0.05	—[a]	—[a]	—[a]
V	TP	7	2.14	2.14	1.71	+0.14	−0.29	−0.14	—[a]	—[a]	—[a]
	Others	21	1.85	2.29	1.86	.00	−0.29	−0.10	4	7	10

[a] Did not receive feedback.
[b] One group did not complete postsession questionnaires.

"more than usual" during this period while all but one of the other group members felt that they had talked "less than usual" or "about the same"; (3) 8 of 9 *TP*s responded that the feedback lights had "helped" them during the second discussion while the others were split between feelings of being "helped" and being "hindered."

Experiments II and III

In Experiment I red and green lights were distributed to the *S*s on the basis of the *E*s' intuitive judgments as to what behaviors should be encouraged or discouraged. It was thought that such a procedure would be most effective in bringing about the desired changes in the behavior of the *S*s. When the effectiveness of this procedure was demonstrated, the question arose as to how crucial were the *E*s' choices of which behaviors to reinforce in producing the observed effect. Did the *TP*'s increase in sociometric status result from an increase in certain categories of verbal output, or was it simply the result of his talking more in general? Experiments II and III represent an attempt to answer this question by eliminating the *E*s' judgments from the administering of the lights. Fifty-six undergraduate *S*s were assigned to 14 four-man groups. Seven groups were run in each experiment.

Experiment II

Procedure. Experiment II was an exact replication of Experiment I in terms of the general procedure followed. The only modification was in the manner in which the red and green lights were administered to the *S*s during their second case discussion. All "feedback" lights were administered automatically by a preprogrammed event-controlling unit which was activated by the same switches used to record the *S*s' verbal output. In this way it was possible to make the lights contingent upon the *S*s' talking without regard to its content.

The program unit was connected to a 25-position stepping switch which moved to the next position with the recording of each discrete utterance by any of the *S*s. Each *S* had a fixed sequence of 25 events programmed for him: he could receive a green light, a red light, or no lights each time he talked. *TP* received a "leadership encouraging" schedule of 15 green lights with the remaining 10 positions blank. A separate timing device was connected to the *TP*'s circuit which delivered a red light to him for every 45 seconds of continuous silence. The other three *S*s received identical "followership encouraging" schedules consisting of 7 red lights, 2 green lights, and 16 blanks. These two schedules were intended to approximate the schedules administered in Experiment I in terms of both absolute number of lights and ratios of red to green.

Instructions regarding the onset of the "feedback lights" prior to the second discussion were the same as in Experiment I. Subjects also filled out the same sociometric questionnaire after each of three discussions and the same postexperimental questionnaire as were administered in Experiment I.

Results. Although it was the intention of the *E*s to provide *S*s with schedules of red and green lights which at least approximated those received by their counterparts in Experiment I, this objective was not achieved. The actual mean numbers of lights received by the *S*s in both experiments are shown in Table 4. It is obvious that all *S*s in Experiment II received considerably fewer lights of both kinds than did the comparable *S*s in Experiment I.

This deficit appears to have been mainly due to the fact that the programmed schedules were simply too sparse, parti-

Table 4

Number of Lights Received

Experiment		TP	M-1	M-2	M-3
I	Green	38.1	15.2	15.1	13.8
	Red	7.6	7.8	9.6	9.3
II	Green	15.4	1.7	1.7	0.4
	Red	5.3	9.7	6.0	3.3
III	Green	38	15	16	14
	Red	7	8	10	9
IV	Green	14.0	—	—	—
	Red	5.0	—	—	—
V	Green	—	7.9	7.9	5.1
	Red	—	6.4	7.7	5.6

cularly in terms of green lights. There is also, however, a methodological problem inherent in the design of this study. In order for the *TP* to receive green lights, it was necessary for him to talk. If the programmed schedule of green lights was insufficient to produce a sizable increase in his talking over time, then this placed an obvious limitation on the number of green lights he would receive over the course of the entire discussion.

The major results of Experiment II are presented in Table 1. When compared with *TP*s in the Control groups, it can be seen that even making the green lights contingent upon sheer talking produces an increase in both the sociometric rankings received from others and verbal output. These increases are not, however, as great as those obtained in Experiment I.

From the first to the second discussion the *TP* shows a significant increase in sociometric rankings received from others

and a significant ircnease in taking time. These gains in sociometry and talking time are maintained by the *TP* to a significant extent throughout the third discussion.

Unfortunately, the fact that fewer lights were given to the *S*s in Experiment II than to the *S*s in Experiment I makes it impossible to give an unequivocal answer to the question of how much the *E*s' judgments contributed to the over-all effect. It does appear safe to conclude, however, that such judgments as were being made in Experiment I were at least not indispensible in producing significant changes in both verbal behavior and sociometric rankings.

Experiment III

Procedure. As a second method of eliminating the *E*s' judgments from the administration of lights, seven groups of *S*s received red and green lights on a time-contingency basis. A leadership schedule was derived by averaging the number of red and green lights received by TPs in Experiment I within each successive 5-minute interval and then distributing this number randomly over an equal period of time. In a like manner a different schedule was derived for M-1, M-2, and M-3 on the basis of the average number of lights received by their counterparts in Experiment I.

These schedules were administered manually by a single E who viewed a large clock with a sweep-second hand in conjunction with the four schedules written out on large sheets of cardboard. This procedure allowed Ss to receive the same number and ratio of lights received in Experiment I, but without regard to whether or not they were talking at the time. In all other respects, the procedure was the same as that followed in Experiment I.

Results. Table 4 shows the numbers of lights received by all Ss in Experiment III. It can be seen that these numbers correspond to the averages of Experiment I.

The changes in sociometric status and verbal output that resulted from this procedure were no greater, and in some cases were smaller, than those obtained in the control groups (see Table 1).

EXPERIMENTS IV AND V

The experiments described thus far have all involved an attempt to alter the verbal behavior of all four group members. This procedure consisted of essentially two operations: (1) an attempt to increase the TP's output by rewarding his talking and punishing him for being silent, and (2) an attempt to decrease the other members' output by punishing their talking and rewarding their silence. Although these two operations can be conceptualized separately, they did not function independently in the experiments reported above. The behavior change of the TP in Experiments I and II may have been due to one or the other of these two techniques, or to an interaction of the two.

In order to determine the independent effects of these two operations, two additional experiments were conducted. Experiment IV provided only the TP with feedback, while Experiment V provided only the three nontarget Ss with feedback.

Experiment IV

Procedure. To provide only the TP with feedback during the second discussion, it was necessary to instruct the other three members of the group in such a way that they would not anticipate any feedback while at the same time instructing the TP in the usual manner. To achieve this, two sets of written instructions were prepared and were passed out to the group just prior to the second discussion. The instructions that the TP read were a written version of the standard instructions given to all Ss in the experimental condition of Experiment I. The other three Ss were given a written version of the control instructions of Experiment I. Both sets of instructions were carefully prepared to appear identical in terms of location of paragraph indentations, margins, and other typographical aspects. No Ss in any of the groups reported awareness of this difference in the instructions.

A single E administered the red and green lights to the TP in the same manner that they were given to the TP's in Experiment I. No explicit attempt was made to replicate the mean numbers of each kind of light given in Experiment I.

Results. The sociometric and verbal output measures for Experiment IV show virtually no changes over the three discussions and do not differ from the results obtained in the control condition (Table

1). The mean number of lights received by the *TP* are reported in Table 4. In comparison with the figures for Experiment I, the number of green lights received by the *TP*s is much smaller. This was due mainly to the fact that the *TP*s did not markedly increase their verbal output in the second discussion.

Experiment V

Procedure. This experiment was essentially the complement of Experiment IV. Instead of encouraging the *TP* to talk more, the procedure of Experiment V consisted of discouraging the other three members of the group and withholding all feedback from the *TP*. Written instructions were again used to instruct the *S*s differentially with regard to the administration of feedback in the second discussion. The *TP* received the control version while the other three were given the experimental version.

The *E* who administered the feedback lights to the three nontarget *S*s followed the same general rules that were observed in Experiment I in attempting to decrease their verbal output in the second discussion.

Results. The TPs in Experiment V increased slightly in sociometric ranking and verbal output from the first to the second discussion (Table 1). None of these increases were significant, however. As shown in Table 4, the nontarget *S*s received slightly fewer red lights and about half as many green lights as did the nontarget *S*s in Experiment I.

Discussion

The results of Experiment I clearly demonstrate that the procedure used is an effective method of changing the verbal output of selected group members in a desired direction. Furthermore, changes in the sociometric structure of the group are highly correlated with verbal output changes ($r = .84$). It had been anticipated that a crucial element necessary for the success of this manipulation was the manner in which the experimenters determined the appropriate times to reinforce group members. Therefore, the results of Experiment II were somewhat surprising in that the programmed machine produced not only an increase in the *TP*'s verbal output, but also a significant rise in his sociometric status.

One possible explanation for the similarity in the results of Experiments I and II is that the same general class of behaviors was being reinforced by both the experimenters and the programmed machine. Although there are no data to confirm this notion, it was the opinion of the experimenters that all discussions were relatively homogeneous in content and highly task-oriented, with very few irrelevant or disruptive statements being made by any of the participants. This being the case, it seems reasonable to assume that the majority of the *TP*s' statements that were reinforced in both Experiments I and II were task relevant in nature, and, therefore, that an increase in such verbal output would result in higher sociometric rankings for the *TP*s.

Some indirect support for this contention is provided by Oakes (1962), who used a reinforcement technique similar to the one described in this report in an attempt to determine which of the twelve Bales' categories of response are most susceptible to reinforcement. His findings show that only one of these categories, "giving opinion, evaluation, analysis, expresses feeling, wish," could be increased significantly during a group discussion. It should be noted that more than 50% of the total responses were coded in this one category. These findings appear to coincide with our contention that discussion content was both relevant to the case discussion and homogeneous across groups. Therefore, it is not surprising that the experimenter function of selecting statements to "reinforce" in Experiment I is not critical in the alteration of group structure. At the same time, the results of Experiment III indicate that lights must be contingent upon verbal behavior to be effective. Receiving encouraging lights at predetermined intervals did not prove sufficient to significantly alter the initial group structure.

The technique which was used successfully to modify group structure can be considered as two separate operations. One operation consisted of positively reinforcing or encouraging the target person to step up his verbal output. A complementary operation was employed simultaneously to depress the verbal output of the other group members except when they complied or agreed with the *TP*. It could be argued that one or the other of these two operations alone might account for most of the behavioral and sociometric changes. Experiments IV and V were designed to test the independent effects of each of these two component techniques. The results suggest that both operations are necessary to produce modification of the group behavior. The ineffectiveness of either operation used separately indicates that without some encouragement a quiet group member will not spontaneously increase his output when other members are artificially depressed; and conversely it is not enough to encourage a quiet individual to participate more unless "room" is provided for his increased verbal output. It is also possible that when both techni-

ques are employed, agreeing and complying behaviors of other group members may increase and provide additional social reinforcement for the *TP*.

The previously mentioned high correlation between sociometric rankings and total talking time deserves further consideration. Given a situation in which four strangers are brought together, allowed to interact for a brief period, and then asked to evaluate one another on characteristics such as "best ideas," "guidance," and "leadership," one might expect that sheer amount of talking would be a salient factor in determining these evaluations. It would be misleading, however, to conclude that such a high correlation between talking and sociometry always obtains in group situations, or that talking, regardless of its quality or appropriateness, always leads to the perception of good ideas and leadership ability. Such a hypothesis would have to be tested under a wider variety of situations than the present experimental design affords. For instance, other group members may rate a talkative man highly on "best ideas" if he is perceived as talking a great deal because he had earned encouragement from expert evaluators. On the other hand, others may not positively evaluate a talkative man's ideas if they are aware that experimenters are manipulating rather than evaluating his behavior. These considerations have been explored by Hastorf *et al.* (1964).

The results of Experiments I and II show that the increase in the *TP*'s verbal output from the first to the second discussion is partly carried over to the third period when the lights are not used. The question of how long the effect lasts and whether or not it will generalize to other similar situations is unanswered. A series of experiments to test the perseveration and generalization of these effects is in progress.

If *TP* gains in sociometry and talks more, some one person or combination of other participants must lose sociometric votes and talk less. Because of this "degrees of freedom" restriction, it is of some interest to explore the dynamics of the change situation. For instance, one might ask which group member(s) loses when *TP* gains. It would be reasonable to predict that each man loses sociometric votes and talking time in proportion to what he has to lose, i.e., *M-1*, the man who was originally ranked the highest, would lose the most, and *M-2* and *M-3* should lose

proportionally less. An analysis of ratings received by *M-1*, *M-2*, and *M-3* (Table 5) shows that in Experiment I, *M-1*'s losses alone account for *TP*'s gains. In Experiment II, although *M-1* suffers the greatest loss, *M-2* also talks somewhat less and receives lower ratings on the questionnaires.

It might also be asked if the increase in the *TP*'s sociometric rank from the first to the second discussion was largely due to the other members assigning lower ranks to themselves. This would result in an artificial elevation of the *TP*'s rank. The data were analyzed with all self-rankings eliminated and each subject's ratings of

Table 5

SOCIOMETRIC RANK AND VERBAL OUTPUT CHANGES FROM DISCUSSION
PERIOD 1 TO DISCUSSION PERIOD 2

Experiment		*TP*	*M-1*	*M-2*	*M-3*
Control	Sociometric rank[a]	+0.24	−0.12	−0.35	+0.25
	Verbal output (%)	+2.9	−2.3	−3.9	+3.3
I	Sociometric rank	+1.53	−0.72	−0.61	−0.31
	Verbal output (%)	+21.3	−15.7	−5.0	−0.7
II	Sociometric rank	+1.05	−0.36	−0.56	−0.05
	Verbal output (%)	+13.7	−10.3	−7.1	+3.6
III	Sociometric rank	+0.32	+0.06	−0.32	+0.10
	Verbal output (%)	+0.6	−2.3	−0.2	+2.1
IV	Sociometric rank	+0.29	−0.45	+0.11	−0.08
	Verbal output (%)	+1.3	−3.5	+1.7	+0.6
V	Sociometric rank	+0.42	−0.14	−0.38	+0.08
	Verbal output (%)	+5.0	−4.8	−1.3	+1.2

[a] Total positive and negative sociometric changes are not necessarily equal because self-rankings have been excluded from the averages which are presented in Table 1.

the other group members reranked from 1 to 3. This analysis revealed substantially the same pattern of results as those presented in Table 1.

Two opposing hypotheses may be entertained regarding the *TPs'* affective response to the experimental manipulation. It could be predicted that participants who are rewarded for talking will gain more satisfaction from the discussion and will generalize some of this affect to the case problem, or alternatively that the *TP* will feel uncomfortable in the unfamiliar role of a high participator. The postsession questionnaire results clearly support the former prediction in that *TPs* enjoyed participating in the second discussion and indicated strong preference for the second case problem. During the first discussion, before any lights were administered, high participators showed no more preference for the case than did low participators.

In summary, the experiments described above provide a workable technique for the alteration of verbal output and sociometric structure in a group situation and define some of the necessary conditions to obtain such changes.

Two problems emerge that are of significance to the understanding of social interaction. The first relates to the perseveration and the generalization of behavior change. What are the conditions under which behavior change would perseverate and generalize to other conditions? We have obtained evidence of some perseveration to a sessoin which immediately followed the acquisition session. An important variable in this respect is the way in which the *TP* himself views the situation. We would hypothesize that the more an individual perceives changes in his behavior as being self-caused and not the result of external forces (in Heider's (1958) sense of the word), the more likely he will maintain some of this behavior change.

The second general problem concerns the perception and evaluation of one person's behavior change by others. In the experiments described above when a *TP's* verbal output was markedly changed, the other group members attributed high quality to the output. It is our hypothesis that observers who are able to see the rewarding or punishing lights would be more likely to attribute the change in behavior to the influence of the lights and would thus be less willing to attribute such qualities as leadership to the *TP*.

REFERENCES

AIKEN, E. G. "Interpersonal Behavior Changes Perceived as Accompanying the Operant Conditioning of Verbal Output in Small Groups." *Technical Report Number II.* Western Behavioral Sciences Institute, 1963.

BACHRACH, A. J., CANDLAND, D. K., and GIBSON, J. T. "Group Reinforcement of Individual Response Experiments in Verbal Behavior." In Irwin A. Berg and Bernard M. Bass (Eds.), *Conformity and Deviation.* New York: Harper, 1961. Pp. 258–285.

BALES, R. F. *Interaction Process Analysis: A Method for the Study of Small Groups.* Cambridge, Mass.: Addison-Wesley Co., Inc., 1950.

HASTORF, A. H. "The 'Reinforcement' of Individual Actions in a Group Situation." In L. Krasner and L. P. Ullmann (Eds.), *Research in Behavior Modification.* New York: Holt, 1964.

HASTORF, A. H., KITE, W. R., GROSS, A. E., and WOLFE, LYN J. "The Perception and Evaluation of Behavior Change." Unpublished Manuscript. Stanford University, 1964.

HEIDER, F. *The Psychology of Interpersonal Relations.* New York: Wiley, 1958.

OAKES, W. F. "Reinforcement of Bales' Categories in Group Discussion." *Psychol. Rep.*, 1962, 11, 427–435.

OAKES, W. F., DROGE, A. E., and AUGUST, B. "Reinforcement Effects on Participation in Group Discussion." *Psychol. Rep.*, 1960, 7, 503–514.

PEPINSKY, P. N., HEMPHILL, J. K., and SHEVITZ, R. N. "Attempts to Lead, Group Productivity, and Morale under Conditions of Acceptance and Rejection." *J. Abnorm. Soc. Psychol.*, 1958, 57, 47–54.

PERFORMANCE EXPECTATIONS AND BEHAVIOR IN SMALL GROUPS*

Joseph Berger and Thomas L. Conner

When given a collective task to accomplish, a group of strangers will evolve patterns of interaction that clearly reflect differences in power and prestige among the members. Some members will be more active than others, exercise more influence than others, and be rewarded more often than others. It is our purpose to set down in formal axiom form some of the processes that underly such patterns of inequalities and that account for their maintenance.

Bales and his associates found in their observation of *ad hoc* college student discussion groups that, through time, marked inequalities develop in the overall rates of initiation of activity by each member.[1] Further, they found that those who ini-

* Joseph Berger and Thomas L. Conner, "Performance Expectations and Behavior in Small Groups," *Acta Sociologica*, 12 (1969), 186–98. Reprinted by permission.

Research for this paper was supported in large part by grants from the National Science Foundation (NSF G-13314, G-23990, GS-1170) and by a grant from the National Institute of Mental Health (MH 16580—01). We would like to acknowledge the help given us at various stages of this investigation by Bernard P. Cohen, Hamit Fisek, Robert E. Muzzy, J. Laurie Snell, Murray Webster, and Morris Zelditch, Jr.

[1] R. F. Bales, F. L. Strodtbeck, T. M. Mills, and Mary E. Roseborough, "Channels of Communication in Small Groups" *American Sociological Review*, 16, 1951, pp. 461–468, R. F. Bales, "The Equilibrium Problem in Small Groups" in T. Parsons, R. F. Bales, and E. A. Shils, *Working Papers in the Theory of Action* (Glencoe: The Free Press, 1953), pp. 111–161; R. F. Bales, and P. E. Slater, "Role Differentiation in Small Decision-Making Groups," in T. Parsons, R. F. Bales, *et al., Family Socialization and Interaction Process* (Glencoe: The Free Press, 1955), pp. 259–306; C. Heinicke and R. F. Bales, "Development Trends in the Structure of Small Groups," *Sociometry*, 16, 1953, pp. 7–38.

tiate activity most frequently also receive activity most frequently and tend to be ranked highest by group members on the criteria of who had the best ideas, who guided the group discussion, and who demonstrated leadership. Norfleet found similar regularities in her examination of adult discussion groups which met together over a period of three weeks.[2] Ratings, by the members, of those individuals seen as having contributed most to the "productivity" of the group became concentrated, with a high degree of agreement, on a few individuals. Those who were rated as the best contributors also tended to be high on both initiation and receipt of interaction.

These investigations indicate that a cluster of correlated inequalities develop in discussion groups. If we assume that the "guidance" ratings reflect primarily successful influence and that the "best ideas" and "contribute to productivity" ratings reflect judgments of ability at the discussion task, then the cluster of inequalities includes at least initiation of activity, receipt of activity, task ability, and social influence.

The characteristics of these groups and their activities which we believe were crucial to the formation of inequalities were that:

a) they were given a collective task to accomplish;

b) it was reasonable to think of members having differential capacity to contribute to completing the task;

c) the completion of the task was of central importance to the members.

Under pressure to complete the task

successfully, those thought to be more able were given more opportunities to contribute (questions, inquiring glances, etc.) and were allowed to exercise more influence both in terms of persuading others and having contributions accepted; and, since the members of these groups were originally undifferentiated in status, judgments about ability were based on evaluations of contributions early in the discussions.

Harvey[3] and Sherif, White, and Harvey[4] found in groups with an already established power and prestige ordering that expectations for quality of future performance on the group's task and positive evaluations of past performance were correlated with the power and prestige ordering. Whyte found very similar things were true of the bowling activities of a street corner gang.[5] Our interpretation of these investigations is that performance expectations directly reflect beliefs that members hold about task ability, and that those thought to be more able were more likely to be perceived as having performed well.

The set of relationships we have inferred from the above investigations are only gross "tendencies" and correlations. Presumably there are processes in the social interaction that takes place in task performing groups that underly these tendencies. We have only hinted at what

---

[2] B. Norfleet, "Interpersonal Relations and Group Productivity," *Journal of Social Issues*, 4, 1948, pp. 66–69.

[3] O. J. Harvey, "An Experimental Approach to the Study of Status Relations in Informal Groups", *American Sociological Review*, 18, 1953, pp. 359–367.

[4] M. Sherif, B. J. White, and O. J. Harvey, "Status in Experimentally Produced Groups," *American Journal of Sociology*, 60, 1955, pp. 370–379.

[5] W. F. Whyte, *Street Corner Society: The Social Structure of an Italian Slum* (Chicago: University of Chicago Press, 1943).

some of the processes might be. Our task now is to set down systematically what these processes are and how they combine to produce differences in activity rates, influence, etc.

I. THE STRUCTURE OF INTERACTION

Our analysis applies to a group of at least two persons who have a task to accomplish together. We assume the members are all oriented toward successful, collective completion of the task in a finite time period. The group is thus assumed to be "task focused" and "collectively oriented".

As such a group attempts to complete their task, they partition their activities into the completion of a series of smaller "tasks" or subtasks. For example, if the group has met together to consider their budget for some coming period of time, they may partition their meeting into review of the previous budget, consideration of future needs, and construction of a new budget. These in turn will be broken down into smaller and smaller questions. This, of course, is not a "rational" process in the sense that subtasks are explicitly defined before they are discussed. Rather, it is a process that takes place as the group proceeds, and in "natural" settings the division of the task into subtasks is a product and not a precondition of the interaction.

In most cases the division of the task into subtasks results in a series of "smallest" subtasks which can be defined by a fundamental sequence of behaviors that is repeated for each subtask. The nature of this sequence is considered in detail below. For our present purposes it will suffice to indicate that the sequence begins with the presentation of an idea or suggestion

or fact (perhaps preceded by a question) to which the members must react, and the sequence ends with consensus (probably only public consensus) on the quality of the idea or acceptability of the suggestion or accuracy of the fact.

For the sake of clarity let us label the larger task the group must accomplish by T and the set of smallest subtasks by t_1. Our conception, then, of the interaction process is that the group proceeds from dealing with t_1 to dealing with t_2 to dealing with t_3, etc., however they have defined the t's for themselves, and that the completion of T has been accomplished when all of the t's have been dealt with.

Kinds of Behavior

In analyzing the interaction in task performing groups we will pay attention only to certain kinds of behavior and only to certain characteristics of those kinds of behavior. Our focus is upon "task" behavior as opposed to "social-emotional" or "process" behavior.[6] That is, we exclude from analysis behavior that is related exclusively to social and emotional relationships in the group. So, for example, behavior aimed at increasing morale or commitment to the task, or smoothing tension, or establishing friendship does not fall within the scope of our theory.

We begin, as Bales and others have, by dividing all of the behavior which is reasonably classified as social into small units called *acts*. An act is usually a simple verbal sentence but could be a gesture, a look, or some other form of non-verbal communication. More strictly, an act is the smallest unit of social behavior that can be

---

[6] Bales, *op. cit.*

classified within our system. Any behavior that is not an instance of one of our concepts is, of course, ignored. The kinds of acts we are primarily concerned with are *action opportunities, performance outputs,* and *reward actions.*

An *action opportunity* is a request for an activity, such as when x asks y a question, or x looks inquiringly at y. For our purposes an action opportunity may be directed at a particular person or not, and may specify the kind of activity requested or not. We will also be interested in the initiator of an action opportunity and, if it is directed, the receiver of an action opportunity. A *performance output* is an act which is an attempt to solve or partially solve a subproblem. Included would be giving information or facts, and providing suggestions or ideas. As with *action opportunities, performance outputs* may be directed at a particular person or not, and both the initiator and the receiver are of interest. A *reward action* is any act which communicates the evaluation of a performance output, such as agreeing with a suggestion, concurring with a fact, or disputing an idea.[7] A reward action may also be directed or undirected and have both an initiator and receiver. As well, it may be either positive or negative in content.

Cognitive Constructs

The above terms are all observable behaviors. Not all of the terms of our theory are observable, however. Some of them refer to unobservable cognitions that persons may have that are related to the kinds of observable behavior we are concerned with. The first of these is the concept *performance expectation,* which is a general belief or anticipation about the quality of future performance outputs. Performance expectations are ordinarily in a one-to-one relation to beliefs about task ability. Those high in ability will be expected to perform well, and vice versa. We will be concerned with whether the expectations are held for self or other(s) and will usually deal only with relative expectations, that is, rankings rather than some concept of absolute expectations.

A *unit evaluation* is a momentary evaluation of whatever composes the unit. By momentary we mean the evaluation is relatively temporary rather than enduring, thus leaving out sentiments such as liking, loving, hating, etc. The unit evaluated can be either a performance output or a person. Evaluation of a performance output would be thinking a fact is accurate, an idea unsound, or a suggestion acceptable. Evaluation of a person would be thinking some *person* made a good suggestion or presented a good idea. Obviously an evaluation of a person and of his performance are rarely going to differ, but which gets evaluated first may be of importance, such as when the quality of a performance is decided upon by referring first to the performer. We will distinguish only positive and negative evaluations.

Defined Terms

The terms above are all really primitive terms whose meaning is given by general understanding and example. Other terms that we use can be formally defined using

[7] The term "reward action" usually has a broader meaning than what we intend here. We are concerned only with those acts in which one actor communicates to another his acceptance or rejection of specific performance outputs.

the primitive terms. We will now briefly state them for later use.

Acceptance of an action opportunity occurs when an action opportunity is directed at some person x and he responds with some other categorizable behavior such as a performance output. Otherwise the action opportunity is *declined*. If some person x initiates a performance output, then an *influence attempt* is a negative reward action directed at x accompanied with an alternative or counter performance output. *Acceptance of an influence attempt* is any change of the evaluation of a performance output following an influence attempt.

II. Informal Characterization of the Interaction

Let us imagine that some group of persons, all strangers of equal status, come together to collectively complete some task —say a discussion problem. As they concern themselves with their task, they are continually initiating performance outputs and giving others action opportunities. As this takes place they are also engaged in evaluating each other's performance outputs and communicating these evaluations with reward actions. During the early phases of this process we believe that most of this behavior takes place in a random manner—particularly the distribution of action opportunities and whether these opportunities are accepted. However, as the members continue to interact, evaluations of performances become significant, and under some circumstances become the bases for a socially known ranking of the members by task ability—a ranking of performance expectations. Should this happen, it will markedly affect the future

behavior of the members. Specifically, it will affect who is given action opportunities, who will on his own initiate performance outputs, whose performance outputs are positively or negatively evaluated, and who will be influenced by whom. We further believe that the patterning of these behaviors will in general maintain the performance expectation ranking and that there are several processes by which behavior inconsistent with the rankings is "explained away" and hence has no significance for altering the ranking.

III. Sequences of Kinds of Behavior

Our analysis rests upon two fundamental assumptions. First, that the behavior that takes place concerning any particular subtask[8] is patterned. Kinds of behavior follow each other in specifiable orders. Second, that the likelihoods of certain kinds of behavior will differ by the position of persons in the performance expectation ranking. We will deal with the former here and delay the latter till the next section.

Let us imagine that we are examining a group as it is ready to begin working on a particular subtask. We will analyze what takes place from the standpoint of some arbitrary reference person, call him p. He faces a decision at this point. If he decides to act, he may initiate either a performance output or an action opportuntity; or if someone else acts, he may receive an action opportunity or not. These four events—p initiates a perform-

---

[8] Henceforth, when we write "subtask" we mean "smallest subtask".

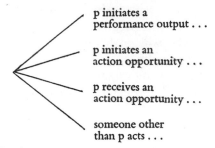

p initiates a
performance output . . .

p initiates an
action opportunity . . .

p receives an
action opportunity . . .

someone other
than p acts . . .

Fig. 1.

ance output, p initiates an action opportunity, p receives an action opportunity, or someone else acts—are mutually exclusive and exhaustive at this time. We will represent the situation at this point by a simple tree diagram as shown in Figure 1. As we continue the analysis we will add further branches to the tree.

If p initiates a performance output, a specifiable pattern of possibilities will follow. He may initiate a second performance output, but that would be the start of a new subtask and we want to confine ourselves to those behaviors relevant to the present subtask. What will follow p's performance—either immediately or eventually—is an evaluation-influence process. Others in the group will now be considering how to evaluate p's performance. To simplify the analysis, for the moment assume that the only members of the group

are p and q. If q reacts positively to p's performance—p receives a positive reward action from q—then consensus has been achieved and work on the subproblem has been completed. If q reacts negatively—p receives an influence attempt from q—then consensus will be achieved only if one of p and q changes his mind. P may change his mind right away or counter with an influence attempt directed at q. Eventually, however, if p and q are strongly committed to completing the larger task T, they will reach consensus—that is, one of them will be influenced.

Suppose now that the group has three members, p, o, and q, and that p's performance is still up for evaluation. Now, whether p is influenced or not depends upon the evaluations of both o and q. Either o or q or both may initiate an influence attempt toward p and precipitate the necessity for further discussion before consensus is achieved. Further, o and q may attempt to influence each other by persuading the other to change an already expressed evaluation.

We will specify the parts of the evaluation-influence process as follows. Following p's performance output he may receive one or more positive reward actions only, or he may receive at least one negative reward action. In the former cir-

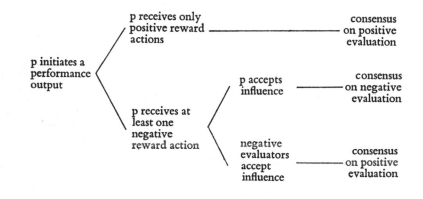

p initiates a
performance
output

p receives only
positive reward
actions ———————— consensus
on positive
evaluation

p receives at
least one
negative
reward action

p accepts
influence ———— consensus
on negative
evaluation

negative
evaluators
accept
influence ———— consensus
on positive
evaluation

Fig. 2.

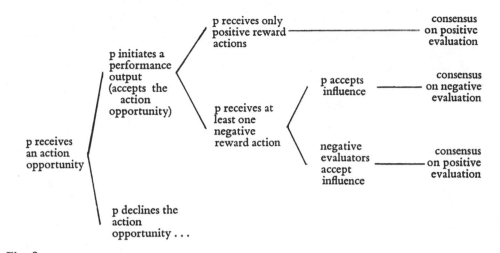

Fig. 3.

cumstances, consensus is achieved; in the latter circumstance, the question of whether p is influenced or whether those who expressed negative evaluations are influenced must be resolved. When p is influenced, there is consensus on the negative evaluation. When he is not, there is consensus on the positive evaluation. Figure 2 shows the tree diagram of the evaluation-influence sequence.

Returning to Figure 1, if p receives an action opportunity he must decide whether to respond or not by initiating a performance output. If p initiates a performance output after having been given an action opportunity, that is, accepts the opportunity, all behavior during and after that sequence will be the same as when p initiates a performance without an action opportunity. If p declines the action op-

Fig. 4.

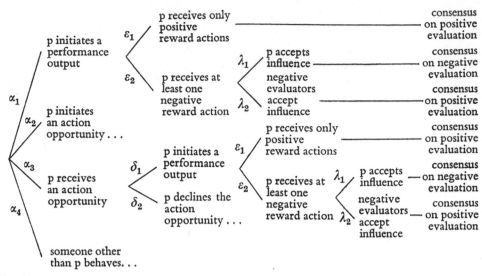

Fig. 5.

portunity, then presumably someone else, say q, will initiate a performance output. But our description of the interaction will not change; only the reference person will change. Figure 3 below shows the sequence when p has received an action opportunity.

Figures 1, 2, and 3 together describe the entire set of behavior possibilities that define a subtask.[9] Figure 4 shows the tree diagram which contains all the possibilities.

IV. The Ranking of Performance Expectations

Probability Axioms

Let us now consider a group of n individuals, $p_1, p_2, \ldots p_n$, each ranked by

---

[9] The notion of a smallest subtask defined by sequences of behavior is an analytic construct and it is not assumed that the behavioral elements of a subtask will necessarily occur within a contiguous temporal unit.

expected level of performance at their collective task T. We assume that this expectation structure is regarded by the group as relevant to task completion, that there is one ability or a perfectly correlated collection of abilities that define the ranking, and that there is complete agreement on the ranking by all members.

As the members begin work on some substask t_k, the sequences of behavior possibilities in Figure 4 describe their activity. The selection of a branch in the tree by any particular person is not completely capricious, however. His selection will depend upon his performance expectation ranking, and, we believe, will be probabilistically determined. Thus, we assume that a well defined probability, ranging from 0 to 1, exists corresponding to each possibility in the sequence of possibilities of Figure 4 and that for any particular possibilities the probabilities associated with each member of the group will be ordered. Figure 5 shows the probabilities in question.

The assertions below directly order the

value of α_1, α_3, ε_1, δ_1, and λ_2. In all cases, it will be asserted that persons higher in the ranking of expected performance will have larger values of the probability being considered. This means that where the probabilities being considered refer to one branch of a two branch part of Figure 5, the probabilities for the second branch are being inversely ordered to the ranking of expected performance.

The first axiom concerns α_1. It asserts that the higher a person's expectation rank, the more likely he is to initiate an unrequested performance output at the beginning of a subtask.

Axiom 1. If p_i is ranked higher than p_j on expected performance, than p_i is more likely than p_j to initiate a performance output at the beginning of any subtask t_k.

Once a person performs, the question of performance evaluation arises. Axiom 2 states that the higher a person's expectation rank the more likely he is to receive a positive reward action from any particular other person. It follows from that axiom that the higher a person's expectation rank the more likely he is to receive only positive reward actions for any given performance output.

Axiom 2. For any given performance output, if p_i is ranked higher than p_j on expected performance, than p_i is more likely to receive a positive reward action than is p_j.

If a member receives at least one negative reward action, the person who is lower in expectation rank should be influenced more often. Axiom 3 asserts this.

Axiom 3. For any given number of influence attempts, if p_i is ranked higher than p_j on expected performance, then p_j is more likely to accept influence than p_i.

If at the start of a subproblem t_k, all members refrain from initiation of a performance output, then an action opportunity will almost certainly be initiated. The allocation of action opportunities should be related to the expectation structure.

Axiom 4. For any subtask t_k, if p_i is ranked higher than p_j on expected performance, p_i is more likely than p_j to receive an action opportunity.

And finally, not only are higher ranking members more likely to receive action opportunities, they are also more likely to accept them.

Axiom 5. For any subtask t_k, if p_i is ranked higher than p_j on expected performance, then p_i is more likely to accept an action opportunity at the beginning of t_k.

Some Consequences

To further display the nature of this axiom structure as well as illustrate its use, we now consider two fairly direct consequences of these asertions. These consequences are also of substantive interest in their own right.

1. Performance Outputs

The likelihood of a person making a performance output is determined by the likelihood that he initiates a performance output without being requested, the likelihood that he is requested to perform, and the likelihood that he performs when he is requested. The probability that he initiates a performance output without a prior action opportunity is α_1; that he is requested to perform is α_3; and that he responds to an action opportunity is δ_1. Thus the probability that a person initiates a performance output is

$$\alpha_1 + \alpha_3 \delta_1.$$

Since α_1 (Axiom 1), α_3 (Axiom 4), and δ_1 (Axiom 5) are all larger for higher ranked persons, it follows that for p_i ranked higher than p_j,

$$(1.1) \quad (\alpha_{1i} + \alpha_{3i} \delta_{1i}) > (\alpha_{1j} + \alpha_{3j} \delta_{1j}).$$

That is, *the higher the rank of a person in the expectation ranking, the greater the likelihood that he will make performance outputs.*

2. Acceptance of Performance Outputs

Whether or not a given performance output is accepted (positive consensus on evaluation of the performance output) depends both upon the reaction to it (whether all positive or some negative) and upon the outcome of the influence struggle in the case of at least one negative reaction. The probability that a person's performance output is accepted has four additive components:

1. $\alpha_1 \varepsilon_1$
2. $\alpha_1 \varepsilon_2 \lambda_2$
3. $\alpha_3 \delta_1 \varepsilon_1$
4. $\alpha_3 \delta_1 \varepsilon_2 \lambda_2$

Components 1 and 3 are directly ranked by the axioms, but components 2 and 4 are not ranked by anything in the formulation up to now. So an additional assumption is required before the probability of having a performance output accepted can be ranked.

A substantively reasonable assumption is that the success of higher ranked persons at influencing others compensates for the higher frequency of received influence attempts for a given performance of lower ranked persons. Thus,

$$(1.2) \quad \lambda_{2i}/\lambda_{2j} > \varepsilon_{2j}/\varepsilon_{2i}.$$

From (1.2) and the anxioms, we have:
Theorem 1. For p_i ranked higher than p_j on expected performance.

a. $\alpha_{1i} \varepsilon_{1i} > \alpha_{1j} \varepsilon_{1j}$
b. $\alpha_{1i} \varepsilon_{2i} \lambda_{2i} > \alpha_{1j} \varepsilon_{2j} \lambda_{2j}$
c. $\alpha_{3i} \delta_{1i} \varepsilon_{1i} > \alpha_{3j} \delta_{1j} \varepsilon_{1j}$
d. $\alpha_{3i} \delta_{1i} \varepsilon_{2i} \lambda_{2i} > \alpha_{3j} \delta_{1j} \varepsilon_{2j} \lambda_{2j}$

If Theorem 1 is true, then *the acceptance of performance outputs is ranked by performance expectations.*

3. Maintenance of Expectation

Theorem 1 plays a fundamental role in the maintenance of ranking structures based on performance expectations. The four assertions of the theorem represent *sufficient* conditions for such a structure to remain unchanged. So if all four conditions held for all pairs of members, no change of positions in the ranking structure would be anticipated. However, these conditions are undoubtedly not the minimum conditions *necessary* for maintenance. Some amount of violation of them would probably be tolerated without resultant change.

The role of the four conditions in maintaining expectation structures follows from their role in the creation of such structures. We believe that if for some p_i and p_j, initially not distinguished by expected performance, p_i, emerged as having had more performance outputs accepted than p_j, then p_i would be ranked higher by the group than p_j on expected performance. In other words, evaluations of past performances are the basis for expectations about future performances, and once such expectations are established, evaluations of present performances are crucial to the maintenance of those expectations.

V. AN EXPERIMENT

We will present experimental evidence in support of the assertion that if p_i is ranked higher than p_j on expected performance, then p_i is less likely to accept influence, Axiom 3. The experimental situation was constructed so that who initiates performance outputs and action opportunities, who receives action opportunities, the number of consecutive performance outputs, and the number of influence attempts per performance have all been controlled and fixed. Performance expectations for two persons were manipulated and acceptance of influence was examined as a dependent variable.

The experiment consisted of two parts, called phase 1 and phase 2. Two subjects participated in each experiment. In phase 1 they were both publicly given fictitious scores on a test which was purported to measure their ability at the phase 2 task. This was the manipulation of performance expectations. In phase 2 they were required on repeated occasions (i.e., trials) to select one of two alternatives as the correct answer to a word association problem. The selection of a correct answer had two stages. Every time a subject was presented with a set of alternatives, he first made a preliminary selection and exchanged information with his partner as to which alternative each initially selected. The subjects could not verbally communicate nor even see each other but indicated their choices to the experimenter and each other using a system of lights and push-button switches. Following the initial choice, each made a private final choice taking the information he had received from the other into account. The purpose of this initial choice—final choice sequence was defined as seeing how well they worked together "as a team". They were told, moreover, that their final decision would be evaluated in terms of a "team score". The team score was simply the sum of the number of "correct" final decisions which each made, with no record kept of the relative contributions of each. The requirement that subjects make a communicated initial choice is equivalent to their having been given a mandatory action opportunity, and the choice itself constitutes a performance output. Thus action opportunities could not be un-

equally distributed nor could a subject decline to make a performance output.

To create the possibility for each subject to accept influence from the other and to standardize receipt of influence attempts, the experimenter controlled the exchange of initial choice information. Except for three trials of the total of twenty-five (6, 13, 20), the subjects were led to believe that they initially disagreed. They had to decide each time whether "he's right and I'm wrong," which would be a change of evaluation and hence acceptance of influence, or whether "I'm right and he's wrong," which would be nonacceptance of influence.

The phase 2 task problems consisted of sets of words such as the one shown below.

YESTERDAY
(A)   (B)
TA-KIN   TU-SAK

Subjects were instructed that the non-English words in the bottom row were phonetic spellings from a language unknown to them but that one of the words had the same meaning as the English word given. They were told that by comparing the sounds of the non-English words with the meaning of the English word they could decide which word was correct. The ability to do this was called "Meaning Insight Ability." Both the ability and the language, of course, were fictitious. Subjects were shown a total of twenty-five different word sets.

Each word set was selected, on the basis of a pretest, so as to represent as ambiguous a choice as possible. Only those word sets which elicited selection of one alternative 40–60 percent of the time when shown to approximately 100 pretest subjects were used in the task sequence. The order of presentation of the word sets was randomized.

The manipulation of competence at "Meaning Insight," hence the manipulation of performance expectations, was accomplished in phase 1 by showing the subjects a series of twelve words sets very similar to those described above. In each of these word sets the role of the English and non-English words was reversed as in the example below.

LU-BOYEL

(A)   (B)

LOVE   SOFTNESS

Subjects were given fictitious scores for their choices on those twelve word sets. Their scores were interpreted to them as representing rare occurrences and as being either superior or poor, so that each subject was led to believe either that he was exceptionally good or exceptionally bad, and either that his partner was exceptionally good or exceptionally bad. Hence, there were four performance expectation conditions:

(a) high self, low other
(b) high self, high other
(c) low self, low other
(d) low self, high other

It was predicted that the rate of acceptance of influence would be greatest in condition (d), least in (a), and that conditions (b) and (c) would have the same rate.

The subjects were 162 Stanford University male undergraduates who volunteered from various university classes. They were paid $1.25 per hour for participating. Forty-two were eliminated from the analysis for becoming suspicious or failing to accept one or more of the manipulations in the experiment.

Table 1 presents the mean proportion of final choices, for all trials, where subjects in each condition declined to accept influence (i.e., their final choice was the same as their initial choice).

It is clear that the data confirm the order predicted by the theory and that those who were expected to perform relatively better declined to accept influence more.

The above ordering also holds true throughout the series of trials. Figure 6, shown below, is a graph of the proportion of non-acceptance of influence for blocks of three trials.

The rates for all conditions are constant, they never overlap [except, of course, for

Table 1

PROPORTION OF FINAL CHOICES WHERE SUBJECTS DECLINED TO ACCEPT INFLUENCE

Condition	Proportion	Number
high self, low other	.78	29
high self, high other	.67	31
low self, low other	.65	32
low self, high other	.44	28

(b) and (c)], and the ordering is as predicted. It is especially interesting to note how similar conditions (b) and (c) are. The curves very clearly suggest that in this situation, at least, relative, not absolute, performance expectations affect acceptance of influence.

VI. SUMMARY

We began this paper with some speculations from the literature that power and prestige orderings in small groups are related to participation rates, distributions

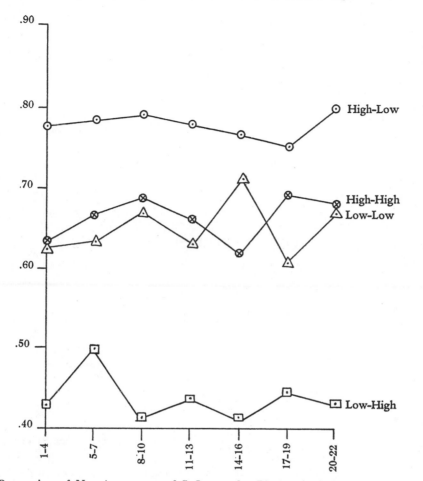

Fig. 6. Proportion of Non-Acceptance of Influence for Blocks of Three Trials.

of rewards and evaluations, and to exercise of influence. We formalized these speculations in a set of axioms which describe the process of problem solving interaction in small groups. Experimental evidence was presented which confirms one assertion—that a person expected to perform well relative to another person will accept influence less than one expected to perform poorly relative to a second person.

What remains to be done is to gather additional evidence for other assertions of the theory and for specific derivations from the theory. The experimental situation described can be easily modified to carry out such experiments. In addition to providing evidence for the theory, such experiments should lead to refinement of the theory and more precise statements of its axioms.

5

External Status Characteristics and Internal Group Structure

SOME CONSEQUENCES
OF POWER DIFFERENCES IN DECISION-MAKING
IN PERMANENT
AND TEMPORARY THREE-MAN GROUPS*

E. Paul Torrance

INTRODUCTION

Most of the sociological and social psychological studies of the consequences of power differences in decision-making have necessarily been concerned either with communities,[1] large organizations,[2] tem-porary groups,[3] or artificially created laboratory groups with but brief histories of interaction.[4] The present study deals with decision-making in small permanent groups with uniform, well-established, and clear-cut power structures (power being defined as the influence exerted by one person over another). A number of studies of decision-making in formal organizations suggest that the effects of power differences may be due as much to patterns of

* E. Paul Torrance, "Some Consequences of Power Differences in Decision-Making in Permanent and Temporary Three-Man Groups," *Research Studies*, State College of Washington, 22 (1954), 130–40. Reprinted by permission.

[1] F. Hunter, *Community Power Structure* (Chapel Hill: University of North Carolina Press, 1953).

[2] D. C. Pelz, *Power and Leadership in the First-Line Supervisor* (Ann Arbor, Mich.: Institute for Social Research, University of Michigan, 1951).

[3] T. Mills, "Power Relations in Three-Person Groups," *American Sociological Review*, XVIII (August, 1953), 351–356.

[4] H. H. Kelley, "Communication in Experimentally Created Hierarchies," *Human Relations*, IV (No. 1, 1951), 39–56.

behavior developed as a result of interaction as to the presence of power itself.[5] For this reason, a second aspect of the present study is a comparison of the decision-making behavior of permanent groups with that of similarly constituted temporary groups.

It was expected that, as a result of their prior interactions, the permanent groups would differ from the temporary groups in that they would have more strongly established patterns of interaction in line with the power structure, stronger tendencies to self-preservation, and less ability to change their behavior to meet the requirements of tasks different from their usual task. However, it was expected that even in the temporary groups behavior would still be conditioned by the expectations associated with each "office" or "position," because the members would still differ in the same way in regard to "actual power." It was hypothesized that the differences in power associated with official positions would detract from the quality of decisions in both permanent and temporary groups. It was also hypothesized, however, that the consequences of power differences would be lessened in the temporary groups, and that these groups would make better decisions in situations where consideration of the judgments of all members would be likely to contribute to the quality of the decision. Finally, it was hypothesized that in a situation threatening the survival of the group, the permanent groups would more frequently make decisions strengthening the group's cohesiveness and preserving its integrity.

SUBJECTS

It was found that B-26 combat crews were particularly well suited to the purposes of the study. A B-26 crew is composed of three men: a pilot, a navigator, and a gunner. The pilot as the aircraft commander has final authority to make crew decisions regardless of difference in rank. The navigator is a commissioned officer and may even outrank the pilot; he makes many decisions and as a commissioned officer may exercise certain power over the gunner, an enlisted man. However, he may be overruled by the pilot and in many ways occupies a status inferior to that of the pilot. The gunner, of course, as an enlisted man, is definitely the "low man on the totem pole" and has relatively little power over the two officers.

The permanent crews studied herein had been together for several months and had reached the final stage of their crew training prior to entering combat. The temporary groups were drawn from the same type of personnel. They were, however, regrouped so that no man was in a group with a member of his regular crew. For each set of three crews, the following pattern was followed in the regrouping.

Crew A: Pilot 1, Navigator 2, Gunner 3;
Crew B: Pilot 2, Navigator 3, Gunner 1;
Crew C: Pilot 3, Navigator 1, Gunner 2.

EXPERIMENTAL DESIGN

Each of the 62 permanent and 32 temporary crews was given four decision-

---

[5] C. Heinicke and R. F. Bales, "Developmental Trends in the Structure of Small Groups," *Sociometry*, XVI (February, 1953), 7–38; D. Cartwright and A. Zander, *Group Dynamics Research and Theory* (Evanston, Ill.: Row, Peterson, 1953).

making problems varying in nature and difficulty. Both individual and group decisions were required. The procedures used in reaching the decisions were observed and recorded, using Bales's categories.[6]

The first problem was the Maier Horse-Trading Problem:[7] "A man bought a horse for $60 and sold it for $70. Then he bought it back for $80 and sold it for $90. How much money does he make in the horse-trading business?"

Each individual was first asked to write his solution on a slip of paper without conferring with anyone. Crew members were then asked to confer to reach a mutually agreeable crew decision.

The second problem required the subjects to estimate the number of dots on a 16" × 21" card with 3,155 black dots scattered evenly but not geometrically over a white background. The card was exposed for 15 seconds, and each subject wrote his individual estimate on a slip of paper. They were then asked to come to a group decision concerning the best estimate. Finally, each man was again asked to write on a slip of paper the number of dots he personally *really* thought there were.

The picture of the conference group in the Michigan Group Projection Sketches[8]

was used in the third problem. The subjects were instructed to write a five-minute story about the picture. They were asked to write what they thought was going on in the picture, what had been going on, and what the outcome would be. After the individual stores had been collected, the subjects were asked agree upon and write, within a ten-minute limit, a crew story about the same sketch.

The fourth problem was a simulated survival situation in which the crew was to assume that it had been downed in enemy territory. After two days, one of the crew is slowing down the attempt to reach safe territory, estimated to be about 40 miles away. He has developed severe blisters on his feet and feels that he is nearing exhaustion. He does not believe that he can continue and urges the other two men to go ahead without him. The crew was instructed to designate one member to act as the man giving up, and to make its decision as it would in an actual situation.

After the four decision-making problems, a very brief questionnaire regarding the subjects' reactions to the fourth decision-making situation was administered, along with a question concerning their feelings about being transferred to another crew.

---

[6] R. F. Bales and F. L. Strodtbeck, "Phases in Group Problem-Solving," *Journal of Abnormal and Social Psychology*, XLVI (October, 1951), 485–495.

[7] N. R. F. Maier and A. R. Solem, "The Contribution of a Discussion Leader to the Quality of Group Thinking: the Effective Use of Minority Opinions," *Human Relations*, V (No. 3, 1952), 277–288.

[8] W. E. Henry, "Group Projection Sketches for the Study of Small Groups," *Journal of Social Psychology*, XXXVIII (February, 1951), 77–102.

ANALYSIS OF RESULTS

1. The Horse-Trading Problem

Three different answers are most often given on the Horse-Trading Problem: $0, $10, and $20. If any member of the group has the correct answer, the solution is usually so simple and obvious that his answer is readily accepted, if it is really considered by the group. This makes it

Table 1

PERCENTAGES OF FAILURES TO INFLUENCE TO ACCEPT CORRECT ANSWER
ON HORSE-TRADING PROBLEM IN PERMANENT VS. TEMPORARY CREWS

	Permanent Crews (N = 62)	Temporary Crews (N = 32)
Pilots	6%	0%
Navigators	20%	10.5%
Gunners	37%	12.5%

very easy to determine influence and failure to influence. For example, in one crew, the pilot's answer was $0, the navigator's was $20, and the gunner's was $10. The crew correctly decided upon $20. It may thus be assumed that the navigator influenced the decision. If the crew had decided upon $10, it might have been assumed that the gunner influenced the crew to accept an incorrect answer while the navigator failed to influence the crew to accept a correct answer. If two members had the same answer as the crew answer, both were credited. If all three had the same answer, no one was credited.

In the permanent crews, 31 per cent of the pilots, 50 per cent of the navigators, and 29 per cent of the gunners had the correct answer. Among these, as shown in Table 1, the pilots were most successful and the gunners least successful in influencing the crew to accept their correct solutions. Only 6 per cent of the pilots, as compared with 20 per cent of the navigators and 37 per cent of the gunners, failed to influence the crew to accept their solutions when they had the correct answer (differences all significant at the 5 per cent level of confidence).

When temporary crews are compared with permanent crews, it is found that the temporary crews had a higher percentage of correct answers than did the permanent crews (78.2 per cent against 60.4 per cent with the difference singificant at the 10 per cent level of confidence). Some understanding of the dynamics emerges when failure to influence is analyzed by crew position as shown in Table 1. In the temporary crews, the effects of status differences seem to have been diminished and all members whatever their position failed less frequently to influence when they had the correct answer (significant at better than the 10 per cent level of confidence for all positions).

These findings support the contention of Heinicke and Bales[9] that in groups with a history of interaction, the opinions and suggestions of high status members tend to be accepted and these individuals do not have to do much to win their points, while suggestions of members of less importance are often passed over. In short, both the exercise and acceptance of power is stabilized in the permanent groups.

2. The Dot Test

To permit a more adequate discussion of results, treatment of the Dot Test data will be omitted. The chief contribution

---

[9] C. Heinicke and R. F. Bales, *op. cit.*

of these data is the revelation of a consistent tendency for individuals of higher status to accept the group's decision more fully than did those of lower status. Members of the temporary groups also tended to accept the group's decision more fully than did the members of the permanent groups.

3. The Conference Story

Since individuals wrote their stories about the conference-group sketch before the crew story was prepared, it is possible to develop an influence index for each person. In each case, the five most salient aspects of each group story were identified; then the individual stories were checked for the presence of these same five features. If all five indicators were common to the crew and individual stories, a score

of "5" was assigned; if four were common, a score of "4" was given; et cetera. If four or five were common, it was considered that the individual had exerted a strong influence on the crew's decision. If three elements were common, the individual was considered to have exerted "some influence." Less than three common aspects was considered as evidence of little or no influence.

The results, shown in Table 2, indicate that the members of permanent crews influenced the crew's decision according to the power structure (differences significant at better than the 5 per cent level of confidence).

Permanent and temporary crews also were compared on the basis of the percentages of those who exerted little or no influence, or failed to influence. The results, presented in Table 3, indicate the

Table 2

CONSEQUENCES OF POWER DIFFERENCES IN PERMANENT GROUPS IN
INFLUENCING DECISION CONCERNING STORY ABOUT CONFERENCE GROUP

	Percentages		
Degree of influence	Pilot	Navigators	Gunners
Strong influence	59.6	38.5	0
Some influence	23.4	26.9	23.2
Little or no influence	17.0	34.6	76.8
Total	100.0	100.0	100.0

Table 3

COMPARISON OF FAILURE TO INFLUENCE CONFERENCE-GROUP STORY DECISION
IN PERMANENT VS. TEMPORARY CREWS

	Permanent Crews (N = 62)	Temporary Crews (N = 32)
Pilots	17.0%	9.4%
Navigators	34.6%	25.0%
Gunners	76.8%	53.1%

same trend in temporary as in permanent crews. A striking fact is that there is again a consistent tendency for fewer in all positions to fail to influence the decision (difference for gunners significant at the 5 per cent level of confidence).

Differences in perceptions of group functioning as measured by content analyses of the stories are too complex to be discussed in this paper, but one aspect of this analysis supports the hypothesis that the low status member of the group does not feel free to disagree and therefore withholds his ideas. In the permanent crews only 46 per cent of the gunners, as compared with 70 per cent of the navigators and 72 per cent of the pilots, perceived disagreement in the conference group (difference significant at the 5 per cent level of confidence). Contrariwise, in the temporary groups, the gunners perceived as much disagreement as did the other members of the crew.

4. The Survival Problem

In the survival problem, influence was studied through participation analysis and the questionnaire administered after the crew decision. Both amount and type of participation were considered. Amount of participation was computed by counting the interactions credited to each individual. The navigators contributed 40.7 per cent of the total participations, in contrast to 34.1 and 25.2 per cent for pilots and gunners, respectively (differences significant at the 1 per cent level of confidence). On account of operational difficulties, comparable data for temporary groups are not available.

The interaction process is most clearly represented by the percentage in each position who acted one or more times in each category of the Bales system. The results indicate that certain types of interaction tend to characterize the occupants of each position. The pilots show more solidarity; give more suggestions, opinions, evaluations, and information; do more asking for suggestions and less withdrawing from the field (differences all significant at about the 10 per cent level of confidence or better). The navigators do more disagreeing (significant at the 5 per cent level of confidence). The gunners manifest less show of solidarity; offer fewer suggestions and opinions; give less orientation and information; do less asking for suggestions; and show more tension and withdrawal from the field (differences significant at about the 10 per cent level of confidence or better).

It would appear that these behaviors may be regarded as typical of the three different status levels. The pilot as the "official leader" is the one who feels most responsible for maintaining the solidarity of the group and least able to afford to withdraw from the field. He must move the group forward by asking for and giving suggestions. The navigator evidently has enough power and feels secure enough to disagree and to try to influence the group's decision, even though he may not have enough power to get his suggestions accepted. The gunner, on the other hand, feels responsible for neither the solidarity of the group nor the solution of the group's problem. His appears to be a somewhat dependent role, in keeping with the expectation common to many formal groups that individuals in the lower ranks are not supposed to contribute to the planning and decision-making activities of the organization.

Responses to the decision-making ques-

Table 4

CONSEQUENCES OF POWER DIFFERENCES IN PERMANENT GROUPS ON DECISION-MAKING BEHAVIOR, ACCORDING TO INDIVIDUAL DECLARATIONS

Attitude and behavior	Percentages		
	Pilots	Navigators	Gunners
Made little effort to influence decision	43.8	28.1	55.3
Had most influence on decision	41.7	8.8	0.0
Complete agreement with decision	77.1	59.6	52.6
Complete satisfaction with decision	89.6	86.0	84.2

tionnaire are summarized in Table 4. According to their own reports, the pilots and gunners made less effort to influence the crew's decision than the navigators (significant at the 1 per cent level of confidence). Very few, however, felt that they had influenced the decision greatly (difference in percentages between pilots and navigators significant at the 1 per cent level of confidence). None of the gunners felt that they had greatly influenced the decision. Probably as a result, fewer of the gunners and navigators completely agreed with the decision (difference significant at the 1 per cent level of confidence).

To obtain information concerning the effects of status position regarding attraction to the group, the subjects were also asked how they felt about being transferred to another crew. Of the navigators. 28.1 per cent, as compared with 8.3 per cent of the pilots and 10.5 per cent of the gunners, stated that it would not matter greatly if they were transferred (difference between navigators and pilots and gunners combined significant at the 1 per cent level of confidence). This is an indication of the navigator's relatively weak attraction to the crew and suggests that his needs are being less well satisfied in

the group. The gunners, on the other hand, seem to be better satisfied with their membership in the crew, even though they make little effort to influence crew decisions and have little influence. It might be inferred that they have accepted their low status more completely than the navigators have.

Temporary and permanent groups can be compared in regard to the characteristics of the decisions submitted. The results of categorization of the decisions indicate that the temporary groups more frequently made sequential decisions which might require testing and revision. The meaning of this becomes clearer when it is noted that more of the permanent crews decided to keep the ailing member with them in spite of all circumstances. They simply did not entertain the notion that this might not be possible. Their decisions were, therefore, presented as final and not needing future revision to keep them in harmony with the reality of events. Of the permanent crews, 93.7 per cent manifested much concern for keeping the crew together, whereas only 71.8 per cent of the temporary crews showed such a concern. The permanent crews also tended to mention provision for first aid and attempts to bolster the ailing member's morale. This finding might be accepted in support of Cartwright and Zander's[10] hypothesis that willingness to endure pain or frustration for the group may be a possible indication of the group's cohesiveness. It is also likely that more pressure is felt to appear cohesive when one is in the company of one's own crew. These data do not answer questions concerning the quality of the decisions. The willingness to endure pain or frustration for the group may in some instances be taken too far and result in blindness to the realities of the situation.

DISCUSSION

It must be recognized that crew position is the only status variable with which this study has dealt. Crew position, however, appears to be the most potent of these variables and in the crews studied is fairly congruent with other status variables such as age and military rank. In the fairly rare cases in which close status congruency did not exist, observers noted the obvious effects of other status variables. In one crew, the navigator and pilot were of the same military rank, but the navigator was 10 years older than the pilot. In a second crew, the navigator was a major and the pilot was a first lieutenant. In a third, the navigator held a doctoral degree and had been a member of the faculty of a major university, while the pilot had completed only one year of college. In all three cases, it was quite obvious that the navigator was the most influential member of the group in the test situations.

It should also be explained that the finding that temporary crews make better decisions than permanent crews in certain situations does not constitute an argument against the value of crew integrity. Rather, it should constitute an argument for training crews to change their behavior to meet the requirements of different situations. The pilot may be an excellent leader for the group while the plane is in the air, but this does not mean that he will be the most adequate leader if the plane crashes and the crew is faced with the problem of surviving. The pilot may be the most authoritative on air operations, but another member may be more authoritative in regard to living off the land and finding the way to safety. It also illustrates the need for training crews to consider the opinions and judgments of all its members in situations in which there are no real authorities in the crew.

The finding that permanent groups more frequently than temporary groups express willingness to make sacrifices in order to keep the crew intact has interesting implications. In most cases, this tendency is likely to have survival value, as has repeatedly been shown in the analysis of group survival experiences.[11] The fact, however, that this tendency seems to block the making of sequential decisions might have negative survival value in certain extreme conditions in which the preservation of crew integrity would endanger the chances of survival of the whole crew.

An important problem in regard to the

10 D. Cartwright and A. Zander, *op. cit.*

11 E. P. Torrance, "The Behavior of Small Groups under the Stress Conditions of Survival," *American Sociological Review* (to be published).

position of the navigator is revealed by the fact that he tries hard to influence the group's decisions without too much success, together with the fact that he feels less strongly attracted to the group. The findings of this study are consistent with those reported by Festinger, *et al.*[12]—that a member is likely not to be attracted to a group in which he feels that others will probably disagree with his opinions.

---

[12] L. Festinger, *et al.*, "The Influence Process in the Presence of Extreme Deviates," *Human Relations*, V (No. 4, 1952), 327–346.

Finally, a possible implication for small-group research should be pointed out. Although a similar pattern of influence is found in temporary and permanent groups, the degree of status influence differs. It must be remembered that this occurred in spite of the fact that the rearranged crews were still composed of a pilot, a navigator, and a gunner who still possessed different degrees of power. This would suggest the need for conducting studies in permanent groups with various types of power structure as a supplement to studies of temporary groups with artificially created hierarchies.

SOCIAL STATUS
IN JURY DELIBERATIONS*

*Fred L. Strodtbeck, Rita M. James,
and Charles Hawkins*

Occupational specialization has two distinguishable effects. First, it increases productivity and, second, it provides the basis for a status hierarchy. It is less commonplace to think of role differentiation in face to face groups as arising from a similar economic process and resulting in

---

* Fred L. Strodtbeck, Rita M. James, and Charles Hawkins, "Social Status in Jury Deliberations," *American Sociological Review*, 22 (December 1957), 713–19. Reprinted by permission.

similar status differences. For groups to define and achieve their goals, they must control the use of their primary group resource, their common time together. Only one, or, at most, a few persons can talk at any given instant and be understood. Who talks and how much he talks is, within limits, determined by the reactions of the remainder of the group to the speaker. Acts that are perceived as relevant to the solution of the group's problems are generally favorably received and the responsible speaker is encouraged to continue. Over the long run participation tends to become differentiated with a small fraction of the group's members accounting for most of the participation.

For the purposes of the present study into the relationships between occupation and selected aspects of role differentiation, it is desirable that the focus of the small group discussion not be that narrowly circumscribed by status prerogatives. For example, a group of officers and enlisted men discussing military problems or a group of doctors and nurses discussing a medical problem would not provide the circumstance we require. A greater presumption of equality is desired.

In the jury situation there is not only the wide-spread norm that group members should act toward one another as equals but also the reinforcement of the presumption of equality by the requirement that the verdict be unanimous. Equal and responsible participation in the deliberation is an institutionalized expectation. Therefore, if there is evidence that the status differences of the larger community become manifest in the deliberation, then it may be expected that a similar generalization of status will be found in other interactional contexts where hierarchical considerations are more prominent.

It is essential for our study that wide background differences be present within the juror population. This is assured by the fact that in metropolitan areas such as Chicago, St. Louis, and Minneapolis where our experimental jury research has been conducted, jurors are selected by a random process from voting registration lists. The resultant jury pool population compares closely with the expected population computed from census reports, al-

though there are several known sources of bias. Lawyers, doctors, teachers, policemen, and other local and federal employees, including elected officials, are excused from jury service. Aliens, foreign visitors, recent migrants and persons under 18, who are not eligible to vote, do not appear on the jury lists. Finally, men who operate "one man" businesses and prospective jurors with pressing personal problems can ordinarily have their jury service deferred or cancelled. The net effect is that the professions and the very low education and occupation groups are slightly under-represented.

Occupations are classified in four groups: proprietors, clerical, skilled, and labor. "Proprietor" includes the census category[1] of Proprietors, Managers, and Officials as well as professionals such as architects, accountants, and engineers who are not excluded from service. "Clerical" and "skilled" categories correspond to the census categories and "labor" subsumes the census categories semi-skilled workers, non-farm laborers and servant classes. Farm owners and laborers are absent from our populations, and retired persons have been classified by their occupations prior to retirement. Women are classified by their stated occupations, except that housewives are classified by their husbands' occupations.

Previous studies indicate that power and participation in face to face situations are related to status. Caudill[2] observed the

---

[1] Alba M. Edwards, *Bureau of the Census Alphabetical Index of Occupations by Industries and Social-Economic Groups*, Washington, D.C.: U.S. Department of Commerce, 1937.

[2] William Caudill, *The Psychiatric Hospital*

daily exchange of information at administrative conferences among the staff of a small psychiatric hospital and found that the relative participation by the director of the service, the residents, the head nurse, the nurses, and the occupational therapist were ordered by their statuses in the hospital even though the lower status persons ordinarily spent more time with the patients. Torrance[3] used nonmilitary problems but found that pilots, navigators, and gunners recognized a power hierarchy in the contrived situation which paralleled that ordinarily in effect in airship operation. Strodtbeck[4] demonstrated that the greater economic and religious power of Navaho in contrast with Mormon women was reflected in their greater power in husband-wife decision-making. More pertinent, perhaps, is a study[5] relating to the continuation in jury deliberations of a strong emphasis by women on expressive and integrative acts. The components that had been found descriptive of women's role in family interaction situations were found to characterize women's roles in jury deliberations.

It is important to stress that while the related studies are consistent insofar as they suggest a parallel between generalized

status and status in face to face systems, they do not provide a firm basis for generalizing to the situation at hand, at least in terms of the measure of correspondence. In Torrance's experiment the pilots probably dominated to a lesser degree in the experimental situation than they would have when the airship was in operation. Thus, while the ordering was preserved, it was undoubtedly attenuated. In the present case, what differences are to be expected? Relations between roles like pilot-gunner and clerical worker-laborer are not equally clear in the interaction differences they imply. There is no compelling reason to believe that clerical workers and laborers will have had sufficient experience together to evolve a stable pecking order. Further, once jurors have completed their deliberations, there is no expectation of continued relations that would provide opportunity for external status differences to become manifest. If status differences are present in the jury room, it is almost certain that they arise in part because the varied requirements of the deliberation re-create within the jury the need for the differential experiences associated with status. Whether or not the determinants from the external system are great enough to become apparent in a one to two hour deliberation is the empirical question we seek to answer.

---

as a Small Society, Cambridge: Harvard University Press, 1957.

[3] E. P. Torrance, "Some Consequences of Power Differences on Decision Making in Permanent and Temporary Three-Man Groups," Research Studies, Pullman: State College of Washington, 1954, 22, pp. 130–140.

[4] F. L. Strodtbeck, "Husband-Wife Interaction Over Revealed Differences," American Sociological Review, 16 (August, 1951), pp. 141–145.

[5] F. L. Strodtbeck and R. D. Mann, "Sex Role Differentiation in Jury Deliberations," Sociometry, 19 (March, 1956), pp. 3–11.

Source of Data

Mock jury deliberations were conducted in which the participants were jurors drawn by lot from the regular jury pools of the Chicago and St. Louis courts. The jurors listened to a recorded trial, deliberated, and returned their verdict—all under the customary discipline of bailiffs of the court. The jury deliberations were recorded, fully transcribed, and scored in terms of interaction process categories.

This paper is based primarily upon 49 deliberations for which interaction process analysis has been carried out. Although further work is in process on more than 100 additional deliberations which have been collected by the project during the past three years, the present report is final in that further interaction process analysis of the type here reported is not contemplated. Two civil trials were used as the basis for the deliberations. In the first (29 deliberations), the plaintiff, a secretary, seeks compensation for injuries incurred in a two-car collision, and in the second (20 deliberations), a young child seeks compensation for facial disfigurement incurred in a fire alleged to have been caused by a defective vaporizer. A total of 49 × 12, or 588 different jurors were involved. Data on 14 vaporizer cases and 28 recent experimental trials are utilized in other portions of the paper. In total, data from 91 juries are used in the examination of different status effects.

Table 1

OCCUPATIONAL STATUS OF 49 JURY FOREMEN

Occupation	Expected*	Observed	Index
Proprietor	9.73	18	185
Clerical	15.03	15	100
Skilled	9.56	8	84
Labor	14.68	8	54

* Computed under assumption that foremen will be proportional to portion of sample in the given occupation.

selection of a foreman was quickly and apparently casually accomplished. There was no instance in which mention of any socio-economic criteria was made, but this is not to say that socio-economic criteria were not involved. For example, Table 1 shows that some foremen were selected from all strata, but the incidence was three and a half times as great among proprietors as among laborers. In addition, although the details are not given in the table, tabulation shows that only one-fifth as many women were made foreman as would be expected by chance.

SELECTING A FOREMAN

After the jury listened to the case, they were told to select their foreman and begin their deliberation. In more than half of the deliberations, the foreman was nominated by one member and then quickly accepted by the remainder of the group. In about a third of the deliberations the man who opened the discussion and sought either to nominate another, or to focus the group's attention on their responsibility to select a foreman, was himself selected foreman. However, in all instances the

RELATIVE PARTICIPATION

The deliberations were recorded with two microphones to facilitate binaural identification of individual participants. The protocols were fully transcribed, and from the protocol each speaker's contributions were unitized into discrete acts. These acts are roughly the equivalent of a simple declarative sentence. Identification of the speaker was checked with the original observer's notes and scoring was done by an assistant with the aid of the recording plus indications of nonverbal gestures made by the original observer.

Table 2

PERCENTAGE RATES OF PARTICIPATION IN JURY DELIBERATION BY OCCUPATION AND SEX OF JUROR

Sex	Occupation				
	Proprietor	Clerical	Skilled	Laborer	Combined
Male	12.9	10.8	7.9	7.5	9.6
	(81)	(81)	(80)	(107)	(349)
Female	9.1	7.8	4.8	4.6	6.6
	(31)	(92)	(28)	(62)	(213)
Combined	11.8	9.2	7.1	6.4	8.5
	(112)	(173)	(108)	(169)	(562)*

* Numbers of jurors are shown in parentheses. Twenty-six of 588 jurors from the 49 juries used were not satisfactorily classified by occupation and are omitted.

Since there are 12 persons in the jury, one-twelfth or 8⅓ per cent, of the total acts is the pro rata percentage for each juror's acts. This provides the base-line against which the effects of external status may be appraised. The higher the average participation of an occupational group, the greater their relative share of the common resource of time. It may be seen in Table 2 that in all occupations males talked more than females and the amount of participation was sharply differentiated between higher than expected values for proprietors and clerical workers and lower than expected values for skilled and unskilled laborers.

While the moderately differing values in Table 2 are averages based upon the scores of more than 500 persons, within any particular deliberation, there was a very steep differentiation between the most and least-speaking jurors. For example, in 82 per cent of the juries the top three participators account for one-half or more of the total acts with the remainder distributed among the other nine members. It is to be emphasized that the averages of Table 2 are descriptive of the relative participation of the occupation and sex groups, but do not reflect the wide variation within a jury.

One of the sources of differences in participation within the jury may be attributed to the election of one member to play the role of foreman. The foreman was responsible for approximately one-fourth of the total acts, and as previously shown, was more frequently selected from the higher status groups, but when foreman scores were eliminated the average participation values were as follows: proprietor, 8.9; clerical, 7.0; skilled, 6.3; labor, 5.9. The gap between clerical and skilled workers is narrower but the rank order is unchanged.[6]

The latent premise in the study of participation is that high participation indicates greater ability to influence others

---

[6] A further check was made on the effects of being on a jury with differing numbers of one's own occupation group. For juries in which at least two of each occupational group are present, the values are quite similar to Table 2, and while there is some tendency for higher status persons to talk more when they are alone, or in a marked minority, further corrections have minor effects.

Table 3

AVERAGE VOTES RECEIVED AS HELPFUL JUROR BY OCCUPATION AND SEX

Sex	Occupation				
	Proprietor	Clerical	Skilled	Laborer	Combined
Male	6.8	4.2	3.9	2.7	4.3
	(113)	(108)	(115)	(143)	(479)
Female	3.2	2.7	2.0	1.5	2.3
	(34)	(116)	(36)	(76)	(262)
Combined	6.0	3.4	3.5	2.3	3.6
	(147)	(224)	(151)	(219)	(741)*

* This number includes 14 additional cases for which interaction process scores are not available.

in keeping with the actor's goals. Earlier research supports such an interpretation for *ad hoc* problem-solving groups and for families. Further evidence is available from the present research. Jurors were asked before the deliberation what, if anything, they would award the plaintiff. A detailed examination of pre-deliberation awards of the individual juror with the subsequent group awards in 29 deliberations reveals that the more active jurors shifted their pre-deliberation positions less than less active jurors, in the process of agreeing with the group verdict.[7] This interpretation of the relation between participation and influence or status level may be documented by comparing the average predeliberation award by occupational group with the jury verdict. The correlations are as follows: proprietor .50, (P < .05); clerical .11; skilled .29; labor .02. Members from the same occupational group sometimes initially favored different verdicts, and in this case not all the members of this group achieved their desired outcome. Nonetheless, the proprietors showed a significant correlation between

their average and the jury verdicts. This result, which separates proprietors from other occupations, corresponds to the participation values after they have been corrected by eliminating the foreman. Since our content analyses clearly show that foremen were more neutral in the discussion of how much money to award the plaintiff than other high participating jurors, the corrected participation values are probably a more satisfactory measure of influence in the damage award discussion.

The meaning of levels of participation may be viewed from still another perspective. After the deliberation, the jurors were asked to answer a battery of questions reporting their personal satisfaction with the quality of the deliberation and the tone of interpersonal relations. The level of an individual's satisfaction was positively correlated with the level of his own participation (r = .52, P < .05). The involvement that high participation represents in the jury is not unlike the investment in the affairs of the larger community by higher status persons; both are instruments for group-derived satisfactions.

As a further commentary upon the interpretation of participation levels, responses to the post-deliberation question,

---

[7] Allen Barton, "Persuasion and Compromise in Damage Awards," December, 1956. Unpublished ms.

"Who do you believe contributed most to helping your group reach its decision?" were tabulated by occupation of the target person. The average number of helpfulness votes received by occupation groups (see Table 3) closely parallels the participation by occupation groups (see Table 2). The correlation between votes received and participation is about .69 when sets of individual values are correlated. Male clerical workers get slightly fewer votes than their participation would appear to warrant and male skilled workers get slightly more, but the overwhelming impression is that votes received as a helpful juror, like participation, influence, and satisfaction parallels status differentiation in the larger society.

PERCEIVED FITNESS AS JURORS

Where is the quality of justice to be found? The Courts Martial reform, which permitted enlisted men to request other enlisted men for their trial panels, was largely nullified by their preference to leave their cases in the hands of officers. How do jurors react? A departure from

random selection might tend toward over-selection the higher ocupations as it had in the helpfulness nominations, or, as one might predict in terms of class theory, departure from randomness might be in the direction of heightened choice for the chooser's own occupation. How these counter tendencies might be balanced is a question for which we have no theoretical answer and therefore must investigate empirically.

In an effort to probe deeper for evidence of class identifications, the following question was asked of 28 juries.

> The jury pool is made up of people from all walks of life. However, if a member of your family were on trial and you had your choice, which of the following kinds of people would you prefer to make up the majority of the jurors who would hear your case?
>
> (Business and professional people; clerical and white collar workers; skilled workers; unskilled workers.)

The expected values, determined by assuming that each status group is equally likely to be chosen, have been divided into the observed values and the resultant ratio multiplied by 100 to give the index numbers shown in Table 4. All groups, except

Table 4

CHOICE OF JUROR IF MEMBER OF RESPONDENT'S FAMILY WERE ON TRIAL, BASED UPON OCCUPATION STEREOTYPES (PRO RATA EXPECTED IS 100)*

Respondent's Occupation	Preferred Occupation			
	Proprietor	Clerical	Skilled	Laborer
Proprietor (63)	241	95	51	13
Clerical (107)	206	112	71	11
Skilled (72)	172	55	139	33
Laborer (76)	126	42	147	84

* These data were collected from jurors in our 28 most recent experimental juries. See fn. 8.

Table 5

CHOICE OF JUROR IF RESPONDENT WERE ON TRIAL, BASED UPON
DELIBERATION EXPERIENCE (PRO RATA EXPECTED IS 100)*

Respondent's Occupation	Preferred Occupation			
	Proprietor	Clerical	Skilled	Laborer
Proprietor (78)	169	110	119	39
Clerical (129)	145	100	101	75
Skilled (74)	147	104	84	73
Laborer (120)	162	100	112	74

* The expected values used to form the index numbers have been determined by assuming that each person distributes his four choices under conditions that give an equal chance of each of the 11 fellow juror's being chosen. For example, for 2 proprietors, 4 clerical, 2 skilled, and 4 labor, the expected distribution of the 8 proprietor votes would be 2/11(B), 3/11(B), 4/11(B) and 8/11(B). It is assumed that no fellow juror can be chosen twice by the same subject. The expected and observed choices for individuals on one jury are combined by status groups and accumulated for the 20 vaporizer cases were asked this form of the question, so the 411 responses come from a potential population of (29×12)+(20×6), or 468.

laborers, would prefer to have a member of their family tried before a jury, the majority of whose members were proprietors. Like other groups, laborers were also upwardly oriented in their preference rank but their first choice was skilled workers, then proprietors. Clerical and skilled workers chose persons from their own occupation group as their second choice. All groups except laborers ranked laborers last. Laborers placed themselves third and clerical persons last. It is to be stressed that Table 4 represents the choice of jurors in terms of occupational stereotypes. It is what a member of one occupational group perceives in terms of his generalized conception of his own and other occupational groups.

We also asked jurors to choose "four of your fellow jurors whom you would best like to have serve on a jury if you were on trial." This latter question asks jurors not for generalized conceptions of other occupational groups but for evaluations of particular persons. We wished to know if the selections when jurors chose on the basis of face to face contact were similar or different from stereotype choices.[8] If a prototype of a social system had grown during deliberation, jurors might come to regard one another more in terms of performance in the task at hand than in terms of general social status. It was also possible for the deliberation to reveal status-based ideologies that would open latent schisms. The data suggest that differences were ordinarily not magnified by the deliberation and the jurors came to be convinced that a just job had been done. The special thrust of the question "If a member of your family were on trial" could have sensitized jurors to think in terms of personal interests rather than abstract

---

[8] The stereotype juror preference question was not asked the juries in Table 5. The 28 juries of Table 4 are a wholly different set, so that the possible bias of face to face choices by the prior administration of the stereotype choices is avoided.

principles such as competence or justice. Heightened sensitivity of personal interests could have caused respondents to turn away from those who had been the arbiters of consensus in their deliberation.

Table 5 shows a preference for proprietors but at a somewhat lower level. More detailed effects of the face to face experience in contrast with the response to occupational categories may best be illustrated by subtracting Table 4 from Table 5. It is to be noted that while Tables 4 and 5 are based on different populations, the respondents in both cases are random samples from the population available in successive weeks in the jury pool.

When Table 4 is subtracted from Table 5 (see Table 6) a positive value in the matrix represents an increase in index value associated with the face to face experience. The boldface diagonal shows that "down group" choices were lower at each occupation level, particularly among proprietors and skilled laborers. That is, choices after the deliberation experience are not determined by a narrow "interest group." In addition, all values above the main diagonal are positive. That is, face to face experience caused lower status persons to be evaluated more highly. As shown below the main diagonal, proprietors were reduced in the evaluation of clerical and skilled workers and increased in the evaluation of laborers; clerical persons were rated more highly by both skilled workers and laborers; and laborers decreased their former preference for skilled workers. The lower range of index values in the face to face situation arises in part from the effects of forcing the distribution of 4 votes among the 11 jurors who were members of the respondent's particular jury. Notwithstanding this flattening ef-

fect, it still appears that the face to face experience (1) results in fewer proprietor and skilled worker "own group" choices; and (2) brings the choice gradients into smoother conformity with the observed contribution of each status group to the deliberation.

DISCUSSION

July deliberations have been used to examine the intersection of occupational status and sex with the typically small group measures of participation, influence, satisfaction, and perceived competence. The null assumption that there is no relation between these modes of classification can be safely rejected. Men, in contrast with women, and persons of higher in contrast with lower status occupations have higher participation, influence, satisfaction and perceived competence for the jury task.

The present study does little to explain the cause of this differentiation. Insofar as selection of the foreman may be taken as a guide to more general expectations concerning desirable attributes for the jury

Table 6

CHANGE IN INDEX VALUE ASSOCIATED WITH DELIBERATION EXPERIENCE (VALUE OF TABLE 4 SUBTRACTED FROM TABLE 5)

| Respondent's Occupation | Preferred Occupation | | | |
	Pro-prietor	Cleri-cal	Skilled	Laborer
Proprietor	−72	15	55	26
Clerical	−61	−12	30	64
Skilled	−35	49	−55	40
Laborer	36	58	−35	−10

task, it appears that the foreman is expected to be a male, preferably, a male of higher occupational status. Although we know of no empirical studies, we assume that the business discipline and related experiences of higher status occupations involve both substantive knowledge, and interactional skills that may be used during the deliberation. Hence, in the competition for the available deliberation time, higher status males may rise to prominence because their comments are perceived to have greater value. On the other hand, since the cues of status—dress, speech, and casual references to experiences—are easily read, the differentiation may in part be explained by these expectations instead of actual performance.

Jurors who used more of the group's scarce resource, their common time together, were perceived by respondents to be the jurors desired if they were on trial. This finding suggests that whatever the criteria used by the groups to regulate the contributions of their members, these criteria were broadly held. The differential distribution of speaking time was achieved without serious violation of developing group norms. Further, face to face experience, in contrast with occupational stereotypes, tended to smooth post-meeting choices into a gradient parallel to both activity rates and status. These findings and others reported constitute a preliminary clarification of the small group process within the deliberation.

While our data do little to illuminate *how* differentiation arises, the status gradients emerge clearly in as brief a time as the one or two hour discussions under study. Though careful study will be required to determine the degree to which one may generalize from status in the larger social system to a particular interaction context, the demonstration of the continuity of status in the present case should be noted in any theory directed to the description of the process of status affirmation and maintenance.

STATUS CHARACTERISTICS AND
SOCIAL INTERACTION*

Joseph Berger, Bernard P. Cohen, and Morris Zelditch, Jr.

ABSTRACT

This paper deals with the small groups literature on status organizing processes in decision-making groups that are initially differentiated by one or more external status characteristics. The main result in this literature is that when members of task-oriented groups differ with respect to some status characteristic, such as age, sex, race, occupation, or education, such characteristics determine the distribution of participation, influence, and prestige among members. This effect is independent of the existence of any prior, culturally-established belief in the relevance of the status characteristic to the task. To explain this result, we assume that status characteristics determine evaluations of and performance-expectations for individuals in the group and that such evaluations and expectations in turn determine the distribution of participation, influence, and prestige. In this paper we stipulate conditions sufficient to produce such an effect. Further, to explain the fact that the effect is independent of prior cultural belief in the relevance of the status characteristics, we assume that status characteristic becomes relevant in any situation except one in which it is culturally known *not* to be relevant, new expectations forming that are consistent with evaluations and expectations previously associated with the status characteristic. Direct experimental tests provide support for each of the assumptions in this explanation independently of the others. Subsequent work, therefore, has been devoted to refining and extending the theory. The most important result of this subsequent work is that, given two equally relevant status characteristics, individuals combine all inconsistent status information rather than reducing its inconsistenty. If this result survives further experimental tests, it provides a straightforward basis for extending the theory to multicharacteristic status situations.

* Research for this paper was supported by grants from the National Science Foundation (GS 1170), the Advanced Research Projects Agency, Department of Defense (DAHC15 68 C 0215), and a special research fellowship to Joseph Berger by the National Institutes of Health. We would particularly like to acknowledge the advice and assistance at various stages in this research by Bo Anderson, Tom Conner, Paul Crosbie, Hamit Fisek, Lee Freese, Joan Kiker Kruse, Ron Kruse, Bill McKeown, Jim Moore, and Marjorie Seashore.

STATUS CHARACTERISTICS AND SOCIAL INTERACTION

1. Background and Statement of the Problem

The purpose of the present paper is to study the ways in which status characteristics organize social interaction. The problem with which we are concerned is one of the older problems in sociology. By 1908 Simmel was already saying that, "The first condition of having to deal with somebody at all is to know with *whom* one has to deal" (Simmel, 1908; quoted from Wolff, 1950, 307, italics in the original). While one might know with whom one had to deal from direct knowledge of the particular individual, Simmel observed that one might also know with whom one had to deal from a knowledge of his status category (Simmel, 1908; in Wolff, 1959, 344–5). Twenty years after Simmel's *Soziologie*, Park already took for granted a conception of interaction in which an individual, on encountering another, classified the other in terms of status categories such as age, sex, and race, attributed to the other characteristics associated with his social type, and organized his conduct towards the other on the basis of such stereotyped assumptions (Park, 1928).

A considerable number of investigations in what is conventionally regarded as the "small groups" literature deal with this problem: That is, there are a considerable number of investigations in which some interaction measure, such as participation or influence, is observed in groups the members of which differ in age, sex, race, occupation, or some similar status category. For example, Caudill finds that

positions in the occupational hierarchy of a psychiatric hospital determine participation rates in ward rounds. The ward administrator participates more than the chief resident, the chief resident more than other residents, the most passive resident more than the most aggressive nurse (Caudill, 1958, ch. 10). Or Torrance finds that positions in a B-26 air crew determine influence over decisions made by the group. Pilots are more able to influence decisions than navigators, navigators more than gunners; and this is true even when the pilot's opinion is by objective standards incorrect; true also, even when the task of the group has nothing much to do with the activities of B-26 air crews (Torrance, 1954). In juries, it is found that sex and occupation determine participation, election to foremanship, and evaluation of competence as juror (Strodtbeck, James and Hawkins, 1958; Strodtbeck and Mann, 1956). In biracial work groups it is found that whites initiate more interactions than blacks, they talk more to other whites than to blacks, and even blacks talk more to whites than to other blacks (Katz, Goldston, and Benjamin, 1958; Katz and Benjamin, 1960). Similar findings are reported in over a dozen investigations between 1950 and 1965 alone. (In particular see, in addition to the above references, Croog, 1956; Heiss, 1962; Hoffman, Festinger, and Lawrence, 1954; Hurwitz, Zander and Hymovich, 1960; Leik, 1963; Mishler and Tropp, 1956; Zander and Cohen, 1955, and Ziller and Exline, 1958.)

Our objectives are *first*, to examine what all this research adds up to; that is, to formulate a more general description of the phenomenon as it is regularly found in a variety of concretely different settings and circumstances. *Second*, to explain the results of this research; that is, to show them as consequences of some more general theory. For this purpose, part of the present paper is devoted to the construction of the required theory. *Third*, given this theoretical formulation, to review research designed to test, refine, and extend it.

2. Abstract Empirical Generalization of the Results of Research on the Effect of Status Characteristics on Interaction in Decision-Making Groups.

While our problem is old, and the relevant research extensive, it is difficult to say what it all adds up to. The difficulty lies in two directions: First, there is no very precise conceptualization of the relevant variables. All the investigations that concern us involve status differences, but none of them provide any very precise notion of what a status difference is. They all involve some form of participation, prestige, or influence, but none of them provide any very precise notion of how these things are related to each other. Second, the concrete differences in these studies are very great, so that it is difficult to decide just what systematic import they have. The status differences with which they deal involve in some cases formal positions in a hierarchy (chief of a service, resident, nurse; pilot, navigator, gunner); in some cases personal reputations (prestige as experts on mental hygiene); in some cases status in the community or society (occupation, age, sex, race). The dependent variable is sometimes participation rates, sometimes influence over decisions, sometimes perceptions of abilities, sometimes evaluations of

performance. The greatest differences of all are in the task and interaction conditions investigated: From the estimation of the number of dots on a card to discussion of damage awards in a jury trial; from conferences among professionals to coalition games; from familiar tasks, intimately related to the purposes of the group (mental hygiene specialists holding a mental hygiene conference) to tasks utterly foreign to their purposes (air crews constructing a story from a projective stimulus).

Nevertheless, these investigations have a number of common elements. First, they all deal with *some* form of status difference. Furthermore, all the status categories employed in these investigations, however different in concrete detail, have at least two properties in common: (1) Differences in status always appear to imply differential evaluations of individuals. (2) Differences in status always provide the basis for inferring differences in one or more other capacities or characteristics possessed by the individual. The assumptions made about the individual on the basis of his status category appear to be of two kinds: Specific expectations are formed about the specific abilities relevant in the situation of interaction itself; often, also, more general expectations are apparently formed about capacities of the sort that might extend over many distinct kinds of situations. For example, assumptions might be made, on the one hand, about the ability to solve a mathematical puzzle; on the other hand, about intelligence. (To fix terminology, a characteristic that is differentially evaluated and implies possession of other characteristics is a *status characteristic*; a status characteristic from which one infers very general assumptions about individuals is a *diffuse* status characteristic.)

Second, almost all of the aspects of interaction important in these studies can be conceptualized in terms of four kinds of observable behavior: (1) Individuals either give or do not give *action opportunities* to others; that is, they either do or do not distribute chances to perform, as when one individual asks another for his opinion. (2) Given an action opportunity, individuals either do or do not contribute a *performance output* to the interaction of the group. (3) Given a performance output, others evaluate it positively or negatively; given that they evaluate it positively or negatively, they either communicate a *reward action* to another or they do not. Finally, (4) as a consequence of exchanging views with respect to the task, it sometimes happens that one individual is *influenced* by another; that is, one individual changes his mind as a result of discovering a difference of opinion with another, or he does not. All four are highly intercorrelated: (Bales and Slater, 1955). Strodtbeck found performance outputs highly correlated with influences (Strodtbeck, 1951). Therefore, though there are great differences from one investigation to another in which dependent variable is the focus of analysis, it is reasonable to regard them all as different behavioral consequences of one underlying structure and to regard them as related functions of that structure. (Collectively, these four kinds of interaction can be called the *observable power and prestige order of the group*.)[1]

Third, though the tasks, settings, and interaction conditions in these studies are concretely very different, in all cases the individuals in the group are collectively oriented to a common task. Usually the task requires that the group make a decision; there is some belief that there is a right and a wrong, or a good and a bad decision; and the purpose of the group is to make the right or good decision. In coming to the right decision it is typically the case that it is legitimate to use another person's opinion as the basis of one's own opinion if one believes that the other is right. Hence, one may say that members of the group are looking for the right or good answer, either from themselves or from others. (Our terminology will be: A task that is defined as having a right and a wrong, or a good and a bad answer, if the right or good answer is defined as "success" and the wrong or bad answer as "failure," is a *valued* task; a task in which it is either necessary or legitimate to use *whatever* opinion one believes is right, whether the opinion of another or oneself, is a *collective* task. A group oriented to a collective, valued task is a *task-focused* or a *task-oriented* group.)

It is important to note some respects in which these investigations differ. While we propose to ignore differences in concrete details, they differ also in more abstract and general ways, and it is particularly in these more abstract differences that one sees the power of the generalization we hope to abstract from them. An investiga-

---

[1] In some cases the dependent variable is not one of these behaviors, but is some behavior which can be shown to be dependent on them. For example, in Zander and Cohen (1955) the dependent variable is relative satisfaction with the group experience, apparently due to action opportunities and reward actions received by the higher status individuals.

tion like Caudill's study of hospital ward rounds involves a status structure embedded in the formal organization of the hospital, and one that is immediately and obviously defined as relevant to what takes place in ward rounds. But Torrance's study of air crews shows that the formal status structure operates not only in respect to its established purposes (such as solving an air crew survival problem), but even in respect to a totally non-relevant task (constructing projective stories). Furthermore, Hurwitz, Zander, and Hymovitch (1960) show that informal status structures are as powerful as formally instituted ones in determining power and prestige orders. Thus, the effect of the status characteristic does not depend on formal sanctions and supports, nor on the access to resources that official position provides. Nor is it necessary that the status structure evolve out of the interaction of members of the group, for Strodtbeck shows the same effects though his juries are *ad hoc*. (Indeed, there is some evidence to show that categories like age, sex, occupation, education, and race work best when the group has *not* had a long history of interaction as a group [Leik, 1963]). Thus, in all these investigations there is a status structure, but it is sometimes formal and sometimes informal, sometimes has prior associations with the task of the group and sometimes not.

Because the concrete differences in these investions are so great, it requires a rather high level of abstraction to say what they have in common; but once conceded this level of abstraction, it requires only a single empirical generalization to summarize the principal findings of all of them:

> When a task-oriented group is differentiated with respect to some external status characteristic, this status difference deter-

mines the observable power and prestige order within the group whether or not the external status characteristic is related to the group task.

3. The Problem of Explanation and Construction of a Theory.[2]

To this point, the analysis yields an abstractly formulated empirical generalization; our purpose now is to explain it. The problem is to derive it from some more general theoretical formulation. To be useful, that is to increase understanding of this phenomenon and provide a basis for refining and extending knowledge of it, this theory should satisfy at least the following four requirements: (1) It should stipulate at least the sufficient conditions under which a status organizing process occurs. (2) It should specify what it is about status characteristics that determines behavior. (3) It should specify what behaviors in fact are determined by status characteristics. (4) It should describe the mechanisms by which status characteristics determine behavior. Hence, our purpose now is to construct a theoretical formulation satisfying these four requirements.

We will formulate this theory from the point of view of an actor, p, oriented to at least two social objects, himself p', and another, o. We assume p to be in the following situation: There exists a task, T, with at least two outcomes, T_a and T_b, which are *differentially evaluated*: One

---

[2] The theory presented here is part of a more comprehensive research program concerned with expectation-states processes. In general terms, this program consists of a number of theoretical formulations which are concerned with the problem of how expectation-states are formed and how they determine behavior in *different types* of social situations. (See Berger, et al, [Eds], forthcoming.)

state is positively and one negatively evaluated one is defined as "success" and the other "failure." The individuals for whom T is a task are task-focused, that is, they are motivated to achieve the positively-evaluated state and avoid the negatively-evaluated state. The task is such that individuals facing the task are *collectievly-oriented*, that is, it is both legitimate and necessary to take behavior of others into account. It is assumed that possessing the state x of some performance characteristic C* increases the individual's likelihood of achieving "success" at the task while possessing the complimentary state of C* increases the individual's likelihood of "failure" at the task. In other words, C* is *instrumental* to T. (For purposes of simplifying analysis, we treat all characteristics as dichotomies. Hence the characteristic C* has only the states C_a* and C_b*. If they are differentially evaluated, we say that one is positively and one negatively evaluated.) Who possesses the state x of C* may not be known to p. Call a task situation having these properties S*. We assume that in S* the social objects p' and o are described by states of a diffuse status characteristic, D, and only D. A characteristic is a diffuse status characteristic for p if it has three properties: First, p believes that it is better to possess one state of D than another; that is, the states of D are *differentially valued*. Second, p associated with the states of D one or more *specific expectations* for behavior. Thus, he may expect that college professors speak a pure form of English or that Jews are very studious. The set of all such specific expectations associated with the state D_x we will denote γ. The states in γ, like the states of D, are valued, either positively or negatively. Third, p associates with each state x of D a *general expectation state*, GES_x;

for example, that people who possess the state D_x are smart or moral. Where a specific expectation is one that is applicable to a defined situation or class of situations, for a general expectation no specified situation or class of situations is defined. The belief that officers are gentlemen is an expectation of this kind. GES_x is an evaluated state, and has the same value as the state D_x with which it is associated.

Because diffuse status characteristics play so central a role in our theory, we restate the ideas just given in terms of a formal definition:

> *Definition 1.* Diffuse status characteristic D is a *diffuse status characteristic* if and only if
>
> 1. The states of D are differentially evaluated, and
> 2. to each state x of D there corresponds a distinct set γ_x of states of specific, evaluated characteristics associated with D_x, and
> 3. to each state x of D there corresponds a distinct general expectation state, GES_x, having the same evaluation as the state D_x.

The task situation S*, then, is a situation in which there is a valued task, T; there is a characteristic C* instrumental to T; individuals are task-focused and collectively-oriented; and they possess the states of one, and only one, diffuse status characteristic D.

Status characteristics are not automatically brought into play simply by being present in the situation: An important theoretical task, therefore, is to characterize the class of social situations in which status characteristics do operate to govern what takes place. That is, we must formulate conditions under which it is in fact the case that the behavior of individuals in regard to each other is based on the specific and general conceptions that are associated with the status characteristic they possess. When it is true for a given situation that the behavior of individuals is based on the status-associated conceptions they have of one another, we speak of the status characteristic being *activated*:

> *Definition* 2. (Activation) D is activated in S* if and only if p attributes in S* the states GES_x and/or the sets of states γ_x to p' and o which are consistent with their states of D.

(By *consistent* we mean that the states have the same evaluation. Thus the positively evaluated general expectation state is consistent with the positively evaluated state of D.) The definition says what we mean by saying behavior in a specific situation is based on status-associated conceptions is that p, in that situation, attributes to self and other the same evaluations and expectations that p attributes to the status classes of which self and other are members. If p is a female who believes that males know more than females about anything legal, then we say that for p sex is activated in juries if p believes that specific male jurors, say Smith, Jones, and Brown, know more than she does about anything legal.

We now want to describe the conditions under which a status characteristic is activated. But there have been almost no studies of activation, and we know almost nothing about the conditions under which the evaluations and expectations associated with a class of persons come to be applied to specific individuals in specific situations.[3] There are certainly situations in which some, at least, of the status characteristics that might be used to organize interaction in fact are not: But what conditions are necessary to bring them into play? Because we do not know, the present formulation is based on giving one set of conditions that we do know are sufficient; but does not claim that these conditions are exhaustive or are necessary. That is, we do not preclude the possibility that other conditions also activate a status characteristic, and that these conditions might be much more general than those we assume here. What we claim for our first assumption is that, whatever other conditions will activate a status characteristic, it is *at least* brought into play if, first, p is in situation S* and, second, (keeping in mind that there is just one D in S*) if D is a *social basis of discrimination* between p' and o; if, that is, p' and o possess different states of D.

> *Assumption* 1. (Activation) Given S*, if D in S* is a social basis of discrimination between p' and o then D is activated in S*.

(Note that none of the pejorative implications of "discrimination" belong to our use here, nor is it even implied that p discriminates for or against someone in his actions. That he does or does not do so we intend to derive from other features of the situation; it does not follow tautologically from assumption 1.) The substantive import of assumption 1, taken in conjunction with the way in which we have defined and limited S*, is that a status characteristic is brought into play, *at least*, in situations that are task situations, in which no prior expectations for the task or affectual relations among group members have been established, and

---

[3] Leik's research is exceptionally interesting in this regard. It suggests that the extent to which a status characteristic is brought into play in a given situation is affected (negatively) by the extent of prior acquaintance of the group members (Leik, 1963).

in which a status characteristic discriminates some group members from others. In effect, this way of formulating the conditions of activation raises for further theoretical and experimental work such problems as whether and to what extent D is activated, for example, in purely social-emotional situations; whether and to what extent D is activated in equal status situations; whether all or only some status characteristics are activated in multi-characteristic status situations. (The latter two conditions are considered below in Section 5.)

If a status characteristic is activated in situation S* there are two possible situations to consider: First, the performance characteristic C* that is instrumental to the task in S* may have some prior association with D. For example, a male and a female may be required to perform a mechanical task. Both may assume that the male has greater mechanical ability than the female, because the status characteristic and task ability are probably conventionally associated. Second, the performance characteristic that is instrumental to the task in S* may have no prior association with D. For example, a pilot and a gunner may be required to construct a fantasy from an ambiguous projective stimulus (Torrance, 1954). The ability to construct a fantasy is probably not an ability conventionally associated, as a matter of established cultural belief, with air crew status.

In the first case, the activation of the status characteristic is sufficient to determine the assumptions p makes about the specific abilities of p' and o: P associates with states of C* with the states of D; and has attributed them to p' and o in this situation. The definition of the immediate situation therefore is a fairly straightforward matter.

In the second case, the way in which the structure of the situation comes to be defined is less clear. For if the characteristic instrumental in S* has no prior association with the status characteristics visible in it, how will differences in status imply anything for behavior? What is at issue is the relevance of the status characteristic in the particular situation; where by *relevance* we mean that if p believes o to possess a given state of D, then p expects that o will also possess a given state of C.

The assumption we make about relevance is a strong one: We believe that in this situation the members of the group act as if the burden of proof is on showing that the status characteristic is *not* relevant; in other words, that it becomes relevant unless p specifically *knows*, as a matter of prior belief, that it is not a basis for making inferences about the characteristic C*. It is possible of course, for prior belief to establish the *independence* of two characteristics: For example, p might have a well-formed belief that athletic ability and academic status are independent. Given this belief, p will not be willing, nor believe himself able, to infer from the fact that p' is a professor and o a student *either* that p' is better than o *or* o better than p' as a basketball player. Two characteristics that are socially defined as independent are, in the language of our theory, *dissociated*. We assume that the status characteristic must be dissociated from the task characteristic required in S* if the status characteristic is to be irrelevant to it. Faced with a new task characteristic in a new situation, one about which p has formed no prior beliefs, nothing bars p from seeing the status characteristic as relevant. If nothing bars the status characteristic from being relevant, it will in our view become relevant; it will be used as a social basis for defining the new situation. (This property of D may be called its *expansive* property, and the process by which it defines new situations the *burden of proof* process).[4]

In formulating our assumptions about this process, we take note of the fact that if a status characteristic is activated in situation S*, its *components* will consist of a state x of D, which is an evaluated state; an evaluated set of specific characteristics γ_{x},; and a state x of GES, an evaluated general expectation state. Given S* and the activation of D, p possesses or has had attributed to him one set of these components, say D_x, γ_x, and GES_x; o possesses or has had attributed to him a second set of these components, say $D_{\bar{x}}$, $\gamma_{\bar{x}}$, and $GES_{\bar{x}}$. Furthermore, the two sets have different evaluations. With respect to these components, we assume that:

> *Assumption* 2. (Burden of proof) If D is activated in S* and has not been previously dissociated from C*; and if there is no other social basis of discrimination between p' and o; then at least one of the components of D will become relevant to C* in S*.

This assumption is quite general, permitting a number of different mechanisms by which D becomes relevant to C*: The evaluation of a state, GES, D itself, or even one of the states in γ might become the basis for forming expectations in S*. The important point is that if they have not been previously associated with the characteristic instrumental in S*, but at the same time have not previously been socially defined as independent of it, then one or more of the components of the activated status characteristic become relevant to C*.

That the components of D are relevant in S* means that p believes he can make assumptions about the performance he can expect from p' and o based on a knowledge of one or more of these components. Such assumptions are here called *performance expectations*. A performance expectation is a general belief or anticipation about the quality of future performance outputs. Performance expectations are ordinarily in a one-to-one relation to beliefs about task ability. Those high in ability will be expected to perform well; those low in ability will be expected to perform poorly. Such expectations are important: For previous work shows that it is reasonable to explain the clustered inequalities that emerge in decision-making groups in terms of underlying differences in performance-expectations (see Berger and Snell, 1961; Berger and Conner, 1969). Therefore, explaining inequalities in decision-making groups can be viewed as a problem in explaining how performance-expectations are formed, how they differentiate, how they change, or how they are maintained. In the case of equal status groups, i.e., groups not initially different in status, how they form and are maintained can be explained in part by certain features of the social situation of p—that a decision is required, that disagreements emerge in the group, that resolution of these disagreements tends to create some broader and more enduring expectations about who, in the future, can be expected to be right or wrong about such matters. In the case of groups that are initially differentiated in status, however, there

---

[4] The social conditions under which the burden of proof process does *not* operate, or its effect is modified, are clearly a crucial theoretical and empirical problem which requires further research. It would be of interest to know, for example, to what extent the effect of an initially non-relevant but activated status characteristic is modified given that task-expectations *already exist* in a particular social situation.

exists already a basis for forming such expectations: The status characteristic, D. P has already made some assumptions, based on D, about what p' and o are like; from these assumptions he makes some further inferences about what p' and o are like in this particular situation, even if it is a new kind of situation about which no prior assumptions are incorporated in D.

What expectations does p form? Assumption 2 claims that p expects p' and o to possess some state of C*. It remains to say what state of C* p expects this to be. The most reasonable assumption is that the formation of performance-expectations in the particular situation is consistent with whatever knowledge p believes himself already to possess about p' and o. By *consistent* we mean that all the evaluations of the components of the situation that come to be associated in the mind of p are similar. The components of the activated D (D_x itself, GES_x, and γ_x) are either positively or negatively evaluated. The states of C* that are instrumental to T are also positively evaluated, because the outcomes to which they are instrumental are themselves positively or negatively evaluated. We assume p to behave in such a way as to make the relations among all these evaluations as consistent as he can:

Assumption 3. (Assignment) If any of the components of an activated D are relevant to C*, p will assign states of C* to self and other in a consistent manner.

Given assignment of states of C* to p' and o, we believe the behavior of p to be determined. The kind of behavior that concerns us we have referred to in section 2 as the *observable power and prestige order*. It will be recalled that this order is composed of four kinds of behavior:

(1) *action opportunities* which are requests by one individual for activity from another, such as a question, or an inquiring look, offering an opportunity to make some sort of contribution to the task; (2) *performance outputs*, which are attempts to make a contribution to accomplishment of the task, such as providing suggestions, offering facts; (3) *reward actions*, which are communicated evaluations made of performance outputs or persons, as when one individual agrees with another, or praises another, or disputes the idea of another; (4) *influence*, which is a change of evaluation or opinion as a consequence of disagreement with another. (Greater detail on the interaction process involving such behavior is given in Berger and Conner, 1969).

We say that position A is higher than position B in the observable power and prestige order if an actor occupying position A as compared to position B is more likely to receive action opportunities, more likely to initiate performance outputs (with or without being given action opportunities), more likely to have his performance outputs positively evaluated, and less likely to be influenced in the case of a disagreement with another. Further, the greater the distance between positions A and B, the greater the difference in the likelihood of initiating and receiving these behaviors.

We now relate self and other performance expectation states to p's power and prestige position in the group. We do this by assuming that the higher the expectations an individual holds for self relative to other (the greater his expectation advantage), the higher his power and prestige position.

Assumption 4. (Basic Expectation Assumption) If states of C* are assigned by p to himself and o consistent with the states of an activated D, then p's position relative to o in the observable power and prestige order will be a direct function of p's expectation advantage over o.

Because we are dealing with dichotomies, we can think of performance-expectation states as either high or low. Therefore, the performance-expectation state of p relative to o is one of four possible states: High-high, high-low, low-high, or low-low. The expectation advantage of p relative to o for these four possible states is positive for the state high-low, zero for the states high-high and low-low, and negative for the state low-high. Thus, if p holds a low-high expectation state while o holds a high-low expectation state in S*, assumption 4 claims that they interact in the following manner: P is more likely to give o action opportunities than o will give p; p is less likely to initiate performance outputs than o (with or without being given an action opportunity); p is more likely to communicate positive reward actions to o than o is to p; and if there is a disagreement, p is more likely to yield to the influence of o than o is to p. (For more detailed development of reasons for making this assumption, see Berger and Conner, 1969).

Basic Result. (Order-equivalence of Status Definitions) Given S*, and a D that has not been culturally associated with or dissociated from C*, then p's position relative to o in the observed power and prestige order will be a direct function of their relative states of D, provided any of the following is true in S*:

(1) if D is the only social basis of discrimination;

(2) if D is the only social basis of discrimination and has been activated;

(3) if D is a social basis of discrimination, has been activated, and any of the components of D are relevant to C*;

(4) if D is a social basis of discrimination,

has been activated, and states of C* have been assigned to states of D in a consistent manner;

and for a diffuse status characteristic, $\hat{D}$, whose states have been culturally associated in a consistent manner with states of C*,

(5) if $\hat{D}$ is a social basis of discrimination and has been activated.

This result claims, essentially, that the effect of a status characteristic is independent of the amount of status definition that has initially taken place in S*. Line (1) is a situation that initially is only minimally defined; that is, there is initially no relation between states of D, states of C*, and expectations for p's behavior. In more specific terms, this is a situation where the only thing that the members of the group know is that p' is a D_a and o is a D_b and that this status difference has not been culturally associated with or dissociated from their immediate task. Line (4) on the other hand is initially, before the process has begun, already maximally defined; that is, task-expectations are initially assigned to p' and o that are consistent with their states of D. More specifically, this is a situation where what is initially known or believed is that p' is a D_a and o is a D_b; that this specific p' is superior to this specific o on a set of characteristics $C_1, C_2, \ldots C_n$ (some of the members of the set γ of characteristics associated with D); and also that this specific p' is superior to this specific o with respect to C*, the characteristic instrumental to their immediate task. Line (5) also describes a situation which is initially maximally defined, but in this case the maximal definition has been brought about by the fact that, by cultural belief, differences in task-expectations have been previously associated with status differences. That is, members of the group know that p' is a D_{ab} and that o is a D_b; that this particular p′ is superior to this particular o on a set of characteristics C_1, C_2, ... C_n (some of the members of the set γ of characteristics associated with D), *and* believe that C*, the characteristic instrumental to their task, is included in this set. The basic result claims the equivalence of these status situations: The distribution of action opportunities, performance outputs, reward actions, and influence is in all of them ordered in terms of relative states of D. This result does not claim that the magnitude of the differences between high and low positions in the power-prestige order is necessarily the same in all cases; increasing amounts of status definition may strengthen the effect. But the order of the differences between high and low states of D is preserved. Furthermore, this effect does not depend on whether or not states of C* were previously associated with states of D. In line (5) our basic result covers a case in which there is a prior association of D and C*; but in lines (1)–(4) no prior association of D and C* is assumed. Again, our basic result claims these situations are equivalent: The distribution of action opportunities, performance outputs, reward actions, and influence will be ordered in both cases in terms of relative states of D.

That the theory explains the results of previous experiments should be evident from the order-equivalence result, which covers them all. The only objection one might make to this claim is that the conditions stipulated by the theory are simpler than those found in previous experiments, so that it requires a good deal of interpretation of them to match theory to experiment. This objection is valid, and is one reason for subjecting the theory to more direct tests, which are described in section 4. But this objection aside, the results of these experiments follow from the concepts and assumptions of our theory in what is otherwise a fairly straightforward manner.

Furthermore, the theory as formulated satisfies the requirements we laid down for it at the outset: It describes in a precise manner what it means for status to organize interaction. It identifies the aspects of behavior that can be said to be organized by status characteristics; it identifies the properties of a status characteristic that can be said to do the work of organizing this behavior; it describes the mechanisms through which the process takes place; it stipulates conditions sufficient for the status-organizing process to occur.

4. Direct Experimental Tests of the Theory.

While we argue that our theory enables us to explain much that is known about the status organizing process as it occurs in task-oriented groups this argument involves considerable interpretation of what is taking place in the wide variety of situations in which this process has been investigated. These experiments are typically more complex, involving more features than is necessary, according to our theory, to activate the status organizing process. This makes such experiments easily subject to several alternative explanations. Furthermore, they are not systematically informative for the whole range of situations in which, according to our theory, status organizing processes will take place. It is thus incumbent on us to obtain more direct tests of our theory under conditions involving no more and no less than those stipulated by our theory.

In this section we describe two such tests. Both take place in a standardized experimental situation the techniques and procedures of which are designed to operationalize the conditions of the theory and the components of an observable power and prestige order.[5]

This situation has two phases, a manipulation phase and a decision-making phase:

In the manipulation phase, subjects are put into one or another expectation-state, either by testing their ability directly or by providing them with status information. Subjects are always of identical status. They are not permitted to see each other during the experiment, so that control over the status information they possess is complete. If both have the state D_x, each subject is informed that one of them is D_x, but the other has some other state of D. For example, if both are Air Force staff sargeants, each is told that one is a staff sargeant and the other is a captain; or that one is a staff sargeant and the other an airman third class. Each subject assumes that the other subject is the one who possesses the other state of D.

In the decision phase, pairs of subjects repeat n identical decision-making trials, each of which has the following structure: Each trial requires a binary choice. The choice is made in three stages, the first of which is an initial choice between alternatives made independently by each subject, without knowing the choice of his partner. Subjects then communicate their initial choices to their partner, after which they each independently make a final choice. The next trial then begins.

Subjects are instructed to make what they feel to be the correct preliminary choice and, after having taken information from the other subject into consideration, to make what they feel is the correct final choice. It is repeatedly emphasized that it should be of no importance whether initial choices coincide with final choices, that using advice from others is both legitimate and necessary, and that it is primarily important that subjects make a correct *final* choice.[6]

The task consists of a sequence of almost identical stimuli, each of which is a large rectangle made up of smaller rectangles, some black and some white. The subject is to decide whether there is more white area or more black area in each rectangle.[7] The stimuli are in fact so chosen that the task is ambigious: The probablity of a white-response for each stimulus is close to .50 and the decision on any given trial is independent of the decision on the preceding trial. However, the subject is told that in each case there is a correct response, and success at the task is defined in terms of a set of standards giving scores (number of correct responses) typically attained by subjects like themselves. The ability required by

---

[5] In this section we describe only experiments in which status information is manipulated. The experimental situation, however, was developed originally by Berger for the purpose of studying both the emergence and the effects of performance-expectations. See Berger

and Conner, 1969, or Berger, Conner and McKeown, 1969.

[6] Various methods have been used to operationalize collective orientation. For example, sometimes it has been left to the instructions to emphasize the legitimacy of taking advice, sometimes subjects have been given scores as a team, and sometimes the two have been combined. For the procedures used in team scoring, see Berger and Cornner, (1969).

[7] See Moore, 1965. Other tasks have been used (see, for example, Berger and Conner, 1969) as well as variants of this one (see, for example, Berger and Fisek, 1970).

the task is described by the experimenter as "contrast sensitivity" or "spatial judgment" ability and subjects are told it is not related to artistic or mathematical ability. In other words, an attempt is made to define the situation in such a way that the ability is one with respect to which they have no prior expectations.

Communication between subjects is completely manipulated by the experimenter. This is accomplished by an Interaction Control Machine (ICOM) consisting of subject-consoles, a host experimenter panel, and a master control unit. Each subject, partitioned off so that he is unable to see any other subject, sits in front of a subject-console on which he finds various buttons and lights. Decisions are made by pushing the buttons; information is comminicated by observing the lights. All circuits pass through the master control unit, so that the experimenter is capable of manipulating communication from subject to subject.

The structure of the experimental trial, together with the control exercised through the use of ICOM, makes action opportunities and performance outputs of all subjects equal; all reward actions, that is, all communicated evaluations, and therefore all disagreements or agreements among subjects, are controlled by ICOM. A precise measure of the power nad prestige position of the subject is obtained by studying the probability that one subject influences another. If the subject changes his final choice, he is said to make an *O- response*; if he does not change his final choice, he is said to make an *S-* or *stay*, response. The probability of an S-response measures the exercise of influence in the situation.

A post-session interview follows he manipulation and decision-making phases.

This interview is used to eliminate subjects who are definitely suspicious, and claim to act on their suspicions; to eliminate subjects who have some other basis for differentiating themselves from their partner besides the status characteristic— who, for example, manage to see the other subject, when the other is from a visible minority group; and to eliminate subjects who are unable to understand the instructions, or do not hear or understand the status manipulations of the experiment.

The first experiment that represents a test of the status characteristics theory was carried out by Moore (1968), using the standardized experimental setting described above. Moore found that subjects who believed that they had more education than their partner had a higher probability of an S-response, i.e., were less readily influenced, than those who believed they had a lower educational status. Furthermore, and perhaps more important, Moore found no significant difference between subjects for whom the task ability was already associated with the status characteristic and those for whom it was not.

For this experiment, Moore used 85 junior college students. In the case of 45 of them, Moore informed them that one of the two subjects participating in the experiment was from the junior college from which both in fact came, while the other was from a nearby high school. This created a high-low condition; that is, both subjects believed that they had the higher state of the status characteristic, while their partner had the lower state. In the case of the remaining 40 subjects, Moore informed them that one of the two subjects participating was from the junior college from which both came, but the other was from a nearby four-year private university, Stanford. This created a low-high condition. In addition, of the 45 high-low subjects, 22 were informed that it had already been found that those from the junior college consistently did better at the task they were to perform than subjects from the nearby high school. Similarly, of the 40 low-high subjects 20 were informed that it had already been found that those from Stanford consistently did better at such tasks. These two instructions experimentally created an association between the status and performance characteristics in the experimental situation. Moore found that if a performance-characteristic is previously associated with a status characteristic, and the status characteristic disrciminates between p' and o, the probability that S yields to the influence of his partner is an inverse function of his status. If the performance-characteristic is not previously associated with a status characteristic, but not dissociated from it, the probability that a subject yields to the influence of his partner is again an inverse function of his status, and in fact to about the same degree. Thus, two of the predictions derivable from the theory are confirmed by this experiment.

The burden of proof assumption is perhaps the strongest assumption of the status characteristics theory, and it would be desirable if possible to isolate it for direct tests, independently of the theory's remaining assumptions. This in fact can be accomplished if (1) activation can be induced experimentally and (2) there is independent evidence confirming the assignment and basic expectation assumptions. For if we were to fail to find differences in the probability of an S-response between high-low and low-high subjects, and had ourselves assured that

activation had taken place, then our failure could not be attributed to the activation assumption; nor, if we had independent evidence in favor of the assignment and basic expectation assumptions, could we attribute our failure to the remaining assumptions of the theory. Clearly it would be the burden of proof assumption that would require reformulation.

The same reasoning can in fact be extended to each assumption of the theory in turn: For example, if we experimentally induce both activation and relevance, any failure to find differences in the probability of an S-response between high-low and low-high subjects could be attributed only to a failure of either the assignment or basic expectation assumptions. But in fact, a good deal of earlier work confirms the basic expectation assumption; therefore, the difficulty must be in the assignment assumption if any difficulty is found at all.

This sort of reasoning led to the following experiment: One hundred and eighty Air Force staff sergeants were informed either that one of the two subjects participating in the experiment was a staff sergeant and the other was an airman third class; or else one was a staff sergeant and the other a captain. (In all cases the partner was said to be from a unit sufficiently distant from the subject's own unit to eliminate direct command relations as a factor in the experiment.) Subjects were chosen on the basis of army general classification scores in such a way that their scores were about average; and 58 of them were told that the army general classification score of their patrner was higher or lower, whichever was consistent with their relative rank. The purpose of this treatment was to experimentally induce activation. Another 57 were told not

Table 1

PROPORTION, MEAN NUMBERS OF S-RESPONSES, AND STANDARD DEVIATION

Condition*	Number of Subjects	S-responses		
		Proportion	Mean	Standard Deviation
Assignment: High-low	28	.88	33.5	4.7
Assignment: Low-high	29	.74	28.2	5.0
Burden of Proof: High-low	28	.82	31.1	3.3
Burden of Proof: Low-high	30	.74	27.7	5.9
Activation: High-low	31	.81	30.7	3.6
Activation: Low-high	34	.75	28.7	6.8

* Conditions are labelled according to the assumption directly tested by the condition, and putative air force ranks of p and o—sergeant-airman (High-low) and sergeant-captain (Low-high).

only their partner's score, relative to their own, but also that previous work had shown that individuals with higher army classification scores performed better in contrast sensitivity tests. The purpose of this treatment was to experimentally induce relevance. The remaining 65 subjects were told nothing except the putative rank of their partner. We made no effort to directly induce differences in performance-expectations. Sufficient confirmation had been provided by previous experiments to give us great confidence in the basic expectation assumption (see particularly Berger and Conner, 1969).

If all four assumptions of the theory hold, then the probability of an S-response should be greater for subjects who believe their partner is an airman third class than for those who believe he is a captain, regardless of the amount of additional information the subject is given about himself and his partner. In Table 1 we see that high-low subjects consistently have higher probabilities of an S-response than low-high subjects. Nor does the amount of additional information given materially increase the effect of the treatment in the

case of low-high subjects i.e., subjects who believed their patrner was a captain. More complete status definition has some effect in the case of the high-low subjects —i.e., those who believed their patrner was an airman third class. Possibly this reflects the greater doubt expressed by subjects in post-session interviews, that sergeants differed very much from younger enlisted men in ability; the further information serving, presumably, to remove such doubts.[8] The basic results, nevertheless, provide confirmation for each assumption of the theory independently of the others.

5. Refinement and Extension of the Theory.

Further research on the theory of status characteristics and expectation states has been conditioned in large part by two purposes: First, to *refine* the theory, in the sense of increasing its precision. Second, to *extend* the theory, in the sense of increasing its generality. Both go beyond

---

[8] For additional results and further analysis, see Cohen et al, (forthcoming.)

what is conventionally called testing the theory: To *test* a theory is to confirm or disconfirm some hypothesis that in a strict sense derives from it. The experiments described in section 4 are in this sense properly called tests of the theory. But for the most part, the research with which we are now concerned does not test hypotheses that in any rigorous sense derive from the theory. The theory, however, provides the *basis* for this research, in the sense that its problems come to be posed because of the theory, and the concepts and theoretical arguments employed to deal with these problems stem from the theory. Thus, the theory guides and organizes this research and its results show as modifications in the way the theory is formulated.

We will describe six further experiments, the six falling into three basic groups: The first group of experiments equates, as well as differentiates, the statuses of individuals. The second makes specific (as opposed to diffuse) status characteristics that are initially irrelevant relevant to a group's task. The third provides subjects with information about multiple statuses, some of which is inconsistent.

(1) *Equating p′ and o.* The theory as originally formulated was concerned to explain the consequences of status differences on interaction. In formulating its scope, situations in which all individuals in the group were alike, as for example one finds in Bales' groups, were ruled out. No assumptions were made about whether individuals would form expectations for equal ability if they felt they were equal in status to others in the group; but it was tacitly supposed that, in any case, a status characteristic that did not discriminate between p′ and o (such as sex in an all-male group) would not dampen the effect of one that did (such as educational differences in an all-male group.) Furthermore, in formulating the burden of proof process, the effect of the process was made to depend on the absence of any information discriminating between p′ and o other than D itself—for other information might be inconsistent with D or might already have defined the situation independently of D, both of which were beyond the scope of the theory. But in formulating this condition, it was again assumed that information equating p′ and o would not inhibit the effect of D on the observed power and prestige order of the group.

These tacit assumptions about the effect of equal status are called into question by the results of an experiment by Seashore. The original purpose of Seashore's experiment was to study incongruent status situatinos. For this purpose, Seashore had white female junior college students work on the contrast sensitivity task with what were said to be black female Stanford students. To isolate the effect of incongruent statuses, three control conditions were employed: (1) Subjects were informed that 0 was a white female Stanford student of the same age as the subject; (2) 0 was a white female junior college student of the same age as the subject; or (3) 0 was a black female junior college student of the same age as the subject. The relevant status information was communicated by allowing the subject to see, in filling out a form, the form previously filled out by 0 showing 0's name, age, sex, race, and school. Subjects were equated on all status characteristics not intended to produce differences in the behavior of the subject in the situation; for assumption 2 could be interpreted as claiming that the effect

of the status characteristic would be inhibited only if other status information
discriminated between p' and o.

Seashore found no differences between
treatments (Seashore, 1968). While there
had been a number of departures in procedure in the Seashore experiment, any
of which might have accounted for the
difference between her results and previous
results such as those described in section 4,
Cohen, Kiker, and Kruse reasoned that
Seashore had activated statuses that equated subjects, and the effect of equating
subjects was to reduce the effect of the
differentiating status characteristic on the
probability of an S-response. They therefore replicated Seashore's experiment, using as conditions: (1) White female junior
college students who were informed that
O was black, but who were given no other
information about O; (2) or who were
informed that O was black and of the same
age as the subject; (3) or who were informed that O was a Stanford student,
but were given no other information about
O; or (4) who were informed that O was
a Stanford student of the same age as the
subject. This experiment confirmed the
hypothesis that equating subjects reduces
the effect of a differentiating characteristic
on the probability of an S-response.

This result implies that for the burden
of proof process to be maximally effective,
not only must there be no other characteristic inconsistent with or prior to D,
that also discriminates between p' and o;
there must also be no other characteristic
that equates p' and o. It should be observed that this does not imply, as would
seem likely on first sight, that the activation assumption is similarly restricted in
scope. For Seashore experimentally induced activation of equal status information, and it does not follow that if

subjects are left to choose for themselves
from multiple sources of status information that equal statuses will have the same
effect. This remains to be seen from
further experiments.

In an effort to extend the scope of the
status characteristic expectations states
formulation, Berger and Fisek (1969)
constructed a generalization of this theory. This generalization sought to describe
the operation of specific as well as diffuse
status characteristics and the operation of
multiple status characteristics in task situations. The experiments described in (2)
and (3) below primarily arose out of an
attempt to refine and answer questions
posed in developing this generalization.

(2) *Effect of other kinds of status elements.* A specific status characteristic is
one the states of which are differentially
evaluated and from which one believes it
possible to infer some other attributes of
p' and o. It differs from a diffuse status
characteristic only in not implying any
general expectation state. The theory as
originally formulated does not deal with
such characteristics; it deals only with
diffuse status characteristics and, indeed,
tacitly treats the general expectation state
as one of the principal mechanisms by
which diffuse status characteristics become
relevant in situations never previously defined by p. While there is no evidence to
disprove this, there is evidence to show
that, under certain circumstances, specific
as well as diffuse status characteristics can
be made relevant in situations to which
they have no prior relevance.

Berger, *et al.* (1970) have shown that
one can make a specific status characteristic relevant, even if it has no prior
association with the characteristic instrumental to a task, if it is made the basis

for allocating rewards to p' and o. This happens even though allocation of rewards on the basis of the irrelevant characteristic is made to look quite arbitrary. The investigation required a two-experiment design: In the first experiment, subjects were tested for their *meaning insight* ability, an intuitive ability, that makes it possible for some individuals to know which of two non-English words is the same in meaning as a comparison English word. (The ability, of course, is artificially created by the experimenter; for details, see Berger and Conner, 1969). In the second experiment, in which the same subjects participated, they were told that it was customary to give 25¢ per trial to subjects with high contrast sensitivity, the ability required by the experimental task, and 10¢ per trial to subjects with low contrast sensitivity, as rewards for their respective contributions to the group effort. As the experimenters were very pressed for time, they could not test subjects for contrast sensitivity; but because they wanted to keep the conditions of this study fairly comparable to the conditions of their other studies, they would pay the subjects on the basis of the only information they did know, the meaning insight scores they knew the subjects had been given from the previous experiment in which it was known they had participated. Thus, there is a characteristic, C_1, nonrelevant to the task; a characteristic, C_2, instrumental to the task; and a reward that is supposed to be associated with the ability that is instrumental to the task. When the reward is instead given on the basis of the nonrelevant characteristic, the nonrelevant characteristic determines the probability of an S-response in the experiment.

A similar two-experiment design has been used by Freese to show that given three specific characteristics, say C_1, C_2, and C_3, if subjects believe that C_1 and C_2 are positively correlated they make inferences about the task characteristic C_3 from C_1. On the other hand, if they believe C_1 and C_2 are inversely correlated they do not. Freese first tested subjects on their meaning insight ability. They were then informed either that one could also infer, if one had high meaning insight ability, that one also had high *social prediction* ability or else that it was known that individuals with high meaning insight ability had low social prediction ability. (Social prediction ability is the ability to predict behavior in complex social situations.) The experiment then ended, but subjects were asked to participate in a second experiment in which the contrast sensitivity task was used. Meaning insight ability predicted the probability of an S-response for subjects in the contrast sensitivity situation if it was positively correlated with social prediction ability, but not if the two were negatively correlated.

These two experiments show that, under certain circumstances, other status elements of the situation as well as the diffuse status characteristic are capable of defining it; and they may go some way, too, to clarifying what it is about the diffuse status characteristic that accounts for its "expansive" properties.

(3) *Multiple-characteristic status situations*. Where two or more status characteristics are activated in a situation, the possibility arises that they are inconsistent; it is about such situations that most theories of status characteristics have been written (see, for example, Hughes, 1945

or Lenski, 1956). It is typically assumed that such situations are tense and awkward, but it is not so clear how they are resolved. Does the individual define the situation with respect to just one characteristic, neglecting, suppressing, or denying the significance of the other? One might suppose this from a balance theory, in which inconsistency must in some manner be reduced. Or does the individual combine all the information made available to him, in a sense "averaging" it over all characteristics, forming expectations for self and other that are somewhere in between those formed if both characteristics are high or both low?

Two experiments by Berger and Fisek, (1970), and Berger, Fisek, and Crosbie (1970), show that subjects combine information rather than balance it. These experiments artificially construct two equally-weighted specific status characteristics, each of which is made equally relevant to the contrast sensitivity task. When they are made inconsistent, subjects are found to have a probability of an S-response lower than those who are consistently high, but higher than those who are consistently low (Berger and Fisek, 1970). Furthermore, a subject who is high on one characteristic and low on another has a lower probability of an S-response when his partner is high on both characteristics than when his partner is low on one but high on the other characteristic (and similarly for the obverse case,) (Berger, Fisek, and Crosbie, 1970). This further supports the finding that a combined hierarchy is formed on the basis of inconsistent status information.

The significance of these two experiments is, of course, that they provide the basis for greatly extending the generality of the original theory; for it now becomes possible, in fact, to extend the theory to situations defined by any number of characteristics.

6. *Summary and conclusion.*

The research described in this paper can be summarized in terms of the following stages:

(1) The first stage was one in which an abstractly formulated empirical generalization was constructed from an analysis of the dozen or so investigations reported between 1950 and 1965 of the distribution of participation, prestige, and influence in decision-making groups that are initially different in age, sex, occupation, education, race, or similar social categories: When task-oriented groups are differentiated with respect to some external status characteristic, the differences between individuals in status determine the observable power and prestige order of the group, whether the status characteristic is previously associated with the task or not.

(2) In the second stage of this research, a theory was formulated that explains this generalization. The theory explains it by attributing to status characteristics differential evaluations, differential specific expectations, and differential general expectations. These three properties are called into play when two or more individuals are committed to some outcome, must take each other into account in bringing this outcome about, and have no other or no prior basis for inferring who is better able to achieve this outcome. They are called into play even if no prior association exists between status characteristics and instrumental-task characteristics, just so long as nothing positively stands in the way of making a connection

between the two. Becoming in this way relevant to the immediate task situation, expectations for performance in the particular situation are formed that are consistent with the components of the status characteristic. Once formed, such performance-expectations are known to determine the distribution of opportunities to perform, the rate of performance outputs, the likelihood that a performance output is positively rewarded, and the exercise of influence.

(3) The third stage has involved direct experimental tests of the assumptions made by this explanation. The logical structure of the argument makes it possible to test each of them independently of the other. These direct experimental tests have provided confirmation for the basic assumptions of the status characteristics formulation.

(4) The fourth stage has been one concerned with the refinement and extension of the theory. Further experiments show that: (a) Under certain circumstances, other status elements can become the basis for organizing the distribution of power and prestige in the group. (b) Given information about two relevant characteristics, subjects combine this information, even if it is inconsistent; creating a hierarchy of power and prestige that places inconsistent individuals between those consistently high and those consistently low. (c) Information that equates the status of subjects is combined with other information in the same manner; so that under certain circumstances, if subjects are equal in status this reduces the effect on the power and prestige order of status characteristics that discriminate between them.

(5) The fifth stage, now in progress, is concerned with organizing further work on the status-expectation process: This we believe involves reformulating the theory so as to account for the results of the experiments that were designed to refine and extend the theory.

REFERENCES

BALES, R. F., F. I. STRODTBECK, T. M. MILLS, and M. E. ROSEBOROUGH, "Channels of Communication in Small Groups," *American Sociological Review*, 16 (1951) 461–68.

BALES, R. F., and P. SLATER, "Role Differentiation in Small Decision Making Groups," in Parsons, T. and R. F. Bales, *Family, Socialization and Interaction Process* (Glencoe, Illinois: The Free Press), 1955.

BERGER, J., and J. L. SNELL, "A Stochastic Theory for Self-Others Expectations," *Technical Report* #1, (Stanford, California: Laboratory for Social Research), 1961.

BERGER, J., and T. CONNER, "Performance-Expectations and Behavior in Small Groups," *Acta Sociologica*, 12 (1969) 186–98.

BERGER, J., T. CONNER, and W. McKEOWN, "Evaluations and the Formation and Maintenance of Performance Expectations," *Human Relations*, 22 (1969) 481–82.

BERGER, J., and H. FISEK, "Consistent and Inconsistent Status Characteristics and the Determination of Power and Prestige Orders," *Sociometry*, 33 (1970) 287–304.

BERGER, J., H. FISEK, and P. CROSBIE, "Multi-Characteristic Status Situations and The Determination of Power and Prestige Orders," *Technical Report* #35 (Stanford, California: Laboratory for Social Research), 1970.

BERGER, J., and H. FISEK, "An Extended Theory of Status Characteristics and Expectation States," unpublished manuscript, Stanford California, 1969.

BERGER, J., H. FISEK, and L. FREESE, "Paths of Relevance and the Determination of Power and Prestige Orders," unpublished manuscript, Stanford, California, 1970.

BERGER, J., T. CONNER, and H. FISEK (eds.), *Expectation States Theory: A Research Program*, forthcoming.

CAUDILL, W., *The Psychiatric Hospital as a Small Society*, (Cambridge, Massachusetts: Harvard University Press), 1958, Chapter 10.

COHEN, B. P., J. BERGER, and M. ZELDITCH, JR., *Status Conceptions and Power and Prestige*, forthcoming.

COHEN, B. P., J. KIKER, and R. KRUSE, "The Formation of Performance Expectations Based on Race and Education: A Replication," *Technical Report* #30, (Stanford, California: Laboratory for Social Research), 1969.

CROOG, S. H., "Patient Government: Some Aspects of Participation and Social Background on Two Psychiatric Wards," *Psychiatry*, 19 (1956) 203–7.

FREESE, L., *The Generalization of Specific Performance Expectations*, unpublished Ph.D. dissertation, (Stanford, California), 1969.

HEISS, J. S., "Degree of Intimacy and Male-Female Interaction," *Sociometry*, 25 (1962), 197–208.

HOFFMAN, P. J., L. FESTINGER, and D. H. LAURENCE, "Tendencies Toward Group Comparability in Competitive Bargaining," *Human Relations*, 7 (1954) 141–59.

HUGHES, E. C., "Dilemmas and Contradictions of Status," *American Journal of Sociology*, 50 (1945) 353–59.

HURWITZ, J. I., A. F. ZANDER, and B. HYMOVITCH, "Some Effects of Power on the Relations Among Group Members," in Cartwright, D., and A. Zander, (eds.) *Group Dynamics*, (New York: Harper & Row) 1960, 448–56.

KATZ, IRWIN, GOLDSTONE, and BENJAMIN, "Behavior and Productivity in Bi-Racial Work Groups," *Human Relations*, 11 (1958) 123–41.

KATZ, IRWIN, and L. BENJAMIN, "Effects of White Authoritarianism in Bi-Racial Work Groups," *Journal of Abnormal and Social Psychology*, 61 (1960) 448–56.

LEIK, ROBERT K., "Instrumentality and Emotionality in Family Interaction," *Sociometry*, 26 (1963) 131–45.

LENSKI, G., "Social Participation and Status Crystallization," *American Sociological Review*, 21 (1956) 458–64.

MISHLER, E. G., and A. TROPP, "Status and Interaction in a Psychiatric Hospital," *Human Relations*, 9 (1956) 187–205.

MOORE, J., "Development of the Spatial Judgment Experimental Task," *Technical Report* #15 (Stanford, California: Laboratory for Social Research), 1965.

MOORE, J., "Status and Influence in Small Group Interactions," *Sociometry*, 31 (1968) 47–63.

PARK, R. E., "Bases of Race Prejudice," *The Annals*, 140 (1928) 11–20.

SEASHORE, MARJORIE, *The Formation of Performance Expectations for Self and Other in an Incongruent Status Situation*, unpublished Ph.D. dissertation, (Stanford, California), 1968.

SIMMEL, G., *Sociologie, Untersuchungen über die Formen der Vergeselschaftung* (Leipzig, Germany: Verlag von Duncker und Humblot) 1908, in Wolff, K., *The Sociology of Georg Simmel*, (Glencoe, Illinois: The Free Press).

SIMMEL, G. op cit., in Wolff, K., *Essays on Sociology, Philosophy and Aesthetics*, (New York: Harper & Row), 1959, 344–45.

STRODTBECK, F. L., "Husband-Wife Interaction Over Revealed Differences," *American Sociological Review*, 16 (1951) 468–73.

STRODTBECK, F. L., and R. D. MANN, "Sex Role Differentiation in Jury Deliberations," *Sociometry*, 19 (1956) 3–11.

STRODTBECK, F. L., R. M. JAMES, and C.

HAWKINS, "Social Status in Jury Deliberations," in Maccoby, E. E., T. M. Newcomb,
and E. L. Hartley (eds.), *Readings in
Social Psychology*, 3rd Ed. (New York:
Henry Holt and Company) 1958, 379–88.

TORRANCE, E. P., "Some Consequences of
Power Differences on Decision Making in
Permanent and Temporary Three-Man
Groups," *Research Studies*, State College
of Washington, #22 (1954) 130–40.

ZANDER, A., and A. R. COHEN, "Attributed
Social Power and Group Acceptance: A
Classroom Experimental Demonstration,"
Journal of Abnormal Social Psychology, 51
(1955) 490–92.

ZILLER, R. C., and R. V. EXLINE, "Some
Consequences of Age Heterogeneity in Decision-Making Groups," *Sociometry*, 21
(1958) 198–201.

6

The Effects
of Status Incongruency

STATUS CONGRUENCE AND
COGNITIVE CONSISTENCY*

Edward E. Sampson

In the following paper, we present a theoretical framework, referred to as a theory of expectancy congruence, which attempts to integrate the sociological literature on status crystallization[1] and the psychological literature on cognitive consistency. The paper will be organized into several major sections. The first section discusses the theory and research dealing with status crystallization. The second briefly outlines psychological developments in the area of cognitive consistency. The next section presents our theory of expectancy congruence, integrating the material of the first two sections. We conclude by examining further aspects of the theory and by re-examining the status crystallization literature in light of the theory of expectancy congruence.

APPROACHES TO STATUS CONGRUENCE

For many years, sociologists and social psychologists have been interested in social class or social status, as an independent and as a dependent variable in their theory and research.[2] The approaches of Max

* Edward E. Sampson, "Status Congruence and Cognitive Consistency," *Sociometry*, 26 (1963), 146–62. Reprinted by permission of the American Sociological Association.

[1] In this paper, we shall use the terms status crystallization, status equilibration, and status congruence to refer to the same phenomena: the degree of correspondence across various dimensions of status ranking.

[2] See for example, Urie Bronfenbrenner,

Weber[3] and more recently of Parsons[4] and of Lenski[5] have emphasized that a given individual may be ranked in many different systems of stratification. This observation has suggested the importance of examining the relationships that exist between these systems or dimensions as well as the second-order relationships with other social and psychological variables. It is to be noted that this approach differs from that discussed by Warner and Lunt[6] and Centers,[7] who were mainly

concerned with discovering which dimensions provided the best indicator of an individual's "real" social class or which combination or weighting of dimensions was most predictive of behavior. By contrast, this newer emphasis attempts to discover the consequences of differential placement along the various ranking dimensions, by utilizing an index of differential ranking as a major independent variable.

Research using this latter approach has been reported by Lenski,[8] Adams,[9] and Exline and Ziller.[10] Lenski's work relates an index of status crystallization to the individual's political attitudes, whereas the research reported by Adams and by Exline and Ziller relates this index to small group morale and productivity.[11] In order to provide a concrete basis on which to build our theoretical framework, we shall briefly summarize some of the most relevant theory and research involving the status variable.

Lenski examined four status systems—

"Socialization and Social Class Through Time and Space," in Eleanor E. Maccoby, Theodore M. Newcomb, and Eugene L. Hartley, editors, *Readings in Social Psychology*, New York: Henry Holt, 1958, pp. 400–425. Richard Centers, *The Psychology of Social Classes*, Princeton University Press, 1949; August B. Hollingshead and Frederick C. Redlich, *Social Class and Mental Illness*, New York: John Wiley & Sons, 1958; Daniel R. Miller and Guy E. Swanson, "The Study of Conflict," in Marshall R. Jones, editor, *Nebraska Symposium on Motivation*, Lincoln, Neb.: University of Nebraska Press, 1956; Robert R. Sears, Eleanor E. Maccoby and Herry Levin, *Patterns of Child Rearing*, Evanston, Ill.: Row, Peterson & Co., 1957; and W. Lloyd Warner and Paul S. Lunt, *The Social Life of a Modern Community*, New Haven: Yale University Press, 1941; and *idem., The Status System of a Modern Community*, New Haven: Yale University Press, 1942.

[3] Max Weber, "Class, Status, Party," in Hans H. Gerth and C. Wright Mills, translators and editors, *From Max Weber: Essays in Sociology*, New York: Oxford University Press, 1946.

[4] Talcott Parsons, "An Analytical Approach to the Theory of Social Stratification," Ch. 7, *Essays in Sociological Theory, Pure and Applied*, Glencoe, Ill.: Free Press, 1949.

[5] Gerhard Lenski, "Status Crystallization: A Nonvertical Dimension of Social Status," *American Sociological Review*, 19 (August, 1954), pp. 405–413.

[6] Warner and Lunt, *op. cit.*

[7] Centers, *op. cit.*

[8] Lenski, *op. cit.*

[9] Stuart Adams, "Status Congruency as a Variable in Small Group Performance," *Social Forces*, 32 (October, 1953), pp. 16–22.

[10] Ralph V. Exline and Robert C. Ziller, "Status Congruency and Interpersonal Conflict in Decision-making Groups," *Human Relations*, 12 (April, 1959), pp. 147–162.

[11] It is to be noted that the variable of status crystallization or congruence may be considered a characteristic of the social structure and a characteristic of a particular unit of that structure, e.g. an individual. That is, one may meaningfully speak of the extent to which a given social organization—e.g. a small group, an organization, or a society—has evolved a crystallized or congruent status structure; and one may also speak of the extent to which a given person's status positions are crystallized or congruent.

income, occupation, education, and race or ethnic position—computing an index of crystallization across these dimensions for a sample of individuals. A person who ranked in similar positions across the dimensions was referred to as "high crystallized," while a person who ranked differently across the dimensions (regardless of the pattern) was referred to as "low crystallized." Lenski related this index of crystallization to expressed political attitudes and behavior, finding that liberal attitudes were positively related to low crystallization. He interpreted his findings as suggesting that the low crystallized person was dissatisfied with the present state of affairs, felt frustrated, and sought social change. This was in contrast to the satisfaction and relative lack of frustration of the highly crystallized person. This finding and interpretation seem to imply what Benoit-Smullyan[12] referred to as a status equilibration tendency; that is, a tendency for a person's position in one hierarchy to match his position in another. It is also akin to the point made by Homans[13] in his discussion of the costs incurred from a condition of status incongruence. It suggests that differential ranking—at least on the four dimensions which Lenski selected—is an undesirable, costly state, giving rise to pressures to move towards a state of congruence or equilibrium. We shall have reason to deal in more detail with this point when we relate this material to the literature in psychology dealing with a principle of cognitive consistency, especially Festinger's theory of cognitive dissonance.[14]

Adams computed an index of status congruence for a group of air crews on dimensions such as age, rank, amount of flight time, education, length of service, etc. His findings indicated that air crews with high congruence were characterized by their increasing friendship, greater mutual trust, and greater intimacy as compared to low congruent crews. In interpreting his results, Adams, like Lenski, turned to the dissatisfaction and frustration of the individuals in incongruent positions, who thereby considered themselves inappropriately placed within their group. These individuals were more apt to manifest behaviors which would be disruptive to their group. Again, the implication is that congruence is the desired, pleasant, nondisruptive state, both for the individual and for the group of which he is a member.

Exline and Ziller experimentally varied the status congruence of the individuals in small discussion groups on the dimensions of voting power and task ability. Their findings indicated that congruent groups were more congenial and showed greater discussion agreement than incongruent groups. The authors further suggested that if their situation had permitted it, there was an indication that the incongruent groups would have changed towards a congruent status structure. Thus, once again, we have the implication that incongruence is undesirable and that there are tendencies towards the development of congruent status structures within groups.

[12] Emile Benoit-Smullyan, "Status, Status Types, and Status Interrelations," *American Sociological Review*, 9 (April, 1944), pp. 151–161.

[13] George C. Homans, *Social Behavior: Its Elementary Forms*, New York: Harcourt, Brace & World, Inc., 1961.

[14] Leon Festinger, *A Theory of Cognitive Dissonance*, Evanston: Row, Peterson, 1957.

Although it was not presented in this context, the findings and interpretation of a study by Kleiner, Parker, and Taylor[15] are also relevant. They hypothesized a relationship between the level of aspiration-level of achievement discrepancy and the incidence of mental illness. Their rationale suggested that this discrepancy produced frustration and stress for the individual, who responded by a flight into illness. They used educational rank as a measure of the individual's level of aspiration, and occupational rank as a measure of achievement. The discrepancy of which they speak, therefore, is an index of status congruence as employed, for example, by Lenski. Furthermore, the postulation of frustration as a reaction to this discrepancy directly parallels Lenski's interpretation and is consistent with the findings and interpretation of the small group studies of Adams and of Exline and Ziller. It is interesting to note, however, that whereas Lenski suggests and empirically finds that this state of frustration leads to active attempts to change the system (e.g. liberal political attitudes and behavior), Kleiner suggests and generally finds that it leads to a higher incidence of mental illness. Both approaches, however, suggest that incongruence is an undesirable state and that individuals will attempt to cope with it in some manner. Different coping techniques therefore become another issue of relevance in the further examination of this variable. Some persons may be expected to reduce status

incongruence by means of flight into fantasy and illness (Kleiner); whereas others may attempt to reduce it by means of active efforts to change the social system or their relation to it (Lenski).[16]

Continuing our examination of relevant literature, it is valuable to take note of a distinction which Bales has made in his theory and supported by his research findings.[17] Although Bales presented his material in a somewhat different context, as with the work of Kleiner, there is a similarity to the variable of status congruence that demands further exploration. In general, Bales has distinguished between task leaders and socioemotional

---

[15] As reported in an unpublished dittoed note seen by the author while at the Research Center for Group Dynamics of the University of Michigan in 1960.

[16] Is this not also a point which is implied by Merton? Cf. Robert Merton, *Social Theory and Social Structure*, Glencoe, Ill.: Free Press, 1957. His formulation of five different types of responses to the discrepancy between societal goals and sanctioned means to attain these goals may be considered as expressing the manner by which persons located in different segments of the social system are expected to react to status incongruence. "Conformity" is a response of those persons who presently occupy congruent status positions, while "innovation," "ritualism," "retreatism," and "rebellion" represent responses of persons in incongruent positions. Retreatism or withdrawal, including a psychotic reaction, thus becomes comparable to the response suggested by Kleiner, while rebellion, or actively seeking to change the system, becomes comparable to the response suggested by Lenski.

[17] Robert F. Bales, "Adaptive and Integrative Changes as Sources of Strain in Social System," in A. Paul Hare, Edgar F. Borgatta, and Robert F. Bales, editors, *Small Groups*, New York: Knopf, 1955, pp. 127–131; and "Task Roles and Social Roles in Problem-solving Groups," in Eleanor E. Maccoby, Theodore M. Newcomb, and Eugene L. Hartley, editors, *Readings in Social Psychology*, New York: Henry Holt, 1958, pp. 437–447.

leaders within small discussion groups. He suggests that it is difficult for the same person to fulfill both functions, each of which is necessary for the group to continue operating effectively. Bales' method for identifying the task specialist and the socioemotional specialist involves ranking group members according to various categories of participation or interaction. Thus the most active individual (i.e. the most highly ranking) on giving suggestions and orientation may be identified as the task specialist, while the highest ranking individual on giving positive emotion or support may be identified as the socioemotional leader.

At first glance, it appears that the Bales' finding that it is *unusual* for the same person to head both ranks (i.e. fulfill both types of functions) is opposed to the previous findings which indicated the existence of a tendency toward status congruence. This is an instance of a person who ranks high on one dimension and low on another: obviously, therefore, it is an instance of status incongruence. However, as treated by Bales, this is not an undesirable state, but rather appears to be the more typical, felicitous condition of small group functioning. This finding may mean simply that one cannot rank *high* on both dimensions, but implies nothing about an incongruity for other ranks; or it may mean that differential ranking is *not necessarily* incongruent and undesirable. Assuming this latter point is correct, there is a particularly significant conclusion to be drawn: differential ranking does not *by itself* produce status incongruence and tendencies towards congruence. Although the preceding authors (e.g., Lenski, Adams, Exline and Ziller, and Benoit-Smullyan) have implied that differential

ranking defines status incongruence and produces desires or pressures towards change, we would like to anticipate our later theoretical development at this point by briefly suggesting an alternate proposal.

It appears that the meaningful sense in which rank positions may be said to be incongruent and that tendencies towards status equilibration exist does not occur with *any* discrepancy between the positions, but rather, with any discrepancy that implies inconsistent expectations for the behavior of the occupants of the positions. This consideration suggests that it is not the mere location on a status hierarchy that is important, but rather the expectations connected with that location. It further implies that a given individual may occupy a low rank in one hierarchy and a high rank in another and *not* be under pressure to change, if there is a consistency between the expectations coincident with those two positions. And finally, it implies that the dimensions which have been selected for research by Lenski, by Adams, by Exline and Ziller, and by Kleiner, are dimensions in which there is a high correspondence between positional discrepancy and expectational inconsistency, even though this apparently is not the case for the two major dimensions of which Bales speaks. And, in fact, Bales' theory points out that the inconsistency exists among the expectations connected with similar ranking on both dimensions rather than with differential ranking on each.

All of the preceding, much of which we shall develop further in the following sections, suggests the importance of empirical research directed towards identifying the nature of the expectations which correspond to the different ranking systems of a society, organization, or group, and towards identifying the mechanisms by which these expectations are shaped and altered to be congruent with the changing needs of the society, organization, or group.

Theories of Cognitive Consistency

There has been a growing interest in psychology in the cognitive factors involved in behavior. The focus of the attitude change theories of Katz and Stotland,[18] Osgood, Suci, and Tannenbaum,[19] and Rosenberg, Hovland, McGuire, Abelson, and Brehm,[20] has involved a principle of cognitive consistency. In general terms, the individual is seen as motivated to maintain consistency among his cognitions or aspects of his cognitions, and attitude change may be brought about by introducing an inconsistency among certain of these elements.

The approach to interpersonal behavior suggested by Heider[21] and formalized by Cartwright and Harary,[22] as well as the approaches of Newcomb[23] and of Festinger,[24] are also similar in their emphasis on individual tendencies towards maintaining cognitive balance, symmetry, or consonance. Zajonc[25] summarizes many of these similarities in his recent review.

Each of the approaches has supported its theoretical orientation with empirical evidence suggesting that people apparently do establish relationships between themselves and others that could be characterized as balanced or symmetric or that persons do act in a manner designed to reduce dissonance.

The cognitive units tending towards consistency which these theories typically discuss include sets of attitudes towards persons and objects, two sets of attitudes or beliefs, and expectations and behavior. It is this final cognitive unit of expectation, and specifically Festinger's theory with which we shall deal further.

Festinger[26] has suggested that one form of cognitive dissonance involves a discrep-

[18] Daniel Katz and Ezra Stotland, "A Preliminary Statement to a Theory of Attitude Structure and Change," in Sigmund Koch, editor, *Psychology: A Study of a Science, V. 3*, New York: McGraw-Hill, 1959.

[19] Charles E. Osgood, George J. Suci, and Percy H. Tannenbaum, *The Measurement of Meaning*, Urban, Ill.: University of Illinois Press, 1957.

[20] Milton J. Rosenberg, Carl I. Hovland, William J. McGuire, Robert P. Abelson, and Jack W. Brehm, *Attitude Organization and Change: An Analysis of Consistency Among Attitude Components*, New Haven: Yale University Press, 1960.

[21] Fritz Heider, "Attitudes and Cognitive Organization," *Journal of Psychology*, 21 (January, 1946), pp. 107–112; and *The Psychology of Interpersonal Relations*, New York: Wiley, 1958.

[22] Dorwin Cartwright and Frank Harary, "Structural Balance: A Generalization of Heider's Theory," *Psychological Review*, 63 (September, 1956), pp. 277–293.

[23] Theodore M. Newcomb, "An Approach to the Study of Communicative Acts," *Psychological Review*, 60 (November, 1953), pp. 393–404; and "Individual Systems of Orientation," in Sigmund Koch, editor, *Psychology: A Study of a Science, V. 3*, New York: McGraw-Hill, 1959.

[24] Festinger, *op. cit.*

[25] Robert B. Zajonc, "The Concepts of Balance, Congruity, and Dissonance," *Public Opinion Quarterly*, 24 (Summer, 1960), pp. 280–296.

[26] Festinger, *op. cit.*

ancy between expectation and occurrence. Thus persons who expect that the world will end on a particular day experience dissonance when that day comes and passes and the world continues to exist.[27] Similarly, one can interpret the findings of Aronson and Mills,[28] showing greater attraction to a group with a severe initiation ceremony as compared with one less severe, in terms of the discrepancy between expectation or belief and occurrence. It would be dissonant to maintain the belief that one endured so severe an initiation for so unimportant a group; therefore, the group must be highly attractive and important. We would add that this must be so, of course, because one has the *underlying expectation* that high effort, high embarrassment, high severity of initiation, etc. goes with high reward. In order to maintain this underlying expectation, one alters his valuation of the group. That is to say, the person maintains that the expected relationship between hard work (severity of initiation, etc.) and reward is positive. Thus, when given a situation involving hard work, he completes this relation according to expectation by positing high reward value to the object, group, person, etc. This is referred to by Festinger as an example of maintaining consonance.

We shall now expand this idea by assuming that it is useful to deal with the psychological tendencies towards cognitive consistency in terms of expectancy units. Persons can then be characterized by their tendencies to maintain a consistency among expectations. That is, they function cognitively so as to maintain a consistency among the various expectations which they hold and between expectation and occurrence.

STATUS INCONGRUENCE,
EXPECTANCY INCONGRUENCE,
AND COGNITIVE DISSONANCE

We are now in a position to deal with the sociological variable of status congruence in the same terms we have selected for discussing the psychological tendencies towards cognitive consistency. To complete this step, we must first deal with the relationship between rank position and expectation. Let us make the assumption that one aspect of each position—or set of positions—along a given status dimension consists of certain expectations for the behavior of the occupant of that position. Thus, for example, a person ranking high in eduction may meaningfully be said to have certain expectations held by others and by himself for his behavior. A similar parallel between rank position and expectation can be drawn for other dimensions along which persons can be ranked. It is to be noted that this assumption is analogous to that made in role theory in speaking of positions in the structure of society and expectations connected to these positions.[29]

[27] Leon Festinger, Henry W. Riecken, and Stanley Schachter, "When Prophecy Fails," in Eleanor E. Maccoby, Theodore M. Newcomb, and Eugene L. Hartley, editors, *Readings in Social Psychology*, New York: Henry Holt, 1958, pp. 156–163.

[28] Elliot Aronson and Judson Mills, "The Effect of Severity of Initiation on Liking for a Group," *Journal of Abnormal and Social Psychology*, 59 (July, 1959), pp. 177–181.

[29] See Theodore R. Sarbin, "Role Theory," in Gardner Lindzey, editor, *Handbook of Social Psychology, V. 1*, Cambridge: Addison-Wesley, 1954.

By the preceding assumption, we have now drawn a complete parallel between a condition of status incongruence and a condition of expectancy incongruence, or cognitive dissonance in Festinger's terminology.

Let us be a bit more specific on this point by examining two status dimensions, A and B, and the *underlying expectation* specifying the nature of the relationship to be expected between A and B. It is possible to speak of various positions or ranks along dimension A (R_{1A}, R_{2A}, ... R_{An}), and various positions or ranks along dimension B (R_{1B}, R_{2B}, ... R_{nB}). Corresponding to each position along A are certain expectations pertaining to the behavior of the occupant of that position (e_{R1A}, e_{R2A}, ... e_{RnA}). A similar situation exists for each position along B. The underlying expectation is seen as linking the rank positions of A and B including their corresponding expectations.

Let us next define inconsistency or incongruity between A and B in a manner parallel to Festinger's definition of dissonance:[30] That is, A implies not B. We then conclude that when the underlying expectation maintains that A and B are positively related such that if R_{1A} then R_{1B} an instance in which we find R_{1A} and R_{5B} is an instance of status incongruence (as typically used to refer to differential rank positions) *and* an instance of expectancy incongruence or dissonance. However, when the underlying expectation maintains that A and B are negatively related such that if R_{1A}, then R_{5B}, an instance in which we find R_{1A} and R_{5B} is an instance of status incongruence (as defined by differential ranking), but is

not an instance of expectancy incongruence or dissonance. Assuming a tendency towards congruence, we expect change in the former case but not in the latter. Thus we arrive at the point suggested earlier in our consideration of Bales; mere difference in rank position does not necessarily function as Lenski and the others have posited.

To summarize, we have suggested that one can treat the sociological variable of status congruence in the same terms useful in treating psychological theories of cognitive consistency, specifically, in terms of a more general theory of expectancy congruence.

TOWARDS AN EXPECTANCY CONGRUENCE MODEL OF INTERPERSONAL BEHAVIOR

We shall continue our examination of the general principle of expectancy congruence by presenting and discussing some of the assumptions underlying the model. In developing the model itself, we employ assumptions that are similar to those employed by G. H. Mead[31] and to those suggested as the basis for the A-B-X model of Newcomb[32] and the communication and social motivation models of Festinger.[33] We begin with a set of assumptions within a functionalist framework. From these

---

[30] Festinger, *op. cit.*

[31] George H. Mead, *Mind, Self, and Society*, Chicago: University of Chicago Press, 1934.

[32] Newcomb, *op. cit.*

[33] Leon Festinger, "Informal Social Communication," *Psychological Review*, 57 (September, 1950), pp. 271–282; and "Motivation Leading to Social Behavior," in Marshall R. Jones, editor, *Nebraska Symposium on Motivation*, Lincoln, Neb.: University of Nebraska Press, 1954.

assumptions, we derive certain implications for the functioning of individuals and of collectivities. Basically, we attempt to derive conclusions which pertain to intraindividual and interindividual pressures towards cognitive consistency (expectancy congruence). Thus, this model is seen as relevant to psychological theories of individual cognitive behavior as well as to social psychological theories of group and collective behavior. As previously, our aim is to deal with the variable of status congruence as an example of the operation of this model. To this end we conclude this article with a brief consideration of the findings of the initial studies cited by Lenski, Adams, and Exline and Ziller in the context of the expectancy congruence model.

We should warn the reader at this point that we are not presenting the following as a formally derived theory with primitives, postulates, theorems, etc. But rather, we shall endeavor to discuss our propositions in a logical manner without presenting the more elegant outlines of a formal theory. We shall number our major paragraphs in order to provide easier reference and to emphasize the logical order of the propositions.

1. Let us begin with the central assumption that one of the basic requirements of individual and collective survival—in other words, a requirement basic to the continued existence of a social order—is a degree of coordination among the actions of two or more persons involved in any particular interaction situation. This assumption implies each individual's necessary dependence on other individuals for his own survival.

2. Let us next assume that among other factors, this coordination itself requires a degree of anticipatory knowledge about the behavior which may be expected of the other participants in the particular interaction situation. This knowledge permits the regulation of one's own behavior vis-à-vis the others with whom one is interacting. We shall further assume that this anticipatory knowledge exists within the person (P) in the form of expectations about his and the other's (O's) behavior.[34] These assumptions are similar to those advanced many years ago by G. H. Mead[35] and presently supported by those working in role theory.[36]

3. Over time, and we assume, through a series of child and adult experiences including intentional instruction, incidental learning, and learning of a trial-and-error sort, individuals (and larger units, including groups, organizations, and societies) develop a model of their physical and their social world. This model is assumed to contain the expectations, hypotheses, or hunches the individual maintains about his own behavior, the behavior of other persons, and about the physical environment. For purposes of this paper, we shall not deal with the expectations involving the physical environment, but rather shall concentrate solely upon those involving one's self and other persons—i.e., the social environment.

This "world view" is similar to what

---

[34] It is important to note that we are not implying that this anticipatory knowledge is necessary for a cooperative as contrasted with a competitive interaction situation. An expectation about the other's behavior must be maintained, whether this other be friend or foe.

[35] Mead, *op. cit.*

[36] See for example, Merton, *op. cit.*; Sarbin, *op. cit.*; and Tamotsu Shibutani, *Society and Personality*, Englewood Cliffs, N.J.: Prentice-Hall, Inc., 1961.

those in the area of person perception have discussed in terms of the individual's cognitive system or theory of personality.[37] It is also similar to what has been referred to as the individual's "cognitive map" of his world.[38] In many respects, it is also comparable to what Bruner has referred to in his discussion of the individual's development of models and strategies for dealing effectively with his environment.[39]

When the unit we deal with his not the individual, but the group, organization, or society, we may speak of the norms, the values, and the ideology of the collectivity as being parallel to the individual's world view, model, or strategy. In point of fact, much of the individual's own model is a socially shared model of expectations, commonly treated under the rubric of "norms."

4. We next assume that an internally consistent or reliable model is more useful in the coordination of interactions than an unreliable model. That is, a set of expectations which is internally consistent provides the individual and the collectivity with potentially nonconflicting organizations of the social environment and thus provides relatively nonconflicting guidelines for action and interaction.

It also seems plausible to maintain that not only is an internally consistent set of expectations useful, but also, a valid set is more useful to the individual and the collectivity than an invalid set. By validity, we refer to the match or fit between expectation and input. A model or set of expectations which fits or matches the input from the environment within a tolerated range of error permits better coping with the environment, and thus, better coordination of action and interaction.[40]

---

[37] Leonard Berkowitz, "The Judgmental Process in Personality Functioning," *Psychological Review*, 67 (March, 1960), pp. 130–142; Jerome Bruner, David Shapiro and Renato Tagiuri, "The Meaning of Traits in Isolation and in Combination," in Renato Tagiuri and Luigi Petrullo, editors, *Person Perception and Interpersonal Behavior*, Stanford, Calif.: Stanford University Press, 1958; and Edward E. Jones and John W. Thibaut, "Interaction Goals as Bases of Inference in Interpersonal Perception," in Renato Tagiuri and Luigi Petrullo, editors, *Person Perception and Interpersonal Behavior*, Stanford, Calif.: Stanford University Press, 1958.

[38] Edward C. Tolman, "Cognitive Maps in Rats and Men," from, *Collected Papers in Psychology*, Berkeley: University of California Press, 1951.

[39] Jerome S. Bruner, "The Cognitive Consequences of Early Sensory Deprivation," in Philip Solomon, Philip E. Kubzansky, P. Herbert Leiderman, Jack H. Mendelson, Richard Trumbull, and Donald Wexler, editors, *Sensory Deprivation*, Cambridge: Harvard University Press, 1961.

[40] We further suggest that there are individual differences not only with respect to expectations, but also with respect to tolerance of error or mismatch. To use the language of statistics, persons may be seen to vary in their tolerance of the discrepancy between the expected and the observed occurrence of an event. Some persons may find satisfaction with a p-value (probability that one would be incorrect in stating that there is no difference between what was expected and what was observed) of .50 or higher, while others may demand p-values approaching the .05 level. Additionally, it seems plausible to maintain that these p-values not only differ across persons, but within a given person across situations. For example, in a situation in which knowledge about the other's behavior is particularly important (such as for one's own survival), a p-value of .001 or less may be seen as necessary; whereas, in other less important situations, the same individual may demand a less stringent level of significance.

The material in psychology which deals with tolerance of ambiguity and which relates this

(See Festinger's treatment of a similar point in the 1954 Nebraska Symposium on Motivation.)

Based on the assumed necessity for a reliable and a valid model of the environment for the coordination of interaction, we postulate the existence of tendencies towards the achievement and maintenance of both an internally consistent and an externally valid set of expectations. We refer to the preceding as the *principle of expectancy congruence*. Because we are speaking of a consistency among expectations as well as between expectation and environmental input, this principle refers to these two distinguishable types of congruence.

Some Important Aspects
of the Principle
of Expectancy Congruence

1. One aspect of this principle is comparable to the concern of the various psychological theories of cognitive consistency which we previously discussed.

2. Another aspect, and one which is of greater immediate concern in this article, suggests that individual tendencies towards expectancy congruence give rise to socially communicated, interpersonal pressures for one's self and others to present pictures of themselves which are congruent with what

is expected. When others behave in a manner which is congruent with our expectations for them, we are better able to coordinate our actions and interactions with them, i.e., our model provides an accurate picture of the social environment.

Furthermore, O's deviation from expectation is a condition which is particularly painful to P, as he can no longer so easily coordinate his and O's actions. Deviation of any kind (e.g., disagreement in opinion, belief, or attitude) does not necessarily give rise to these pressures, but rather, only *unexpected* deviation has this effect. Therefore, the fact that two friends disagree in opinion would not in and of itself produce pressures toward agreement as some theories would suggest.[41] In fact, there may be no pressures towards agreement, but instead pressures towards maintaining disagreement if this state is congruent with what each expects, e.g., with the underlying expectation. That one may empirically find pressures towards opinion agreement between two friends suggests that this is the expected state. Where agreement is not found, however, this may be as balanced, symmetric, and felicitous a state as a state of agreement, if it conforms to expectation. What has been referred to as "an agreement to disagree" basically reflects this underlying expectation to which we are referring.

3. In an analogous manner, deviation of a group member from the group's opinion on an issue will produce pressures towards uniformity of opinion,[42] only when this deviation is also a deviation

---

tolerance to certain personality traits or cognitive styles is of obvious relevance in this context. Cf. for example, Jack Block and Jeanne Block, "An Interpersonal Experiment on Reactions to Authority, *Human Relations*, 5 (January, 1952), pp. 91–98; Else Frenkel-Brunswik, "A Study of Prejudice in Children," *Human Relations*, 1 (July, 1948), pp. 295–306; and Abraham H. Maslow, "The Authoritarian Character Structure," *Journal of Social Psychology*, 18 (November, 1943), pp. 401–411.

[41] Cartwright and Harary, *op. cit.*; Heider, *op. cit.*; and Newcomb, *op. cit.*

[42] Stanley Schachter, "Deviation, Rejection, and Communication," *Journal of Abnormal and Social Psychology*, 46 (September, 1951), pp. 190–207.

from expectation for that particular group member. Implied in this model therefore is the possibility of certain group members' holding opinions discrepant from other group members but under no pressure to change, because this state is congruent with expectations for those members. Note the difference between this derivation and that of the Festinger-Schachter model,[43] which suggests that pressures operate towards uniformity of opinion as a function of the increasing discrepancy of a member's opinion from the group's opinion. We are suggesting that it is not necessarily a uniformity of opinion that is sought and towards which pressures are directed, but rather, a conformity to expectation. Therefore, homogeneity of opinion is not necessarily the desired end state; congruence with expectation is. Where the underlying expectation or group norm maintains that all group members without exception should have the same opinion, then opinion deviation is an instance of deviation from expectation, and pressures towards expectancy congruence are brought to bear on group members.

4. There is one further aspect of this model which must be discussed before examining the relationship between it and the earlier research and theory on the variable of status congruence. Assuming that each individual potentially is the locus of a multiplicity of expectations for his behavior, some of which may be incongruent with one another, we can examine the consequences of this condition within the context of the principle of expectancy congruence. One of the first and most obvious consequences involves the

individual's own efforts to achieve and maintain a congruence among these various expectations for his behavior. These efforts would direct our attention to the aspect of role theory which is discussed under the title of role conflict. This presents an instance of an individual under conflicting expectations. We shall not deal with this consequence, but rather shall examine the consequences of this state for others with whom P interacts.

According to the expectancy congruence principle, P will be the recipient of socially communicated pressures from various O's to achieve and maintain a congruence among the expectations for his behavior. To the extent that P presents multiple faces to these others (because he is subject to multiple expectations), they too will be in an undesirable situation and will seek to change it towards a picture of P which is congruent, e.g. which is uni-faced rather than multi-faced. Therefore, P will be under pressures from others to present a picture of himself which is consistent.[44] He finds himself in a situation which is *doubly* unpleasant. In the first place, multiple, incongruent expectations may make it difficult for him to maintain a consistent picture of himself; and in the second place,

---

[43] Festinger, *op. cit.*, 1950, 1954; and Schachter, *op. cit.*

[44] We do not intend to ignore the possibility that O may achieve congruence by changing his own set of expectations rather than by applying pressures to P. We recognize this as a distinct possibility, but wish to pursue the consequences of the interpersonal approach in this article. We would suggest that the pressures of which we speak are nearly always communicated in varying degrees of obviousness in all interpersonal situations, e.g., from a lifted eyebrow, to a subtle glance, to a spoken word. And, we would add, this occurs most often prior to P's changing his own expectations about O.

multiple, incongruent expectations may make it difficult for others to interact with him and to coordinate their behavior with his.

An example presented to the author by a student in an interviewing course may make the above problem clearer. This student was a nurse who had two major aspects to her role. One aspect dictated that she be a strict supervisor of a group of nursing trainees. The second aspect, on the other hand, dictated that she be a warm, compassionate counsellor, helping the trainees handle any particularly difficult interpersonal problems they faced. She recognized a problem in relating to the trainees, as she would not easily co ordinate the different, incongruent expectations demanded as aspects of this nurse-role. We would further suggest that this situation of multiple, disparate expectations is *equally* a problem for all those trainees interacting with her. Each time they confront her they must ask themselves, "Which hat is she wearing?" "Is she the strict supervisor with punitive powers; or is she the warm, compassionate, understanding counsellor?" Until this question is answered by them, they are unable to relate to her and to coordinate their actions with hers. Thus the multiple, incongruent expectations are a problem for all participants in the interaction situation, and, as we have suggested, lead to pressures on the part of both interactants to achieve and maintain a state in which the expectations centering about P are congruent with one another: a state of expectancy congruence.

Let us simplify the preceding and continue to refer to a person in a situation of multiple, incongruent expectations as a multi-faced person (note the colloquial use of "two-faced" in this context) and

then examine this approach a bit further. Assuming, as we have done, that a multi-faced person is undesirable to himself personally and to those with whom he interacts, what happens in those groups and organizations in which a certain degree of "multi-facedness" is required? In other words, some key persons in a group or organization may have as part of their roles the necessary characteristic of being multi-faced. Thus, for example, the bureaucrat may be forced to show one face to his fellow workers and another face to his clients or to his family. The question then becomes one of investigating the means whereby such key personnel are given supports by their group or organization that enable them and others to continue functioning in this manner. An organization may have formal and informal rules that serve to insulate the key man from encountering those persons who may see his many faces; and similarly, there may be rules that serve to limit the nature of the contact between those various persons. Thus, formal lines of communication and stresses towards impersonal relationships within some groups and organizations may be most helpful in this respect.

INTERPERSONAL PRESSURES TOWARDS STATUS CONGRUENCE

We are now in a position to conclude our presentation by reexamining the research and theory on the variable of status congruence using the model just discussed.

The major findings involving the variable of status congruence suggest that incongruence in status ranks is an undesirable state as it leads to frustration and a desire for change. It was left relatively unexplained as to why this should be and why tendencies towards status equilibration, crystallization, or congruence should exist. According to the expectancy congruence model, however, an explanation is readily available. Both P and O find incongruence undesirable and frustrating in that it hinders their necessary coordination of interaction. With incongruence, the world is unorganized and difficult to cope with; thus both P and O seek to achieve and maintain a congruence of status positions, i.e., a congruence of expectations. Placing one's self and others into status positions is one means of ordering the social environment to facilitate coordinated interaction. Therefore, both intrapersonal and interpersonal effort is directed towards a congruence of expectations, a condition which is found with a congruent status structure.

Another aspect of the status congruence research and theory suggests that groups having a high degree of status incongruence are characterized by lack of mutual trust, reduced friendliness, and at times, by reduced productivity. From the model which we have suggested, each of these findings can be easily explained.

As we have seen, both P and O find congruence of expectation a desirable state and are subject to pressures to attain this state. To the extent that change towards congruence is impaired or impossible— that is, to the extent that an individual cannot change his positions within a given ranking system towards congruence with his other rank positions, or, to the extent that the group cannot develop a congruent status structure for its members—there will be dissastifaction and continued frustration. The Adams finding reporting that

groups high in status congruence showed a greater degree of mutual trust, greater friendship, and greater intimacy than groups low in status congruence is a reflection of this state of affairs. The multifaced individual (the status or expectancy incongruent individual) quite obviously is the kind of person that one would find difficult to trust, be friendly, and intimate with. And, by extension, it is not surprising that a group having a large number of such persons (a group low in status congruence) should be characterized as Adams has done.

It is now only one step further to explain the reduction in productivity that occurs within low congruent groups. Given the inconsistency in expectations for the other's behavior, this reduction may stem very simply from each individual's inability easily to coordinate his behavior with the behavior of others of his group. Or, this reduction may stem from the group's lack of cohesiveness, increase in tension, and increased concern with group maintenance rather than task problems. Such a group may expend much of its effort on achieving a congruence or a consistency of expectations, or working to defend against the apparent inconsistencies which exist, and thus have little energy remaining to devote to the task. Their "hidden agenda" of congruence-seeking and incongruence-defending, therefore, may readily serve to reduce their productive efficiency.

To summarize, we have suggested that the conditions necessary for the continuation of the social order, which are also the conditions necessary for the continuation of the individual who is at all points dependent on that social order, include at minimum an anticipatory knowledge of the behavior which may be expected of the other participants in a given interaction situation. The organization of this anticipatory knowledge into a model of expectations about the social and physical environment, and the demands for an internally consistent and an externally valid model provide the basic framework for deriving predictions about individual and group behavior, and for explaining the already existing theory and research on the variable of status congruence.

Coordinating status position with expectation and status congruence with expectancy congruence permits one to discuss status equilibration or status congruence tendencies within individuals and within social structures in terms of the more general principle of expectancy congruence. The effects of low status congruence for the individual as well as for the group—e.g., dissatisfaction, lowered productivity, lowered cohesiveness—become a function of the problems involved in coordinating one's behavior with the behavior of others in a situation which is characterized by multiple and conflicting expectations for one's and the other's behavior.

STATUS CONGRUENCE AND EXPECTATIONS*

Arlene C. Brandon

When persons are ranked on status dimensions such as income, education, occupation and ethnic origin the results may either be a similarity of ranks across dimensions (status congruence) or a dissimiliarity of ranks (status incongruence). Status congruence as a basic component of social certitude[1] contributes to the development of stable expectation for behavior—a prerequisite for smooth interpersonal interaction. Status incongruence, on the other hand, prevents the attainment of social certitude by introducing conflicting expectations into the situation, thereby decreasing the ease with which interpersonal harmony may be reached.

A number of studies have demonstrated that status incongruence is detrimental to smooth interaction. Thus, in comparison to congruent individuals, incongruent individuals desire a change in the social order and vote more liberally,[2] withdraw

* Arlene C. Brandon, "Status Congruence and Expectations," *Sociometry*, 28 (1965), 272–87. Reprinted by permission of the American Sociological Association.

[1] George C. Homans, *Social Behavior, its Elementary Forms*, New York: Harcourt, Brace and World, Inc., 1961.

[2] Gerhard E. Lenski, "Status Crystallization: A Non-Vertical Dimension of Social Status," *American Sociological Review*, 19 (August, 1954), pp. 405–13.

from social situations,[3] and tend to have more psychosomatic symptoms;[4] while members of incongruent groups are less efficient[5] and feel less attracted to the other group members than do members of congruent groups.[6]

These studies, which utilized Lenski's[7] pioneering but rather simple model, defined incongruence as any discrepancy of ranks across dimensions without clearly stating whether the dimensions were conceptualized as independent or as linked to each other. Because this statement is absent in all of the studies one is led to believe that the dimensions were assumed to be unrelated and that incongruence could then be defined simply as a dissimilarity of ranks regardless of the dimensions used. Such a model, which says in effect, the greater the incongruence the greater the difficulty in interaction, is not adequate for dealing with a number of questions, for example, will incongruence on any one set of dimensions have the same effect on some dependent variable as incongruence on another set of dimen-

sions? Is there a range of incongruence such that difficulty exists only outside that range? Is congruence at a low level psychologically as rewarding as congruence at a high level? Are there situations in which incongruence might be pleasurable and sought?

This paper is not directly aimed at these particular questions; its intent, rather, is to demonstrate that by clarifying the concept of status congruence these questions and others may be handled more fruitfully in the future than they can be now. The clarification in this paper will be to dissect out of status congruence the effect of expectations which link the dimensions to each other, and then to demonstrate that the predictive usefulness of status congruence may be increased if these expectations are taken into consideration.

Sampson's[8] theoretical article was devoted to just this question of expectation. He suggested that instead of defining incongruence as any rank pattern that is not completely consistent across dimensions, as the Lenski model does, one must first determine whether such consistency is expected by the persons involved. If consistency is not expected then a divergence from consistency should not be defined as incongruent because social certitude has not been abused. If, on the other hand, consistency is expected, but does not exist then social certitude stands threatened because of the introduction of contradictory expectations for behavior. As an example of Sampson's clarification of the Lenski model let us assume that dimensions x, y, and z have been used;

---

[3] Gerhard E. Lenski, "Social Participation and Status Crystalization," *American Sociological Review*, 21 (August, 1956), pp. 458–64.

[4] Elton F. Jackson, "Status Consistency and Symptoms of Stress," *American Sociological Review*, 27 (August, 1962), pp. 469–80.

[5] Stuart Adams, "Status Congruency as a Variable in Small Group Performance," *Social Forces*, 32 (October, 1953), pp. 16–22.

[6] Ralph V. Exline and Robert C. Ziller, "Status Congruence and Interpersonal Conflict in Decision-Making Groups," *Human Relations*, 12 (April, 1959), 147–62. Still other dependent variables have been used by A. Zaleznik, C. R. Christensen and F. J. Roethlisberger, *The Motivation, Productivity and Satisfaction of Workers*, Boston: Harvard University, 1958.

[7] Lenski, *op. cit.*

[8] Edward E. Sampson, "Status Congruence and Cognitive Consistency," *Sociometry*, 26 (June, 1963), pp. 146–62.

then according to the Lenski model, a person ranking 1, 1, and 4 respectively would be as incongruent as another person ranking 1, 4, and 1. Sampson, however, would suggest that there might be a strong expectation by the persons involved linking dimensions x and y to each other, and a weaker expectation linking either to z; therefore, no statement about the existence of incongruence could be made until these expectations were clarified. If it turns out that these particular expectations existed (x and y: neither to z) then the ranks 1, 1, and 4 are a congruent set of ranks and 1, 4, 1 are not. Thus the two models would state different predictions: Lenski, ignoring the implicit expectations between dimensions, would expect the same results from either set of ranks; while Sampson, utilizing expectation as a basis for the definition of incongruence, would expect different results from the two sets of ranks.

If the inclusion of expectation is a refinement over the earlier model of incongruence, then an experiment pitting one model against the other should lead to differences in predictive accuracy. A fair test of the two models would be to predict to the same kind of dependent variables as have been previously studied in a similar kind of situation. Thus, a laboratory experiment as previously used by Exline and Ziller[9] has been designed and the predictions are to such variables as enjoyment of the group experience, and other satisfaction variables which have been measured in the past. For convenience these positive kinds of experiences will be referred to as "positive affect" and will include all of the "good" things that go

on in a group. The opposite, more negative aspects will be referred to as "negative affect." Hypotheses will be stated such that "high score" refers to an expression of positive affect while "low score" refers to a more negative expression.

METHOD

Three dimensions were chosen such that the first and second, and first and third, were linked by a relatively strong expectation of positive correlation, while a weaker expectation linked the second and third dimension. These dimensions were, personal status, job difficulty, and leadership position. It was assumed (a validation of this assumption will be discussed in a later section) that job and status were linked by an expectation of positive correlation; and that status and leadership position were similarly linked; while job and leadership were assumed to be linked less strongly than either of the other two. Three groups were arranged so that each person was ranked on each dimension. Five possible patterns of rankings (called conditions) were designed and six groups included under each condition.

Design of the Experiment

Given three individuals, each ranked on three dimensions, one may derive a variety of rank matrices. In this experiment, where two sets of dimensions are linked by strong expectation of positive correlation (personal status and job responsibility; personal status and leadership position), five possible matrices exist. Each individual may show: (1) consistent ranks across all three dimensions (Completely Consistent), (2) inconsistent ranks across all dimensions (No Consistency), (3) consistent ranks only on the two dimensions linked by an expectation of positive correlation: Job and Personal Status (Expected Consistency), (4) consistent ranks only on

---

[9] Exline and Ziller, *op. cit.*

Table 1

FIVE EXPERIMENTAL CONDITIONS BASED ON THREE STATUS DIMENSIONS

Experimental Condition	Personal Status	Job	Leadership Position
1. Completely Consistent (CC)	Older male (1) Younger male (2) Female (3)	Cutter (1) Draftsman (2) Folder (3)	Group representative (1) Understudy (2) No position (3)
2. No Consistency (NC)	Older male (1) Younger male (2) Female (3)	Folder (3) Cutter (1) Draftsman (2)	Understudy (2) No position (3) Group representative (1)
3. Expected Consistency (3EC)	Older male (1) Younger male (2) Female (3)	Cutter (1) Draftsman (2) Folder (3)	No position (3) Group representative (1) Understudy (2)
4. Expected Consistency (4EC)	Older male (1) Younger male (2) Female (3)	Folder (3) Cutter (1) Draftsman (2)	Group representative (1) Understudy (2) No position (3)
5. Unexpected Consistency (UC)	Older male (1) Younger male (2) Female (3)	Folder (3) Cutter (1) Draftsman (2)	No position (3) Group representative (1) Understudy (2)

NOTE: The numbers in parentheses indicate the rank value of that position.

the two dimensions linked by an expectation of positive correlation: Personal Status and Leadership Position (Expected Consistency) and (5) consistent ranks on those two dimensions linked only weakly by an expectation (Unexpected Consistency). Table 1 shows the actual composition of each condition.

Briefly, the Lenski model will predict a positive monotonic relationship between consistency and congruent affect, while Sampson's Expectancy Theory[10] will predict that this relationship holds only if consistency is in line with expectation. The following experimental hypotheses can thus be generated:

Experimental Condition	Expectancy Congrunce	Lenski Model
1. Completely Consistent (CC)	CC will score as well as both EC conditions	CC will score higher than any other condition
2. No Consistency (NC)	NC will score as low as UC	NC will be the lowest scoring condition
3. Expected Consistency 3 (3EC)	3EC will score equal to CC and 4EC, and higher than NC and UC	3EC will score equal to 4EC and UC and lower than CC
4. Expected Consistency 4 (4EC)	4EC will score equal to CC and 3EC, and higher than NC and UC	4EC will score equal to 3EC and UC and lower than CC
5. Unexpected Consistency (UC)	UC will score equal to NC and lower than CC or either EC	UC will score equal to both EC and lower than CC

---

[10] Sampson, *op. cit.*

Manipulation of Status Dimensions

Personal Status

Highest rank assigned to male graduate student; second rank assigned to male undergraduate student; third rank assigned to female undergraduate. Personal status was controlled through selection rather than experimental manipulation.[11] Subjects were hired through the University Placement Center and paid the usual hourly rate. Applicants were screened by the Center to meet the age, sex and year in school requirement of the experiment. Each group consisted of two males, differing from each other by at least two years in school and one in age or vice versa, and a female closer in age and year in school to the younger male than to the graduate male. The median age for the graduate student male was 23 with a range from 20 to 36; the median for the undergraduate male was 19 with a range from 17 to 26 and the median for the female was 20 with a range from 17 to 24.[12]

Leadership Position

Rank 1 assigned to the group representative; rank 2 to the understudy to the

group representative; rank 3 assigned to the person who does not receive a position on this dimension. Basically, the goal of the leadership manipulation was to rank group members on leadership relative to each other. The technique for establishing this ranking consisted of two main steps.

1. Measurement of leadership position: The actual measurement was purportedly based on a five minute story written about TAT cards # 5, 10, and 15, which were presented to the subject shortly after they entered the experimental room. At the end of this time, an assistant entered the room and collected the material; the experimenter explained that the stories would be scored and the results presented shortly.

2. Criteria for choosing the leader: The group members had been told at the Placement Center and reminded again during the experiment that future work might be available for them if they did well in their group tasks. Furthermore, it was explained that many groups would be needed for this future work which would consist of testing and interviewing subjects individually and that a liaison officer between the subject group and the experimenter would be needed to handle the administrative duties. The liaison person could be employed only if his group scored well enough on the task to qualify for future work. The person chosen must be popular, easygoing, and responsible, and the experimenter emphasized the need for an individual who could get along well with others over any other criteria. Since, in his administrative duties, the liaison would have increased responsibility over the other subjects who were simply being tested and interviewed, he would be paid more than those who were being tested. It was made clear that this pay difference would exist only in the proposed future sessions, not in the

---

[11] It has been suggested that the Personal Status dimension could have been manipulated by using two confederates and only one experimental subject. Although such a procedure would have been "cleaner," data would have been available from only one person instead of the entire group. In order to gain group data it was decided to risk some noise in the manipulation of this dimension.

[12] Further details are available in, Arlene C. Brandon, "The Relevance of Expectation as an Underlying Factor in Status Congruence," unpublished Ph.D. dissertation, University of California, Berkeley, 1964.

present experiment. Subjects were told that they could not volunteer for the job but that the assignment would be based on the analysis of the stories written to the TAT cards. The person with a purportedly greater leadership position was assigned the title of group representative, the second most competent person the title of understudy, and the least competent person was ignored.

Job Difficulty

Highest rank assigned to the Cutter; second rank assigned to the Draftsman; third rank to the Folder. Three jobs differing in difficulty and responsibility were assigned to the group members. In order to insure that each individual played an equal part in the fate of the group a work context was established. The three group members were told to imagine themselves as factory workers producing high quality items. Each item that met the experimenter's standards would be purchased for $100.[13] A completed item consisted of three parts: A cut, drawn, and folded part. The written standards given to the group members called for each item to be as perfect as possible e.g., all drawn lines were to be absolutely straight, all cut edges to be completely smooth. If, however, items were submitted for inspection which did not meet the experimenter's standards the group would be fined $150 for each faulty item. Since each group possessed enough raw materials for only 18 items the maximum score was 1800, and it was possible for a group to obtain a positive, negative, or zero score.

It was possible, however, for the group to prevent penalties by eliminating faulty items immediately upon production instead of presenting them for inspection. Upon doing so, they would naturally reduce their total possible maximum score, since they were not allowed any more raw material than the original 18. The higher their final score, that is, the more the items bought by the experimenter, the more likely they were to receive further employment, for only those groups who scored above the median score for all groups would be eligible for later employment. Subjects were not told the numerical value of the median score though they were told that no group ever made 18 items and it was suggested that the median might even be as low as 2. Each job was then demonstrated and described by the experimenter.

The Cutter's job was to cut out a pattern, six layers thick, with a large paper cutter; any slip with the paper cutter would ruin six pieces at one time. The Draftsman's job was to draw three three-inch squares at one time using carbon paper and ruler. The Folder's job was to fold one piece of paper at a time into quarters.[14] Clearly each job differed in responsibility since each individual could ruin different amounts of materials with one wrong move. It was emphasized that if the Folder folded 18 items but the Cutter cut none, the group had nothing to sell.

---

[13] Sums as large as $100 never changed hands nor did the subjects believe such an exchange would occur, $100 being simply equivalent to 100 points. The monetary designation was used only because it made sense within the factory framework.

[14] For details of the materials used and instructions given see Brandon, *op. cit.*

General Procedure

As soon as the subjects entered the experimental room the TAT cards were presented, the stories written and then taken out of the room by the experimenter's assistant. Subjects were asked their name, age, year in school, and major (manipulation of personal status dimension), and told about the possibility of future work and the necessity for choosing a leader to be called the group representative. The first questionnaire was then distributed, the purpose of this questionnaire being to check on the manipulation of some of the independent variables, e.g., desirability of group representative's job, perceived linkage between status and job, and also perceived linkage between status and leadership potential. While the subjects were answering this questionnaire the assistant returned to the experimenter the card which supposedly contained the subject's ranking on the leadership dimension. These rankings were read to the group upon completion of the questionnaire (manipulation of leadership position).

The jobs were described and demonstrated and assigned to each group member (manipulation of job responsibility). Subjects were allowed to question the experimenter and all but the Folder permitted some practice. At the completion of the practice period, the practice items were discarded and the raw material distributed: the Cutter received three packs of six papers each, the Draftsman six packs of three papers each, and the Folder 18 pieces of paper. Also on the table were the paper cutter, masking tape, ruler, T-square and pencils.

Before the start of the work session sub-jects were reminded that they must decide which pieces they wished to discard and which to submit for inspection, and that the decision was to be made by the entire group. Subjects were given three work periods of ten minutes, each separated by three three-minute rest periods. Within the work periods they were allowed to work, talk, and do anything except change jobs or do another person's job; while in the rest periods they were to stop work. It was emphasized that discussion was allowed in both the rest and work periods.

The experimenter left the room during the thirty-three minute work period. Upon her return she did not examine the group's products but immediately distributed the second questionnaire designed to measure the dependent variables.[15] At the completion of the questionnaire the subjects were interviewed about their perception of the purpose of the experiment, which was then explained in detail.

VALIDATION OF INDEPENDENT VARIABLES

This section will present data relevant to the assumed ordering within each of the three dimensions and to the expectations linking the dimensions to each other.

Validation of Personal Status Variable

The question concerning this dimension is whether subjects use age, sex, and year

---

[15] Other measures taken were observations of the group interaction by observers and a content analysis of the tape recordings of the work sessions. Due to poor reliability and external events which made it necessary to use

in school as criteria for differentiating personal status. The experimental subjects themselves could not be questioned on this matter because such questions might bring these variables into such sharp focus that they would become aware of their status differences and relate these to the experimental procedure. Therefore, an independent sample of twenty-eight undergraduate non-psychology majors were given the following descriptions presented in this order: 23 year old male, senior; 20 year old male, junior; 20 year old female, sophomore. The subjects were asked to rank these hypothetical subject persons on the amount of "status" they possessed in the subject's eyes and in the eyes of people in general. The older male received the rank of one, seventy-five per cent of the time ($\chi^2 = 16.89$, p $<$ .001),[16] the younger male received the rank of two, seventy-eight per cent of the time ($\chi^2 = 22.65$, p $<$ .001) and the female received the rank of three, eighty-nine per cent of the time ($\chi^2 = 33.69$, p $<$ .001). Thus, ample evidence exists to validate the manipulation of this dimension.

Validation of Job Responsibility and Difficulty

At the conclusion of the work session the experimental subjects were asked to

rank the jobs in terms of responsibility. Cutter was ranked as the most responsible job by ninety-seven per cent of the subjects; Draftsman as second most responsible by ninety-two per cent; and Folder as least responsible by ninety-four per cent —giving strong evidence that the manipulation of job responsibility was in the intended direction.

Validation of Leadership Position

It seemed likely that subjects would rather be ranked high in leadership potential than low; therefore, the subjects should prefer the job of group representative to any other position. On the first questionnaire, before the group representative was announced and before the jobs were described, the following questions were asked: "How much do you want to be group representative? How much do you want to be understudy? How much do you want no job at all?" Answers were on a seven point scale; the score of *seven* indicated an interest in the job and the score of *one* indicated no interest.

Analyses revealed that the group representative was seen as a significantly more desirable job than the job of understudy (t $=$ 2.81, p $<$ .01) and than no job at all (t $=$ 2.75, p $<$ .01). The job of understudy was not seen as more desirable than no position at all. These results reveal only that the job of group representative can be differentiated from the other two positions, thus although a hierarchy exists on this dimension it is not

---

data from only one observer, neither of these measures differentiated conditions. Further details are available in Brandon, *op. cit.*

[16] It was assumed in calculating χ^2 that if Personal Status were unrelated to Job Difficulty or Leadership Position, that when asked to rank persons on these dimensions the choices would be made at random; each person would be expected to receive approximately one third of

the choices. The significant χ^2 calculated for each person (2 d.f., corrected for continuity) reveal that the choices were not dictated by chance alone.

as sharp a hierarchy as on the other two dimensions.

Validation of Expectations Linking Dimensions to Each Other

The following questions were asked on the first questionnaire before the subjects knew the nature of the jobs and before the assignment of group representative was announced.

"Who should have the most difficult job in the group? Who should have the easiest job in the group? Who should be the group representative?" When presented with these questions the subjects only knew each other's name, age, year in school, and major field of study. Most subjects violently objected to answering such questions, for they rightly claimed insufficient information. Although the subjects claimed that they were just guessing, analyses show that their answers were not random. The older male was perceived as being most appropriate for the most difficult job in the group ($\chi^2 = 21.7$, $p < .001$) and the female as most appropriate for the easiest job ($\chi^2 = 12.17$, $p < .01$). These results demonstrate that personal status and job responsibility are linked by an expectation of positive correlation, as hypothesized. The older male was also perceived to be most appropriate for the job of group representative ($\chi^2 = 6.03$, $p < .05$), thus linking personal status with leadership position.

To check whether or not the dimensions of Job and Leadership were associated less frequently than either the dimensions of Job and Status or Status and Leadership, fifteen undergraduate non-psychology majors, nonexperimental subjects who had not previously been questioned were asked: "What percentage of time do you think Job and Leadership are associated? Job and Status? Leadership and Status?" The terms were roughly defined and subjects were told to use the common sense notion of the terms and to rank the associations as they would be ranked by the population at large.

The percentage figures given by the subjects were transformed into rankings: the highest percentage given the rank of 1 and the lowest given the rank of 3. If the association between Job and Leadership were ranked third—that is, if these two attributes were seen by the subjects as being less often associated than the other two combinations—the result was scored as tending to confirm the assumption. If the Job and Leadership association received some other rank, the result was scored as tending to disconfirm the assumption. Eleven out of fifteen persons assigned the lowest percentage of association to the combination of Job and Leadership ($p < .05$).

In summary, evidence has been presented which establishes the psychological significance of the variables from which congruent and incongruent combinations were developed: personal status, job responsibility, and leadership position. There was also a widely shared expectation among the subjects that personal status and job responsibility should go together and a somewhat less prevalent, though still modal, expectation that leadership and personal status should go together. From the judgments of the auxiliary sample it may be assumed that the expectation of a positive association between leadership and job responsibility was less shared within the experimental groups than were the other two expectations.

Results

All self report data were gathered from the second questionnaire completed by the subjects at the end of the work session. All questions were answered on a seven point scale and scored so that *seven* indicated high positive affect and low negative affect while *one* indicated low positive affect and high negative affect.[17]

The first question used to measure attitude towards the group experience was a ten-item semantic differential in which adjectives (such as happy-sad; or angry-calm) were used to describe subjects' feelings during the work period. Table 2 reveals that the subjects in the congruent condition 4EC (Expected Consistency) experienced significantly more positive affect than subjects in the NC (No Consistency) condition and slightly more than subjects in UC (Unexpected Consistency) condition. The other conditions do not differ from each other. The relative ordering of conditions should be noted here for a similar pattern of results will emerge over other measures. The pattern shows that both EC conditions, which contain rankings in line with expectation, form a high scoring cluster while conditions NC and UC, neither of which contain rankings in line with expectation, form a low scoring cluster. Condition CC (Completely Consistent), which is part of the high scoring cluster on this particular measure, will be seen to be unstable in its relative position across other measures (the Completely Consistent condition will be discussed in a later section).

---

[17] The author would like to express her thanks to Sheldon Berkowitz and Wayne Sailor, who were invaluable aids in the analysis of the data.

Two questions were used to measure felt and perceived tension and hostility in the group. When asked "How much tension was there in the group?" subjects in the No Consistency (NC) condition and Unexpected Consistency condition (UC) reported more tension than subjects in the Expected Consistency (EC) conditions, with NC differing significantly from both EC conditions at the .02 level or less, and condition UC differing from 3EC but only at the .07 level. The Completely Consistent condition scores between these two clusters but does not differ significantly from either.

When asked, "How much tension or hostility did you feel?" a similar pattern of results occurs; subjects in the NC and UC conditions report experiencing significantly more tension than subjects in both EC conditions (.05 or less); again CC remains between the two clusters but this time differs from 3EC at the .10 level.

Subjects were also asked how pleasant they found the group experience (see Table 2). The answer to this question reveals an even more dramatic pattern. Subjects in NC scored significantly lower (.02 or less) than *every* other condition and even lower than UC, its usual partner on such measures. Again, however, the relative ordering of conditions remains the same.

Interest in Group Productivity

Although actual productivity measures would have been desirable, the nature of the tasks made such measures unfeasible. Since the success of the group depended on each individual's contribution of a certain number of "perfect" items, the greatest challenge was for the Cutter. His task was so difficult that the majority of

Table 2

MEAN SCORES ON GROUP AFFECT (HIGH SCORE=HIGH POSITIVE AFFECT)

Affect Measure	Expected Consistency (4EC)	Expected Consistency (3EC)	Completely Consistent (CC)	Unexpected Consistency (UC)	No Consistency (NC)
		Experimental Conditions			
1. Total semantic differential	49.61[c,d]	45.88	47.00	44.11[d]	43.00[c]
2. How much tension or hostility was there in the group	5.72[b]	5.88[a,d]	5.11	5.05[d]	4.22[a,b]
3. How much tension or hostility did you feel	5.76[a,c]	5.72[a,c]	4.83	4.16[a]	4.55[c]
4. How pleasant was the group atmosphere	5.94[a]	5.72[a]	5.78[a]	5.56[b]	4.33[a,b]
5. How much did you care whether the items were up to standards	5.11	5.72[a]	4.88	5.22[d]	4.11[a,d]

NOTE: Because there were specific hypotheses concerning the dependent variables, "t" test rather than analyses of variance were employed (two-tailed tests). Means sharing a common superscript are significantly different at the following levels: $a = p < .01$; $b = < .02$; $c = < .05$; $d = .07$. The comparison in every case is between a mean with an underlined letter (thus, for example, the means of 5.94 and 5.72 in line 4 are not significantly different; they are compared with the mean of 4.33).

Cutters cut only one packet (6 items) successfully in the thirty-three minute work period. Frequently one or two packets were ruined and discarded before a success was reached. Thus there was virtually no range of productivity for the Cutter; the task was so difficult that individual differences disappeared and all persons did equally well. Similarly, there was no performance range for the Folder; all persons folded eighteen items unless they voluntarily stopped work when it became obvious that the Cutter was not going to produce any items. The Draftsman's productivity was more variable than either of the others; but this variability seemed dependent on the sex of the Draftsman. Females, who were ignorant of the workings of the T square, produced much less and had a more difficult time than did males, who were familiar with the materials.

Since the nature of the tasks made it impossible to measure actual productivity, interest in productivity was measured instead. Subjects were asked, "How much did you care whether items were up to standards and passed inspection?" Answers were on a seven point scale, 7 indicating that the subject cared very much about the items and 1 that he cared very little. Again subjects in both EC conditions scored highest and subjects in conditions NC and UC lowest, while CC scored slightly less than 3EC (see Table 2).

In summary, then, on six measures of attitude toward the group experience a definite pattern of responses emerge. By ranking each condition on each of these

Table 3

RANK ORDER OF FIVE EXPERIMENTAL CONDITIONS ON
FIVE MEASURES OF AFFECT

Affect Measures	Experimental Conditions				
	4EC	3EC	CC	UC	NC
Total semantic differential	1	3	2	4	5
How much tension or hostility did you feel	1	2	3	5	4
How much tension or hostility was there in the group	1	3	2	4	5
How much did you care whether the items were up to standards	3	1	4	2	5
How pleasant was the group atmosphere	1	3	2	4	5
Sum of ranks	7	12	13	19	24

NOTE: Rank 1=high positive affect; Rank 5=low positive affect.

measures, the pattern can be brought into sharp focus. Thus, the condition scoring highest on any one measure (high positive affect) is given the rank of 1, and the condition scoring lowest (low positive affect) the rank of 5. The sum of these ranks reveals two clusters, with the Completely Consistent condition falling between them. Table 3 shows that subjects experiencing the highest amount of positive affect are in the conditions which contain dimensions linked by an expectation of positive correlation (EC) while subjects experiencing the least amount of positive affect are in conditions which contain either no linkage (NC) or unexpected linkage (UC). The results seem to favor the predictions made by Expectancy Theory.

DISCUSSION

The discussion will focus first on the predictions made by the Lenski model and then Expectancy Theory.

The Lenski model of status congruence predicted that on measures of positive affect the five experimental conditions should be ordered as follows: CC > 3EC = 4EC = UC > NC. That this exact order never occurred has been shown in Table 3.

The crucial test of the Lenski model comes in the comparison of condition UC with both conditions 3EC and 4EC. All three conditions contain the same absolute amount of rank consistency, that is, consistency on two out of the three dimensions. Since the pure amount of consistency is equal, the prediction is that all three conditions should score equally well on measures of positive affect, but the data do not support this prediction. It has been demonstrated that both Expected Consistency (EC) conditions scored significantly higher than Unexpected Consistency condition on the total semantic differential, and on measures of felt and perceived tension. Therefore, equal consistency of ranks does not result in equality of positive affect. The comparison of those three conditions suggests that consistency *in line with expectation* as found in the EC conditions, rather than consistency *per se*, increases the subject's reported feelings of positive affect.

Expectancy Theory predicted that the experimental conditions would be ordered as follows: CC = 3EC = 4EC > UC = NC. Except for the Completely Consistent condition, which will be discussed in the next section, this prediction reflects the actual results.

The two EC conditions never scored significantly different from each other although UC scored higher than NC across many measures, this was significant only on perceived pleasantness. Most impressive, however, is the clear dichotomy of the high and low scoring clusters (see Table 3), which leads to the suggestion that status congruence is a more accurate predictor of positive affect within a group if the expectations between dimensions are considered.

Neither the Lenski model nor Expectancy model, however, adequately predicted the location of the Completely Consistent condition (CC). The former predicted that it would score highest on measures of positive affect while the latter predicted that it would score equal to the EC conditions. In point of fact, CC usually scored somewhere between the two clusters, rarely differing significantly from either.

As a *post hoc* explanation for this development, opposing forces preventing CC from clearly falling into either cluster may be hypothesized. The first force which moves CC towards the high scoring cluster of congruent conditions is the linkage of expected dimensions; this is "distributive justice."[18] The second force that moves CC towards the lower end of the scoring continuum is "distributive jealousy."[19]

Distributive justice[20] exists when costs and rewards are distributed in a manner called "fair or just" by the persons involved. Thus fairness and justice exist when expectations are confirmed and costs and rewards are as they "should be." In the experiment reported here, the subjects considered it fair and just that the older male hold the most responsible job and the female the least responsible job. In some cases, however, no standards of fairness or justice obtained; for example, in this study, leadership was not strongly associated with the job responsibility dimension—it was not *more* fair for the group to associate leadership with one particular rank on the job dimension than any other. When the standards of "fairness" can no longer be used, the concept of distributive justice becomes important. Justice implies that whenever fairness cannot be defined, the costs and rewards which are to be distributed should be distributed equally among all persons. For example, since leadership rank is not expected to be linked with any particular job rank, then leadership should be assigned such that persons who have a low rank on the other dimensions will be compensated by being given more leadership.

Distributive justice has two aspects: first, and most crucial, is that justice be attained; second, and less crucial, although still important, is equality—that those

---

[18] Homans, *op. cit.*

[19] The term distributive jealousy is used to indicate a lack of distributive justice.

[20] Homans, *op. cit.*

Table 4

FORCES TOWARDS GROUP HARMONY IN EACH EXPERIMENTAL CONDITION

Experimental Condition	Existence of Justice (++)	Equitable Distribution of Resources (+)	Total forces towards harmony (Maximum: 3) (Minimum: 0)
Expected Consistency (4EC)	++	+	3
Expected Consistency (3EC)	++	+	3
Completely Consistent (CC)	++	—	2
Unexpected Consistent (UC)	—	+	1
No Consistency (NC)	—	+	1

NOTE: The pluses are taken as an ordinal scale because it has been hypothesized that the existence of justice is a *more* important contributor to group harmony than is the equitable distribution of resources. The distribution of these forces, which very in each experimental condition, has been diagrammed above.

items whose distribution are not dictated by notions of justice be distributed equally. In this study, the two components of distributive justice existed in varying degrees in the conditions. In the Completely Consistent condition, and in both Expected Consistency conditions, justice existed; in No Consistency, both EC and Unexpected Consistency equality existed, for ranks on dimensions were equally distributed among persons. If it is assumed that the attainment of justice is more important to the group than the equitable distribution of resources, the forces on each condition may be diagrammed; the attainment of justice will be indicated by ++ and the equitable distribution of resources by +. These symbols indicate the amount of force towards group harmony. The total score for each condition shown in Table 4 indicates the emergence of two clusters: Conditions 3EC and 4EC on the upper end of the scoring range and conditions UC and NC on the lower end, while CC falls in a central position. This is the same clustering effect previously found when all of the conditions were ranked on measures of positive affect.

In CC the equality aspect of distributive justice was unequivocally ignored, for in this condition, the older male held all the desirable positions and the female held none. The few rewards which could have been shared among group members—for example, the desirable position of high job responsibility or the position of leadership —were not shared but were concentrated on one member. To quote from Homans,[21] "The more to a man's disadvantage the rule of distributive justice fails of realization, the more likely he is to display the emotional behavior we call anger" (p. 75).

It must be remembered that CC does not differ significantly from the other conditions, thus there is no statistical significance to explain. The purpose of this analysis is only to offer a suggestion as to why CC was slightly different from the congruent conditions. Distributive jealousy was probably not a strong or powerful reaction, yet its mere existence made CC less pleasant than either of the other congruent conditions.

---

[21] *Ibid.*

From the analysis of CC, it seems likely that consistency of ranks should not be used when the consistency is not demanded by expectation. If consistency is not expected or if it is immaterial, then its presence may lead to a new development in the group—for example, distributive jealousy which may undermine smooth group interaction.

In general, the results of this study indicate that status incongruence is a more accurate predictor of positive affect within a group if it is defined as a dissimilarity of ranks which is opposed to expectation, rather than being defined as simply any discrepancy from complete consistency Dissimilarity of ranks *per se* is too simple a model of status congruence; and the implicit expectations linking the dimensions to each other must be taken into account before incongruence can be said to exist.

CONSISTENT AND INCONSISTENT STATUS CHARACTERISTICS AND THE DETERMINATION OF POWER AND PRESTIGE ORDERS*

Joseph Berger and M. Hamit Fisek

It has long been known that previously established status characteristics act as important determinants of the emergent power and prestige order in small task-oriented groups (see, for example, Torrance, 1957; Katz, Goldston, and Benjamin, 1958). Previous research specifically directed to this problem has shown that the resultant task behavior of the group members who are differentiated on a single status characteristic or evaluative dimension, external to the group's task, will reflect their relative states of this characteristic: Group members with the highly evaluated state of the differentiating characteristic will exercise greater influence on the task outcome than those with the less highly evaluated state of the characteristic. This has been demonstrated to occur when the differentiating characteristic is of a diffuse nature, such as educational level and military rank, *whether or not* this

* Research for this paper was supported by grants from the National Science Foundation (GS 1170) and the Advanced Research Projects Agency, Department of Defense (DAHC15 68 C 0215). We would particularly like to acknowledge the assistance of Paul Crosbie in the presentation of the results of this study. We would also like to acknowledge the help given us at various stages of this investigation by Bo Anderson, Bernard P. Cohen, M. Zelditch, Jr., Karen Cook, Sandra Costello, Libby Ruch, and Jerry Talley. Reprinted by permission of the American Sociological Association from *Sociometry*, 33, No. 3 (September 1970).

characteristic is initially relevant to the group's task (Moore, 1968; Cohes, Berger, and Zelditch, forthcoming). It has also been demonstrated to occur when the differentiating characteristic is a specific status characteristic instrumental to the group's task (Berger and Conner, 1969).

In explaining these and related results, Berger and Conner (1969) argue that the members of task-oriented groups come to develop through time stable conceptions of the performance capacities of each other. These conceptions, or performance expectations, are beliefs about the relative task abilities of individuals that the members of the group come to hold. Typically these expectations will be differentiated; that is, they will be conceptions of inequalities in the task abilities of the group members. If differentiated, these performance expectations legitimate and determine differences in the power and prestige positions that develop in the group: inequalities in opportunities to perform, in performance rates, in evaluations of members' contributions, and in the relative influence of the different members on the decisions of the group. In this sense the group's ordering of power and prestige positions is said to be a function of a structure of performance expectations its members come to hold. In the situation where the members of a task group are differentiated in terms of a diffuse status characteristic (age, sex, occupation, etc.), such differentiation provides a basis in terms of which these performance expectations are formed. That is, distinctions in task expectations come to coincide with the evaluational distinctions on the status characteristic (Berger, Cohen, and Zelditch, 1966). In the case where the members of a task group are differentiated in terms of a specific status characteristic, task ex-

pectations are provided by the performance conceptions already associated with the characteristic. Thus, through their relation to performance expectations, differentiating status characteristics (diffuse or specific) determine the ordering of power and prestige positions in the task-oriented group.[1]

An obvious extension of this line of research is to the problem of multicharacteristic status differentiation—that is, to the situation in which the members of the task-oriented group are differentiated on two or more status characteristics, each of which is instrumental to their task, and each of which carries information on expected performance capacities. The determination of power and prestige orders appears to be a straightforward matter when the distribution of two or more status characteristics is consistent—that is, when the members of the group possess similarly evaluated states of the characteristics each of which is providing congruent information about an individual's performance capacities. In this case the power and prestige order of the group should be a direct function of the distribution of the states of the characteristics. The relationship between the group's power and prestige order and its differentiating status characteristics appears much less clear, however, when the distribution of these characteristics is inconsistent. This is the situation where at least one of the members of the group possesses dissimilarly evaluated states of the characteristics and

---

[1] For an application of the expectation argument to the situation where the members of the task-oriented group are not initially differentiated in terms of a specific or diffuse social characteristic, see Berger, Conner, and McKeown (1969) and Fisek (1969).

these are providing incongruent or contradictory performance information, e.g., that an individual has "high" performance capacities and at the same time "low" performance capacities with respect to the group's task. Here we may ask how the actors cognitively define such inconsistencies, and what are the consequences of such definitions for their behavior in the group. This is the theoretical issue with which we are concerned. Putting the matter more generally, we may state our problem as follows: Given that the members of a task-oriented group are differentiated on two or more socially valued characteristics instrumental to their task and which are allocated in a consistent or inconsistent manner, how will the members of such groups form performance expectations, and how will these expectations be related to the group's power and prestige order?

Before proceeding with our analysis, it should be noted that our theoretical problem ties in with another line of research that has long been of considerable interest to sociologists, that concerned with status equilibration or congruency (Lenski, 1956; Homans, 1961; Zelditch and Anderson, 1966). Traditionally, however, this research has focused on *diffuse* status characteristics and on the operation of these characteristics in more general settings than those of immediate interest to us. In this connection it should also be noted that Sampson (1963) has presented a theoretical framework for analyzing status congruencies that has many similarities to our own approach.

In the next section a theoretical structure is developed within which our problem is restated, and what appear to be at least two alternative answers are formulated. We then present an experiment designed to discriminate between these alternatives, and then evaluate these theoretical alternatives in the light of our findings.

THEORETICAL CONSIDERATIONS

To facilitate our analysis of this problem we shall conceptualize it in terms of a simplified theoretical structure. Although this theoretical structure is simplified, we believe it contains those elements that are important and relevant to the processes with which we are concerned.

We imagine a group containing two or more actors. However, we view the group from the point of view of one actor, say p. Strictly speaking, the other actors are objects of orientation to p. For purposes of experimental study we confine our attention to two persons, p and o.

P and o are engaged in the solution of some task, which for simplicity we view as having only two outcomes, "success" or "failure." The task may be almost any kind of activity involving a series of contributions or problem solving attempts by one or more of the actors. Moreover, the members of the group are committed to the successful completion of the task, and it is both legitimate and crucial for them to take each other's behavior into account in order to achieve this outcome. In this sense, the group is "task focused," and its members are "collectively oriented" in solving their problem.

We assume that there exist in this situation a number of *specific status characteristics*. A *characteristic*, C, is some aspect or property of an individual that might be used to describe him. For C to be a *status characteristic*, we require that it consist of at least two states which are differentially evaluated in terms of honor, esteem, desirability. For C to be a *specific status characteristic*, specific performance expectations must be associated with its states. These are beliefs about how an individual possessing a given state of C will perform in defined or specified task situations. For example, mathematical ability may function as a specific status characteristic. We distinguish different levels of this characteristic, we associate differential social values to these levels (positive and negative), and we associate beliefs about the different performance capacities of individuals possessing the different states of the characteristic. Again for purposes of simplifying our analysis, we assume that there exist just two such characteristics in our situation, C_1 and C_2. Each characteristic involves two states that are differentially evaluated—one positively and the other negatively—and associated with these states are the beliefs that individuals possessing them also possess, respectively, "high" and "low" performance capacities with respect to a task for which these characteristics are relevant. In the situation of interest to us, we assume that it is given that p and o know that they are differentiated (possess different states) with respect to C_1 and C_2, that these status characteristics are relevant to their task, and that they are of equal weight. Within this framework we can now consider how different distributions of the states of these status characteristics are related to different possible power and prestige orders that might emerge in the group.

The first case to be considered is that involving a consistent distribution of the states of the characteristics. Here the states of the characteristics possessed by each individual have the same or consistent evaluations. That is, all positively evaluated states are possessed by one individual, and all negatively evaluated states are possessed by the second. As already noted, this case would appear to present no new theoretical issues when compared with the situation in which there is a single characteristic (diffuse or specific) which differentiates the member of the group. We assume that given two or more differentiating status characteristics relevant to the group's task, if these characteristics are allocated in a consistent manner, their effect on the group's power and prestige order will be similar to that of a single differentiating characteristic. The actor who possesses the positively evaluated states will hold a higher position on the power and prestige order than the actor who possesses the negatively evaluated states. The first individual will receive more action opportunities, make more performance outputs, be more likely to have these positively evaluated, and exercise more influence than the second individual.

The case where there is an inconsistent distribution of differentiating characteristics is considerably more complex. This is the situation where at least one of the group members, p or o, possesses states of the characteristics that do not have consistent evaluations—for example, p possesses the positively evaluated state of C_1 and the negatively evaluated state of C_2. Here the actor has two bases for forming his performance expectations, and these are providing contradictory information. The information provided by one characteristic is that p has a "high" performance capacity relative to o on this task, while that conveyed by the second is that he has a "low" performance capacity relative to o on the task. We assume that p comes to cope with this problem, and that through the operation of some particular cognitive mechanism he comes to form performance expectations that enable him to effectively interact in the situation. Further, we assume that the cognitive mechanism that operates to determine the formation of performance expectations in this case will also be operative in the situation where the distribution of status characteristics is consistent. Thus in determining which mechanism operates in the case of inconsistent distributions, we are trying to determine more generally how expectations will form in situations in which two or more status characteristics are task-significant.

On theoretical grounds, two alternative modes of cognitively defining the situation seem possible. The first, which we shall call a "balancing" mechanism, is based on some of the general ideas to be found in the literature on cognitive consistency theories (Heider, 1946; Newcomb, 1953). Applying this line of thinking to our problem, we reason that the actor p will tend to cognitively balance his situation so as to form performance expectations for self and other that correspond with a distribution of states of characteristics that is consistent or univalent for each individual. In the case where the distribution of the states of characteristics is such that each actor already possesses consistently or univalently evaluated states, p will form his expectations based on the actual distribution of status characteristics. In the case where the distribution of status characteristics is inconsistent, p is expected to cognitively alter the situation. For example, if p possesses the positively evaluated state of C_1, and the negatively evaluated state of C_2, we might find him using only one of these characteristics as the basis on which he forms his task expectations. The particular manner of bal-

ancing the situation is likely to depend upon the context of the specific situation. However, what is important is that according to this line of reasoning, the actor will form expectations that correspond to a perceived distribution of states that is consistent or univalent for each individual. Consequently, in terms of the conditions of our problem, where only two states are distinguished on C_1 and C_2, different distributions of these characteristics will result in p's forming one of two expectation states for self and other—either "high" or "low." Through the operation of the balancing mechanism, different distributions will be reduced to a unique balanced structure.[2]

The second mode of cognitively defining the situation that we consider is one which we shall refer to as a "combining" mechanism. The ideas involved here are loosely associated with those from information and decision-making theories. According to this mechanism, the actor essentially operates as an information processing system, taking into account all information available to him as regards the relevant status characteristics and the task in the situation. Thus in forming expectations for self and other, p will use the information provided by both characteristics. In a manner which we cannot as yet precisely describe, he will combine the performance information given by each of these characteristics in forming *resultant* expectation states. In the case where p is confronted with a consistent distribution of equally

---

[2] More generally, this argument leads us to expect that the number of different expectation states p can form is limited to the number of differentially evaluated states distinguished on the status characteristics possessed by the members of his group.

weighted social characteristics, the resultant expectations that he forms will simply reflect the "high" and "low" performance conceptions associated with the states of these characteristics. In the case where p is confronted with an inconsistent distribution of these states—say, a group member has "high" performance capacity on C_1 and "low" on C_2—the resultant expectation he will form is for some state lying between "high" and "low": an "average" level state. Thus under this mechanism, the combined expectations that p will form for self and other can assume a large number of different values ranging from "high" to "low" and depending on the particular distribution of the characteristics in the situation.

Since there are no clearcut theoretical grounds to favor one or the other of these cognitive defining mechanisms, we have designed and conducted an experiment to enable us to discriminate between them. The experiment was designed to correspond with the simplified theoretical structure developed in this section.

THE EXPERIMENT

The experimental situation consisted of two phases. In the first phase we created two specific status characteristics and assigned states of these characteristics to two subjects. In the second phase, we put the subjects in a standardized experimental situation where we could measure each subject's likelihood of being influenced by the other subject. This measure of influence was used as the indicator of the power and prestige position of the individual in the group.

Upon their arrival at the experimental laboratory, the subjects were led to separate rooms and given two written tests. These tests were designed to establish two fictional abilities or specific status characteristics on which the subjects could be differentiated. One test, called the "Meaning Insight Ability" test, was said to measure "meaning insight," a basic ability of the individual. This test contained fictional word association problems which involved matching an English word with the supposed phonetic spellings of two non-English words from a language unknown to the subjects. For each problem, the subject was asked to determine which of the two non-English words had the *same meaning* as the English word. The other test, called the "Relational Insight Ability" test, was said to measure "relational insight," another basic ability. This test also contained word association problems. These involved matching the supposed phonetic spelling of a Japanese word with two "ancient Japanese ideographs." For each problem, the subject was asked to determine which of the two ideographs had the *same pronunciation* as that given by the phonetic spelling, independent of their meanings. Each of the tests contained twenty problems. Prior experience with these tests show them to be sufficiently vague and yet believable to enable the experimenter to induce a subject's belief and confidence in almost any score. Thus they provide an efficient means for creating and randomly assigning states of specific status characteristics.

Having completed the tests, the subjects were led to the experimental room and seated in individual booths. Once seated, the apparent purpose of the experiment was explained. They were told that they would be working on a group decision-making task. The task, called a "Contrast Sensitivity" task, involved the visual judgment of a series of slides. Each slide consisted of two rectangular patterns, one above the other, and each pattern was composed of a different arrangement of small black and white squares. The problem, they were told, was to decide for each slide which of the two patterns, the top or the bottom, contained the greater area of white. Like the two ability tests, this task was also constructed to be ambiguous, so there were no right answers; both patterns in each slide contained the same area of white. Previous standardization work with the task indicated that the actual probability of picking either pattern was approximately .5 for each slide (Ofshe and Simpson, forthcoming). To control for any lack of homogeneity between stimulus slides, the order of presentation was randomized by selecting a random starting stimulus for each group while the actual sequence was maintained from experiment to experiment.

The status characteristics were introduced by telling the subjects that since they would be working together as a group, it would be helpful for them to know as much as possible about each other. They were told that the purpose of the tests they had taken earlier was to provide them with this information. In order to establish relevance between the characteristics and the task, Meaning Insight Ability and Relational Insight Ability were represented as being highly correlated with Contrast Sensitivity and with each other. They were told that people with high Meaning Insight and high Relational Insight Ability usually do quite well on the Contrast Sensitivity problems, and people without these abilities usually do poorly. Furthermore, in an attempt to make the two abilities seem equally relevant, the tests themselves, in terms of their intrinsic prop-

erties, were constructed so as to be quite dissimilar from the Contrast Sensitivity task.

At this point the subjects' scores on the two tests were reported to them. The reporting of the scores was the main experimental manipulation—in fact, the only experimental manipulation which was used to create different conditions. We created three different conditions on the basis of the reported scores. Conditions I and II, which we designate as HH–LL and LL–HH (the first two letters indicate the states of C_1 and C_2 that p possessed, and the last two letters indicate the states that o possessed), were run simultaneously. In each group one subject was assigned to the HH–LL condition and the other to the LL–HH condition. This assignment was random. In these groups the subjects were told that one of them (the subject assigned to the HH–LL condition) had gotten a score of 19 out of a possible 20 on the Meaning Insight Ability test and a score of 18 out of a possible 20 on the Relational Insight Ability test, while the other subject (the subject assigned to the LL–HH condition) had gotten a score of 9 on the Meaning Insight Ability test and a score of 8 on the Relational Insight Ability test. These scores were interpreted for the subjects in terms of a chart of national standards. The standards define a score between 16 and 20 to be a superior performance, one between 11 and 15 to be an average performance, and one between 0 and 10 to be a poor performance. Thus the scores for the HH–LL subjects were interpreted as representing superior scores for self and poor scores for other, while those for the LL–HH subjects were interpreted as representing poor scores for self and superior scores for other.

In Condition III, which we designate

as HL–LH, both members of the group were given inconsistent score patterns. The scores reported showed that one of the subjects had scored 19 on the Meaning Insight Ability test and 8 on the Relational Insight Ability test, while the other subject had scored 9 on the Meaning Insight Ability test but had scored 18 on the Relational Insight Ability test. These scores were reported as being "unsual" to the subjects. The particular inconsistent score patterns were randomly assigned.

In performing the Contrast Sensitivity task, the procedure was for each subject to give an initial opinion of the correct answer, to be able to see the other person's initial opinion, and then to make a final decision. The subjects were told that this exchange of information on initial opinion was part of the group decision-making procedure and might be helpful to their own solutions of the problems. Actually, this exchange was controlled and was built into the experiment to provide the opportunity for exercising influence. All communication between the subjects occurred through the panels of an interaction control machine. One of these panels was located on each of the subjects' desks, and it allowed the subject to indicate his initial choice by pressing one of two buttons, to subsequently see the other person's initial choice on a signal light, and to indicate his final decision. These panels also allowed an experimental assistant in a separate room to control the information on the other person's choice. That is, the subjects could be made to see an agreeing or disagreeing initial choice from the other person independently of the other person's actual choice. To operationalize collective orientation, it was emphasized to the subjects that they should not hesitate to change their initial choice if that helped

them to get the right answer, that the utilization of advice and information from others was both legitimate and reasonable in this situation, and that it was primarily important that they make a correct *final* choice.[3]

The experiment was run for twenty-five trials or Contrast Senstivity slides. Twenty of these trials were controlled disagreements or "critical" trials in which both subjects thought they were disagreeing with each other. The five agreement trials were also controlled; these were randomly distributed for each group, with one agreement included in each successive block of five trials. The reason for this high proportion of disagreements was to force the subjects to differentiate themselves on task performance.

After the experiment, the subjects were given a questionnaire to fill out. Upon completion of the questionnaire, they were taken to separate rooms and extensively interviewed. The purpose of the questionnaire and interview was to determine the effectiveness of the experimental manipulations and to gather information on the cognitive sets of the subjects at the end of the experiment.

A total of 91 subjects took part in the experiment. These were all male students from local junior colleges. They were recruited on a volunteer basis and were paid for their participation. Of the total number of subjects taking part in the experiment, 15 have been eliminated from the

---

[3] In these expectation-states experiments, "collective orientation" has been operationalized either by a technique of instructional emphasis (such as in this study) or by a technique involving instructional emphasis and a "team scoring" procedure as in Berger and Conner (1969).

analysis of the results. These subjects were excluded for violating one or more of the initial conditions of the experiment, as determined in the post-experimental questionnaires and interviews. The following criteria were used as bases for exclusion:

1. *Suspicion:* If a subject became suspicious of any of the experimental manipulations he was eliminated from the sample. This category also included subjects who had previously read about deception experiments and thought the present experiment similar to them, and also subjects who had heard from others that the study involved deception.

2. *Extraneous bases of differentiation between subjects:* If any particular set of circumstances provided a subject with a basis of differentiation between himself and the other apart from the experimental manipulation, then he was eliminated from the sample. Thus, all visible minority group members were eliminated from the sample. Previous acquaintance between the two group members also resulted in their being eliminated from the sample.

3. *Failure of experimental manipulation:* Subject who were unable to understand the instruction, who were confused as to what was happening in the experiment and/or did not understand crucial parts of the instructions such as the relation of the test to the Contrast Sensitivity task, were eliminated from the sample.

Of the total, 76 remained in the sample: 26 in the HH–LL condition; 26 in the HL–LH condition; and 24 in the LL–HH condition. The predictions and results for these subjects are presented in the following section.

Predictions and Results

Our measure of an individual's power and prestige position was the rate at which he accepted influence, given a disagreement with other. This was operationalized as the proportion of "stay-responses" made by a subject over the twenty critical trials of the experiment. A subject's response was coded as a "stay-response" if his final decision was the same as his initial choice, and was coded as a "change-response" if his final decision coincided with his partner's initial choice. What are the specific predictions which follow from the balancing and combining arguments for the different conditions in this experiment?

The argument for the balancing mechanism for this situation is that all subjects will hold either high expectations for self and low for other, or low for self and high for other; and these will correspond with a perceived distribution of states of characteristics that is consistent or univalent for each individual. Power and prestige positions will then be directly determined by these expectation structures. For subjects in the HH–LL or LL–HH conditions consistent distributions of states of characteristics are already given for each individual in the situation. The expectation structures which respectively correspond to these distributions are high-self, low-other and low-self, high-other. Consequently, we would expect subjects in the HH–LL condition to be less influenced and thus have a higher rate of stay-responses than subjects in the LL–HH condition. If the balancing argument is correct, subjects in the HL-LH condition would also form expectations that correspond to a perceived distribution of states of characteristics that is consistent or univalent to each individual. For this to occur, the subjects in this situation would probably select only one of the characteristics as a basis for their expectations. As a consequence, individual subjects in this condition would form either high-self, low-other or low-self, high-other expectation structures. Thus we would expect individual subjects in the HL–LH condition to have a rate of stay-responses similar to subjects in either the HH–LL or the LL–HH condition. Ideally, if the balancing mechanism were also operating in a uniform manner for the HL–LH subjects, we should find the overall proportion in the inconsistent condition approximating the proportions in one of the two consistent conditions. However, since this may not be true, and we have no way of predicting the direction of the cognitive balance taken by inconsistent subjects— either to forming high-self, low-other or low-self, high-other expectation structures —we might find the overall proportion of stay-responses in the inconsistent condition diverging from the proportions in the consistent conditions. To the extent that the divergence occurs, however, we would definitely expect to find bi-modality—that is, some subjects with response rates similar to the HH–LL subjects, and others with response rates similar to the LL–HH subjects.

For the multi-characteristic situations in which the distribution of states is consistent, HH–LL and LL–HH, the combining mechanisms argument leads to the same predictions as those of the balancing mechanism. Under the assumptions of this argument, the individual uses all the information available concerning the distribution of states of characteristics in forming expectation states for self and other. These expectation states are an "average" or some combining function of states of characteristics he and the other possess. Thus in the situation where the information conveyed to the individual is that he is high on two equally weighted charac-

teristics and the other is low on these characteristics, the HH–LL condition, the individual is expected to form a high-self, low-other expectation structure. Similarly, under this argument the individual in the LL–HH condition is expected to form low-self, high-other expectations. Again assuming that the individual's power and prestige position is a direct function of his expectation structure, we expect to find a higher rate of stay-responses for individuals in the HH–LL condition as compared to those in the LL–HH condition. However, for subjects in the HL–LH condition, the predictions from the combining mechanism argument are markedly different from those we were led to by the balancing mechanism argument. In this condition subjects are expected to form expectation states that combine the information that they are high on one characteristic and low on a second equally weighted characteristic. The result is that the subject holds expectations for an "average" performance level relative to the task—somewhere between high and low. Therefore, the expectation structure for subjects in this condition should be "average" for self and "average" for other. Again assuming that the individual's power and prestige position is a direct function of his expectation structure, this argument leads us to expect that the overall proportion of stay-responses for these subjects will be markedly different from those in the HH–LL or LL–HH conditions, and in fact should be in between the rates in these conditions. Further, this line of reasoning leads us to expect that the distribution of the number of stay-responses per subject should be uni-modal and similar to the distributions in the other two conditions. In short, the combining argument

Table 1

PROPORTION, MEAN NUMBER OF STAY-RESPONSES, AND VARIANCE

Condition	Number of Subjects	Stay-Responses		
		Proportion	Mean	Variance
HH-LL	26	.821	16.42	4.73
HL-LH	26	.661	13.23	5.62
LL-HH	24	.533	10.67	10.23

predicts that the HL–LH condition will be characterized by a rate of stay-responses that is peculiar to itself.

The experimental results are presented in Table 1. This table shows the proportions, mean number of stay-responses, and variances for subjects in each of the three conditions.

To begin with, it is to be observed that the data presented provide clear support for the primary prediction, common to both the balancing and combining arguments, that the rate of stay-responses for subjects in the HH–LL condition will be greater than the rate of stay-responses for subjects in the LL–HH condition. The actual proportion of stay-responses averaged for all subjects in the HH–LL condition is 0.82, as compared to 0.53 for subjects in the LL–HH condition. The difference is strikingly large. Application of the Mann-Whitney U test gives the probability of obtaining this difference on the basis of chance alone as considerably less than .001, as reported in the first row of Table 2. It seems reasonable to conclude that when the distribution of states of two specific status characteristics is consistent, this distribution tends to order the power and prestige structure of the group such that the actor who possesses the highly evaluated states of the characteristics is less likely to accept influence than the actor who possesses the less highly evaluated states of the characteristics.

Secondly, it is to be observed that the proportion of stay-responses for the subjects in the HL–LH condition is 0.66. This value is almost exactly in the middle of the spread between the values for the HH–LL and the LL–HH conditions. Applying the Mann-Whitney U test to the

Table 2

RESULTS OF MANN-WHITNEY U TEST APPLIED TO
DIFFERENCES BETWEEN CONDITIONS

Conditions Tested	Test Statistics		
	U	Z	P
HH-LL vs. LL-HH	27.0	5.068	.00003
HH-LL vs. HL-LH	87.5	3.923	.00005
LL-HH vs. HL-LH	123.0	2.805	.02270

differences between the HL–LH and the HH–LL conditions we get the result reported in the second row of Table 2— that the likelihood of obtaining this difference on the basis of chance alone is considerably less than .001. Application of the same test to the difference between the HL–LH and the LL–HH condition yields the result that the obtained difference could have been produced by chance alone with a probability of less than .05. There seems to be little question that the HL–LH condition produces a different rate of stay-responses from either the HH–LL or the LL–HH conditions. These results are fully consistent with the predictions from the combining mechanism argument: that the rate of accepting influence for subjects in the inconsistent condition will differ markedly from the rates of either of the consistent conditions and that this rate in fact will be in between the rates of the other two conditions.

This analysis, however, does not completely eliminate the balancing mechanism argument. This argument admits the possibility that the direction of cognitive balance may not be uniform and that some subjects in this condition may balance in the direction of forming high-self, low-other expectations while others balance in the direction of forming low-self, high-other states. If this occurred, the resultant mean proportion of stay-responses for these different types of subjects could turn out to be an average of the rates found in the consistent conditions. However, if this did occur, there should be evidence for it in the distribution of stay-responses in the inconsistent condition.

Looking at the variance of the number

Table 3

The Frequency Distribution of the Number of Stay-Responses Per Subject

Number of Stay-Responses	HH-LL	HL-LH	LL-HH
4			X
5			
6			X
7		X	XXXX
8			X
9			X
10		X	X
11		XXX	XXXXX
12	XX	XXXXXX	XXX
13	X	XXX	XX
14	X	XXXX	XX
15	XXXXX	XXXX	XX
16	XX	XX	X
17	XXXXXXX	X	
18	XXXX	X	
19	XX		
20	XX		

of stay-responses, as reported in the fourth column of Table 1, we see that the variance for the HL–LH condition is 5.62. Although this value is larger than that for the HH–LL condition, which is 4.73, this difference cannot be considered striking. Indeed, comparing the variance of the HL–LH condition with that of the LL–HH condition, which is 10.23, we see that it is considerably less than that obtained for this particular consistent condition. In order to examine additional data relevant to this problem, we present in Table 3 the frequency distribution of the number of stay-responses for all three conditions.

Examining the data for subjects in the HL–LH case, we find no indications of bi-modality in this distribution. As a matter of fact, the distribution for the HL–LH case and the distribution for the HH–LL case look remarkably similar. The only change between the conditions seems to be a linear transformation of the mean.[4] Thus we find no support for the argument that the observed rate of stay-responses is due to an aggregation across two populations of subjects balancing in different directions.

We conclude that the data obtained from this experiment clearly favor the combining mechanism argument. The subjects of this experiment do indeed seem to be operating on the information given to them about the states of the specific status characteristics each of them possesses in forming task expectations for self and other in such a way as to use and combine all the information that is available to them. Thus in the case where the distribution of the states of the characteristics is inconsistent they tend to combine the states of the two characteristics so as to form "average" states.

There is one point worth noting as regards the generality of this conclusion. The inconsistent case we have investigated is both inconsistent and "symmetric." It is symmetric in the sense that looking at each actor separately we find that he possesses one positively and one negatively evaluated state. Further, it is symmetric in the sense that the distributions for the two actors are "mirror images" of each other. It is conceiveable that while the balancing mechanism does not operate in this case, it does operate where there already exists some status "edge" or advantage that provides a particular direction along which balancing can occur. Such a situation would be inconsistent and non-symmetric: one in which all the group members do not possess a matched and equal number of positively and negatively evaluated states. We are at present conducting a study to determine what are the properties of emergent power and prestige orders in such situations.

---

[4] Since all the subjects in the LL–HH condition were placed in a consistent low state to begin with, the relatively high variance in this condition cannot be taken as evidence for the balancing mechanism argument insofar as it applies to the problem of multiple characteristics. Rather, this high variance is believed to reflect the tension and resulting unstable behavior produced by the cumulative effect of the two low ability manipulations employed in this condition.

SUMMARY

We started our investigation with the problem: Given that the members of a task-oriented group are differentiated with respect to two or more status characteristics instrumental to their task, how is the distribution of these characteristics related to the group's power and prestige order?

A theoretical analysis of this problem led us to the issue of how expectations are formed, and in particular how they are formed when the distribution of status characteristics is inconsistent. We have considered two alternative mechanisms which may be operating in the formation of expectations in multi-characteristic task situations. The first, which we have referred to as a balancing mechanism, postulates that the actor cognitively defines the situation so as to form expectation states that correspond with a perceived distribution of states of characteristics that is consistent or univalent for each individual. For the situation we considered, the operation of this mechanism would result in p's assigning one of two expectations states to self and to other—either "high" or "low." The second cognitive process we considered is one we have referred to as a combining mechanism. This postulates that the actor forms his expectations by combining or averaging the performance information contained in the states of the status characteristics possessed by self and other. For our situation of concern, the operation of this mechanism would result in p's assigning to self and to other one of a large number of different expectations ranging from "high" to "low" and depending upon the particular distribution of status characteristics. In any event, once p has formed expectations, whether through the operation of a balancing or combining mechanism, his power and prestige position is assumed to be directly determined by his self-other expectation structure.

We designed and conducted a study, built around a standardized experimental situation, in an attempt to discriminate between the two alternative mechanisms. The study consisted of two phases, in the first of which we established and assigned the states of two specific status characteristics to two actors who in the second phase were put in a standardized experimental situation where we could measure the power and prestige ordering that developed. The experiment consisted of three conditions: In the first condition (consistent), a subject who was high on both characteristics was paired with one who was low on both characteristics; in the second condition (consistent), a subject who was low on both characteristics was paired with one who was high on both characteristics; and in the third condition (inconsistent), a subject who was high on one characteristic but low on the second was paired with one who was low on the first characteristic and high on the second. The balancing and the combining mechanisms make different predictions as to the behavior of subjects in the third condition.

The results of our experiment clearly conform to the predictions made from the combining argument. The rate at which subjects in the inconsistent condition accepted influence was significantly different from and in between the corresponding rates for subjects in the consistent conditions. It is also clear that this is not due to aggregating results over subjects who were behaving in radically different ways. We conclude that our experimental results strongly support the combining mechanism argument with following reservation: It may be that a situation involving a symmetric distribution of characteristics is a special one with particular properties. We are now in the process of investigating this phenomenon in a situation involving non-symmetric distribution of the states of the characteristics in order to determine whether this is indeed the case.

REFERENCES

BERGER, J., B. P. COHEN and M. ZELDITCH, JR., "Status Characteristics and Expectation States." Pp. 29–46 in J. Berger, M. Zelditch, Jr., and Bo Anderson (eds.), *Sociological Theories in Progress*, Vol. I. Boston: Houghton Mifflin, 1966.

BERGER, J., T. L. CONNER and W. L. McKEOWN, "Evaluations and the Formation and Maintenance of Performance Expectations." *Human Relations*, 22 (December 1969), 481–502.

BERGER, J., and T. L. CONNER, "Performance Expectations and Behavior in Small Groups" *Acta Sociologica*, 12 (1969): 186–198.

COHEN, B. P., J. BERGER and M. ZELDITCH, JR., *Status Conceptions and Power Prestige.* Forthcoming monograph.

FISEK, M. H., *The Evolution of Status Structures and Interaction in Task Oriented Discussion Groups.* Unpublished Ph.D. dissertation, Department of Sociology, Stanford University, 1969.

HELDER, F., "Attitudes and Cognitive Organization." *Journal of Psychology*, 21 (1946): 107–112.

HOMANS, G. C., *Social Behavior: Its Elementary Forms.* New York: Harcourt, Brace and World, 1961.

KATZ, I., J. GOLDSTON and L. BENJAMIN, "Behavior and Productivity in Bi-Racial Work Groups." *Human Relations*, 11 (1958): 123–141.

LENSKI, G. E., "Social Participation and Status Crystallization." *American Sociological Review*, 21 (August 1956): 458–464.

MOORE, J. C., JR., "Status and Influence in Small Group Interactions." *Sociometry*, 31 (March 1968): 47–63.

NEWCOMB, T., "An Approach to the Study of Communicative Acts." *Psychological Review*, 60 (1953): 393–404.

OFSHE, R., and J. H. SIMPSON, "Contrast Sensitivity: A Task for Use in Controlled Interaction Experiments." Forthcoming technical report, Laboratory for Social Research, Stanford University.

SAMPSON, E. E., "Status Congruence and Cognitive Consistency." *Sociometry*, 26 (1963): 146–162.

TORRANCE, E. P., "Some Consequences of Power Differences on Decision-Making in Permanent and Temporary Three-Man Groups." *Research Studies*, State College of Washington, 22 (1954): 130–140.

ZELDITCH, M., JR., and Bo ANDERSON, "On the Balance of a Set of Ranks." Pp. 244–268 in J. Berger, M. Zelditch, Jr. and Bo Anderson (eds.), *Sociological Theories in Progress*, Vol. I. Boston: Houghton Mifflin, 1966.

7

Non-Vertical
Social Organization

GROUP STRUCTURE AND THE NEWCOMER:
AN EXPERIMENTAL STUDY
OF GROUP EXPANSION*

Theodore M. Mills

What determines how the newcomer becomes related to the group? In this paper we report results of an experimental test of some factors and suggest their implication for the sociology of small groups.

The occurrence of the newcomer is frequent and familiar: the new neighbor, the recruit, the immigrant, the freshman,

the trainee, the new executive, etc. When we include the newborn, it is clear that continued social existence is impossible without newcomers, and without effective processes of amalgamation. The arrival of an outsider changes the situation both for him and for the group, setting in motion reactions to the change and processes of mutual adjustment which may or may not be satisfactory in their outcome. In any concrete case these processes are probably complex, being subject to the interaction of a number of variables, such as age of the group, its function in the larger society, its relation to other groups, its organization, how members in the initial group feel about one another, what the new person seems like, or is like, why he comes, etc. One aim in studying these processes

* Reprinted from Theodore M. Mills in collaboration with Anders Gauslaa, Yngvar Løchen, Thomas Mathiesen, Guttorm Nørstebø, Odd Ramsøy, Sigurd Skirbekk, Olav Skårdal, Liv Torgersen, Birger Tysnes, and Ørjar Øyen, *Group Structure and the Newcomer: An Experimental Study of Group Expansion* (Oslo: Universitetsforlaget, 1957), by permission of Universitetsforlaget. Copyright © 1957 by The Norwegian Research Council for Science and the Humanities.

is to reduce the problem to simpler terms. Another is to explore group properties. Often, through analysis of reactions to change, properties inherent but not evident in the group—and in this case in the newcomer—may be brought to light.

Some discussions of the question emphasize the point of view of the newcomer, such as Simmel's description of the stranger[1] and Schuetz's analysis of strains as the stranger becomes more or less integrated in a society.[2] In another context Simmel identifies chiefly with members of the group as he describes the likely reactions of an intimate pair to the appearance of a third party;[3] and von Wiese takes essentially the same point of view in his analysis of the expansion of the triad.[4] Freud and subsequent psychoanalytic writers write from within the group when they trace the impact of the newborn child upon the older child and upon the father.[5] We take the theoretical position—possibly shared by these writers—that the process is the result of interaction between factors associated with the group and factors associated with the newcomer.

However, in our experiment we test only one set of factors—those associated with the structure of the original group.

Our questions are: How does the structure of relationships in the initial group affect the relationship that develops between the newcomer and group members? And how does the position of a given member in the structure affect his relationship with the newcomer? Actually, our experimental question is even more limited than this. Since we vary group structure and a given person's place in it by using two role-players interacting with a "naive" subject, our dependent variable is the newcomer's relationship with the single "naive" subject rather than with all group members. Moreover, we select only one characteristic of group structure (but we believe a basically important one); namely, the degree to which each of the three members accepts, and feels accepted by, the others. This characteristic we call emotional integration, or, for brevity, integration. The single characteristic of a person's position is the degree to which he feels accepted or rejected by other group members. As we test these variables, other important factors mentioned above are held as nearly constant from group to group as possible.

THE FIRST HYPOTHESIS

The first hypothesis and its alternative are extrapolations from Freud, and from Simmel and von Wiese, respectively. From their discussions of the family and two and three person groups, we derive hypotheses which may hold for a wider variety of situations, including small groups in a laboratory. Needless to say, since we do not test their propositions in their settings

[1] G. Simmel, "Der Fremde," in *Soziologie*, 2nd printing (München and Leipzig: Verlag von Dunker und Humblot, 1922), pp. 509–12. See also K. H. Wolff, ed., *The Sociology of Georg Simmel* (New York: The Free Press, 1950), pp. 402–8.

[2] A. Schuetz, "The Stranger," *The American Journal of Sociology*, XLIX, No. 6 (May, 1944), 499–507.

[3] *Op. cit.*, Chaps. 2, 3, and 4.

[4] Leopold von Wiese and Howard Becker, *Systematic Sociology; on the Basis of the Beziehungliehre and Gebildelehre of Leopold von Wiese* (New York: Wiley, 1932), pp. 525–27.

[5] Sigmund Freud, *The Complete Psychological Works of Sigmund Freud*, ed. James Strachey, Vol. XVII (London: Hogarth, 1955).

we intend neither to prove nor to disprove them. Instead, we test how well the generalizations, rooted in their discussions but made by us, hold in the laboratory.

Freud and subsequent psychoanalytical investigators have found that one of the more significant events in the life cycle is the arrival of a new brother or sister. Hostility toward the infant and a wish to throw him out is often found in the older child. Hostility on this occasion may be a universal reaction,[6] though its intensity and the way it is handled probably vary considerably. Adding the assumption, which we believe is consistent with psychoanalytical tradition, that the child who feels relatively secure in his emotional attachments to father and mother will feel less hostility than one who feels less secure, our first hypothesis is:

> A member of the initial group who feels accepted by others is more likely to develop a congenial relationship with a newcomer than a member who feels isolated from and rejected by the others.

The alternative to this hypothesis derives from Simmel's and von Wiese's discussions of the expansion of the dyad and triad. Simmel argues that two people who have an intimate and warm relationship will, when confronted with a newcomer, feel and express hostility toward him and that he will reciprocate. In this case, contrary to the first hypothesis, rejection is from secure members. Presumably, rejection is more likely than had the pair been in conflict.

---

[6] The connection between this phenomenon and Miller and Dollard's frustration-aggression hypothesis depends, of course, upon the nature of the attachment of older child to the mother. See J. Dollard *et al.*, *Frustration and Aggression* (New Haven: Yale Univ. Press, 1939).

Von Wiese utilizes Simmel's principle in his discussion of the expansion of the triad: "What is really normal (in terms of frequency distribution) [for the triad] is that two of the members are more intimate with each other than they are with the third, and . . . frequently . . . two members become allies . . . and . . . relegate the third to an inferior rank." "In many instances the underprivileged member seeks to strengthen his position by forming alliances outside the triad. He . . . finds a new partner, so that *a new pair is formed*. The triadic group has been transmuted into a double pair. . . ."[7]

If a genuine interacting unit of four persons is formed by this expansion, the double pair pattern forms only because the accepted members have rejected the newcomer, the isolated member has welcomed him and in each case the new member has reciprocated. This view is based on Simmel's and von Wiese's principles, and it constitutes our alternative to the first hypothesis.

THE SECOND HYPOTHESIS

The second hypothesis (and its alternative) concerns the total patterns of emotional ties in the group. It is based upon the premise that a fully integrated group —where emotional ties between all members are positive—has richer resources for handling successfully the problem of integration entailed in assimilating a new member than do groups which already have within them negative relationships, or from one point of view, unresolved

---

[7] Von Wiese and Becker, *op. cit.*, pp. 525–27.

problems of integration.[8] Our hypothesis is that:

> The degree of integration in the initial group—the proportion of emotional ties that are congenial—increases the probability that a positive relationship will be established with the newcomer.

The alternative to this hypothesis derives from the common observation that a close "in-group" resents an intruder— like Simmel's intimate pair, and like Becker's folk society which he says has "... self-imposed mental and social isolation vis-à-vis the stranger; there is a deep dislike of the person who concretely represents the forces of change."[9] This alternative, then, is that full integration decreases the probability that a positive relationship will be developed with the newcomer; partial integration—where at least one member is isolated—increases it.

In summary, according to the first and second hypotheses, we expect the warmest relationship to develop when the original members are friendly, the coolest when they are in conflict. In partially integrated groups, we expect a warm relationship to develop between the newcomer and those who already have friends in the group, and a cool relationship to develop in respect to those who are initially rejected. According to the alternative hypotheses, on the other hand, we expect the warmest relationship to develop with a rejected member and the coolest to occur when the initial members are friendly.

In the next section we describe how the newcomer is introduced into the group, how we use role-playing to vary systematically feelings of acceptance and group integration, and how we match the first subject and the newcomer on certain characteristics. We report the effectiveness of the role-playing, present our measures and our experimental design, and show how we test the hypotheses.

INTRODUCING THE NEW MEMBER

A visitor arriving before a typical experimental session would find six members of the research team assembled in a small observation room. Two are sitting close to a one-way screen preparing sheets for scoring behavior according to Bales' technique,[10] one tests the tape recorder, one—the experimenter—readies instructions, questionnaires, etc., and the other two check each other on details, for they have just changed from civilian clothes to military uniforms. When all is ready, these, the role-players, leave by the back door and are followed later by the experimenter. Lights are dimmed; visible through the screen is a larger room with a table, four chairs, several cabinets and a microphone in the center of the table.

The experimenter enters with three soldiers—the disguised role-players and a naive subject. He explains the aim of investigating how groups solve problems, explains the one-way screen, the observers, the tape-recorder, the microphone and

---

[8] Though this proposition is not made in Talcott Parsons, Robert F. Bales, and Edward Shils' *Working Papers in the Theory of Action* (New York: The Free Press, 1935), it is based upon their argument.

[9] Howard Becker, *Through Values to Social Interpretation* (Durham, N.C.: Duke Univ. Press, 1950), p. 50.

[10] Robert F. Bales, *Interaction Process Analysis* (Reading, Mass.: Addison-Wesley, 1950).

what is expected of them. There will be two tasks, each lasting 25 minutes; for the first there will be three members of the group and for the second, four. The task is to tell a single dramatic story weaving together three pictures,[11] which will be shown for 20 seconds. The group is to work together on the story. An award will be given to the group producing the best drama. After questions and clarification the discussion begins.

In observing the group processes carefully, the visitor would become aware of the gradual appearance and the eventual crystallization of a definite pattern of relationships between the three men. He may find the subject and one role-player interpreting the pictures in very much the same way, developing a dramatic theme which seems satisfying to both. The other role-player sees something else in the pictures, wanting some other hero, some other ending. By the time the task is over and the members have had a five-minute break for informal talk, the visitor would see that what was agreement on the story has deepened to personal warmth and that disagreement has grown to dislike. In this the visitor finds the end-product of our attempt to establish, artificially but convincingly, a particular group structure in which the naive subject has a given degree of acceptance and the group as a whole is integrated at a specified level. As explained below, the visitor would find other structures on other occasions.

Following the five-minute break, the men fill out questionnaires. From the sub-

---

[11] H. A. Murray, *Thematic Apperception Test* (Cambridge, Mass.: Harvard Univ. Press, 1943).

ject's answers we learn whether his perceptions and feelings correspond to the desired pattern and we learn how he feels about a new member joining the group. In the meantime, the newcomer, having been introduced to the others, reports in writing how he feels about entering an established group.

The second task session begins. Explanations and instructions are repeated and the group starts working on the second story about another set of pictures. For about five minutes the role-players maintain attitudes and types of behavior that re-affirm the relationships of the first session. Gradually they withdraw so that whatever relationship seems natural between the first subject and the newcomer may develop. Withdrawal is only partial, for they return act for act, agreement for agreements, etc.

When time is up, the experimenter asks the role-players to retire to another room —the withdrawal of the two role-players is of course made to appear incidental— and gives the subjects questionnaires much like those filled out earlier by the first subjects.

Although the experimental run is over, there remains the critically important "cooling-out" period, during which the subjects are made fully aware of the experimental procedures and are encouraged to release whatever tension this new view generates. Calling in the role-players, the experimenter explains the precise purpose and methods of the study. Role-players identify themselves, explain their roles, how their behavior fits the design of the experiment and how on other occasions they act different roles. They encourage the subjects to re-live with them from this new viewpoint the important events in the discussions. The "cooling-out" process differs from subject to subject and may take from 15 to 45 minutes. The subjects are paid and asked not to discuss their experience with anyone. Our brief report cannot go into the complications and functions of "cooling-out"—functions for the role-players, the research team as a whole, as well as for the subjects—we simply note that one of our chief aims is to make perfectly clear why deception is used and to show precisely where it is and is not used. The other is to permit catharsis, especially for the subjects.

ESTABLISHING DIFFERENCES BETWEEN GROUPS IN PERSONAL ACCEPTANCE AND IN GROUP INTEGRATION

Our visitor found one pattern in the first session. It is through the use of four patterns that we control the two independent variables.

In Pattern I, which we call the *all positive*, the role-players create as nearly as possible a feeling of complete acceptance between all three. How the subject feels about the pictures, what he wants and needs the story to be, become the baseline for their reactions, their comments, and their suggestions. From the indications he gives, they build up the group's culture so that it mirrors his attitudes, values and preferences. They move from this level to personal warmth, regardless of what is being talked about. The subject is fully accepted in a well-integrated group.

In Pattern II—the *all negative*—the role-players develop a disorganized group, where no two are in agreement and where in time there is antipathy between all. Natural idiosyncrasies in projections are amplified; whatever baseline for agreement there might have been is erased; and compromise or submission is discouraged. From this state of confusion and failure in the task they shift to deeper hostility in the subsequent informal period. The subject, like the others, is rejected in a disintegrated group.

In the other two patterns, two members are in coalition against the third. In Pattern III the subject is *out* of the coalition (rejected); in IV he is *in* the coalition (accepted). Both patterns are partially integrated. Our hypothetical visitor saw Pattern IV.

To summarize, role-players create four types of patterns in the first session: Two in which the subject is *accepted*; two in which he is rejected. One is *fully* integrated, one *malintegrated* and two are *partially* integrated.

EFFECTIVENESS OF ROLE-PLAYING

The role-players were effective in almost three-fourths of their attempts (27 out of 38). They trained for two and a half months. They practiced upon themselves and upon preliminary subjects, each player taking all roles in all patterns, learning to work with partners, learning the behavior that strengthens or weakens a pattern and gaining skill in adapting quickly to different types of subjects. In spite of training, however, one-fourth of the attempts were failures—a proportion we have come to expect. When the role-playing is beyond the superficial level, actor's feelings are directly involved. Disturbances of the day or session before may press to be played out during the session, altering or destorying the desired pattern. The actor may really like the subject to whom he must be hostile, or vice versa. Basically compatible partners may on occasions be unable to make "hostility" convincing, or players with unresolved problems between them may find cooperation even in being hostile too much to achieve. Moreover, feelings of guilt associated with deception and fear of omnipotence associated with success, when out of perspective, often press against effective assumption of the role. These and other problems lead us to expect a number of failures in any long series of runs.

They also make it advisable to decide before the analysis of results what constitutes a satisfactory run. For inclusion as an experimental case, we require that the desired pattern be unquestionably apparent in *both* the observers' records of supportive and non-supportive behavior during the session and in the subject's picture of the emotional ties between the three members.

The observers' records are summarized by calculating the *rate of support* from each member to the others. Based upon the interaction process analysis scores, it is defined and calculated as follows:

The rate at which member 1 supports member 2, for example, is given by the equation:

$$\text{Rate}_{12} = \frac{A_{12} - D_{12}}{B_2 + C_2}$$

Where A_{12} is the frequency of suportive acts (Bales' categories 1, 2, and 3) initiated by member 1 and directed to member 2.

D_{12} is the frequency of non-supportive acts (categories 10, 11, and 12) initiated by member 1 and directed to member 2. B_2 and C_2 combined is the frequency of instrumental acts (categories 4 through 9) initiated by member 2 regardless of their recipients.

As an illustration, the rates for one of the experimental groups are as follows (case no. 44, the subject-*in*-coalition pattern):

Support from	Support to		
	Subject	Ally	Isolate
Subject	—	.38	−.16
Ally	.36	—	−.42
Isolate	−.34	−.39	—

The second basis for assessing the role-playing is, as we have said, the subject's picture of the emotional ties between members which is obtained from his answer to this question:[12]

Sometimes people agree with each other but at the same time they may not like each other. In other cases people may disagree, yet like each other. We would like to know how the members of your group liked each other.

You will be given detailed instructions by the experimenter. He will tell you how to use the following scale:
—3 disliked him strongly
—2 disliked him somewhat
—1 disliked him more than liked him
1 liked him more than disliked him
2 liked him somewhat
3 liked him very much.

(The experimenter explains how to use the scale in completing the following matrix):

---

[12] The question is a modification of Tagiuri's relational analysis; see R. Tagiuri, "Relational Analysis: An Extension of Sociometric Method with Emphasis upon Social Perception," *Sociometry*, XV (1952), 91–104.

	A	B	C
Person A[a] likes/dislikes	—	3	−2
Person B likes/dislikes	3	—	−3
Person C likes/dislikes	−3	−3	—

[a] A is subject, B is ally, and C is isolate in this particular case.

The subject's answers from case no. 44 are inserted for illustration. From the support rates described above and the subject's assessment of who likes whom it is apparent that case no. 44 is fully acceptable. Overt interaction shows the two-against-one pattern; the subject's feelings toward others and his perceptions of how they feel, reflect it perfectly.

A total of 38 sessions were run. Our design has 8 cells; four patterns times two sets of role-players. Though 27 of the 38 sessions met our criteria, their distribution was uneven so that one cell had only two satisfactory cases. Since our supply of subjects was exhausted, we accepted one case that failed to meet all the criteria in order to have three cases in each cell, or a total of 24 experimental cases. The average support rates for these are shown in Table 1; and, the average "liking" ratings are shown in Table 2. Examination of the support rates shows that the desired patterns are evident in all sets of cases. The same is true for "liking." We believe we have four distinctly different types of structures which vary in the degree to which the subject is accepted and in the degree of group integration. Moreover, we are convinced that the subjects perceive and act according to the desired patterns.

How First Subject and Newcomer Are Matched

In our design the purpose in matching subjects is to reduce the between-persons and between-groups error due to personality and social factors. First subject and newcomer are matched on sex, age, current role in the Norwegian society and on basic tendencies in interacting with others, as measured by Schutz's FIRO test.[13]

Schutz's test was given to 539 Norwegian army recruits who had been in the service from one to four months. Using scores from five Guttman scales, Schutz classifies a respondent as *personal, counterpersonal,* or *over-personal.* Using scores from three other scales, he classifies him as *counterdependent* or *dependent.* By personal he means that the person has no deepseated anxiety about being accepted by others; by counter-personal, that he does and that he handles it by keeping others enough at a distance so that they have little opportunity for rejecting him; by over-personal he means that the person has anxiety and that he manages it by closely engaging others. By independent he means that the person has no basic conflict concerning authority figures or in assuming an authority role; by counterdependent, that he does and that he tends to attack authority or authorized rules; by dependent, that he has conflict and that he handles it by being overly submissive to authority and to rules, depending more upon them than upon himself. Schutz's test also classifies individuals on *assertiveness,* from low to high.

On personal-ness and on dependence, the sample of 539 subjects are classed as shown in Table 3. Only those individuals classed as personal and dependent were

---

[13] William C. Schutz, *FIRO: A Three-Dimensional Theory of Interpersonal Behavior* (New York: Holt, Rinehart & Winston, 1958).

Table 1

AVERAGE SUPPORT RATES DURING FIRST SESSIONS:
BEST SIX SESSIONS IN EACH PATTERN

	Who supports whom[a]					
Pattern	S–R₁	S–R₂	R₁–S	R₁–R₂	R₂–S	R₂–R₁
I All positive	**.24**	**.21**	**.30**	**.25**	**.26**	**.16**
II All Negative	−.02	−.16	−.28	−.35	−.35	−.45
III S *Out* of Coalition	−.03	−.06	−.19	**.37**	−.45	−.33
IV S *In* Coalition	**.32**	−.11	**.39**	−.30	−.31	−.24

[a] S is subject; R₁ is first role-player, and R₂ is second role-player. Where the support rate should be high, the figure is in boldface.

Table 2

AVERAGE RATINGS BY THE SUBJECT OF WHO LIKES WHOM:
BEST SIX SESSIONS IN EACH PATTERN

	Who likes whom[a]					
Pattern	S–R₁	S–R₂	R₁–S	R₁–R₂	R₂–S	R₂–R₁
I All Positive	**2.3**	**2.7**	**2.0**	**2.0**	**2.2**	**2.5**
II All Negative	−1.3	−0.2	−1.8	−1.8	−1.7	−1.2
III S *Out* of Coalition	1.3	1.2	−1.0	**2.8**	−0.2	**2.8**
IV S *In* Coalition	**2.5**	−0.3	**1.8**	−1.5	−0.8	−1.7

[a] For meanings of S and R, see Table 1. When ratings should be high, the figure is in boldface.

Table 3

SELECTED RESULTS OF FIRO TEST 539 SUBJECTS

	Personal-ness				
Dependence	Counter-personal	Personal	Over-personal	Uncertain	Total
Counter-dependent	25	29	17	33	104
Dependent	45	101	35	146	327
Uncertain	19	31	16	42	108
Total	89	161	68	221	539

used as experimental subjects (figure in italics). Particular pairs of subjects were, in addition, matched on assertiveness. Later in the experimental run, but not systematically, pairs were also matched on the linguistic region of their home resiednce, and subjects very low on assertiveness and intelligence (data from army records) were eliminated. Members in a given pair were stationed at different training camps, there being two widely separated ones in the Oslo area.

Measures of the Dependent Variable

The relationship between first subject and newcomer is considered to approach full congeniality when there is positive anticipation by the first subject, active and supportive behavior while working together, and while being "free" together, and, finally, mutual liking of one another. We shall describe our measures of these characteristics detail.

Anticipated Value

Immediately after being introduced to the newcomer the first subject is asked to reply to the following question:

> "Another member joins the group. How will his arrival alter the possibility of your ideas and opinions being incorporated into the final group decision?
> 1. Greatly decrease the chances
> 2. Decrease them somewhat
> 3. Increase them somewhat
> 4. Greatly increase the chances"

From number one through number four, the answers are scored: —2, —1, +1 and +2.

Behavior in a Working Group

For this we take two measures during the second session: 2) the rate of interaction between subjects (as the inverse of avoidance) and b) mutual support between them. Both are derived from interaction process analysis scores. The first

is the average number of acts directed toward one another divided by the average initiations by all members.[14] The second is the average support rate between the two subjects which is explained above.[15]

Behavior While Alone

In the "free period," when the role-players have been withdrawn and the subjects are left with nothing to do, we again measure their rate of activity and their supportive behavior. Interaction is calculated this time by counting the number of seconds of overt behavior and dividing by the total time they are left together.

Liking of One Another

As stated above, at the end of the second session subjects fill in a liking

---

[14] This ratio is used to offset any pacesetting tendencies the role-players might have had.

[15] Two reliability tests were made between interaction process analysis observers. The first was done on the raw frequency of acts of a given category originating from a given member and directed toward another given member during the discussion period. Scores were plotted on Mosteller-Tukey binomial probability paper. For 10 sessions selected at random we found that agreement between scorers could be entirely due to chance. This poor reliability on raw scores is due chiefly to the fact that one observer tallied more scores in all categories than the other.

In the second test we correlated the support rates. Since the rate is a ratio of several sets of a single observer's scores it is less affected by total number of scores. The product-moment correlation coefficient for 96 support rates from 10 sessions selected at random is +.69. With this degree of agreement, we consider the average between the rates of the two observers a good estimate of supportive behavior in the groups.

Table 4

EXPERIMENTAL DESIGN

	Teams of role-players	
Pattern during first session	A	B
I All Positive	case 1	case 4
Subject accepted ;	2	5
group fully integrated	3	6
II All Negative	7	10
Subjects rejected ;	8	11
group malintegrated	9	12
III Subject *Out* of Coalition	13	16
Subject rejected ;	14	17
group partially integrated	15	18
IV Subject *In* Coalition	19	22
Subject accepted ;	20	23
group partially integrated	21	24

matrix which, except for the additional row and column for the newcomer, is the same as the one presented earlier to the first subject and illustrated above. To estimate from their ratings the degree of mutual liking, we use the following ratio:

$$\frac{1 \text{ plus first's rating of second plus second's rating of first}}{1 \text{ plus the difference between their ratings of one another}}$$

THE EXPERIMENTAL DESIGN

Our experimental design, shown in Table 4, is set up for analysis of variance,

the two principle sources of variance we are interested in being (a) the characteristics of the pattern in the initial group and (b) the role-playing teams. Cases have been re-numbered for the reader's convenience.

TESTING THE HYPOTHESES

A note about how we test the hypotheses is necessary. If personal acceptance in the previous group does in fact lead to a more congenial relationship, we should expect more positive readings in

	Patterns			
Structural characteristics	I	II	III	IV
1. To what extent is there full, *positive integration ?*	full	none	partly	partly
2. Is there sufficient agreement for *successful* completion of tasks ?	yes	no	yes	yes
3. Are relationships *heterogeneous*—some positive, some negative ?	no	no	yes	yes
4. Is the subject *accepted* by someone else ?	yes	no	no	yes

Pattern IV than in Pattern III. This comparison affords a clean test, for in other characteristics, such as degree of integration, sufficient agreement to reach a decision, heterogeneity of relationships (some positive, some negative) the two patterns are identical. Testing the second hypothesis, on group integration, is less straightforward. We cannot, for example, conclude from a comparison of fully integrated and malintegrated patterns how the variable operates because some of the other properties just mentioned, including personal acceptance, also differ. To see how a test is possible in spite of this interdependence we first examine the characteristics of all four patterns as shown above.

Though there is interdependence, it is evident that no two patterns are alike in all characteristics. This means that we may infer which variables or simple combinations of variables account for any observed rank order in congeniality. For example, if the relationship in Pattern IV is more positive than in Pattern III (indicating the predicted effect of acceptance) but if in addition we find that Pattern I is still more positive than IV and that Pattern II is more negative than III, we can conclude that personal acceptance and group integration interact to produce the greatest likelihood of a positive relationship. In fact, this is what is predicted by the first and second hypotheses. No other set of differences will enable us to reject the null hypotheses, and this set cannot be accounted for by the effects of the other structural characteristics listed above. Therefore, providing the first hypothesis holds, we test the second hypothesis by testing specifically for the following rank order in congeniality of relationship between first subject and newcomer:

Pattern	Rank order
I	1
II	4
III	3
IV	2

Correspondingly, the alternative hypotheses are tested in terms of given rank orders. Since the hypotheses do not contend that complete interaction exists between acceptance and group integration, there are a greater number of rank orders, which if observed enable us to reject the null hypotheses. The principal ones are:

Pattern	Rank orders		
I	4	3	4
II	3	4	2
III	1	1	1
IV	2	2	3

Results

We now follow in chronological order the development of the relationship between a member of the initial group and the newcomer. As we come to each measure we present the means for the four patterns, the relevant results from the analysis of variance and our conclusions regarding the two hypotheses and their alternatives. We do not report the breakdown of means by role-playing teams because in no case were teams a significant source of variance.

Anticipated Value. We find that the subject *out of* the coalition values the newcomer the most; the subject in a fully integrated group the least. From Pattern I through IV, the rank order is 4, 3, 1, 2, differences between the four means being significant at the .05 level. The results, we see, are contrary to the first and second hypotheses and in line with the alternative hypotheses. Being accepted by someone in the initial group lessens the value of the newcomer and this is accentuated when all members accept each other. In this instance, before the two persons interact, and from the point of view only of the first subject, the evidence supports the principle derived from Simmel and von Wiese.

The Working Relationship. Actually working together is a different matter. Results show that having an ally in the previous group leads to a *better* working relationship. In itself, the state of integration of the group makes no difference. Instead, another group characteristic mentioned above, namely, heterogeneity of ties, interacting with acceptance, constitutes the second important factor. This means that one works best with the newcomer when one has had, and has, an ally and some other member of the group has been, or is, rejected. One works least well when the group has been disorganized—when all members reject one another. From Pattern I through IV, the average activity rates are .28, .16, .21, and .38; the average support rates are .14, − .18, .01, and .28, the differences between the latter means being significant at the .01 level. Since the two measures are associated we take the more definite set of differences (support rates) as an estimate of the relationship. Pattern IV is more positive than Pattern III, which means that while other variables are constant, personal acceptance leads to a more congenial working relationship.

What is the effect of group integration? It cannot be a positive factor because support is lower when there is complete integration (Pattern I) than when there is only partial integration (Pattern IV).

On the other hand, it cannot be a negative factor because support is lower when there is malintegration (Pattern II) than when it is partial (Pattern III). Our conclusion is that it makes no important difference. Do any of the other structural properties mentioned above? Group success does not, because even though Pattern II is unsuccessful and significantly lower in support than the others, there is a significant difference between two successful patterns (I and IV).

We suggest that *heterogeneity of relationships* along with *personal acceptance* accounts for the major observed differences. Results show that the most positive relationship exists when there are both positive and negative ties and the first subject is accepted (IV). The least positive relationship exists when ties are homogeneous and the subject is rejected (II).

Conclusion: For the first hypothesis, which involves personal acceptance, we reject both the null and alternative hypotheses. For the second, involving group integration, we do not reject the null hypothesis. Integration is indeterminate. We conclude that a) personal acceptance/ rejection and b) heterogeneity/homogeneity of the emotional ties are the two important variables. It is perhaps of interest that relativity of acceptance is not symmetrical: being relatively better off than others induces a positive relationship, but being relatively deprived does not induce the most unsatisfactory one.

How Subject and Newcomer Interact When Alone. As we might expect, when the role-players are withdrawn and when there is no task before them, the subjects interact differently. From Pattern I through IV, the average activity rates are 73.5, 66.8, 87.5, and 88.4; the average support rates are .23, .31, .29, and .40, the differences between these latter means being significant at the .05 level, except between Patterns II and III. We see, first, that activity and support are not associated as they were in the working group. The subjects in the homogeneous patterns (I and II) are relatively passive; while those in the heterogeneous groups are more active. Neither this nor the observed rank order in support is expected from either set of hypotheses. It is true that support is higher in Pattern IV than in III, indicating (in line with the first hypothesis) that acceptance leads to a positive relationship, but the effect is not general, for support is lower in Pattern I (where there is acceptance) than in two patterns where there is rejection. Analysis shows that neither personal acceptance, nor integration, nor heterogeneity, nor group success determine the difference. . . .

How Subjects Feel about Each Other. Using the sociometric rating and the ratio described in the previous section, an analysis of variance test shows no significant differences between pairs of subjects in the four patterns. For this measure we reject no null hypotheses.

How Satisfied the Subjects Are with Their Group Experience. Since items in the satisfaction questionnaire we used[16] refer to what happened in the group as a whole rather than specifically to the

relationship between subjects, we do not use the data as a test of our hypotheses. We simply present the scores to give a fuller picture of how the subjects feel in the working group. From Pattern I through IV, average secores for the first subject are 58, 40, 41 and 54; average scores for the newcomer are 52, 43, 56 and 53, with differences in the first set significant at the .05 level, except for Patterns II and III, and differences in the second set also significant at the .05 level, except for Patterns I and IV. In three of the patterns the scores follow the support rates fairly closely: satisfaction is high and mutual in Patterns I and IV and low and mutual in Pattern II. In Pattern III the subject is dissatisfied while the newcomer is more satisfied than in any other type of group. This difference is probably due to the fact, which we shall refer to later, that the newcomer rejects the subject out of the coalition (just as the others do), joining their coalition.

Conclusion. The general conclusion from our results is that, with expansion of a group, the emotional ties between members of the initial group help determine how the new person will fit in. The obvious note in this should not cover up several important implications. The first is that the organization of the whole group, as well as the particular place a member has in it, makes a difference. How you work with a new member is determined as much by how others react to *each other* as it is influenced by how they

---

[16] Sample items taken from the Bales' Satisfaction Questionnaire (unpublished): "Some of the participants were too aggressive," "I felt like a guinea pig." The subject is asked to check one of six responses from strongly agreed

to strongly disagreed. Responses are weighted arbitrarily and the sum of checked responses constitutes the satisfaction score. A high score indicates high satisfaction.

feel toward you. The second is that, at least in shifting from three to four persons, there apparently exists no structural tendency associated with the foursome (two-against-two, for example) that erases the effects of the ties in the previous threesome.

In more detail, what can be concluded about the effect of the two independent variables in our hypotheses? In respect to personal acceptance, our results show that, in anticipation of the newcomer, it *decreases* his expected value; that, in the actual working group, it *increases* the probability of a positive relationship; and, finally, it *increases* this probability when they are alone, providing ties in the original group were heterogeneous. Group integration *reduces* the anticipated value of the newcomer, but it has no important effect one way or another in the working group or in the "free" period. The variable either plays a tertiary role or no significant role at all. In its place as an important group characteristic is *heterogeneity*. It interacts with personal acceptance, *increasing* the probability of a positive working relationship. Neither these three variables, nor any other that we have tested, affects significantly our measure of the mutuality of liking between old member and newcomer.

If we take the working relationship as an estimate of how old member and newcomer get along in a group—as an estimate superior to anticipations alone and to interaction when the role-players are not present—the results show, to repeat, that a) the *acceptance* of a given member by others and b) the *heterogeneity* of the emotional ties in the initial group interact to produce a higher probability of a congenial relationship. In our experi-

ment this case is represented by Pattern IV. Here the first subject is a member of a coalition against a third person; on arrival the newcomer is welcomed into and joins the coalition, rejecting the isolate.

Discussion

As noted above, Simmel's proposition that acceptance in the pair increases the probability of a negative relationship with the newcomer is, in effect, applied by von Wiese to the expansion of the triad. His application is under a special set of conditions which we do not duplicate experimentally. For one thing, the isolate in our experiment is not free to "seek out" a partner. Secondly, the experimental group is a single working unit, whereas it is not clear whether von Wiese has in mind this kind of group—or whether he refers to semi-detached pairs with no more than three persons interacting at any one time. With these differences in conditions making a direct test of his argument impossible, we can only say that in our setting we find no evidence whatever that the group separates into two pairs. On the contrary, when the situation is most ripe —when the threesome is split two-against-one and when the isolate says he would *value* a partner—the newcomer makes the simple choice of joining the *others*, who (we find from the reactions in Pattern IV) welcome him, if for no other reason than to avoid a two-two split which might jeopardize their positions. Our evidence is that the coalition pattern in the threesome develops into the three-against-one split. Moreover, we believe that in a working group, even in the relatively unusual case where the isolate is given the prerogative of choosing the new group member, it would take a strong positive relationship indeed to stand up against the contrary forces which tend to keep the isolate an isolate.

Our evidence is that we cannot generalize from Simmel's proposition to the expansion of the triad. We do not know if the proposition holds for the expansion of the dyad, but if it does we must ask whether the dynamics of expansion in the two cases might not be fundamentally different, or, in some respects, even opposite. Is the tendency in one case according to Simmel's proposition and in the other case according to the contrary principle derived from Freud?

With this question in mind, let us examine more closely such expansion of the triad as involves the variable of heterogeneity, a variable that neither Simmel nor Freud discusses. First, let us assume that acceptance and heterogeneity operate for all group members of the triad as they do for the experimental subject; second, let us assume, for the moment, that the way one member relates to the newcomer does not materially affect how another will relate to him. Noting that from the present point of view Patterns III and IV are identical, and applying our findings, the structures develop into the four-person patterns shown in the accompanying figure.

In each case the prior pattern is visible in the subsequent structure. Moreover, other structural characteristics mentioned above remain essentially the same; homogeneity/heterogeneity, degree of integration, potential for success, etc. These facts suggest a simple but general principle of expansion; namely, *given a clear group organization and the addition of a new*

member, a set of forces operates which tends to preserve, with the minimum alteration, the essentials of the state of organization before the addition.[17] Within "organization" should be included both the pattern of internal ties and the relationship of the group to the external situation. Acceptance of the newcomers in the first pattern maintains the group's homogeneity and its integration; rejection in the disorganized group maintains disorganization; and absorption of the newcomer into the coalition maintains the balance of power within a coalition and keeps the isolate an isolate.

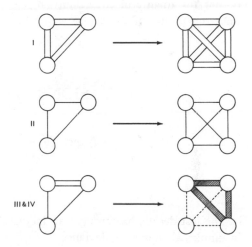

Fig. 1. Tendencies in the structural development from three- to four-person groups. Strongest positive is indicated by shaded double lines; strongest negative by solid single line, and moderate negative by dotted line.

---

[17] See Parsons, Bales and Shils, *op. cit.*, pp. 99–103, for the related question of the conditions of equilibrium.

Now it is just this principle that apparently does not operate when the third member is added to the dyad. True, the congeniality of the pair is still visible in the new coalition pattern, but the group property of homogeneity changes to heterogeneity and full integration to partial. Some obvious but unique properties of the dyad become relevant. Heterogeneity cannot exist in the dyad. In our use of the term, even if positive cathexis exists but is not reciprocated, we consider the relationship incongenial, negative, and therefore homogeneous. Groups of all other sizes can be either heterogeneous or homogeneous. The second obvious point is that the quality of the relationship defines the nature of the group as a whole.

If rejecting the newcomer is the way to maintain the former positive tie, the very process of maintenance undermines the integrative and homogeneous character of the group. If Simmel is right, the preservation principle does not operate. Were it operating the new group would be "all positive."

For these reasons, we suggest that if Simmel is correct, the principles of expansion for the dyad are basically different from those of the triad. Moreover, it appears that the lower limit for the operation of the preservation principle is the increase from three to four members. We see no compelling reason at this time to suggest an upper limit.

INVASIONS OF PERSONAL SPACE*

Nancy Jo Russo and Robert Sommer

The last decade has brought an increase in empirical studies of deviance. One line of investigation has used the case study approach with individuals whom society has classified as deviants—prostitutes, drug addicts, homosexuals, mental patients, etc. The other approach, practiced less frequently, has involved staged situations in which one individual, usually the investigator or one of his students, violates the norm or "routine ground" in a given situation and observes the results.[1] The latter approach is in the category of an experiment in that it is the investigator himself who creates the situation he observes and therefore has the possibility of systematically varying the parameters of social intercourse singly or in combinations. From this standpoint these studies have great promise for the development of an experimental sociology following the model set

---

* Nancy Jo Russo and Robert Sommer, "Invasions of Personal Space," *Social Problems*, 14 (1966), 206–14. Reprinted by permission.

[1] See for example Harold Garfinkel, "Studies of the Routine Grounds of Everyday Activities," *Social Problems*, 11 (Winter, 1964), pp. 225–250.

down by Greenwood.[2] With topics such as human migration, collective disturbance, social class, the investigator observes events and phenomena already in existence. Control of conditions refers to modes of observations and is largely on an *ex post facto* statistical or correlational basis. On the other hand, few staged studies of deviance have realized their promise as experimental investigations. Generally they are more in the category of demonstrations, involving single gross variations of one parameter and crude and impressionistic measurement of effect without control data from a matched sample not subject to the norm violation. Of more theoretical importance is the lack of systematic variation in degree and kind of the many facets of norm violation. The reader is left with the impression that deviancy is an all-or-none phenomenon caused by improper dress, impertinent answers, naive questions, etc. It cannot be denied that a graduate student washing her clothes in the town swimming pool is breaking certain norms. But we cannot be sure of the norms that are violated or the sanctions attached to each violation without some attempt at isolating and varying single elements in the situation.

The present paper describes a series of studies of one norm violation, sitting too close to another individual. Conversational distance is affected by many things including room density, the acquaintance of the individuals, the personal relevance of the topic discussed, the cultural backgrounds of the individuals, the personalities of the individuals, etc.[3] There are a dozen studies of conversational distance which have shown that people from Latin countries stand closer together than North Americans,[4] eye contact has important effect on conversational distance,[5] introverts stand farther apart than extraverts,[6] friends place themselves closer together than strangers,[7] and so on, but there is still, under any set of conditions, a range of conversational distance which is considered normal for that situation. Several of these investigators, notably Birdwhistell,[8] Garfinkel,[9] Goffman,[10] and Sommer[11] have described the effects of intruding into this distance or personal space that surrounds each individual. The interest shown in the human spacing mechanisms as well as the possibilities of objective measurement of both norm violation and defensive postures suggests that this is an excellent area in which to systematically study norm violations.

The present paper describes several studies of invasions of personal space that

---

[4] Edward T. Hall, "The Language of Space," *Landscape*, 10 (Autumn, 1960), pp. 41–44.

[5] Michael Argyle and Janet Dean, "Eye-Contact, Distance, and Affiliation," *Sociometry*, 28 (September, 1965), pp. 289–304.

[6] John L. Williams, "Personal Space and its Relation to Extraversion-Introversion," unpublished M.A. thesis, University of Alberta, 1963.

[7] Kenneth B. Little, "Personal Space," *Journal of Experimental Social Psychology*, 1 (August, 1960), pp. 237–247.

[8] Birdwhistell, R. L. *Introduction to Kinesics*, Washington, D.C.: Foreign Service Institute, 1952.

[9] Garfinkel, *op. cit.*

[10] Erving Goffman, *Behavior in Public Places*, Glencoe, Ill.: The Free Press, 1963.

[11] Robert Sommer, "Studies in Personal Space," *Sociometry*, 22 (September, 1959), pp. 247–260.

---

[2] Ernest Greenwood, *Experimental Sociology*, New York: Kings Crown Press, 1945.

[3] Edward T. Hall, *The Silent Language*, Garden City, N.Y.: Doubleday, 1959.

took place over a two-year period. The first was done during the summer of 1963 in a mental hospital. At the time it seemed that systematic studies of spatial invasions could only take place in a "crazy place" where norm violation would escape some of the usual sanctions applied in the outside world. Though there is a strong normative control system that regulates the conduct of mental patients toward one another and toward staff, the rules governing staff conduct toward patients (except cases of brutality, rape, or murder), and particularly higher status staff, such as psychiatrists, physicians, and psychologists, are much less clear. At times, it seems that almost anything can be done in a mental hospital provided it is called research and one can cite such examples as psychosurgery, various drug experiments, and recent investigations of operant conditioning as instances where unusual and sometimes unproven or even harmful procedures were employed with the blessings of hospital officialdom. To call a procedure "research" is a way of "bracketing" it in time and space and thus excluding it from the usual rules and mores. This is one reason why we supposed that spatial invasions would be more feasible inside a mental hospital than outside. We had visions of a spatial invasion on a Central Park bench resulting in bodily assault or arrest on a sex deviant or "suspicious character" charge. It seemed that some studies of norm violation were deliberately on a one-shot basis to avoid such difficulties. After the first study of spatial invasions in a mental hospital had been completed, however, it became apparent that the method could be adapted for use in more typical settings. We were then able to undertake similar intrusions on a systematic basis in a university library without any untoward consequences,

though the possibilities of such problems arising were never far beyond the reaches of consciousness in any of the experimental sessions.

METHOD

The first study took place on the grounds of Mendocino State Hospital, a 1500-bed mental institution situated in parklike surroundings. Most wards were unlocked and many patients spent considerable time outdoors. In wooded areas it was common to see patients seated underneath trees, one to a bench. Because of the easy access to the outside as well as the number of patients involved in hospital industry, the ward areas were relatively empty during the day. This made it possible for the patients to isolate themselves from other people by finding a deserted area on the grounds or remaining in the almost empty wards. The invasions of personal space took place both indoors and outdoors. The victims were chosen on the basis of these criteria: the victim would be a male, sitting alone, and not engaged in any clearly defined activities such as reading, card playing, etc. All sessions took place near the long stay wards, which meant that newly-admitted patients were largely omitted from the study. When a patient meeting these criteria was located, E walked over and sat beside the patient without saying a word. If the victim moved his chair or moved farther down the bench, E would move a like distance to keep the space between them about six inches. There were two experimental conditions. In one, E sat alongside a patient and took complete notes of what ensued. He also jiggled his keys occasionally and looked at the patient in order to assert his dominance. In the second experimental condition, E simply sat down next to the victim and, three or four times during the 20 minute session, jiggled his keys. Control subjects were selected from other patients seated at some distance from E but still within E's visual field. To be eligible for the control group, a patient had to be sitting by himself and not reading or otherwise engaged in an activity as well as be visible to E.

Each session took a maximum of twenty minutes. There were 64 individual sessions with different patients, 39 involved the procedure in which E took notes and 25 involved no writing.[12] One ward dayroom was chosen for additional, more intensive observations. During the daylight hours this large room was sparsely populated and the same five patients occupied the same chairs. These patients would meet Esser's[13] criteria of territoriality in that each spent more than 75 per cent of his time in one particular area.

RESULTS

The major data of the study consist of records of how long each patient remained seated in his chair following the invasion. This can be compared with the length of time the control patients remained seated. Figure 1 shows the cumulative number of patients who had departed at each one-minute interval of the 20 minute session. Within two minutes, all of the controls were still seated but 36 per cent of the experimental subjects had been driven away. Within nine minutes fully half of

---

[12] Four incomplete sessions are omitted from this total. On two occasions a patient was called away by a nurse and on two other occasions the session was terminated when the patient showed signs of acute stress. The intruder in Study One was the junior author, a 35 year old male of slight build. It is likely that invasions by a husky six-footer would have produced more immediate flight reactions.

[13] Aristide H. Esser, *et al.*, "Territoriality of Patients on a Research Ward," *Recent Advances in Biological Psychiatry*, Vol. 8, in Joseph Wortis (ed.), New York: Plenum Press, 1965.

the victims had departed compared with only 8 per cent of the controls. At the end of the 20 minute session, 64 per cent of the experimental subjects had departed compared with 33 per cent of the controls. Further analysis showed that the writing condition was more potent than the no-writing condition but that this difference was significant only at the .10 level ($\chi^2 = 4.61$, df $= 2$). The patient's actual departure from his chair was the most obvious reaction to the intrusion. Many more subtle indications of the patient's discomfort were evident. Typically the victim would immediately face away from E, pull in his shoulders, and place his elbows at his sides. Mumbling, irrelevant laughter, and delusional talk also seemed to be used by the victim to keep E at a distance.

Repeated observation of the same patients took place on one particular ward where the patients were extremely territorial in their behavior. Five patients generally inhabited this large room and sat in the same chairs day after day. There were gross differences in the way these particular territorial patients reacted to the writer's presence. In only one case (S_3) was E clearly dominant. At the other extreme with S_1 and S_2, it was like trying to move the Rock of Gibraltar. E invariably left these sessions defeated, with his tail between his legs, often feeling the need to return to his colleagues and drink a cup of coffee before attempting another experimental session. S_5 is a peculiar case in that sometimes he was budged but other times he wasn't.

STUDY TWO

These sessions took place in the study hall of a university library, a large room with high ceilings and book-lined walls.

The room contains fourteen large tables in two equal rows. Each table is 4 × 16 feet, and accommodates six chairs on each long side. Because of its use as a study area, students typically try to space themselves as far as possible from others. Each victim was the first female sitting alone in a pre-determined part of the room with at least one book in front of her, two empty chairs on either side (or on one side if she was at the end of the table), and an empty chair across from her. An empty chair was also required to be across from E's point of invasion. The second female to meet these criteria and who was visible to E served as a control. The control was observed from a distance and no invasion was attempted. Sessions took

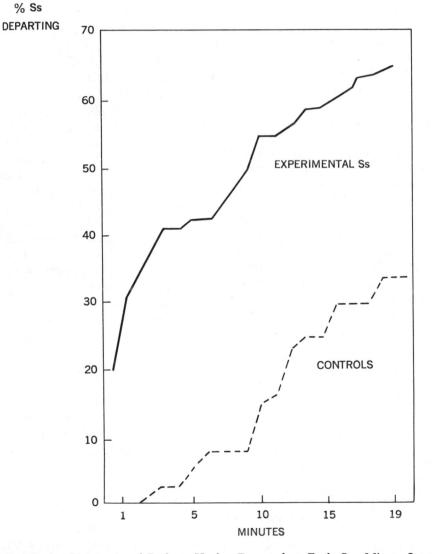

Fig. 1. Cumulative Percentage of Patients Having Departed at Each One-Minute Interval.

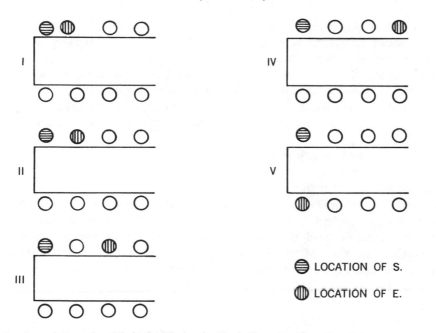

Fig. 2. Seating of Intruder Vis-à-vis Victim in Each Experimental Condition.

place between the hours of 8–5 on Mondays through Fridays; because of time changes between classes and the subsequent turnover of the library population, the observations began between 5 and 15 minutes after the hour. There were five different experimental conditions.

Condition I: E walked up to an empty chair beside an S, pulling the chair out at an angle, and sat down, completely ignoring S's presence. As E sat down, she unobtrusively moved the chair close to the table and to S, so that the chairs were approximately within three inches from one another. The E would lean over her book, in which she surreptitiously took notes, and tried to maintain constant shoulder distance of about 12 inches between E and S. To use Crook's[14] terms,

E tried to maintain the arrival distance, and to keep the S from adjusting to a settled distance. This was sometimes difficult to do because the chairs were 18½ inches wide and an S would sometimes sit on the other half of her chair, utilizing its width as an effective barrier. However, E tried to get as close to the Ss as possible without actually having any physical contact. If the S moved her chair away, E would follow by pushing her chair backward at an angle and then forward again, under the pretense of adjusting her skirt. At no time did she consciously acknowledge S's presence. In this condition E took detailed notes of the S's behavior, as well as noting time of departure.

Condition II: E went through the same procedure, except instead of moving the adjacent chair closer to S, E sat in the

---

[14] J. H. Crook, "The Basis of Flock Organization in Birds," in W. H. Thorpe and O. L. Zangwill (eds.), *Current Problems in Animal*

Behaviour, Cambridge: Cambridge University Press, 1961, pp. 125–149.

adjacent chair at the expected distance, which left about 15 inches between the chairs or about two feet between the shoulders of E and S.

Condition III: One empty seat was left between E and S, with a resulting shoulder distance of approximately three and a half feet.

Condition IV: Two empty seats were left between E and S with a resulting shoulder distance of about five feet.

Condition V: E sat directly across from S, a distance of about four feet.

In all conditions E noted the time of initial invasion, the time of the S's departure (or the end of the thirty minute session, depending on which came first), and any observable accommodation to E's presence such as moving books or the chair. For the controls E noted the time the session began and the time of the C's departure if it occurred within thirty minutes after the start of the session.

Results

Figure 3 shows the number of subjects remaining after successive five minute periods. Since there was no significant difference between the scores in Conditions 2–5, these were combined in the analysis.

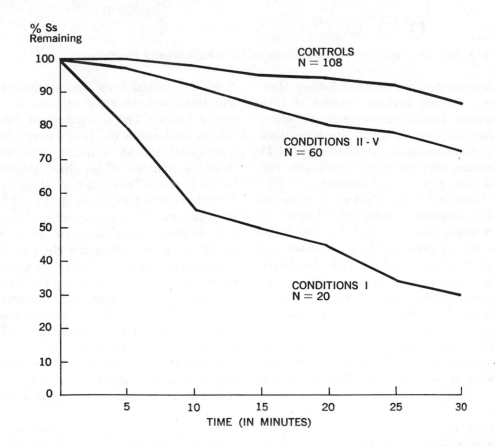

Fig 3. Per cent of Victims Remaining at Each Five Minute Interval after the Invasion.

At the end of the thirty minute session, 87 per cent of the controls, 73 per cent of the Ss in the combined conditions remained, compared to only 30 per cent of the experimental Ss in Condition I. Statistical analysis shows that Condition I produced significantly more flight than any of the other conditions, while there was a slight but also significant difference between the combined conditions (2–5) and the control condition. Although flight was the most clearly defined reaction to the invasion, many more subtle signs of the victim's discomfort were evident. Frequently an S drew in her arm and head, turned away from E exposing her shoulder and back, with her elbow on the table, her face resting on her hand. The victims used objects including books, notebooks, purses, and coats as barriers, and some made the wide chair into a barrier.

Discussion

These results show clearly that spatial invasions have a disruptive effect and can produce reactions ranging from flight at one extreme to agonistic display at the other. The individual differences in reacting to the invasion are evident; there was no single reaction among our subjects to someone "sitting too close." The victim can attempt to accommodate himself to the invasion in numerous ways, including a shift in position, interposing a barrier between himself and the invader, or moving farther away. If these are precluded by the situation or fail because the invader shifts positions too, the victim may eventually take to flight. The methods we used did not permit the victim to achieve a comfortable *settled distance*. Crook[15] studies the spacing mechanisms in birds, and found three component factors that maintain individual distance, which he defined as the area around an individual within which the approach of a neighboring bird is reacted to with either avoidance or attack. A number of measurements may be taken when studying individual distance— the arrival distance (how far away from settled birds a newcomer will land), settled distance (the resultant distance after adjustments have occurred), and the distance after departure. The conditions in Study One and in Condition I of the second study called for E to maintain the arrival distance, and to keep the victim from adjusting to a settled distance. In these conditions, the victim was unable to increase the arrival distance by moving away (since the invader followed him down the bench in Study One and moved her chair closer in Study Two), and the greatest number of flight reactions was produced by these conditions. McBride,[16] who has studied the spatial behaviors of animals in confinement, has found that avoidance movements and turning aside are common reactions to crowding, particularly when a submissive animal is close to a dominant animal. Literally the dominant bird in a flock has more space and the other birds will move aside and look away when the dominant bird approaches. Looking away to avoid extensive eye contact was also a common reaction in the present studies. This probably would

---

[15] Crook, *op. cit.*

[16] Glen McBride, *A General Theory of Social Organization and Behaviour*, St. Lucia: University of Queensland Press, 1964; also McBride, *et al.*, "Social Forces Determining Spacing and Head Orientation in a Flock of Domestic Hens," *Nature*, 197 (1963), pp. 1272–1273.

not have occurred if a subordinate or lower status individual had invaded the personal space of a dominant or higher status individual. There was also a dearth of direct verbal responses to the invasions. Only two of the mental patients spoke directly to E although he sat right beside them, and only one of the 80 student victims asked E to move over. This is some support for Hall's view that "we treat space somewhat as we treat sex. It is there but we don't talk about it."[17]

We see then that a violation of expected conversational distance produces, first of all, various accommodations on the part of the victim. The intensity of his reaction is influenced by many factors including territoriality, the dominance-submission relationship between invader and victim, the locus of the invasion, the victim's attribution of sexual motives to the intruder (in this case all victims and intruders were like-sex individuals), etc. All of these factors influence the victim's definition of the situation and consequently his reaction to it. In the present situation the first reaction to the invasion was accommodation or adaptation: the individual attempted to "live with" the invasion by turning aside,

interposing a notebook between himself and the stranger, and pulling in his elbows. When this failed to relieve the tension produced by the norm violation, flight reactions occurred.

There are other elements in the invasion sequence that can be varied systematically. We have not yet attempted heterosexual invasion sequences, or used invaders of lower social standing, or explored more than two unusual and contrasting environments. We are making a start toward using visual rather than spatial invasions, in this case starting at a person rather than moving too close to him. Preliminary data indicate that visual invasions are relatively ineffective in a library where the victims can easily retreat into their books and avoid a direct visual confrontation. There are many other types of intrusions, including tactile and olfactory, that have intriguing research potentialities. It is important to realize that the use of staged norm violations permits these elements to be varied singly and in combination, and in this sense to go beyond the methods of *ex post facto* or "natural experiments" or single-point demonstrations. It is noteworthy that the area of norm violation provides one of the most fruitful applications for the experimental method.

---

[17] Hall, *The Silent Language, op. cit.*

EFFECTS OF SIZE AND
TASK TYPE ON GROUP PERFORMANCE
AND MEMBER REACTIONS*

J. Richard Hackman and Neil Vidmar

Many of the most obvious—and most potent—determiners of group behavior are, ironically enough, also among the least investigated and least understood in the group psychology field. Several reviewers (e.g., Golembiewski, 1962; Collins and Guetzkow, 1964; McGrath and Altman, 1966) have documented the dearth of systematic knowledge about two such factors: group size and the nature of the group task.

Clearly, both group size and task characteristics should make differences in the ways people interact in groups and in the kinds of reactions they have to the group experience. The scattered empirical work which has involved these variables documents this contention. Thomas and Fink (1963) reviewed 31 studies of group size. They concluded that while research on size has not been carried out in a very systematic fashion, the variable is an important one in understanding group behavior. The potency of task effects on group behavior has been demonstrated in

the work of Breer and Locke (1965), Morris (1966), and Hackman (1968).

The present research is an attempt to assess systematically the effects which group size and task characteristics—considered both separately and in combination —have on group performance and member reactions. Six group sizes and three types of tasks are used. In addition, the generality of the findings is examined by comparing data collected in two different laboratory settings. The focus of the research may be summarized by three general questions which are discussed separately below.

How does group size relate to group performance and member reactions? Previous results regarding the effects of size on group performance have not been altogether consistent. A review of the literature by Thomas and Fink (1963) indicated that quality of performance and productivity were positively related to group size under some conditions and in no instances were smaller groups superior. Measures of speed, however, showed no difference or favored smaller groups.

As Thomas and Fink suggest, the inconsistency of results may derive from aspects of the research methodologies which were used. For example, many studies

* J. Richard Hackman and Neil Vidmar, "Effects of Size and Task Type on Group Performance and Member Reactions," *Sociometry*, 33 (1970), 37–54. Reprinted by permission of the American Sociological Association.

have not varied size in complete sequence over a wide range, making it difficult to discern the exact relationship between size and performance. Further, studies varied widely in the kinds of tasks which were used. Such task heterogeneity across studies could easily obscure size-performance relationships if, in fact, task characteristics interact with size in affecting performance.

This study attempts to overcome some of the difficulties which have plagued earlier studies by using groups of all sizes between two and seven members, and by dealing with task characteristics in a systematic fashion. In addition, group performance is assessed on seven independent dimensions (described below) to permit a more detailed analysis of how group size affects performance. Use of solution quality or speed as the only performance criteria (as has been done in many previous studies) may not fully reveal the complexity of performance effects attributable to group size.

Data regarding the effects of group size on member reactions are relatively more clear than results relevant to performance. Thomas and Fink (1963), Golembiewski (1962), and Deutsch and Rosenau (unpublished, 1963), all conclude that the smaller the group, the more a member will be satisfied with the group discussion and his part in it. The latter authors report that for a human relations problem "... the size of the group had ... an inverse effect on the group members' own satisfaction with it. As size increased, communication difficulties increased and the group members felt they had less influence on each other, that they were more inhibited in expressing their views, and that the group worked less cooperatively on the task" (p. 3). Many of the negative reactions of the members to larger groups

may stem from the difficulties which these groups have in organizing themselves. As size increases, there is a tendency for groups to form sub-groups or cliques and for more division of labor to occur (Golembiewski, 1962; Hare, 1952). As Berkowitz (cited in Thomas and Fink, 1963) notes, the cohesion of the total group drops under such conditions.

Nevertheless, the findings of Slater (1958) show that members may also react negatively if the group is too small. Slater suggests that members find groups of size five most satisfying. In smaller groups the members appear to feel that the group is too "intimate" and that they cannot express disagreements. Consistent with this interpretation, Bales and Borgatta (1955) and O'Dell (1968) found that members of smaller groups tend to feel more tension, but at the same time express less hostility. In both studies groups of size two were found to be especially strongly characterized by high tension and low hostility.

This study attempts to replicate the Slater findings, using an instrument which should provide additional insight into the factors which differentiate the kinds of satisfaction experienced by members in various sizes of groups.

How do certain task characteristics relate to group performance and member reactions? Previous research has shown that both the pattern of group interaction and the nature of group products are strongly determined by characteristics of group tasks. In particular Morris (1966), Hackman (1968), and Kent and McGrath (1969) have documented the effects of three "types" of intellective group tasks on group process and performance. In all three studies, however, the data were collected from three-person groups.

This study attempts to extend the generality of the previous findings by examining the relationship between task type (described below) and performance characteristics for groups of different sizes. In addition, the effects of task type on member reactions to the group are assessed.

Do group size and task type interact in determining group performance and member reactions? There are good empirical and theoretical reasons to expect that group size and task factors interact in affecting what happens in groups. Roby and Lanzetta (1958) have pointed out that different tasks may require different behaviors (i.e., have different "critical demands") for successful performance. Small groups may have an advantage over large groups in meeting some of these demands (e.g., high levels of coordination among members), while the reverse may be true for other demands (e.g., generation of a large pool of heterogeneous ideas). Steiner (1966) has presented several models of group performance which deal with such size-task interactions in considerable detail.

The present study attempts to determine, for "intellective" group tasks, whether group performance and member reactions are substantially influenced by the interaction between size and task type.

METHOD

Independent Variables

Three independent variables were incorporated into the research design. They are: group size, type of task, and experimental laboratory.

Group size. Six different sizes of groups were used, ranging from size two through size seven.

Task type. The three task "types" identified

by Hackman (1968) served as another factor in the study design. All of the tasks required the group to produce a written passage (or "product") and hence may be characterized as requiring intellective (as opposed to motor) activties on the part of group members. None of the tasks has a unique solution.

Production tasks call for the production and presentation of ideas, images, or arrangements (e.g., "Write a story about this inkblot," or "Describe this mountain scene"). *Discussion tasks* call for evaluation of issues, usually with a requirement of group consensus (e.g., "What makes for success in our culture?" or "Should birth control pills be made available without prescription?"). *Problem solving* tasks require members to spell out a course of action to be followed to resolve some specific problem (e.g., "How should a person go about attaching pictures to walls without scarring the walls?" or "How could you safely change a tire on a busy expressway at night?")

Since previous results (e.g., Kent and McGrath, 1969) have shown that differences among specific tasks control at least as much behavioral variance as differences among specific groups of subjects, a total of 36 different tasks (12 of each of the three types) was used. By using a large number of specific tasks, the generality of obtained results is enhanced. In addition, the possibility that differences associated with task type are, in fact, due to characteristics of the specific tasks used is diminished.

The tasks used were approximately equivalent in difficulty and in familiarity to the subjects. Effects associated with the specific tasks were statistically accounted for in the analysis of variance.

Experimental laboratory. The experiment was run simultaneously at two institutions (Yale University and the University of Illinois, Urbana) using male undergraduates at each institution as subjects. Subjects at the University of Illinois were obtained from the introductory psychology subject pool and were required to participate; subjects at Yale were volunteers recruited from the student body at large and paid $1.25 per hour for participa-

Table 1

ITEMS ON THE MEMBER REACTION QUESTIONNAIRE

1. This group was too small (in number of members) for best results on the task it was trying to do.
2. This group was too large (in number of members) for best results on the task it was trying to do.
3. This group made the best use of its time solving the task.
4. I felt tense and uncomfortable in the group on this task.
5. There was too much competition among the group members.
6. There were considerable differences of ability and competence among the members of this group.
7. There was much disagreement among the members of the group on this task.
8. Some people in the group talked too much.
9. *I* talked too much.
10. Considering the entire problem-solving session, my opinion was given adequate consideration by the other group members.
11. There was a definite leader in the group.
12. My group *needed* a strong leader to keep it on the track.
13. My group was creative on this task.
14. I felt inhibited from expressing my feelings during the group discussion.
15. There was sufficient time to work on the task.
16. I think my group set forth a high quality written solution to this task.
17. I had considerable influence in determining my group's final written solution to the task.
18. Rather than one unified group, it seemed the group worked in sub-groups or as individuals on this problem.
19. I was interested in this problem.
20. How much influence did the group have on your personal, final ideas about what would be a good solution to the task?
    (a great deal of influence, considerable influence, moderate influence, little influence, almost no influence).

tion. The experimental instructions were given to the subjects by Hackman at Yale and Vidmar at Illinois.

Considerable care was taken to ensure that all other aspects of the experimental methodology under the experimenters' control were as nearly identical as possible for the two laboratories. Thus, the differences between the laboratories were probably considerably less substantial than those which exist among most small group studies reported in the literature. By including the experimental laboratory as a factor in the study design, it is possible to test the approximate "lower bound" of inter-study generalizability. If substantive results in the present study should not generalize across the two laboratories, important questions must be raised about the process of comparing and generalizing findings from totally unrelated investigations.

Dependent Variables

Two classes of dependent variables were used in the study: member reactions to the

Table 2

GROUP SIZE EFFECTS ON PERFORMANCE AND MEMBER REACTIONS

Group Product Characteristics	Group Size						F-ratio[a]
	2	3	4	5	6	7	
Action orientation	4.41	4.14	4.18	4.03	4.02	3.92	0.61
Length	4.69	3.38	3.91	3.47	3.86	3.68	2.11
Originality	3.70	3.29	3.66	3.40	3.52	3.90	0.84
Optimism	4.38	4.13	4.25	3.90	3.84	4.16	1.21
Quality of presentation	4.37	4.16	4.04	3.91	3.85	4.07	0.48
Issue involvement	4.27	3.85	3.88	3.88	3.94	4.24	1.35
Creativity	4.24	3.84	3.99	3.90	4.06	4.13	1.01
Member Reactions[b]							
1. Group too small	2.85	2.46	2.35	2.25	2.02	1.95	3.00*
2. Group too large	2.04	2.32	2.76	2.99	3.79	3.69	12.38**
3. Made best use of time	5.37	4.70	4.37	4.39	3.91	4.25	6.45**
5. Too much competition	1.74	2.18	2.42	2.63	2.90	2.82	5.88**
6. Considerable differences in ability	2.32	2.97	3.28	3.52	3.90	4.29	11.86**
7. Much disagreement	2.06	2.72	2.77	3.03	3.35	3.20	6.54**
8. Some members talked too much	2.21	2.52	2.81	2.92	3.27	3.66	4.79**
10. My opinion considered	5.69	5.36	5.01	5.30	4.78	4.86	4.70**
14. I was inhibited	1.94	2.05	1.98	2.14	2.56	2.31	2.56*
17. I influenced the solution	5.17	4.63	4.50	4.08	3.93	4.06	13.45**
18. Not unified: subgroups	2.18	2.70	2.95	3.37	3.32	3.29	5.77**
20. Group influenced me	2.93	2.74	2.91	2.66	2.53	2.57	2.62**

[a] $df = 5, 60$.
[b] Only items relating significantly to group size are included.
* $p < .05$.
** $p < .01$.

group experience and characteristics of the written products prepared by the groups.

Member reactions.[1] A questionnaire was administered to each group member imme-diately after each task. It consisted of 20 items dealing with a diversity of possible reac-tions to the group experience. The items were derived from previous investigations and from *a priori* speculation about the effects of group size, task type, and their possible interactions. Each item was accompanied by a seven-point Likert-type scale anchored on the respective ends by "not at all true" and "very true." Scores for each subject on each item were averaged across group members, and the mean group scores per item were used in the

---

[1] Many related studies in the literature use the term "member satisfaction." The present authors prefer the term "member reactions" because both this study and previous studies have asked for descriptive reactions as well as the evaluative responses which the term "satis-faction" implies.

analysis. The items are presented in Table 1.

Group product measures. Primary measures of the characteristics of the written group products were six descriptive dimensions developed by Hackman, Jones, and McGrath (1967). The dimensions are (a) action orientation—the degree to which a product states or implies that a specific or general course of action should be, might be, or will be followed; (b) length; (c) originality—the degree to which a product is fresh and unusual (not necessarily good or creative) as opposed to obvious and mundane; (d) optimism—the degree to which the general point of view or tone of a product can be characterized as "positive" or optimistic as opposed to "negative" or pessimistic; (e) quality of presentation—evaluation of the grammatical, rhetorical, and literary qualities of a product; and (f) issue involvement—the degree to which a product takes or implies a particular point of view regarding some goal, event, issue, or procedure.

In addition, the global creativity of each product was assessed. Numerical scores on all seven dimensions were obtained for each product, by a seven-pile sorting procedure described in detail by Hackman et al. (1967). Reliabilities of the dimension scores used in the analyses ranged from .77 to .96, with a median reliability of .85.

Design

The study used a 6 × 3 × 2 (size × task type × laboratory) analysis of variance design with task as a repeated measure. Six groups of each of the six sizes were run at each laboratory. Hence a total of 72 groups were used, 36 at each institution. (Total N was 324 subjects.) Each experimental group worked on three tasks, one of each of the three types. Order of presentation of each task type was completely counterbalanced throughout the design.

Procedure

Up to 35 subjects were run at each experimental session. Subjects were randomly as-signed to groups of the various sizes. An attempt was made to run at least one group of each size at each session, but the plan was modified from time to time to accommodate the number of subjects present at a particular session.

Groups were allowed 15 minutes per task. When the time had elapsed, the groups were told to stop working on the task and were asked to complete the Member Reaction Questionnaire. When all members had finished the questionnaire, the group immediately began the next task. After three tasks had been completed, subjects reconvened for a discussion of the experiment and then were dismissed.

RESULTS

Size Effects on Performance and Member Reactions

The relationships between group size and the dependent variables are summarized in Table 2. Size was not significantly related to the measures of performance characteristics, although dyads were higher than groups of other sizes on six of the seven product dimensions. Size was significantly related to 12 of the 20 member reaction items.

Consistent with the findings of previous studies, there was more dissatisfaction with group processes as size increased. The larger the group size, the more members complained that the group was too large for effective task performance. Larger groups were seen as being highly competitive, as having considerable disagreement, and as showing disunity. Members reported feeling that some individuals talked too much in the larger groups and that they themselves felt inhibited from expressing their feelings. Considerable differences in ability and competence were seen as characterizing the larger groups.

Although individuals in smaller groups tended to feel that the groups were too small for best results, they also felt more personally involved in them. They indicated more often that their own opinions were considered by other members, that they personally influenced the solution, and that they in turn were more influenced by other group members. Finally, members of smaller groups felt that the group operated more efficiently and made better use of its time than did members of larger groups.

formance and member reactions are summarized in Table 3. Task type was significantly and substantially related to all seven product dimensions, and was significantly related to 10 of the 20 member reaction items.

The relationships between task type and performance replicate the findings of Hackman (1968) and of Kent and McGrath (1969) almost perfectly. Products from production tasks were very original, tended to be lengthy, had high literary quality, and were generally pessimistic or

Table 3
TASK EFFECTS ON PERFORMANCE AND MEMBER REACTIONS

Group Product Characteristics	Task Type		Problem Solving	F-ratio[a]
	Production	Discussion		
Action orientation	2.96	3.17	6.22	102.69**
Length	4.42	3.31	3.77	10.71**
Originality	4.87	3.24	2.62	58.83**
Optimism	3.49	3.77	5.06	45.36**
Quality of presentation	4.34	4.26	3.61	5.53**
Issue involvement	2.39	5.20	4.44	98.65**
Creativity	4.35	3.85	3.88	4.03**
Member Reaction[b]				
1. Group too small	2.13	2.44	2.37	3.30*
2. Group too large	3.23	2.90	2.66	8.80**
3. Made best use of time	4.34	4.36	4.79	4.95**
5. Too much competition	2.62	2.43	2.29	3.43*
12. Group *needed* strong leader	3.56	3.21	2.98	7.90**
13. Group was creative	4.94	4.05	4.26	15.81**
14. I was inhibited	2.26	2.20	2.03	3.23*
15. Was sufficient time	3.79	4.47	4.30	4.31*
18. Not unified: subgroups	3.17	3.02	2.72	5.04**
20. Group influenced me	2.90	2.62	2.65	7.17**

[a] $df = 5.60$.
[b] Only items relating significantly to task type are included.
* $p < .05$.
** $p < .01$.

Task Effects on Performance and Member Reactions

The effects of task type (production, discussion, and problem solving) on per-

negative in tone. In addition, products from production tasks were highest on overall "creativity." Products from discussion tasks were characterized by high issue involvement, and also tended to have high literary quality. Products from problem solving tasks were especially high on action orientation and were the most optimistic or positive in tone. Problem solving products tended to be low in quality of presentation.

Quite different reactions to the performance process itself (as indicated by the member reaction items) were elicited by the three types of tasks. Group members reported experiencing considerable "process" difficulty in working together on production tasks. These tasks (which call for the generation and presentation of new ideas) elicited feelings that there was too much competition among individuals and that a strong leader was needed to "keep the group on the track." Size was a problem for groups working on production tasks; there were many complaints that the group was too large for effective performance on production tasks and few complaints that it was too small. Nevertheless, group members reported that the group had considerable influence on their own feelings about the solution and that they were especially creative on the task; and the assessment of the group products bears out this contention.

When working on discussion and problem solving tasks, members generally reported a more relaxed atmosphere than was the case for production tasks. Discussion tasks yielded feelings that there was sufficient time to work on the solution but, in comparison to the other task types, that the group was less creative.

Group members working on problem solving tasks reported that they were able to work together more effectively than did individuals working on the other types of tasks. For example, groups split into subgroups less frequently; members reported feeling less inhibited about expressing their opinions; there was less noticeable compe-

tition among members; and members felt that the group made relatively good use of its time.

Interactions between Group Size and Task Type

Contrary to expectations, there were no significant interactions between group size and task type on the performance measures and only one involving member reactions. Members working on production and on discussion tasks reported higher levels of disagreement (item 7) in the group as size increased, whereas the level of disagreement was low and fairly constant across size for problem solving tasks. This finding is, of course, consistent with the generally low level of problems with group process reported by members working on problem solving tasks.

Laboratory Effects

For the seven measures of performance characteristics, there was one significant main effect involving experimental laboratory, two interactions between group size and laboratory, and four interactions between task type and laboratory. For the 20 member reaction items, there were seven significant main effects involving experimental laboratory and eight interactions between task type and laboratory. There were no interactions between size and laboratory.

DISCUSSION

The Uniqueness of Size Two

Early in the century, Simmel (1902) pointed out, on a conceptual level, the uniqueness of two-person groups, and recent empirical studies by Bales and Borgatta (1955) and O'Dell (1968) have demonstrated the special character of interaction in dyads.

The present data provided an opportunity to determine whether members of dyads react differently to the group experience than do members of groups of other sizes, and to see if the performance of dyads differs from that of larger groups.

To determine whether or not dyads were unique in the present study, the difference in mean score (ignoring sign) between dyads and triads was compared to the average difference between means for all other adjacent sizes (i.e., 3 vs. 4, 4 vs. 5, 5 vs. 6, and 6 vs. 7) on all dependent variables. For 13 of the 27 dependent variables the difference between dyads and triads was more than twice as large as the average difference between other adjacent sizes. Further, analyses comparing the scores of dyads to the average scores of all other groups showed that 11 of the 13 differences were statistically significant ($p < .05$, two-tailed).[2] The nature of the obtained differences is discussed below.

Dyads scored substantially higher than other groups on four of the seven product dimensions: action orientation, length, issue involvement, and creativity. These dimensions all are likely to be influenced by the general level of task-relevant activity in the group, which suggests members of dyads may have been more heavily invested in the performance process than were members of other groups.

Data from the Member Reaction Ques-

tionnaire tend to support the above interpretation. Members of dyads reported substantially more often than members of other groups that the group had made good use of its time, that each member had had considerable influence in determining the group solution, and that a high quality solution had been produced. Coordination problems were conspicuously absent in dyads. Members very infrequently reported that there were high levels of competition or disagreement between members, that they had talked too much, that they had worked as individuals rather than together on the task, or that a strong leader was needed to keep the group on the task. Finally, despite all of these positive reactions, members of dyads still reported more often than members of other groups that the group was too small for best performance.[3]

In sum, it appears that dyads in the present study were substantially different from groups of other sizes both in performance characteristics and in reactions of members to the group experience. Dyads showed a higher level of intensity in performance, were especially well satisfied with the group experience, and reported a decided lack of coordination difficulties.

What Is the Optimal Group Size?

Research by Slater (1958) suggests one straightforward means of estimating the "optimal" group size—simply determine what size group members prefer. Although both Hare (1952) and Slater find a general increase in dissatisfaction as size in-

---

[2] For all 27 dependent variables, the dyad-triad difference averaged about 1.8 times as large as differences between other adjacent sizes. Multiple comparisons showed dyads to be significantly different from the combined means of sizes 3–7 on 18 of the 27 variables.

[3] The findings of Bales and Borgatta (1955) and of O'Dell (1968) suggest that members of dyads experience more tension and exhibit less antagonism than members of other groups. Contrary to the implications of the earlier stud-

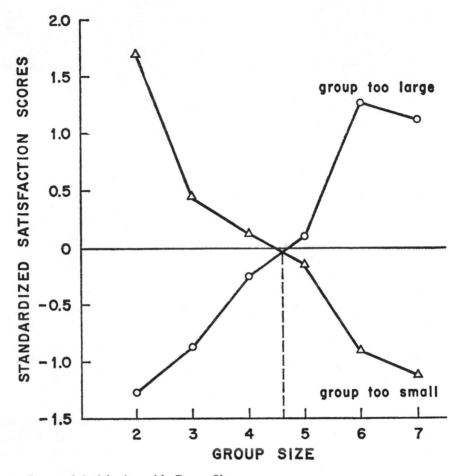

Fig. 1. Reported Satisfaction with Group Size.

creases (a finding replicated by this study), Slater further proposes that five-person groups may be optimal.[4] The reason, Slater suggests, is that smaller groups are

too intimate and members may be inhibited from expressing disagreements in them.

The present data allow reexamination of Slater's conclusion. Items one and two of the Member Reaction Questionnaire ("the group is too small"; "the group is too large") reflect two opposing types of general dissatisfaction with the group size. If item scores are standardized (assuming interval data) and the data is plotted on a graph with size on the abcissa and satisfaction on the ordinate, the intersection of the two items will indicate the

---

ies, members of dyads in this study did not report feeling more tense and uncomfortable than members of other groups. Data directly relevant to the level of expressed antagonism were not available in this study.

[4] It should be noted, however, that studies by Ziller (1957) and Miller (reported by Thomas & Fink, 1963) found no consistent relationship between size and member satisfaction.

point of optimal reported satisfaction with the size of the group. Since neither task type nor laboratory interacted with size, the data were averaged across these variables before converting to standard scores. The results are shown in Figure 1. Consistent with Slater's finding, optimal satisfaction with size is found between four and five members. Slater's groups were from a single population and worked only on "human relations" tasks; the conclusion may now be generalized over three types of intellective tasks and two laboratory populations.

Yet the finding that members are most comfortable with groups of size four or five is, in some ways, inconsistent with other data from the same people. According to items on the Member Reaction Questionnaire, members of dyads were clearly the most satisfied, and dissatisfaction increased, in approximately linear fashion, from size three to size seven. Further, the middle-sized groups (i.e., sizes three through five) were *less* creative than the dyads or the relatively large groups. Why, then, should members of these groups report that they are the most satisfied with the size of their groups?

It may be that members of smaller groups feel unusually "exposed" and, while in fact they experience few objective difficulties in working together, they are still vaguely uncomfortable. The present data do not, unfortunately, address this possibility. The data are clear for larger groups. In these groups, members are unhappy, and the reasons center around the coordination difficulties they encounter (see Table 2). Yet even if the above line of reasoning is valid, we must explain why performance tended to be less adequate in middle-sized groups than in dyads and in very large groups.

One possibility is that middle-sized groups are, in a sense, too comfortable for their own good. It appears that members of dyads may have responded to their "exposure" by pouring their energies into task performance. And, since there are very few coordination problems in these groups, the result was relatively good performance.

Although coordination and conflict *was* more of a problem for large groups, any detrimental effects associated with these difficulties may have been more than offset by three compensating factors. First, there are obviously more resources available to bring to bear on the task in a larger group than in a smaller one. Secondly, members in the larger groups reported that the coordination problems tended to be dealt with by breaking the groups into subgroups—in effect, solving the coordination problems by doing away with much of the need to coordinate. Finally, whatever conflicts about ideas and solutions that were present in the larger groups may themselves have been conducive to task performance (Hoffman, 1965).

Thus, it may be that groups of four and five, while most comfortable to group members, do *not* provide the conditions (either dyads' feelings of being "exposed" or conflict-and-coordination problems of large groups) which can provide an impetus for effective task performance. The question of the "optimal" group size is a complex one. The present data strongly suggest that it is *not* simply the size with which group members feel most comfortable.

The Importance of Task Characteristics

The substantial effects of task type on performance replicate the findings of Hackman (1968) and Kent and McGrath (1969), and show that the effects are equally as potent in groups larger and smaller than the triads used in the earlier studies. To further understanding of the nature of these task effects, it may be helpful to examine in more detail the differences in member reactions associated with working on tasks of the three types.

It will be recalled that production tasks resulted in more reports of tension and conflict among members than did other types, that discussion tasks led to a somewhat more "relaxed" atmosphere, and that problem solving tasks resulted in perceptions that members were working together relatively effectively. Why should this be so?

Different types of tasks require, or at least encourage, different patterns of member behavior. Morris (1966), for example, has shown that the three task types result in substantially different emphases in the group interaction process. Production tasks, since they demand "divergent" thinking of group members, probably encourage members to propose their *own* ideas and solutions to the problem. For college students, thinking new thoughts may be a very personal activity, and one that is not done very often (or probably very well) in groups. Thus, working on production tasks in groups may well lead to high levels of tension, competition, and what Hoffman (1965) has called "ideational conflict." And, as Hoffman suggests, such conflict can be *conducive* to creative problem solving since it prevents groups from quickly centering on a single alternative and encourages the integration of various suggestions. This, perhaps, can help explain the coincidence of high levels of process difficulty with high product creativity for groups working on production tasks. Moreover, Hoffman suggests that positive feelings are generated when conflict is resolved in a creative manner,

which perhaps accounts for the reports by members working on production tasks that their solution *was* creative and that they had been considerably influenced by other group members.

The interpersonal tensions which characterized groups working on production tasks tended not to be present for problem solving tasks. This is not surprising for two reasons. First, problem solving tasks (which call for preparation of instructions about actions to be taken) probably do not encourage the type of divergent thinking which typifies production tasks, and which, appearently, can lead to tension and conflict. Second, individuals may be much more competent working in groups on problem solving tasks than they are on production tasks. The planning and coordinating activities called for by problem solving tasks are very similar to what takes place in "real world" committees, with which most of the present subjects undoubtedly had had abundant experience. Thus, the group members may have worked together on problem solving tasks more effectively in part because they simply had had more experience performing "problem solving" tasks in groups in their daily lives.

Finally, there is some indication that group members may have been "seduced" by the discussion tasks. Members reported that they felt they had plenty of time to work on these tasks, and that they did not feel their solutions were very creative (a report which was, in fact, borne out by the performance data). Discussion tasks require group members to discuss and evaluate an issue, often one of societal importance. This kind of activity is a familiar one to most individuals (and perhaps especially so for college students), and one which is usually engaged in for the intrinsic satisfactions that the dis-

cussion provides. Thus, the groups working on discussion tasks may have simply
"taken it easy" and enjoyed the interaction, with solution quality suffering as a
result.

All of the above interpretations assume
of course that group performance and
member reactions result from an *interaction* between the demands of the tasks and
the characteristics of the individuals performing them. Task characteristics, taken
alone, probably cannot be very potent in
determining member reactions to the
group experience or characteristics of the
group output. Given the magnitude of the
task effects obtained in this research,
further investigation of the means by
which the interaction between task characteristics and performer characteristics
takes place would seem to be well worthwhile. Until such studies are done, of
course, the generalizability of the present
results beyond the subject populations employed remains open to question.

Interactions between Group Size and Task Type

Only one significant interaction between
group size and task type was obtained,
although it had been expected that substantial interactions would occur. Reexamination of the literature and theoretical
arguments summarized earlier in this
paper has revealed, however, that in almost every case reported, interactions between size and task characteristics have
involved broader differences among tasks
than those used here (e.g., intellective vs.
motor tasks, or clerical vs. creative tasks).
It may be that the reason no interactions
were obtained in the present study is that
the "critical demands" of the three types
of intellective tasks used were so similar
that different sized groups did not have

differential advantages in meeting them.

Thus, the present results should not be
interpreted as evidence that task characteristics and size do not interact *in general;*
rather, they suggest that such interactions
may not be of very substantial magnitude
within the domain of intellective tasks.
Further investigation of the kinds of tasks
which do give rise to interaction effects
would seem warranted—both to learn
more about the substantive nature of such
effects, and because their identification
should considerably facilitate efforts to
locate those dimensions which are of
greatest importance in describing differences among tasks themselves.

Differences between Experimental Laboratories

A large number of significant main effects and interactions were obtained involving the two experimental laboratories
where the research was run (Yale University and the University of Illionis).

Groups run at Yale tended to have
more severe difficulties with interpersonal
processes than did Illinois groups. Yale
subjects more often reported that their
groups were too large to be effective, that
there was too much competition and disagreement among members, and that
there was too little time to complete the
task. Members of Illinois groups indicated
that they felt their solutions were of higher
quality and more creative than did Yale
subjects, but on the objective performance measures Yale solutions tended to
be superior. The differences between Yale
and Illinois groups on many measures
were especially pronounced for subjects
who worked on production type tasks,
and usually were quite small for subjects
who dealt with problem solving tasks.

It appears that differences in personality and performance style between students at the two universities may be at least partly responsible for the obtained between-laboratory main effects and interactions. The two student bodies undoubtedly differ in important respects —both because of different admissions policies and because of different interpersonal norms which may characterize the two social systems. For example, unpublished research by Chris Argyris (personal communication) has shown Yale students to exhibit especially high levels of interpersonal competitiveness and mistrust in small group interaction. Such a tendency would, of course, be consistent with the high levels of process difficulty reported by members of Yale groups in the present study.

Factors other than differences in student characteristics may have been responsible for the obtained between-laboratory findings. In particular, how subjects were recruited for participation (volunteers vs. conscriptees), ecological factors (e.g., room size, furniture, seating arrangements), or expectancies of subjects and of experimenters may have affected the results. These possibilities are examined (and the between-laboratory findings are discussed in more detail) in a separate report.

What deserves emphasis here is the fact that, despite a concerted attempt to minimize inter-laboratory differences in research procedure, substantial main effect and interactions involving the two laboratories were obtained. How comparable, then, are the findings of two investigators who are entirely out of contact with one another, whose work overlaps only in that they are studying the same substantive variables? What specific aspects of the research procedure or setting are causally responsible for the obtained

between-laboratory differences? How is it that factors which are often so subtle as to be unnoticed can account for more dependent variable variance than do the major "substantive" variables of interest?

Until answers to questions such as these begin to be formulated, the generalizability of much small group research would appear, as suggested by McGrath and Altman (1966), to be very much a live issue.

REFERENCES

BALES, R. F. and E. F. BORGATTA, "Size of Group as a Factor in the Interaction Profile." In A. P. Hare, E. F. Borgatta and R. F. Bales, *Small Groups.* New York: Knopf, 1955.

BREER, P. E. and E. A. LOCKE, *Task Experience as a Source of Attitudes.* Homewood, Illinois: Dorsey, 1965.

COLLINS, B. E. and H. A. GUETZKOW, *A Social Psychology of Group Processes for Decision-making.* New York: Wiley, 1964.

DEUTSCH, M. and N. ROSENAU, "The Effects of Group Size and Group Task upon Productivity and Member Interaction." Unpublished, 1963.

GOLEMBIEWSKI, R. T., *The Small Group: An Analysis of Research Concepts and Operations.* Chicago: University of Chicago Press, 1962.

HACKMAN, J. R., "Effects of Task Characteristics on Group Products." *Journal of Experimental Social Psychology* 4 (1968): 162–187.

HACKMAN, J. R., L. E. JONES and J. E. McGRATH, "A Set of Dimensions for Describing the General Properties of Group-Generated Written Passages." *Psychological Bulletin* 67 (1967): 379–390.

HARE, A. P., "Interaction and Consensus in Different Sized Groups." *American Sociological Review* 17 (1952): 261–267.

HOFFMAN, L. E., "Group Problem Solving." In L. Berkowitz, *Advances in Experimental Social Psychology*, Vol. 2, New York: Academic Press, 1965.

KENT, R. N. and J. E. McGRATH, "Task and Group Characteristics as Factors Influencing Group Performance." *Journal of Experimental Social Psychology* 5 (1969): 429–440.

McGRATH, J. E. and I. ALTMAN, *Small Group Research: A Synthesis and Critique of the Field*. New York: Holt, 1966.

MORRIS, C. G., "Task Effects on Group Interaction." *Journal of Personality and Social Psychology* 4 (1966): 545–554.

O'DELL, J. W., "Group Size and Emotional Interaction." *Journal of Personality and Social Psychology* 8 (1968): 75–78.

ROBY, T. B. and J. T. LANZETTA, "Considerations in the Analysis of Group Tasks." *Psychological Bulletin* 55 (1958): 88–101.

SIMMEL, G., "The Number of Members as Determining the Sociological Form of the Group." Part I: *American Journal of Sociology* 8 (1902): 1–46; Part II: *American Journal of Sociology* 8 (1902): 158–196.

SLATER, P. E., "Contrasting Correlates of Group Size." *Sociometry* 21 (1958): 129–139.

STEINER, I. D., "Models for Inferring Relationships between Group Size and Potential Productivity." *Behavioral Science* 11 (1966): 273–283.

THOMAS, E. J. and C. F. FINK, "Effects of Group Size." *Psychological Bulletin* 60 (1963): 371–384.

VIDMAR, N. and J. R. HACKMAN, "Inter-Laboratory Generalizability of Small Group Research: An Experimental Study." *Journal of Social Psychology*, in press, 1969.

ZILLER, R. C., "Group Size: A Determinant of the Quality and Stability of Group Decisions." *Sociometry* 20 (1957): 165–173.

THE DEVELOPMENT
OF TASK AND SOCIAL-EMOTIONAL
ROLE DIFFERENTIATION*

Peter J. Burke

The line of research reported here deals with the emergence in group interaction

* Peter J. Burke, "The Development of Task and Social-Emotional Role Differentiation," *Sociometry*, 30 (1967), 379–92. Reprinted by permission of the American Sociological Association.

of two specialized leadership roles: one administering to the task needs of the group (directing, summarizing, providing ideas, etc.) the other alleviating the frustration, disappointments and hostilities which arise in interaction. Following Bales and Slater we refer to the persons playing these roles respectively as the task leader (specialist) and the social-emotional leader (specialist).[1] The separation of leadership functions into two distinct roles played by separate individuals is called task and social-emotional role differentiation. Our aim in this paper is to extend the theory of task and social-emotional role differentiation as developed by Bales and his co-workers so that *conditions* for the development of differentiated roles can be hypothesized, tested, and specified.

Bales and Slater have hypothesized that a process of role differentiation takes place along task and social-emotional dimensions in group interaction. Very briefly, their ideas are:[2]

1. In any group's attempt to reach a goal through interdependent, coordinated activity, acts designed to achieve the goal (task acts) give rise to tension and hostility (social-emotional problems). When one person engages in task acts, another is thereby denied the opportunity; in reaching decisions, some ideas are selected over other ideas; some departure from equality of participation must occur because not everyone can act at the same time. Meaningful coordination requires an inequality of participation in task actions.

2. When there is inequality, the person who is highly active in the task area is the primary source of change and of tension and is consequently the target of some hostility. It is his action which deprives action opportunities to others and forces them to adjust their behavior and ideas to accomplish the task.[3]

3. Because the task leader (the person most active in the task area) is himself the principal source of tension, it is unlikely that he would be effective in resolving this tension, and, if the tension is to be reduced, someone other than the task leader must assume a role aimed at the reduction of interpersonal hostilities and frustrations.

4. The result, therefore, is the development of task and social-emotional role differentiation.

5. The tendency toward the differentiation of task and social-emotional roles is quite generalized, depending not upon any gross differences between persons, upon pre-existing cultural prescriptions, or upon any particular task demand, but rather upon fundamental social processes common to all social systems.[4]

---

[1] Cf. Robert F. Bales and Philip E. Slater, "Role Differentiation in Small, Decision Making Groups," in Talcott Parsons and Robert F. Bales, eds., *Family, Socialization and Interaction Process*, Glencoe: The Free Press, 1955, pp. 259–306; Philip E. Slater, "Role Differentiation in Small Groups," *American Sociological Review*, 20 (1955), pp. 300–310; Robert F. Bales, "Task Status and Likeability as a Function of Talking and Listening in Decision Making Groups," in Leonard D. White, ed., *The State of the Social Sciences*, Chicago: The University of Chicago Press, 1956, pp. 148–161; Robert F. Bales, "Task Roles and Social Roles in Problem Solving Groups," in E. Maccoby, T. Newcomb and E. Hartley, eds., *Readings in Social Psychology*, New York: Henry Holt and Co., 1958 (3rd edition), pp. 437–447.

[2] The above summary is based primarily on the references in Note 1.

[3] Bales presents several possible explanations for this. The first, based upon psychoanalytic theory, is that there may exist a "tendency to transfer whatever negative attitudes there may be toward authority to any person who begins to achieve prominence or high status." A second is that "the person who takes the lead in finding some solution to the problem will generally threaten some values held dear by some members of the group and may collect by displacement the negative effect generated by the general value conflict, as well as that due to the disturbance he directly provokes." A third alternative suggested is that "it is very difficult to make substantial contributions [in small discussion groups] without talking a great deal, and overtalking may be resented by other members as a threat to their own status and a frustration of their own desire to talk." Bales, *op. cit.*, 1956, p. 152. Slater, *op. cit.*, emphasizes the second of these explanations, while Bales presents evidence supporting the third.

[4] Bales and Slater, *op. cit.*, p. 300.

More recently, however, several authors have commented that the tendency toward differentiation of task and social-emotional roles, rather than being a very generalized, nearly universal tendency, may be somewhat unique to particular situations and conditions. It has been suggested that in order to generalize the above theory to conditions outside the laboratory, it must be supplemented by the consideration of additional factors such as group size,[5] the degree of familiarity of the group members with each other,[6] the degree of task-orientation of the group members,[7] the degree of legitimacy or acceptability in the group of instrumental, task oriented behavior, and the degree to which the leader is legitimated.[8]

With respect to the factor "legitimacy of leadership," for example, Verba has argued that in a group with a legitimate leader (that is one who is accepted by other group members) task and social-

emotional role differentiation is less likely to develop. The legitimate leader does not have to prove himself to his group, at least not to the extent that an emergent leader in a laboratory group does.[9] The legitimate leader does not have to use power openly and directly to validate his position; he can contribute to the group as the task and situation demand.[10] But the emerging, non-legitimate leader must make use of every opportunity to validate his position. He must strive almost continuously to engage in task relevant activities and in so doing he violates expectations, and poses a threat to the group. For this reason an emergent leader would engage in less expressive-supportive activity, and would tend to alienate members, creating social-emotional problems and a disliking of himself, thereby bringing about differentiation along task and social-emotional lines. On the other hand, the legitimate leader would have time and

---

[5] George Levinger, "Task and Social Behavior in Marriage," *Sociometry*, 27 (1964), pp. 433–448.

[6] Robert K. Leik, "Instrumentality and Emotionality in Family Interaction," *Sociometry*, 26 (1963), pp. 131–145.

[7] Richard D. Mann, "Dimensions of Individual Performance in Small Groups under Task and Social-Emotional Conditions," *Journal of Abnormal and Social Psychology*, 62 (1961), pp. 674–682.

[8] Sidney Verba, *Small Groups and Political Behavior*, Princeton, N.J.: Princeton University Press, 1961. Two other factors which Verba suggests may influence the development of differentiation in laboratory groups are (1) the values typically held by college students (the usual subjects in these experiments) which make them hostile to instrumental, directive behavior, and (2) the fact that the task in laboratory groups is set by the experimenter rather than by the members and under such conditions the members are likely to react

negatively to task actions. These factors are viewed by Verba as contributing to a conflict in the group between maintaining both "instrumental effectiveness and a satisfactory affective tone in the group." S. Verba, *op. cit.*, pp. 144–150.

[9] See, for example, Christoph Heinicke and Robert F. Bales, "Development Trends in the Structure of Small Groups," *Sociometry*, 16 (1953), pp. 7–38, and Hugh Philip and Dexter Dunphy, "Developmental Trends in Small Groups," *Sociometry*, 22 (1959), pp. 162–174.

[10] For a discussion of the effects of the task and situation on the nature of the leadership provided in groups see Amatai Etzioni, "Duel Leadership in Complex Organization," *American Sociological Review*, 30 (1965), pp. 688–698; Robert D. Rossel, "Dual Leadership in Complex Organizations: An Empirical Test," unpublished manuscript, December, 1966; Philip M. Marcus, "Expressive and Instrumental Groups: Toward a Theory of Group Structure," *American Journal of Sociology*, 66 (1960), pp. 54–59.

energy to engage in expressive-supportive activity; there would be few social-emotional problems, and less tendency for him to be disliked.[11] Consequently there would be little or no differentiation.

If these ideas are true, then Verba and others have identified a set of variables or conditions impinging upon relationship between task activity and social-emotional activity such that differentiation would by no means be a "universal" tendency. To extend the Bales-Slater theory of task and social-emotional role differentiation, we should begin to test some of these ideas and systematically include those which are upheld as conditions in the statement of the theory. It is the purpose of this paper to present a test of one of these hypothesized conditions for the development of role differentiation: the degree of legitimacy or acceptability in the group of task oriented behavior. However, before we do this let us look a little more closely at the work of Bales and Slater, in order to clarify their ideas on the nature of role differentiation.

Implicit in the theory are three views of role differentiation which ought to be distinguished. First, that of Bales, as a condition such that one person in the group is rated highest on task performance, but is not as well liked as others in the group (he is not highest on "likeability").[12] Second, that of Slater, as a condition such that the person who is rated highest on task performance shows less concern than others in the group for internal social-emotional problems, and is less supportive in his response to the others around him.[13]

The third view is an alternative way of conceptualizing Slater's orientation. On the one hand, we may talk about two specialized roles in the group: one serving instrumental functions, the other serving expressive functions. This is the usual notion of role differentiation. On the other hand, we may talk about the psychological incompatibility of these two modes of behavior which results in a person's specializing in one or the other of these modes of behavior, finding it difficult or impossible to engage in both types. All three of the above views of role differentiation hinge upon the idea of an underlying incompatibility between the task and expressive orientations, and it is the "inherentness" of this incompatibility which is being questioned.[14]

In summary, we wish to extend the ideas of Bales and Slater on the conditions leading to task and social-emotional role differentiation. To do this we conceptualize the social-emotional leadership role as being composed of behaviors aimed at the reduction of frustration and interpersonal hostilities in the group, and we ask under what conditions (why) does an inequality of participation in task actions (the task leader by definition engaging in more than anyone else) lead to a disliking of the task leader, lead to less social-emotional activity on the part of the task leader, lead to a separation of the role of task specialist from the role of social-emotional specialists (all three of these phenomena being variously conceived as forms of task and social-emotional role differentiation)?

---

[11] Cf. Robert D. Rossel, *op. cit.*, Herman Turk, "Instrumental and Expressive Ratings Reconsidered," *Sociometry*, 24 (1961), pp. 76–81, and Philip M. Marcus, *op. cit.*

[12] Bales, *op. cit.*, 1956, Cf. also Bales, *op. cit.*, 1958.

[13] Slater, *op. cit.*, 1955, pp. 308–309.

[14] Slater, *op. cit.*, pp. 308–309.

Our working hypothesis is that the legitimation of task activity in a group (a) prevents high task performance on the part of one member (or alternatively high inequality of task performance) from violating the expectations of group members and leading to a disliking of the high task contributor, and (b) frees the task specialist from having to concentrate heavily on task activity in order to prove himself, and allows him freedom to engage in social-emotional activity if he is inclined.[15]

PROCEDURES

Groups

Twenty-one groups composed of undergraduate students enrolled in introductory courses in sociology met, as part of a course requirement concerned with the study of social control, to discuss a human relations case-study of a juvenile delinquent (Johnny Rocco).[16] The groups, consisting of either four or five members, met in a "small groups laboratory" equipped with one-way mirrors and sound recording equipment.[17] They were seated around a hexagonal table and copies of the case-study were distributed. After sufficient time to read the case, the copies were collected and the participants were instructed to analyze and discuss the case focusing upon the questions "Why were the individuals involved in the case behaving as they were?" and "What, if anything, should be done about it?" The participants were told they would have 30 minutes to discuss the case. At that point, if there were no further questions, the experimenter told them to begin and then left the room.

Measures

After the discussion, the participants rated each other and themselves, using a 10 point scale, on 11 items designed to measure task leadership performance and social-emotional leadership performance (See Figure 1). These ratings were averaged for each person rated, and the averages were standardized within each group, across the members, to have a zero mean. This was done in order to eliminate ideosyncratic differences in the average level of ratings from individual to individual. These scores were then factor analyzed and two orthogonal factors accounting for 82 per cent of the variance were retained and rotated to simple structure.[18] The first

---

[15] Slater, *op. cit.*, p. 307, ties the idea of compulsiveness to personality predispositions and finds that strong task leaders who were members of low status consensus groups tended to have more authoritarian (F scale) personalities than strong task leaders who were members of high status consensus groups. This fits the pattern discussed above if we view status consensus as evidence of legitimated, differentiated task participation. Where high task participation is not legitimated, a person would have to be somewhat compulsive to ignore the norms and go ahead and engage in a high degree of task activity.

[16] Stanley Schachter, "Deviation, Rejection, and Communication," in D. Cartwright and A. Zander, eds., *Group Dynamics*, Evanston: Row, Peterson and Co., 1960 (second edition) pp. 260–285.

[17] The original plan was to have all groups of size five, however, extra persons were not scheduled for each meeting to assure that a pool of five would always be there. Consequently 11 groups are of size 4.

[18] The Biomedical Computing Program BMD03M (General Factor Analysis) was used for this. W. J. Dixon, ed., *BMD Biomedical Computing Programs*, Health Sciences Com-

Figure 1

FACTOR ANALYSIS OF RESPONSES TO POST-SESSION QUESTIONNAIRE

Item	Loadings I (Task)	II (Social-Emotional)
*1. Providing "fuel" for discussion by introducing ideas and opinions for the rest of the group to discuss	.87	.43
**2. Doing most to guide the discussion and keep it moving effectively	.83	.50
*3. Joking and kidding, finding the potentially humorous implications in this discussion	.54	.54
4. Doing most to keep relationships between members cordial and friendly	.40	.83
5. Making most attempts to influence the group's opinion.........	.80	.37
6. Being the most successful in influencing the group's opinion......	.79	.44
*7. Providing clarification, getting the discussion to the point by getting terms defined, and pointing out logical difficulties	.75	.51
**8. Most liked...	.43	.61
9. Standing out as the leader in the discussion.......................	.86	.43
*10. Making tactful comments to heal any hurt feelings which might arise in the discussion	.37	.85
**11. Providing the best ideas for the discussion	.85	.43

* Adapted from James A. Davis, *Great Books and Small Groups*, New York: The Free Press of Glencoe, Inc., 1961.
** Adapted from R. F. Bales and P. E. Slater, *op. cit.*

factor, accounting for 50 per cent of the variance, included the "task" items and was labeled *Task Leadership Performance*. The second factor, accounting for 32 per cent of the variance, included the social-emotional items and was labeled *Social-Emotional Leadership Performance*. These factors will frequently be referred to as the "task factor" and the "social-emotional factor."

Factor scores on these two factors were then generated for each and every member, thus providing the measures of task leadership performance and social-emotional leadership performance.[19] On the basis of these scores the task leader (person in each group with highest task factor score) and the social-emotional leader (person in each group with the highest social-emotional factor score) of each group were designated.[20] Also from these

puting Facility, Department of Preventive Medicine and Public Health, School of Medicine, University of California, Los Angeles, 1965.

[19] The factor analysis provides a weighting technique for combining the scores (ratings) of similar items into a composite score (factor score) on each of the two dimensions.

[20] This measure of social-emotional leadership performance differs from that of Bales and Slater by focusing directly on the expressive functioning of the members rather than on the degree to which they are liked—a possible consequence of handling social-emotional problems.

factor scores, several additional measures were obtained. As a measure of the inequality of participation on the task dimension we used the variance among the task factor scores of the members of each group (task variance) and as an alternative measure, the task factor score of the task leader (task score). This latter measure makes sense if we remember that the sum of the task scores in each group is zero, so that to the extent that the task leader's score is up, someone else's score must be down. As the measure of task and social-emotional role differentiation we used a measure of dissimilarity between the roles of task leader and social-emotional leader described as follows:

Using the task and social-emotional factors as orthogonal axes of a Cartesian coordinate system, the locations of task and social-emotional leaders (or of any of the group members) may be plotted. (See example in Figure 2.) The degree of task and social-emotional role differentiation of a group may then be defined as the linear graph-distance separating the point on the graph representing the task leader of that group from the point on the graph representing the social-emotional leader of that group. At one extreme, if the task leader and the social-emotional leader are the same person, the distance is zero and there is no differentiation. At the other extreme the two points are on opposite sides of the graph and there is some maximum amount of differentiation of the perceived role behavior of the two leaders. In general, the degree of differentiation

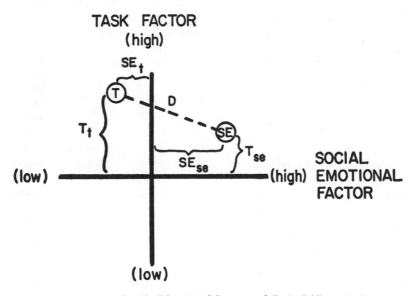

Fig. 2. Representation of the Graph Distance Measure of Role Differentiation*.

* T represents the position of the task leader, T_t representing his task score, SE_t representing his social-emotional score. SE represents the position of the social-emotional leader, T_{se} representing his social-emotional score. The distance, D,

$$= \sqrt{(T_t - T_{se})^2 + (SE_t - SE_{se})^2}$$

shows the graph distance separating the two points and represents the amount of task and social-emotional role differentiation.

will be somewhat between these two extremes.

Our measure of the legitimation of task activity comes from observer ratings of the groups on the extent to which the members displayed, in their interaction, an acceptance of what might be termed a "task ethic": the extent to which they were concerned about performing their task of discussing the case, arriving at conclusions, arriving at a consensus, avoiding distractions which might occur, assessing their relation to the goal at various stages, etc. Concern for and acceptance of this "task ethic," was taken as evidence of the legitimacy of task activity in the group and the groups were divided into two categories: High Task Legitimacy and Low Task Legitimacy. There was agreement on the classification of 18 (87 per cent) of the cases between two independent observers and on the three cases where there was not agreement the author's judgement was used to finally classify the group.

RESULTS

Before discussing findings relevant to the hypotheses, it is appropriate to ask to what extent there is comparability between the measurement procedures of Bales and Slater and those of the present study. To answer this question we present a comparative set of data using both the Bales-Slater procedures and those of the present study.

1. *Identification of the "task leader."* Following the Bales-Slater procedures, the member of each group who achieved the highest average ranking on the item "providing the best ideas" may be identified as the task leader. Using the present procedures, the person with the highest task factor score may be designated as task leader. To what extent do these two procedures yield the same result? Table 1 presents information on the correspondence of the outcomes of the two sets of procedures. As can be seen, there is considerable—though not unanimous—correspondence between the two methods. In 17 of the 21 cases there was perfect agreement, and of the four on which there was disagreement, three were only one step off.

2. *Identification of the "social-emotional leader."* Again, following the Bales-Slater procedures, the member of each group who achieved the highest ranking average on the item "best liked" may be identified as a social-emotional leader. The person receiving the largest social-emotional factor score, using the present methods, may similarly be designated as the social-emotional leader. Table 2 shows the degree of correspondence between the

Table 1

AGREEMENT BETWEEN BALES-SLATER PROCEDURES AND THE PRESENT
PROCEDURES FOR IDENTIFYING THE TASK LEADER

	Complete Agreement	One Step Deviation	Two or More Step Deviation	Total
Number of Cases	17	3	1	21
Per Cent	81	14	5	100

Table 2

AGREEMENT BETWEEN BALES-SLATER PROCEDURES AND THE PRESENT
PROCEDURES FOR IDENTIFYING THE SOCIAL-EMOTIONAL LEADER

	Complete Agreement	One Step Deviation	Two or More Step Deviation	Total
Number of Cases	12	5	4	21
Per Cent	57	24	19	100

results obtained by the two procedures. As can be seen, the degree of agreement in identifying social-emotional leaders is not as great as the degree of agreement in identifying task leaders. There are only 12 cases of perfect agreement, and of nine on which there is disagreement, five are one step off, and four are more than one step off.

Though the agreement here is far from perfect, it must be remembered that a certain amount of disagreement was anticipated with our shift in measurement procedures to capture Slater's conception of the social-emotional role in terms of active concern for internal social-emotional problems. Looking at the results of the factor analysis (Figure 1) we see that the primary source of disagreement in the results of the two methods can be attributed to the fact that the item "most liked" does not load as highly on the social-emotional factor as do some other items. (The degree of correlation between the item "most liked" and the social-emotional factor is only .61, whereas, for example, the item "making tactful comments" correlates .85 with the social-emotional factor.) Social-emotional leadership, as defined in the factor analysis, and as we set out to define it, is concerned with the active reduction of interpersonal conflict and hostility. Such behavior may result in a person being well liked, as Bales

suggested, however, the item "most liked" then is only an indirect measure of the performance of expressive functions in a group.

In summary, on the task dimension, our methods give results quite close to those obtained using the methods of Bales and Slater, giving confidence we are measuring the same phenomena. On the social-emotional dimension, the results of the two methods differ somewhat. The differences, however, appear to be the result of the fact that Bales and Slater have measured social-emotional leadership only indirectly while the present methods attempt to measure the phenomena more directly. We turn now to results relevant to the hypotheses.

3. *Inequality of Task Participation and Liking of the Task Leader.* One of the working hypotheses stated that the legitimation of task activity in a group prevented inequality of task performance from leading to a disliking of the high task contributor (the task leader). Table 3 presents data relevant to a test of this hypothesis. We see in that table, for groups of low task legitimation, there is a negative relationship between inequality in task performance and liking of the task leader (as measured by item 8 of the questionnaire). The correlation using task variance as a measure of task inequality is $-.73$ ($p < .05$), while the correlation

Table 3

CORRELATIONS BETWEEN MEASURES OF INEQUALITY OF TASK PARTICIPATION AND MEASURES OF TASK AND SOCIAL-EMOTIONAL ROLE DIFFERENTIATION, BY DEGREE OF LEGITIMATION OF TASK PARTICIPATION

	High Task Legitimation Groups (N=10)		
	Liking of Task Leader[b]	SE Score of Task Leader[b]	Role Differentiation (Graph Distance)
Task Variance[a]	.03	.11	.11
Task Score[a]	−.13	−.14	.04
	Low Task Legitimation Groups (N=11)		
	Liking of Task Leader[b]	SE Score of Task Leader[b]	Role Differentiation (Graph Distance)
Task Variance[a]	−.73*	−.78*	.64*
Task Score[a]	−.43†	−.74*	.79*

* $p<.05$.
† $p<.10$.
[a] Correlations between task variance and task score are: For high task legitimation groups +.81 ($p<.05$); for low task legitimation groups: +.79 ($p<.05$).
[b] Correlations between liking of the task leader and social-emotional score of the task leader are: for high groups +.51 ($p<.10$); for low groups +.71 ($p<.05$).

using leader's task score as a measure of inequality is − .43 ($p < .10$). For groups with high task legitimation, however, there is no correlation between either measure of inequality of task participation and liking of the leader. These findings are consistent with the hypothesis, and it is clear that task legitimation mediates the effects of inequality of task participation, at least in terms of the degree of liking of the task leader.

4. *Inequality of Task Participation and Role Differentiation. Case I.* The second working hypothesis stated that legitimation of task activity in a group frees the task specialist from having to concentrate heavily on task activity in order to prove himself to the group, and allows him freedom to engage in social-emotional activity if he is so inclined. This hypothesis really speaks to some intrapsychic process for which we have no evidence. However, if such a process occurs, there will be cer-

tain behavioral outcomes and it is the perception of these that we have measured. We may deduce from this hypothesis, then, that there will be a negative relationship between the task score of the task leader and the social-emotional score of the task leader *in the low task legitimation groups*, but not in the high task legitimation groups. Table 3 also presents data relevant to this hypothesis. We note there is a negative correlation (− .74 $p < .05$) between the task and social-emotional factor scores of task leaders in the low legitimation groups, while there is essentially no correlation between these measures in the high task legitimation groups. Again we find support for the hypothesis: concentration on task activity in low task legitimation groups prevents the task specialist from engaging in social-emotional activity. No such relationship, however, exists in the high task legitimation groups.

We may additionally note here that our

alternative measure of inequality of task participation (task variance) is also negatively related to the social-emotional score of the task leader $(-.78; p < .05)$ in the low task legitimation groups, indicating the effect of certain *social* factors in addition to the hypothesized intrapsychic process. This can perhaps be more clearly seen by noting that the partial correlation between task variance and social-emotional score of the task leader, controlling for task score of the task leader, is equal to $-.46$ $(p < .10)$. In those groups in which there is an inequality of task participation, the social-emotional score of the task leader is depressed an amount over and above any decrease due to his own task score. To understand this, it must be noted that a high task variance, when we control for the level of task specialist's task score, indicates that someone else also has a high task score (though of course not as high as the task specialist's score). This pattern is what we would expect if the task specialist and someone else were in competition for the role of task leader, and such competition may be expected to detract from the task specialist's social-emotional contributions. If there is a certain amount of defensiveness involved on the part of the task leader about his task position which causes a reduction in his social-emotional score, we may speculate from the above data, that this defensiveness is brought about not only by his own position in the hierarchy of task outputs, but also by the relative position of others who may be in competition with him for the task leadership position.

5. *Inequality of Task Participation and Role Differentiation. Case II.* We turn now to the last alternative conception of role differentiation: the degree to which the role or task leader differs from that of social-emotional leader (using our graph distance measure). This conception of differentiation is obviously more sociological than the previous, being defined as a relationship between two roles rather than a relationship between two components of a single role. Again, the hypothesis states that as task inequality goes up there arise, in the condition of low task legitimation, social-emotional problems, which, if they are to be handled, must be handled by someone other than the task leader (we assume that the person who has primary "responsibility" for this will be the social-emotional specialist). The result will be high role differentiation as defined by our graph distance model. Table 3 presents data relevant to a test of this hypothesis. We see that in the low task legitimation groups both measures of inequality of task participation are positively related to differentiation. The correlation between the task score of the task leader and differentiation is $+ .79$ $(p < .05)$, while the correlation between task variance and differentiation is $+ .64$ $(p < .05)$. In the high task legitimation condition, there is essentially no correlation between either measure of task inequality and differentiation. Again, the hypothesis is supported. However, to understand this last result a little more fully, let us look at what is involved in these correlations.

Differentiation in the graph distance model has been defined as

$$D = \sqrt{(T_t - T_{se})^2 + (SE_t - SE_{se})^2}$$

where T_t is the task score of the task leader; T_{se} is the task score of the social-emotional leader; SE_{se} is the social-emotional score of the task leader; and SE_{se} is the social-emotional score of the social-emotional leader. The hypothesis suggests that in the low task legitimation groups, there is a certain complementarity in the behaviors of the task and social-emotional leaders which does not necessarily exist in the high task legitimation groups. Specifically, that as task inequality goes up (either T_t or task variance), the social-emotional leader engages in more social-emotional activity and less task activity to handle the social-emotional problems which emerge in the low task legitimation groups. Although not all of the correlations are significant, the low task legitimation groups do show this complementary nature of the task and social-emotional roles to a greater extent than do the high task legitimation groups, and, taken with the findings of section four above, the overall result is the observed correlation between inequality of task paraticipation and role differentiation in the low task legitimation groups.

SUMMARY

We began with the task of attempting to extend the theory of task and social-emotional role differentiation as developed by Bales and Slater along certain lines suggested by Verba. Such role differentiation was hypothesized to result from the inequality of participation in task activity under the condition that high task participation is not legitimated by social circumstances. It was found that:

1. Inequality of task participation is corelated with a disliking of the task leader under conditions of low task legitimacy, but not under conditions of high task legitimacy.
2. High task participation on the part of the task leader and competition over the task leader's role is associated with a reduction of the amount of social-emotional participation on the part of the task leader under conditions of low task legitimation, but

not under conditions of high task legitimation.
3. Inequality of participation in the task area is associated with the emergence of distinct task and social-emotional roles in conditions of low task legitimation, but not in conditions of high task legitimation.

These results strongly suggest that the factor "legitimation of task activity," as evidenced by the group members' acceptance of the propriety and efficacy of task activity, mediates between inequality of task participation and the development of task and social-emotional role differentiation (as variously conceived), and for this reason the theory of role differentiation is not complete without its inclusion. The following restatement of the Bales-Slater theory is an attempt to include this factor:

1. In any group's attempt to reach a goal through interdependent, coordinated activity, acts designed to achieve the goal (task acts) give rise to tension and hostility *if they go beyond the legitimate, expected level* (and thus constitute a threat).
2. Subject to the condition given in No. 1 above, when there is an inequality of participation in the task area, the person who is most highly active is the primary source of *undesired, non-legitimate* change and is consequently the target of some hostility.
3. The person who is *illegitimately* high in task participation is likely to be preoccupied with task action and, therefore, to engage in little social-emotional activity.
4. Because the task specialist is himself the principal source of tension it is unlikely that he would be effective in resolving this tension, and, if the tension is to be reduced, someone other than the task leader must assume a role aimed at the reduction of interpersonal hostilities and frustrations.
5. The result, therefore, subject to the conditions given in Nos. 1, 2, and 3 above, is the development of task and social-emotional role differentiation.

III

POWER PROCESSES
IN SMALL GROUPS

8

The Exercise of Power

POWER-DEPENCENCE RELATIONS*

Richard M. Emerson

Judging from the frequent occurrence of such words as *power, influence, dominance* and *submission, status* and *authority*, the importance of power is widely recognized, yet considerable confusion exists concerning these concepts.[1] There is an extensive literature pertaining to power, on both theoretical and empirical levels, and in small group[2] as well as large community contexts.[3] Unfortunately, this already large and rapidly growing body of research has not achieved the cumulative character desired. Our *integrated* knowledge of power does not significantly surpass the conceptions left by Max Weber.[4]

This suggests that there is a place at this moment for a systematic treatment of social power. The underdeveloped state of this area is further suggested by what appears, to this author, to be a recurrent flaw in common conceptions of social power; a flaw which helps to block adequate theoretical development as well as

* Richard M. Emerson, "Power-Dependence Relations," *American Sociological Review*, 27 (1962), 31–41. Reprinted by permission.

[1] See the Communications by Jay Butler and Paul Harrison on "On Power and Authority: An Exchange on Concepts," *American Sociological Review*, 25 (October, 1960), pp. 731–732. That both men can be essentially correct in the points they make yet fail to reconcile these points, strongly suggests the need for conceptual development in the domain of power relations.

[2] Among many studies, see Ronald Lippitt, Norman Polansky, Fritz Redl and Sidney Rosen, "The Dynamics of Power," *Human Relations*, 5 (February, 1952), pp. 37–64.

[3] Floyd Hunter, *Community Power Structure*, Chapel Hill: University of North Carolina Press, 1953.

[4] Max Weber, in *The Theory of Social and Economic Organization*, New York: Oxford University Press, 1947, presents what is still a classic formulation of power, authority, and legitimacy. However, it is characteristic of Weber that he constructs a typology rather than an organized theory of power.

meaningful research. That flaw is the implicit treatment of power as though it were an attribute of a person or group ("X is an influential person." "Y is a powerful group," etc.). Given this conception, the natural research question becomes "Who in community X are the power *holders*?" The project then proceeds to rank order persons by some criterion of power, and this ordering is called the *power-structure*. This is a highly questionable representation of a "structure," based upon a questionable assumption of *generalized power*.[5]

It is commonly observed that some person X dominates Y, while being subservient in relations with Z. Furthermore, these power relations are frequently intransitive! Hence, to say that "X has power" is vacant, unless we specify "over whom." In making these necessary qualifications we force ourselves to face up to the obvious: power is a property of the social relation; it is not an attribute of the actor.[6]

_____

[5] See Raymond E. Wolfinger, "Reputation and Reality in the Study of 'Community Power'," *American Sociological Review*, 25 (October, 1960), pp. 636–644, for a well taken critical review of Floyd Hunter's work on these very points. The notion of "generalized power" which is not restricted to specific social relations, if taken literally, is probably meaningless. Power may indeed be generalized across a finite set of relations in a power network, but this notion, too, requires very careful analysis. Are you dealing with some kind of halo effect (reputations if you wish), or are the range and boundary of generalized power anchored in the power structure itself? These are questions which must be asked and answered.

[6] Just as power is often treated as though it were a property of the person, so leadership, conformity, etc., are frequently referred to the personal traits of "leaders," "conformers," and

In this paper an attempt is made to construct a simple theory of the power aspects of social relations. Attention is focused upon characteristics of the relationship as such, with little or no regard for particular features of the persons or groups engaged in such relations. Personal traits, skills, or possessions (such as wealth) which might be relevant to power in one relation are infinitely variable across the set of possible relations, and hence have no place in a general theory.

THE POWER-DEPENDENCE RELATION

While the theory presented here is anchored most intimately in small group research, it is meant to apply to more complex community relations as well. In an effort to make these conceptions potentially as broadly applicable as possilbe, we shall speak of relations among *actors*, where an actor can be either a person or a group. Unless otherwise indicated, any relation discussed might be a person-person, group-person or group-group relation.

Social relations commonly entail *ties of mutual dependence* between the parties. A *depends* upon B if he aspires to goals or gratifications whose achievement is facilitated by appropriate actions on B's part. By virtue of mutual dependency, it is more or less imperative to each party that he be able to control or influence the other's conduct. At the same time, these ties of mutual dependence imply that each party is in a position, to some degree, to grant or deny, facilitate or hinder, the other's

_____

so on, as if they were distinguishable types of people. In a sociological perspective such behavior should be explicitly treated as an attribute of a relation rather than a person.

gratification. Thus, it would appear that the power to control or influence the other resides in control over the things he values, which may range all the way from oil resources to ego-support, depending upon the relation in question. "In short, *power resides implicitly in the other's dependency.* When this is recognized, the analysis will of necessity revolve largely around the concept of dependence.[7]

Two variables appear to function jointly in fixing the dependence of one actor upon another. Since the precise nature of this joint function is an empirical question, our propostion can do no more than specify the directional relationships involved:

> *Dependence (Dab).* The dependence of actor A upon actor B is (1) directly proportional to A's *motivational investment* in goals mediated by B, and (2) inversely proportional to the *availability* of those goals to A outside of the A-B relation.

In this proposition "goal" is used in the broadest possible sense to refer to gratifications consciously sought as well as rewards unconsciously obtained through the relationship. The "availability" of such goals outside of the relation refers to alternative avenues of goal-achievement, most notably other social relations. The costs associated with such alternatives must be included in any assessment of dependency.[8]

If the dependence of one party provides the basis for the power of the other, that power must be defined as a potential influence:

> *Power (Pab).* The power of actor A over actor B is the amount of resistance on the part of B which can be potentially overcome by A.

Two points must be made clear about this definition. First, the power defined here will not be, of necessity, observable in every interactive episode betwen A and B, yet we suggest that it exists nonetheless as a potential, to be explored, tested, and occasionally employed by the participants. Pab will be empirically manifest only *if* A makes some demand, and only *if* this demand runs counter to B's desires (resistance to be overcome). Any operational definition must make reference to *change* in the conduct of B attributable to demands made by A.

Second, we define power as the "resistance" which can be overcome, without restricting it to any one domain of action. Thus, if A is dependent upon B for love and respect, B might then draw A into criminal activity which he would normally resist. The reader might object to this formulation, arguing that social power is in fact restricted to certain channels. If so, the reader is apparently concerned with "legitimized power" embedded in a social structure. Rather than begin at this more evolved level, we hope to derive legitimized power in the theory itself.

The premise we began with can now be stated as Pab = Dba; the power of A over B is equal to, and based upon, the dependence of B upon A.[9] Recognizing the

---

[7] The relation between power and dependence is given similar emphasis in the systematic treatment by J. Thibaut and H. H. Kelley, *The Social Psychology of Groups*, New York: John Wiley and Sons, 1959.

[8] The notion of "opportunity costs" in economics is a similar idea. If an employee has alternative employment opportunities, and if these opportunities have low associated cost (travel, etc.), the employee's dependence upon his current employer is reduced.

---

[9] In asserting that power is based upon the dependency of the other, it might appear that we are dealing with *one* of the bases of power ("reward power") listed by John R. P. French,

reciprocity of social relations, we can represent a power dependence relation as a pair of equations:

$$Pab = Dba$$
$$Pba = Dab.$$

Before proceeding further we should emphasize that these formulations have been so worded in the hope that they will apply across a wide range of social life. At a glance our conception of dependence contains two variables remarkably like supply and demand ("availability" and "motivational investment," respectively).[10] We prefer the term *dependency* over these economic terms because it facilitates broader application, for all we need to do to shift these ideas from one area of application to another is change the motivational basis of dependency. We can speak of the economic dependence of a home builder upon a loan agency as varying directly with his desire for the home, and hence capital, and inversely with the "availability" of capital from other agencies. Similarly, a child may be dependent upon another child based upon motivation toward the pleasures of collec-

tive play, the availability of alternative playmates, etc. The same generic power-dependence relation is involved in each case. The dependency side of the equation may show itself in "friendship" among playmates, in "filial love" between parent and child, in "respect for treaties" among nations. On the other side of the equation, I am sure no one doubts that mothers, lovers, children, and nations enjoy the power to influence their respective partners, within the limit set by the partner's dependence upon them.

Finally, because these concepts are meant to apply across a wide variety of social situations, operational definitions cannot be appropriately presented here. Operational definitions provide the necessary bridge between generalizing concepts on the one hand, and the concrete features of a specific research situation on the other hand. Hence, there is no *one* proper operational definition for a theoretical concept.[11]

BALANCE AND IMBALANCE

The notion of reciprocity in power-dependency relations raises the question of equality or inequality of power in the relation. If the power of A over B (Pab) is

---

Jr. and Bertram Raven, "The Bases of Social Power," *Studies in Social Power*, D. Cartwright, editor, Ann Arbor, Michigan: Institute for Social Research, 1959. However, careful attention to our highly generalized conception of dependence will show that it covers most if not all of the forms of power listed in that study.

[10] Professor Alfred Kuhn, Department of Economics, University of Cincinnati, has been working on a theory for power analysis soon to be published. The scheme he develops, though very similar to the one presented here, is put together in a different way. It is anchored more tightly to economic concepts, and hence its implications lead off in different directions from those presented below.

---

[11] Many different operational definitions can serve one theoretical concept, and there is no reason to require that they produce inter-correlated results when applied in the same research situation. While the controversies surrounding "operationalism" have now been largely resolved, there remains some confusion on this point. See, for example, Bernice Eisman, "Some Operational Measures of Cohesiveness and Their Interrelations," *Human Relations*, 12 (May, 1959), pp. 183–189.

confronted by equal opposing power of B over A, is power then neutralized or cancelled out? We suggest that in such a balanced condition, power is in no way removed from the relationship. A pattern of "dominance" might not emerge in the interaction among these actors, but that does not imply that power is inoperative in either or both directions. A *balanced* relation and an *unbalanced* relation are respectively as follows:

$$\begin{array}{ccc} Pab = Dba & & Pab = Dba \\ \| \quad\quad \| & & \vee \quad\quad \vee \\ Pba = Dab & & Pba = Dab \end{array}$$

Consider two social relations, both of which are balanced, but at *different levels* of dependence (say Loeb and Leopold, as compared with two casual friends). A moment's thought will reveal the utility of the argument that balance does not neutralize power, for each party may continue to exert profound control over the other. It might even be meaningful to talk about the parties being controlled by the relation itself.

Rather than cancelling out considerations of power, receiprocal power provides the basis for studying three more features of power-relations: first, a power advantage can be defined as Pab minus Pba, which can be either positive or negative (a power disadvantage) ;[12] second, the *cohesion* of a relationship can be defined as the average of Dab and Dba, though this definition can be refined;[13] and finally, it opens the door to the study of balancing operations as structural changes in power-dependence relations which tend to reduce power advantage.

Discussion of balancing tendencies should begin with a concrete illustration. In the unbalanced relation represented symbolically above, A is the more powerful party because B is the more dependent of the two. Let actor B be a rather "unpopular" girl, with puritanical upbringing, who wants desperately to date; and let A be a young man who occasionally takes her out, while dating other girls as well. (The reader can satisfy himself about A's power advantage in this illustration by referring to the formulations above.) Assume further that A "discovers" this power advantage, and, in exploring for the limits of his power, makes sexual advances. In this simplified illustration, these advances should encounter resistance in B's puritanical values. Thus, when a power advantage is *used*, the weaker member will achieve one value at the expense of other values.

In this illustration the tensions involved in an unbalanced relation need not be long endured. They can be reduced in either of two ways: (1) the girl might reduce the psychic costs involved in continuing the relation by redefining her moral values, with appropriate rationalizations and shifts in reference group attachments; or (2) she might renounce the value of dating, develop career aspirations, etc., thus reducing A's power. Notice that the first solution does *not* of necessity alter

12 J. Thibaut and H. H. Kelley, *op. cit.*, pp. 107–108.

13 This definition of cohesion, based upon dependency, seems to have one advantage over the definition offered by Leon Festinger, *et al.*, *Theory and Experiment in Social Communication*, Ann Arbor: Research Center for Group Dynamics, University of Michigan Press, 1950. The Festinger definition takes into account only one of the two variables involved in dependency.

the unbalanced relation. The weaker member has sidestepped one painful demand but she is still vulnerable to new demands. By contrast, the second solution alters the power relation itself. In general, it appears that an unbalanced relation is unstable for it encourages the use of power which in turn sets in motion processes which we will call (a) cost reduction and (b) balancing operations.[14]

Cost Reduction

The "cost" referred to here amounts to the "resistance" to be overcome in our definition of power the cost involved for one party in meeting the demands made by the other. The process of cost reduction in power-dependence relations shows itself in many varied forms. In the courting relation above it took the form of alteration in moral attitudes on the part of a girl who wanted to be popular; in industry it is commonly seen as the impetus for improved plant efficiency and technology in reducing the cost of production. What we call the "mark of oppression" in the character structure of members of low social castes (the submissive and "painless" loss of freedom) might well involve the same power processes, as does the "internalization of parental codes" in the socialization process. In fact,

---

[14] The "tensions of imbalance," which are assumed to make an unbalanced relation unstable, are closely related to the idea of "distributive justice" discussed by George C. Homans, *Social Behavior: Its Elementary Forms*, New York: Harcourt, Brace and World, Inc., 1961. All of what Homans has to say around this idea could be fruitfully drawn into the present formulation.

the oedipal conflict might be interpreted as a special case of the tensions of imbalance in a power-dependence relation, and cost reduction takes the form of identification and internalization as classically described. "Identification with the aggressor" in any context would appear to be explainable in terms of cost reduction.

In general, *cost reduction* is a process involving change in values (personal, social, economic) which reduces the pains incurred in meeting the demands of a powerful other. It must be emphasized, however, that these adjustments do not necessarily alter the balance or imbalance of the relation, and, as a result, they must be distinguished from the more fundamental *balancing operations* described below. It must be recognized that cost reducing tendencies will take place even under conditions of balance, and while this is obvious in economic transactions, it is equally true of other social relations, where the "costs" involved are anchored in modifiable attitudes and values. The intense cohesion of a lasting social relation like the Loeb-Leopold relation mentioned above can be attributed in part to the cost reduction processes involved in the progressive formation of their respective personalities, taking place in the interest of preserving the valued relation. We suggest that cost reducing tendencies generally will function to deepen and stabilize social relations over and above the condition of balance.

Balancing Operations

The remainder of this paper will deal with balancing processes which operate through changes in the variables which define the structure of the power-dependence relation as such. The formal notation adopted here suggests *exactly four generic types* of balancing operation. In the un-

$$Pab = Dba$$
balanced relation $\lor \quad \lor$, balance can
$$Pba = Dab$$

be restored either by an increase in Dab or by a decrease in Dba. If we recall that *dependence* is a joint function of two variables, the following alterations will move the relation toward a state of balance:

1. If B reduces motivational investment in goals mediated by A;
2. If B cultivates alternative sources for gratification of those goals;
3. If A increases motivational investment in goals mediated by B;
4. If A is denied alternative sources for achieving those goals.

While these four types of balancing operation are dictated by the logic of the scheme, we suggest that each corresponds to well-known social processes. The first operation yields balance through motivational withdrawal by B, the weaker member. The second involves the cultivation of alternative social relations by B. The third is based upon "giving status" to A, and the fourth involves coalition and group formation.

In some of these processes the role of power is well known, while in others it seems to have escaped notice. In discussing any one of these balancing operations it must be remembered that a prediction of which one (or what combination) of the four will take place must rest upon analysis of conditions involved in the concrete case at hand.

In the interest of simplicity and clarity, we will illustrate each of the four generic types of balancing operation in relations

among children in the context of play. Consider two children equally motivated toward the pleasures of collective play and equally capable of contributing to such play. These children, A and B, form a balanced relation if we assume further that each has the other as his only playmate, and the give-and-take of their interactions might well be imagined, involving the emergence of such equalitarian rules as "taking turns," etc. Suppose now that a third child, C, moves into the neighborhood and makes the acquaintance of A, but *not* B. The A-B relation will be thrown out of balance by virtue of A's decreased dependence upon B. The reader should convince himself of this fact by referring back to the proposition on dependence. Without any of these parties necessarily "understanding" what is going on, we would predict that A would slowly come to dominate B in the pattern of their interactions. On more frequent occasions B will find himself deprived of the pleasures A can offer, thus slowly coming to sense his own dependency more acutely. By the same token A will more frequently find B saying "yes" instead of "no" to his proposals, and he will gain increased awareness of his power over B. The growing self-images of these children will surely reflect and perpetuate this pattern.

OPERATION NUMBER ONE: WITHDRAWAL

We now have the powerful A making demands of the dependent B. One of the processes through which the tensions in the unbalanced A-B relation can be reduced is *motivational withdrawal* on the part of B, for this will reduce Dba and Pab. In this illustration, child B might lose some of his interest in collective play under the impact of frustrations and demands imposed by A. Such a withdrawal from the play relation would presumably come about if the other three balancing operations were blocked by the circumstances peculiar to the situation. The same operation was illustrated above in the case of the girl who might renounce the value of dating. It would seem to be involved in the dampened level of aspiration associated with the "mark of oppression" referred to above.

In general, the denial of dependency involved in this balancing operation will have the effect of moving actors away from relations which are unbalanced to their disadvantage. The actor's motivational orientations and commitments toward different areas of activity will intimately reflect this process.

OPERATION NUMBER TWO: EXTENSION OF POWER NETWORK

Withdrawal as a balancing operation entails subjective alterations in the weaker actor. The second operation takes place through alterations in a structure we shall call a *power network*, defined as two or more *connected* power-dependence relations. As we have seen in our illustration, when the C-A relation is connected through A with the A-B relation, forming a simple linear network C-A-B, the properties of A-B are altered. In this example, a previously balanced A-B relation is thrown out of balance, giving A a power advantage. This points up the general fact that while each relation in a network will involve interactions which appear to be independent of other relations in the network (e.g., A and B are seen to play together in the absence of C; C and A

in the absence of B), the internal features of one relation are nonetheless a function of the entire network. Any adequate conception of a "power structure" must be based upon this fact.

In this illustration the form of the network throws both relations within it out of balance, thus stimulating one or several of the balancing operations under discussion. If balancing operation number two takes place, *the network* will be extended by the formation of new relationships. The tensions of imbalance in the A-B and A-C relations will make B and C "ready" to form new friendships (1) with additional children D and E, thus lengthening a linear network, or (2) with each other, thus "closing" the network. It is important to notice that the lengthened network balances some relations, but not the network as a whole, while the closed network is completely balanced under the limiting assumptions of this illustration. Thus, we might offer as a corollary to operation number two: Power networks tend to achieve closure.[15]

If the reader is dissatisfied with this illustration in children's play relations, let

---

[15] The notion of closed versus open networks as discussed here can be directly related to research dealing with communication networks, such as that reported by Harold J. Leavitt, "Some Effects of Communication Patterns on Group Performance," *Journal of Abnormal and Social Psychology*, 46 (January, 1951), pp. 38–50, in which the limiting assumptions involved in this discussion are fully met by experimental controls. In discussing those experiments in terms of the concepts in this theory we would consider each actor's dependence upon other actors for *information*. A formal treatment of such networks is suggested by A. Bavelas, "A Mathematical Model For Group Structure," *Applied Anthropology*, 7 (Summer, 1948), pp. 16–30.

A be the loan agent mentioned earlier, and B, C, . . . N be home builders or others dependent upon A for capital. This is the familiar monopoly situation with the imbalance commonly attributed to it. As a network, it is a set of relations connected only at A. Just as the children were "ready" to accept new friends, so the community of actors B, C, . . . N is ready to receive new loan agencies. Balancing operation number 2 involves in all cases the *diffusion* of dependency into new relations in a network. A final illustration of this principle can be found in institutionalized form in some kinship systems involving the extended family. In the case of the Hopi, for example, Dorothy Eggan has described at length the diffusion of child dependency among many "mothers," thus draining off much of the force of oedipal conflicts in that society.[16] We have already suggested that oedipal conflict may be taken as a special case of the tension of imbalance, which in this case appears to be institutionally handled in a manner resembling operation number two. This is not to be taken, however, as an assertion that the institution evolved as a balancing process, though this is clearly open for consideration.

It is convenient at this juncture to take up balancing operation number 4, leaving number 3 to the last.

OPERATION NUMBER FOUR: COALITION FORMATION

Let us continue with the same illustration. When the B-C relation forms, closing

---

[16] Dorothy Eggan, "The General Problem of Hopi Adjustment," *American Anthropologist*, 45 (July–September, 1943), pp. 357–373.

the C-A-B network in the process of balancing, we have what appears to be a coalition of the two weaker against the one stronger. This, however, is not technically the case for A is not involved in the B-C interactions; he simply exists as an alternative playmate for both B and C.

The proper representation of coalitions in a triad would be (AB)-C, (AC)-B, or (BC)-A. That is, a triadic network reduces to a coalition only if two members unite as a single actor in the process of dealing directly with the third. The difference involved here may be very small in behavioral terms, and the distinction may seem overly refined, but it goes to the heart of an important conceptual problem (the difference between a closed "network" and a "group"), and it rests upon the fact that two very different balancing operations are involved. The C-A-B network is balanced through the addition of a third relation (C-B) in operation number two, but it is still just a power network. In operation number 4 it achieves balance through collapsing the two-relational network into one group-person relation with the emergence of a "collective actor." Operation number two reduces the power of the stronger actor, while number 4 increases the power of weaker actors through collectivization. If the rewards mediated by A are such that they can be jointly enjoyed by B and C, then the tensions of imbalance in the A-B and A-C relations can be resolved in the (BC)-A coalition.

In a general way, Marx was asking for balancing operation number 4 in his call to "Workers of the world," and the collectivization of labor can be taken as an illustration of this balancing tendency as an historic process. Among the balancing operations described here, coalition formation is the one most commonly recognized as a power process. However, the more general significance of this balancing operation seems to have escaped notice, for the typical coalition is only one of the many forms this same operation takes. For this reason the next section will explore coalition processes further.

The Organized Group

We wish to suggest that the coalition process is basically involved in all organized group functioning, whether the group be called a coalition or not. We believe this illuminates the role which power processes play in the emergence and maintenance of group structure in general.

In the typical coalition pattern, (AB)-C, A and B constitute a collective actor in the sense that they act as one, presenting themselves to their common environment as a single unit. A coalition, as one *type* of group, is characterized by the fact that (a) the common environment is an actor to be controlled, and (b) its unity is historically based upon efforts to achieve that control. Now, all we need do to blend this type of group with groups in general is to *dehumanize* the environmental problem which the group collectively encounters. Thus, instead of having the control of actor C as its end, the group attempts to control C in the interest of achieving X, some "group goal." Now, if C also aspires toward X, and if C is dependent upon the group for achieving X, C might well be one of the group members—any member. Thus, in a three-member group we have three coalition structures as *intra*group relations, each representable as ([AB]-C)-X, with A, B and C interchangeable.

The situation involved here is reminiscent of the rapidly forming and reforming coalitions in unconsolidated children's play groups. As the group consolidates, these coalitions do not drop out of the picture; they become stabilized features of group structure, and the stabilization process is identical with "norm formation." In fact, the demands made by (AB) of C in the power process within ([AB]-C) are exactly what we normally call *group norms* and *role-prescriptions*. Such norms are properly viewed as the "voice" of a collective actor, standing in coalition against the object of its demands. This reasoning suggests an idealized conception of group structure, based upon two types of collective demands:

(1) *Role-Prescriptions.* Specification of behavior which all group members expect (demand) of one or more but not all members.

(2) *Group Norms.* Specifications of behavior which all group members expect of all group members.

Certain actions, when performed by some member or members, need not be performed by all other members to properly facilitate group functioning. These will tend to be incorporated in role-prescriptions, which, taken together, provide a division of labor in a role structure. Roles are defined and enforced through a consolidation of power in coalition formation. Likewise with group norms. Thus, the structure of a group (its norms and prescriptions) will specify the makeup of the coalition a member would face for any group-relevant act he might perform.

This conception of group structure is idealized in the sense that it describes complete consensus among members, even to the point of group identification and internalization of collective demands (members expect things of themselves in the above definitions). Balancing operations, along with cost reduction, should move group structure toward this ideal.

AUTHORITY

It should be clear that in introducing conceptions of group *structure* we have in no way digressed from our discussion of power *processes*, for the emergence of these structural forms is attributed directly to operation number four, closely resembling coalition formation. Even the most formalized role-prescription is properly viewed as the "voice" of all members standing as a coalition in making its demand of the occupant of the role. Whenever a specific member finds occasion to remind another member of his "proper" job in terms of such prescriptions, he speaks with the *authority* of the group behind him; he is "authorized" to speak for them. In this sense, every member has authority of a kind (as in civil arrest), but authority is usually used to refer to power vested in an office or role. The situation is basically the same, however, in either case. The occupant of such a role has simply been singled out and commissioned more explicitly to speak for the group in the group's dealings with its members. That authority is *limited* power follows from logical necessity when role-prescriptions are treated as they are here. A dean, for example, can force faculty member A to turn in his grades on time because the demand is "legitimate," that is, supported by a coalition of all other faculty members joining with the dean in making the demand. If that dean, however, were to employ sanctions in an effort to induce that member to polish the dean's private car, the "coalition" would immediately re-form around the faculty member, as

expressed in role-prescriptions defining the boundary of "legitimate power" or authority. The dean's authority is power contained and restricted through balancing operation number four, coalition formation.

The notion of legitimacy is important, for authority is more than balanced power; it is *directed* power which can be employed (legitimately) only in channels defined by the norms of the group. A person holding such authority is commissioned; he does not simply have the right to rule or govern—he is obliged to. Thus, authority emerges as a transformation of power in a process called "legitimation," and that process is one special case of balancing operation number four.[17]

---

[17] The process of legitimation has sometimes been described as a tactic employed by a person aspiring to power or trying to hold his power, rather than a process through which persons are granted restricted power. For example, C. Wright Mills states: "Those in authority attempt to justify their rule over institutions by linking it, as if it were a necessary consequence, with widely believed in moral symbols, sacred emblems, legal formulae. These central conceptions may refer to good or gods, the 'vote of the majority,' 'the will of the people,' 'the aristocracy of talent or wealth,' to the 'divine right of kings,' or to the allegedly extraordinary endowments of the ruler himself. Social scientists, following Weber, call such conceptions 'legitimations,' or sometimes 'symbols of justification.' " (*The Sociological Imagination*, New York: Oxford University Press, 1959, p. 36). Whether we view the process of legitimation in the context of the *formation* of such collective conceptions, or in the context of calling upon them to justify action, the process is fundamentally that of mobilizing collective support to oppose those who challenge power. Power so supported is authority, and the process fits the general model of coalition formation.

Earlier in this section we referred to the common phenomenon of rapidly forming and re-forming coalitions in children's play groups. Our reasoning suggests that it is precisely through this coalition processes that unifying norms emerge. These fluctuating coalitions can be taken as the prototype of organized group life wherein the tempo of coalition realignment is accelerated to the point of being a blur before our eyes. Stated more accurately, the norms and prescriptions define implicitly the membership of the coalition which would either support or oppose any member if he were to perform any action relevant to those norms.

OPERATION NUMBER THREE: EMERGENCE OF STATUS

One important feature of group structure remains to be discussed: status and status hierarchies. It is interesting that the one remaining balancing operation provided in this theory takes us naturally to the emergence of status ordering. Operation number three increases the weaker member's power to control the formerly more powerful member through increasing the latter's motivational investment in the relation. This is normally accomplished through giving him status recognition in one or more of its many forms, from ego-gratifications to monetary differentials. The ego-rewards, such as prestige, loom large in this process because they are highly valued by many recipients while given at low cost to the giver.

The discussion of status hierarchies forces us to consider *intra*-group relations, and how this can be done in a theory which treats the group in the singular as *an* actor. The answer is contained in the idealized conception of group structure outlined above. That conception implies that every intra-group relation involves at once every member of the group. Thus, in a group with members A, B, C, and D, the relations A-B, A-C, etc. do not exist. Any interactions between A and B, for example, lie outside of the social system in question unless one or both of these persons "represents" the group in his actions, as in the coalition pattern discussed at length above. The relations which do exist are (ABCD)-A, (ABCD)-B, (ABCD)-C and (ABCD)-D as a minimum, plus whatever relations of the (ABCD)-(AB) type may be involved in the peculiar structure of the group in question. Thus, in a group of N members we have theoretical reason for dealing with N *group-member* relations rather than considering all of the $\frac{N(N-1)}{2}$ possible member-member relations. Each of these group-member relations can now be expressed in the familiar equations for a power-dependence relation:

$$Pgm_i = Dm_ig$$
$$Pm_ig = Dgm_i.$$

To account for the emergence of a status hierarchy within a group of N members, we start with a set of N group-member relations of this type and consider balancing operations in these relations.

Let us imagine a five member group and proceed on three assumptions: (1) *status* involves differential valuation of members (or roles) by the group, and this valuation is equivalent to, or an expression of, Dgm_i; (2) a member who is highly valued by the group is highly valued in other *similar* groups he belongs to or might freely join; and (3) all five members have the same motivational investment in the group at the outset. Assumptions 2 and 3 are empirical, and when they are true they imply that Dgm and Dmg are inversely related across the N group-member relations. This in turn implies a state of imbalance of a very precarious nature so far as group stability is concerned. The least dependent member of a group will be the first to break from the group, and these members are precisely the most valued members. It is this situation which balancing operation number three alleviates through "giving status" to the highly valued members, thus gaining the power to keep and control those members.

These ideas are illustrated with hypothetical values in Table 1, with imbalance represented as power advantage (PA). Balancing operations will tend to move PA toward zero, as shown in column 6 after the highly valued members A and B have come to depend upon the group for the special rewards of status, and in column 9 after the least valued members D and E have withdrawn some of their original motivational investment in the group. The table presents three stages in status crystallization, and the process of crystallization is seen as a balancing process. The final stage (columns 7, 8, and 9) should be achieved only in groups with very low membership turnover. The middle stage might well be perpetual in groups with new members continually coming in at the lower levels. In such "open" groups, status striving should be a characteristic feature and can be taken as a direct manifestation of the tensions of imbalance. In the final stage, such strivers have either succeeded or withdrawn from the struggle.

Among the factors involved in status ordering, this theory focuses attention upon the extreme importance of the *availability* factor in dependency as a determinant of status position and the values employed in status ordering. In considering Dgm (the relative value or importance the group attaches to member roles), it is notably difficult to rely upon a functional explanation. Is the pitcher more highly valued than the center fielder because he is functionally more important or because good pitchers are harder to find? Is the physicist valued over the plumber because of a "more important" functional contribution

Table 1

HYPOTHETICAL VALUES SHOWING THE RELATION BETWEEN DGM AND DMG IN A GROUP WITH FIVE MEMBERS

	Before Balancing			After Operation #3			After Operation #1		
Member	1 Dgm	2 Dmg*	3 PAgm**	4 Dgm	5 Dmg	6 PAgm**	7 Dgm	8 Dmg	9 PAgm**
A	5	1	−4	5	5	0	5	5	0
B	4	2	−2	4	4	0	4	4	0
C	3	3	0	3	3	0	3	3	0
D	2	4	2	2	4	2	2	2	0
E	1	5	4	1	5	4	1	1	0

* Assuming that all members have the same motivational investment in the group at the outset, and that highly valued members (A and B) are valued in other groups as well.
** Power Advantage PAgm=Dmg–Dgm.

to the social system, or because physicists are more difficult to replace, more costly to obtain, etc.? The latter considerations involve the availability factor. We suggest here that the *values* people use in ordering roles or persons express the dependence of the system upon those roles, and that the *availability* factor in dependency plays the decisive part in historically shaping those values.[18]

CONCLUSION

The theory put forth in this paper is in large part contained implicitly in the ties of mutual dependence which bind actors together in social systems. Its principal value seems to be its ability to pull together a wide variety of social events, ranging from the internalization of parental codes to society-wide movements, like the collectivization of labor, in terms of a few very simple principles. Most important, the concepts involved are subject to operational formulation. Two experiments testing certain propostions discussed above led to the following results:

1. Conformity (Pgm) varies directly with motivational investment in the group;
2. Conformity varies inversely with acceptance in alternative groups;
3. Conformity is high at both status extremes in groups with membership turnover (see column 5, Table 1),

4. Highly valued members of a group are strong conformers *only if* they are valued by other groups as well. (This supports the notion that special status rewards are used to hold the highly valued member who does not depend heavily upon the group, and that in granting him such rewards power is obtained over him.);
5. Coalitions form among the weak to control the strong (balancing operation number three);
6. The greatest rewards within a coalition are given to the less dependent member of the coalition (balancing operation number three, analogous to "status giving").

Once the basic ideas in this theory have been adequately validated and refined, both theoretical and empirical work must be extended in two main directions. First, the interaction process should be studied to locate carefully the factors leading to *perceived* power and dependency in self and others, and the conditions under which power, as a potential, will be employed in action. Secondly, and, in the long run, more important, will be study of *power networks* more complex than those referred to here, leading to more adequate understanding of complex power structures. The theory presented here does no more than provide the basic underpinning to the study of complex networks. There is every reason to believe that modern mathematics, graph theory in particiular,[19] can be fruitfully employed in the analysis of complex networks and predicting the outcome of power plays within such networks.

---

[18] "Motivational investment" and "availability," which jointly determine dependency at any point in time, are functionally related through time. This is implied in our balancing operations. While these two variables can be readily distinguished in the case of Dmg; they are too intimately fused in Dgm to be clearly separated. The values by which a group sees a given role as "important" at time 2, evolve from felt scarcity in that role and similar roles at time 1.

---

[19] F. Harary and R. Norman, *Graph Theory as a Mathematical Model in the Social Sciences.* Ann Arbor: Institute for Social Research, 1953. An effort to apply such a model to power relations can be found in John R. P. French, Jr., "A Formal Theory of Social Power," *The Psychological Review*, 63 (May, 1956), pp. 181–194.

POWER-DEPENDENCE RELATIONS:
TWO EXPERIMENTS*

Richard M. Emerson

In this paper we report two experimental studies, one dealing with conformity, the other exploring *coalitions* in the triad. While both of these topics have received considerable separate attention in the literature, they are presented together in this paper because the separate findings may involve a single body of principles comprising a theory of balancing tendencies in *power-dependence relations.*[1]

The first study was performed well before the theory of power relations was formulated. In this article we present first the data from that study, along with its original rationale, and we then examine those data in terms of the subsequent theory of power. Finally, a second experiment is reported, designed explicitly to test predictions from the theory.

FIRST STUDY: STATUS INSECURITY AND CONFORMITY

Sherif,[2] Asch,[3] and others have shown that subjects submit to social influence under certain laboratory conditions. Typi-

cally, such experiments employ temporary *aggregates* of subjects, among whom no established social relations exist. Hence, in an effort to explain subject behavior, attention tends to be focused upon attributes of persons rather than attributes of interpersonal relations.[4] By contrast, this study was designed to explore interpersonal determinants of conformity or submission to social influence in structured groups, under controlled laboratory conditions.

Three hypotheses were being tested. *Submission* to *group influence* varies directly with (1) *motivation* toward participation in the group, (2) intensity of group *expectations*, and (3) *status insecurity*. (Status insecurity was defined simply as "uncertainty of acceptance or continued acceptance in status position.") Hypothesis 1 was adapted from the work of Festinger and associates.[5] Hypothesis 2,

---

* Richard M. Emerson, "Power-Dependence Relations: Two Experiments," *Sociometry*, 27 (1964), 282–98. Reprinted by Permission of the American Sociological Association.

[1] Richard M. Emerson, "Power-Dependence Relations," *American Sociological Review*, 17 (February, 1962), pp. 31–41.

[2] Musafer Sherif, "A Study of Social Factors

in Perception," *Archives of Psychology*, Number 187 (July, 1935).

[3] Solomon E. Asch, "Effects of Pressure Upon the Modification and Distortion of Judgment," in Dorwin Cartwright and Alvin Lander, editors, *Group Dynamics*, New York: Row, Peterson and Company, 1953, pp. 151–162.

[4] John H. Rohrer, "The Influence of Personality Structure on Interpersonal Behaviors," *Annual Technical Report*, ONR Contrast N ont-475(01), March 1, 1953.

[5] Leon Festinger, Stanley Schachter and

while commonplace, would underlie the differentiated structure of influence in role-systems. The rationale for hypothesis 3 was largely implicit: since the rewards of group participation are mediated by position in group relations, uncertainty of position makes gratification problematic, producing a cautious, compliant orientation in role-behavior.

Method

To achieve the objectives of this study, it was necessary to find a fairly large number of groups, all very much alike in size and structure, and small enough to be studied in a laboratory situation. With the cooperation of the Minneapolis Boy Scout organization, twenty Boy Scout patrol groups took part. The study was organized as a "distance judging contest," with patrol groups as the competing units.

These twenty patrols, averaging five members each, made up four Boy Scout troops. After a questionnaire had been administered to the entire troop, patrols were taken to the laboratory one at a time to take part in judging tasks. In a completely darkened room, the patrol saw two pinpoints of light about six feet apart and twenty feet away. After ten seconds the right hand light went out, leaving only one light. After ten more seconds a third light came on about midway between the first two, and remained for ten seconds. All stimulus lights then went off and each scout tried to estimate the location of the third light, relative to the two framing lights, on a continuum numbered from 0 (left light) to 100 (right light).

This procedure was repeated five times as *practice trials*, and continued through fifteen more *official trials*. Members' estimates were private, but it was understood that scores would be made public after the task was finished.

Conformity Measure. After each official trial, the experimenter gathered all estimates of light position, went through the motions of averaging them, and then announced a *fictitious group average* before the next trial. Based on considerable pretesting with light settings and announced averages, plausible averages were presented which were nonetheless clearly in conflict with sensory evidence. Conformity was measured as change in behavior toward the fictious "group norm." Figure 1 presets light settings and fictitious averages across all trials.

Motivational Commitment. The initial questionnaire contained a sociometric question, calling for four ordered choices, directed toward any scout in the Troop. In addition, five items were included concerning motivational commitment to the patrol group.[6]

Level of Group Expectation. After the five practice trials, subjects were asked to rate each scout on a five-point scale, indicating how well the group expected that scout to perform in the contest. These ratings were averaged for each subject.

Status Insecurity. In the laboratory ses-

Kurt Back, *Theory and Experiment in Social Communication*, Ann Arbor: Research Center for Group Dynamics, University of Michigan, 1950.

---

[6] A Guttman scale was used without collapsing response categories, yielding a coefficient of reproducibility of .82 across the subjects in this study. The items were derived, with some modification, from a similar scale worked up by Harold H. Kelley and Edmond H. Volkart, "The Resistance to Change in Group Anchored Attitudes," *American Sociological Review*, 17 (August, 1952), pp. 453–65.

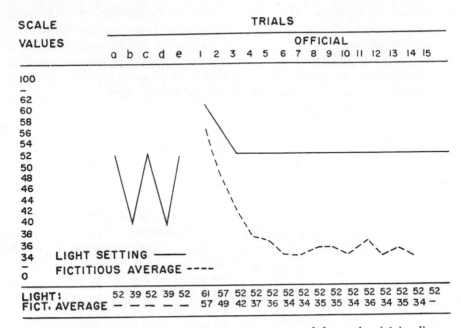

| SCALE | TRIALS |
| VALUES | OFFICIAL |

Fig. 1. Light setting and fictitious group averages announced for each trial in distance judging.

sion, the first "judging task" asked the subject to guess which scouts might have chosen him in the sociometric question by checking a "yes" or a "no" after each scout's name. In addition, he indicated his certainty or uncertainty about each guess on a four-point scale. These certainty-uncertainty self-ratings were averaged across all ratings.

Validation of Measures. (1) Patrols scoring high on motivation tend to make sociometric choices within the patrol, $r = .42$. (2) There was intersubject reliability in expectation ratings, by F test, and level of group expectation correlates with sociometric status, $r = .53$. (3) An attempt to validate the status insecurity measure against reciprocated sociometric choices failed to provide validation.

Finally, the validation of our measure of conformity, the dependent variable, in-

volved an experimental treatment. After the tenth official trial, the laboratory assistant returned with "results" for the practice trials, "just to let them know how well they were doing." In ten groups, chosen at random, each member received a card saying "You did very well in practice. Better than most." In the other ten groups the card read "You did not do very well in practice. Not as well as most." If change in behavior is attributable to social influence via the fictitious "group norm," conformity scores should decrease and increase in these groups respectively. They did so quite dramatically ($p < .01$, by Fisher's exact test).

To nullify the effect of this validation treatment upon conformity scores, *absolute conformity* was transformed into *relative conformity*, in standard deviation units, standardizing scores with experimental treatments.

Table 1

ANALYSIS OF VARIANCE FOR 20 GROUPS ON INITIAL ESTIMATES AND CONFORMITY

Source of Variation	Sum of Squares	df	Mean Square	F
Initial Estimates				
Between	1575.0	19	82.8	.67
Within	9822.3	79	124.3	—
Total	11397.3	98		
Conformity				
Between	603.5	19	31.8	1.76*
Within	1423.6	79	18.0	—
Total	2027.1	98		

* $.01 < p < .05$.

Results

Table 1 presents a simple analysis of variance for twenty groups on conformity, with and without the influence of the fictitious average. Conformity is subject to a "group effect" in this study, a subject's conformity score being a function of the group he belongs to. We must ask if these between-group variations in conformity are attributable to member motivation. Table 2 presents correlations among group means on conformity, motivation, percent of choices made within the group, and choices received from outside of the group.

These correlations confirm hypothesis 1. Conformity varies directly with motivation. *In addition,* patrols whose members receive choices from outside the group obtain little conformity from their members. We will return to this point!

Hypothesis 2 asserts that conformity varies directly with level of group expectation. Since expectation increases with status ($r = .53$, N = 88) we expect to find status differentials reflected in conforming

Table 2

CORRELATIONS AMONG GROUP MEANS ON CONFORMITY, MOTIVATION,
SOCIOMETRIC CHOICES WITHIN THE GROUP, AND CHOICES
RECEIVED FROM OUTSIDE THE GROUP

Variable	Correlation*			
	1	2	3	4
1. Conformity	—	.60	.42	—.57
2. Motivation	.60	—	.42	—.33
3. Within-group choices (percent)	.42	.42	—	—.60
4. Out-group choices received	—.57	—.33	—.60	—

* N = 20 patrol groups.

Table 3

Mean Conformity Scores for Class Intervals* on Sociometric Status Inside and Outside the Group**

Status Inside the Group	Status Outside the Patrol Group					
	0 to 4		4 to 9		10 plus	
		(n)		(n)		(n)
0 to 3	.49	15	.37	8	−.35	4
4 to 11	.15	18	−.22	9	−.27	9
12 plus	−.42	13	−.34	6	.20	10

* Class intervals were selected to distribute n's as equally as possible, while preserving as many intervals as possible.
** Six subjects were not included for insufficient data.

behavior. However, we found no significant relation between expectation and conformity, despite the commonplace character of this hypothesis. But what of status and conformity?

Correlations in Table 2 suggest that the source of sociometric status (in-group or out-group choices received) may make a difference. Hence, Table 3 presents mean conformity for cross-classified status sources. In general, subjects receiving few choices from either source are strong conformers. Subjects receiving many choices from *one* but not *both* sources do not conform. Subjects receiving many choices from both sources conform. This is interaction between status sources in Table 3 shows up as a curvilinear relation between conformity and total status in Table 4! Conformity is found at status extremes.

Discussion

How are these findings to be explained? One interpretation of high status conformity can be eliminated at once. It is sometimes suggested that such conformity is not real, since leaders *set* the norms they

"conform" to.[7] However, in this study the experimenter set the norm.

The author initially thought that "status

Table 4

Mean and Standard Deviation of Conformity Scores by Class Intervals on Total Sociometric Status*

Sociometric Status	N	Mean	SD
0 to 3	12	.68	1.05
4 to 7	11	.28	.90
8 to 11	19	.13	.67
12 to 15	14	−.41	1.06
16 to 19	9	−.47	.91
20 to 23	8	−.46	1.12
24 to 27	6	−.21	.98
28 to 31	6	−.11	.78
32 plus	6	.47	.66

* Eight subjects were not included for insufficient data.

[7] Carl J. Hovland, Irving L. Janis and Harold H. Kelley, *Communication and Persuasion*, New Haven: Yale University Press, 1953, pp. 150.

Table 5

CORRELATIONS BETWEEN CONFORMITY, SOCIOMETRIC STATUS, LEVEL OF
EXPECTATION AND MOTIVATION FOR SUBJECTS CLASSIFIED AS
CENTRAL OR PERIPHERAL GROUP MEMBERS

| | | Sociometric Status | | | | | | |
| | | Peripheral (N=56) | | | Central (N=32) | | | |
Variable	(1)	(2)	(3)	(4)	(1)	(2)	(3)	(4)
1. Conformity	—	−.37	.15	.29	—	.33	.35	.47
2. Status	−.37	—	.18	.03	.33	—	.33	.21
3. Expectation	.15	.18	—	−.01	.35	.33	—	.36
4. Motivation	.29	−.03	−.01	—	.47	.21	.36	—

insecurity" might provide the answer. Marginal members might be uncertain of acceptance in the group, and high status members might be uncertain of maintaining status at a level where competition is intense. Our measure of status insecurity, however, failed to correlate either with status or conformity. The doubtful validity of that measure might be used as an "out," but serveral revised forms of the measure all failed.

An alternative rationale involves a different dynamic at the two status extremes. The peripheral member, who might "know his position" all too well, is nonetheless in a *weak* position, and his behavior might be accordingly deferential. By contrast, the high status member might see his position as defined in part by high group expectations (as indeed it is in these data). Hence, he might "conform" not out of deference but as a "responsible leader," receptive to group demands.[8]

---

[8] Ferenc Merei, "Group Leadership and Institutionalization," in Eleanor Maccoby. Theodore Newcomb, and Eugene Hartley, editors, *Readings in Social Psychology*, New York: Henry Holt and Company, 1958, pp. 522–32.

To examine this approach, we divide the subjects into *low* and *high* status groups, using the apex of the conformity curve as a cutting point, and perform linear analysis within each group (see Table 5). We find that *level of expectation* does in fact correlate a little with conformity, and only among the higher status subjects. In addition, we find *motivation* correlated higher with conformity among these subjects. (High status members score higher on motivation, but not significantly so.)

Thus, there are some data suggesting that conformity may be attributable to different sources at the two status extremes, but the leads are tenuous indeed. However, there is one variable in these data which demands attention—*source of sociometric status*. The conforming high status members derive status from out-group choices (Tables 3 and 4). Members with comparable in-group status, who receive few out-group choices, are the strongest deviates in the study! (Table 3).

To summarize, the data suggest that conformity is related to (1) motivation, (2) low in-group status in the absence of out-group status, and (3) high in-group status *if* accompanied by high out-group status.

POWER-DEPENDENCE RELATIONS

In the year following the above study, a theory of power relations was slowly formulated without any special reference to the above findings. It was initially designed to account for processes in large-scale social movements, such as the rise of organized labor, and it was first applied in a study of attitude change in intergroup relations.[9] When it was presented as a step toward a general theory of power (see footnote 1), it was noticed for the first time that it might provide an organized explanation for the data presented above.

> The central ideas in the theory can be summarized as follows:
>
> *Power (Pab)*. The power of actor A over actor B is the amount of resistance on the part of B which can potentially be overcome by A.[10]
>
> *Dependence (Dab)*. The dependence of actor A upon actor B is (1) directly proportional to A's *motivational investment* in goals mediated by B, and (2) inversely proportional to the *availability* of those goals outside the A-B relation.
>
> *(Pab = Dba)*. The power of A over B is equal to, and based upon, the dependence of B upon A.

The entire theory revolves around these three notions. Since power is based upon the other's dependence, most of the analysis concerns the two variables which determine dependency.

[9] Richard M. Emerson, "Power Relations and Attitude Change," *The Journal of Human Relations*, 4 (Summer, 1956), pp. 11–25.

[10] The term "actor" refers either to a person or a group (a collective actor) wherever it occurs.

Recognizing the reciprocal character of social relations, involving *mutual* dependency, a *power-dependence relation* is represented as a set of two equations. The relation may be either

$$\text{balanced} \begin{pmatrix} \text{Pab} = \text{Dba} \\ \| \qquad \| \\ \text{Pba} = \text{Dab} \end{pmatrix} \text{ or}$$

$$\text{unbalanced} \begin{pmatrix} \text{Pab} = \text{Dba} \\ \vee \qquad \vee \\ \text{Pba} = \text{Dab} \end{pmatrix}.^{[11]}$$

It is argued that a power balance does not neutralize power, for the relation may be balanced at different *levels* of reciprocal power, leading to a conception of cohesion in social relations or groups.

In an unbalanced relation someone has a *power advantage* (PA) represented as PAab = Pab—Pba. This theory hypothesizes that unbalanced power relations are inherently unstable, generating "tensions of imbalance"[12] which set in motion one or several "balancing operations." A *balancing operation* is a change in the power-

[11] In an attempt to overcome the cumbersome problem of describing reciprocal ego-alter relations, we adopt the formal notation of symbols and subscripts. Pab is read as "the power of A over B," etc. An important feature of this theory is that power is treated as an attribute of a reciprocal A-B *relation* rather than an attribute of a person.

[12] The instability of unbalanced relations can be traced to (a) the fact that any *use of power* will by definition arouse psychological conflict in the recipient, and (b) when power is not actually used, parties nonetheless feel vulnerable in their excessive dependency. The subject involved in an unbalanced relation will likely see the relation as lacking what Homans has called *distributive justice* (George C. Homans, *Social Behavior: Its Elementary Forms*, New York: Harcourt, Brace and World, 1961, pp. 72–78). A study of that concept will show that it can be coordinated closely with the conditions of balance and imbalance.

dependence relation which moves PA toward zero. It follows from the above propositions that exactly four balancing operations exist:

1. WITHDRAWAL. Decreased *motivational investment* on the part of the weaker member.
2. NETWORK EXTENSION. Increased *availability* of goals for the weaker member outside the relation (extension of the "power network" through formation of new relations).[13]
3. STATUS GIVING. Increased *motivational investment* on the part of the stronger member.
4. COALITION FORMATION. Decreased *availability* of goals outside of the relation for the stronger member ("coalition formation," or collapsing a power network).

While these four operations are suggested logically, they appear to correspond with well-known social processes as suggested by the descriptive names chosen for them. The rest of the theory presented earlier explores some of the implications of these balancing operations in the emergence of group structure, the conversion of power into "authority" and the formation of status hierarchies. Perhaps the most interesting feature of the theory is the concept of "availability" of rewards through alternative social relations, for this notion makes possible a fairly rigorous conception of *power networks*. Change in such structures can be deduced, and from changes in one relation, subsequent changes throughout the network can be deduced.

In the above study of conformity (submission to group influence) we are concerned with a set of n group-member power relations in a group of size n.[14] Conformity should be a function of the member's dependence upon the group. Thus, it should vary directly with *motivational commitment*, and inversely with *availability* of gratification from alternative sources. If sociometric choices received from outside the group are taken as an index of availability, we can deduce the relationships found in Table 2 and the top row of Table 3.

Turning to *status* and conformity, we confront the group's dependence upon the member, in the reciprocal power-dependence relation. The relative power of members (freedom to deviate with impunity?) should increase with *in-group status*, as shown in the left column of Table 3. However, this relation is reversed when high out-group status (*availability*) is added, as shown in the right hand column of Table 3. How can this interaction between *status* and *availability* be explained in our theory?

Balancing Operation 3: Status Giving. In Table 6 we present hypothetical values for a group of five persons. In column 1, members are ordered in terms of Dgm_i, the dependence of the group upon the member. Since the group's dependence upon the contributions of a member is closely related to the group's collective "valuation" of that member or the role he occupies, column 1 can be considered an incipient status order.

Now, *assume* that the highly valued members happen to be valued by other similar groups, thus reducing their dependence upon the group in question. When this is the case, Dgm and Dmg are

---

[13] A *power network* is defined as two or more connected power-dependence relations. A *network* is not to be confused with *group*. The former is a set of relations among actors. The latter *is* an actor. For a full discussion of this point, see the original article on power-dependency relations.

[14] We are *not* concerned with a set of n(n-1)/2 member-member relations, for reasons discussed in the earlier paper.

Table 6

HYPOTHETICAL RELATIONS BETWEEN DGM AND DMG BEFORE AND AFTER
BALANCING IN A FIVE MEMBER GROUP

	Unbalanced			After Operation 3			After Operation 1		
Member	1 Dgm	2 Dmg	3 PAgm*	4 Dgm	5 Dmg	6 PAgm*	7 Dgm	8 Dmg	9 PAgm*
A	5	1	−4	5	5	0	5	5	0
B	4	2	−2	4	4	0	4	4	0
C	3	3	0	3	3	0	3	3	0
D	2	4	2	2	4	2	2	2	0
E	1	5	4	1	5	4	1	1	0

* Power Advantage (PAgm) = Dmg−Dgm.

inversely related across members, producing a precarious state of imbalance (Column 3). The most valued members would be the most difficult to control, the first to drop out of the group, etc.

Our theory predicts that balancing operations will produce changes, with power advantages converging on zero. Four operations are theoretically possible, but only one of them is feasible at the high status level, in the situation under discussion. That one is number 3, "status giving." Its effect is to increase the dependence of the otherwise independent member, through granting him the special rewards of high status (e.g., prestige, salary increase, etc.). By so doing, the group can keep and control its valued members. In terms of the data presented above, it is most important to note that this balancing operation should effect *only* those members who (a) are highly valued by the group, and (b) are highly valued by other similar groups. Hence, this theory predicts a curvilinear relation between status and conformity, *if and only if* high status members have "status" in alternative groups. This is exactly what the data in Tables 2 and 3

seem to suggest. The crucial variable appears to be the *availability* factor in dependence.[15]

---

[15] In predicting conformity on the part of high status members under specific conditions, we in no way contradict the notion that these members have more power than other members of the group. Column 4 in Table 6 clearly shows this. As stated above, balance does not neutralize power. The complex relations involved here have generated conflicting hypotheses concerning the relation of status and conformity. Our theory would predict vastly different relationships in different group situations, as Table 6 indicates. For a discussion of status and conformity hypotheses, see Carl I. Hovland, Irving L. Janis, and Harold H. Kelley, *Communication and Persuasion*, New Haven: Yale University Press, 1953, pp. 149–150. Some of the studies pertinent to our hypothesis are: Harold H. Kelley and Edmond H. Volkart, "The Resistance to Change of Group Anchored Attitudes," *American Sociological Review*, 17 (August, 1952), pp. 453–465; James E. Dittes and Harold H. Kelley, "Effects of Acceptance upon Conformity to Group Norms," *Journal of Abnormal and Social Psychology*, 53 (July, 1956), pp. 100–107; H. L. Wilensky, *Intellectuals in Labor Unions*, Glencoe, Ill.: The Free Press, 1956, pp. 228–

This has been an *ex post facto* account. However, the theory presented was not designed specifically for these data, nor with these data in mind. The dynamics which this theory imputes to conformity patterns among the Boy Scouts are the same dynamics we see in other settings (e.g., the relation between outside "job-offers" and status advancement in academic and business institutions). Sometimes these dynamics are brought to the level of strategy in overt "power-plays," while otherwise they remain implicit, unrecognized by the participants.

SECOND STUDY: COALITION FORMATION AND "STATUS GIVING"

Our effort to account for conforming behavior by high status group members in terms of a balancing process has a major shortcoming. The data do not show balancing *in process*. An experiment which does isolate the process of "status giving" as such, along with other balancing tendencies, should strengthen the discussion a little.

Among the four balancing operations in this theory, operation # 4 is most commonly recognized as a power process, best illustrated by the coalition. Study 2 will examine coalitions in the triad, predicting that among three equally feasible unions, coalitions will form in a selective manner producing balance in the relations among actors. In addition, Study 2 will present further evidence relating to operation # 3,

"status giving." It will show that the *least* dependent member of a coalition will be given the *larger* share of the rewards within the forming coalition.

Research Setting

Theodore Caplow presented a theory of coalitions in the triad,[16] predicting which coalitions will occur based upon the initial distribution of power among members of the triad.

Vinacke and Arkoff[17] conducted a simple experiment to test Caplow's predictions. Three subjects played a game in which each player was assigned a number (initial "power"), and when a die was thrown all players advanced around the board a number of steps equal to the product of their own "power" and the value on the die. The first player around the board won points. Any two players could form a partnership, pool their power, and advance as one. Partners could divide their winnings (points) as they chose. The numbers assigned to players as initial power provided the six power conditions considered by Caplow:

	A	B	C	
1.	1	1	1	A=B=C
2.	3	2	2	A>B, B=C, A<(B+C)
3.	1	2	2	A<B, B=C
4.	3	1	1	A>(B+C), B=C
5.	4	3	2	A>B>C, A<(B+C)
6.	4	2	1	A>B>C, A>(B+C)

[16] Theodore A. Caplow, "A Theory of Coalitions in the Triad," *American Sociological Review*, 21 (August, 1956), pp. 489–493.

[17] W. Edgar Vinacke and Abe Arkoff, "An Experimental Study of Coalitions in the Triad," *American Sociological Review*, 22 (August, 1957), pp. 406–414.

230; John W. Thibaut and Harold H. Kelley, *The Social Psychology of Groups*, New York: John Wiley and Sons, 1959, pp. 251–52.

It is important to note that each triad studied was exposed to all six power conditions throughout a series of trials, but winnings were *not* cumulated across trials.

The predictions and the results were essentially in accord with the theory under study here. The "balancing" effect of coalition formation is reflected in the tendency for the weaker members to unite and win. However, examination of these "power" conditions suggests that conditions 1, 2, 3, and 5 are identical so far as real power is concerned. In 5, for example, a coalition will prevent A from winning all points. But if a coalition does form, *all* members including A have equal incentive for being in it and it matters not with whom they coalesce. The determinants of power in our theory suggest a power balance in all the above conditions, save 4 and 6 where no coalition is expected anyway. A prediction of coalitions *from the structure of power* relations would simply assert that "some" coalition will form in conditions 1, 2, 3, and 5; no coalitions in 4 and 6. The predictions actually made (and largely borne out) in Vinacke's study must be based upon the *"sense of power"* associated with these numbers by irrational subjects, the "sense of justice" the numerical values evoke, etc. In short, the experiment reveals the habits-of-mind brought by the subjects, rather than the structure of power relations among them.[18]

---

[18] Thibaut and Kelley, in their excellent discussion of power, have also noted this point concerning the Vinacke study. In all of these conditions—"the weaker ones are weaker only with respect to initial weight, which signifies only the power they would possess if everyone acted independently. All are equal in power when coalitions are permitted." See John Thibaut and Harold H. Kelley, *The Social Psychology of Groups*, New York: John Wiley and Sons, 1959, pp. 217–18.

In the following study we employ the same game situation used by Vinacke and Arkoff, modified at significant points, to demonstrate balancing processes more clearly.

The Experiment

Fourteen triads were recruited from Introductory Sociology classes, and each played a "game of skill and chance" in the laboratory. The game consisted of 20 trials, with 100 points to be won in each trial and *accumulated* throughout the game. At the end of the game there were a "winner", "runner-up," and a "loser" in each triad. We are dealing with a network among three competing players.

At the start of each trial each subject drew a disk at random with a number on it, and when a die was thrown all would move around a board according to the product of their number and the value of the die. As soon as numbers were drawn, partnerships could be formed, winnings to be distributed in any multiple of five (to facilitate cumulating scores). A partnership was considered a single player, and ties between players would result in fifty points to each player.

Among the twenty trials there were three trial types, defined in terms of the numbers on the disks used for that trial:

Trial Type 1.   3   1   1
Trial Type 2.   3   2   1
Trial Type 3.   3   3   3

These three conditions have no important relation to the "power" conditions in the Vinacke study. Type 1 encourages no coalition, and amounts to a gift of 100 points given out to some player at random. Its function is to maintain imbalance among players in amount of winnings throughout the game. Trial type 2 pre-

Table 7

DATA SHEET FOR ONE TRIAD DURING A TWENTY-TRIAL GAME

Trial	( )	Trial Type A	B	C	Cumulated Score A	B	C	Points Won A	B	C
1	(1)	1	1	3	—	—	—	—	—	100
2	(3)	3	3	3	—	—	100	50	50	—
3	(2)	3	1	2	50	50	100	60	40	—
4	(1)	1	3	1	110	90	100	—	100	—
5	(2)	1	2	3	110	190	100	40	—	60
6	(3)	3	3	3	150	190	160	50	—	50
.	...	.	.	.	...	...	...	..	..	..
.	...	.	.	.	...	...	...	..	..	..
18	(3)	3	3	3	590	520	590	—	80	20
19	(2)	2	1	3	590	600	610	25	25	50
20	(3)	3	3	3	615	625	660	50	50	—
					Final Score			665	675	660

sents the subjects with a very complex bargaining situation (when taken alongside cumulated scores at any point in the game) and it was included only to keep the game lively and the subjects aroused. Finally, trial type 3 makes any one of the three coalitions equally feasible. *Coalition formation was studied in trials of type 3, with power distributions anchored in the accumulated scores.* Large accumulated winnings represent *previous* power advantage.

Throughout the 20 trials the three trial-types were alternated. The structure of the experiment can best be summarized by presenting the tabular record for one of the actual triads in Table 7.

Hypotheses

In our game situation, *previous* power advantage is reflected in cumulated winnings. To study the balancing tendency of coalitions we must compare the variance in cumulated winnings before and after coalition formation. Prior to each

trial cumulated winnings will fall into one of four patterns. For each pattern we predict that the most frequent coalition will be the one which produces the largest reduction in variance among accumulated scores. Assuming equal distribution of winnings within coalitions, we have the following pre-coalition conditions and predicted coalitions:

1. A>B>C   (Not AB; BC more than AC)
2. A=B>C   (Not AB; AC or BC)
3. A>B=C   (Only BC)
4. A=B=C   (Balance—no prediction)

Balancing Operation #3. When a coalition forms, what determines the distribution of rewards within that coalition? This question takes us to operation #3, the same one involved in high status conformity in Study 1, seen now in a different setting. Consider the 18th trial in Table 7, where A has accumulated 590 points, B has 520, and C has 590. Assuming the predictions above are sound, there is a strong pressure for either the AB or BC coalition to form. Now, B "belongs" to both of these incipient groups, and hence

Table 8

THE BALANCING EFFECT OF COALITIONS IN THE TRIAD

Pre-Coalition Condition	N	Coalitions Formed		P**
A>B>C	35	(AB+AC) 9	(BC)* 26	.0000
A=B>C	14	(AB) 2	(AC+BC)* 12	.1101
A>B=C	49	(AB+AC) 3	(BC)* 46	.0000

* Coalitions which produce balance in cumulative winnings.
** Binomial probabilities, based upon $(.66+.33)^{35}$, $(.33+.66)^{14}$ and $(.66+.33)^{49}$, respectively.

his dependence upon either A or C as a potential partner is lower than the dependence of the partner, giving B a power advantage *within* whichever partnership he chooses. The player with the lowest cumulative score at the start of the trial has a power *advantage* in that trial. *If he exercises that power he can demand a larger share of the points.*[19] In trial 18 he did just that. Giving additional points to the less dependent member in this study is analogous to giving high status rewards to a valued (and less dependent) member in the previous study. In both cases, the *availability* factor in dependence is the crucial variable.

The situation in trial 18 can be generalized for all coalitions in the study by the hypothesis; when rewards are divided unequally the effect will be reduced variance in cumulative winnings (i.e, a balancing effect).

---

[19] Power (Pab) was defined at the outset as "the resistance on the part of B which can be potentially overcome by A." In this research setting, "resistance overcome by A" can be measured as "extra points given to A."

Results

There were 98 trials of type 3 within which coalitions were studied. These trials were first classified into the four *pre-coalition conditions* based upon cumulative scores at the beginning of the trial.[20] Table 8 presents the obtained frequencies for each coalition possibility in each condition. This table shows quite clearly that coalitions tend to form in such a way as to equalize the outcome among players. When one player gains an advantage, the power structure shifts to reduce that advantage through coalition formation. The nine exceptions in the A > B > C condi-

---

[20] Two judges were given these cumulative scores and instructed to classify each set, *impressionistically*, into one of four categories (A>B>C; A=B>C; A>B=C; and A=B=C). The two judges had initial agreement on all but seven of the 98 sets, and these seven were resolved by coin-toss. The frequencies were 35, 14, 49, and O, respectively. Trial type 1 was intended to minimize the occurrence of the A=B=C condition. This, plus the fact that judges ignored absolute magnitudes, accounts for the total absence of that condition.

tion were all AC coalitions as predicted above. In the three exceptions in the A > B = C condition, A received much less than half of the points, showing that the BC coalition was strongly favored in these three cases as well.

Turning to the distribution of rewards within coalitions, we predicted that unequal divisions would have a balancing effect through reducing the variance in winnings among players. We can go further and predict the coalition situations in which unequal divisions will occur. Each of the 98 coalitions formed can be analyzed for balance or imbalance within the coalition. Thus, if A = 640, B = 640, and C = 520, either AC or BC coalition would form, and either one will be out of balance in C's favor. Unequal division of reward should occur in such unbalanced coalitions, and the larger share should go to the stronger member of the coalition.

Table 9

THE BALANCING EFFECT OF DIVISION OF REWARDS WITHIN COALITIONS

Coalitions	Division of Rewards	
	Even	Uneven
Balanced	44	2
Unbalanced	26	26*

* The larger proportion went to the stronger member in all 26 cases.
** Chi Square = 22; p < .001.

Table 9 presents the data properly classified. There were 28 unequal divisions of reward within coalitions, 26 of which occurred in unbalanced coalitions. The larger share of winnings went to the stronger member in all 26 cases. However, there were 26 unbalanced coalitions in which rewards were evenly divided. Power is a *potential* (see the definition of power above) which might not be recognized or acted upon.

SUMMARY AND CONCLUSION

In a previous article, a theory of power-dependence relations was presented, based upon the proposition that power derives from the other's dependency. The theory presents a definition of balance and imbalance in power relations and relational networks, and proceeds to analyze balancing processes. Four generic types of *balancing operations* are suggested by that theory.

We have presented here experimental findings pertaining to three points in that theory. First, the power to influence an actor is based upon his dependency, which in turn is directly proportional to his motivational investment in goals mediated by the power holder, and inversely proportional with the availability of those goals outside of the relationship. Second, the balancing effect of coalition formation (balancing operation #4 in the theory) is shown in a rather simple game situation.

The third finding concerns balancing operation #3, which increases the dependence of the stronger party through increasing his motivational investment in the relation. This operation was called "status giving" in the theory, and the emergence of status hierarchies in group structure was attributed to this balancing process. In the first study, employing natural groups with established status orders, a curvilinear relation was found between status of member and power of group over member. This curvilinear relation seems explainable, after the fact, as a result of balancing operation #3, but these data do not show that process *in process*. In the second study, the same balancing operation is seen in a totally different context. When both A and B desire to form a coalition primarily with C, C gains a power advantage in the (unbalanced) AC relation. He is given additional points to increase his "motivational investment" in joining that relation. The same situation holds by analogy in the first study. A high-status member of a Boy Scout patrol, *if desired as a member by other patrols*, is given special "status rewards" which bind him to his home patrol. In both studies the crucial variable appears to be the "availability" of rewards through alternative relations in a power network.

Among the avenues for continued research within this theoretical framework two are immediately suggested: (1) study of the interaction process in determining the conditions under which power is recognized and acted upon by the participants, as well as the strategy and tactics employed; and (2) study of the properties of more complex relational networks or power "structures." The latter will involve research carrying the principles of this theory out of the small group laboratory and into complex community structure. The two experiments reported here illustrate the use of "small groups" as a research setting (rather than a substantive area) for the study of principles which, hopefully, are not limited to small groups. While the empirical findings in such small group studies cannot be generalized beyond the laboratory, the theoretical principles under study can and should be general in character.

SOME CONDITIONS OF OBEDIENCE AND DISOBEDIENCE TO AUTHORITY*

Stanley Milgram

The situation in which one agent commands another to hurt a third turns up time and again as a significant theme in human relations. It is powerfully expressed

* Stanley Milgram, "Some Conditions of Obedience and Disobedience to Authority," *Human Relations*, 18 (1965), 57–75. Reprinted by permission of Plenum Publishing Company Ltd.

in the story of Abraham, who is commanded by God to kill his son. It is no accident that Kierkegaard, seeking to orient his thought to the central themes of human experience, chose Abraham's conflict as the springboard to his philosophy.

War too moves forward on the trial of an authority which commands a person to destroy the enemy, and perhaps all organized hostility may be viewed as a theme and variation on the three elements of authority, executant, and victim.[1] We describe an experimental program, recently concluded at Yale University, in which a particular expression of this conflict is studied by experimental means.

In its most general form the problem may be defined thus: if X tells Y to hurt Z, under what conditions will Y carry out the command of X and under what conditions will he refuse. In the more limited form possible in laboratory research, the question becomes: if an experimenter tells a subject to hurt another person, under what conditions will the subject go along with this instruction, and under what conditions will he refuse to obey. The laboratory problem is not so much a dilution of the general statement as one concrete expression of the many particular forms this question may assume.

One aim of the research was to study behavior in a strong situation of deep consequence to the participants, for the psychological forces operative in powerful and lifelike forms of the conflict may not be brought into play under diluted conditions.

This approach meant, first, that we had a special obligation to protect the welfare

and dignity of the persons who took part in the study; subjects were, of necessity, placed in a difficult predicament, and steps had to be taken to ensure their well-being before they were discharged from the laboratory. Toward this end, a careful, post-experimental treatment was devised and has been carried through for subjects in all conditions.[2]

TERMINOLOGY

If Y follows the command of X we shall say that he has obeyed X; if he fails to carry out the command of X, we shall say that he has disobeyed X. The terms *to obey* and to *disobey*, as used here, refer to the subject's overt action only, and carry

---

[1] Consider, for example, J. P. Scott's analysis of war in his monograph on aggression:

'... while the actions of key individuals in a war may be explained in terms of direct stimulation to aggression, vast numbers of other people are involved simply by being part of an organized society.

'... For example, at the beginning of World War I an Austrian archduke was assassinated in Sarajevo. A few days later soldiers from all over Europe were marching toward each other, not because they were stimulated by the archduke's misfortune, but because they had been trained to obey orders.' (Slightly rearranged from Scott (1958), *Aggression*, p. 103.)

[2] It consisted of an extended discussion with the experimenter and, of equal importance, a friendly reconciliation with the victim. It is made clear that the victim did not receive painful electric shocks. After the completion of the experimental series, subjects were sent a detailed report of the results and full purposes of the experimental program. A formal assessment of this procedure points to its overall effectiveness. Of the subjects, 83.7 per cent indicated that they were glad to have taken part in the study; 15.1 per cent reported neutral feelings; and 1.3 percent stated that they were sorry to have participated. A large number of subjects spontaneously requested that they be used in further experimentation. Four-fifths of the subjects felt that more experiments of this sort should be carried out, and 74 per cent indicated that they had learned something of personal importance as a result of being in the study. Furthermore, a university psychiatrist, experienced in outpatient treatment, interviewed a sample of experimental subjects with the aim of uncovering possible injurious effects resulting from participation. No such effects were in evidence. Indeed, subjects typically felt that their participation was instructive and enriching. A more detailed discussion of this question can be found in Milgram (1964).

no implication for the motive or experiential states accompanying the action.[3]

To be sure, the everyday use of the word *obedience* is not entirely free from complexities. It refers to action within widely varying situations, and connotes diverse motives within those situations: a child's obedience differs from a soldier's obedience, or the love, honor, and *obey* of the marriage vow. However, a consistent behavioral relationship is indicated

in most uses of the term: in the act of obeying, a person does what another person tells him to do. Y obeys X if he carries out the prescription for action which X has addressed to him; the term suggests, moreover, that some form of dominance-subordination, or hierarchical element, is part of the situation in which the transaction between X and Y occurs.

A subject who complies with the entire series of experimental commands will be termed an obedient subject; one who at any point in the command series defies the experimenter will be called a *disobedient* or *defiant* subject. As used in this report, the terms refer only to the subject's performance in the experiment, and do not necessarily imply a general personality disposition to submit to or reject authority.

Subject Population

The subjects used in all experimental conditions were male adults, residing in the greater New Haven and Bridgeport areas, aged 20 to 50 years, and engaged in a wide variety of occupations. Each experimental condition described in this report employed 40 fresh subjects and was carefully balanced for age and occupation-

---

[3] *To obey* and *to disobey* are not the only terms one could use in describing the critical action of Y. One could say that Y is cooperating with X, or displays conformity with regard to X's commands. However, cooperation suggests that X agrees with Y's ends, and understands the relationship between his own behavior and the attainment of those ends. (But the experimental procedure, and, in particular, the experimenter's command that the subject shock the victim even in the absence of a response from the victim, preclude such understanding.) Moreover, cooperation implies status parity for the co-acting agents, and neglects the asymmetrical, dominance-subordination element prominent in the laboratory relationship between experimenter and subject. *Conformity* has been used in other important contexts in social psychology, and most frequently refers to imitating the judgments or actions of others when no explicit requirement for imitation has been made. Furthermore, in the present study there are two sources of social pressure: pressure from the experimenter issuing the commands, and pressure from the victim to stop the punishment. It is the pitting of a common man (the victim) against an authority (the experimenter) that is the distinctive feature of the conflict. At a point in the experiment the victim demands that he be let free. The experimenter insists that subject continue to administer shocks. Which act of the subject can be interpreted as conformity? The subject may conform to the wishes of his peer or to the wishes of the experimenter, and conformity in one direction means the absence of conformity in the other. Thus the word has no useful refer-

ence in this setting, for the dual and conflicting social pressures cancel out its meaning.

In the final analysis, the linguistic symbol representing the subject's action must take its meaning from the concrete context in which that action occurs; and there is probably no word in everyday language that covers the experimental situation exactly, without omissions or irrelevant connotations. It is partly for convenience, therefore, that the terms *obey* and *disobey* are used to describe the subject's actions. At the same time, our use of the words is highly congruent with dictionary meaning.

al types. The occupational composition for each experiment was: workers, skilled and unskilled: 40 per cent; white collar, sales, business: 40 per cent; professionals: 20 per cent. The occupations were intersected with three age categories (subjects in 20s, 30s, and 40s, assigned to each condition in the proportions of 20, 40, and 40 per cent respectively).

THE GENERAL LABORATORY PROCEDURE[4]

The focus of the study concerns the amount of electric shock a subject is willing to administer to another person when ordered by an experimenter to give the 'victim' increasingly more severe punishment. The act of administering shock is set in the context of a learning experiment, ostensibly designed to study the effect of punishment on memory. Aside from the experimenter, one naïve subject and one accomplice perform in each session. On arrival each subject is paid $4.50. After a general talk by the experimenter, telling how little scientists know about the effect of punishment on memory, subjects are informed that one member of the pair will serve as teacher and one as learner. A rigged drawing is held so that the naïve subject is always the teacher, and the accomplice becomes the learner. The learner

is taken to an adjacent room and strapped into an 'electric chair.'

The naïve subject is told that it is his task to teach the learner a list of paired associates, to test him on the list, and to administer punishment whenever the learner errs in the test. Punishment takes the form of electric shock, delivered to the learner by means of a shock generator controlled by the naïve subject. The teacher is instructed to increase the intensity of electric shock one step on the generator on each error. The learner, according to plan, provides many wrong answers, so that before long the naïve subject must give him the strongest shock on the generator. Increases in shock level are met by increasingly insistent demands from the learner that the experiment be stopped because of the growing discomfort to him. However, in clear terms the experimenter orders the teacher to continue with the procedure in disregard of the learner's protests. *Thus, the naïve subject must resolve a conflict between two mutually incompatible demands from the social field. He may continue to follow the orders of the experimenter and shock the learner with increasing severity, or he may refuse to follow the orders of the experimenter and heed the learner's pleas. The experimenter's authority operates not in a free field, but against ever-mounting countervailing pressures from the person being punished.*

A few technical points need to be considered before the findings of the study are described. For the purpose of delivering shock, a simulated shock generator is used, with 30 clearly marked voltage levels that range from 15 to 450 volts (and each activated by one of 30 individual lever switches set in a horizontal line). The naïve subject is given a sample shock of

---

[4] A more detailed account of the laboratory procedure can be found in Milgram (1963). A similar and independently evolved experimental procedure, employing a shock generator, victim, and learning task, was reported by Buss (1961). Buss used the technique for studying aggression, not obedience, and did not make use of the fundamental measure employed in the present study: break-off points. His investigation promises to be a useful complement to the present research.

45 volts to convince him of the authenticity of the instrument. The generator bears verbal designations that range from 'Slight Shock' to 'Danger: Severe Shock'.

The responses of the victim are standardized on tape, and each protest is coordinated to a particular voltage level on the shock generator. Starting with 75 volts the learner begins to grunt and moan. At 150 volts he demands to be let out of the experiment. At 180 volts he cries out that he can no longer stand the pain. At 300 volts he refuses to provide any more answers to the memory test, insisting that he is no longer a participant in the experiment and must be freed. In response to this last tactic, the experimenter instructs the naïve subject to treat the absence of an answer as equivalent to a wrong answer, and to follow the usual shock procedure. The experimenter reinforces his demand with the statement: 'You have no other choice, you must go on!' (This imperative is used whenever the naïve subject tries to break off the experiment.) If the subject refuses to give the next higher level of shock, the experiment is considered at an end. A quantitative value is assigned to the subject's performance based on the maximum intensity shock he administered before breaking off. Thus any subject's score may range from zero (for a subject unwilling to administer the first shock level) to 30 (for a subject who proceeds to the highest voltage level on the board). For any particular subject and for any particular experimental condition the degree to which participants have followed the experimenter's orders may be specified with a numerical value, corresponding to the metric on the shock generator.

This laboratory situation gives us a framework in which to study the subject's reactions to the principal conflict of the experiment. Again, this conflict is between the experimenter's demands that he continue to administer the electric shock, and the learner's demands, which become increasingly more insistent, that the experiment be stopped. The crux of the study is to vary systematically the factors believed to alter the degree of obedience to the experimental commands, to learn under what conditions submission to authority is most probable, and under what conditions defiance is brought to the fore.

PILOT STUDIES

Pilot studies for the present research were completed in the winter of 1960; they differed from the regular experiments in a few details: for one, the victim was placed behind a silvered glass, with the light balance on the glass such that the victim could be dimly perceived by the subject (Milgram, 1961).

Though essentially qualitative in treatment, these studies pointed to several significant features of the experimental situation. At first no vocal feedback was used from the victim. It was thought that the verbal and voltage designations on the control panel would create sufficient pressure to curtail the subject's obedience. However, this was not the case. In the absence of protests from the learner, virtually all subjects, once commanded, went blithely to the end of the board, seemingly indifferent to the verbal designations ('Extreme Shock' and 'Danger: Severe Shock'). This deprived us of an adequate basis for scaling obedient tendencies. A force had to be introduced that would strengthen the subject's resistance to the experimenter's commands, and reveal individual differences in terms of a distribution of break-off points.

This force took the form of protests

from the victim. Initially, mild protests were used, but proved inadequate. Subsequently, more vehement protests were inserted into the experimental procedure. To our consternation, even the strongest protests from the victim did not prevent all subjects from administering the harshest punishment ordered by the experimenter; but the protests did lower the mean maximum shock somewhat and created some spread in the subject's performance; therefore, the victim's cries were standardized on tape and incorporated into the regular experimental procedure.

The situation did more than highlight the technical difficulties of finding a workable experimental procedure: it indicated that subjects would obey authority to a greater extent than we had supposed. It also pointed to the importance of feedback from the victim in controlling the subject's behavior.

One further aspect of the pilot study was that subjects frequently averted their eyes from the person they were shocking, often turning their heads in an awkward and conspicuous manner. One subject explained: 'I didn't want to see the consequences of what I had done.' Observers wrote:

> ... subjects showed a reluctance to look at the victim, whom they could see through the glass in front of them. When this fact was brought to their attention they indicated that it caused them discomfort to see the victim in agony. We note, however, that although the subject refuses to look at the victim, he continues to administer shocks.

This suggested that the salience of the victim may have, in some degree, regulated the subject's performance. If, in obeying the experimenter, the subject found it necessary to avoid scrutiny of the victim, would the converse be true? If the victim were rendered increasingly more salient to the subject, would obedience diminish? The first set of regular experiments was designed to answer this question.

IMMEDIACY OF THE VICTIM

This series consisted of four experimental conditions. In each condition the victim was brought 'psychologically' closer to the subject giving him shocks.

In the first condition (Remote Feedback) the victim was placed in another room and could not be heard or seen by the subject, except that, at 300 volts, he pounded on the wall in protest. After 315 volts he no longer answered or was heard from.

The second condition (Voice Feedback) was identical to the first except that voice protests were introduced. As in the first condition the victim was placed in an adjacent room, but his complaints could be heard clearly through a door left slightly ajar, and through the walls of the laboratory.[5]

---

[5] It is difficult to convey on the printed page the full tenor of the victim's responses, for we have no adequate notation for vocal intensity, timing, and general qualities of delivery. Yet these features are crucial to producing the effect of an increasingly severe reaction to mounting voltage levels. (They can be communicated fully only by sending interested parties the recorded tapes.) In general terms, however, the victim indicates no discomfort until the 75-volt shock is administered, at which time there is a light grunt in response to the punishment. Similar reactions follow the 90- and 105-volt shocks, and at 120 volts the victim shouts to the experimenter that the shocks are becoming painful. Painful groans are heard on administrations of the 135-volt shock, and at 150 volts the victim cries out, 'Experimenter, get me out of here! I won't be in the experiment any more! I refuse to go on!' Cries of this type continue

The third experimental condition (Proximity) was similar to the second, except that the victim was now placed in the same room as the subject, and 1½ feet from him. Thus he was visible as well as audible, and voice cues were provided.

The fourth, and final, condition of this series (Touch-Proximity) was identical to the third, with this exception: the

---

with generally rising intensity, so that at 180 volts the victim cries out, 'I can't stand the pain', and by 270 volts his response to the shock is definitely an agonized scream. Throughout, he insists that he be let out of the experiment. At 300 volts the victim shouts in desperation that he will no longer provide answers to the memory test; and at 315 volts, after a violent scream, he reaffirms with vehemence that he is no longer a participant. From this point on, he provides no answers, but shrieks in agony whenever a shock is administered; this continues through 450 volts. Of course, many subjects will have broken off before this point.

A revised and stronger set of protests was used in all experiments outside the Proximity series. Naturally, new baseline measures were established for all comparisons using the new set of protests.

There is overwhelming evidence that the great majority of subjects, both obedient and defiant, accepted the victims' reactions as genuine. The evidence takes the form of: (a) tension created in the subjects (see discussion of tension); (b) scores on 'estimated pain' scales filled out by subjects immediately after the experiment; (c) subjects' accounts of their feelings in post-experimental interviews; and (d) quantifiable responses to questionnaires distributed to subjects several months after their participation in the experiments. This matter will be treated fully in a forthcoming monograph.

(The procedure in all experimental conditions was to have the naïve subject announce the voltage level before administering each shock, so that—independently of the victim's responses—he was continually reminded of delivering punishment of ever-increasing severity.)

victim received a shock only when his hand rested on a shockplate. At the 150-volt level the victim again demanded to be let free and, in this condition, refused to place his hand on the shockplate. The experimenter ordered the naïve subject to force the victim's hand onto the plate. Thus obedience in this condition required that the subject have physical contact with the victim in order to give him punishment beyond the 150-volt level.

Forty adult subjects were studied in each condition. The data revealed that obedience was significantly reduced as the victim was rendered more immediate to the subject. The mean maximum shock for the conditions is shown in *Figure 1*.

Expressed in terms of the proportion of obedient to defiant subjects, the findings are that 34 per cent of the subjects defied the experimenter in the Remote condition, 37.5 per cent in Voice Feedback, 60 per cent in Proximity, and 70 per cent in Touch-Proximity.

How are we to account for this effect? A first conjecture might be that as the victim was brought closer the subject became more aware of the intensity of his suffering and regulated his behavior accordingly. This makes sense, but our evidence does not support the interpretation. There are no consistent differences in the attributed level of pain across the four conditions (i.e. the amount of pain experienced by the victim as estimated by the subject and expressed on a 14-point scale). But it is easy to speculate about alternative mechanisms:

Empathic cues. In the Remote and to a lesser extent the Voice Feedback condition, the victim's suffering possesses an abstract, remote quality for the subject. He is aware, but only in a conceptual sense, that his actions cause pain to another person; the fact is apprehended, but not felt. The

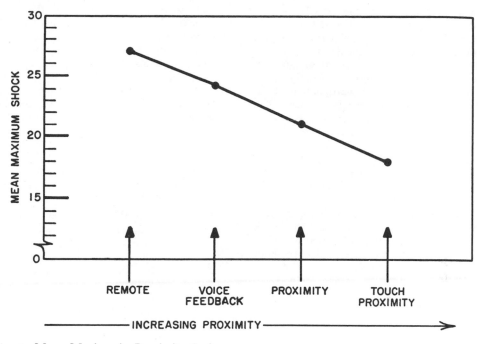

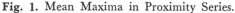

Fig. 1. Mean Maxima in Proximity Series.

phenomenon is common enough. The bombardier can reasonably suppose that his weapons will inflict suffering and death, yet this knowledge is divested of affect, and does not move him to a felt, emotional response to the suffering resulting from his actions. Similar observations have been made in wartime. It is possible that the visual cues associated with the victim's suffering trigger empathic responses in the subject and provide him with a more complete grasp of the victim's experience. Or it is possible that the empathic responses are themselves unpleasant, possessing drive properties which cause the subject to terminate the arousal situation. Diminishing obedience, then, would be explained by the enrichment of empathic cues in the successive experimental conditions.

Denial and narrowing of the cognitive field. The Remote condition allows a narrowing of the cognitive field so that the victim is put out of mind. The subject no longer considers the act of depressing a lever relevant to moral judgement, for it is no longer associated with the victim's suffering. When the victim is close it is more difficult to exclude him phenomenologically. He necessarily intrudes on the subject's awareness since he is continuously visible. In the Remote conditions his existence and reactions are made known only after the shock has been administered. The auditory feedback is sporadic and discontinuous. In the Proximity conditions his inclusion in the immediate visual field renders him a continuously salient element for the subject. The mechanism of denial can no longer be brought into play. One subject in the Remote condition said: 'It's funny how you really begin to forget that there's a guy out there, even though you can hear him. For a long time I just concentrated on pressing the switches and reading the words.'

Reciprocal fields. If in the Proximity condition the subject is in an improved position to observe the victim, the reverse is also true. The actions of the subject now come under proximal scrutiny by the victim. Possibly, it is easier to harm a person when he is unable to observe our

actions than when he can see what we are
doing. His surveillance of the action directed against him may give rise to shame,
or guilt, which may then serve to curtail
the action. Many expressions of language
refer to the discomfort or inhibitions that
arise in face-to-face confrontation. It is
often said that it is easier to criticize a man
'behind his back' than to 'attack him to
his face'. If we are in the process of lying
to a person it is reputedly difficult to 'stare
him in the eye'. We 'turn away from others
in shame' or in 'embarrassment' and this
action serves to reduce our discomfort. The
manifest function of allowing the victim of
a firing squad to be blindfolded is to make
the occasion less stressful for him, but it
may also serve a latent function of reducing the stress of the executioner. In short,
in the Proximity conditions, the subject
may sense that he has become more salient
in the victim's field of awareness. Possibly
he becomes more self-conscious, embarrassed, and inhibited in his punishment of
the victim.

Phenomenal unity of act. In the Remote
conditions it is more difficult for the subject to gain a sense of *relatedness* between
his own actions and the consequences of
these actions for the victim. There is a
physical and spatial separation of the act
and its consequences. The subject depresses
a lever in one room, and protests and cries
are heard from another. The two events
are in correlation, yet they lack a compelling phenomenological unity. The structure of a meaningful act—*I am hurting a
man*—breaks down because of the spatial
arrangements, in a manner somewhat analogous to the disappearance of phi phenomena when the blinking lights are spaced
too far apart. The unity is more fully
achieved in the Proximity conditions as
the victim is brought closer to the action
that causes him pain. It is rendered complete in Touch-Proximity.

Incipient group formation. Placing the
victim in another room not only takes him
further from the subject, but the subject
and the experimenter are drawn relatively
closer. There is incipient group formation
between the experimenter and the subject,
from which the victim is excluded. The

wall between the victim and the others
deprives him of an intimacy which the
experimenter and subject feel. In the Remote condition, the victim is truly an outsider, who stands alone, physically and
psychologically.

When the victim is placed close to the
subject, it becomes easier to form an
alliance with him against the experimenter.
Subjects no longer have to face the experimenter alone. They have an ally who is
close at hand and eager to collaborate in
a revolt against the experimenter. Thus,
the changing set of spatial relations leads
to a potentially shifting set of alliances over
the several experimental conditions.

Acquired behavior dispositions. It is
commonly observed that laboratory mice
will rarely fight with their litter mates.
Scott (1958) explains this in terms of
passive inhibition. He writes: 'By doing
nothing under . . . circumstances [the ani-
mal] learns to do nothing, and this may
be spoken of as passive inhibition . . . this
principle has great importance in teaching
an individual to be peaceful, for it means
that he can learn not to fight simply by
not fighting.' Similarly, we may learn not
to harm others simply by not harming
them in everyday life. Yet this learning occurs in a context of proximal relations with
others, and may not be generalized to that
situation in which the person is physically
removed from us. Or possibly, in the past,
aggressive actions against others who were
physically close resulted in retaliatory
punishment which extinguished the original
form of response. In contrast, aggression
against others at a distance may have only
sporadically led to retaliation. Thus the
organism learns that it is safer to be aggressive toward others at a distance, and
precarious to be so when the parties are
within arm's reach. Through a pattern of
rewards and punishments, he acquires a
disposition to avoid aggression at close
quarters, a disposition which does not extend to harming others at a distance. And
this may account for experimental findings
in the remote and proximal experiments.

Proximity as a variable in psychological
research has received far less attention

than it deserves. If men were sessile it would be easy to understand this neglect. But we move about; our spatial relations shift from one situation to the next, and the fact that we are near or remote may have a powerful effect on the psychological processes that mediate our behavior toward other. In the present situation, as the victim is brought closer to the man ordered to give him shocks, increasing numbers of subjects break off the experiment, refusing to obey. The concrete, visible, and proximal presence of the victim acts in an important way to counteract the experimenter's power and to generate disobedience.[6]

CLOSENESS OF AUTHORITY

If the spatial relationship of the subject and victim is relevant to the degree of obedience, would not the relationship of subject to experimenter also play a part?

There are reasons to feel that, on arrival, the subject is oriented primarily to the experimenter rather than to the victim. He has come to the laboratory to fit into the structure that the experimenter—not

---

[6] Admittedly, the terms *proximity, immediacy, closeness,* and *salience-of-the-victim* are used in a loose sense, and the experiments themselves represent a very coarse treatment of the variable. Further experiments are needed to refine the notion and tease out such diverse factors as spatial distance, visibility, audibility, barrier interposition, etc.

The Proximity and Touch-Proximity experiments were the only conditions where we were unable to use taped feedback from the victim. Instead, the victim was trained to respond in these conditions as he had in Experiment 2 (which employed taped feedback). Some improvement is possible here, for it should be technically feasible to do a proximity series using taped feedback.

the victim—would provide. He has come less to understand his behavior than to *reveal* that behavior to a competent scientist, and he is willing to display himself as the scientist's purposes require. Most subjects seem quite concerned about the appearance they are making before the experimenter, and one could argue that this preoccupation in a relatively new and strange setting makes the subject somewhat insensitive to the triadic nature of the social situation. In other words, the subject is so concerned about the show he is putting on for the experimenter that influences from other parts of the social field do not receive as much weight as they ordinarily would. This overdetermined orientation to the experimenter would account for the relative insensitivity of the subject to the victim, and would also lead us to believe that alterations in the relationship between subject and experimenter would have important consequences for obedience.

In a series of experiments we varied the physical closeness and degree of surveillance of the experimenter. In one condition the experimenter sat just a few feet away from the subject. In a second condition, after giving initial instructions, the experimenter left the laboratory and gave his orders by telephone; in still a third condition the experimenter was never seen, providing instructions by means of a tape recording activated when the subjects entered the laboratory.

Obedience dropped sharply as the experimenter was physically removed from the laboratory. The number of obedient subjects in the first condition (Experimenter Present) was almost three times as great as in the second, where the experimenter gave his orders by telephone. Twenty-six subjects were fully obedient in the two first condition, and only 9 in the second (Chi square obedient *vs.* defiant in the two conditions, 1 d.f. $= 14.7$; $p <$ .001). Subjects seemed able to take a far stronger stand against the experimenter when they did not have to encounter him face to face, and the experimenter's power over the subject was severely curtailed.[7]

Moreover, when the experimenter was absent, subjects displayed an interesting form of behavior that had not occurred under his surveillance. Though continuing with the experiment, several subjects administered lower shocks than were required and never informed the experimenter of their deviation from the correct procedure. (Unknown to the subjects, shock levels were automatically recorded by an Esterline-Angus event recorder wired directly into the shock generator; the instrument provided us with an objective record of the subjects' performance.) Indeed, in telephone conversations some subjects specifically assured the experimenter that they were raising the shock level according to instruction, whereas in fact they were repeatedly using the lowest shock on the board. This form of behavior is particularly interesting: although these subjects acted in a way that clearly undermined the avowed purposes of the experiment, they found it easier to handle the conflict in this manner than to precipitate an open break with authority.

Other conditions were completed in which the experimenter was absent during the first segment of the experiment, but reappeared at the point that the subject definitely refused to give higher shocks when commanded by telephone. Although he had exhausted his power via telephone, the experimenter could frequently force further obedience when he reappeared in the laboratory.

Experiments in this series show that the physical *presence* of an authority is an important force contributing to the subject's obedience or defiance. Taken together with the first experimental series on the proximity of the victim, it would appear that something akin to fields of force, diminishing in effectiveness with increasing psychological distance from their source, have a controlling effect on the subject's performance. As the victim is brought closer, the subject finds it harder to administer shocks to him. When the victim's position is held constant relative to the subject, and the authority is made more remote, the subject finds it easier to break off the experiment. This effect is substantial in both cases, but manipulation of the experimenter's position yielded the more powerful results. Obedience to destructive commands is highly dependent on the proximal relations between authority and subject.

TENSIONS

The description of final scores does not fully convey the character of the subjects' performance, and it would be useful to interrupt our reporting of quantitative relationships to remark on the subjects' general reaction to the situation.

One might suppose that a subject would simply break off or continue as his conscience and temperament dictated. Yet this is very far from what happened. There were powerful reactions of tension and

---

[7] The third condition also led to significantly lower obedience than this first situation, in which the experimenter was present, but it contains technical difficulties that require extensive discussion.

emotional strain in a substantial proportion of the participants. Persons were observed to sweat, tremble, stutter, bite their lips, and groan as they found themselves increasingly implicated in the experimental conflict. Some sense of the subjects' mood can be gotten from a transcript of their remarks at break-off point. Here are the remarks of two defiant subjects:

Is he banging? . . . Is he hurt out there? Well, I don't want to be responsible for anything that happens to him. No, I can't go on with it. I don't know whether he's all right or not. I mean he may have a heart condition or something; I wouldn't feel right doing it. He's banging for help. He's evidently in trouble or he wouldn't bang . . . I don't see any sense to this to knocking him out or something. I just can't see it.

(Subject refuses to administer shocks)
[*Subject 0108*]

The man is banging. He wants to get out . . . I'm sorry. If the man wants to get out I'd just as soon stop . . . I don't want to administer any more [extremely excited] . . . I will gladly refund the check, but I will not harm this man . . . I'm sorry, I will not give him any more if he obviously wants to get out. There is no money in the world that will make me hurt another individual. [*Subject 010X*]

And here is a transcript from an obedient subject. He began the experiment calmly, but became increasingly tense as the experiment proceeded. After administering the 150-volt shock, he began to address the experimenter in agitated tones:

150 volts delivered. You want me to keep going?
165 volts delivered. That guy is hollering in there. There's a lot of them here. He's liable to have heart condition. You want me to go?
180 volts delivered. He can't stand it! I'm not going to kill that man in there!

You hear him hollering? He's hollering. He can't stand it. What if something happens to him? . . . I'm not going to get that man sick in there. He's hollering in there. You know what I mean? I mean I refuse to take responsibility. He's getting hurt in there. He's in there hollering. Too many left here. Geez, if he gets them wrong. There's too many of them left. I mean who is going to take responsibility if anything happens to that gentleman?
[*The experimenter accepts responsibility.*] All right.
195 volts delivered. You see he's hollering. Hear that. Gee, I don't know. [*The experimenter says: 'The experiment requires that you go on.'*]—I know it does, sir, but I mean—hugh—he don't know what he's in for. He's up to 195 volts.
210 volts delivered
225 volts delivered
240 volts delivered. Aw, no. You mean I've got to keep going up with the scale? No sir. I'm not going to kill that man! I'm not going to give him 450 volts! [*The experimenter says: 'The experiment requires that you go on.'*]—I know it does, but that man is hollering in there, sir . . .

Despite his numerous, agitated objections, which were constant accompaniments to his actions, the subject unfailingly obeyed the experimenter, proceeding to the highest shock level on the generator. He displayed a curious dissociation between word and action. Although at the verbal level he had resolved not to go on, his actions were fully in accord with the experimenter's commands. This subject did not want to shock the victim, and he found it an extremely disagreeable task, but he was unable to invent a response that would free him from *E*'s authority. Many subjects cannot find the specific verbal formula that would enable them to reject the role assigned to them by the experimenter. Perhaps our culture does not provide adequate models for disobedience.

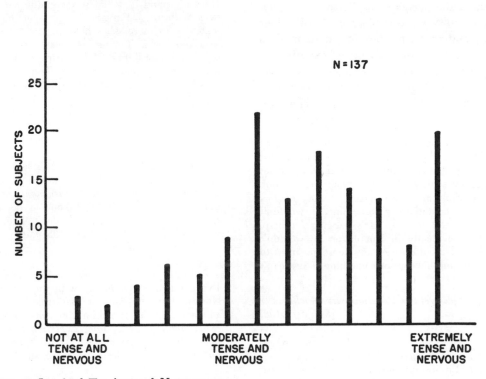

Fig. 2. Level of Tension and Nervousness.

Figure 2 shows the self-reports on 'tension and nervousness' for 137 subjects in the Proximity experiments. Subjects were given a scale with 14 values ranging from 'Not at all tense and nervous' to 'Extremely tense and nervous'. They were instructed: 'Thinking back to that point in the experiment when you felt the most tense and nervous, indicate just how you felt by placing an X at the appropriate point on the scale.' The results are shown in terms of mid-point values.

One puzzling sign of tension was the regular occurrence of nervous laughing fits. In the first four conditions 71 of the 160 subjects showed definite signs of nervous laughter and smiling. The laughter seemed entirely out of place, even bizarre. Full-blown, uncontrollable seizures were observed for 15 of these subjects. On one occasion we observed a seizure so violently convulsive that it was necessary to call a halt to the experiment. In the post-experimental interviews subjects took pains to point out that they were not sadistic types and that the laughter did not mean they enjoyed shocking the victim.

In the interview following the experiment subjects were asked to indicate on a 14-point scale just how nervous or tense they felt at the point of maximum tension (*Figure 2*). The scale ranged from 'Not at all tense and nervous' to 'Extremely tense and nervous'. Self-reports of this sort are of limited precision, and at best provide only a rough indication of the subject's emotional response. Still, taking the reports for what they are worth, it can be seen that the distribution of responses spans the entire range of the scale, with the majority of subjects concentrated at the center and upper extreme. A further breakdown showed that obedient subjects reported themselves as having been slightly more tense and nervous than the defiant subjects at the point of maximum tension.

How is the occurrence of tension to be interpreted? First, it points to the presence of conflict. If a tendency to comply with authority were the only psychological force operating in the situation, all subjects would have continued to the end and there would have been no tension. Tension, it is assumed, results from the simultaneous presence of two or more incompatible response tendencies (Miller, 1944). If sympathetic concern for the victim were the exclusive force, all subjects would have calmly defied the experimenter. Instead, there were both obedient and defiant outcomes, frequently accompanied by extreme tension. A conflict develops between the deeply ingrained disposition not to harm others and the equally compelling tendency to obey others who are in authority. The subject is quickly drawn into a dilemma of a deeply dynamic character, and the presence of high tension points to the considerable strength of each of the antagonistic vectors.

Moreover, tension defines the strength of the aversive state from which the subject is unable to escape through disobedience. When a person is uncomfortable, tense, or stressed, he tries to take some action that will allow him to terminate this unpleasant state. Thus tension may serve as a drive that leads to escape behavior. But in the present situation, even where tension is extreme, many subjects are unable to perform the response that will bring about relief. Therefore there must be a competing drive, tendency, or inhibition that precludes activation of the disobedient response. The strength of this inhibiting factor must be of greater magnitude than the stress experienced, else the

terminating act would occur. Every evidence of extreme tension is at the same time an indication of the strength of the forces that keep the subject in the situation.

Finally, tension may be taken as evidence of the reality of the situations for the subjects. Normal subjects do not tremble and sweat unless they are implicated in a deep and genuinely felt predicament.

BACKGROUND AUTHORITY

In psychophysics, animal learning, and other branches of psychology, the fact that measures are obtained at one institution rather than another is irrelevant to the interpretation of the findings, so long as the technical facilities for measurement are adequate and the operations are carried out with competence.

But it cannot be assumed that this holds true for the present study. The effectiveness of the experimenter's commands may depend in an important way on the larger institutional context in which they are issued. The experiments described thus far were conducted at Yale University, an organization which most subjects regarded with respect and sometimes awe. In postexperimental interviews several participants remarked that the locale and sponsorship of the study gave them confidence in the integrity, competence, and benign purposes of the personnel; many indicated that they would not have shocked the learner if the experiments had been done elsewhere.

This issue of background authority seemed to us important for an interpretation of the results that had been obtained thus far; moreover it is highly relevant to any comprehensive theory of human obedience. Consider, for example, how closely our compliance with the imperatives of others is tied to particular institutions and locales in our day-to-day activities. On request, we expose our throats to a man with a razor blade in the barber shop, but would not do so in a shoe store; in the latter setting we willingly follow the clerk's request to stand in our stockinged feet, but resist the command in a bank. In the laboratory of a great university, subjects may comply with a set of commands that would be resisted if given elsewhere. *One must always question the relationship of obedience to a person's sense of the context in which he is operating.*

To explore the problem we moved our apparatus to an office building in industrial Bridgeport and replicated experimental conditions, without any visible tie to the university.

Bridgeport subjects were invited to the experiment through a mail circular similar to the one used in the Yale study, with appropriate changes in letterhead, etc. As in the earlier study, subjects were paid $4.50 for coming to the laboratory. The same age and occupational distributions used at Yale, and the identical personnel, were employed.

The purpose in relocating in Bridgeport was to assure a complete dissociation from Yale, and in this regard we were fully successful. On the surface, the study appeared to be conducted by RESEARCH ASSOCIATES OF BRIDGEPORT, an organization of unknown character (the title had been concocted exclusively for use in this study).

The experiments were conducted in a three-room office suite in a somewhat run-down commercial building located in the downtown shopping area. The laboratory was sparsely furnished, though clean, and marginally respectable in appearance.

When subjects inquired about professional affiliations, they were informed only that we were a private firm conducting research for industry.

Some subjects displayed skepticism concerning the motives of the Bridgeport experimenter. One gentleman gave us a written account of the thoughts he experienced at the control board:

> ...Should I quit this damn test? Maybe he passed out? What dopes we were not to check up on this deal. How do we know that these guys are legit? No furniture, bare walls, no telephone. We could of called the Police up or the Better Business Bureau. I learned a lesson tonight. How do I know that Mr Williams [the experimenter] is telling the truth...I wish I knew how many volts a person could take before lapsing into unconsciousness...
>
> [*Subject 2414*]

Another subjects stated:

> I questioned on my arrival my own judgment [about coming]. I had doubts as to the legitimacy of the operation and the consequences of participation. I felt it was a heartless way to conduct memory or learning processes on human beings and certainly dangerous without the presence of a medical doctor.
>
> [*Subject 2440 V*]

There was no noticeable reduction in tension for the Bridgeport subjects. And the subjects' estimation of the amount of pain felt by the victim was slightly, though not significantly, higher than in the Yale study.

A failure to obtain complete obedience in Bridgeport would indicate that the extreme compliance found in New Haven subjects was tied closely to the background authority of Yale University; if a large proportion of the subjects remained fully obedient, very different conclusions would be called for.

As it turned out, the level of obedience in Bridgeport, although somewhat reduced, was not significantly lower than that obtained at Yale. A large proportion of the Bridgeport subjects were fully obedient to the experimenter's commands (48 per cent of the Bridgeport subjects delivered the maximum shock *vs.* 65 per cent in the corresponding condition at Yale).

How are these findings to be interpreted? It is possible that if commands of a potentially harmful or destructive sort are to be perceived as legitimate they must occur within some sort of institutional structure. But it is clear from the study that it need not be a particularly reputable or distinguished institution. The Bridgeport experiments were conducted by an unimpressive firm lacking any credentials; the laboratory was set up in a respectable office building with title listed in the building directory. Beyond that, there was no evidence of benevolence or competence. It is possible that the *category* of institution, judged according to its professed function, rather than its qualitative position within that category, wins our compliance. Persons deposit money in elegant, but also in seedy-looking banks, without giving much thought to the differences in security they offer. Similarly, our subjects may consider one laboratory to be as competent as another, so long as it *is* a scientific laboratory.

It would be valuable to study the subjects' performance in other contexts which go even further than the Bridgeport study in denying institutional support to the experimenter. It is possible that, beyond a certain point, obedience disappears completely. But that point had not been reached in the Bridgeport office: almost half the subjects obeyed the experimenter fully.

FURTHER EXPERIMENTS

We may mention briefly some additional experiments undertaken in the Yale series. A considerable amount of obedience and defiance in everyday life occurs in connexion with groups. And we had reason to feel in the light of many group studies already done in psychology that group forces would have a profound effect on reactions to authority. A series of experiments was run to examine these effects. In all cases only one naïve subject was studied per hour, but he performed in the midst of actors who, unknown to him, were employed by the experimenter. In one experiment (Groups for Disobedience) two actors broke off in the middle of the experiment. When this happened 90 per cent of the subjects followed suit and defied the experimenter. In another condition the actors followed the orders obediently; this strengthened the experimenter's power only slightly. In still a third experiment the job of pushing the switch to shock the learner was given to one of the actors, while the naïve subject performed a subsidiary act. We wanted to see how the teacher would respond if he were involved in the situation but did not actually give the shocks. In this situation only three subjects out of forty broke off. In a final group experiment the subjects themselves determined the shock level they were going to use. Two actors suggested higher and higher shock levels; some subjects insisted, despite group pressure, that the shock level be kept low; others followed along with the group.

Further experiments were completed

using women as subjects, as well as a set dealing with the effects of dual, unsanctioned, and conflicting authority. A final experiment concerned the personal relationship between victim and subject. These will have to be described elsewhere, lest the present report be extended to monographic length.

It goes without saying that future research can proceed in many different directions. What kinds of response from the victim are most effective in causing disobedience in the subject? Perhaps passive resistance is more effective than vehement protest. What conditions of entry into an authority system lead to greater or lesser obedience? What is the effect of anonymity and masking on the subject's behavior? What conditions lead to the subject's perception of responsibility for his own actions? Each of these could be a major research topic in itself, and can readily be incorporated into the general experimental procedure described here.

LEVELS OF OBEDIENCE AND DEFIANCE

One general finding that merits attention is the high level of obedience manifested in the experimental situation. Subjects often expressed deep disapproval of shocking a man in the face of his objections, and others denounced it as senseless and stupid. Yet many subjects complied even while they protested. The proportion of obedient subjects greatly exceeded the expectations of the experimenter and his colleagues. At the outset, we had conjectured that subjects would not, in general, go above the level of "Strong Shock'. In practice, many subjects were willing to administer the most extreme shocks available when commanded by the experimenter. For some subjects the experiment provides

an occasion for aggressive release. And for others it demonstrates the extent to which obedient dispositions are deeply ingrained, and are engaged irrespective of their consequences for others. Yet this is not the whole story. Somehow, the subject becomes implicated in a situation from which he cannot disengage himself.

The departure of the experimental results from intelligent expectation, to some extent, has been formalized. The procedure was to describe the experimental situation in concrete detail to a group of competent persons, and to ask them to predict the performance of 100 hypothetical subjects. For purposes of indicating the distribution of break-off points judges were provided with a diagram of the shock generator, and recorded their predictions before being informed of the actual results. Judges typically underestimated the amount of obedience demonstrated by subjects.

In *Figure 3*, we compare the predictions of forty psychiatrists at a leading medical shool with the actual performance of subjects in the experiment. The psychiatrists predicted that most subjects would not go beyond the tenth shock level (150 volts; at this point the victim makes his first explicit demand to be freed). They further predicted that by the twentieth shock level (300 volts; the victim refuses to answer) 3.73 per cent of the subjects would still be obedient; and that only a little over one-tenth of one per cent of the subjects would administer the highest shock on the board. But, as the graph indicates, the obtained behavior was very different. Sixty-two per cent of the subjects obeyed the experimenter's commands fully. Between expectation and occurrence there is a whopping discrepancy.

Why did the psychiatrists underestimate the level of obedience? Possibly, because

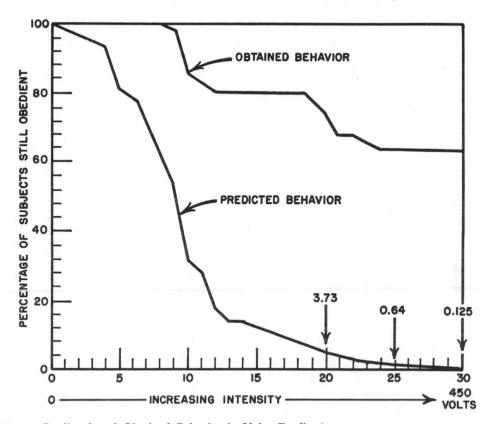

Fig. 3. Predicted and Obtained Behavior in Voice Feedback.

their predictions were based on an inadequate conception of the determinants of human action, a conception that focuses on motives *in vacuo*. This orientation may be entirely adequate for the repair of bruised impulses as revealed on the psychiatrist's couch, but as soon as our interest turns to action in larger settings, attention must be paid to the situations in which motives are expressed. A situation exerts an important press on the individual. It exercises constraints and may provide push. In certain circumstances it is not so much the kind of person a man is, as the kind of situation in which he is placed, that determines his actions.

Many people, not knowing much about the experiment, claim that subjects who

go to the end of the board are sadistic. Nothing could be more foolish as an overall characterization of these persons. It is like saying that a person thrown into a swift-flowing stream is necessarily a fast swimmer, or that he has great stamina because he moves so rapidly relative to the bank. The context of action must always be considered. The individual, upon entering the laboratory, becomes integrated into a situation that carries its own momentum. The subject's problem then is how to become disengaged from a situation which is moving in an altogether ugly direction.

The fact that disengagement is so difficult testifies to the potency of the forces that keep the subject at the control board.

Are these forces to be conceptualized as individual motives and expressed in the language of personality dynamics, or are they to be seen as the effects of social structure and pressures arising from the situational field?

A full understanding of the subject's action will, I feel, require that both perspectives be adopted. The person brings to the laboratory enduring dispositions toward authority and aggression, and at the same time he becomes enmeshed in a social structure that is no less an objective fact of the case. From the standpoint of personality theory one may ask: What mechanisms of personality enable a person to transfer responsibility to authority? What are the motives underlying obedient and disobedient performance? Does orientation to authority lead to a shortcircuiting of the shame-guilt system? What cognitive and emotional defenses are brought into play in the case of obedient and defiant subjects?

The present experiments are not, however, directed toward an exploration of the motives engaged when the subject obeys the experimenter's command. Instead, they examine the situational variables responsible for the elicitation of obedience. Elsewhere, we have attempted to spell out some of the structural properties of the experimental situation that account for high obedience, and this analysis need not be repeated here (Milgram, 1963). The experimental variations themselves represent our attempt to probe that structure, by systematically changing it and noting the consequences for behavior. It is clear that some situations produce greater compliance with the experimenter's commands than others. However, this does not necessarily imply an increase or decrease in the strength of any single definable motive. Situations producing the greatest

obedience could do so by triggering the most powerful, yet perhaps the most idiosyncratic, of motives in each subject confronted by the setting. Or they may simply recruit a greater number and variety of motives in their service. But whatever the motives involved—and it is far from certain that they can ever be known—action may be studied as a direct function of the situation in which it occurs. This has been the approach of the present study, where we sought to plot behavioral regularities against manipulated properties of the social field. Ultimately, social psychology would like to have a compelling *theory of* situations which will, first, present language in terms of which situations can be defined; proceed to a typology of situations; and then point to the manner in which definable properties of situations are transformed into psychological forces in the individual.[8]

Postscript

Almost a thousand adults were individually studied in the obedience research, and there were many specific conclusions regarding the variables that control obedience and disobedience to authority. Some of these have been discussed briefly in the preceding sections, and more detailed reports will be released subsequently.

There are now some other generalizations I should like to make, which do not derive in any strictly logical fashion from the experiments as carried out, but which, I feel, ought to be made. They are formulations of an intuitive sort that have

---

[8] My thanks to Professor Howard Leventhal of Yale for strengthening the writing in this paragraph.

been forced on me by observation of many subjects responding to the pressures of authority. The assertions represent a painful alteration in my own thinking; and since they were acquired only under the repeated impact of direct observation, I have no illusion that they will be generally accepted by persons who have not had the same experience.

With numbing regularity good people were seen to knuckle under the demands of authority and perform actions that were callous and severe. Men who are in everyday life responsible and decent were seduced by the trappings of authority, by the control of their perceptions, and by the uncritical acceptance of the experimenter's definition of the situation, into performing harsh acts.

What is the limit of such obedience? At many points we attempted to establish a boundary. Cries from the victim were inserted; not good enough. The victim claimed heart trouble; subjects still shocked him on command. The victim pleaded that he be let free, and his answers no longer registered on the signal box; subjects continued to shock him. At the outset we had not conceived that such drastic procedures would be needed to generate disobedience, and each step was added only as the ineffectiveness of the earlier techniques became clear. The final effort to establish a limit was the Touch-Proximity condition. But the very first subject in this condition subdued the victim on command, and proceeded to the highest shock level. A quarter of the subjects in this condition performed similarly.

The results, as seen and felt in the laboratory, are to this author disturbing. They raise the possibility that human nature, or—more specifically—the kind of character produced in American democratic society, cannot be counted on to insulate its citizens from brutality and inhumane treatment at the direction of malevolent authority. A substantial proportion of people do what they are told to do, irrespective of the content of the act and without limitations of conscience, so long as they perceive that the command comes from a legitimate authority. If in this study an anonymous experimenter could successfully command adults to subdue a fifty-year-old man, force on him painful electric shocks against his protests, one can only wonder what government, with its vastly greater authority and prestige, can command of its subjects. There is, of course, the extremely important question of whether malevolent political institutions could or would arise in American society. The present research contributes nothing to this issue.

In an article titled 'The Dangers of Obedience', Harold J. Laski wrote:

'... civilization means, above all, an unwillingness to inflict unnecessary pain. Within the ambit of that definition, those of us who heedlessly accept the commands of authority cannot yet claim to be civilized men.

'... Our business, if we desire to live a life, not utterly devoid of meaning and significance, is to accept nothing which contradicts our basic experience merely because it comes to us from tradition or convention or authority. It may well be that we shall be wrong; but our self-expression is thwarted at the root unless the certainties we are asked to accept coincide with the certainties we experience. That is why the condition of freedom in any state is always a widespread and consistent skepticism of the canons upon which power insists.'

REFERENCES

BUSS, ARNOLD H., *The Psychology of Aggression*. New York and London: John Wiley, 1961.

KIERKEGAARD, S., *Fear and Trembling* (1843). English edition, Princeton: Princeton University Press, 1941.

LASKI, HAROLD J. (1929). "The Dangers of Obedience," *Harper's Monthly Magazine* 159, June, 1–10.

MILGRAM, S., "Dynamics of Obedience: Experiments in Social Psychology," Mimeographed Report, *National Science Foundation*, January 25, 1961.

MILGRAM, S., "Behavioral Study of Obedience," *J. Abnorm. Soc. Psychol.* 67, 371–8.

MILGRAM, S., "Issues in the Study of Obedience: A Reply to Baumrind," *Amer. Psychol.* 19 (1964), 848–52.

MILLER, N. E., "Experimental Studies of Conflict," in J. McV. Hunt (Ed.), *Personality and the Behavior Disorders.* New York: Ronald Press, 1944.

SCOTT, J. P., *Aggression.* Chicago: University of Chicago Press, 1958.

A COMPARATIVE TEST
OF THE STATUS ENVY, SOCIAL POWER,
AND SECONDARY REINFORCEMENT THEORIES
OF IDENTIFICATORY LEARNING*

Albert Bandura, Dorothea Ross, and Sheila A. Ross

Although it is generally assumed that social behavior is learned and modified through direct reward and punishment of instrumental responses, informal observation and laboratory study of the social learning process reveal that new responses may be rapidly acquired and existing behavioral repertoires may be considerably changed as a function of observing the behavior and attitudes exhibited by models (Bandura, 1962).

The latter type of learning is generally labeled "imitation" in behavior theory, and "identification" in most theories of personality. These concepts, however, are treated in the present paper as synonymous since both encompass the same behavioral phenomenon, i.e., the tendency for a person to match the behavior, attitudes, or emotional reactions as exhibited by actual or symbolized models. While the

---

* Albert Bandura, Dorothea Ross, and Sheila A. Ross, "A Comparative Test of the Status Envy, Social Power, and Secondary Reinforcement Theories of Identificatory Learning," *Journal of Abnormal and Social Psychology*, 67 (1963), 527–34. Copyright 1963 by the American Psychological Association, and reproduced by permission.

defining properties of identification are essentially the same in different personality theories, a host of divergent learning conditions have been proposed as the necessary antecedent variables for matching or identificatory behavior (Bronfenbrenner, 1960; Freud, 1946; Freud, 1924, 1948; Kagan, 1958; Klein, 1949; Maccoby, 1959; Mowrer, 1950; Parsons, 1955; Sears, 1957; Whiting, 1960).

In the experiment reported in this paper predictions were derived from three of the more prominent theories of learning by identification, and tested in three-person groups representing prototypes of the nuclear family. In one condition of the experiment an adult assumed the role of controller of resources and positive reinforcers. Another adult was the consumer or recipient of these resources, while the child, a participant observer in the triad, was essentially ignored. In a second treatment condition, one adult controlled the resources; the child, however, was the recipient of the positive reinforcers and the other adult was assigned a subordinate and powerless role. An adult male and female served as models in each of the triads. For half the boys and girls in each condition the male model controlled and dispensed the rewarding resources, simulating the husband dominant family; for the remaining children, the female model mediated the positive resources as in the wife dominant home. Following the experimental social interactions the two adult models exhibited divergent patterns of behavior in the presence of the child, and a measure was obtained of the degree to which the child subsequently patterned his behavior after that of the models.

According to the *status envy theory* of identification recently proposed by Whiting (1959, 1960), where a child competes unsuccessfully with an adult for affection, attention, food, and care, the child will envy the consumer adult and consequently identify with him. Whiting's theory represents an extension of the Freudian defensive identification hypothesis that identificatory behavior is the outcome of rivalrous interaction between the child and the parent who occupies an envied consumer status. While Freud presents the child as in competition with the father primarily for the mother's sexual and affectional attention, Whiting regards any forms of reward, material and social, as valued resources around which rivalry may develop. The status envy theory thus predicts that the highest degree of imitation by the child will occur in the experimental condition in which the rivalrous adult consumes the resources desired by the child, with the consumer adult serving as the primary object of imitation.

In contrast to the envy theory, other writers (Maccoby, 1959; Mussen & Distler, 1959; Parsons, 1955) assume that the controller, rather than the consumer, of resources is the main source of imitative behavior. The *power theory* of social influence has received considerable attention in experimental social psychology, though not generally in the context of identification theories.

Social power is typically defined as the ability of a person to influence the behavior of others by controlling or mediating their positive and negative reinforcements. French and Raven (1959) have distinguished five types of power based on expertness, attractiveness, legitimacy, coerciveness, and rewarding power, each of which is believed to have somewhat differential effects on the social influence process. For example, the use of threat or coercion, in which the controller derives power from his ability to administer punishments, not only develops avoidance behavior toward the controller but also decreases his attractiveness and hence his effectiveness in altering the behavior of others beyond the immediate social influence setting (French, Morrison, & Levinger, 1960; Zipf, 1960). The use of reward power, in contrast, both fosters approach responses toward the power figure and increases his attractiveness or secondary reward value through the repeated association of his attributes with positive reinforcement. Attractiveness is assumed to extend the controller's power over a wide range of behavior (French & Raven, 1959).

In the present investigation power based upon the ability to dispense rewards was manipulated experimentally. In accordance with the social power theory of identification, but contrasting with the status envy hypothesis, one would predict that children will reproduce more of the behavior of the adult who controls positive reinforcers, than that of the powerless adult model, and that power inversions on the part of the male and female models will produce cross-sex imitation.

The *secondary reinforcement theory* of identification, which has been alluded to in the discussion of social power through attractiveness, has been elaborated in greatest detail by Mowrer (1950, 1958). According to this view, as a model mediates the child's biological and social rewards, the behavioral attributes of the model are paired repeatedly with positive reinforcement and thus acquire secondary reward value. On the basis of stimulus generalization, responses which match those of the model attain reinforcing value for the child in proportion to their similarity to those made by the model. Conse-

quently, the child can administer positively conditioned reinforcers to himself simply by reproducing as closely as possible the model's positively valenced behavior. This theory predicts that the experimental condition in which the child was the recipient of positive reinforcements will yield the highest imitation scores with the model who dispensed the rewards serving as the primary source of imitative behavior.

METHOD

Subjects

The subjects were 36 boys and 36 girls enrolled in the Stanford University Nursery School. They ranged in age from 33 to 65 months, although the variability was relatively small with most of the ages falling around the mean of 51 months.

An adult male and female served as models in the triads so as to reproduce possible power structures encountered in different types of family constellations. A female experimenter conducted the study for all 72 children.

Design and Procedure

The subjects were assigned randomly to two experimental groups and one control group of 24 subjects each. Half the subjects in each group were males, and half were females.

High rewarding power was induced experimentally through the manipulation of material and social reinforcements, and the use of verbal structuring techniques. While accompanying the child to the experimental room, for example, the experimenter informed the child that the adult who assumed the role of controller owned the nursery school "surprise room," as well as a fabulous collection of play materials. After introducing the child to the controller, the experimenter asked whether the child may play in the surprise room. The controller explained that he was on his way to his car to fetch some of his most attractive toys, but the experimenter and the child could proceed to the room where he would join them shortly. As the controller left, the experimenter commented on how lucky they were to have access to the controller's play materials.

On the way to the experimental room they met the other adult who insisted on joining them but the experimenter informed her that she would have to obtain permission from the controller since he owned the room, and it was doubtful whether sufficient play materials were available for both the adult and the child. This brief encounter with the other adult was designed primarily to create the set that rewards were available to one person only and thereby to induce rivalrous feelings over the controller's resources.

As soon as the experimenter and the child arrived in the experimental room, they sat down at a small table and played with the few Lincoln Logs and two small cars that were provided. A short time later the other adult appeared and announced that the controller also granted her permission to play in the room.

The controller then entered carrying two large toy boxes containing a variety of highly attractive masculine and feminine toys, a colorful juice dispensing fountain, and an ample supply of cookies. As soon as the controller appeared on the scene, the experimenter departed.

For children in the Adult Consumer condition, the adult who assumed the role of consumer requested permission to play with the articles and the controller replied that, since the child appeared to be occupied at his table, the consumer was free to use the play materials. This monopolistic move by the consumer adult left the child stranded at a table with two relatively uninteresting toys.

During the 20-minute play session, the controller offered the consumer, among other things, miniature pinball machines, mechanical sparkling toys, kaleidoscopes, dolls, and actively participated with the consumer in dart games and other activities. To add to the credibility of the situation, both the controller and consumer devoted most of their attention to articles, such as the pinball machine and dart game, which could be used in adult appropriate activities. Throughout the interaction the controller was most helpful, supportive, and generous in dispensing social reinforcers in the form of praise, approval, and positive attention. The consumer, in turn, commented frequently on the controller's highly attractive resources so as to further enhance the controller's rewarding status. The consumer also verbalized considerable positive affect characteristic of a person experiencing positive reinforcements.

Approximately half way through the session, the controller remarked, "Say, you look hungry. I have just the thing for you." He then brought forth the soda fountain dispenser, poured colorful fruit juices into paper cups and served them to the consumer along with a generous supply of cookies. While the consumer was enjoying his snack, the controller turned on a "TV-radio" that played a nursery melody while a revolving dial displayed a series of storybook scenes.

Toward the end of the session, the controller informed the consumer that he will be leaving on a shopping trip to San Francisco that afternoon, and asked the consumer if there was anything special she would like him to buy for her. The consumer requested a super two-wheel bicycle, a high status object among the nursery school children. The controller promised to purchase the bicycle along with any other items the consumer might think of before the controller departed for the city.

The procedure for the Child Consumer condition was identical with that described above except the child was the recipient of the material rewards and the social reinforcement. During the session the other adult sat at the opposite end of the room engrossed in a book, and was totally ignored by the controller. In discussing the prospective San Francisco shopping trip, the controller mentioned to the child that he was planning to visit some toy stores in the city that afternoon, and asked for suggestions of attractive toys he might purchase for future play sessions with children.

For half the boys and girls in each treatment condition the male model controlled and dispensed the resources, simulating the husband dominant family; for the remaining children the female model mediated the positive resources in the wife dominant home.

At the completion of the social interaction session the controller announced that he had a surprise game in his car that the three of them could play together. The controller then asked the other adult to fetch the experimenter to assist them with the game, and as soon as the adult departed, the controller removed the toys and assembled the imitation task apparatus.

Imitation Task

The imitation task was essentially the same two-choice discrimination problem utilized in an earlier experiment (Bandura & Huston, 1961), except the response repertoires exhibited by the models were considerably extended, and the procedure used in the acquisition trials was somewhat modified.

The apparatus consisted of two small boxes with hinged lids, identical in color and size. The boxes were placed on stools approximately 4 feet apart and 8 feet from the starting point. On the lid of each box was a rubber doll.

As soon as the other adult returned with the experimenter, the controller asked both the child and the experimenter to be seated in the chairs along the side of the room, and the other adult to stand at the starting point, while the controller described the game they were about to play. The controller then explained that the experimenter would hide a picture sticker in one of the two boxes and the object of the game was to guess which box contained the sticker. The adults would

have the first set of turns, following which the child would play the guessing game.

The discrimination problem was employed simply as a cover task that occupied the children's attention while at the same time permitting observation of the models as they performed divergent patterns of behavior during the discrimination trials in the absence of any set to attend to or learn the responses exhibited by the models.

Before commencing the trials, the controller invited the other participants to join him in selecting a "thinking cap" from hat racks containing two identical sets of four sailor caps, each of which had a different colored feather. The controller selected the green feathered hat, remarked, "Feather in the front" and wore the hat with the feather facing forward. The other model selected the yellow feathered hat, commented, "Feather in the back," and placed the hat on her head with the feather facing backward. The child then made his choice from the four hats in the lower rack and it was noted whether he matched the color preference, hat placement, and the verbal responses of the one or the other model.

The models then went to the starting point, the child returned to his seat, and the experimenter loaded both boxes with sticker pictures for the models' trials.

During the execution of each trial, each model exhibited a different set of relatively novel verbal and motor responses that were totally irrelevant to the discrimination problem to which the child's attention was directed. At the starting point the controller stood with his arms crossed, but at the experimenter's warning not to look, the controller placed his hands over his eyes, faced sideways, and asked, "Ready?" The other model stood with his arms on his hips, then squatted with his back turned to the boxes, and asked, "Now?"

As soon as the experimenter gave the signal for the first trial, the controller remarked, "Forward march" and began marching slowly toward the designated box repeating, "March, march, march." When he reached the box he said, "Sock him," hit the doll aggressively off the box, opened the lid and yelled, "Bingo," as he reached down for the sticker. He then remarked, "Lickit-sticket," as he pressed on the picture sticker with his thumb in the upper-right quadrant of a 24 × 24 inch sheet of plain white paper that hung on the wall immediately behind the boxes. The controller terminated the trial by replacing the doll facing sideways on the container with the comment, "Look in the mirror," and made a final verbal response, "There."

The other model then took her turn and performed a different set of imitative acts but equated with the controller's responses in terms of number, types of response classes represented, structural properties, and interest value. At the starting point, for example, she remarked, "Get set, go" and walked stiffly toward the boxes repeating "Left, right, left, right." When she reached the container she said, "Down and up," as she lay the doll down on the lid and opened the box. She then exclaimed, "A stickeroo," repeated, "Weto-smacko," and slapped on the sticker with the open hand in the lower-left quadrant of the sheet of paper. In terminating the trial, the model lay the doll on the lid of the container with the remark, "Lie down," and returned with her hands behind her back, and emitted the closing remark, "That's it."

The two sets of responses were counterbalanced by having the models display each pattern with half the subjects in each of the three groups.

The models performed alternately for four trials. At the conclusion of the fourth trial the controller explained that he had to check some materials in his car and while he and the other model were away the child could take his turns. Before they departed, however, the experimenter administered a picture preference test in which the models were asked to select their preferred picture from six different stickers pasted on a 5 × 8 inch card,

after which the child was presented a similar card containing an identical set of stickers and requested to indicate his preference.

In addition to the introductory block of four trials by the models, the child's 15 total test trials were interspersed with three two-trial blocks by the models. The models were always absent from the room during the child's test series. This procedure was adopted in order to remove any imagined situational restraints against, or coercion for, the child to reproduce the models' responses. Moreover, demonstrations of delayed imitation in the absence of the model provides more decisive evidence for learning by means of imitation.

The models always selected different boxes, the right-left position varying from trial to trial in a fixed irregular order, and the controller always took the first turn. Although the models received stickers on each trial, the child was nonrewarded on one third of the trials in order to maintain his interest in the cover task.

At the beginning of each of the blocks of subjects' trials, the experimenter administered the picture preference test and the selection of stickers that matched the models' choices was recorded. In addition, on the eighth trial the models removed their hats and hung them in different locations in the room. If the child removed his hat during the session and placed it along side one or the other of the model's hats, this imitative act was also scored.

At the completion of the imitation phase of the experiment, the children were interviewed by the experimenter in order to determine whom they considered to be the controller of resources, and to assess their model preferences. The latter data were used as an index of attraction to the models. In addition, for the children in the adult consumer condition, the session was concluded by providing them the same lavish treatment accorded their adult rival.

Children in the control group had no prior social interaction with the models but participated with them in the imitative learning

Table 1

MEAN NUMBER OF IMITATIVE RESPONSES PERFORMED BY SUBGROUPS OF CHILDREN IN THE EXPERIMENTAL TRIADS

Subjects	Objects of imitation			
	Male Controller	Female Consumer	Female Controller	Male Consumer
Girls	29.00	9.67	26.00	10.00
Boys	30.17	18.67	22.33	16.17
Total	29.59	14.17	24.17	13.09
	Controller	Ignored	Controller	Ignored
Girls	22.00	16.17	31.84	22.17
Boys	29.17	16.67	26.83	34.50
Total	25.59	16.42	29.34	28.34

phase of the study. The experimenter assumed complete charge of the procedures and treated the models as though they were naive subjects. The control group was included primarily to determine the models' relative effectiveness as modeling stimuli. In addition, the models alternated between subjects in the order in which they executed the trials so as to test for the possibility of a primacy or a recency of exposure effect on imitative behavior.

Imitation Scores

The imitation scores were obtained by summing the frequency of occurrence of the postural, verbal, and motor responses described in the preceding section, and the hat, color, and picture preferences that matched the selections of each of the two models.

The children's performances were scored by three raters who observed the experimental sessions through a one-way mirror from an adjoining observation room. The raters were provided with a separate check list of responses exhibited by each of the two models, and the scoring procedure simply involved checking the imitative responses performed by the children on each trial. In order to provide an estimate of interscorer reliability, the per-

formances of 30% of the children were recorded simultaneously but independently by two observers. The raters were in perfect agreement on 95% of the specific imitative responses that they scored.

RESULTS

The control group data revealed that the two models were equally effective in eliciting imitative responses, the mean values being 17.83 and 20.46 for the male and female model, respectively; nor did the children display differential imitation of same-sex $(M = 22.30)$ and opposite-sex $(M = 18.50)$ models. Although children in the control group tended to imitate the second model $(M = 22.21)$ to a somewhat greater extent than the one who performed first $(M = 16.08)$ on each trial, suggesting a recency of exposure effect, the difference was not of statistically significant magnitude $(t = 1.60)$.

Table 1 presents the mean imitation scores for children in each of the two experimental triads. A $2 \times 2 \times 2 \times 2$ mixed factorial analysis of variance was com-

Table 2

SUMMARY OF THE ANALYSIS OF VARIANCE OF THE IMITATION SCORES

Source	df	MS	F
Between subjects	47	310.17	
Sex of subjects (A)	1	283.59	<1
Sex of controller model (B)	1	128.34	<1
Adult versus child consumer (C)	1	518.01	1.61
A×B	1	23.01	<1
A×C	1	1.76	<1
B×C	1	742.59	2.31
A×B×C	1	21.10	<1
Error (b)	40	321.49	
Within subjects	48	113.24	
Controller versus other model (D)	1	2,025.84	40.61***
A×D	1	297.51	5.96*
B×D	1	237.51	4.76*
C×D	1	396.09	7.94**
A×B×D	1	256.76	5.15*
A×C×D	1	19.52	<1
B×C×D	1	23.02	<1
A×B×C×D	1	184.00	3.69
Error (w)	40	49.88	

* $p < .05$.
** $p < .01$.
*** $p < .001$.

puted on these data in which the four factors in the design were sex of child, sex of the model who controlled the resources, adult versus child consumer, and the controller versus the other model as the source of imitative behavior.[1] As shown in Table 2, the findings of this study clearly support the social power theory of imitation. In both experimental treatments, regardless of whether the rival adult or the children themselves were the recipients of the rewarding resources, the model who possessed rewarding power was imitated to a greater degree than was the rival or the ignored model ($F = 40.61$, $p < .001$). Nor did the condition combining resource ownership with direct reinforcement of the child yield the highest imitation of the model who controlled and dispensed the positive rewards. The latter finding is particularly surprising since an earlier experiment based on two-person groups (Bandura & Huston, 1961), demonstrated that pairing of model with positive reinforcement substantially enhanced the occurrence of imitative behavior. An examination of the remaining significant interaction effects together with the postexperimental interview data suggest a possible explanation for the discrepant results.

The differential in the controller-other model imitation was most pronounced

[1] The assistance of Eleanor Willemsen with the statistical computations is gratefully acknowledged.

when the male model was the controller of resources ($F = 4.76$, $p < .05$), particularly for boys. In fact, boys who were the recipients of rewarding resources mediated by the female model tended to favor the ignored male as their object of imitation. In the postexperiment interview a number of boys in this condition spontaneously expressed sympathy for the ignored male and mild criticism of the controller for not being more charitable with her bountiful resources (for example, "She doesn't share much. John played bravely even though she didn't even share.... She's a bit greedy.").

As a partial check on whether this factor would tend to diminish the differential imitation of the two models, six children—three boys and three girls—participated in a modified Child Consumer treatment in which, halfway through the social interaction session, the ignored adult was informed that he too may have access to the playthings. He replied that he was quite content to read his book. This modified procedure, which removed the rivalry and the exclusion of the model, yielded four times as much imitation of the controller relative to the model who was ignored by choice.

The significant triple interaction effect indicates that the differential in the controller-other model imitation was greatest when the same-sex model mediated the positive reinforcers, and this effect was more pronounced for boys than for girls.

The data presented so far demonstrate that manipulation of rewarding power had produced differential imitation of the behavior exhibited by the two models. In order to assess whether the dispensing of positive reinforcers in the prior social interaction influenced the overall level of matching responses, the imitation scores in each of the three groups were summed across models and analyzed using a Sex $\times$ Treatment design.

The mean total imitative responses for children in the Child Consumer, Adult Consumer, and the Control group were 50.21, 40.58, and 37.88, respectively. Analysis of variance of these data reveals a significant treatment effect ($F = 3.37$, $.025 < p < .05$). Further comparisons of pairs of means by the t test, show that children in the child rewarded condition displayed significantly more imitative behavior than did children both in the Adult Consumer treatment ($t = 2.19$, $p < .05$), and those in the Control group ($t = 2.48$, $p < .02$). The Adult Consumer and Control groups, however, did not differ from each other in this respect ($t = .54$).

The model preference patterns were identical for children in the two experimental conditions and, consequently, the data were combined for the statistical analysis. Of the 48 children, 32 selected the model who possessed rewarding power as the more attractive, while 16 preferred the noncontrolling adult. The greater attractiveness of the rewarding model was significant beyond the .05 level ($\chi^2 = 5.34$). The experimental triad in which boys were the recipients of positive reinforcers while the male model was ignored, and the female consumer-girl ignored subgroup, contributed the highest preference for the noncontrolling adult.

In addition to the experimental groups discussed in the preceding section, data are available for 9 children in the Adult Consumer condition, and for 11 children in the Child Consumer treatment who revealed, in their postexperiment interviews, that they had actually attributed rewarding power to the ignored or the consumer adult despite the elaborate experimental

Table 3

IMITATION AS A FUNCTION OF ATTRIBUTED REWARDING
POWER TO THE MODELS

Treatment condition	Objects of imitation			
	Female controller	Male non-controller	Male controller	Female non-controller
Adult consumer	24.0	12.3	29.8	14.6
Child consumer	18.2	6.7	35.5	16.2

manipulations designed to establish differential power status. A number of these children were firmly convinced that only a male can possess resources and, therefore, the female dispensing the rewards was only an intermediary for the male model (for example, "He's the man and it's all his because he's a daddy. Mommy never really has things belong to her. . . . He's the daddy so it's his but he shares nice with the mommy. . . . He's the man and the man always really has the money and he lets ladies play too. John's good and polite and he has very good manners.") This view of resource ownership within the family constellation was often directly reinforced by the mothers (for example, "My mommy told me and Joan that the daddy really buys all the things, but the mommy looks after things."). Children who attributed the resource ownership to the consumer or ignored female model had considerable difficulty in explaining their selection (for example, "I just knowed it does. . . . I could tell, that's how."), perhaps, because the power structure they depicted is at variance with the widely accepted cultural norm.

As shown in Table 3, models who were attributed rewarding power elicited approximately twice as many matching responses as models who were perceived by the children as possessing no control over the rewarding resources. Because of the small and unequal number of cases in each cell, these data were not evaluated statistically. The differences, however, are marked and quite in accord with those produced by the experimentally manipulated variations in power status.

DISCUSSION

To the extent that the imitative behavior elicited in the present experiment may be considered an elementary prototype of identification within a nuclear family group, the data fail to support the interpretation of identificatory learning as the outcome of a rivalrous interaction between the child and the adult who occupies an envied status in respect to the consumption of highly desired resources. Children clearly identified with the source of rewarding power rather than with the competitor for these rewards. Moreover, power inversions on the part of the male and female models produced cross-sex imitation, particularly in girls. The differential readiness of boys and girls to imitate behavior exhibited by an opposite-sex model are consistent with findings reported by Brown (1956, 1958) that boys show a decided preference for the masculine role, whereas, ambivalence and masculine role preference are widespread among girls. These findings probably reflect both the differential cultural tolerance for cross-sex behavior displayed by males and females, and the privileged status and relatively greater positive reinforcement of masculine role behavior in our society.

Failure to develop sex appropriate behavior has received considerable attention in the clinical literature and has customarily been assumed to be established and maintained by psychosexual threat and anxiety reducing mechanisms. Our findings strongly suggest, however, that external social learning variables, such as the distribution of rewarding power within the family constellation, may be highly influential in the formation of inverted sex role behavior.

Theories of identificatory learning have generally assumed that within the family setting the child's initial identification is confined to his mother, and that during early childhood boys must turn from the mother as the primary model to the father as the main source of imitative behavior. However, throughout the course of development children are provided with ample opportunities to observe the behavior of both parents. The results of the present experiment reveal that when children are exposed to multiple models they may select one or more of them as the primary source of behavior, but rarely reproduce all the elements of a single model's repertoire or confine their imitation to that model. Although the children adopted many of the characteristics of the model who possessed rewarding power, they also reproduced some of the elements of behavior exhibited by the model who occupied the subordinate role. Consequently, the children were not simply junior-size replicas of one or the other model; rather, they exhibited a relatively novel pattern of behavior representing an amalgam of elements from both models. Moreover, the specific admixture of behavioral elements varied from child to child. These findings provide considerable evidence for the seemingly paradoxical conclusion that imitation can in fact produce innovation of social behavior, and that within the same family even same-sex siblings may exhibit quite different response patterns, owing to their having selected for imitation different elements of their parents' response repretoires.

The association of a model with non-contingent positive reinforcement tends to increase the incidence of imitative behavior in two person groups (Bandura & Huston, 1961), whereas the addition of a same-sex third person who is denied access to desired rewards may provoke in children negative evaluations of the rewarding model and thereby decreases his potency as a modeling stimulus. These two sets of data demonstrate how learning principles based on an individual behavior model may be subject to strict limitations, since the introduction of additional social variables into the stimulus complex can produce significant changes in the functional relationships between relevant variables.

REFERENCES

BANDURA, A. "Social Learning Through Imitation." In M. R. Jones (Ed.), *Nebraska Symposium on Motivation: 1962*. Lincoln: Univer. Nebraska Press, 1962. Pp. 211–269.

BANDURA, A., and HUSTON, ALETHA C. "Identification as a Process of Incidental Learning." *J. Abnorm. Soc. Psychol.*, 1961, 63, 311–318.

BRONFENBRENNER, U. "Freudian Theories of Identification and Their Derivatives." *Child Developm.*, 1960, 31, 15–40.

Brown, D. G. "Sex-Role Preference in Young Children." *Psychol. Monogr.*, 1956, 70 (14, Whole No. 421).

Brown, D. G. "Sex-Role Development in a Changing Culture." *Psychol. Bull.*, 1958, 55, 232–242.

French, J. R. P., Jr., Morrison, H. W., and Levinger, G. "Coercive Power and Forces Affecting Conformity." *J. Abnorm. Soc. Psychol.*, 1960, 61, 93–101.

French, J. R. P., Jr., and Raven, B. "The Bases of Social Power." In D. Cartwright (Ed.), *Studies in Social Power*. Ann Arbor, Mich.: Institute for Social Research, 1959. Pp. 150–167.

Freud, Anna. *The Ego and the Mechanisms of Defense*. New York: International Univer. Press, 1946.

Freud, S. "The Passing of the Oedipus-Complex." In, *Collected Papers*. Vol. 2. London: Hogarth Press, 1924. Pp. 269–282.

Freud, S. *Group Psychology and the Analysis of the Ego*. London: Hogarth Press, 1948.

Kagan, J. "The Concept of Identification." *Psychol. Rev.*, 1958, 65, 296–305.

Klein, Melanie. *The Psycho-Analysis of Children*. London: Hogarth Press, 1949.

Maccoby, Eleanor E. "Role-Taking in Childhood and its Consequences for Social Learning." *Child Develpm.*, 1969, 30, 239–252.

Mowrer, O. H. "Identification: A Link Between Learning Theory and Psychotherapy." In, *Learning Theory and Personality Dynamics*. New York: Ronald Press, 1950. Pp. 69–94.

Mowrer, O. H. "Hearing and Speaking: An Analysis of Language Learning." *J. Speech Hear. Disord.*, 1958, 23, 143–152.

Mussen, P., and Distler, L. "Masculinity, Identification, and Father-Son Relationships." *J. Abnorm. Soc. Psychol.*, 1959, 59, 350–356.

Parsons, T. "Family Structure and the Socialization of the Child." In T. Parsons and R. F. Bales (Eds.), *Family, Socialization, and Interaction Process*. Glencoe, Ill.: Free Press, 1955. Pp. 35–131.

Sears, R. R. "Identification as a Form of Behavioral Development." In D. B. Harris (Ed.), *The Concept of Development*. Minneapolis: Univer. Minnesota Press, 1957. Pp. 149–161.

Whiting, J. W. M. " Sorcery, Sin, and the Superego: A Cross-Cultural Study of Some Mechanisms of Social Control." In M. R. Jones (Ed.), *Nebraska Symposium on Motivation: 1959*. Lincoln: Univer. Nebraska Press, 1959. Pp. 174–195.

Whiting, J. W. M. "Resource Mediation and Learning by Identification." In I. Iscoe and H. W. Stevenson (Eds.), *Personality Development in Children*. Austin: Univer. Texas Press, 1960. Pp. 112–126.

Zipf, Sheila G. "Resistance and Conformity under Reward and Punishment." *J. Abnorm. Soc. Psychol.*, 1960, 61, 102–109.

THE INEFFECTIVENESS OF PUNISHMENT
POWER IN GROUP INTERACTION*

*Norman Miller, Donald C. Butler,
and James A. McMartin*

Reward and punishment are two major forms of social control. Though discussions of social power often refer to other bases of control, e.g., expert power, or referent power (French and Raven, 1960), these dimensions probably depend heavily on the ability to deliver reward and punishment. At first glance we might expect control over either punishment or reward to provide equal advantages to those who possess it. Thus in group interaction we might expect that in comparison to those with no power, those with high power to punish would do as well as those with high power to reward in inducing others to bestow desired commodities upon them. Of course, those with no power could not expect to induce anyone to help them achieve their ends, except perhaps through eliciting such social responses as pity, compassion, domination, etc.

While this analysis appears to have an *a priori* validity, considerations of notions such as exchange (Homans, 1958; Thibaut

and Kelley, 1959; Blau, 1964), reciprocity (Gouldner, 1960) and equity (Adams, 1964) suggest another outcome. They imply quite distinct rather than comparable outcomes for those with high punishment power and those with high reward power. They imply that social behavior will elicit "just returns." Those with high reward power should indeed get what they desire because their own behavior is "generous," "altruistic," etc. Contrariwise, those with high punishment power should have difficulty obtaining their end. They too should get their just desserts but in their case their desserts are aversive stimuli. Thus an exchange analysis implies that not only will they not do as well in obtaining their desired ends as those with high reward power, but furthermore they might also be expected to be even less effective than those with no power whatsoever.

Another argument for asymmetry in the roles of reward and punishment power might be drawn from the differences between reward and punishment in their effects on the learning and maintenance of individual behavior (Skinner, 1953; Estes, 1944). In general, mild punishment seems to be less permanent in its effect and more likely to produce unwanted

---

* Noman Miller, Donald C. Butler, and James A. McMartin, "The Ineffectiveness of Punishment Power in Group Interaction," *Sociometry*, 32 (1969), 24–42. Reprinted by permission of the American Sociological Association.

emotional behavior than does reward. Furthermore, while punishment may act to depress a specific prior response, the behavior which it elicits may be hard to specify. On these grounds we might expect a user of reward to be more effective in generating specifically desired behavior from others than a user of punishment. In terms of the features of this experiment, this implies that a person who relies on reward as a mode of influence would obtain more rewards and fewer punishments from others than a person who relies on punishment. In other words, even though the person who relies on punishment hopes to control the environment (other people) so as to obtain rewards, he may simply elicit punishing responses in return.

Consistent with the predictions generated by either the exchange theory or behavior theory analysis, previous research has suggested a difference between reward and punishment power. In a previous experiment (Butler and Miller, 1965b), we argued that knowledge of a group member's reward power was more useful than knowledge of his punishment power in predicting characteristics of his interpersonal interaction. Three sources of evidence supported this conclusion. (1) A general law was proposed which relates (a) a subject's relative receipt of the rewards dispensed by a group to (b) a subject's reward power $(\pi+)$ relative to the mean $\pi+$ of the group $(\bar{\pi}+)$. This law holds regardless of fluctuations in punishment power. Furthermore, this law has received more extensive confirmation in a study of five man groups (Miller and Butler, 1968), which examined ten different power structures. (2) A comparison of selected cells of the design in which target subjects possessed

equal reward power, but different punishment power, revealed no difference in other subjects' attempts to reward these two types of target subjects. Furthermore, there was a similar lack of difference in behavior toward the two types of target subjects in terms of number of punishments addressed to them. (3) A subject's reward power $(\pi+)$ was shown to be not only an excellent predictor of the number of rewards others addressed to him, but it also predicted the number of punishments addressed to him better than his punishment power $(\pi-)$. It is important to note, of course, that points 2 and 3 above are more speculative than 1 and should probably be considered as hypotheses.

At any rate, translated into the considerations of the present study, the points above suggest that a manipulation of reward power will have a more potent effect than a comparable manipulation of punishment power. Thus, the present study attempts to assess more directly the relative effect of differences in reward and punishment power.

An individual's power was manipulated by controlling the conditional probability of successfully completing a communicative act (having a reward or punishment delivered to a target to which one had addressed it). In this experiment this means that when subjects attempted to send others rewards or punishments (tickets on which they imprinted a plus or minus) their likelihood of having their "message" delivered was controlled by the experimenter. This definition of power may on first consideration appear somewhat unrelated to common conceptions of the term. While not wishing to place ourselves in a position which compels us to incorporate the totality of the layman's connotative meaning of a term into our own definition, an example may indicate that our operationalization of "power" does conform more closely to common understandings than may initially be apparent. In the setting of an advanced Political Science graduate seminar on foreign affairs, consider the behavior of group members when a new graduate student attempted to make some point during the discussion. On the other hand, consider the reaction in the same setting if (former) President Johnson (who happened to be sitting-in that day) attempted to make the identical point. The beginning graduate is likely to be interrupted, cut short, or even censor himself partway through his delivery. In contrast, Johnson is likely to be very carefully attended to, without any risk of interruption even if he were making the identical point. From our stance, the difference in ease ("likelihood") with which one's message is transmitted amounts to (reflects) a difference in power.

The experimental design permits both within-group and between-group comparisons of the two modes of social control. It employs the same simplified form of social interaction we have used in the past (Butler and Miller, 1965a and 1965b).[1] It allows each person the option of sending other group members a reward or punishment (a positive or negative "message") on each of a series of trials. Each person's "pay-off" at the end of the interaction is the algebraic sum of his receipts from others, that is, the number

of positive receipts minus the number of negative receipts.

METHOD

Design

Table 1 presents the experimental design. For each subject in a group, both reward power $(\pi+)$ and punishment power $(\pi-)$ were experimentally controlled. A subject's reward power $(\pi+)$ refers to the experimenter-assigned probability that his attempts to communicate rewards would be successful. Likewise, a subject's punishment power $(\pi-)$ refers to the experimenter-assigned probability of his successful communication of punishments. For either type of power, the probability that a subject's communication would be delivered was constant regardless of to whom the communication was addressed. Furthermore, a given subject's power was constant throughout the experiment. Thus the restrictions imposed on each subject can be specified listing his $\pi+$ and $\pi-$ (viz. $\pi+/\pi-$). Six three-man groups were assigned to each of the six power structures. As seen in Table 1, the power structures differed in the total amount of power available in the group (see column labeled "pooled power"), and the type of power $(\pi+$ or $\pi-)$ on which individual members within each group differed (see differences within each row). This latter manipulation resulted in two major experimental blocks. Thus, within structures I, II, and III, the members posessed different amounts of reward power $(\pi+)$. For comparisons *between* these structures, however, the average reward power in the group $(\pi+)$ was constant. (In other words, within each of these groups, members differed in reward power but the group themselves only differed in the average amount of punishment power). For groups IV, V, and VI, just the opposite was the case. Within each structure $\pi+$ was constant and members of a single structure differed only in their punishment power $(\pi-)$. *Between* these three structures only $\pi+$ varied.

---

[1] This same form of interaction (Flament and Apfelbaum, 1966) and other similar forms of simplification have become increasingly popular in studies of group interaction (Kelley et al, 1962).

Table 1
The Experimental Design

Group Structures	N^a	Ratio of Reward to Punishment Power ($\pi+/\pi-$) for Individuals with Low Power, Medium Power, and High Power within Each Group			Average Power of Group		
		Low Power	Medium Power	High Power	Reward Power ($\bar{\pi}+$)	Punishment Power ($\bar{\pi}-$)	Pooled Power
Punishment power ($\pi-$) is constant within groups and ($\bar{\pi}-$) varies between groups.							
I	6	.0/.0	.5/.0	1.0/.0	.5	.0	.25
II	6	.0/.5	.5/.5	1.0/.5	.5	.5	.50
III	6	.0/1.0	.5/1.0	1.0/1.0	.5	1.0	.75
Reward power ($\pi+$) constant within groups and ($\bar{\pi}+$) varies between groups.							
IV	6	.0/.0	.0/.5	.0/1.0	.0	.5	.25
V	5	.5/.0	.5/.5	.5/1.0	.5	.5	.50
VI	5	1.0/.0	1.0/.5	1.0/1.0	1.0	.5	.75

^{a} N= the number of groups run under a particular power structure.

Subjects

The subjects were 108 male undergraduates at Yale University who partially met a requirement of an introductory psychology course by volunteering. They were randomly assigned to groups and positions within a group.

Procedure

The apparatus and procedure was similar to those described previously (Butler and Miller, 1965). The essential features were as follows. Subjects sat in isolated booths and interacted with two other strangers. Each subject had a supply of tickets identifiable as his by color. He was free on each of 200 trials to send a reward or punishment (+ or —) to whomever he chose (except himself). The subjects produced a reward by writing a "+" on a blank ticket and a punishment by writing a "—." These marks were the only content of each "message" they sent. Each person's task was to distribute tickets so as to get others to send pluses to him. Subjects were not told about the power manipulation imposed within or between groups. The task was presented as individualistic competition (i.e., do as well as you can). Thus subjects were not focused on competition within the group.

RESULTS

An overall measure of a subject's effectiveness in getting others to reward him would be the number of positive minus the number of negative messages he received (i.e., his payoff). However, this number depends on (a) the $\pi+$ and $\pi-$ of the other subjects who were sending messages to him, as well as (b) the actual behavior of these other subjects. Since part (a) is controlled by the experimenter, only part (b) is a true dependent variable. In other words, for any given subject the relative numbers of plus and minus messages that he received from a particular other subject depended not only on what that other subject addressed to him, but also on that other subject's $\pi+$ and $\pi-$. Therefore, the number of messages *addressed to* a person was chosen as the response measure rather than the number *received*. The number of messages addressed to subjects ignores the *experimenter-determined* feature of whether a sent message was in fact received. Furthermore, the full data of who sent what to whom was collapsed into three measures of individual behavior: (a) the mean number of positive messages addressed to a person from other subjects per trial (P+), (b) the mean number of negative messages addressed to a person from other subjects per trial (P—), and (c) the mean number of positive messages sent by a subject per trial (S+). Since measure (c) is equal to one minus the mean number of negative messages sent by a subject per trial, negative messages sent by subjects need not be analyzed.

Group behavior was analyzed by summing measures of individual behavior within the replications of each structure. Thus, group response measures that are analogous to the individual (person) response measures can readily be derived by summing measures of individual behavior. For instance, $\bar{P}+$ equals the mean number of positive messages addressed to others within the group per trial. The group measures analogous to individual measures are $\bar{P}-$, $\bar{S}+$, and $\bar{S}-$. However, for between-group comparisons, it is important to note that within the limits of rounding and recording errors, equivalent but opposite effects are found for total $(\bar{P}+)$ and $(\bar{P}-)$ since for all groups these two measures must sum to the same

Table 2

ANALYSIS OF VARIANCE OF POSITIVE MESSAGES SENT[a]

Source	d.f.	MS	F	p
Total	101			
Between Structures	33			
A. Type of power varied within the structure	1	371.98	<1	
B. $\bar{\pi}$ of a structure	2	9914.12	2.62	$.05<p<.10$
A×B	2	67418.12	17.79	$<.001$
Residual (Error)	28	3789.37		
Within Structures				
C. π within a structure	2	9832.92	10.34	$<.001$
A×C	2	21754.63	22.87	$<.001$
B×C	4	625.63	<1	
A×B×C	4	2170.72	2.29	$.10<p<.25$
Residual (Error)	56	891.27		

[a] $\bar{p}+$ (for between-structure effects) and $p+$ (for within-structure effects).

constant. Furthermore, for between-group comparisons the value computed for *messages addressed to* ($\bar{P}$) must equal the value for messages sent by ($\bar{S}$).

Between-Structure Effects

Group behavior will be examined first. An analysis of variance was performed on the number of positive messages (P+) p addressed in different power structures (see the "Between-Structure" portion of Table 2).[2] As expected, the interaction of the mean power of a structure (see column labeled "Pooled" in Table 1) with type of power that varies between structures ($\pi-$ versus $\pi+$) was highly significant ($F = 17.79$; d.f. $= 2/28$; $p < .001$). This interaction, as shown in Figure 1,

indicates that with higher levels of reward power more positive messages are sent (and received), whereas with higher levels of punishment power fewer positive and hence more negative messages are sent (and received).[3]

To test the more specific prediction based on our previous results that reward power is a more powerful determinant of group behavior than punishment power, the magnitudes of the slopes of the two lines in Figure 1 were compared. This was done by means of an interaction t test (Walker and Lev, 1953: 159), which compares the differences between the high and low points of the two lines. Since the *a priori* prediction is directional, a one-tailed test was employed. The t of 1.21, (d.f. $= 28$) only approaches significance ($p < .07$ one-tailed). A similar analysis,

---

[2] One replication was discarded from structures V and VI because of experimenter errors in controlling subject's π values. Therefore, unweighted means analyses of variance were performed on the data.

[3] The percentages in Figure 1 are equivalent to raw counts because the total number of messages sent is constant for all groups (*viz.* 600).

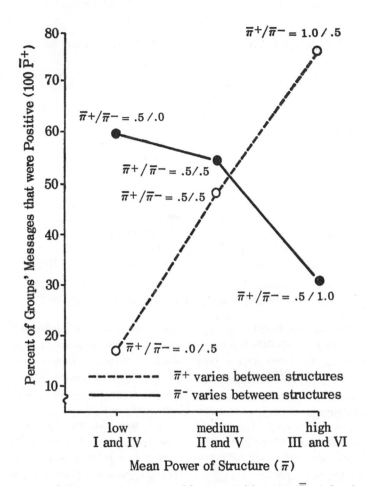

Fig. 1. The per cent of the groups' messages with were positive ($100 \ \overline{P}+$) for the six conditions. The solid line represents groups with $\overline{\pi}+$ held constant at .5, and the dashed line groups with $\overline{\pi}-$ held constant at 5.

however, on data from the first 50 trials was highly significant ($t = 5.27$, d.f. $= 28$, $p < .001$). Taken together these results suggest that for groups, punishment power is initially a much less potent determinant of the overall or average behavior in the group than reward power, but with continued interaction, the significance of this difference between the two types of power dissipates. Nevertheless, inspection of the means in the final trial block shows that

the differences, although less significant, were of comparable magnitude to those in the first 50 trials. The reason why the differential effectiveness of reward power as opposed to punishment power lessens as trials progress can be traced to the increasing development of idiosyncratic differences from group to group, even though they are in the same experimental condition. In other words, the fact that the differential potency of the two types of power loses significance is attributable to an increase across trials in the variability of group behavior within each of the power structures. Comparison of the variance in trial block 1 and trial block 4 across all six structures yields a t of 2.17 (d.f. = 32, $p < .025$ one-tailed) and confirms this interpretation.

The overall data for $\bar{P}+$ could be interpreted as indicating that groups learn to use the type of power they possess. Groups which differ in punishment power but possess equal reward power, use punishment at a level commensurate with the punishment power available. Similarly, groups which differ in reward power but possess equal punishment power, use reward in correspondence with the amount of reward available. One problem with this interpretation however, is that the use of reward and punishment is not independent. In other words, manipulation of punishment power could conceivably affect only the tendency to use reward. The differences in use of punishment may simply reflect the fact that the experimental situation permits no alternative. If a subject chooses to send fewer rewards his only alternative is to use more punishments. A design in which another response class was available, such as "not responding" or sending a "neutral message" would clarify this situation. However, even if the first problem were eliminated a second problem still exists. Namely, this interpretation cannot account for the differential potency of reward power as opposed to punishment power.

The between group data, however, could be explained by behavior theory, applied to groups as a whole, as follows. Groups whose members have a higher average reward power are more effective in getting each other to send rewards, due to the manipulative capacity of reinforcement. Groups which have higher punishment power, however, simply elicit punitive replies more often. This distinction between *reinforcement* and mere *cueing* will be discussed more fully later.

Within-Structure Effects

Messages Addressed to a Subject. Analysis of within-structure effects of π on P+ discloses a pattern of outcomes consistent with the between-structure findings. The significant A $\times$ C interaction ($F = 22.87$; d.f. = 2/56; $p < .001$) in the "Within-Structure" portion of the analysis of variance presented in Table 2 is directly analogous to the previously discussed "Between-Structure" interaction (A $\times$ B). In this instance, however, it is the π of *individuals within each structure* which interacts with the type of power varied within the structure (reward or punishment). The interaction (shown in Figure 2) shows that more positive messages are addressed to persons with high reward power and fewer to those with high punishment power.

The between-group effects presented in the previous section could not be comfortably translated into an equity or exchange analysis in that these theories imply an exchange between two or more interacting persons or groups and the groups in this experiment did not interact with another group or party. However, their application to differences in the outcome for within-structure comparisons is relatively straight-forward. As would be expected, from both behavior and exchange theories, with increments in an individual's $\pi+$, more rewards are addressed to him, whereas with increments in $\pi-$ fewer rewards are addressed to him.

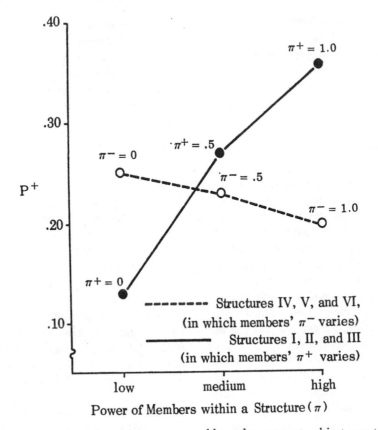

Fig 2. The mean number of positive messages addressed to a target subject per trial by other subjects in his group (P+) as a function of the target subject's power within the group. The solid line represents individuals in the groups in which members differ in power to reward ($\pi+$) and the dashed line those who differ in power to punish ($\pi-$).

From the standpoint of our initial predictions, however, the more important consideration is the comparative slopes produced by within-group manipulations of reward and punishment power. The prediction of greater potency for reward power as compared to punishment power was clearly confirmed (interaction $t = 2.32$, d.f. $= 19$, $p < .025$ one-tailed).[4]

Whereas for between-group data, an analysis of rewards addressed to group members ($\bar{P}+$) is necessarily identical to an analysis of punishments ($\bar{P}-$), the corresponding response measures in within-structure analyses P+ and P— are

---

[4] Once again, this interaction t-test compares the respective differences between the endpoints of the two lines in Figure 2. It shows that

comparable manipulations $\pi+$ and $\pi-$ do not have equivalent strengths of effect. It is not just that they have different directions of effect on P+, but rather, that given their particular direction, differences in $\pi+$ have greater impact than differences in $\pi-$.

partially independent. In an analysis which parallels that of Table 2, the within-structure effects show results for P— opposite to, but essentially consistent with, those presented above for P+. Fewer negative messages were addressed to those with higher reward power whereas more were addressed to those with higher punishment power ($F = 4.12$, d.f. $= 2/56$, $p < .05$). Thus, in terms of both P+ and P— high punishment power appears to be more of a handicap than an advantage, in that more negative messages were addressed to those with high π—. However, in contrast to the differential potency of reward and punishment power on P+, no significant difference between the slopes was found for P—.[5]

Messages Sent by a Subject. Analysis of messages sent by persons in different power positions also shows an interaction between a person's level of power and the type of power that contributes to his power position within the group ($F = 5.34$, d.f. $= 2/56$, $p < .01$). Figure 3 presents this interaction. As shown, the least powerful group member behaves similarly regardless of whether group members differ in reward or punishment power. However, this is not true for the moderate and high power members. When group members differ in punishment power, the high power person uses more reward than the other group members. When group members differ in reward power, the person with

intermediate power uses reward more frequently than the other group members.

These data can be fitted into an exchange or behavior theory analysis of the experimental situation, as follows. The person with high punishment power (π— $= 1.0$) receives relatively few punishments from others in his group because the design of this study imposes a restriction on the π— of the others in his group; they had either little (π— $= .5$) or no (π— $= .0$) power to reach him with punishments. Since he receives few punishments, he is not inclined to reply in kind. On the other hand, the person with high reward power (π+ $= 1.0$), sends more punishments because the design of this study handicaps the others in his group by allowing them little (π+ $= .5$) or no (π+ $= .0$) power to reach him with rewards.

If one assumed that subjects will learn to use that type of power which they possess, linear (but oppositely directioned) effects would be expected in Figure 3. As seen, however, this does not occur; the high power person in the two types of structures deviates from this linear pattern. As indicated above, the reversal in the two curves at the high power positions can be directly accounted for in terms of what they receive from the other group members, which, in a sense, is an artifact of the design. Thus, while the reversals of the curves in Figure 3 are consistent with either exchange or behavior theory, they do not support the proposition that subjects learn to use whichever type of power they possess. The unacceptability of that hypothesis also follows directly from the ineffectiveness of punishment power; greater amounts resulted in less success in inducing others to send rewards. By what mechanism would a person learn to

---

[5] The fact that both $\bar{\pi}$— and π— clearly produced differences in P+ as well as P— provides strong disconfirmation of our initial hypothesis about the effects of punishment power. This speculation, derived from our previous studies and presented primarily as point (2) in paragraph four of the introduction must now be discarded.

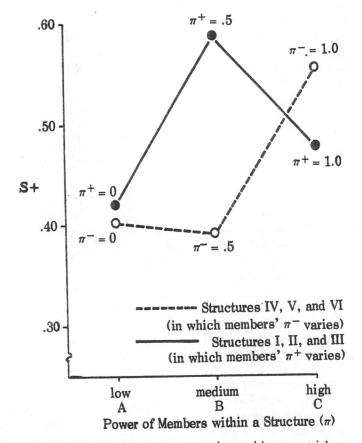

Fig 3. The mean number of positive messages sent by a subject per trial, as a function of his power within the group. The solid line represents innividuals in the groups in which members differ in power to rewards $(\pi+)$ and the dashed line those who differ in power to punish $(\pi-)$.

use a controlling device which does not control?

Relative Effectiveness Within Structures

Though the game was presented to subjects as "individualistic competition" (viz., "do the best you can"), its essentially competitive character may nevertheless have intruded into and perhaps even pervaded the interaction. Each person's goal in the interaction was to obtain as many "pluses" from others as possible.

If a subject was extremely competitive, some of the facets of the various strategies which may have occurred to him would take on different meaning than they might if he were accepting the "individualistic competition" instructions wholeheartedly. Thus, he may note that to the extent that he attempts to influence others via reward, his influence attempts inflate the payoff of others. Consequently, relative to others, his own outcome suffers to the extent that he relies on reward. If instead he can successfully influence others via punishment, not only is he ahead, but relatively, he is even further ahead in that his punishment puts other group members behind. Messick and Thorngate (1967) have demonstrated the importance of such relative gains. Thus, another approach to the within-structure data is to consider the *relative effectiveness* of group members.

To derive an individual effectiveness score for each member, the difference between the rewards addressed to a person (P+) and those he sent to others (S+) was added to the difference between the punishments he sent to others (S−) and the punishments addressed to him by others (P−). This index (P+ − S+) + (S   P) reflects a person's achieve-

ment of ends relative to his cost (where cost is measured by the other person's potential gain). Analysis of variance of these effectiveness scores yields a significant interaction between a member's power (π) within the structure and the type of power that varies within the structure ($F = 12.07$; d.f. $= 2/56$; $p < .01$). These results are pictured in Figure 4.

As seen by comparing Figure 4 to Figure 2, the form of the interaction parallels the outcome for P+. However, it is important to note that the data in Figure 4 represents a clear departure from equitable exchange. If equitable exchange operated within structures, net rewards addressed to a person would equal his net

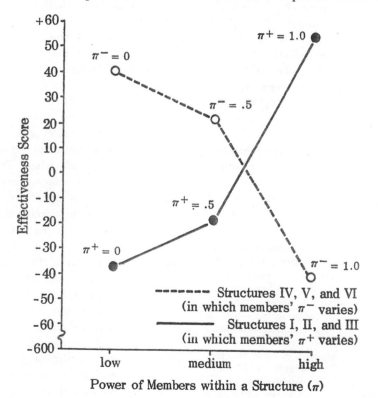

Fig 4. "Net effectiveness" as a function of power within the group. The solid line represents individuals in the groups in which members differ in reward power and the dashed line those who differ in power to punish ($\pi-$).

cost and all members would obtain an effectiveness score of zero. Thus Figure 4 depicts deviations from equitable exchange. When a person's $\pi+$ is high relative to other group members he is sent more than his just desserts whereas when his $\pi-$ is high relative to others he is sent less than he "fairly" deserves.

These results can be handled by behavior theory. The departure from equity can be accounted for by (1) the control possibilities inherent in reinforcement and (2) the aversive function of negative messages. The more positive messages a person successfully transmits, the more chance he has to get more than his share in return. Subjects who send positives but do not get through so often (e.g., $\pi+ = .5$), have less chance to manipulate others, and so on. For fixed $\pi+$, a large $\pi-$ has the opposite influence on effectiveness. The more $\pi-$ a person has, the more often his ill-chosen negative messages will find their target and elicit a negative reply, which lowers his effectiveness. Thus the experimental conditions result in more effectiveness for high $\pi+$ than his own responses "deserve," and in less effectiveness for high $\pi-$.[6]

---

[6] While these results are intriguing, it must be noted that in another sense, the data of Figure 4 do not represent "effectiveness" in that the index employed uses "messages addressed to" rather than "messages actually received" as one of its components. When an index is derived by incorporating the latter component, there are no significant within-group effects. However, such a "true effectiveness" score necessarily contains experimenter effects (the independent variables) as well as subject behavior. Consequently, its meaning is difficult to interpret.

Discussion

One very simple finding of this study is that the possession of greater amounts of reward power results in more attempts by others to be rewarding whereas greater amounts of punishment power produces just the opposite result. Others tend to be less rewarding (and more punishing). This opposite direction of effect produced by reward and punishment power presents little problem for either behavior theory or the various versions of exchange theory. On the other hand, this outcome seems contrary to a naive, common sense psychology in that we tend to think of those with more substantial coercive or punitive resources as being *better* able to obtain what they want (in this case, rewards). The resolution of this "disconfirmation" of common sense may of course lie in the relatively nonpunitive nature of the punishment power in the present study. That is, a ticket with a minus on it may not be particularly aversive. A more likely alternative, however, is that the effectiveness of punishment power rests on its non-use. Indeed, when Thibaut and Kelley (1959: 119) suggest that those with high power use it sparingly, they may well be thinking predominantly of punitive or coercive power. In this experiment, high punishment (or reward) power did not exist merely as a threat, but rather, was reflected in actual differences in *use* of the two response alternatives.

A second and more important finding of this study is the differential potency or effectiveness of comparable manipulations of reward and punishment power. Though greater reward power facilitates one's attempts to induce others to be rewarding (whereas greater punishment power is a hindrance), the facilitating effect of a given increment in reward power is greater than the hindering effect of a comparable increment in punishment power.[7] This outcome does appear troublesome for exchange or equity theories in that in their present form they do not appear to possess any mechanism whereby this difference in the potency of the two modes of control could be derived. Of course, one could argue that the present data are inappropriate for those versions of exchange theory whose propositions are primarily "perceptual" (Thibaut and Kelley, 1959; Adams, 1965). Thus, for a more appropriate test of these theories, subjects would be asked to estimate the number of pluses and minuses they thought ("perceived") they had distributed and received. However, Homans' (1958) version of exchange theory is stated in more behavioral terms and consequently the present data should be relevant to it. Furthermore, there should be some relevance even for the more perceptual theories in that perceptual data would be highly (though not perfectly) correlated with behavioral data.

---

[7] In terms of the preceding discussion, it is important to point out that for the data of this experiment there is no easy way to determine just what it is in a given person's behavior that is being rewarded or punished by the "messages" that are transmitted. This is one of the consequences of an experiment in which subjects truly interact; the subject himself determines what is rewarded or punished. For precise knowledge of what it is that is being rewarded or punished (and the consequences of doing so) one would have to run a simulated interaction experiment in which the experimenter (and not the subjects) administers the rewards and/or punishments.

On the other hand, there are at least three ways in which behavior theory can handle the differential potency of reward and punishment power. (1) Our preferred interpretation postulates a dual cue and reinforcement function for rewards but simply a cue function for punishments. In other words, both rewards and punishments tend to elicit a matching response from the target person. This cue function results in no (or little) permanent modification in overall tendency to use either response. In addition, however, rewards also have a reinforcing function which does modify the operant probability of using rewarding responses.

(2) A second, somewhat related explanation postulates reinforcing functions for both reward and punishment power, but in order to account for the differential potency of the two, stipulates different critical thresholds (levels of π) as necessary for eliciting the reinforcement mechanism. In this case, reward reinforces whatever response preceded it whereas punishment reinforces other responses which didn't precede it. That is, punishment has a suppressing function. It suppresses whatever response preceded or elicited it (probably another person's punishing response) *by* reinforcing other responses. And in this experiment, the only other responses available were either (a) sending a reward or (b) simply not responding and responding instead to the other person. Thus, punishments might at least in part operate to reinforce the sending of rewards. However, while the consequence of different reinforcement thresholds for $\pi+$ (and $\pi-$ and/or the split reinforcing function of $\pi-$) would result in different slopes for $\pi+$ and $\pi-$, this mechanism could not by itself explain

the different *direction* of effect produced by increases in the two types of power. Thus, it would be necessary here too to add a cue function for punishment power which is stronger than the reinforcement function and would thereby generate increments in P− (and decrements in P+) when $\pi+$ is raised. The reinforcing effect of punishment power would simply act to reduce or somewhat minimize the cue function.

(3) A third possibility stresses a cueing function for reward and punishment power and ignores differential reinforcement functions. Indeed, stated in extreme form, reinforcement mechanisms need not be introduced at all. The greater potency of $\pi+$ as compared to $\pi-$ could be due to (a) an initial response bias toward using rewards (which may of course ultimately rest on reinforcement mechanisms operating in prior times or circustances) or (b) upon lower thresholds for noticing rewards as opposed to punishments. In choosing between these two, the response bias hypothesis is supported by early trial data of this and several of our prior studies. Contrariwise, our intuition as well as recent work in signal detection lead us to suspect that if anything exactly the opposite is true in respect to differential noticing of rewards and punishments— namely, since punishments typically have a lower frequency of occurrence against the background of events, they are *more* easily noticed.

These various "explanations" can only be sketched here due to limitations of space. Furthermore, their detailed application to the present data may not be as direct as we have implied. For instance, pluses may have still a third function. They may serve as negative reinforcers in that the receipt of a plus necessarily means the absence of a minus. (This potential property of pluses may be more easily detectable in a procedure which allowed subjects more than these two sole response alternatives). Likewise, it may be important to distinguish between the effects of nonresponding and neutral responding. Receiving no communication from a person on a particular trial may have a different effect than receiving a neutral communication from which both rewarding and punishing properties are absent.[8]

Besides testing the validity of the various explanatory mechanisms proposed above, a variety of other questions await answers from future studies. (1) Would different levels of "effectiveness" be obtained with instructional sets other than the individualistic competition induced in this study? Instructions designed to engage more competitive motives (intragroup competition) or more altruistic motives might interact quite differently with experimental manipulations of π or $\bar{\pi}$. (2) In the present experiment, subjects were unaware of their own power position within the structure. In real life one ordinarily knows one's position within the group. This is often even true when one enters a new group.

---

[8] It is also important to note that while the results for comparisons between-group and comparisons among individuals within groups are comparable in this study, it may be inappropriate to conclude that they necessarily reflect the same process. That is, it is both psychologically as well as logically possible that the effects of manipulations of $\bar{\pi}$ could invoke different mechanisms than manipulation of π. For instance, it is conceivable that the reinforcing function could work *comparatively* within groups, yet lead to no between-group differences among groups which differ markedly in $\bar{\pi}$.

One knows the amount of brass on one's own as well as everyone else's shoulders. One knows the titles in front of one's name or the valued resources that one can marshal to aid the group in attaining its goal. Perhaps prescience of one's position interacts with experimental manipulations of power to yield outcomes quite different from those obtained in this experiment. For instance, it is conceivable that higher levels of $\pi-$ would not be disadvantageous if everyone knew the group power structure. Then, it might be possible for those with high $\pi-$ to use it sparingly. (3) The interpretive limitations imposed by the availability of only two response alternatives (reward and punishment) has already been mentioned. In order to develop an index of the use of reward relative to receipts, a third response alternative is necessary. (4) Other focuses of interest are the effects of the amount of resources individuals possess. Experimentation on the effects of manipulating power via the magnitudes of feedback in addition to quality, via available ranges of feedback, or via other bases of power (e.g., expertise) would all be interesting.

REFERENCES

ADAMS, J. S., "Inequity in Social Exchange." Pp. 267–297 in L. Berkowitz (ed.), *Advances in Experimental Social Psychology.* New York: Academic Press, 1965.

BLAU, P. M., Exchange and Power in Social Life. New York: Wiley, 1964.

BUTLER, D. C. and N. MILLER, "Power to Reinforce as a Determinant of Communi-

cation." *Psychological Reports* 16 (June 1965): 705–709.

——, "Power to Reward and Punish in Social Interaction." *Journal of Experimental Social Psychology* 1 (November 1965): 311–322.

ESTES, W. K., "An Experimental Study of Punishment." *Psychological Monographs,* 57, #263, 1944.

FLAMENT, C. and E. APFELBAUM, "Elementary Processes of Communication and Structuration in a Small Group." *Journal of Experimental Social Psychology* 2(October 1966): 376–386.

FRENCH, J. R. and B. RAVEN, "The Bases of Social Power." in Cartwright, D. and A. Zander (eds.), *Group Dynamics.* New York: Row, Peterson, 1960.

GOULDNER, A. W., "The Norm of Reciprocity." *American Sociological Review* 25 (April 1960): 161–178.

HOMANS, G. C., "Social Behavior as Exchange." *American Journal of Sociology* 63 (May 1958): 597–606.

KELLEY, H. H., J. W. THIBAUT, R. RADLOFF, D. MUNDY, "The Development of Cooperation in the Minimal Social Situation." *Psychological Monographs* 76, #538, 1962.

MESSICK, D. M. and W. B. THORNGATE, "Relative Gain Maximization in Experimental Games." *Journal of Experimental Social Psychology* 3 (January 1967): 85–101.

MILLER, N. and D. BUTLER, "Social Power and Communication in Small Groups." *Behavioral Science.* 1968.

SKINNER, B. F., *Science and Human Behavior.* New York: Macmillan, 1953.

THIBAUT, J. W. and H. H. KELLEY, *The Social Psychology of Groups.* New York: Wiley, 1959.

WALKER, H. M. and J. LEV, *Statistical Inference.* New York: Holt, Rinehart and Winston, 1953.

APPROACHES TO AGGRESSION AS A SOCIAL BEHAVIOR[1]

Patricia Barchas

At a time when there is increasing agreement that the biology of an organism is both a determinant of and determined by the experiences of the organism, it seems appropriate to consider the general problem of biological correlates of social behaviors. A number of basic social processes may be rooted in biology, i.e., may be biologically part of the interacting repertoire of an organism. Examples of such processes are certain rank phenomena, dominance, deference, affiliation, as well as certain types of aggressive behavior. We will examine the relation of biological to social behaviors by focusing upon aggression, a phenomenon which though not a unitary concept has received enough attention for data and conceptual frameworks to have been developed. After presentation of conceptual approaches to aggression, we will present some correlates to aggression in animals as these may be related to aggression in man. Studies are cited for example and illustration rather than for complete coverage.

We will be considering aggression as the outcome of conflict which is interpersonal in nature, broadly following the definition of Carthy and Ebling, "An animal acts aggressively when it inflicts, attempts to inflict or threatens to inflict damage on another animal. The act is accompanied by recognizable behavioral symptoms and definable physiological changes." (Carthy & Ebling, 1964, p. 1). The aggressive act as it occurs in a social group is a dramatic and to some extent easily observable behavior in terms of frequency, duration and intensity. We are concerned with aggression which takes place in a social context, the minimum requirements being that there is an actor who commits the aggressive act and a recipient or target for the act.

There are several conceptual frameworks. They differ in part with reference to the aspects of aggression which are emphasized, in motivational or biological assumptions, in their predictive value, and in the directives for research suggested.

EVOLUTION

The first vantage point to be considered has great popular appeal and is broad enough to include many kinds of inquiry. It is that of evolution, in which man is viewed as having evolved from a similar biological basis as the Old World monkeys and apes, and as having evolved through

[1] Supported in part by ONR grant N00014-67-A-0112-0027 and PHS grants MH 13,259 and MH 16,632.

the pressures of selection a biology suitable for the hunting-gathering conditions under which evolution took place. In this view, one of the most important traits that evolved is the emotions of man: rage is an emotion and aggression is an outcome of that emotion. The approach to aggression through evolution is expressed by Hamburg and Washburn: "Man enhanced the biological base modified by the great development of the social brain and language. Aggression may be increased by early experience, play and rewards of the system. Individuals' aggressive actions are determined by biology and experience." (Hamburg, 1961, 1963).

In the context of evolution, then, man is seen as a biological organism whose range of behaviors is, in part, determined by his biology but is modifiable by experience. The argument suggests that there is in man a biologically inherent capacity for aggression presumably based in the "old" part of the brain (the limbic system). Modification by experience suggests that the "new" part of the brain, the "social brain" (the cortex) has influence over the emotional part (Hamburg, 1962, 1963), and that by experience (learning) this influence may be increased. The directives for research would seem to be to define specifically what the biological determinants of aggression are—in the brain or in the periphery—under what conditions they come into play, how modifiable they are by experience. Predictively, the evolutionist suggests that man will aggress but does not state under what conditions he will aggress or when the inherent capacity is loosed. Dr. David Hamburg (Hamburg, 1971) has suggested specific conditions which appear to raise the probability of aggression in free-ranging chimps and baboons, particularly in the presence of scarce resources.

The vantage point of evolution is attractive because it permits a wide range of speculation and interests. It is not, however, necessary to subscribe to the theory of evolution in order to pursue biological questions relating to aggression. Much work has been done by biologists who note the similarity of man and animals without attempting to explain that similarity. These workers use nonhuman organisms as a viable model with which to explore hypotheses. This approach is in some ways similar to work which uses computer simulation to study human cognition. Such an approach is essentially analogic and necessitates hypotheses which are specific enough to permit specification of critical properties which must be present in the model.

PSYCHOANALYTIC

A second vantage point which has also become part of the popular culture is the psychoanalytic. Here also aggression is considered to be an inherent, if mysterious, part of man's nature. There is posited a constant state, need or drive for aggressive activity. This has been termed an hydraulic model in which the need piles up and spills over into action (Berkowitz, 1962). Alternatively, one may visualize a bubble of gas rising to the surface of a liquid. The suggestion is that if it cannot get to the surface it will form with other bubbles of gas to eventually erupt. The expression of the aggressive urge is presumably mutable, through socialization and adequate resolution of developmental stages of growth. Any aggressive act is explained after the fact by referral to the need. The predictive value of the model is limited: one may predict that aggression will occur over the life span of an individual. The target of aggression, the conditions of aggression, the manner of aggression, and the intensity of aggression cannot be predicted in advance.[2,3] The directives of this model would be to find, presumably in the brain, the biological correlate(s) of the posited energy for aggressive activity and to our knowledge this has not been done.[4]

It should be noted that there is no evidence to support "catharsis," the idea of draining off aggressive energy. In fact, there is evidence that expression of aggression increases the probability that the organism will again express aggression.[5]

FRUSTRATION LEADS TO AGGRESSION

Still another vantage point comes from the Dollard-Miller hypothesis that frustra-

tion leads to aggression (Dollard et al., 1939). The essence of the argument is that, as an organism moves toward a goal it is likely to aggress if frustrated in obtaining that goal and will choose as its preferred target for aggression the frustrator, or will displace the aggression onto another object. This view locates aggression in the context of interaction with the environment given that the actor wants to move, or is moving, toward a goal. Anything that obstructs the path will cause frustration which is likely to be expressed as aggression toward the obstruction. If direct expression is prohibited, one may see displacement. In this model, conditions for aggression and target of aggression are broadly specified. Intensity of drive toward the goal is implied. Here we have a predictive model which can account for some, but not all, types of aggression. The motivational assumption centers around goal achievement. There is no particular biological assumption, although it would be consistent with the model to postulate that under conditions of frustration, there are biological changes which give rise to or accompany the aggressive act. In terms of biologically oriented research, the directives are to establish the physiological correlates to frustration and to aggression.

ETHOLOGY

Another vantage point comes from the work of the ethologists (Hinde, 1966;

---

[2] It should be noted that linked to the psychoanalytic view are such interesting ideas as identification with the aggressor and sublimation, which may have importance outside of the model described.

[3] It may be that gifted practitioners can use the analytic framework for predictive or therapeutic purposes. However, their ability to do so is not easily transferred to the less gifted.

[4] From this and similar untested models of aggression, one finds suggestions that sports and war may drain off aggressive energy and should be so utilized, and one may observe nursery schools in which children are encouraged to express aggression, under the hypothesis that it will otherwise be unresolved, etc.

[5] It may be that the term catharsis refers to two entities. In the analytic view catharsis "cleanses" the system of a self generating ag-

gressive energy. In experimental situations, catharsis is meant to "cleanse" the system of a readiness to aggress induced by frustration or other aversive stimuli. It is the latter condition that fails to decrease the probability of aggression in experimental settings.

Lorenz, 1963). This line of thinking suggests that, in lower animals at least, aggressive behavior comes as a specific response by the animal to particular stimuli or releasers in the environment, this being genetically laid down. The reaction is less if the animal is in low arousal condition and stronger if the animal is in a high arousal condition. The ethologists' approach underlines the necessity of paying attention to, at least with lower organisms, quite specific external cues as releasers of behavior. They argue, in terms of displacement, that if arousal is strong in an animal and if the specific external cue is present and if there is no avenue for direct expression of behavior, then it will spill over into a displacement activity. In this model, prediction of aggression is possible if (1) the arousal state of the animal is specified and (2) if salient releasers are specified. This model has inherent biological assumptions in that the biological conditions of low arousal or high arousal presumably could be specified. Directives for research from this model would be to specify the releasers for each organism, to specify the biological measure of arousal, and to differentiate the physiology of arousal from the physiology of aggression. The question here is whether there is a general arousal which may be, but not necessarily expressed by aggressive behavior, or whether there is a specific "aggressive" arousal which must be so expressed.

Berkowitz combines the frustration-leads-to-aggression model with the ethologist's approach, specifically setting these against the psychoanalytic model and finds that such a combination accounts for a great deal of the data with which he is concerned (Berkowitz, 1962). He argues that the psychoanalytic model, assuming a constant internal driving force, does not pay sufficient attention to the role of specified external stimuli. Viewing the frustration-leads-to-aggression hypothesis in light of the ethologist's findings, Berkowitz reinterprets frustration as deriving as much from the interruption of the behavioral sequence as from block-age of goal attainment. He broadens frustration to include any aversive stimuli. Berkowitz emphasizes learning and learning theory, thereby permitting himself to address process questions and to ask refined questions about the mutability of aggression. Though not explicitly suggested by the model, the idea of looking for biological measures of aggression is consistent with Berkowitz. He would be alert to differentiating not only arousal from aggression, but specific arousal physiology from (a) general arousal, and (b) learning.

SOCIAL LEARNING

Bandura's work on social learning suggests that any number of positive or negative stimuli can lead to increased arousal in the animal. Dependent upon what the individual has learned, and upon what he anticipates the consequence of his actions to be, the individual may emit behavior within his repertoire. In other words, both arousal and the behavior subsequent to arousal are socially induced. The behavioral repertoire of individuals is learned, and the emitted behavior is conditioned by the consequence anticipated. In Bandura's model, arousal is general. Biologists working with this model would be directed to find measures of arousal, and to check the hypothesis of general arousal against that of specific arousal.

Each of the above frameworks emphasizes the actor who aggresses, determinants of the aggression being located in long-term biological propensity and/or in short-term response to the environment. Learning may modify the response. The target of aggression is given only incidental attention. The effect of the group on the aggressor and of aggression on the group is immediately approachable with the ideas of Berkowitz and Bandura. It is our view that these conceptual framework are not mutually exclusive, but that some are more helpful than others as bases for asking answerable questions.

Stimulus Conditions

A question of interest which is raised by several of the frameworks for viewing aggression, is whether man is programmed to respond aggressively to certain conditions, to certain stimuli in the environment. Whereas the ethologists have found that in lower animals the stimuli may be very explicit (e.g., a shape), one would expect that in the higher mammals, such as the primates and humans which are noted for their greater plasticity, the conditions would be more general.

Hamburg, putting together a wealth of clinical observations on humans and field studies on baboons and chimpanzees, cites eight conditions under which he feels aggression is likely (Hamburg, 1971). We feel that in so doing he is perhaps delineating some of the basic stimuli which in the higher mammal elicit a propensity for aggression. The conditions Hamburg cites deal with the following areas: food; caring for an infant; acts of dominance; redisplacement of aggression, as when an animal has been aggressed against and

then aggresses against another in turn; failure of compliance to social cues; some oddity, physical or behavioral; dominance over time; and consort pairs. He states that the presence of scarce resources raises the probability of aggressive behavior. In addition to these, Hamburg recognizes certain developmental patterns in which aggression occurs, e.g., males in adolescence. These may be areas which cue aggression in the higher apes, man included. Several of the areas seem to be insufficient to cue aggression alone. For example, food must be present when the animal is hungry.

Two of Hamburg's conditions are supported by laboratory data on initiation of interaction in groups of three rhesus. Within each group, the animals were matched closely for age, sex, condition, weight, housing and time in captivity (Barchas, 1971). The data follows the first hour of interaction of these groups of feral animals. In terms of aggression the pattern is quite clear; over half of the aggressive acts occur within the first ten minutes of interaction, around the period where the status ordering or the dominance ordering is being worked out, and a third of the remaining acts of aggression occur at the end of the hour when food is produced, thus suggesting that at least two of Hamburg's areas hold up in a laboratory situation. A third area suggested by Hamburg is also supported by this data, for rating of the remaining acts of aggression in context permits the interpretation that most, if not all, were induced by either misapplication or misunderstanding of the cues, as when an animal approaches for affiliation.

Making the point that aggression is generally stimulus-bound, Kenneth Moyer

(Moyer, 1969) approaches the same question and suggests several classes of aggression on the basis of the stimulus characteristics which will evoke aggression. These are: predatory, intermale, fear-induced, irritable, territorial defense, maternal and instrumental. The difference between Moyer's classification of aggressive acts and Hamburg's may be viewed as the difference between a laboratory-based investigator and a clinical field worker. It is of interest to note the areas of overlap in these systems, as they may suggest non-situation based stimuli.

BIOCHEMICAL SYSTEM OF AROUSAL

There are biochemical systems of arousal which have been associated with aggression. These systems are adrenal steroid hormones, thyroid hormones and the adrenal catechol hormones (epinephrine, norepinephrine). Each has a different role in terms of the rapidity with which the systems are turned on and off and the different turnover rates which determine how long the system remains an active force within the organism. The biochemical systems and associated fighting behavior may apparently be influenced by such factors as the genetic strain of the animal, whether the animal has been housed in isolation or in groups of varying size, the socialization process, learning and drugs. It would appear that these biochemical systems are sensitive to any number of environmental experiences and may alter short- and long-term arousal (Barchas et al., 1971).

Stolk, Conner, Levine and Barchas (Stolk et al., 1970), using shock-induced aggression in a laboratory, have investigated the effects of drugs upon rats when they have been housed under different circumstances. (This is a situation in which aggression is induced by giving paired rats shocks to the feet.) Among other things, they found that brain norepinephrine (which may act as a transmitter between nerve cells in the brain) has a faster turnover in the isolated animals and that the isolated animal shows more irritability and more aggressive behavior than do animals housed normally or in crowded situations. They have also found that rubidium chloride, a drug known to effect brain norepinephrine by increasing its turnover, increases aggressive behavior in isolated animals. If indeed brain norepinephrine is related to the expression of aggression, it is of interest that the same laboratory has found strain differences, i.e., genetic differences, in the level of the enzymes which make norepinephrine.

In these studies using the shock induced aggression situation it has been found that there are marked differences in the neurochemical changes in the animals depending upon whether they are administered shocks to the feet in an isolated condition, or are given the same number of shocks in the presence of another animal, in which case they are able to fight. Interestingly, the fighting animals show less increase in the steroid stress hormones. The results taken together suggest that: (1) the social situation can markedly affect the neurochemistry of the brain, (2) there may be different effects at the time of fighting and a few hours later, and (3) the changes in neurochemistry may alter the likelihood of further expression of certain social behaviors. The need for further neurochemical investigation of aggressive behavior has been previously emphasized by J. Barchas (Barchas, 1967). It would be of interest to use conditions utilized by social psychologists in terms of biochemical effects.

Shock induced fighting may be analogous to the stimuli which elicits aggressive behavior in lower animals as described by the ethologists. It remains to be demonstrated whether there are similar changes in brain functioning when the animal is faced with "naturally occurring stimuli," and whether the changes are due to conditioning or learning itself rather than to fighting. Clearly, behavior affects the biochemistry of the brain. In this situation, several "behaviors" are occurring. If we are interested in aggression specifically, then we must distinguish the brain changes which are due to aggression from those which are due to learning and habituation.

ISOLATION, HOUSING, AND EARLY STIMULATION

A number of investigators have found that the isolated mouse is very aggressive. Bruce Welch (Welch, 1965) explains the aggressiveness in part by saying that the isolated animal is more responsive to *any* cue, is generally more irritable given *any* input, and therefore *any* behavior would likely be maximized subsequent to isolation. In line with Welch's studies, Bunney (1971) has found that DOPA (dihydroxyphenylalanine), a drug, increases aggressive tendencies and also increases manic behavior. Here we have additional evidence that increase of aggression, at least through artificial means, goes hand-in-hand with an increase in general excitability. James P. Henry (Henry et al., 1967) and his group have found, con-

sistently with Welch's data, that mice which were isolated early in life reacted to social stimuli with much more hypertension and with more fighting of a serious nature than did mice which receive social stimulation from birth. He uses the term habituation, saying that the mice were exposed to social stimulation from birth and were able to habituate to the stimuli.

There are conflicting data on the effect of housing on the aggressiveness of animals, Welch (Welch & Welch, 1965) having found that the isolated mouse, when placed in social context, was more aggressive than the grouped animal, and that the grouped animal was more aggressive than the animal which lived in an over-populated situation. Others, however, have found that the over-populated, dense living situation produces a high level of aggressivity. Christian and Davis (Christian & Davis, 1964) present data to this effect. Two factors may influence these findings. One is, of course, the strain of mouse used, which was different in the studies, for it is well known that strain differences can produce differences in many types of behavior. The second factor and the one of interest to us here, is the fact that Welch's animals were raised in a constant living situation which generally was not the case for the other studies. The physiological and behavioral data on early experiences would suggest that an animal which was raised in a small group and then later placed in an over-populated area would be expected to react differently than an animal which was raised in the over-populated area.

Clear evidence on the effect of early stimulation of mice pups on later reactions, both behaviorally and hormonally, is given in Levine's work (Levine, 1960, 1962). Using three groups of mice pups, rearing some with the mother, some in isolation, and some in isolation but being handled once a day, he observed the animals two years later, there having been no intervening manipulations or differences in housing. Levine found that the animal which was reared with a small amount of stimulation of handling once a day had a far greater repertoire of responses than did the animal which was not handled during that period. The animal reared in isolation tended to have an all-or-none response, as opposed to a moderated response of the animals which had had stimulation. The data is fairly clear that animals in isolation, raised there or placed there, have difficulty coping.

One might think of the hormone and neuroregulator (compounds which may act as transmitters between nerve cells) systems as being emotostats which are set, some in response to early experiences and others in response to more recent experiences. It may be that the emotostats equip the animal to react appropriately to given amounts of stimulation, such as that which he experiences early, and that stimulation which is either above or below the range of the emotostat cannot be easily handled by the animal. Saslow and Blackly (Saslow & Blackly, 1964) make a similar point, saying that the social situation inevitably leads to repetitive stimuli. Hence, if the symbolic experience is responsible for physiological response and, if by reason of early experience, habituation cannot occur, then when the organism is finally placed in a social situation it will receive an unending series of hypothalmic arousals whose severity is determined by its own interstate.

It would appear then that early experiences, at least if they are gross enough, can affect the way in which an animal reacts to his social environment. Whether early experiences bear a direct relation to aggression or whether the relation to aggression is through a general arousal system is unclear. It is clear that other general biological differences affect both arousal and aggression. Evidence for this comes from two sorts of research, one is strain differences and the other is sex differences within the same strain.

STRAIN DIFFERENCES

Working with dogs, Scott (Scott, 1958) found that when the puppies of an aggressive breed and a docile breed were raised under differing conditions, the strain differences could indeed be modified by the early experiences. For example, the aggressive pup which was raised with a docile mother, 'though less aggressive than the littermates who were raised with the docile mother, was more aggressive than the docile pups raised with the docile mother. It will be remembered that there are strain differences, at least in the mice, in the levels of the enzymes which make norepinephrine, a compound associated with aggressive arousal.

SEX DIFFERENCES

There is considerable evidence, women's lib to the contrary, that there are marked differences between the sexes with regard to aggressive behavior as well as other behaviors (Hamburg & Lunde, 1966). Experimental and field observations on Old World monkeys and great apes taken together suggest that the males do have an aggressive predisposition, presumably based on genetic factors mediated by hormonal effects on brain differentiation and muscle growth, which may be further developed through social learning. The young male (Harlow, 1962) has a greater proclivity for aggressive play and there are indications (DeVore, 1965; Jay, 1965) that young females show considerably greater interest in infants than do young males, and young females generally appear more motivated toward grooming behavior than do young males. Hamburg and Lunde (Hamburg & Lunde, 1966) raise the question whether such differences in infantile response patterns may be mediated by hormonal effects on brain during fetal life. Additional evidence along this line comes from experiments in which young animals are administered hormones of the opposite sex with behaviors following more closely the hormone than the apparent biology of the animal (Hamburg & Lunde, 1966). The young female who has been given male sex hormones, becomes more aggressive, among other changes in behavior.

Clearly, there are at least two ways of looking at correlations of level of hormones or other compounds and behavior. One way is to look at the concomitant fluctuation in the level of the hormone and the performance of a particular kind of behavior in a very immediate way; the other is the developmental correlation in which the presence of a hormone in adequate amounts during an early critical period may have consequences throughout the life-span, even when the hormone is no longer present or is present in much smaller quantity. Here again we have the implicit idea of an emotostat being set.

IMMEDIATE EXPERIENCES

What are some examples of the immediate experiences which result in an increase in aggressive tendencies, and which

also have been shown to vary biological compounds within the animal? As a first instance, we may take the reproductive cycle of the female during which there is hormonal changing of the body with potential resultant irritability which may emerge as aggression (Hamburg & Lunde, 1966). Another instance comes from the observations that groups of rhesus living in cities rather than in rural areas, or living in rural areas where either food or space is curtailed, exhibit more aggression within the group (Jay, 1965). This is compatible with the observation that when rhesus groups are subjected to various pressures—whether they be trapping, harassment, high instance of infectious disease, lack of food, or lack of space—they exhibit tension which is followed or accompanied by aggressive acts (Jay, 1965). Still another instance comes from the findings that animals and humans which have been sleep deprived exhibit irritability which in some cases may be interpreted as an increase in aggression as well (Morden et al., 1968).

Such data suggest that tension itself may lead to aggression. Perhaps the frustration leads to aggression hypothesis may be viewed as a special case of this idea wherein frustration of access to a goal object leads to tension which may lead to aggression. Also, perhaps some of the psychoanalytic material may be viewed as thwarted desires resulting in tension which may then be expressed as aggression. (It should be clear that both animals and humans develop quite different learned habits in different environments and some behaviors which are classified as aggressive may actually be habits.)

It would appear that aggression may follow any situation which is either stressful or arousing to an animal, and aggression per se may be one alternative for reaction to the situation. A balance or homeostasis approach would suggest that there is a range of arousal which animals find appropriate and that they will react to stress or to arousing situations so as to maintain their appropriate range. Mason (Mason, 1962) suggests that there is data which support the hypothesis that infant clinging has the function of reducing stress within the infant. One might view aggression, amongst other behaviors, as acting to reduce the stress within an organism. Given social learning and socialization one might suggest that the organism learns to meet certain types of stress with certain types of aggression.[6] In a general state of stress or arousal, the animal could well respond to specific cues in the environment as determinants of behavior. For example, Berkowitz has shown that for humans the presence of a culturally defined object, such as a gun, increases the probability of aggression (Berkowitz, 1962).

STATUS CONSIDERATIONS

Traditionally it has been assumed that one function of dominance and deference relationships or the status ordering in general is to control aggression. Certainly, status relationships often appear to have this effect.[7] In higher monkeys and apes and in humans, the status ordering in newly formed groups emerges rapidly with differentiation being quickly established, that differentiation being stable for the duration of the interaction (Barchas, 1971). This is also true when the animals or humans are matched as closely as possible in terms of age and sex, weight and condition (for the animals), and educational level, race and background (for the humans). Differentiation occurs within the first fifteen minutes of interaction. Such matching minimizes the observable effect following from the interpretation that dominance is assigned solely according to characteristics of the animals. Further when animals were regrouped, so that three dominant animals, three second ranking, and three least dominant were together, they showed the same pattern (Barchas, 1971).

Welch has found gross physiological differences in mice from ongoing groups according to whether they are dominant or subordinate (Welch & Welch, 1966). The physiology is grossly different enough for the investigators to determine on basis of the physiology in double blind experiments whether the animal was dominant or whether the animal was subordinate.

---

[6] For example, Isaac Barchas (1971) suggests that the most common reason the people fighting is fear of being hurt.

[7] There are at least two types of relations which seem to enter into making up a status relationship in a group: one of these is the dominance relationship in which the dominant animal has priority of access to desired objects;

the other is the deference relationship in which the deferring animal gives priority to another animal. These are frequently seen in a group as reciprocal in which the dominant animal will receive submissive gestures from the subordinate animal. In general, one may conceive of dominance and deference as relationships as existing between two animals with the entire group being ranked in terms of dominance relationships. It is not clear and, in fact, there is evidence to the contrary that dominance and deference are always reciprocal, meaning that the most dominant animal is not necessarily the least deferent animal and vice versa.

Bach and Bogdinoff (Bach & Bogdinoff, 1964) in their paper on plasma lipid responses to leadership, conformity and deviation, make points which are consistent with Welch's ideas. Using peripheral measures, they found that it was "well established that specific characteristics of group interaction do modify differentially the physiological responses of our subjects," and again even within the confines of the laboratory, sociological forces have turned out to be significant determinants of the process of lipid mobilization. It would appear that the relationship of sociological forces and biology are bidirectional.

Aggressions occur relatively frequently between members of primate groups who hold adjacent positions in the status hierarchy (Carpenter, 1965). It could be argued that there is not enough differentiation in terms of status for expectations to clearly govern interaction and that the possibility of misconstruing approach responses is magnified. It is also true that there may simply be more interaction amongst members of a group who hold adjacent positions.

CHANGES IN STATUS ORDERINGS

Observations have been made of groups in which the high status animal is removed. When the leader is removed sequentially, the group becomes unstable and one may observe higher instances of aggression (Carpenter, 1965).

Zitrin (Zitrin, personal communication), in an unpublished study performed 30 years ago, was interested in the pecking hierarchy of chickens, which is known to be linear and transitive. In an effort to discover something of the characteristics

which made the most dominant chicken dominant, he removed the dominant bird and disguised it by giving it different marks on its face, thus setting up a situation in which he could distinguish whether it was the behavior of the bird itself or the reaction of the other members which caused the dominance. The dominant bird retained its usual stance, behaviors, etc. and presumably did not know that it was disguised. However, in its disguised state, the other birds attacked it as a newcomer despite its efforts to maintain dominance and it descended in the dominance hierarchy. To my knowledge, this experiment has not been done with any higher animals but certainly supports the idea that the position of high status is at least as much a matter of reaction of those lower in the hierarchy as the actions of the dominant bird. Status control of aggression, then, is dependent upon lower, as well as higher ranking individuals.

Another example of change in status comes from Marsden (Marsden, 1968). Following up Cofford and Sades' work which showed that the social rank of mothers may strongly influence the rank of their offspring, he explored the question of whether changes in social rank amongst mothers in a small confined group of rhesus resulted in changes in patterns of agonistic behavior in their offspring. The findings were, in general, that the hierarchy of the offspring directly reflected the rise or fall of the ranks of the mother and that the agonistic responses of the infant coincided with that of the mother.

Masserman, Wecken and Wolf (Masserman et al., 1968) studying social relationships and aggression in rhesus monkeys (18 young adult rhesus monkeys) found that the presence of a familiar cagemate raised an animal's dominance with respect to strangers and that in groups of unfamiliar animals, submissives, particularly females, gained status by enlisting the aid of dominant others. They found that aggression was more frequent and of longer duration in group trials than among pairs and attributed under one situation an increase in aggression to a smaller test area. Space has repeatedly been found to be important in frequency of aggression.

Whether changes in status, longer or short term, occasion physiological changes has not been determined, but would seem plausible on the basis of other evidence we have discussed.

SUMMARY

The material discussed suggests that there is a strong interaction between social environment and biology. It would seem that the social environment may affect both the long and short term biology of animals, and that biology becomes a determinant of the range of actions and reactions the animal may have in further environmental encounters.

A question central to most approaches to aggression revolves about the inner state of the organism, the readiness of the organism to aggress. This may be a general or specific arousal state: one or the other is required by each approach. In some cases, readiness to aggress is self-generating and in others depends upon perception of external stimuli. We have suggested a system of "emotostats" in which early experience sets range of reaction and later experience sets specific reaction to stimuli. It seems clear that emitted behavior depends on both external and internal stimuli, and that processing of stimulation is in part biologically determined.

REFERENCES

BARCHAS, ISAAC. Personal communication, 1971.

BARCHAS, J., STOLK, J., CIARANELLO, R., and HAMBURG, D., "Neuroregulatory Agents and Psychological Assessment," in *Psychological Assessment* Vol. 2, P. McReynolds (editor). Palo Alto, California: Science and Behavior Books, 1971 in press.

BARCHAS, J. "Comments on Biogenic Amines," in *Regulation of Behavior in Aggression and Defense*, C. Clements and D. Lindsly (editors). California: University of California Press, 1967.

BARCHAS, PATRICIA. "Emergence of Dominance and Deference Structures in Rhesus." Unpublished dissertation, Stanford University, 1971.

BERKOWITZ, L. *Aggression: A Social Psychological Analysis*. New York: McGraw-Hill, 1962.

BOGDONOFF, M., KLEIN, R., BACK, K., NICHOLS, C., TROYER, W., and HOOD, T. "Effect of Group Relationship and the Role of Leadership Upon Lipid Mobilization," *Psychosom. Med., 26*: 710–719 (1964).

BUNNEY, W. E. JR., BRODIE, H. K. H., MURPHY, D. L., and GOODWIN, F. K. "Studies of alpha-methyl-para-tyrosine, L-dopa, and L-tryptophan in Depression and Mania," *Amer. J. Psychiat. 127*: 872–881 (1971).

CARPENTER, C. R. *Naturalistic Behavior of Nonhuman Primates*. Pennsylvania: Pennsylvania State University Press, 1965.

CARTHY, J. D., and EBLING, F. J. *The Natural History of Aggression*. New York: Academic Press, 1964.

CHRISTIAN, J. J., and DAVIS, D. E. "Endocrines, Behavior and Population," *Science 146*: 1550–1560 (1964).

DAVIS, DAVID E. "The Physiological Analysis of Aggressive Behavior," in *Social Behavior and Organization Among Vertebrates*, W. Etkin (editor). Chicago: University of Chicago Press, 1964.

DEVORE, I. (editor). *Primate Behavior*. New York: Holt, Rinehart, & Winston, 1965.

DOLLARD, J., MILLER, N., DOOB, K., MOWRER, O., and SEARS, R. *Frustration and Aggression*. New Haven: Yale University Press, 1939.

HALL, K. R. L. "Aggression in Monkey and Ape Societies," in *Primates: Studies in Adaptation Variability*, Phyllis C. Jay (editor). New York: Holt, Rinehart, & Winston, 1968.

HAMBURG, D. "Relevance of Recent Evolutionary Changes to Human Stress Biology," in *Social Life of Early Man*, S. Washburn (editor). New York: Wenner-Grend Foundation for Anthropological Research, 1961.

HAMBURG, DAVID A. "Recent Advances in Biological Sciences Pertinent to the Study of Human Behavior," in *Science and Psychoanalysis*, Vol. V, J. H. Masserman (editor). New York: Grune and Stratton, Inc., 1962, pp. 37–53.

HAMBURG, D. "Emotions in Perspective of Human Evolution," in *Expression of the Emotions in Man*, Peter Kuafb (editor). New York: International Universities Press, 1963.

HAMBURG, DAVID A. "Psychobiological Studies of Aggressive Behavior," *Nature, 230*: 19–23 (1971).

HAMBURG, DAVID A., and LUNDE, DONALD. "Sex Hormones in Development of Sex Differences in Human Behavior," in *Development of Sex Differences*, E. Maccoby (editor). Stanford, California: Stanford University Press, 1966, pp. 1–24.

HARLOW, H. "The Heterosexual Affectional System in Monkeys," *Amer. Psychol., 17*: 1 (1962).

HENRY, JAMES P., MEEHAN, JOHN P., and STEPHENS, PATRICIA M. "The Use of Psychosocial Stimuli to Induce Prolonged Systolic Hypertension in Mice," *Psychosom. Med., 29*: 408–432, 1967.

HINDE, ROBERT. *Animal Behavior: A Synthesis of Ethology and Comparative Psychology*. New York: McGraw-Hill, 1966, pp. 270–290.

JAY, P. "Field Studies," in *Behavior of Nonhuman Primates, Modern Research Finds*, A. Schrier, H. Harlow, and F. Stottnitz (editors). New York: Academic Press, 1965, pp. 525–591.

LEVINE, S. "Stimulation in Infancy," *Sci. Amer., 202*: 81–86, 1960.

LEVINE, S. "The Psychophysiological Effect of Early Stimulation," in *Roots of Behavior*, E. L. Bliss (editor). New York: Hoeber Medical Division, 1961.

LORENZ, KONRAD. *On Aggression*. New York: Harcourt, Brace & World, Inc., 1963.

MASON, W. A. "Socially Mediated Reduction in Emotional Response of Young Rhesus Monkeys," *J. Abnom. Soc. Psychol., 60*: 100–104, 1960.

MASSERMAN, J. H., WECHKIN, S., and WOOLF, M. "Social Relationships and Aggression in Rhesus Monkeys," *Arch. Gen. Psychiat., 18*: 210–213, 1968.

MARSDEN, H. M. "Agonistic Behavior of Young Rhesus Monkeys After Changes Induced in Social Length with Their Mothers," *Anim. Behav., 16*: 38–44, 1968.

MORDEN, B., CONNOR, R., MITCHELL, G., DEMENT, W., and LEVINE, S. "Effects of Rapid-Eye-Movement (REM) Sleep Deprivation on Shock Induced Fighting," *J. Physiol. Behav., 3*: 425–432, 1968.

MOYER, K. E. "Kinds of Aggression and Their Physiological Basis," *Commun. in Behav. Biol., Part A, 2*: 65–87, 1968.

SASLOW, G., and BLACKLY, P. H. "Introduction. In Timberline Conference on Psychophysiologic Aspects of Cardiovascular Disease," *Psychosom. Med., 26*: 409, 1964.

SCHACTER, S., and SINGER, J. E. "Cognitive, Social, and Physiological Determinants of Emotional State," *Psychol. Rev., 69*: 379–397, 1962.

SCOTT, J. P. Aggression Chicago: University of Chicago Press, 1958.

SCOTT, J. P. "Critical Periods in the Development of Social Behavior in Puppies," *Psychosom. Med., 20*: 42–54, 1958.

SCOTT, J. P. "The Effects of Early Experience on Social Behavior and Organization," in *Social Behavior and Organization Among Vertebrates*, William Ethin (editor). Chicago: University of Chicago Press, 1964.

STOLK, J., CONNER, R., LEVINE, S., and BARCHAS, J. "Brain Catecholamine Metabolic and Shock-Induced Fighting Behavior in Rats: Differential Effects of Shock and Fighting on the Neurochemical Response to a Common Stimulus." In preparation.

WASHBURN, S., and HOWELL, F. "Human Evolution and Culture," in *The Evolution of Man*, S. Lax (editor). Chicago: University of Chicago Press, 1960, pp. 33–56.

WELCH, B. L. "A Psychophysiological Response to the Mean Level of Environmental Stimulation: A Theory of Environmental Integration," in *Medical Aspects of Stress in the Military Climate*, D. McK. Rioch (editor). Washington, D.C.: U.S. Government Printing Office, 1965, pp. 778–814.

WELCH, B. L., and WELCH, A. S. "Effect of Grouping on the Level of Brain Norepinephrine in White Swiss Mice," *Life Sci., 4*: 1011, 1965.

WELCH, B. L., and WELCH, A. S. "Graded Effects of Social Stimulation Upon d-amphetamine Toxicity, Aggressiveness and Heart and Adrenal Weight," *J. Pharmacol. Exp. Ther., 151*: 331, 1966.

ZIRTRIN, ARTHUR. *Personal communication*, 1970.

THE EFFECTIVENESS OF PACIFICIST STRATEGIES IN BARGAINING GAMES*

Gerald H. Shure, Robert J. Meeker, and Earle A. Hansford

You begin with the relations between might and right, and this is assuredly the proper starting point for our inquiry. But, for the term "might," I would substitute a tougher and more telling word: "violence." In right and violence, we have today an obvious antinomy.

* Gerald H. Shure, Robert J. Meeker, and Earle A. Hansford, "The Effectiveness of Pacificist Strategies in Bargaining Games," *Journal of Conflict Resolution*, 9, No. 1 (1965), 106–17. Copyright 1965 by the University of Michigan. Reprinted by permission.

This quotation from Sigmund Freud's essay, "Why War?" points to the heart of the puzzling contradiction between our assertion of ethical principles, which repudiate violence, and the basis on which they too frequently rest—warfare, threats, and hostilities. To the pacifist, the inherent conflict and moral bankruptcy that is involved in using these means to promote justice lead not only to our current international deadlock but to a profound ethical dilemma. He believes we cannot repudiate violence as immoral and at the same time resort to it without violating our basic psychological integrity. To avoid such corruption he eschews the use of any form of violence, harmful coercion, or threats of these.

We shall not argue with the social idealism or morality reflected in the nonviolent approach, but rather shall direct ourselves to the task of identifying some of the essential features of these alternatives to violence and exploring the extent and conditions of their effectiveness. As Janis and Katz (1959) have shown, these approaches, largely based upon ethical principles, contain a rich matrix of hypotheses about the constructive forces in man and society, hypotheses that are worthy of investigation and that have been relatively unexplored by the social scientist. There are, of course, significant differences among such movements as passive resistance, nonresistance, nonviolent direct action, satyagraha, and others, which are all generally classified as nonviolence movements. We shall not attempt to review or catalogue these differences. An excellent major step toward such an undertaking has already been made by Gene Sharp (1959). In our series of studies we shall ignore many of the qualifications and distinctions which characterize the real-life versions of these movements, and we shall not attempt to distinguish conceptually between the uses of force and resistance that constitute instances of violence or nonviolence. These are major issues that require study and analysis, but we shall sidestep them to pursue our more limited aims.

In an earlier series of experiments (Meeker, Shure, and Moore, 1964; Shure, Meeker, and Moore, 1963), we investigated the effects of providing bargainers with equivalent threat capabilities. A series of hypotheses was tested that concerned threat availability and psychological factors in conflict escalation. Among other results, we found that the pairing of a cautious, well-intentioned bargainer with an aggressive bargainer led to greater loss and disruption of negotiations than occurred between pairs of equally belligerent bargainers. The current series of studies was initiated in an attempt to identify those features of conciliatory bargaining that prove to be helpful or detrimental to the realization of cooperative bargaining outcomes, and to specify the range of circumstances that influence these features.

In an initial conceptual analysis three types of conciliatory bargainers were identified and selected for further study: the ethically motivated cooperator, the irresolute or timid cooperator, and the resolute or strategic cooperator. This paper reports on a pacifist version of the ethically motivated cooperator. We recognize that our use of the term pacifist does not coincide with common usage, but we retain it because it does have the advantage of familiarity and affords us a simple name for referring to the Ss (subjects) in our study who, among other beliefs, reject violence as a means for resolving issues. As will soon become apparent, the pacifist S lives up to his namesake rather better than many of his counterparts outside the laboratory.

This paper, then, will report on the measured effectiveness of pacifist bargaining strategies as studied under the controlled conditions of laboratory experimentation. On the face of it, this proposition has an untoward sound. Pacifism doesn't seem to belong in a laboratory and the mere prospect of its being there deserves some preliminary comment.

In one respect the whole enterprise seems profane. The emphasis on "measured effects" suggests that a basically moral concept is somehow being subjected to a test solely on the basis of its practical effectiveness. We recognize that practical effectiveness is not the sole criterion, and, for many, not even the essential criterion by which pacifism should be judged, but we point out that it is seldom, if ever, totally irrelevant as a consideration. Indeed, pacifists are as convinced of the ultimate efficacy of their approach as of its moral correctness.

Granting that we should study the problem, the restrictive atmosphere of a laboratory hardly seems like an appropriate or even an adequate setting for a demonstration of pacifism. The main advantage, as with any laboratory study, is control. In the case of pacifist behavior this assumes added importance. Outside the laboratory there is virtually no opportunity to gather systematic behavioral evidence on the effectiveness of pacifist strategies. This is not necessarily for want of pacifists. There are, to be sure, an increasing number of people who advocate nonviolent means of social and political action; there are even some who practice what they advocate. The difficulty is in measuring their effectiveness. Pacific methods as practiced are seldom pure in form. It is seldom that an individual pacifist or a pacifist group is solely responsible for setting a given social or political policy. It is therefore difficult to say how much belongs to Martin Luther King and how much to Malcolm X, how much to the march on Washington and how much to the Cambridge riots. A mixture of nonviolence and threat may be effective, but it is not pacifism.

As with most experimental studies, there are also the obvious limitations. To transport the phenomenon from the street into the laboratory one must abstract, compress, and simplify until one reaches some satisfactory compromise between a fully representative situation and a manageable one. In the present case, the situation is completely wrested from the larger questions and rich complexities of international and national politics to the complex simplicities of an interpersonal bargaining situation. The lack of pressure from the larger social scene, frequently a critical factor in the pacifist's appeal, and the vagueness of the appropriate institutional norms are the two most general and obvious limitations of our laboratory situation. These are limitations of some importance and must be duly noted in qualifying our results.

Since pacifism has never, to our knowledge, been placed in the laboratory before, and since our particular representation of it is of considerable importance in interpreting the results, we should like to describe our study in some detail. Let's turn to the immediate problem of providing a conflict situation within which the pacifist's response may be distinguished. There can be conflict situations in which no singularly pacifist response can be made. In fact, of all the conflict situations generated by bargaining theories and studies of bargaining behavior, few, if any, afford an opportunity for a uniquely pacifist response. How, then, do we create a confrontation between a pacifist and an intractable adversary in our experimental situation?

PROCEDURE

In our experimental situation, *S*s are told that they are going to perform as operators in a communication system (see

Figure 1). Their task is to transmit messages. At the beginning of each work period, Ss are given a five-unit message to transmit. Transmission of a message can be accomplished only by inserting the message unit, letter by letter, into a communication channel. Only completely inserted messages are transmitted.

Each S is informed that he is assigned to a communication channel that will also be used by one other S. This channel, common to a pair of Ss, has a total storage capacity of six units (message units are stored in the channel until all five units are inserted into the channel). Upon successful insertion of the fifth unit, the complete message is transmitted and the channel storage is emptied of the transmitted units. It then becomes available for the other operator to transmit his message. However, the six-unit channel storage limitation prevents concurrent transmission of messages by both Ss. Only one S can transmit first.

The Ss perform their task during work periods made up of 15 opportunities for joint action (called "turns"). During each turn, an S chooses from one of two action alternatives: inserting a letter unit into channel storage or withdrawing a letter unit from channel storage. This latter action also permits the S to pass or take no action if he has not already inserted. Thus an S can successfully insert a complete message into the channel in five turns if the spaces in the channel are not already occupied. To do so requires that the other S not try to transmit simultaneously but wait for the first S to complete his transmission.

If both attempt to do so—whenever their insertions exceed the channel capacity of six units—an "overload" results. This is a costly situation, since the S is charged operating costs for each of the turns that is expended until his message is transmitted. Thus it is to the S's advantage to transmit his message first and with as little overload trouble as possible. In this feature lies the source of potential conflict and cooperation. Since each S temporarily needs exclusive use of five of the six channel units to transmit his message, the Ss have to work out an arrangement for effective channel utilization. In the event that neither operator is willing to relinquish use of the channel temporarily to allow the other to go first, a deadlock will occur; under such a state of mutual interference, turns are wastefully expended and both operators suffer losses. Under these conditions, three relationship patterns may emerge: dominance–submission, in which one operator continually uses the channel first and the other transmits second; sharing, in which the operators adopt an alternating pattern of transmitting first and second from one period of operation to the next; or continued mutual interference.

THE ESSENTIAL FEATURES OF THE TACIT BARGAINING SITUATION

This basic situation is one which we have used in other bargaining research. It is interpersonal, repetitive, and capable of generating conflict and cooperation. It can also be a source of great involvement to the Ss because successful transmission is rewarded by actual monetary payment. For all that, this type of situation is not yet sufficient for a well-defined pacifist–adversary confrontation. In order to achieve this, we need to incorporate the following additional features: (1) the means of bargaining control must involve the availability of an ethically questionable means, preferably physical violence; (2) we need

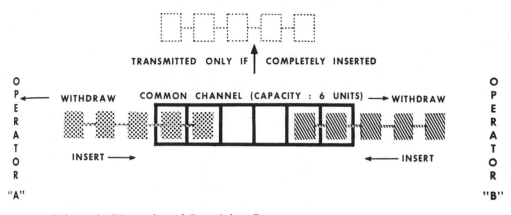

Fig. 1. Schematic Illustration of Bargaining Game.

aggressive bargainers who will use this means to gain a bargaining advantage; (3) this advantage should be incompatible with the *prima facie* claims for a fair share by the pacifist; (4) the situation should be so contrived that, if the pacifist employs resistance, the aggressor can achieve his ends only by using means that cause physical harm; and finally, (5) we need a threatening or hostile action that is available to the pacifist but that he refuses to employ even though his adversary uses means that cause him physical pain.

We translated these requirements into the conditions of our laboratory situation by modifying its rules and moves as follows. In addition to earning more money, the operator who transmits his message first in the current operating period acquires an additional power move, which he may employ in the subsequent work period. This move, called a JOLT BACK action, enables him to override the other operator. In effect, the possessor who employs his JOLT BACK can push back the other operator's inserted units and thereby guarantee himself first transmission. Repeated use of this move enables one bargainer to perpetuate his domination as long as he is willing to do so. It is important to note that this power move is not

initially available but is acquired by one bargainer or the other *within* the bargaining relationship, and that the initial acquisition of the move can only occur with the tacit consent of the other bargainer.

Introduction of this power move greatly increases the role that trust plays in initiating a cooperative resolution. To let the other S go first is essentially to hand over control of one's future fate to him with the adverse possibility that he may never hand it back. Great as this risk may be, the alternative is a mutually dysfunctional deadlock, since someone must go first on each work period or neither can earn anything.

While some of our Ss might identify the continued use of the JOLT BACK action as an unwarranted exercise of power, others might see it as a necessary act in the face of the unmeasurable risk associated with giving it up. In either case, we also wished the move to carry with it the onus of unfairness of means—both as a potential source of moral concern for the user and as a basis for rejection of its use as an immoral and violent act by our pacifist. We tried to achieve this by pairing the use of the JOLT BACK action with the administration of a painful electric shock to the other S. With this modification and the resistance of our pacifist, the self-per-petuating use of force by the JOLT BACK action requires the user to shock the other operator repeatedly if his domination is contested. A sample shock was adminis-tered to each S by the experimenter to demonstrate the effect of the JOLT BACK action.

Given this conflict situation, modified by the introduction of a move which af-fords a sustained power advantage to the S willing to inflict physical pain, we felt we had now provided for a meaningful pacifist response. Let us follow our play-ers through a few hypothetical work peri-ods. In the first period the pacifist makes a cooperative gesture by letting the other operator go first. By taking this initiative, he demonstrates he is acting not out of weakness but rather in a spirit of coopera-tion and trust. In the next work period the pacifist, in keeping with a claim to a "fair" division of earnings, will now wish to take his turn transmitting first. However, his adversary now has the means of control-ling the next encounter. Assuming that he plans to exploit his power advantage, he will, if necessary, use his JOLT BACK action to perpetuate his domination. What does our pacifist do? He can avoid being shocked by waiting for the dominator to transmit first. Instead, the pacifist de-monstrates his resistance by entering units into the channel, and standing in the way of the dominator. By presenting himself in this way, period after period if neces-sary, the pacifist forces the dominator to use his JOLT BACK action if he wishes to maintain his position. For the pacifist there is no difference in monetary costs between standing in the path and waiting on the sidelines; the difference is simply and solely in terms of forcing the adver-

sary to employ violence and through this, presumably, to recognize the pacifist's claim to a fair share of the payoff.

Through this act of passive resistance, the pacifist obliges the other operator to do something unethical and dramatically symbolizes that domination is wrong. While a change of status cannot be wrested from the possessor of the JOLT BACK, through this behavior or any other available action, the pacifist is provided with one additional response which en-hances the clarity of his commitment to nonviolence. The action simply provides an opportunity for each player to shock the other side. While this shock action does not effect the position of either bar-gainer in the channel, it does afford a means of threat or retaliation for the operator who otherwise has no direct way to influence the dominating operator. The pacifist, of course, does not shock or threaten to shock the other operator and thus further conveys his commitment to nonviolence.

THE SIMULATED PACIFIST AND THE SUBJECT UNDER PRESSURE

This then is our laboratory bargaining situation. Next, of course, we need to bring our pacifists and aggressors into our situation for a confrontation. As one might guess, even among the American college sophomore species, that self-replenishing reservoir of Ss for psychological experi-ments, pure forms of the subspecies *homo pacifist* are hard to come by. We have settled instead for a programmed pacifist, who behaves just as we have indicated. By simulating the performance of one member, we also avoid the obscuring ef-fects of the unique patterns of interaction that evolve between two live players. As a result, the data obtained permit more adequate comparison and summarization at intermediate and critical stages of the experiment.

With each incoming S our simulated pacifist makes an initial demonstration of good faith by letting the other man go first; he always makes the claim that alternation is fair; if he meets an aggressor, he invariably stands in the way to force the use of violence until his claim is responded to; and finally, he himself never resorts to retaliation with electric shock. To face this simulated pacifist, we dip into the pool of college freshmen and sophomores for our real Ss. Now it is obvious that, even if the college student is not typically a pacifist, neither is he overwhelmingly an aggressive dominator. To encourage as many as possible to adopt this role, each S is placed on a three-man team; the other team members are programmed confederates who are presumably performing other essential team tasks and are to share equally in the money that the S earns as operator and representative of his team in confronting the other team operator. Before the first trial, and after the second and fourth trials, these "teammates" send messages to the S to persuade him to adopt a dominating strategy. The team is also given an opportunity to choose their payoff level for the game by a majority vote. The teammates invariably vote for a payoff favoring a dominating strategy in perference to one more favorable to cooperation. All of the incoming Ss receive these same sets of pressures encouraging the adoption of a dominating orientation. The S, of course, is still free to do whatever he decides during the task itself and the teammates cannot interfere with his decisions.

The experiments described are carried out in the System Development Corporation research laboratory, using the Philco 2000 computer and computer-tied TV consoles and associated switch-insertion facilities. Twenty-four Ss are concurrently paired against the simulated pacifist. Ss send messages (moves, bids, threats, offers) to their paired opponents by making switch insertions. These are processed by the computer and then the results are displayed on the receiver's TV console. Computer programs assist in umpiring moves, providing displays of game-relevant information, and recording all moves, messages, and times. We also have our computer perform as 24 standardized, yet flexible, interviewers. Between game messages and moves, computer-generated questions based on the Ss' particular responses interrogate the players to elicit amplifying subjective information on the bases of their actions, their current intentions and expectations, their perception of the opponent, etc. As already noted, the computer is also programmed to assume the roles of the S's two teammates as well as the pacifist's role. By simulating the pacifist's behavior, we achieve a rigorously controlled representation of this bargaining style in the context of flexibility of detailed behavior.

Results

Let us turn now to some of our results. One of the first questions we asked was what our Ss planned to do before beginning their first encounter with their pacifist adversary or their own teammates— before having an opportunity to interact with anyone. Recall that a cooperative move involves serious risk of loss of bar-

gaining power and that a domination attempt may initiate a stalemate of mutual
losses and exchanges of electric shock. Of
the 143 Ss, slightly more than half (75)
indicated that they planned to dominate
from the outset; two Ss planned to settle
for less than half, and the remaining 66
Ss planned to try to share the profits
equally. However, following the first four
trials (including the period of pressure
from other team members toward domination and the initial exposure to the
pacifist's behavior), 54 of the 68 Ss who
planned to cooperate had changed to a
strategy of dominant behavior, and four
who planned to dominate were now co-
operating. Over this period, the shift away
from cooperation was significantly greater
than the shift toward it. Thus, urged on
by their teammates, about four-fifths of
the Ss who planned to cooperate had
changed to dominating behavior in which
they knowingly shocked our resisting pacifist at least twice each trial. As meager
consolation to those who are about to
despair over our students' basic humanity,
18 of our Ss (about one-eighth) refused
to employ the shock in any of the work
periods.

What happened to the remaining 125
dominators? How effective was the pacifist's appeal in converting them? By experiment's end, 40 additional Ss had
adopted an alternating pattern; the other
85, approximately two-thirds, continued to
dominate and shock. Considering that approximately 48 percent of our total number of Ss began with plans to cooperate
and that we ended up with only 39 percent
cooperating, the overall effectiveness of the
pacifist's strategies cannot be considered
impressive. Taken at face value, it would
even appear that many potential recruits
to cooperation may have been *lost* rather
than *gained*.

WHY WAS THE PACIFIST'S STRATEGY RELATIVELY INEFFECTIVE?

While of considerable interest, these
summary findings, by themselves, tell us
little about the situational factors and psychological processes associated with player
intractability or conversion to a cooperative stance. We should like to attempt to
understand more completely why our pacifist did not persuade two-thirds of the Ss.

To help structure our search for answers, let us identify some of the tactics of
persuasion employed by our pacifist and,
by doing so, perhaps we can better isolate
those failures of strategy that limited his
success. The first thing the pacifist must
establish is that the situation is not a simple contest of wills and that some outcomes are inherently unjust and/or rest
upon immoral means. To make this point,
the pacifist should force the recognition on
the part of the adversary that by dominating he is maintaining an unfair advantage
and is doing so by immoral means. The
pacifist should also establish that his cooperative behavior is not due to personal
submissiveness, weakness, or cowardice—
without this, the adversary is again left
free to define the situation as a simple
contest of wills in which he is, flatteringly
enough, superior. And finally, to assuage
any fears of recrimination and suspicions
of duplicity, the pacifist should give his
adversary every reassurance and guarantee
possible. In summary, the pacifist's tactics
aim to induce in his adversary a recognition of the unfairness of his claims and the
immorality of his means, to establish his
own personal resolve, and to give reassurance that he has acted and will act in
good faith.

While the pacifist's behavior in the task
is intended to communicate these points,
a number of experimental manipulations

were employed to increase the clarity with which each of them would be represented. Let us see, then, to what extent the pacifist succeeds in satisfying these conditions for persuading his adversary through his actions and in the context of additional experimental manipulations.

A factor that might be expected to exert a considerable influence on the pacifist's appeal would be the opportunity for direct exchanges of messages above and beyond that afforded by information tacitly communicated in game moves. Thus, in one experimental manipulation, the opportunity for *operators* to exchange additional messages either is or is not available. When available, the communication period is interposed between some of the working periods. (In the first part of the experiment, operator communications were permitted following work periods 5, 6, and 7.) In his messages, the pacifist amplifies on the intentions behind his actions. He states his conciliatory intent, presents a statement of fair demands, and emphasizes his refusal to use the shock and his intention to force the other to shock him if he is going to remain unfair.

The comparisons of Ss in the two conditions were statistically significant on two counts. First, all Ss who switched from dominating to sharing during work period 6, 7, or 8 (the periods following operator-to-operator messages) were in the communication condition and received these messages. No Ss in the noncommunication condition were converted during this period. Second, dominating Ss in the communication condition (as evidenced by responses to computer interrogations) thought it more likely than those in the noncommunication condition that the pacifist was trying to make them feel guilty or embarrass them and that he was trying to trick or deceive them. These results suggested that the person-to-person communications made the moral issue more salient. However, this salience had two opposite effects. For a limited number of Ss, it produced the desired conversion, but for many others, their resolve to dominate was strengthened, or at least rationalized, by attributing trickery to the motives of the pacifist.

As a second feature of our experimental design, we manipulated the experimental conditions related to the matter of projecting the pacifist's character and motives to his adversary. Common sense and many studies have shown that prior knowledge of and acquaintance with an individual exercise an influence over the interpretation that is made of his behavior. In our laboratory situation, Ss did not know with whom they would be paired as adversaries, believing only that their opposite number would be selected from among the other 23 students receiving instruction. Furthermore, their interaction in the context of the task was limited to game moves communicated via television and switch buttons. Was the pacifist's behavior likely to be perceived less clearly under these conditions of minimal knowledge than if the S received additional personal information about him? Furthermore, would such perceptions influence the S's interpretation of and responses to the pacifist? To answer this question, we had all Ss fill out personal information questionnaires. These were presumably exchanged with the opposing operator either at the beginning of or midway into the experiment. In fact, all Ss received personal information for the programmed pacifist which was designed to project an image of a Quaker who is morally committed to principles of nonviolence. Before the initiation of the work periods, and either with or without the benefit of this material, Ss characterized their bargaining adversary on eight semantic differential rating scales. Chi-square comparisons of the initial ratings made by Ss with and without this personal information showed that the Ss who exchanged this information perceived the pacifist as significantly more moral, wiser, more peaceful, and more honest—and even braver and stronger. Thus the initial exposure to this information clearly succeeded in conveying and establishing a favorable image of the pacifist—an image that should serve to reduce the ambiguity of intentions that his game behavior communicated. Did this factor influence the overall frequency of a favorable response to the pacifist's appeal? Not in the slightest. Chi-square tests showed that Ss receiving prior personal knowledge showed no greater tendency toward cooperative behavior in the ensuing trials. On the face of it this was a puzzling and unexpected result. To compound our puzzlement, we found that the mid-game semantic differential ratings of the pacifist were essentially identical for Ss in the communication and noncommunication conditions, although a significantly greater shift toward cooperation had already occurred in the condition where communications were previously exchanged. Together these results suggest that more than a clear picture and favorable image of the pacifist is necessary for an effective appeal, and that the significant shift to cooperation in the communication condition was not achieved by providing more information about the pacifist.

Consider one additional variation of the pacifist bargaining strategy. Supposing that an S had been shocking the pacifist, and even supposing that he admitted this was wrong or at least morally questionable, he might still have faced a problem. He may have wondered whether he could afford to cooperate at this point; he may have hesitated for fear of recrimination. At this point, then, it should have been effective if the pacifist could assuage his fears by giving him some guarantee or overt reassurance against retaliation. To test this we provided one-half of the Ss with a mid-game opportunity to "give up" or reject future acquisition of the harmful actions (the JOLT BACK and electric shock) for the remainder of the work periods. The pacifist always did so. Thus roughly half of the dominators faced a "disarmed" pacifist while the other half faced a pacifist who had had no opportunity to disarm. The manipulation had no effect. Again we were puzzled.

Why did the intended reassurance of the act of "disarmament" fail to induce more dominators to convert? Strangely enough, because it apparently was irrelevant. On various occasions when dominators were queried by the computer on why they believed the pacifist did not employ his shock, only 5 to 13 percent cited fear as a reason, whereas about half believed he refrained from using his shock action out of principle. Reassurance, then, was apparently not a factor, since these are approximately the same percentages found in the converted group.

The results for these three experimental manipulations suggest that when the pacifist fails it is not primarily because he fails to project a clear image of his intentions. Naively we had assumed that the various manipulations would only serve to strengthen the pacifist's case—the personal profile information, the availability of communication, the opportunity to forego harmful actions—all of these would ostensibly contribute to the effectiveness of the pacifist's bargaining strategy. Behind this lay the assumption that the pacifist would more than likely benefit from anything that served to bring his character, his claims, and his commitments into sharper focus. Our results suggest that this assumption needs to be questioned or at least seriously qualified. While the pacifist appeal can persuade some adversaries away from their initial positions, and it does influence a small proportion to do so, particularly under the condition of personal communications, it also fails to influence many Ss who plan to dominate. But beyond these obvious alternatives it may have another effect; it may encourage exploitation among Ss who otherwise do not entertain such plans prior to interacting with the pacifist.

Let us pursue this somewhat further by considering the following effects which knowledge of the adversary produced. In replying to a postexperimental question, 78 percent of all Ss indicated that the personal information about the pacifist had a significant influence on their strategy. Even among the unremitting dominators only about one-fourth indicated this information had negligible or no influence. While the influence among those who are converted to cooperation is readily understandable, what is the nature of this self-acknowledged influence among the intractable dominators?

Two possibilities suggest themselves. First, though the dominators refuse to give up their control, they may continue to dominate with greater reluctance and an increased sense of guilt, caused by the knowledge that they are shocking somebody who isn't likely to shock back. To check this possibility, an index of reluctance to shock (the use of the *insert* action on turns when the JOLT could have been employed) was calculated and used as a

manifest expression of experienced guilt. Only 14.5 percent of the intractable dominators made a sustained effort (on more than two trials) to avoid shocking the operator facing them; about 45 percent made no effort to avoid shocking the other operator by first testing to see whether he would back out voluntarily. Thus, for the dominators, the influence of knowledge did not lead to increased manifest guilt in more than a small percentage cases, if indeed it accounted for any of this guilt.

A second possibility is that the information on the pacifist may be used as a basis for adopting and maintaining an exploitative attitude. Before the initiation of the work periods, Ss were given an opportunity to vote for one of two payoffs that determine their potential earnings in each work period. Other things being equal, voting for the low payoff is less risky—Ss do not lose as much money if they go second or reach an impasse. With the high payoff they earn more if they successfully dominate, but they lose more if they get into trouble or go second. Before the start of bargaining and with no knowledge of the other operator, only 37 percent of the dominators voted for the payoff which favors a successful dominating strategy. At mid-game, half of our Ss were afforded the opportunity to vote to revise their payoff for the remainder of the game. What did our Ss do? On their second vote, in those conditions where a second vote took place, 94 percent of the dominators voted for this payoff. Reassured by their knowledge of the pacifist that they could dominate with impunity, they did not soften their demands but planned for continued exploitation. The pacifist's tactics apparently invite exploitation and aggression even among those who do not begin with such intentions.

The judgment that many bargainers—some initially cooperative—end up exploiting the pacifist is harsh and unflattering, but it is supported by a configuration of indices based on both objective behavior and on amplifying subjective ratings made by the Ss themselves. Furthermore, the failure of conversion does not arise from misperception of the pacifist's intention or fear of reprisal. While suspicious to some extent, our Ss were not holding back because of the Orwellian dictum that "Saints should always be judged guilty until they are proven innocent." Clarification of pacifist intentions does not lead to a greater number of conversions.

These findings, of course, must be viewed from the perspective of the restrictive conditions of our experiment. The Ss were operating under considerable pressure from their "teammates" to dominate. Although the real-life counterpart of such pressure is a factor with which the pacifist appeal frequently must contend, it will be of considerable interest to see what happens when such pressure is absent. Furthermore, our pacifist is a pure type—absolute in his commitment to principles of nonviolence. Thus he does not avail himself of some of the adjunct coercive techniques used by many resistance groups. The situation also narrowly limits the bargainers' options and permits little or no opportunity for intermediate resolution; there are no available means of gradually expanding limited areas of mutual agreement or of cooperative initiatives where risk is less than all-or-none. Social norms, sanctions, and pressures are vague and ill-defined for the Ss. There are, then, some rather stringent qualifications within which our results must be phrased.

But for all this we have at least made a bench mark for additional experimentation in the area of cooperative strategies in bargaining. While the pacifist's limited success may be attributable to the recognized limitations of our situation—the purity of his bargaining style, the sparseness of the bargaining space, and especially the absence of societal pressures—we may duly note that this tells us something about the limitations of pacifist strategies as well as about our restrictive conditions. Thus, if we need to enrich our situation to find those conditions necessary for effectiveness, this also helps us to see more clearly the qualifications for nonviolent bargaining strategies. Through systematic modifications in both environment and cooperative strategies in our future research, we hope to map out some of the limits and bases for the effectiveness of strategies based on cooperative rather than dominating intent.

As for the findings themselves, no summary on our part could match a commentary on the use of force written in 1929 by theologian Reinhold Niebuhr:

> Where there is a great inequality of physical advantage and physical power, it is difficult to establish moral relations. Weakness invites aggression. Even the most intelligent and moral individuals are more inclined to unethical conduct with those who are unable to offer resistance to injustice than with those who can. . . .
>
> It is obviously possible to resist injustice without using physical force and certainly without using violence. . . . But it seems that the world in which we live is not so spiritual that it is always possible to prompt the wrong doer to contrition merely by appealing to his conscience. . . . .

References

Janis, I. L., and D. Katz. "The Reduction of Intergroup Hostility: Research Problems and Hypotheses," *Journal of Conflict Resolution*, 3, 1 (Mar. 1959), 85–100.

MEEKER, R. J., G. H. SHURE, and W. H. MOORE, JR. "Real-Computer Studies of Bargaining Behavior: The Effects of Threat upon Bargaining," *AFIPS Conference Proceedings, 1964 Spring Joint Computer Conference*, Vol. 25, 115–23.

SHARP, G. "The Meanings of Non-Violence:

A Typology (Revised)," *Journal of Conflict Resolution*, 3, 1 (Mar. 1959), 41–66.

SHURE, G. H., R. J. MEEKER, and W. H. MOORE, JR. "Human Bargaining and Negotiation Behavior: Computer-based Empirical Studies. I. The Effects of Threat upon Bargaining." System Development Corporation Document TM-1300/000/00, June 25, 1963.

THE EFFECTIVENESS OF PACIFIST STRATEGIES: A THEORETICAL APPROACH*

Richard Ofshe

The question of the power of pacifist behavior to produce cooperative responses in conflict situations has recently been raised by several researchers (Laws, 1965; Shure et al., 1965; Deutsch et al., 1967; Meeker and Shure, 1969; and Vincent and Tindell, 1969) and has been the subject of a number of comments (Rapoport et al., 1965 and Rapoport, 1969). The researches that have been reported to date are best described as exploratory in nature. The majority of the investigations have been directed toward the development of a standardized experimental situation and the empirical exploration of

a number of possible relationships.[1] Although the experiments demonstrate that it is possible to investigate pacifist behavior under controlled laboratory conditions and that certain naive expectations about the effects of pacifist strategies are incorrect,

* Richard Ofshe, "The Effectiveness of Pacifist Strategies: A Theoretical Approach," *Journal of Conflict Resolution*, 15, No. 2 (June 1971), 261–69. Copyright 1971 by the University of Michigan. Reprinted by permission.

[1] The experiments conducted by Shure et al. (1965), Meeker and Shure (1969) and Vincent and Tindell (1969) were conducted under relatively similar experimental conditions. These experiments are distinguished from those of Lave (165) and Deutsch et al. (1967) since they had certain procedural similarities and incorporated the necessity of using physical violence in order to overcome the pacifist. The latter experiments did not require the use of physical violence. Although the results of the Lave and Deutsch et al. researches bear on the question of the effectiveness of pacifist strategies, the primary interest here will be in results of experiments conducted in the Shure et al. (1965) format.

their results are of only limited value in the analysis of pacifist behavior as a strategy in conflict situations. There are two reasons for this. The first is that no attempt has been made to generate a theoretical analysis of the strategy which leads to predictions that may be empirically investigated. Lacking such an analysis, the experiments cannot be evaluated as a set of investigations all of which bear on a theory and hence each result must be considered independently, with the consequence that each is of diminished value. The second reason is that it happens to be the case that the particular line of research that is currently being pursued focuses on those aspects of the pacifist strategy which are of relatively little importance to the question of the strategy's power.

In this paper an attempt will be made to provide a theory which identifies some of the conditions under which pacifist strategies are effective and explains why they are effective. In order to accomplish this it will be necessary to first provide an organization of the existing literature, identify certain crucial structural variables that have so far been ignored and develop an argument for the position that those aspects of the pacifist's strategy that have been considered are not the aspects of the pacifist's behavior that are most likely to be related to the success of the strategy.

It will be convenient to employ some simple notation in the presentation of the organization of the existing literature and in the development of the theory. The important elements of the pacifist-strategy experimental situation can be represented by four symbols: E, S, P, and O. The symbols E and S will be used in the traditional fashion to denote the experimenter

and the subject. P will be used to denote the pacifist. In the experiments that have been reported, there have been two types of Os. In some cases O has been defined as a team or cohort which S represents in the game against P (Shure et al., 1965). In other cases, O is simply an audience in the form of an observer who is senior in age to S and will interview him after the experiment (Meeker and Shure, 1969). It should also be noted that in some experiments O is missing entirely. That is, there is no mention of a team or cohort nor of an audience with whom S will interact in the future (Lave, 1965; Deutsch et al., 1967; Meeker and Shure, 1969; and Vincent and Tindell, 1969).

The research setting in which the bulk of the experiments have been conducted (the pacifist-strategy experiment) is a laboratory experimental situation in which S is made to believe that he is participating in a two-person, non-zero sum, iterated game with P. In fact, S interacts with a robot who is either resident in a computer or whose actions are performed by a confederate of the experimenter. In all cases the robot's strategy is determined prior to the start of the game and is in no way affected by S's behavior. The game is structured such that on each of a series of plays S and P must compete for control of a communication channel and hold it long enough to complete a transmission.[2] A payoff is awarded for each successful transmission. One player can prevent the other from completing the transmission by also attempting to use the channel and

---

[2] There is no substantive content to the message. The transmission problem simply provides a context in which to create conflict between S and P.

thereby blocking it. If a message is not transmitted during a given play of the game a stalemate results and no payoffs are made. The players also compete for possession of a power advantage which, if obtained, permits the holder to force his opponent to unblock the channel. Whenever the power advantage is employed it is the case that the player who is being forced to vacate the channel simultaneously receives a painful electric shock. The power advantage and the shock cannot be separated.

In the game, *P* always permits *S* to obtain the power advantage and win on the first trial. *P* then attempts to use the channel on the second play. If *S* forces him out of the channel *P* repeats his attempt to use the channel on the next trial. If *S* again forces *P* out of the channel, *P* continues to make his claim for a share of the payoffs by continuing to attempt transmission on each subsequent trial. Clearly, there is a simple solution to the game. *S* and *P* can alternate winning trials. *S*'s choice dilemma is whether to cooperate (alternate) or dominate (win every play) through the use of his power advantage and electric shock.

Variations on the basic research situation include the presence of an audience in different forms; various changes in *P*'s behavior designed to demonstrate his staunch pacifist position and claim that the alternating strategy is just; providing *P* with the ability to retaliate which he either gives up, threatens to use or actually uses; and providing *S* with progressively greater amounts of information about *P*'s background (such that he is a Quaker).

The reported experiments have dealt with the demonstration that changes in *S*'s behavior can be produced by changes in the *O* or *P* variables. The relationships that have been investigated are represented in the graph in Figure 1.

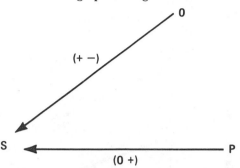

Fig. 1. Causal Effects on the Behavior of *S*. A directed line indicates the relationship between independent and dependent variables. The signs associated with each line summarize the effects on *S*'s aggressive behavior of changes in the independent variables.

The available experimental results concerning the effects of changes in either the *O* or *P* variable can be summarized as follows. The presence or absence of *O* and changes in *O*'s character produce significant changes in the behavior of *S*. In the Meeker and Shure (1969) experiments, three levels of cooperative behavior were produced by manipulating the *O* variable. The results of these manipulations were that the greatest proportion of cooperative behavior by *S* occurs under conditions in which an audience is present but is non-interfering. The Meeker and Shure data also reveal a decrease in *S*'s level of cooperative behavior when there is no mention of an audience and *S* is not the representative of a team, that is, *O* is simply absent. Finally, the lowest level of cooperative behavior is produced under conditions in which a cohort is present and is applying pressure for aggressive behavior. (The graphs reporting the relevant data are presented in Figure 2.) Obviously, the experimental condition that

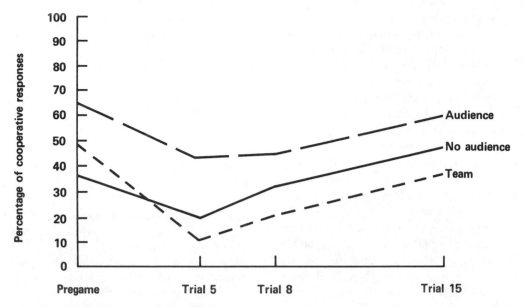

Fig. 2. Effects of Manipulations of the O Variable. This figure is based on data reported in Meeker and Shure (1969).

is missing from this series is one in which a cohort is present and attempts to influence S to move to a cooperative strategy. In light of the available evidence, it seems likely that this condition would produce a greater level of cooperative behavior than is produced in the condition in which a passive audience is merely present.

The reasonable conclusion from this data is that S's behavior is substantially affected by social pressure applied in the form of direct influence attempts or in the form of a passive social conscience. Given that the *no cohort–no audience* (O absent) condition is identified as the baseline condition, the $(+ -)$ designation associated with the O–S relation in Figure 1 can be read as indicating that appropriate changes in the O variable can produce either increases or decreases in the level of S's aggressive behavior.

The effects on S of changes in the P variable have been investigated in several

experiments in which either the pacifist belief structure underlying P's behavior is revealed in progressively greater detail or P's behavior is modified in a number of different fashions. In a series of experiments, Deutsch et al. (1967) investigated the effects of different robot strategies on S's aggressive behavior. Comparison of the effects of the display of a pacifist strategy with the effects elicited in a control condition reveals that the pacifist strategy elicits no more cooperative behavior than does the strategy used in the control condition (Deutsch et al., 1967, p. 358). The result of Lave's (1965) experiment also shows the pacifist strategy to be ineffective. Ss tended to exploit pacifist players.

Shure et al. (1965) report on the effects of displaying a pacifist behavior strategy as well as on the effects of differences in the degree to which S possesses knowledge of the moral stance underlying P's actions. The display of a pacifist strategy produces a massive shift (54 out of 68 Ss) toward aggressive behavior on the part of individuals who planned initially to play in a cooperative fashion. A very minor shift (4 out of 75 Ss) was produced in the behavior of individuals who planned initially to dominate. In other variations of the basic experiment, Ss were given different amounts of information about the pacifist's moral position and the pacifist, who was initially given the ability to retaliate, disarmed himself during the game. These variations produced no significant changes in the behavior of Ss. The single manipulation of the P variable that produced a singificant effect was the introduction of persuasive communication subsequent reactions of Ss who received directly from P to S. Comparison of the communications from P with those who did not receive persuasive messages reveals that the only conversions to cooperation came from the group that was exposed to the communication. The effect of communications from P to S was, however, mixed. For the majority of Ss, those who were playing the dominant strategy and were not converted to the cooperative strategy by the communication from P, the effect of the communication was to produce a negative reaction to the pacifist. Shure et al. (1965) report that those in the communication condition who were not converted

> thought it more likely than those in the noncommunication condition that the pacifist was trying to make them feel guilty and embarrass them and that he was trying to trick or deceive them (p. 113–14).

Vincent and Tindell (1969) conducted an experiment in which in one condition a pacifist who had the power to retaliate was made to warn S that he would retaliate against aggression and in a second

condition actually did retaliate whenever shocked by S. P never administered a shock except in response to S's aggressive act. The result of this experiment was that the condition in which P only warned that he would retaliate produced about the same proportion of Ss choosing to apply physical violence against the pacifist as did the experiments conducted by Shure and his associates (1965). The condition in which the pacifist reacted to aggression with an aggressive response produced significantly more aggressive behavior from S than did the *warning but no action* condition.

In summary, it has been found that in a situation of conflict of interest between two individuals, the progressive disclosure of one individual's moral position as a pacifist, the pacifist's use of overt gestures of good faith, and his active rejection of the means of violence have the effect of producing either no substantial change in his opponent's aggressive behavior or result in increased aggression. The $(O+)$ designation associated with the P–S relation in Figure 1 is intended to denote that the results of variations in experimental conditions from nondisplay to display of pacifist behavior, from no retaliation to retaliation and from limited knowledge to greater knowledge produce either no substantial change or an increase in the level of S's aggressive behavior.

The primary focus of research on pacifist strategies has been on the effects of changes in P's behavior and on the effects of differences in the extent of S's knowledge about P. The experiments that were performed on the effects of variations in O were in response to criticisms (Rapoport et al., 1965 and Deutsch et al., 1967) that all of the original experiments by Shure and his associates were conducted under conditions in which S was urged to dominate by his teammates. The results of the reported experiments suggest that pacifist strategies have little to recommend them as strategies in conflict situations.

There is one important structural characteristic present in all of the experiments that has been overlooked and one characteristic of conflict situations in which pacifist strategies are attempted that has been missed and therefore excluded from the experimental situation. The argument that will be developed below will rest on the premises that the characteristic of the experiments that has been overlooked is vital in the analysis of their results and that the characteristic of conflict situations that has been excluded from the situation is the crucial variable which determines the success of pacifist strategies.

First, consider the structural characteristic of the experimental situation that has been overlooked in the analysis of the conflict. This is the presence of the experimenter. Although any effects introduced by E are present in all of the experiments, recognition of the possibility that E may be influencing S's behavior is a first step in explaining the apparently anomolous results of the experiments. In terms of paths of influence on S, the structure of the experiment may be represented as in Figure 3.

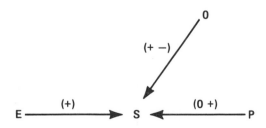

Fig. 3. Channels of Influence to S in the Pacifist-Strategy Experiment.

It is reasonable to regard the presence of E (that is, S's knowledge of E's expectations for his behavior) as acting to influence S to adopt a competitive strategy and that this influence is present despite any other manipulations that are introduced.[3] There is ample evidence that supports the contention that individuals participating in experiments operate with a commitment to contribute to "science" and attempt to perform the *role* of "subject" in an acceptable fashion. Orne's researches (1962, and Orne and Evans, 1965) and Milgram's (1965) study of obedience are the classic examples of this effect. They each demonstrate that the role of participant in an experiment has a powerful effect on an individual's behavior. In the context of the pacifist-strategy experiment it is reasonable to suppose that Ss define proper role performance as calling for competition with P and for attempting to *win* in the conflict.

Recognition of the possible influence of the experimenter's role relationship with S necessitates a reappraisal of the manipulations of the O variable. For example, in the cohort condition the effect of the teammate's urging to dominate could be interpreted as a manipulation that reinforces E's influence. The fact that there is still considerable aggressive behavior on S's part in the conditions in which no O is present can be accounted for simply as a result of E's influence on S. Also, the result that the presence of an observer who will interview S after the experiment produces a decrease in S's aggressive behavior can be accounted for by postulating that the presence of the observer serves

---

[3] Deutsch et al. (1967) also suggest this effect of E's presence, but do not develop the argument further.

as a cue to S that the expectation for his performance is more complicated than it appears on the surface and hence the definition of his role as subject is open for interpretation. Under this condition S will be more sensitive to general social norms prescribing equitable behavior and more responsive to pacifist appeals.

The argument being advanced here is that the crucial variable necessary to explain S's performance in the pacifist-strategy experiment as it is presently constructed is the clarity with which S perceives his role to be defined. The more ambiguous the definition, the more S will tend to express a preference for playing the cooperative strategy, since this strategy is consistent with norms that typically apply to interactive siutations.

It is important to recognize that S is constrained by his social role and hence has little freedom of action if the role is clearly defined. It is not surprising that Ss are relatively unresponsive to the pacifist appeal when the role of "subject" in an experiment on gaming and conflict is defined in a straightforward fashion and no cues to any alternative definition are provided. The reason that the clarity of S's perception of his role as subject is a crucial variable is that this role definition places S in a position of conflict of interest with P that is not defined solely by the monetary payoffs for which they are competing. The requirements of S's role conflict with P's desires. Ss are in a position analogous to that of a police officer who is ordered to remove peaceful sit-in demonstrators from a building. Within the boundaries defined by his role, the officer has relatively little freedom of choice. His only realistically possible response to the pacifist character of the demonstrator's actions can be in terms of how he goes

about his job. If under these circumstances the officer chooses to act with minimum force, the pacifist's strategy has produced a positive response. To say that the pacifist strategy fails unless the officer removes his badge and resigns on the spot rather than remove the demonstrators is unrealistic and suggests a misunderstanding of what pacifist strategies are designed to accomplish.

Although the argument advanced above accounts for the results of the pacifist-strategy experiments, it, together with the experiments themselves, is of relatively little importance in the identification of conditions under which pacifist strategies will affect the outcome of conflicts. The reason that the experiments contribute little to the analysis of pacifist strategies is that they investigate the effects of manipulations of the wrong variables. The selection of the P–S and O–S relations indicates a failure to recognize where the potential power of the pacifist's behavior is located.

The situation chosen as the research setting is a reasonable analogue to the social structure in which pacifist appeals are made. For example, S and P are in direct interaction and from S's position there is a conflict of interest between them. S's conflict of interest with P has two components. First, there is a payoff available to S if he overcomes P. In addition, S must operate within the boundaries of a social role in which he is the representative, the agent, of E and sometimes of O. The definition of S's role calls for a certain outcome to his interaction with P. The existing evidence indicates that S's behavior is controlled by the expectations of E and the expectations and actions of O. It is possible to interpret the reported data in terms of a hypothesis that it is largely S's perception of his role that creates a conflict of interest for him and therefore determines his unresponsiveness to P's behavior.

Although it has not been considered explicitly, the experimental situation includes another potential influence channel through which the pacifist's strategy might operate. The channel, which is typically present in "real world" situations in which pacifist appeals are made, is the one from the pacifist to an audience which may or may not be directly involved in the conflict between the pacifist and the other party. That is, the P–O relation.[4]

It can be argued that since S's behavior is defined by a social role, the potential of a pacifist appeal as a strategy in the conflict situation lies in the extent to which the pacifist is able to affect the audience that can control S. The problem for the pacifist is to elicit action from O. The O position in the experiment can be made to serve as an analogue for the different types of audiences to which pacifist appeals are typically directed. The theory that will be developed below will attempt to relate the different characteristics of audiences to the probabilities of their members' responding to pacifist appeals.

The argument made previously was that it is the extent of his conflict of interest with P that determines S's respon-siveness to P's behavior. This argument can be applied to the P–O relationship and can be used to identify situations in which O will be differentially sensitive to P's pacifist appeal. The general premise of the argument is that the greater the conflict of interest between an individual and a pacifist, the less the likelihood that the individual will respond to the pacifist's moral appeal. The structural variable that differentiates S and O is that S's social position produces a role-determined conflict of interest with P and specifies a limited set of possible reactions to P from which S must choose. For O, there is no clearly defined social role, either in the experiment or in the "real world," that produces a conflict of interest with P and constrains O's behavior such that he has relatively little freedom of action. There are, however, a number of structural considerations that determine the extent to which O will find himself with a greater or lesser economically-based conflict of interest with P and hence will cause him to be differentially sensitive to P's pacifist appeals.[5]

If the experimental situation is considered as an analogue to the structure of conflict situations in which pacifist appeals are attempted, there are at least three different sets of relations with S and P that can be created for O which cor-

---

[4] Up to this point, the symbol O has been used to represent a supposed team or observer that was introduced as a variable in the pacifist-strategy experiment. From this point forward, O should be considered to denote an individual whose relations with P and S are subject to manipulation across treatment conditions and whose behavior is to be predicted. O is a subject in the experiment.

[5] Obviously, the actual effectiveness of the pacifist strategy in any "real world" situation will depend on the distribution of O's who occupy different positions in the audience that is informed about the conflict between S and P. The question being addressed here is that of the identification of conditions under which pacifist appeals will be successful, not how frequently these conditions obtain naturally or how they may be brought about.

respond to the relations between audiences and combatants in "real world" conflict situations in which pacifist strategies are employed. The three different sets of relations that can be used to define *O*'s position create three different levels of conflict of interest and therefore should produce three different degrees of sensitivity to pacifist appeals.[6]

The first of the three positions that *O* might occupy is one in which *S* acts directly in *O*'s interest in that *O*'s payoffs vary directly with *S*'s payoffs. This set of relations should produce the smallest degree of receptivity to the pacifist appeal of any of the three sets of relations to be considered. Given even this condition, however, the likelihood of *O*'s responding favorably to a pacifist appeal should be inversely related to the magnitude of the conflict of interest between *O* and *P*. For example, assume that in the context of an experimental situation similar to the standard research situation *O* is the subject and *S* is a confederate of the experimenter. The situation could be manipulated such that *O* believes that *S* and *P* are to play a competitive game, *O* is to advise *S* on strategy in the game, and *O* will receive a share of *S*'s winnings. *O*'s task in the experiment is simply to advise *S* on the manner in which to play the game. It would be possible to manipulate the intensity of *O*'s conflict of interest

with *P* by manipulating the amount of the payoff for a win across treatment conditions. As the amount of the payoff increases, the probability of *O*'s advising *S* to play cooperatively should decrease.

The situation described above creates relations between *O* and *P* and *O* and *S* that are analogous to the relations that define the position of a citizen of a country that is a colonial power, who derives direct economic benefits from one of its colonies, and who is confronted with a conflict between the colonial administration and the nationals of the colony. The nationals desire independence and are using pacifist techniques in their struggle.

The second of the three positions that *O* might occupy is one in which he receives no benefit from *S*'s success in the conflict with *P*. In this case, *O*'s position is analogous to that of a neutral observer such as in the case of a citizen of a country that has no colonial interests and is made aware of the pacifist appeal of nationals who are seeking independence from a colonial power. The required relations between *O* and *S* and *O* and *P* could be created in the context of the modified experimental situation by manipulating a situation in which *S* is to engage in the game with *P*, *O* observes the game, and *O* is to advise *S* on strategy. *O* is paid a fixed sum for his participation in the experiment which is in no way dependent on *S*'s success in the game. If the conflict of interest argument is correct, the probability that *O* advises *S* to play cooperatively under these conditions should be higher than the probability obtained under any of the conditions defined for the case discussed above.

The third position that could be defined for *O* for which the conflict of interest argument yields a straightforward predic-

---

[6] If one wished to consider the effectiveness of pacifist strategies relative to non-pacifist strategies, it would be a simple matter to design control conditions for each of the treatment conditions that are to be considered in which *P* played a non-pacifist strategy. The effects of this difference (pacifist—non-pacifist) on *O*'s behavior could then be determined for each level of conflict of interest that is created.

tion is one in which O and P share a commonality of interest in that O's payoffs are related to P's success. Of the three conditions that have been defined, this one should produce the greatest responsiveness (i.e., probability of advising S to play cooperatively) to pacifist appeals. In this case O occupies a position that is analogous to the position of the nationals of a colony who are not themselves engaged in conflict with the controlling foreign power but stand to gain if the pacifist's strategy is successful. The conflict of interest argument leads to the recognition that one of the possible strengths of pacifist strategies might be in their ability to mobilize the support and action of members of an audience who would benefit from the pacifist's actions but would not be induced to act under less dramatic circumstances. If a pacifist's behavior appears to be able to produce a mass movement (not itself necessarily pacifist in character) it will probably result in success at inducing cooperative behavior from the adversary. The success of the strategy might not, however, be for the reasons that the pacifist would prefer.

The conflict of interest hypothesis suggests an additional condition under which pacifist strategies might be expected to be differentially effective. Consider the following case. O is in a position in which he is formally independent of both S and P and has no direct economic interest in the success of either party (as in the second case described above). Under this condition O's receptivity to pacifist appeals is likely to be affected by the extent to which he perceives himself to share some important characteristic with either S or P. Although O has no true conflict of interest with either party in the P–S

interaction, he should be differentially sensitive to P's appeal depending on whether or not be is able to identify with one of the two parties. For example, if O possesses a status characteristic that differentiates him from one of the parties to the conflict and generates a bond of psychological equivalence with the other party, his reaction to the pacifist's appeal should be systematically affected. Instances of factors on which it would be reasonable to expect identifications to be made are characteristics such as membership in a minority group when P and S differ in this regard, even if O is a member of a different minority group than either of the parties to the conflict. Also, if O were in a position in which he benefited from the colonial interests of his country and S were the representative of a different colonial power, it is likely that O would be less responsive to the pacifist's appeal than if he had no economic involvement in his country's colonies.

The hypotheses developed in this paper have attempted to relate a structural variable (conflict of interest) that partially defines the relations between an audience and the combatants in conflicts in which one of the parties adopts a pacifist strategy to the probability that a member of the audience will be responsive to the pacifist's appeal. The variable that has been considered in this paper is only one of a set of variables that are likely to affect this response probability. The other major variables that will likely be useful in explaining the behavior of audience members are those of the specific context and specific content of the pacifist's appeal. The researches on pacifist behavior that have been conducted to date have been concerned with manipulations of only the most gross characteristics of the pacifist's behavior and have been minimally concerned either with the issues involved in the conflict in which the pacifist participates and/or with the more subtle aspects of the pacifist's strategy. Little attention has been given to the questions of effects on the audience's responsiveness to pacifist appeals of differences in the issues that precipitate the conflict between the pacifist and his opponent, the particular set of actions that the pacifist chooses to employ in stating his claim and the types of arguments that the pacifist directs toward the audience. These are the characteristics of the pacifist's strategy that make it a unique strategy in conflict situations. They should be investigated in order to identify the characteristics of social situations and stimulus inputs that determine when appeals to moral principles will be effective in producing action on the part of individuals for whom the moral principles are usually of minimal salience.

An attempt has been made in this paper to introduce certain structural concepts (role and position) and the variable of conflict of interest in order to develop a formulation that takes into account the fact that the behaviors of participants in conflict situations in which pacifist appeals are made are affected by both social and psychological considerations. Although the tack taken in this has been the treatment of relations between pairs of elements involved in the conflict situation (P and S, or P and O, or O and S) it should be recognized that this is only a first and inadequate step. The pairs of elements in the situation must be recognized to be interconnected and to constitute a system. The social situation in which pacifist strategies are

typically employed is composed of sets of relations that must be considered simultaneously if the final outcome of the action of any participant is to be predicted. Obviously, it is possible to decompose the situation into a number of discrete independent and dependent variables, and obviously it is necessary to establish that one variable affects another in a specified fashion using standard experimental techniques. It is also obvious that utilization of only this approach will prove inadequate for the investigation of the topic of pacifist strategies. At minimum it will be necessary to work both theoretically and empirically with situations in which it is possible for P to affect O and S, and for O to act to affect S.[7] Given an experimental situation in which parameters such as payoffs, P's actions and the content of P's communications to O and S can be manipulated by the experimenter and influence processes can operate in a manner analogous to "real world" conditions, it should be possible to conduct meaningful research on issues such as the effectiveness of different variants of pacifist techniques and on issues such as the relative effectiveness of pacifist and non-paci-

---

[7] The pacifist conflict situation is no more complicated than other social situations in which a number of participants interact and are each affected by different sets of variables and one another's actions. The coalition and prisoner's dilemma games are similar situations. It has been shown elsewhere (cf., Ofshe and Ofshe, 1970) that both situations can be decomposed through experimental control, that causation can be established and measurements of the effects of independent variables obtained, and that these measurements can be used to predict the behavior of all participants in the complex situation and hence the behavior of the complex interaction systems themselves.

fist techniques under a variety of social conditions.

REFERENCES

DEUTSCH, M., Y. EPSTEIN, D. CANAVAN, and P. GUMPERT. "Strategies of Inducing Co-operation: An Experimental Study," *Journal of Conflict Resolution*, 11, 3 (Sept., 1967), 345–60.

LAVE, L. "Factors Affecting Co-operation in the Prisoner's Dilemma," *Behavioral Science*, 10, 1 (Jan., 1965), 26–38.

MEEKER, R. and G. SHURE. "Pacifist Bargaining Tactics: Some 'Outsider' Influences," *Journal of Conflict Resolution*, 13, 4 (Dec., 1969), 487–93.

MILGRAM, S. "Some Conditions of Obedience and Disobedience to Authority," *Human Relations*, 13, 1 (Feb., 1965), 57–76.

OFSHE, L., and R. OFSHE. *Utility and Choice in Social Interaction*, Englewood Cliffs, N.J.: Prentice-Hall, 1970.

ORNE, M. "On the Social Psychology of the Psychological Experiment," *American Psychologist*, 17, 7 (July, 1962), 776–83.

ORNE, H., and F. EVANS. "Social Control in the Psychological Experiment," *Journal of Personality and Social Psychology*, 1, 3 (March, 1965), 189–200.

RAPOPORT, A. "Editorial Comment," *Journal of Conflict Resolution*, 13, 4 (Dec., 1969), 485–86.

RAPOPORT, A., M. SHUBIK and R. THRALL. "Editorial Comment," *Journal of Conflict Resolution*, 9, 1 (March, 1965), 66–67.

SHURE, G., R. MEEKER and E. HANSFORD. "The Effectiveness of Pacifist Strategies in Bargaining Games," *Journal of Conflict Resolution*, 9, 1 (March, 1965), 106–117.

VINCENT, J., and J. TINDELL. "Alternative Cooperative Strategies in a Bargaining Game," *Journal of Conflict Resolution*, 13, 4 (Dec., 1969), 494–510.

9

Group Control of Deviance

DEVIATION, REJECTION, AND COMMUNICATION*

Stanley Schachter

The phenomenon of "group standards," uniformities of behavior and attitudes resulting from interaction among members of a group, is a widely documented finding in the social sciences. The gang studies of Shaw (9, 10), Thrasher (14), Whyte (16), and Zorbaugh (18) point up the existence of group codes and group standards. Community studies such as the Yankee City Series (15) or the Middletown books (5, 6) are in large part concerned with social conformities resulting from group membership and interaction.

In psychological circles interest in group standards was probably first stimulated by the experiments of Sherif (11, 12), which demonstrated the convergence of judgments as a function of group interaction.

Sherif's approach has been chiefly that of restricting experimental work to small, carefully designed laboratory studies of perceptual phenomena. The principles derived have then been extended to more complex social phenomena. Others have studied these more complex social phenomena directly: several factory studies have demonstrated the existence of group standards about production level among industrial workers (2, 17); Newcomb (8) has found in a college community similarities of political attitudes which can plausibly be interpreted as group standards; Merei (7) has demonstrated that group standards arise in children's play groups and serve to increase the "strength" of the group.

The means by which the group imposes and maintains conformity have been an area of speculation. It has been suggested that non-conformity results in rejection from the group. Thrasher (16, p. 291) says: "Opinion in the gang manifests its

* Stanley Schacter, "Deviation, Rejection, and Communication," *Journal of Abnormal and Social Psychology*, 46 (1951), 190–207. Copyright 1951 by the American Psychological Association, and reproduced by permission.

pressure in the variety of methods through which group control is exerted, such as applause, preferment and hero-worshipping as well as ridicule, scorn, and ostracism ... the member who has broken the code may be subjected to a beating or in extreme cases may be marked for death." Sherif and Cantril (13, p. 321) state: "Just as good members of any organized group uphold the values or norms of the group, ... so the good members of gangs become conscious of their own norms and react violently against deviants and nonconformists."

The present study is concerned with the consequences of deviation from a group standard. Its immediate background is a study by Festinger, Schachter, and Back (4) of the relationships between group structure and group standards. Findings pertinent to the present study will be briefly reviewed.

1. Within each social group in a housing community there was homogeneity of attitude toward a community-wide problem. Among these groups, however, there was marked heterogeneity of attitude.
2. There was a high positive correlation between cohesiveness of the social group (measured by per cent of in-group sociometric choices) and strength of the group standard (measured by per cent of conformers to the standard).
3. Within a social group, deviates from the group standard received far fewer sociometric choices than did conformers.

The theory developed to explain these findings is as follows: Within any social group, pressures operate toward uniformity of attitude. The origins of such pressures are at least twofold: social reality and group locomotion.

Social reality. On any issue for which there is no empirical referent, the reality of one's own opinion is established by the fact that other people hold similar opinions. Forces exist to establish uniformity and thus to create "reality" for the opinion.

Group locomotion. Uniformity may be necessary or desirable for the group to locomote toward its goal. Locomotion will be facilitated if all members agree on a particular path to the goal.

The strength of the pressures toward uniformity that a group can exercise on its members will vary with the *cohesiveness* of the group and the *relevance* of the issue to the group. "Cohesiveness" is defined as the total field of forces acting on members to remain in the group. Stemming from cohesiveness is the property called the "internal power of the group," which is defined as the magnitude of change the group can induce on its members. The degree of internal power will be equal to the magnitude of the force on the member to remain in the group. If we assume that all groups are attempting to induce the same amount, we can derive that there will be fewer deviates from a group standard in highly cohesive groups than in less cohesive groups.

"Relevance" refers to the ordering, in terms of importance to the group, of the activities over which the internal power of the group extends. The conceptual dimension along which we can order particular activities as relevant or irrelevant to a particular group still remains unclear. There appear to be three possible bases for such ordering: the importance of the activity for group locomotion, the value which the group places upon the activity, and some hierarchy of needs common to group members in their roles as group members. Whatever the basis for ordering, we may anticipate that a group will exercise greater influence over relevant than over irrelevant activities.

It is assumed that there is a parallel between the process of induction and actual communication; that is, communication is the mechanism by which power is exerted. Therefore, one method by which deviation from a group standard may be maintained is cutting off the deviate from communication with the group. Lack of communication may result from little initial contact between the individual and the group or rejection from the group. In the latter case, if the magnitude of the change that the group attempts to induce is greater than the force on the individual to stay in the group, the deviate will want to leave the group, and/or the group will tend to push the deviate out of the group.

The present study is specifically concerned with the rejection of a deviate by the group. It is probable that not all groups reject to the same degree and that rejection is a consequence of deviation on only certain kinds of issues. To delineate more carefully some of the conditions affecting rejection, this experiment examines the effect of degrees of cohesiveness of the group and relevance of the issue on the degree of rejection of a deviate. The effects of these variables on communication and induction within the groups are also studied.

The Experiment

The experiment was conducted as the first meeting of a club. Four types of clubs were set up, each representing a different degree and combination of cohesiveness and relevance. In each club paid participants deviated from and conformed to an experimentally created group standard. Discussion in each club was systematically observed. At the end of each meeting members were nominated for committees, and sociometric questionnaires were filled out. These served as measures of rejection.

The four types of clubs set up were case-study, editorial, movie, and radio clubs. There was a total of 32 clubs, eight of each type. Each club had from five to seven members and three paid participants who were perceived as fellow club members. All of the subjects (Ss) in the clubs were male college students.

In a typical meeting, after preliminary introductions, each club member read a short version of the "Johnny Rocco" case (3), the life history of a juvenile delinquent, which ended as Johnny was awaiting sentence for a minor crime. The case was presented as that of a real person. The leader of the club, in all instances the experimenter (E), asked the members to discuss and decide the question, "What should be done with this kid?" The discussion was guided by a seven-point scale made up of alternative suggestions ordered along a love-punishment dimension. Point 1 presented the "all-love" viewpoint, point 7 the "all-punishment" viewpoint. Between these extremes were graded variations of the two points of view.[1] This scale was used to point up the differences of opinion within the group. It was introduced to the club members as a convenient device for learning everyone's position and for channelizing discussion.

After reading the case, each club member announced the position on the scale that he had chosen. Then the three paid participants in each club announced their positions. One

---

[1] For example, point 3 read: "He should be sent into an environment where providing Johnny with warmth and affection will be emphasized slightly more than punishing him, but discipline and punishment will be frequent if his behavior warrants it." For purposes of brevity the revised case study and the complete love–punishment scale are omitted from this paper. Interested readers may obtain copies by writing to the author.

paid participant, the "deviate," chose a position of extreme deviation and maintained it throughout the discussion; the second, the "mode," chose and maintained the modal position of group opinion; and the third, the "slider," chose the position of extreme deviation but allowed himself to be gradually influenced, so that at the end of the discussion he was at the modal position.

The case was written sympathetically to ensure that the deviate paid participant would be a deviate. In all clubs almost all members chose positions on the scale emphasizing love and kindness (positions 2–4), and the deviate chose the position of extreme discipline (position 7).

The discussion, limited to 45 minutes, was largely a matter of thrashing out differences of opinion among club members. After 20 minutes the leader took a census to ensure that everyone was fully aware of everyone else's position. He took no part in the discussion except to answer the few questions directed to him. At the end of the discussion a final census was taken. Then the leader turned the discussion to the future of the club. At this time the committee nomination blanks and sociometric questionnaires were filled out.

After each meeting the Ss were told that this had been an experiment and not a club, and the purposes of the experiment and the various devices used were fully explained. The Ss were asked not to disclose the true nature of these "clubs." There was no indication that anyone gave away the experiment.

How the Variables, Cohesiveness and Relevance, Were Produced

"Cohesiveness" has been defined as the total field of forces acting on members to remain in the group. The greater the valence of the group for its members, the greater the cohesiveness. Valence of the group derives from at least two sources, the attractiveness of the activities the group mediates and the attractiveness of the members of the group. In this experiment two degrees of cohesiveness were produced by manipulating the attractiveness of the activities mediated by the groups.

Subjects were recruited for club membership from economics classes at the University of Michigan. The case-study and editorial clubs were described to half of these classes. The case-study clubs were purportedly being set up at the request of a group of lawyers, judges, and social workers to advise on the treatment and disposition of delinquents, sex offenders, etc. The editorial clubs were supposedly being organized at the request of a new national magazine to advise on feature articles, format, policy, etc. Interested students filled out a blank indicating which club they were interested in joining, and checked two rating scales noting the extent of their interest in each club. These were four-point scales—"not interested at all," "only mildly interested," "moderately interested," and "extremely interested."

The movie and radio clubs were described to the other half of these classes. The movie clubs were purportedly being set up for a local theatre. The club members were to see films and decide which ones the theatre could successfully program. Radio clubs were supposedly being formed to serve a similar market research function for a local radio station. Students indicated their interest in these two clubs in the manner described above.

The case-study and movie clubs were high cohesive groups, made up of students who had checked between "moderately" and "extremely interested" on the scales for these clubs. The editorial and radio clubs were low cohesive groups, made up of students who indicated high interest in joining the case-study or movie clubs and little or no interest in joining the editorial or radio clubs.[2] Students

---

[2] A subject did not know which of the two clubs he had come to until the meeting was under way.

becoming members of clubs they were interested in joining made up the high cohesive groups. Those becoming members of clubs they were not interested in joining made up the low cohesive groups. In short, cohesiveness is defined here in terms of the valence of the activity.[3]

"Relevance" has been defined as an ordering of group activities along a dimension of "importance" to the group. Two degrees of relevance were produced experimentally. In one case, Ss were concerned with an activity corresponding to the purpose of the club. In the other case, Ss were concerned with an activity which had nothing to do with the purpose of the club.

Case-study and editorial clubs discussed a case study and a feature article, respectively. Movie and radio clubs discussed issues foreign to the purpose of the clubs; each began with an appropriate subject but was diverted to a side issue. The movie clubs saw a 15-minute film, and the radio clubs listened to a 15-minute recording. Then the leader introduced the observer as someone who had written up the Johnny Rocco case and wanted the help

Table 1

MEAN RATINGS ON SIGN-UP SHEETS

Group	Case-Study	Editorial
Hi Co Rel	3.27	2.20
Lo Co Rel	3.33	1.71
	Movie	Radio
Hi Co Irrel	3.53	2.24
Lo Co Irrel	3.34	1.59

---

[3] This may seem a rather restricted definition of cohesiveness. Back (1), however, has demonstrated that cohesiveness, no matter what its source, can be considered a unitary concept. Whether cohesiveness is based on friendship, the valence of the activity mediated by the group, or group prestige, the consequences of increasing cohesiveness are identical.

of the group to discuss what should be done with him. The group was assured that this had nothing to do with the club and would never happen again. With some enthusiasm from the paid participants, the group always agreed to discuss the case.

To make constant the time of interaction among Ss, radio and movie clubs were chosen as a setting for the irrelevant issue. The Ss were unable to interact while looking at a movie or listening to a recording. Therefore, their discussion time was the same as that of Ss discussing relevant issues.

To compare data obtained in the four types of clubs, it was necessary that the content be constant. This was done by using the "Johnny Rocco" case and the love—punishment scale in all the clubs. In case-study clubs, "Johnny Rocco" was the case for the day. In editorial clubs, "Johnny Rocco" was part of a feature article on juvenile delinquency. In movie and radio clubs, "Johnny Rocco" was the irrelevant issue. In all clubs the scale was the basis for discussing, "What should be done with the kid?"

In summary, there were four kinds of clubs, each reproducing a different combination of the experimental variables, as follows:

1. High cohesiveness—relevant issue (*Hi Co Rel*): Case-Study Club
2. Low cohesiveness—relevant issue (*Lo Co Rel*): Editorial Club
3. High cohesiveness—irrelevant issue (*Hi Co Irrel*): Movie Club
4. Low cohesiveness—irrelevant issue (*Lo Co Irrel*): Radio Club

In the procedure used there are two possible sources of selective error. (1) Possibly students interested in the case-study and editorial clubs were selectively different from those attracted to the movie and radio clubs. However, more than 80 per cent of the students addressed asked to join one of the clubs. More than 90 per cent of these expressed preferences for case-study or movie clubs. (2) Students assigned to case-study and movie clubs rated editorial and radio clubs slightly more favorably than students assigned to editorial and radio clubs. Possibly students in case-study and movie clubs were more attracted to the idea of a club, any kind of club. This factor, however, probably had little effect on experimental results. In the degree of rejection of the deviate, no difference was found in high cohesive groups between students who rated the nonpreferred activity high and those who rated it low.

The Validity of the Manipulation of Cohesiveness

The manipulation of cohesiveness began with the canvassing for *S*s and their assignment to clubs on the basis of preliminary interest ratings. This method of assignment is summarized in Table 1, were figures were obtained by assigning numerical values to the four points of the rating scale. "Not interested at all" has the value 1; "extremely interested" has the value 4; and the two intermediate points, the values 2 and 3. The figures are the mean ratings of each club made by all *S*s assigned to a particular experimental condition. There is a marked difference between *S*s in high and low cohesive groups in their ratings of the clubs to which they were assigned. In the low cohesive conditions, all but two *S*s rated the clubs in which they were placed between "not interested at all" and "only mildly interested." In the high cohesive conditions, all but two *S*s rated the clubs in which they were placed between "extremely interested" and "moderately interested."

How successful was this method in manipulating cohesiveness? At the end of each meeting, each *S* filled out a cohesiveness questionnaire designed to determine his intentions toward the club. There were three questions: (1) Do you want to remain a member of this group? (2) How often do you think this group should meet? (3) If enough members decide not to stay so that it seems this group might discontinue, would you like the chance to persuade others to stay?

Table 2 summarizes the data from this questionnaire and shows marked differences between high and low cohesive groups. In high cohesive groups 101 of the 102 *S*s wanted to continue their memberships; in low cohesive groups only 62 of 96 *S*s wanted to do so. There are differences, too, between *S*s in the two conditions who wanted to remain in their clubs. Such *S*s in low cohesive groups wanted to meet less often and were less willing to persuade others to stay in the club than were *S*s in high cohesive groups. The manipulation was clearly successful in producing groups with different degrees of cohesiveness.

The Paid Participants

The three paid participants in each group were perceived as fellow club members. Like the *S*s, they were male undergraduates. In each meeting, in each condition, they played three roles, deviate, mode, and slider. The deviate adopted the position of extreme discipline and maintained it throughout the discussion. The mode championed that position which the modal number of members supported. If during the meeting the modal position shifted, he shifted. The slider began as an extreme deviate (position 7) and during the meeting moved step by step to the modal position.

The mode and slider roles were controls. The deviate and the mode provided evidence of the effect of deviation as contrasted to conformity. Comparison of the slider and the deviate tested whether rejection was a result of having at one time, but no longer, championed a deviate position, or of simply maintaining deviancy against all attempted influence.

The three roles were systematically rotated among four paid participants so that each played each role twice in each experimental condition. To assure constancy from meeting to meeting, rules of behavior guiding the paid participants in any role were carefully defined. (1) Each paid participant had to speak once

Table 2

BREAKDOWN OF ANSWERS TO THE COHESIVENESS QUESTIONNAIRE

Group	N	Question 1 Want to remain member?		Question 2 Frequency of meetings?		Question 3 Want to induce others to stay in club?	
		Yes	No	Once or twice a week	Once every 2, 3, or 4 weeks	Yes	No
Hi Co Rel	53	98%	2%	61%	39%	73%	19%
Lo Co Rel	50	68	32	54	46	51	34
Hi Co Irrel	49	100	0	73	27	61	35
Lo Co Irrel	46	61	39	36	64	21	71

every five minutes. If during any five-minute interval no one addressed a remark to him, he initiated a communication. (2) Where possible, all communications made by the paid participants, whether initiated or in response to someone, were rephrasings of the position he was maintaining at the time. (3) When it was impossible simply to rephrase the position, the paid participants at the deviate position were permitted two standard arguments: (a) Despite the fact that Johnny was shown love and affection, he went back to stealing. (b) It could not be said that discipline would not work, since it had not consistently been applied to Johnny.

Measures of Rejection

After the discussion the leader introduced the subject of the club's future and proposed a plan by which a functioning group could be organized. To expedite such organization, each member filled out three mimeographed sheets: a committee nomination blank, a sociometric test, and the cohesiveness questionnaire described earlier.

Committee nominations. Three committees were set up, differing with respect to interest of the work, importance of the assigned functions, and delegated responsibility for club

activities. They were called the Executive, Steering, and Correspondence Committees. In each club, the job of each committee was defined in much the same way, but with slightly different content. The Executive Committee was to decide what the group should discuss, to act as liaison agent between the club and its sponsoring agency, and to determine club policy. The Steering Committee was to prepare and present discussion materials and determine discussion procedure. The Correspondence Committee was to perform secretarial functions.[4]

The *S*s were instructed to nominate persons whom they considered most capable of handling the work of each committee. They were not to nominate themselves or the same person for more than one committee. The number of members on each committee was manipulated so that no matter what number were present in any particular group, everyone

---

[4] To check on whether or not jobs on these committees actually did vary in attractiveness, in several of the groups the members were asked to write their own names next to those committees in which they were most interested. Most requested the Executive Committee, a few the Steering, and none the Correspondence Committee.

had to nominate everyone else present for some committee. When ten people were present, each member nominated three people for each committee; when nine people were present, only two people were nominated for the Correspondence Committee; and, when eight people were present, two people were nominated for the Steering Committee and two for the Correspondence Committee. The importance or unimportance of the committees to which the paid participants were nominated serves as an index of acceptance or rejection.

The Sociometric Test. Subjects were informed that it might become necessary to reduce the number of club members or to break up the group and portion out its members to one of the other clubs, and that therefore it would be helpful to know which people would like to remain together. They were asked to rank everyone present in order of preference for remaining in the same group with themselves. In contrast to committee nomination instructions, the emphasis here was on congeniality. These data provide a sociometric index of rejection.

The Observation Schedule

An observer, introduced as a friend interested in what the club was doing and who could be imposed upon to take notes, recorded the following aspects of the group process: (1) who spoke to whom; (2) the length, in time, of the communication; (3) whether the speaker attacked or supported the position of the person to whom he spoke; (4) whether a communication, even if not addressed to a person at a specific position, implied approval or disapproval of this position; and (5) whether the speaker talked about experiences from his own or his friends' personal histories.

Rationale

The setup described, while constituting a reasonably well controlled experimental situa-

tion, represented for the Ss a real-life situation. What was for E a method of manipulating a variable was for S a club he was interested in joining. The measuring instruments were conventional methods of electing officers; and so on. In short, the experiment was fitted within a social framework completely consistent with the idea and operation of a club with no sacrifice of experimental control. The rationale for this procedure was the assumption that it would be possible to reproduce the variables and phenomena under study with greater intensity in a purportedly "real-life situation" than in a laboratory setup that was identified as such. It is possible to produce complex social phenomena in laboratory experiments. Which procedure is more "effective" in the study of particular social phenomena can only be determined by additional investigation.

THE THEORETICAL RELATIONSHIPS AMONG COHESIVENESS, RELEVANCE, AND REJECTION

The theory presented in the introduction can now be expanded to make specific derivations as to the degree of rejection anticipated in each experimental condition. The theory states that there are pressures toward uniformity of behavior and attitude among members of most social groups. If differences of opinion exist within a group, forces will arise on the members to restore uniformity. A number of corrective tendencies will develop; for example, pressures develop to change the opinions of members of the group holding opinions different from one's own opinion to coincide more closely with those of other group members; a tendency develops to decrease one's dependence on deviant members as appropriate reference points in establishing the reality of one's own opinion. In any group where differences of opinion exist probably all of these tendencies exist and are, we shall say, simultaneously a function of the total pressures toward uniformity. In the present experimental situation where almost all *S*s were of similar opinions and there was only one deviate, it seems reasonable to suggest that the predominant tendencies acting on group members were the pressures to change the opinion of the deviate, and the tendency to decrease dependence on the deviate as a point of reference for establishing social reality.

A. *Pressures to change (Pch)* refer to the magnitude of pressures acting on group members to change a deviant opinion to conform more closely with their own. We make these assumptions about the relationship of *Pch* with the variables cohesiveness, relevance, and state of opinion:

1. *With increasing difference of opinion the magnitude of* Pch *should increase.*

If uniformity exists, *Pch* should have zero magnitude. As group opinion departs more and more from uniformity, *Pch* should correspondingly increase.

2. *With increasing cohesiveness, the magnitude of* Pch *should increase. At any point along a scale of difference of opinion,* Pch *should be greater for high than for low cohesive groups.*

Pressures to uniformity arise in part from a need for social reality within an appropriate reference group. A cohesive group, in which membership is valued, can be considered a more important reference group than a low cohesive group in which membership is not particularly cherished. Therefore, we can anticipate that pressures to uniformity will be greater in high than in low cohesive groups.

3. *With increasing relevance of issue, the magnitude of* Pch *should increase.*

Any set of activities can be ordered along some dimension of "importance" (relevance) for a particular reference group. It is plausible to assume that for activities which are of importance to the group, greater pressures to change will exist than for activities which are unimportant.

B. *Dependence (Dep)* refers to the extent to which members of a group rely on one another as reference points in establishing social reality. We make these assumptions about the relationships of dependence with the variables cohesiveness, relevance, and state of opinion:

1. *With increasing difference of opinion the magnitude of* Dep *will decrease.*

If opinions are identical, dependence will be high. When persons have different opinions, it is unlikely that they will depend on one another to establish the reality of their opinions.

2. *With increasing cohesiveness, the magnitude of* Dep *will increase.*

Members of a high cohesive group (a valued and important reference group) will more dependent on one another than will members of a low cohesive group.

3. *With relatively small differences of opinion the magnitude of* Dep *will increase with increasing relevance of issue. As difference of opinion increases,* Dep *for relevant issues decreases more rapidly than* Dep *for irrelevant issues, and a point of zero* Dep *will be reached with less difference of opinion for relevant than for irrelevant issues.*

The more "important" an issue to a particular group, the greater the extent to which group members depend on one another for social reality. On relevant issues, it will be more important that the reference group which establishes social reality have similar opinions than on less relevant issues. Therefore, dependence should decrease more rapidly with increasing perceived difference and reach the point of zero dependence earlier for highly relevant issues than for irrelevant issues.

These relationships are presented graphically in Figure 1. The rising *Pch* curves and falling *Dep* curves with increasing difference of opinion express assumptions A_1 and B_1 above. The greater magnitude of high cohesive than of low cohesive

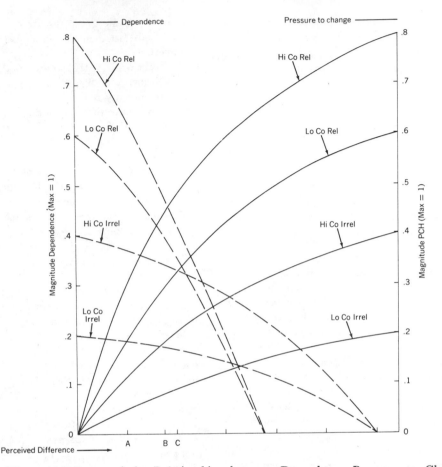

Fig. 1. Theoretical Curves of the Relationships between Dependence, Pressures to Change, and Cohesiveness, Relevance, and Perceived Difference of Opinion.

curves (relevance held constant), and of relevant than of irrelevant *Pch* curves (cohesiveness held constant), expresses assumption A₂, A₃, and B₂. At low levels of perceived difference with cohesiveness held constant, the magnitude of relevant *Dep* curve is greater than that of irrelevant *Dep* curves. Curves for relevant conditions drop at a faster rate and reach the point of zero dependence with far less perceived difference than do curves for irrelevant conditions. This is an expression of assumption B₃.

For each condition, the maxima of the

Pch and *Dep* curves are of the same magnitude. We assume that the maxima of both factors are similarly a function of total pressures to uniformity. The scale of magnitude along the ordinate of this graph has maximum = 1. The values assigned are, of course, arbitrary and purely illustrative.

From these curves we can make predictions concerning the interrelationships among cohesiveness, relevance, and degree of rejection.

We shall coordinate rejection to the amount of pressures to change that do not find public expression. The amount of pressures that do find public expression we call communication. Dependence defines the proportion of pressures to change that can be expressed. Multiplying these two factors, therefore, gives the amount of pressures that will actually be exerted.[5]

$$Comm = Pch \times Dep$$

Rejection, then, which is defined as the amount of pressures not exerted, is computed by multiplying Pch by the quantity $(1 - Dep)$.

$$Rej = Pch \times (1 - Dep)$$

The number 1 represents maximum dependence, the point at which all Pch will be communicated. The greater the pressures and the smaller the dependence, the greater the rejection. In effect, this formula suggests that rejection requires relatively little dependence on a person and, at the same time, relatively high pressures to change him. If pressures to change are high but dependence is high, rejection will be relatively slight. If dependence is low but there are no pressures to change, rejection will not occur.

Applying this formula to the postulated curves in Figure 1, we find these relationships. At point A in this figure:

$$Pch \times (1-Dep) = Rej$$
Hi Co Rel $.300 \times (1-.650) = .105$
Lo Co Rel $.185 \times (1-.513) = .090$
Hi Co Irrel $.110 \times (1-.375) = .069$
Lo Co Irrel $.050 \times (1-.185) = .041$

At point B where the perceived difference is somewhat greater:

$$Pch \times (1-Dep) = Rej$$
Hi Co Rel $.437 \times (1-.487) = .224$
Lo Co Rel $.295 \times (1-.409) = .174$

Hi Co Irrel $.175 \times (1-.341) = .115$
Lo Co Irrel $.075 \times (1-.175) = .062$

These trends become clear: (1) As perceived difference increases, the degree of rejection in each of these conditions will increase. (2) At any point beyond zero, along the axis of perceived difference:

Rej in *Hi Co Rel* > *Rej* in *Lo Co Rel*
Rej in *Hi Co Irrel* > *Rej* in *Lo Co Irrel*
Rej in *Hi Co Rel* > *Rej* in *Hi Co Irrel*
Rej in *Lo Co Rel* > *Rej* in *Lo Co Irrel*[6]

Thus, the set of assumptions determining the shapes of these curves leads to these experimental predictions: (*a*) Persons in the mode and slider roles (who at the end of a meeting are close to zero perceived difference) will be rejected less (if at all) than will persons in the deviate role. (*b*) From experimental condition to condition the degree of rejection of persons in the deviate role will vary in the order noted in trend 2 above. With cohesiveness constant, rejection will be greater in relevant than in irrelevant groups. With relevance constant, rejection will be greater in high than in low cohesive groups.

RESULTS

The post-meeting nominations for committees and the sociometric rankings of all club members provide two indices of

---

[5] This theory of communication will be developed and expanded in the following section.

[6] It is impossible to make an exact prediction about relative rejection between the *Lo Co Rel* and *Hi Co Irrel* conditions. Though the curves imply *Rej* in *Lo Co Rel* > *Rej* in *Hi Co Irrel*, this was done purely for illustrative simplicity. We have, of course, no way of determining the relative contributions of cohesiveness and relevance in a comparison to *Lo Co Rel* and *Hi Co Irrel* conditions.

rejection, i.e., nominations to the less important committees and relatively low sociometric rankings.

Sociometric Rankings

At the end of each meeting the members of each club ranked everyone in the order of his desirability as a fellow club member. The instructions emphasized congeniality and compatibility as the basis for ranking. The lower the ranking, the greater the rejection.

Table 3 presents mean sociometric rankings of each paid participant in each condition. Each figure in the table is the mean of the mean sociometric rankings in each group. The N for each figure is 8, the number of groups in each condition. Since the groups varied in size from eight to ten members, all rankings were corrected to equivalent scores by adopting the nine possible rankings in a group of ten people as a basic scale and correcting rankings in smaller groups to equivalent scores. The mean rank in every group is 5.

Table 3

MEAN SOCIOMETRIC RANKINGS OF THE PAID PARTICIPANTS

Group	Deviate	Mode	Slider
Hi Co Rel	6.44	4.65	5.02
Lo Co Rel	5.83	4.70	4.56
Hi Co Irrel	6.51	4.68	4.44
Lo Co Irrel	5.67	3.83	5.03

These relationships emerge from Table 3: (1) In any condition, mean rankings of either mode or slider are considerably below mean rankings of the deviate. All mode-deviate differences are significant by a t-test at the 7 per cent level of confidence or better. Clearly, a penalty of

relative rejection is imposed on a deviate. (2) There are no significant differences in rankings of either the mode or slider when comparisons are made between conditions.[7] The variables of cohesiveness and relevance have no effects on group evaluation of individuals who are at, or who adopt, the group norms. (3) The deviate is rejected more strongly in high than in low cohesive groups. Between rankings in high and low cohesive groups, the t is significant at the 12 per cent level for the difference between Hi Co Rel and Lo Co Rel, and at the 1 per cent level for the difference between Hi Co $Irrel$ and Lo Co $Irrel$.[8] As predicted, greater cohesiveness produces greater rejection.

There is, however, no immediate evidence that the variable, relevance, affects the degree of rejection. The mean sociometric rankings of the deviate in the relevant and irrelevant condition, with cohesiveness constant, are about the same. This may be attributed in part to the fact that the measurement is a relative one, indicating only an individual's relative preference for one person over another, with no indication of the absolute intensity of like or dislike. There is, however, some indication of the relative intensities of the ratings in each condition. Occasionally a subject refused to fill in the sociometric sheet, or simply put in numbers in sequence, explaining that he was unable to discriminate among the people present. Random ranking implies that there was no genuine basis on which to express pre-

---

[7] The largest difference, that between the Hi Co $Irrel$ and Lo Co $Irrel$ conditions for the mode, is significant by t-test at only the 28 per cent level.

[8] In all tests of significance mentioned in this section, the group rather than the individual was considered the unit.

ference. If, therefore, any one experimental condition has a significantly greater
number of random rankings than do the
others, it may be inferred that, in general,
all rankings in this condition were made
with less basis for expressing preference
and imply less intensity of like or dislike
than in a condition where random responses are rare. More than twice as many
random rankings were made in irrelevant
conditions as in relevant. Of all subjects,
16 per cent ranked randomly in the irrelevant conditions and 6.8 per cent in the
relevant conditions. This difference is
significant by chi-square with 1 *d.f.* at the
2 per cent level. There were no significant
differences between *Hi Co Rel* and *Lo Co
Rel* or between *Hi Co Irrel* and *Lo Co
Irrel*. Though mean rankings are about
the same for relevant and irrelevant conditions, random rankings of the deviate
seem to imply less strong feelings of rejection in the irrelevant groups.

These sociometric data are in the directions predicted. (1) Paid participants in
the mode and slider roles were not rejected; as deviates they were definitely
rejected. (2) There is greater rejection of
the deviate in high than in low cohesive
groups. (3) Though sociometric rankings
of the deviate are about the same for
relevant and irrelevant conditions, random
sociometric rankings indicate that the intensity of rejection in irrelevant conditions
was less than in relevant conditions.

Assignment to Committees

With instructions emphasizing competence for the job, the members of each
club nominated people for membership on
the Executive, Steering, and Correspondence Committees. Rejection is coordinated to assignment to the least desirable
committee. The Executive was the most

Table 4

PERCENTAGE OF SUBJECTS ABOVE
CHANCE ASSIGNING " MODE "
TO COMMITTEES

Group	Executive	Steering	Correspondence
Hi Co Rel	−4.56	+6.76	−2.22
Lo Co Rel	−9.83	+20.15	−10.44
Hi Co Irrel	−0.08	+6.85	−6.93
Lo Co Irrel	+3.70	+3.70	−8.07

Table 5

PERCENTAGE OF SUBJECTS ABOVE
CHANCE ASSIGNING " SLIDER "
TO COMMITTEES

Group	Executive	Steering	Correspondence
Hi Co Rel	+1.76	−5.93	+4.16
Lo Co Rel	+7.32	−7.86	+0.50
Hi Co Irrel	−4.97	+4.38	+0.39
Lo Co Irrel	+2.69	−3.52	+0.16

Table 6

PERCENTAGE OF SUBJECTS ABOVE
CHANCE ASSIGNING " DEVIATE "
TO COMMITTEES

Group	Executive	Steering	Correspondence
Hi Co Rel	−14.00	−8.34	+22.31
Lo Co Rel	−17.58	−7.81	+25.26
Hi Co Irrel	−16.41	+4.83	+11.44
Lo Co Irrel	+10.16	−9.40	−1.30

attractive committee and the Correspondence the least attractive.

Tables 4, 5, and 6 present the data on
the assignment of paid participants in the
mode, slider, and deviate roles to the three
committees. All figures in each table represent the percentage, above or below
chance expectancy, of all *S*s in each con-

dition who assigned the various roles to the different committees. In Table 4, the mode was nominated for the Executive Committee by 4.56 per cent less than we would expect if nominations in the *Hi Co Rel* condition had been made on some randomly determined basis. Varying group sizes, affecting the probability of any one person being assigned to a particular committee, necessitated computation of chance expectancies.

The standard errors of all chance percentages are close to 6.20.[9] Any score greater than 10.23 is significant at the 10 per cent level; greater than 12.90 is significant at the 5 per cent level; and greater than 15.93 is significant at the 1 per cent level. If the 5 per cent level is accepted, Table 5 reveals no significant fluctuations from chance in assigning the slider to any one particular committee. Similarly, for the mode, in Table 4, we find only one score that departs significantly from chance, assignment of the mode to the Steering Committee in the *Lo Co Rel* condition. With the large number of scores obtained, this may be interpreted as a chance fluctuation. There is no indication of systematic rejection for the mode or slider roles.

Table 6 for the deviate presents a completely different picture. In all conditions, except *Lo Co Irrel*, the deviate is over-nominated for the Correspondence Committee and under-nominated for the

---

[9] This score was computed using $\sqrt{\dfrac{pq}{n}}$, the customary formula for computing the standard error of a percentage. Since the number of cases varied slightly from condition to condition, and P varied slightly with the number of people in each group, the standard error 6.20 is a convenient approximation. The obtained standard errors for each committee in each condition are all quite close to this figure.

Executive Committee. Deviation results in assignment to a relatively peripheral position in the role structure of the group. Not only is the deviate considered relatively undesirable as a fellow club member, but also least capable of handling the important jobs in the club.

The degree of rejection, however, is affected by the experimental variables. Rejection is greater in both relevant conditions than in the irrelevant conditions. A *t*-test with 30 *d.f.* yields significance at the 2 per cent level of confidence for this difference. Differences between the degree of rejection in high cohesive groups and low cohesive groups, however, are less clear-cut. Although there is a difference between high and low cohesive irrelevant conditions significant by *t*-test at the 10 per cent level, there is no difference between the two relevant conditions. This is clearly inconsistent with theoretical expectations. Possibly the committee assignment measure should also be considered a relative measure that gives no indication of intensity of feeling. It is plausible that, though there is no difference between high and low cohesive relevant groups in the percentage of people assigning the deviate to the Correspondence Committee, the intensity of rejection is greater in high than in low cohesive groups. In contrast to the sociometric ranking, however, no *S* had difficulty in making these judgments, and there is no evidence of random assignment to committees. This may possibly be attributed to the different natures of the measures. A judgment of fitness for a particular job is a fairly everyday matter. Decisions about which people should be in or out of a group appear to be a more unusual sort of judgment to make.

Except for this single inconsistency, the data support the predictions. Neither the mode nor the slider was rejected. In all

conditions except *Lo Co Irrel*, where we anticipated very little rejection, the deviate was over-nominated for the Correspondence Committee. Rejection of the deviate was greater in the relevant than in the irrelevant conditions, and greater in the *Hi Co Irrel* than in the *Lo Co Irrel* condition.

THE PROCESS OF COMMUNICATION

The previous section has treated the relationships between experimental manipulations and post-meeting measurements. This section relates the processes of induction and communication, as they occurred during the meetings, to the experimental variables, cohesiveness and relevance, and to the postmeeting measurements.

We shall consider communication, the process of one person talking to another, as the mechanism of induction, i.e., the means by which influence is exerted. There are, of course, other reasons why people communicate, but within the confines of this experiment and theory, we shall largely limit ourselves to communication as influence.

From the theoretical elaboration of "pressures to uniformity," specific derivations may be made about certain aspects of the patterns of communication that occurred in these meetings. Let us first relate the constructs, *Pch* and *Dep*, to the occurrence of communication.

1. Pressures to change others mean pressures to influence others, which we will consider identical with pressures to communicate. Our earlier assumptions may, therefore, be extended to communication pressures. The pressures to communicate to a deviate will rise with increasing perceived difference, increasing cohesiveness, and increasing relevance.

2. Dependence refers to the extent to which a person relies on another person or group of persons to establish social reality. It defines the proportion of pressure to change that can actually find public expression. Actual communication, then, is a function of both *Dep* and *Pch*, with dependence modifying the proportion of pressures to change that will be expressed publicly. Actual communication is formulated as $Comm = Pch \times Dep$.

In Figure 2, the heavily dotted lines, constructed by making the proper multiplications at each point, represent the magnitude or frequency of actual communication that should be directed at positions with different degrees of perceived difference in the four experimental conditions.[10] This figure is the same as Figure 1, with the curves for predicted communication added.

Let us examine more closely the meaning of "perceived difference." It refers to the phenomenological difference between two people rather than to the absolute difference between two points on the love-punishment scale. Two people may be at position 4 on the scale and perceive the difference between themselves and someone at position 7 as of very different orders of magnitude. We shall postulate that in

---

[10] The coordination of rejection to the amount of pressures that are not publicly expressed can be demonstrated graphically in Figure 2. At any point along the axis of perceived difference, rejection is equal to the difference between the height of the appropriate derived curve of actual communication and the height of the corresponding curve for *Pch*.

This relationship is simply stated algebraically:

$$Rej = Pch \times (1 - Dep)$$
$$= Pch - Pch \times Dep$$
$$Comm = Pch \times Dep$$
$$\therefore \ Rej = Pch - Comm$$

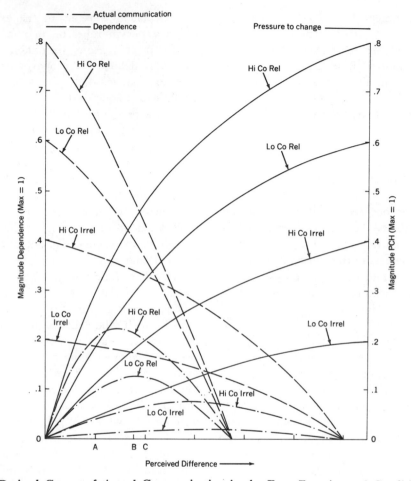

Fig. 2. Derived Curves of Actual Communication in the Four Experimental Conditions.

this experiment perceived differences increased with discussion. In all club meetings the question, "How much do we really differ?" was frequently discussed, and attempts were made to reduce the distance between points on the scale. The deviates, however, were specifically instructed to resist attempts to minimize differences between themselves and people at other positions. The assumption that perceived difference increases with discussion seems reasonable, therefore, in this situation.

Accepting this assumption, we may say that the dotted curve of communication in Figure 2 represents the actual pattern of communication during the course of the meeting. From these considerations a number of testable derivations may be about the frequency and pattern of communication to each paid participant in each condition.

Communication Patterns to the Deviate

A prediction previously developed was that rejection will increase with increasing perceived difference. Therefore, people who strongly reject the deviate perceive a greater difference between themselves and the deviate than do pople who do not reject. In Figure 2, point C represents the position of a rejector at the end of a meeting, point B the position of a mild rejector, and point A the position of a non-rejector. If perpendiculars are projected from these points, they intercept the communication curves at different relative positions.

If we accept the assumption that perceived difference increases with discussion time, and postulate that points C, B, and A in Figure 2 represent, respectively, the end-of-the-meeting perceptions of people who reject the deviate strongly, reject mildly, and do not reject, then we must

say that the curves of actual communication up to points C, B, and A represent the patterns of communication from these three kinds of people to the deviate during the course of the meeting. In Figure 3 these predicted curves of communication, projected from Figure 2, are drawn for these three kinds of people for each experimental condition. These curves are specific predictions about the pattern and magnitude of communication to the deviate.

In Figure 3 the ordinate represents the amount of communication during the meeting, and the abscissa, the flow of time from zero to 45 minutes. A point on these curves represents the amount of communication that will be addressed to the deviate at a particular time in the course of the meeting by either the people who reject him strongly, reject mildly, or do not reject. All curves start slightly above the zero point, for it seems likely that even at the beginning of a meeting there is some perception of difference.

In the *Hi Co Rel* condition, the communication curve of non-rejectors increases continuously throughout the meeting. The curve of strong rejectors reaches a peak during the meeting and then declines continuously; and the mild rejectors' curve reaches a peak somewhat later and then declines. In all other conditions, all communication curves to the deviate rise continuously throughout the meeting.

The data testing these derivations are presented in Table 7. The meeting is here divided into ten-minute intervals and communications to the deviate during each interval tallied. The three categories of rejectors are determined by sociometric rankings of the deviate. Non-rejectors ranked the deviate from 1.0–3.72; mild rejectors from 4.0–7.92; and strong rejectors between 8 and 9. The figures in the

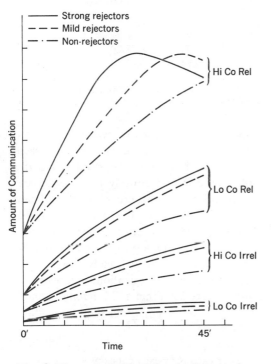

Fig. 3. Theoretical Curves of Communications from Strong Rejectors, Mild Rejectors, and Non-Rejectors to the Deviate in the Four Experimental Conditions.

Table 7

MEAN NUMBEER OF COMMUNICATIONS ADDRESSED TO " DEVIATE " DURING
THE COURSE OF THE MEETING BY SUBJECTS WITH DIFFERENT
POST-MEETING REACTIONS TO HIM

Group	N	Time Interval in Minutes			
		5–15*	15–25	25–35	35–45
Hi Co Rel					
Non-rejectors	13	1.15	0.92	2.15	1.54
Mild rejectors	15	0.40	1.27	1.87	0.86
Strong rejectors	25	0.68	1.60	1.52	0.76
Lo Co Rel					
Non-rejectors	13	0.38	0.54	0.84	0.46
Mild rejectors	22	0.58	0.50	1.23	1.73
Strong rejectors	15	0.26	0.47	1.27	2.99
Hi Co Irrel					
Non-rejectors	9	1.32	1.44	0.99	2.44
Mild rejectors	20	1.15	1.35	1.55	1.20
Strong rejectors	20	0.75	1.15	1.60	3.42
Lo Co Irrel					
Non-rejectors	16	1.69	1.69	2.34	2.12
Mild rejectors	15	1.47	0.94	2.20	3.74
Strong rejectors	15	1.20	0.74	2.47	2.87

* Because the first few minutes of many meetings were concerned with technical problems and deciding just what was to be done, data from the 0–5 time interval are not reported.

table represent the total number of communications in each time interval made by all people in each rejector category, divided by the number of people in this category.

Let us examine first the data for the *Hi Co Rel* groups in Table 7. The strong rejectors reach their peak of communication to the deviate in the 15–25 minute interval and then decline steadily. The difference between the peak interval and the final time interval is significant at better than the 1 per cent level.[11] Mild rejectors reach their peak somewhat later, in the 25–35 minute interval, and then decline. The difference between this peak

and the final time interval is significant at the 3 per cent level. Non-rejectors seem to reach a peak and then decline, but this difference is due entirely to one case and is significant at exactly the 50 per cent level of confidence. The data, then, essentially parallel theoretical expectations.

In the other experimental conditions the theory anticipates a steady rise in the number of communications addressed to the deviate by either mild, strong, or non-rejectors. The remaining data in Table 7

---

[11] All of the level of significance reported with this set of data were obtained by tabulat-

ing for each S in each category whether or not the number of communications he had addressed to the deviate was higher in one time interval than in the interval with which it was being compared. Probabilities were then computed by means of binomial expansion.

Table 8

MEAN NUMBER OF COMMUNICATIONS ADDRESSED TO THE " MODE " AND
" SLIDER " DURING THE COURSE OF THE MEETING

Group	N	Time Interval in Minutes			
		5–15	15–25	25–35	35–45
Hi Co Rel					
Mode	53	0.13	0.06	0.06	0.10
Slider	53	0.53	0.55	0.21	0.17
Lo Co Rel					
Mode	50	0.06	0.10	0.14	0.22
Slider	50	0.30	0.20	0.20	0.20
Hi Co Irrel					
Mode	49	0.18	0.16	0.37	0.12
Slider	49	0.79	0.47	0.20	0.04
Lo Co Irrel					
Mode	46	0.14	0.15	0.13	0.45
Slider	46	0.72	0.63	0.41	0.30

indicate that this is essentially correct. In six of these nine breakdowns, the number of communications to the deviate rises continuously, and differences between the last two time intervals are significant at the 12 per cent level or better for all but the rising *Lo Co Irrel* curves. In three cases (non-rejectors in *Lo Co Rel* and *Lo Co Irrel*, mild rejectors in the *Hi Co Irrel*) there is a slight drop in the final interval. None of these drops is significant.

The theoretical derivations seem as well corroborated as can be anticipated with the relatively small number of cases involved. Most of the curves rise, and the only significant declines are the predicted ones.

Communication Patterns to the Mode and Slider

The position of the mode on the scale of perceived difference in Figure 2 should be at zero, the point of no perceived difference between himself and most of the others in the group. At this point $Pch = 0$, and dependence is at a maximum. There should therefore be no communications to the mode during any meeting in any experimental condition. This conclusion, however, must be qualified by two considerations. (1) As a rule, most, but not all, of the members of any one club were at the modal position. There were slight differences, therefore, between the mode and a few members of the group. (2) A paid participant in the modal role was required to speak once every five minutes. Courtesy would probably demand an occasional response.

We may anticipate, then, that the curve of communication to the mode in all experimental conditions should be a low straight line, parallel to the horizontal time axis. In Table 8, we see that this is the case. The figures in this table are computed on the same basis as those in the previous table. In all conditions only a very small number of communications was addressed to the mode at any time.

Fluctuations from a straight line are all within the range of chance expectancy.

Theoretically, communications to the slider present a more complicated picture, for it is impossible to predict exactly the interaction between perceived difference and decreasing absolute difference. But it is reasonable to suggest that communications to the slider should be at about the same level as to the deviate until the slider makes his first shift, and then communications should gradually decrease until by the end of the meeting they are at about the same level for both the slider and the mode. The data presented in Table 8 essentially substantiate these expectations. About 15 minutes after the meeting started the slider shifted from 7 to 5, and finally adopted the modal position between the 35- and 40-minute marks. In all experimental conditions, communications to the slider are at first considerably above the level of communication to the mode and then decline steadily to the level of the mode in the final time interval.[12]

The Frequency of Communication

From the theoretical considerations previously formulated, additional derivations can be made about the magnitude or absolute amounts of communication in each experimental condition. It may be predicted, from the curves of communication in Figure 3, that the amount of communication to the deviate will decrease from *Hi Co Rel* condition to *Lo Co Rel* to *Hi Co Irrel* to *Lo Co Irrel*. And, since the distribution of positions on the love-punishment scale is the same from condition to condition, it may also be anticipated that the mean amounts of communication for meetings, within each condition, will vary in the same order. The data collected with the present observation schedule are, however, inadequate to substantiate or disprove these derivations. It has been postulated that the magnitude of pressures to uniformity are greater on relevant than on irrelevant issues, in high than in low cohesive groups. These derivations will hold *only* for communications that arise from pressures to uniformity, and we can say nothing about communications that arise from other sources. However, people communicate for numberless reasons beyond that of restoring uniformity of opinion. It seems a reasonable assumption that the more irrelevant an issue, the greater will be the number of communications that have sources other than pressures to uniformity. If this analysis of the differences between the discussions of relevant and irrelevant issues is correct, supporting evidence must be found in areas other than the directions and amounts of communication.

Differences between the communication process in relevant and irrelevant conditions are shown in Table 9. Communications in the relevant groups tended to be longer. Slightly more than 30 per cent of all communications in the relevant groups were long communications (more than 30 seconds), and only 21 per cent were long

---

[12] In the first time interval, though the number of communications to the slider is considerably higher than that to the mode, comparison with Table 7 reveals that the number of slider-directed communications is consistently lower than that to the deviate. Probably this is an artifact of the slider role. In preparing to shift position, the slider probably tended to be somewhat less extreme and emphatic in his defense of position 7.

Table 9

INTERRUPTIONS, PAUSES, PERSONAL REFERENCES, AND LONG COMMUNICATIONS IN ALL CONDITIONS

	Hi Co Rel	Lo Co Rel	Hi Co Irrel	Lo Co Irrel
Per cent long communications	28	33	25	17
Mean interruptions per meeting	67.71	29.86	78.71	82.00
Total pauses	1	1	3	7
Personal history references	18	14	5	8

in the irrelevant condition.[13] In addition, discussion in these two conditions went at a different clip. There were far more interruptions in irrelevant than in relevant groups.[14] An interruption is defined as any attempt to break into a speech before it is completed. Oddly enough, in the face of the greater number of communications and the more rapid clip in irrelevant groups, there was a greater number of pauses in the discussions of the irrelevant groups. Though there was no systematic notation of pauses, the observer noted all particularly long, uncomfortable intervals when no one had anything to say. In short, there were marked differences in the character of discussion in the two conditions. Discussion in irrelevant groups might be characterized as cocktail party conversation, fast, brief, clipped, and in bursts; discussion in the relevant groups resembled the board meeting, slow, even-paced, long, and well considered.

Consistent with these characterizations of the process of the meeting are the additional data presented in Table 9 on the relative frequency of personal history references. Reference to personal history may be considered evidence of real involvement in the discussion. In relevant groups, there were more than two and a half times as many personal references as there were in irrelevant groups.[15] Not only were the discussions of the irrelevant groups more glib, but also apparently more superficial.

The marked differences in the manner of relevant and irrelevant groups indicate that communications in irrelevant groups resulted in good part from sources other than pressures to uniformity. The data, therefore, do not serve as an adequate test of the derivations concerning the relative amounts of communication in the various conditions.

SUMMARY

A set of assumptions has been developed which defines the relationships of the con-

---

[13] This difference has a $t = 2.06$, which with 30 *d.f.* is significant at the 5 per cent level.

[14] The difference between mean number of interruptions in relevant and irrelevant groups is significant at better than the .001 level of significance, with $t = 5.74$ for 30 *d.f.* These measures of interruption and length of communication are relatively independent. Rank order correlations between the two are only $+.39$ in the irrelevant condition and $+.45$ in the relevant condition.

[15] The difference yields a t of 1.89, which with 30 *d.f.* is significant at the 8 per cent level.

structs dependence and pressures to change, to cohesiveness, relevance, and state of opinion. Both communication and rejection have been coordinated to these constructs. Dependence defines the proportion of the pressures to change that can find public expression, and communication is defined as:

$$Comm = Pch \times Dep'$$

Rejection is coordinated to the amount of pressures to change which are not exerted and is defined as:

$$Rej = Pch \times (1 - Dep)$$

These coordinations and the assumptions defining *Pch* and *Dep* allow us to make a number of predictions as to the results of the experiment. Predictions about rejection and the evidence supporting them will be reviewed briefly.

1. *Persons in the mode and slider roles will be rejected less (if at all) than will persons in the deviate role.*

On both the sociometric and committee assignment measures there was no evidence that either the mode or slider was rejected. The deviate, on the other hand, was rejected in all experimental conditions except *Lo Co Irrel*. Where the magnitudes of both *Dep* and *Pch* are low, we anticipate relatively little rejection. Thus, in the *Lo Co Irrel* condition, the sociometric ranking of the deviate was only slightly above the mean, and he was not overnominated for the correspondence committee.

2. *With cohesiveness held constant, rejection will be greater in relevant groups than in irrelevant groups.*

(*a*) On the committee assignment measure the deviate was assigned to the Correspondence Committee to a far great-

er extent in the relevant groups than in the irrelevant groups.

(*b*) Though sociometric rankings of the deviate are about the same for the relevant and irrelevant conditions, there is evidence from random sociometric rankings that the intensity of rejection is greater in the relevant than in the irrelevant conditions.

3. *With relevance held constant, rejection will be greater in high cohesive than in low cohesive groups.*

(*a*) The mean sociometric ranking of the deviate was considerably higher in both high cohesive conditions than in the corresponding low cohesive conditions.

(*b*) On the committee assignment measure the deviate was nominated to the Correspondence Committee to a greater extent in the *Hi Co Irrel* than in the *Lo Co Irrel* condition. There is no difference, however, between the *Hi Co Rel* and the *Lo Co Rel* conditions. This inconsistency may be explained in terms of the relative nature of the measure. Here, too, the intensity of rejection may be stronger in *Hi Co Rel* than in *Lo Co Rel* groups. There is no immediate evidence, however, to support this argument.

Predictions about patterns of communication follow:

1. *In the* Hi Co Rel *condition, the amount of communication addressed to the deviate by non-rejectors should increase continuously throughout the meeting. Strong rejectors should reach a peak of communication during the meeting and then decline continuously and mild rejectors should reach a peak somewhat later and then decline.*

2. *In all other experimental conditions, communications to the deviate from strong mild, or non-rejectors should increase continuously throughout the meeting.*

3. *In all experimental conditions, there should be relatively few communications addressed to persons in the modal role and no increase in communications during the meeting.*

4. *In all conditions, communications to the slider should decrease during the meeting as the slider shifts from a deviate to a modal position.*

The data essentially substantiated all of these predictions. The theory leads to other predictions about the relative magnitudes of communication in each experimental condition. These derivations, however, hold only for communications arising from pressures to uniformity. Since in irrelevant conditions many communications arose from other sources, it is impossible to test these derivations.

REFERENCES

1. BACK, K. W. "The Exertion of Influence Through Social Communication." Unpublished Doctor's dissertation, Massachusetts Institute of Technology, 1949.

2. COCH, L., and FRENCH, J. R. P., JR. "Overcoming Resistance to Change." *Hum. Relat.*, 1948, 1, 512–532.

3. EVANS, J. "Johnny Rocco." *J. Abnorm. Soc. Psychol.*, 1948, 43, 357–383.

4. FESTINGER, L., SCHACHTER, S., and BACK, K. *Social Pressures in Informal Groups: A Study of a Housing Community.* New York: Harper, 1950.

5. LYND, R. S., and LYND, H. M. *Middletown, A Study in Contemporary American Culture.* New York: Harcourt, Brace, 1929.

6. LYND, R. S., and LYND, H. M. *Middletown in Transition.* New York: Harcourt, Brace, 1937.

7. MEREI, F. "Group Leadership in Institutionalization." *Hum. Relat.*, 1941, 2, 23–39.

8. NEWCOMB, T. M. *Personality and Social Change.* New York: Dryden Press, 1943.

9. SHAW, C. R. (Ed.) *Brothers in Crime.* Chicago: Univ. of Chicago Press, 1938.

10. SHAW, C. R. *The Jack Roller.* Chicago: Univ. of Chicago Press, 1939.

11. SHERIF, M. "A Study of Some Social Factors in Perception." *Arch. Psychol., N. Y.,* 1935, No. 187.

12. SHERIF, M. *The Psychology of Social Norms.* New York: Harper, 1936.

13. SHERIF, M., and CANTRIL, H. *The Psychology of Ego-Involvements.* New York: Wiley, 1947.

14. THRASHER, F. M. *The Gang.* Chicago: Univ. of Chicago Press, 1927.

15. WARNER, W. L., and LUNT, P. S. *The Social Life of a Modern Community.* New Haven: Yale Univ. Press, 1941.

16. WHYTE, W. F. *Street Corner Society.* Chicago: Univ. of Chicago Press, 1943.

17. ZANDER, A., and CHABOT, J. Unpublished study.

18. ZORBAUGH, H. W. *The Gold Coast and the Slum.* Chicago: Univ. of Chicago Press, 1929.

ON "STATUS-LIABILITY"*

*James A. Wiggins, Forrest Dill,
and Richard D. Schwartz*

In the past, several empirical investigations have concerned themselves with the effect of the status of a frustration- or interference-agent on the aggression or punishment he receives from those he frustrated. In experimental investigations, Worchel and Reiser found that verbal aggression toward a frustration-agent decreased with his increasing status (faculty vs. student; captain vs. private).[1] Similarly, in a correlational study, Cohen found that in hypothetical situations aggression toward a frustration-agent decreased with his status (authority figures vs. peers).[2] The rationale in each case was that a

high-status individual could counter-aggress or punish if aggressed against. Schwartz and Skolnick found similar results in the differential sanctioning of lower-class unskilled workers charged with assault and medical doctors accused of malpractice.[3] In an experimental investigation, Hollander found that status (past task competence) protected a frustrating nonconformist from punishment (lost influence), a phenomenon he called "idiosyncrasy credit."[4]

At the same time, only one investigation has attempted to vary simultaneously the status of the interference-agent and the intensity of the frustration. In a correlational study, Graham *et al.* found that in hypothetical situations the strength of the positive relationship between frustration-intensity and aggression toward the frustration-agent decreased as the latter's status increased (and if the frustration-agent was a parent, the relationship completely disappeared).[5]

* James A. Wiggins, Forrest Dill, and Richard D. Schwartz, "On 'Status-Liability'," *Sociometry*, 28 (1965), 197–209. Reprinted by permission of the American Sociological Association.

[1] P. Worchel, "Catharsis and the Relief of Hostility," *Journal of Abnormal and Social Psychology*, 55 (March, 1957), pp. 238–243; M. Reiser, R. Reeves, and J. Armington, "Effect of Variations in Laboratory Procedure and Experiments Upon Ballistocardiogram, Blood Pressure, and Heart Rate in Healthy Young Men," *Psychosomatic Medicine*, 17 (1955), pp. 185–199.

[2] A. Cohen, "Social Norms, Arbitrariness of Frustration, and Status of the Agent of Frustration in Frustration-Aggression Hypothesis," *Journal of Abnormal and Social Psychology*, 51 (March, 1955), pp. 222–226.

[3] R. Schwartz and J. Skolnick, "Two Studies of Legal Stigma," *Social Problems*, 10 (Fall, 1962), pp. 133–142.

[4] E. Hollander, "Competence and Conformity in the Acceptance of Influence," *Journal of Abnormal and Social Psychology*, 61 (April, 1960), pp. 365–370.

[5] F. Graham, W. Charwat, A. Honig, and P. Weltz, "Aggression as a Function of the

The purpose of the present investigation is to examine this relationship experimentally. Three levels of interference-intensity and two levels of status are used in the experiment. The former is conceived as the degree to which a group member's behavior decreases the probability of the group achieving its goal. The three levels range from behavior having little effect on the probability of goal-achievement (low interference-intensity) to behavior appreciably decreasing the probability of goal-achievement (medium interference-intensity) to behavior practically eliminating the possibility of goal-achievement (high interference-intensity). Following Hollander, "status" is conceived as a group member's past competence at group tasks. In order to isolate the effect of high status more exactly, the experiment examines the difference between "high" and "medium status" as opposed to the more usual concern with "high" and "low status."

The specific propositions tested are:

1. The greater the interference-intensity the greater the punishment of the interference-agent.

2. The greater the status of the interference-agent the less the punishment he receives.

3. The relationship between punishment and the status of the interference-agent is negative under low- and medium-interference and positive under high-interference.

Proposition 3 in the major focus of the investigation. It asserts that the group members will show little inclination to punish a high-status interference-agent as long as he does not step too far out of bounds. As long as there is still hope of achieving the group goal, the group will bear with him because of (1) his past

performance and (2) their future need of his services. However, if his behavior interferes to the degree that group's goal is jeopardized, the members will punish him more than a lower-status member who interferes to the same degree. The rationale for this "status-liability" proposition will be treated in the discussion section below.

METHOD

Experimental Setting

Thirty four-person groups were randomly assigned to one of six experimental variations by the use of a die. The subjects were student volunteers from psychology and sociology classes in the summer session at Northwestern University.

The subjects were ushered into the experimental room and each settled in an enclosed working space. Although subjects were unable to see one another, the experimenter could observe all subjects from his position at a table in the middle of the room. The subjects were read the following instructions:

When you volunteered to participate in this experiment, you couldn't have known that you stood to gain some money as well as two hours of credit for participating in it. I can now tell you that your group is one of twelve groups which are in competition for a prize of $50. The competition for this $50 prize operates very simply; the group with the highest scores on the five tasks that you are about to undertake wins the $50.

(More extemporaneously, they were told the following:) In actuality, you are competing with one other group. Your group is the last in one complete series of twelve groups which are competing for the $50. The other eleven groups have been completed. Since

Attack and the Attacker," *Journal of Abnormal and Social Psychology*, 46 (May, 1951), pp. 512–520.

yours is the last group in this series, you will know what score you will have to beat to win the $50 and at the end of this session we will know whether your group has won the $50.

(Returning to the more obvious reading of instructions:) We are specifically interested in some factors which affect task performance in a competitive setting, and you will probably be able to see what these factors are as the experiment progresses. If not, I'll explain them to you at the end of the experiment.

The design of the experiment is quite simple. Each of you will work five tasks of varying degrees of difficulty and of varying natures. You will be graded on how well you perform these tasks. Following your completion of each task, they will be collected and graded as quickly as possible. The tasks have been constructed with this in mind: each is easily graded by means of a scoring key. When I have finished scoring the particular task, I will give you your scores on a scoresheet, which I will replicate here on the blackboard. You will notice that the scoresheet will also contain some information of importance to you: the best scores that any one of the previous groups in your series has achieved on each of the tasks. By comparing your group's performance with these scores, you will be able to estimate your group's chances of winning the $50. (Extemporaneously: Since yours is the last group in this series, you are assured of winning the $50 if your group accumulative score at the end of the five tasks is higher than the score of the other group.) If, at the end of the five tasks your score is lower than the score of the best group, you will still be eligible for a second prize of $15. If you should win either prize, the money will be sent to you within a week.

On the scoresheet, I will list your individual performances as well as the total score of your group on each task. Two things should be noted about this scoring procedure. First, the scores that I post will be standardized to a perfect score of 20 for each task. This procedure is followed so that each task will be comparable with each other task in terms of arriving at a total score across all five tasks. No task is worth more than another task. Thus, for example, on the first task, there are 75 items. A person who answers all 75 items correctly would receive a standardized score of 20. A person who gets 45 items right would receive a standardized score of 12. The other tasks work exactly the same way. The second thing about these scores is that you will be primarily interested in the accumulative score of your group. On the blackboard, you will notice that the accumulative score of the best group after the first task is 63, the accumulative score after the second task is 93, after the third task it is 128, and so on. (Extemporaneously: If your final group accumulative score is the least bit higher than the best accumulative score—that is, higher than the 222 score achieved by this group—then you will win the $50.) Each of you will be designated by a letter, A, B, C, or D. As this has not been done on the basis of your sitting order, you will not know which individual is designated by a particular letter.

After the scores for each of the tasks has been posted, you will each be given a short questionnaire form and a distribution sheet to complete. The questionnaire concentrates on the factors in which I am interested and is a very important part of the experiment. It is urgent that you answer the items as honestly as possible, since the worth of the experiment depends to a great extent on your honest answers. Equally important is the distribution sheet which you will fill out. On this distribution sheet, you will be asked how you would divide the $50 should your group win it. Your honesty and accuracy is as important to you as to us as the distribution you designate will actually determine what share of the $50 each group member will receive. This will be determined by the average of the distributions indicated by each of you.

One final point. While we are grading your tasks, you are to work on a special task. This task will have nothing to do with your competition for the $50. However, it is an important aspect of this study.

Now are there any questions?

After the answering of any questions, the subjects turned to the first task.

Task #1: A six-minute, 75 word, synonym-antonym test.

Task #2: A four-minute, 200 item, number-translation test in which a code number was to be added to all odd numbers and subtracted from all even numbers.

Task #3: A six-minute, 20 item, logic and math test.

Task #4: A ten-minute, 25 item, reading-comprehension test.

Task #5: A four-minute, 500 item, symbol-for-number substitution test.

Intervening task: A task to construct different shapes from several pieces of cardboard.

The Manipulation of the Independent Variables

The variable of interference was manipulated by the cheating of a fictitious subject and the resulting removal of points from the group score. During task #4, the experimenter interrupted the subjects and in a somewhat emotional and confused manner told the subjects the following:

On this last task, I had to stop the task early because I observed Member C looking back to the first page consistently through the period.... As carefully specified in the instructions this is against the rules ... (after some pondering, he began again) In fairness to the other groups in this series, I think I should subtract some points from your score. I think ... (so many points) is fair enough. This is difficult to judge as it has never happened before. (The written instructions for task #4 specified that one could not look back at the first page.)

Now, there was no Member C. Although there were four subjects and letters A, B, C, and D were used in reporting performance, none of the subjects was actually lettered C. Instead there were two A's, one B, and one D. Of course, the subjects were not aware of this. The intensity of the interference was manipulated by the number of points that were subtracted from the group score. In the low-intensity variation, 4 points were subtracted (leaving the group only 4 points behind the "best group"); in the medium-intensity variation, 20 points were subtracted (at the same time leaving the group 20 points behind the "best group"); and in the high-intensity variation, 36 points were subtracted (and leaving the group 36 points behind the "best group"). The latter deficit was virtually impossible to make up on the last task.

The variable of status was manipulated by the use of standardized scores given to each group member. The scores were such that one member usually received about two-thirds of a perfect score (high status); two members received about one-half of a perfect score (medium status); and one member received about one-third of a perfect score (low status). Which group member received which score was determined by their actual rank order on their performance on the first task. The fictitious member C was assigned to either the "high status" or "medium status" position in order to effect the desired manipulation. The scores were then manipulated so that each subject maintained the same rank on all five tasks. The ambiguity of the scoring procedures and the standardization of all scores to a maximum score of 20 maintained the authenticity of the scores.

Measurements

The effectiveness of the independent variables was measured by two items on the post-task questionnaire. "Perceived status" was measured by the following item:

Who has the greatest ability to affect the group's chances of winning the competition from this point on? List the members by their letters in the appropriate categories shown below.

a. High ability	_____	(3)
b. Medium ability	_____	(2)
c. Low ability	_____	(1)

"Perceived interference-intensity" was measured by the following item:

How did the performance of the other group members on the last task affect your group's chances of winning the competition? List the members by their letters in the appropriate categories shown below.

a. Helped a lot	_____	
b. Helped some	_____	
c. Helped a little	_____	
d. Neither helped nor hindered	_____	(1)
e. Hindered a little	_____	(2)
f. Hindered some	_____	(3)
g. Hindered a lot	_____	(4)

The dependent variable, "punishment," was independently measured by the following items:

How do you feel about the other persons? List each one of them by their letters in the appropriate categories below:

a. Strongly like	_____	(1)

b. Like	_____	(2)
c. Indifferent	_____	(3)
d. Dislike	_____	(4)
e. Strongly dislike	_____	(5)

If you were to participate again in a similar experiment, how would you feel about participating with friends of your own choosing rather than the present members of the group? List the members of the group by their letters in the appropriate categories below.

a. Would strongly favor friend of my own choosing rather than members(s)	_____	(5)
b. Would prefer friend of my own choosing rather than member(s)	_____	(4)
c. Have no preference	_____	(3)
d. Would prefer group member(s)	_____	(2)
e. Would strongly favor group member(s)	_____	(1)

In the spaces provided alongside the letters, indicate how much of the total reward you wish to allocate to each member—including yourself. Please use percentages, e.g., 40%, 30%, etc. Be sure that the total adds up to 100%.

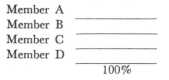

Member A	_____
Member B	_____
Member C	_____
Member D	_____
	100%

This last index was considered the principal index of punishment. The index scores obtained at the end of task #4 were used in the analysis.

RESULTS

The Effectiveness of the Independent Variables

Table 1 shows the average scores of the "perceived status" index for the six ex-

Table 1

MEAN PERCEIVED STATUS SCORE FOR ALL EXPERIMENTAL VARIATIONS

Status of Interference-Agent	Interference-Intensity			Total Mean
	(1) High	(2) Medium	(3) Low	
High	2.9	3.0	2.8	2.9
Medium	1.9*	1.8*	1.8*	1.8*
Total mean	2.4	2.4	2.3	—

* Differences between High and Medium status statistically significant at P<.05 using the t-Test (for all cells, N=20).

perimental variations just prior to the interference manipulation. The average index score is 2.9 in the high-status variation and 1.8 in the medium-status variation. The between-variation difference is statistically significant beyond the .05 level. The differences between the interference-intensity variations are not significant.

Table 2 shows the average scores of the "perceived interference-intensity" index for the six experimental variations just after the interference manipulation. The average index score is 3.8 in the high-intensity variation, 2.9 in the medium-intensity variation, and 1.6 in the low-intensity variation. The between-variation differences are statistically significant beyond the .05 level. The differences between the status variations are not significant.

The Tests of the Propositions

Punishment increases as interference-intensity increases. Tables 3, 4, and 5 show the mean scores of the punishment indices for the six experimental variations. The total mean scores for the three inter-ference-intensity variations are presented in the last row of each table. The difference between the high- and low-interfer-ence variation is statistically significant using each of the three indices. The dif-ference between the high- and medium-interference variations is significant using two of the indices. The difference between the medium- and low-interference varia-tions is insignificant using each of the three indices.

Punishment decreases as the status of the interference-agent increases. The total

Table 2

MEAN PERCEIVED INTERFERENCE SCORE FOR ALL EXPERIMENTAL VARIATIONS

Status Interference-Agent	Interference-Intensity			Between-Variation Differences			Total Mean
	(1) High	(2) Medium	(3) Low	1–2	2–3	1–3	
High	3.9	2.9	1.5	1.0*	1.4*	2.4*	2.8
Medium	3.6	2.8	1.7	0.8*	1.1*	2.9*	2.7
Total mean	3.8	2.9	1.6	0.9*	1.3*	2.2*	—

* Statistically significant at p<.05 using the t-Test.

Table 3

MEAN DISLIKE SCORE FOR ALL EXPERIMENTAL VARIATIONS

Status of Interference-Agent	Interference-Intensity			Between-Variation Differences			Total Mean
	(1) High	(2) Medium	(3) Low	1–2	2–3	1–3	
High	4.8	2.6	2.0	2.2*	0.6	2.8*	3.1
Medium	3.8	3.7	2.9	0.1	0.8*	0.9*	3.5
Between-status difference	1.0*	−1.1*	−0.9*	—	—	—	—
Total mean	4.3	3.2	2.4	1.1*	0.8	1.9*	—

* Statistically significant at $p < .05$ using the t-Test. The status-interference interaction is statistically significant at $p < .05$ ($F = 3.49$) using the analysis of variance test.

mean scores of the punishment indices for the two status variations are presented in the last column of Tables 3, 4, and 5. Using each of the three punishment indices, the small between-variation differences are in the predicted direction but each fails to reach statistical significance.

The relationship between punishment and the status of the interference-agent is negative under low- and medium-interference and positive under high-interference. As shown in Table 3, the first punishment index (disliking) shows differences between the high- and medium-status variations that are statistically significant for all three interference variations.

In both the low- and medium-interference variations, the punishment score is higher for the medium-status interference-agent. In the high-interference variation, the punishment score is higher for the high-status interference-agent. An analysis of variance test shows an F value with $p < .05$ for the status-interference interaction. As shown in Table 4, the differences for the second punishment index (non-participation), between the high- and medium-status variations, are insignificant for all three interference variations. As shown in Table 5, the differences for the third punishment index (reward distribution), the principal index, are statistically significant for all three interference variations.

Table 4

MEAN NON-PARTICIPATION SCORE FOR ALL EXPERIMENTAL VARIATIONS

Status of Interference-Agent	Interference-Intensity			Between-Variations Differences			Total Mean
	(1) High	(2) Medium	(3) Low	1–2	2–3	1–3	
High	4.6	3.9	2.8	0.7	1.1*	1.8*	3.8
Medium	4.6	4.1	3.6	0.5	0.5	1.0*	4.1
Total mean	4.6	4.0	3.2	0.6	0.8	1.4*	—

* Statistically significant at $p < .05$ using the t-Test.

Table 5

MEAN REWARD-DIFFERENTIATION SCORE FOR ALL EXPERIMENTAL VARIATIONS

Status of Interference-Agent	Interference-Intensity			Between-Variation Differences			Total Mean
	(1) High	(2) Medium	(3) Low	1–2	2–3	1–3	
High	08	32	36	−24*	−04	−28*	25
Medium	16	17	25	−01	−08*	−09*	19
Between-status difference	−08*	15*	11*	—	—	—	06
Total mean	12	24	30	−12*	−06	−18*	—

* Statistically significant at $p < .05$ using the t-Test. The status-interference interaction is statistically significant at $p < .05$ ($F = 4.65$) using analysis of variance test.

As with the first punishment index, in both the low- and medium-interference variations, the punishment score is higher for the medium-status interference-agent. In the high-interference variation, the punishment is again higher for the high-status interference-agent. An analysis of variance yields an F value with $p < .05$ for the status-interference interaction.

To look at the data within status variations and across interference variations clarifies the picture. Within the high-status variation, the first and third indices show a significant increase in punishment from the low-interference variation to the high-interference variations and from the medium-interference variation to the high-interference variation. They do not show a significant increase in punishment from the low- to the medium-interference variation. Within the medium-status variation, the same indices show a significant increase in punishment from the low- to the medium-interference variation and from the low- to the high-interference variation. They do not show a significant increase in punishment from the medium- to the high-interference variation. The only significant difference demonstrated by the second index is the increase in punishment from the low- to the high-interference variation. This is found in both the high- and medium-status variations.

DISCUSSION

The interesting finding in this study is the evidence that high status persons are punished less for minor, but more for major, interference than middle status persons. In analysis of variance terms, there is a significant interaction between status and interference in determining punishment. Interactive relationships, in this case, are of special interest because they indicate that a variable which works one way under a given condition works the opposite way when the condition is changed. In seeking an explanation, we must ask what it is about the change in condition which reverses the effect of the variable. Why, in this case, does an increase in interference change high status from a shield to a target?

The problem can best be approached by breaking it into two questions. Why are persons of high status relatively free of penalties when they make a minor or moderate error? Why are they punished more severely than persons of middle status for a major error?

There are several possible explanations of the cloak afforded by high status. Persons who have contributed unusually well to the group in the past may have earned the gratitude of the group, which is usually expressed by giving them extra rewards. This seems especially likely in a situation, such as the experimental one, where the basis for evaluation is largely limited to quantitative scores on a single scale representing contributions to the group goal. In this situation, if not generally, punishment for interference with these goals can be imposed only by a reduction in these rewards, an action which would run counter to the response of expressing appreciation. Therefore, it may be reasonable to suppose that this interference would be discounted as long as it still left interferer as the highest single contributor to the group. In the condition of low interference, this was the case. The high status person had, by the end of the third trial, contributed about 12 points more to the group score than did any of the other participants. By the end of the fifth session, it could be anticipated that he would have contributed in all about 20 "extra" points. Against this total contribution, the loss of four points would still leave him as the outstanding contributor. If his fellow members operated on the principle of distributive justice, they would have a continuing basis for rewarding him differentially.

This explanation does not work as satisfactorily for the reaction to medium interference, however. There, the loss to the group (20 points) was sufficient to wipe out the differential contribution of the

high status person even if he continued to perform as well in the final trials as he had in the first three. Yet he is penalized little more for medium interference than he was for low. He continues to be protected by his high status.

Involved here may well be some subtler social processes. The high status person may benefit from the sentiment of respect which is associated with a demonstration of skill. One is reminded of the answer given to Dickens when he asked about the respect in which a particular American was held, despite the fact that he was known by all to be a blackguard: "Well, sir, he is a smart man."

Underlying such a sentiment may well be the perception that such persons can retaliate against those who punish them. The fear of retaliation might be heightened in the situation, since punishment had to be called for by the individual without his knowing whether the same decision would be made by others in the group. (The fear of retaliation against the individual might have been lessened by uncertainty as to whether the punitive judgments would be disclosed at the end of the session, but the possibility was left open. Even if the realistic danger of disclosure were eliminated, habits learned in other situations might have generalized to this one.) Another form of retaliation which might have been feared is that the high status person would diminish his potential contribution to the group on the final trial. Since his efforts had been demonstrated to be important to the group, there would be good reason to avoid such an effect as long as victory was still possible. Moreover, retaliation by the punished person—in addition to hurting the group more because of the skill of the high status man—might have been considered more likely. In a society which does award idiosyncrasy credits, high status persons accept them as their due. When they are denied, as they would be by severe punishment in this case, a sense of injustice is to be expected. A characteristic reaction to perceived injustice is alienation from the group and retaliation against it. Whatever their own perceptions of justice, the other members of the group might accordingly refrain from punishment if only to keep the group in the running.

Most of these considerations would not serve to protect the high status person where his interference ruins the chance of group success. In this situation, his action had the effect of wiping out his great contribution. Even if he continued to score as he had in the past, his net contribution would be about the same as that of the lowest scorer. It would hardly merit gratitude. Also, retaliation against the punitive individual would be less likely, since everyone in the group would be more likely to punish the offender. (It might also be less serious if the offender were conceived to have lost moral stature as a result of the censure implied in the larger penalty imposed by the experimenter.) Retaliation against the group, through lessened effort on the next trial, would be meaningless since the group had lost its chance of winning already. Thus, gratitude, distributive justice, and the fear of retaliation would not afford the high-status person protection from punishment where his interference destroyed the chance of group success.

Thus, the above factors possibly explain the decrease in the protection afforded by high status, but they do not

necessarily explain the *intensity* of the punishment received by an individual of high status relative to that received by those of lesser status. What about respect for skill, the kind of sentiment Dickens described? It may be less of an asset than at first appears. When it serves the perceived interest of the group, it may heighten acceptance and offset minor failings. When it stands alone, it may work the other way. Homans suggests just such an interaction. "Indeed a man who 'could' supply a service, in the sense that the signs associated with him resemble those of other men who have supplied the service, but who does not in fact supply it, will not reap approval but resentment. He had deprived his fellows of an expected reward."[6] The process is beautifully illustrated in Britten's opera, *Peter Grimes*. The hero, a fisherman who ventures farther and catches more fish for himself than others in the village, is hounded to death for this reason.

There is some social science research which supports this view. Evience of considerable personal dislike of doctors was discovered in a questionnaire study by Gamson and Schuman.[7] A striking finding in that study was that dislike correlated directly with respect. Similar conclusions were reached in the small group studies by Borgatta, Bales and Slater. They discovered that, with the rare exception of the "great man," persons skilled at provid-

---

[6] G. Homans, *Social Behavior: Its Elementary Forms*, New York: Harcourt, Brace & World, Inc., 1961, p. 148.

[7] W. Gamson and H. Schuman, "Some Undercurrents in the Prestige of Physicians," *American Journal of Sociology*, 68 (January, 1963), pp. 463–470.

ing good ideas or guiding the group were unable to remain or become best-liked and, on the contrary, were disproportionately disliked.

A second possible explanation involves yet another notion of distributive justice, one which suggests that an individual is punished in proportion to the rewards he has received in the past. An individual who has already been awarded more for his contributions to the group should be "fined" more for deviations which seriously jeopardize the group's chances of achieving its goal.

This notion may or may not be supported by the rationale that small punishments will not effectively alter the behavior of an individual who has accumulated great rewards and can therefore "afford" to take some losses. Only correspondingly large punishments can possibly serve this function. Therefore, an individual who has reaped large rewards for major contributions to the group may reap correspondingly large punishments for major depletions.[8]

In many social situations, punitive tendencies toward persons of high status are likely to be obscured by a variety of factors, such as the ones we have discussed. Accordingly, behavior toward such persons tends to be deferential. Where high status is disentangled from these protective factors, however, it appears to establish its possessor as a preferred target for aggression. To the student of revolutions, this conclusion will come as no surprise. The justification for investigating it further in the laboratory lies in the possibility of isolating the process by which it occurs and understanding its consequences more fully.

---

[8] An analysis of the data showed that the high-status person was given an average proportion of the $50 that was significantly higher than that given to the middle-status person through tasks 1, 2, and 3. The other two indices did not show such differences.

IV

LEADERSHIP
AND GROUP
DECISION MAKING

10

Leadership

LEADER'S CONTRIBUTION
TO TASK PERFORMANCE IN COHESIVE
AND UNCOHESIVE GROUPS*

Fred E. Fiedler and W. A. T. Meuwese

Although a group or a team may be frequently less efficient than individuals working alone (Faust, 1959; McCurdy & Lambert, 1952; Shaw, 1932) when taken on a per man-hour basis, teamwork is essential where the task precludes individuals from independent action. A single individual cannot operate a submarine or represent three widely divergent viewpoints. One of the leader's main functions is the effective use and coordination of his team members' skills and abilities.

Interestingly enough, practically no

* Fred E. Fiedler and W. A. T. Meuwese, "Leader's Contribution to Task Performance in Cohesive and Uncohesive Groups," *Journal of Abnormal and Social Psychology*, 67 (1963), 83–87. Copyright 1963 by the American Psychological Association, and reproduced by permission.

work has been published on the specific conditions under which efficient utilization of the leader's or his group members' abilities takes place. We have generally assumed that a good group simply consists of abler members than a poor group. Leaders tend to be chosen from among those most competent to perform the job they are to supervise. The present paper attempts to show that the leader's ability to contribute to the task depends to a considerable extent on the cohesiveness of his group.

The underlying hypothesis deriving from earlier work (Fiedler, 1958) can be described as follows. The leader's ability to contribute to the group's productivity requires that the group's structure enable him to communicate effectively with all members, and that the members be willing to follow the directions of the leader.

It is probably also necessary that the leader is free to devote his influence to the task rather than having to direct his efforts mainly toward group maintenance. From empirical evidence (Back, 1951; Fiedler, 1958) it may be inferred that these conditions are fulfilled if there is a certain degree of *cohesiveness* in the group. In this paper a group is defined to be cohesive if one or both of the following conditions are present in the group: the members feel attracted to the group, the members are adjusted to the group and free of interpersonal tension. Both of these conditions can be assessed by questionnaires administered to the group members.

We shall here examine data which were obtained in four different studies. The analyses were based on the assumption that a correlation between some person's ability or achievement score and some measure of his group's performance provides a measure of the individual's direct influence on the group's task performance.

The major operational hypothesis to be tested was that: The leader's ability score will correlate positively with a measure of group effectiveness in cohesive groups, but not in uncohesive groups.

METHOD AND RESULTS

Tank Crew Study

A study was conducted on 25 Army tank crews which participated in an experiment comparing tank equipment (Fiedler, 1955). Each crew consisted of five enlisted men, viz., a tank commander (TC) who was the formal leader of the group, a gunner (G), a driver (D), a loader (L), and a bow gunner (BG). All crews remained intact during the course of the study.

Each crew was assigned to work with five different models of tanks and each tank test entailed driving toward, recognizing, and hitting five different targets. A combined criterion was developed which estimated the probability that a tank performing in this manner would emerge victorious in a duel with a similar tank. This score was based on the

Table 1

CORRELATIONS (rho) OF ARMY GENERAL CLASSIFICATION TEST (AGCT)
AND PROFICIENCY SCORES WITH TANK CREW CRITERIA
$(N=8)$

Group	TC	G	D	L	BG
	AGCT score				
Cohesive	26	05	52	76**	59
Uncohesive	−21	−29	20	23	−21
	Proficiency score				
Cohesive	94***	38	94***	47	49
Uncohesive	−21	−38	−66*	43	−23

Note.—TC=Tank commander, G=Gunner, D=Driver, L=Loader, BG=Bow gunner.
  * $p<.10$, two-tailed.
 ** $p<.05$, two-tailed.
*** $p<.01$, two-tailed.

number of seconds required for each of the three subtasks; time to travel to the target, time to recognize the target, and time to hit the target. Army General Classification Test (AGCT) scores as well as individual proficiency scores were obtained for all crew members prior to the experiment.

The sample was divided into the eight most cohesive and the eight least cohesive groups on the basis of sociometric choices which were obtained from crew members at three points in the experiment. As can be seen from Table 1, Column 1, the contribution of the leader is greater in cohesive groups. This trend emerges most clearly when proficiency scores are utilized.

Although this was not hypothesized, it can also be seen from Table 1 that the ability of the other crew members generally correlated positively in cohesive teams while zero or negative relations were found in uncohesive teams.

B-29 Bomber Crews

A second set of crew performance and individual proficiency data were obtained in the course of a study on B-29 bomber crews (Fiedler, 1955). These crews, each consisting of five officers and six enlisted men, were in training at Randolph Air Force Base during the Korean war in 1951.

Ground School Grades (GSG) were available for several crew members. These grades reflect with reasonable accuracy the crew member's competence on his crew tasks. According to research of the Air Force Crew Research Laboratory at Randolph Field, one of the best objective measures of crew effectiveness was the "Radar Bomb Score circular error average" (RBS). The reliability of this score was estimated to be .45 (Knoell & Forgays, 1952).

Several measures were obtained which indicate the cohesiveness or attractiveness of the

Table 2

CORRELATIONS (rho) OF INDIVIDUAL GROUND SCHOOL GRADES AND RADAR BOMB SCORES UNDER DIFFERENT CONDITIONS OF ATTRACTION TO GROUP (Cohesiveness)

| | Cohesiveness | | | | | |
| | High | | Low | | Very low | |
Group	N	r	N	r	N	r
Officers						
Aircraft commander	6	67	7	85*	4	−40
Pilot	6	70	7	43	5	30
Bombardier	5	80	7	22	5	−30
Radar operator	5	48	6	41	5	30
$\bar{r}$		66		48		−02
Enlisted						
Radio operator	5	−20	7	47	5	−18
Left gunner	5	−30	7	−01	5	10
Right gunner	5	−78	7	−87**	5	−70
$\bar{r}$		−43		−14		−26

* $p < .05$, two-tailed.
** $p < .01$, two-tailed.

crew. These were the crew members' ratings of confidence in the aircraft commander, liking for the aircraft commander, liking for crew members, and feeling of crew effectiveness. The median intercorrelation of these measures was .59 and the ratings were, therefore, combined.

On the basis of these combined cohesiveness or attractiveness scores, the crews were divided into those having high, low, and very low attractiveness to crew members.[1] Table 2 presents the correlation of ground school scores with the radar bomb score criterion.

The officers' proficiency score correlated positively with radar bomb scores in high and low cohesiveness conditions, but not in very low cohesive groups. The proficiency of the enlisted men correlated zero or negatively with the criterion. In essence, therefore, these findings support those obtained on Army tank crews. This analysis also suggests the possibility that not only the leader's proficiency, but also the proficiency of the key members, in this case the officers, can influence group effectiveness only in cohesive teams.

Research on Antiaircraft Artillery Crews

A study was conducted by Hutchins and Fiedler (1960) on antiaircraft artillery crews, each of which consisted of 8–12 enlisted men. AGCT scores were gathered on all available personnel. As was the case in other studies, complete data could not be obtained from all crews in the sample because of sickness, temporary leaves, or duty assignments away from the site of testing.

Crew performance scores were based on crew rankings by officers in charge of companies and platoons. These rankings correlated with objective target acquisition and performance scores which were the accepted crew

---

[1] Data for "medium cohesive" crews were too incomplete to be of use.

Table 3

CORRELATION (rho) OF AGCT WITH EFFECTIVENESS IN GROUPS HIGH, MEDIUM, AND LOW ON LEADER'S AND MEMBER'S GENERAL ARMY ADJUSTMENT SCORE

	High	Medium	Low
	Leader's GAA score		
	(N=6)	(N=9)	(N=9)
AGCT leader	84*	−21	23
AGCT members	24	−37	−17
	Member's GAA score		
	(N=8)	(N=8)	(N=8)
AGCT leader	57	26	−05
AGCT members	−48	−01	−07

Note.—Seventeen groups were omitted from the analysis because of missing data.
* $p < .05$, two-tailed.

performance criteria indicating that the guns were accurately aimed on the targets.

The General Army Adjustment (GAA) scores which are indices of morale and crew attractiveness served to indicate the cohesiveness of the group. The groups were divided into crews high, medium, and low on these two criteria. The AGCT score of the leader and the average AGCT score of the members were correlated with the crew's effectiveness. The results are presented in Table 3.

Again, it can be seen that the leader's AGCT score correlates with performance in cohesive crews (high GAA) but not in uncohesive crews. Member AGCT, on the other hand, does not correlate with crew performance in either cohesive or uncohesive groups.

Research on Group Creativity

The last study to be described was intended to identify leader attitudes which are conducive to group creativity (Fiedler, Meuwese,

& Oonk, 1961). This investigation was conducted in the Netherlands and utilized 32 Catholic and 32 Calvinist university students. Each subject participated in two groups: once in a four-man team having homogeneous membership, and once in a team consisting of two men from each religion. In 16 of the groups the experimenters appointed a chairman, while the other 16 groups worked as "informal" teams.

Table 4

Correlations (rho) between Group Creativity and Analogies Scores

Analogies score of:	"Cohesive" No destructive critic (N=14)	"Uncohesive" Destructive critic (N=17)
Informal leader	51*	24
Group members	−02	18

Note.—In one group it was impossible to determine the informal leader on the basis of the sociometric questions.
* $p < .05$, one-tailed.

The task consisted in devising three different stories from the same TAT card, either Card 11 or 19. The creativity expressed in these stories was judged by two raters on the basis of a manual. The correlation between the two judges' ratings was .81 for Card 11 and .88 for Card 19.

A 14-item Analogies test[2] was administered to all subjects and we are here concerned with the relation of performance on this short intelligence test and group creativity. The groups were divided into those which seemed tense and unpleasant and thus uncohesive, and

---

[2] Constructed by J. C. van Lennep, University of Utrecht. This test is similar in form and content to the Miller Analogies Test.

those which were relaxed and at ease, hence cohesive. This was inferred from sociometric questions which asked the subjects to name individuals who were "destructively critical." The informal leader of the group was determined by means of sociometric questions, e.g., "Which of the group members had most influence on the opinions of others?"

Correlations between creativity and informal leader's Analogies scores and member's average Analogies scores are presented in Table 4.

Here again, we find that the leader's intelligence influences the group performance most in cohesive, pleasant groups. The informal leader has little direct influence in groups which are relatively uncohesive. It can thus be concluded that this analysis also confirms the hypothesized relationship.

Significance of Results

To assess the combined probability that this series of results could have been obtained by chance, a set of four independent cases was formed, consisting of the *smallest* correlations for each separate sample from Table 5 in which the main results of this study are summarized. The combined probability for these four samples, computed according to Jones and Fiske (1953), was below the .01 level, one-tailed test.

Discussion

The results clearly confirm the hypothesis that a leader directly influences the effectiveness of the group only if the group is cohesive. This relationship was found in four entirely different studies and it thus seems to be fairly general.

The results do *not* indicate that the leader does not have *power* in uncohesive

Table 5

CORRELATIONS OF LEADER'S ABILITY WITH GROUP EFFECTIVENESS

Study	Ability score	Effectiveness criterion	Cohesiveness criterion	Correlation (rho)			
				Cohesive groups	N	Un-cohesive groups	N
Army tank crews	AGCT	Probabllity of winning a battle	Sociometric	.26	8	−.21	8
Army tank crews	Proficiency rating	Probability of winning a battle	Sociometric	.94**	8	−.21	8
B-29 bomber crews	Ground School	Radar bomb score	Liking for the group	.67	6	−.40	4
Antiaircraft artillery crews	AGCT	Ratings	Leader's Army Adjustment score	.81*	6	.23	9
Antiaircraft artillery crews	AGCT	Ratings	Member's Army Adjustmcnt score	.57	8	−.05	8
Dutch creativity study	Analogies score	Creativity ratings	Presence of destructive critic	.54*	14	.24	17

* $p < .05$.
** $p < .01$.

groups. He may or may not have power; but if he does, he exerts it in a way that is not directly reflected in the group's product. Thus, the leader of an uncohesive group may be forced into a position in which it is necessary to exert influence mainly on the maintenance of the group. Cohesive groups probably do not require as much of the leader's effort to maintain the group as would be the case in uncohesive groups. The leader may, therefore, be able to influence the level of group task performance by contributing directly to the solution of the problem.

REFERENCES

BACK, K. "Influence Through Social Communication." *J. Abnorm. Soc. Psychol.*, 1951, 46, 9–23.

FAUST, W. L. "Group Versus Individual Problem-Solving." *J. Abnorm. Soc. Psychol.*, 1959, 59, 68–72.

FIEDLER, F. E. "The Influence of Leader-Keyman Relations on Combat Crew Effectiveness." *J. Abnorm. Soc. Psychol.*, 1955, 51, 227–235.

FIEDLER, F. E. *Leader Attitudes and Group Effectiveness.* Urbana: Univer. Illinois Press, 1958.

FIEDLER, F. E., MEUWESE, W. A. T., and OONK, SOPHIE. "An Exploratory Study of Group Creativity in Laboratory Tasks." *Acta Psychol.*, Amsterdam, 1961, 18, 100–119.

HUTCHINS, E. B., and FIEDLER, F. E. "Task-Oriented and Quasi-therapeutic Rolc Functions of the Leader in Small Military Groups." *Sociometry*, 1960, 23, 393–406.

JONES, L. V., and FISKE, D. W. "Models for Testing the Significance of Combined Results." *Psychol. Bull.*, 1953, 50, 375–382.

KNOELL, DOROTHY, and FORGAYS, D. G. "Interrelationships of Combat Crew Performance in the B-29." *USAF Hum. Resour. Res. Cent., Res. Note*, 1952, CCT 52–1.

McCURDY, H. G., and LAMBERT, W. E. "The Efficiency of Small Human Groups in the Solution of Problems Requiring Genuine Cooperation." *J. Pers.*, 1952, 20, 478–494.

SHAW, MARJORIE E. "A Comparison of Individuals and Small Groups in the Rational Solution of Complex Problems. *Amer. J. Psychol.*, 1932, 44, 491–504.

LEADERSHIP AND CRISES*

Robert L. Hamblin

The purpose of this paper is to report a laboratory investigation of two hypotheses about leadership during crises, namely: leaders have more influence during periods of crisis than during noncrisis periods, and groups tend to replace their old leader with a new leader if the old leader does not have a solution to a crisis problem.

THEORY

Crises

All groups, whether they are large or small, powerful or weak, have the possibility of experiencing a crisis, *an urgent situation in which all group members face a common threat*. A common crisis experienced by family groups is the reduction or loss of income through unemployment, sickness, or death. Religious groups may face crises of persecution. Political parties usually experience a crisis in every election or, if there is lack of electoral machinery, in every revolution. Nations face a crisis in every sudden economic depression or inflation and in every attack by another nation. A crisis is a generic social experience.

There have been a number of field and laboratory studies of group behavior during crises. Stouffer, *et al.*, have studied the reaction of troops to the crisis of battle (20). Durkheim has studied the influence of religious, economic, and political crises on suicide rates and social integration (5). Hovland and Sears (12), Marshall (13), and Moore (15) have studied some social effects of economic crises at the societal level. Also, there have been numerous laboratory studies.[1] However, only in Mar-

* Robert L. Hamblin, "Leadership and Crises," *Sociometry*, 21 (1958), 322–35. Reprinted by permission of the American Sociological Association.

[1] For references to most of these studies, see (8) and (10).

shall's study is there an investigation of the effects of crises on leadership.

Leadership

When most people think of leadership or leaders they think of traits. This may be because of a psychological bias in our culture where aspiring Ben Franklins attempt to develop the traits of a leader as a means of ascending the ladder of success. Consistent with this bias, social scientists have conducted a number of studies in an attempt to isolate the crucial traits of leaders. These attempts have been abortive, not in the sense that each investigator was unable to isolate crucial traits that separated the leaders from the nonleaders, but rather that few commonalities appeared among the crucial traits isolated in the different studies. The brave souls (2, 19) who have tried to synthesize the results of these studies have become discouraged with the trait approach to the study of leadership and have evidently communicated this discouragement quite effectively as most psychologists seem to be abandoning it (4, pp. 535–550; 7; 16, pp. 328–340).

Modern Machiavellis have followed an alternative approach which has been more fruitful. An interest not in what leaders *are* (traits) but in what *successful* leaders *do* has led them to study in experimental situations the effects of a number of different leadership procedures. (The Lewin-Lippitt-White-Autocracy Democracy experiment is, perhaps, the best known of these studies.) Although their substantive findings are important, a significant scientific "breakthrough" was achieved by this group in their development of reliable observational techniques for measuring interaction variables including leadership or influence.

These observational techniques led to the discovery that the leader-follower dichotomy is quite misleading in that influence is almost always distributed, sometimes quite evenly, among group members. That is, the activities of the leader, the high influencer, differ only in degree from the activities of the nonleaders.

This discovery that influence is widely distributed has led in turn to an interest in situational variables which affect the distribution of influence. In particular, the effect of size on the distribution of influence has been investigated several times (1, 9, 11, 14). The present study represents a continuation of this interest in situational variables which affect the distribution of influence. The situational variable here is the "crisis" versus the "noncrisis" situation.

However, there is another important finding from these observational studies which is important in understanding this experiment. After isolating a number of leadership functions, investigators have discovered that a group may have more than one leader at a time. Different members may take the lead in fulfilling different group functions. One member may have the most substantive influence, that is, the most ideas adopted as to how to solve the group's environmental problems. He is called the substantive or task leader. Another member may influence the group the most in coordinating the activities of the various members into a cooperating whole. He is called a procedural leader. Another group member may have the most influence in helping group members handle their emotions and thus in maintaining group cohesion. He is called the socioemotional leader. (Of course, a single individual may at the same time be the task, procedural, and socioemotional leader.[2]) In this experiment we are concentrating on the investigation of substantive leadership since the crisis problem is an environmental problem.

The Hypotheses

The first hypothesis (the centralization hypothesis) came from Weber's writings on bureaucracy. Bureaucracies are intricate mechanisms developed to foster the complete centralization of substantive influence in the hands of one man, the director of the bureau. The hundreds and sometimes thousands at the lower levels are supposed to follow the orders of the director in solving the bureau's environmental problems.

Weber assumes that bureaucracies develop when complex problems requiring the coordinated efforts of a vast number of people have to be solved in a very limited time, such as when an army is in battle. Of course, complex problems, coordinating the efforts of vast numbers, and limited time add up to urgency or time pressure. Bureaucracy (and, perhaps, more generally, centralization of influ-

---

[2] Using data from his interaction categories, together with data from a postexperiment questionnaire, Bales discovered a tendency for one member to become what he called the task leader and another member to become the socioemotional leader. His data indicate that the task leaders were high both on substantive and procedural influence. However, using a set of influence categories which may be more sensitive, we found an increasing tendency for one member to become the substantive leader and another to become the procedural leader as group size increases (9).

ence) occurs because, as Weber points out, "Precision, speed, unambiguity ... reduction of friction ... are raised to an optimum point ..." (6).

As noted above, an essential characteristic of all crises is urgency or time pressure. Hence, from Weber's writings we are led to expect that influence may be more centralized (that the high influencer would have relatively more influence) in crisis than in noncrisis periods.

The second hypothesis (the replacement hypothesis) comes from a working assumption of almost every student of modern politics that a leader (or party) will be voted out of power if he (or it) fails to cope successfully with any serious domestic or international crisis.

Of course, there are some crisis problems for which humans have no known solution. But even in these crises the leader is expected to be replaced. In a study of national politics from 1824 to 1924, Marshall (13) presents rather striking data which support this assumption. From 1824 to 1924 the economy of the United States was predominantly agricultural and agricultural economies usually suffer an economic crisis during periods of drought. Marshall's data show that in 11 out of 13 elections where rainfall was below average during the four years prior to election, the party in power was voted out of office. His data also show that in 11 out of 12 elections where rainfall was above average during the four years prior to elections, the political party in power remained in office.

It is a long way from national political parties to the high influencer in a laboratory group and it is a long way from economic crises experienced by nations to an experimentally produced crisis experienced by *ad hoc* groups of three in a laboratory. But if the assumption or principle is general it should apply. Hence, the hypothesis that groups tend to replace their old leader with a new leader if the old leader does not have a solution to the crisis problem.

METHOD

The Experimental Groups

The experiment reported herein involves the before-after observations of twelve three-person groups in a crisis situation and twelve more three-person groups in a control situation. However, this experiment was preceded by two rather elaborate pretests which together involved the observation of an additional 60 groups. It took us this long to work out the measurement problems encountered as well as to acquire the courage to produce a crisis that was severe enough to be valid or, for that matter, interesting.

The participants were either personal acquaintances of the experimental staff or residents of a housing development for married students. Ages ranged between twenty-five and thirty years. Half of the participants were men; the other half women. To reduce barriers to cooperation, participants composing any given experimental group were of the same sex and of approximately the same age.

The Experimental Situation

The experimental task involved a modified shuffleboard game which lasted about 30 minutes.[3] Each group of participants was ushered into the experimental room, shown the experimental equipment, and given a general but very incomplete idea about the nature and rules of the game. They were told that

---

[3] For a rather complete set of the instructions used in this experiment see (10).

they were to discover the rules themselves by trying different things and by watching a light board. A red light would flash every time a rule was violated and a green light would flash every time a score was made.

The participants were told that they would be competing with high-school students who had previously participated in a similar experiment; that their cumulative scores and the average cumulative scores of the high-school students would be posted for each of six, 5-minute playing or task periods into which the game was divided. To ensure their ego involvement the experimenter said:

> ... the ability to analyze a rather complex situation is the important skill in this game. I have seen many groups work very hard to make many successful shots only to lose most of the points gained through penalties because they failed to learn the ... rules. For this reason we expect mature college graduates to do better than high-school students. If you do get more points, however, you will have to work hard; these high-school students did.

These instructions were evidently successful for the average group behaved as though they were in a tournament. They rushed, ran, and not infrequently shouted. Most groups were visibly satisfied as they mastered the rules and as their scores began to exceed those of the high-school students. The groups were not given the scores they actually earned, however. The threat that would have been experienced by some of the groups who did not do so well as the high-school students had to be avoided. Hence, standard scores were given. These standard scores exceeded the high-school scores by a small but comfortable margin at the end of the first half, or experimental Period 1.

By the end of Period I the average group had learned most of the rules and, hence, was making numerous successful shots as indicated by the frequent flashing of the green lights and the before-mentioned lead over the high-school scores. The participants presented a picture of self-satisfaction and confidence.

The situation during the last half, or experimental Period II, remained about the same for the control groups. They usually worked hard consolidating their lead over the high-school students and their scores continued to exceed the scores of the high-school students by an ever-widening margin. But the situation changed markedly for the crisis groups. The self-satisfaction and confidence they exhibited at the end of Period I was that "which goeth before a fall."

The Crisis

The crisis was produced by changing the rules of the game. Procedures that were permissible before the change were now against the rules; procedures that were against the rules now became permissible. Lights had been used in teaching the participants the original rules and they could be used in indicating the changes. As the participants saw it, they were receiving red lights for doing the very things for which they had been receiving green lights. But this was not all. As soon as the participants learned a new rule and received a green light, the rule was changed again. The new effect was that the participants were unable to earn a single score during the last three periods. Since high-school groups were control groups, their scores continued to increase during the last half. Of course, the members of the crisis groups did not know this. As they saw it, their leads vanished, and then their scores fell farther and farther behind those of their rivals.

In the context of the self-satisfaction and confidence at the end of Period I, the switch in Period II to failure of previously successful procedures, the inability to find new procedures that were permanently successful, and the ever-increasing margin of failure in the scores during Period II proved quite effective in producing threat or frustration. The crisis groups looked more frustrated and they engaged in much more aggression than did the control groups during the last half. (The difference in the frequency of observed aggression was significant beyond the .05 level.[4]) Also after the experimental session was over, the crisis groups were very hostile. It took a long, permissive discussion and all the skill the experimenters had to reduce this hostility. However, after discussing the experimental procedures, purpose, and results, most of the participants in the crisis groups acted happy and proud that they had received the "full treatment." Even so, there were some who went away wearing hostile expressions.

But our real fear in this final experiment was not that the threat might not be severe enough but that it would be so severe that the situation would seem hopeless rather than urgent, that the crisis groups would simply withdraw. Not one group gave up, however. Until the end the members of all crisis groups continued to search for, find, and test new procedures. Hence, the situation was evidently both threatening and urgent.

Measurement

As mentioned above, the leadership variable used in this study involves substantive influence or ideas for solving the environmental problems which are adopted by the group.

The environmental problem directly involved in the crisis was to determine the rules by trying different procedures for playing the game and by watching the flashing lights. In attempting to solve the problem, the participants would usually suggest different procedures to be tested. In addition, as the different procedures were tested, the participants would suggest that certain rules were in effect. Not all these suggestions or ideas for solving the environmental problem were adopted by the group. If either or both of the other participants did cooperate in the test of a suggested procedure, a unit of influence was scored. (Most of the suggested procedures

---

[4] For the details of this finding, see (10).

were tried and tested by all participants, as the flashing lights were ambiguous enough to make a multiple test desirable.) Also, a unit of influence was scored when a rule was suggested but not immediately tested if there were some agreement, an absence of disagreement, and subsequent conformity to the rule.

An observation form was developed with a column for each participant and a column for "comments." Each time a participant suggested a procedure to the group for testing, or suggested a rule, a "/" was placed in his column in a new row, and a word or two was placed in the same row in the "comments" column to help the observer recall the suggestion if its adoption was delayed. If a suggestion was actually adopted (as indicated above) the "/" was changed to an "X" and was counted as a unit of substantive influence. Scripts were used in training the observers and it was possible to reduce the reliability error to less than 10 per cent.[5]

The basic data were used to calculate two standard measures—influence ratios and acceptance rates.

A given member's influence ratio for a given period represents his raw influence score (the number of accepted substantive suggestions) divided by the average of the raw influence scores of the other group members. For example, if during Period I the high influencer has a raw influence score of 10 adopted suggestions and the other members have scores of 3 and 2 accepted suggestions, then the influence ratio for the high influencer would be 4. He would have four times more influence than the average of the other group members.

A given member's acceptance rate for a given period is simply the proportion of his suggestions that were accepted during that period. For example, if during Period I the high influencer made 15 suggestions and of these 10 were accepted, then his acceptance rate would be .67, indicating that two thirds or 67 per cent of his suggestions were accepted by the group.

A very influential leader probably has both a high influence ratio and a high acceptance rate. But of the two, the influence ratio seems to be the more stable and the more crucial indication of leadership. Hence, the leader or high influencer is always the participant with the highest influence ratio except in the case of a tie. Then the tying participant with the highest acceptance rate is the high influencer.

Results

The Centralization Hypothesis

High influencers have more influence during periods of crisis than during periods of noncrisis.

As indicated above, influence ratios and acceptance rates are standard measures of influence. Also, the crisis groups experienced a crisis during Period II but the control groups did not. Hence, the most obvious implication of the centralization hypothesis is that during Period II the high influencers in the crisis groups should have higher influence ratios and higher acceptance rates than the high influencers in the control groups.

The mean influence ratios for the high influencers during Period II are 3.3 for the crisis groups and 3.0 for the controls. The difference is in the predicted direction, but the probability is .07 which is greater than .05 where the null hypothesis could be rejected.[6]

---

[5] A description of the computation of the reliability error as well as the training methods used in reducing the reliability error are found in (10).

[6] This and all the other probabilities of alpha errors (except the one noted in Table 1) were calculated using the Mann-Whitney U test

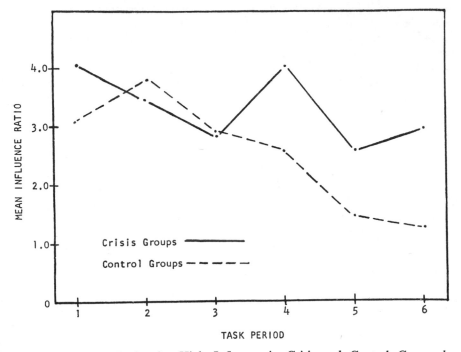

Fig. 1. Mean Influence Ratios for High Influence in Crisis and Control Groups by Task Periods.

NOTE: Differences between crisis and control groups are significant for periods 4, 5, and 6 (beyond .05 level).

The mean acceptance rates for the high influencers during Period II are .44 for the crisis groups and .43 for the controls. The probability of an alpha error exceeds .50.[7] Hence, the data, when tabulated by experimental periods, do not support the centralization hypothesis.

Of course, the data could also be used to calculate the influence ratios and the acceptance rates for the high influencers during each of the six task periods. Since the task periods 4, 5, and 6 correspond

(17, pp. 116–126). The data meet all the assumptions of this distribution-free statistic.

[7] The term "Type-I error" is sometimes used to refer to an alpha error or the rejection of a null hypothesis when it is in fact true.

to Period II, another obvious implication of the centralization hypothesis is that during task periods 4, 5, and 6, the high influencers in the crisis groups should have higher influence ratios and higher acceptance rates than the high influencers in the control groups.

The differences in the mean influence ratios shonw in Figure 1 support the centralization hypothesis. In addition to their being in the right direction, the probability is sufficiently small to reject the null hypothesis.

The differences in the mean acceptance rates in Figure 2 support the centralization hypothesis. The differences are in the expected direction for task periods 5 and 6. The probability is sufficiently small to

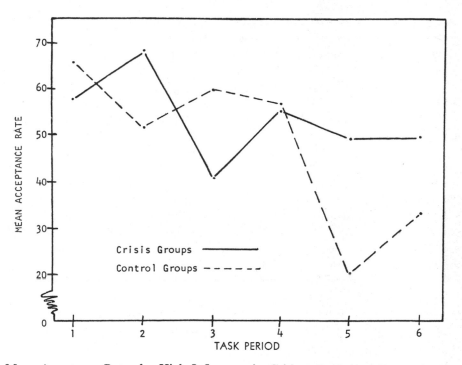

Fig. 2. Mean Acceptance Rates for High Influencers in Crisis and Control Groups by Task Periods.

NOTE: Differences between crisis and control groups are significant for period 5 and 6 (.05 level).

reject the null hypothesis. However, this is not true for period 4. The difference, although it is not significant, is not even in the predicted direction. This indicates that the difference in influence ratios of the high influencers in the crisis and control groups is due to a lack of suggestions on the part of the high influencers in the control groups rather than a decreased suggestibility on the part of their fellow participants.

But why should the data support the centralization hypothesis when tabulated by task period but not support it when tabulated by the longer experimental period? The reason is the replacement of the old leaders by the new leaders which is discussed below.

The evidence indicates that replacement does not occur immediately but only after the old leader fails to solve the crisis problem. The old leader usually has a high influence ratio and acceptance rate at first, usually during period 4, but from that point on has a relatively low influence ratio and acceptance rate. The new leader has a low influence ratio and acceptance rate at first but then has a relatively high influence ratio and acceptance rate for the remaining task periods. Thus tabulating the data for the entire experimental period (Period II) gives the old and the new leaders' influence ratios and acceptance rates not for the time each were leaders but for the time they were both leaders and nonleaders. Therefore, tabulating the data by the longer experimental period is inappropriate or, at least, less appropriate than tabulating the data by the shorter task periods.

One last thing before discussing the evidence for the replacement hypothesis. In Figures 1 and 2 notice the high influence ratios and acceptance rates for the first three task periods. They are as high as the influence ratios and the acceptance rates of the crisis groups for the last three task periods. Although unintentional, we evidently created crises for both the control and crisis groups for these first three periods. Certainly, in retrospect, a common threat was present (they might not do so well as the high-school students) and the situation was urgent (they had only 30 minutes to learn the rules and make 150 points.) Hence, it may be that

the control groups were in a noncrisis situation only during the last three task periods.

The Replacement Hypothesis

A group tends to replace its old leader with a new leader if the old leader does not have an obvious solution to the crisis problem.

Of course the most obvious way to test this hypothesis is simply to count the number of crisis and control groups where the leaders or high influencers did and did not change from Period I to Period II. These data, shown in Table 1, support the replacement hypothesis.

However, the data in Table 1 tell but a meager part of the story. A more adequate way to show what happened is to

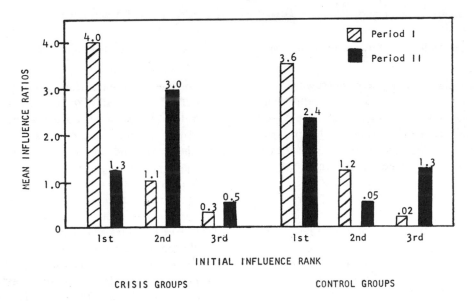

Fig. 3. Mean Influence Ratios by Initial Influence Rank of Members of Crisis and Control Groups by Experimental Periods.

NOTE: Change from Period I to Period II is significantly different for participants in crisis and control groups whose initial influence rank was second and third (.05 level).

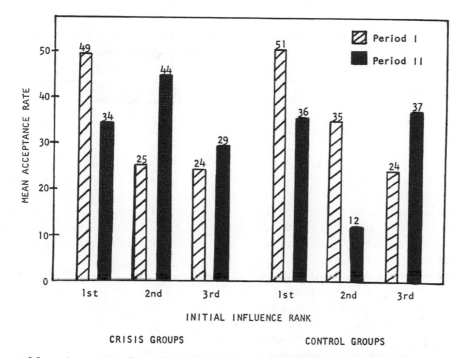

Fig. 4. Mean Acceptance Rates by Initial Influence Rank of Members of Crisis and Control Groups by Experimental Periods.

NOTE: Change from Period I to Period II is significantly different for participants in crisis and control groups whose initial influence rank was second (.05 level).

tabulate the influence ratios and the acceptance rates of the participants by their initial influence ranks for Period I and Period II. This shows what happened during Period II to the influence ratios and the acceptance rates of the participants who ranked first, second, and third in influence during Period I. These data appear in Figures 3 and 4.

The data in Figure 3 do, of course, support the replacement hypothesis. It appears that the participants who initially were second in influence rank became the new leaders in the crisis groups. That is, in fact, what happened. The participants who were initially second in influence rank became the new leaders in every one of the nine cases where the leader was re-

placed. This did not happen in the control groups. The participants who were initially second in influence rank either tied for third or became third in influence rank in Period II in ten of the twelve control groups. Also it was the participants who were initially third in influence rank that became the new leaders in the three cases where the leaders were replaced in the control groups.

The mean acceptance rates in Figure 4 tell a similar story except that the differential increase in acceptance rates of the participants who initially ranked third in influence is not significant.

The data in Figures 3 and 4 combine to suggest that a struggle for influence was waged in both the crisis and control

Table 1

REPLACEMENT OF LEADERS IN THE CRISIS AND CONTROL GROUPS

	Leader replaced	Leader not replaced
Crisis groups	9	3
Control groups	3	9

(Chi square, one-tailed test, corrected for continuity, P less than .05)

groups. During Period I, the participants who ranked first and second in influence evidently vied with one another for the top position. In the crisis groups the crisis evidently caused the participants who originally ranked second to become dominant. The participants who ranked third remained quite isolated. In the control groups, however, the participants who initially ranked first were able to maintain their position of dominance evidently by forming a coalition with the participants who initially ranked third, perhaps, by giving them support. This evidently froze out the participants who initially ranked second.

These results are somewhat at variance with those of Mills (14). Mills concluded that three-person groups normally develop into a coalition of two and an isolate, and that Simmel's (18, pp. 165–178) *tertius gaudens* (an influence structure where two powerful units are vying with one another for the support of a weak third unit) is rare. Unfortunately, we do not have the support and opposition data to determine exactly what the coalition structure was. But it is rather obvious that the control groups do exemplify the *tertius gaudens* and, in three cases, the *tertius*, initially the weakest of the three units involved, became the high influencer. It is also very doubtful that the participants initially ranked first and second in the

crisis groups actually formed a coalition, at least in the nine cases where replacement occurred. However, in the three cases where replacement did not occur, a coalition may have existed between the participants who initially ranked first and second.

Of course, our experimental situation differs considerably from Mills'. There were a number of factors present which could, conceivably, account for the differential results.

1. *Time pressure.* Our situation was designed to be urgent, and, in general, it was probably much more urgent than was Mills' situation.

2. *Threat.* It was almost entirely absent from Mills' experiment.

3. *Objectivity.* In our experiment, the flashing lights gave the participants rather objective criteria for making decisions. This, of course, was not true in Mills' experiment.

At this point it is impossible to say which, if any, of these factors were responsible for the differential results. Further experimentation is required. However, these results do highlight the importance of attempts to isolate the conditions which produce different influence and coalition structures. Theory such as that developed by Caplow (3) and experiments such as the one conducted by Vinacke and Arkoff (21) are indicated by the results.

Summary

The purpose herein was to report a laboratory investigation of two hypotheses about leadership during crises, namely: leaders have more influence during periods of crisis than during non-crisis periods, and groups tend to replace their old leader with a new leader if the old leader does not have an obvious solution to a crisis problem. Twenty-four groups were brought into a laboratory situation. Twelve experienced an apparently genuine crisis where there was no solution to the crisis problem. Data from an observational measure of influence give support to both hypotheses.

References

1. Bales, R. F., "The Equilibrium Problem in Small Groups," in T. Parsons, R. F. Bales, and E. A. Shils (eds.), *Working Papers in the Theory of Action*, Glencoe, Ill.: Free Press, 1953, 111–162.

2. Bird, C., *Social Psychology*, New York: Appleton-Century, 1940.

3. Caplow, T., "A Theory of Coalitions in the Triad," *American Sociological Review*, 1956, 21, 489–493.

4. Cartwright, D., and A. Zander, *Group Dynamics*, Evanston, Ill.: Row, Peterson, 1956.

5. Durkheim, E., *Suicide*, Glencoe, Ill.: Free Press, 1951.

6. Gerth, H. H., and C. W. Mills, *From Max Weber: Essays in Sociology*, New York: Oxford University Press, 1946.

7. Gouldner, A. W. (ed.), *Studies in Leadership*, New York: Harper, 1950.

8. Hamblin, R. L., and J. A. Wiggins, "Suggestibility, Imitation, and Recall Dur-

ing a Crisis," *Midwest Sociologist*, 1957, 20, 26–32.

9. Hamblin, R. L., "An Experimental Study of the Relationship of Communication, Power Relations, Specialization, and Social Atmosphere to Group Size," Ph.D. Dissertation, University of Michigan (Mic. 55–1362).

10. Hamblin, R. L., "Group Integration During a Crisis," *Human Relations*, 1958, 11, 67–76.

11. Hare, P., "A Study of Interaction and Consensus in Different Sized Groups," *American Sociological Review*, 1952, 17, 261–267.

12. Hovland, C. I., and R. R. Sears, "Minor Studies in Aggression: VI, Correlations of Lynchings with Economic Indices," *Journal of Psychology*, 1949, 9, 301–310.

13. Marshall, R., "Precipitation and Presidents," *The Nation*, 1927, 124, 315–316.

14. Mills, T. M., "Power Relations in Three-Person Groups," *American Sociological Review*, 1953, 18, 351–356.

15. Moore, B., "A Comparative Analysis of Class Struggle," *American Sociological Review*, 1945, 10, 21–37.

16. Sanford, F. H., "The Followers Role in Leadership Phenomena," in G. F. Swanson, *et al.*, (eds.), *Readings in Social Psychology*, New York: Holt, 1952.

17. Siegel, S., *Nonparametric Statistics for the Behavior Sciences*, New York: McGraw-Hill, 1956.

18. Simmel, G., *The Sociology of Georg Simmel*, K. H. Wolff (ed.) Glencoe, Ill.: Free Press, 1950.

19. Stogdill, R. M., "Personal Factors Associated with Leadership: A Survey of the Literature," *Journal of Psychology*, 1948, 25, 35–71.

20. Stouffer, S. A., *et al., The American Soldier: Combat and Its Aftermath,*

Princeton N.J.: Princeton University Press, 1949.

21. VINACKE, W. E., and A. ARKOFF, "An Experimental Study of Coalitions in the Triad," *American Sociological Review*, 1957, 22, 406–414.

SOME CONDITIONS AFFECTING THE USE OF INGRATIATION TO INFLUENCE PERFORMANCE EVALUATION*

Edward E. Jones, Kenneth J. Gergen, Peter Gumpert, and John W. Thibaut

The worker-supervisor relationship may be, and fruitfully has been (for example, Thibaut & Kelley, 1959), conceived as a power relationship in which an exchange of behavior products is involved. Put most simply, the worker exchanges his productive effort for such tangible rewards as wages or such intangible ones as approval and promotion prospects. The supervisor in various ways controls the giving of these rewards so as to provide optimal incentives for effective worker performance. The supervisor is said to have superior power essentially because he can help or hurt the worker more than the latter can help or hurt him. Unless his talents are in great demand elsewhere and barriers to mobility are minimal, the worker is more dependent on the supervisor than vice versa.

Because of his relative dependence, the worker is motivated to comply with the supervisor's directives and must learn and accept the latter's criteria of performance evaluation. Having done so, he is then in a position to maintain his outcomes at a high level by performing in line with these criteria. By mastering the task, then, the worker in effect exerts counterpower on the supervisor and may narrow the range of outcomes received to those at the positive end of the potential span of outcomes.

While the worker may thus effectively control the supervisor through his own operations within the task system, this means of control or counterpower is not always available. A worker who lacks appropriate talent might be unable to meet the supervisor's standards, or those standards might themselves be so ambiguous that the route to positive outcomes is obscure. In such circumstances, we

* Edward E. Jones, Kenneth J. Gergen, Peter Gumpert, and John W. Thibaut, "Some Conditions Affecting the Use of Ingratiation to Influence Performance Evaluation," *Journal of Personality and Social Psychology*, 6 (1965), 613–25. Copyright 1965 by the American Psychological Association, and reproduced by permission.

might expect to find attempts to control the supervisor occurring outside the task system itself (cf. Blau, 1954). Thus the ineffective or bewildered worker might attempt to present himself in a positive manner to bias the supervisor in his favor. This would effectively increase the worker's outcomes only when the supervisor was himself uncertain about good and bad performance or otherwise free to choose among competing standards in evaluating a complex task.

The present investigation was directed to some of these alternative ways of influencing a supervisor. It attempted to explore some of the conditions affecting the adoption of attraction-seeking strategies in a performance setting. For convenience these strategies are referred to under the rubric of *ingratiation*, which refers to those witting and unwitting attempts to manage an impression so as to increase one's attractiveness to a particular other (Jones, 1964). The basic position of the present paper is that such strategies of ingratiation may be identified in work situations where the supervisor cannot be readily controlled through the task system, and the supervisor has some freedom to develop and modify his standards of performance evaluation. The specific form that ingratiation takes is expected to be a function of the cues provided by the supervisor concerning his own values and interpersonal orientation.

The psychology of ingratiation has only recently begun to receive attention as an experimental problem. In a study closely related in method to the present ones, Jones, Gergen, and Jones (1963) investigated the differential use of ingratiation tactics as a function of status in an undergraduate ROTC unit. In that study, experimentally induced pressures to make an attractive impression led all subjects to show greater opinion conformity to the target, led the high-status subjects to become more modest in describing themselves, and the low-status subjects to become more favorable in their ratings of the target. These same three tactical classes—opinion conformity, self-presentation, and other enhancement—were included as dependent variables in the present study. While these types of communication do not exhaust the tactical possibilities of ingratiation, they cover an extensive proportion of the terrain and provide convenient possibilities for quantitative measurement.

Having thus set the stage and introduced the players, we may now consider in more concrete detail the problems and opportunities created in the present experiment. Picture a worker who has just been introduced to a rather vague, complex, and ambiguous task. The task involves a series of similar problems which he is required to solve on a trial-by-trial basis. He quickly learns that the problems are soluble, but his own prospects for solving them are clearly not good: a supervisor, whom he has only briefly met, provides a pattern of outcomes indicating poor performance over a series of practice problems. Through a plausible experimental arrangement, the worker is led into a controlled interaction with the supervisor. They exchange opinions about important and trivial issues, exchange self-ratings, and end up trading evaluative ratings of each other. This controlled interaction provides an opportunity for the worker to try to impress the supervisor if he is so inclined. What conditions are likely to entice the worker to put this opportunity to use?

As forecast by the foregoing discussion, the degree of supervisory freedom in developing and applying standards of evaluation seems critical. Thus in the experiment the worker either learns that the supervisor is free to decide after each trial whether a solution is correct, or that he is committed to a series of problem solutions which he has worked out in advance. In the former case there exists a possibility of biasing the supervisor's decisions in the worker's favor; no such possibility exists in the latter case. The general prediction would be, then, that ingratiation should occur when the supervisor is potentially open to influence but not when he is restricted to preestablished criteria in his decisions to reward or punish.

But if ingratiation does occur, what form is it likely to take and how may it be identified? Common experience suggests that ingratiation attempts occur when the prospects for success (that is, creating an attractive impression) outweigh the risks of failure. These prospects are determined both by the surrounding conditions of interaction and the apparent characteristics of the target person. Furthermore, the characteristics of the target person should actually shape the form of ingratiation once it occurs. In the present experiment, the worker received one of two patterns of preinformation about the supervisor's beliefs and values. The worker was either led to believe that the supervisor, in his leader role, especially valued togetherness, accommodation, and worker solidarity or that he was only concerned with effective performance and cared not about the frills of group cohesiveness and personal styles which contribute to it.

Knowing this much, we can predict some of the more likely variations in impression management as a function of the supervisor's openness to influence and his personal views about the leadership

role. The most confident prediction is that opinion conformity or agreement between worker and supervisor should be greatest when the latter is open to influence and values accommodation, least when he is open to influence but competence and performance are admired. Under the latter circumstances, a show of independence provides some evidence of competence through the associative relationship which presumably links competence to assertiveness and self-confidence. When the supervisor is not open to influence, conformity should be moderate and more in the nature of cognitive readjustment than instrumental opinion change.

The prediction with respect to self-presentation was not so clear. The most reasonable expectation was that those subjects exercising the ingratiation option would show that they too valued whatever personal attributes were stressed by the supervisor and attempt to convince the supervisor that they possessed these attributes in fair degree. While the first part of this prediction was open to straightforward test (subjects were asked to check those attributes they considered important), the second part raises difficulties. It seems likely that blatant self-advertisement is not very winning as an ingratiation tactic, and it is difficult for a person to establish his affability or his competence through self-declaration alone. With trepidation, then, it was predicted that subjects would describe themselves more positively on attributes admired by the supervisor than on attributes belittled by him, and that this tendency would be especially strong when the supervisor was potentially open to influence.

With respect to the third dependent variable, other enhancement, it was predicted that subjects in the open-to-influence conditions would be more favorable in their supervisor ratings than those in the closed conditions. This was expected to be especially true on those personal attributes known to be prized by the supervisor.

METHOD

Subjects

A total of 50 undergraduate male volunteers participated as experimental subjects. Recruited from the introductory psychology course at the University of North Carolina, all but 7 of these subjects had previously completed a Campus Opinion Survey in a group testing session. This questionnaire served as the base-line measure for infering opinion conformity in the experiment, and thus analysis on this dependent variable was perforce restricted to those who had completed the survey. All data from 4 of the remaining subjects were discarded either because the subjects were clearly suspicious or because they obviously misunderstood experimental instructions. A total of 39 subjects were thus available for investigating opinion conformity, while 46 subjects provided usable data for the remaining analyses.

Procedure

Subjects appeared for the experiment in pairs and were introduced to an experimental accomplice identified as a graduate student in the School of Business Administration. The subjects were informed that they were to be players in a game designed to simulate the features of a real business concern. The graduate student was to serve as the supervisor in the game. He was to evaluate the performance of the two subjects and to give or take away points accordingly.

The experimenter then explained that the period would be divided into three parts. First there was to be a practice session in which the subjects would learn how the game was

played. Then there was to be a "get-acquainted" session in which the subjects and the supervisor would get to know each other a little better as persons. Finally, the game was to be played for points. While the final game was continually referred to as the climax of the experiment, the task toward which everything else was to lead, it was not actually played.

Variation in Conditions of Supervisory Judgment. All subject pairs were then told that the supervisor had previously looked over some relevant literature in preparation for his judging task. However, for approximately half of the pairs the experimenter emphasized both to the subjects and to the supervisor that the information was general in its implications and, he said, turning to the supervisor,

> these materials ... won't give you the specific information you need in order to evaluate the other's decisions in the game. You'll just have to wait until you hear each worker's answer each time, and then use your best judgment in awarding points.

Because of the implied freedom of the supervisor to make on-the-spot decisions, this instructional variation will hereafter be called the open-judgment, or merely open condition.

The remaining subject pairs were told, on the other hand, that the materials which the supervisor had been studying prior to their arrival provided much of the data on which the answers could be based. In addition, subjects in this, the closed-judgment or closed condition were told,

> He has already recorded his answers to each of the practice problems and also to each of the problems in the game to be played for real. ... These will serve as the correct answers and each of your responses will be judged right or wrong in terms of whether they match the supervisor's sheet or not.

After the open or closed variation had been induced, the supervisor was taken to an adjoining room to finish looking over the materials.

Practice Session. The experimenter then proceeded to outline the remainder of the procedure. The subjects would be placed in individual booths and each would be provided with a manual of practice problems, a set of message forms, and a scoring sheet. The manual would contain 14 sets of four advertising slogans, each set consisting of slogans which concerned a different consumer product (for example neckties, washing machines, skin cream). It would be the task of each subject to rank the four slogans in each set in terms of their probable effectiveness in increasing sales for the product in question. This ranking was to be recorded on a message blank to be carried by the experimenter to the supervisor. The latter would then communicate to each subject, via a microphone, the number of points won or lost on that trial. Although the subjects would not be competing in any formal way, each would be allowed to hear the number of points he won or lost as well as the outcome of the other subjects.

In order to provide a meaningful incentive for doing well in the game, the subjects were further told that the research was sponsored by the American Advertising Council, and that each subject would be paid according to the number of points he received during the game. Each subject would be credited with $1 at the outset, but each could win up to $10 if the supervisor approved of his choices. It was emphasized that the supervisor had not been informed about the monetary significance of the points he would award, allegedly because this might cause him to be over-generous in his ratings. As the game proceeded, the subjects were to use the scoring sheets to keep abreast of their gains and losses.

The subjects were then led to their respective booths and each was assigned a letter by which he was to be identified during the remainder of the procedure. Both subjects were assigned the letter A and both were led to believe that the other subject was B. The sets of slogans in the practice session were of two distinct types, and the scoring sheets were organized to emphasize the fact: one group

of slogans were for use in magazine and newspaper media, the remainder were for use with radio and television. As the subjects proceeded through the sets of slogans, each found (by prearrangement) that he was earning many points on the radio and television slogans but actually losing on the magazine and newspaper items. In addition, each was led to believe that the other subject was doing well on the magazine and newspaper slogans but doing poorly on the radio and television items. At the end of the practice session the experimenter announced that because of time limitations the actual game would concern only one of the two types of slogans. By a rigged coin toss he then indicated that in the real game only magazine and newspaper items would be used.

This elaborately controlled sequence of events was designed to serve a number of purposes. The subject had to be led to expect that he would do poorly in the real game and thus could not effectively control his outcomes by successful task performance. The fact that the other subject would probably do well in the real game presumably added some edge to the subject's motivation. And yet, each subject actually had done as well as the other on the average item of the practice game; while he was inferior on one sort of item, he was superior on the other sort. It was hoped that this arrangement would serve to minimize the personal failure implications of performance on the practice problems and inhibit such defensive reactions as autistic distortion of expected outcomes. Since his prospects were in the end determined by an arbitrary coin toss, there was presumably no ready target for blame and the subject was free to make the best of a bad situation.

Get-acquainted Pseudointeraction. As indicated above, a get-acquainted message exchange was interposed between the practice game and the "real" game which was allegedly to climax the experiment. This exchange of personal information was introduced, according to the experimenter, in order to make the game a more valid simulation of a real business organization where

> performance ... involves many complicated social factors. An organization can be set up to work in a certain way, but how it actually works is often affected by how the people who work together feel about each other, their mutual understanding, and so on.

The experimenter attempted to justify the artificial arrangement for the interaction by arguing that a controlled exchange of messages would make it easier to keep track of the "acquaintance process," and insure that each subject had an equal opportunity to give the supervisor information about himself.

To begin the get-acquainted session, the experimenter told the subjects that they would be able to listen over the sound system as he asked the supervisor a few questions about himself. After this, each subject would be given detailed instructions about an exchange of written messages between himself and the supervisor. The experimenter then left the room and turned on a tape recording of an interview between himself and the supervisor. Cross-cutting the variation in conditions of supervisory judgment (open versus closed), a variation in the supervisor's expressed values about leadership was introduced at this point. The general format of the interview was the same in all conditions: the supervisor was asked to discuss his thoughts on the relationship between a supervisor and his worker, to state his views on personnel selection in industry, and to comment on general criteria for determining salary differentials and promotion. The supervisor's tape-recorded response to these problems differed radically in the two halves of the subject sample.

Half of the subjects heard an interview in which the supervisor continually emphasized the "human" side of business. In his comments he stressed such factors as the spirit of cooperation, the importance of getting along with others, considerateness, and understanding. Competence and performance motivation

were simply not mentioned in his discussion of relevant considerations, though they were not explicitly belittled. In view of the emphasis on accommodation and social solidarity pervading the interview, the supervisor in this condition is hereafter referred to as Sol. The remaining subjects were exposed to interview responses in which the supervisor stressed the quality and quantity of job performance above all else. The only important personal characteristics that should be considered in selecting and evaluating workers were those associated with talent and perseverance. A man's thoughts and feelings and reactions off the job were clearly his own business. In view of the emphasis on performance and productivity characterizing the interview, the supervisor in this condition is hereafter referred to as Prod. The Sol-Prod variation was chosen to reflect extreme versions of leader orientations often distinguished in the literature on role differentiation in small groups. Bales and Slater (1955), for example, contrast the

> person who symbolizes the demands of task accomplishment and [the] person who symbolizes the demands of social and emotional needs [p. 304]

and suggest that this fundamental differentiation occurs in all social systems.

The pseudointeraction which followed the interview actually involved an exchange of questionnaires between each subject and the supervisor. Since the questionnaire responses of the subject provided the main dependent variable data of the study, the nature of the questionnaires will be discussed in that context.

Measures of Opinion Conformity, Self-Presentation, and Other Enhancement

Each subject completed in the same sequence a self-rating questionnaire to be transmitted to the supervisor, a shortened version of the same opinion questionnaire he had completed earlier in the semester, and finally rated the supervisor on the same questionnaire form used for the self-ratings. He was led to believe that the supervisor was filling out the opinion questionnaire while he, the subject, was rating himself; the supervisor was filling out his self-rating form while the subject was indicating his opinions; and both were evaluating each other during the final phase of the exchange. It is important to remember that the subject was aware of the supervisor's opinions at the time he recorded his, the subject was aware of how the supervisor had rated himself before the subject rated him, and all questionnaire responses were made with the clear understanding that they would be transmitted to the supervisor.

The self-description rating form consisted of 20 pairs of attributive antonyms. Each personal attribute was separated from its opposite by three 12-point scales. On the first of these scales the subject was to rate himself, on the second he was to indicate his ideal along that dimension, and the third scale was to be left for the supervisor's use. Subjects were also asked to check those antonym pairs which they considered "especially important personal characteristics." While each item was quite clearly evaluative in connotation (that is, was composed of a favorable and an unfavorable antonym), the items fell in two predetermined content classes. Half of the items dealt with qualities connoting *affability*, warmth, or affectionateness (for example, friendly versus aloof, likable versus not likable), while the other half were more obviously centered around judgments of *respect* (for example, efficient versus inefficient, strong versus weak). Eighteen independent raters had previously classified the items as affability or respect attributes with near-unanimous agreement on the items finally chosen. The 20 items were presented in mixed order as far as content was concerned and the position of the more socially desirable attribute varied unsystematically from left to right on the page.

The opinion questionnaire consisted of 20 items taken from the 50-item Campus Opinion Survey which most of the subjects had completed earlier in the semester. From the initial battery of items, the 10 items judged by the class to be most "important" as a determiner of personal attractiveness and the 10 judged to be least important were combined to comprise the final shortened opinion questionnaire. Each of the 20 items was separated by two 12-point scales along which agreement or disagreement could be expressed. When he received the opinion questionnaire, each subject found that the supervisor had already used the first of the two scales to indicate his agreement or disagreement with the item statement. The subject was thus to use the second scale and return the completed questionnaire to the supervisor via the experimenter.

The opinions presented as the supervisor's had been especially prepared in advance for each subject. Working from the subject's own Campus Opinion Survey responses, the supervisors' opinion ratings were so arranged that: for half of the important and half of the unimportant items the supervisor's responses were the same as those which the subject had earlier given; on three of the important and three of the unimportant items, the supervisor disagreed with the subject's previous opinions by 6 scale points; on two of the important and two of the unimportant items, the supervisor disagreed with the subject's prior opinions by 3 scale points. The pattern of agreement and disagreement was the same for all subjects, so that the same item in the same position was always an agree, a 3-disagree, or a 6-disagree item. The overall effect of this procedure was to confront the subject with opinions from the supervisor which agreed with his own on many of the items (assuming little change from the previous testing) but showed some or much disagreement on other statements varying in importance.

The other description form was identical in appearance to the self-description rating form. The ideal and self-scales were already filled in, presumably by the supervisor, and the subject was left with the task of evaluating the supervisor on the same dimensions before the form was returned to him. Again by prearrangement, Sol's ideal and self-ratings were slightly closer to the positive antonym on the affability items than the respect items, and Prod's ratings were slightly closer to the positive end on respect than affability items. The mean and standard deviation of supervisor self-ratings (that is, his overall favorability in rating himself) was the same for both Sol and Prod.

A final questionnaire was also administered to inquire into the subject's "private" impressions of the supervisor, his view of the experimental setting, and his awareness of opportunities for social influence. The subjects were then told that the experiment was completed, informed of the true purpose of the experiment and of the deceptions involved, and requested not to discuss the experiment with classmates. Each received $2 for his cooperation.

RESULTS

Effectiveness of Inductions

Open-closed judgment variation. Before examining the results relevant to the main experimental predictions, it is first necessary to establish the extent to which the two independent variables were successfully manipulated. The open-closed judgment variable was, of course, intended to have complex cognitive and motivational effects. To pursue all the evidence on these would carry us directly to an analysis of the pseudointeraction data. At a minimum, however, it was essential that the subjects properly understood and were able to recall the nature of the task situation for which they were preparing throughout the experiment. In the postexperimental questionnaire all subjects were asked to indicate whether the supervisor was to grade their answers (administer points) in terms of a set of previously developed solutions or whether he was free to decide on each trial whether a given answer merited credits or debits. A total of four subjects, in three conditions, were eliminated because they did not choose the alternative appropriate to their experimental condition, thus indicating gross inattention or confusion. The results for

Table 1

MEAN RATINGS OF THE SUPERVISOR FOLLOWING THE SOLIDARITY VERSUS THE PRODUCTIVITY INTERVIEW

| | Condition | | | | | | |
| | Solidarity | | | Productivity | | | |
Trait	Open	Closed	Total	Open	Closed	Total	$p$diff.
Cold (versus warm)	6.55	6.27	6.42	7.43	5.90	6.67	*ns*
Weak (versus strong)	5.73	6.36	6.05	3.43	4.80	4.12	.01
Incompetent (versus competent)	3.82	3.55	3.69	2.79	2.80	2.80	.05
Permissive (versus demanding)	5.54	5.54	5.50	2.79	3.80	3.30	.001
Intolerant (versus tolerant)	5.09	3.82	4.46	7.14	5.60	6.37	.01[a]
Tenderhearted (versus tough-minded)	7.09	6.91	7.00	5.14	5.00	5.07	.001
Unfair (versus fair)	3.73	3.82	3.78	4.07	3.20	3.64	*ns*
Not likable (versus likable)	4.27	3.91	4.09	5.57	4.20	4.89	*ns*

Note.—Higher scores signify greater attribution of first listed trait in each pair.
[a] The difference between open and closed conditions is also significant ($p < .05$).

Table 2

CONFORMITY ON DISCREPANT ITEMS (TOTAL, IMPORTANT ONLY) AS A
FUNCTION OF SUPERVISOR VALUE AND JUDGMENT CONTEXT

	Means[a]			
	All discrepant items		Important items	
	Solidarity	Productivity	Solidarity	Productivity
Open	20.78	28.40	9.67	15.20
Closed	27.60	25.60	14.70	13.10

Analysis of variance summary

	All discrepant items			Important items		
Source	df	MS	F	df	MS	F
Open-closed (A)	1	4.04		1	2.15	
Solidarity-productivity (B)	1	7.80		1	3.86	
A×B	1	23.04	2.47	1	12.71	4.34*
Error	35	9.34		35	2.93	

[a] The lower the score, the greater the agreement with the supervisor.
* $p < .05$.

these subjects were in line with their incorrect self-assignment and not with the actual instructions to which they had been exposed. The overall effect of the differential instructions, then, was clearly as intended for more than 90% of the subjects.

Going a step beyond this minimal validation of the open-closed variation, we might ask whether the open condition in fact aroused more explicit concern with the impression created than did the closed condition. There is little indication from a set of four questionnaire items that subjects were aware of such a concern and willing to report it to the experimenter. Subjects in the two open conditions did express slightly more interest in being liked and admired by the supervisor, but not significantly more. It is not clear whether such an interest is always difficult to admit, whether judgmental openness

never aroused self-conscious desires to impress the supervisor, or whether such desires were aroused initially but had declined by the time of the postexperimental questionnaire. We shall return to this question in considering, later, individual differences in response to the experimental inductions.

Supervisor values. While it might be expected that the subjects' impressions of the supervisor would be influenced by their own behavior during the experiment, gross differences in the pattern of postexperimental ratings should still have distinguished between personal attributes implied by an emphasis on solidarity versus those implied by an emphasis on productivity. Table 1 presents the mean ratings of the supervisor as a function of his expressed values, along with the probability levels of significant mean differences. From the results in this table it is clear that the two taped interviews succeeded in conveying divergent information about the supervisor and that subjects typically used this information to construct quite different impressions of him. As expected, relative to the productivity-oriented supervisor (Prod) the solidarity-oriented supervisor (Sol) was seen as more permissive, more tolerant, and more tenderhearted. The expected difference in ratings of warmth, however, was not significant. It is perhaps not surprising that subjects saw Prod as stronger and more competent than they saw Sol. Sol, on the other hand, was better liked than Prod though not reliably so. The perceived differences between the two supervisors were, thus, largely differences on the attributes specifically emphasized in the interviews and do not seem to be strongly mediated by an evaluative halo effect.

Opinion Conformity as an Ingratiation Tactic

A major hypothesis of the present study concerned the interactive impact of both independent variables on the degree to which subjects conform to the supervisor's opinions. Specifically, it was predicted that subjects in the open-judgment conditions would conform more to Sol and less to Prod than would subjects in the closed conditions. As detailed above, conditions for estimating the degree of conformity were established by having the supervisor appear to transmit bogus opinion ratings, some of which were systematically discrepant from the earlier expressed opinions of the subject. The subject was instructed to respond to each of the supervisor's opinions with his own, degree of conformity being measured as the proximity of subject and supervisor on the discrepant items.

As Table 2 shows, the resulting means fell into the pattern predicted by the conformity hypothesis but the analysis portion of Table 2 indicates that the crucial interaction did not approach significance. It may be recalled, however, that the message exchange involved both "important" and "unimportant" issues (as determined by the normative judgments of the population from which the present subject sample was drawn). While conformity on unimportant items showed a slight (and nowhere near significant) trend in line with the hypothesis, conformity on important items resulted in a significant interaction (Table 2). Consistent with the greater statistical significance obtained when important items only were considered, subjects in the open-solidarity condition do conform more on important versus unimportant items relative to all other subjects ($p < .10$). Thus, subjects in this crucial cell seem to attach a special meaning to the more important opinion items—whereas all subjects show a moderate and similar degree of conformity on unimportant items, open-solidarity subjects show a distinctive tendency to conform on the important items.

One difficulty with measuring conformity by summing the ultimate discrepancies between the supervisor's and the subject's opinion ratings is that much of the resulting variance may reflect opinion changes occurring prior to the experiment—that is, between taking the before measure in the classroom and being confronted with the supervisor's opinions. It was possible for drastic changes on individual items to obscure the overall pattern of conformity or nonconformity. It was decided, there-

Table 3

OPINION CONFORMITY:
MEASURE OF MOVEMENT TOWARD
SUPERVISOR

Movement index means[a]		
	Judgment context	
	Open	Closed
Solidarity	8.9	6.9
Productivity	6.7	7.6

Analysis of variance summary			
Source	df	MS	F
Open–closed (A)	1	.31	
Solidarity–productivity (B)	1	.57	
A×B	1	2.09	5.08*
Error	35	.41	

[a] The higher the score, the greater the incidence of movement toward the supervisor. For each subject, each of the 20 discrepant items was assigned a score of +1 for movement toward the supervisor and a 0 otherwise.
* $p < .05$.

fore, to limit the contribution of individual opinion items and to assign each subject a score based on the frequency of his conformity as inferred by the direction of prepost change. Disregarding the magnitude of this change, a score of 1 was assigned for each rating falling between the prerating and 2 points beyond the supervisor's rating; all other items were simply assigned a 0. The decision to include movement slightly beyond the supervisor's rating seemed psychologically reasonable and was an a priori decision. The choice of 2 points beyond, rather than 1 or 3, was arbitrary. This method reduces substantially the within-cell variance, the predicted interaction is clearly significant ($p < .05$), and interpretation does not

need to be restricted to the important items.

Positivity of Self-Presentation

Prior to the exchange of opinion messages, subjects were instructed to describe themselves to the supervisor via a 20-item rating scale composed of evaluative personal attributes in antonym form. The content of these attributes had been preselected so that half of them connoted qualities relevant to judgments of respect or admiration for personal strength and competence (respect items) while the remaining half centered around qualities of friendliness and approachability (affability items). The apparent congruence between these two categories of item content and the qualities emphasized by the two supervisors was, of course, deliberately contrived. It was expected that the open-judgment context would give rise to ingratiating self-presentations in the particular areas stressed as important by the subject's supervisor.

It will be recalled that subjects both rated themselves and indicated their ideal position on each antonym. They were also instructed to check attribute pairs they considered especially important in determining the attractiveness of others. As mentioned in the introductory section, a clear expectation was that those subjects in the open conditions would show that they too valued whatever personal attributes were stressed by the supervisor. The most direct means to this end was, presumably, for the subject to attach more importance to these attributes.

Turning to the results, solidarity subjects did emphasize the importance of affability items whereas productivity subjects attached more importance to respect items ($p_{\text{diff}} = .01$). While this differential emphasis was more marked in the open treatments, the interaction between judgment condition and supervisor values was not significant. This suggests that the subjects' conceptions of important attributes were shaped by the supervisor's comments during the interview, but there was no clear evidence that the subjects used agreement with the supervisor's standards to win his favor.

The remaining issue concerns evidence that the subjects in the open conditions tried to convince the supervisor that they in fact possessed the admired attributes. It was predicted that subjects would describe themselves more positively on attributes admired by the supervisor than on attributes ignored or belittled by him, and that this tendency would be especially strong when the supervisor was potentially open to influence. This prediction was proposed with some hesitance in view of the fact that a person does not necessarily convince others that he is, say, "noble" by constantly extolling his own nobility. But a study by Jones, Gergen, and Davis

Table 4

FAVORABILITY OF SELF-PRESENTATION (IDEAL AND SELF-RATINGS ON RESPECT AND AFFABILITY ATTRIBUTES)

| | Experimental condition | | | | |
| | Open | | Closed | | Significant |
Y	Solidarity	Productivity	Solidarity	Productivity	comparison
Affability					
Self	35.64	38.50	37.18	33.60	—
Ideal	21.91	25.00	25.63	25.00	—
Respect					
Self	39.91	34.86	47.00	35.40	S vs. P**
Ideal	22.09	15.86	25.00	16.20	S vs. P***
Total					
Self	75.55	73.36	84.18	69.00	—
Ideal	44.00	40.86	50.63	41.20	—
Respect-affability	4.27	−3.64	9.82	1.80	S vs. P**
discrepancy[a]					O vs. C*
Self-ideal discrepancy					
Affability	13.73	13.50	11.55	8.60	—
Respect	17.82	19.00	22.00	19.20	—
R—A[b]	4.09	5.50	10.27	10.60	O vs. C*

[a] The lower the score the greater the tendency to describe self positively on respect (relative to affability) items.

[b] The lower the score the greater the tendency to describe self (relative to ideal) positively on respect (relative to affability) items.

* $p < .05$.
** $p < .01$.
*** $p < .001$.

(1962) showed that female subjects became more self-enhancing when instructed to create a good impression. In a subsequent study by Jones et al. (1963), low-status ROTC students became more self-enhancing when instructed to win the favor of higher status students, except on those items judged to be especially important. Because of the variation of perceived item importance as a function of experimental treatment in the present study, the effects of importance on self-ratings could not be meaningfully studied.

Table 4 presents the mean values of both ideal and self-ratings on respect and affability attributes; the lower the value, the closer the ideal or self-rating to the positive or favorable end of the scale. Several features of this rather complex table deserve comment. First of all, there is no reliable tendency for subjects to describe themselves favorably on all items or on affability items as a function of either judgmental context or supervisor values. When the analysis is restricted to respect attributes, however, there is a strong effect of the Sol-Prod variable on both ideal and self-ratings. When confronted with a supervisor who has previously emphasized performance and competence, subjects locate their ideal selves closer to the scale extremes represented by such trait names as efficient, original, well-organized, and levelheaded. In addition, they present themselves as actually having more of these characteristics when communicating to Prod.

While these systematic variations in respect to item ratings are of interest in their own right, reflecting as they do an implicit tailoring of the presented self to accommodate the characteristics of another, there is no evidence in the raw data of

Table 4 that this accommodation serves as an ingratiation tactic. That is, the tendency to model themselves after the supervisor seems no greater in the open than in the closed conditions.

An unexpected finding was that those subjects confronting Sol described themselves more positively on respect items in the open than in the closed condition ($p < .06$). To the extent that this is a reliable difference, it might be argued that when there is no direct effect of the supervisor's admiration of respect attributes (such as occurred in the Prod conditions), the context of supervisory judgment does affect respect item self-ratings. In the Prod conditions, in other words, the impact of the supervisor's values may have been powerful enough to override the weaker effects of openness to influence.

A notable (if unavoidable) weakness in the present design is its "after-only" nature. The final ratings of self and ideal are a compound of current subjective state, self-conscious strategy, scale interpretation, and other sources of idiosyncratic response bias. This is, probably, the reason why there is such excessive variability in the self-presentation scores. In an effort to get a clearer picture of the experimental effects less contaminated by these sources of response bias, the following procedure was followed as a way of using each subject as his own control. Since there were no systematic differences in either ideal or self-ratings on affability items, and since affability self-ratings were moderately correlated with respect self-ratings (r's ranging from .431 to .784), each subject was assigned a score representing favorable self-rating on respect items minus favorable self-rating on affability items. The resulting R—A difference score serves as an index of his tendency to describe himself positively on respect relative to affability items. This provides, then, a relative emphasis score and also controls for each subject's tendency to restrict himself to a particular region of the scale.

Placing these R—A scores in a factorial design yields two significant main effects: the Sol-Prod variation is highly significant and judgmental context also has a reliable effect (see Table 4). Thus not only do subjects show a general tendency to place a relative stress on their respectworthy qualities when confronted with a task-oriented, performance-centered supervisor, they also stress respect qualities when in a position to influence the supervisor to act in their behalf.

A final point needs to be considered before leaving the self-presentation results. It has been noted that both ideal and self-ratings on respect items were clearly affected by the supervisor's characteristics. This suggests that the Sol-Prod variable influenced in a general way how the scale should be used, but did not affect the relative placement of ideal and self-ratings. It is as if the supervisor, through his interview responses, defined for the subject what is "good"—it is good to be extremely competent, strong, cool-headed, etc.—but he did not affect how the subject saw himself relative to maximal goodness. The open-closed variable, on the other hand, did affect this placement of self relative to ideal so that subjects presented themselves as more competent, etc., when more strongly motivated (in the open conditions) to impress the supervisor with their worthiness.

This reasoning is supported by the last row of Table 4, where a final self-ideal discrepancy index is shown. Since the effects of shifting both ideal and self-ratings canceled each other out, only the open-closed variable remained significant.

It should be emphasized that the obtained pattern of self-presentation results was not predicted in detail. In particular, there was at the outset no theoretical reason to expect systematic variations in respect items but not affability items. It is also clear that the open-closed variables had weak effects on most indices of self-presentation, reaching substantial proportions only with a derived index of self-enhancement on respect minus affability items. Nevertheless, the significant findings reported seem provocative, and their implications will be discussed below.

Other Enhancement

As in the previous study by Jones et al. (1963), the final portion of the interchange between subjects and supervisor involved ratings of the supervisor on the same sheet on which he had presumably rated himself. These ratings were presumably to be transmitted to the targets of evaluation. In the earlier study, low-status subjects showed a greater tendency than high-status subjects to evaluate their partners positively, and this was especially true when instructions emphasized the importance of compatibility. No such differential tendency was observed in the present study. That is, contrary to experimental expectations subjects in the open conditions were not more favorable in their transmitted ratings of the supervisor than those in the closed conditions. Nor were there any more subtle effects depending on the content of the items, etc. Rating variability was extremely high, and it may be that the experimental inductions had lost their potency by the time that the "other ratings" took place.

DISCUSSION

Subjects in the present study were either presented with or denied the opportunity to improve their outcomes by ingratiating themselves with the supervisor. Provision of this opportunity was implicit in the conditions which allegedly permitted the supervisor to judge each solution attempt as it was offered by the subject. Denial of this opportunity was implicit when the supervisor was allegedly committed to a set of predetermined answers in rewarding or punishing the subject's solution attempts. In the latter conditions, we would expect the subjects to be relatively unconcerned with the personal impression they may be making on the supervisor, whereas this type of concern should be heightened in the conditions of open or uncommitted supervisory judgment. The way in which this concern might manifest itself was more or less an open question, though it seemed clear that the tactics of managing a favorable impression would vary with the values and other personal attributes characterizing the supervisor. For this reason, quite different information was conveyed to subjects in the solidarity versus the production treatment, designed to emphasize radically different supervisor attitudes and orientations.

The most specific and theoretically obvious prediction involved the differential use of opinion conformity as an ingratiation tactic. It was predicted that conformity would be greatest in the open-solidarity condition and least in the open-productivity condition, the two closed conditions falling in between. The results generally support this prediction, though the degree of support depends on the particular measure employed. If one totals the item discrepancies between subject and supervisor ratings, then the interaction is significant only with the more "important" items. If one merely classifies each item as movement toward the supervisor versus residual, the interaction is significant with both unimportant and important items. Insofar as the importance distinction is worth taking seriously, it does seem reasonable to suggest that issues generally viewed as important are more useful than trivial ones for emphasizing agreeableness as well as for emphasizing independence.

The theoretical interpretation of the predicted interaction assumes that subjects in both open conditions have a special concern with being liked or admired, but that they must proceed to implement this concern in different ways. Subjects in the open-solidarity condition are invited by circumstances and the nature of the target to employ conformity for strategic purposes. Subjects in the open productivity condition, on the other hand, are confronted with a person who seems to devalue opinion agreement as such and circumstances seem to point away from conformity as a tactic for impressing the supervisor. Some interesting, if tentative, correlational data seem to support this interpretation. Those subjects who expressed an interest in being attractive to the supervisor (as measured by a series of items on the postexperimental questionnaire) showed a special tendency to respond differently as a function of the supervisor's expressed values. In the solidarity conditions, the correlation between conformity and attraction motivation was .434; in the productivity conditions the correlation between the same two variables was —.179. In spite of the small samples involved, the difference between these correlations is almost significant ($p < .10$) suggesting that wanting to be liked leads to conformity only when the target person himself seems to value accommodation and togetherness. With a few qualifications, then, the results fit the argument developed in the introductory section: the openness of supervisory judgment provides the incentive to concentrate on creating an attractive impression; the supervisor's own emphasis on effective interpersonal relations points out the appropriate path of impression management.

The tenuous but provocative self-presentation results also merit some discussion. It is apparent that self-descriptions on traits connoting interpersonal warmth and congeniality were unaffected by the experimental variables. Ideal ratings on these traits were similarly unaffected. This is quite surprising in view of the solidarity supervisor's explicit emphasis on the value and importance of such traits in work groups. In comparison, the stated values of the supervisor had a clear effect on ratings of traits connoting competence and personal power. Both self-descriptions and ideal ratings were more favorable in the productivity conditions. The fact that both sets of ratings were more positive suggests that respect attributes are evaluated relative to a shifting standard, a standard quite sensitive to the value attached to competence and performance by a supervisor. Ideal and self-evaluations on affability attributes may be more firmly anchored in each individual's past experiences with others. Many subjects may have entered the experimental situation with the conviction that too much friendliness and warmth is a bad thing and this conviction was little influenced by the promptings of the solidarity supervisor.

Of greater theoretical interest was the tendency for subjects in the open conditions to present themselves as closer to their ideal on respect than on affection items—relative to the subjects in the closed conditions. For whatever reason, subjects in the open conditions were more anxious to impress the supervisor with their competence than their affability. Under the circumstances, if the supervisor could be led to have respect for the subject's judgment, he might begin to assign more points for the latter's solution attempts. Such an increase in respect could, of course, have no such effect in the closed conditions. Impressing the open judge with one's competence seems to be a more direct way to influence his judgment than presenting oneself as affable, and (by inference at least) dependent. It would be interesting to explore the possible conditions under which self-advertised dependence (placing onself at another's mercy) would become a strategy to influence performance evaluation.

The expectation that subjects in the open conditions would "flatter" the supervisor—especially on those attributes he has stressed as valuable—was not confirmed by the data. It may be true that rating the supervisor in a complimentary way is viewed as a risky or inopportune strategy of influence. In our considered judgment, however, the open-closed induction had probably lost much of its strength before the final rating scales were administered. Not only had a fair amount of time elapsed since the instructions had emphasized this variable, but there were probably growing suspicions that the "real" game would never be played. Apropos of this suggestion that the induction had lost its strength by the time subjects were asked to rate their supervisors, there is evidence in the postexperimental questionnaire that at least in the crucial open-solidarity condition, those who remained interested in making themselves attractive *did* evaluate the supervisor more positively. In the open-solidarity condition only, a questionnaire measure of attractiveness motivation showed a firm positive correlation with favorability of ratings ($r = .636$); in the other conditions the correlation between the same two indexes ranged from $-.131$ to $+.082$. Perhaps if the open-to-influence induction had been stronger, the former correlation would have been lower and the tendency for subjects in the open-solidarity condition to flatter would have been more uniform.

REFERENCES

BALES, R. F., and SLATER, P. E. "Role Differentiation in Small Decision-Making Groups." In T. Parsons and R. F. Bales (Eds.), *Family Socialization and Interaction Process.* Glencoe, Ill.: Free Press, 1955. Pp. 259–306.

BLAU, P. M., "Patterns of Interaction Among a Group of Officials in a Government Agency." *Human Relations*, 1954, 7, 337–348.

JONES, E. E. *Ingratiation: A Social Psychological Analysis.* New York: Appleton-Century-Crofts, 1964.

JONES, E. E., GERGEN, K. J., and DAVIS, K. E. "Some Determinants of Reactions to Being Approved or Disapproved as a Person." *Psychological Monographs*, 1962, 76 (2, Whole No. 521).

JONES, E. E., GERGEN, K. J., and JONES, R. G. "Tactics of Ingratiation Among Leaders and Subordinates in a Status Hierarchy." *Psychological Monographs*, 1963, 77 (3, Whole No. 566).

THIBAUT, J. W., and KELLEY, H. H. *The Social Psychology of Groups.* New York: Wiley, 1959.

11

Group Decision Making

COLLECTIVE BEHAVIOR
IN A SIMULATED PANIC SITUATION*

Harold H. Kelley, John C. Condry, Jr., Arnold E. Dahlke,
and Arthur H. Hill

The experiments reported here are concerned with the behavior exhibited by a collection of persons when they are suddenly confronted with an imminent danger and provided with a means of escape that is limited and for which they do not possess any prior organized mode of use. Because the escape avenue permits only one person at a time to escape, they are contriently interdependent (Deutsch, 1949). One person's use of the escape route reduces the likelihood that the remaining individuals will be able to escape. Furthermore, simultaneous attempts to use

the route reduce its effectiveness. Under these conditions, the escape efforts of the individuals may be orderly, permitting the maximum number possible for the available time to traverse the escape route. Or, the escape efforts may be disorderly and characterized by "traffic jams" which waste time and reduce the number who succeed in escaping. We are concerned here with some of the factors which affect the extent to which the collection's behavior is incoordinated. It can be seen that we are examining a collective situation very similar to that studied by Mintz in his widely known experiment (1951) which Brown (1954), in his excellent review of the literature on mass phenomena, has described as a laboratory paradigm of an escape mob.

Although not in complete agreement, writers on panic before Mintz had tended

* Harold H. Kelley, John C. Condry, Jr., Arnold E. Dahlke, and Arthur H. Hill, "Collective Behavior in a Simulated Panic Situation," *Journal of Experimental Social Psychology*, 1 (1965), 20–54. Reprinted by permission of Academic Press, Inc.

to emphasize *perceived danger* and *mutual influence* (suggestion, contagion, mimicry) as the key factors in the development and spread of incoordinated and nonadaptive "panic" behavior. In the emotional state induced by the threat of the impending danger, individuals were thought to become more suggestible and, hence, more influenced by the example of others' behavior and less governed by ordinary critical thought processes, moral codes, etc. Taking issue with this view, Mintz emphasized that persons are merely reacting to the reward structure of the situation. As long as escape is orderly, each sees that his interests lie in continuing to cooperate with others. However, when a few individuals begin to create a disturbance in the use of the exit, the others will recognize the threat to their own escape and see that their only hope lies in themselves trying to push through. Thus, the individual is no less rational or moral in the panic than in any other situation. He is always in pursuit of his own interests and acts on the basis of his current estimates of where these lie. In this analysis, Mintz is most sharply in conflict with the earlier views on the question of the role of perceived danger. Mintz explicitly denies that intense fear (or emotional excitement, as he often refers to it) is responsible for nonadaptive group behavior.

While the originality of Mintz's work must be acknowledged, several major criticisms can be made of his procedure and conceptualization. The most important of these is that his method cannot be considered to test the effects of danger. The subjects were promised small monetary rewards, ranging from 10¢ to 25¢, for escaping (withdrawing their cones from within a large bottle) in time, and even smaller fines, from 1¢ to 10¢, for failing

to do so. It is difficult to believe that the results from this situation shed much light on behavior under conditions of high stress. To argue, as Mintz does, that intense fear is shown not to be important because even in its absence there occurs "behavior analogous to that occurring in panics" is to overlook the possibility that collective incoordination may have a variety of quite different causes.

A second criticism, first noted by Brown (1954), is that Mintz's analysis of incoordination is only a partial one. It starts at a point in time when a disturbance or jam has already begun. It does not face the problem of the *origination* of the first jam-producing escape attempts.

A third criticism is that the behaviors of Mintz's subjects do not seem to provide apt illustrations of his view that even under the press of the "panic," individuals continue to act in a thoughtful manner. This view certainly provides no explanation of why a subject should, on seeing two other cones jammed in the bottleneck, nevertheless immediately proceed to try to remove his own cone. This is particularly difficult to understand in view of the fact that he had just been given a convincing demonstration that only one cone can be removed at a time.

Finally, if we look to Mintz's study for practical recommendations about how to reduce incoordination in danger situations (and practical implications are surely one goal of science), none is forthcoming. Among his several experimental variations, the only one in which the amount of incoordination was markedly reduced involved group goals (surpassing the performance of a group from another university) rather than individual ones (gaining individual rewards and avoiding individual fines). Limited to this result one would be forced to conclude that incoordination is more or less inevitable when members of a collectivity are oriented toward their separate personal goals, and that improvement is possible only when these orientations are supplanted by the identification with success of the total group. This provides a totally misleading emphasis. Surely there must be some factors within the individual reward-fine situation that have important effects upon the amount of jamming. The present criticism is that Mintz's work fails to reveal these and, worse, implies that none of any significance exists.

The present experiments were designed to pursue the question of the factors and processes underlying incoordination in the interdependent escape situation. As will be seen, the theoretical analysis and experimental proceedures were planned to meet some of the above objections to Mintz's work. The analysis deals with the origin as well as the spread of escape attempts, the latter being cast in terms of a more modern theory of social influence. The experimental procedures deal exclusively with the case where "selfish" individual interests predominate and focus upon some of the factors within that setting which affect the collectivity's success. Most important among these is degree of threat or danger. Levels of threat as high as seemed experimentally feasible were examined and compared with the absence of threat.

We shall first consider the general conceptual framework, and then the methods and results of the three experiments in turn.

THEORETICAL ANALYSIS

It would seem that a complete account of collective performance in the interdependent escape situation would include (1) a conception of what constitutes a "solution"[1] to the problem posed for the collectivity and (2) a theory of individual behavior in the escape situation. The first would specify an ideal pattern for the various participants' behavior, and the second would suggest the factors determining the extent to which this pattern would be realized.

The nature of the solution in this case is easy to specify. It is what the participants would try to arrange if they had full knowledge of the problem and time to analyze, discuss, and agree upon a method for coping with it. They would plan, obviously, a queue. The first person in the queue would use the escape route first while the others waited, the second would use it next, and so on down the line. The concept of queue affords a criterion against which to evaluate the performance of the collectivity. This criterion is used implicitly when "time to escape" or "jamming" are employed as proficiency measures. Both increase with increasing departures from an orderly queueing procedure.

To say that the participants might *try* to form and maintain a queue is not, of course, to say they would succeed in doing so. It is instructive to consider why their plan might break down. The answer is that certain persons in the queue would not be satisfied with the positions they were allotted and would try to occupy positions closer to the head of the line.

---

[1] "Solution" is used here in the same sense as in the outline of the 1952 edition of the *Readings in Social Psychology* by Swanson, Newcomb, and Hartley (1952). The Mintz study was placed in part II dealing with collective problem-solving and in a subsection entitled "Behavior in the absence of collective solutions."

In doing so, they would interfere with the escape of persons with higher priorities and consequently waste time for the queue.

This suggests something about the conditions under which a queue might spontaneously develop and persist, even, as in the case under study, in the absence of prior opportunities for planning. A queue would be likely to develop if there were great variability among the individuals in their attitudes toward the situation—in how urgent they felt the necessity of escape to be. Given heterogeneity of attitudes, the person feeling the greatest urgency would go first while the others more or less willingly waited, followed by the person with the next greatest concern, and so on, with the individual most indifferent to the threatened danger being willing to wait until the end of the line. An orderly queue would also be likely to develop if all participants held attitudes of indifference. In this case, some time might be lost while all waited for someone else to go first, but assuming a general weak incentive for leaving the situation (as in a practice fire drill), this type of time wasting would probably be of little importance. They certainly would not waste time with jams.

The distribution of attitudes most obviously detrimental to the development and maintenance of a queue is that of uniformly high felt urgency. If all judge the danger to be imminent and intolerable, and are, consequently, highly desirous of immediate escape, all will seek the head of the queue and none will be willing to accept positions toward the rear.

This analysis assumes that a person's behavior with respect to attempting immediate escape vs. waiting for others to escape depends upon his assessment of the situation, i.e., his attitude toward it. Accordingly, the key factor mediating the success or failure of a collectivity is the *distribution* of these attitudes. If they are concentrated at the high urgency end of the scale, either being so from the outset or becoming so during the escape period, the occurrence of orderly queueing is unlikely. We must consider, therefore, factors that will bias the initial distribution toward the anxious extreme or that will make for shifts in that direction.

The latter eventuality, that the distribution of attitudes may shift toward the high urgency end of the scale, implies changes in individuals' evaluations of the situation as a result of events in the early stages of the escape period. Let us briefly consider how this might occur. One possibility is that the person's estimate of the likelihood of successful escape may change as time passes, and particularly as time is wasted by jamming. In this case, the actions of the other *indirectly* affect his attitudes through changing the characteristics of the situation in several crucial respects, viz., the time left and the apparent inefficiency of time use.

A second possibility, and one much more familiar to the social psychologist, is that the actions of others *directly* affect his attitudes. Much of what is known from research on interpersonal influence suggests that the conditions in the typical interdependent escape situation are highly appropriate for such influence to occur. The situation is an *ambiguous* one, difficult for the individual to assess. The information available is unclear with regard to how dangerous the threatened consequences are and their imminence. The situation is also an *important* one. He must make some sort of judgment and decide upon his action regarding the escape, and the wisdom of this action may have important consequences for him. Finally, the situation permits *communication* among the participants. Information about others' evaluations is communicated to the individual through their verbal behavior and escape actions, or in our experiments where verbal communication is ruled out, through their behavioral examples alone. Given these conditions of ambiguity, importance, and communication, individuals will be influenced by one another and this influence process will operate to produce a uniformity or concentration of attitudes. The entire process can be conceptualized in terms of a group powerfield that produces similarity among the participants in their life spaces, as suggested by French (1944), or in terms of pressures toward uniformity, as described by Festinger (1950).

In brief, we are arguing that the distribution of attitudes toward the escape situation is the critical factor in the performance of the collectivity. If this distribution is initially, or later becomes, concentrated at the end of the attitude continuum reflecting high concern and feelings of urgency about escape, the spontaneous formation and maintenance of an orderly queue will not be possible. Each variable in the escape situation may then be examined for (1) its possible effect upon the initial distribution of attitudes, and (2) its possible contribution to changes in these attitudes during the course of the escape process.

In the experiments to be described, we have studied four experimental variables. The first is the *threatened penalty* for failure to escape. With increasing magnitude of penalty, increased concentration in the state of high concern can be ex-

pected for several different reasons. First, the most direct and obvious effect is that the greater the threat, the greater the number of participants who will be highly concerned (and realistically so) and desire to be first in the escape queue. Second, as a byproduct of the first effect, the higher threat will produce more time-wasting jams which will demonstrate to initially unconcerned persons that successful escape through waiting is less promising than they might have thought. Third, as an additional byproduct of the first, the greater number of escape attempts generated by high threat will constitute a greater volume of communication conveying the evaluation of the situation as one requiring urgent action. Fourth, in addition to being more numerous, these communications may also exert more influence upon the other participants because of the heightened importance of the situation, following Festinger's (1950) hypothesis that pressures toward uniformity increase as the issue becomes more important. The last three points all refer to ways in which high threat may increase the likelihood that initially less concerned persons will be swayed toward greater concern by the behavior of those attempting escape. For all these various reasons, the threat of large penalties for failure to escape should produce more incoordination than the threat of small penalties.

The second factor is *size* of the collectivity. The effect of size is likely to be, in part, purely mathematical: the greater the number of persons involved, the greater the likelihood that two or more will feel a similar degree of high urgency, attempt to escape at the same time, and prevent each other from doing so. In addition, size may have a preinteraction psychological effect: the more people involved, the more likely are members to judge the available time (whatever it is estimated to be) to be insufficient and, hence, early escape to be important. Finally, as outgrowths of the above effects, large group size may be expected to produce second-order effects during the interaction which are similar to those suggested above for high threatened penalty. The high rate of escape attempts and jams will act to change the attitudes of other participants, through providing new information about the situation (regarding the time available and efficiency of time use) and through communicating evaluations of the situation that may influence the initially unconcerned or undecided. All these considerations indicate that large collectivities should show greater incoordination in their escape efforts than small ones.

Our third and fourth experimental variables were formulated explicitly in terms of the social influence process occurring during interdependent escape. The third variable is the individual's *susceptibility to social influence:* whether he is "set" to take his cues from the other participants and be influenced by them, or to be independent and make up his own mind about the situation. The former should increase the concentration or homogenization of views and the latter should retard it. The effect of this would be expected to depend upon what initial attitude is prevalent within the collectivity. If the distribution is initially weighted toward the high concern end, being oriented toward basing one's evaluation upon others' behavior should make for numerous and rapid shifts toward that end, with highly detrimental consequences for group coordination.

Our fourth and final experimental variable is the *availability of confidence re-*

sponses. This might be viewed in terms of anti-panic leadership (Brown, 1954). It is often true in danger situations that the highly confident and calm people have no way to express their evaluation of the situation in a manner as dramatic and unequivocal as are the behaviors (i.e., the escape attempts) of the highly concerned person. Under these conditions, the actions of the latter are likely to catch the attention of the less worried or uncertain participants, and, in the absence of counter-balancing examples from the opposite extreme, sway them in the direction of high concern. The analogy might be drawn to a group discussion where the proponents of only one extreme viewpoint can find words to express their position. The tendency would be for the opinion distribution to shift toward the expressed position. In our basic experimental situation, each person has only two response options: to wait or to attempt to escape. Therefore, the most confident persons are not distinguishable from other "waiters" who may be quite worried but still willing, at least momentarily, to wait. In a special three-response condition, an additional action was provided whereby individuals could indicate their confidence and willingness to let others go first. On the assumption that use of this response would prevent concentration at the anxious end of the attitude continuum, it was predicted that collective coordination would be greater than in the two-response condition.

GENERAL PROCEDURE

In the three experiments to be reported, the situation and procedure were essentially the same from one to the next. In all cases, the Ss came to a laboratory at a scheduled time and were seated in separate booths or rooms. They were not able to see and were not permitted to speak to one another during the experiment. Upon being seated, each one had electrodes, for delivering shock, attached to the first and third fingers of his non-preferred hand.

The experiment was described as a study of behavior under threat, the situation being one where a number of people have to use a single, limited exit to escape from an impending danger within a limited time. The threatened penalty for failure to escape was, in most cases, one or more painful electric shocks. The fact that only one person at a time could escape was made clear by explanation and demonstration.

While the details differed from one experiment to the next, in all cases the S could see signal lights showing his own position vis-à-vis the danger situation and similar lights showing the position of each of the other Ss. At the beginning of a trial, each one's light indicated he was in "danger." By making a simple response (turning or pressing a switch), a person could attempt to escape. When he did so, he changed the color of the signal lights corresponding to him, and in this manner his escape attempt was made visible to all the others (and himself, as well). When one S, and only one, has his escape switch "on" for a brief time (3 seconds in all cases), his signal lights turned green, which indicated for all to see that he had succeeded in escaping from the danger. Interdependence in escape was introduced by the fact that if two or more Ss had their escape switches "on" at the same time, none could escape and they all remained in danger. In other words, one person had to have sole and uninterrupted

occupancy of the escape "route" for a 3-second period if he was to escape. Successful escapes were shown to the Ss (with illustrations of the 3-second period but without labeling its duration) as were mutual interferences or "jams."

Following these instructions, the experimental trials were run, E giving "start" and "stop" signals to provide a standard time period for escape. After the trials, the Ss were given posttrial questionnaires followed by a "catharsis" session in which the experiment was explained, justification was given for subjecting them to threat, and they were permitted to ask questions and air their feelings. Finally, they were asked not to discuss the experiment with other potential Ss, a request to which they all agreed and with which they apparently complied.

Although it was designed to create the same type of "bottleneck" situation, there are essential differences between the apparatus used in these experiments and that used by Mintz (1951). First, the Ss in these experiments were isolated from one another, there being little possibility for visual or verbal contact during the trial. This provided better control of the interpersonal variables that might operate in such a situation. Since an S could not tell the identity of persons attempting to escape, such variables as personality impressions and clues as to social status could not affect his reactions to these events.

A second essential difference is in the use of electronic equipment. In Mintz's study it was possible for the cones to jam tightly in the bottleneck and delay the trial while they were being dislodged. This was not possible in this experiment. The escape and interdependence were controlled by electronic circuits which enabled a jam to be disentangled merely by the participants' releasing their escape switches. Thus, the time loss due to jams was entirely under the control of the participants. Further, it was possible to obtain precise data on the process of escape. When any S pressed his escape switch, this action was automatically recorded on an Esterline-Angus operations recorder. This enabled the E to return to the data and ascertain such things as how many jams occurred and for what duration, which members were involved in each jam, the exact pattern of events leading to jams, etc.

The latter aspect of our apparatus also enabled us to use a different measure of group incoordination than Mintz had employed. He reports only whether or not a jam developed within each of the collections in his various experimental conditions. We used as the basic dependent variable the percentage of persons succeeding in escaping during a standard time period. This particular measure, although easily determined and interpreted, seems rather crude at first glance. It was chosen when two other more refined measures were found to be highly correlated with it. The first such measure, termed "man-seconds," was the sum over the various Ss of the time each one spent in the danger situation until his escape or, if he failed to escape, until the end of the trial. It reflects (inversely) not only the number of persons who succeeded in escaping, but how soon in the trial they did so. A second measure, termed "jam-seconds," was the sum over the various Ss of the time each one had his escape switch "on" while one or more others also had theirs "on." In other words, it reflects the length of jams and the number of persons contributing to them. These two indices and the percentage of persons escaping during the first trial were derived from the data obtained in Experiment III. Linear relationships were found among the three variables, and the percentage of persons escaping yielded product moment correlations of -0.97 and -0.92, respectively with "man-seconds" and "jam-seconds" $(N = 40$ in each case). This was taken as sufficient reason for using the simple percentage of escapes as our sole measure of group coordination.

It may further be noted that in two of the experiments (I and III), the Ss were put through three successive trials. Throughout this paper we rely exclusively upon data from the first trial. This decision is based upon recognition of the difficulties involved in interpreting the behavior on the later trials created by such probable factors as incredulity (when a promised threat is not delivered), practice effects, and physiological changes (when drugs are used as in Experiment I).

EXPERIMENT I[2]

Procedure

Design and Subjects. The first experiment to be reported[3] dealt with two of the factors discussed earlier: (1) magnitude of the threatened penalty and (2) size of the collectivity. The three magnitudes of penalty used will be referred to as *low threat, medium threat,* and *high threat.* Collections of *four, five, six,* and *seven* Ss were employed. Each collection was composed of Ss of the same

[2] This experiment was conducted by Dahlke in the Laboratory for Research in Social Relations, University of Minnesota.

sex, either all males or all females. Thus, the design was a $3 \times 4 \times 2$ factorial design with two collections assigned to each condition. It can be seen that the total number of collections was 48 and the total number of *S*s, 264. The collection is the unit upon which statistical analysis is based.

Collections in the low- and medium-threat conditions were studied during one quarter of the academic year, and those in the high-threat condition, during the following quarter. All *S*s were drawn from the same supply source, namely, introductory psychology students at the University of Minnesota who had indicated a willingness to participate in psychological experiments. Because they receive two extra points on their final examination grade for each hour of experimental participation, about 90% of the students enrolled in the introductory classes express willingness to serve as experimental *S*s and are placed in a common subject pool. For the low- and medium-threat conditions, *S*s were selected from this pool simply on the basis of their conformity to sex and scheduling requirements. They were notified by postcard of the time and place of the experiment, but no inkling was given of its nature. Insofar as possible, the various conditions were run in random order, but exceptions were made when fewer *S*s appeared than had been scheduled.

The selection of *S*s for the high-threat condition was based upon an additional criterion. In order to insure that no harmful effects would result from the injection of epinephrine, the records of *S*s meeting the sex and schedule requirements were cleared with the University's Student Health Service. Only those persons judged to be able to withstand the

injection without any possibility of ill effects (and this was the vast majority) were contacted for the experiment.

Apparatus. The *S*s were seated in booths which enabled them to see the *E* at the front of the room but not one another. Mounted in front of each was an escape switch which they were to move when they wished to escape. A large panel of lights, placed in the front of the room so that all *S*s could see it, displayed the actions of all the participants. By watching the light panel, each *S* could determine what every other *S* was doing at any point in time, whether each had succeeded in escaping, etc.

The light panel displayed a column of three colored lights for each *S*. At the start of the experiment, a white light was "on" in each column indicating that each person was in "danger." When an *S* moved his escape switch to the right, a red light appeared in his column on the panel indicating an attempted escape. If the escape was successful, a green light appeared in his column. The columns were labeled A through D (or up to G, if necessary) but in mixed order. Each *S* knew his own letter and therefore could readily locate the column of lights displaying his actions and fate. While he could see the three to six columns corresponding to the other *S*s, because of the mixed order of the labels, he could not determine which of them corresponded to any particular other booth or *S*. Thus, even though he may have formed an impression of another *S* and noted his booth location, the individual could not tell which lights indicated the other's actions.

The time necessary for a single *S* to escape was 3 seconds, provided no other *S*s attempted to escape during this time. If two or more attempted to escape at the same time, all remained in the "red" condition and none escaped until all but one person had released their escape switches, and he had sole possession of the "red" (the "escape route") for 3 continuous seconds. The 3-second and jam rules were applied by a research assistant

---

[3] The three experiments are presented in logical order rather than in the order in which they were performed. The third one reported here was actually the first in the series. It was followed, in order, by the ones described here as Experiments I and II.

located in an adjoining control room.[4] Guided by a metronome beat at half-second intervals and possessing a light panel similar to that visible to the Ss, the assistant turned on a given S's green light when the S alone had his escape light on for 3 uninterrupted seconds. When the green light showing successful escape was turned on, that S's switch was deactivated so that his subsequent actions had no effect on the lights or upon others' escape attempts.

The time allowed for the entire collection to escape was determined by the flow of red-colored water from one large water bottle into another, in a water version of an hour-glass type timer. This was done so the Ss would have no reliable index of the length of time available but at the same time would have a vivid reminder that time was "running out." The Ss were told:

"The time you have in which to escape is the time required for the water to flow from the top bottle of these two to the bottom bottle. I merely reverse their positions. When all of the water has left the top bottle, I will announce that time is up."

The amount of water in the bottles was varied to provide twice as much time as was minimally necessary for the given number of Ss to escape. Thus, with the minimum escape time of 3 seconds per person, a maximally efficient four-man group would require 12 seconds, and was therefore allowed 24 seconds. With the same rule, five-man groups were allowed 30 seconds; six-man groups, 36 seconds; and seven-man groups, 42 seconds. The Ss were not told how long they would have, their only clue to this being the volume of water present in the bottles at the start.

Instructions. When the Ss entered the experimental room, they were seated and instructed not to talk. In the medium- and high-threat conditions, electrodes were taped to the first and third fingers of each one's non-preferred hand, and the E determined each one's "shock threshold." He also delivered two fairly strong shocks (one of approximately 40 volts, 60-cycle ac, and the other of about 50 volts) and noted the S's reactions to them. These "data" were referred to later when the Ss were threatened with more severe shocks. Following this, Ss in the high-threat condition were given a subcutaneous injection of epinephrine by a physician[5] while E gave the following explanation:

"The shot you are getting is a neutral solution. Last quarter we were interested in what effect Vitamin B would have in this experimental situation, so we injected all our subjects with vitamin B. When we analyzed our results we couldn't determine whether they were due to the vitamin or just to getting the shot itself. So, we are now using you as 'control' subjects and are giving you a completely neutral solution. This will have no physiological effects —it is completely neutral."

The Ss in the low-threat condition were not attached to electrodes and received neither shocks nor injections.

After the above preliminaries, the basic instructions were given. The experiment was described as part of an investigation supported by a federal agency for the purpose of studying the "alarming increase in the rate of deaths and injuries occurring in civilian disasters" and of solving the problem of the "causative factors" in these situations. The Ss were told:

---

[4] We are indebted to Lee A. Borah, Jr., for his careful performance of this task.

[5] The dosage and procedure here were identical with those used by Schachter and Singer (1962). The dosage was ½ cc of a 1:1000 solution of Winthrop Laboratory's Suprarenin. We are indebted to Dr. Abelardo Mena, M.D., for giving the injections and providing the necessary safeguards in the event any S had overreacted to the injection or the drug.

"The result we obtain will make a very important contribution to its solution. I'd like to ask all of you for your utmost cooperation. You people are going to be placed in a (danger) situation and given a limited amount of time to escape. However, it takes a short, but definite time interval for any one individual to escape. If another person tries to escape at the same time, he will become, so to speak, jammed in the exit, and neither will be able to escape. Such jams will waste some of the time available for escape." (The word "danger" was omitted from the instructions given the low-threat *S*s.)

The *S*s were then shown how to use the apparatus, and demonstrations were given of an escape, jam, and resolution of a jam. Guided by *E*'s directions, two persons tried to escape at the same time and a jam was demonstrated. Then, one was directed to release his switch and the other's escape was shown. Then the former was permitted to escape. The time allowed for the entire group to escape was explained as above.

In addition, the medium- and high-threat *S*s were told:

"I have called this a danger situation because those of you who do not escape before the time is up will receive a painful electric shock as a result of not escaping. Just a few moments ago, we determined a "shock threshold" for each of you. We went through all the trouble of getting these measurements because we want to be able to give you the most painful and uncomfortable shock we can, without seriously hurting you in any way. I want to be completely honest with you and tell you exactly what you are in for. Those of you who do not escape will receive a series of extremely painful shocks. They'll be a lot more painful than the ones we gave you a few moments ago—they're going to hurt. But we must do this to impress upon you the uncomfortable consequences of not escaping. By combining the value of your shock threshold with your ability to discriminate between two shocks at a higher level, we have been able to estimate how

much shock would be dangerously harmful to you. We're not going to give you that amount, of course, but we are going to get as close to it as we possibly can. Those of you who do not escape will have to face the consequences of as painful and uncomfortable a shock as we can give."

Finally, all groups were told:

"About this time in past sessions of this experiment some people expressed a desire to leave, after finding out what it was all about. But I'm afraid I can't allow this. . . . However, I would like you to indicate on these questionnaires how you feel about being in the experiment and whether or not you feel like leaving at this time."

The pretrial questionnaire was given to *S*s in all conditions. This required them to state whether they felt like leaving the experiment, to rate their feelings about being in the experiment on a six-point scale from "extremely calm" to "extremely uneasy," and to estimate how many of their group would succeed in escaping. Immediately following these questions, the first trial was run. In the medium- and high-threat conditions, the *S*s who did not escape this time were told they would be shocked after the last trial in the series, and a second trial was run. The same procedure was repeated for a third trial after which the *S*s were given a final questionnaire. Needless to say, they were never given the threatened shocks. The final phase of the procedure was a "catharsis" session and request for secrecy.

The reader will note particularly the difference between the three threat conditions. The *low-threat S*s faced no penalty for failing to escape. The instructions simply indicated they were to try to escape during the limited time period. The *medium-threat S*s were shown convincingly that they could be given electric shocks, and they were threatened with the penalty of as painful shocks as possible (without harming them) if they failed to escape. The *high-threat S*s were in the same situation except that they had heard the threat of painful shocks from 7 to 10 minutes after having received the injection of epinephrine. This was assumed to make for a higher level of anxiety on the theory, as stated by Schachter and Singer (1962), that the strength of an emotional reaction is a joint function of the external stimulus conditions (the same threat for our medium- and high-threat Ss) and the degree of excitation of the sympathetic nervous system (higher for the high-threat Ss because of the injection). Schachter's pretests had shown that the sympathetic effects of the given dosage of epinephrine begin within 3–5 minutes after the injection and last for at least 10 minutes. The timing of our procedure made it highly likely that all Ss were experiencing symptoms often associated with danger (speeded heart rate and involuntary tremor) during the time they were being told of the painful consequences of failure to escape and during the escape trials.

Results

As a check upon the efficacy of the threat manipulations, the Ss in all conditions were asked, in the pretrial questionnaire, if they wished to leave the experiment. The results are presented in Table 1. Because the data did not vary with size, the numbers expressing a wish to leave are shown only for the males and females within each threat condition. It can be seen that considerably fewer males indicated a desire to leave, and in general, the results indicate a difference between the threat conditions. The high-threat groups do not differ greatly from the medium-threat groups, but there is a sizable difference between low threat and the other two conditions.

There are forty-four Ss in each of the six cells in Table 1. It can be seen that we succeeded in creating enough concern on the part of the females in the medium

Table 1

NUMBER OF SUBJECTS EXPRESSING DESIRE TO LEAVE EXPERIMENT BEFORE FIRST TRIAL (EXPERIMENT I)

| | Threat condition | | |
Sex	Low	Medium	High
Males	0	3	4
Females	2	12	11

and high conditions that one in four was willing to sacrifice whatever time and energy investment had been made in coming to the experiment in order to withdraw from it.

A further check upon the threat manipulations is provided by the pretrial ratings of uneasiness. As in the case of the data above, these ratings did not vary systematically with size so the averages are presented in Table 2 only by sex and threat. A rating of 1 signified that S felt completely calm; 2, relatively calm; 3, a little uneasy; 4, quite uneasy; 5, very uneasy; and 6, extremely uneasy. An analysis of variance of these ratings (based on the average ratings for each of the 48 collections) yielded a significant sex effect ($p < .001$), threat effect ($p < .001$), and interaction between sex and threat ($p <$

Table 2

AVERAGE RATINGS OF UNEASINESS BEFORE FIRST TRIAL (EXPERIMENT I)

| | Threat condition | | |
Sex	Low	Medium	High
Males	1.96	3.46	3.32
Females	2.22	3.55	4.38

.025). It can be seen that the pattern of results is generally similar to that for the number of Ss wishing to leave the experiment. Orthogonal comparisons for the three degrees of threat show that the high and medium conditions combined are significantly higher than the low one ($p <$ .005), but the high condition is not significantly higher than the medium one. The highest degree of concern about the threatened penalty is shown by the female Ss in the high condition. Their uneasiness is significantly higher there than that of the males in the same conditions ($p <$ .01) and than their own uneasiness in the medium condition ($p < .01$). Apparently adding the epinephrine injection to the threat of shock produced no increment in the anxiety level of the males but did so for the females. This evidence incidentally provides a confirmation of the Schachter and Singer (1962) theory for the females but not for the males.

Table 3 presents the analysis of variance for the escape data for the first trial, based upon the percentage of persons escaping in each collection during the allotted time. Percentage is used, of course, to enable comparison of the different sized collections. It can be seen that all three main effects are significant, but none of the interaction terms is. The averages for the sex and threat conditions are shown in Table 4 for easy comparison with the uneasiness ratings in Table 2. It can be seen that the percentage escaping declines as threat increases. Orthogonal comparisons among the three conditions, similar to those made for the pretrial uneasiness ratings, yield approximately similar results. High- and medium-threat conditions combined differ significantly from low threat ($p < .05$), and the difference between high and medium threat is of borderline significance ($p < .10$). Females succeed in escaping less frequently than do males. Although the sex-by-threat interaction term is not significant, the females seem more affected by the increase in threatened penalty, consistent with the pattern of results on their reported feelings of uneasiness in Table 2.

In brief, it appears that incoordination of interdependent escape increases as the

Table 3

ANALYSIS OF VARIANCE FOR PERCENTAGE ON FIRST TRIAL (EXPERIMENT I)

Source	Sum of squares	Degrees of freedom	Mean square	F ratio	p
Threat	44.178	2	22.089	4.710	<.025
Sex	60.345	1	60.345	12.861	<.005
Size	65.646	3	21.882	4.660	<.025
Threat × Sex	9.004	2	4.502	<1	
Threat × Size	22.739	6	3.790	<1	
Sex × Size	21.299	3	7.100	1.513	
Threat × Sex × Size	28.377	6	4.730	1.008	
Error	112.627	24	4.692		
Total	364.215	47			

threatened penalty increases. The correspondence between the pattern of escape results (in Table 4) and that of the pretrial ratings of uneasiness (in Table 2) suggests that this effect is probably mediated by the emotional reactions of anxiety or concern which are stronger in the higher threat conditions and particularly so for the female Ss.

The average percentage escaping varies with size in the following manner: in collections of 4, 77% escape on the average; in collections of 5, 57% escape; in collections of 6, 31% escape; and in collections of 7, 49% escape. These results are generally consistent with our expectations that incoordination would increase with increasing size. It should be noted that over the range of four to six, the average *number* of persons escaping declines, even though the time permitted for escape increases. These averages, for sizes four through seven, respectively, are 3.09, 2.84, 1.83, and 3.42.

The relatively high rate of escape in the seven-man collections is, of course, quite unexpected. That this result is not adventitious is shown by the similar result obtained by Hill from the data reported below in Experiment III. He used the same apparatus as in the present experiment and had seven real Ss and two

Table 4

AVERAGE PERCENTAGE ESCAPING ON
FIRST TRIAL (EXPERIMENT I)

Sex	Threat condition		
	Low	Medium	High
Males	79	69	60
Females	59	42	11

simulated ones. For present purposes, the latter may be disregarded because they never contributed to jams. The degree of threat, as will be shown later, was probably at about the medium threat level of the present experiment. Hill's collections yielded an average percentage of escape of 53% which is quite close to the value for the seven-man collections in the present experiment (49%).

What are the possible explanations of this unexpected effectiveness of the seven-man groups? A close consideration of the procedure used, both in this experiment and Experiment III, suggests one possibility. It will be recalled that the time allowed for the collection to escape was controlled by the flow of water from one large bottle into another. The larger the group, the more water needed in the bottle. The large volume of water necessary for the seven-man group may have been sufficiently impressive in appearance to give a degree of confidence in the adequacy of the allotted time that the smaller groups did not have. In other words, for the seven-person collections, the time may have been seen as sufficient to enable everyone to escape, this perception reducing the urgency of the need to be "first in line."

Contradicting this suggestion is the absence of any evidence of greater pretrial concern (in the ratings of uneasiness) or greater pretrial optimism (in the estimates of number who will escape) within the seven-man groups. However, it may still have been true that the reassuring effect of the large volume of water developed only after the trial began when the rate of flow became known. Experiment II was designed to eliminate this possible effect of the timing device.

EXPERIMENT II[6]

This experiment was conducted to provide further evidence on the effect of size but without the possibly contaminating effects of clues provided the Ss as to the amount of time allotted for escape. In general, the procedure was similar to that of Experiment I except that the water-bottle timer was replaced by a tone which increased in pitch every few seconds, thus portraying the passage of time without giving any information as to when it would terminate.

Procedure

Design and Subjects. Only size of the collection and sex of Ss were varied. A single degree of threat was used throughout that was approximately equal to the medium threat condition in Experiment I. Again, collections of four, five, six, and seven persons were used, each one being composed entirely of males or females. Six collections of each sex were used for each size, yielding 48 in all and requiring 132 male and 132 female Ss. These were undergraduates at UCLA recruited from the introductory psychology classes by a standard procedure used for most psychological experiments. This consists of circulating through the class a sign-up sheet which indicates the number and type of subjects needed and the time and place of the experiment. No indication was given of the specific nature of the experiment. Collections in the various conditions were scheduled in a random order, but departures from this order were made when fewer Ss than planned appeared for an experimental session.

Apparatus. A shift in locale of the experiment necessitated constructing new apparatus. While it was quite different physically from that used in Experiment I, it was functionally identical. Each S sat before his own private console (light panel). In the top center of this was mounted a single combination push-button-indicator light unit. Below it, arrayed across the bottom of the panel, were six similar switch-light units.[7] The latter served simply as signal lights indicating to S what the other six persons (in seven-man collections) were doing and their success in escaping (if any). The top center switch-light unit served the dual purpose of showing S his state (whether in danger, attempting escape, or having escaped) and of providing him with his means of attempting escape (by merely pressing the push-button switch). At the beginning of a trial, all signal lights were red indicating that all Ss were in danger. When S pressed his escape switch it turned yellow indicating an attempted escape. One of the lights in the bottom row, the one corresponding to the S, also turned yellow on each of the other consoles. After 3 seconds, if no other person interfered, the escape switch (and corresponding lights on the other consoles) turned green indicating a successful escape. If more than one S pressed the escape switch at the same time, both the red and yellow indicate lights appeared, indicating a jam. This combination of lights appeared on the escape switch of each person contributing to the jam and also on the indicator lights cor-

---

[6] This experiment was conducted by Condry in the Department of Psychology, University of California, Los Angeles.

[7] These units are Micro Switch Series 2 combination push-button switch and indicator light devices, manufactured by Micro Switch, Freeport, Illinois. The switch components (catalog 67 number 2D64) have a two-circuit, double-break arrangement of the contacts. The indicator units (catalog 67 number 2C6) contain four lamp sockets which, with split display screens, make possible eight two-color combinations.

responding to each contributor in the bottom row of lights all other consoles. Thus, every S could tell not only that there was a jam but which other Ss were involved in it. In general, each S had complete information about his own and each other person's actions and fate. (However, because of a scrambled relation between seating position and position of lights on the consoles, the S could not tell which light corresponded to any other given participant.)

The timing and interdependency rules were applied automatically by electronic circuits. This system also deactivated a person's switch when he escaped so he could no longer interfere with the others. With collections smaller than seven, the unused switches and lights were, of course, deactivated from the outset.

The passage of time was signalled by a tone, increasing in pitch every few seconds. The Ss were told:

"On each trial you will all start at red, and your object is to escape (that is, to go to green) before the end of the trial is reached. When I say 'go' the trial will begin, and when I say 'stop' the trial will be over. During this time, to show you that time is passing, we'll play a tone that will sound like this. (He plays sample.) When I say 'go' the tone will start and it will slowly rise up the scale as you heard. When time is up, it will stop and I will stop and I will say 'stop.' At the end of the trial, only those people whose lights are green will have successfully escaped."

Thus, the amount of time available for the collection to escape was totally ambiguous, and there was certainly no basis for Ss in the seven-man collections to feel any more confidence in their ability to escape than those in any other size groups. The amount of time actually allotted depended upon the size of the collection, exactly as in Experiment I.

Instructions. When the Ss came to the experimental session they were seated in front of their individual consoles so that they could not easily see the consoles of others. (They were in separate small rooms for the most part and always at least back-to-back.) They were instructed not to look at each other nor to talk during the session. Electrodes were taped to the first and third fingers of their nonpreferred hands. The statement of the purpose of the experiment was identical with that of Experiment I. After being told that they would be placed in a danger situation from which they were to attempt to escape, the use of the equipment and the time signal were described and demonstrated. The demonstrations were somewhat more elaborate than in Experiment I, all Ss participating in jams and eventually being permitted to escape.

The penalty for nonescape was described as a series of painful shocks. In describing these, E said:

"I don't like to have to give you these shocks, but in an experiment such as this it is necessary. To show you we will indeed give you the shock and to give you some idea of what type of shock to expect, just before we start the trial I will give you a *mild* sample shock. This will give you some idea of what is to come, but let me stress that the final shock will be much stronger."

After these instructions, the Ss were given a mild shock (40 volts, 100 cps), and the trial was immediately begun. The purpose of this procedure was to confront the Ss with the threat and then immediately put them into the escape situation. It was felt that by dropping them more suddenly into the action situation they would have less time to think about what to do and whether or not E was being truthful. (In order to achieve this, the pretrial questionnaire, which in the prior experiment had required several minutes lapse between the threat and the actual escape trial, was not used.) The pretrial shock was given because pilot data indicated Ss were more convinced they would really be shocked after the trial if they were given a mild one before it started.

After the trial was run (and only one trial

was used), the *S*s were given a posttrial questionnaire and a catharsis session. The former contained the same uneasiness rating as did Experiment I's pretrial questionnaire.

Results

For reasons given in the preceding paragraphs, the uneasiness ratings were obtained only after the trial was over, the *S*s being asked to indicate how they felt a few moments earlier, before the trial began. Nevertheless, these ratings provide our only basis for comparing the level of concern in this experiment with that in the previous one. An analysis of variance of the ratings yielded no significant size effect and only a significant sex difference ($p < .01$) with the male average being 3.79 and the female average, 4.33. Thus, as in Experiment I, the female *S*s are somewhat more concerned. The level of uneasiness indicated by these means seems most like that induced by the high-threat condition of the preceding experiment. This seems rather high in terms of a comparison of the procedures used in the two studies but is consistent with the generally high level of incoordination in the present study which, as will be seen below, also resembles that of the high-threat condition of Experiment I.

The average percentages escaping in the various conditions are given in Table 5. An analysis of variance of these results yields a significant sex difference ($p < .05$). As in Experiment I, the males have a higher rate of escape than the females. The analysis of variance of the data as presented in Table 5 does not yield a significant size effect ($p < .10$). It can be seen that the size trend from the female collections is very irregular, but even with these puzzling aberrations, there seems to be a clear difference between the four- and five-man collections, on the one hand, and the six- and seven-man collectinos on the other. A comparison of these two halves of the size continuum yields a significant difference ($p < .05$). By combining males and females, the percentage escaping varies with size in the manner shown in bottom line of Table 5. These percentages correspond to the following average *number* of persons for the sizes four through seven, respectively: 1.92, 2.50, 1.33, and 1.50. In other words, in the larger collections, even though more time and potential escapes are available, fewer persons succeed in escaping.

When these results are compared with those of Experiment I, it is observed that the general rate of escape is lower in the present case. As noted above, this is consistent with the questionnaire data indicating that a higher level of uneasiness

Table 5

AVERAGE PERCENTAGE ESCAPING ON FIRST TRIAL (EXPERIMENT II)

| Sex | Size | | | | Total |
	Four	Five	Six	Seven	
Males	67	63	42	24	49
Females	29	37	3	19	22
Total	48	50	22	21	35

was achieved in this study than in the earlier one (considering all three levels of threat there).

Comparing the size trends for the two experiments, a sharp discrepancy occurs for seven-man collections where the rate of escape is markedly lower in the present data. It appears that when the clues as to available time are removed, the unexpected efficiency of the seven-man groups disappears, and the time required per escape tends to increase with group size. However, there is still a suggestion that the seven-man groups do not experience as much difficulty as the trend over the smaller groups would lead one to expect. We will discuss this later.

Experiment III[8]

Although this experiment was conducted before the two just reported, in a sense it should have followed them. In showing the important contributions the factors of threat and size make to incoordinated collective behavior, Experiments I and II can be regarded as providing a partial validation of our laboratory setting as a simulation of natural panic situations. It then becomes appropriate to seek within the experimental setting factors that, given high threat and large size, make for more or less incoordination. Such factors might be particularly relevant in generating practical ideas about the reduction of

---

[8] This experiment was conducted by Hill in the Laboratory for Research in Social Relations, University of Minnesota. It constituted the research upon which he based a dissertation submitted to the graduate faculty of the University of Minnesota in partial fulfillment of the requirements for the Ph.D.

panic behavior even in situations which, from the point of view of danger and size, are particularly prone to it.

The choice of factors for investigation here stems from the social influence analysis of the interdependent escape situation, outlined earlier. The central argument is that escape will be more coordinated when heterogeneity of the participants' initial assessments of the danger can be maintained, or at least, when they can be prevented from becoming concentrated in the state of high concern.

Susceptibility to social influence is one factor that should be related to homogenization of attitudes. An individual who is sure of the accuracy of his own assessment of the situation should be less susceptible to pressures toward uniformity than a person less sure of his own evaluation of the situation. Groups composed of individuals who are independent of social influence would be expected to maintain more successfully their original heterogeneity of assessment and action, with its concomitant advantages for escape.

The second factor investigated here is the availability of confidence responses. In the two preceding experiments, only two responses were available to *S*s, the responses of *attempting* escape and of *waiting*. Members who were confident that they would be able to escape later had no way to express this confidence to the other group members and, hence, no way to influence the unsure participants. An unsure person will use social reality as a basis for his evaluation of the danger in the situation and will look to see how others have assessed the danger in order to decide how he, himself, should react. Because the more confident persons are unable to communicate their assessments of the situation, the unsure one knows only that his fellows are either waiting passively like himself or fighting to escape. Consequently, his evaluations are likely to be influenced in the negative direction. Escape becomes embraced as the appropriate behavior and he too begins to push and fight to get out through the exit.

The provision of a special response with which the confident, unworried person can signal his assessment of the situation —a response that is easy to make, socially acceptable, and highly distinctive and recognizable—would be expected to lead to significant changes in the collection's behavior. Faced with distinctive responses made by both his more anxious and his less anxious colleagues, the uncertain individual should be able to obtain more complete information about how others regard their probable outcomes. He is less likely to be swept toward one extreme of the response continuum in a nonadaptive struggle to escape.

Procedure

Design and subjects. A $2 \times 2 \times 2$ experimental design was used, the three factors being susceptibility to social influence (high vs. low), response availability (two responses vs. three), and sex. Data for forty collections are reported, five comprised entirely of males and five of females in each of the four basic experimental conditions. Allocation within sex was by the method of random blocks.

The Ss were drawn from summer session classes at the University of Minnesota. Appointments were made by telephone on the evening immediately preceding the experimental session. In the low susceptibility condition, after the S agreed to come at the desired time, he was told:

"Fine! This is a group experiment. In this experiment we are able to estimate

accurately how you will perform. On the basis of a few pieces of key information from your record we predict that *you* will do well. We try to make the groups up of people of differing abilities, and good people are harder to get, so that your being able to come makes my task of scheduling easier."

For Ss scheduled for the high susceptibility condition no comparable comments were made, and in no case was any other information given about the nature of the experiment.

Apparatus. The apparatus was identical to that used in Experiment I, with two notable exceptions. First, although seven Ss came for each experiment, there were two extra booths, one at each end of the row, which were left empty. The Ss were unaware these end booths were unoccupied, and the actions of Ss supposedly in them were represented on the light panel, so the participants thought the collection consisted of nine persons. The reason for these "simulated Ss" will be explained later. Second, the escape switch sometimes had an added function. As in the first experiment, when it was centered, at the start, a white light was on indicating "danger," and when it was moved to the right, the red "escape attempt" light went on. In the three-response condition, however, the S could also move the escape switch to the left and turn on a yellow light. This was used as a signal of confidence and willingness to wait. Accordingly, the column of lights for each S contained a yellow light in addition to the other three. Otherwise the color coding of the lights was the same as in the first experiment where white meant "danger," red meant "attempt to escape," and green meant "successful escape." The two columns of lights corresponding to the two empty booths were manipulated from a neighboring control room.

The passage of time was signaled by the flow of colored water from one bottle to another as in Experiment I. The group was given 50 seconds to escape, 42 for the seven real

*S*s and 4 seconds each for the two simulated *S*s (see next section).

In the front of the room was an impressive looking "shock machine" with wires running to each booth where two electrodes were attached to the first and third fingers of the *S*s' nonpreferred hands. Although no shocks were delivered, the purpose of this machine was to make the threat of shock a real and meaningful danger.

Use of simulated subjects. A test of our ideas about the effects of a confidence response requires that there be a range of confidence within the collections. To insure that confident persons were represented it was decided to include in each group two simulated *S*s who, in the two response condition, would wait passively until all others had escaped (if this should occur) before they would attempt to escape. In the three-response condition they would express their confidence immediately and maintain this until all other group members had escaped, and only then would they proceed to escape. By this means it was possible to insure heterogeneity of expressed evaluation in the three-response condition. The simulation was carried out by leading the seven *S*s to believe that nine of them were present (it being almost impossible to tell that the two empty booths were unoccupied) and by having the assistant in the control room manipulate the two extra columns of lights, following the rules described above. In only two of the forty collections in the experiment was there a single individual who expressed suspicion about the number of *S*s present.

Instructions. The majority of the instructions were the same as those given in the two experiments already described. The *S*s were told they would be placed in a danger situation and that their task was to escape. The nature of the situation was explained, and escapes, jams, and "confidence" responses were demonstrated (the last, in the three-response condition only.) The penalty for not escaping was described as a painful but safe

electric shock which would be delivered at the end of the experiment. No sample shocks were given.

High susceptibility was established by telling the *S*s that although a number of them had been present before and knew how the situation operated, the instructions were being repeated for the few who had not been there previously. This was reinstated at the end of the instructions by saying:

> Those of you who have been here before have a good idea of what is the best way to behave in this situation. For those of you who have not been here before, it would probably be best if you *watch carefully* what others are doing to help you decide the course of action which gives you the greatest chance of getting out. You can see what the other, more experienced people are doing by watching their lights up here."

Of course, none of the group members had been in the situation before, but the purpose was to make all group members feel less expert in the task than others in the group, and hence, more susceptible to the influence of the others' examples.

The *low susceptibility* manipulation, which had been introduced at the time of making the appointment, was reinstated at the beginning of the instructions as follows:

> "As I mentioned to two of you on the telephone when I called you for this experiment, we expect you two to perform well. You two should not be swayed by the way others are reacting to the situation. Make up your own minds and be independent in deciding how to deal with the situation."

At the end of the instructions they were again reminded that they should "make up their own minds." Each person, of course, was supposed to assume that he was one of the two special *S*s. This was an attempt to decrease susceptibility to social influence.

In the three-response condition, after escapes and jams had been explained and before any demonstrations had been given, the use of the extra response was explained as follows:

"This, therefore, is a situation in which consideration and politeness count. Some people have to be considerate of others and let them go first or no one will get out. By turning your switch to the left you will turn on the yellow light in the top row of your column. This signals that you have confidence that the group can escape, and you are willing to wait and let someone else escape. Thus, when you turn switch to the left and hold it there you are indicating that you do not intend to escape immediately and that someone else should go ahead and use the exit."

Immediately before the first trial was run, the *S*s were asked to write down their estimates of how many of the nine would escape before the time limit; three trials were then run. As in the procedure outlined for Experiment I, *S*s who did not escape each time were told they would be shocked after the series of trials was over. After completion of the third trial the *S*s were given a questionnaire and then informed that no shocks would be given. A catharsis session and pledge to secrecy concluded the experiment.

Results

Level of Concern. The measuring instruments used in this experiment provided no pretrial measure of uneasiness. The postexperimental questionnaire contained three questions relevant to concern. These, along with the most apt characterizations of the typical answers, are as follows: (1) "How afraid are you of electric shocks?", typically answered with "some" which fell between "very little" and "a great deal"; (2) "How sure were you during the experiment that you would be shocked if you failed to escape?", typically answered with "sure I would" which fell between "didn't know" and

"very sure I would"; and (3) "How much did you worry about getting shocked today?", typically answered with "a little" which fell between "not at all" and "some." On all three questions females were significantly more concerned than males ($p < .01$ in each case). No differences were found between the response availability conditions. On the first question, high-susceptibility collections reported greater fear of shock ($p < .02$); on the second there was no susceptibility difference; and on the third, the high-susceptibility condition again indicated more worry ($p < .01$).

These results do not permit a comparison of level of concern with the other experiments, although one is inclined to believe it is somewhat lower in the present case. As in the preceding instances, females express more concern than males. (However, contrary to the other sets of data, they are *not* less efficient in escaping, as we shall see in a moment.) The variation in concern between the two susceptibility treatments would create problems for the analysis were it not for the fact that there is no relationship between a total score derived from these three questions (for each collectivity) and percentage escaping ($r = 0.08$). This makes it seem unlikely that differences in concern between the different experimental conditions could have affected the escape results. Hence, comparisons holding concern constant were not made. It should be noted that the lack of correspondence between this measure and success of escape is also inconsistent with the results from the preceding experiments.

Effect of Number of Available Responses. Table 6 shows the average number and the average percentage (the latter based

Table 6

AVERAGE NUMBER AND PERCENTAGE ESCAPING ON FIRST TRIAL (EXPERIMENT III)

Susceptibility to influence	Number of available responsés					
	Two-responses		Three-responses		Total	
	Number	Percentage	Number	Percentage	Number	Percentage
High	2.5	36	6.4	91	4.4	63
Low	2.2	31	4.3	61	3.2	46
Total	2.3	33	5.3	76	3.8	54

on the seven real Ss) escaping on the first trial in each of the four experimental conditions. No sex difference in rate of escape was found, so the data for males and females have been combined in this table. A three-way analysis of variance (responses × susceptibility × sex) revealed that the only source of variance differing significantly from chance was number of responses ($F = 9.62$, $p < .005$), there being more escapes in the three-response than in the two-response condition. This is strong support for our hypothesis that providing means for the more confident participants publicly to express their feelings increases the success of the collective escape effort.

Effect of Susceptibility to Influence. It must first be asked whether the manipulation of susceptibility, which was a matter of differential instructions, was successful. Of three items in the postexperimental questionnaire designed to check this, two indicate partial success while the third fails to differentiate the high- and low-susceptibility groups. High-susceptibility Ss rated themselves significantly more "influenced by what others did" ($p < .05$) and less competent and able to "perform well on this task in comparison with others

in the group" ($p < .01$). Mean ratings of amount of attention paid to "what others were doing" were identical for high and lows.

From Table 6 and the analysis of variance reported above, it can be seen that the susceptibility factor does not have a simple over-all effect on success of escape. Although there is not a significant interaction term in the analysis of varaince, the pattern of averages in Table 6 suggests that high susceptibility particularly promotes successful coordination when the confident members are able to express their feelings. This suggests the further possibility that the effects of susceptibility may depend upon the nature of the behavior and feelings that are predominant within the collection at the beginning of the trial. If the general tenor of feeling in the group is one of great concern, high susceptibility should make for spread of this feeling and a concentration of the Ss in the high concern state which is hypothesized to be detrimental to successful escape. On the other hand, if the predominant initial feeling is one of confidence, high susceptibility should lead to the opposite effect.

To test this idea, we resorted to a measure of pretrial optimism for each collection based on the participants' estimates, made immediately before the trial began, of how many of the nine persons would escape. A complication arose when this estimate was found to be significantly higher (i.e., optimism was higher) in the high susceptibility condition than in the low ($p < .01$). Thus, optimism as well as susceptibility to influence was apparently manipulated by the instructions.[9] Because this seems like a situation in which peoples' expectations would tend to be self-confirming (cf. Merton, 1957, on the self-fulfilling prophecy), we might expect more escapes to occur in the more optimistic groups. Indeed, this was the case. The average optimism score within each collection was found to be correlated with the percentage of *S*s who escaped ($r = 0.34$ which, for $N = 40$, is significant at the .05 level).

These results complicated the task of examining the effects of high vs. low susceptibility while holding constant initial optimism. We proceeded as follows: the median of the average estimates of number who would escape was 5.43. The 19 collections whose average estimate was above this figure were termed *high* in optimism, and the 21 collections at or below this median were termed *low*. A cross tabulation was then made of optimism and susceptibility. The correlation between the two variables is reflected in the fact that the largest frequencies appear in the High-High and Low-Low

cells. Because of this pattern, it was necessary to analyze the resulting set of data with an approximate method for the analysis of variance for unequal *N*'s (Walker and Lev, 1953, pp. 381–382). A further complication was presented by the fact that within the high susceptibility condition, nine of the ten three-response groups were above the median in optimism, and within the low-susceptibility condition, only three of the ten three-response groups were so.[10] Hence, differences due to response availability would have the effect of generating an interaction in the analysis. To eliminate this source of error, the number escaping was corrected for response availability. The mean number escaping in the three-response condition (5.3) was 3.0 greater than that in the two-response condition (2.3), so three escapes were added to each two-response entry. With this correction, Table 7 was obtained. The analysis of variance of Table 7 revealed no difference between susceptibility conditions or between levels of optimism, but there was a significant interaction between optimism and susceptibility ($p < .01$). As one would expect, when initial optimism is high the number escaping is greater in the high-susceptibility condition than in the low, but when the initial level of optimism is low, the number escaping in

---

[9] On close examination of the instructions, it makes sense that the high-susceptibility *S*s were more optimistic: most *S*s except themselves were said to be experienced in the situation. In the low-susceptibility condition only *S* and one other person supposedly had the special talent; none had experience.

[10] This reflects the fact that optimism is somewhat higher in the three-response condition ($p < .10$). However, this was shown not to account for the difference between the two- and three-response conditions. The latter yielded a significantly higher rate of escape even when optimism was held constant. Thus, we can be sure that the positive effect of the three-response condition is not mediated by initially high optimism.

Table 7

SUSCEPTIBILITY DIFFERENCES IN AVERAGE NUMBERS ESCAPING[a] ON FIRST
TRIAL, WITH OPTIMISM HELD CONSTANT (EXPERIMENT III)

Susceptibility to influence	Level of optimism		Total
	High	Low	
High	7.1	3.2	5.9
	($N=14$)	($N=6$)	($N=20$)
Low	3.8	4.8	4.6
	($N=5$)	($N=15$)	($N=20$)
Total	6.2	4.3	5.2
	($N=19$)	($N=19$)	($N=40$)

[a] The number escaping in each collection was corrected, as described in the text, to eliminate differences due to response-availability conditions.

the low-susceptibility condition is greater than in the high.

DISCUSSION

Our results show fairly convincingly that the higher the threatened penalty for failure to escape, the greater is the incoordination (the less successful are the escape attempts). That this effect is mediated by emotional reactions to the threat is suggested by the fact that conditions in which self-ratings of uneasiness are high tend also to be those in which escape is least successful. This holds true for the three threat conditions in Experiment I, for females vs. males in Experiments I and II, and for the general level of escape in Experiment I vs. II. The exception to this pattern occurs in Experiment III where, although the females express greater concern about getting shocked (on the posttrial questionnaire), they are no less successful in escaping than the males.

The effect of size upon incoordination is less clear. Let us disregard for the moment the puzzling results for the seven-man collections in Experiment I and treat the data as indicating a general decrease in success of escape with increasing size. Do our results contain any clues as to why this trend occurs? It will first be recalled that increasing size had no effect on pretrial ratings of uneasiness in Experiment I or upon similar posttrial ratings (made of pretrial feelings) in Experiment II. These results suggest that size did not have the preinteraction psychological effect we had thought it might, namely, that the available time would be judged less adequate for the larger collections (with resulting heightened concern). In the case of Experiment I this may reflect the special condition of the procedure in which a pretrial clue as to the available time, which varied by size, was provided by the water bottles serving as timers. However, the similar results from Experiment II where this clue was absent suggest this special condition had little effect insofar as the relation between size and *pre*trial feelings are concerned. Although the retrospective nature of the rating data in Experiment II argues for some caution in their interpretation, the lack of relation between size and rated uneasiness there and in Experiment I suggests that size has its effect *after* the trial gets under way.

Beyond suggesting the inapplicability of the pretrial effect above, our data provided only one further clue as to the basis of the size effect, one that is consistent with a simple mathematical account of the consequences of increasing size. The number of seconds required for each escape (on the average) was determined for each size by simply dividing the number of seconds allotted collections of that size by the average number of escapes (as listed in the *Results* sections for Experiments I and II). These average times were then plotted against the number of ways it is possible for jams to occur for each size. The formula for the latter is $2^n - n - 1$ for size n, which yields 11 for size four (six possible dyads, four possible trios, and one quartet), 26 for size 5, 57 for size 6, and 120 for size 7. The resulting plot is shown in Fig. 1. The data from Experiment I are represented by I's, those from Experiment II by II's, and the single data point from Experiment III by a III. It can be seen that the points from Experiment I for sizes 4, 5, and 6 fall close to a straight line. This also happens to be a line that would intersect the ordinate at a point close to what the escape time would be for a one-person "collection," shown in Fig. 1 by a "T." This "collection" would be incapable of creating jams (i.e., $2^n - n - 1 = 0$) and should be able to achieve an escape time per person of only slightly more than 3 seconds (3 seconds plus reaction time). For these sizes in Experiment I, then, time per escape seems to be a direct function of the number of possible ways jams can occur.

Unfortunately, the data points from Ex-

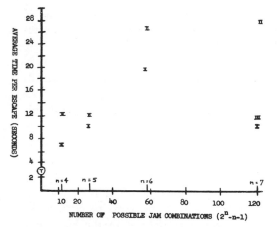

Fig. 1. Average time per escape as a function of number of possible jam combinations (all experiments).

periment II do not conform to this simple linear relation that seems to fit the first three points from Experiment I so well. While incoordination seems generally to increase with size in Experiment II, it is not at all clear what the probable shape of the function is. While the simple mathematical function suggested by Experiment I remains an intriguing hypothesis, further evidence is needed to determine whether (or when) a more complex function characterizes the relationship.

To return to the data with regard to seven-man collections, the difference in rates of escape for these collections between Experiments I and III on the one hand and II on the other suggests that the information provided by the water bottles in the former experiments served to facilitate coordination. However, the rate of escape for these groups even in Experiment II seems higher (time per escape being lower as in Fig. 1) than one would expect from a simple extrapolation of the results from the smaller collections.

One intriguing possible explanation is

that recognition of the large number of persons who are potential candidates for use of the escape route leads some of them to give up hope of escaping. In this manner, the large group becomes functionally a smaller one. Then, as those who do attempt to escape succeed in doing so, the initially pessimistic become aroused to make attempts.

Possibly consistent with the first part of this argument is the finding that the pretrial estimates of the number that will escape, when expressed as percentages of the number of persons in the collections for which the estimates were made, tend to decline with increasing size. The data from Experiment I yield average estimates of 71% for four-man collections, 68% for five, 68% for six, and 65% for seven. Experiment III provides estimates made for nine-man collections which average 62%.

This trend might suggest that the perceived likelihood of escape declines with increasing size. On the other hand, as noted before, there is no increase in feelings of uneasiness with increasing size. The estimate of number who will escape may not reflect expectations about one's own success but merely about the fate of the collectivity. Thus, a person may estimate that few will escape but, at the same time, feel confident that he will be one of those who do. His escape attempt will then be vigorous despite his gloomy outlook for the collectivity. That this is common is suggested by data from Experiment III where an analysis was made of the correlation within each group between the individuals' optimism and their positions in the escaping queue. The evidence, significant at between the .10 and .05 level, is that the least optimistic tend to escape first.

The discussion of the last two paragraphs, in which we have proposed there may be a direct relation between a person's expectations about the likelihood of escape and his attempts to do so, suggests a distinction that perhaps should have been made earlier. This is between (1) perceived danger and (2) perceived likelihood of escape. Our discussion of the role of assessments of the situation and homogenization of attitudes was intended to be cast entirely in terms of the first factor. However, the latter factor must not be overlooked. Indeed, it was one of Mintz's (1951) major points in support of his general de-emphasis of the role of danger that, even though perceived danger is extremely high, if there is seen to be little chance of avoiding it, there will be little panic. This is the substance of the argument we have suggested (but not proved) for the seven-man groups: that some of them see so little chance of escape (at least, initially) that they effectively reduce the size of the group by their passivity in regards to escape. In general, it might be fruitful to consider these two factors as acting together multiplicatively to determine the frequency and vigor of escape attempts. If *either* perceived danger or perceived likelihood of escape are low, there will be few escape attempts. Only if both are high will the individual be oriented strongly toward attempting escape. The analysis in this paper has assumed implicitly that perceived likelihood of escape is moderately high and, in that context, has dealt with the effects of the distribution of assessments of the danger.

Experiments I and III provide data that might be considered relevant to the factor of perceived likelihood of escape: the pretrial estimate of how many would escape which we have referred to as an index of optimism. In both experiments this is positively correlated with the number who actually do escape (.40 for Experiment I and .34 for III, both significant at $p < .05$). This might be taken as evidence for the assertion above, that escape attempts are more frequent and vigorous when perceived likelihood of escape is high. However, the terms in the correlation do not correspond well to those in the theoretical statement. The relation of *escape attempts* to *actual escapes* is obviously a complex one, actual escapes being infrequent if none attempt to escape, but also, under conditions of interdependence, if too many attempt it. Similarly, as noted above, our optimism index may not reflect accurately the perceived likelihood of the individual's own escape. In short, the present data do not seem to be adequate to the task of disentangling and evaluating the role of the factors of perceived danger and perceived likelihood of escape.

The results of Experiment III suggest in several ways that it is fruitful to analyze the interdependent escape situation in terms of social influence processes and pressures toward uniformity. While the effects of our experimental manipulations of susceptibility to influence were complex, they display an eminently reasonable pattern when account is taken of initial level of concern. With high concern (low optimism), collective coordination is most adequate when persons are oriented toward disregarding each other's behavior. With low initial concern (high optimism), the opposite is true: coordination is most adequate when the participants are oriented to pay attention to each other. Another way to view this interaction is in terms of the correlation between predic-

tions of escape and actual escapes under the two susceptibility conditions.[11] This correlation is .50 for the high-susceptibility condition (significantly different from zero with $p < .025$) and $-.30$ in the low-susceptibility condition (not significant). The difference between the two correlations is significant at the .02 level. Thus, the self-fulfilling prophecy effect is evidenced when susceptibility is high but not when it is low.

This result obviously has interesting but complex implications for preparing collectivities to cope successfully with interdependent escape problems. If they can be trained to have high confidence in their joint ability to escape, it is best also to teach them to be highly responsive to each other's actions. However, the latter training will be quite detrimental if they get into a situation in which their initial general level of confidence is low.

Turning to the effects of providing a means of expressing confidence during the escape period, the three-response condition was predicted to yield a higher rate of escape. This prediction was based on the assumption that a concentration of attitudes in states of high concern is detrimental to coordination of escape attempts and that availability of the confidence response would serve to maintain heterogeneity of evaluations or, at least, to prevent their converging toward the anxious states. The experimental evidence from

---

[11] The number of escapes was corrected to eliminate differential effects of the two- vs. three-response conditions, as explained earlier in the text. It must also be noted that the correlations were calculated over collections, between the *average* estimate and the number escaping, both expressed as percentages of the number in the collection.

Experiment III indicates clearly that superior coordination was achieved when the confidence response was available. To determine the basis of this effect, the data were first examined to determine whether heterogeneity of evaluations played a role in superiority. No relationship was found between within-collection *variance* on the (pretrial) optimism or (posttrial) anxiety measures and the number escaping. The lack of relationship here casts some doubt upon the interpretation that successful escape is mediated by heterogeneity. However, serious doubts must be raised about the relevance of these measures, particularly on the grounds that they may not reflect the distribution of evaluations *during* the escape period.

It is possible that the provision of three responses made the subjects more confident before the trial began and, hence, more able to escape. However, as already reported, a comparison of the response availability conditions holding initial optimism constant still yielded superiority for the three-response conditions, so this explanation seems improbable.

The possibility also exists that provision of an extra response permits better coordination of escape attempts. For example, it may be possible to resolve disagreements about position in the queue by using only the yellow ("confidence") and white ("in danger") lights without causing a jam. Thus, the participants might decide who is to be next while one of their number is in the process of escaping. The experimental records fail to support this view. There were very few groups in which the white light received any substantial use for the purpose of coordination in the three-response condition. Subjects who used the confidence light seemed then to go directly to escape (red) without waiting in the "white" state at all.

The most likely explanation of the effect of the confidence response is that the evidence of confidence it made possible reduced anxiety, increased willingness to wait, and hence reduced the amount of jamming that occurred. In other words, the public signs of confidence shifted the entire distribution of assessments toward the low anxiety end of the scale. In the low-susceptibility condition where the group members were presumbaly paying less attention to each other, the available public signs might be expected to make little difference, and there is some support for this. The difference between the two response conditions is smaller (although not significantly so) in the low-susceptibility condition than in the high.

The clear implication of Experiment III is that a bias in the availability of distinctive responses leads to a correspondingly biased shift in the distribution of opinion within the collectivity. That bias in available responses is not uncommon in interdependent escape settings is suggested by a close examination of Mintz's experiment and many of the real life situations it is intended to simulate. These typically provide a dramatic way for the most frightened persons to make known their evaluations of the situation (viz., the escape response) but fail to provide a single, equally distinctive response for persons who are least frightened by the threat. To be sure, there is often available a repertoire of possible responses for the latter, but there are restraints against many of these (e.g., inhibitions about making one's self conspicuous) and there is no *single* response that is highly practiced and obviously relevant. Hence, for reasons of restraint and conflict, the most confident individuals often fail to respond and their inactivity renders them indistinguishable from the middle range of persons who are most uncertain about the matter. The situation resembles, then, a group discussion in which only persons of one extreme persuasion are permitted to voice their views. The result of this seems obvious: uncertain individuals will be swayed toward the one extreme and the rate of homogenization will be much faster than if both extremes had been represented equally forcibly.

A similar explanation can probably be given for the general acceptance of extreme types of behavior in other situations in which there exists a bias in the availability of distinctive responses (e.g., in the generation of fads, fashions, and crazes). Or, to take the case of extreme political behavior, there are usually people who feel strongly that the behavior represented is undesirable. They seek for some distinctive means of dramatizing their opposition in the hope that they can swing the balance away from what they regard as inappropriate behavior. However, they often have no means of presenting their view that is as distinctive and dramatic as that of their "extremist" opponents. Here too, then, we have an example of a biased response situation in which persons at one end of an opinion continuum are not differentiated behaviorally from those with more neutral views. The present evidence would seem to indicate that lack of a distinctive and recognizable response for those of one extreme position leads to an eventual concentration of opinion at the opposite end of the scale in a portion that is not representative of the range of evaluations initially present in the group.

SUMMARY

Three experimental studies of interdependent escape, based on a laboratory simulation of one type of panic situation,

have been reported. Each collection of subjects was given a limited amount of time to escape from an imminent danger, but they were able to escape only one at a time. The major findings from the experiments are:

(1) As threatened penalty for failure to escape increases, the percentage of persons who succeed in doing so declines.

(2) As size of the collection increases, the percentage escaping declines. This may also be stated as an increase in the time required per escape with increasing size. There remains considerable ambiguity about the shape of this function.

(3) If members of the collection are oriented toward taking their behavioral cues from each other, as compared with an orientation toward making their behavioral decisions independently of one another, the effect upon escape may be either a deleterious one (when at the outset there is generally little optimism about escape) or a salutary one (when the general level of initial optimism is high.)

(4) The availability of a distinctive response for the public expression of confidence greatly increases the percentage of persons who succeed in escaping.

The results are taken as indicating the fruitfulness of analyzing the interdependent escape situation is terms of present-day concepts and principles of social influence.

REFERENCES

BROWN, R. W. "Mass Phenomena." In G. Lindzey (Ed.), *Handbook of Social Psychology.* Cambridge, Mass.: Addison-Wesley, 1954. Pp. 833–876.

DEUTSCH, M. "A Theory of Cooperation and Competition." *Human Relations*, 1949, 2, 129–152.

FESTINGER, L. "Informal Social Communication." *Psychol. Rev.*, 1950, 57, 271–282.

FRENCH, J. R. P., JR. "Organized and Unorganized Groups Under Fear and Frustration." *Univ. Iowa Studies Child Welfare,* 1944, 20, 229–308.

MERSON, R. K. *Social Theory and Social Structure.* (2nd ed.). Glencoe, Ill.: Free Press, 1957.

MINTZ, A. "Non-Adaptive Group Behavior." *J. Abnorm. Soc. Psychol.,* 1951, 46, 150–159.

SCHACHTER, S., and SINGER, J. E. "Cognitive,

Social, and Physiological Determinants of Emotional State." *Psychol. Rev.,* 1962, 69, 379–399.

SWANSON, G. E., NEWCOMB, T. M., and HARTLEY, E. L. *Readings in Social Psychology.* (2nd ed.). New York: Henry Holt, 1952.

WALKER, HELEN M., and LEV, J. *Statistical Inference,* New York: Henry Holt, 1953.

GROUP INFLUENCE
ON INDIVIDUAL RISK TAKING*

Michael A. Wallach, Nathan Kogan, and Daryl J. Bem

What are the effects of group interaction on risk and conservatism in decision making? By risk and conservatism we mean the extent to which the decision maker is willing to expose himself to possible failure in the pursuit of a desirable goal. Consider the situation in which several individuals working separately arrive at a series of decisions, and then are brought together to arrive at a group consensus regarding those decisions. What relationship should one expect to find between the individual decisions and the group consensus?

———————
* Michael A. Wallach, Nathan Kogan, and Daryl J. Bem, "Group Influence on Individual Risk-Taking," *Journal of Abnormal and Social Psychology,* 65 (1962), 75–86. Copyright 1962 by the American Psychological Association, and reproduced by permission.

On the basis of prior experimental studies of individual and group judgment (e.g., Schachter, 1951; see also the section on group pressures and group standards in Cartwright & Zander, 1960, pp. 165–341), we should predict an averaging effect, i.e., group decisions randomly distributed around the average of the pre-discussion individual decisions. Such an effect would seem to imply a process of mimimizing individual losses, or mimimizing the maximum individual concession. The cited studies report that inducements toward compromise and concession seem to be exerted most strongly toward group members whose initial individual views are most deviant from the central tendency.

An equally, if not more, compelling alternative hypothesis is that the group discussion will lead to increased conservatism, relative to the average of the prior individual decisions. One may cite the observations of Whyte (1956), among others, concerning the outcomes of conferences and meetings in bureaucratic organizations. Whyte argues that the use of committees and teams in the management of business and other kinds of enterprises leads inexorably to an inhibition of boldness and risk taking, a concentration on the conservative course when a choice must be made between more and less risky courses of action. How are such effects to be explained? First, it may be that the very nature of the group process or atmosphere encourages such a trend: there may be a fear, for example, of appearing foolhardy to others. Alternatively, or in addition, it is possible that the mechanism underlying an increase in conservatism is one of greater influence being exerted within the group by members whose individual conservatism tendencies are stronger. These two interpretations are not incompatible, of course, since the group process, if encouraging of conservatism, will enhance the influence of the initially more conservative members.

Finally, consideration should be given to the remaining and least likely possibility—that group interaction will eventuate in increased risk taking relative to the average of the prior decisions of the group members working separately. In this regard, Osborn (1957) has reported that group interaction may lead to quite radical, bold, problem solutions. While Osborn claims that special conditions must exist if such effects are to be observed, attempts to produce such conditions experimentally (Taylor, Berry, & Block, 1958) have yielded no evidence whatever for the so-called "brainstorming" phenomenon. Thibaut and Kelley (1959, pp. 267–268)

discuss the conflicting evidence on this issue. We might, in passing, also mention mass or crowd phenomena, in which extreme actions taken by groups are well beyond the capacities of the members of such groups considered individually (Brown, 1954; Turner & Killian, 1957). The relevance of such mass phenomena to group decision making in a laboratory context, however, is probably quite remote. In sum, increased risk taking as a consequence of group interaction appeared to us to be the least feasible of the three possibilities discussed above.

An examination of the literature reveals little experimental research which addresses itself explicitly to the problem of the present investigation. Lonergan and McClintock (1961) report that membership in an interdependent group led to no significant move toward greater conservatism or risk taking in a betting situation involving monetary gain or loss. Since the group situation was so structured that a consensus was not required, however, this experiment is not directly relevant to the aims of the present study. Hunt and Rowe (1960) report no difference between three-person groups and individuals in riskiness of investment decisions. However, the brevity of the group interaction (15 minutes) and the disruptive influence of having the various groups meet within sight of each other in a large room render their results inconclusive. Atthowe (1961), comparing individual and dyadic decisions in the choice of the better of two alternative wagers, found greater conservatism in the dyadic decisions. But the relevance of this result to the problem at hand is called into question when we learn that the alternative wagers were presented to the subjects as "problems taken from the mathematical reasoning section of an advanced intelligence test and arranged as wagers" (p. 115). This could well contribute to a conservative strategy.

We turn, finally, to a study by Stoner (1961), which provides the starting point for the research to be reported. Using male graduate students of industrial management as subjects, Stoner observed that a group consensus regarding degree of risk to be taken in resolving a "life dilemma" situation deviated from the average of prediscussion decisions in the direction of greater risk taking. These results took us by surprise. We wondered whether the finding could be generalized to other subject populations, whether it was an enduring effect, and whether it might have anything to do with relationships between risk taking and perceived group influence.

One issue that arises in interpreting Stoner's (1961) study concerns the effect that expectations about one's role might have on the results. Thus, a group of male graduate students of industrial management might make more risky decisions qua group than would each such student individually—the result obtained by Stoner—because the presence of their peers reminds each that one of the positively sanctioned attributes of the business manager role which they occupy or aspire to occupy is a willingness to take risks in their decision making. Stoner's use of a male business school sample, therefore, leaves open the possibility that his results may be a function of this particular group's self-assigned professional role alone. It also is possible that a group of males, regardless of their professional role, might make more risky decisions when gathered together because the presence of other males serves as a reminder that one of the expected indications of manliness in our society is a willingness to be bold and

daring in decision making. Conversely, a group of females might make more conservative decisions when gathered together, or at least might fail to shift in a risky direction, since risk taking tendencies are not likely to be mutually reinforced in groups for whom risk is not a positive social value (see, e.g., Komarovsky, 1950; Milner, 1949; Wallach & Caron, 1959).

In the present experiment, we shall employ samples of male and female undergraduates enrolled in a liberal arts curriculum at a large state university. If the effects observed by Stoner (1961) are found to hold for both of the above samples, this would constitute strong evidence for the generality of the phenomenon and its independence of occupational and sex role considerations. Furthermore, the use of previously unacquainted subjects whose ascribed status is initially equal will insure that whatever effects are obtained cannot be attributed to an association between initially high or low status, on the one hand, and risk or conservatism, on the other. If initial status levels were unequal, low status individuals might simply adopt the standards of those whose status is high —an outcome which would tell us nothing about the effect of group interactional processes as such on individual risk taking.

One should distinguish initially ascribed status from status indices (e.g., perceived influence and popularity) derived from the group experience. Since such indices may bear some relation to initial risk taking level, the necessary sociometric-type judgments will be obtained.

Finally, evidence will be presented with regard to the following two questions: Is the group induced effect on risk taking limited only to the group member's over compliance in the group setting or does it also extend to his covert acceptance when he makes postgroup decisions as an individual (see Festinger, 1953; Kelley & Thibaut, 1954)? To what extent are group effects on individual decision making relatively enduring or short-lived?

METHOD

Assessment of Level of Conservatism or Risk Taking

The instrument used for assessing level of conservatism or risk taking, as developed in some of our prior research (Kogan & Wallach, 1961; Wallach & Kogan, 1959, 1961), is called an "opinion questionnaire" and contains descriptions of 12 hypothetical situations. The central person in each situation must choose between two courses of action, one of which is more risky than the other but also more rewarding if successful. For each situation the subject must indicate the lowest probability of success he would accept before recommending that the potentially more rewarding alternative be chosen. The probabilities listed are 1, 3, 5, 7, and 9 chances of success in 10, plus a final category (scored as 10) in which the subject can refuse to recommend the risky alternative no matter how high its likelihood of success.

The situations were so designed as to cover a wide range of content, and may be summarized as follow:

1. An electrical engineer may stick with his present job at a modest but adequate salary, or may take a new job offering considerably more money but no long-term security.

2. A man with a severe heart ailment must seriously curtail his customary way of life if he does not undergo a delicate medical operation which might cure him completely or might prove fatal.

3. A man of moderate means may invest some money he recently inherited in secure "blue chip" low return securities or in more risky securities that offer the possibility of large gains.

4. A captain of a college football team, in the final seconds of a game with the college's traditional rival, may choose a play that is almost certain to produce a tie score, or a more risky play that is almost certain to produce a tie score, or a more risky play that would lead to sure victory if successful, sure defeat if not.

5. The president of an American corporation which is about to expand may build a new plant in the United States where returns on the investment would be moderate, or may decide to build in a foreign country with an unstable political history where, however, returns on the investment would be very high.

6. A college senior planning graduate work in chemistry may enter university X where, because of rigorous standards, only a fraction of the graduate students manage to receive the PhD, or may enter university Y which has a poorer reputation but where almost every graduate student receives the PhD.

7. A low ranked participant in a national chess tournament, playing an early match which the top-favored man, has the choice of attempting or not trying a deceptive but risky maneuver which might lead to quick victory if successful or almost certain defeat if it fails.

8. A college senior with considerable musical talent must choose between the secure course of going on to medical school and becoming a physician, or the risky course of embarking on the career of a concert pianist.

9. An American prisoner-of-war in World War II must choose between possible escape with the risk of execution if caught, or remaining in the camp where privations are severe.

10. A successful businessman with strong feelings of civic responsibility must decide whether or not to run for Congress on the ticket of a minority party whose campaign funds are limited.

11. A research physicist, just beginning a 5-

year appointment at a university, may spend the time working on a series of short-term problems which he would sure to solve but which would be of lesser importance, or on a very important but very difficult problem with the risk of nothing to show for his 5 years of effort.

12. An engaged couple must decide, in the face of recent arguments suggesting some sharp differences of opinion, whether or not to get married. Discussions with a marriage counselor indicate that a happy marriage, while possible, would not be assured.

The response categories are arrayed from chances of 1 in 10 upward for the odd items and in the reverse order for the even items, thus, counter balancing for any possible order preference effect in choice of probability level. An overall conservatism-risk taking score is derived by adding the scores for the separate items. The larger this score, the greater the subject's conservatism.

Our prior research, cited above, yielded split-half Spearman-Brown reliability coefficients ranging from .53 to .80 for various age and sex samples, suggesting that the instrument possesses satisfactory internal consistency. The results of the present experiment will provide evidence, furthermore, of high test-retest reliability.

Regarding the instrument's construct validity as a risk taking measure, our earlier studies, cited above, have yielded findings consistent with a risk taking interpretation. For example, degree of conservatism as measured with the present instrument increases with age from young adulthood to old age for both males and females, and increases with degree of subjective probability of personal failure in a motor skill game with actual motor skill controlled.

Experimental Condition

Subjects. The subjects were invited to participate in an experiment which would take no longer than 2 hours and for which re-

muneration would be provided. Six subjects were scheduled for any one time, with every effort being made to insure that previously acquainted persons were not signed up for the same session. A total of 167 subjects participated in the experimental condition—14 all-male groups and 14 all-female groups.[1] The subjects were liberal arts students enrolled in summer session courses at the University of Colorado in Boulder.

Prediscussion Individual Decisions. The experiment was run in a seminar room around a very long table. For the initial administration of the questionnaire, subjects took alternate seats with the experimenter at one end. The six subjects were requested to read the instructions to the questionnaire and to look over the first item. The experimenter then emphasized two points in further standard instructions: that the more risky alternative is always assumed to be more desirable than the safer course, if the former should prove successful; that the odds which the subject marks indicate the lowest odds the subject would be willing to take and still advise the central figure to give the risky alternative a try. The subjects were told there was no time limit, that they should consider each of the 12 situations carefully, and that they could return to an earlier question if they wished to. The conservatism-risk instrument then was filled out individually by each of the six subjects in a group administration session that took about 20 minutes. To avoid giving any of the sub-

---

[1] Of the 14 male groups, 13 contained six subjects each, and one contained five subjects. A subject in one of the six-person male groups misunderstood instructions for the prediscussion individual decisions, so that his decision scores were removed prior to analysis. All 14 of the female groups contained six subjects each. A subject in each of 2 female groups misunderstood instructions for the prediscussion individual decisions, so that the decision scores of these two females were removed prior to analysis.

jects the feeling that they were being rushed, the questionnaires were not collected until all had finished.

Group Discussion and Consensual Group Decisions. Without having had any prior expectation that they would be requested to discuss their decisions, the six subjects were then asked to move together into a discussion group at one end of the table. They now each were given another copy of the questionnaire, and a stand-up cardboard placard with the identification letter K, L, M, N, O, or P on it was placed before each subject. The experimenter then told them that the questionnaire now before them was the same one they just finished taking. They had taken it, he continued, to familiarize them with all the situations and to give them some idea where they might stand on each. Now he wanted the group to discuss each question in turn and arrive at a unanimous decision on each. This time they could not return to a question, but rather had to discuss each one until the group decision was reached before going on to the next. When the group reached its decision on a question, all subjects were to mark it on their questionnaires in order to have a record. The group would be completely on its own, the experimenter not participating in the discussion at all.

The experimenter then retired to the other end of the table in order to be as far from the group as possible. A question that often arose before discussion had started was what to do if a deadlock occurs. The experimenter's standard reply was:

> Most groups are able to come to some decision if those who disagree will restate their reasons, and if the problem is reread carefully.

Most groups succeeded in reaching a unanimous decision on most items, although an occasional deadlock did occur on one or another item. The group discussions were of such a nature as to indicate that the participants were highly involved in the decision tasks.

Postdiscussion Individual Decisions. After the discussion was over, the experimenter proceeded to ask the group members to spread apart for some further individual work and to take their questionnaires and identification placards with them. In standard instructions, he requested them to go back over the situations and indicate their own present personal decisions with a "P." He noted that while in some cases the subjects may have agreed with the group decision, in other cases they may have disagreed with it. In the former cases the P would be placed on the same line as the check mark; in the latter cases, on a different line.

While the consensual decisions by the group would indicate the public effect of the discussion process, the private postdiscussion decisions made once again on an individual basis would indicate whether the discussion process had influenced covert acceptance as well as public compliance.

Rankings for Influence and Popularity. After the postdiscussion individual decisions had been made, a ranking sheet was passed out to each subject requesting that he rank everyone in the group (identified by their letter placards), including himself, in terms of how much each influenced the final group decision. Then each subject was requested to rank everyone in the group (except, of course, himself) in terms of how much he would like to become better acquainted with each.

The rankings for influence provided the information needed for examining possible relationships between strength of individual risk taking or conservatism tendencies, on the one hand, and degree of influence in the group, on the other. If such relationships existed, it seemed to be of interest to determine whether they were specific to perceived influence or would prove to be dependent upon the subject's popularity; hence the second set of rankings.

Secrecy Instructions. After the ranking sheets were collected, the experimenter told the group that the research would be carried out in coming weeks, and that they could now appreciate why it would be important for the content of the experiment to be kept secret, since a person who even knew that the group would be discussing the same questions which he had filled out individually would have a tendency to mark logically defensible answers instead of his true opinion, etc. The subjects therefore all were sworn to secrecy. Various indications suggest that the pledge was faithfully kept.

Post-postdiscussion Individual Decisions. A further session of individual decision making took place approximately 2–6 weeks later for some subjects. These subjects individually were given the conservatism-risk questionnaire a third time and were asked to reconsider the situations. The standard instructions emphasized that the experimenter was not interested in testing the subject's memory, but rather wanted the subject truly to *reconsider* each situation. The instructions thus oriented the subjects away from simply trying to recall their prior decisions. Each subject was paid for this further work.

CONTROL CONDITION

Subjects. Control subjects were obtained in the same way as the experimental subjects, and likewise received remuneration for their work. The controls were signed up to participate in two sessions: the first to last about 20 minutes; the second, exactly 1 week later, to last about 15 minutes. A total of 51 subjects participated in the control condition— 24 males and 27 females. Like the experimental subjects, the controls were liberal arts students enrolled in summer session courses at the University of Colorado in Boulder.

First Individual Decision Session. The first session was identical to the prediscussion individual decision part of the experimental condition. From six to eight subjects of the same sex, scheduled for the same time, filled out

the conservatism-risk instrument while sitting together in physical conditions identical to those of the experimental subjects and at approximately the same time of day as the experimental subjects had worked. Exactly the same instructions were provided as had been given the experimental subjects.

After the first session, the control subjects were sworn to secrecy. They also were told that they would be taking a similar questionnaire the next week, and that it was extremely important that they not discuss it with one another nor with anyone else, since such discussion might affect the way they filled out next week's questionnaire.

Second Individual Decision Session. The same control subjects who had participated in a particular first individual decision session came back exactly 1 week later. After checking that no discussion had taken place in the intervening week among the controls, the experimenter handed out new copies of the questionnaire and explained that this questionnaire was identical to the one taken last week. Each subject was requested to go back over the situations and reconsider them, the experimenter emphasizing that he was not interested in testing the subject's memory but rather wanted the subject truly to *reconsider* each situation. The instructions were so designed, therefore, as to dissuade the subject from assuming that the most socially acceptable thing to do would be to try to make the same decisions that he had made a week ago. Change was encouraged rather than discouraged. Control subjects were sworn to secrecy again at the end of the second session.

RESULTS

Consensual Group Decisions Compared with Prediscussion Individual Decisions

Tables 1 and 2 examine, for male and female groups, respectively, the significance of the conservatism difference between the

Table 1

SIGNIFICANCE OF CONSERVATISM DIFFERENCE BETWEEN MEAN OF PREDISCUSSION
INDIVIDUAL DECISIONS FOR A GROUP'S MEMBERS AND GROUP'S
CONSENSUAL DECISION: MALES

Item	Mean difference[a]	Number of groups[b]	t
All combined	−9.4	14	6.46****
1	−1.0	14	4.34****
2	−0.2	14	<1.00
3	−1.1	13	2.19*
4	−1.8	13	6.18****
5	+0.1	13	<1.00
6	−1.2	13	3.35**
7	−2.0	14	9.64****
8	−1.1	14	1.97
9	−1.0	10	3.67**
10	−0.4	13	<1.00
11	−1.1	12	4.37***
12	+0.8	11	2.34*

[a] In Tables 1, 2, 3, 4, 6, and 7, a negative difference signifies a risky shift, a positive difference signifies a conservative shift.

[b] In Tables 1 and 2, number of groups for an item is less than 14 when one or more groups deadlocked on that item. Any deadlocked item is, of course, not included when calculating scores for all items combined.

    * $p < .05$.
    ** $p < .01$.
    *** $p < .005$.
    **** $p < .001$.

mean of the prediscussion individual decisions made by the members of each group and that group's consensual decisions. The basic test is carried out using the total conservatism score, which consists of all 12 item scores combined. Tests also are carried out for each item separately.

In the case of the total score, a group's difference score is the sum of the 12 unanimous group decision scores minus the average of the prediscussion total individual decision scores for the six members.[2]

Since larger scores indicate greater conservatism, a negative difference (or score decrease) indicates a shift in the risky direction. A t test is used to determine whether the 14 difference scores for the groups of each sex are significantly different from zero (McNemar, 1955, pp. 108–109).[3] These total score data indicate a move in the risky direction significant beyond the .001 level for the 14 male groups, and a move in the risky direction significant beyond the .005 level for the

---

[2] Any deadlocked item is, of course, not included in either term for the group in question.

[3] All significance levels cited in this study are based on two-tailed tests.

14 female groups. Furthermore, the degree of shift is not significantly different for the two sexes.

In the case of the scores for a single item, a group's difference score consists of the unanimous group decision on that item minus the average of the prediscussion individual decision scores on that item for the six members. Once again a negative difference or score decrease indicates a shift in the risky direction, and a *t* test is applied to determine wether the difference scores for all groups that reached a unanimous decision on the item in question are significantly different from zero. For both the male and female groups, we find that 10 of the 12 items show shifts in the risky direction, 7 of them significant in each case. Five of those 7 are the same for both sexes. Only 2 items show any indication for either sex of not sharing in

the general shift toward greater risk taking: Items 5 and 12. It should be noted that these two items exhibited, in our previous research, the lowest correlations with the overall risk-conservatism score, suggesting that they are relatively impure measures of the psychological dimension being tapped by the other 10 items.

In sum, the evidence from Table 1 and 2 indicates a strong move toward greater risk taking when groups arrive at unanimous decisions, compared with the risk levels ventured by the same persons in prediscussion individual decisions. Furthermore, this move toward greater risk taking obtains for females as well as for males.

A further question concerns the extent to which the risky shift is consistent from one group to another. Consider one example of several consistency tests that have been conducted, all of which yield highly

Table 2

SIGNIFICANCE OF CONSERVATISM DIFFERENCE BETWEEN MEAN OF PREDISCUSSION INDIVIDUAL DECISIONS FOR A GROUP'S MEMBERS AND GROUP'S CONSENSUAL DECISION: FEMALES

Item	Mean difference	Number of groups	*t*
All combined	−9.4	14	3.91***
1	−1.0	13	4.17***
2	−0.6	14	1.65
3	−0.4	14	1.12
4	−1.4	14	2.60****
5	+0.7	14	1.80
6	−0.8	13	2.63****
7	−2.0	12	3.21**
8	−1.7	14	5.26*****
9	−0.8	12	1.19
10	−1.5	13	3.18**
11	−0.9	13	2.28*
12	+0.6	6	2.00

* $p < .05$.
** $p < .01$.
*** $p < .005$.
**** $p < .025$.
***** $p < .001$.

similar results. Suppose we define a group as showing a risky shift from prediscussion individual decisions to consensual group decisions if the difference score for its total score, as defined above, is a negative one. Fourteen out of 14 male groups and 12 out of 14 female groups are found to move in the risky direction, both results being very significant by a sign test. Such a finding demonstrates, therefore, that the risky shift phenomenon is quite consistent across groups.

Postdiscussion Individual Decisions Compared with Prediscussion Individual Decisions

In Tables 3 and 4 we present, once again for male and female groups, respectively, the significance of the difference between

the mean of the prediscussion individual decisions and the mean of the postdiscussion individual decisions made by the members of each group. The basic test once again is provided by the total conservatism score, but tests also are presented for each item separately.

For the total score, a group's difference score consists of the average of the postdiscussion total individual decision scores for the members minus the average of the prediscussion total individual decision scores for the same members. Negative difference scores again indicate risky shifts, and a t test is applied to determine whether the 14 difference scores for the groups of each sex are significantly different from zero. We find, once again, a shift in the risky direction significant beyond the .001 level for the 14 male groups, and a risky

Table 3

SIGNIFICANCE OF CONSERVATISM DIFFERENCE BETWEEN MEAN OF PREDISCUSSION INDIVIDUAL DECISIONS FOR A GROUP'S MEMBERS AND MEAN OF POSTDISCUSSION INDIVIDUAL DECISIONS FOR A GROUP'S MEMBERS: MALES

Item	Mean difference	Number of groups	t
All combined	− 10.4	14	9.12****
1	− 1.0	14	4.32****
2	− 0.6	14	2.87*
3	− 1.1	14	3.04**
4	− 1.7	14	8.14****
5	+ 0.1	14	<1.00
6	− 1.1	14	3.79***
7	− 1.8	14	7.80****
8	− 1.1	14	3.54***
9	− 1.1	14	3.99***
10	− 0.3	14	<1.00
11	− 0.8	14	4.36****
12	+ 0.1	14	<1.00

   * $p<.02$.
  ** $p<.01$.
 *** $p<.005$.
**** $p<.001$.

Table 4

SIGNIFICANCE OF CONSERVATISM DIFFERENCE BETWEEN MEAN OF PREDISCUSSION
INDIVIDUAL DECISIONS FOR A GROUP'S MEMBERS AND MEAN OF
POSTDISCUSSION INDIVIDUAL DECISIONS FOR A GROUP'S
MEMBERS: FEMALES

Item	Mean difference	Number of groups	t
All combined	−8.2	14	3.67**
1	−0.9	14	5.09**
2	−0.7	14	2.67*
3	−0.6	14	2.58***
4	−1.4	14	3.40**
5	+0.6	14	1.85
6	−0.8	14	2.90*
7	−1.7	14	3.56**
8	−1.2	14	4.44****
9	−0.5	14	<1.00
10	−0.7	14	1.95
11	−0.9	14	2.89*
12	+0.7	14	3.66**

* $p < .02$.
** $p < .005$.
*** $p < .025$.
**** $p < .001$.

shift significant beyond the .005 level for the 14 female groups. As before, the degree of shift is not significantly different for the two sexes.

Turning to the scores for each separate item, a group's difference score consists of the average of the postdiscussion individual decision scores on that item minus the average of the prediscussion individual decision scores on that item. With a negative difference score indicating a risky shift and a t test applied to indicate whether the 14 difference scores for each sex on an item are significantly different from zero, we find that 9 of the 12 items show separate significant shifts in the risky direction for the male groups (with one additional item shifting nonsignificantly in the same direc-

tion), and that 8 of the 12 items show separate significant shifts toward greater risk taking for the female groups (with two additional items shifting nonsignificantly in that direction). The 8 items showing significant risky shifts for the females are among the 9 showing significant risky shifts for the males. Items 5 and 12 one again are the only ones for either sex showing any indication of not sharing in the general shift toward greater risk taking found in both sexes.

There is clear evidence, therefore, that postdiscussion individual decisions exhibit a strong move toward greater risk taking when compared with prediscussion individual decisions arrived at by the same persons, and do so for both sexes. The

Table 5

COMPARABILITY OF EXPERIMENTAL AND
CONTROL SUBJECTS IN INITIAL
CONSERVATISM AND AGE

Subject	Males		Females	
	M	N	M	N
	Mean Initial Overall Conservatism			
Experimental	66.9	82[a]	65.6	82[a]
Control	68.3	24	64.6	27
t	0.41		0.34	
	Mean Age			
Experimental	20.7	82[b]	20.3	84
Control	21.0	24	20.7	27
t	0.41		0.67	

[a] Initial overall conservatism scores were a-vailable for 164 of the experimental subjects. See Footnote 2 in text.

[b] One subject forgot to list his age, and one group contained five rather than six subjects.

group discussion process, in other words, seems to have an effect on private attitudes (postdiscussion individual decisions) that is just as significant as its effect on publicly expressed views (unanimous group decisions).

Once again we may inquire about the extent to which the risky shift is consistent from group to group. Several consistency tests have been carried out, all yielding highly similar results. As an example, suppose we define a group as exhibiting a shift in the risky direction from prediscussion to postdiscussion individual decisions if the difference score for its total score, as defined in this section, is a negative one. Fourteen out of 14 male groups and 12 out of 14 female groups are found to shift in the risky direction, both results being quite significant by a sign test. Such a finding demonstrates, therefore, that the risky

shift phenomenon is quite consistent across groups in regard to covert acceptance as well as overt compliance.

Control Subjects

To insure that the move toward greater risk taking just described actually is a result of the group discussion process, we must turn to the findings for the control subjects. The comparability of control and experimental subjects is indicated in Table 5. We note that, in the case both of males and females, the experimental and control subjects have approximately the same initial total conservatism scores, and are approximately the same in age.[6] Item-by-item comparisons of experimental and control subjects of each sex on initial conservatism scores also were carried out and show that controls and experimentals within sex obtain highly similar scores.

In Tables 6 and 7 we present, for male and female control subjects, respectively, the significance of the difference between decisions made during the first and the second sessions. It will be recalled that one week intervened between these two sessions, and that instructions for the second session requested the subjects not to try simply to remember what they had marked before, but to reconsider their decisions. It is evident that the total conservatism score shows no shift from first to second session for either sex. Turning to the separate tests carried out on each item, we find that none of the 12 items shows a significant shift for the males, and

---

[6] It might also be mentioned that, in confirmation of earlier findings (Wallach & Kogan, 1959, 1961), there is no sex difference in intial total conservatism scores for either the experimental or the control subjects.

Table 6

SIGNIFICANCE OF CONSERVATISM
DIFFERENCE BETWEEN FIRST AND
SECOND DECISIONS BY MALE
CONTROL SUBJECTS

Item	Mean difference	Number of subjects	t^a
All combined	+1.5	24	<1.00
1	+0.4	24	<1.00
2	−0.3	24	<1.00
3	+0.3	24	<1.00
4	+0.8	24	2.00
5	−0.4	24	1.06
6	0.0	24	<1.00
7	+0.4	24	1.03
8	+0.5	24	1.63
9	−0.1	24	<1.00
10	+0.1	24	<1.00
11	+0.1	24	<1.00
12	−0.4	24	1.42

^{a} All t values ns.

Table 7

SIGNIFICANCE OF CONSERVATISM
DIFFERENCE BETWEEN FIRST AND
SECOND DECISIONS BY FEMALE
CONTROL SUBJECTS

Item	Mean difference	Number of subjects	t
All combined	−2.2	27	1.26
1	−0.4	27	<1.00
2	−0.2	27	<1.00
3	−1.0	27	2.61*
4	−0.4	27	1.12
5	−0.3	27	<1.00
6	−0.2	27	<1.00
7	0.0	27	<1.00
8	0.0	27	<1.00
9	+0.2	27	<1.00
10	+0.3	27	1.03
11	−0.3	27	<1.00
12	+0.1	27	<1.00

* $p < .02$.

only 1 of the 12 items shows a significant shift for the females. When no group discussion and achievement of group consensus intervenes, then, there is no systematic shift toward to the findings for the control subjects. The greater risk taking or greater conservatism, and this despite instructions that encourage shifts by emphasizing that we are not interested in the subjects' memories.

The data for the control subjects also provide us with an opportunity for determining the test-retest reliability of the conservatism-risk instrument, with one week intervening and under instructions that encourage change rather than constancy. For the 24 male subjects, the product-moment correlation coefficient between total conservatism scores in the first and second sessions is .78. For the 27 female subjects, the same correlation coefficient is .82. Test-retest reliability of the instrument, therefore, is quite high.

Prediscussion Risk Taking and Influence in the Group

Our data concerning perceived influence within the group consisted in each individual's ranking of all group members, including himself, in terms of how much each influenced the group's decisions. A first question to ask of these influence rankings is: How consistent are they from member to member within a group? To determine the degree of agreement among a group's members in their rankings of one another for influence, Kendall's coefficient of concordance (Siegel, 1956, pp.

Table 8

DEGREE OF AGREEMENT AMONG GROUP MEMBERS IN RANKINGS OF ONE ANOTHER FOR INFLUENCE[a]

	Males			Females	
Group	N	W	Group	N	W
1	6	.64**	1	6	.85**
2	6	.55**	2	6	.61**
3	6	.74**	3	6	.31
4	6	.72**	4	6	.79**
5	6	.70**	5	6	.47**
6	6	.50**	6	6	.67**
7	5	.56*	7	6	.13
8	6	.50**	8	6	.59**
9	6	.62**	9	6	.59**
10	6	.66**	10	6	.69**
11	6	.66**	11	6	.83**
12	6	.55**	12	6	.80**
13	6	.54**	13	6	.70**
14	6	.73**	14	6	.30

[a] Kendall's coefficient of concordance.
* $p < .05$.
** $p < .01$.

229–238) was applied to each group's influence rankings. If the members of a group agree regarding who among themselves are more influential and who less so, then W will be significantly large. Table 8 presents the results of these tests for all 28 groups. It is evident that agreement in influence rankings is quite high: the degree of agreement is significant for all 14 of the male groups, and for 11 of the 14 female groups.

Given this high agreement among group members in their rankings of one another for influence, an approximate overall estimate of degree of influence for a given group member was obtained by averaging the influence ranks that had been assigned to that person by all members of the group (including that person). The lower the average, the greater that subject's perceived influence (i.e., the higher the assigned influence ranks for that person). These average influence scores for the subjects of each sex were correlated with the initial total conservatism scores obtained by the same subjects. The resulting product-moment correlation coefficients are shown in Table 9. They are significant beyond the .005 and .05 levels for the 82 males and the 82 females, respectively: persons higher in initial risk taking are rated as having more influence on the group decisions.

Average popularity scores for each group member were constructed by averaging the popularity rankings assigned by all the other members of the group. We note in Table 9 that there emerges a very strong relationship between this average popularity score and the average influence score for both the male and the female group members: persons rated high in influence also tend to be rated high in popularity. This general relationship has, of course, been known for some time (see, e.g., Back, 1951; Horowitz, Lyons, & Perlmutter, 1951; Tagiuri & Kogan, 1960), so that our obtaining it here increases our confidence in the respective measures being used to assess influence and popularity. It is further evident in Table 9, however, that degree of initial risk taking is *not* related to degree of popularity within the group for either sex.

Finally, we also find from Table 9 that risk taking and influence are significantly related for each sex when popularity ratings are held constant. The partial correlation coefficients are significant beyond the .01 and .02 levels for the males and females, respectively. It is evident, there-

Table 9

PRODUCT-MOMENT CORRELATIONS AMONG INITIAL CONSERVATISM,
INFLUENCE, AND POPULARITY[a]

	Males (N=82)[b]	Females (N=82)[b]
	r	r
Initial overall risk taking and influence	.32****	.22*
Initial overall risk taking and popularity	.15	−.04
Influence and popularity	.72*****	.54*****
Initial overall risk taking and influence, popularity held constant[c]	.30***	.28**

a Small score values signify greater, risk taking, greater influence, and greater popularity.

b While all influence and popularity scores are based on the 167 subjects in the experimental condition, the correlations are based on the 164 of those subjects for whom initial overall risk taking scores were available.

c Partial correlation coefficients.

    * $p<.05$.
   ** $p<.02$.
  *** $p<.01$.
 **** $p<.005$.
***** $p<.001$.

fore, that the relationships obtained for both sexes between degree of initial risk taking and degree of influence on group decisions are not dependent upon members' popularity.

Maintenance of the Risky Shift over a Subsequent Period of Time

An interesting further question concerns the extent to which the shift toward greater risk taking, which we have found to result from group discussion, is maintained over a subsequent period of time. We were able to gather evidence on this point for males but not for females. In the case of the former, but not in the case of the latter, a random sample of subjects from the original groups could be obtained for further study. The 22 males who were available for further work were approximately evenly distributed among the 14 original male groups. After a time interval of roughly 2–6 weeks had elapsed since the group session, these subjects individually were given the conservatism-risk questionnaire a third time, as described in the section on procedure.

The comparability of the random male subsample of 22 to the original male experimental condition sample of 82 is evident from the following data on total conservatism scores. The mean prediscussion total conservatism score was 66.9 for the sample of 82, and also was 66.9 for the subsample of 22. The mean postdiscussion total conservatism score, in turn, was 56.6 for the whole sample and 56.2 for the subsample. The t test of the difference scores had yielded a t significant beyond the .001 level ($t = 9.12$) for the whole sample, and it also yielded a t significant beyond the .001 level ($t = 4.70$) for the subsample.

Turning now to the total conservatism scores obtained by this subsample when they took the questionnaire again 2–6 weeks after the group discussion (call these scores the "post-postdiscussion" individual decisions), the mean score is 54.6. The mean of the difference scores obtained by subtracting each subject's prediscussion total conservatism score from his post-postdiscussion total conservatism score is − 12.3, with a t test of these difference scores yielding a t value of 4.92 ($p < .001$), hence indicating a risky shift from the prediscussion individual decisions to the post-postdiscussion individual decisions. The mean of the difference scores obtained, in turn, by subtracting each subject's postdiscussion total conservatism score from his post-postdiscussion total conservatism score is only − 1.6, and a t test of these difference scores is not significant, hence indicating no further change from the postdiscussion individual decisions to the post-postdiscussion individual decisions. Item-by-item analyses tell the same story: the only significant item shifts are risky ones, and they are as strong from prediscussion to post-postdiscussion sessions as they are from prediscussion to postdiscussion sessions.

In sum, the data available on the point indicate that the shift in the risky direction found to occur as a result of the group discussion process is maintained over a subsequent period of time.

DISCUSSION AND CONCLUSIONS

The following conclusions may be drawn from the preceding evidence

1. Unanimous group decisions concerning matters of risk show a shift toward greater risk taking when compared with prediscus-sion individual decisions made by the same persons and concerning the same matters. This holds both sexes.

2. Postdiscussion individual decisions that follow unanimous group decisions exhibit the same kind of shift toward greater risk taking as appears in the group decisions. This is the case for both sexes. Covert acceptance as well as overt compliance, thus, are affected in the same manner by the discussion process.

3. This shift toward greater risk taking as a result of the discussion process is still maintained when 2–6 weeks have elapsed since the discussion occurred. Evidence on this point was available only for males.

4. No shift in risk taking level of individual decisions occurs over time in the absence of the discussion process. This holds for both sexes.

5. There is a positive relationship between degree of risk taking in prediscussion individual decisions and the extent to which group members are perceived by one another as influencing group decisions. This relationship is specific to judgments of influence, in that it obtains when judgments of popularity are held constant, and also no relationship is found between prediscussion individual risk taking and the extent to which group members are judged to be popular. These statements all hold for both sexes.

The present study indicates, then, that group interaction and achievement of consensus concerning decisions on matters of risk eventuate in a willingness to make decisions that are more risky than those that would be made in the absence of such interaction. Furthermore, although initial ascribed status levels of the group members are equal, it is found that persons with stronger individual risk taking proclivities tend to become more influential in the group than persons who are more conservative. Two alternative interpretations of these findings can be suggested; one more group centered, the other more person centered: It is possible that there is at work in these groups a process of diffusion or spreading of responsibility as a result of knowing that one's decisions are being made jointly with others rather than alone. Increased willingness to take risk would eventuate from this decreased feeling of personal responsibility. That initial risk taking and judged influence within the group are positively related could well occur as a consequence of this process, since one of its effects would be for the views of high risk takers to be given more weight by the rest of the group. Alternatively, the fact that high risk takers exert more influence may be a cause of the group's movement toward greater risk taking. It is possible that high risk takers are also more likely to take the initiative in social situations. Of course, these two interpretations are not necessarily mutually exclusive. Both of them may contribute to the group effect.

That females as well as males show the same change toward greater risk taking as a result of the group interaction condition, and that the samples of both sexes were liberal arts university students, renders it unlikely that the results can be explained on the basis of reinforcement by others of one's expectation as to whether one's appropriate role is to be more or less of a risk taker. We noted earlier that Stoner (1961) found a move toward greater risk taking in group as compared to individual decision making by male graduate students of industrial management, and we pointed out that this result might be accounted for in terms of the professional role that they had assigned themselves by becoming graduate students in a business school. Presence of peers might be expected to increase the salience of their business manager role, and a

greater willingness to take risks in decision making might well be perceived as one of the attributes of that role. Such a role expectation interpretation is ruled out for the present study, however, through our use of liberal arts students as subjects. In addition, the possibility of explaining the results in terms of males' perceiving their appropriate role as one of willingness to be bold and daring, and being reinforced in this view by interaction with other like-minded males, is ruled out by the present study's obtaining the same results for females as for males. This outcome would not be expected if the findings depended on sex linked role expectations as to whether one should be more risky or more conservative. This outcome also, of course, rules out interpretation in terms of any possible sex linked differences in major fields of study.

That the group induced move toward greater risk taking in individual decisions is still maintained 2–6 weeks after the discussion, provides evidence, incidentally, which supports Lewin's (1947) view that "group carried" attitudinal changes maintain themselves (see also Pelz, 1958).

REFERENCES

ATTHOWE, J. M., JR. "Interpersonal Decision Making: The Resolution of a Dyadic Conflict." *J. Abnorm. Soc. Psychol.*, 1961, 62, 114–119.

BACK, K. W. "Influence Through Social Communication." *J. Abnorm. Soc. Psychol.*, 1951, 46, 9–23.

BROWN, R. W. "Mass Phenomena." In G. Lindzey (Ed.), *Handbook of Social Psychology.* Vol. 2. *Special Fields and Applications.* Cambridge, Mass.: Addison-Wesley, 1954. Pp. 833–876.

CARTWRIGHT, D., and ZANDER, A. (Eds.) *Group Dynamics.* (2nd ed.) Evanston, Ill.: Row, Peterson, 1960.

FESTINGER, L. "An Analysis of Compliant Behavior." In M. Sherif and M. O. Wilson (Eds.), *Group Relations at the Crossroads.* New York: Harper, 1953. Pp. 232–255.

HOROWITZ, M. W., LYONS, J., and PERLMUTTER, H. V. "Induction of Forces in Discussion Groups." *Hum. Relat.*, 1951, 4, 57–76.

HUNT, E. B., and ROWE, R. R. "Group and Individual Economic Decision Making in Risk Conditions." In D. W. Taylor (Ed.), *Experiments on Decision Making and Other Studies.* Arlington, Va.: Armed Services Technical Information Agency, 1900. Pp. 21–25. (Technical Report No. 6, AD 253952)

KELLEY, H. H., and THIBAUT, J. W. "Experimental Studies of Group Problem Solving and Process." In G. Lindzey (Ed.), *Handbook of Social Psychology.* Vol. 2. *Special Fields and Applications.* Cambridge, Mass.: Addison-Wesley, 1954. Pp. 735–785.

KOGAN, N., and WALLACH, M. A. "The Effect of Anxiety on Relations Between Subjective Age and Caution in an Older Sample." In P. H. Hoch and J. Zubin (Eds.), *Psychopathology of Aging.* New York: Grune and Stratton, 1961. Pp. 123–135.

KOMAROVSKY, MIRRA. "Functional Analysis of Sex Roles." *Amer. Sociol. Rev.*, 1950, 15, 508–516.

LEWIN, K. "Frontiers in Group Dynamics." *Hum. Relat.*, 1947, 1, 2–38.

LONERGAN, B. G., and McCLINTOCK, C. G. "Effects of Group Membership on Risk-Taking Behavior." *Psychol. Rep.*, 1961, 8, 447–455.

McNEMAR, Q. *Psychological Statistics.* (Rev. ed.) New York: Wiley, 1955.

MILNER, ESTHER. "Effects of Sex Role and Social Status on the Early Adolescent Personality." *Genet. Psychol. Monogr.*, 1949, 40, 231–325.

OSBORN, A. F. *Applied Imagination.* New York: Scribner, 1957.

PELZ, EDITH B. "Some Factors in 'Group Decision.'" In Eleanor E. Maccoby, T. M. Newcomb, and E. L. Hartley (Eds.), *Readings in Social Psychology.* (3rd ed.) New York: Holt, 1958, Pp. 212–219.

SCHACHTER, S. "Deviation, Rejection, and Communication." *J. Abnorm. Soc. Psychol.*, 1951, 46, 190–207.

SLEGEL, S. *Nonparametric Statistics for the Behavioral Sciences.* New York: McGraw-Hill, 1956.

STONER, J. A. F. "A Comparison of Individual and Group Decisions Involving Risk." Unpublished master's Thesis, Massachusetts Institute of Technology, School of Industrial Management, 1961.

TAGIURI, R., and KOGAN, N. "Personal Preference and the Attribution of Influence in Small Groups." *J. Pers.*, 1960, 28, 257–265.

TAYLOR, D. W., BERRY, P. C., and BLOCK, C. H. "Does Group Participation When Using Brainstorming Facilitate or Inhibit Creative Thinking?" *Admin. Sci. Quart.*, 1958, 3, 23–47.

THIBAUT, J. W., and KELLEY, H. H. *The Social Psychology of Groups.* New York: Wiley, 1959.

TURNER, R. H., and KILLIAN, L. M. (Eds.) *Collective Behavior.* Englewood Cliffs, N. J.: Prentice-Hall, 1957.

WALLACH, M. A., and CARON, A. J. "Attribute Criteriality and Sex-Linked Conservatism as Determinants of Psychological Similarity." *J. Abnorm. Soc. Psychol.*, 1959, 59, 43–50.

WALLACH, M. A., and KOGAN, N. "Sex Differences and Judgment Processes." *J. Pers.*, 1959, 27, 555–564.

WALLACH, M. A., and KOGAN, N. "Aspects of Judgment and Decision Making: Interrelationships and Changes with Age." *Behav. Sci.*, 1961, 6, 23–36.

WHYTE, W. H., JR. *The Organization Man.* New York: Simon and Schuster, 1956.

COMPONENTS OF GROUP RISK TAKING*

Allan I. Teger and Dean G. Pruitt

Since Stoner (1961) first demonstrated that groups have a tendency to take greater risks than individuals, many studies have shown similar results over many tasks and conditions (Bem, Wallach, and Kogan, 1965; Marquis, 1962; Wallach and Kogan, 1965; Wallach, Kogan, and Bem, 1962; Wallach, Kogan, and Bem, 1964). The standard method for studying this effect consists of two steps. The subjects are first asked to make individual decisions on a series of problems in which it is possible to take greater or lesser risk. They are then placed in a group situation and required to discuss and make a group decision on the same problems. The difference between the mean level of risk taken initially by the individuals and the mean of their later group decisions is termed a "shift." If there is change toward greater risk, it is termed a "risky shift." A risky shift is almost always found.

Various theories have been put forward to explain this risky shift, and evidence has been brought to bear on some of them. The hypothesis that a value of risk in male society produces the shift was ruled out

---

* Allan I. Teger and Dean G. Pruitt, "Components of Group Risk Taking," *Journal of Experimental Social Psychology*, 3 (1967), 189–205. Reprinted by permission of the Academic Press, Inc.

when Wallach *et al.* (1962) found a risky shift among women. Bem *et al.* (1965) demonstrated that the effect is not due to an expectation of sympathy from others in the event of failure, since those who expected others to be present during possible failure took less risk rather than more risk.

Wallach and Kogan (Wallach *et al.*, 1962; Wallach and Kogan, 1965) have theorized that the risky shift is due to a spread of responsibility. According to these authors, the fact that others are present to share the responsibility if failure occurs allows each group member to feel less personal blame for a possible failure. With less fear of failure, the group members feel free to take greater risk. While this theory has not been tested directly, Wallach and Kogan (1965) have developed evidence which they consider relevant to the conditions under which a risky shift occurs and hence the conditions underlying diffusion of responsibility (since they consider this to be the immediate antecedent of the risky shift). These authors found no difference in risky shift between groups that had to reach a consensus and groups that only had to engage in a discussion. Hence, they conclude that the risky shift results from some element of group discussion. They also found that simple acquaintance with the prior decisions made by other group members, without a group discussion, produced no risky shift. Hence, they conclude that the risky shift is due to some element of group discussion other than the exchange of information about preferences. They suggest that the "affective bonds formed in discussion" facilitate a diffusion of responsibility onto other group members and, hence, encourage a shift toward risk. As will be shown later, there are problems with the findings upon which this conclusions is based.

Brown's (1965) "value theory" is the major alternative to that advanced by Wallach and Kogan. According to this theory, cultural norms cause people initially to label most decision problems of the kind used in this research as warranting either a "risky" or a "cautious" approach. Such problems are said by Brown to generate a "value of risk" or a "value of caution." The implications of these labels are differently interpreted, so that in the actual initial decision, some people take more risk than others on an item. The risky shift occurs only with items that generate a value of risk. It is due, in part, to an exchange of information about initial decision during the group discussion. As a result of this exchange, most group members discover that the other members of their group have taken as much or more risk than themselves on a problem. Consequently, they begin to wonder whether their behavior is actually in line with the value of risk that they have adopted. While they thought that they were being quite risky in their initial decision, comparison with others suggests that they were taking only an average level of risk (or less). Hence, they become more risky on the second decision, in an effort to conform to the value of risk as newly interpreted.

The risky shift also results in part from persuasive communication. If most members of the group agree that risk is the correct value for the problem under consideration, then most of the reasons and justifications brought out in the discussion will favor risk. The subjects will then hear additional reasons why risk, is correct, moving them further toward the value of risk, and causing them to take even greater risk.

According to Brown, the same two mechanisms should produce a shift away from risk on problems that generate a value of caution.

Brown's theory is supported tangentially by two lines of evidence: (1) Hinds (1962) has found that subjects typically believe that they are taking more risk than the average man in their initial decision. This supports the assumption that people are trying to be risky in these decisions. (2) Two of the decision problems that have been used in most of the studies in this area consistently show a shift *away from risk*, and Nordhøy (1962) has developed other items that produce a similar "cautious shift."[1] This evidence suggests the need for a theory which, like Brown's, accounts for shifts away from risk as well as risky shifts.

Kogan and Wallach (1967) have criticized Brown's theory as being inconsistent with one of their research findings cited above: that simple acquaintance with the views of other group members, in the absence of discussion, produced no risky shift. Brown's theory is vulnerable

---

[1] However, the consistency of the cautious shift on Nordhøy's items is somewhat in doubt, according to a personal communication from Donald Marquis.

to this criticism, since he assumes that exchange of information about initial decisions causes people to revise their interpretation of the value of risk and, therefore, to shift toward greater risk. However, the validity of this research finding is in doubt, as will now shown.

This finding (Wallach and Kogan, 1965) was based on an experimental condition in which the subjects silently exchanged information on their answers to the decision problems. The problems were dealt with one by one as follows: Each group member made a tentative decision, which was posted by the experimenter for everyone to see. Another round of choices was then made and posted, and this procedure was continued until consensus was achieved. No risky shift was found.

The validity of this result is in question, because the method employed appears to encourage group convergence on the mean of the initial decisions in two ways: (a) The groups were required to reach consensus. Under normal conditions, such a requirement would cause many members to stand fast and argue for their own viewpoints in an effort to sway the others in their direction. But in this case, the subjects were not permitted to communicate. Hence, the only strategy for achieving consensus that may have seemed available to many subjects was to move toward the other group members, i.e., toward the group average. (b) The subjects were told that their recommendations "should consist of what you think the group *can* agree on and what you think the group should agree on." Given these instructions, it is not surprising that a risky shift failed to materialize, since the initial mean is the most obvious point on which the group "can agree.

Not only is the finding based on this

questionable method relevant to the adequacy of Brown's theory; it is also, as was mentioned earlier, the basis for Wallach and Kogan's conclusion that affective bonds formed in the discussion underlie the risky shift. Hence, this finding is of considerable theoretical importance and deserves replication with a more adequate methodology. Such replication was one of the major purposes of the present study.

This study was also designed to determine whether discussion will produce a greater risky shift than simple information exchange.[2] The earlier study by Wallach and Kogan also examined this issue, but it deserves to be looked at again in light of the criticism just given of their method. Wallach and Kogan would undoubtedly predict that discussion will produce more risky shift than information exchange, since discussion should permit the development of affective bonds that facilitate a diffusion of responsibility. Brown would probably also make the same prediction, since discussion provides everything that information exchange provides *plus* an opportunity for the presentation of reasons and justifications for taking risk, which may move people further toward the value of risk.

A third purpose of the study was to examine the relationship between the initial level of risk taken on a decision problem and the risky shift on that problem. One interpretation of Brown's theory would

---

[2] This and the prior statement of purpose are worded in a way that assumes we are dealing with problems that elicit a value of risk. This is because of a history of risky shift in most of the problems used in the study. Problems that elicit a value of caution should show some cautious shift under information exchange and a greater cautious shift under discussion.

lead to the prediction of a positive correlation between these variables. This follows from the assumption that the value of risk or caution elicited by a problem will affect the initial decision on that problem as well as the subsequent shift. Problems that elicit a value of risk should show a risky initial decision and a shift toward risk; problems that elicit a value of caution should show a conservative initial decision and a shift away from risk. Hence, the prediction of a correlation between these variables. Wallach and Kogan's theory does not yield a prediction about this issue, since it does not deal with differences between decision problems.

The final aim of the study was to examine the relationship between group size and the extent of the risky shift. Both theories would probably agree that a larger discussion group should produce a greater risky shift. Wallach and Kogan might argue that this is due to the increased ability to shift responsibility in a larger group, while Brown night hold that more information is brought out in a larger group to support the initial value produced by the problem.

METHOD

Subjects

A total of 165 male undergraduates at the University of Delaware took part in the experiment. All were volunteers for experiments on decision making and were paid for their time. They were assigned at random to the various conditions and participated in groups of from 3 to 5 students.

Measure of Risk Taking

The decision task was the choice dilemma questionnaire devised by Wallach and Kogan

(1959, 1961) and used in many of their studies. It consists of twelve items, each of which requires the subject to give advice to a hypothetical person who is faced with a difficult decision. The subject must decide whether to advise the person to take a risky or a nonrisky alternative. If the risky alternative is chosen, he must also decide the minimum odds of success which should be demanded before choosing that alternative. In all items, the risky alternative involves a better outcome than the nonrisky alternative *if it is successful*. If the risky alternative is not successful, then the nonrisky alternative would be preferable. A preference for higher risk is indicated by choice of the risky alternative with lower odds of success. The lowest risk would be indicated by a choice of the nonrisky alternative.

All of the items are sufficiently ambiguous that the subject is forced to make some assumptions. This prevents an obvious solution for optimal gain. The questions cover a wide range of topics, with the stakes varying from money, to life, to a victory in a chess game. An example of one of the items is shown below.[3]

1. Mr. A, an electrical engineer, who is married and has one child, has been working for a large electronics corporation since graduating from college five years ago. He is assured of a lifetime job with a modest, though adequate salary, and liberal pension benefits upon retirement. On the other hand, it is very unlikely that his salary will increase much before he retires. While attending a convention, Mr. A is offered a job with a small, newly founded company which has a highly uncertain future. The new job would pay more to start and would offer the possibility of a share in the ownership if the company survived the competition of the larger firms.

Imagine that you are advising Mr. A. Listed below are several probabilities or

---

[3] For the complete set of items, see Kogan and Wallach (1964).

odds of the new company proving financially sound. Please check the lowest probability that you would consider acceptable to make it worthwhile for Mr. A to take the new job.
—The chances are 1 in 10 that the company will prove financially sound.
—The chances are 3 in 10 that the company will prove financially sound.
—The chances are 5 in 10 that the company will prove financially sound.
—The chances are 7 in 10 that the company will prove financially sound.
—The chances are 9 in 10 that the company will prove financially sound.
—Place a check here if you think Mr. A should *not* take the new job no matter what the probabilities.

Initial Decisions for All Conditions

The subjects were seated around a large circular table. A tape recording of the instructions was played to them. They were told to

... Decide what advice you would give a person who must make the choice depicted in the problem.... You will be given several choices. You must pick the best choice.... You are to pick the *lowest* probability of success that he should accept. You should always assume that of the two alternatives, the one which is the most doubtful of being successful would be the best if it was successful.... Think of yourself as an advisor to the person in the problem. Think of yourself as being in a position where the person must take the advice that you give him....

They were also told that after they had made all of their decisions, the decisions would be played off on a roulette wheel so that they could see whether their decisions might have brought success or failure in reality. It was explained that the outcome would not affect their pay or anything else, but would just give them an idea of how the odds they picked might have turned out.

After the presentation of the instructions they were given copies of a booklet containing a brief resumé of the instructions, the 12 choice dilemma items, and a final questionnaire to assess their confidence in their answers to the 12 items. They were told to take approximately 15 minutes to finish the questionnaire, but were allowed to take as long as necessary to finish. They were instructed not to discuss the items. The experimenter monitored the room by means of a hidden microphone to make certain that there was no discussion.

After all subjects had finished making their initial decisions, the booklets were collected and the second phase of the experiment was begun. In this phase the groups of subjects were assigned at random among one control and three experimental conditions.

Conditions I and II

The subjects were told that their first decisions had been for practice to familiarize them with the items. A second set of taped instructions was then presented, as follows:

... Discuss these problems as a group, one problem at a time. We would like you to try and arrive at a unanimous decision if possible, on each problem. If you are unable to arrive at a unanimous decision after discussing the problem, do not be concerned. We will average the decisions that each one of you makes, and this average will be considered the group's decision.... Please do not feel bound by what you marked as your decision on the practice booklet. Whether or not you change or how much you change is not important. What is important is that you discuss each problem seriously and reconsider each answer carefully.

The subjects were each given a new question booklet for reference and an answer sheet on which to make their final answers. It was explained that the group decisions, rather than the earlier individual decisions, would be played off on the roulette wheel. Before the experimenter left the room he stated that there was a microphone in the ceiling and that the discussion would be tape recorded.

After the discussion session was finished, the subjects completed a rating scale to determine their perceived responsibility for the group decisions.

The instructions and procedures were the same for both condition I and condition II, the only difference between the two conditions being the size of the group. Condition I (larger groups) contained five groups of five subjects each, and five groups of four subjects each, while condition II (small groups) contained ten groups of three subjects each.

Condition III

As in condition I and II, the subjects were told that their initial decisions had been for practice. In this condition they were asked to "compare notes" with each other and then make new, final decisions. Discussion was not permitted. Instead, each subject was given a package of cards, showing the various possible choices such as 1/10, 3/10, and so forth. Going around the table in order, each subject held up a card indicating his choice on the item under consideration. This was done for three full rounds. The subjects were instructed as follows:

... Consider what you are doing as a form of discussion. You are each getting an opportunity to compare your initial decision with that of others. You are also given a chance to change your decisions if you wish to.... Feel free to change your answers at any time. For example, if after the second vote you wish to change your answer, merely hold up a different card indicating your new decision for the third vote. Remember, if this were the usual form of discussion, many of you would change your answers for various reasons during the course of the discussion. Always consider your own decision in light of others' decisions, but in the end do whatever you think is the best. You do not have to reach a consensus.... Please do not feel bound by what you marked as your decision on the practice booklet. Whether or

not you change or how much you change is not important. What is important is that you reconsider each answer carefully.

The subjects were given booklets of the items for reference, and answer sheets for their final decisions. The use of the roulette wheel at the end was explained as in conditions I and II. There were five groups of five subjects each and five groups of four subjects each, as in condition I.

Control Condition

The control subjects were told that their initial decisions were for practice and then were asked to make new final decisions. The reason for this procedure was explained as follows:

... Up until now you have had no guidelines by which to make your decisions. Possibly by reconsidering each problem after having seen it before, you will have a better idea of the kind of decision that you would like to make.... Please do not feel bound by what you marked as your decision on the practice booklet. Whether or not you change or how much you change is not important. What is important is that you reconsider each answer carefully.

These final decisions, they were told, would be played off on the roulette wheel. No mention was made of a group, as in this condition it was the subjects' individual final decisions, made independently, which would be recorded. The subjects were run in groups similar to the ones in the other conditions, although the groups size varied. The total number of subjects was equal to five groups of five subjects and five groups of four subjects as in conditions I and III.

Final Procedure

In all cases the subjects who made their initial decision together were the same as those who comprised a group for later interaction. No subjects entered or left after the first phase of the experiment had begun. After the initial decisions were made and the second set of instructions administered, approximately 25–30 minutes remained for making the final decisions. The amount of time for the final decisions was approximately the same for all groups in all conditions. The experimenter was never in the room with the subjects except to distribute and collect materials and to administer instructions. The experimenter monitored the group at all times by means of a microphone. Only during the discussion periods of conditions I and II were the subjects aware of the microphone. After the final decisions were made, the experimenter played off all of the decisions on the roulette wheel.

Results

The responses of the subjects were initially coded as the number of chances in ten that they would accept. This score was then subtracted from ten to get a "risk score" in which a higher number represents greater risk. The basic shift measure was computed by subtracting the risk score on the initial decision from the risk score on the second. The larger this difference, the greater the shift toward risk.

According to Brown's theory there are two major types of decision items, those that produce a tendency toward risk and those that produce a tendency toward caution. In the Wallach, Kogan, and Bem study (1962) items No. 5 and 12[4] of the choice dilemmas failed to show the risky

---

[4] Number 5 requires a decision about whether to advise a business executive to build a factory in a country where the government may nationalize foreign investments. Number 12 requires a decision about whether to advise marriage for a couple who have experienced some disagreements.

shift. These items are presumably examples of the cautious type and, hence, were expected to show a shift toward caution rather than toward risk. They were therefore analyzed separately.

Risk Taking on the Ten Items for Which a Risky Shift Was Predicted

The average risky shift in each condition is summarized in Table 1. These numbers represent the total risky shift for the ten items, averaged across groups in each condition. The most important comparisons among these conditions are between the average risky shift in each experimental condition and the average risky shift in the control condition. These results are summarized in Table 2.

The results shown in the first row of Table 2 reveal a significant risky shift for the larger (four- and five-man) discussion groups. This is in line with the findings of Stoner (1961), Wallach et al. (1962), Wallach and Kogan (1965), and others. On the other hand, row two indicates that the smaller (three-man) discussion groups failed to show a significant risky shift.

The third row of Table 2 reveals that there was a significant risky shift condition III, where the groups were able to compare notes regarding their decisions but were not allowed to discuss the items or decisions. This result is contrary to that of Wallach and Kogan (1965), and is presumably due to the fact that the present subjects were not instructed to try to reach consensus as were those in the Wallach and Kogan study.

An orthogonal comparison method was used for contrasting condition I with condition II and condition Ia with condition Ib. The results showed a significantly greater amount of risky shift in the larger

Table 1

MEAN RISKY SHIFT IN EACH CONDITION FOR THE TEN "RISK" ITEMS

Condition	N	Mean risky shift[a]	SD
I Discussion	10	7.85	4.28
Ia (groups of size 5)	5	9.76	3.29
Ib (group of size 4)	5	5.94	4.73
II Discussion (groups of size 3)	10	1.41	5.07
III Information exchange	10	3.13	2.98
IIIa (groups of size 5)	5	2.92	3.30
IIIb (groups of size 4)	5	3.34	2.98
Control	10	.06	2.40

[a] Summed over the ten "risk" items.

Table 2

DIFFERENCE IN RISKY SHIFT BETWEEN CONTROL CONDITION AND EACH EXPERIMENTAL CONDITION FOR THE TEN RISK ITEMS

Comparisons	Mean difference	df	t	p (two-tailed)
I vs. control	7.79	18	4.99	.01
II vs. control	1.35	18	.76	n.s.
III vs. control	3.07	18	2.52	.05

(four- and five-man) discussion groups (condition I) than in the smaller (three man) discussion groups (condition II $(F = 9.81$, 1 and 17 df, $p < .01)$. This result is not surprising, as condition I showed a significant level of risky shift as compared with a control, which condition II did not. This trend toward greater risky shift in larger groups continued when Ia and Ib were compared $(F = 1.73$, 1 and 17 df, $p < .25)$. Five-man groups (Ia) showed a greater shift toward risk than four-man groups (Ib), though this trend was not significant.

Conditions I and II were comparable in having five groups of five subjects and five groups of four subjects. Hence, a 2 × 2 analysis of variance could be performed.

A significant difference in amount of risky shift was found between these conditions $(F = 8.58$, 1 and 16 df, $p < .01)$, indicating that the risky shift is greater when discussion is allowed than when only an exchange of information on decisions is permitted. The interaction between group size and condition was suggestive but not statistically significant $(F = 1.73$, 1 and 16 df, $p < .25)$.

Risk Taking on the Two Items for Which a Cautious Shift Was Predicted

The two items (Nos. 5 and 12) that were left out of the major analyses because of their past failure to exhibit a risky shift were analyzed separately. The

Table 3

MEAN RISKY SHIFT IN EACH CONDITION FOR THE TWO NON-RISK ITEMS

Condition	N	Mean risky shift[a]	SD
I Discussion	10	−.50	1.04
Ia (groups of size 5)	5	−.76	1.06
Ib (groups of size 4)	5	−.24	1.07
II Discussion (groups of size 3)	10	.11	1.52
III Information exchange	10	−.69	1.04
IIa (groups of size 5)	5	−1.28	1.21
IIIb (groups of size 4)	5	−.10	.34
Control	10	−.32	1.43

[a] Summed over the two non-risk items.

average total risky shift on these items for the groups in each condition is presented in Table 3. Note that almost all of the means are in a negative direction, indicating a shift toward a more cautious choice after the group situation.

These items were subjected to the identical analyses performed on the risky items, but no significant differences were found, possibly as a result of the unreliability of data that are based on only two items.

Comparison Between the Decision Items

Table 4 gives the average initial risk and risky shift for each of the 12 decision problems[5] under the four main conditions. In Table 5 are shown correlations across items between initial risk and risky shift, based on the data from Table 4. One part of Table 5 is based on all 12 items, the other on the ten that usually show a risky shift (i.e., all except Nos. 5 and 12).

The coefficients for all of the experi-

---

[5] The numbers in this table correspond to those used by Kogan and Wallach (1961).

mental conditions in Table 5 are positive, indicating that items which elicit riskier initial decisions produce a greater risky shift. These coefficients are quite large for this kind of data, and most are statistically significant. It is important to note that such results could not be due to self-correlation, regression, or a ceiling effect, since all such effects would produce negative correlations. The negative coefficients shown for the control group may be due to such effects.

The results shown in Table 5 are compatible with Brown's theory, which would attribute such positive correlations to the operation of a third common factor: the value of risk or conservatism elicited by each item. Such a value presumably determines both the initial level of risk and the extent of risky shift. However, another possible way of explaining these results would be to assume that the two variables being correlated are causally related, i.e., that the initial level of risk taken by any person on any item somehow determines the extent of his subsequent risky shift. If this were true, then one would expect to find positive correlations between these

Table 4

Mean Initial Risk and Risky Shift for Every Item

Item No.	Condition I		Condition II		Condition III		Control	
	Initial risk	Risky shift	Initial risk	Risky shift	Initial risk	Risky shift	Initial risk	Risky shift
1	4.68	1.48	4.74	.46	4.15	.68	4.68	−.02
2	3.92	.32	3.47	−.27	2.84	−.11	3.95	.01
3	4.32	1.20	4.23	−.52	3.86	1.02	3.42	.50
4	5.86	1.47	6.13	.51	5.80	.62	5.64	−.09
5	1.85	−.07	2.10	.57	2.21	−.32	2.14	−.38
6	4.39	.84	4.10	.43	4.67	.23	4.49	−.11
7	5.87	1.29	5.55	.92	5.53	.28	5.15	.01
8	3.77	.16	3.07	−.60	2.70	−.29	3.00	.26
9	5.07	.62	4.71	.02	4.75	.48	4.59	−.34
10	4.10	−.24	3.28	.12	3.83	.02	3.75	−.11
11	5.54	.71	4.84	.46	5.23	.21	5.04	−.26
12	1.87	−.43	2.44	−.46	2.11	−.37	1.95	.05

Table 5

Correlation between Initial Risk and Risky Shift Across Items

	Across all 12 items		Across the 10 risk items	
	r	p	r	p
Condition I	.78	.01	.64	.05
Condition II	.51	n.s.	.77	.01
Condition III	.67	.05	.47	n.s.
Control	−.19	n.s.	−.60	n.s.

two variables *across groups* within each item.[6] Such correlations were computed for the three experimental conditions and, by way of contrast to assess the impact of regression and self-correlation, for the control groups. There were 48 coefficients in

all, one for each of the 12 items in the four conditions. The 12 coefficients under each condition were then averaged, using z scores; and the results are shown in Table 6. All four average r's are close to zero, and none is statistically significant by a signed rank test. Hence, it appears that there is no relationship between the initial risk taken by a person and the extent of his risky shift. Therefore, the most appropriate interpretation of the correlations shown in Table 5 would appear to be that initial risk and risky shift are both greatly affected by the nature of the item, as implied by Brown's theory.

Convergence Shift

The extent to which the members of a group agree on the answer to a problem can be called "convergence." The variance estimate (s^2) calculated over the members of a group for a given problem can be used as an inverse measure of convergence. This has the advantage of be-

---

[6] If individuals who take greater initial risk show greater risky shift, then groups whose members take greater initial risk should show greater risky shift.

Table 6

AVERAGE CORRELATIONS BETWEEN
INITIAL RISK AND RISKY SHIFT
ACROSS GROUPS WITHIN ITEMS

	Average r (computed from z)	p
Condition I	−.07	n.s.
Condition II	.115	n.s.
Condition III	−.237	n.s.
Control	−.322	n.s.

Note. $N = 10$ groups per coefficient.

ing unaffected by group size, which was of course a variable in this experiment. The difference between the convergence on the initial decision and the convergence on the second can be termed "convergence shift." As a measure of this variable, we used the variance estimate on the initial decision minus the variance estimate on the second. This reflects the extent to which a group moves toward agreement on an item.

No interesting results were found for the measure of initial convergence, but convergence shift was related to other variables. The main data on the latter variable are shown in Table 7. As might be expected, the convergence shift in all three experimental conditions was significantly greater than that in the control condition, where the subjects did not interact. The difference in amount of convergence shift among the various sizes of discussion group was negligible, but condition I (discussion) showed a significantly greater convergence shift than condition III (information exchange) ($F = 32.18$ 1 and 16 df, $p < .001$).

A correlational analysis revealed, for condition I, a significant positive relationship between initial risk and convergence shift ($r < .63$, $N = 12$, $p < .05$) and between risky shift and convergence shift ($r = .68$, $N = 12$, $p < .05$). The comparable statistics were: for condition II, $r = .28$ and $− .42$, and for condition III, $r = .37$ and .08. None of these was statistically significant.

Confidence and Perceived Responsibility

A correlational analysis showed that confidence in the initial decision was not related to initial risk or to risky shift. The

Table 7

MEAN CONVERGENCE SHIFT IN EACH CONDITION FOR ITEMS

Condition	N	Mean convergence shift	SD
I Discussion	10	3.96	1.53
Ia (groups of size 5)	5	4.51	2.13
Ib (groups of size 4)	5	3.42	1.50
II Discussion			
(groups of size 3)	10	4.08	1.85
III Information exchange	10	1.77	2.56
IIIa (groups of size 5)	5	1.44	1.22
IIIb (groups of size 4)	5	2.10	1.10
Control	10	.44	.74

measure of confidence used here was a rating scale in which the subject indicated his over-all confidence in all 12 decisions. Stoner (1961) also found no relationship between confidence and risk when he measured this variable separately on each item both before and after the group decision.

In the two conditions where discussion was allowed (conditions I and II), the subjects were asked to assess the amount of responsibility that they felt for the group decision. The responsibility felt in the larger groups was not significantly different from that felt in the smaller ones ($t = .21$, $df = 18$).

DISCUSSION

Exchange of Information

The results of this study appear to confirm the criticism that was made of the Wallach and Kogan (1965) study. With an improved methodology, a risky shift was found in groups that were not permitted to engage in a discussion but whose members could only exchange minimal information about their prior decisions. This finding is evidence against the assertion by Wallach and Kogan that group discussion is the "necessary and sufficient condition, for occurrence of the shift toward risk, and against their associated viewpoint that the risky shift grows exclusively out of the affective bonds that develop among the members of a group in the give and take of discussion. This finding is compatible with one part of Brown's (1965) value theory. Brown asserts that acquaintance with the decisions of others leads many group members to conclude that they are not sufficiently adhering to the value of risk, which causes them to be-

come more risky in their subsequent decisions.

Discussion

A greater risky shift was found in the discussion condition than in the information exchange condition. This finding is in line with the thinking of Wallach and Kogan as well as with that of Brown, but for different reasons. The former authors would probably attribute it to the opportunity afforded by a discussion for the development of affective bonds, while the latter would probably point out that discussion provides a better opportunity for group members to acquaint one another with the arguments in favor of the value of risk. Since the discussion condition is compared with an information exchange condition that does not encourage a convergence on the prior group mean but does demonstrate a risky shift, the present test of the discussion variable is stronger than that in the Wallach and Kogan (1965) study.

Differences Between Decision Problems

As in other studies, a shift away from risk was observed in most conditions for problems Nos. 5 and 12, though statistical significance could not be demonstrated for this shift when these 2 items were examined separately. The importance of considering individual decision problems is, however, clearly shown by the high correlations that were found between initial risk and risky shift, across items.

These correlations are compatible with Brown's value theory. One would expect an item that elicits an initial value of risk to produce relatively risky initial decisions and an item that elicits an initial value of caution to produce relatively cautious inital decisions. Since, according to Brown, the former kind of item also produces a risky shift and the latter a conservative shift, a positive correlation is insured. That positive correlations were found across the ten risk items as well as the full 12 items suggests the need for a slight modification of Brown's theory. Presumably all ten of the risk items elicit a value of risk. Hence, the variance reflected in these correlations must be attributed to differences in the strength of or adherence to the value of risk. In other words, in some sense, the value of risk or caution may be a continuous variable, ranging from strong risk to strong caution.[7]

The relationship that was found between initial risk and risky shift is not peculiar to the present study. A reanalysis of the Stoner (1961) data revealed a significant positive correlation ($r = .61$, $N = 12$, $p < .05$) between the initial risk and the risky shift across items. A significant positive correlation ($r = .71$, $N = 12$, $p < .01$) was also found when the initial risk for each item reported by Wallach and Kogan (1961) was correlated with the risky shift reported by Wallach *et al.* (1962). It was necessary to use data from two studies by these authors because no one study reported both statistics.

Though a high positive correlation between these variables is found in three studies, it does not necessarily follow that the decision problems produce the same initial level of risk and risky shift in all

three studies. Indeed, problem No. 5, which produced a cautious shift in the Wallach and Kogan studies and under most conditions of the present study, produced a relatively high initial risk and a risky shift in the Stoner study. A possible explanation for this discrepancy may lie in the relationship between the subject matter of this problem and the background of Stoner's subjects. Stoner's subjects were students in a school of industrial management and presumably accustomed to dealing with risk in business ventures. Problem No. 5 concerns a businessman who must decide whether to build a factory in a country that may nationalize all foreign investments. It is not surprising that such subjects would attach a value of risk to such an item, although ordinary college students appear to attach to it a value of caution.

The line of reasoning just presented suggests that Brown's theory should be expanded so that the background of the subject as well as the nature of the problem is seen as determining the value given to a problem.

Group Size

The present study contains strong evidence that group size is positively related to the extent of the risky shift. A minimal risky shift was found in groups of size three, a moderate shift in groups of size four, and a large shift in groups of size five. This finding is compatible with the two major theories in this field: Brown can accommodate this finding by assuming that more arguments favoring the initial value of risk are brought out in a larger group; Wallach and Kogan, by asuming that a larger group permits greater spread

---

[7] This notion is really implicit in Brown's second mechanism, that the presentation of arguments favoring the value of risk moves people *toward* this value.

of responsibility. The latter interpretation might be called into question by our failure to find any differences between larger and smaller groups in the amount of responsibility felt for the group decision. However, this evidence is somewhat weak because the validity of our responsibility measure has not been been established, and it is quite possible that such a self-description is highly affected by social desirability considerations.

Though a statistically significant risky shift was not found for groups of three (condition II), it would probably be a mistake to assume that no shifts were taking place, because high (and in one case significant) positive correlations were found for this condition between initial risk and risky shift, just as in the other conditions. The nature of the effect in this condition is somewhat mystifying.

Theories of the Risky Shift

Taking an overview of the findings reported in this study. Brown's theory seems to come off better than that of Wallach and Kogan. The case made by the latter authors for the exclusive importance of emotional bonds generated in discussion seems clearly mistaken. While the importance which they give to diffusion of responsibility is not directly examined in this study, the irrelevance of this hypothesis to the findings about differences between decision problems is damaging In particular, the diffusion-of-responsibility hypothesis suffers by having no apparent relevance to the strong correlations that we found between initial risk and risky shift. On the other hand, Brown's value-of-risk theory clearly implies all of the findings in this study.

REFERENCES

BEM, D. J., WALLACH, M. A., and KOGAN, N. "Group Decision Making Under Risk of Aversive Consequences." *Journal of Personality and Social Psychology*, 1965, 1, 453–460.

BROWN, R. *Social Psychology*. New York: The Free Press, 1965.

HINDS, W. C. "Individual and Group Decisions in Gambling Situations." Unpublished master's thesis, Massachusetts Institute of Technology, School of Industrial Management, 1962.

KOGAN, N., and WALLACH, M. A. *Risk Taking: a Study in Cognition and Personality.* New York: Holt, Rinehart, and Winston, 1964.

KOGAN, N., and WALLACH, M. A. "Risk Taking as a Function of the Situation, the Person, and the Group." In *New Directions in Psychology III*. New York: Holt, Rinehart, and Winston, 1967.

MARQUIS, D. G. "Individual Responsibility and Group Decisions Involving Risk." *Industrial Management Review*, 1962, 3, 8–23.

NORDHØY, F. "Group Interaction in Decision-Making Under Risk." Unpublished master's thesis, Massachusetts Institute of Technology, School of Industrial Management, 1962.

STONER, J. A. F. "Comparison of Individual and Group Decisions Involving Risk." Unpublished master's thesis, Massachusetts Institute of Technology, School of Industrial Management, 1961.

WALLACH, M. A., and KOGAN, N. "Sex Differences and Judgment Processes." *Journal of Personality*, 1959, 27, 555–564.

WALLACH, M. A., and KOGAN, N. "Aspects of Judgment and Decision Making: Interrelationships and Changes with Age." *Behavioral Science*, 1961, 6, 23–36.

WALLACH, M. A., and KOGAN, N. "The Roles of Information, Discussion, and Consensus in Group Risk Taking." *Journal of Experimental Social Psychology*, 1965, 1, 1–19.

WALLACH, M. A., KOGAN, N., and BEM, D. J. "Group Influence on Individual Risk Taking." *Journal of Abnormal and Social Psychology*, 1962, 65, 75–86.

WALLACH, M. A., KOGAN, N., and BEM, D. J. "Diffusion of Responsibility and Level of Risk Taking in Groups." *Journal of Abnormal and Social Psychology*, 1964, 68, 263–274.

THE
CLASSIC
EXPERIMENTS

V

THE ASCH EXPERIMENT

EFFECTS OF GROUP PRESSURE
UPON THE MODIFICATION AND DISTORTION
OF JUDGMENTS*

S. E. Asch

We shall here describe in summary form the conception and first findings of a program of investigation into the conditions of independence and submission to group pressure. . . .

Our immediate object was to study the social and personal conditions that induce individuals to resist or to yield to group pressures when the latter are perceived to be *contrary to fact*. The issues which this problem raises are of obvious consequence for society; it can be of decisive importance whether or not a group will, under certain conditions, submit to existing pressures. Equally direct are the consequences for individuals and our understanding of them, since it is a decisive fact about a person whether he possesses the freedom to act independently, or whether he characteristically submits to group pressures.

The problem under investigation requires the direct observation of certain basic processes in the interaction between

individuals, and between individuals and groups. To clarify these seems necessary if we are to make fundamental advances in the understanding of the formation and reorganization of attitudes, of the functioning of public opinion, and of the operation of propaganda. Today we do not possess an adequate theory of these central psycho-social processes. Empirical investigation has been predominantly controlled by general propositions concerning group influence which have as a rule been assumed but not tested. With few exceptions investigation has relied upon descriptive formulations concerning the operation of suggestion and prestige, the inadequacy of which is becoming increasingly obvious, and upon schematic applications of stimulus-response theory.

The bibliography lists articles representative of the current theoretical and empirical situation. Basic to the current approach has been the axiom that group pressures characteristically induce psychological changes *arbitrarily*, in far-reaching disregard of the material properties of the given conditions. This mode of thinking has almost exclusively stressed the slavish submission of individuals to group forces, has neglected to inquire into their possibilities for independence and for productive

---

* S. E. Asch, "Effects of Group Pressure Upon the Modification and Distortion of Judgments," in *Groups, Leadership, and Men*, ed. H. Guetzkow (Pittsburgh: Carnegie Press Publishers, 1951), pp. 177–90. Reprinted by permission.

relations with the human environment, and has virtually denied the capacity of men under certain conditions to rise above group passion and prejudice. It was our aim to contribute to a clarification of these questions, important both for theory and for their human implications, by means of direct observation of the effects of groups upon the decisions and evaluations of individuals.

The Experiment and First Results

To this end we developed an experimental technique which has served as the basis for the present series of studies. We employed the procedure of placing an individual in a relation of radical conflict with all the other members of a group, of measuring its effect upon him in quantitative terms, and of describing its psychological consequences. A group of eight individuals was instructed to judge a series of simple, clearly structured perceptual relations—to match the length of a given line with one of three unequal lines. Each member of the group announced his judgments publicly. In the midst of this monotonous "test" one individual found himself suddenly contradicted by the entire group, and this contradiction was repeated again and again in the course of the experiment. The group in question had, with the exception of one member, previously met with the experimenter and received instructions to respond at certain points with wrong—and unanimous—judgments. The errors of the majority were large (ranging between ½″ and 1¾″) and of an order not encountered under control conditions. The outstanding person—the critical subject—whom we had placed in

the position of a *minority of one* in the midst of a *unanimous majority*—was the object of investigation. He faced, possibly for the first time in his life, a situation in which a group unanimously contradicted the evidence of his senses.

This procedure was the starting point of the investigation and the point of departure for the study of further problems. Its main features were the following: (1) The critical subject was submitted to two contradictory and irreconcilable forces— the evidence of his own experience of an utterly clear perceptual fact and the unanimous evidence of a group of equals. (2) Both forces were part of the immediate situation; the majority was concretely present, surrounding the subject physically. (3) The critical subject, who was requested together with all others to state his judgments publicly, was obliged to declare himself and to take a definite stand vis-à-vis the group. (4) The situation possessed a self-contained character. The critical subject could not avoid or evade the dilemma by reference to conditions external to the experimental situation. (It may be mentioned at this point that the forces generated by the given conditions acted so quickly upon the critical subjects that instances of suspicion were rare.)

The technique employed permitted a simple quantitative measure of the "majority effect" in terms of the frequency of errors in the direction of the distorted estimates of the majority. At the same time we were concerned from the start to obtain evidence of the ways in which the subjects perceived the group, to establish whether they became doubtful, whether they were tempted to join the majority. Most important, it was our object to establish the grounds of the subject's independence or yielding—whether, for example, the yielding subject was aware of the effect of the majority upon him, whether he abandoned his judgment deliberately or compulsively. To this end we constructed a comprehensive set of questions which served as the basis of an individual interview immediately following the experimental period. Toward the conclusion of the interview each subject was informed fully of the purpose of the experiment, of his role and of that of the majority. The reactions to the disclosure of the purpose of the experiment became in fact an integral part of the procedure. We may state here that the information derived from the interview became an indispen-

sable source of evidence and insight into the psychological structure of the experimental situation, and in particular, of the nature of the individual differences. Also, it is not justified or advisable to allow the subject to leave without giving him a full explanation of the experimental conditions. The experimenter has a responsibility to the subject to clarify his doubts and to state the reasons for placing him in the experimental situation. When this is done most subjects react with interest and many express gratification at having lived through a striking situation which has some bearing on wider human issues.

Both the members of the majority and the critical subjects were male college

Table 1

Lengths of Standard and Comparison Lines

Trials	Length of Standard Line (in inches)	Comparison Lines (in inches)			Correct Response	Group Response	Majority Error (in inches)
		1	2	3			
1	10	8¾	10	8	2	2	—
2	2	2	1	1½	1	1	—
3	3	3¾	4¼	3	3	1*	+¾
4	5	5	4	6½	1	2*	−1.0
5	4	3	5	4	3	3	—
6	3	3¾	4¼	3	3	2*	+1¼
7	8	6¼	8	6¾	2	3*	−1¼
8	5	5	4	6½	1	3*	+1½
9	8	6¼	8	6¾	2	1*	−1¾
10	10	8¾	10	8	2	2	—
11	2	2	1	1½	1	1	—
12	3	3¾	4¼	3	3	1*	+¾
13	5	5	4	6½	1	2*	−1.0
14	4	3	5	4	3	3	—
15	3	3¾	4¼	3	3	2*	+1¼
16	8	6¼	8	6¾	2	3*	−1¼
17	5	5	4	6½	1	3*	+1½
18	8	6¼	8	6¾	2	1*	−1¾

* Starred figures designate the erroneous estimates by the majority.

students. We shall report the results for a total of fifty critical subjects in this experiment. In Table 1 we summarize the successive comparison trials and the majority estimates.

1. There was a marked movement toward the majority. One-third of all the estimates in the critical group were errors identical with or in the direction of the distorted estimates of the majority. The significance of this finding becomes clear in the light of the virtual absence of errors in control groups the members of which recorded their estimates in writing. The relevant data of the critical and control groups are summarized in Table 2.

2. At the same time the effect of the

Table 2

DISTRIBUTION OF ERRORS IN EXPERIMENTAL AND CONTROL GROUPS

Number of Critical Errors	Critical Group* (N=50) F	Control Group (N=37) F
0	13	35
1	4	1
2	5	1
3	6	
4	3	
5	4	
6	1	
7	2	
8	5	
9	3	
10	3	
11	1	
12	0	
Total	50	37
Mean	3.84	0.08

* All errors in the critical group were in the direction of the majority estimates.

majority was far from complete. The preponderance of estimates in the critical group (68 per cent) was correct despite the pressure of the majority.

3. We found evidence of extreme individual differences. There were in the critical group subjects who remained independent without exception, and there were those who went nearly all the time with the majority. (The maximum possible number of errors was 12, while the actual range of errors was 0–11.) One-fourth of the critical subjects was completely independent; at the other extreme, one-third of the group displaced the estimates toward the majority in one-half or more of the trials.

The differences between the critical subjects in their reactions to the given conditions were equally striking. There were subjects who remained completely confident throughout. At the other extreme were those who became disoriented, doubt-ridden, and experienced a powerful impulse not to appear different from the majority.

For purposes of illustration we include a brief description of one independent and one yielding subject.

Independent

After a few trials he appeared puzzled, hesitant. He announced all disagreeing answers in the form of "Three, sir; two, sir"; not so with the unanimous answers. At trial 4 he answered immediately after the first member of the group, shook his head, blinked, and whispered to his neighbor: "Can't help it, that's one." His later answers came in a whispered voice, accompanied by a deprecating smile. At one point he grinned embarrassedly, and whispered explosively to his neighbor: "I always disagree—darn it" During the questioning, this subject's constant refrain was: "I called them as I saw them, sir." He insisted that his estimates were right without, however, committing himself as to whether the others were wrong, remarking that "that's the way I see them and that's the way they see them." If he had to make a practical decision under similar circumstances, he declared, "I would follow my own view, though part of my reason would tell me that I might be wrong." Immediately following the experiment the majority engaged this subject in a brief discussion. When they pressed him to say whether the entire group was wrong and he alone right, he turned upon them defiantly, exclaiming: "You're *probably* right, but you may be wrong!" To the disclosure of the experiment this subject reacted with the statement that he felt "exultant and relieved," adding, "I do not deny that at times I had the feeling: 'to heck with it, I'll go along with the rest.'"

Yielding

This subject went with the majority in 11 out of 12 trials. He appeared nervous and somewhat confused, but he did not attempt to evade discussion; on the contrary, he was helpful and tried to answer to the best of his ability. He opened the discussion with the statement: "If I'd been the first I probably would have responded differently"; this was his way of stating that he had adopted the majority estimates. The primary factor in his case was loss of confidence. He perceived the majority as a decided group, acting without hesitation: "If they had been doubt-

ful I probably would have changed, but they answered with such confidence." Certain of his errors, he explained, were due to the doubtful nature of the comparisons; in such instances he went with the majority. When the object of the experiment was explained, the subject volunteered: "I suspected about the middle—but tried to push it out of my mind." It is of interest that his suspicion was not able to restore his confidence and diminish the power of the majority. Equally striking is his report that he assumed the experiment to involve an "illusion" to which the others, but not he, were subject. This assumption too did not help to free him; on the contrary, he acted as if his divergence from the majority was a sign of defect. The principal impression this subject produced was of one so caught up by immediate difficulties that he lost clear reasons for his actions, and could make no reasonable decisions.

A FIRST ANALYSIS OF INDIVIDUAL DIFFERENCES

On the basis of the interview data described earlier, we undertook to differentiate and describe the major forms of reaction to the experimental situation, which we shall now briefly summarize.

Among the *independent* subjects we distinguished the following main categories:

(1) Independence based on *confidence* in one's perception and experience. The most striking characteristic of these subjects is the vigor with which they withstand the group opposition. Though they are sensitive to the group, and experience the conflict, they show a resilience in coping with it, which is expressed in their continuing reliance on their perception

shake off the oppressive group opposition. and the effectiveness with which they

(2) Quite different are those subjects who are independent and *withdrawn*. These do not react in a spontaneously emotional way, but rather on the basis of explicit principles concerning the necessity of being an individual.

(3) A third group of independent subjects manifest considerable tension and *doubt*, adhere to their judgments on the basis of a felt necessity to deal adequately with the task.

The following were the main categories of reaction among the *yielding* subjects, or those who went with the majority during one-half or more of the trials.

(1) *Distortion of perception* under the stress of group pressure. In this category belong a very few subjects who yield completely, but are not aware that their estimates have been displaced or distorted by the majority. These subjects report that they came to perceive the majority estimates as correct.

(2) *Distortion of judgment.* Most submitting subjects belong to this category. The factor of greatest importance in this group is a decision the subjects reach that their perceptions are inaccurate, and that those of the majority are correct. These subjects suffer from primary doubt and lack of confidence; on this basis they feel a strong tendency to join the majority.

(3) *Distortion of action.* The subjects in this group do not suffer a modification of perception nor do they conclude that they are wrong. They yield because of an overmastering need not appear different from or inferior to others, because of an inability to tolerate the appearance of defectiveness in the eyes of the group. These subjects suppress their observations and voice the majority position with awareness of what they are doing.

The results are sufficient to establish that independence and yielding are not psychologically homogeneous, that submission to group pressure (and freedom from pressure) can be the result of different psychological conditions. It should also be noted that the categories described above, being based exclusively on the subjects' reactions to the experimental conditions, are descriptive, not presuming to explain why a given individual responded in one way rather than another. The further exploration of the basis for the individual differences is a separate task upon which we are now at work.

EXPERIMENTAL VARIATIONS

The results described are clearly a joint function of two broadly different sets of conditions. They are determined first by the specifis external conditions, by the particular character of the relation between social evidence and one's own experience. Second, the presence of pronounced individual differences points to the important role of personal factors, of factors connected with the individual's character structure. We reasoned that there are group conditions which would produce independence in all subjects, and that there probably are group conditions which would induce intensified yielding in many, though not in all. Accordingly we followed the procedure of *experimental variation*, systematically altering the quality of social evidence by means of systematic variation of group conditions. Secondly, we deemed it reasonable to assume that behavior under the experimental social pressure is significantly related to certain basic, relatively permanent characteristics of the individual. The investigation has moved in both of these directions. Because the study of the character-qualities which may be functionally connected with independence and yielding is still in progress, we shall limit the present account to a sketch of the representative experimental variations.

The Effect of Nonunanimous Majorities

Evidence obtained from the basic experiment suggested that the condition of being exposed *alone* to the opposition of a "compact majority" may have played a decisive role in determining the course and strength of the effects observed. Accordingly we undertook to investigate in a series of successive variations the effects of *nonunanimous* majorities. The technical problem of altering the uniformity of a majority is, in terms of our procedure, relatively simple. In most instances we merely directed one or more members of the instructed group to deviate from the majority in prescribed ways. It is obvious that we cannot hope to compare the performance of the same individual in two situations on the assumption that they remain independent of one another. At best we can investigate the effect of an earlier upon a later experimental condition. The comparison of different experimental situations therefore requires the use of different but comparable groups of critical subjects. This is the procedure we have followed. In the variations to be described we have maintained the conditions of the basic experiment (*e.g.*, the sex of the subjects, the size of the majority, the content of the task, and so on) save for the specific factor that was varied. The following were some of the variations we studied:

1. *The presence of a "true partner."* (a) In the midst of the majority were *two* naive, critical subjects. The subjects were separated spatially, being seated in the fourth and eighth positions, respectively. Each therefore heard his judgment confirmed by one other person (provided the other person remained independent), one prior to, the other subsequently to announcing his own judgment. In addition, each experienced a break in the unanimity of the majority. There were six pairs of critical subjects. (b) In a further variation the "partner" to the critical subject was a member of the group who had been instructed to respond correctly throughout. This procedure permits the exact control of the partner's responses. The partner was always seated in the fourth position; he therefore announced his estimates in each case before the critical subject.

The results clearly demonstrate that a disturbance of the unanimity of the majority markedly increased the independence of the critical subjects. The frequency of pro-majority errors dropped to 10.4 per cent of the total number of estimates in variation (a), and to 5.5 per cent in variation (b). These results are to be compared with the frequency of yielding to the unanimous majorities in the basic experiment, which was 32 per cent of the total number of estimates. It is clear that the presence in the field of *one other* individual who responded correctly was sufficient to deplete the power of the majority, and in some cases to destroy it. This finding is all the more striking in the light of other variations which demonstrate the effect of even small minorities provided they are unanimous. Indeed, we have been able to show that a unanimous majority of three is, under the given conditions, far more effective than a majority of eight containing one dissenter. That critical subjects will under these conditions free themselves of a majority of seven and join forces with one other person in the minority is, we believe, a result significant for theory. It points to a fundamental psychological difference between the condition of being alone and having a minimum of human support. It further demonstrates that the effects obtained are not the result of a summation of influences proceeding from each member of the group; it is necessary to conceive the results as being relationally determined.

2. *Withdrawal of a "true partner."* What will be the effect of providing the critical subject with a partner who responds correctly and then withdrawing him? The critical subject started with a partner who responded correctly. The partner was a member of the majority who had been instructed to respond correctly and to "desert" to the majority in the middle of the experiment. This procedure permits the observation of the same subject in the course of transition from one condition to another. The withdrawal of the partner produced a powerful and unexpected result. We had assumed that the critical subject, having gone through the experience of opposing the majority with a minimum of support, would maintain his independence when alone. Contrary to this expectation, we found that the experience of having had and then lost a partner restored the majority effect to its full force, the proportion of errors rising to 28.5 per cent of all judgments, in contrast to the preceding level of 5.5 per cent. Further experimentation is needed to establish whether the critical subjects were responding to the sheer fact of being alone, or to the fact that the partner abandoned them.

3. *Late arrival of a "true partner."* The critical subject started as a minority of one in the midst of a unanimous majority. Toward the conclusion of the experiment

one member of the majority "broke" away and began announcing correct estimates. This procedure, which reverses the order of conditions of the preceding experiment, permits the observation of the transition from being alone to being a member of a pair against a majority. It is obvious that those critical subjects who were independent when alone would continue to be so when joined by another partner. The variation is therefore of significance primarily for those subjects who yielded during the first phase of the experiment. The appearance of the late partner exerts a freeing effect, reducing the level to 8.7 per cent. Those who had previously yielded also bcame markedly more independent, but not completely so, continuing to yield more than previously independent subjects. The reports of the subjects do not cast much light on the factors responsible for the result. It is our impression that having once committed himself to yielding, the individual finds it difficult and painful to change his direction. To do so is tantamount to a public admission that he has not acted rightly. He therefore follows the precarious course he has already chosen in order to maintain an outward semblance of consistency and conviction.

4. *The presence of a "compromise partner."* The majority was consistently extremist, always matching the standard with the most unequal line. One instructed subject (who, as in the other variations, preceded the critical subject) also responded incorrectly, but his estimates were always intermediate between the truth and the majority position. The critical subject therefore faced an extremist majority whose unanimity was broken by one more moderately erring person. Under these conditions the frequency of

errors was reduced but not significantly. However, the lack of unanimity determined in a strikingly consistent way the *direction* of the errors. The preponderance of the errors, 75.7 per cent of the total, was moderate, whereas in a parallel experiment in which the majority was unanimously extremist (*i.e.*, with the "compromise" partner excluded), the incidence of moderate errors was reduced to 42 per cent of the total. As might be expected, in a unanimously moderate majority, the errors of the critical subjects were without exception moderate.

The Role of Majority Size

To gain further understanding of the majority effect, we varied the size of the majority in several different variations. The majorities, which were in each case unanimous, consisted of 16, 8, 4, 3, and 2 persons, respectively. In addition, we studied the limiting case in which the critical subject was opposed by one instructed subject. Table III contains the means and the range of errors under each condition.

With the opposition reduced to one, the majority effect all but disappeared. When the opposition proceeded from a group of two, it produced a measurable though small distortion, the errors being 12.8 per cent of the total number of estimates. The effect appeared in full force with a majority of three. Larger majorities of four, eight, and sixteen did not produce effects greater than a majority of three.

The effect of a majority is often silent, revealing little of its operation to the subject, and often hiding it from the experimenter. To examine the range of effects it is capable of inducing, decisive variations of conditions are necessary. An indication of one effect is furnished by the following variation in which the conditions of the basic experiment were simply reversed. Here the majority, consisting of a group of sixteen, was naive; in the midst of it we placed a single individual who responded wrongly according to instructions. Under these conditions the members of the naive majority reacted to the lone dissenter with amusement and disdain. Contagious laughter spread through the group at the droll minority of one. Of significance is the fact that the members lack awareness that they draw their strength from the majority, and that their reactions would change radically if they faced the dissenter individually. In fact, the attitude of derision in the majority turns to seriousness and increased respect as soon as the minority is increased to three. These observations demonstrate the role of social support as a source of power

Table 3

ERRORS OF CRITICAL SUBJECTS WITH UNANIMOUS MAJORITIES
OF DIFFERENT SIZE

Size of majority	Control	1	2	3	4	8	16
N	37	10	15	10	10	50	12
Mean number of errors	0.08	0.03	1.53	4.0	4.20	3.84	3.75
Range of errors	0–2	0–1	0–5	1–12	0–11	0–11	0–10

and stability, in contrast to the preceding investigations which stressed the effects of withdrawal of social support, or to be more exact, the effects of social opposition. Both aspects must be explicitly considered in a unified formulation of the effects of group conditions on the formation and change of judgments.

The Role of the Stimulus-Situation

It is obviously not possible to divorce the quality and course of the group forces which act upon the individual from the specific stimulus-conditions. Of necessity the structure of the situation moulds the group forces and determines their direction as well as their strength. Indeed, this was the reason that we took pains in the investigations described above to center the issue between the individual and the group around an elementary and fundamental matter of fact. And there can be no doubt that the resulting reactions were directly a function of the contradiction between the objectively grasped relations and the majority position.

These general considerations are sufficient to establish the need of varying the stimulus-conditions and of observing their effect on the resulting group forces. We are at present conducting a series of investigations in which certain aspects of the stimulus-situation are systematically altered.

One of the dimensions we are examining is the magnitude of discrepancies above the threshold. Our technique permits an easy variation of this factor, since we can increase or decrease at will the deviation of the majority from the given objective conditions. Hitherto we have studied the effect of a relatively moderate range of discrepancies. Within the limits of our procedure we find that different magnitudes of discrepancy produce approximately the same amount of yielding. However, the quality of yielding alters: as the majority becomes more extreme, there occurs a significant increase in the frequency of "compromise" errors. Further experiments are planned in which the discrepancies in question will be extremely large and small.

We have also varied systematically the structural clarity of the task, including in separate variations judgments based on mental standards. In agreement with other investigators, we find that the majority effect grows stronger as the situation diminishes in clarity. Concurrently, however, the disturbance of the subjects and the conflict-quality of the situation decrease markedly. We consider it of significance that the majority achieves its most pronounced effect when it acts most painlessly.

SUMMARY

We have investigated the effects upon individuals of majority opinions when the latter were seen to be in a direction contrary to fact. By means of a simple technique we produced a radical divergence between a majority and a minority, and observed the ways in which individuals coped with the resulting difficulty. Despite the stress of the given conditions, a substantial proportion of individuals retained their independence throughout. At the same time a substantial minority yielded, modifying their judgments in accordance with the majority. Independence and yielding are a joint function of the following major factors: (1) The character of the stimulus situation. Variations in structural clarity have a decisive effect: with diminishing clarity of the stimulus-conditions the majority effect increases. (2) The character of the group forces. Individuals are highly sensitive to the structural qualities of group opposition. In particular, we demonstrated the great importance of the factor of unanimity. Also, the majority effect is a function of the size of group opposition. (3) The character of the individual. There were wide, and indeed, striking differences among individuals within the same experimental situation. The hypothesis was proposed that these are functionally dependent on relatively enduring character differences, in particular those pertaining to the person's social relations.

BIBLIOGRAPHY

ASCH, S. E. "Studies in the Principles of Judgments and Attitudes: II. Determination of Judgments by Group and by Ego-Standards." *J. Soc. Psychol.*, 1940, 12, 433–465.

———. "The Doctrine of Suggestion, Prestige and Imitation in Social Psychology." *Psychol. Rev.*, 1948, 55, 250–276.

ASCH, S. E., BLOCK, H., and HERTZMAN, M. "Studies in the Principles of Judgments and Attitudes. I. Two Basic Principles of Judgment." *J. Psychol.*, 1938, 5, 219–251.

COFFIN, E. E. "Some Conditions of Suggestion and Suggestibility: A Study of Certain Attitudinal and Situational Factors Influencing the Process of Suggestion." *Psychol. Monogr.*, 1941, 53, No. 4.

LEWIS, H. B. "Studies in the Principles of Judgments and Attitudes: IV. The Operation of Prestige Suggestion." *J. Soc. Psychol.*, 1941, 14, 229–256.

LORGE, I. "Prestige, Suggestion, and Attitudes." *J. Soc. Psychol.*, 1936, 7, 386–402.

MILLER, N. E. and DOLLARD, J. *Social Learning and Imitation.* New Haven: Yale University Press, 1941.

MOORE, H. T. "The Comparative Influence of Majority and Expert Opinion." *Amer. J. Psychol.*, 1921, 32, 16–20.

SHERIF, M. "A Study of Some Social Factors in Perception." *Arch. Psychol.*, N.Y., 1935, No. 187.

THORNDIKE, E. L. *The Psychology of Wants, Interests, and Attitudes.* New York: D. Appleton-Century Company, Inc., 1935.

A STUDY OF NORMATIVE
AND INFORMATIONAL SOCIAL INFLUENCES
UPON INDIVIDUAL JUDGMENT*

Morton Deutsch and Harold B. Gerard

By now, many experimental studies (e.g., 1, 3, 6) have demonstrated that individual psychological processes are subject to social influences. Most investigators, however, have not distinguished among different kinds of social influences; rather, they have carelessly used the term "group" influence to characterize the impact of many different kinds of social factors. In fact, a review of the major experiments in this area—e.g., those by Sherif (6), Asch (1), Bovard (3)—would indicate that the subjects (Ss) in these experiments as they made their judgments were *not* functioning as *members* of a group in any simple or obvious manner. The S, in the usual experiment in this area, made perceptual judgments in the physical presence of others after hearing their judgments. Typically, the S was *not* given experimental instructions which made him feel that he was a member of a group faced with a common task requiring cooperative effort for its most effective solution. If

"group" influences were at work in the foregoing experiments, they were subtly and indirectly created rather than purposefully created by the experimenter.

HYPOTHESES

The purpose of this paper is to consider two types of social influence, "normative" and "informational," which we believe were operative in the experiments mentioned above, and to report the results of an experiment bearing upon hypotheses that are particularly relevant to the former influence. We shall define a *normative social influence* as an influence to conform with the positive expectations[1] of another.[2] An *informational social influence* may be

---

* Morton Deutsch and Harold B. Gerard, "A Study of Normative and Informational Social Influences upon Individual Judgment," *Journal of Abnormal and Social Psychology*, 51 (1955), 629–36. Copyright 1955 by the American Psychological Association, and reproduced by permission.

[1] By positive expectations we mean to refer to those expectations whose fulfillment by another leads to or reinforces positive rather than negative feelings, and whose nonfulfillment leads to the opposite, to alienation rather than solidarity; conformity to negative expectations, on the other hand, leads to or reinforces negative rather than positive feelings.

[2] The term *another* is being used inclusively to refer to "another person," to a "group," or to one's "self." Thus, a normative social influence can result from the expectations of oneself, or of a group, or of another person.

defined as an influence to accept information obtained from another as *evidence* about reality. Commonly these two types of influence are found together. However, it is possible to conform behaviorally with the expectations of others and say things which one disbelieves but which agree with the beliefs of others. Also, it is possible that one will accept an opponent's beliefs as evidence about reality even though one has no motivation to agree with him, per se.

Our hypotheses are particularly relevant to normative social influence upon individual judgment. We shall not elaborate the theoretical rationales for the hypotheses, since they are for the most part obvious and they follow from other theoretical writings (e.g., 4, 5).

Hypothesis I

Normative social influence upon individual judgments will be greater among individuals forming a group than among an aggregation of individuals who do not compose a group.[3]

------

[3] Generally one would also expect that group members would be more likely to take the judgments of other group members as trustworthy evidence for forming judgments about reality and, hence, they would be more susceptible to informational social influence than would nongroup members. The greater trustworthiness usually reflects more experience of the reliability of the judgments of other members and more confidence in the benevolence of their motivations. However, when group members have had no prior experience together and when it is apparent in both the group and nongroup situations that the others are motivated and in a position to report correct judgments, there is no reason to expect differential susceptibility to informational social influence among group and nongroup members.

That is, even when susceptibility to informational social influence is equated, we would predict that the greater susceptibility to normative social influence among group members would be reflected in the greater group influence upon individual judgment. This is not to say that individuals, even when they are not group members, may not have some motivation to conform to the expectations of others— e.g., so as to ingratiate themselves or so as to avoid ridicule.

Hypothesis II

Normative social influence upon individual judgment will be reduced when the individual perceives that his judgment cannot be identified or, more generally, when the individual perceives no pressure to conform to the judgment of others.

Hypothesis III

Normative social influence to conform to one's own judgment will reduce the impact of the normative social influence to conform to the judgment of others.

Hypothesis IV

Normative social influence to conform to one's own judgment from another as well as from oneself will be stronger than normative social influence from oneself.

Normative social influence from oneself to conform to one's own judgment may be thought of as an internalized social process in which the individual holds expectations with regard to his own behavior; conforming to positive self-expectations leads to feelings of self-esteem or self-approval while nonconformity leads to feelings of anxiety or guilt. In general, one would expect that the strength of these internalized self-expectations would reflect the individual's prior experiences with them as sources of need satisfaction —e.g., by conforming to his own judgments or by self-reliance he has won approval from such significant others as his parents. As Hypothesis IV indicates, we believe that contemporaneous social pressure to conform to one's own judgment may supplement, and perhaps be even stronger than, the individual's internalized pressure to conform to his own judgment.

Two additional hypotheses, dealing with the effect of difficulty of judgment, are relevant to one of the experimental variations. They follow:

Hypothesis V

The more uncertain the individual is about the correctness of his judgment, the more likely he is to be susceptible to both normative and informational social influences in making his judgment.

Hypothesis VI

The more uncertain the individual is about the correctness of the judgment of others, the less likely he is to be susceptible to informational social influence in making his judgment.[4]

---

[4] Although we have no data relevant to this hypothesis, we present it to qualify Hypothesis V and to counteract an assumption in some of the current social psychological literature. Thus, Festinger (5) has written that where no physical reality basis exists for the establishment of the validity of one's belief, one is dependent upon social reality (i.e., upon the beliefs of others). Similarly, Asch (2) has indicated that group influence grows stronger as the judgmental situation diminishes in clarity. The

METHOD

Subjects. One hundred and one college students from psychology courses at New York University were employed as *S*s. The study was defined for the *S*s as an experimental study of perception.

Procedure. We employed the experimental situation developed by Asch (1) with certain modifications and variations which are specified below. For detailed descriptions of the procedures utilized by Asch and replicated in this experiment, Asch's publication should be consulted. The basic features of the Asch situation are: (*a*) the *S*s are instructed that they are participating in a perceptual experiment, wherein they have to match accurately the length of a given line with one of three lines; (*b*) correct judgments are easy to make; (*c*) in each experimental session there is only one *naive S*, the other participants, while ostensibly *S*s, are in fact "stooges" who carry out the experimenter's instructions; (*d*) each participant (i.e., the naive *S* and the stooges) has to indicate his judgments publicly; (*e*) on 12 of the 18 perceptual judgments the stooges announce wrong

---

implication of Hypothesis VI is that if an individual perceives that a situation is objectively difficult to judge—that others as well as he experience the situation in the same way (i.e., as being difficult and as having uncertainty about their judgments)—he will not trust their judgments any more than he trusts his own. It is only as his confidence in their judgments increases (e.g., because he deems that agreement among three uncertain judges provides more reliable evidence than one uncertain judge) that the judgments of others will have informational social influence. However (at any particular level of confidence in the judgment of others), one can predict that as his confidence in his own judgment decreases he will be more susceptible to normative social influence. With decreasing self-confidence there is likely to be less of a commitment to one's own judgment and, hence, less influence not to conform to the judgments of others.

and unanimous judgments, the errors of the stooges are large and clearly in error; (*f*) the naive *S* and the stooges are in a face-to-face relationship and have been previously acquainted with one another.[5]

To test the hypotheses set forth in the foregoing section, the following experimental

------

[5] Inspection of the Asch situation would suggest that informational social influence would be strongly operative. As Asch has put it (2, p. 461):

> The subject knows (a) that the issue is one of fact; (b) that a correct result is possible; (c) that only one result is correct; (d) that the others and he are oriented to and reporting about the same objectively given relations (e) that the group is in unanimous opposition at certain points with him.

He further perceives that the others are motivated to report a correct judgment. In such a situation, the subject's accumulated past experience would lead him to expect that he could rely on the judgments of others, especially if they all agreed. That is, even if his eyes were closed he might feel that he could safely risk his life on the assumption that the unanimous judgments of the others were correct. This is a strong informational social influence and one would expect it to be overriding except for the fact that the subject has his eyes open and receives information from a source which he also feels to be completely trustworthy—i.e., from his own perceptual apparatus. The subject is placed in strong conflict because the evidences from two sources of trustworthy information are in opposition.

In the Asch situation, it is apparent that, in addition to informational social influence, normative social influence is likely to be operating. The naive *S* is in a face-to-face situation with acquaintances and he may be motivated to conform to their judgments in order to avoid being ridiculed, or being negatively evaluated, or even possibly out of a sense of obligation. While it may be impossible to remove completely the impact of normative social influence upon any socialized being, it is evident that the Asch situation allows much opportunity for this type of influence to operate.

variations upon Asch's situation were employed:

1. *The face-to-face situation.* This was an exact replication of Asch's situation except for the following minor modifications: (*a*) Only three stooges, rather than eight, were employed;[6] (*b*) the *S* and the stooges were unacquainted prior to the experiment; and (*c*) two series of 18 judgments were employed. In one series (the visual series), the lines were physically present when the *S* and the stooges announced their judgments; in the other series (the memory series), the lines were removed before any one announced his judgment. In the memory series, approximately three seconds after the lines were removed the first stooge was asked to announce his judgment. The sequences of visual and memory series were alternated so that approximately half the *S*s had the memory series first and half had the visual series first.

2. *The anonymous situation.* This situation was identical with the face-to-face situation except for the following differences: (*a*) Instead of sitting in the visual presence of each other, the *S*s were separated by partitions which prevented them from talking to each other or seeing one another; (*b*) Instead of announcing their judgments by voice, the *S*s indicated their judgments by pressing a button; (*c*) No stooges were employed. Each *S* was led to believe he was Subject No. 3, and the others were No. 1, No. 2, and No. 4. He was told that when the experimenter called out "Subject No. 3" he was to indicate his judgment by pressing one of three buttons (A, B, or C) which corresponded to what he thought the correct line was. When an *S* pressed a given button, a corresponding bulb lit on his own panel and on a hidden master panel. Presumably the appropriate bulb also lit on the panels of each of the other *S*s, but, in fact, the bulbs on any *S*'s panel were not connected to the buttons

------

[6] Asch found that three stooges were about as effective in influencing the *S*s as eight.

of the other *S*s. When the experimenter called for the judgments of Subject No. 1, of Subject No. 2, and of Subject No. 4, a concealed accomplice manipulated master switches which lit bulbs on each of the *S*'s panels that corresponded to judgments presumably being made by these respective *S*s. Subjects No. 1, No. 2, and No. 4 were, in effect, "electrical stooges" whose judgments were indicated on the panels of the four naive *S*s (all of whom were Subject No. 3) by an accomplice of the experimenter who manipulated master switches controlling the lights on the panels of the naive *S*s. The pattern of judgments followed by the "electrical stooges" was the same as that followed by the "live stooges" in the face-to-face situation. (*d*) In providing a rationale for being labeled Subject No. 3 for each of the naive *S*s, we explained that due to the complicated wiring setup, the *S*'s number had no relation to his seating position. Implicitly, we assumed that each *S* would realize that it would be impossible for the others to identify that a judgment was being made by him rather than by any of two others. However, it is apparent from postexperiment questionnaires that many of the *S*s did not realize this. It seems likely that if we had made the anonymous character of the judgments clear and explicit to the *S*s, the effects of this experimental variation would have been even more marked.

3. *The group situation.* This situation was identical to the anonymous situation except that the subjects were instructed as follows:

This group is one of twenty similar groups who are participating in this experiment. We want to see how accurately you can make judgments. We are going to give a reward to the five best groups— the five groups that make the fewest errors on the series of judgments that you are given. The reward will be a pair of tickets to a Broadway play of your own choosing for each member of the winning group. An error will be counted any time one of you makes an incorrect judgment. That is, on any given card the group can make as many as four errors if you each judge incorrectly or you can make no errors if you

each judge correctly. The five groups that make the best scores will be rewarded.

4. *The self-commitment variation.* This variation was employed in both the face-to-face and anonymous situations. In it, each *S* was given a sheet of paper on which to write down his judgment before he was exposed to the judgments of the others. He was told not to sign the sheet of paper and that it would not be collected at the end of the experiment. After the first series of 18 judgments, the *S*s threw away their sheets. The *S*s did not erase their recorded judgments after each trial as they did in the Magic Pad self-commitment variation.

4A. *The Magic Pad self-commitment variation.* This variation was employed in the anonymous situation. In it, each *S* was given a Magic Writing Pad on which to write down his judgment before he was exposed to the judgments of the others. After each *S* had been exposed to the judgment of the others and had indicated his own judgment, he erased his judgment on the Magic Writing Pad by lifting up the plastic covering. It was made convincingly clear to the *S* that only he would ever know what he had written down on the pad.

5. *The public commitment variation.* This variation was employed in both the face-to-face situation and in the anonymous situation. In it, the *S*s followed the same procedure as in the self-commitment variation except that they wrote down their initial judgments on sheets of paper which they signed and which they knew were to be handed to the experimenter after each series of 18 judgments.

RESULTS

The primary data used in the analysis of the results are the errors made by the *S*s which were in the direction of the errors made by the stooges. We shall present first the data which are relevant to our hypotheses; later we shall present other information.

Hypothesis I

The data relevant to the first hypothesis are presented in Table 1. The table presents a comparison of the anonymous situation in which the individuals were motivated to act as a group with the anonymous situation in which there was no direct attempt to induce membership motivation; in both situations, no self or public commitment was made. The data provide strong support for the prediction that the normative social influence upon individual judgments will be greater among individuals forming a group than among individuals who do not compose a group. The average member of the group made more than twice as many errors as the comparable individual who did not

participate in the task as a member of a group.

Qualitative data from a postexperimental questionnaire, in which we asked the S to describe any feelings he had about himself or about the others during the experiment, also support Hypothesis I. Seven out of the fifteen Ss in the "group" condition spontaneously mentioned a felt obligation to the other group members; none of the individuals in the nongroup condition mentioned any feeling of obligation to go along with the others.

Hypothesis II

To test the second hypothesis, it is necessary to compare the data from the

Table 1

MEAN NUMBER OF SOCIALLY INFLUENCED ERRORS IN INDIVIDUAL
JUDGMENT AMONG GROUP MEMBERS AND AMONG NONMEMBERS

Experimental Treatment	N	Memory Series	Visual Series	Total
Group, anonymous, no commitment	15	6.87	5.60	12.47
Nongroup, anonymous, no commitment	13	3.15	2.77	5.92
			p values*	
		.01	.05	.001

* Based on a *t* test, using one tail of the distribution.

Table 2

MEAN NUMBER OF SOCIALLY INFLUENCED ERRORS IN INDIVIDUAL JUDGMENT
IN THE ANONYMOUS AND IN THE FACE-TO-FACE SITUATIONS

Situation	No Commitment				Self-Commitment				Public Commitment			
	Visual	Memory	Total	N	Visual	Memory	Total	N	Visual	Memory	Total	N
Face-to-face	3.00	4.03	7.03	13	.92	.75	1.67	12	1.13	1.39	2.52	13
Anonymous	2.77	3.15	5.92	13	.64	.73	1.37	11	.92	.46	1.38	13

face-to-face and anonymous situations among the individuals who were otherwise exposed to similar experimental treatments. Tables 2 and 3 present the relevant data. It is apparent that there was less social influence upon individual judgment in the anonymous as compared with the face-to-face situation. This lessening of social influence is at the .001 level of statistical confidence even when the comparisons include the "commitment variations" as well as both the visual and the memory series of judgments. The interaction between the commitment variations and the anonymous, face-to-face variations, which is statistically significant, is such as to reduce the over-all differences

Table 3

p VALUES* FOR VARIOUS COMPARISONS OF SOCIALLY INFLUENCED ERRORS IN THE ANONYMOUS AND FACE-TO-FACE SITUATIONS

Comparison	Total Errors
A vs. F	.001
A vs. F, no commitment	.001
A vs. F, self-commitment	.10
A vs. F, public commitment	.001
Interaction of commitment with A-F	.01

* p values are based on t tests, using one tail of distribution, derived from analyses of variation.

Table 4

p VALUES* FOR VARIOUS COMPARISONS OF SOCIALLY INFLUENCED ERRORS IN THE DIFFERENT COMMITMENT TREATMENTS

Comparison	Total Errors	Errors on Visual Series	Errors on Memory Series
No commitment vs. public commiment, F	.001	.01	.001
No commitment vs. self-commitment, F	.001	.01	.001
Self-commitment vs. public commitment, F	.01	NS	NS
No commitment vs. self-commitment, A	.001	.01	.01
No commitment vs. public commitment, A	.001	.01	.002
Self-commitment vs. public commitment, A	NS	NS	NS

* p values are based on t tests, using one tail of the distribution, and derived from the analyses of variation.

Table 5

MEAN NUMBER OF SOCIALLY INFLUENCED ERRORS IN JUDGMENTS IN THE ANONYMOUS SITUATION AS AFFECTED BY THE COMMITMENT VARIATIONS

No Commitment				Magic Pad Self-Commitment				Self-Commitment				Public Commitment			
Visual	Mem-ory	Total	N	Visual	Mem-ory	Total	N	Visual	Mem-ory	Total	N	Visual	Mem-ory	Total	N
2.77	3.15	5.92	13	1.63	2.27	3.90	11	.64	.73	1.37	11	.92	.46	1.38	13

between the anonymous and face-to-face situation; the differences between the face-to-face and the anonymous situations are most strongly brought out when there is no commitment. Similarly, if we compare the anonymous and face-to-face situations, employing the memory rather than the visual series, the effect of the normative influence upon judgments in the face-to-face situation is increased somewhat, but not significantly. That is, as we eliminate counter-normative influences (i.e., the "commitment") and as we weaken reality restraints (i.e., employ the "memory" rather than "visual" series), the normative influences in the face-to-face situation operate more freely.

The support for Hypothesis II is particularly striking in light of the fact that, due to faulty experimental procedure, the "anonymous" character of the anonymous situation was not sufficiently impressed on some of the Ss. For these Ss, the anonymous situation merely protected them from the immedite, visually accessible pressure to conform arising from the lifted eyebrows and expressions of amazement by the stooges in the face-to-face situation. Complete feeling of anonymity would probably have strengthened the results.

Hypotheses III and IV

Tables 4, 5, and 6 present results showing the influence of the different commitment variations. The public and the self-commitment variations markedly reduce the socially influenced errors in both the face-to-face and anonymous situations. In other words, the data provide strong support for Hypothesis III which asserts that normative social influence to conform to one's own judgment will reduce the impact of the normative influence to conform to the judgment of others.

The data with regard to the influence of self-commitment are ambiguous in implication since the results of the two self-commitment variations—i.e., the "Magic Pad self-commitment" and the "self-commitment—are not the same. The first self-commitment variation produced results which are essentially the same as the public commitment variation, markedly reducing socially influenced errors. The Magic Pad self-commitment variation produced results which were different from the no commitment variation, reducing the errors to an extent which is statistically significant; however, unlike the first self-commitment variation, the Magic Pad self-commitment was significantly less effective than the public commitment in reducing socially influenced errors.

Our hunch is that the Ss in the first self-commitment variation perceived the commitment situation as though it were a public commitment and that this is the explanation of the lack of differences between these two variations. That is, writing their judgments indelibly supported the belief that "others can see what I have written." The Ss in the Magic Pad self-commitment variation, on the other hand, were literally wiping their initial judgments away in such a manner that they would be inaccessible to anyone. Hence, in the Magic Pad variation, the normative influences to conform to one's own judgment had to be sustained by the S himself. Normative influences from the S's self (to be, in a sense, true to himself) were undoubtedly also operating in the noncommitment variation. What the Magic Pad did was to prevent the S from distorting his recollection of his independent judgment after being exposed to the judgments of the others. Further, there is a theoretical basis for assuming that the commitment to a judgment or

Table 6

p VALUES* FOR VARIOUS COMPARISONS OF SOCIALLY INFLUENCED
ERRORS IN THE DIFFERENT COMMITMENT VARIATIONS

Comparison	Total Errors	Errors on Visual Series	Errors on Memory Series
No commitment vs. Magic Pad self-commitment	.05	NS	NS
Magic Pad self-commitment vs. self-commitment	.005	NS	.05
Magic Pad self-commitment vs. public commitment	.001	NS	.01

* *p* values are based on *t* tests using one tail of the distribution.

decision is increased following the occurrence of behavior based upon it. Hence, the behavior of writing one's judgment down on the Magic Pad makes the original decision less tentative and less subject to change. However, it is apparent that this internally sustained influence to conform with one's own judgment was not as strong as the combination of external and self-motivated influences. These results support our fourth hypothesis.

Hypothesis V

Table 7 presents a comparison of the errors made on the visual and on the memory series of judgments. It is apparent that the *S*s were less influenced by the judgments of others when the judgments were made on a visual rather than on a memory basis. It is also evident from the data of Table 2 that the differences between the visual and memory series were reduced or disappeared when the *S*s wrote down their initial, independent judgments. These results support our fifth hypothesis which asserts that the more uncertain the individual is about the correctness of his judgment, the more likely he is to be susceptible to social influences in making his judgment. Further support comes from the questionnaire data. Out of the 90 *S*s who filled out questionnaires, 51 indicated that they were more certain of their judgment when the lines were visually present, 2 were more certain when they were absent, and 39 were equally certain in both instances.

Table 7

SOCIALLY INFLUENCED ERRORS IN INDIVIDUAL JUDGMENTS AS AFFECTED
BY THE STIMULUS TO BE JUDGED (VISUAL OR MEMORY)

	N	Mean Number of Errors	"*p*" value
Errors on visual series	99	2.20 ⎱	.005*
Errors on memory series	99	2.60 ⎰	
Total errors when visual series was first	51	4.12 ⎱	.005
Total errors when memory series was first	48	5.71 ⎰	

* Based on a *t* test of differences between visual and memory series for each subject.

Being exposed first to the memory series rather than the visual series had the effect of making the Ss more susceptible to social influence upon their judgments throughout both series of judgments. In other words, an S was more likely to make socially influenced errors on the memory series and, having allowed himself to be influenced by the others on this first series of judgments, he was more likely to be influenced on the visual series than if he had not previously participated in the memory series. It is as though once having given in to the social influence (and it is easier to give in when one is less certain about one's judgment), the S is more susceptible to further social influences.

DISCUSSION

A central thesis of this experiment has been that prior experiments which have been concerned with "group" influence upon individual judgment have, in fact, only incidentally been concerned with the type of social influence most specifically associated with groups, namely "normative social influence." Our results indicate that, even when normative social influence in the direction of an incorrect judgment is largely removed (as in the anonymous situation), more errors are made by our Ss than by a control group of Ss making their judgments when alone.[7] It seems reasonable to conclude that the S, even if not normatively influenced, may be influenced by the others in the sense that the

judgments of others are taken to be a more or less trustworthy source of information about the objective reality with which he and the others are confronted.

It is not surprising that the judgments of others (particularly when they are perceived to be motivated and competent to judge accurately) should be taken as evidence to be weighed in coming to one's own judgment. From birth on, we learn that the perceptions and judgments of others are frequently reliable sources of evidence about reality. Hence, it is to be expected that if the perceptions by two or more people of the same objective situation are discrepant, each will tend to re-examine his own view and that of the others to see if they can be reconciled. This process of mutual influence does not necessarily indicate the operation of normative social influence as distinct from informational social influence. Essentially the same process (except that the influence is likely to be unilateral) can go on in interaction with a measuring or computing machine. For example, suppose one were to judge which of two lines is longer (as in the Müller-Lyer illusion) and then were given information that a measuring instrument (which past experience had led one to believe was infallible) came up with a different answer; certainly one might be influenced by this information. This influence could hardly be called a normative influence except in the most indirect sense.

While the results of prior experiments of "group" influence upon perception can be largely explained in terms of nonnormative social influence, there is little doubt that normative influences were incidentally operative. However, these were the casual normative influences which can

---

[7] Asch (2) reports that his control group of Ss made an average of considerably less than one error per S.

not be completely eliminated from any human situation, rather than normative influences deriving from specific group membership. Our experimental results indicate that when a group situation is created, even when the group situation is as trivial and artificial as it was in our groups, the normative social influences are grossly increased, producing considerably more errors in individual judgment.

The implications of the foregoing result are not particularly optimistic for those who place a high value on the ability of an individual to resist group pressures which run counter to his individual judgment. In the experimental situation we employed, the S, by allowing himself to be influenced by the others, in effect acquiesced in the distortion of his judgment and denied the authenticity of his own immediate experience. The strength of the normative social influences that were generated in the course of our experiment was small; had it been stronger, one would have expected even more distortion and submission.

Our findings, with regard to the commitment variations, do, however, suggest that normative social influences can be utilized to buttress as well as to undermine individual integrity. In other words, normative social influence can be exerted to help make an individual be an individual and not merely a mirror or puppet of the group. Groups can demand of their members that they have self-respect, that they value their own experience, that they be capable of acting without slavish regard for popularity. Unless groups encourage their members to express their own, independent judgments, group consensus is likely to be an empty achievement. Group process which rests on the distortion of

individual experience undermines its own potential for creativity and productiveness.

SUMMARY AND CONCLUSIONS

Employing modifications of the Asch situation, an experiment was carried out to test hypotheses concerning the effects of normative and informational social influences upon individual judgment. The hypotheses received strong support from the experimental data.

In discussion of our results, the thesis was advanced that prior studies of "group" influence upon individual judgment were only incidentally studies of the type of social influence most specifically associated with groups—i.e., of normative social influence. The role of normative social influence in buttressing as well as undermining individual experience was considered.

REFERENCES

1. ASCH, S. E. "Effects of Group Pressure upon the Modification and Distortion of Judgments." In H. Guetzkow (Ed.), *Groups, Leadership and Men.* Pittsburgh: Carnegie Press, 1951. Pp. 177–190.

2. ASCH, S. E. *Social Psychology.* New York: Prentice-Hall, 1952.

3. BOVARD, E. W. "Group Structure and Perception." *J. Abnorm. Soc. Psychol.*, 1951, 46, 498–505.

4. DEUTSCH, M. "A Theory of Cooperation and Competition." *Hum. Relat.*, 1949, 2, 129–152.

5. FESTINGER, L. "Informal Social Communication." *Psychol. Rev.*, 1950, 57, 271–282.

6. SHERIF, M. "A Study of Some Social Factors in Perception." *Arch. Psychol.*, 1935, 27, No. 187.

SOCIAL SUPPORT, DISSENT, AND CONFORMITY*

Vernon L. Allen and John M. Levine

The importance of group consensus on conformity is clearly demonstrated by the impact of a single dissenter's presence in the group. Asch's (1951) research dramatically demonstrates the effect of dissent on conformity. When one stooge dissented from the incorrect group by giving the correct answer, conformity decreased significantly from approximately 32 per cent to 5 per cent. This type of dissent—when one person disagrees with the group by giving the correct response—provides social support for the subject who also responds correctly.

The role of veridical dissent in reducing conformity has important theoretical implications for understanding the group's effect on individual behavior. Asch (1951) noted that two factors are present in this situation, either of which might be responsible for the observed reduction in conformity: (1) presence of a partner agreeing with the subject (social support), and (2) lack of group unanimity or consensus. If the social support of a partner were the crucial factor in this situation, in order to reduce conformity the dissenter would have to give the specific response that the subject privately believed or per-

ceived to be correct. But, if merely breaking the group's consensus were the critical variable, a dissenter's disagreement with the group—whether or not his answer were correct and agreed with the subject's private judgment—would be sufficient to decrease conformity.

To test these alternative explanations, Asch (1955) had one confederate answer even more incorrectly than the incorrect group in an experiment requiring subjects to match a standard line with one of three comparison lines. In this condition of erroneous dissent, conformity was reduced from 32 percent to 9 per cent; the decrease was nearly as great as that produced by the presence of a veridical dissenter (social support). From these results, Asch concluded that breaking the group's consensus was the major factor responsible for conformity reduction in the veridical dissent condition.

Asch's conclusion can be questioned on both theoretical and methodological grounds. First, a methodological problem in the experiment makes hazardous the comparison of results from the veridical dissent condition with the erroneous dissent condition. The degree of extremeness of the group norm was confounded across the two conditions. In the veridical dissent condition, the group's answer was extremely incorrect on one-half of the pressure trials and moderately incorrect on the other half. In the erroneous dissent

* Vernon L. Allen and John M. Levine, "Social Support, Dissent, and Conformity," *Sociometry*, 31 (1968), 138–49. Reprinted by permission of the American Sociological Association.

condition, however, the group's answer was moderately incorrect on all pressure trials. Previous research indicates that amount of conformity is a direct function of extremeness of the group norm (Helson et al., 1958; Tuddenham, 1961); thus, conformity reduction in the erroneous dissent condition may have been caused partially by the group norm being less extreme in this condition than in the veridical dissent condition.

The moderately incorrect location of the group norm in the erroneous dissent condition was unavoidable in Asch's study. Only three comparison lines were used; with the dissenter choosing the most incorrect alternative, the group could only give the moderately incorrect answer. In the present study this methodological problem was avoided by locating the group norm at a constant position on a nine-point scale in all conditions, rather than varying the group's position across the veridical dissent and the erroneous dissent conditions.

Asch's conclusion can also be questioned on the basis of theory and everyday observation. In real-life situations, conformity often is not reduced when a more extreme response breaks group unanimity; on the contrary, increased adherence to the group norm sometimes results. For example, a person who privately opposes a government policy may feel more pressure to support the policy after hearing it opposed by someone holding a position more extreme than the popular one. Two theoretical approaches would predict more conformity in this situation. From a role theory viewpoint, extreme dissent makes more salient the role of the deviant. Since negative expectations are commonly associated with the deviant role, enhanced pressure toward conformity would result (Allen, 1965). Judgmental theory (Sherif

and Hovland, 1961) would also predict more conformity under the extreme dissent condition. A dissenter holding a position more extreme than the group establishes a more distant anchor point. By comparison with the extreme anchor, the group's position would appear moderate and reasonable, resulting in increased conformity. Finally, the generality of Asch's results can be questioned. Even if erroneous dissent does reduce conformity on visual items, as Asch found, this reduction may be limited to objective items. On subjective items such as opinions, erroneous dissent may be ineffective. On ambiguous or subjective material, an extreme position may be seen as more acceptable and plausible than in the case of material having objectively correct answers. In the present study the range of stimulus content is increased by using opinion and information items, in addition to visual perceptual items.

The purpose of the present study is to determine the effectiveness of several types of dissent as means of reducing conformity on both objective and subjective material. In the veridical dissent condition, another group member always gives the correct answer, in agreement with the subject's private perception; in other dissent conditions, one person disagrees with the group but does not give the answer that the subject believes to be correct or appropriate. The influence on conformity of amount of dissent, as well as direction of dissent, is investigated.

METHOD

Design

Five experimental conditions were used. In four of these conditions, one person, answering

Table 1

RELATION OF THE DISSENTER TO THE GROUP IN THE FIVE CONDITIONS

Experimental Condition	Dissenter's Response
1. Consensus	No dissent
2. Veridical dissent	Correct or popular
3. Extreme erroneous dissent	Much more incorrect or unpopular than the group
4. Slight veridical dissent	Slightly more correct or popular than the group
5. Slight erroneous dissent	Slightly more incorrect or unpopular than the group

fourth in a group of five, dissented from the erroneous responses of three other subjects. Responses of the three subjects who answered first, second, and third, remained constant across all conditions. The response of person four, the dissenter, deviated from the group in direction and degree as shown in Table 1.

An example will illustrate the dissenter's average distance from the group on the nine-point response scale. Assume that the correct or modal answer for an item is three. The unanimous answer of the simulated group, always placed at the 95th percentile of the standardization group, would be six. In the veridical dissent condition, the dissenter would answer three, the correct or popular answer. In the extreme erroneous dissent condition, the dissenter would give response nine—clearly more incorrect than the incorrect group response of six. The dissenter's response in the two slight dissent conditions deviates from the group by one scale point: the dissenter would give answer five in the slight veridical dissent condition and answer seven in the slight erroneous dissent condition.

In the consensus condition, all four simulated subjects gave the same incorrect or unpopular answers on the critical trials that were given by the first three subjects in the four dissent conditions.

Apparatus

The apparatus was a Crutchfield-type electrical signaling device (Crutchfield, 1955). It consists of five adjacent booths containing signal lights and answer switches, a master control panel in an adjoining room, and a slide projector operated by remote control. The subjects are led to believe, by instructions and practice trials, that signal lights in their booths indicate responses of the other four persons in the group. Actually, lights in all booths are controlled by the experimenter from a master panel. The subjects believe that one member of the group answers in each of the five positions; however, all subjects answer last (fifth) on all trials. The same simulated group responses are presented to all five subjects. In this way, the simulated group can be made either to agree or disagree with the subject's private judgments.

Procedure

Seated in the five booths, subjects were instructed to make accurate judgments on perceptual, information, and opinion items projected on a screen in front of the room. Use of the apparatus was explained and four practice trials were given, during which each subject's order of answering varied. During the practice trials, subjects called out their answers aloud so that all subjects could verify that the lights correctly indicated other subjects' responses. The subjects were told that during the experiment each subject would keep the same position throughout all trials, e.g., one subject would always answer first, another would always answer second, etc. The experimenter left the room and presented the experimental slides by remote control. All subjects answered in position five, and all observed the same sequence of simulated group responses which were controlled by the experimenter. A short questionnaire and careful debriefing followed the experiment.

Stimuli

Stimuli were of three types: perceptual items requiring visual judgment (e.g., "Which of the numbered arcs was taken out of the circle?"), general information items (e.g., "In thousands of miles, how far is it from San Francisco to New York"), and opinion items (e.g., "Most young people get too much education."). Each stimulus had nine alternative answers, corresponding to the nine switches on the panel. Visual and information items were answered by using the number below each switch (1 through 9). For the opinion items, the switches were labeled on a continuum from "very strongly disagree" (switch 1) to "very strongly agree" (switch 9).

Of the 45 items used, 18 were critical, or group pressure, items; six each of visual, information, and opinion. On these critical items, the norm of the simulated group was placed at the 95th percentile of responses given by a standardization group. The standardization group was composed of persons answering alone without seeing responses of others. For information and opinion items, the standardization group was 300 introductory psychology students. The Tuddenham, et al. (1956) standardization group was employed for visual items. The remaining 27 stimuli were neutral items on which the simulated group gave popular correct answers across all conditions. On both critical and neutral items, the group was unanimous on one-half of the trials and variable on one-half. On unanimous items all simulated subjects gave the same answer. On variable items, simulated subjects gave one of two answers which differed by one point on the response scale.

The order of stimulus presentation was balanced in four ways. The 45 slides were divided into blocks of 15 with each block containing six critical and nine neutral items. Second, the critical items were separated by two or three neutral stimuli. Third, the three types of stimuli (visual, information, and opinion) were counterbalanced within each block of 15. Finally, unanimous and variable trials were counterbalanced.

Subjects

The subjects were 165 student volunteers from an introductory psychology class at the University of Wisconsin. Students earned credits applicable to their class grade by participating as subjects. Data from 20 subjects were discarded because their clear statements in the post-experimental questionnaire indicated knowledge of the deception. Five randomly chosen subjects of the same sex were always tested together as a group. Approximately the same number of males and females were assigned to each of the five conditions.

Method of Analysis

For each subject a mean conformity score was computed for each of the three types of items. To ascertain initial responses, a pre-experimental questionnaire containing critical opinion and information items, along with many buffer questions, was administered in class to all potential subjects at the beginning of the semester. Since this procedure was not feasible for visual items, modal responses of the Tuddenham, et al. (1956) standardization group were used as initial scores. Mean conformity scores were computed by summing the algebraic differences between initial responses and responses given in the group situation and dividing by the number of items used for each subject. Six items of each type were almost always employed in calculating the mean conformity score of each subject. But when the subject's initial answer on a critical trial was as extreme or more extreme than the simulated answer this item was not used in calculating the mean conformity score, since the subject did not receive group pressure. Only 81 of 1884 initial information and opinion scores (4.3 per cent) fell at or beyond the simulated group norm.

To assess the effects of the various types of dissent on conformity, each experimental (dissent) condition must be compared with the consensus condition. The appropriate statistic for comparing several experimental conditions with a single control is Dunnett's test (Winer, 1962); this test maintains the level of Type I error for the summary decision regarding comparisons of all experimental conditions with the control.

RESULTS

Perception of Dissent

It is essential to ascertain whether subjects recognized that the dissenter agreed with them in the veridical dissent condition and that he disagreed with the group in the other dissent conditions. Information relevant to the experimental manipulation of dissent was obtained from the post-experimental questionnaire. On one item subjects were asked whether anyone in the group tended often to agree with them. Table 2 shows the percentage of subjects who identified the dissenter as the person who frequently agreed with them. As data in Table 2 show, subjects more often correctly perceived the presence of a partner in the veridical dissent condition than in the other conditions. Combining male and female data in Table 2, difference among the conditions was significant at less than the .01 level ($x^2 =$ 46.96).

A majority of subjects in the veridical dissent condition was aware of having a partner (93 per cent of males and 73 per

Table 2

PERCENTAGE OF SUBJECTS IN THE NONUNANIMOUS CONDITIONS WHO PERCEIVED THE DISSENTER AGREEING WITH THEM

Condition	Male % N	Female % N
Veridical dissent	93 (15)	73 (15)
Extreme erroneous dissent	7 (14)	7 (14)
Slight veridical dissent	23 (13)	27 (15)
Slight erroneous dissent	20 (10)	8 (13)

cent of females). Only one male and one female reported the dissenter as agreeing with them in the extreme erroneous dissent condition. These data, then, reflect a quite accurate perception of the situation. A few subjects in the slight veridical dissent and slight erroneous dissent conditions also identified the dissenter as having agreed with them. For subjects in the veridical dissent condition, this report was sometimes accurate; the distribution of subjects' initial responses did show an overlap on some items with the dissenter's answer.

Data from the post-experimental ques-

Table 3

PERCENTAGE OF SUBJECTS IN THE (NONPARTNER) DISSENT CONDITIONS WHO PERCEIVED THE DISSENTER DISAGREEING WITH THE GROUP

Condition	Male % N	Female % N
Extreme erroneous dissent	29 (14)	50 (14)
Slight veridical dissent	8 (13)	0 (15)
Slight erroneous dissent	10 (10)	8 (13)

tionnaire were also used to determine whether subjects correctly perceived that the dissenter disagreed with the group. Table 3 presents results for the three dissent conditions in which the dissenter did not give the correct or modal responses. Combining male and female data in Table 3, difference among the three conditions was significant at less than the .01 level ($x^2 = 13.97$).

Fifty per cent of the females and 29 per cent of the males correctly identified the dissenter as having often disagreed with the group in the extreme erroneous dissent condition. In spite of the great distance of the dissenter's responses from the correct or modal answer, only half the females and less than one-third of the males identified the dissenter. The result may be due to subjects' perceiving agreement between the dissenter's answer and the group's response because both disagreed strongly with the subject's own position. Even fewer subjects perceived the dissenter as disagreeing with the group in the slight dissent conditions. In summary, these data show, as expected, that more subjects correctly perceived the dissenter as disagreeing with the group in the extreme erroneous dissent condition than in the two slight dissent conditions.

Conformity

Mean conformity scores on each of the three types of items in the five conditions are shown in Table 4. Male and female data are combined in Table 4, since no significant sex differences emerged. Inspection of the table reveals that veridical dissent reduced conformity on all three types of items, as compared with the consensus condition. The veridical dissent con-

dition significantly reduced conformity for visual items ($t = 4.56$, $p < .01$) and opinion items ($t = 3.10$, $p < .01$).[1] Conformity scores on information items were lower in the veridical dissent condition than in the consensus condition, but the difference failed to reach statistical significance.

The effect on conformity of the extremely erroneous dissenter can be seen in the third row of Table 4. Relative to the amount of conformity in the consensus conditions, conformity was significantly reduced in the extreme erroneous dissent condition on visual items ($t = 3.61$, $p < .01$).[2] Notice that on opinion items there was a slight and nonsignificant decrease in conformity in the extreme erroneous dissent condition. The mean conformity score was .82 for the extreme erroneous dissent condition and .45 for the veridical dissent condition, indicating that veridical dissent was approximately twice as effective in reducing conformity as extreme erroneous dissent. For information items conformity was not significantly reduced in the extreme erroneous dissent condition. In fact, here conformity was slightly higher than in the consensus condition (.66 vs. .64). We had expected that the extreme erroneous dissent condition would

---

[1] All Dunnett's t tests reported are two-tailed.

[2] It should be mentioned that for males amount of reduction in conformity on visual items in the extreme erroneous dissent condition was as great as that found in the veridical dissent condition (.32 and .30, respectively). For females, however, the veridical dissent condition reduced conformity on visual items somewhat more than the extreme erroneous dissent condition (.18 and .38, respectively).

Table 4

MEAN CONFORMITY SCORE

Condition	N	Type of Item		
		Visual	Information	Opinion
Consensus	36	.755	.644	1.079
Veridical dissent	30	.244	.445	.447
Extreme erroneous dissent	28	.351	.665	.823
Slight veridical dissent	28	.661	.562	.765
Slight erroneous dissent	23	.616	.684	.844

Note: Date are combined for males and females.

increase conformity, but only this single instance of a slight increase was found.

Results for the two conditions involving slight dissent from the group are also shown in Table 4. Both the slight dissent conditions produced, in general, small but nonsignificant decreases in conformity on all three types of items, as compared with the consensus condition. In addition, the slight veridical dissent and slight erroneous dissent conditions did not differ significantly in amount of conformity.

In summary, veridical dissent significantly reduced conformity on visual and opinion items but not on information items. The extreme erroneous dissent condition reduced conformity on visual items only. Neither of the slight dissent conditions significantly reduced conformity.

Emotional Reactions

One item from the post-experimental questionnaire measured subjects' emotional reactions to the group pressure situation on a 12-point scale ranging from "calm and relaxed" to "disturbed and upset." Table 5 presents means for subjects' reports of their feelings during the experiment. Both males and females re

Table 5

MEANS FOR SUBJECTS' REPORTED FEELINGS DURING THE EXPERIMENT

Condition	Male	Female
Consensus	3.07	2.43
Veridical dissent	2.33	1.47
Extreme erroneous dissent	2.93	2.43
Slight veridical dissent	3.00	2.80
Slight erroneous dissent	3.20	3.77

Note: "Calm and relaxed" = 1; "disturbed and upset" = 12.

ported feeling calmer and more relaxed in the veridical dissent condition than in the consensus condition. Difference between the consensus condition and the veridical dissent condition was statistically significant for females ($t = 2.31$, $p < .05$), but not for males ($t = 1.08$). Means for the other conditions did not differ significantly from the consensus condition; in several dissent conditions subjects were slightly more disturbed and upset than in the consensus condition. It should be noted, however, that in general subjects were only minimally upset; means of all conditions were located toward the "calm and relaxed" end of the scale. Of course, though upset, subjects may have been reluctant to admit that they were disturbed by the procedure.

DISCUSSION

Our results support Asch's (1955) findings on the type of item that he used: for visual perceptual items both the veridical dissent and extreme erroneous dissent conditions significantly reduced conformity. On opinion items, however, only the veridical dissent condition significantly decreased conformity.

Contrary to our expectation, extreme erroneous dissent did not increase conformity; the effect of extreme erroneous dissent was shown, however, to depend on the nature of the stimulus material. Therefore, we must question Asch's general conclusion that breaking group consensus is the crucial variable responsible for reducing conformity when the social support of a partner (veridical dissent) is provided.

Before discussing these findings, a word should be said about the lack of a significant decrease in conformity for information items in the veridical dissent condition. One explanation for this result is that the amount of conformity obtained in the consensus condition was not great enough, when compared with the reduction caused by veridical dissent, to produce a statistically significant difference. Information items were quite easy for subjects, a fact probably responsible for low conformity in the consensus condition. Previous research had reported a strong correlation between conformity and item difficulty (Coleman, et al., 1958).

Now let us consider why the presence of an extreme erroneous dissenter reduces conformity on visual items but not on opinions. Our explanation is based on the different implications of group unanimity for objective and subjective material. Persons hold strong expectations that group members will agree on matters of physical reality which are amenable to objective verification, such as length of lines. Only one objectively correct answer exists for visual discriminations, and a group's responses on such judgments are expected to be unanimous and correct. Lack of group consensus on visual items implies that the group's perception of physical reality is unreliable and therefore should not be taken as a basis for making perceptual judgments. Hence, in the extreme erroneous dissent condition nonconformity on visual items would result from the subject's rejecting the majority as an acceptable reference group and relying instead on his own perception of physical reality.

On opinion items other people's responses serve as the sole index of reality —social reality—because objective bases for evaluation of the correctness or appropriateness of an answer do not exist (Festinger, 1954). Although visual items have only one objectively correct answer, for opinion items there are many equally reasonable and correct answers. Thus, lack of group consensus does not have the same implication for opinions as for visual judgments. Some degree of variability among group members is to be expected on subjective material, unlike the situation for visual items. Therefore, in spite of lack of unanimity on opinion items, the group is not rejected as a social referent. In the extreme erroneous dissent condition, conformity on opinions is perhaps not significantly reduced because the group is still employed as an index of social reality.

A second theoretical consideration is suggested by our findings: do different psychological mechanisms also account for conformity reduction on objective and subjective items in the veridical dissent condition? Recall that our data showed that only veridical dissent significanly reduced conformity on opinion items; merely breaking group consensus by extreme erroneous dissent was not sufficient. The mechanism primarily responsible for the effectiveness of veridical dissent on opinion items is apparently the emotional comfort of having a partner with whom to face the opposing group. Supporting this suggestion are results of subjects' emotional reactions during the experiment. In the veridical dissent condition, subjects reported feeling more calm and relaxed than in the other conditions. In contrast with results for opinion items, results for visual items showed that conformity was significantly reduced by *both* veridical dissent and extreme erroneous dissent. Since conformity was effectively reduced in both conditions in the case of visual items, breaking the group's consensus appears to be the critical factor involved. We suggested earlier that lack of consensus on visual items might lead to rejection of the group as a reference group. In accord with this analysis, the effectiveness of veridical dissent on visual items might be associated with rejection of the group standard, rather than with the emotional comfort of having a partner.

We have suggested that different psychological mechanisms could be responsible for the effectiveness of veridical

dissent on objective (visual) and on subjective (opinion) items. One kind of data relevant to testing the hypothesis would consist of subjects' ratings of the group's competence on visual and opinion items under conditions of group unanimity and nonunanimity. Difference in relative competence of the group on visual and opinion items should be greater in nonunanimous conditions (extreme erroneous dissent and veridical dissent) than in the unanimous condition, if rejection of the group on visual items occurs in the nonunanimous conditions as we suggest. Results from an unpublished experiment by the authors—replicating the present study in part—lend some support to this prediction.

Although our data suggest that social support deriving from veridical dissent is necessary for reduction of conformity on opinion items, the role of dissent per se should not be entirely discounted. Evidence indicates that mere dissent does make a slight contribution. Results showed that the presence of an extreme erroneous dissenter slightly reduced conformity on opinion items. Moreover, a small reduction in conformity occurred in the slight veridical dissent and the extreme erroneous dissent conditions, which is consistent with Asch's (1951) finding for a compromise partner. The insignificant reduction in conformity in the slight dissent conditions is not caused by failure to perceive that the dissenter deviated from the group. Even when the dissenter was clearly perceived by most subjects, as in the extreme erroneous dissent condition, conformity was not significantly reduced on opinion items. In view of these data, we can safely say that on subjective material the breaking of group consensus has a minor and nonsignificant effect, the magnitude of which is negligible compared with the impact of the social support of a veridical dissenter.

REFERENCES

ALLEN, V. L., "Conformity and the Role of the Deviant." *Journal of Personality* 33 (December 1965): 584–597.

ASCH, S. E., "Effects of Group Pressure Upon the Modification and Distortion of Judgment." Pp. 177–190 in H. Guetzkow (ed.), *Groups, Leadership, and Men.* Pittsburgh: Carnegie Press, 1951.

———, "Opinions and Social Pressure." *Scientific American* 193 (November 1955): 31–35.

COLEMAN, J. F., BLAKE, R. R., and MOUTON, J. S., "Task Difficulty and Conformity Pressures." *Journal of Abnormal and Social Psychology* 57 (July 1958): 120–122.

CRUTCHFIELD, R. S., "Conformity and Character." *The American Psychologist* 10 (May 1955): 191–198.

FESTINGER, L., "A Theory of Social Comparison Processes." *Human Relations* 7 (May 1954): 117–140.

HELSON, H., BLAKE, R. R., and MOUTON, J. S., "An Experimental Investigation of the Effectiveness of the 'Big Lie' in Shifting Attitudes." *Journal of Social Psychology* 48 (August 1958): 51–60.

SHERIF, MUZAFER, and CARL I. HOVLAND, *Social Judgment.* New Haven: Yale University Press, 1961.

TUDDENHAM, R. D., "The Influence Upon Judgment of the Apparent Discrepancy Between Self and Others." *Journal of Social Psychology* 53 (February 1961): 69–79.

TUDDENHAM, R. R., MACBRIDE, P., and ZAHN, V., "Studies in Conformity and Yielding." I. Development of standard experimental series–1. Contract NR 170–159, Group Psychology Branch, Office of Naval Research, 1956.

WINER, B. J., *Statistical Principles in Experimental Design.* New York: McGraw-Hill, 1962.

VI

COMMUNICATION NETWORK
EXPERIMENTS

COMMUNICATION PATTERNS
IN TASK-ORIENTED GROUPS*

Alex Bavelas

When the nature of a task is such that it must be performed by a group rather than by a single individual, the problem of working relationships arises. One of the more important of these relationships is that of communication. Quite aside from a consideration of the effects of communication on what is generally called "morale," it is easily demonstrated that for entire classes of tasks any hope of success depends upon an effective flow of information. But on what principles may a pattern of communication be determined which will in fact be a fit one for effective human effort? Administrative thinking on this point commonly rests upon the assumption that optimum patterns of communications for a task-group may be derived from the specifications of the task to be performed. Students of organization, however, have pointed out repeatedly that working groups—even if one considers only communications relevant to the work being done—invariably tend to depart from formal statements of

the patterns to be employed. One may take the view that this departure is due to the tendency of groups to adjust toward that class of communication patterns which will permit the easiest and most satisfying flow of ideas, information, and decisions. In groups which are free of outside control, it is clear that the interaction patterns which emerge and stabilize are products of the social process within the group. A group which exists as a part of a larger organization, however, seldom has the freedom to make such an adjustment. In most organizations the maintenance of the stated—and presumably optimum—patterns of communication is regarded as a first principle of effective performance. It is easy to understand this tendency of administration to inhibit changes in formal communication patterns. One need only remember how intimate the relation is between communication, control, and authority.

In these organizational situations, the imposed patterns of communication may determine certain aspects of the group process. This raises the question of how a fixed communication pattern may affect the work and life of a group. Do certain patterns have structural properties which may limit group performance? May it be that among several communication pat-

* Reprinted from *The Policy Sciences*, edited by Daniel Lerner and Harold D. Lasswell with the permission of the publishers, Stanford University Press. Copyright 1951 by the Board of Trustees of the Leland Stanford Junior University.

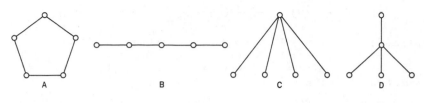

Fig. 1.

terns—*all logically adequate for the successful completion of a specified task*—one will result in significantly better performance than another? What effects might pattern, as such, have upon the emergence of leadership, the development of organization, and the degree of resistance to group disruption?

These questions have prompted a series of exploratory studies which have grown into a program of research. The findings are incomplete at present, but are of interest in their possible implications. In this chapter, the attempt will be made to describe the areas of present experimental activity and the general direction which the work is taking.

SOME GEOMETRIC PROPERTIES OF COMMUNICATION PATTERNS

If we consider who may communicate with whom in a task-group, without regard for the nature or medium of the communication, we can ask a number of simple but important questions. Let us vary the ways in which five individuals are linked[1] to one another (it being under-

stood that every individual in the group will be linked to at least one other individual in the same group). What different kinds of communication patterns may we produce, and how may we describe quantitatively the differences between them? Obviously, this would more properly be an exercise for a topologist. For the social scientist it is more to the point to ask, "What differences among these patterns appear (quite intuitively) to be of a kind that would affect human beings in some way?" If we look at the patterns shown in Figure 1, we find that intuitive notions come easily—perhaps, too easily. Students commonly remark, upon seeing patterns *C* and *D* for the first time, that pattern *C* is "autocratic," while pattern *D* is a typical "business set-up." Actually, of course, in so far as linkage goes they are identical, the only difference being the arrangement of the dots on this paper. Among patterns *A*, *B*, and *C*, however, we may point to some real differences. For instance, in pattern *A* each individual can communicate with two others in the group directly—that is, without relaying a message through some other person. In patterns *C* and *D* there is only one individual in the group who can communicate directly with all the others.

To make another comparison, any individual in pattern *A* can communicate with any one of the others with no more than a single "relay." In pattern *B*, two individuals must relay messages through

---

[1] For the purpose of this discussion, if individual *p* is linked to individual *q* it will mean that *p* may communicate to *q*, and that *q* may communicate to *p*—that is, the link is symmetrical.

p——————q——————r——————s——————t
4.0   5.7   6.7   5.7   4.0

p to q $=1$	q to p $=1$	r to p $=2$	s to p $=3$	t to p $=4$
p to r $=2$	q to r $=1$	r to q $=1$	s to q $=2$	t to q $=3$
p to s $=3$	q to s $=2$	r to s $=1$	s to r $=1$	t to r $=2$
p to t $=4$	q to t $=3$	r to t $=2$	s to t $=1$	t to s $=1$
p to all $= 10$	q to all $=7$	r to all $=6$	s to all $=7$	t to all $= 10$

Fig. 2.

three others in order to communicate with each other.

In a sense, the comparisons just made involve the notion of "distance" between individuals in a pattern. If we adopt some method of counting the "distances" between individuals, we can make some statements regarding differences between and within patterns. In Figure 2 a method of counting is illustrated as applied to pattern B in Figure 1. The summation of all internal distances for pattern B is 40 ($\Sigma d_{x,y} = 40$). In a similar way, we find that the same summation for pattern A is 30 and for pattern C, 32. (Fig. 3 shows the tabulations of distances in pattern C.)

Turning to the question of differences among positions in the same pattern, we see clearly that position q in the pattern shown in Figure 2 is different from posi-

tion p in the same pattern. One aspect of this difference is shown by the tabulation in Figure 2: $d_{p,x} = 10$, $d_{q,x} = 7$. Position q in Figure 2 has a total distance of 7, just as position q in Figure 3. In this case the distance from q to all others does not differentiate between the two positions. Yet we cannot but feel from an inspection of the patterns that there is a difference between the two q positions. We could, of course, point to the fact that in one case q has two "neighbors" and in the other case has only one. But let us consider further the question of distance as such. Since the two patterns in question have different $\Sigma d_{x,y}$ values, it may help if we express the distance "q to all others" in a relative manner. One way of doing this is to calculate for each position the value of the expression:

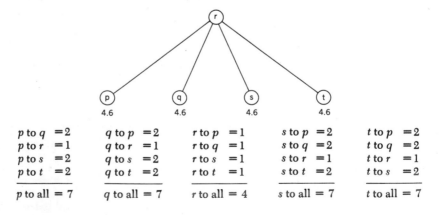

p to q $=2$	q to p $=2$	r to p $=1$	s to p $=2$	t to p $=2$
p to r $=1$	q to r $=1$	r to q $=1$	s to q $=2$	t to q $=2$
p to s $=2$	q to s $=2$	r to s $=1$	s to r $=1$	t to r $=1$
p to t $=2$	q to t $=2$	r to t $=1$	s to t $=2$	t to s $=2$
p to all $= 7$	q to all $= 7$	r to all $= 4$	s to all $= 7$	t to all $= 7$

Fig. 3.

$$\frac{\Sigma d_{x,y}}{\Sigma d_{q,x}}.$$

For position q in Figure 2, this quantity would be equal to 5.7; for position q in Figure 3, the quantity would be equal to 4.6. In Figure 4 are shown such similar values for each of the positions in pattern A of Figure 1.

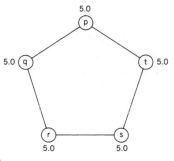

Fig. 4.

If we were to summarize the preceding discussion, we could say that comparisons between two patterns might be made on the basis of "dispersion" (sum of internal distances) defined as $\Sigma d_{x.y}$; and that comparisons between positions within the same pattern might be made on the basis of "relative centrality" defined as $\dfrac{\Sigma d_{x,y}}{d_{q,y}}$ (the sum of all internal distances of the pattern divided by the total sum of distances for any one position in the pattern).

OPERATIONAL POSSIBILITIES OF PATTERNS

Let us turn now to the question of how these patterns of communication might be used by a group. Any sensible discussion of "operation" must, of course, be in terms of some specified task. A simple but interesting one would be the following: each of five subjects is dealt five playing cards from a normal poker deck and has the task of selecting from his hand the one card which, together with the four cards similarly selected by the other four subjects, will make the highest-ranking poker hand possible under these conditions.[2] The cards may not be passed around, but the subjects may communicate over the indicated channels, in the particular pattern being tested, by writing messages.

It is clear that pattern B in Figure 1 may be operated in a number of ways, or "operational patterns." Two of the possible operational patterns for communicating necessary information are shown in Figure 5. Obviously, it is possible for pattern B to be so operated that the subject in any one of the five positions will be the one to have all the necessary information first (and presumably decide which card each subject should select). There are no linkage strictures which would force a given method of operation into use. We might ask, however, whether there are differences in efficiency between different operational patterns. Two measures of efficiency come naturally to mind: the number of messages required for task completion, and the time required for task completion.

With respect to the number of messages required, it is possible to make a general statement. In terms of the task given above, one may say that each of the subjects has in his possession one-fifth of the information necessary for a solution. Also, all of the information must at some time be present at one position in the pattern.

---

[2] We assume subjects with perfect knowledge of poker-hand ratings.

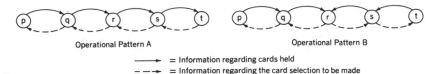

Operational Pattern A　　　　　　　Operational Pattern B

——————▶ = Information regarding cards held
— — —▶ = Information regarding the card selection to be made

Fig. 5.

It can be shown that four messages are necessary and sufficient to accomplish this. Since each subject must know the correct card for him to select, an additional four messages will be required. One may say, therefore, that for any patterns with *symmetrical linkage* the number of messages required will be equal to $2(n-1)$, where n stands for the total number of positions, and that this requirement is completely independent of the linkage pattern as such.

With respect to the time it would take to reach a solution in different patterns, we have a somewhat different situation. We must, of course, for any general discussion of speed of solution assume some standard unit of time to be associated with a message.[3] Let t equal the time it takes for information to go from one person to another when they are linked, i.e., when they occupy neighboring positions in the pattern.

(Before going on to a consideration of the patterns under discussion, a relationship between t and the number of individuals in a group should be pointed out. If any linkage pattern is allowed, then it may be stated that the minimum time for solution will have the following relation to the number of individuals in the pattern:

$$t^{min} = x + 1 \quad \text{when} \quad 2^x < n \leqslant 2^{x+1}.$$

This relationship leads to some rather interesting conclusions. Let us consider two groups with unrestricted linkage—one group of nine members and one group of sixteen members. With a task such as that of selecting the best poker hand, the minimum time necessary for completion would be the same for both groups, although in the first case we would have nine individuals each possessing one-ninth of the information, and in the second each with one-sixteenth of the information.)

With t defined in this way it is easy to see that operational pattern A in Figure 5 will require 8 time units, while operational pattern B in the same figure will require 5 time units. Obviously, when more than one message is sent in the same time unit, time is saved. However, if individual p sends a message simultaneously with individual r (as in Fig. 6), his message to q

Fig. 6.

cannot possibly contain the information contained in the message from r. We can expect, therefore, that in certain patterns time will be saved at the expense of messages; and doing the task in minimum messages will involve the use of more time units. This is nicely illustrated by pattern A in Figure 1. In this pattern the problem may be done in as few as 3 time units, but

---

[3] This is not intended to exclude the possibility that in certain patterns "morale" effects will materially affect the speed with which an individual might perform.

to do this requires 14 messages; if the problem is done in 8 messages (the fewest possible), the number of time units required increases to 5.

Some Experiments with Selected Patterns

An analysis such as this must sooner or later lead to the question: "Granted that a kind of difference has been demonstrated between one pattern and another, is it a difference which will make a difference?" Such a question can be answered only by experiment. Without attempting a detailed account, a brief mention of two experimental studies would be helpful here.

Sidney Smith conducted an experiment[4] at Massachusetts Institute of Technology with eight groups of college students using patterns *A* and *B* shown in Figure 1. He gave his groups a task which in its essentials was similar to the poker-hand problem described earlier. Instead of playing cards, each subject was given a card upon which had been printed five symbols taken from among these six: $\bigcirc \, \triangle \, * \, \square \, + \, \diamondsuit$. While each symbol appeared on four of the five cards, only one symbol appeared on all five cards. Each group's task was to find the common symbol in the shortest time possible. In each subject's cubicle was a box of six switches, each switch labeled with one of the six symbols. The task was considered finished when each member of the group indicated that he knew the common symbol by throwing the appropriate switch. The switches operated a board of lights visible to a laboratory assistant who recorded individual and group

times and errors (an error being the throwing of an incorrect switch). The subjects communicated by writing messages which could be passed through slots in the cubicle walls. The slots were so arranged that any desired linkage pattern could be imposed by the experimenter. No restriction whatever was placed upon the content of the messages. A subject who had the "answer" was at liberty to send it along. The cards upon which the messages were written were coded so that a reconstruction of the communicatory activity could be made.

Each experimental group worked on fifteen successive problems. The same six symbols were used throughout, but the common symbol varied from trial to trial. Four groups worked in pattern *A*, and four other groups worked in pattern *B*. No group worked in more than one pattern.

Of the detailed analysis which Smith made of the experimental data, only two findings will be presented here: errors, and the emergence of recognized leaders (see Table 1 and Fig. 7).

Table 1

Error Category	Pattern A	Pattern B
Average total errors	14.0	7.0
Average group errors	5.0	1.5

Total errors = number of incorrect switches thrown.

Group errors = number of problems which on completion contained at least one error.

(All figures are averages from the performance of four groups in each pattern. Each group did 15 problems.)

With respect to the emergence of recognized leadership, Smith had each of his subjects answer a questionnaire immedi-

---

[4] Unpublished; manuscript in preparation.

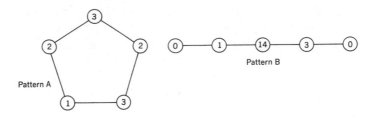

Pattern A

Pattern B

Fig. 7. The number at each position shows the total number of group members (in the four groups in that pattern) who recognized the individual in that position as the leader.

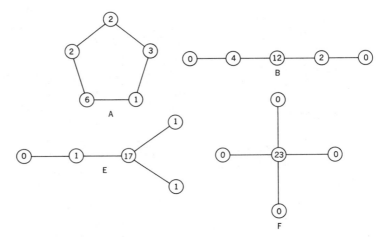

Fig. 8. Emergence of recognized leaders.

ately after the end of the fifteenth trial. One of the questions read: "Did your group have a leader? If so, who?" The answers are shown in Figure 7.

While no good theory could be formulated for the differences in numbers of errors, the findings suggested that the individual occupying the most central position in a pattern was most likely to be recognized as the leader. Also, from observation of the subjects while they worked, it appeared that morale was better in pattern *A* than in pattern *B*, and that the morale of the individuals in the most peripheral (least central) positions of pattern *B* was the poorest.

In order to explore these possibilities further, Harold Leavitt did a more de-

tailed study[5] of the same two patterns plus two others. The four patterns he uesd are shown in Figure 8. Leavitt used the same problems and the same experimental setting used by Smith. His findings on errors and leadership recognition are presented in the same form as Smith's data (Table 2 and Fig. 8).

Leavitt's findings considerably strengthen the hypothesis that a recognized leader (under the conditions of the experiment) will most probably emerge at the

---

[5] For a detailed account of this experiment, see Harold J. Leavitt, "Some Effects of Certain Communication Patterns on Group Performance" (Ph.D. dissertation, Massachusetts Institute of Technology, 1949).

Table 2

Error Category	Patterns			
	A	B	E	F
Average total errors	17	10	3	10*
Average group errors . . .	3	2	1	1

* Leavitt attributes almost all of this error figure to one of the five pattern *F* groups which became confused over the meaning of one member's method of reporting his information.

position of highest centrality. His findings also lend some support to the hypothesis that errors may be related to pattern properties.

In addition to errors and leadership, Leavitt was interested in the question of morale differences between and within patterns. His subjects were asked two questions to which they responded by ratings from 0 (very unfavorable) to 10

(very favorable). The data are given below in averages of all ratings for subjects in the same pattern (Table 3):

In order to check the hypothesis that morale differences exist within patterns and are related to relative centrality, the following analysis of the responses to the same two questions was made (Table 4). The ratings of men who occupied the most peripheral positions in patterns *B*, *E*, and *F* were averaged together; the ratings made by men in the most central positions of the same three patterns were also averaged together. All ratings made by subjects in pattern *A* were omitted from these calculations for the obvious reason that no one is most central or most peripheral in that pattern.

On the basis of a detailed study of all the data yielded by his experiments, Leavitt makes the following comments:

Table 3

Questions	Average Rating by Pattern			
	A	B	E	F
How much did you like your job?	6.6	6.2	5.8	4.7
How satisfied are you with the job done?	8.0	5.8	6.0	5.4

Table 4

Questions	Average Rating by Position in Pattern	
	For 35 individuals in the most peripheral positions*	For 15 individuals in the most central positions†
How much did you like your job?	3.2	8.8
How satisfied are you with the job done?	4.6	7.8

* As represented here (black dots):

† As represented here (black dots):

Pattern F[6] operated as expected in all five cases. The peripheral men sent their information to the center where the answer was arrived at and sent out. This organization usually evolved by the fourth or fifth trial and was maintained unchanged throughout the remaining trials.

Pattern E operated so that the most central man got all the information and sent out the answer. Organization evolved more slowly than in pattern F, but, once achieved, was just as stable.

Pattern B was not as stable as patterns E and F. Although most of the times the answer was sent out by the individual in the most central position, this function was occasionally performed by one of the men on either side of him. Organization was slower to evolve than in patterns E and F.

Pattern A showed no consistent pattern of organization. Subjects, for the most part, merely sent messages until they received or could work out the answer themselves.

A PROPOSED EXPERIMENT USING THE SAME PATTERNS BUT A DIFFERENT TASK

In the Leavitt experiment, the normal behavior of a subject in working toward a solution was to send to the others a list of the five symbols appearing on his card. Occasionally, however, something quite different would occur. The subject would send, instead, the one symbol (out of the total six symbols)[7] which was *not* on his card. The advantages of this method in saving time and avoiding possible error are obvious. In a sense this procedure is a "detour" solution of the problem confronting the subject. The whole task situation was such as to suggest strongly the straightforward action of sending along the symbols one had, rather than the symbol one had not. Although the frequency of occurrence of this insight was fairly even in the groups, its adoption by the groups as a method of work was not. It was used by two of the five groups in pattern A, by one of the five groups in pattern B, and by none of the groups in patterns E and F. While these differences could not be demonstrated to be significant, they excited considerable speculation. In individual psychology it has been shown repeatedly that an individual's frame of reference may be such as to effectively inhibit the solving of a problem requiring a detour. With the groups in question the insight invariably occurred to some member or members. Why, then, did it not spread throughout the group in every case? Might it be that in certain communication patterns the probability of effective utilization of the insights that occur is greater than in others? It was felt that if a more suitable task could be devised, some relationship between the occurrence and utilization of insights and communication pattern might be uncovered.

A task has been constructed which seems to be a step in the right direction. Preliminary trials with it are encouraging. The task consists essentially of forming squares from various geometric shapes. In Figure 9 are shown the fifteen pieces which make up the puzzle and how they go together to form five squares.

Out of these shapes, squares may be made in many ways. Some of the possible combinations are: $c\,c\,a\,a$, $e\,a\,a\,a\,a$, $e\,a\,a\,g$, $f\,f\,a\,a\,a\,a$, $f\,f\,c\,a$, $f\,f\,g\,a\,a$, $i\,c\,a$, etc. However, if, using all fifteen pieces, five squares

---

[6] In this quotation, pattern letters used in Figure 9 have been substituted for the letters used in Leavitt's report.

[7] He could see all six symbols on his box of six switches.

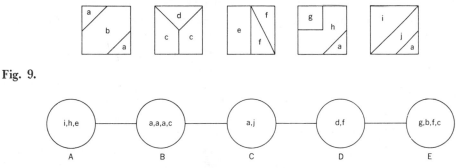

Fig. 9.

Fig. 10.

must be constructed, there is only one arrangement that can succeed—that shown in Figure 9. In the experimental situation the pieces are distributed among the five subjects. They are told that the task will be successfully completed when each subject has a square before him and no unused pieces. Messages and pieces may be passed along open channels.

The initial distribution of the pieces may be made so that the probability of "bad" squares being formed is increased ("bad" squares being any which, perfect in themselves, make a total of five squares impossible). A possible distribution is given in Figure 10.

As can be seen, the pieces with which an individual starts may suggest a particular composition. Or, the pieces an individual starts with may suggest nothing at all and therefore be speedily traded. Let us look at the situation at position *A* in Figure 10. The pieces *i*, *h*, *e* do not readily suggest a combination of themselves. We may assume that the subject will pass one of the three to position *B*. At position *B*, however, the situation is quite different. The combinations *a*, *c*, *e* or *a*, *a*, *a*, *h* or *a*, *c*, *i* all form squares which if completed will lead to group failure, so that any piece received from position *A* merely suggests

possible "wrong" squares. In preliminary trials the "bad" squares appear with great regularity. The point of the experiment is what happens, once these deceptive "successes" occur. For an individual who has completed a square, it is understandably difficult to tear it apart. The ease with which he can take a course of action "away from the goal" should depend to some extent upon his perception of the total situation. In this regard, the pattern of communication should have well-defined effects.

A formal experiment using this task has not yet been done. Preliminary runs (making use of various communication patterns and concerned primarily with experimental method) have revealed, however, that the binding forces against restructuring are very great, and that, with any considerable amount of communication restriction, a solution is improbable.

CONCLUDING REMARKS

The studies so briefly discussed in this chapter, if they do nothing more, suggest that an experimental approach to certain aspects of social communication is possible and that, in all probability, it would be practically rewarding. Although the problem of effective communication is an old one, recent trends are bringing to it a new sense of urgency. More and more it is becoming clear that any fundamental advance in social self-understanding must rest upon more adequate intercommunication. In areas where effective and highly integrated social effort is required, the problem is particularly critical. This is nowhere better illustrated than in scientific work. In many fields, it has become impossible to think in other terms than research teams. These groups, aside from the ordinary problems of communication which attend organization, face a whole new set of problems arising from the current emphasis upon "security." In practice, security is invariably translated into "communication restriction." In a sense, the experiments discussed above explore precisely this question: what happens to the performance and morale of working groups when communication is restricted in one way rather than in another?

The experimental evidence is provocative. Generalization at such an early stage of work is dangerous, but one is tempted to make a tentative step. It would seem that under the conditions imposed in the experiments, differences between certain patterns very probably exist. The differences most clearly revealed by the experiments are with respect to (a) the location, in the pattern, of recognized leadership; (b) the probability of errors in performance; and (c) the general satisfaction of group members.

Further, we note that in patterns with a high, localized centrality, organization evolves more quickly and is more stable, and errors in performance are less. At the same time, however, morale drops. It is conceivable that poor morale would, in the long run, affect stability and accuracy negatively. The experimental runs of fifteen trials conducted by Smith, if extended to a larger number trials, might well begin to show this effect.

More speculative, at present, is the question of the occurrence and utilization of insight. The preliminary trials with the "five squares" puzzle, while few, are dramatic. Every group succeeded in forming two, or three, or four squares. But the ability to restructure the problem, to give up the partial successes, varied widely from pattern to pattern. If the indications of the few experimental runs that have been made to date are any guide, both occurrence and utilization of insight will be found to drop rapidly as centrality is more and more highly localized. In one group, the individual to whom the necessary insight occurred was "ordered" by the emergent leader to "forget it." Losses of productive potential, in this way, are probably very common in most working groups, and must be enormous in the society at large.

COMMUNICATION STRUCTURE, DECISION STRUCTURE, AND GROUP PERFORMANCE*

Mauk Mulder

In the classical Bavelas-Leavitt research on communication structures in task-performing groups it was found that so-called wheel or star groups (cf. fig. 1) worked faster, needed a smaller number of messages and made less errors than circle groups (2, 8). Results were exactly similar in a replication of Leavitt's experiment by us with Dutch subjects (10). In these experiments the task of the group was to identify by means of written communication a symbol, held in common by all group members.

The topological structure determines, according to Leavitt (8), the better performance of the wheel groups. "Centrality," as a measure of "closeness" of an individual position to all other positions in the structure, is also a measure of the "availability of all information," which is necessary for the solving of the group problem. The most central position in the wheel, closest to all other positions, is most likely to get the answer first. This answer-getting potential is very different from the

one in the circle, where all members have an equal opportunity to collect all information and to solve the problem.

Quite contrary, however, were experimental results found by Shaw (12, 13). When solving "simple" problems (Leavitt-type) his wheel groups required less time than the circle groups (although the difference failed to reach significance). But his circle groups were faster than the wheel groups for so-called "complex" problems (for an example, see below).

In his theoretical explanation Shaw suggests that the differences found between the structures are due to the "availability of information" (with regard to simple problems) and to the "possibility of contributions" from all members of the group (complex problems).

"When simple problems are to be solved the availability of information is of primary importance. Thus, the wheel should be faster than the circle because the wheel pattern has the effect of designating which *S* will perform the function of identifying the common symbol. As the complexity of the problem increases, however, the possibility of contributions from all members of the group becomes much more important. This is true because some S's are more capable than others of solving such problems quickly, and because part solutions can be delegated to various positions,

* Mauk Mulder, "Communication Structure, Decision Structure, and Group Performance," *Sociometry*, 23 (1960), 1–14. Reprinted by permission of the American Sociological Association.

thereby compensating in part for the effects of "saturation." With complex problems, then, the wheel should be slower than the circle because the *central person becomes saturated* (i.e. because the optimal output level is exceeded) and because it sometimes forces the weakest person in the group to function in the leadership role" (13; cf. also 4).

However, the difference between the so-called simple and complex problems is a difference in degree rather than in kind and does not prepare us beforehand for the complete reversal appearing in Shaw's results. Is it then possible to explain the seemingly quite contrary findings of Leavitt and Shaw in one theory, without using the "substantial" concepts of "complexity" and "simplicity" of problems as basic in such a theory?

A characteristic common to the theories of both Leavitt and Shaw seems to be that too much emphasis is laid on the *topological* structure. "Availability of information," "contributions from all members" and "saturation" are *directly* derived from the networks (wheel and circle). However, the topological structure does not determine what really happens, but only what is possible.

Predictions (on "time" and "amount of communication") derived from the topological structure are not validated by the data reported by Leavitt and, for a comparable task, by Heise and Miller (8, 7). Furthermore Guetzkow and Simon, and Flament demonstrated that in different topological structures the developing organization determines the speed of groups when solving Leavitt-type simple problems (5, 6, 3).

This paper attempts to demonstrate that the decision structure, not the topological structure, determines the task performance of a group.

THEORY

Decision Structure

In task-performing groups there is exchange of information items. But besides that, several decisions by individual members have to be made. Among these are the decision to collect all needed information before passing it on; the decision to make a problem solution for one's self, etc. We introduce the construct "decision structure" as referring to: "who makes decisions for whom," and hypothesize that *groups with a more centralized decision structure will be capable of better group performance, because the contributions of the individual group members can be integrated by the person in the central "position" (the leader position).* The theory is restricted to situations in which two or more persons perform a *group task*, as in our experiment in which information, initially divided over all members, must be used to solve the problem.

In contrast to the topological structure, which does not change in time and whose parts are never modified by each other, the decision structure must *develop*. This is only logical, but a very important consequence hereof may be clarified.

A *more centralized structure* is in general characterized by *"vulnerability."* In the case of a centralized interaction structure (referring to "who interacts with whom") a high proportion of the total interaction goes through one of the group members. A disturbance in the functioning of this central position will have a radical effect, because this effect will be spread quickly through the total group and it will be very difficult to send the information flow via other positions.

The manifestation of vulnerability will

be a result of the pressure exerted on the central position and its resistance against this pressure.

By *pressure* we mean heavy input and output requirements, such as requests for information or for explanation, by peripheral group members. The capacities, motives and access to resources of the central person determine whether he accepts the "imperatives" in these messages, or opposes them. By *resistance* we mean this relative degree of opposition which may be mobilized versus attempted inductions. An example would be the central person's refusing to send the requested separate information and instead collecting information until he can make the problem solution. Thus would begin the centralization of the decision processes.

It is our opinion that negative effects of vulnerability will become manifest when a centralized interaction structure fails to sufficiently develop toward a strongly centralized *decision structure*. In experiments such as Leavitt's and Shaw's newly formed groups start new tasks. If they fail to develop centralized decision structures we expect that, in the beginning of the "work phase," groups with a more centralized interaction structure (wheel groups) will perform no more effectively and eventually may perform less well than do less centralized (circle) groups. Now Shaw's experimental group tasks differ in an essential way from those of Leavitt and Guetzkow. While the latter groups solved fifteen problems, the former performed only three or four tasks.[1] The opportunity

for the centralized decision structure to develop itself is considerably smaller in Shaw's experiments because of the smaller number of problems (which also leads to a shorter work period).

There is support for this theory in reported data. In Shaw's experiments half, or less than half, of the wheel groups develop into strongly centralized decision structures in which a central person makes the solution and sends it out, while in the experiments by Leavitt, Guetzkow and the present writer all wheel groups develop into such "central" groups. In the temporal analyses of these latter investigators and others, the weak start of wheel groups is apparent (8, 5, 9, 10).

With regard to the seemingly controversial results for "simple" and "complex" problems, it does not seem correct to state that "the wheel allows for better performance with simple problems, the circle with complex ones," but that the more centralized decision structures, which developed in Leavitt's groups solving 15 problems, enabled a better performance. Furthermore, the *gradual* difference between simple and complex problems has the effect, simply, that the development of the more centralized decision structure takes more time (i.e., problems) with the complex problems than with the simple ones.

An operational definition of the decision structure is as follows.

In the experimental groups a person (e.g. the central person in the wheel) may function as a mere "relayer" or as an "integrator." In the latter case he may make the decision not to pass the messages he

---

[1] Another crucial difference concerns the size of the groups (number of positions): Shaw's groups are smaller. This variable has been studied by the present writer in an experiment, reported in 11. In this publication it is also explained why the three-position circle and other totally interconnected structures are inadequate for testing Shaw's participation-theory.

receives, but to withhold them till he himself can make the problem solution and then he may (a) send the solution to other group members or (b) send the solution plus all necessary information in one message to other group members or (c) send all necessary information in one message to other group-members.

The "centrality index," which measures the degree of centralization of the decision structure, is based on communication acts of these three "types," all of them referring to decisions which have consequences for other group members.

The "decision centrality index" (D.C.I.) is computed in this way: As a first step, for each person in the group, it is necessary to compute how many persons are supplied by this person with messages of type (a), (b) or (c). This is done by a precise analysis of the communication-content.[2] Second, the scores of all "positions" in the group are summed up. Third, the *proportion* of every "position" is calculated by dividing his individual score by the total score. The last step is to calculate the *difference* between the "position" with the highest proportion and the "position" with the next highest. Thus the "decision centrality index" (D.C.I.) gives a measure of the centralization of the decision structure on *one* "position" (the "leader"). It may vary from 0 to 1.00.

Hypotheses

The theory is laid down in the following hypotheses.

1. To the extent that the decision structure of groups is centralized, the groups will give a better performance in their group tasks.[3]

The specific hypotheses to test in the present experiment are:

1a. To the extent that the decision structure of groups is more centralized, the group task will be performed faster.

1b. To the extent that the decision structure of groups is more centralized, the quality of the task performance will be better.

1c. To the extent that the decision structure of groups is more centralized, the group task will be performed more efficiently.

Performance per time-unit is measured by the time the group needs to solve its problem. The quality of performance is defined here by the number of errors made by the group during the task accomplishment. Efficiency is defined by the number of messages the group needs to solve the problem.

2. To the extent that a structure is more centralized, it is characterized by a greater "vulnerability." The vulnerability will manifest itself when the pressure exerted on the central position of the structure is greater than its resistance.

In our experimental design, the wheel groups start with a centralized *interaction* structure, but they do not immediately develop a centralized decision structure.

---

[2] In this operation type (b)- and (c)-content, although *in principle different*, are given the same weight (=1), because when all information is put together on one sheet, the solution of this *experimental task* can be read off easily. Type (a)-content is weighted double (=2) because here the person who sends out the solution does not allow for *any* participation in the solution by the "receiver."

[3] It is understood that the groups accept as their task to work as fast as possible. Should the group goal be: "to work slowly and badly," more centralized groups should perform this task "better."

We expect then that, during the beginning of the work period, the resistance of the center will be smaller than the pressure on it. Specific hypotheses:

2a. To the extent that the interaction structure in groups is more centralized, the group task will be performed relatively more slowly during the beginning period of the work.

2b. To the extent that the interaction structure in groups is more centralized, the quality of the group task will be relatively poorer during the beginning period of the work.

2c. To the extent that the interaction structure in groups is more centralized, the group task will be performed relatively less efficiently during the beginning period of the work.

These hypotheses can be tested in the experiment, by comparing the performance of more centralized (wheel) groups and less centralized (circle) groups, during the first part of the work-period (for instance, in the first two problems) and in the last period of the work (last two problems).

Shaw has found that the "corrective power" (determined by comparing the number of corrected errors with the total number of errors) is smaller in wheel than in circle groups. This is in agreement with the vulnerability hypothesis, so the specified hypothesis can be formulated:

2d. To the extent that the interaction structure is more centralized, the "corrective power" of the group will be smaller.

PROCEDURE

The Experimental Groups

In the present experiment two topological structures of four positions are investigated: wheel and circle. (cf. fig. 1.)

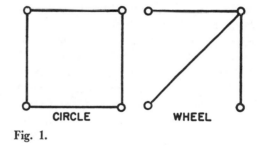

Fig. 1.

Twenty-six groups were run, 13 for each "structure." The subjects were students of Leiden University in their first year. They were naive in this type of experiment and were instructed to work as a group as fast as possible. Subjects of a given group were not acquainted with each other prior to the experiment; instructions for the experiment were given them after they were seated together. They were told who could communicate with whom, but the structure was not made explicit.

The Experimental Situation

The subjects were told that we wanted to investigate how fast groups can solve certain abstract problems. Five problems had to be solved; the writer would have preferred more problems, to allow for the complete development of the decision structure, but this was the maximum possible in the time the subjects had available. The problems were the "complex" ones Shaw had used. The following is an example:

A small company is moving from one office-building to another. It must move four kinds of equipment: (a) chairs, (b) desks, (c) filing-cabinets and (d) typewriters. How many trucks are needed to make the move in one trip?

The eight items of information needed

to solve the problem are that the company owns a total of 12 desks, 48 chairs, 12 typewriters, 15 filing-cabinets, and that one truckload can take 12 typewriters, or 3 desks, or 5 filing-cabinets, or 24 chairs.

The statement of the problem was typed completely on each of four separate cards and each of the eight items of information was typed on a separate card. Each subject was given one of the problem cards; the information was equally divided over the group members. For completion of the group task each subject has to know the problem solution.

The subjects were seated around a circular table, so that each was separated from the next by a vertical partition from the center to the table's edge. The partitions had slots permitting subjects to push written message cards to the persons on either side of them.

To allow for communication to the other members of the group, a four-layered quadrilateral box was placed at the center of the table. The box was placed so that the partitions just touched each of the four points of the quadrangle. Each of the four resulting work spaces was painted a different color. The subjects were supplied with blank message cards whose colors matched those of their work spaces. Any message sent from a booth had to be on a card of the booth's color.

Measurement

When the group had solved the problems, each subject was asked to fill out a questionnaire, in which mainly measurements of satisfaction and leadership were made. The most important data in this experiment, however, were time scores, communication units and errors. These could be directly observed during the session or analyzed from the material afterwards.

Results

First we will report results of analyses of circle versus wheel data, bearing especially on the "development hypotheses" (2a., 2b., 2c.) but also on 1a., 1b. and 1c.

Then we will report results of analyses based on the degree of centralization of the decision structure during the last phase of the work. Only hypotheses 1a., 1b., and 1c. will be tested in these analyses.

With regard to the development of the group structure, the decision centrality index of the wheel groups during the last two problems is .51; that of the circle groups is .24. This difference is significant (Mann Whitney U Test: $p < .01$ one-tailed test).[4] For the *first* phase of the work period, no such difference occurs. Each position's proportion of the total *interaction* remains the same during the work period, both in the wheel groups and in the circle groups. Thus the interaction structure does not appear to develop in wheel or circle groups.

Wheel Versus Circle

In Table 1, data on the speed of the work performance are reported.

The increase in "superiority" of the wheel appears clearly from the data in the last row. In the beginning of the work

---

[4] Since the data satisfied few of the assumptions of normal-distribution methods, only "distribution-free" methods have been used. Results will be stated for a one-tail test, since they test directional predictions. For more details on this study cf. 11.

Table 1*

MEAN TIME PER PROBLEM (FOR TOTAL GROUP) IN MINUTES

	First Problem	Second Problem	Third Problem	Fourth Problem	Fifth Problem	All Problems
Circle	13.95	8.70	6.60	6.55	7.25	8.61
Wheel	16.27	9.92	6.13	5.85	5.88	8.81
Circle minus Wheel	−2.32	−1.22	+0.47	+0.70	+1.37	

*Note: 13 circle groups are compared with 13 wheel groups. The interaction between structure and problem sequence is significant (Kendell's Tau=1.0, p=.01).

period, the circle groups are faster than the wheel groups, but the difference decreases. In a later phase the relation is reversed, and then the difference increases. Thus hypothesis 2a is strongly supported.

Hypothesis 1a is not confirmed. Although the wheel groups are faster in the fourth and fifth problems, the difference fails to reach significance.

In Table 2, data on the quality of the performance are reported.

It appears that 60 per cent of all wheel errors are made in the first two problems, 19 per cent in the last two. For the circle these figures are, respectively, 40 per cent and 44 per cent. This difference between wheel and circle groups is large and significant. Hypothesis 2b is thus strongly supported by these findings.

The same holds for hypothesis 1b. In the last phase of the work period, the wheel groups make fewer errors than the circle groups.

With regard to errors, hypothesis 2d is also strongly supported by the data. In the circle groups, 29 errors are corrected from a total of 57 errors; in the wheel, only 13 are corrected from a total of 53. The difference is significant (Chi-square: $p < .01$).

In Table 3, data on the efficiency of the task performance are reported.

Again the superiority of the wheel increases steadily from first to fifth problem. Hypothesis 2c has found strong support.

While the difference is not statistically significant in the first phase of the work period, it increases to such an extent that,

Table 2*

ERRORS PER PROBLEM

	First Problem	Second Problem	Third Problem	Fourth Problem	Fifth Problem	All Problems
Circle	9	15	8	7	18	(57)
Wheel	20	12	11	4	6	(53)

*Note: The difference between wheel and circle in the 2×5 table is significant at the .05 level (likelihood ratio test of the independence hypothesis).
The differences between wheel and circle in the fifth problem and in the fourth and fifth problems together are significant at the .05 level (Chi square, with correction for continuity).

Table 3*

MEAN NUMBER OF MESSAGES, PER PROBLEM, PER POSITION

	First Problem	Second Problem	Third Problem	Fourth Problem	Fifth Problem	All Problems
Circle	8.20	7.08	5.88	5.75	6.28	(6.64)
Wheel	7.15	5.68	3.63	3.43	3.38	(4.65)
Circle minus Wheel	+1.05	+1.40	+2.25	+2.32	+2.90	

*Note: The interaction between structure and problem sequence is significant (Tau = 1.0, p = .01).

The difference between wheel and circle is not significant in the first problem; it is significant at the .01 level in the last problem (Mann Whitney U test).

in the later phases, it is large and significant. Thus hypothesis 1c also is strongly supported.

D.C.I. in Last Phase

We now turn to the second set of analyses, based on the degree of centralization of the decision structure achieved by the groups in the last problem. For every group, the decision centrality index during the last problem was calculated; then the wheel groups were divided in two classes, containing the six more-centralized and the six less-centralized wheel groups; the same was done with the circle groups.

Results of these analyses are reported in Table 4.

It will be noted in Table 4 that the subclasses of wheel and circle groups varied substantially in degree of centralization of decisions. The less centralized six among both wheel and circle groups achieved only a low level of centralization, while

Table 4*

DECISION CENTRALITY INDEX, SPEED, QUALITY, AND EFFICIENCY, ON LAST (FIFTH) PROBLEM

	n (1)	D.C.I. (2)	Time to Solve (3)	Errors (4)	Messages per Position (5)
More-centralized wheel groups (W_1)	6	.85	4.01	0	2.46
Less-centralized wheel groups (W_2)	6	.17	7.88	5	4.21
More-centralized circle groups (C_1)	6	.54	5.79	4	4.88
Less-centralized circle groups (C_2)	6	.07	8.84	12	7.46

*Note: Within the table, differences in D.C.I., time and messages are tested with the Mann Whitney U test. The difference in errors is tested with Fisher's exact test.

Results are for one-tail test, except the D.C.I.-comparison of W_2 versus C_1.

Significance of differences:	P < .01	P < .05
W_1–W_2,	Col. 2, 3, 5	———
W_2–C_1,	2	Col. 3
C_1–C_2,	2, 5	3
W_1–C_2	4, 3, 5	———

Table 5*

MEAN NUMBER OF SENT MESSAGES, PER POSITION, IN LAST PROBLEM

Central position $W_1 = 4.67$	Peripheral positions $W_1 = 1.72$
Central position $W_2 = 7.17$	Peripheral positions $W_2 = 3.22$
Circle position $\quad = 6.17$	

*Note: Differences are tested with Mann Whitney U Test (one-tail-test).
The difference between central positions in W_1 and central positions in W_2 is significant at the .05 level. The difference between peripheral positions in W_1 and peripheral positions in W_2 is significant at the .01 level.

the more centralized six achieved a substantial level, even among circle groups. Indeed, the C_1 groups show a significantly higher level than the W_2 groups.

The time data are according to prediction on the basis of the decision centrality index: groups with a more centralized decision structure are faster, as is apparent from the large and significant differences between W_1 groups and W_2 groups, C_1 and C_2 and W_1 and C_2. The most important datum, however, is that the circle groups with a more centralized decision structure (C_1) needed considerably less time than the less centralized wheel groups (W_2). From these findings it may be concluded that the decision structure is the primary determinant of the speed of performance. The more centralized the decision structure, the faster is the group's performance. Hypothesis 1a is thus strongly supported by these experimental results.

The number of errors decreased with increasing decision centrality index (Tau: $p < .05$) but some differences are extremely small. Only the difference between the most centralized groups (W_1) and the least centralized ones (C_2) was significant. These results give support to hypothesis 1b.

With regard to number of messages, a large difference exists between W_1 and C_2. Also, within the topological structure, an increasing decision centrality index leads to a decreasing amount of communication. But C_1 groups did not need fewer messages than W_2 groups. Hypothesis 1c is supported, but the degree of centralization of the interaction structure also exerts some influence on the *amount* of communication.

Some of our data on the distribution of communication over the different "positions" within the group are very relevant in connection with Shaw's concept of "saturation." In the wheel groups, the central person sends out a mean of 8.7 messages per problem, the "peripherals" 3.3. One may question whether the central person does not exceed the optimal output level. He may do so in the beginning (mean number of messages = 13.6) but definitely does not at the end (mean = 6.2). Here his communication activity is not different from that of circle members (cf. Table 3). Table 5 presents further crucial data bearing on this problem.

Persons in the center position of the decision structure in W_1 *send out* fewer messages than central persons in W_2 (and less than circle members, although this difference is not significant). The number of messages they receive is made up of the number the peripherals send. Thus it appears from the table that the central persons in W_1 also *receive* fewer messages than central persons in W_2. These relations do not change when a correction is made for time differences. Thus the communication activity (input and output) of the central position even decreases when centralized decision structures develop, and the saturation hypothesis must be rejected.

DISCUSSION

In early studies in this field, stress was laid on the topological structure as a determinant of group performance. Guetzkow and Simon, and Flament, however, already demonstrated that, when *simple* problems are solved, the *speed* of the group's performance is determined by the organization which the group develops.[5]

A theory by Shaw states that "availability of information" determines the performance of groups when simple problems are solved, but that for more complex problems the possibility of contributions from all members becomes much more important. Groups which allow for participation of all group members should perform complex tasks faster than groups where this is not the case. Shaw tested this theory by a comparison between groups with a topological circle structure and groups with a wheel (star) structure. The latter structure may be called a centralized interaction structure, since all interaction is "to" or "from" a central position. The former structure should permit more participation of all members.

---

[5] Simon and Guetzkow refer to "optimal organizations." In their *conclusions* they do not distinguish the decision structure from the interaction structure (cf. 6 and also for more elaboration on this point 11).

The present theory is quite the reverse. It states that a high degree of centralization of the decision processes leads to better group performance.

Shaw assumes a sharp, "substantial" difference between simple and complex problems. This difference, however, is one of gradation. In our opinion the essential point is that, irrespective of the complexity of the problem, *integration* of the group process is necessary. When two or more persons work on the same task, so that the work of each of them is only a part of the "total," the integration of their contributions is a basic condition for a good end performance. When decision structure refers to "who makes decisions for whom," integration is secured to an optimal degree by a strongly centralized decision structure. The central person can then integrate the contributions of all individual members.

The theory is confirmed by the experimental results. In a number of our groups, a centralized decision structure developed during the work period, even though it was relatively short. These groups performed their tasks with more speed, fewer errors and more efficiency than groups where centralization of the decision processes did not develop to such an extent.

In Shaw's participation theory it is hypothesized that, as a consequence of centralization processes, the central person would become "saturated" because the optimal output level would be exceeded. Our data, however, demonstrate that, in groups where a more centralized decision structure develops, the central position is not characterized by a greater communication input or output, but rather by a smaller one. Thus the saturation hypothesis proves to be incorrect.

The data also demonstrate that the development of a centralized decision structure (and, consequently, a better group performance) is to a very considerable degree independent of the topological structure or the interaction structure. But *if* the centralized decision structure develops on the basis of a centralized interaction structure, this leads to some special consequences. More centralized structures are in general characterized by a greater "vulnerability." By this is meant that a disturbance in the functioning of the central position will quickly disturb the functioning of the total group. Now we hypothesized that in groups with a centralized interaction structure (as the wheel groups in the experiment) such disturbances in the functioning of the central positions should occur *in the beginning* of the experimental sessions. Then the input and output requirements of the central position would be such that he could not meet them. This would lead to negative results for the group's performance.

This hypothesis, which may explain some of Shaw's results, is also confirmed by our results. The more centralized interaction structures demonstrate a greater vulnerability at the beginning of the work, which leads to negative performance results. The development of centralized decision structures appears to cancel these initial negative effects radically.

SUMMARY

This paper reported a laboratory investigation testing two hypotheses about group structure and group performance. The first hypothesis was that the more centralized the decision structure of groups, the better will be the group's performance in regard to speed, quality and efficiency. The second hypothesis stated that more centralized structures are generally characterized by "vulnerability," which leads to negative performance results as long as centralized *decision* structures have not developed. These hypotheses were confirmed by the results of an experiment in which groups of four persons solved so-called complex problems.

REFERENCES

1. BAVELAS, A., "A Mathematical Model for Group-Structures," *Applied Anthropology*, 1948, 7, 16–30.

2. BAVELAS, A., "Communication Patterns in Task-Oriented Groups," in D. Cartwright and A. Zander (Eds.), *Group Dynamics*, New York: Row-Peterson, 1953, 493–506.

3. FLAMENT, C., "Changements de Rôles et Adaptation à la Tâche dans les Groupes de Travail Utilisant Divers Réseaux de Communication," *L'Année Psychologique*, 1956, 2, 411–431.

4. GILCHRIST, J. C., M. E. SHAW, and L. C. WALKER, "Some Effects of Unequal Distribution of Information in a Wheel-Group Structure," *Journal of Abnormal and Social Psychology*, 1954, 49, 554–556.

5. GUETZKOW, H., "Organizational Development and Restrictions in Communications," Dittoed paper, Carnegie Institute of Technology, 1951 (108 pp.).

6. GUETZKOW, H., and H. A. SIMON, "The Impact of Certain Communication Nets upon Organization and Performance in Task-Oriented Groups," *Management Science*, 1955, 1, 233–250.

7. HEISE, G. A., and G. A. MILLER, "Problem Solving by Small Groups Using Various Communication Nets," *Journal of Abnormal and Social Psychology*, 1951, 46, 327–335.

8. LEAVITT, H. J., "Some Effects of Certain Communication Patterns on Group Per-

formance," *Journal of Abnormal and Social Psychology*, 1951, 46, 38–50.

9. Luce, R. D., J. Macy, L. S. Christie, and D. H. Hay, "Information Flow in Task Oriented Groups," Technical Report No. 264, 1953, Research Laboratory of Electronics, Massachusetts Institute of Technology.

10. Mulder, M., "Groepsstructuur en Gedrag," *Nederlands Tijdschrift voor de Psychologie*, 1956, 11, 85–133.

11. Mulder, M., "Group-Structure and Group-Performance," *Acta Psychologica*, 1959, 15.

12. Shaw, M. E., "Some Effects of Unequal Distribution of Information upon Group Performance in Various Communication Nets," *Journal of Abnormal and Social Psychology*, 1954, 49, 547–553.

13. Shaw, M. E., "Some Effects of Problem Complexity upon Problem Solution Efficiency in Different Communication Nets," *Journal of Experimental Psychology*, 1954, 48, 211–217.

TASK DEPENDENCY OF ORGANIZATIONAL CENTRALITY: ITS BEHAVIORAL CONSEQUENCES

Claude Faucheux and Kenneth D. Mackenzie*

A substantial number of experimental studies have attempted to explore the relations among group organization, task, and performance. Following the works of Bavelas (1950) and Leavitt (1951), a number of experiments have manipulated the communication network given to the group and measured their relative efficiency and satisfaction with various tasks. However, results from these studies are not always easy to interpret. For instance, Leavitt (1951), Guetzkow and Simon (1955), and Cohen, Bennis, and Walkon (1961) find that, for a simple task like the common-symbol task, a highly centralized communication structure (a wheel) is more conducive to high group performance than a less centralized network. On the other hand, Shaw (1951a, 1951b) and Shaw and Blum (1965) report that for a more complex task a less centralized network (a circle) seems to be more efficient. However, Guetzkow and Dill (1957) and Guetzkow and Simon (1955) argue that one reason why different networks vary in efficiency is the influence exerted by the network's restrictions on the ability of the groups to develop adequate organizations. He shows that when intertrial free discussion is allowed, groups quickly develop an organization capable of coping with the

* Claude Faucheux and Kenneth D. Mackenzie, "Task Dependency of Organizational Centrality: Its Behavioral Consequences," *Journal of Experimental Social Psychology*, 2 (1966), 361–75. Reprinted by permission of Academic Press, Inc.

networks and perform equally well in all of them. Along a similar line, Mulder (1960) argues that only the decision structure is important and demonstrates that a centralized decision structure leads to better results than a less centralized one, even for Shaw's so-called "complex" task. He shows that circles have superior performance to wheels in the beginning trials, but that this difference tends to decrease and reverse itself in the final trials of a longer series.

One cannot be surprised, therefore, by the pessimistic conclusions of Glanzer and Glaser's (1961) survey of the literature, namely, that at the present time there is no simple answer as to the effect of the structure of a group on its efficiency. Some of the difficulties lie in the interference between the imposed network and organizational development. In this sense, the manipulation of the communication network does no more than manipulate the organizational constraints on the group attempting to solve a given problem. The organization structure *per se* is neither manipulated nor controlled adequately, since in an all-channel many different organization structures can develop. For example, an all-channel can develop into a wheel. And we know that a wheel network is not necessarily the most conducive environment for a centralized organization, which often develops faster in an all-channel. One way to overcome these difficulties is to treat the organization as a dependent variable.

But in treating the organization as a dependent variable one is immediately faced with another difficulty, which lies in the definition of the nature of the task. We have seen how the simplicity-complexity dimension can be deceiving. Some attempts have been made to understand

and control the nature of the task, the most remarkable being by Roby and Lanzetta (1958). But as Zajonc (1965, p. 71) pointed out:

> ... however up to now their classification appears not to have had a pronounced theoretical influence, probably because the vast majority of tasks used in small group research simply defy a parametric analysis in terms proposed by Roby and Lanzetta and possibly in any other terms as well.

Flament's (1963, 1965) work can be interpreted as an attempt to overcome the difficulty pointed out by Zajonc (1965), by describing the task requirement in terms of graph theory, and to predict performance according to the degree of isomorphism between task and structure. Another approach in specification of the dimension of tasks is the work of Shaw (1963), using Thurstone and Chave attitude-scaling technique with graduate students in psychology as the judges.

Despite the difficulties in determining the dimensions or procedures to differentiate tasks along a continuum, it is possible to distinguish between a routine deductive task and a nonroutine inferential task. Therefore, it should be possible to establish the existence of the impact of organizational task on organizational structure and performance by examining the behavior under the impact of two series of tasks: a series of simple routine tasks and a series of complex problem-solving tasks. In order to do this, as Lorge *et al.* (1958) point out, the group must be given sufficient time to emerge from an *ad hoc* group to a functioning organization with relatively stable, differentiated roles. But the fact that it usually takes time for groups to emerge implies that the organizational structure is changing. One of the co-authors (Mackenzie, 1964 and Mackenzie and Huysmans, 1965) has worked on studies where such change is the rule rather than the exception. If the structure is changing as the group emerges, then it is not clear that organizational structure can be an independent variable unless the proper restrictions are imposed. It makes more sense to treat organization structure as a dependent rather than as an independent variable.

In an earlier experiment one of the authors (Faucheux and Moscovici, 1960) considered the group organization as a variable dependent on the nature of the task and as an intervening variable between task and performance. Two types of task were used. One was of a "deductive" nature: the solution required only the strict application of a set of rules and a correct sequence of deductions. The other task was of an "inferential" nature since it required the generation of all possible combinations of a *set* of elements, combinations which could not be deduced and had to be inferred. The members were absolutely free to communicate to each other and the communications were entirely tape-recorded. From the communication matrices it was possible to decide whether or not the group was "centralized." Twelve groups of four members had to perform both tasks: half of them the deductive task first, the other half the inferential task first. The results show that the groups tended to develop a centralized organization in the deductive task and a noncentralized one in the inferential task. The few groups who failed to centralize in the deductive task performed less well than those who centralized, and similarly the groups who centralized in the inferential task performed less well than those who did not. These latter groups

developed an identical organization of three differentiated roles.

The experiment reported in the present paper is similar to the French experiment in that the task was manipulated as the independent variable and the organization treated as a dependent one; however, it differs on several points. First, an index of centrality, developed by one of the authors (Mackenzie, 1966), provides a precise measure of centrality which allows a better analysis of the organizational development over time and trial by trial. Second, a method for a more detailed content analysis of the communications, which provides a better understanding of the different activities in which the members engage themselves, was developed by one of the authors (Mackenzie, 1964, Mackenzie and Huysmans, 1965, and Mackenzie and Frazier, 1966). Third, the tasks were different. The inferential type of task was not purely inferential and required some coordination, but it had the advantage over the French experiment of permitting repeated performances of similar tasks. The inferential task was developed from the mathematical results of a paper by one of the authors (Mackenzie, 1967), and will be discussed in the next section. Fourth, only written communications were allowed. Fifth, in the French experiment the task could be performed by individuals; whereas in the CIT experiment, the information was distributed among the members, which made interactions necessary in order to solve the problem.

In this paper we want primarily to demonstrate (a) the task dependency of organizational centrality and (b) how the organization structure and behavior act as an intervening variable between task and performance. In addition, we hope to suggest the potentialities of a new approach to organizational psychology.

METHOD

Subjects were taken from the undergraduate population at Carnegie Institute of Technology. There were fourteen groups of five members each. Each group had to perform two series of tasks. Task A, the minimum-list-of-symbols task, was primarily deductive in nature. Task B, the network decomposition task, mainly required inferences.

Half of the groups performed a series of eight A tasks, followed by a series of four B tasks. The other groups were first given four B tasks, followed by eight A tasks. The average group spent 80 minutes on the series of A tasks and 142 minutes on the series of B tasks.

The subjects were told that the average group needed 4 hours for the entire experiment and that they would be paid for 4 hours regardless of how long they took to complete the experiment. Four groups exceeded the 4 hours, and three groups were not able to complete all eight of the A tasks because one or more of the members had to leave.

After receiving their instructions for the first series of tasks, the subjects were assigned to five different booths which isolated them visually. All communications were written on colored paper forms. Each subject had a different color. The subjects were provided carbon paper for copies to be sent to other members. There were no restrictions placed on content of the messages. The experimenters delivered all messages after stamping the time and message number.

The subjects received a coffee break between the two series of tasks. During the coffee break discussion of the experiment was forbidden. After the coffee break, the subjects were instructed in their second series of tasks.

At the end of the experiment, the subjects completed a questionnaire.

Description of the Tasks

Task A—Minimum List of Symbols. The group had to find the smallest complete set of different symbols (minimum list) distributed among them. The group had a correct solution only if all members sent the experimenter a correct list in the same order.

Four types of symbols were used: digits, letters, colors, or simple geometric symbols. The type of symbol varied from trial to trial and all four were used, but each subject received the same type on a given trial.

The minimum-list-of-symbols task required that the subjects share their information, compiling a minimum list of symbols, and checking to see that all had the same list.

Task B—Network Decomposition Task. Each of the subjects was given a list of arcs from a five-point graph. The first step was to construct the network from the arcs; to do this the subjects had to share their information and infer the correct total graph which integrated all the information distributed among the members. The second step was to decompose the total graph into two subgraphs which had to be wheels, circles, or all-channels. In this experiment there were up to three possible correct decompositions, and the subjects did not know how many correct solutions existed. The subjects had to check the total graph and generate, check, and share the subgraphs. The subgraphs had to be compiled for the total solution and shared. The decomposition of the graph was very difficult and required inferences by the group. The average group spent 35 minutes per B task. Tasks A and B are illustrated in Fig. 1.

Dependent Measures

Index of Centrality. An index of centrality developed by one of the authors (Mackenzie, 1966b) was used to compute the individual centralities and group centrality for each trial. The centrality index is based on the group's communications incidence matrix, where each

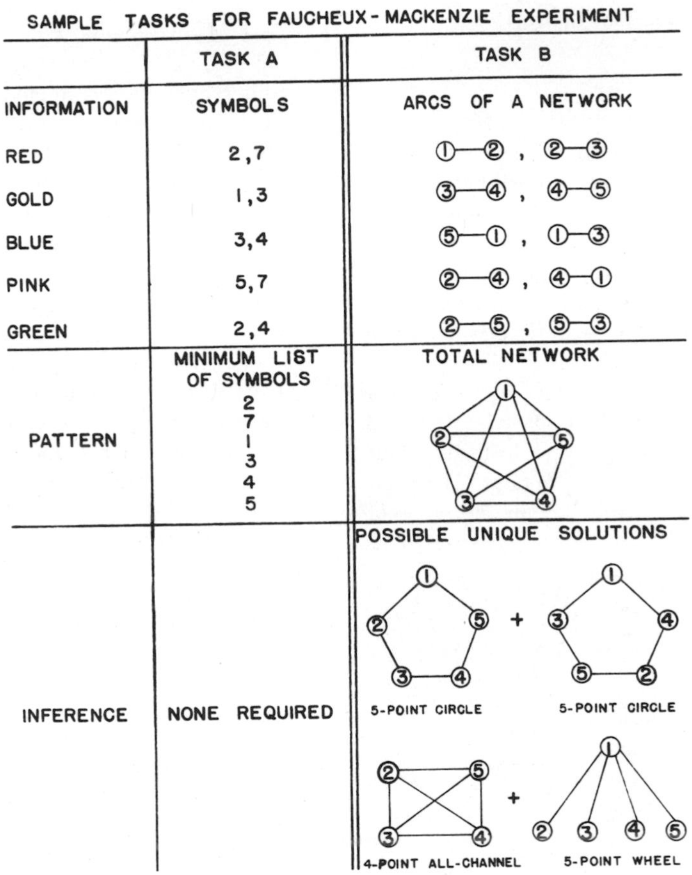

SAMPLE TASKS FOR FAUCHEUX-MACKENZIE EXPERIMENT

	TASK A	TASK B
INFORMATION	SYMBOLS	ARCS OF A NETWORK
RED	2,7	①—② , ②—③
GOLD	1,3	③—④ , ④—⑤
BLUE	3,4	⑤—① , ①—③
PINK	5,7	②—④ , ④—①
GREEN	2,4	②—⑤ , ⑤—③
PATTERN	MINIMUM LIST OF SYMBOLS 2 7 1 3 4 5	TOTAL NETWORK
INFERENCE	NONE REQUIRED	POSSIBLE UNIQUE SOLUTIONS 5-POINT CIRCLE + 5-POINT CIRCLE 4-POINT ALL-CHANNEL + 5-POINT WHEEL

Fig. 1.

entry is the fraction of the total number of the group's messages sent by one participant to another. The index is so constructed that it is zero for the homogeneous all-channel and unity for the homogeneous wheel. A graph is homogeneous if all nonzero entries in the matrix are equal. The centrality index, then, is based on actual communication patterns rather than upon the mere availability of communication channels. The centrality index allowed us to monitor the actual communications structure from trial to trial.

Performance. The primary measure of performance was the mean number of errors per trial. The error rate reflected the *accuracy* of the group's performance. We also computed the mean number of messages per trial and the mean time to reach the correct solution for each trial. The mean number of messages and mean time per trial were used to compare within task performances but not to compare performances between tasks, since the two types of tasks were different and required a different amount of time and number of messages per trial. We also calculated the mean of messages per minute, which was used as an estimate of the *efficiency* of communication. The lower the number of messages per minute, the greater the *economy* in communication or the lower the redundancy.

Subjective Evaluations. At the end of the experiment the subjects completed a questionnaire in which they were asked to evaluate on a nine-point scale such things as the group performance, their own performances, their relative liking of each task, and to what extent the group members took appropriate roles needed by the group.

Content Analysis of the Communications. The centrality indices reflected only the communication patterns in terms of the numbers of messages sent and received. By using the method of one of the authors (Mackenzie, 1964), based on set theory, a detailed content analysis was made on the written messages. All messages were coded into 288 task-oriented categories, consisting of 32 activities with 9 subcategories (called "elements") for the type of statement made about each activity. There were also 63 nontask-oriented categories consisting of 7 activities with 9 social subcategories. We also coded time, message numbers, identification of sender and receiver, trial numbers, group numbers, and the symbol or arc content of each message. The activities ranged from a "communication

about one arc or symbol" to "communications concerning the goal of minimizing the number of messages." Examples of subcategories (elements) are decisions, requests, suggestions, or instructions. Each message was first broken down into its activities and then these into elements. The nontask-oriented communications ranged from a "nontask-oriented communication about the experiment staff" to "jabberwocky" in which nonsense communications were coded. Examples of nontask-oriented subcategories include "shows solidarity," "shows antagonism," "agreement or approval."

RESULTS

Centrality

As expected, we found sharp differences in centrality between tasks (Table 1). We found a tendency for the group to centralize on the eight A tasks, but there was no noticeable upward or downward trend over the four B trials.

Using standard regression techniques, we performed the following calculations:

(i) For the groups performing the A tasks first, we regressed the centrality of the groups against *trial number* and *total elapsed time* for both the A tasks and the B tasks. This gave us four regressions.

Table 1

MEAN CENTRALITIES OF EXPERIMENTAL GROUPS

Task	Task performed first	Task performed second	Mean for all trials
Task A	.665[a]	.617	.645
Task B	.298[b]	.395	.340

[a] The differences between means for all three columns are significant at the 0.001 level.

[b] The difference between means for the first two columns (the order in which a series of tasks was performed) is nonsignificant for the A tasks ($t = 0.74$) but significant for the B tasks ($t = 2.18$, $p < .05$).

(ii) For the group performing the B tasks first, we regressed the centrality of the groups against *trial number* and *total elapsed time* for both the A tasks and the B tasks. This gave us four regressions.

We found (Table 1) that for the A tasks the mean centrality was not affected by the order of performance, and that there was a slight but significant difference for the B tasks ($t = 2.18$, $p < .05$). The result for the B tasks raised the question of the effect on the centrality of the second series of tasks due to the first series of tasks. In order to test for such an effect, we computed the amount of variance in the second series of tasks about the regression line for the first series of tasks for both trial number and total elapsed time. We found the following:

(i) By using the trial-number regressions, the B tasks accounted for only 25% of the variance in the A tasks and the A tasks accounted for none of the variance in the B tasks (in fact the variance actually increased).

(ii) By using the total elapsed time regressions, the B tasks accounted for none of the variance in the A tasks and the A tasks accounted for none of the variance in the B (in fact the variance actually increased in both cases).

We conclude, therefore, that the organization structure depends upon the nature of the task, and the organization structures for the two tasks are different *and* independent.

Among the fourteen groups performing the A tasks only three did not centralize completely in a wheel structure, while the other eleven centralized on the average between the fourth and fifth trials. The mean trial number for centrality was 4.4 when A's were performed first and 4.5 when A's were performed second. By examining the graph of trial numbers versus

centrality for each group of A tasks, ten of the eleven groups exhibited the same pattern. One can see a regular increase over the first few trials and then a sudden jump in centrality to 1.0 (that of a wheel), followed by a plateau reflecting the stabilization in a wheel structure. Only two groups manifested a slight decrease in centrality on the eighth trial.

Among the seven groups performing A first, six centralized in a wheel, and when confronted with B tasks all decentralized immediately on the first B task (mean decrease in centrality was 0.623). Among the seven groups performing A last, three did not complete all eight tasks because, having already exceeded the 4 hours, one of their members had to leave to meet other obligations. One of these three groups centralized and the other two did not.

The centrality for the B tasks was significantly lower than for the A tasks and no trend was noticeable over the four trials. The inferential component in the task inhibited a greater centralization. This supports our hypothesis that the degree of centralization of a group is determined by the nature of the task. As we shall see later, though the low variance in centrality within the B tasks does not permit any conclusion about the relation between centrality and performance, there are some significant relationships between centrality and the subjective evaluation of performance.

Performance

A Tasks. Before considering the performance in the A tasks, let us remember that three groups (Groups 14, 9, and 10) were not able to complete the eight trials: these groups were performing the A tasks, and when they had exceeded the 4 hours some of their members had to leave to meet external obligations. Table 2 contains the performance measures of these three groups, plus another (Group 19) which completed all eight trials but failed to centralize. We can see that the performances of Groups 9 and 10 were relatively poor compared to those of Group 14, which centralized on the sixth and last trial, and Group 19. Let us compare the performance of the three groups that did not centralize with the performance of the eleven others before their centraliza-

Table 2

PERFORMANCE MEANS FOR THOSE GROUPS NOT COMPLETING ALL EIGHT
A TASKS OR WHO DID NOT CENTRALIZE

Group designation	Mean No. of messages per trial	Mean time per trial	Mean No. of messages per minute	Mean No. of errors per trial	Mean centrality in A trials	No. of completed trials
14[a]	20.0	5.67	3.65	0.18	.466	6
9[b]	45.5	7.40	6.12	1.00	.315	5
10	56.0	9.75	5.73	1.75	.147	4
19	37.0	11.00	3.36	0.13	.441	8

[a] Groups 14, 9, 10, started with task B and Group 19 started with task A. Group 14 centralized on trial 6. The other three groups did not centralize.

[b] The mean number of messages per trial, mean number of messages per minute, and mean number of errors per trial were higher ($p<.05$) for groups 9 and 10 than for 14 and 19. In addition the mean centrality was significantly lower for Groups 9 and 10.

Table 3

PERFORMANCE MEANS FOR BOTH TASKS ACCORDING TO CENTRALITY

Experimental situation	Mean No. of messages per trial	Mean time per trial	Mean No. of messages per minute	Mean No. of errors per trial
Groups that never centralized on A tasks (9, 10, 19)	43.9	9.60**[a]	5.22	.76***[b]
Precentralization data for groups that eventually centralized on A tasks	32.6	10.50**	3.11	.32*
Postcentralization data on A tasks	10.4	4.00	2.07	.13
All B tasks	81.2	35.5	2.45	.66**

[a] The differences between all six pairs of means in each column are significant at .05, except the pairs marked by asterisks where * means $p<.10$ and ** means $p>.10$. Thus 21 out of a possible 24 pairs of means are significantly different at .05.

[b] This number has three asterisks since the pair (.76, .32) is significantly different at 0.10; but the pair (.76, .66) is not significantly different at 0.10.

tion (Table 3): the former sent more messages per trial ($t = 1.95$, $p < .05$), their communication efficiency (in terms of messages per minute) was lower ($t = 2.85$, $p < .005$), and the number of errors per trial was greater ($t = 1.41$, $p < .10$). If we look at the groups who did centralize and compare their performances before and after centralization, we find again the same trends: after centralization the number of messages, the time and the number of errors per trial fell significantly. Clearly performance increased in the A tasks when the groups centralized.

B Tasks. In the A tasks there was a clear distinction between the groups that did not centralize and those that did. For the groups that centralized, it was very simple to distinguish between pre-jump and postjump trials. There were no such clear distinctions for the B trials. We could not discriminate performance differences according to the centrality index, partly because of the low mean and variance for the B tasks and partly because of the difficulty in interpreting the meaning of low centrality. The interpretation problem is discussed in the summary and discussion section. However, for all four performance measures (Table 3) there exist significant differences between the A and B tasks.

It is clear that for the most part the Task A data are not directly comparable in any meaningful sense with Task B data because the tasks are different. The one possible exception is the number of messages per minute, which is a measure of communication efficiency. For the B tasks the number of messages per minute was significantly higher than for the postcentralization A trials ($t = 10.8$, $p < .005$), but significantly lower than for the precentralization A trials ($t = 5.07$, $p < .005$) and the noncentralized groups on A trials ($t = 8.20$, $p < .005$). It is therefore possible to conclude that, in terms of communication efficiency, the B groups performed less well than the centralized A groups and better than the precentralized and noncentralized groups.

Subjective evaluations. The final questionnaire permitted us to obtain data on the subjective evaluation by the subjects of their relative liking of each task, and to what extent they thought the members in their group took the roles they felt were required.

Group-performance evaluation. Since the A tasks required centralization for greater efficiency, we expected that the greater the centralization of a group, the higher would be the evaluation of its performance by the members. Inversely, since the B tasks required more participation from all the members (therefore less centralization) in order to generate all possible solutions, we expected that the lower the centralization, the higher would be the group-performance evaluation. These expectations were supported by the data: we found a significant positive correlation (.817, $p < .05$) between average centrality (mean of the postjump trials, or the mean of all trials if the group did not centralize) and the mean group-performance evaluation for the A tasks, and a negative correlation ($-.365$, $p > .05$) for the B tasks. Although this last correlation did not reach a satisfactory level of significance, the difference between the two coefficients was highly significant.

Personal-performance evaluation. By the same reasoning, there should be a positive correlation for the B tasks between the evaluation of one's own performance and one's evaluation of group performance, and a negative correlation for the A tasks. The A tasks required very little personal performance unless the subject was in the most centralized position, but the B tasks required a high performance level by each subject. The correlation was significantly positive for the B tasks (.087, $p < .05$) and negative for the A tasks ($-.419$, $p < .05$). Again, the difference between these two coefficients was significant.

Liking of the tasks. Since average individual participation was inversely related to centralization, and the B tasks presented more of an intellectual challenge, one would expect a greater liking for the B tasks than for the A tasks. This assumption was supported by the findings ($t = 2.61$, $p > .02$).

Role-fulfillment evaluation. Another interesting finding was that for both tasks there was a significant and positive correlation between the group-performance evaluation and the extent to which members felt that the appropriate roles had been taken in the group ($r = .702$ for A tasks and .687 for B tasks, both $p < .05$). However, only for the A tasks did we find a positive correlation between this evaluation of role fulfillment and group centrality ($r = .852$, $p < .05$); there was no significant correlation for B ($r = .076$). This demonstrates that different roles were expected in the two different tasks.

Content Analysis

As mentioned earlier, the number of messages sent and received (upon which the centrality index is based) does not tell the complete story. It is also necessary to analyze the content of the messages. The size of our data does not permit, in this paper, a thorough content analysis; therefore, we shall analyze a subset of the data dealing directly with organizational centrality. In our content analysis we had one activity dealing with a con-

Table 4

ORGANIZATIONAL CONTENT OF COMMUNICATIONS

Experimental situation	No. of elements per trial[a] concerning organizing for greater efficiency	No. of elements per trial concerning the designation of one or more coordinators
Groups that never centralized on A tasks	4.30*[b]	2.40*
Precentralization data for groups that eventually centralized on A tasks	6.43*	7.42
Postcentralization data on A tasks	0.00	0.05
All B tasks	3.39†	3.68*

[a] The number of elements is identical to the number of statements unless the statement is a compound statement, in which case the number of elements is the same as the number of parts.

[b] The differences between all six pairs of means in each column are significant below .05 except those pairs marked by an asterisk * or a dagger †. This number has both an asterisk and a dagger because the pairs of means (4.30, 6.43), and (4.30, 3.39) are not significantly different. In this table nine out of the twelve possible pairs of means are significantly different at .05.

cern for organizing for greater efficiency and two activities for the group's discussion about the designation of one or more coordinators (Table 4).

We found a significant difference between the groups who did not centralize and the others before their centralization in the A tasks. The latter communicated more than the former about the designation of a coordinator ($t = 2.35$, $p < .05$). However, there was no significant difference in the average number of statements (elements) about organizing for greater efficiency. Thus the groups that centralized were more concerned with the designation of a coordinator and equally interested in efficiency. This suggests that perhaps one of the reasons some groups did not centralize was their relative lack of communication about selecting a coordinator about whom they would centralize.

After the groups centralized, the number of communications, for the A tasks, concerning organizing for greater efficiency and the designation of one or more coordinators, fell essentially to zero. The differences are significant at the .001 level. This finding is supported by the results of the questionnaire where, for the A tasks, there is a high correlation between centrality, group performance, and feelings that members took the appropriate roles. If the group had not been performing well (efficiency) or if members felt that appropriate roles had not been taken, then there should have been statements to this effect.

If we now make the same comparison between the A groups and B groups, we find significant differences between the B tasks and the precentralized A tasks ($t = 2.08$, $p < .05$ for efficiency and $t = 2.85$, $p < .01$ for coordinators) but no significant difference between B tasks and the noncentralizing groups in the A tasks.

SUMMARY AND DISCUSSION

Our first objective was to determine the influence of the nature of the task upon the organization of a group. Our data demonstrate clearly that the A tasks (which were of a routine deductive nature) led towards centralization while the B tasks (which were nonroutine and had some inferential components) did not lead toward centralization.

Our second objective was to determine how organization structure acts as an intervening variable between task and performance. The results clearly show how a more centralized organization was conducive to a better performance with the A tasks. However, we did not find so clear a relationship for the centrality data in the B tasks. There are at least two explanations. The first is technical: the variance in centrality for the B tasks is low (the adjusted standard error is 0.147). A second and more substantive reason is the fact that a low centrality group does not necessarily mean an organized group and certainly does not explain what kind of organization it has, if any. One can see four distinct possibilities in interpreting low centrality:

(1) A *stable, differentiated* organization where the roles of the participants differ from each other on each trial and the role of each participant does not change over time.

(2) A *flexible* organization where members take appropriate roles as needed. Such an organization can be characterized by different roles among the participants on a given trial, with the role of each participant changing from trial to trial.

(3) A *chaotic* organization where the roles of the members are not different on a given trial and where the roles of the participants vary from trial to trial.

(4) A *uniform* organization where the roles

of the members are not different on a given trial and where the roles of the participants do not vary from trial to trial.

Only a detailed content analysis of the messages in terms of the activities can permit us to decide which kind of organization is behind the overall centrality of the group.

Moreover, the subjective evaluations by the members of their performance and of the group activities support our reasoning concerning the task dependency of organizational centrality.

The evidence presented in this paper, in our opinion, supports strongly the idea that treating organization structure as a dependent variable is a necessary condition for further development of experimental research in organizational behavior. In order to do so we shall need more insight into the determinants of organizational behavior and a more refined methodology to measure the dependent dimensions.

REFERENCES

BAVELAS, A. "Communication Patterns in Task-Oriented Groups." *Journal of Accoustical Society of America*, 1950, 22, 725–730.

COHEN, A., BENNIS, W., and WALKON, G. "The Effects of Continued Practice on the Behavior of Problem-Solving Groups." *Sociometry*, 1961, 24, 416–431.

FAUCHEUX, C., and MOSCOVICI, S. "Etudes sur la Créativité des Groupes: II—Tâche, Structures des Communications et Réussite." *Bulletin du Cerp*, 1960, IX, 11–22.

FLAMENT, C. *Applications of Graph Theory to Group Structure*. Translated by Pinard, M., Breton, R., and Fontaine, F. Englewood Cliffs, N.J.: Prentice-Hall, 1963.

FLAMENT, C. *Reseaux de Communication et Structures de Groupe*, Paris: Dunod, 1965.

GLANZER, M., and GLASER, R. "Techniques for the Study of Group Structure and Behavior: II. Empirical Studies of the Effects of Structure in Small Groups." *Psychological Bulletin*, 1961, 58, 1–27.

GUETZKOW, H., and DILL, W. R. "Factors in the Organizational Development of Task-Oriented Groups." *Sociometry*, 1957, 20, 175–204.

GUETZKOW, H., and SIMON, H. A. "The Impact of Certain Communication Nets Upon Organization and Performance in Task-Oriented Groups." *Management Science*, 1955, 1, 233–250.

LEAVITT, H. J. "Some Effects of Certain Communication Patterns on Group Performance." *Journal of Abnormal and Social Psychology*, 1951, 46, 38–50.

LORGE, I., FOX, D., DAVITZ, J., and BRENNER, M. "A Survey of Studies Contrasting the Quality of Group Performance and Individual Performance," 1920–1957. *Psychological Bulletin*, 1958, 55, 337–372.

MACKENZIE, K. D. *Mathematical Theory of Organizational Structure*. Ph.D. thesis, Berkeley: University of California, 1964.

MACKENZIE, K. D. "Structural Centrality in Communications Networks." *Psychometrika*, 1966, 31, No. 1, March, 1966.

MACKENZIE, K. D. "Decomposition of Communication Networks." *Journal of Mathematical Psychology*, 1967, 4, No. 1, February, 1967, in press.

MACKENZIE, K. D., and FRAZIER, G. D. "Applying a Model of Organization Structure to the Analysis of a Wood Products Market." *Management Science* (Series B), 12, April, 1966.

MACKENZIE, K. D., and HUYSMANS, J. H. B. M. "A Formal Analysis of a Group Decision-Making Experiment." Working Paper No. 11, Ford Foundation Project in Organizational Behavior, Graduate School of Industrial Administration, Carnegie Institute of Technology, Pittsburgh, Pennsylvania, March, 1965.

MULDER, M. "Communication Structure, Decision Structure, Communication, and Group Performance." *Sociometry*, 1960, 23, 1–14.

ROBY, T. B., and LANZETTA, J. T. "Work Group Structure, Communication, and Group Performance." *Sociometry*, 1956, 19, 105–113.

ROBY, T. B., and LANZETTA, J. T. "Considerations in the Analysis of Group Tasks." *Psychological Bulletin*, 1958, 55, 88–101.

SHAW, M. E. "Some Effects of Problem Complexity Upon Problem Solution Efficiency in Different Communication Nets." *Journal of Experimental Psychology*, 1954a, 48, 211–217.

SHAW, M. E. "Some Effects of Unequal Distribution of Information Upon Group Performance in Various Communication Nets." *Journal of Abnormal and Social Psychology*, 1954b, 49, 547–553.

SHAW, M. E. "Scaling Group Tasks: A Method for Dimensional Analysis." Technical Report No. 1, 1963, University of Florida, Contract NR 170–266, Nonr-58 (11), Office of Naval Research.

SHAW, M. E., and BLUM, J. M. "Group Performance as a Function of Task Difficulty and the Group's Awareness of Member Satisfaction." *Journal of Applied Psychology*, 1965, 151–154.

ZAJONC, R. B. "The Requirements and Design of a Standard Group Task." *Journal of Experimental Social Psychology*, 1965, 1, 71–88.

VII

GAMING EXPERIMENTS

12

The Prisoner's Dilemma

FACTORS AFFECTING CO-OPERATION IN THE PRISONER'S DILEMMA*

Lester B. Lave

INTRODUCTION

The Prisoner's Dilemma is a 2-person situation in which each player must forsake the possibility of maximizing his own (short-run) profit to enjoy the greatest payoff (maximize long-run profit). An example is the decision of a duopolist to maintain the high price of his rival. Either firm would gain a considerable short-run advantage by cutting price. The inducement to cut price becomes even stronger after the other firm has done so, but if both firms resort to price-cutting, the profits of both will fall.

This situation is illustrated below in Figure 1. Here Firm A must decide whether to choose strategy 1 (maintain a high price) or strategy 2 (cut price); Firm B must also choose between these alternatives. The consequences of these actions are noted in the matrix. If both firms choose to maintain their prices (strategy 1), both win 3. If one firm decides to cut price (strategy 2) while the other maintains price (strategy 1), the former firm will make 10 while the latter firm loses 5. Finally, if both decide to cut price, both lose 3.

In an appropriate institutional setting this situation can form the basis of many economic conflicts from duopoly problems to bargaining over tariffs (Lave, 1962). It can also serve as a rather general model of conflict for the psychologist. The situation has been abstracted into a game of strategy for experimental treatment. These experiments have shown the Prisoner's Dilemma to be an extremely delicate situation in which apparently subtle changes in conditions give rise to wide differences in the collusion or competition found. Although it seems clear that a large number of

* Reprinted from *Behavioral Science*, Volume 10, No. 1, 1965, by permission of James G. Miller, M.D., Ph.D., Editor.

elements are involved in the decision of a subject about whether or not to establish co-operation, except for Deutsch (1962) little work has been reported that has specifically set out to find what these elements are. The present series of experiments attempts to investigate three possible factors that are both important and easily amenable to experimental treatment.

Firm B

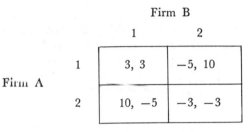

Fig. 1. The Prison's Dilemma (Matrix 5). The first payoff in each square goes to Firm A, the second to Firm B.

Three Factors Affecting Co-Operation

Number of trials. The first critical element in producing co-operation in the Prisoner's Dilemma is the number of trials the game will be repeated. With an unknown rival and a 1-trial game, it is difficult to imagine the wisdom of choosing strategy 1. The single-trial situation eliminates both the possibility of future co-operation and the possibility of punishing a rival for noncooperative action in the one trial.

The number of trials to be played can make the matrix more dramatic and co-operation more practical. Consider two games where the payoffs in the second are n times those in the first. The second game is to be played for a single trial while the first game will be played for n trials. The two games are equivalent in the formal sense that the amount of money each player can win is equal in both games (or

the expected values of the two games have the same range across different opponents). However, the games are quite different with respect to negotiating co-operation and the division of payoffs. The expected values of the two games are not equal for a given rival, since certain forms of behavior can induce co-operation or competition. When a game is iterated, it is possible to display behavior that induces or stifles co-operation; it is possible to use the choices in the game to communicate with each other. The tacit, rudimentary form of this communication takes time, no matter how dramatic the matrix nor how well disposed the two players. With an unknown rival, a single trial can never serve to establish co-operation; there is not time for a response to one's choice. Before he makes his choice, a player cannot know that his rival seems willing to co-operate. Moreover, in order to gain co-operation, there should be sufficient trials so that the risk of loss, of unsuccessful negotiation, seems small in comparison with the possible gain. Thus, the longer the game, the more likely it is that a stable co-operation solution is achieved.

Earlier work (Lave, 1960) conjectured that, within a narrowly defined group, the expected value of attempting co-operation (choosing strategy 1) exceeded that of doing nothing (choosing strategy 2) when the number of trials, n, was large enough so that $k(d - b) < n(a - d)$ (see Figure 2). As argued below, $d - b$ is the loss for an unsuccessful attempt to co-operate, while $a - d$ is the difference between the payoffs for co-operating and for competing with the rival. The parameter that summarizes the subject population is k and was found to be about three for a population of Reed College undergraduates. Since the subjects of the present

Player B

		1	2
	1	a, a'	b, c'
Player A	2	c, b'	d, d'

Again, the first payoff in each square goes to Player A, the second to Player B.

Payoffs:		a	b	c	d
Matrix:	1	3	−100	4	−3
	2	3	−75	4	−3
	3	3	−50	4	−3
	4	3	−5	4	−3
	5	3	−5	10	−3
	6	2.5*	−5	10	−3

Fig. 2. Matrices Used in Experiments. Note: Figure 1 illustrates Matrix 5.

* If both players choose strategy 1 in Matrix 6, Player A receives a payoff of 2 while Player B receives a payoff of 5.

experiments are also undergraduates of comparable intelligence, we presume k to take on a value of about three for these experiments.

Payoffs. The second critical element affecting co-operation is conjectured to be the specific numerical entries in the matrix relative to one another. It seems likely that, as the entries vary, co-operation can be made easier to achieve initially, easier to stabilize on, etc. The six matrices used in these experiments are described in Figure 2. In particular, we might hypothesize that the larger b is with respect to a, the more difficult it will be for a subject to decide to attempt co-operation. Picture a subject deciding whether to show that he wishes to co-operate by choosing strategy 1 when his rival has not yet shown any signs of being co-operative. This player is almost surely faced with at least one trial at payoff b, the lowest payoff in the matrix. (The larger this loss, the more reluctant a player will be to attempt co-operation.)

Second, we might expect that the larger c is with respect to a, the greater will be the pull away from co-operation and the less likely it will be that a pair will settle on stable co-operation. The payoff c is the value of "double-crossing" one's partner once co-operation at 1, 1 has been achieved.

Third, we might expect that the smaller d is with respect to a, the more likely it would be that a subject will attempt to achieve co-operation at 1, 1. From the way the matrix is defined, a is the reward for co-operation while d is the penalty for nonco-operation after both players have evolved a stable position at either co-operation or competition. The factor $a − d$ then measures the incentive to establish co-operation. The incentives leading to co-operation can be summarized in the hypothesis stated above, that subjects will attempt to co-operate when the number of trials is large enough so that $3(d − b) < n(a − d)$. For these experiments, d was never varied.

Finally, we might expect that a move toward asymmetric payoffs as shown in matrix 6 will strongly affect co-operative behavior. When players co-operate in matrix 6, Player A receives only 2 while Player B receives 5. It was hypothesized that such an asymmetry would disrupt the game and greatly reduce the amount of co-operation achieved. Players would be attempting to settle the question of how payoffs should be divided as well as whether they wanted to achieve co-operation.[1] Since players are not permitted to

---

[1] In a summary of results from small-group experiments, Berelson and Steiner (1964, p.

talk to each other, they can only communicate by their choices in the game. There is a necessary ambiguity under these conditions when a player A chooses strategy 2 in order to achieve more equal payoffs: Is he giving up co-operation for all time or simply modifying the pattern under which he is willing to co-operate? (Since a player's choices are the way in which he indicates whether a distribution of the payoffs is satisfactory, it is possible that the bargaining process might never terminate. Until bargaining terminates, there is no compelling reason to predict that subjects will go to a Pareto optimal point [Bishop, 1960].)

Schelling has conjectured that there will be a tendency for simple, obvious, probably symmetric solutions to occur in games, especially as the problems of co-ordination are emphasized and those of bargaining played down (1960, p. 54). He has also conjectured that the assumption of symmetry is not always a good one in bargaining situations (1960, p. 267). In the case of the asymmetric matrix, the former conjecture might be formalized as the hypothesis that subjects will probably fall into co-operating at 1, 1 and disregard the asymmetry or perhaps find some equally simple way which would yield symmetric payoffs. The latter conjecture might be formalized as the hypothesis that subjects will not insist on equal payoffs if

it seems likely that doing so will cost a fair amount of money.

The other player. The third critical factor involves the characteristics of the subject a player is paired with. In order to find the extent of co-operation, some of these experiments were run with subjects paired with each other. But a more interesting and time-saving procedure involves running a subject against some fixed behavior pattern played by a stooge. Such planned behavior patterns allow intensive investigation of the power of certain strategies to induce collusion or the hope of collusion in a subject.

Four behavior patterns were distilled from earlier experiments. To aid in remembering these patterns, they were given colorful names. The first pattern, Stalin, involves always playing strategy 2 (the nonco-operative strategy) no matter what the subject plays. Khrushchev played strategy 2 constantly, except for an occasional sally over to strategy 1. The third stooge, Coolidge, played strategy 1 only after the subject had played strategy 1 four times and was choosing it a fifth time. The final stooge was Gandhi, who always chose strategy 1.

While these stooges are archetypes of subjects' behavior patterns, it is possible to cite a logical, consistent explanation for each pattern. Stalin has a utility function that indicates an enormous loss if he should ever play strategy 1 while the other player chooses strategy 2. His loss would be so high that he is willing to forego the possibility of earning money by co-operating. A player choosing a Stalin pattern believes his opponent is both powerful and malevolent, and so he protects himself against the worst. He chooses a strategy to minimize his maximum possible loss: the minimax strategy.

---

353) note that "At least in American studies, and on tasks requiring collaborative activity, co-operative groups are more cohesive and more personally satisfying than internally competitive ones, and their performance is more homogeneous and usually more effective." Applied to matrix 6 the proposition might be interpreted to say that the asymmetry has emphasized the conflict between players to the detriment of the goal of the group to form a coalition against the experimenter.

Khrushchev is a slightly more flexible Stalin who is taking advantage of the knowledge he obtains from his opponent's reactions. He is not especially concerned about being double-crossed, he is only concerned with maximizing his relative payoff, i.e., his payoff minus his opponent's playoff. It seems likely that after a very few attempts, the Khrushchev pattern can involve too many strategy 1's and come out with a lower absolute (or even relative) payoff than Stalin.

Coolidge is simply an extremely cautious player. He does want to co-operate and make money, but he is suspicious of his partner until the partner has shown good intentions. The Coolidge pattern defines good intentions as willingness to go almost bankrupt in the attempt to signal co-operation.

The last pattern, Gandhi, was particularly prevalent among Harvard undergraduates. They analyzed the game and concluded that the only way the pair could make money was by co-operating. This immediately led them to the conclusion that they should never play anything except strategy 1. These subjects would have played only strategy 1's throughout, but they were slightly suspicious of the experimental situation and so concluded, in those cases where they were not answered with strategy 1's, that the game was somehow rigged (which was not always so).

Three Conjectures Concerning Subjects' Behavior

There are three further conjectures concerning subjects' behavior that might be mentioned since some small amount of evidence can be brought to bear on them. (1) A subject's experience in the game is likely to influence the way he plays in the future. In a few cases a second game was run at the conclusion of the first game to examine this assumption. (2) Different subjects should exhibit different behavior patterns in the game. A first approach to measuring these differences involves using subjects from three universities and conjecturing that the population within each university is homogeneous while that between universities is different. (3) A subject's behavior should change if he knows the exact number of trials in the game. Luce and Raiffa (1957) demonstrate in a proof by backward induction that no matter how long the game, if subjects are told the number of trials, collusion is not as good for one player as choosing strategy 2; collusion is said to be dominated. This process of fixing on strategy 2 for the last trial and extending the logic back to the first trial has been found unlikely to occur in practice beyond a trial or two from the end. One can avoid the proof by backward induction by a simple change in the conditions of the game: tell players that the game will end after trial n with probability p. Both ways of ending the game are used in these experiments, and an attempt is made to evaluate further the practical importance of the Luce-Raiffa proof.

Comments on Experimental Methodology

Two variations in procedure which have been incorporated into these experiments should be commented upon, since there may be questions about their effect and desirability. The first involves paying subjects substantial sums of money for the game so that their earnings depend on their winnings in the game. Evidence presented earlier (Lave, 1960) showed that there were substantial differences in behavior depending on whether subjects were actually paid or were merely told to "imagine that the money made a difference to them." In the present series of experiments, subjects often questioned the experimenters on the subject of money and apparently small differences in payoff were noticed. Many subjects caught small errors in the payoffs and wanted them rectified immediately. There was also much concern over the total payoff.

The second concerns some reported experiments (Fouraker & Siegel, 1963; Siegel & Fouraker, 1960; Suppes & Carlsmith, 1962) which have instructed subjects to behave as if each were a large oligopolistic firm, a major nation in world affairs, or some such. A game such as the Prisoner's Dilemma might be set up in terms of prices set, quantities sold, people killed, etc. Such a setup tends to give the experiment an air of the parlor game: the subject cannot fully comprehend what he is to do, whom he is to please, or what he is to maximize. But a more serious difficulty might result. The subject is told to behave as if he were the "President of U.S. Steel" or the "President of the United States." Such an injunction can hardly be followed except through a subject's individual (almost certainly naive) conception of the way he thinks Roger Blough or Lyndon Johnson behaves. Thus, a subject behaves as he imagines someone else acts and not the way he himself would act. The result can only be a tendency toward confused behavior with the subject never sure what is expected of him and playing according to inconsistent principles. If one uses college sophomores as subjects, one should at least get the behavior of college sophomores, not the be-havior that college sophomores imagine is typical of Lyndon Johnson.

One illustration of the failure, when using college students, to understand that they are motivated and behave as college students is contained in Siegel and Fouraker (1960, p. 100): "In the present series of experiments, only one pair of subjects failed to reach a contract. This statistic is startling, when considered in the light of the frequency with which negotiations are broken off under other circumstances. Apparently the disruptive forces which contribute to the rupture of some negotiations were at least partially controlled in our sessions." Since they were paying their subjects about $5 for less than two hours of gaming, an alternative explanation might note that the levels of payoffs were so high that, with a wide range of acceptable payoffs, there was only the matter of somehow dividing the money. In their terminology, the subject's level of aspiration was below the range of possible payoffs.

EXPERIMENTS: METHOD

Twelve series of experiments were conducted in the spring of 1963 using undergraduates of Harvard University, Massachusetts Institute of Technology, and Northeastern University. Subjects were hired through advertisements in the school newspapers. The advertisements stated that subjects would take part in a bargaining experiment that had reference to international politics and that pay would depend on performances in the game. Subjects were given a standard instruction sheet with appropriate changes for the different matrices used and an appended paragraph when they were to play more than a single game.

The instruction sheet informed subjects that

they were to play a bargaining game and that the $5 which they had been given ($4 was used in games with types 4, 5, and 6 matrices, see below) was theirs, but had to be used to cover any losses incurred during the game. The only goal mentioned in the instructions enjoined subjects to maximize their winnings since everything they won would be part of their earnings. The instruction sheet went on to present the matrix to be used, to state the number of trials the game would be played, and to explain the numbers in the matrix so that subjects would know the payoffs for each combination of strategies in the game. After a subject had made his choice, he was given a slip of paper stating: "You chose strategy ( ) while the other player chose strategy ( ). Thus you win (or lose) ( )¢ while the other player wins (or loses) ( )¢." He was then paid or charged the appropriate amount. Subjects recorded their strategy choices on a sheet which had a place for recording, if they chose, the strategy choices of their rival. Subjects were asked to write a brief explanation of each choice they made.

As in a previous game (Lave, 1962) when the number of trials was large, subjects were allowed to fill out a superstrategy telling how they would behave for the remainder of the game. Such a procedure became available only after a large number of trials. What it became apparent that almost all subjects wanted to fill out this superstrategy, it was suggested that everyone write it out. In only eight cases out of 84 (9.5 per cent) did subjects wish to continue playing and prefer not to write a superstrategy.

Table 1 lists the number of subjects taking part in each of the experiments performed. These experiments were performed in twelve sessions lasting approximately two hours each. Every attempt was made to prevent the earlier experiments from contaminating those that came later: One school was taken at a time, subjects were asked not to tell others about the game, and not more than four weeks elapsed between the beginning and end of experiments at one school or more than seven weeks between the beginning and end

Table 1

NUMBER OF SUBJECTS IN EACH SITUATION

Number of Trials by Stooges	Matrix				
	1–2	3	4	5	6
Over 100 Trials					
Stalin-Coolidge	14	1, 16*	1		
Khrushchev		16*			
Gandhi					
Paired		32, 16†	14		
50 Trials					
Stalin-Coolidge			9		
Khrushchev			5		
Gandhi			6	4	
Paired			10	6	16
25 Trials					
Stalin-Coolidge		6			
Khrushchev					
Gandhi					
Paired	14				
15 Trials					
Stalin-Coolidge					
Khrushchev					
Gandhi					
Paired		6	6	6	18*

* Second game.
† Northeastern University subjects.

of all experiments. There was no evidence of contamination.

RESULTS

The first factor hypothesized to affect co-operation, the number of trials in the game, can be tested in matrices 1–2, 3, and 4. (A preliminary-analysis revealed that behavior in the first two matrices was the same and so they were aggregated throughout these analyses.) Table 2 shows the percentage of players attempting co-operation in games using these matrices when the number of trials was varied from over 100 to 50, 25, and 15. It was hypothesized that players would attempt co-oper-

Table 2

PLAYERS ATTEMPTING CO-OPERATION

Matrix	No. Trials	Dummy or Pairs	Percentage of Players Choosing One or More Strategy 1's	Critical No. of Trials	Percentage of Players Deviating From Hypothesis
1–2	Over 100	Coolidge	85.7 (12/14)	45	14.3
3	Over 100	Pairs	100 (28/28)	24	0
3	25	Stalin	66.7 (4/6)	24	33.3
3	25	Pairs	85.7 (12/14)	24	14.3
3	15	Pairs	50 (3/6)	24	50
4	Over 100	Pairs	100 (28/28)	1	0
4	50	Stalin	100 (9/9)	1	0
4	50	Pairs	100 (10/10)	1	0
4	15	Pairs	100 (6/6)	1	0

ation if the number of trials were such that $3(b - d) < n(a - d)$ (see Figure 2). Nine tests are presented in the table along with the percentage of players in each experiment who contradicted the hypothesis. The hypothesis is substantiated in five cases, only 14 per cent of the players deviated from it in another two cases, and the two exceptions show deviations of 33 per cent and 50 per cent. In all, only nine players out of 101 contradicted the hypothesis. However, these tests were generally not near the critical area. The data must be conceived to be generally in favor of the hypothesis, although they do not prove it.

In examining the effect of entries in the matrix on co-operation (factor 2), we hypothesized that the smaller b, the more attempts would be made toward co-operation and the smaller c, the more stable would be co-operation once it had been achieved. In going from matrix 1 to matrix 4 the size of b is reduced successively from -100 to -5, while other factors are held constant. Table 2 shows the percentage of subjects attempting co-

operation (defined as choosing one or more strategy 1's) in these matrices. In the games with more than 100 trials, the percentage of subjects attempting co-operation increases from 85.7 per cent to 100 per cent in moving from matrix 1–2 to matrix 4. The 15-trial games also support the hypothesis, although none of the tests seem to be sensitive ones.

Figure 3 presents a comparison of matrices 4 and 5 where c was changed from 4 to 10. The matrix shows that, as hypothesized, co-operation is more unstable in matrix 5, although the effect is not very large. (Note that all pairs arrived at co-operation at least momentarily and that any deviation from complete co-operation is due to instability.) The apparent difference is further diminished by the fact that one pair gained co-operation in matrix 5 by alternately double-crossing, i.e., 1, 2; 2, 1; 1, 2: .... Thus, the curve for matrix 5 is higher than shown. A purer test of this question is presented below in connection with the Gandhi stooge.

It was hypothesized that asymmetry

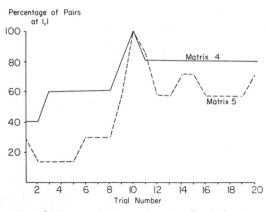

Fig. 3. Effect of Increasing the Incentive to Double-Cross (Matrices 4 and 5, 50 Trials).

would cause a drop in the percentage of pairs co-operating since players would spend effort worrying about the way payoffs should be split. In games with 50 trials, there was 57.5 per cent co-operation in matrix 5 and 50 per cent co-operation in matrix 6. Subjects did spend time trying to indicate what were acceptable

splits, and three patterns of co-operation emerged. In the first, subjects stayed with the conventional 1, 1 and forgot asymmetries in the payoffs; only one pair was satisfied with this solution. In the second pattern, subjects alternately double-crossed each other: 1, 2; 2, 1, 2; . . . to get an expected value of 2 and ½ cents per trial; two pairs found this second pattern an acceptable solution. Finally, one pair settled on the optimal way of gaining equal payoffs: they played five trials at 1, 1 and then played 2, 1 for the sixth trial to achieve an expected value of 3 and ⅓ cents per trial. The outstanding feature of the asymmetric game is that subjects failed to understand each other's signals and had the greatest difficulty settling on some stable form of co-operation.

The fixed behavior patterns (factor 3) provided more systematic evidence on reactions of players to given strategies. The Stalin dummy can be used to give some idea of the number of strategy 1's subjects

Table 3

NUMBER OF PLAYERS CHOOSING n STRATEGY 1'S

Matrix	Number of Strategy 1's Chosen													Total Number of Players Choosing Strategy 1
	0	1	2	3	4	5	6	7	8	9	10	11	12	
Stupid or malevolent opponent ⎧ 1–2 (Coolidge) (over 100 trials)	2	1	2	1	4	4*								14
4 (Stalin) (50 trials)	0	0	0	1	4	1	1	2						9
4 (Khrushchev) (50 trials)	0	0	0	0	0	0	1	1	0	1	1	1		5
4 (Gandhi) (50 trials)						1							5	6

Stalin average number of 1's = 4.89.
Khruschev average number of 1's = 7.6.
* Number of players choosing 5 or more strategy 1's.

were willing to choose when faced with a partner who is either too stupid or too malevolent ever to choose a strategy 1. (The Coolidge pattern is identical with the Stalin pattern until the fifth choice of strategy 1. The patterns are not analyzed separately here.)

Table 3 presents a comparison between the reactions of subjects to such a stupid or malevolent partner for two matrices: 1–2 and 4. In order to hold constant the attractiveness of co-operation, matrices 1–2 were run with more than 100 trials while matrix 4 was run with 50 trials (thus, they should be strictly comparable so far as the number of trials is concerned if the previous hypothesis about the effect of the number of trials is correct). The medium number of strategy 1's chosen is the same, four, for both matrices 1–2 and matrix 4. The principal difference is that subjects are strung out toward the bottom in the former matrix. Thus, the median amount of co-operative behavior toward a stupid player was the same in both the high-loss matrices (1 and 2) and in the low-loss matrix (4).

The table also presents a comparison between the reactions of players to different types of given strategies, holding other variables constant. Within the context of matrix 4 in a 50-trial game, subjects reacted to Stalin, Khrushchev, and Gandhi. The goal of the Khrushchev pattern is to maximize payoff relative to the rival's. Therefore, when his opponent starts to write him off as nonco-operative, the Khrushchev stooge plays a strategy 1 to stir his rival's hopes. Figure 4 shows the percentage of players choosing strategy 1 in a second game when one group is confronted with Stalin and another with Krushchev. Note that players react strongly to Khrushchev's hint that he may be

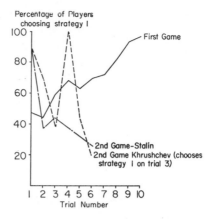

Fig. 4. Comparison of Behavior in First and Second Games (Matrix 3, Over 100 Trials).

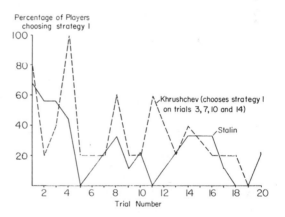

Fig. 5. Stalin vs. Khrushchev (Matrix 4, 50 Trials).

willing to co-operate. Figure 5 shows a comparison between these two behavior patterns in matrix 4 with a 50-trial game. Again, Khrushchev appears to stimulate his rival strongly to play strategy 1. However, by the fourth time Khrushchev chooses strategy 1, his rival refuses to react at all. Table 3 shows that the mean response for the Khrushechev pattern is about three higher than for the Stalin pattern, thus both making a case for Khrushchev's effectiveness and pointing

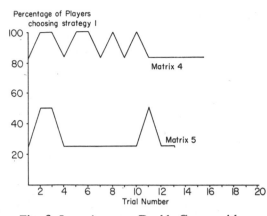

Fig. 6. Incentive to Double-Cross with a Gandhi Pattern (Matrices 4 and 5, 50 Trials).

out that after the second time he loses this effectiveness.

If the rationale behind the Gandhi pattern strategy were correct, we would expect to find all subjects co-operating with the stooge within a short time. Figure 6 shows the percentage of players choosing strategy 1 in matrices 4 and 5 in 50-trial games. Note that the curves reach an initial high and then decline as players discover that their partner would choose only strategy 1. As a matter of fact, any player who ever initially double-crossed Gandhi after co-operation was achieved eventually played only strategy 2. The pattern fails at maximizing absolute pay-offs, but even worse, fails at maximizing cooperation. Note that Figure 6 sharply differentiates between matrices 4 and 5, thus showing the greater pull toward double-crossing of the latter matrix.

DISCUSSION

We can pursue the three principal factors affecting co-operation in a slightly stronger context by restating the hypotheses to predict the *achievement* of co-operation, rather than attempts at co-operation. The first factor would then predict that the amount of achieved cooperation would rise as the number of trials increases. Figure 7 presents the percentage of pairs co-operating at 1 , 1 in matrix 3 when the number of trials was changed successively from over 100 trials to 25 and then 15. The amount of co-operation falls slightly in the reduction to 25 trials and then is reduced to zero in the 15-trial games. Figure 8 presents the percentage of pairs co-operating in matrix 4 when the number of trials is reduced from over 100 to 50 and then to 15. Figure 9 presents the percentage of pairs at 1 , 1 in matrix 5. These three figures generally support the hypothesis that the amount of achieved co-operation is directly related to the number of trials in the game.

For matrix 3 the percentage of pairs co-operating seems to bear an inverse relation to the number of trials; the shorter the game, the more co-operation is evidenced. A *post hoc* explanation of this

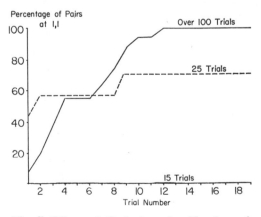

Fig. 7. Effect of Reducing the Number of Trials (Matrix 3, Over 100, 25, and 15 Trials).

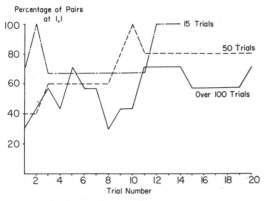

Fig. 8. Changes in Co-operation Due to Reducing the Number of Trials (Matrix 4, Over 100, 50, and 15 Trials).

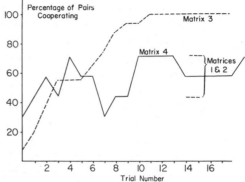

Fig. 10. Effect of Changing Matrix Entries (Matrices 1–2, 3, and 4, Over 100 Trials).

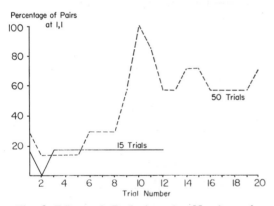

Fig. 9. Effect of Reducing the Number of Trials (Matrix 5, 50 and 15 Trials).

tendency might point out that with shorter games there is less chance to mend any damage that might have been done by attempting to exploit a rival early in the game. Thus, the shorter the game, the less we might expect players to double-cross once they had achieved co-operation. However, the argument seems tenuous. Figure 8 contains no evidence for this hypothesis in matrix 4, and there is no evidence from matrix 6 which would support the conclusion. It seems likely that

all three curves in Figure 8 differ only by some random factor.

The second factor is transformed into hypotheses about the relationship between matrix entries and achieved co-operation. Figure 10 presents the percentage of players co-operating in matrices 1–4 in games with more than 100 trials. The first two matrices present some difficulty since they were used only with stooges and not with paired subjects. Given the difficulty of co-ordinating, it seems safe to assume that if two players were willing to play two or more strategy 1's, they would have succeeded in co-operating. Since 11 of 14 subjects fit into this category, we might have expected five pairs to arrive at co-operation. Even using the more strict criterion of three attempts at co-operation, only five players fail to qualify. Thus, it seems likely that between 43 and 71 per cent of the pairs would have arrived at co-operation in the first two matrices.

In matrix 3 all of the subjects arrived at stable co-operation. In matrix 4 only 70 per cent of the pairs colluded at any one time, and a smaller number must have arrived at stable co-operation. On the other hand, every pair arrived at 1, 1 at some time or other. Extending the hypothesis that more subjects would attempt co-operation as the magnitude of b decreased to a hypothesis that the amount of stable co-operation would increase seems fraught with difficulties. The relation holds for the reduction of b from $1 to $.50, but fails in the further reduction to $.05. The behavior might be explained by noting that with the large loss, subjects were reluctant to risk choosing strategy 1 initially. But, if they did risk it, they never deviated from co-operation once it had been attained. With the small-loss game, subjects were quite willing to risk indicating they wanted to co-operate, but had no good mechanism for enforcing co-operation once it had been temporarily attained. Thus, b serves not only as a bar to co-operation as hypothesized, it serves as a means of enforcing co-operation.

Lawrence Fouraker suggests that matrices 1, 2, and 3 would not be Prisoner's Dilemmas if the entries were in utility rather than monetary terms. Certainly the utility of winning 4 cents is not going to be much greater than the utility of winning 3 cents. His point offers another explanation of why co-operation in these matrices was centered around the problem of attaining the co-operative point with no suggestion of moving away from (1 , 1) once it was attained. On the other hand, co-operation in the other three matrices centered around the problem of staying at 1 , 1.

It was conjectured that subjects would find this experiment a learning situation and behave quite differently in a second game. Measuring the difference is complicated here since the second game was not completely comparable to the first

one. Players were paired in the first game and so reinforced their desire to arrive at a stable co-operative solution. The second game paired subjects with stooges who either chose no strategy 1's (Stalin) or chose only one strategy 1 (Khrushchev). Figure 4 presents a comparison of behavior in the two games. With Stalin or Khrushchev as a partner, it is inevitable that the number of attempts at co-operation must be biased downward and quickly fall to zero. The figure indicates that players in the second game were much more optimistic on the first trial; they demanded co-operation immediately. The number of strategy 1's they continued to play indicates they were willing to gamble much money on achieving co-operation. Thus, learning did occur and players were reinforced by the first game.

These experiments provided a first test of differences between subjects since three universities in the Boston area provided the subjects for these experiments. Figure 11 presents the percentage of pairs from each university group co-operating in games using matrix 3 with more than 100 trials. Note that Harvard and M.I.T.

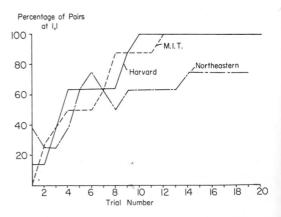

Fig. 11. Comparison of Subjects from Three Universities (Matrix 3, Over 100 Trials).

subjects exhibit very similar behavior patterns while subjects from Northeastern University present quite a different picture. We did not attempt to investigate any of the many explanations that might account for this difference, but merely noted it and drew the conclusion that the Harvard and M.I.T. populations could be aggregated for the analysis.

In those games where less than 100 trials were to be played the subjects were told the exact number of trials in the game and so had the opportunity to end co-operation on the last trial or at some time before the end of the game. Table 4 lists the incidence of double-crossing in the paired games with specifically announced end points. The logic of the situation would have players never co-operating, since they would have decided to double-cross on the last trial and have extended the logic all the way back to the first trial. The table shows double-crossing to be concentrated in the last trial, although there are a few instances in earlier trials. Thus, the evidence agrees with previous experiments that double-crossing does not extend far back from the end of the game and that the process of backward induction is not nearly as powerful as the Luce-Raiffa (1957) argument might indicate.

The behavior exhibited toward Gandhi hinted that there is a period of feeling out a partner, of making sure that he has no obvious weakness. If weaknesses are found they will be exploited. This hypothesis can be tested by seeing whether, with some exceptions, co-operation is more likely to be stable if it is achieved only after some exploration of the possibilities. Figure 12 presents the number of non-1, 1 choices before the first 1 , 1 choice and, on the other axis, the number of non-1, 1 choices after the first 1 , 1 choice. The figure is dominated by two polar cases: first there are those pairs that took some time to reach 1 , 1 and then remained there; then there are those pairs that came to a 1 , 1 solution immediately and then deviated shortly afterwards. Only a few cases occur where the pairs reached immediate agreement and stayed there; these cases are rarer than might have been expected. It appears that easy victory is not always to be looked for.

Scodel (1962) reports a series of experiments where subjects attempted to maximize their relative payoffs rather than their absolute payoffs. Scodel hypothesized that such behavior would be general since it was observed in spite of efforts to find a matrix that would promote co-

Table 4

DOUBLE-CROSSING BY MATRIX

Matrix Type	Number Trials	Number Subjects	Number at (1 , 1)	Double Crossing		Double Crossing			
				Number	Per cent	On Last Trial	$n-1$	$n-2$	$n-3$
3	25	14	10	6	60	6			
4	50	10	8	2	25	2			
	15	6	6	3	50	3			
5	50	14	9	5	56	3	1		1
	15	6	2	1	50			1	

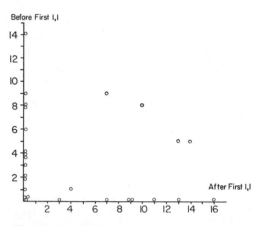

Fig. 12. Tradeoffs Between Nonco-operation Before and After First 1 , 1.

operation. Matrices 3 and 4 fit in with his definition and although there was some evidence that a low value of b and a small number of iterations produced nonco-operative results essentially similar to Scodel's, there was no substantial evidence that players were maximizing any utility other than their own money payoff.

Throughout these experiments, subjects seemed to regard each other as equals and demanded at least equal payoffs. In the asymmetric game, for example, subjects insisted on at least equal payoffs though it cost them a great deal of money to do so. In all the paired games, subjects insisted on probing for possible weaknesses in their partners; and every time a weakness was discovered, it was exploited. One additional way of viewing this sort of behavior would be to look at the subject who first indicates that he wishes to co-operate by playing a strategy 1. It is altogether possible that this subject will be taken advantage of and exploited continually, since he obviously has committed himself to co-operation. His opponent might occasionally double-cross once co-operation has been achieved, or be slow to learn to co-operate initially. Table 5 shows the difference in the number of strategy 1's played by the first subject who tried to signal co-operation and those played by

Table 5

TEST OF LEADERSHIP ROLE

Matrix	Number Trials	Number Pairs Considered*	Mean Excess Number Strategy 1 Choices Made by Leader†	Mean Excess Number Strategy 1 Choices Made by Leader Ignoring Initial Choice‡
3	100	20	.700	−.300
3	25	4	+1.000	0
3	15	3	+2.000	+1.000
4	100	5	+1.400	+.400
4	50	3	+1.333	+.333
4	15	1	+4.000	+3.000
5	50	5	+.800	−.200

* Only those pairs are considered where one of the players chose strategy 1 before the other player, i.e., only those pairs where there was a leader.

† Derived by taking the difference between the total number of strategy 1's chosen by the follower and the number chosen by the leader and dividing by the number of pairs.

‡ Previous column neglecting the initial trial in which the leader chose his first strategy 1.

his rival. Notice that, when we discount the initial attempt, the initial co-operator plays no more strategy 1's in general than his rival. Thus, again there is evidence that players insisted on equality and refused to allow themselves to be exploited.

CONCLUSION

The data were consistent with the hypothesis that subjects attempt co-operation when the number of trials is large enough that $3(b - d) < n(a - d)$. Subjects also attempt co-operation more often as b is decreased from 100 to 5 and deviate from temporary co-operation as the c is increased. The amount of achieved co-operation is a direct function of the number of trials and an inverse function of the size of b, although the latter relation is complicated by the dual role of b since it also serves to enforce stable co-operation. Thus, the amount of co-operation decreases in the further reduction of b from 50 to 5.

The fixed behavior patterns utilized as stooges in the game concentrated the information about subjects' reactions to certain strategies of interest. The Stalin pattern showed the reactions of subjects to cautious or malevolent partners. The Khrushchev pattern indicated that players will be greatly encouraged by the smallest sign that their previously cautious partner may wish to co-operate. Finally, the Gandhi pattern indicated that subjects engaged in rather costly searches for weaknesses in their rivals and, where a weakness was found, immediately exploited it.

Subjects tended to demand payoffs which were at least equal to those of their partners and generally double-crossed in the last few trials of the game, bargained so much that they generally failed to

arrive at co-operation in the asymmetric matrix, and refused to take on a consistent role of leader in ensuring co-operation. The general behavior might be described as sharply competitive while still attempting to co-operate to the extent of earning a positive payoff.

REFERENCES

BERELSON, B., and STEINER, G. *Human Behavior; An Inventory of Scientific Findings.* New York: Harcourt, 1964.

BISHOP, R. "Duopoly: Collusion or Warfare?" *Amer. Econ. Rev.*, 1960, 50, 933–967.

DEUTSCH, M. "Co-operation and Trust: Some Theoretical Notes." In M. Jones (Ed.), *Nebraska Symposium on Motivation.* Lincoln: Univ. of Nebraska Press, 1962. Pp. 275–319.

FOURAKER, L., and SIEGEL, S. *Bargaining Behavior.* New York: McGraw-Hill, 1963.

LAVE, L. *Applications of the Theory of Games to Economics.* Unpublished A.B. dissertation, Reed College, 1960.

LAVE, L. "An Empirical Approach to the Prisoner's Dilemma." *Quart. J. Econ.*, 1962, 76, 424–436.

LUCE, R. D., and RAIFFA, H. *Games and Decisions.* New York: Wiley, 1957.

SCHELLING, T. *The Strategy of Conflict.* Cambridge: Harvard Univ. Press, 1960.

SCODEL, A. "Induced Collaboration in Some Non-Zero-Sum Games. *J. Conflict Resolution*, 1962, 6, 334–340.

SIEGEL, S., and FOURAKER, L. *Bargaining and Group Decision Making.* New York: McGraw-Hill, 1960.

SUPPES, P., and CARLSMITH, J. "Experimental Analysis of a Duopoly Situation from the Standpoint of Mathematical Learning Theory." *Internat. Econ. Rev.*, 1962, 2, 60–78.

INDUCING TRUST:
A TEST OF THE OSGOOD PROPOSAL*

Marc Pilisuk and Paul Skolnick

Charles Osgood's "Suggestions for Winning the Real War with Communism" (1959) first contained a proposal later detailed in *An Alternative to War or Surrender* (Osgood, 1962) as "graduated reciprocation in tension reduction." Apart from its intended significance in suggesting a way out of the cold war, "graduated reciprocation in tension reduction" states a theory of the step-by-step evolution of interparty conflict. The theory has particular relevance to the origins of variability—individual or group—which determine conflict outcomes. It is built upon the premise that individual initiative, even in the absence of coercive sanction, can prescribe the behavior of both parties in a conflict situation.

The major contention of the Osgood thesis is that psychological processes working against the possibilities of a complete rapprochement, or a disarmament agreement in the cold-war case, might be overcome by reversing the essentially unilateral steps by which the arms race continues to accelerate. Instead of small graduated increments in armaments, or threatening moves, which tend to be reciprocated ad infinitum, Osgood proposed a set of small, unilateral, conciliatory overtures each preceded by an announcement and carried out without guarantee of reciprocal overtures. After several such moves, none really sacrificing security, reciprocation leading to a reversal of the arms-suspicion deadlock could be anticipated.

Amitai Etzioni in his article on "The Kennedy Experiment" outlines events of the "thaw" period following the Cuban missile crisis which seem to conform, in a general way, to Osgood's thesis (Etzioni, in press). But the international arena provides too little control for a test of a theory which, in the more general statement, purports to speak to the underlying process of conflict. The laboratory provides opportunity for greater control and has provided the setting for a number of studies dealing with the consequence of unilateral initiatives.

An experimental literature has gradually developed on the effects of unilateral position and/or unilateral moves upon bilateral behavior. Deutsch and Krauss (1960) developed a trucking game in which they found that a unilateral power position was detrimental to cooperation. Raser and

* Marc Pilisuk and Paul Skolnick, "Inducing Trust: A Test of the Osgood Proposal," *Journal of Personality and Social Psychology*, 8 (1968), 121–33. Copyright 1968 by the American Psychological Association, and reproduced by permission.

Crow, using the international simulation, found that acquisition of a unilateral power advantage (acquisition of an invulnerable weapon) tended to increase the incidence of aggressive actions (Raser & Crow, 1964). Both of these studies were related more to the converse of the Osgood proposition, that is, to the effects of acquiring unilateral power rather than to effects of unilateral conciliation. But another study, using a cleverly devised game of unequal power, tested the effectiveness of a completely pacifist strategy on the part of the player in the weaker position. The strategy proved ineffective in generating mercy from the stronger player (Shure, Mecker, & Hansford, 1965). Again this speaks only obliquely to the proposal in question which called for modest steps toward unilateral disarmament.

While the advantages of manipulation and control are common to these studies, some of the designs are obviously too complex to permit a sequence of controlled experiments systematically varied in detail over a range of circumstances. But the theory under consideration is related to a very simple paradigm. The theory in its general statement applies to all conflict between two contestants in circumstances where mutual distrust prevents finding a mutually satisfactory outcome and where the parties have identifiable moves with payoffs dependent upon these moves. The Prisoner's Dilemma game meets these criteria and provides a most appropriate setting for control.

The basis of interest in the Prisoner's Dilemma situation derives from the significance of the conflicting motivations represented by the two alternatives. The D (defection) choice assures a player of minimal loss (if the other player should also choose D) and maximal gains (should

the other player choose C, cooperation). The C choice can be justified only by mutual consideration for the well-being of both players. Such consideration is better served by mutual cooperation which provides small gains to both. As a player controls only his own choices, his selection of the C response reflects his own trust or, in repeated plays, his desire to induce trust in the other's behavior. Conversely, suspicion leads to the choice of defection which, when mutual, is detrimental to both players.

A rather extensive literature on the Prisoner's Dilemma game is reviewed by Rapoport and Orwant (1962), by Gallo and McClintock (1965), and by Rapoport and Chammah (1965). Those Prisoner's Dilemma studies using a contrived adversary provide the clearest tests for the consequences of a unilateral patterning of moves upon cooperation. A variety of false-feedback conditions have been used in the Prisoner's Dilemma including the following types:

1. Total unilateral cooperation: The stooge cooperates without regard to the subject's actual moves (Rapoport & Chammah, 1965; Solomon, 1960).

2. Total unilateral defection: The stooge defects without regard to the subject's moves (Solomon, 1960).

3. Random feedback: The stooge cooperates or defects according to a random schedule again without regard to the subject's behavior. The probability of a C or D move is preset and remains the same for every trial (Bixenstine, Potash, & Wilson, 1963b; Marlowe, Gergen, & Doob, 1966).

4. Matching strategies: Here the stooge matches the actual performance of the subject in "tit-for-tat" fashion. The matching may be of the subject's current move or of his previous one. In the latter case a player who defected on one trial would be faced with defection on the subsequent

trial. In such strategies the level of co-operation by the stooge is entirely contingent upon the subject's own performance (Komorita, 1965).

5. Partial reinforcement strategy: This lies between the random and matching strategies, for in it the stooge's responses to particular moves are randomly selected but with one probability for a subject's co-operative moves and a different probability for his defecting moves. Hence, one can predetermine the proportion of times co-operation will be rewarded or defection punished, for example, 85% of subject's cooperative moves are met by the C response while perhaps 60% of subject's D responses are met by defection (Pylyshyn, Agnew, & Illingsworth, 1966; Komorita, 1965).

The matching strategies are categorically distinct from all others in their sensitivity to the play of the real player. This type of contingency is apparently conducive to cooperation (Komorita, 1965). One finding on an entirely non-contingent feedback, that is, on the effectiveness of 100% cooperation, is that the martyr stooge, over a lengthy sequence of trials, evokes two very different responses. About half the subjects take continuous advantage of the stooge while the other half come to a level of complete cooperation themselves (Rapoport & Chammah, 1965). This contrasts with the Shure et al. (1965) study of pacifist strategies, but again is peripheral to the idea of graduated reciprocation. Komorita studied a modified Prisoner's Dilemma adding a third choice for one of the players which permitted the inflicting of a heavy punishment to the other. In this way he demonstrated that unilateral restraint by the party who was alone equipped with a punitive option served to increase the rate of cooperation (Komorita et al., 1967).

The conventional two-choice Prisoner's Dilemma game permits a player to convey to his patrner an intention to engage in cooperative behavior. For him to do this, however, he must engage in cooperative behavior himself, and there is an immediate cost associated with the behavior if his partner has not chosen, at the same time, to do likewise.[1]

In the extended form of the Prisoner's Dilemma game (Pilisuk & Rapoport, 1964a, 1964b) the opportunity for conveying a change in one's intentions is made easier by the possibility of engaging in partially cooperative behaviors which would prove less costly to the initiator at payoff time. On the other hand, these less costly gestures might be viewed more as a "come on" than as a sincere indicator of the desire to achieve mutual cooperation. A way of further increasing the separation between conveying intentions and the cost associated with displaying one's intentions is provided for in the extended form. By virtue of the fact that the decision of how far to cooperate is enacted only gradually, it is possible to permit each player to inspect the performance of the other at some time prior to the terminal payoff. This opportunity for inspection may be used, with varying degrees of honesty, to give an indication of one's intended level of cooperation.

In addition, the entire game can be set in the simulated surrounding of an arms

---

[1] The conventional two-choice Prisoner's Dilemma game is played without direct communication between opposing players. This need not be the case and an important methodological contribution for the conduct of controlled communication of basic options and intentions in game experiments is seen in the development of the interaction screen (Sawyer & Friedell, 1965).

race—disarmament dilemma. The units of cooperation are conversions from missiles to factories, the terminology of weapons' disparity and economic productivity are used to describe the payoff matrix, and one's apparatus is described as a country.[2] This context contains the rudiments needed to test the "graduated reciprocation in tension" proposal, that is, disarming moves of specified sizes, preceded by a demonstration of intentions and repeated over a series of trials. In one study, using the extended Prisoner's Dilemma, it was found that in those pairs where both players had taken a substantial unilateral initiative, at some point early in the course of play, the prognosis for mutual cooperation was very good (Pilisuk, Potter, Rapoport, & Winter, 1965). Another study using the extended game permitted an announcement of intentions prior to actual behavior. Where integrity of these announcements occurred, increases in cooperative behavior tended to follow. However, there was a marked tendency to make deceptive use of the communication opportunity which tended to work against cooperation (Pilisuk, Winter, Chapman,

& Haas, 1967). Hence, there are limiting conditions under which an earlier finding that communication induces cooperation (Deutsch, 1958) would appear to hold.

These studies still fail to provide a direct test of the Osgood thesis. The limitation is inherent in the use of natural pairs which did not provide cases of a single player consistently making small, conciliatory overtures preceded each time by an indication of intention to do so. Subjects made gestures at odd times of various sizes and with varying degree of integrity of prior announcement. Contrived feedback could correct this. The present study contrasts the conduciveness to cooperation (or disarmament in the particular game) of two types of false feedback and of the presence or absence of an opportunity to communicate intentions via an inspection procedure. The two feedback conditions are a matching strategy and a conciliatory strategy. The latter leads in the direction of cooperation by small steps while remaining entirely contingent upon the subject's behavior. The hypothesis relevant to the Osgood proposal is that the conciliatory strategy when combined with honest communication will produce the greatest amount of cooperation.

---

[2] Effects resulting from the use of such labels have been reported in Pilisuk, Potter, Rapoport, and Winter, 1965. The use of arms-race terminology adds connotative meanings to the previously described "inspection" procedure. In the arms-control debate, inspection refers to a verification procedure on the reduction of armaments. In the present study the inspection procedure refers only to a peek at an adversary's armament level *before* the time when such a glimpse is useful for verification purposes. Since the word inspection is used in instructions to subjects, it is again used in this report. It must be understood, however, that it functions here as a form of prior announcement of intention and not as a verification procedure.

METHOD

One-hundred and twelve subjects participated in this experiment. The subjects were male student volunteers from the University of Michigan and Purdue University. The actual monetary rewards that the subjects received were dependent upon game outcomes. All subjects were led to believe that they were playing in pairs (some were actually playing against a "simulated other"), and acquaintances were not paired. An experimental session ordinarily contained four simultaneously performing pairs.

Subjects were seated at a table with a partition separating each subject from the others. The experiment was then explained as a simulation of international relations. Each subject had a board in front of him with five levers on it. Each lever exposed a picture of a missile on the left, or a factory on the right. Subjects started every trial with five missiles showing. A move consisted of converting zero, one, or two of the levers from missiles to factories or back again.

There were five moves in every trial but only the state following the last move had a payoff associated with it. Subjects received information of their adversary's performance level by a light signal after the fifth move of every trial. A subject was instructed to refer to his payoff matrix to determine how much money he and the other player had won or lost on that trial. Specific examples of the payoff matrix were illustrated to be certain that the task was understood. Subjects played the game described for 25 repeated trials but

NUMBER OF MISSILES OTHER PERSON HAS LEFT

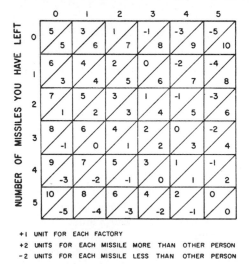

+1 UNIT FOR EACH FACTORY

+2 UNITS FOR EACH MISSILE MORE THAN OTHER PERSON

−2 UNITS FOR EACH MISSILE LESS THAN OTHER PERSON

Fig. 1. Payoff matrix shown to subjects. (Number to left of diagonal is payoff to subject. Number to right of diagonal is payoff to other player.)

were not informed of how many trials they were to play. After the experiment, subjects were asked to fill out a questionnaire.

The principle of payoff is given by the simple rule that a subject is rewarded for his conversion of missiles to factories, punished doubly for the degree that he has disarmed in excess of his opponent's level, and rewarded doubly for his missile superiority.[3] The complete matrix of payoff values, exactly as it is shown to the subjects, is presented in Figure 1.

While there are 6×6 contingent outcomes, the basic paradigm of the mixed motive Prisoner's Dilemma game is preserved. On any given trial a subject earns more the more highly he is armed, *regardless* of the armament level of his adversary. Yet, as in the more conventional two-choice game, mutual defection (armament in this case) reduces substantially the earnings of both parties and disarmament is advantageous to precisely the degree that it is mutual.

While instructions employed the terminology of countries, weapons, and economic units, no preference is expressed for either the armed or the disarmed state. Instructions carefully avoid any reference to goals of the task which might be inferred from such terms as game, competition, cooperation, winning, maximize earnings, etc. Subjects were left to infer from the matrix of outcomes their own purposes of play. Payoffs in actual money were presented after the experiment at the value of 1¢ per unit of the matrix.

The experiment was a factorial design in which three variations of the pattern of other's cooperation were crossed with the presence or absence of an inspection on the third move of each trial (see Figure 2). The natural pair experiment played without inspection has already been described. In the inspection conditions, the experimental pro-

---

[3] The payoff principle is expressed in the following formula: If players A and B expose F_a and F_b factories, respectively, and receive payoffs P_a and P_b, respectively, then [1] $P_a = 2 F_b - F_a$ and [2] $P_b = 2 F_a - F_b$.

FEEDBACK

INSPECTION			
	PAIRS WITH INSPECTION N=24	MATCHING WITH INSPECTION N=16	CONCILIATORY WITH INSPECTION N=16
	PAIRS WITHOUT INSPECTION N=24	MATCHING WITHOUT INSPECTION N=16	CONCILIATORY WITHOUT INSPECTION N=16

Fig. 2. Experimental design.

cedure was modified to inform each subject, by means of a lighting device, just how many missiles the other player had after the third move of every trial. It should be noted here that inspection performance, occurring at the third move, is not strictly binding. In the subject's two remaining moves he may still change four of his five units from the state displayed at inspection. In the two false-feedback conditions which used inspections, the artificial subject demonstrated at inspection the precise number of missiles to be shown on his fifth or payoff move, that is, the stooge used his inspection move with absolute integrity.

The two types of contrived feedback used in this experiment will be called matching and conciliatory. In the matching conditions two missiles were always given as the opponent's armament level for the first trial and thereafter the number of missiles the subject himself showed on Trial n was revealed as the number shown by the opponent for Trial $n+1$. In the conciliatory conditions, feedback (opponent's performance) was also two missiles for the first trial but thereafter the opponent's performance on Trial $n+1$ was one missile less than the subject had shown on the previous trial. The central prediction was that honest inspection and conciliatory behavior would increase cooperation (disarmament), that is, that the Osgood proposal would work.[4]

The authors further hypothesized (*a*) that for comparable conditions the conciliatory feedback would produce more cooperation than either the matching feedback or the natural condition, (*b*) that the matching strategy in turn would be more conducive to cooperation than the natural pair conditions (as in Komorita, 1965), and (*c*) that when feedback was constant, the conditions providing an opportunity for communication via inspection would produce greater cooperation. In other words, in addition to the success of the Osgood proposal significant main effects were predicted for the presence of contrived feedback and for the presence of inspection in all contrived feedback conditions.

Results

The major findings may be organized under three subheadings: (*a*) indexes of cooperation across conditions, (*b*) change in cooperation over time, and (*c*) utilization of the inspection move.

[4] The Osgood proposal is richer than this brief description would indicate. While the conciliatory condition meets some aspects of the graduated reciprocation thesis, the matching strategy is also similar to the proposal in its responsiveness to both the belligerent and friendly overtures of the other party. It is on the issue of initiatives that the conciliatory strategy is used here as the closer simulation of the Osgood strategy.

Cooperation Across Conditions

The most obvious index of cooperation is the gross number of missiles converted to factories at payoff time. The missile averages, or gross rates of noncooperation taken over all 25 trials, are seen in Figure 3. The results of an analysis of variance performed on these data are presented in Table 1. As predicted, the anova showed a significant feedback main effect ($p < .001$). In comparison with behavior in the natural pairs playing without inspection, the matching condition produced significantly more cooperation ($t = 5.79$; $df = 38$; $p < .001$).[5] The conciliatory condition also produced significantly more cooperation than occurred in the natural pairs ($t = 4.41$; $df = 38$; $p < .001$), but the differences between matching and conciliatory were not significant.

The difference in cooperation between natural and programmed conditions is even more pronounced in the games which offered opportunity for communication of intention via inspection. Here, total disarming reached an average level of only .8 (out of five possible units) in the natural pairs, which is significantly less cooperative than the 2.6 units average of the matching condition ($t = 5.5$; $df = 38$; $p < .001$). Again the matching condition was not distinguished significantly from the conciliatory condition. Clearly both forms of contrived feedback, matching and conciliatory, induced cooperation beyond what is ordinarily forthcoming in such circumstances, and this major effect is present regardless of the presence or absence of an opportunity for communication via inspection.

---

[5] All significance levels reported for *t* tests are two-tailed.

The question of whether the presence of inspection itself has discernible effects is not yet answered. The issue is important since inspection provided the only form of opportunity to convey intentions to the other party. Obviously the inspection condition has a somewhat different meaning in the natural and artificial conditions. In both artificial conditions one of the players (the stooge) conveyed his final or payoff move with absolute integrity. In the natural condition the use of inspection was left entirely up to the subjects. In the natural pairs, the presence of an inspection opportunity significantly reduced the amount of cooperation ($t = 3.16$; $df = 46$; $p < .001$).

The artificial conditions suggest an interesting interaction. Contrary to our hypothesis, honest inspection was not uniformly conducive to cooperation. The source of feedback by inspection interaction ($F = 2.85$; $p < .056$) suggests that inspection tends to improve cooperation in the conciliatory condition but weakens it in the matching condition and in the natural pairs. While this only approaches significance, we do report the finding recalling that the Osgood proposal for graduated reciprocation in tension reduction calls for combining an honest prior announcement of intention before each move with a regular progression of small conciliatory moves.

A more subtle index of cooperation takes into account the tendency of pairs of players to polarize or "lock-in" at near total levels of cooperative or competitive responses. The following measure defines criterion groups on the basis of terminal performance, the state of cooperation to which a pair had evolved toward the culmination of the experimental session. Continuing a practice of previous studies

Table 1

OVERALL ANALYSIS OF VARIANCE FOR EFFECTS OF VARIATIONS OF
FEEDBACK AND INSPECTION UPON MISSILE
(NONCOOPERATION) RATIO

Source	SS	MS	F ratio
Feedback (A)	31651.37500000	15825.687500	10.92***
Inspection (B)	4387.52343750	4387.523438	3.03*
A×B	8263.32031250	4131.660156	2.85**
Error	153683.58593750	1449.845139	

* $p < .10$, $df = 1/106$.
** $p < .056$, $df = 2/106$.
*** $p < .001$, $df = 2/106$.

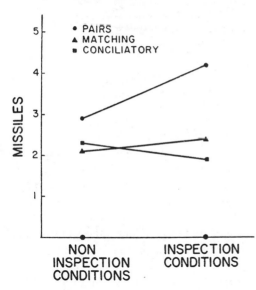

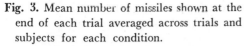

Fig. 3. Mean number of missiles shown at the end of each trial averaged across trials and subjects for each condition.

(Pilisuk et al., 1965) every pair of players was classified into one of three discrete categories in accordance with the performance of both players during the last five trials of an experimental session containing 25 trials.[6] The pairs are labeled

Dove (cooperators), Hawk (noncooperators) and Mugwumps (intermediate). A pair was labeled Dove if (*a*) both players showed four or more factories for each of the last five trials, and (*b*) if none of the subjects had less than 22 factories (more than three missiles) over these same trials. The Hawk criteria are completely symmetrical. A Hawk pair was so designated if (*a*) neither player had less than four missiles (more than one factory) on any one of the last five trials, and (*b*) none of the subjects totaled less than 22 missiles (more than three factories) over these same five trials. The third and intermediate group, Mugwumps, contain all the remaining pairs who failed to meet the conditions for classification as either Dove or Hawk. These groupings, while arbitrary, provide for stringent differentiation between cooperators (Doves) and noncooperators (Hawks).

The essential feature of these criteria is that they provide not only for a measure of pair, as opposed to individual, performance but also that they reflect a fact

---

[6] Classification for the pair is automatically given by the one real subject in the false-feed-back conditions where the stooge copied the subject's behavior.

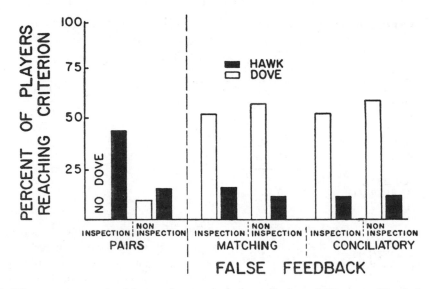

Fig. 4. The percentage of subjects who reached the criterion of Dove or Hawk for the six conditions.

about the data on cooperativeness in non-zero-sum games, that is, that it is likely to become increasingly polarized over repeated trials with the two players coming to achieve either the mutually competitive or the mutually cooperative state and to become set in it.

The particular criteria chosen are selected to provide continuity with earlier work (Pilisuk et al., 1965). In actual fact these criteria which were designed to measure *pair* performance could produce artifacts when one of the pair members is a preinstructed stooge. The probability that two players making random choices will fall into one of the two groups is less than 10^{-5}. The probability that a single player making random responses will meet criterion is still quite low but is certainly greater in the false-feedback conditions. Here a subject reaching Dove or Hawk criterion himself assures the selection of the pair into the category. The apparent difference in meanings of Dove and Hawk criterion groups under natural and false-feedback conditions is tempered by the lock-in phenomenon. This lock-in or tendency of members of natural pairs to come to play very much like one another at or near one of the poles of cooperation is repeated in our natural conditions. The percentages of players achieving Dove, Hawk, and Mugwump criteria in each of the six conditions are shown in Figure 4.

It can readily be seen that both false-feedback conditions produce significantly more Doves (at least 50% of players meet the Dove criterion in all false-feedback conditions) than in the comparable conditions using natural pairs. Using both actual number of missiles shown and criterion group, it appears that players receiving false feedback were more co-operative than players receiving real feed-back.

Time Course of Cooperation

What subjects do on the very first trial may be predictive of their amount of co-operation in later trials.[7] The current experiment finds slight support for this observation by obtaining a correlation of .3 between number of missiles on the first move and total number of missiles for the four false-feedback conditions (correlation is significant at the .01 level). The same correlation for the natural pairs (.18) is not significant. In natural games, ran-domly matched players tend to arrive at

quite close levels of cooperation leaving most of the variance to be accounted for by player interaction and little by predis-posing tendencies.

After the first move, a player has a his-tory of experience which becomes a major factor in determining his subsequent deci-sions (Pilisuk et al., 1965). Changes in cooperative behavior which develop in the course of the experiment are depicted in Figures 5 and 6. The points represent missile levels for nonoverlapping trial blocks of five trials each.

The findings suggest a gradual decline in armament levels in five of the six con-ditions. Only the natural pairs with in-spection were apparently becoming still less cooperative at the end of the experi-ment. This calls into question exactly how honest were the demonstrations of inten-tion in the natural circumstances which will be discussed shortly. It is obvious here, however, that the mere existence of a channel for communication of intention is

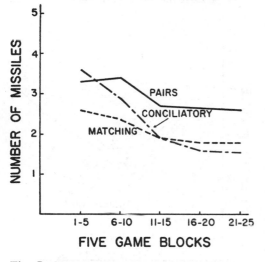

Fig. 5. Changes in cooperation or disarma-ment levels over time in noninspection conditions.

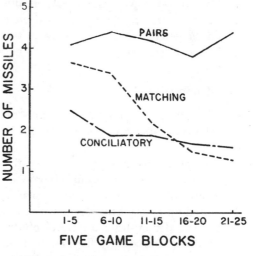

Fig. 6. Changes in cooperation or disarma-ment levels over time in inspection con-ditions.

[7] Terhune (1965), using a two-choice game, found a not quite significant trend between first-trial cooperation and subsequent coopera-tion.

not, by itself, conducive to trust. This has been noted in previous findings as well (Pilisuk et al., 1967b).

Cooperation in the conciliatory condition appears to increase from the start, perhaps with an added boost from the addition of honest inspection, but it appears to level off as the average value approaches one missile. Here an artifact introduced by the conciliatory strategy may be operating. For instance, where a subject takes cognizance of the fixed nature of his adversary's strategy, he (the subject) then gains optimal rewards from a strategy of retaining one missile on every trial. He may, in fact, come upon this one missile strategy inadvertently and stick to it because of the rewarding character without even realizing the nature of the other's strategy. That this is the case is evidenced by another piece of data, namely, that not one subject in the conciliatory condition could state, at the end, the principle of the "one-less" conciliatory strategy used by his adversary. We cannot say, at this point, whether the armament decline would have continued as rapidly if this artifact were removed.

Use of Inspection

The inspection point, where present, was the only opportunity for a player to exchange information with his opposite number prior to the payoff move. In this experiment, inspection occurred only on the third of five moves and a player, permitted up to two conversions per move, could thus demonstrate any level of disarmament (from zero to five) he desired. After this opportunity for demonstration of intentions, the player has two remaining moves in which he might still change as many as four out of his five units from factory to missile or the reverse. Hence,

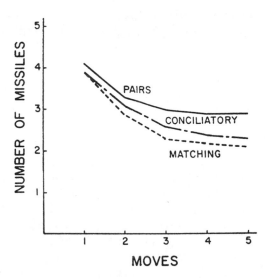

Fig. 7. Average number of missiles shown on every move for the noninspection conditions.

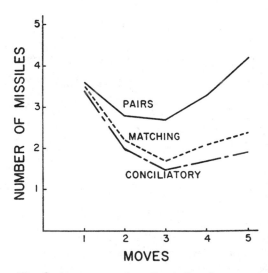
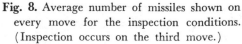

Fig. 8. Average number of missiles shown on every move for the inspection conditions. (Inspection occurs on the third move.)

the performance at inspection has necessary implications only for those displaying total armament or total disarmament and even for these cases, the implications for final performance are slight. When the inspection move has such necessary implications for the payoff move, we call the inspection binding. The significance of the performance at inspection was essentially a demonstration or nonbinding promise of intention. It could be matched identically by the player's subsequent performance at the payoff trial (as was done by the stooge in the false feedback conditions). It could be a promise overfulfilled at pay-

off time, as happened on occasion, or it could be used to demonstrate a higher level of intention to disarm than actually followed. This latter discrepancy may be taken as an index of deception.

A typical progression of play in conditions without inspections changed markedly when the third move was open as an inspection. The results of the average performance levels on the first through fifth moves is shown for the three non-

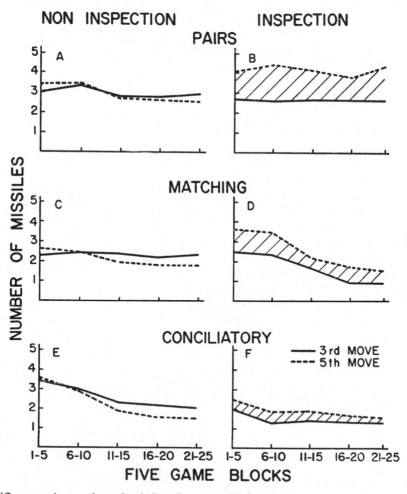

Fig. 9. Differences in number of missiles shown on third and fifth moves. (For inspection conditions the shaded area represents amount of deception.)

inspection conditions in Figure 7 and for the three inspection conditions in Figure 8.

The comparison of noninspection with inspection conditions is obvious. In the typical noninspection circumstance a player moves directly from his original state of five missiles to his terminal state. In the typical inspection game a player disarms somewhat to the point of inspection and rearms somewhat in his remaining moves. This difference is found in the conciliatory and matching conditions as well as with the natural pairs.

Using the decreased level in cooperation after inspection as an index of deception, it is possible to plot the amount of deception within five-game trial blocks. The amount of deception is shown as the gray areas in Figure 9, b, d, and f.

The mean discrepancy between displayed level at inspection and at terminal performance again shows a consistent use of the inspection opportunity for deceptive purposes. The natural pairs provide a base against which to measure the effects of the experimental variation in other's strategy upon the integrity of the subject's performance. This contrast suggests that an opponent who uses his inspection opportunity to display his precise intentions with integrity may be having a beneficial effect upon the integrity of the subject himself. Perhaps the clearest way to demonstrate this is with frequency data which indicate the number of times a particular promise was fulfilled, that is, demonstration at inspection was either maintained or over-fulfilled by still greater

disarmament at the payoff trial. These data are shown for each inspection condition, broken down by five-game trial blocks in Figure 10.

The results of a trend analysis performed on the data confirm a tendency across conditions to use the inspection opportunity with increasing integrity, ($F = 27.83$; $p > .001$).[8] It is instructive to contrast the integrity change in the matching-inspection condition, Figure 10, with the terminal cooperation rate for the same condition over the same trial blocks, Figure 6. Subjects started using the inspection opportunity deceptively 63% of the time during the first trial block of the

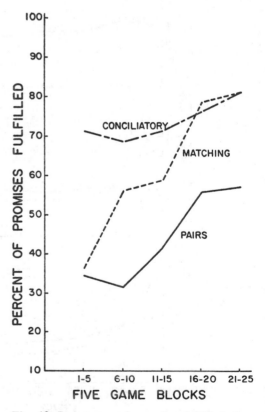

Fig. 10. Percentage of promises fulfilled (integrity on inspection move).

---

[8] An unweighted means analysis of variance to test for linear trend was used for a two-factor (trial blocks versus condition) 5×3 design (see Winer, 1962, p. 377).

matching condition. Here, the matching stooge using absolutely honest demonstrations of intention apparently induced a very sharp reduction in the level of deception as well as an increase in the level of cooperation. Unfortunately, for purposes of comparison, the conciliatory group was essentially honest from the start.

DISCUSSION

The primary results of the study indicate that both matching and conciliatory strategies increase cooperation over the rate naturally found in this experimental game. The Osgood proposal for combining small, consistent, unilateral overtures of good intention with an honest prior announcement of moves does apparently produce markedly more cooperation than is found in the natural state but only a marginal and contingent increase over the rate found in a comparable matching strategy.

The interaction effect cited, that is, increased cooperation resulting from honest inspection in combination with the conciliatory strategy, was not found where criterion groups were used as the index of cooperation. This may represent an artifact produced by the payoff matrix where a rigid conciliatory strategy is employed. In the conciliatory condition, as previously mentioned, it was possible for a player to secure maximum rewards by less than maximum cooperation. A player consistently converting four missiles to factories would be consistently met by an adversary disarming completely and would stand to win more this way than if he were cooperating at any other level. The discovery of such an optimal state may have served to curtail any tendency to increase

cooperation beyond that point. Hence, several players who might otherwise have met the Dove condition detected this peculiar option and fell slightly short of the cooperation level needed for Dove classification. The interpretation is supported by data comparing the rates of cooperation of the matching and conciliatory strategies over time. The conciliatory strategies produce a rapid rise in cooperation which levels at close to the optimum state.

It seems also possible that the conciliatory strategy may have been most useful in inducing movement toward cooperation, but that once the advantages of mutual cooperation have grown apparent that a tit-for-tat strategy will serve to push it all the way. Such combined strategies are certainly worth trying but a third possibility remains, namely that nonpunitive sensitivity to partner's behavior, a variable shared by both conciliatory and matching strategies, is the critical factor which overrides the minor variations found between them.

The results which dealt with the absolute integrity of announcement of intention through inspection suggested that the addition of inspection might be differentially favorable to cooperation, that is, favorable only in the conciliatory condition. Subjects in the conciliatory condition were asked whether they thought the inspection opportunity made a difference in their strategy. Fourteen of 16 felt that the inspection made a difference in their own performance. The same number felt that inspection contributed to cooperation. In the natural condition where cooperation was substantially lower (and the inspection was frequently used deceptively), subjects most frequently felt that the inspection made a difference in the direction of reducing cooperation. There may be some cognitive congruity operation occurring here with the subject's tendency to see consistency between his own final cooperation level and the experimental conditions present at the time.

In the matching strategy the prior announcement of moves appears actually to decrease the amount of cooperation. We did find that the initial reaction to this condition was apparently to be unresponsive to the integrity of the stooge, that is, not to match the stooge in his integriy until later in the time course when the mutual cooperative pattern started to emerge. Without the trusting set (introduced by the conciliatory condition) the presence of an adversary who honestly signals his moves but does not take any cooperative initiatives (only responds to cooperative gestures) may be taken as a temptation for taking advantage of this adversary who has not made known any cooperative intentions of his own. In the conciliatory condition, however, the stooge makes cooperative gestures in addition to responding to the subject's gestures, and the addition of honest communication calls attention to the trustful intentions. This conclusion must be considered as tentative because of the marginal significance of the interaction effect reported above ($p >$ .056).

It should be reiterated that the inspection move was not a pure signal of intention. This is important, for communication, once considered the panacea for distrust, is itself a many faceted phenomenon. In this particular study it was possible to make a very modestly binding show of intentions. By showing total disarmament at inspection one could expose himself to loss in that he could only enact an 80% rearmament in the two remaining moves

before payoff. This places a very particular significance on the display of total cooperation at inspection. It also leaves ground for suspicion of motives in the display of less than total cooperation. In an analogous study where total retraction was possible, where the inspection move was purely signal, we found the communication to inhibit lock-in but not to increase total cooperation. But in another condition of that study, a more binding inspection where full disarmament at inspection meant at least 50% disarmament at payoff, the result was first a decrease but then a very sharp increase in mutual cooperation (Pilisuk et al., 1967b). There is obvious need for control on the nature of the communication variable. Osgood's proposal that communication be precise, honest, and placed before each move assists in definition. The degree to which it can be made to appear binding also appears important. The only other evidence bearing upon the hypothesis came when we asked subjects at the end if they would trust the other person. All 16 subjects in the conciliatory group said "yes" in contrast to 62–75% in the other false-feedback conditions and still fewer in the natural groups. Only 7 of 24 subjects in the natural pair inspection condition said they would trust the other party.

In designing the false-feedback situation we were frankly concerned that both matching and conciliatory conditions would be too obvious. We feared not only that the patterns would be discovered but that this would happen sufficiently early in the sequence to arouse suspicions in the subjects regarding the deception. The actual recognition of the pattern proved more difficult than originally anticipated. About half of the subjects saw no formula at all governing the pattern of the preprogrammed other. Of those who did see a plan in the other person's behavior it was often represented by a rather simplified statement like "he stayed armed most of the time to try to win." The dependence of stooge strategy on one's own offered some interesting and perhaps projective insights into the attribution of motives. One subject in the conciliatory condition stated the strategy of the other was to stay mostly armed so he himself reacted by staying armed and "did him one better." Not one of 64 subjects facing either the matching strategy or the conciliatory strategy could satisfactorily state the principle of his adversary's strategy. Whatever effects on the subject's behavior transpired, they were achieved without the mediation of precise awareness of the strategy. In other words, it does not appear to be absolutely necessary to give public announcement or to let the adversary know the overall plan of strategy, or even for the adversary to perceive the strategy accurately in order for the strategy to be effective.

The Osgood proposal is certainly not tested definitively in a single study. From this study we find support for the effect of honest prior announcement of moves in interaction with conciliatory steps as productive of cooperative behavior. From the studies reviewed in the introduction, it seems fair to conclude that complete unilateral martyrdom and trust are, at least under some conditions, ineffective in inducing cooperation. The studies also show that unilateral reliance upon power, or threatening moves tends to beget belligerence rather than conciliation. Between the extremes of overt reliance upon belligerent or threatening moves and complete conciliation and trust there lies a strategy of moves which is most effective in the reduc-

tion of intergroup hostility. As a first approximation, the Osgood proposals remain a tenable candidate for such a pattern of moves. Why such proposals are not more frequently or more arduously tested in the field is a question which goes beyond the scope of this paper.

REFERENCES

BIXENSTINE, V. E., POTASH, H. M., and WILSON, K. V. "Effects of Level of Cooperative Choice by the Other Player on Choices in a Prisoner's Dilemma Game: Part I." *Journal of Abnormal and Social Psychology*, 1963, 66, 308–313. (a)

BIXENSTINE, V. E., POTASH, H. M., and WILSON, K. V. "Effects of Level of Cooperative Choice by the Other Player on Choices in a Prisoner's Dilemma Game: Part II." *Journal of Abnormal and Social Psychology*, 1963, 67, 139–147. (b)

DEUTSCH, M. "Trust and Suspicion." *Journal of Conflict Resolution*, 1958, 2, 267–279.

DEUTSCH, M., and KRAUSS, R. M. "The Effect of Threat upon Interpersonal Bargaining." *Journal of Abnormal and Social Psychology*, 1960, 181–189.

ETZIONI, A. "The Kennedy Experiment." *Western Political Quarterly*, 1967, 20, 361–380.

GALLO, P. S., and McCLINTOCK, C. "Cooperative and Competitive Behavior in Mixed Motive Games." *Journal of Conflict Resolution*, 1965, 9, 68–78.

KOMORITA, S. S. "Cooperative Choice in a Prisoner's Dilemma Game." *Journal of Personality and Social Psychology*, 1965, 2, 741–745.

KOMORITA, S. S., SHEPOSH, J. P., and BRAVER, S. L. "Power, the Use of Power, and Perceived Intentions in a Two-Person Game." Unpublished manuscript, Wayne State University, 1967.

MARLOWE, D., GERGEN, K. J., and DOOB, A. N. "Opponent's Personality, Expectation of Social Interaction, and Interpersonal Bargaining." *Journal of Personality and Social Psychology*, 1966, 3, 206–213.

OSGOOD, C. E. "Suggestions for Winning the Real War with Communism." *Journal of Conflict Resolution*, 1959, 3, 295–325.

OSGOOD, C. E. *An Alternative to War or Surrender*. Urbana, Ill.: University of Illinois Press, 1962.

PILISUK, M., POTTER, P., RAPOPORT, A., and WINTER, J. A. "War Hawks and Peace Doves: Alternate Resolutions of Experimental Conflicts." *Journal of Conflict Resolution*, 1965, 9, 491–508.

PILISUK, M., and RAPOPORT, A. "A Non-Zero-Sum Game Model of Some Disarmament Problems." In, *Peace Research Society; Papers I*. Tokyo: International Academic Press, 1964. (a)

PILISUK, M., and RAPOPORT, A. "Stepwise Disarmament and Sudden Destruction in a Two-Person Game: A Research Tool." *Journal of Conflict Resolution*, 1964, 8, 36–49. (b)

PILISUK, M., SKOLNICK, P., THOMAS, K., and CHAPMAN, R. "Boredom Versus Cognitive Reappraisal in the Development of Cooperative Strategy." *Journal of Conflict Resolution*, 1967, 11, 110–116. (a)

PILISUK, M., WINTER, J. A., CHAPMAN, R., and HAAS, N. "Honesty, Deceit, and Timing in the Display of Intentions." *Behavioral Science*, 1967, 12, 205–215. (b)

PYLYSHYN, Z., AGNEW, N., and ILLINGWORTH, J. "Comparison of Individuals and Pairs as Participants in a Mixed-Motive Game." *Journal of Conflict Resolution*, 1966, 10, 211–220.

RAPOPORT, A., and CHAMMAH, A. M. *Prisoner's Dilemma*. Ann Arbor: University of Michigan Press, 1965.

RAPOPORT, A., and ORWANT, C. "Experimental Games: A Review." *Behavioral Science*, 1962, 7, 1–37.

RASER, J. R., and CROW, W. J. WINSAFE II: "An International Simulation Study of Deterrence Postures Embodying Capacity to Delay Response." La Jolla, Calif.: Western Behavioral Science Institute, 1964. (mimeo)

SAWYER, J., and FRIEDELL, M. F. "The Interaction Screen: An Operational Model for Experimentation on Interpersonal Behavior." *Behavioral Science*, 1965, 10, 446–460.

SHURE, G. H., MEEKER, R. J., and HANSFORD, E. A. "The Effectiveness of Pacifist Strategies in Bargaining Games." *Journal of Conflict Resolution*, 1965, 9, 106–117.

SOLOMON, L. "The Influence of Some Types of Power Relations Upon the Level of Interpersonal Trust." *Journal of Abnormal and Social Psychology*, 1960, 61, 223–230.

TERHUNE, K. W. "Psychological Studies of Social Interaction and Motives (Siam). Phase 1. Two-Person Gaming Study." Cornell Aeronautical Laboratory Technical Report #VX-2018-G-1, 1965.

WINER, B. J. *Statistical-Principles in Experimental Design*. New York: McGraw-Hill, 1962.

OPPONENT'S PERSONALITY, EXPECTATION OF SOCIAL INTERACTION, AND INTERPERSONAL BARGAINING*

David Marlowe, Kenneth J. Gergen, and Anthony N. Doob

The analysis of bargaining behavior within the context of two-person games has been the subject of considerable research in recent years. In contrast to an early concern with economic and mathematical considerations (Luce & Raiffa, 1957), recent investigations have emphasized the interpersonal aspects of the bargaining situation. These latter studies view bargaining as a special instance of social interaction amenable to analysis within the framework of experimental social psychology. Deutsch and Krauss (1960), for example, studied the effects of unilateral and bilateral threat on the ability of persons to reach agreement in a simulation game; Scodel, Minas, Ratoosh, and Lipetz (1959) and Minas, Scodel, Marlowe, and Rawson (1960) examined bargaining behavior in a two-person game under varying communication conditions, payoff values, and opponent strategies; Deutsch (1958) related bargaining be-

havior to the variables of trust and suspicion; and Solomon (1960) investigated the influence of various power relationships on bargaining strategies. The focus in the majority of these studies has been on the degree to which a person will cooperate with or exploit an opponent under varying stimulus conditions. In general, these investigations seem to indicate that unless cooperative strategies are fostered through special experimental instructions or intersubject communication, persons will choose to compete with one another and will play in such a way as to maximize the difference between their own and their partner's payoffs.

Given the recent trend toward viewing economic bargaining as a form of social interaction, it has been only natural to seek personality and attitudinal correlates of bargaining behavior. Using a two-person game of the prisoner's-dilemma format, Deutsch (1960) reported that authoritarians (as measured by the F Scale) tended to be less trusting of the other player and to make more uncooperative choices. Marlowe (1963) found that passive-dependent persons were disposed to respond to unconditionally cooperative behavior with cooperation on their own part. And Lutzker (1960) reported that

* David Marlowe, Kenneth J. Gergen, and Anthony N. Doob, "Opponent's Personality, Expectation of Social Interaction, and Interpersonal Bargaining," *Journal of Personality and Social Psychology*, 3 (1966), 215–21. Copyright 1966 by the American Psychological Association, and reproduced by permission.

internationally minded as compared to isolationists were more cooperative in a two-person game. Though few in number, such experimental studies are consistent in indicating that reliable differences in bargaining behavior are associated with personality predispositions of the players.

The present investigation sought to continue and broaden the emphasis on the social aspects of the bargaining situation by concentrating on two variables which are basic to most social relationships. When two persons are engaged in a real-life bargaining transaction, there are at least two types of information which are focal in determining the course of the relationship. First, we generally form at the outset of the relationship some impression of the kind of person with whom we are dealing. These impressions may determine to a large degree the type of behavior manifested towards another person (cf. Davis, 1962; Gergen & Jones, 1963). Second, one's estimate of the longevity of a relationship may also play an important role. For example, Thibaut and Kelley (1959) have discussed the fact that persons are often more revealing to total strangers than to close friends; Gergen and Wishnov (1965) have explored the effects of varying the degree of anticipated interaction on the way in which a person will present himself to another.

The variable of interaction anticipation would seem to have special significance for the area of interpersonal bargaining. The vast majority of bargaining studies have been conducted under conditions in which subjects expected no future confrontation with their opponents. However, in everyday relationships, persons seldom find themselves in the highly transient bargaining arena best characterized, perhaps, by the New York Stock Exchange.

More typically, people expect to "live" with their behavior, and expect to defend and discuss it in ongoing relationships. This paper, then, reports on two investigations which sought to relate bargaining behavior in a two-person game to the variables of the perceived personality of the opponent[1] and expectation of future interaction with the opponent.

In the first investigation (Experiment I) the aim was simply to demonstrate that when bargaining with a predominantly cooperative other, persons will play more cooperatively when expecting to be confronted by this other than when no post-bargaining interaction is anticipated. Here it was reasoned that the exploitation of another person who is trying to be cooperative is socially undesirable behavior. Thus a face-to-face meeting with an exploited partner would create embarrassment, if not arouse guilt for the subject. Hence, it was felt that subjects would feel a stronger disposition to do the gracious thing and cooperate when they expected to be confronted with their behavior.

Given that the expectation of future interaction will induce greater cooperation, Experiment II attempted to show that interaction anticipation would have quite different effects on bargaining behavior depending on the perceived personality characteristics of the opponent. At least one major dimension along which persons often characterize others is that of egotism versus humility. As Gergen and Wishnov

---

[1] Although the term "opponent" has traditionally been used to refer to the participants in two-person games, in many instances the term is misleading. In this study, as in many others, the notion of a game or competition is never specifically introduced to the subjects by the experimenter.

(1965) have reasoned, interacting with an egotist can often be threatening, and at the outset tends to reduce one's power in a social relationship. The optimum strategy for restoring power when bargaining with an egotist would seem to be successful competition. It was further felt that this tactic would most likely occur when further interaction was anticipated. There would seem to be less need to restore one's power in a relationship which is seen to be short-lived. It was hypothesized then that when dealing with a partner who describes himself in grandiose terms, the direct effects of anticipated interaction (Experiment I) would not hold. Rather, it was expected that when bargaining with an egotistical other the anticipation of further interaction would lead to *greater* exploitation of the partner.

On the other hand, a person who is seen to be self-effacing and humble seems to elicit quite different reactions. Such a person often evokes feelings of pity and nurturance on the part of others. To exploit such a person would give rise to feelings of guilt. Under public scrutiny, the exploitation of such a person would also be conspicuously undesirable. However, it is also just such a person who invites exploitation. The person who displays only his shortcomings lays himself open to the other's advantage. The variation in anticipated interaction should make an important difference concerning which of these two reactions predominates. Feelings of guilt and the undesirable features of exploitation should be particularly salient when further interaction is expected. On the other hand, when one will not be held responsible for his behavior, or have to face his victim, the invitation to exploitation should be accepted. It was thus felt that when dealing with a self-effacing

other, the findings of the initial experiment would be replicated even more dramatically. That is, when further interaction is anticipated, little exploitation should take place; when no further interaction is expected, exploitation should be maximal. The hypothesis for Experiment II can thus be summarized as follows: When interacting with a predominantly cooperative other, with anticipation of further interaction, subjects will exploit this other to a greater degree if he is seen to be egotistical than if he is seen to be self-effacing; when no further interaction is anticipated, the reverse will be true.

Experiment I

This experiment was designed to study the effects of an anticipated social interaction on bargaining behavior. The specific hypothesis was that subjects who bargain with an expectation of later meeting their opponent will make significantly more cooperative choices than persons who bargain with no expectation of later meeting their opponent.

Method

Subjects. Twenty-three college males, all freshmen at Harvard University, participated in the experiment. Students were chosen at random from the university directory and asked to serve in a study of bargaining and decision making. Virtually all the students contacted agreed to serve. The subjects were informed that they would be paid a minimum of $1.50 for their time, and that they would "have an opportunity to make more money."

Procedure. Subjects participated in the experiment in groups ranging in size from four to six. Upon arriving at the experimental site each subject was seated at a large table. The table was partitioned in such a way that subjects could neither see, signal, nor otherwise communicate with each other. The experiment was described by the experimenter as focusing on the way in which persons make decisions when bargaining with each other under restricted conditions. Subjects were told that each would be working with a partner, ostensibly one of the other subjects at the table. A series of decisions were to be made by each subject and his partner, and as a result of these decisions various amounts of money could be made. During these instructions and those which followed the experimenter never used such words as "win," "lose," "beat," "game," "opponent." In this way it was hoped that the arousal of strictly competitive motives could be avoided.

Subjects were then introduced to what has formally been termed a non-zero-sum game. Such a game can be contrasted with the zero-sum game in which there is no possibility for players to increase their payoffs through cooperation. Subjects were told that they would be faced with a number of decision trials and that on each trial they would be required to choose between pressing either a black or a red button. Each subject was led to believe that his partner would simultaneously be deciding which of the two buttons to press. On each trial there were thus four possible combinations which could occur for any subject pair. Subjects were then introduced to a payoff matrix which was posted in front of each subject and which displayed the amounts of money each would obtain for each of the four combinations. It was explained to the subjects that if on any trial both partners chose red, each would receive $.01; if both chose black each would receive $.03; if one chose red and the other chose black, the first would receive $.05 and the second would receive nothing. As can be seen, this game is of the standard "prisoner's-dilemma" variety (cf. Rapoport & Orwant, 1962).

After the game had been thoroughly explained, half of the subject groups (confrontation condition) were told:

In the past we have found that we can learn much more about what went on if we have each pair of subjects meet with me to discuss why they behaved as they did. So, after we have finished here, you will meet with the person you bargained with to discuss why you behaved as you did.

For the remaining subject pairs these instructions were omitted (no-confrontation condition).

The apparatus used to conduct the game was similar to that devised by Crutchfield (1955) to study conformity behavior. With this equipment the subjects' choices register on the experimenter's panel. By throwing various switches the experimenter can inform each subject of the choice which his partner has made, and at the same time also indicate the resultant payoff. The experimenter can, of course, supply the subjects with inaccurate information and announce whatever choices the concerns of the study demand. The present experiment consisted of 30 trials. On 24 of these trials each subject was informed that his partner had chosen "Black" (the cooperative choice). The "partner's" Red choices were randomly distributed over Trials 4–30. Each subject was thus led to believe that his partner was playing a predominantly cooperative game, and was thus faced with a dilemma. He could select Black and thereby maximize joint gain ($.03 each), or he could press Red and exploit his partner's good intentions ($.05 for him and nothing for his partner). Inasmuch as it was the only choice which avoided the maximization of joint gain, the number of trials on which the subject selected Red served as a measure of exploitation.

After the game had been terminated all subjects were supplied with an adjective check list containing 81 adjectives arranged in alphabetical order. Subjects were asked to place a check by those 10 adjectives which they felt best described their partner. After completing the check list subjects in the confrontation condition were informed that they would not have to meet their partner because, "we are short of time and have collected enough data." After paying the subjects what they had earned in the game and for their participation in the experiment, the subjects were allowed to depart.

Results and Discussion

The mean number of Red (exploitative) choices made by the subjects in the no-confrontation conditions was 24.5 ($n = 12$), as compared to a mean of 19.1 in the confrontation condition ($n = 11$). The difference between these means is significant beyond the .05 level ($t = 2.34$).[2] Thus, in line with the prediction, subjects who expected to discuss their behavior after bargaining were significantly less exploitative (or more cooperative).

It was ventured above that the exploitation of a well-intentioned other, combined with the knowledge that one will be confronted by this other, leads to anticipatory guilt or embarrassment and thus the avoidance of exploitation. However, this explanation depends on the supposition that subjects did, indeed, perceive the partner as well-intentioned. Although four out of every five choices which the partner made were cooperative, there is an alternative way in which such choices might have been viewed by the subjects. The persistent selection of Black could have been seen as an attempt on the partner's part to seduce the subject into choosing Black, with the partner then intending to defect to Red. However, a perusal of the adjectives used to describe the partner indicates that this latter way of viewing the partner was very unlikely. The five adjectives most frequently checked as being descriptive of the partner were: persistent, conservative, dependable, naive,

and generous. Those most infrequently checked were: treacherous, tolerant, tactful, neat, and greedy.

It would seem, then, that the disposition to act more equitably under conditions of confrontation serves to enhance one's public image. In the no-confrontation condition whatever guilt or embarrassment is aroused is largely personal and not in itself sufficient to inhibit exploitation. This result is reminiscent of the findings in the area of conformity and social influence which indicate that behavioral conformity is enhanced under conditions of public surveillance (Argyle, 1957; Mouton, Blake, & Olmstead, 1956).

EXPERIMENT II

Experiment I indicated that under circumstances in which no information is available regarding the person with whom one is bargaining, there is a tendency for subjects to be more exploitative when they anticipate no postbargaining confrontation. One personality dimension which should interact significantly with a variation in interaction anticipation is egotism versus humility. This consideration lent itself to a 2×2 factorial design with the cross-cutting dimensions of opponent's personality (egotistical versus humble) and interaction anticipation (confrontation versus no confrontation). The procedure for this experiment was highly similar to that of Experiment I, but may be compared in the following respects:

Subjects. The subjects were 44 Harvard freshmen recruited in the same manner as those used in Experiment I. Care was taken to obtain subjects not living in the same dormitories as those previously used. Eleven subjects were assigned at random to each of the four experimental conditions.

Procedure. Subjects were again seated at the partitioned table and told that the experi-

---

[2] All tests of significance reported are two-tailed.

ment dealt with various aspects of bargaining and decision making. However, in addition, the experimenter indicated that he was interested in some of the social aspects of bargaining and that each subject would be asked to describe himself on a set of forms which would then be given to his partner to examine. In this manner, subjects were told, they would each be able to form some sort of impression of the person with whom they would be bargaining.

All subjects were then provided with a 14-item questionnaire. Nine of these items were in the form of 12-point rating scales anchored at the extremes with such phrases as "clear-thinking"–"fuzzy-minded," and "efficient"–"inefficient," etc. The remaining items were taken from the Janis and Field (1959) self-esteem scale. A representative item was, "In general, how confident do you feel about your abilities?" Subjects answered on a 5-point scale which ranged from "very" to "not at all." Subjects were asked not to place their names on the questionnaires.

After the questionnaires were completed and collected, each subject was provided with either one of two especially prepared questionnaires which ostensibly had been filled out by his partner. These questionnaires were intended to create either the impression that the partner was egotistical or that he was extremely humble or modest. The first nine items on the questionnaire had earlier been given to an independent group of undergraduates. From the ratings made by this group it was possible to establish modal response patterns for the various scales. For the present experiment the questionnaire for the egotistical partner was prepared in such a way that the scale points checked were always closer to the positive end of the scale than the modal responses by 2 scale points. On the other hand, the self-ratings for the "humble partner" always differed from the modal responses by 2 scale points toward the negative end of the scale. On the self-esteem measure the egotistical partner always endorsed the most extreme positive position, while the

humble partner always endorsed the most negative position on each of the five items.

After the subjects had been given an opportunity to read the ratings made by their supposed partners, they were given a six-item questionnaire on which they were to rate their impression of their partner. These ratings were not to be seen by the partner. Half of the subject groups were then given the same instructions that subjects in the confrontation condition had been given in Experiment I. The remaining subject groups received no such instructions.

The game used in this experiment was identical to that used in the initial experiment, and the subjects again found their partner to be almost persistently cooperative. After the game was completed, subjects were given the same six-item questionnaire filled out just prior to the game and asked to consider again their impressions of their partner. The session was terminated in the same manner as the initial experiment.

Results

Before examining the results regarding subjects' bargaining behavior, it is appropriate to ask whether the attempt to manipulate the subjects' perception of the partner's personality was effective. The first imprssion ratings, made by the subjects immediately after being exposed to self-ratings supposedly made by their partner, provide a direct check on the effectiveness of this manipulation. These impression ratings were made on a number of 12-point scales. Two of these scales ("self-centered versus humble" and "modest versus conceited") referred specifically to the intended personality induction. Combining the ratings made on these two scales, the mean ratings of subjects facing the egotistical partner were compared by a t test with the mean ratings of those expecting to interact with a humble partner

($n = 22$ for both groups). With a range of possible scores from 2 to 24, the former group obtained a mean of 22.05, whereas the mean for the latter group was only 6.36. The difference between these means is highly significant ($t = 19.7$, $p < .00001$). Quite clearly, the manipulation of perceived personality was effective.

Turning to the major results, it will be recalled that an interaction between perceived personality and expectancy of interaction was predicted. More specifically, it was hypothesized that when expecting a postexperimental confrontation, subjects would exploit the egotistical partner more than the humble partner, but that when no further interaction was anticipated the reverse would be true. The dependent variable in Experiment II (as in Experiment I) was the number of exploitative (Red) choices made by subjects over the 30 trials. Figure 1 presents the mean number of Red choices made in the four conditions, while Table 1 contains the results of an analysis of variance performed on this data. As can be seen in Table 1, there

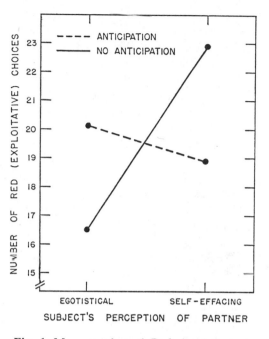

Fig. 1. Mean number of Red (exploitative) choices for subjects in Experiment II.

Table 1

ANALYSIS OF VARIANCE OF EXPLOITATIVE CHOICES IN EXPERIMENT II

Source	df	MS	F
Confrontation (A)	1	1.21	<1
Partner personality (B)	1	73.05	2.12
A×B	1	158.07	4.58*
Error	40	34.48	

* $p < .05$.

were no significant main effects due to either the perceived personality or the confrontation variables. As anticipated, however, there is a significant personality confrontation interaction ($p < .05$). Con-

sulting Figure 1, it can be seen that the configuration of the means lends full support to the major hypothesis. Subjects cooperated more with a humble person they expected to meet than with one they did not expect to meet; when the partner was an egotist, however, there was greater cooperation if they did not expect to interact with him.

An analysis of the pre-post change scores of subjects' perceptions of the partner revealed several additional facts. These six rating scales were arranged so as to form three distinct perceptual clusters: egotism, independence, and likability. An analysis of the prescores on these three dimensions indicated no significant differences between confrontation and no-confrontation subjects within either condition of perceived personality. In other words, as would be hoped, there were no systematic differences in the way the partner was seen at the outset of the bargaining task which resulted from the variation in confrontation. Second, it was also found that in addition to seeing their partner as more egotistical (as discussed above), subjects facing the egotistical partner also saw him as significantly ($p < .05$) less likable prior to the bargaining task. This finding confirms those of Pepitone (1964).

Finally, whereas the perception of the humble partner was found to be virtually unaltered as a result of the bargaining experience, such was not the case with the egotistical partner. As a result of bargaining with the egotistical partner, subjects came to see him as significantly ($p < .025$) less egotistical, less independent ($p < .025$), and more likable ($p < .05$). In short, it seemed that regardless of confrontation, the predominantly cooperative behavior of the partner in this condition was seen as inconsistent with the personality traits ascribed to him initially. The cooperative behavior, in effect, appeared to alter the subjects' perception so that at the termination of the experiment the perceived differences between the egotistical and humble partner was much less marked (though still significant at beyond the .01 level with regard to perceived egotism). One might be led to speculate that had the game gone on indefinitely, the differences in exploitation due to initial perceived personality might have eventually washed out.

DISCUSSION

The results of Experiment I indicate quite clearly that when no personal information is available concerning the person with whom one is bargaining, and

this other plays a predominantly cooperative game, there is a greater tendency to exploit this other when not expecting a later confrontation. The findings from Experiment II, however, modify this picture substantially. When personal information becomes available regarding the other, this information may indeed reverse the role of the confrontation variable. Specifically, when the other person is perceived to be egotistical and self-centered, he is *more* likely to be exploited when future interaction is anticipated than when it is not.

The prediction of this latter finding was based on the assumption that a boastful other tends to force those with whom he interacts into an undesirable low status position. This state of affairs can be described as an imbalance in displayed power, and may be reacted to by attempts to redress the imbalance. In the Gergen and Wishnov (1965) study, for example, subjects faced with an egotist began describing themselves in an extremely positive manner and would not reveal shortcomings. However, it would appear that the need to redress an imbalance in displayed power is less powerful when the interaction is seen to be short-lived. The expectancy of being confronted by an egotist who may have been very exploitative would seem to be an intimidating experience, demanding the defensive reaction of exploitation. In line with this speculation, there was a tendency for female subjects in the Gergen and Wishnov study to magnify their positive features to a greater extent when future interaction with the egotist was anticipated. The male subjects in the present experiment seem to have demonstrated a similar tendency to an even greater extent through their differential exploitation of the egotist as a function of their expectancy of confrontation.

Turning to the subjects' reactions to the humble partner, interpretation of the results raises certain difficulties. It was initially speculated that the self-effacing partner would instigate two opposing tendencies for subjects: the humility of the partner would cause them to feel embarrassed if they engaged in exploitation, and yet this same humility would increase the likelihood that monetary rewards could be obtained through exploitation. It was hypothesized that the variation in confrontation would split these tendencies in such a way that embarrassment would become more salient when interaction was anticipated, and exploitation would become more attractive when there was no possibility of being held responsible for one's actions.

Some check on these speculations can be obtained by comparing the amount of exploitation of the humble partner in Experiment II with the degree to which the partner about whom nothing was known in Experiment I was exploited. In Experiment II all the factors operating to produce the results of Experiment I should be present in addition to those created by the knowledge of the partner's humility. If the above speculations are correct, in Experiment II there should have been more exploitation in the no-confrontation condition and less in the confrontation condition than found in Experiment I. Consulting the results of the two experiments, it is found that these expectations are only partially verified. In the confrontation conditions the results were in the anticipated direction; when the partner was seen as humble the mean number of Red button presses was 18.9, whereas it was 19.1 when there was no personal information available. On the other hand, in the no-confrontation condition when the partner was seen as humble the mean was 22.9; when there was no information available it was 24.5. The indication is that the humble partner tended to elicit fewer exploitative choices regardless of expectancy of confrontation. Although this tendency does not reach statistical significance, it does cast some doubts on the speculation that the humble other invites exploitation when he does not have to be confronted. If anything, the results seem to suggest that there is a generalized pity felt for the humble other, and this feeling manifests itself across conditions. These results have some parallel in the Gergen and Wishnov (1965) finding that subjects would, out of commiseration, reveal more of their negative features to a self-derogating other regardless of whether they expected a long-term relationship or not.

One might raise questions about the relationship of this study, as well as others done in a bargaining context, to more general forms of human behavior. Is the two-person game, in other words, not too rarefied for the results to be translated into useful and cogent principles of social interaction? For those who believe bargaining behavior to be sufficiently intriguing in and of itself, this question may be of little moment. However, one of the major intents of the present study was to highlight the relationship between pure experimental games and more broadly pervasive social factors. In one sense, the experimental game thus becomes a useful vehicle for testing out ideas concerning social interaction. Regarding the present experiment, it is not difficult to think of social situations which have conceptual similarities. One might be led to predict, for example, the reactions of peers in a business organization to each other. In such organizations one is often faced with the choice of competitive exploitation versus cooperation for mutual benefit. The present experiment would suggest at least two important factors, namely, perceived personality and amount of anticipated interaction, which would determine which of these choices would be made.

REFERENCES

ARGYLE, M. "Social Pressure in Public and Private Situations." *Journal of Abnormal and Social Psychology*, 1957, 54, 172–175.

CRUTCHFIELD, R. S. "Conformity and Character." *American Psychologist*, 1955, 10, 191–198.

DAVIS, K. E. "Impressions of Others and Interaction Context as Determinants of Social Interaction in Two Person Discussion Groups." Unpublished doctoral dissertation, Duke University, 1962.

DEUTSCH, M. "Trust and Suspicion." *Journal of Conflict Resolution*, 1958, 2, 267–279.

DEUTSCH, M. "Trust, Trustworthiness, and the F Scale." *Journal of Abnormal and Social Psychology*, 1960, 61, 138–140.

DEUTSCH, M., and KRAUSS, R. M. "The Effect of Threat on Interpersonal Bargaining." *Journal of Abnormal and Social Psychology*, 1960, 61, 181–189.

GERGEN, K. J., and JONES, E. E. "Mental Illness, Predictability, and Affective Consequences as Stimulus Factors in Person Perception." *Journal of Abnormal and Social Psychology*, 1963, 67, 95–104.

GERGEN, K. J., and WISHNOV, BARBARA. "Others' Self-Evaluations and Interaction Anticipation as Determinants of Self-Presentation." *Journal of Personality and Social Psychology*, 1965, 2, 348–358.

JANIS, I. L., and FIELD, P. B. "Sex Differences and Personality Factors Related to Persuasibility." In C. I. Hovland and I. L. Janis (Eds.), *Personality and Persuasibility*. New Haven: Yale Univer. Press, 1959. Pp. 55–68.

LUCE, R. D., and RAIFFA, H. *Games and Decisions*. New York: Wiley, 1957.

LUTZKER, D. R. "Internationalism as a Predictor of Cooperative Behavior." *Journal of Conflict Resolution*, 1960, 4, 426–430.

MARLOWE, D. "Psychological Needs and Cooperation vs. Competition in a Two-Person Game." *Psychological Reports*, 1963, 13, 364.

MINAS, J. S., SCODEL, A., MARLOWE, D., and RAWSON, H. "Some Descriptive Aspects of Two-Person, Non-Zero-Sum Games. Part II." *Journal of Conflict Resolution*, 1960, 4, 193–197.

MOUTON, JANE, S., BLAKE, R. R., and OLMSTEAD, J. A. "The Relationship Between Frequency of Yielding and Disclosure of Personal Identity." *Journal of Personality*, 1956, 24, 339–347.

PEPITONE, A. *Attraction and Hostility*. New York: Atherton Press, 1964.

RAPOPORT, A., and ORWANT, C. "Experimental Games: A Review." *Behavioral Science*, 1962, 7, 1–37.

SCODEL, A., MINAS, J. S., RATOOSH, P., and LIPETZ, M. "Some Descriptive Aspects of Two-Person Non-Zero-Sum Games." *Journal of Conflict Resolution*, 1959, 3, 114–119.

SOLOMON, L. "The Influence of Some Types of Power Relationships and Game Strategies on the Development of Interpersonal Trust." *Journal of Abnormal and Social Psychology*, 1960, 61, 223–230.

THIBAUT, J. W., and KELLEY, H. H. *The Social Psychology of Groups*. New York: Wiley, 1959.

13

A Two-Person
Bargaining Game

STUDIES OF INTERPERSONAL BARGAINING*

Morton Deutsch and Robert M. Krauss

INTRODUCTION

A *bargain is* defined in Webster's Unabridged Dictionary as "an agreement between parties settling what each shall give and receive in a transaction between them"; it is further specified that a bargain is "an agreement or compact viewed as advantageous or the reverse." When the term "agreement" is broadened to include tacit, informal agreements as well as explicit agreements, it evident that bargains and the processes involved in arriving at bargains ("bargaining") are pervasive characteristics of social life.

The definition of "bargain" fits under

sociological definitions of the term "social norm." In this light, it may be seen that the experimental study of the bargaining process and of bargaining outcomes provides a means for the laboratory study of the development of certain types of social norms. It is well to recognize, however, that bargaining situations have certain distinctive features which, unlike many other types of social situations, make it relevant to consider the conditions which determine whether or not a social norm will develop as well as to consider the conditions which determine the nature of the social norm if it develops. Bargaining situations highlight for the investigator the need to be sensitive to the possibility that, even where cooperation would be mutually advantageous, shared purposes may not develop, agreement may not be reached, interaction may be regulated antagonistically rather than normatively.

* Morton Deutsch and Robert M. Krauss, "Studies of Interpersonal Bargaining," *Journal of Conflict Resolution*, VI (1962), 52–76. Copyright 1962 by the University of Michigan. Reprinted by permission.

The essential features of a bargaining situation exist when:

1. both parties perceive that there is the possibility of reaching an agreement in which each party would be better off, or no worse off, than if no agreement is reached;
2. both parties perceive that there is more than one such agreement which could be reached; and
3. both parties perceive each other to have conflicting preferences or opposed interests with regard to the different agreements which might be reached.

Everyday examples of a bargaining situation include such situations as: the buyer —seller relationship when the price is not fixed; the husband and wife who want to spend an evening out together but have conflicting preferences about where to go; union–management negotiations; drivers who meet at an intersection when there is no clear right of way; disarmament negotiations.

From our description of the essential features of a bargaining situation it can be seen that, in terms of our prior conceptualization of cooperation and competition (Deutsch, 1949), it is a situation in which the participants have mixed motives toward one another: on the one hand, each has interest in cooperating so that they reach an agreement; on the other hand, they have competitive interests with regard to the nature of the agreement they reach. In effect, to reach agreement the cooperative interest of the bargainers must be strong enough to overcome their competitive interests. However, agreement is not only contingent upon the *motivational* balances of cooperative to competitive interests but also upon the situational and cognitive factors which would facilitate or hinder the recognition or invention of a bargaining agreement that reduces the opposition of interest and enhances the mutuality of interest.[1]

The discussion of the preceding paragraph leads to the formulation of two general, closely related propositions about the likelihood that a bargaining agreement will be reached.

1. Bargainers are more likely to reach an agreement, the stronger are their cooperative interests in comparison with their competitive interests in relationship to each other.
2. Bargainers are more likely to reach an agreement, the more resources they have available for the recognition or invention of potential bargaining agreements and the more resources they have for communication to one another once a potential agreement has been recognized or invented.

From these two basic propositions and additional hypotheses concerning the conditions which determine the strengths of the cooperative and competitive interests and the amount of available resources, we believe it is possible to explain the ease or difficulty of arriving at a bargaining agreement. We shall not present a full statement of these hypotheses here but shall instead turn to a description of a series of experiments that relate to Proposition 1.

Experiment I

The first experiment to be reported here was concerned with the effect of the availability of threat upon bargaining in a two-person experimental bargaining

---

[1] Schelling, in a series of stimulating papers on bargaining (1957, 1958), has also stressed the "mixed motive" character of bargaining situations and has analyzed some of the cognitive factors which determine agreements.

game we have devised.[2] Threat is defined as the expression of an intention to do something which is detrimental to the interests of another. Our experiment was guided by two assumptions about threat:

1. If there is a conflict of interest and a means of threatening the other person exists, there will be a tendency to use the threat in an attempt to force the other person to yield. This tendency will be stronger, the more irreconcilable the conflict is perceived to be.

2. If threat is used in an attempt to intimidate another, the threatened person (if he considers himself to be of equal or superior status) will feel hostility toward the threatener and will tend to respond with counter-threat and/or increased resistance to yielding. We qualify this assumption by stating that the tendency to resist will be greater, the greater the perceived probability and magnitude of detriment to the other and the lesser the perceived probability and magnitude of detriment to the potential resistor from the anticipated resistance to yielding.

The second assumption is based upon the view that to allow oneself to be intimidated, particularly by someone who does not have the right to expect deferential behavior, is (when resistance is not seen to be suicidal or useless) to suffer a loss of social face and, hence, of self-esteem; and that the culturally defined way of maintaining self-esteem in the face of attempted intimidation is to engage in a contest for supremacy *vis-à-vis* the power to intimidate or, minimally, to resist intimidation. Thus, in effect, it can be seen that the use of threat (and if it is available to be used,

there will be a tendency to use it) should strengthen the competitive interests of the bargainers in relationship to one another by introducing or enhancing the competitive struggle for self-esteem. Hence, from Proposition 1, it follows that the availability of a means of threat should make it more difficult for the bargainers to reach agreement (providing that the threatened person has some means of resisting the threat). The preceding statement is relevant to the comparison of both of our experimental conditions (described below) of threat, *bilateral* and *unilateral*, with our experimental condition of *nonthreat*. We are hypothesizing that a bargaining agreement is more likely to be achieved when neither party can threaten the other, than when one or both parties can threaten the other.

It is relevant now to compare the situations of bilateral threat and unilateral threat. For several reasons, it seems likely that a situation of bilateral threat is less conducive to agreement than is a condition of unilateral threat. First, the sheer likelihood that a threat will be made is greater when two people rather than one have the means of making the threat. Secondly, once a threat is made in the bilateral case, it is likely to evoke counterthreat. Withdrawal of threat in the face of counterthreat probably involves more loss of face (for reasons analogous to those discussed above in relation to yielding to intimidation) than does withdrawal of threat in the face of resistance to threat. Finally, in the unilateral case, although the person without the threat potential can resist and not yield to the threat, his position *vis-à-vis* the other is not so strong as the position of the threatened person in the bilateral case. In the unilateral case, the threatened person may have a worse

---

[2] The game was conceived and originated by the senior author; the junior author designed and constructed the apparatus employed in these experiments. We gratefully acknowledge the expert advice of R. E. Kudlick in the design of the electrical circuitry employed.

outcome than the other whether he resists or yields; while in the bilateral case, the threatened person is sure to have a worse outcome if he yields but he may insure that he does not have a worse outcome if he does not yield.

Method

Subjects (Ss) were asked to imagine that they were in charge of a trucking company, carrying merchandise over a road to a destination. For each trip they completed they made $.60, minus their operating expenses. Operating expenses were calculated at the rate of one cent per second. So, for example, if it took thirty-seven seconds to complete a particular trip, the player's profit would be $.60–$.37 or a net profit of $.23 for that particular trip.

Each subject was assigned a name, Acme or Bolt. As the "road map" (see Figure 1) indicates, both players start from separate points and go to separate destinations. At one point their paths coincide. This is the section of road labeled "one-lane road." This section of road is only one lane wide; this means that two trucks, heading in opposite directions, could not pass each other. If one backs up the other can go forward, or both can back up, or both can sit there head-on without moving.

There is another way for each subject to reach the destination on the map and this is labeled the "alternate route." The two players' paths do not cross on this route, but the alternate is 56 per cent longer than the main route. Subjects were told that they could expect to lose at least $.10 each time they used the alternate route.

At either end of the one-lane section there is a gate which is under the control of the player to whose starting point it is closest. By

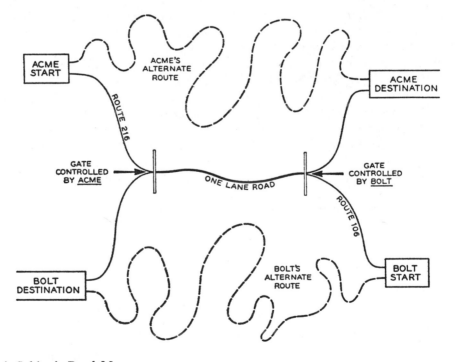

Fig. 1. Subject's Road Map.

closing the gate, one player can prevent the other from traveling over that section of the main route. It is the use of the gate which we will call the threat potential in this game. In the bilateral threat potential condition (*Two Gates*) both players had gates under their control. In a second condition of unilateral threat (*One Gate*) Acme had control of a gate but Bolt did not. In a third condition (*No Gates*) neither player controlled a gate.

Subjects played the game seated in separate booths positioned so that they could not see each other but both could see the experimenter. Each *S* had a "control panel" mounted on a $12'' \times 18'' \times 12''$ sloping-front cabinet (see Figure 2). The apparatus consisted essentially of a reversible impulse counter which was pulsed by a recycling timer. When the *S* wanted to move her truck forward she threw a key which closed a circuit pulsing the "add" coil of the impulse counter which was mounted on her control panel. As the counter cumulated, the *S* was able to determine her "position" by relating the numbers which had been written in on her "road map." Similarly, when she wished to reverse, she would throw a switch which activated the

"subtract" coil of her counter, thus subtracting from the total on the counter each time the timer cycled.

S's counter was connected in parallel to counters on the other *S*'s panel and on *E*'s panel. Thus each player had two counters on her panel, one representing her own position and the other representing the other player's. Provision was made in construction of the apparatus to cut the "other player's" counter out of the circuit, so that each *S* knew only the position of her own truck. This was done in the present experiments.

The only time one player definitely knew the other player's position was when they had met head-on on the one-way section of road. This was indicated by a traffic light mounted on the panel. When this light was on, neither player could move forward unless the other moved back. The gates were controlled by toggle switches; panel-mounted indicator lights showed, for both subjects, whether each gate was open or closed.

The following "rules of the game" were stated to the *S*s:

1. A player who stated out on one route and

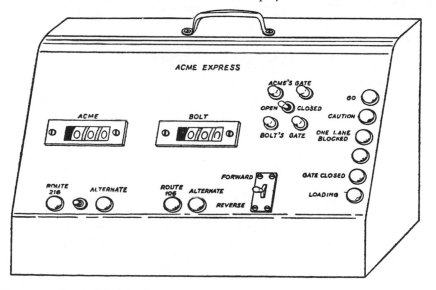

Fig. 2. Subject's Control Panel.

wished to switch to the other route could do so only after first reversing and going back to the start position. Direct transfer from one route to the other was not permitted except at the start position.

2. In the conditions where Ss had gates, they were permitted to close the gates only when they were traveling on the main route. (That is, they were not permitted to close the gate while on the alternate route or after having reached their destinations.) However, Ss were permitted to open their gates at any point in the game.

Ss were taken through a number of practice exercises to familiarize them with the game. In the first trial they were made to meet head-on the one-lane path; Acme was then told to back up until she was just off the one-lane path and Bolt was told to go forward. After Bolt had gone through the one-lane path, Acme was told to go forward. Each continued going forward until each arrived at her destination. The second practice trial was the same as the first except that Bolt rather than Àcme backed up after meeting head-on. In the next practice trial, one of the players was made to wait just before the one-way path while the other traversed it and then was allowed to continue. In the next practice trial, one player was made to take the alternate route and the other was made to take the main route. Finally, in the Bilateral and Unilateral Threat conditions the use of the gate was illustrated (by having the player get on the main route, close the gate, and then go back and take the alternate route). The Ss were told explicitly with emphasis that they did *not* have to use the gate. Before each trial in the game the gate or gates were in the open position.

The instructions stressed an individualistic motivational orientation. Ss were told to try to earn as much money for themselves as possible and to have no interest in whether the other player made money or lost money. They were given $4.00 in poker chips to represent their working capital and told that after each trial they would be given "money" if they

made a profit or that "money" would be taken from them if they lost (i.e., took more than 60 seconds to complete their trip). The profit or loss of each S was announced so that both Ss could hear the announcement after each trial. Each pair of subjects played a total of twenty trials; on all trials, they started off together. In other words, each, trial presented a repetition of the same bargaining problem. In cases where subjects lost their working capital before the twenty trials were completed, additional chips were given them. Subjects were aware that their monetary winnings and losses were to be imaginary and that no money would change hands as a result of the experiment.

Sixteen pairs of subjects were used in each of the three experimental conditions. The Ss were female electrical and supervisory personnel of the New Jersey Bell Telephone Company who volunteered to participate during their working day.[3] Their ages ranged from 20 to 39, with a mean of 26.2. All were naive to the purpose of the experiment. By staggering the arrival times and choosing girls from different locations, we were able to insure that our subjects did not know with whom they were playing.

Results[4]

The best single measure of the difficulty experienced by the bargainers in reaching an agreement is the sum of each pair's profits (or losses) on a given trial. The higher the sum of the payoffs to the two players on a given trial, the less time it took them to arrive at a procedure for sharing the one-lane path of the main

---

[3] We are indebted to the New Jersey Bell Telephone Company for their cooperation in providing subjects and facilities for this experiment.

[4] We are indebted to M. J. R. Healy for suggestions concerning the statistical analysis of these data.

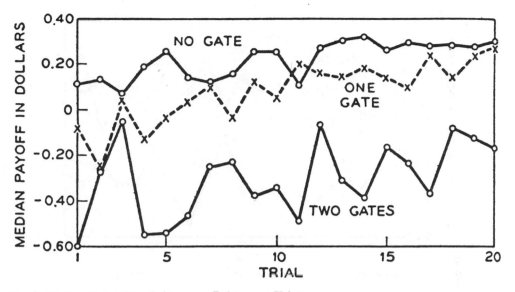

Fig. 3. Median Joint Payoff (Acme + Bolt) over Trials.

Table 1

MEAN PAYOFFS SUMMATED OVER THE TWENTY TRIALS

	Means			Statistical Comparisons: p Values[1]			
Variable	(1) No Threat	(2) Unilateral Threat	(3) Bilateral Threat	Over-all	(1) vs. (2)	(1) vs. (2)	(2) vs. (3)
Summed Payoffs (Acme+Bolt)	203.31	−405.88	−875.12	0.01	0.01	0.01	0.05
Acme's Payoff	122.44	−118.56	−406.56	0.01	0.10	0.01	0.05
Bolt's Payoff	80.88	−287.31	−468.56	0.01	0.01	0.01	0.20

[1] Evaluation of the significance of over-all variation between conditions is based on an F test with 2 and 45 df. Comparisons between treatments are based on a two-tailed t test.

route. (It was, of course, possible for one or both of the players to decide to take the alternate route so as to avoid a protracted stalemate during the process of bargaining. This, however, always resulted in at least a $.20 smaller joint payoff if only one player took the alternate route, than an optimally arrived at agreement concerning the use of the oneway path.)

Figure 3 presents the medians of the summed payoffs (i.e., Acme's plus Bolt's) for all pairs in each of the three experimental conditions over the twenty trials.[5] These

---

[5] Medians are used in graphic presentation of our results because the wide variability of means makes inspection cumbersome.

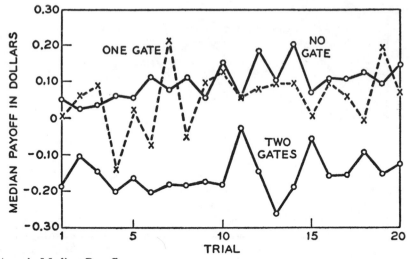

Fig. 4. Acme's Median Payoff.

results indicate that agreement was least difficult to arrive at in the No Threat condition, was more difficult to arrive at in the Unilateral Threat condition, and exceedingly difficult or impossible to arrive at in the Bilateral Threat condition. (See also Table 1).

Figure 4 compares Acme's median profit in the three experimental conditions over the 20 trials; while Figure 5 compares Bolt's profit in the three conditions. (In the Unilateral Threat condition, it was Acme who controlled a gate and Bolt who did not.) It is evident that Bolt's as well

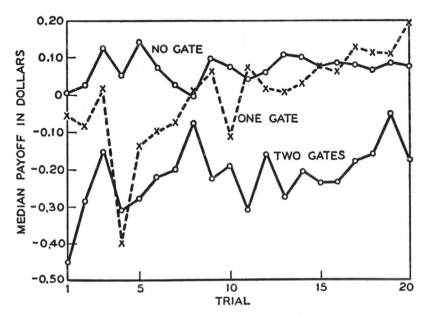

Fig. 5. Bolt's Median Payoff.

as Acme's outcome is somewhat better in the No Threat condition than in the Unilateral Threat condition; Acme's as well as Bolt's outcome is clearly worst in the Bilateral Threat condition. (See Table 1 also.) However, Figure 6 reveals that Acme does somewhat better than Bolt in the Unilateral condition. Thus, if threat-potential exists within a bargaining relationship it is better to possess it oneself than to have the other party possess it. However, it is even better for neither party to possess it. Moreover, from Figure 5, it is evident that Bolt is better off not having than having a gate even when Acme has a gate: Bolt tends to do better in the Unilateral Threat condition than in the Bilateral Threat condition.

To provide the reader with a more detailed description of what went on during the bargaining game, we present a synopsis of the game for one pair in each of the three experimental treatments.

No Threat Condition

Trial 1. The players met in the center of the one-way section. After some back-and-forth movement Bolt reversed to the end of the one-way section, allowing Acme to pass through, and then proceeded forward herself.

Trial 2. They again met at the center of the one-way path. This time, after moving back and forth deadlocked for some time, Bolt reversed to start and took the alternate route to her destination, thus leaving Acme free to go through on the main route.

Trial 3. The players again met at the center of the one-way path. This time, however, Acme reversed to the beginning of the path, allowing Bolt to go through to her destination. Then Acme was able to proceed forward on the main route.

Trial 5. Both players elected to take the alternate route to their destinations.

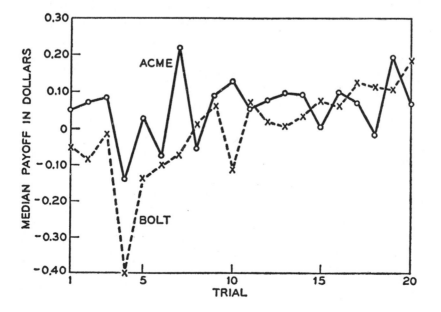

Fig. 6. Acme's and Bolt's Median Payoff in Unilateral Threat Condition.

Trial 7. Both players took the main route and met in the center. They waited, deadlocked, for a considerable time. Then Acme reversed to the end of the one-way path allowing Bolt to go through, then proceeded through to her destination.

Trials 10 through 20. Acme and Bolt fall into a pattern of alternating who is to go first on the one-way section. There is no deviation from this pattern.

The only other pattern which emerges in this condition is one in which one player dominates the other. That is, one player consistently goes first on the one-way section and the other player consistently yields.

Unilateral Threat Condition

Trial 1. Both players took the main route and met in the center of it. Acme immediately closed the gate, reversed to "start" and took the alternate route to her destination. Bolt waited for a few seconds, at the closed gate, then reversed and took the alternate route.

Trial 2. Both players took the main route and met in the center. After moving back and forth deadlocked for about fifteen seconds, Bolt reversed to the beginning of the one-way path, allowed Acme to pass, and then proceeded forward to her destination.

Trial 3. Both players started out on the main route, meeting in the center. After moving back and forth deadlocked for a while, Acme closed her gate, reversed to "start" and took the alternate route. Bolt, meanwhile, waited at the closed gate. When Acme arrived at her destination she opened the gate, and Bolt went through to complete her trip.

Trial 5. Both players took the main route, meeting at the center of the one-way section. Acme immediately closed her gate, reversed and took the alternate route. Bolt waited at the gate for about ten seconds, then reversed and took the alternate route to her destination.

Trial 10. Both players took the main route and met in the center. Acme closed her gate, reversed and took the alternate route. Bolt remained waiting at the closed gate. After Acme arrived at her destination, she opened the gate and Bolt completed her trip.

Trial 15. Acme took the main route to her destination and Bolt took the alternate route.

Trials 17, 18, 19 and 20. Both players took the main route and met in the center. Bolt waited a few seconds, then reversed to the end of the one-way section allowing Acme to go through. Then Bolt proceeded forward to her destination.

Other typical patterns which developed in this experimental condition included an alternating pattern similar to that described in the No Threat condition, a dominating pattern in which Bolt would select the alternate route leaving Acme free to use the main route unobstructed, and a pattern in which Acme would close her gate and then take the alternate route, also forcing Bolt to take the alternate route.

Bilateral Threat Condition

Trial 1. Acme took the main route and Bolt took the alternate route.

Trial 2. Both players took the main route and met head-on. Bolt closed her gate. Acme waited a few seconds, then closed her gate, reversed to "start," then went forward again to the closed gate. Acme reversed and took the alternate route. Bolt again reversed, then started on the alternate route. Acme opened her gate and Bolt reversed to start and went to her destination on the main route.

Trial 3. Acme took the alternate route to her destination. Bolt took the main route and closed her gate before entering the one-way section.

Trial 5. Both players took the main route and met head-on. After about ten seconds spent backing up and going forward, Acme closed her gate, reversed and took the alternate route. After waiting a few seconds, Bolt did the same.

Trials 8, 9, 10. Both players started out on the main route, immediately closed their gates, reversed to start and took the alternate route to their destinations.

Trial 15. Both players started out on the main route and met head-on. After some jockeying for position, Acme closed her gate, reversed and took the alternate route to her destination. After waiting at the gate for a few seconds, Bolt reversed to start and took the alternate route to her destination.

Trials 19, 20. Both players started out on the main route, immediately closed their gates, reversed to start and took the alternate routes to their destinations.

Other patterns which emerged in the Bilateral Threat condition included alternating first use of the one-way section, one player's dominating the other on first use of the one-way section, and another dominating pattern in which one player consistently took the main route while the other consistently took the alternate route.

Discussion

The results of Experiment I clearly indicate that the availability of a threat potential in our experimental bargaining situation adversely affects the player's ability to reach effective agreements. In terms of our introductory analysis of bargaining as a mixed motive situation (i.e., one in which both competitive and cooperative motivations are acting upon the participants), we can interpret these results as indicating that the existence of threat enhances the competitive aspects of interaction.

These results, we believe, reflect psychological tendencies which are not confined to our bargaining situation: the tendency to use threat (if a means for threatening is available) in an attempt to force the other person to yield when he is seen as an obstruction; the tendency to respond with counter-threat or increased resistance to attempts at intimidation. How general are these tendencies? What are the conditions likely to elicit them? Answers to these questions are necessary before our results can be generalized to other situations. However, we will postpone consideration of the psychological processes which operate in bargaining until we have had an opportunity to examine the results of some further experiments.

EXPERIMENT II

Our discussion thus far has suggested that the psychological factors which operate in our experimental bargaining game are to be found in many real-life bargaining situations. However, it is well to point out an important unique feature of our experimental game: namely, that the bargainers had no opportunity to communicate verbally with one another. Prior research on the role of communication in trust (Deutsch, 1958, 1960; Loomis, 1959) suggests that the opportunity for communication would ameliorate the difficulty bargainers experience in reaching agreement. This possibility was expressed spontaneously by a number of our subjects in a post-experimental interview. It should be noted, however, that the same research cited above (Deutsch, 1960) indicates that communication may not be effective between competitively oriented bargainers.

To test the effect of communication upon bargaining, we undertook an experiment in which subjects were permitted to talk over an intercom hookup. It was further decided to differentiate Bilateral Communication (both parties permitted to talk) from Unilateral Communication (only one party is permitted to talk).

Method

The experimental apparatus, instructions to the Ss and training procedures here were the same as described in Experiment I. In addition, each S was equipped with a headset (earphones and microphone) hooked into an intercom system. The intercom was so constructed the E could control the direction of Ss' communication. This was necessary so that in the Unilateral Communication condition one S was prevented from talking to the other, but both were able to talk to E when necessary. A filter, built into the intercom's amplification system, distorted voice quality sufficiently to make it unlikely that Ss would recognize one another's voices even if they were previously acquainted, without signif-

icantly impairing intelligibility.[6] Ss received the following instructions on communication:

> During the game, when your trucks are en route, you may communicate with each other . . . (Here Ss received instructions on operating the intercom system) . . . In talking to the other player you may say anything you want; or if you don't want to talk you don't have to. You may talk about the game, about what you'd like to happen in the game, what you're going to do, what you'd like the other player to do, or anything else that comes to mind. What you talk about—or whether you decide to talk or not—is up to you.

These instructions were modified in the Unilateral Communication condition to indicate that only one player (Acme) would be permitted to talk. Communication was not allowed between trials; only during the actual "trip" were Ss permitted to talk.

The two levels of our communication variable (bilateral and unilateral) were combined with the three levels of threat employed in the previous study to produce a 2×3 factorial experiment. It was necessary to employ such a design to test the possibility that communication might be differentially effective under different conditions of threat.

Five pairs of Ss were entered randomly into each of six treatment conditions. All were female electrical and secretarial employees of the Bell Telephone Laboratories and were, in most respects, comparable to the New Jersey Bell Telephone employees used in Experiment I. Again, Ss were selected from different work areas and arrival times were staggered to prevent Ss from knowing their partner's identity.

Results

An analysis of variance of Experiment II indicates that our communication vari-

---

[6] In only one group did an S recognize her partner's voice; this group was discarded.

able had no effect on the player's ability to reach effective agreements; however the "threat" variable, as in the first experiment, had a significant effect. It should also be noted that the results of this experiment are not significantly different from the findings of Experiment I, where no communication was permitted. For economy of presentation these cross-experiment comparisons will be included with the results of Experiment III below.

Product-moment correlations were computed between frequency of communication for each pair (the number of trials out of twenty in which one or both Ss spoke) and joint payoff. Both over-all and within the threat conditions no significant relation was observed between frequency of communication and payoff. As will be discussed below, only a minimum of communication did occur and quite likely frequency of communication in this situation was determined by characteristics of the Ss which were irrelevant to the achievement of agreement in the bargaining situation.

An additional finding of interest: it will be recalled that in the Unilateral Threat condition Acme was the player possessing the threat potential. Similarly, in the Unilateral Communication condition, it was Acme who was allowed to talk. To ascertain the effect of this double asymmetry we ran an additional five pairs of Ss in a Unilateral Threat–Unilateral Communication condition in which Bolt was given the opportunity to talk, while Acme still possessed the threat potential. A comparison of this group with the standard Unilateral Threat–Unilateral Communication condition revealed no significant differences between them.

We can also examine the gross frequency of talking in the three threat conditions. Each pair of Ss received a score based upon the number of trials on which one or both players spoke to the other. The mean frequency of communication in the three threat conditions is presented in Table 2a. Most talking occurs in the No Threat condition; the rate of talking in the Unilateral and Bilateral Threat conditions is approximately equal. However, these differences, when tested by a one-way analy-

Table 2

FREQUENCY OF TALKING

Table 2a

Frequency of Talking in the Three Threat Conditions

	No Threat	Unilateral Threat	Bilateral Threat
Mean number of trials on which talking occurred	5.7	3.9	3.3

Table 2b

Frequency of Talking in the Bilateral vs. Unilateral Communication Conditions

	Bilateral Communication	Unilateral Communication
Mean number of trials on which talking occurred	5.8	2.7

sis of variance, are not large enough to permit a rejection of the null hypothesis.

If we examine frequency of talking in the Unilateral vs. Bilateral Communication conditions we find that, in accordance with expectation, significantly more talk occurs in the bilateral condition ($F =$ 31.04, with 1 and 38 d.f.; $p < 0.001$). These means are presented in Table 2b.

We had intended to tape-record our Ss' communications to preserve them for a subsequent content analysis. Unfortunately, breakdowns of the recording equipment and electrical distortions introduced by the bargaining game apparatus rendered this impossible. Thus, except for the impressions gained by E who monitored all communication, these data are lost and any discussion of communication content must necessarily be impressionistic. Modifications of the equipment are presently under way which will correct these difficulties.

In a post-experimental questionnaire and interview we questioned Ss closely in an attempt to ascertain the reason for the paucity of communication. Most of our Ss were at a loss to explain why they did not talk, although almost all acknowledged that they were less than normally talkative. With some probing on E's part, a frequent comment concerned "the difficulty of talking to someone you don't know." Possibly, the communication process normally involves a system of reciprocal expectations by which a speaker has some idea of the effect his words will have on a listener. Even in an encounter between strangers these expectations may be partly derived from such visual cues as appearance, dress, facial expression, etc. All of these cues were absent in the communication between our Ss. Interestingly enough, when Ss were introduced after the experimental session, a great deal of spontaneous

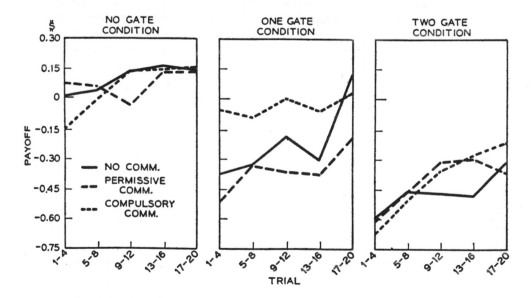

Fig. 7. Mean Joint Payoffs (Acme + Bolt) in the Communication Conditions across the Three Conditons.

chatter ensued. And this was true even of Ss who had not talked at all during the experimental session.

Discussion

It is obvious from the results of Experiment II that the opportunity to communicate does not necessarily result in an amelioration of conflict in our experimental bargaining situation. Indeed, it should be stated that the *opportunity* to communicate does not necessarily result in communication at all. Actually, little communication occurred; most of our Ss did not utilize their opportunity to communicate.

The results of Experiment II are in line with the finding of Deutsch (1960). Apparently the competitive orientation induced by the threat potential in our situation was sufficiently strong to overcome any possible ameliorating effects of communication. In the No Threat condition, where competitiveness is at a minimum, the advantage gained by the use of communication to coordinate effort was offset by the time consumed by talking. It would seem that the coordination problem posed for the Ss by our experimental game was sufficiently simple to be solvable without communication, given the existence of an appropriate motivational orientation. This will be considered further in our discussion of Experiment III.

EXPERIMENT III

Any straightforward interpretation of the effects of communication upon interpersonal bargaining is difficult to make based on the results of Experiment II. This is particularly true in view of the fact that the majority of our Ss did not use the opportunity to communicate that was presented to them. Thus, one may speculate that had our Ss in fact communicated, the outcome of Experiment II might have been quite different.

Studies of collective bargaining procedures suggest one of their important values lies in their ability to prevent disputants from breaking off communication (Douglas, 1958). Newcomb (1948) has used the term "autistic hostility" to denote a situation in which a breakdown, or absence, of communication leads to the exacerbation of interpersonal conflict. Rapoport (1960) has stressed the importance of continued communication in resolving international conflict.

Experiment III was undertaken to test the effect of forced, or compulsory, communication.

Method

The experimental apparatus, instructions to the Ss, and training procedures employed here were the same as in Experiment II. Ss received the following instructions on communication (the italicized portions are those which differ from the instructions used in Experiment II):

> During the game, when your trucks are en route, *you both will be required* to communicate with each other . . . (Here Ss received instructions on operating the intercom system) . . . In talking to the other player you may say anything you want. You may talk about the game, about what you'd like to happen in the game, what you're going to do, what you'd like the other player to do, or anything else that comes to mind. What you talk about is up to you. *But remember, you must any something to the other player on every trip.*

In Experiment III only a Bilateral Communication condition was run, again under three

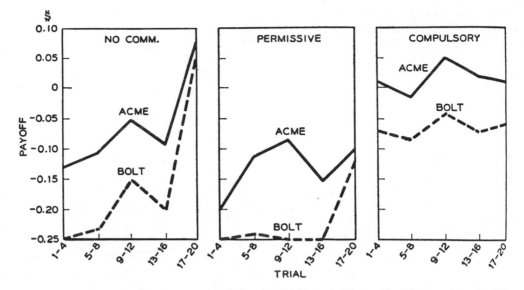

Fig. 8. Acme's and Bolt's Mean Payoffs in the Unilateral Threat Conditon across the Three Communication Conditions.

levels of threat potential. On trials where either *S* failed to talk, they were reminded by *E* at the conclusion of the trial of the requirement that they talk to the other player on every trial. In no group was it necessary to make this reminder on more than four trials.

Ten pairs of *S*s were entered randomly into each of the three treatment conditions, *S*s were drawn from the same pool used in Experiment II; however, none of the *S*s in this experiment had served in the previous one.

Results

We will refer to the form of communication utilized in Experiment II as Permissive Communication; communication in Experiment III will be called Compulsory Communication; in Experiment I, No Communication was involved. Since in Experiment II no differences were found between our Bilateral and Unilateral Communication treatments, we have combined these two categories to increase the *N* of the Permissive Communication group.

Figure 7 presents the mean joint payoffs (summarized as the averages of four-trial blocks for convenience) for all three experiments. (See also Table 3.) The effectiveness of the Compulsory Communication variable is seen in comparison of groups in the Unilateral Threat condition. Here alone, of all the conditions in which gates are present, does performance approach that of *S*s in the No Threat condition. In the Bilateral Threat condition the competitive motivation present seems too great to be overcome, even by the Compulsory Communication treatment. As was noted above, in the No Threat condition coordination was sufficiently simple that communication failed to produce any visible effect.

We can examine more closely performance in the Unilateral Threat condition.

Table 3

MEAN JOINT PAYOFFS (ACME+BOLT) PER TRIAL[1]

	No Threat	N	Unilateral Threat	N	Bilateral Threat	N
Permissive Communication	8.54	(10)	−34.58	(15)	−41.32	(10)
Compulsory Communication	6.09	(10)	−5.14	(10)	−41.73	(10)
No Communication*	10.41	(16)	−22.13	(16)	−47.44	(16)

[1] In an analysis of variance, significant ($p < 0.01$) F ratios were found for the "threat" and "communication" main effect and for the "threat × communication" interaction. Additionally, analysis of trend discloses a significant linear effect over trials ($p < 0.01$) for all groups, with no differences between group trends present.

* Discrepancies between these means and means computed from Table 1 may be attributed to different methods of averaging.

For example, it is possible that the effectiveness of Compulsory Communication as reflected in the joint payoff data is due to an increase in the payoff to Acme (the player possessing a threat potential), without a corresponding increase in Bolt's payoff. In other words, it is possible that Compulsory Communication acts to increase the advantaged player's bargaining power in an asymmetrical situation. Figure 8 breaks down the payoffs of Acme and Bolt in the three communication conditions. Although in all conditions Acme does better than Bolt, the margin of discrepancy does not vary substantially in the three conditions.[7]

An analysis of trend over trials (Grant, 1956) was performed on the data of the three experiments. Over-all, a significant linear component was present, as Figure 7 indicates; however, there were no differences in trend resulting from a partitioning of Ss by the two independent variables or their interactions. This result held true

when the analysis was based on the joint payoff scores and on Acme's and Bolt's scores analyzed separately.

Again, we had intended to record our Ss' conversations for later content analysis. The same technical difficulties discussed above continued to cause difficulty. However, in Experiment III we were somewhat more successful in obtaining complete recordings of a small number of our Ss' conversations. In order to give the reader some notion of the sort of conversations which did take place we present below a transcript for selected trials of three pairs of Ss, one in each of the threat conditions, which were judged to be relatively typical. The numbers in parentheses below each conversation represent the payoff to each player on that trial (in imaginary dollars). Positive numbers represent winnings and negative numbers are losses.

Discussion

In the introduction, we presented our view of bargaining as a situation in which both cooperative and competitive tendencies are present and acting upon the in-

---

[7] A one-way analysis of variance of the algebraic difference in payoff (Acme-Bolt) yields a nonsignificant F ratio.

NO THREAT CONDITION

Trial	Acme	Bolt
1	I'll stop at 5 so you can go through first . . . I'm backing up for you. (0.01)	(0.19)
2	Okay, wait 6 seconds because I had to back up last time. (0.26)	I'll wait for you at 5. (0.10)
6	(0.27)	I'll wait at 5 this time. (0.09)
7	I'll wait for you at 4 or 5. We might as well alternate 'cause I don't see how we'll make any money any other way. (0.03)	Okay, that's true. (0.25)
12	Is it my turn to wait for you? Okay, I couldn't remember whose turn it was. (counting) 13, 14, 15. (0.27)	I'll wait for you this time at 5. Let me know when you reach 15. (0.09)
13	I'll wait for you. Okay. I didn't go on break this morning and boy, am I hungry! I'll make 9 cents and you'll make 27. I started a few seconds too late. (0.07)	All right. I'll let you know at 15. You can start now. (0.26)
16	Okay. I'll count up so you know. 13, 14, 15. There's no way to make money except by compromising this way. Except for the first few times. (0.27)	I'll wait at 5 this time and let me know at 13 also. Okay. Thank you. No, that's the only way and it comes out even that way, usually. Yuh. (0.09)
17	I'll wait at 5. Yeah. Are you from around here? Thank you. I won't ask you any more because I don't know you. (0.03)	Okay. You'll make 9 cents, I'll make 27. Yuh, Summit [a local town]. . . . (counting) 13, 14, 15. Okay. No. (0.26)

Trial	Acme	Bolt
20		I'll wait for you this time.
	Okay. Do you have a watch on?	Yeah.
	What time is it?	Twenty-five after eleven. What number are you on now?
	Twelve.	Okay, (counting) 13, 14.
	(counting) 14, 15. You're such a cooperative partner.	What?
	Nice working for such a cooperative partner.	Oh, nice to work with you, too.
	(0.26)	(0.09)

Unilateral Threat Condition

Trial	Acme	Bolt
1	Do you intend to take the main route?	Um ... I'm taking it, but I've stopped, Are you going to close the gate?
	I've closed it already. I'm going to open it.	You finish yet?
	Yes, I have.	
	(0.26)	(0.05)
2	Yes, I am. I think we're going to meet again. I guess we're met, uh, I'm going to back up.	Are you on the main road? Where are you?
	I'm backing up.	What number are you on?
	Now I'm on 4.	On, all right. I'll go forward.
	I think we met again.	
	(−0.17)	(0.00)
5	My gate's closed.	Uh huh. I noticed.
	It's open now. Oh, we met?	Yes.
	I'm going to reverse.	We met?
	Yes.	Go now.
	I can go?	We'll try.
	No.	No? (laughs)
	Wait a sec. I'll back up some more. Okay. You must almost be there.	
	(−0.12)	(0.06)
6	My gate's closed.	Uh huh. Are you gonna leave it closed?
	No, it's open now. You go . . . Oh. Oh, we met.	I'll go back.

Trial	Acme	Bolt
	Okay.	Try it now.
	Okay, I'm there already.	
	(0.21)	(−0.03)
9	I'll back up.	Okay. I'm there.
	Oh, you're there? You beat me by a hair. I'm only halfway there.	I keep forgetting to push this thing down [probably a reference to switch on intercom].
	Oh.	
	(−0.06)	(0.11)
10	My gate's closed.	Are you there?
	Yes.	All right. You beat me by seven, eight.
	(0.26)	(0.10)
13		Are you there?
	Yeah.	Are you gonna . . . oh, it's open.
	It's open.	
	(0.26)	(0.05)
14	I'll back up.	Try going forward.
	Okay. No.	Not yet?
	You keep coming now.	What, go forward?
	Yeah.	On 15, 16, okay.
	I wonder how many times we're going to play this.	
	(−0.07)	(0.09)
19		Are you going back?
	Yes, are you going forward?	Yes.
	I'm back. There.	Um, no.
	Oh.	
	(0.01)	(0.18)
20		You going forward?
	Uh huh.	What number are you on?
	(counting) 10, 11.	10?
	Okay.	You there?
	Yeah, no, we're blocked.	Oh, I'll go back.
	Are you stopped or going back?	I'm going forward.
	Oh, now you're going forward. Oh, I guess we're okay now.	I'm on 9; are you there?

Trial	Acme	Bolt
	Yeah.	I think I'm glad I'm not a truck driver.
	(0.20)	(—0.01)

BILATERAL THREAT CONDITION

Trial	Acme	Bolt
1	You decide on your route?	I'm taking the main route.
	I am, too.	Oh, we're stopped. What happens now?
	What did you say?	Did you stop?
	Yeah, the lane is blocked completely.	Well, who's going to back up?
	Well, I don't know. You gonna back up this time?	All right. I'll back up.
	All right.	Your gate is locked.
	I know it's locked.	That wasn't very fair.
	Anything's fair.	Well, what are you going to do?
	I don't have to do anything. I'm going to my destination.	This is not funny.
	(laughs)	At your destination?
	No!	I'll never reach mine at this point.
	I've reached mine.	Well?
	Sit tight.	Planned your next route?
	No, have you?	I've got some ideas.
	Thanks a lot.	I'm getting there slowly but surely.
	(laughs)	
	(—0.95)	(—1.87)
2		I've got my plan.
	I've got mine, too.	How're you doing?
	Fine. How are you doing?	Oh, I'm fine. I'm not getting any place fast, though.
	This doesn't move very quick.	Slow trucking.
	That makes two of us.	Where are you now?
	Twenty-seven [on alternate route]. Where are you?	Twenty-four (both laugh). Looks like we both don't trust each other. I'll lose this game.
	(—0.44)	(—0.54)
5	We're stopped. What are we going to do now?	Oh, I backed up the first time. Now it's your turn.
	All right. What are you going to do?	I'm going to take the alternate route.

Trial	Acme	Bolt
	Go right ahead.	Are you going to open your gate?
	No.	What are you going to do now?
	I've got to at least make the loss even.	I hear only one ticking [a reference to noise made by the apparatus].
	(−1.02)	(−0.75)
7		You've got yours closed, too.
	We're both stopped.	Are you going to open your gate?
	Why should I?	I'll do the same next time.
	Is that a threat?	You playing tricks?
	No.	I'll lose five dollars this trip because of you.
	(−1.33)	(−0.75)
9	I see you've got your gate closed. What route are you on?	Why should I tell you?
	Okay, if that's the way you want to play.	No, I'll tell you where I am if you tell me where you are.
	I asked you first.	So am I [sic]. . . . At 17. . . . How far are you?
	I don't believe you.	Have it your way.
	(−1.33)	(−0.75)
13	(Unintelligible)	You had yours closed.
	I think that's my business.	Why don't you open your gate?
	Don't have time.	I'm not getting any place.
	(−0.60)	(−0.23)
14	You have yours shut, too.	What?
	You never let me through.	Let's both open our gates as long as we're going the other way.
	I know you are (sarcastically).	
	(−0.20)	(−0.22)
18	What route are you taking?	(no answer)
	I think we both are going bankrupt.	They [sic] just don't trust each other, right?
	(−0.39)	(−0.50)
20		Your gate's closed again.
	So is yours, so that means you must have taken the alternate route.	Why? What gives you that idea?
	Well, you wouldn't be crazy enough to go to the main route with my gate closed.	Well, maybe I think I can persuade you to open it.

Trial	Acme	Bolt
	You know better than that.	Do I? ... I get the use of these gates all mixed up. I shut mine when I don't want to and, oh, ...
	If I go into the trucking business I'm not going to have gates.	
	(−0.21)	(−0.22)

dividual. From this point of view, it is relevant to inquire as to the conditions under which a stable agreement of any form will develop. However, implicit in most models of bargaining (e.g., Zeuthen, 1930; Stone, 1958; Cervin, 1961; Suppes and Carlsmith, 1961) is the assumption that the cooperative interests of the bargainers will be sufficiently strong to insure that some form of mutually satisfactory agreement will be reached. For this reason, such models have focused upon the form of the agreement reached by the bargainers. Siegel and Fouraker (1960) report a series of bargaining experiments quite different in structure from ours in which only one of many pairs of subjects was unable to reach agreement. Siegel and Fouraker explain this rather startling statistic as follows:

> Apparently the disruptive forces which lead to the rupture of some negotiations were at least partially controlled in our sessions. . . .
> Some negotiations collapse when one party becomes incensed at the other, and henceforth strives to maximize his opponent's displeasure rather than his own satisfaction. . . . Since it is difficult to transmit insults by means of quantitative bids, such disequilibrating behavior was not induced in the present studies. If subjects were allowed more latitude in their communications and interactions, the possibility of an affront–offense–punitive behavior sequence might be increased [p. 100].

In our experimental bargaining situation, the availability of threat clearly made it more difficult for bargainers to reach a mutually profitable agreement. Indeed, Bilateral Threat presents a situation so conflict-fraught that no amount of communication seems to have an ameliorating effect. These tendencies we believe are not confined to our experimental situation. The "affront–offense–punitive behavior sequence" to which Siegel and Fouraker refer, and which we have observed in our experiment, are common attributes of everyday interpersonal conflict. The processes which underlie them have long been of interest to social scientists and an imposing set of theoretical constructs have been employed to explain them.

Dollard *et al.* (1939) have cited a variety of evidence to support the view that aggression (i.e., the use of threat) is a common reaction to a person who is seen as the agent of frustration. There seems to be little reason to doubt that the use of threat is a frequent reaction to interpersonal impasses. However, everyday observation indicates that threat does not inevitably occur when there is an interpersonal impasse. We would speculate that it is most likely to occur when the threatener has no positive interest in the other person's welfare (he is either egocentrically or competitively related to the other); when the threatener believes that the other has no positive interest in his welfare; and when the threatener anticipates either that his threat will be effective or, if ineffective, will not worsen his situation because he expects the worst to happen if he does not use his threat. We suggest that these conditions were operative in our experiment; the subjects were either egocentrically or competitively oriented to one another[8] and they felt that they would not be worse off by the use of threat.

Everyday observation suggests that the tendency to respond with counterthreat or increased resistance to attempts at intimidation is also a common occurrence. It is our belief that the introduction of threat into a bargaining situation affects the meaning of yielding. Although we have no data to support this directly, we will attempt to justify it on the basis of some additional assumptions.

Goffman (1955) has pointed out the pervasive significance of "face" in the maintenance of the social order. In this view, self-esteem is a socially validated system which grows out of the acceptance by others of the claim for deference, prestige and recognition which one presents in one's behavior toward others. Thus, the rejection of such a claim would be perceived (by the recipient) as directed against his self-esteem and one which, in order to maintain the integrity of his self-esteem system, he must react against rather than accept.

One may view the behavior of our subjects as an attempt to make claims upon the other; an attempt to develop a set of shared expectations as to what each was entitled to. Why then did the subjects' re-

actions differ so markedly as a function of the availability of threat? The explanation for this lies, we believe, in the cultural interpretation of yielding (to a peer or subordinate) under duress, as compared to giving in without duress. The former, we believe, is perceived as a negatively valued form of behavior, with negative implications for the self-image of the individual who so behaves. At least partly, this is so because the locus of causality is perceived to be outside the voluntary control of the individual. No such evaluation, however, need be placed on the behavior of one who "gives in" in a situation where no threat or duress is a factor. Rather, we should expect the culturally defined evaluation of such an individual's behavior to be one of "reasonableness" or "maturity." Again, this may be because the cause of the individual's behavior is perceived to lie within the individual.

One special feature of our experimental game is worthy of note: the passage of time, without coming to an agreement, is costly to the players. There are, of course, bargaining situations in which the lack of agreement may simply preserve the *status quo* without any worsening of the bargainers' respective positions. This is the case in the typical bilateral monopoly case, where the buyer and seller are unable to agree upon a price (e.g., see Siegel and Fouraker, 1960; Cervin, 1961). In other sorts of bargaining situations, however (e.g., labor-management negotiations during a strike; inter-nation negotiations during an expensive cold war), the passage of time may play an important role. In our experiment, we received the impression that the meaning of time changed as time passed without the bargainers reaching an agreement. Initially, the passage of time seemed to pressure the players to come to an

[8] A post-experimental questionnaire indicated that, in all three experimental conditions, the Ss were most strongly motivated to win money, next most strongly motivated to do better than the other player, next most motivated to "have fun," and were very little or not at all motivated to help the other player.

agreement before their costs mounted sufficiently to destroy their profit. With the continued passage of time, however, their mounting losses strengthened their resolution not to yield to the other player. They comment: "I've lost so much, I'll be damned if I give in now. At least I'll have the satisfaction of doing better than she does." The mounting losses and continued deadlock seemed to change the game from a mixed motive into a predominantly competitive situation.

The results of Experiments II and III justify, we believe, a reconsideration of the role of communication in the bargaining process. Typically, communication is perceived as a means whereby the bargainers coordinate effort (e.g., exchange bids, indicate positions, etc.). Usually, little emphasis is given to interaction of communication with motivational orientation. Certainly the coordination function of communication is important. However, as Siegel and Fouraker (1960) point out, free communication may also be used to convey information (e.g., threats, insults, etc.) which may intensify the competitive aspects of the situation.

It should be emphasized here that the "solution" of our bargaining problem (i.e., alternating first use of the one-lane section of the main route) is a simple and rather obvious one. Indeed, the sort of coordination of effort required by the game is sufficiently simple to be readily achievable without the aid of communication. (Note that Ss in the No Threat–No Communication conditions did as well as Ss in the two No Threat conditions with communication.) More important than this coordinating function, however, is the capacity of communication to expedite the development of agreements. In this context, agreements serve a function similar to that ascribed by Thibaut and Kelley to the social norm; that is, "...they serve as substitutes for the exercise of personal influence and produce more economically and efficiently certain consequences otherwise dependent upon personal influence processes" (Thibaut and Kelley, 1959, p. 130). Effective communication, by this line of reasoning, would be aimed at the development of agreements or, to state it another way, at a resolution of the competitive orientation which produces conflict in the bargaining situation.

One must grant that our Ss were relatively unsophisticated in the techniques of developing agreements under the stress of competition. Possibly persons who deal regularly with problems of conflict resolution (e.g., marriage counselors, labor–management arbitrators, diplomats, etc.) would have little difficulty in reaching agreement, even under our Bilateral Threat condition.

Another barrier to effective communication lies in the reticence of our Ss. As we noted above, our Ss found talking to an unknown partner a strange and rather uncomfortable experience. This factor alone would limit the possibility of any communication, let alone communication which was effective.

The studies reported here are part of an ongoing program of research on the factors affecting interpersonal bargaining. In an experiment presently under way, we are attempting to develop communication procedures which will be effective in ameliorating conflict in the Bilateral Threat condition. Additionally, in projected studies we intend to investigate the effect of other structural factors on bargaining behavior.

It is, of course, hazardous to generalize from a set of laboratory experiments to the problems of the real world. But our experiment and the theoretical ideas which underlie them can perhaps serve to emphasize some notions which, otherwise, have some intrinsic plausibility. In brief, these are the following: (1) There is more safety in cooperative than in competitive coexistence. (2) The mere existence of channels of communication is no guarantee that communication will indeed take place, and the greater the competitive orientation of the parties *vis-à-vis* each other, the less likely will they be to use such channels as do exist. (3) Where barriers to communication exist, a situation in which the parties are compelled to communicate will be more effective than one in which the choice to talk or not is put on a voluntary basis. (4) If the bargainers' primary orientation is competitive, communication which is not directed at changing this orientation is unlikely to be effective. (5) It is dangerous for bargainers to have weapons at their disposal. (6) Possibly, it is more dangerous for a bargainer to have the capacity to retaliate in kind than for him not to have this capacity, when the other bargainer has a weapon. This last statement assumes that the one who yields has more of his values preserved by accepting the agreement preferred by the other than by extended conflict. Of course, in some bargaining situations in the real world the loss incurred by yielding may exceed the loss due to extended conflict.

REFERENCES

CERVIN, V. B. and HENDERSON, G. P. "Statistical Theory of Persuasion," *Psychological Review*, 68 (1961), 157–66.

DEUTSCH, M. "A Theory of Cooperation and Competition," *Human Relations*, 2 (1949), 129–52.

——. "Trust and Suspicion," *The Journal of Conflict Resolution*, 2 (1958), 265–79.

——. "The Effect of Motivational Orientation upon Trust and Suspicion," *Human Relations*, 13 (1960), 123–40.

DEUTSCH, M. and KRAUSS, R. M. "The Effect of Threat upon Interpersonal Bargaining," *Journal of Abnormal and Social Psychology*, 61 (1960), 181–9.

DOLLARD, J. et al. *Frustration and Aggression.* New Haven, Conn.: Yale University Press, 1939.

DOUGLAS, A. "Peaceful Settlement of Industrial and Intergroup Disputes," *The Journal of Conflict Resolution*, 1 (1957), 69–81.

GOFFMAN, E. "On Face-work," *Psychiatry*, 18 (1955), 213–31.

GRANT, D. A. "Analysis of Variance Tests in the Analysis and Comparison of Curves," *Psychological Bulletin*, 53 (1956), 141–54.

LOOMIS, J. L. "Communication, the Development of Trust and Cooperative Behavior," *Human Relations*, 12 (1959), 305–15.

NEWCOMB, T. R. "Autistic Hostility and Social Reality," *ibid.*, 1 (1947), 69–88.

RAPOPORT, A. *Fights, Games, and Debates.* Ann Arbor, Mich.: University of Michigan Press, 1960.

SCHELLING, T. G. "Bargaining, Communication and Limited War," *The Journal of Conflict Resolution*, 1 (1957), 19–38.

——. "The Strategy of Conflict: Prospectus for the Reorientation of Game Theory," *ibid.*, 2 (1958), 203–64.

SIEGEL, S. and FOURAKER, L. E. *Bargaining and Group Decision Making.* New York: McGraw-Hill, 1960.

STONE, J. J. "An Experiment in Bargaining Games," *Econometrica*, 26 (1958), 286–96.

SUPPES, P. and CARLSMITH, J. M. "Experimental Analysis of a Duopoly Situation from the Standpoint of Mathematical Learning Theory." Applied Mathematics and Statistics Laboratories, Stanford University, 1960. (Mimeo.)

THIBAUT, J. W. and KELLEY, H. H. *The Social Psychology of Groups.* New York: John Wiley & Sons, 1959.

ZEUTHEN, F. *Problems of Monopoly and Economic Warfare.* London: Routledge, 1930.

STRUCTURAL AND ATTITUDINAL FACTORS IN INTERPERSONAL BARGAINING*

Robert M. Krauss

Social psychologists typically postulate two classes of determinants to explain the behavior of interacting persons. One class we will call *structural*. It consists of certain aspects of the social environment in which the interaction is set. Included are such factors as communication networks, status systems, systems of goal interdependence, ecological distributions, etc. In the present experiment we will be concerned with the system of goal interdependence. The other class we will call *attitudinal*. This consists of the perceptual, evaluative, and affective orientations of the interacting individuals toward one another.

It seems usually to be the case that the structural and attitudinal orientations of interacting individuals are mutually supportive. For example, when two individuals are, to use Deutsch's (1949a) term, "promotively interdependent" (that is to say when goal attainment by one increases the probability of goal attainment by the other), it is typically the case that they like, trust, and respect each other (e.g., Deutsch, 1949b; Gottheil, 1955; Lott and Lott, 1960; Mizuhara and Tamai, 1952).

Furthermore, attitudinal orientations established before interaction will affect the character of the subsequent interaction: people who are positively oriented will behave more cooperatively than people who are negatively oriented (see Borah, 1963; Ex, 1959; Rice and White, 1964).

These two sets of findings, taken together, suggest the hypothesis that the relationship between attitudinal and structural orientations is not adventitious, but rather tends toward a preferred equilibrium or "balanced" state. A model for such a process is Heider's (1957) theory of cognitive balance. We will assume that a cooperative structure (i.e., one in which the participants are interdependent in a mutually facilitative way) is in balance with positive interpersonal attitudes and that a competitive structure (i.e., one in which the participants are interdependent in a mutually obstructive way) is in balance with negative interpersonal attitudes. Such an assumption is intuitively plausible

* Robert M. Krauss, "Structural and Attitudinal Factors in Interpersonal Bargaining," *Journal of Experimental Social Psychology*, 2 (1966), 42–55. Reprinted by permission of Academic Press, Inc.

and is not inconsistent with the evidence cited above.

The present study is concerned with interaction in a bargaining game. Bargaining is defined as behavior in a situation having the following characteristics:[1]

1. Both parties have something to gain from reaching an agreement. That is, there is an outcome among the set of outcomes which, if achieved, will leave both bargainers better off than when they started.
2. The situation must contain the possibility of more than one such outcome as is specified above.
3. An outcome profitable to both parties can be effected only by the joint behavior of both parties. And the failure to achieve such an outcome will result in both parties being no better off, or worse off, than they were before bargaining began.
4. Both parties have different preferences among the mutually profitable outcomes.

An important consequence of the structure of bargaining situations is that the participants are mutually interdependent in terms of goal attainment. The concept of mutual interdependence is, of course, not a novel one in social psychology. It lies at the base of Deutsch's (1949a; 1962) theory of cooperation and competition. In Deutsch's theory, cooperative behavior grows out of a structure in which goal attainment by one individual increases the probability of goal attainment by others. Similarly, competitive behavior is induced by a structure in which goal attainment

by one individual decreases the probability of goal attainment by others. However, it is well to note, as Deutsch did, that such simple relations among the goals of interacting persons are the exception rather than the rule in real-life social interaction. More typical are what Schelling (1960) has called "mixed motive" situations—"mixed motive" in the sense that motivations for both cooperative and competitive behavior are simultaneously present.

For the most part, research on bargaining has focused upon the effects of different types of bargaining structures (e.g., see Fouraker and Siegel, 1961; Siegel and Fouraker, 1960; Stone, 1958; Willis and Joseph, 1959). There are, however, a few exceptions to this generalization. Deutsch and Krauss (1960) found that the introduction of a threat potential into a bargaining situation markedly increased the competitive aspect of bargaining behavior. In a second study, the same investigators found a complex statistical interaction between the effects of communication and threat (Deutsch and Krauss, 1962). Where threat was unilateral and communication compulsory, the competitive aspect of bargaining was reduced. However, where threat was bilateral or where communication was not compulsory, the presence of communication had no effect, compared to conditions where no communication was permitted. Also relevant are studies by Borah (1963) and Rice and White (1964).

One may view *inter*personal conflict, implicit in the mixed motive character of a bargaining situation, as a potential source of *intra*personal conflict. When the structure of the relationship and the attitudinal orientation are in balance (i.e., cooperative-positive and competitive-nega-

---

[1] Because the present study is concerned with dyadic bargaining, this definition is formulated in terms of a two-person system. It could readily be extended to multi-person systems such as an oligopoly situation. For a fuller discussion of the properties of bargaining situations, see Boulding (1962) and Schelling (1960).

tive) no conflict exists. However, a state of imbalance (i.e., cooperative-negative or competitive-positive) generates tension which the individual may reduce by moving to a balanced state. Balance may be achieved in one of two ways: by changing the attitude so that it is in balance with the structure or by reorienting the behavior so that it is in balance with the attitude.

One difficulty with applying balance-type theories to specific situations is that it is often difficult to specify in advance which of the available modes of balance is restored by changing the weakest element. However, such an approach poses some problems, since it is difficult to measure in any comparable form the strength of qualitatively different elements, such as structures and attitudes. In such cases the investigator frequently resorts to an experimental manipulation which differentially anchors (i.e., makes differentially resistant to change) one or another of the elements under investigation.

In the present experiment we were able to create positive or negative attitudes on the part of our subjects toward each other by means of an experimental induction. We assumed that an experimentally induced attitude could be strongly anchored and made resistant to change by linking it to the person's self esteem system and that without such a linkage the attitude would be weakly anchored.

The theory employed here predicts that when a participant in a bargaining situation is faced with an imbalance between the structure of his relationship with another individual and his attitude toward that individual, the mode of balance restoration will be determined by the extent to which his attitude is resistant to change. When the attitude is strongly anchored, he will resolve the imbalance by behaving

in a manner consistent with the attitude; when it is weakly anchored, he will resolve it by changing his attitude and behaving in a manner consistent with the structure of his relationship.

In previous experiments subjects who were cooperatively oriented bargained more effectively (i.e., were better able to come to mutually profitable agreements) and used an available means of threat less frequently than did competitively oriented subjects (Deutsch and Krauss, 1960; 1962). In the present experiment it is hypothesized that bargaining effectiveness will be high (1) where the bargaining structure is cooperative and there are no strongly anchored negative attitudes; or (2) where there exist strongly anchored positive attitudes. In effect, we are hypothesizing that bargaining effectiveness will be determined by the interaction of anchoring with the structural and attitudinal factors. Similarly the frequency with which an available means of threat is used will covary with bargaining effectivenness: the more frequently threat is employed the less effective bargaining will be.

METHOD

Overview of Experiment

Eighty pairs of female subjects were randomly assigned to the cells of a $2 \times 2 \times 2$ factorial experiment, consisting of two levels of bargaining structure, Cooperative (Coop.) and Competitive (Comp.); two levels of attitudes, Positive (Pos.) and Negative (Neg.); two levels of attitudinal anchoring, Strong (SA) and Weak (WA). Subjects filled out an opinion questionnaire, then listened to tape recorded task instructions. A fictitious questionnaire, ostensibly belonging to their partner in the experiment, was then distributed. In it, the subject's partner's responses were either similar to or dissimilar from his own. On the basis of this information, subjects were asked to rate each other on an Interpersonal Judgment Scale. They then received instructions designed to produce either strong or weak anchoring of their attitude toward the other player, and the instructions which produced the bargaining structure. Subjects then played a bargaining game for ten trials. Finally, each rated his partner again on the Interpersonal Judgment Scale.

Subjects

One hundred and sixty experimentally-naive female clerical employees of the Bell Telephone Laboratories served as subjects. Their ages ranged from 18 to 35 years, with a mean of about 24. All were high school graduates.

Ten pairs were run in each of the eight cells of a $2 \times 2 \times 2$ factorial matrix. They were assigned randomly to their treatments, with the restriction that the members of a pair had to come from different offices. This was neces-

sary to keep a subject from discovering her partner's identity. Further to prevent identification, their arrival times were staggered by about five minutes.

The Experimental Task

The experimental task consisted of a two-person electromechanical bargaining game. The apparatus has been described in detail in previous publications (Deutsch and Krauss, 1960; 1962) and will only be briefly referred to here. In the game, the participants play the roles of owner-drivers of trucking firms, which carry merchandise over a road from a starting point to a destination. Their profits (paid in imaginary money) are based on the time it takes them to complete a trip—the shorter the time, the greater the profit. If they take too long they can lose money. Their routes are illustrated in Fig. 1. One player ("Acme") travels from the left side of the map to the right, the other ("Bolt") from right to left. One section of their main route is

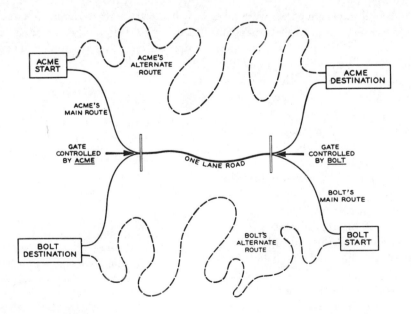

Fig. 1. Subject's Road Map.

common to both—the middle segment labelled "one lane road." As the label implies this section is only wide enough for one truck to go through at a time. Thus, in order to use the Main Routes efficiently the players must work out some method of sharing the one lane section. Of course, the player who is the first to go through the one lane section ends up with the greater profits, since he is able to complete his trip in less time. As the road map indicates, there is another way for the players to reach their destinations, the Alternate Route. However, the length of the Alternate Route is such that its use necessitates a minimum loss of $.10 per trial. Each player also has control of a gate, by use of which he can prevent the other player from passing that point on the main route. The use of these gates constitutes the exercise of threat discussed above. Subjects played the game for a total of ten trials; each trial represented a repetition of the same bargaining problem.

Manipulation of Independent Variables

Structure. Because the structure of the task permits only one player to pass through the one-way section at a time, the experimental task imposes a discrepancy between the positive payoffs obtainable by the subjects on any given trial. This creates the "mixed motive" situation referred to above. The competitiveness of this structure was modified by manipulating the manner in which goal attainment for one subject was affected by the other's goal attainment through a system of bonuses. In the Coop. conditions, each subject received a bonus based on 20 per cent of the other player's profit. That is, 20 per cent of the other player's profit was added to, or 20 per cent of the other's losses was subtracted from, the subject's own profit. In the Comp. condition, the bonus was negative in sign. That is, each player had 20 per cent of the other player's losses added to his own profits.

Attitudes. Positive or negative attitudes were induced by a modification of a technique

developed by Byrne (1961). In the present experiment, each subject received a questionnaire containing 20 statements of opinion and calling for a binary ("agree"–"disagree") response. Shortly thereafter each subject received a questionnaire which ostensibly had been filled out by her partner but which actually had been filled out by the experimenter. In the Pos. conditions, the responses to 17 of the 20 statements in the fictitious questionnaire agreed with the subject's own responses. In the Neg. conditions 17 of the 20 responses disagreed with the subject's own. The subject was asked to use the "other person's questionnaire" to "get a picture of the player" and to "formulate an idea of what she's really like." Then she was asked to rate the other player by filling out a modified version of Byrne's (1961) Interpersonal Judgment Scale. One of Byrne's six items (on personal morality) was omitted. Subjects rated their partner's intelligence, cooperativeness, considerateness, likeability, and desirability as a work partner.

Attitudinal Anchoring. Differential anchoring was achieved by a verbal induction. In the SA condition, subjects were told that they had received sufficient information to form a very accurate picture of the other player and that "the normal, well adjusted individual, the sort of person who understands himself and others and who gets along with people reasonably well" was quite accurate at evaluating others on the basis of this sort of information. The WA instructions simply stated that the information provided was insufficient to form the basis of an accurate judgment. The instructions for the SA and WA conditions were given in an informal and off-handed manner, suggesting that they were not a part of the experiment proper.

Security of Experimental Manipulations

After an experimental session was completed, subjects were informed of the purpose of the experiment and of the deception used in the attitudinal manipulation. Their questions about the experiment were answered at this time. Subjects were requested not to discuss the details of the experiment with their co-workers and questioning revealed no instances of contamination due to violation of this request.

RESULTS AND DISCUSSION

A total of 85 pairs of subjects were run. Five pairs were eliminated from the analysis[2] leaving 80 pairs, ten in each experimental condition.

Effectiveness of the Attitudinal Induction

The effectiveness of the Attitudinal manipulation in creating positive or negative attitudes may be assessed by examining the initial rating on the Interpersonal Judgment Scale. Since the exchange of questionnaires ostensibly took place before the structural or attitudinal anchorage conditions were created, attitudes should be uncontaminated by the other treatment effects. An analysis of variance of the initial ratings on the Interpersonal Judgment Scale indicates large main effects for Attitudes (all five F ratios are significant well beyond the .001 level), with the main effects of the other factors and the interactions not differing significantly from chance.[3] Subjects judge their partners to be more intelligent, cooperative, consider-

ate, likeable, and desirable as a work partner under the positive attitude treatment than under the negative attitude treatment.

Bargaining Effectiveness

The major predictions were concerned with relations between the independent variables and bargaining effectiveness. Bargaining effectiveness is defined as the extent to which the parties jointly maximized the value of their outcomes (see Deutsch and Krauss, 1960; 1962). It will be remembered that payoffs were simple transformation of time (Payoff = 60 minus time in seconds). However, the actual payoffs are contaminated by the Coop.-Comp. manipulation. Therefore, time itself was used as an Index of Bargaining Effectiveness. Since the distribution of time scores was positively skewed a log transformation was performed. A T' score, the Index of Bargaining Effectiveness, is defined as follows:

$$T' = \log_{10}(T - C)$$

---

[2] Two pairs were eliminated because of equipment breakdowns, one because of an error by the experimenter in giving the instructions, one because one of the subjects claimed she was unable to comprehend the instructions, and one because the pair became stalemated for 5 minutes on the first trial.

[3] This is true for all items except Item 2 ("How cooperative do you think this person is?"). For Item 2, the main effects of the other two factors are significant beyond the .05 level. Such a result could be due to a failure in the random assignment procedure or to some systematic variation in the experimenter's behavior, but one would also expect such sorts of contamination to be reflected in the other four items. It seems more reasonable to assume that these effects reflected random variations. Consider the fact that, in all, 35 F tests were performed. Discounting the five tests of the Attitude variable, which produced expected results of a compellingly high order of magnitude, leaves 30 F tests. On a chance basis, with $\alpha = .05$, 1.5 out of 30 tests would be expected to fall within the rejection region.

Table 1

ANALYSES OF VARIANCE OF BARGAINING EFFECTIVENESS, GATE USE AND ATTITUDE CHANGE

Source	1a Bargaining effectiveness (T'_j)			1b Gate use			1c Attitude change		
	df	MS	F	df	MS	F	df	MS	F
1. Structures	1	1.0537	5.052*	1	35.112	4.082*	1	78.40	5.448*
2. Attitudes	1	4.9050	23.518**	1	137.812	16.022**	1	22.50	1.564
3. Anchoring	1	0.0072	0.035	1	7.812	0.908	1	6.40	0.445
1×2	1	0.6137	2.943	1	27.612	3.210	1	13.22	0.919
1×3	1	1.3836	6.634*	1	74.113	8.616**	1	4.22	0.294
2×3	1	1.3852	6.642*	1	49.612	5.768*	1	87.02	6.048*
1×2×3	1	0.1705	0.818	1	30.012	3.489	1	16.90	1.174
Residual	72	0.2086		72	8.601		152	14.39	
Total	79			79			159		

* $p < .05$.
** $p < .01$.

where T is the time (in seconds) to completion of a given trip and C is the minimum possible time minus one. The point effectiveness score (T'_j) of a pair of subjects (a and b) is defined as the sum of their transformed time scores: $T'_j = T'_a + T'_b$. An analysis of variance of the Joint Effectiveness Index (T'_j) summed over ten trials is presented in Table 1a; Table 2a contains the cell means.

We hypothesized that bargaining effectiveness would be determined by the interaction of the anchoring variable with attitude and structure. Inspection of Tables 1a and 2a reveals this to be the case. Of particular interest is the configuration of the interaction effects. The interaction of anchoring and attitude is graphed in Fig. 2 and anchoring and structure in Fig. 3. As Fig. 2 indicates, when anchoring is strong, positive attitudes produce low (i.e., more effective) T'_j scores and negative attitudes produce high T'_j scores. This difference is statistically significant $(t = 5.26, \ p < .01)$. When attitudinal anchoring is weak, the

difference between the positive and negative attitude treatments is not significantly different from zero $(t = 1.59)$. Conversely, as Fig. 3 indicates, where anchoring is weak a cooperative bargaining structure produces significantly more effective bargaining than a competitive structure $(t = 3.39, \ p < .01)$. Under SA no difference is found $(t < 1.0)$.

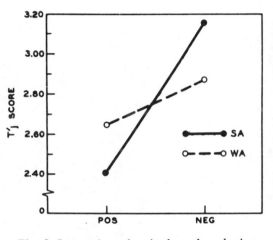

Fig. 2. Interaction of attitude and anchoring on Index of Bargaining Effectiveness (T'_j). (A low score indicates high effectiveness.)

Table 2

CELL MEANS FOR BARGAINING EFFECTIVENESS, GATE USE AND ATTITUDE CHANGE

		2a Bargaining effectiveness (T'_j)[a]		2b Gate use[c]		2c Attitude change[bd]	
	Structure	Pos	Neg	Pos	Neg	Pos	Neg
Strong anchoring	Coop	2.2821	3.3080	1.9	8.5	+0.60	+1.10
	Comp	2.5161	3.0070	3.7	5.5	+0.75	−1.20
Weak anchoring	Coop	2.3556	2.6705	3.4	4.4	−0.30	+1.85
	Comp	2.9310	3.0802	6.6	7.7	−2.10	−0.20

[a] The lower the T'_j score the greater the bargaining effectiveness.
[b] Second rating minus first rating.
[c] $N = 10$ observations (pairs) per cell.
[d] $N = 20$ observations per cell.

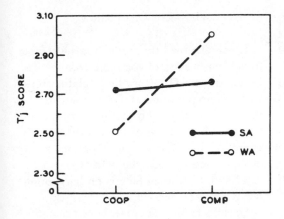

Fig. 3. Interaction of structure and anchoring on Index of Bargaining Effectiveness (T'_j). (A low score indicates high effectiveness.)

duces relatively frequent use. This difference is statistically significant ($t = 4.53$, $p < .01$). When anchoring is weak, the difference between the positive and negative attitude treatments is not significantly different from zero ($t = 1.13$). Similarly, when anchoring is weak, the frequency of gate use is significantly higher in the competitive condition than in the cooperative ($t = 3.50$, $p < .01$). When anchoring is strong, the difference is not significant ($t < 1.0$). The similarity between the findings for Gate Use and the T'_j measure is not surprising since the product moment correlation between these two variables is fairly high ($r = +.73$).

Thus, where attitudes are relatively labile (i.e., WA) the attitudinal effect is attenuated and the reward structure of the task has a determining effect. Where attitudes are relatively resistant to change (i.e., SA), the initial attitude determines the direction of interaction and the effect of the reward structure is minimal.

Use of Gates

Each pair of subjects was assigned a Gate score, based on the number of trials (out of ten) on which one or both players had closed their gates. The results of an analysis of variance of these scores is shown in Table 1b; the cell means are presented in Table 2b.

It was predicted that gate use would vary in the same manner as bargaining effectiveness. Clearly this is the case; significant interactions of attitudinal anchoring with attitude and with bargaining structure are observed. When anchoring is strong, the positive attitude treatment produces relatively infrequent use of gates and the negative attitude treatment pro-

Attitude Change

Subjects' ratings of their partners on the pre- and post-game administration of the Interpersonal Judgment Scale were summed across the five items and the difference of the sums was calculated [Diff = (ΣPost − ΣPre)]. The results of an analysis of variance of these summed differences appear in Table 1c; the associated cell means appear in Table 2c. A significant main effect for structure was obtained. As the cell means indicate, subjects who interacted in a Coop. structure tended to view their partner somewhat more favorably subsequent to their interaction than did subjects in the Comp. conditions. In addition, attitude and anchoring interacted significantly. This interaction is graphed in Fig. 4. From the figure, it is clear that it is the combination of attitude and anchoring which determines the direction of attitude change: with WA, positive attitudes become less positive, negative attitudes become less negative ($t = 2.62$, $p < .01$); when the attitudinal anchor is strong, the difference

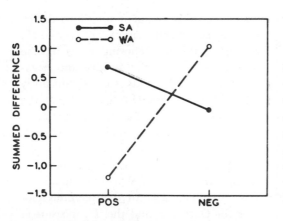

Fig. 4. Interaction of attitudes and anchoring for summed differences between first and second administration of five item Interpersonal Judgment Scale.

in change for positive vs. negative attitudes is nonsignificant ($t < 1.0$).

It is interesting to speculate on the ways in which attitudes may affect interaction in a bargaining situation. One way is by affecting the individual's expectation of the sorts of behavior his partner is likely to emit. Another is by providing a context for interpreting the other person's behavior. As Heider (1957) has pointed out, the interpretation of intention vs. inadvertance, of malevolence vs. benevolence, etc. are complexly determined by the context in which an act occurs. Part of the context is the "inner state" of the actor. Two acts which are objectively identical, committed by two differently perceived individuals, may be responded to in radically different ways. Finally, it seems likely that individuals have developed characteristically different ways of behaving toward positively and negatively evaluated others. Such behavior serves as a cue for the other and is likely to elicit behavior which is consistent with the initial evaluation.

General Discussion

It was assumed that individuals attempt to achieve a state of cognitive balance between the structure of their relationships with others and their affective or attitudinal orientations. From this assumption, and from an analysis of the relevant forces operating in a bargaining situation, a set of hypotheses about the effects of structural and attitudinal factors on bargaining behavior were derived.

In effect, it was postulated that *inter*personal conflict creates a potential situation of *intra*personal conflict. When structures and attitudes are in balance, no intrapersonal conflict exists and the individual is free to behave in an unambivalent manner toward his counterpart. Indeed, his behavior is in a sense "over-determined"; the influence of structures and attitude is mutually reinforcing. However, when these factors are imbalanced, a state of intrapersonal conflict exists which the individual can resolve in one of two ways: by orienting his behavior to make it consonant with his attitude or by changing his attitude so that it is consonant with his behavior. In the present experiment, the mode of balance restoration was determined by the degree of anchorage of the interpersonal attitude: when anchorage was strong the effect of attitude was marked and the effect of structure was minimal; when it was weak this effect was reversed.

Thus it would seem consistent with the balance notion that imbalance between structure and attitude is resolved on an all-or-none basis. The interactions of both attitude and structure with anchoring provide clear evidence on this score. At least within the conditions of the present experiment, it would appear that the attempts of individuals to achieve cognitive balance are sufficiently strong to override certain objective features of their relationships with others.

Bargaining, then, for our subjects consisted at least partly of an attempt to maintain cognitive balance. It may be contended that social structural factors are in general mediated by such psychological processes. That is to say, the orientations which derive from various types of social structures may be viewed as an appropriate set of attitudes, perceptions and expectations held by individuals in that situation. This study has investigated one aspect of the structure of a social relationship, but it seems useful to think of other aspects of structure (e.g., status) as mediated by sets of attitudes which are balanced or congruent with a given structural orientation. Thus one may conceive, on the one hand, of the *behavior* of a low status individual in interaction with one of high status and, on the other, of the *attitudes* of the low and high status individuals which are in a balanced relationship with such behavior. As in the present study, it would be predicted that conflict between behavior and attitude leads either to attitude change or to a reorientation of behavior so as to restore balance.

REFERENCES

BORAH, L. A., JR. "The Effects of Threat in Bargaining: Critical and Experimental Analysis." *Journal of Abnormal and Social Psychology*, 1963, 66, 37–44.

BOULDING, K. E. *Conflict and Defense.* New York: Harpers, 1962.

BYRNE, D. "Interpersonal Attractiveness and Attitude Similarity." *Journal of Abnormal and Social Psychology*, 1961, 62, 713–715.

DEUTSCH, M. "A Theory of Cooperation and Competition." *Human Relations*, 1949, 2, 129–151 (a).

DEUTSCH, M. "An Experimental Study of the Effects of Cooperation and Competition Upon Group Process." *Human Relations*, 1949, 2, 199–231 (b).

DEUTSCH, M. "Cooperation and Trust: Some Theoretical Notes." In M. L. Jones (Ed), *Nebraska Symposium on Motivation.* Lincoln: Univer. of Nebraska Press, 1962.

DEUTSCH, M., and KRAUSS, R. M. "The Effect of Threat Upon Interpersonal Bargaining." *Journal of Abnormal and Social Psychology*, 1960, 61, 181–189.

DEUTSCH, M., and KRAUSS, R. M. "Studies of Interpersonal Bargaining." *Journal of Conflict Resolution*, 1962, 6, 52–76.

EX, J. "The Nature of Contact Between Co-operating Partners and Their Expectation Concerning the Level of Their Common Achievement." *Acta Psychologica*, 1959, 16, 99–107.

FOURAKER, L. E., and SIEGEL, S. "Bargaining Behavior II: Experiments in Oligopoly." The Pennsylvania State Univer., 1961 (mimeo).

GOTTHEIL, E. "Changes in Social Perceptions Contingent Upon Competing or Co-operating." *Sociometry*, 1958, 18, 132–137.

HEIDER, F. *The Psychology of Interpersonal Relations.* New York: Wiley, 1958.

LOTT, BERNICE E., and LOTT, A. J. "The Formation of Positive Attitudes Toward Group Members." *Journal of Abnormal and Social Psychology*, 1960, 61, 297–300.

MIZUHARA, T., and TAMAI, S. "Experimental Studies of Cooperation and Competition." *Japanese Journal of Psychology*, 1952, 22, 121–127.

RICE, G. E., and WHITE, KATHERINE, R. "The Effect of Education on Prejudice as Revealed by a Game Situation." *Psychological Record*, 1964, 14, 341–348.

SCHELLING, T. C. *The Strategy of Conflict.* Cambridge: Harvard Univer. Press, 1960.

SIEGEL, S., and FOURAKER, L. E. *Bargaining and Group Decision Making.* New York: McGraw-Hill, 1960.

STONE, J. J. "An Experiment in Bargaining Games." *Econometrica*, 1958, 26, 286–296.

WILLIS, R. H., and JOSEPH, M. L. "Bargaining Behavior I. Prominence as a Predictor of the Outcome of Games of Agreement." *Journal of Conflict Resolution*, 1959, 3, 102–113.

THE EFFECTS OF NEED TO MAINTAIN FACE ON INTERPERSONAL BARGAINING

Bert R. Brown

Experiments in interpersonal bargaining indicate that unjustified insult, unfair reduction of one bargainer's outcomes by an opponent, or other behavior that poses a threat or damage to "face," usually result in retaliation and mutual loss rather than in cooperative effort (Wilson and Bixenstein, 1964). Experiments by Deutsch and Krauss (1960, 1962) and by Hornstein (1965) support the notion that under certain conditions threat is more likely to result in counterthreat and/or increased resistance to yielding than in compliance. Schelling (1960) and Siegel and Fouraker (1960) argued that a destructive threat-counterthreat-aggression cycle may be brought on by an initial unjust or overly severe threat. There are several reasons why insult, "unfair" reduction of out-

comes, or improper threat may provoke retaliation. One is linked to the notion of "reciprocity." Gouldner (1963) observed that our cultural values emphasize giving back to others an equivalent measure of what has been received from them. This notion adequately explains the "eye for an eye, tooth for a tooth" exchange principle, but does not fully account for the spiraling of aggressive affect also found in conflict situations.

Another explanation, proposed by Deutsch (1961), is that counterthreat and/or resistance will be chosen in response to threat if the threatener is perceived by the threatened as not having the right to expect deference from him. The reason offered by Deutsch is that one will fear a loss of status and self-esteem if he permits himself to be unjustly intimidated. In the face of unjustified threat, the culturally prescribed way of behaving is to challenge the threatener and to engage with him in a contest for supremacy.

Further understanding of retaliation fol-

* Bert R. Brown, "The Effects of Need to Maintain Face on Interpersonal Bargaining," *Journal of Experimental Social Psychology*, 4 (1968), 107–22. Reprinted by permission of Academic Press, Inc.

lowing insult and resistance following threat can be culled from the theoretical writings of Erving Goffman (1955, 1956, 1963). He observed that the "need to maintain face" is another prevalent value in our culture, and he suggested that in the service of this need, people often do things that may be costly to them. Goffman (1955) saw face saving as being so pervasive that "... at each and every moment of interaction, actors are concerned with the question: If I do or do not act in this way or that, will I or others lose face?" (p. 227).

According to Goffman, face-saving behavior is especially apparent (a) in aggressive interchanges, and (b) after one's prestige has been damaged by another in public view. In such conditions, one can save face by demonstrating that he can handle himself and that he is at least equally as capable as his adversary, if not more so. Thus, as Goffman points out, one can ignore a *limited* amount of insult without the avoidance's causing a "loss of face." After a point, one must challenge the offender and seek redress.

That one will often become involved in attempting to demonstrate his capability and strength to his audiences, although it may be *costly*, has direct relevance to interpersonal bargaining. In the present experiment it is assumed that a bargainer acts not only purposively to maximize his own outcome, but also to avoid appearing incapable or foolish to audiences while he is seeking it. This is a broader explanation of bargaining behavior than that posited by the game-theoretic view that rational, economically determined motives will prevail.

A bargainer will generally seek to communicate a positive image of himself to two audiences: (a) the person or persons directly involved in the interchange with

him, and (b) any other audience or "referent" group interested in the outcomes he obtains. The latter may include groups the bargainer represents or in which he holds membership; they may be "real" or imagined, physically present at or absent from the setting in which the bargaining occurs.

Face *saving* and face *restoration* are both expressive of a need to *maintain* face. Operationally, face *saving* in bargaining involves attempts by A to block actions by B which would cause him to appear foolish, weak, and incapable to significant others. Face *restoration* involves attempts by A to seek redress from B who (A believes) has already caused him to look foolish. Such behavior, directed toward reasserting one's capability and strength, generally takes the form of retaliation.

In certain conditions the strength of the need to maintain face may be measured by the *costs* A is willing to bear in his attempt to seek redress from B. Face restoration would thus be evidenced most clearly when a bargainer spends more than he can possibly hope to gain in order to retaliate against another who has exploited him publicly.

The main hypothesis of the present experiment is that retaliation will be more likely and more severe when bargainers receive information from a salient audience that they have been caused to appear foolish by an exploitative other. In contrast, retaliation will be less likely and less severe when they receive information that they looked good—even though exploited—because they played "fair" and honorably.

Secondly, it is hypothesized that an exploited bargainer will be ready to spend *more* to retaliate if he supposes that his opponent is unaware of his costs than if he believes that the other knows them.

We may explain this prediction in the following way: if he attempts retaliation against the one he believes caused him to appear foolish, he will fear looking even worse if he *openly* demonstrates a willingness to damage himself seriously just to "get back at" the other. This formulation suggests not only that a bargainer may be willing to "cut off his nose to save his face" after public exploitation, but also that he may be more content to live with the consequences of his act under the protection of privacy—when he knows that his own costs for retaliation will remain unpublicized.

METHOD

Subjects and Design of Experiment

Sixty adolescent male volunteers (15–17.5 years of age) from New York City public high schools were randomly assigned to conditions in a 2×3 factorial experiment. The independent variables were: (a) "audience feedback" (three levels) and (b) information given to subjects about the other's knowledge of their own costs for retaliating (two levels).

Experimental Situation

All subjects, except for those in control groups, were told that they would be observed and evaluated by an audience (classmates) while participating in a bargaining task. Their classmates were purportedly (but not actually) watching from behind a one-way mirror which opened onto the experimental room. Several procedures were employed to strengthen the credibility of this manipulation. Included among these was the playing of a tape recording of muffled male voices, periodic laughter, shuffling of furniture, etc., behind the mirror during the first ten trials. Subjects were not permitted to see or communicate with the

other participant during the experiment. The subject and his opponent sat on opposite sides of a 6-foot × 6-foot separator panel. Unbeknownst to subjects, the other participant was a confederate (stooge) whose behavior was programmed as highly competitive and exploitative in all conditions of the experiment.

Subjects were systematically exploited in the first ten trials of a 20-trial experiment. Next, all but control subjects received feedback from the "audience" about their appearance during those trials. In the second ten trials, subjects were given the option of retaliating (at costs), or of ignoring their exploitation and thereby increasing their own outcomes. Control subjects were told nothing about being observed and received no feedback.

The Bargaining Task

The task used was a modification of the Deutsch and Krauss (1960) two-person (non-zero sum) trucking game. This task presents a conflict of interest to two bargainers—in order for each to win as much as possible, he must cooperate with the other. Subjects are asked to imagine that they operate trucking companies. Each player must move his truck (with the aid of an electronic device) over a road system to a destination. The faster he completes a trip, the more he will earn. At a "start" signal, the two trucks begin their trips from opposite ends of the road system and move toward each other. There are two routes to the destination—a short, direct route and a longer, more circuitous one. There is a dilemma—a portion of the direct route contains a common pathway which each must use to reach his destination. This section, however, is one lane wide, permitting the passage of only one truck at a time. If both trucks attempt passage through it, they will collide, causing a loss of time and payoff. When a collision occurs at least one player must yield to the other to minimize loss, or both may back down, permitting the other through first. If both refuse to back down, the collision will be prolonged, increasing losses to both. The alternate route contains no common pathway but is twice as long. Its use automatically results in a nominal loss, but permits one to avoid encounters with the other.

Each player is given a "gate" with which he can block the progress of the other indefinitely without affecting the movement of his own truck. In the present experiment the function of the gates was modified; they were used as "toll gates," which on any trial were controlled by only one player. On each trial players were required to either charge the other one of several "tolls" or permit him to pass through without charge. The rules stated that if a toll was charged one could either accept or refuse payment. Acceptance insured passage; refusal meant that one was required to back out of the narrow path immediately and take the longer route. Players were informed that decisions for each trial were irreversible and that they would not be penalized for time spent in making decisions about tolls, since the interval between receiving the *toll announcer card* and sending a *notice of payment* or *refusal to pay card* was electronically timed and subtracted from the total time to completion.

Orientation. Subjects were given an "individualistic" motivational orientation; they were instructed to try to earn as much as possible for themselves and to be unconcerned with the amount earned by the other participant. They were told they could keep whatever they earned (added to or subtracted from a $4.00 real-money "stake" given them at the outset). Their final payoff was determined by the summed earnings on each trial with appropriate adjustments for tolls paid out, tolls collected, and "own" expenses. A series of practice trials was given in which subjects were thoroughly familiarized with the apparatus and the procedures for charging tolls. To eliminate confounding of the results due to subjects' differential awareness of the alternating strategy (in which both players gain), they were tutored in this procedure. A

drawing of lots was prearranged to assure that the stooge "won" control of the gate for the first ten trials, while the subject took control for the last ten.

Stooge's program—first ten trials. The stooge charged high tolls during these trials, causing subjects to lose a sizeable portion of their stake. These tolls were:

Trial number	1	2	3	4	5	6	7	8	9	10
Toll charged by stooge (in cents)	10	30	50	40	30	20	50	40	20	50

The toll charged on each trial was determined by trial number. If a subject avoided the toll gate by taking the alternate route from the outset, the stooge closed the gate anyway, waited a short while, and then proceeded to his own destination without charging a toll. (The stooge's apparatus permitted him to know the whereabouts of the subject's truck at all times, while the latter enjoyed no such advantage.) Avoiding the toll gate in this fashion resulted in a loss of about 15 cents. The stooge, on the other hand, gained approximately 20 cents since his way through the direct route was unobstructed. Refusal to pay a toll after reaching the gate resulted in heavy loss (about 80 cents) because of the increased time needed to back down almost the full length of the direct route. Whenever subjects agreed to pay a toll, the stooge allowed the subject's truck to move through the narrow roadway, ahead of his own.

Following every trial an announcement of the time taken by each to complete the trip was made (corrected for time spent in negotiating toll payment). Subjects were thus confronted with a highly exploitative opponent who caused them heavy losses. This situation was so structured that subjects were free to respond in a number of ways to the stooge's high-handedness—but to no avail.

Stooge's program—second ten trials. The stooge was programmed to travel in the direct route and to pay all tolls he was charged. After paying, he moved directly to his destination. If the subject tried to block, the stooge refused to yield for 30 seconds or until the subject backed up to let him pass. After yielding, the stooge allowed the subject to proceed.

Audience-feedback manipulation. After the tenth trial both the stooge and the subject were handed several sheets, identified by the experimenter as the audience's "evaluations" of them. Blank sheets were given to the stooge, but subjects received one of the two following sets of handwritten feedback: (This procedure was omitted in the control condition.)

"Looked Foolish" Feedback

1. Acme was weak. Bolt made him pay a lot of high tolls and lose.
2. Bolt was out to beat Acme and he really made Acme look like a sucker.
3. Bolt played tricky. He ran rings around Acme and made him lose a lot. Acme looked pretty bad.

"Did Not Look Foolish" Feedback

1. Bolt made Acme pay a lot of high tolls— but Acme looked good because he tried hard and played fair.
2. Bolt was out to beat Acme and make him look like a sucker but Acme played fair and looked good.
3. Bolt was rough and tricky but Acme came out okay because he played it straight.

Subject's toll schedule. Subjects were given the following toll schedule for the second ten trials:

```
Toll you may
  charge      00 10 15 20 30 40 50
Costs to self 00 00 00 10 25 40 60
```

The toll schedule permitted subjects either to retaliate by charging higher tolls, or to maximize their gains by charging smaller ones. Retaliation, however, involved a dilemma: the more severe the retaliation chosen, the higher one's own costs were. Subjects could charge any toll or permit free passage on each trial. That charging higher tolls would reduce their outcomes accordingly was explained to subjects. Tolls were charged by passing a card, with the amount preprinted on it, through a narrow slot in the separator panel. It was through the same slot that subjects had passed a "pay" or "refuse to pay" notice to the stooge.

Knowledge-of-costs manipulations. In one condition the experimenter, in plain view, handed the stooge a paper and told him it was a copy of the subject's toll schedule. The subject therefore knew that the stooge was aware of his costs. In a second condition subjects were assured that the other player would be kept ignorant of their costs. This manipulation was introduced after subjects received the audience feedback. No information was given about (a) whether the audience was told their costs or (b) the stooge's toll costs.

Performance Measures

The main dependent variables were: (a) the number of trials in which subjects charged tolls of more than 15 cents and (b) the amount they spent to charge these tolls. These measures reflect willingness to sacrifice "own" gains for the opportunity to retaliate. In addition, the total payoffs earned by subjects were examined since this measure provides an overall index of bargaining efficiency. The predictions made for this variable parallel those relating to toll-charging behavior.

RESULTS

Comparability of Subjects in the First Ten Trials and Effectiveness of the Experimental Manipulations

Steps were taken, before examining the data bearing on the hypotheses, to determine the comparability of subjects during the first ten trials and to check on the effectiveness of the manipulations. Analyses of variance disclosed no significant differences in total time to reach destination, number of trials on which subjects refused to pay tolls, or number of trials in which subjects avoided the toll gate —that, is traveled the alternate route. Similarly, there were no significant differences in perceptions of the stooge's behavior, as measured by midexperimental questionnaire items, on such dimensions as peaceful–hostile, cooperative–competitive, generous selfish, and yielding–unyielding. The overall means indicated that subjects saw the stooge as competitive and unyielding and moderately selfish and hostile. Finally, the effectiveness of the audience-feedback manipulations was tested by items embedded in the post-experimental questionnaire. These items showed that subjects believed they were under observation by their classmates and that they were strongly influenced by the feedback received. As intended, subjects in the "looked foolish" condition reported that the audience saw them as significantly more "foolish looking" than subjects in the "not foolish" condition. Other differences were all in the expected directions.

Toll-Charging Behavior and Payoffs Earned by Subjects

The main experimental results are shown in Tables 1 and 2. Analysis of variance on the *frequency* with which tolls of more than 15 cents were charged revealed singificant effects of the audience feedback, of other's knowledge of own costs, and of the interaction of these variables. Table 2 shows that subjects who received derogatory feedback retaliated more frequently than both those who received the more favorable feedback and control subjects. Retaliation was less frequent when subjects knew that the other player was informed of their costs than when costs were kept unannounced.

The significant interaction effect was not anticipated, and thus deserves special attention. To pinpoint this effect, the entire set of cell means was evaluated with Duncan's (1955) New Multiple-Range Test. A summary of that analysis is shown in the lower portion of Table 2, which reveals that it was predominantly in the "other ignorant of own costs" condition that the audience-feedback manipulations produced significant differences in the frequency of retaliation. Each of the means differed significantly from the other two.

Table 1

RESULTS OF ANALYSIS OF VARIANCE ON NUMBER OF TRIALS ON WHICH SUBJECTS CHARGED TOLLS INVOLVING COSTS TO SELF

Source	df	MS	F
Audience condition (columns)	2	48.11	15.21**
Other's knowledge of "own" costs (rows)	1	123.26	39.01**
Interaction	2	14.71	4.65*
Error	54	3.16	
Total	59		

* $p < .02$.
** $p < .001$.

In contrast, in the "other knew costs" condition there were no significant differences between either audience-feedback condition and the control condition. This test also shows that the differences in

retaliation between the "looked foolish"/ "other ignorant of costs" condition and the "not foolish"/"other knew costs" condition were highly significant.

In addition to examining the frequency

Table 2

Number of Trials on Which Subjects Charged Tolls Involving Costs to Self

Other's knowledge of subject's costs	Audience condition			
	"Looked foolish" ($\overline{X}$)	"Did not look foolish" ($\overline{X}$)	Control, no feedback ($\overline{X}$)	Overall ($\overline{X}$)
Other knew own costs	2.30	0.90	1.70	1.63
Other ignorant of own costs	7.00	2.20	4.30	4.50
Overall	4.65	1.55	3.00	3.06[a]

Results of t-test comparisons

t (Foolish, not foolish) = 4.00, 38 df, p = $<.01$
t (Foolish, control) = 1.86, 38 df, p = $<.06$
t (Not foolish, control) = 2.37, 38 df, p = $<.025$

Results of multiple-range test[b] (cell means ordered by size)

Not foolish other knew	Control other knew	Not foolish other ignorant	Foolish other knew	Control ignorant	Foolish ignorant
0.90	1.70	2.20	2.30	4.30	7.00

[a] Grand mean.
[b] Any two means not underscored by the same line are significantly different ($p < .05$). Any two means underscored by the same line are not significantly different.

Table 3

Results of Analysis of Variance on Payoffs Expended in Charging Tolls of More Than 15 Cents

Source	df	MS	F
Audience condition (columns)	2	1.06	11.65**
Other's knowledge of "own" costs (rows)	1	3.36	37.33**
Interaction	2	0.51	5.60*
Error	54	0.09	
Total	59		

* $p < .01$.
** $p < .001$.

Table 4

PAYOFFS EXPENDED IN CHARGING TOLLS OF MORE THAN 15 CENTS

Other's knowledge of subject's costs	Audience condition			
	"Looked foolish" $(\overline{X})$	"Did not look foolish" $(\overline{X})$	Control, no feedback $(\overline{X})$	Overall $(\overline{X})$
Other knew own costs	0.23	0.10	0.21	0.18
Other ignorant of own costs	1.03	0.25	0.67	0.65
Overall	0.63	0.17	0.44	0.41[a]
Results of *t*-test comparisons				
t (Foolish, not foolish) = 3.39, 38 df, p = <.01				
t (Foolish, control) = 1.23, 38 df, p = n.s.				
t (Not foolish, control) = 3.00, 38 df, p = <.01				
Results of multiple-range test[b] (cell means ordered by size)				

Not foolish other knew	Control other knew	Not foolish other ignorant	Other knew	Ignorant	Ignorant
.10	.21	.23	.25	.67	1.03

[a] Grand mean.

[b] Any two means not underscored by the same line are significantly different ($p<.05$). Any two means underscored by the same line are not significantly different.

of retaliation, the *amount* that subjects spent to retaliate was studied. These results are shown in Tables 3 and 4. Analysis of variance revealed a pattern of differences similar to that of the "frequency" variable. Since the two measures are correlated, this was not unanticipated. However, a sharpening of the interaction effect was revealed by the Multiple-Range Test and warrants presentation. The lower portion of Table 4 reveals that the effects of audience feedback on expenditures for retaliation (as opposed to its frequency) were observed definitively in both the "other ignorant" and "other informed" of costs conditions. In the latter, subjects who received the "not foolish" feedback spent less to retaliate than either "looked foolish" or control subjects.

We may next examine the effects of the experimental manipulations on overall bargaining efficiency (reflected in the payoffs that subjects earned). Overall payoffs were determined by summing trial payoffs (obtained by subtracting the time to destination on each trial from a base of 60 cents), and making appropriate adjustments for tolls paid out, tolls collected, and "own" costs.

It was predicted that subjects in the "looked foolish" condition would earn less than the other subjects and that those in the "other ignorant of own costs" condition would earn less than those in the "other informed" condition. The results are shown in Tables 5 and 6. Analysis of variance revealed significant differences in payoffs only for the audience-feedback effect. The difference between "other's knowledge of own costs" conditions did not reach significance, but was in the expected direction. The means in Table 6 reveal that subjects receiving the "looked foolish" feedback earned significantly less than the remaining subjects.

The total time subjects took to reach the destination in the second ten trials was studied in order to understand the non-significant difference in payoffs between the "other's knowledge of costs" conditions. Since there were no significant differences in payoffs over the first ten trials, it was deduced that the total payoff differences were probably due to time differences in the latter half of the experiment. Analysis of covariance on this measure (controlled for time in the first ten trials) revealed that "looked foolish" subjects required significantly more time than "not foolish" or control subjects (815 vs. 680 vs. 697 seconds, respectively). These differences could have been caused by (a) use of the alternate route when in control of the toll gate, or (b) lengthy head-on collisions in the second ten trials. Since the alternate route was infrequently used by subjects in those trials, the differences in time, and hence in payoffs, were largely a function of the latter. Since the stooge was programmed to yield only after thirty seconds had elapsed, the number of times he backed down from collisions in the second ten trials is an indicator of the number of "prolonged" collisions, and thus reveals subjects' resistance to the stooge's unobstructed passage. Analysis of variance shows that there were significant differences between audience conditions on this measure, but that none was due to the other manipulations. No significant interaction effect was found.

The means in Table 8 indicate that there were more prolonged collisions in the "looked foolish" condition than in the other audience conditions. Subjects who received the derogatory feedback sought to reduce the stooge's payoff in two ways—by charging him higher tolls and by trying to delay him in the narrow path. Both strategies reflect a willingness to sacrifice own outcomes in order to inflict heavier losses on the other player. Thus, the differences in payoffs reported earlier can be explained by the finding that costlier retaliation (leading to a greater reduction in own payoffs) was caused more by the audience manipulations than by the knowledge-of-costs manipulations.

Table 5

RESULTS OF ANALYSIS OF VARIANCE ON TOTAL PAYOFFS
EARNED OVER TWENTY TRIALS

Source	df	MS	F
Audience condition (columns)	2	30.02	9.77*
Other's knowledge of " own " costs (rows)	1	8.93	2.91
Interaction	2	1.43	<1.00
Error	54	3.07	
Total	59		

* $p < .01$.

Table 6

MEAN PAYOFFS EARNED OVER TWENTY TRIALS

Other's knowledge of subject's costs	Audience condition			
	"Looked foolish" ($\overline{X}$)	"Did not look foolish" ($\overline{X}$)	Control, no feedback ($\overline{X}$)	Overall ($\overline{X}$)
Other knew own costs	−3.92	−1.23	−2.25	−2.46
Other ignorant of own costs	−4.53	−2.54	−2.63	−3.24
Overall	−4.23	−1.89	−2.45	−2.85[a]

Results of *t*-test comparisons
t (Foolish, not foolish = 4.09, 38 *df*, $p = <.01$
t (Foolish, control) = 2.91, 38 *df*, $p = <.01$
t (Not foolish, control) = 1.00, 38 *df*, $p =$ n. s.

[a] Grand mean.

Table 7

RESULTS OF ANALYSIS OF VARIANCE ON NUMBER OF TRIALS ON WHICH THE STOOGE BACKED OUT OF HEAD-ON COLLISION AFTER THIRTY SECONDS

Source	*df*	*MS*	*F*
Audience condition (columns)	2	28.13	4.25*
Other's knowledge of "own" costs (rows)	1	3.75	<1.00
Interaction	2	2.45	<1.00
Error	54	6.62	
Total	59		

* $p < .02$.

Why were subjects in the "looked foolish" condition drawn into such self-destructive bargaining strategies? The suggestion has been made that bargainers attempt to restore face after humiliation by trying to reassert their capability and strength. To test the efficacy of this formulation, subjects were asked how hard they tried to "appear strong" to the other in the second half of the experiment, with responses ranging from "tried very hard" (9) to "didn't try at all" (1). Analysis of variance on this item (shown in Table 9) revealed sharp differences between audience-feedback conditions, but no differences due to the other manipulations or to their interaction. Table 10 shows that concern with "appearing strong" to the other was more prevalent in the "looked foolish" condition than in either the "not foolish" or control groups. It was this potent motivational factor, presumably, that caused humiliated subjects to retaliate against the other player.

Table 8

NUMBER OF TRIALS ON WHICH THE STOOGE BACKED OUT
OF HEAD-ON COLLISION AFTER THIRTY SECONDS

Other's knowledge of subject's costs	Audience condition			
	"Looked foolish" $(\bar{X})$	"Did not look foolish" $(\bar{X})$	Control, no feedback $(\bar{X})$	Overall $(\bar{X})$
Other knew own costs	2.70	0.30	1.60	1.53
Other ignorant of own costs	3.50	1.30	1.30	2.03
Overall	3.10	0.80	1.45	1.78[a]

Results of t-test comparisons
t (Foolish, not foolish) = 2.85, 38 df, p = <.01
t (Foolish, control) = 1.78, 38 df, p = <.06
t (Not foolish, control) = 0.94, 38 df, p = n.s.

[a] Grand mean.

Table 9

RESULTS OF ANALYSIS OF VARIANCE OF EXTENT TO WHICH SUBJECTS TRIED
TO APPEAR STRONG TO THE OTHER PLAYER
DURING THE SECOND TEN TRIALS

Source	df	MS	F
Audience condition (columns)	2	31.02	3.86*
Other's knowledge of "own" costs (rows)	1	7.36	<1.00
Interaction	2	3.05	<1.00
Error	54	8.03	
Total	59		

* $p < .05$.

DISCUSSION

The results of the experiment leave little room for doubt; when bargainers have been made to look foolish and weak before a salient audience, they are likely to retaliate against whoever caused their humiliation. Moreover, retaliation will be chosen despite the knowledge that doing so may require the sacrifice of all or large portions of the available outcomes. Such behavior will be most apparent, however, when bargainers believe that their costs are unknown to their opponent. A significant finding is that humiliated subjects soon discovered a means of retaliation that surpassed the charging of high tolls—by causing head-on collisions and then blocking for prolonged periods, subjects spread the conflict beyond the limits set by the "rules" of the game.

Several factors increased the likelihood

Table 10

EXTENT TO WHICH SUBJECTS TRIED TO APPEAR STRONG TO THE OTHER
PLAYER DURING THE SECOND TEN TRIALS

Other's knowledge of subject's costs	Audience condition			
	"Looked foolish" $(\overline{X})$	"Did not look foolish" $(\overline{X})$	Control, no feedback $(\overline{X})$	Overall $(\overline{X})$
Other knew own costs	6.90	4.60	5.50	5.67
Other ignorant of own costs	8.00	5.80	5.30	6.37
Overall	7.45	5.20	5.40	6.02[a]
Results of *t*-test comparisons				
t (Foolish, not foolish) = 2.54, 38 df, $p = <.02$				
t (Foolish, control) = 2.47, 38 df, $p = <.02$				
t (Not foolish, control) = 0.20, 38 df, $p =$ n.s.				

* Grand mean.

of obtaining support for the hypotheses. Using adolescent subjects, to whom favorable self-presentation is so salient (Erikson, 1963; Coleman, 1961) is one such factor. Another is that subjects received numerous cues indicating that their opponent was much like themselves in several respects. Deutsch (1961) and Borah (1963) have pointed out that intimidation by an "equal" as opposed to a "superior" is more likely to cause resistance.

Of importance, too, is the possibility that while the feedback given to subjects in the "looked foolish" condition served to increase their concern with "looking strong," the "not foolish" feedback may have had an opposite effect. It may have encouraged subjects to focus on increasing their own payoffs rather than on reducing those of the other player. This argument can be supported by acknowledging that the "not foolish" feedback communicated something more to subjects than was originally anticipated; it may not only

have intimated that they were evaluated positively by the audience, but may also have suggested that the stooge was *disfavored* for being high-handed and charging expensive tolls. The "not foolish" feedback placed implicit value on "playing fair" and thereby communicated to subjects what they had best *not* do if they wanted the audience's continued good favor. Thus, it is likely that subjects in the "looked foolish" condition feared a loss of status and consequently of "face" or not retaliating, while in the "not foolish" condition it was retaliation and subsequent audience disapproval that posed the threat to face. Hence face saving was not only responsible for *retaliation* in the "looked foolish" condition, but may also have been responsible for the *restraint* shown in the "not foolish" condition.

Retaliation was clearly regulated by the information that subjects received about the stooge's knowledge of their costs. The effects on retaliation of the *audience's* knowledge of costs would also be important to determine, but were uncontrolled in the present experiment.

The results of the experiment support the hypotheses and therefore imply that the theoretical formulation of the relationship between face saving and bargaining behavior is a workable one. Several alternative explanations require examination, however, before the face-saving rationale can be adopted with confidence.

One possible interpretation is that the retaliation seen in the experiment was caused by a "revenge" motive—by the desire to inflict harm on the other—rather than by a desire to save or restore face atfer exposure to humiliation. The fact that subjects in the "not foolish" condition engaged in significantly less retaliatory behavior than those in the control or "foolish" conditions supports the notion that simple revenge was probably not the *primary* motivating factor. (This was corroborated by postexperimental questionnaire data showing that subjects who "looked foolish" also became more concerned with appearing strong to the stooge than did other subjects.) The latter finding approaches the definition of face restoration advanced earlier—that people will try to reassert their capability and strength after being humiliated even if it may be costly to do so. More importantly, an adequate defense of the revenge interpretation would require an explanation of the differences in toll-charging behavior within the control condition produced by the "knowledge of costs" manipulations. No such explanation can be formulated on the basis of revenge. Subjects intent on pure "harmful vengeance" might reasonably be expected to seek it *regardless*

of the other's knowledge of their costs. Thus, the significant differences in retaliation within the control condition are tied more clearly to the bargainer's "face" vis-à-vis the other, than to revenge.

Yet another hypothesis is that subjects charged high tolls because they were influenced by the "reciprocity" norm already discussed. The notion that one will give back to another an equivalent measure of something received does not explain the results of the experiment sufficiently. Had an eye-for-an-eye, tooth-for-a-tooth value been responsible for the observed retaliation, the differences produced by the manipulations would have been attenuated. Thus it may be deduced that the feedback given to subjects about their appearance, as well as the information they received about their costs, influenced their behavior more than did the stooge's general exploitativeness per se.

The main implications of the reported research are that certain structural components of bargaining situations may prompt negotiators into costly and destructive retaliation after they have been publicly exploited. One variable that strongly affects retaliation is whether or not one's costs have been publicized. Another is the presence of an audience and the feedback it gives about the bargainer's appearance during the engagement. It would be of further value to develop procedures to reveal the extent to which face saving influences behavior in such important areas of human relations as labor–management and international negotiations.

REFERENCES

BORAH, L. A., JR. "The Effects of Threat in Bargaining: Critical and Experimental

Analysis." *Journal of Abnormal and Social Psychology*, 1963, 66, 37–44.

COLEMAN, J. *The Adolescent Society.* New York: Free Press, 1961.

DEUTSCH, M. "The Face of Bargaining." *Operations Research*, 1961, 9, 886–897.

DEUTSCH, M., and KRAUSS, R. "The Effects of Threat on Interpersonal Bargaining." *Journal of Abnormal and Social Psychology*, 1960, 61, 223–230.

DEUTSCH, M., and KRAUSS, R. "Studies of Interpersonal Bargaining." *Journal of Conflict Resolution*, 1962, 6, 52–76.

DUNCAN, D. "Multiple Range and Multiple F Tests." *Biometrics*, 1955, 2, 1–42.

ERIKSON, E. *Childhood and Society.* (2nd ed.) New York: Norton and Co., 1963.

GALLO, P. "Effects of Increased Incentives Upon the Use of Threat in Bargaining." *Journal of Personality and Social Psychology*, 1966, 4, 14–21.

GOFFMAN, E. "On Face Work." *Psychiatry*, 1955, 18, 213–231.

GOFFMAN, E. *The Presentation of Self in Everyday Life.* Edinburgh: Univer. of Edinburgh Press, 1956.

GOFFMAN, E. *Behavior in Public Places.* New York: Free Press, 1963.

GOULDNER, A. "The Norm of Reciprocity: A Preliminary Statement." In E. P. Hollander and R. G. Hunt (Eds.), *Current Perspectives in Social Psychology.* New York: Oxford Univer. Press, 1963. Pp. 269–281.

HORNSTEIN, H. "The Effects of Different Magnitudes of Threat upon Interpersonal Bargaining." *Journal of Experimental Social Psychology*, 1965, 1, 282–293.

KELLEY, H. H. "Experimental Studies of Threats in Interpersonal Negotiations." *Journal of Conflict Resolution*, 1965, 9, 79–105.

SCHELLING, T. C. *The Strategy of Conflict.* Cambridge, Mass.: Harvard Univer. Press, 1960.

SIEGEL, S., and FOURAKER, L. E. *Bargaining and Group Decision Making.* New York: McGraw-Hill, 1960.

WILSON, K. V., and BIXENSTINE, V. E. "Forms of Social Control in Two-Person Two-Choice Games." In M. Shubik (Ed.), *Game Theory and Related Approaches to Social Behavior.* New York: McGraw-Hill, 1964. Pp. 338–358.

VIII

COALITION FORMATION
EXPERIMENTS

AN EXPERIMENTAL STUDY OF COALITIONS
IN THE TRIAD*

W. Edgar Vinacke and Abe Arkoff

Increasing attention has been given to the study of very small interacting groups like the dyad and the triad, models of interaction that are rather easily adapted to experimentation and to theorizing. The three-person situation can be studied in a variety of ways, ranging from the observation of how the members act towards each other[1] to the strict formulation of experimental conditions together with predictions regarding their consequences.[2] A purely rational approach is provided by the theory of games,[3] although there has, as yet, been comparatively incomplete analysis of three-person games.

The point of most interest to social psychologists is the degree to which interaction corresponds to expectations stemming from the perceptions and motives of the participants, compared to those which would ensue from the rational considerations developed by game theorists. The latter base their interpretations upon what would happen were the players to be guided solely by strict adherence to the conditions specified by the rules of the game, and, further, were each player to act according to complete understanding of the final consequences of his play. Clear examples of the difference between

* W. Edgar Vinacke and Abe Arkoff, "An Experimental Study of Coalitions in the Triad," *American Sociological Review*, 22 (1957), 406–14. Reprinted by permission.

[1] For instance, the Bales system for recording interaction could be employed for these very small groups (R. F. Bales, *Interaction Process Analysis: A Method for the Study of Small Groups*, Cambridge: Addison Wesley, 1950). Cf. The effective use of this technique, in Fred L. Strodtbeck, "The Family as a Three-Person Group," *American Sociological Review*, 19 (February, 1954), pp. 23–29.

[2] E.g., as in Theodore M. Mills, "The Coalition Pattern in Three-Person Groups," *American Sociological Review*, 19 (December, 1954), pp. 657–667; in E. Paul Torrance, "Some Consequences of Power Differences in Decision Making in Permanent and Temporary Three-Man Groups," in A. Paul Hare, Edgar F. Borgatta, and Robert F. Bales (editors), *Small Groups: Studies in Social Interaction*,

New York: Knopf, 1955, pp. 482–492; in Strodtbeck, *op. cit.*; see also W. Edgar Vinacke, *The Miniature Social Situation*, Honolulu: University of Hawaii Psychological Laboratory, 1954. The last source gives a thorough treatment of methodological problems in the use of small laboratory groups.

[3] John von Neumann and Oskar Morgenstern, *Theory of Games and Economic Behavior*, Princeton: Princeton University Press, 1944; John C. C. McKinsey, *Introduction to the Theory of Games*, New York: McGraw-Hill, 1952.

purely rational behavior and that which actually occurs in three-person groups is rather difficult to find, although a large amount of research is available on how factors such as status and need operate to influence the character of social interaction. These studies provide ample basis for inferring that there is indeed at least very frequent divergence between what would be expected on *a priori* rational grounds and what really transpires.

It is clear that the differential strength or power characterizing members of the group is a significant factor, one, in fact, that has numerous psychological dimensions not envisaged in game theory. The aim of the present experiment was to determine what actually occurs in three-person groups when the members are initially confronted with a variety of seeming power-relationships to each other. The point of departure was a series of hypotheses proposed by Caplow.[4] He describes situations in which all three participants are equal in perceived power, ones in which one member is seen as much stronger than the other two (even in combination), and ones in which one or two persons are perceptibly stronger (but not so much so that the others in combination would not be more powerful).

After defining the six types of triad, Caplow proposes, as a consequence of logical analysis, that certain kinds of two-person coalitions can be predicted for each type. The six types and the hypotheses derived from them may be formulated as follows where the letters A, B, C denote persons:

Type I (1–1–1):[5] Where $A = B = C$, any combination is equally likely (i.e., there will be no difference in frequency among the alliances AB, AC, BC).

Type II (3–2–2): Where $A > B$, $B = C$, and $A < (B + C)$, the two weaker members will tend to form an alliance (BC will occur more often than AB or AC).

Type III (1–2–2): Where $A < B$ and $B = C$, coalitions including the weaker member are most likely (AB and AC will occur more often than BC).

Type IV (3–1–1): Where $A > (B + C)$ and $B = C$, no coalition is likely.

Type V (4–3–2): Where $A > B > C$ and $A < (B + C)$, the strongest member will least often be involved in coalitions (coalitions AC and BC will occur more often than AB).

Type VI (4–2–1): Where $A > B > C$, and $A > (B + C)$, no coalition is likely. Although additional propositions could be deduced, the present experiment was designed to test the six hypotheses stated above.

One must distinguish between two basic considerations that determine the strategy to be pursued by the members of the groups—let us call them players, since we will be concerned with a game. On the one hand, rational analysis of the final outcome—winning the game—can determine play; that is, a player might act solely in terms of how he can best achieve maximum winnings, in which case he must satisfactorily predict how each of the other two must act in order to win. This

[4] Theodore Caplow, "A Theory of Coalitions in the Triad," *American Sociological Review*, 21 (August, 1956), pp. 489–493.

[5] The figure in parentheses shows the strengthvalue assigned to members of the triad in the present experiment; thus, in Type I, each participant has a strength of "1."

analysis is a concern of the theory of games. On the other hand, play may be determined according to the conditions that obtain at the point where play begins, that is, in terms of how the player interprets the position of himself in relation to the other two players. It is here, apparently, that Caplow's hypotheses apply.

Consider from the first point of view how members must assess the situation. Each player seeks to guarantee that he will win (or be on the winning side). There are only two possibilities in the six types presented above: (a) in Type IV and VI only the strong man can possibly win and (b) in any of the other four types any couple can beat the third member, and, further, no one can win without forming a coalition. This assumes where one is initially stronger that the others will inevitably unite against him, and hence, he, too, must join a coalition in order to win. From this standpoint, alone, the initial power distribution in the case of (b) is meaningless, for, regardless of his own seeming strength, each player must enter a coalition with someone else. If the analysis is carried a step further, it is evident that no one can hope to obtain a greater advantage within the coalition than anyone else, so that not only is every pair equally likely to form a coalition, but every man must agree either to an equal division of the spoils or to give the greater share to his partner. A specific example will illustrate the point. Consider Type V, where initial power is divided on a 4–3–2 basis. It might be supposed that 3 and 2 would join forces because 4 is stronger; yet 4 must reason that exactly this situation would occur, hence, in order to win he must himself form a coalition with either 3 or 2. At the same time, he must anticipate that both 3 and 2 would be unwilling to give him more than 50 per cent of the winnings, because they could get at least that much by joining forces themselves. As a consequence, 4 would inevitably have to offer either 3 or 2 at least 50 per cent. Thus, all three are actually on an equal footing so far as winning is concerned. Exactly the same kind of reasoning applies to Types I, II, and III.

We can conclude, therefore, that only two types are really represented, those where each possible coalition is equally likely (types I, II, III, and V), and those where no coalition would form (Type IV and VI).

Let us turn now to the other factor, that involving the perceptions of the players at the outset of the game. Here, a very different interpretation arises, indeed, the very one proposed by Caplow. In this case, each player acts according to his initially perceived relation to the other two, rather than in terms of the final outcome of the game. There is no need to repeat Caplow's hypotheses, for they are clear enough in this sense.

Only one additional point is essential. Caplow's interpretation is supported by the fact that more reasoning is required in the case of certain participants than for others. For example, it is harder for an initially stronger member to reach the conclusion that relative strengths are irrelevant (Types II, III, and V) than for the other one or two to arrive at this interpretation. In effect, the weaker members can immediately understand the necessity for forming a coalition, whereas the stronger member must go through more complex reasoning to do so. The theory of games, however, would not take this into account, but simply assumes that each player carries out all the steps required to act rationally.

We are left with the conclusion that an actual concrete test of Caplow's hypotheses will constitute a determination of the degree to which persons act according to rational analysis of the outcome of the game or whether they act according to their perceptions of the initial position they hold in relation to the other two. The experiment reported here permits a tentative answer to this question.

METHOD

Ninety male students from an introductory psychology course served as subjects in groups of three, making a total of thirty groups. A simple game situation was devised, in which different patterns of initial strength could readily be established, and yet of sufficient complexity to challenge the interest of the players. Power was varied according to a prearranged plan. There was every indication that the game succeeded in arousing keen interest and strong competition.

Apparatus for the experiment consisted of a modified pachisi board. Only the exterior lanes of the board were used, and the spaces of these lanes were numbered consecutively making a total of 67 spaces. The object of the game was to reach "home" first. The winner was awarded a prize of 100 points. In the event of a coalition, the prize was shared in a manner agreed upon by the allies. A single die, cast by the experimenter, was used. Each player's move was determined by the weight inscribed on the counter he drew from a hopper; he was entitled to move forward the number of spaces equal to his weight times the number shown by the die. All of the players started from the same home base and moved simultaneously, that is, every player moved each time the die was thrown.

At any time during the game, any player, in return for a promise of a specified portion of the prize, could form an alliance with any other player. In this case, the allies immediately pooled their strengths and proceeded to a position equal to their combined acquired spaces; in future throws they moved forward according to their combined weights (times the die). Once an alliance was formed it was considered permanent for that game. Any player could concede defeat when his position appeared hopeless. Instructions presented to each player contained all these details of the game.

Before each game the experimenter, according to a prearranged schedule, placed three counters in the hopper with inscribed weights appropriate to the hypotheses. These weights were as follows:

Type	Weights		
	A	B	C
I. A=B=C	1	1	1
II. A>B, B=C, A<(BC)	3	2	2
III. A<B, B=C	1	2	2
IV. A>(B+C), B=C	3	1	1
V. A>B>C, A<(B+C)	4	3	2
VI. A>B>C, A>(B+C)	4	2	1

Each group of subjects played through three series of games. Each series was composed of six games, one of each type; thus, each group played eighteen games. The serial order of types within each series was arranged according to a Latin square design which varied each type's position in the series systematically and ruled out the effect of the position of types in the series.

Rotation of conditions was by type of initial strength, not necessarily by player, which was left to chance in the drawing of counters. Order of draw was, however, rotated in order among the three participants, so that each drew first, second, and last an equal number of times. Once the draw was completed, each player was called "A," "B," or "C," depending upon the weight he drew. In instances where two or three members had the same weight, designation was by color of the

Table 1

COALITIONS FORMED IN THE SIX TYPES OF POWER-PATTERNS IN TRIADS*

Allies	Type I (1–1–1)†	Type II (3–2–2)	Type III (1–2–2)	Type IV (3–1–1)	Type V (4–3–2)	Type VI (4–2–1)
AB	33	13	24	11	9	9
AC	17	12	40	10	20	13
BC	30	64	15	7	59	8
Total	80	89	79	28	88	30
No Coalition)	10‡	1	11	62	2	60
χ^2	5.43	59.61	12.19	.93	47.07	1.40
d.f.	2	2	2	2	2	2
P	>.05	<.01	<.01	<.70	<.01	<.50

* In all tables, N=90 games for each type.
† The figures in parentheses show the power of the three members, e.g., in Type I, A=1, B=1, and C=1. In computing χ^2, it was assumed that each pair would occur an equal number of times by chance.
‡ There were two three-way coalitions in this type; in a sense these might be considered to be mutual non-aggression pacts.

counter (e.g., in Type I, green was always "A," blue was always "B," and red was always "C").

Finally, it should be noted that once the draw was completed, no further change in advantage was possible except through coalition. The option of "conceding" made it unnecessary to play any longer once the outcome was assured. In point of fact, the winner was decided without any play at all (i.e., the die was not even thrown) in 70 per cent of the games, ranging among types from 64 per cent to 73 per cent). Most of these occurred in the second or third series of games, indicating that players learned to decide the result without play. It may also be that players learned how to play more rationally, with the consequence that Series III may constitute a better test of the hypotheses from the theory of games.

RESULTS

We shall first address ourselves to the hypotheses arising from Caplow's analysis. That is, we shall present the evidence con-

cerning coalitions actually formed in each of the six types of initial power distribution. Then we shall analyze certain other kinds of behavior, and relate the results to expectations derived from the theory of games.

Table 1 gives the distribution of coalitions for each type of triad. The evidence from the present experiment bearing upon Caplow's hypotheses may be summarized as follows:

1. In Type I, all three possible coalitions occurred a large number of times, but coalition AC is under-represented to a degree that approaches significance (P>.05). Detailed analysis failed to disclose any reason for this anomaly, so that it may simply have arisen by chance.[6] We can conclude, tentatively, that the first hypothesis is confirmed. (See, also, Table 2 where no difference occurred among the players with respect to the initiation of alliances.)

---

[6] Note in Table 4 that AC was least frequent in Series I and III, but about as expected in Series II. No apparent reason for this could be identified.

Table 2

MEMBER OF THE TRIAD INITIATING THE OFFER TO FORM A COALITION*

Initiator	Type I (1–1–1)	Type II (3–2–2)	Type III (1–2–2)	Type IV (3–1–1)	Type V (4–3–2)	Type VI (4–2–1)
A	21	17	28	2	18	4
B	26	40	18	32	26	19
C	26	31	27	20	43	26
Total†	73	88	73	54	87	49
χ^2	.69	9.17	2.49	25.33	11.24	15.50
d.f.	2	2	2	2	2	2
P	>.70	.01	<.30	<.01	<.01	<.01

* N=90 games for each type.

† In certain instances it was impossible to decide who initiated the offer, hence N's differ slightly from those in Table 1. There are also offers made when no coalition was formed, especially in Types IV and VI.

2. In Type II, as hypothesized, coalition BC is formed significantly more often than the other two. The second hypothesis is therefore confirmed.

3. In Type III, coalitions AB and AC were predicted as most probable. It is evident that both occur more often than coalition BC, but AC occurs relatively more frequently than AB. In general, the hypothesis is confirmed, but not in a uniform manner.

4. For Type IV it was hypothesized that few coalitions would be formed. The occurrence of only 28 alliances (31 per cent) is significantly less than in Types I, II, III, and V (P<.01). Thus, the fourth hypothesis is confirmed.

5. In Type V, it is quite apparent that the hypothesized result took place; coalition BC occurred most often, with AC next.

6. In Type VI, as in Type IV, it was hypothesized that few coalitions would be formed. Since only 30 alliances (33 per cent) were made (significantly different from Types I, II, III, and V, P<.01), this hypothesis is confirmed. To sum up, it is clear that the results agree very well with preliminary analysis by Caplow.

Turning now to additional points, the present experiment permitted analysis of behavior that accompanied establishment of coalitions, namely, which partner initiated the alliance and what sort of agreement was reached. Table 2 presents evidence pertinent to the initiation of alliances. There was no significant tendency in either Type I or Type III, for any member to propose coalition more often than any other. In the other four types, however, marked differences occurred as to which participant initiated attempts at coalition. In these types it is clear that the players who were initially weakest were most likely to seek alliances, namely, B and C in Type II, B and C in Type IV, B and C in Type V, and B and C in Type VI.

Finally, Table 3 presents the kinds of agreements or "deals" involved in the alliances. It is evident that the kind of perceived power pattern strongly influenced the sort of agreement reached. Where discrepancies in strength were perceptually very pronounced (Types IV and VI), highly disproportionate division of the prize occurred.[7] Where the partners were

---

[7] An analysis not given here shows that the division of the prize agrees significantly with

equal to begin with, or nearly so (Types I and II), equal division was the rule. In situations where one of the participants was weaker than the other two (Types III and V; also Type VI), unequal, but not pronouncedly so, deals were made.

Turning to the alternative hypotheses suggested in the theory of games, the rational considerations we have postulated propose that (a) no coalitions will occur in Types IV and VI, and (b) no differences will occur in the other types in the frequency with which each of the three possible coalitions is formed. The first expectation is generally in agreement with Caplow's hypotheses, but the second is not, except for the initially equal condition of Type I. For Types II, III, and V, therefore, confirmation of Caplow's hypotheses constitutes negative evidence for expectations from game theory. Exceptions run counter to both theories, although the Caplow approach can readily account for them by invoking a variety of psychological and social factors.[8]

Since the results support Caplow very well, we must reject the interpretation, in this instance, in terms of game theory. That is, rather than employing a strategy based upon recognition of the irrelevance of the initial strength relationships, members of triads acted according to their per-

ceptions of these power systems. In Types II, III, and V, to be quite explicit, the expectation that all possible coalitions would occur equally often was not borne out.

There are, however, two additional points to be examined before the hypotheses from the theory of games are finally rejected.[9] First, we can assume that some learning took place from the first to the third series of games, a possible consequence being that players would come to act more rationally (according to analysis of outcome). Second, one might regard those triads that did not act according to game theory as "exceptions" to rational play, and examine the reasons.

With respect to learning, Table 4 presents relevant data. There is no significant difference between Series I and Series III in kinds of coalition formed, so far as Types I, II, III, and V are concerned, i.e., in those situations where strictly rational considerations would result in a tendency for each possible coalition to occur equally often. In short, the experience of playing through two series (60 games) does not teach the players to base their play on outcome, rather than perception of initial strength.

There is, however, a learning effect with respect to the necessity to form coalitions. This is shown in two ways. First, players learn that coalitions are essential in Types I, II, III, and V, since 83 per cent of the non-coalitions for these types occur in

---

the difference in strength of the partners. In Type VI, for example, the deals in the category "1/99 to 29/71" favor "A." The uniformity of this result for other types, also, runs counter to expectations from the theory of games.

[8] For instance, Caplow point out that coalitions in Types IV and VI may result from "extraneous" factors such as an appeal to goodwill. We found that this is often the case.

---

[9] A third point we consider inappropriate, namely, that our situation was not a sufficiently pure test of game theory—that, for example, we might have instructed the subjects in how to analyze outcome. This would be like looking at all four hands in a bridge game.

Table 3

KINDS OF AGREEMENT REACHED IN SIX TYPES OF POWER PATTERNS IN TRIADS*

Division of Prize	Type I (1–1–1)		Type II (3–2–2)		Type III (1–2–2)		Type IV (3–1–1)		Type V (4–3–2)		Type VI (4–2–1)	
	N	Per Cent	N	Per Cent	N	Per Cent	N	Per Cent	N	Per Cent	N	Per Cent
30/50	48	60	62	70	31	39	11	39	41	47	7	28
30/70 to 49/51	25	31	21	24	30	38	3	11	39	44	9	30
1/99 to 29/71	7	9	6	7	18	23	14	50	8	9	14	47
Total	80†	100	89	101	79	100	28	100	88	100	30	100
χ^2	31.64		56.59		3.98		6.96		23.36		2.60	
d.f.	2		2		2		2		2		2	
P	<.01		<.01		<.20		<.05		<.01		<.30	

* N=90 games for each type.
† Two triple coalitions omitted.

Table 4

COALITIONS FORMED IN SIX TYPES OF TRIAD FOR EACH SERIES OF GAMES*

Allies	Series	Type I (1–1–1)	Type II (3–2–2)	Type III (1–2–2)	Type IV (3–1–1)	Type V (4–3–2)	Type VI (4–2–1)
AB	I	9	4	7	4	3	4
	II	10	5	10	5	2	2
	III	14	4	7	2	4	3
	Total	33	13	24	11	9	9
AC	I	3	3	9	2	5	4
	II	9	5	17	4	7	6
	III	5	4	14	4	8	3
	Total	17	12	40	10	20	13
BC	I	11	22	3	7	21	7
	II	9	20	3	0	20	0
	III	10	22	9	0	18	1
	Total	30	64	15	7	59	8
No Coalition	I	7	1	11	17	1	15
	II	2	0	0	21	1	22
	III	1	0	0	24	0	23
	Total	10	1	11	62	2	60

* N=90 games for each type.
Note: There are no statistically significant differences between Series I and III, except for "No Coalition," as pointed out in the text.

Series I, and only 4 per cent occur in Series III. Second, players learn that it is unnecessary to form coalitions in Types IV and VI, since 39 per cent of the non-coalitions occur in Series III, but only 26 per cent in Series I. All but one of the former include the strongest member. This effect agrees with either set of hypotheses, but more with Caplow's, which allows for some coalition in these types.

Consider now the instances that fail to agree with the hypotheses of rational play —the possible "exceptions." A general kind of exception may be noted first. In Table 3 it is shown that a very high proportion of the deals were of the 50/50 variety; of these, in turn, 79 per cent involved no bargaining, i.e., the first offer was accepted. A difficulty arises in the case of these coalitions because we cannot be certain why they took place. According to game theory, we should expect this result, because a 50/50 deal is the best that can rationally be obtained—no player who finds himself in a position to enter this kind of deal would entertain another offer. No bargaining would occur, in this case. Yet, the Caplow analysis also enables us to expect the same result, for in Types I, II, III, and IV there are at least two players who perceive themselves as equal, hence would be reluctant to form disproportionate alliances. Fortunately, a partial test is provided by an analysis of which players formed 50/50 deals. The pattern corresponds precisely with what would be expected from the distribution in Table 4. In the two crucial Types II and III, 50/50 coalitions without bargaining occurred in Series III as follows: Type II with 18 of these alliances —AB 11 per cent, AC 11 per cent, and BC 78 per cent; Type III with 12 of these alliances—AB 8 per cent, AC 33 per cent,

and BC 58 per cent. In sum, the conclusion is warranted that players made deals in accordance with perceived strength, with the result that those having the same weight divided the prize equally, and those having different weights made disproportionate agreements.

Other ways of viewing exceptions are to look at Table 1 for occurrences that depart from an equal distribution (Types I, II, III, and V), or which represent the formation or non-formation of coalitions contrary to hypotheses (Types IV and VI, especially).

An exhaustive analysis of all possible kinds of exceptions failed to disclose any factor that would explain them, save as already mentioned in terms of initial perceptions of strength. Space precludes giving all of these attempts, but one is worth mentioning. Scrutiny of the data reveals only one phenomenon that can confidently be identified as exceptional, namely, the cases where coalitions were formed in Types IV and VI, contrary to both sets of hypotheses. Accordingly, all groups that formed at least one coalition among these six games were compared in detail with those that never established a coalition under these conditions. The latter numbered eight groups; eleven made coalitions in one or two games of these types; and the remaining eleven made coalitions in from three to six of them. A rough index of "irrational" play is thus available, using Types IV and VI as criteria. Judgments of rationality were made for each game of Types I, II, III, and V, based upon what would be expected with complete analysis of outcome. Unfortunately, no significant differences in number of games played rationally in the other four types occurred for the groups playing most rationally on Types IV and VI compared to those groups playing least rationally. Indeed, a game-by-game analysis disclosed the remarkable fact that among the groups which played "irrationally" on all six games of Types IV and VI, one of them played "rationally" on all 12 games of the other four types; among the eight groups which played "rationally" on all six games of Types IV and VI, only one group played "rationally" in the other 12 games.[10]

DISCUSSION

We have suggested that behavior displayed by three persons in a competitive game situation may be considered from either of two points of view. According to one, the game may be played strictly in terms of the final outcome, insofar as this can be determined. Ordinary games depend upon individual skill or luck to make the outcome uncertain, so that winning requires a manipulation of these elements. Under these conditions, although alliances of either a temporary or lasting character may occur, each player strives to overcome all his rivals. In the game-situation utilized in this experiment, however, the element of luck enters solely at the time of the initial drawing of weights; thereafter, the value of the die is exactly the same for all participants at each throw, that is, all move simultaneously.

---

[10] An average of 27 per cent of the games of Types I, II, III, and IV were played "irrationally" by the eight most "rational" groups, compared to 35 per cent by the seven least "rational" groups, using the Type IV–VI criterion. This difference does not even approach statistical significance, employing a t-test.

Ostensibly, skill enters only to the extent that one player can outwit another in establishing an alliance which permits him to be on the winning side. The outcome simply depends upon which pair unites its forces (excluding the times when one man is stronger than the other two in combination). Thus, from this standpoint alone, all other factors are irrelevant—the number of moves specified by the die, the initial weights, and the position of the players during the course of the game. We deduce from purely rational considerations that a strategy based on outcome would actually place each player on an equal footing with each other player. Thus, for the four types of games where alliances are necessary to win, no coalition is any more likely than any other, and, further, no one can assume that he should receive a larger portion of the winnings than his partner.

According to the other view, strategy can be based upon the initial perceptions of the relative strengths of the three players. Under these circumstances, (excluding, again, the straight power types), four different patterns were present, the assessment of which would lead to the notion that winning depends upon balancing one set of weights against another set. In this event, the moves permitted by the value of the die are not immediately seen to be irrelevant (although sooner or later this conclusion is reached, as witnessed by the abandonment of actual play following the setting of coalitions). Further, the initial weights are regarded as anything but irrelevant; on the contrary, coalitions are based upon them, to a very great degree, both in the seeking of a partner and in the kind of division of the winnings agreed upon. The hypotheses proposed by Caplow, it is suggested, pertain to this strategy, actually stating what would be expected were players attending to the initial distribution of strength, rather than to the outcome.

As a test of these two modes of viewing the game, our experiment sustains Caplow's hypotheses, rather than those predicated upon *a priori* analysis of outcome (what has been referred to as "rational" play). This is not to say that members of the triads did not play to win, nor that they did not behave in a fashion to guarantee their winning. Rather it means that players saw their best strategy to lie in manipulating the positions in which they initially found themselves. Such evidence as we were able to obtain indicated that this consideration determined the play of all groups at least some of the time, and most of the groups most of the time. In short, we have no evidence that any group really discovered the strategy based on analysis of outcome.

It must be remembered that people tend to act according to their perceptions of a situation, and not according to what a fully informed theorist might expect. People play games, very often, according to the apparently advantageous strategy rather than the strategy they ought to follow. In our game situation, they played the way they thought they had to play in order to win. It happens, apparently, that they played in terms of the initial distribution of strength, rather than in terms of purely rational analysis of outcome. After the fact, it is really not surprising that our groups behaved as they did, for they simply acted according to their perceptions.

A few remarks may be made about this particular game situation. For one thing, it is evident that, as various persons have pointed out, the triad situation may favor weaker members over those who are initially stronger. (Indeed, according to our analysis in terms of outcome, the initially weakest person may actually be equal to the strongest.) Where play was determined by initial perception of strength, the weakest member was found to be most often a member of the winning coalition; furthermore, his share of the winnings was larger than his strength might seem to warrant, mainly because there was competition for him, because the other players saw him as weaker, hence more readily to be induced into partnership.

Turning to the straight power conditions (Types IV and VI), where one member is stronger than the other two combined, no coalition is likely unless some "extraneous means" is found to persuade the strongest player to enter an alliance, or unless the two weaker members fail properly to assess their position. In the present experiment, although relatively fewer coalitions were formed in these situations than in the others, nevertheless, a substantial number occurred (in 31 per cent and 33 per cent of the games in Types IV and VI, respectively). We have pointed out above that there is a tendency for players to learn not to form coalitions in these types; however, even on the third series of games, coalitions were formed in 20 per cent of the games in Type IV and 23 per cent of the games in Type VI. In fact, learning was more a matter of eliminating coalitions between the two weak players than of avoiding coalitions (see Table 4). If any evidence were needed that players are not guided primarily by "rational" considerations, it is provided by this result. It is true that in some instances, players did not fully understand their actual position, i.e., that the strongest member could win no matter what they did. At other times, however, "extraneous" factors were amply apparent. Appeals were made not to be "greedy," or to oppose a third member who appeared to be successful in a disproportionate number of games, or as a reward for past alliance or promise for future ones. Numerous other factors could be cited, but these are enough to illustrate that even where rational play is easiest to understand, there is no reason to expect that players will act in all instances according to expectation.

Although observed only rarely in this experiment, there were also a couple of instances in which semi-permanent alliances appeared to develop. In particular, one case was noted in which two subjects of an experimental group almost invariably allied against a third. Thus, except when the third player drew invincible power in Type IV or VI, his opponents were assured of a share in the prize. As the games continued, each member of this alliance became increasingly reluctant to make overtures or to entertain offers from the third member of the triad, since to do so would, as each openly expressed it, invite his ally to do likewise, with the result that security would be disrupted. For his part, the third member of the triad attempted to break the alliance, even to the extent of offering to form a coalition when he drew the unbeatable position in Type IV or VI, but to no avail.[11]

---

[11] Personality variables were readily apparent in many other ways, too, which space limitations preclude discussing. Certainly, a situation such as ours is very well suited to the experimental manipulation of motives, attitudes, traits, etc.

SUMMARY AND CONCLUSIONS

A simple game situation was devised to test hypotheses formulated by Caplow pertaining to the formation of coalitions in triads having six patterns of initial strength. The data also were examined in terms of expectations derived from game theory. The two sets of hypotheses were interpreted to stem from perception of initial strength (Caplow) and from analysis of final outcome (game theory). Data were obtained from thirty groups, each playing three games of each type, or 18 in all. Strength was varied by having players draw counters with requisite weights. Conclusions are as follows:

1. Coalitions formed under the conditions of this experiment conformed to Caplow's predictions, and run counter to those based on the theory of games. That is, players appeared to be influenced primarily by perception of their relative strengths at the outset of the game.

2. There was no evidence that players tended to play more in terms of analysis of outcome ("rational" strategy) in later series of games. They did, however, learn when coalitions are either essential or non-essential.

3. The initiation of offers to ally conformed to the initial power patterns of the game. In general, players perceiving themselves as weaker significantly more often initiated offers.

4. The general kinds of agreement reached corresponded closely to perception of initial strength. Bargaining sometimes resulted in alliances that deviated from this relationship, but these departures could also be accounted for in terms of strategy based on perception of initial strength.

COALITIONS IN THE TRIAD: CRITIQUE AND EXPERIMENT*

Harold H. Kelley and A. John Arrowood

Vinacke and Arkoff (4) have presented an experiment which tests some of Caplow's hypotheses (2) about how the relative power of three persons affects the formation of pair coalitions. The situation studied is one in which each person is trying to obtain for himself as much of some valuable but scarce commodity as he can. The three individuals differ in ways relevant to their ability to gain a share of the rewards (referred to as "power"). This work has been especially interesting because of the paradoxical result that with certain distributions of power among the three individuals, in Caplow's words, "the triadic situation often favors the weaker over the strong." Under certain conditions the stronger of the three is at a disadvantage and actually receives the smallest share of the available rewards.

The purpose of the present research is to state with greater precision than heretofore the conditions under which this phenomenon prevails and to test experimentally some of the limits of these conditions. In order to do so, it is necessary to clarify certain ambiguities in the concept of power as used in the Vinacke and Arkoff experiment. This clarification is accomplished through use of the analysis of power provided by Thibaut and Kelley (3).

The problem can best be illustrated by a brief description of the Vinacke and Arkoff procedure. Three subjects play a game in which each moves his counter along the spaces of a game board. The first one to reach the goal receives a prize of 100 points. On successive trials, the experimenter rolls a single die and each player advances a number of spaces determined by the product of two numbers: (a) the number of pips turned up on the die and (b) a "weight," ranging from 1 to 4, which was randomly assigned him at the beginning of the game. For example, in one game player A may have weight 4, player B, weight 2, and player C, weight 1. Since all players start at the same point on the board and move each time the die is cast, the person assigned the largest weight automatically wins. A further rule however, enables any pair of players to form a coalition by combining their weights at any time during the game. When they do so, they are given a single counter placed at a position equal to the sum of the distances the two have attained

* Harold H. Kelley and A. John Arrowood, "Coalitions in the Triad: Critique and Experiment," *Sociometry*, 23 (1960), 231–44. Reprinted by permission of the American Sociological Association.

at that time. On subsequent rolls, they advance according to the sum of their two weights. The formation of a coalition is acknowledged by the experimenter only when the two players have agreed upon how they will divide the 100 point prize, should they receive it; and, once formed, a coalition is indissoluble for the remainder of that game. Thus, the individual or coalition that can mobilize the largest weight automatically wins that game and there is really no need for going through the motions of rolling the die.

The weight each player receives is said to constitute his *power*, but consider this point more closely. In what sense does a player with a weight of 4 have more power than a player with a weight of 2? In the game where the three weights are 4, 2 and 1, the player with the 4 weight has power in the sense that he is able, regardless of the actions of the other two players, to induce his "environment" (the game) to give him the prize. However, in the game with weights 4, 3 and 2, the player with 4 weight can exercise this control over the environment only if the other two players fail to form a coalition. Since any pair can mobilize more weight than the remaining person, each pair has the same amount of power over the third person as does any other pair. The variability in 4's outcomes is as much under the control of the joint actions of the other two players as is the variability in either 2 or 3's outcomes. Hence, as Vinacke and Arkoff point out, the initial weights in the 4–3–2 game are irrelevant with respect to the power a person has in the three-way bargaining situation.

In view of this logical analysis of the objective interdependency relations among the three players, Vinacke and Arkoff's results from the 4–3–2 and similar games are unexpected: The three players treat the weight 4 as if it does yield greater power. As his price for entering a coalition player 4 apparently asks for a lion's share of the prize, because he typically receives more than 50 of the 100 points when he is in a coalition. Furthermore, players 2 and 3 tend to form the majority of the coalitions, presumably because each one can make a better deal with the other than he can with 4. From the point of view of rational analysis, then, the subjects act inappropriately, attributing to 4 a power that he does not in fact possess. The irony of the situation is that this erroneous belief about 4's advantage, which he usually shares, works to his disadvantage in the long run because of his exclusion from coalitions.

The first of the experiments reported below has the purpose of showing that Vinacke and Arkoff's data are, in a sense, spurious. They reflect a misunderstanding of the experimental situation that is not intrinsic to it, but results from the complexity of their total procedure. Confronted with the complexity, subjects erroneously equate initial weights with real power. (Our reasons for believing this erroneous assumption to be a reasonable one, considering the circumstances, are given in the Discussion.) The experimental hypothesis is that with a simpler procedure, subjects will acquire an adequate understanding of the true power relations and act more in accord with a rational analysis of the situation than the Vinacke and Arkoff data would suggest.

The second experiment has the purpose of testing Caplow's hypothesis under conditions where the power differences among the three persons are real rather than illusory. We expect the resulting bias in coalition formation (predominantly between the weaker members) to persist even though subjects are permitted thoroughly to familiarize themselves which the situation. (The limiting conditions under which the Caplow effect can be expected to appear are also described.)

EXPERIMENT I

In the Vinacke and Arkoff procedure, the relationship between weights and power is quite complicated. Each trio of subjects is required to play a series of games in which six different sets of weights are used. In the games played with a given set of values, a player need not have the same weight twice. With some sets of weights (such as 4–2–1) initial weight is relevant to power, and with others (such as 4–3–2) it is not.

In the present experiment, in order to simplify the subjects' task, only one set of weights was used (4–3–2) and each triad was given a lengthy series of trials, each player keeping the same weight throughout. It was expected that, with repeated experience in the single situation, the subjects' analyses of it would come to correspond with the analysis presented above, and their coalition formation and bargaining behavior would be increasingly consistent with an understanding that all players in the game have the same power.

Procedure

Ninety male students, volunteers from an introductory (sophomore) psychology class, served as subjects in thirty experimental triads. There is no reason to believe that the subjects were notably different from Vinacke and Arkoff's. Data were gathered first from 20 triads and, later, from ten additional triads. The first series were given a variable number

of trials (10 to 70 trials, 26 on the average), and in the second series all groups completed 20 trials.

With the exceptions noted above, the experimental procedure followed that of Vinacke and Arkoff as closely as was possible from the available statements of their procedure. A major difference is that, whereas they gave very brief introductory instructions and relied on informal answers to questions to clarify the procedure, we gave rather full formal instructions and tried to minimize the necessity for subjects to ask questions. The subjects were given an individualistic orientation, it being emphasized that each was to accumulate as many points for himself as possible, attempting to maximize his outcomes without regard to those of any other players.

Results

In Table 1 are presented the frequencies of occurrence of the various coalitions. Data from our first and last three trials are presented for comparison with those from Vinacke and Arkoff's three trials in the 4–3–2 condition. They calculated a Chi-square for the 88 instances of coalition formation (excluding the two instances of "no coalition") to determine the likelihood of the departure of the observed distribution from a theoretical distribution in which the three possible coalitions occur equally often. This procedure is not strictly justified, inasmuch as each group of subjects provides three instances of coalition formation, hence the various entries are not independent. However, we present similar Chi-squares in order to provide some basis for comparing the two sets of results.

It appears that the present procedure yields a distribution of coalitions which, although biassed in a manner similar to Vinacke and Arkoff's, is closer to the

Table 1

FREQUENCY OF OCCURRENCE OF VARIOUS COALITIONS IN THE
THREE EXPERIMENTS

	Vinacke and Arkoff's Three Trials		Experiment I					Experiment II			
			First 3 Trials		Last 3 Trials			First 3 Trials		Last 3 Trials	
Coalitions	N	%	N	%	N	%	(Coalitions)	N	%	N	%
2–3	59	66	41	46	37	41	(0–2)	24	53	29	64
2–4	20	22	24	27	26	29	(0–4)	12	27	13	29
3–4	9	10	21	23	27	30	(2–4)	9	20	3	7
No coalition	2	2	4	4	0	..		0	..	0	..
Totals	90	100	90	100	90	100		45	100	45	100

$$\frac{X^2 n = 88}{2df} = 47.07$$

p < .001

$$\frac{X^2 n = 90}{2df} = 2.47$$

.20 < p < .30

$$\frac{X^2 n = 45}{2df} = 22.93$$

p < .001

$$\frac{X^2 n = 86}{2df} = 8.82$$

.01 < p < .02

$$\frac{X^2 n = 45}{2df} = 8.40$$

.01 < d < .02

chance distribution than is theirs. The divergence from the earlier experiment appears even on the first three trials. A comparison of our first three with theirs yields a Chi-square of 8.48, p = .02. (The distribution of first coalitions formed in each triad resembles their distribution most closely, the percentages, in order, being 63, 20 and 17.) These results suggest that, either because of the concentrated experience with the single situation, or perhaps because of greater clarity in the experimental instructions, a number of subjects became aware of the objective power relationships rather early in the game.

From the first to the last trials there is not a significant change in the incidence of the three coalitions, hence we cannot be sure that further experience increased their understanding of the situation. However, this result must be interpreted in the light of the rather limited degree to which

the occurrence of the early coalitions departed from chance. To the extent that subjects achieved an understanding of their relationships very early, further improvement in this respect was limited. Upon examination of the data on a trial-by-trial basis, it is clear that the learning is very rapid, so that after the first three or four trials there is little more than chance exclusion of 4 from coalitions.

In Vinacke and Arkoff's experiment, associated with the tendency for 2 and 3 to be reluctant about forming coalitions with 4, was the tendency for him to receive more than half of the 100 point prize when he did manage to enter a coalition. This effect appears in the early trials of the present experiment and declines, though not significantly so, during its course. During the first three trials, player 4 was a member of a coalition in 26 triads and in 17 of these he managed to come out with more than 50 per cent of the rewards. During the last three trials of the experiment, this was true in only 10 of 29 possible instances. Of the 25 groups in which person 4 was in coalitions during both the first and last three trials, his share of the coalition reward declined in 13 instances, increased in six instances and did not change in the remaining six. Omitting the last six, the difference between the number of decreases and increases yields a p-value of .168 by the Sign test.

There are, then, two behavioral manifestations of the players' perception that 4 has the most power: (a) He is excluded from coalitions and, (b) when he is included in coalitions, he receives more than half the points. When early and later trials are compared, the extent to which 4's frequency of being included increases and the extent to which his percentage winnings per trial decrease provide two indicators of downgrading in the perception of his power. A comparison of the first and last three trials of the experiment reveals that in 18 triads the 4 man was downgraded on both of these indicators or downgraded on one with no change on the other; in six triads, he was upgraded on both indicators or upgraded on one with no change on the other; and in six triads, he did not change on either indicator or was upgraded on one and downgraded on the other. When the last six are omitted from the analysis, the Sign test indicates there was significantly more downgrading than upgrading (p = .026).

On the questionnaire at the end of the experiment all subjects were asked the following open-ended question: "Many subjects believe that 4 is more to be feared, has greater potential, etc. Did you at any time think that this was the case?" All but 14 of the 90 subjects admitted that they at some time had held this belief. This estimate of the extent of the belief, if it errs at all, is probably an underestimate because of the general realization at the end of the experiment of the incorrectness of this view. Most of those admitting to this belief reported having it "at first" or on the first one or two trials. Subjects with the three different weights were equally susceptible to this belief.

The next question asked when the subject realized that no position has any more power than any other and that nobody is justified in asking for more than half the 100 points. Forty-three of the 90 claimed to have realized this before or during the first three trials. Another 33 did not localize their insight so sharply in time. Only 13 admitted they had never realized this. On the basis of their answers to other questions about power relations, preferred position, position likely to win, and ease of bargaining with various positions, another nine subjects were added to the latter category of those who had failed to attain a correct understanding of the situation by the end of the experiment.

In brief, the self-report data suggest that, while some 85 per cent of our subjects believed at some time during the experiment (largely, in the early stages) that the 4 weight carries greatest power, only 25 per cent held this belief at the end of the experiment. As far as we could judge from their answers to questions asked after the experiment, the other 75 per cent had achieved a correct understanding of the power relations and apparently most of them did so during the actual trials of the experiment.

One may ask to what extent this change in belief about power relations reflects the subjects' direct experience with the game, as opposed to their being taught by the small number of their colleagues who had analyzed the situation correctly from the start. To answer this question, a comparison was made between those groups in which, from the sound recordings of the discussion, there appeared to have been some possibility of "teaching," and the remaining groups. There were no differences between the two sets of data either in the amount of learning that took place or in the coalitions formed. Hence, explicit teaching seems not to account for the observed effects.

A final open-ended question asked: "Why do you think that many subjects would believe that 4 is more to be feared, has greater potential, etc.? What is there in the situation that leads to this belief?" The most frequent response, given by 34 of the 90 subjects, dealt with the fact that 4 would win invariably if no coalitions were formed. Another 13 merely stated, without further amplification, that 4 was the largest number. Nine subjects mentioned the mutiplicative aspect of the game, pointing out that multiples of 4 are larger than multiples of 2 or 3. Apparently, the 56 responses in these three categories either discount or overlook the possibility of coalition formation. A fourth category of response deals with 4's "psychological" or "cultural" power. Seventeen of the 90 suggested that it was natural to react to 4's higher weight in the light of their previous experience in games that higher numbers are generally better ones and in everyday life that quantity often has the upper hand. This answer is silent concerning the possibility of coalitions but highlights the stereotype that "more is "better."

It is difficult to evaluate the validity of these post-experiment explanations for the earlier misinterpretation. Because the misperception of 4's power is largely corrected by the end of the experiment, subjects may be somewhat reluctant or even unable to discuss the real basis for their mistaken views. Hence the reasons given by the 22 players who seem never to have realized the true nature of the power situation may be especially valuable indications of the source of the error. Seven of the 22 seemed to believe that coalitions including 4 were somehow more sure of obtaining the prize than were other coalitions or that 4 was the only player capable of bargaining and that the other players had either to accept his terms or receive nothing. We believe it noteworthy that it is only among these 22 players that we find the assertion (made by another seven of them) that a high-weight player is justified in demanding a majority share of the coalition reward because he *contributes more* to the coalition. One might guess that this interpretation figures more prominently in the early reaction to the situation than the overall figures would indicate. The comments about 4's larger number and the multiplicative aspects of the game may well be oblique references to earlier beliefs (which now appear to the subjects as totally unjustified) that the higher weight player makes a greater contribution to coalition success.

EXPERIMENT II

Under the Vinacke and Arkoff procedure, the alternative to being in a coalition on any given trial has the same value (zero) for each player regardless of his weight. Hence, 4's outcomes are as much subject to control through the joint actions of the other two players as are either 2 or 3's outcomes. It is in this sense that 4 has no more power than they. In the present experiment, real power differences aer created by giving the three subjects differential ability to obtain rewards from the game, an ability that can not be attenuated by the actions of the other two persons. This is done by giving each person a specific alternative level of outcomes which he receives if he fails to gain membership in a coalition or if, once in a coalition, he and his partner fail to reach agreement on a division of the spoils. (The bargaining involved in the division of the prize *follows* rather than precedes the choice of coalition partners.) The person with a higher alternative value has high power in the sense that (a) he is less dependent upon getting into a coalition, and (b), during the bargaining following coalition formation, he can hold out for a larger share because he has less to lose if no agreement is reached. The long run effects of the latter, demanding a preponderant share of the reward, are of rather little concern to him because of the first fact. At the same time, factor (b) makes him less desirable than a weaker person as a coalition partner. Hence, we would expect that the poorer a player's alternative, the greater the likelihood of his being included in a pair coalition. Of course, this will be true only when the size of prize given a coalition does *not* increase in proportion to the power of its members. (In the present case, as in the Vinacke and Arkoff procedure, the prize is the same for all coalitions.) It is under these circumstances that Caplow's statement is relevant—that "the weakest member of the triad has a definite advantage, being sure to be included in whatever coalition is formed."

Procedure

Forty-five male students, volunteers from an introductory (sophomore) psychology class, served as subjects in 15 experimental triads. The task was presented as a simple business game in which each player was a corporation chairman, controlling a certain share of the market each month. Each player's object was to accumulate as many points for himself as possible, not to compete but to attempt to maximize his own outcomes without regard to how this might affect the outcomes of the other players. Each subject was randomly assigned a weight—either 4, 2, or 0—which represented the number of points he could earn on each trial if he chose to play the game independently. Any pair of subjects, however, had the option of forming a coalition which was then given one minute to decide in what manner to divide a ten-point prize between them. Coalitions were formed by a series of written choices. At the beginning of each trial, each subject privately indicated the number of the other player with whom he would most like to form a coalition. Reciprocated choices became coalition partners, thereby having the opportunity to attempt to decide how they wanted to divide the ten points between them. The third man, the player *not* in the coalition, was paid off immediately with the number of points equal to his weight or alternative and did not enter into the bargaining for that trial. (If there happened to be no reciprocated choices on a given trial, the subjects were requested to consider the problem again and indicate their choices once more. This procedure was continued until a reciprocated choice appeared. This was necessary on only 43 of the 300 trials. Most of the instances of non-reciprocation were found early in the game.) If the two members of the coalition reached some mutually satisfactory division of the ten points during the minute allotted for bargaining, they then received that number of points as their scores for that trial. If, however, they did not agree before the time limit, they forfeited the ten points and each received the number of points equal to their weights or alternatives. A time limit was placed on the bargaining so that the weaker player could not gain power by stalling and controlling time. Each subject retained the same weight throughout the game, and each triad completed 20 trials.

Although the weights employed in the present study differ from those used in the Vinacke-Arkoff experiment, they are comparable in at least two ways: first, if no coalitions are formed, or if no agreement is reached in the coalitions which are formed, the high-weight man will always win; and second, the coalition is always assured a chance at a larger number of points than is any independent player. For certain analyses, then, we shall consider the present 0–2, 0–4, and 2–4 coalitions as equivalent, respectively, to the

2–3, 2–4, and 3–4 coalitions in the previous experiment.

Results

Table 1 presents the frequencies of occurrence of the various coalitions. Data from the first and last three trials of Experiment II may be compared with those from Vinacke and Arkoff and Experiment I. The relative incidence of the various coalitions for the first three trials of Experiment II does not differ significantly from that of Experiment I. The difference between the two distributions for the last three trials of each experiment is significant at the .01 level with a Chi-square of 10.72. The difference between the two distributions for Experiment II is not significant (Chi-square = 3.48, $p < .20$).

Table 2

MEAN FREQUENCY OF OCCURRENCE OF VARIOUS COALITIONS OVERALL
AND BY HALVES OF EXPERIMENT II WITH COMPARISONS*

Mean Difference per Triad	Overall	First Half of Trials	Second Half of Trials
0–2	12.33	5.67	6.67
0–4	5.20	2.80	2.40
2–4	2.47	1.55	.93
	20 trials	10 trials	10 trials
Mean Difference per Triad			
0–2 > 0–4	7.13	2.87	4.27
	t = 10.62	t = 8.28	t = 9.19
	p < .02	p < .02	p < .02
0–2 > 2–4	9.87	4.13	5.73
	t = 14.68	t = 11.94	t = 12.35
	p < .02	p < .02	p < .02
0–4 > 2–4	2.73	1.27	1.47
	t = 4.07	t = 3.66	t = 3.16
	.02 < p < .10	p = NS	p = NS

* The t values in this table were calculated using the Tukey method for multiple comparisons.

It appears, then, that the present procedure yields a distribution of coalitions which, although departing initially from the Vinacke-Arkoff distribution, does not do so as markedly as does the distribution from Experiment I and comes to approximate the Vinacke-Arkoff distribution far more closely as the trials progress.

The data also suggest that this is not merely an illusory effect which disappears with repeated experience in the situation. Table 2 presents the mean frequencies per triad of the various coalitions, and the significance levels for these differences. The 0–2 coalition occurs significantly more frequently than do either of the other possible pairs, both over the whole series of 20 trials and in both the first and second halves of the experiment; but only over the entire series of trials does the difference between the relative incidence of the 0–4 and 0–2 coalitions approach significance. Moreover, the average frequency of 0–2 coalitions tends to increase from the first to the second half of the experiment, while that of the 2–4 coalitions tends to decrease during the same period (in both instances $.05 < p < .10$, using the ordinary t-test for differences).

Another way of looking at the evidence is in terms of partnership choice data. Each of the positions predominantly chose the lower alternative man as a partner—i.e., 0 chose 2 66 per cent of the time, 2 chose 0 77 per cent of the time, and 4 chose 0 60 per cent of the time. Sign tests show that the results differ significantly from those expected by chance (equally frequent choice of the other two players) at beyond the .05 level in all three cases.

The previous experiments revealed an initial tendency for the 4 man to ask for and receive the majority of points from those coalitions which he did manage to enter. Over the entire series of 20 trials in the present experiment, there was a similar tendency for both 4 and 2 to receive more points than 0 in the 4–0 and 2–0 coalitions respectively (significant at better than the .02 level by the Tukey method for multiple comparisons). The slight tendency for 4 to receive more points than 2 from 2–4 coalitions proved non-significant. The over-all results are duplicated in the first half of the trials for each triad, but largely disappear during the second half—the only significant result remaining in the 4–0 coalition. As expected, on the average 4 received significantly more points per coalition from 0 than he did from 2, as did 2 from 0 over 4. The 0 man was slightly better rewarded by 2 than by 4, and especially during the second half of the game ($.05 < p < .10$). A comparison of first and second half scores reveals that 0's scores per coalition increase significantly ($p < .01$) while 4's scores per coalition decrease slightly ($.05 < p < .10$).

In a questionnaire administered at the end of the experiment the subjects were asked to indicate the following: which weight they would choose as a permanent partner; in general, which weight they believed each of the players should form coalitions with; which weight had the most power; which are the easiest and hardest weights with which to bargain; which weight would win in the long run; and which member, if either, of any coalition is justified in asking for a majority of the points. Their answers reflect the coalition formation and bargaining behavior discussed above. Only five of the 45 subjects, for example, failed to pick the available lower alternative player as a permanent coalition partner. The question: "Which of the three players has the most power?" was asked twice—once early in the questionnaire and once again at the end. At the first asking, four subjects responded that 0 had the most power, three picked 2, 36 chose 4, and two said that there were no power differences. At the later asking, 13 of the subjects who had previously singled out 4 as having power changed their answers to 2. The open-ended explanations accompanying these changes indicate a growing awareness of 2's ability to entice 0 into a coalition although still noting that, *if selected*, 4's higher weight becomes important. In general, however, subjects continue to view power as residing in a higher alternative.

Discussion and Summary

It appears that Winacke and Arkoff's procedure does initially give player 4 an illusory kind of power. In Experiment I, most of the subjects are initially subject to this misperception but apparently achieve a more correct understanding in a few trials. These results are in accord with our general contention that the phenomenon reported by Vinacke and Arkoff is limited to instances where the complexity of the learning task is so great in relation to the amount of contact and experience subjects have with it that they are not able properly to analyze it. In consequence, we witness actions that are "irrational" with respect to the analysis the experimenter makes at his leisure. However, these actions are not necessarily irrational when viewed in the light of the understanding subjects are able to achieve under the pressures of time and task complexity. Incomplete understanding is not to be confused with irrationality.

There are at least two possible interpretations of the initial erroneous attribu-

tion of power to player 4. The first is that the initial attribution of power to 4 reflects a general pessimism about the dependability of cooperative action. Logically, player 4 is more powerful *unless* the others join forces against him. Until one knows that joint action will be instituted dependably, attributing superior power to him is not wholly unwarranted. This interpretation is suggested by the most commonly given explanation for the attribution: 4 has more power because he would win if no coalitions were formed. The declining tendency to attribute power to 4 may reflect a growing confidence that in this situation, at least, cooperative action against him is to be taken for granted.

Another possible interpretation is that our subjects have learned to use a person's potentialities in a field of independent actors as an indication of his ability to contribute to cooperative efforts. This is explicitly suggested by the comments that he makes a larger contribution to any coalition he enters and is consistent with other more general explanations provided by the subjects. In view of their likely experiences with these matters, this conclusion is a highly reasonable one. It is probably true that in everyday situations a person's effectiveness, when everyone is acting for himself, is rather closely related to how much he can add to any joint effort. Thus, the common misperception in the Vinacke and Arkoff situation may reflect a positive correlation in the social environment of the typical subject. The reader may note the similarity of this interpretation to Brunswik's explanation (1) of, for example, the size-weight illusion as reflecting a correlation between size and weight over the universe of objects the person has experienced in his physical environment. In Brunswik's terms, we are suggesting that a person's effectiveness as an individual has "ecological validity" as a cue from which to predict his ability to contribute to joint efforts, and thus enjoys considerable "impression value" or "response-eliciting power." This is the case in the Vinacke and Arkoff situation. In Experiment I, subjects initially utilize this cue extensively, but later learn that it is inappropriate in this situation and hence, its subsequent degree of utilization declines.

The procedure of Experiment II, in contrast to that of Vinacke and Arkoff. appears to create large and lasting power differences among the members of the triad. Given differentially good alternatives to being a coalition or, more important, to acquiescing to a coalition partner's demands, the predicted pattern of coalition formation emerges, and the weakest member of the triad is in the most favored position when it comes to joining pair coalitions. The score and self-report data, however, suggest certain minor trends worth brief consideration. We have noted a tendency for 0's average score per coalition to increase and 4's to decrease. This finding may be taken as an indication that during the course of the trials some 0's are beginning to capitalize on their status as preferred coalition partners by asking for a larger share of the prize and some 4's are recognizing that they must be more generous in dividing the prize if they are to be allowed to enter further coalitions. We have also noted some changes in subjects' perceptions of the most powerful player and in the reasons accompanying their answers. Mention of 2's greater ability to entice 0 into coalitions suggests that some subjects are becoming aware of the truth of Caplow's hypothesis. These findings raise the interesting side problem of how

a high-power individual in a situation with limited communication possibilities would go about establishing trust. Once excluded from coalitions, the high-weight man would probably tend to remain excluded, since unless he could enter a coalition there would be no way for him to demonstrate to the others that he would not use his power against them.

It must be noted that in general 4 tends to accumulate the most points during the game—93 on the average as compared with 86 for 2 and 66 for 0. However, this is probably an artifact of the relative sizes of the alternatives and the prize to be divided. By making the coalition reward larger in relation to the largest weight, one could create a situation in which the highest alternative player would, by reason of his exclusion from coalitions, end up with the smallest accumulated score. However, as the coalition prize becomes larger, the differential power implications of any given set of weights becomes less important.

One might also manipulate the weights and coalition prize in such a manner that the highest alternative player would emerge as the most preferred partner. This is an important point because it indicates the boundary conditions for the phenomena observed in Experiment II. For example, different sizes of rewards might be given to different coalitions. If the various rewards were proportional to the weights of the persons comprising the various coalitions, one would expect no difference in the relative incidence of the three possible types of coalition or even a bias in favor of coalitions including the high-power person. The latter effect would be expected, for example, if the 2–4 coalition received a prize of 12 points, the 0–4 coalition, 8 points, and the 0–2 coalition,

4 points. This would reproduce the situation where the more effective a person is as an independent actor, the more effective is the joint effort to which he contributes. It is not unreasonable to believe that, in many natural situations, joint effectiveness is a direct function (and perhaps even a multipliactive one) of individual effectiveness. In these cases, if the above analysis is correct, coalitions would appear largely among persons of high power. On the other hand, the Caplow effect will appear when coalition effectiveness bears no relation (or a negative one) to the effectiveness of the component members.

REFERENCES

1. BRUNSWIK, E., *Systematic and Representative Designs of Psychological Experiments*, Berkeley: University of California Press, 1949.
2. CAPLOW, T., "A Theory of Coalitions in the Triad," *American Sociological Review*, 1956, 21, 489–493.
3. THIBAUT, J. W., and H. H. KELLEY, *The Social Psychology of Groups*, New York: Wiley and Sons, Inc., 1959, Chapters 7 and 11.
4. VINACKE, W. E., and A. ARKOFF, "An Experimental Study of Coalitions in the Triad," *American Sociological Review*, 1957, 22, 406–414.

A THEORY OF COALITION FORMATION

William A. Gamson

Many novelists as well as political scientists have been fascinated by the intrigues that mark political life. When these intrigues involve not only individuals but also nations we have the stuff of history. This paper deals in a general way with a subject that has been treated specifically by historians and journalists for centuries.

In every historian's description of a revolution, in every political biographer's description of the ascent of his subject, there is a more or less explicit account of the coalitions and alliances which furthered the final outcome. Few areas exhibit less external uniformity. "Politics makes strange bed fellows" we say to express our bewilderment at some new coalition which belies our expectations from past knowledge of the participants.

There are three separate streams of work which have been concerned with the theme. The sociological tributary flows primarily from Simmel,[1] and has focused,

* William A. Gamson, "A Theory of Coalition Formation," *American Sociological Review*, 26 (1961), 373–82. Reprinted by permission.

[1] Georg Simmel, "Significance of Numbers for Social Life" in A. Paul Hare, Edgar F. Borgatta, and Robert F. Bales, editor, *Small Groups*, New York: Knopf, 1955.

in particular, on the relatively simple and manageable three-person group. The triadic relationship has been explored in a series of experimental and theoretical papers by Mills, Strodtbeck, Caplow, and Vinacke and Arkoff.[2]

A second tradition has grown entirely since the end of the Second World War following the publication of von Neumann and Morgenstern's *Theory of Games and Economic Behavior* in 1944.[3] Articles by Shapley and Shubick and by Luce and Rogow on *a priori* power distributions, the von Neumann-Morgenstern "solution" to n-person games and the notion of psi-stability are relevant examples.[4] Both the

small group and the mathematical literature will be discussed in detail following the presentation of the theory.

The third body of work comes from historians and journalists and is primarily descriptive. Not only do these accounts capture much of the drama of coalition formation, but they also serve as a valuable reference point for a theory with descriptive rather than strictly normative ambitions. The accounts of the French National Assembly by Lerner and Aron[5] and by Leites[6] and descriptions of the rise of Hitler and Stalin highlight the dimensions of a theory of coalitions.

Coalitions are temporary, means oriented, alliances among individuals or groups which differ in goals. There is generally little value consensus in a coalition and the stability of a coalition requires *tacit neutrality* of the coalition on matters which go beyond the immediate prerogatives. This makes the pursuit of power itself, i.e., control over future decisions, an ideal basis for coalition formation since it is an instrument for the achievement of widely ranging and even incompatible goals. Two members may realize their mutual goal antagonisms but such decisions lie in the future and the present alliance may make both better able to achieve a wide range of goals not all of which will be incompatible. Power is the currency of politics.

---

[2] T. M. Mills, "Coalition Pattern in Three Person Groups," *American Sociological Review*, 19 (December, 1954), pp. 657–667. F. L. Strodtbeck, "Family as a Three Person Group," *American Sociological Review*, 19 (February, 1954), pp. 23–29. T. Caplow, "A Theory of Coalitions in the Triad," *American Sociological Review*, 21 (August, 1956), pp. 489–493 and "Further Development of a Theory of Coalitions in the Triad," *American Journal of Sociology*, 64 (March, 1959), pp. 488–493. W. E. Vinacke and A. Arkoff, "Experimental Study of Coalitions in the Triad," *American Sociological Review*, 22 (August, 1957), pp. 406–415.

[3] J. von Neumann and O. Morgenstern, *Theory of Games and Economic Behavior*, Princeton, New Jersey: Princeton University Press, third edition, 1953.

[4] L. S. Shapley and M. Shubick, "Method for Evaluating the Distribution of Power in a Committee System," *American Political Science Review*, 48 (September, 1954), pp. 787–792. R. D. Luce and A. A. Rogow, "A Game Theoretical Analysis of Congressional Power Distributions for a Stable Two-Party System," *Behavior Science*, 1 (April, 1956), pp. 83–96. The fine book by R. D. Luce and H. Raiffa, *Games and Decisions*, New York: John Wiley, 1957, contains excellent summaries of work in

---

the theory of games of relevance to social scientists.

[5] D. Lerner and R. Aron, *France Defeats EDC*, New York: Frederick A. Praeger, 1957.

[6] N. Leites, *On the Game of Politics in France*, Rand Corporation: Unedited Advance Copy, 1958.

THE THEORY

Some Definitions

A *decision* is a selection among alternatives. When there are several participants, the selection of any given alternative will distribute rewards among them in a particular fashion. The reward which accrues to any participant or group of participants from a decision is the *payoff*. The payoff may include influence on future decisions.

In any decision, there exists a weight associated with each participant involved such that some critical quantity of these weights is necessary for the decision to be made. We shall call these weights *resources*. They vary with the situation, from military force and industrial capacity in a war to votes in a parliamentary situation to verbal and logical ability in a court of law. One may be able to influence the decision more than his resources would warrant through his strategic position. In fact, this "influence of position" is a primary focus of the theory. The *rules of the game* provide the manner in which the decision may be made; this includes specification of the resources which are relevant to the decision.

A *social unit* is any individual or group which for the duration of the decision follows the same coalition strategy. It might be a state delegation to a political convention, a voting bloc in the United Nations, or an association of retail stores. A *coalition* is the joint use of resources by two or more social units. Once formed, a coalition will frequently meet the definition of a social unit from the period of formation until the decision has been made. A *winning coalition* is one with sufficient resources to control the decision.

The *decision point* is the minimum proportion of resources necessary to control the decision.

Conditions of the Theory

A *full-fledged coalition situation* is one in which the following conditions are present:

1. There is a decision to be made and there are more than two social units attempting to maximize their share of the payoffs.
2. No single alternative will maximize the payoff to all participants.
3. No participant has dictatorial powers, i.e., no one has initial resources sufficient to control the decision by himself.
4. No participant has veto power, i.e., no member *must* be included in every winning coalition.

The first two of these conditions imply that each of the participants has some stake in the outcome—we are not dealing with a null game—and the situation is competitive. Together with condition three, we are assured that a full-fledged coalition situation is an essential game.[7] The portion of condition one which states that more than two social units are involved can easily be derived from the last two conditions. In a one-man group, the participant has dictatorial powers and, in any dyad, either one member is a dictator or each possesses a veto power.

---

[7] An *inessential* game, write Luce and Raiffa, *op. cit.*, p. 185, is one in which "no coalition of players is more effective than the several players of the coalition operating alone ... For every disjoint R and S. V(RUS)= V(R)+V(S) ... Any game which is not *inessential* is called *essential.*" We will call a game strictly essential if the players operating alone always get zero payoff.

While the first three conditions merely remove trivial situations from consideration, condition four places much more severe limits on the generality of the theory. Many interesting situations involving *blocking* coalitions are excluded by this condition for reasons which will become apparent shortly.

However, if the decision point is 50 per cent or less, condition three implies condition four. Then, condition four would be violated if and only if some member controlled more than 50 per cent of the resources; but if this were true, then this member would be a dictator and condition three would be violated.

Parameters of the Theory

To predict who will join with whom in any specific instance, the model requires information on the following:

1. *The initial distribution of resources.* We must know, of course, what the relevant resources are for any given decision and, at some starting point, how much of these resources each participant controls.
2. *The payoff for each coalition.* Every alternative coalition is a partition of the players into classes, and for every such partition we must know the total rewards for each class. In Game Theory, the *characteristic function* of a game is calculated by computing the payoff to any subset of players on the assumption that the complementary set of players will form a coalition. In short, it is postulated that the players assume that every game will reduce to a two-person game. This sometimes gives an unrealistically conservative value for a coalition.

We shall include partitions into more than two classes of players in calculating the payoffs. The same subset may receive one payoff when the complementary set is partitioned in one manner and an entirely different payoff when it is partitioned in a second way. To illustrate, a coalition may be losing and have an estimated payoff of zero if we assume that its opponents will combine but it may be winning on the contrary assumption.

The function which we require appears more complicated than the characteristic function. However, since the theory specifies that only one coalition wins and the payoff to all non-members is zero, in practice we need know only the payoff associated with each possible winning coalition.[8]

Since the rewards will frequently include anticipations of future events, the payoff must reflect differences in the probability of achieving future rewards. To illustrate, the payoff for a coalition at a political convention should reflect the various probabilities that the coalition's candidate will be elected. The payoff for a coalition would be the *expected value* of future decisions—the total payoff from such decisions multiplied by the probability of the coalition's achieving them.

3. *Non-utilitarian strategy preferences.* We must have a rank ordering (with ties allowed) of each participant's inclination to join with every other player *exclusive of that player's control of the resources.* The sources of this non-utilitarian preference will vary depending on the situation: in a small committee, the primary source would probably be interpersonal attraction. In a political convention, we would expect the relative similarity of others' ideology and beliefs to be the principal determinant.

---

[8] Thus, the complete payoff function for any particular game maps every possible coalition into some single value—zero if the coalition is losing and some positive but variable if the coalition is winning.

4. *The effective decision point.* The rules of the game will frequently specify an amount of resources *formally* necessary to control the decision. Yet an amount of resources less than the formal amount may be sufficient to control the decision for all practical purposes. This may occur through considerations which prevent a potentially winning opposition from uniting or through a "bandwagon effect."

For example, in a political convention when a candidate reaches a certain number of votes, close to but still short of a majority, the opposition will "stampede." The decision point in which we are interested is the *effective* rather than the *formal* decision point, although there will be many situations in which these are identical.

If we know the payoff for each coalition, then we can logically deduce the effective decision point. However, in practice the construction of the payoff matrix is dependent on our prior knowledge of this value. In other words, to specify the complete payoff function we must know both whether a coalition has sufficient resources to be winning and how much it will receive. Since separate information is required, we have handled this as an additional constant, but it is not a genuinely independent one.

Additional Definitions and Assumptions

A *minimal winning coalition* is a winning coalition such that the defection of any member will make the coalition no longer winning. The *cheapest winning coalition* is that minimal winning coalition with total resources closest to the decision point. A *payoff class* is a set of payoffs of which the lowest is no more than K per cent less than the highest. The value of K is something which must be determined empirically for a given coalition situation. It specifies, in effect, how large a difference in payoff there must be to make a difference.

The theory applies to full-fledged coalition situations in which we assume the following to be true:

Assumption One: The participants have the same (but not necessarily perfect) information about the initial distribution of resources and the payoff to any coalition.

Assumption Two: Participants do not distinguish between payoffs in the same payoff class.

Assumption Three: Every participant has a rank ordering of non-utilitarian preferences for joining with the other players.

These assumptions and the conditions of the full-fledged coalition situation define the class of games to which the theory is applicable. We can now state the empirical hypotheses of the theory, starting with the general hypothesis:

Any participant will expect others to demand from a coalition a share of the payoff proportional to the amount of resources which they contribute to a coalition.

Any participant, A, estimates the *payoff to himself* from a prospective coalition as a product of the *total payoff* to that coalition and A's expected *share* of that total. The total payoff is known to A and the general hypothesis specifies the share which A will expect to give to others. Thus, A can assign to any prospective coalition a personal payoff value—his proportion of the resources in the coalition multiplied by the total payoff for that coalition.

These values can be assigned to payoff classes of which A will prefer the highest. He does not recognize payoff differences between coalition strategies (prospective coalitions) in the same payoff class. Within any class, he will pursue that coalition strategy whose members have the highest mean rank on his scale of non-utilitarian preferences.

When a player must choose among alternative coalition strategies where the total payoff to a winning coalition is constant, he will maximize his payoff by maximizing his share. The theory states that he will do this by maximizing the ratio of his resources to the total resources of the coalition. Since his resources will be the same regardless of which coalition he joins, the lower the total resources, the greater will be his share. Thus, where the total payoff is held constant, he will favor the *cheapest winning coalition*.

As an illustrative example, let us say that A has 30 per cent of the resources, B has 19 per cent, C has 30 per cent, and D has 21 per cent where the decision point is 51 per cent. For A, the minimal winning coalitions which he must consider are AC and AD. In the former, he will expect 1/2 of the payoff, while in the latter he expects to get approximately 3/5. If they differ in payoff as well, 1/2 of payoff AC may be higher than 3/5 of payoff AD. If these two figures are in the same payoff class, then he will choose to join with the one which he ranks higher on non-utilitarian strategy preference.

Finally, a coalition will form if and only if there are *reciprocal strategy choices* between two participants. To illustrate, let us assume that X's desired coalition in some three-person game is XY, that Y's is XY or YZ, and that Z's favored coalition is XZ. Only X and Y have *reciprocal strategy choices*, i.e. require the other in their *preferred coalition*, and, thus, the coalition XY is predicted by the theory.

The model envisions the process of co-alition formation as a step-by-step process where the participants join two at a time. Once a coalition has been formed, the situation becomes a new one—that is, there is a fresh distribution of resources— and, in the new coalition situation, the original strategies may or may not be appropriate. *If a coalition which forms was predicted by the theory, then each player's original strategy will remain the same.* Thus, if W's preferred coalition was WXY in some game, then if X and Y join, W will still *necessarily* prefer the strategy WXY. If, however, a coalition forms which is an "error" in terms of the theory, the strategy requirements for some players *may* change. Thus, if player W planned to join with X and Y but Y and Z joined, W might now prefer the group YZ to X.

We can now explain why we have excluded games in which some member possesses veto power, i.e., in which condition four of the full-fledged coalition situation is violated. The bargaining situation which is essential for the general hypothesis to be correct is one in which every participant has alternatives. Where one member has veto power, there is no alternative to his inclusion; he could no longer be expected to demand only a proportional share of the payoff.

COALITIONS IN THE TRIAD

Caplow has published two papers on a theory of coalitions in the triad including an evaluation of the experimental evidence.[9] He specified eight types of coalition situations based on the initial distribution of resources. Table 1 reproduces the eight

---

[9] Caplow, 1956, *op. cit.*

Table 1

PREDICTED COALITIONS IN TRIADS OF VARYING INITIAL STRENGTH

Type No.	Distribution of Resources	Predicted Coalition	
		Caplow	Gamson
1	A=B=C	any	any
2	A>B, B=C, A<(B+C)	BC	BC
3	A<B, B=C	AB or AC	AB or AC
4	A>(B+C), B=C	none	none
5	A>B>C, A<(B+C)	BC or AC	BC
6	A>B>C, A>(B+C)	none	none
7	A>B>C, A=(B+C)	AB or AC	Inapplicable
8	A=(B+C), B=C	AB or AC	Inapplicable

types with Caplow's predicted coalition for the continuous situation.

To make our theory applicable to the Caplow situations, we must assume (1) that all winning coalitions have the same payoff, (2) that there are no differences in non-utilitarian strategy preferences, and (3) that the decision point is a simple majority of the resources. It is clear, then, that the prediction from our model will be simply the *cheapest winning coalition* in the applicable situations.

Four of the eight types in Table 1 do not meet the conditions for a full-fledged coalition situation. Types Four and Six represent a dictator situation, and Caplow's prediction for these *inessential* games is also that no coalition will form. Types Seven and Eight fail to meet our fourth condition that no member have veto power for in each of these A must be included in any winning coalition.

In Type One, any coalition will have the same total resources and thus, under the previous assumptions that other things are equal, any coalition would have equal probability. In Type Two, B and C will form a winning coalition, and since A is greater than either B or C, the coalition

BC must be cheaper than either AB or AC. Therefore, our prediction for Type Two agrees with Caplow's.

In Type Three, where A's position is ideal for the role of *tertius gaudens*, the coalitions AB and AC are equal in strength and both are cheaper than the coalition BC. Once again, our prediction corresponds to Caplow's.

Type Five is the only situation in which the two theories differ in their consequences. Caplow finds the following assumptions equally plausible[10]: "The 'chooser' in a triad seeks the maximum advantage or minimum disadvantage of strength relative to his coalition partner" or, "The 'chooser' in a triad seeks to maximize the strength of the coalition in relation to the excluded member." He reasons that the weak man, C, in a Type Five situation, would be sought as a coalition partner by both of the others and could choose on either basis.

Our theory clearly implies the first of these two assumptions. C will prefer the coalition BC to the coalition AC because

---

[10] Caplow, 1959, *op. cit.*

he expects that the stronger A will demand a larger share of the payoff in accordance with his superior resources. The coalition BC is, of course, the cheapest coalition.

Caplow has discussed several experimental studies of triads with the conclusion that they lend some support to his analysis although designed with other purposes in mind. For example, Mills discovered that a subject who was the "odd man" (A) in a Type Three situation tended very slightly to make more efforts to disrupt the coalition between the equals than the subject placed in A's role in a Type Two situation.[11] Caplow concludes that "we would expect less resistance to the 'inevitable' coalition of BC in Type Two than to the improbable, and, therefore, unstable coalition of BC in Type Three."[12]

The most crucial and significant evidence on coalitions in the triad comes from Vinacke and Arkoff who, stimulated by Caplow's first paper, designed an experiment to test the first six of his situations.[13] This experiment is certainly a test of our theory as well, given the earlier predictions of Table 1. Furthermore, in testing the Type Five situation, it provides a comparison at the only point where our predictions differ.

The experimenters had subjects play a parchesi game in which each player's moves were weighted by a numbered counter which he drew from a hopper at the beginning of the game. The weights on these counters represented the six different initial distributions of resources specified by Caplow's theory. Table 2 gives

---

[11] Mills, *op. cit.*

[12] Caplow, 1956, *op. cit.*

[13] Vinacke and Arkoff, *op. cit.*

Table 2

VINACKE AND ARKOFF DESIGN FOR EXPERIMENTAL TEST OF SIX CAPLOW SITUATIONS

Type No.	Description	Weights A	B	C
1	$A=B=C$	1	1	1
2	$A>B, B=C,$ $A<(B+C)$	3	2	2
3	$A<B, B=C$	1	2	2
4	$A>(B+C), B=C$	3	1	1
5	$A>B>C, A<(B+C)$	4	3	2
6	$A>B>C, A>(B+C)$	4	2	1

the weights for each situation. Thirty triads played each game three times with the order arranged to vary systematically the position of the situation in each series.

Vinacke and Arkoff suggested a "game theory" prediction for each of these situations as well, which we shall call the Strict Rationality Theory. They reason that the strictly rational player must realize in a situation such as Type Five that any pair will win, and that if he fails to form a coalition, he can expect his opponents to do so. This reasoning will hold whether one has a weight of two, three, or four, and there is no reason to expect, on rational grounds, that any coalition will form with greater frequency than any other. In fact, this reasoning holds for the first three types as well. In the non-essential types four and six, there is nothing to be gained by forming a coalition and the prediction is that none will take place.

This experiment, then, gives us a chance to compare its results with three different theoretical predictions—Caplow's, Strict Rationality, and our own. In Table 3 we compare these predictions with the actual results of the experiment.

Table 3

RESULTS OF VINACKE-ARKOFF EXPERIMENT WITH THREE THEORETICAL PREDICTIONS

Predicted	1 A=B=C	2 A>B, B=C, A<(B+C)	3 A<B, B=C	4 A>(B+C), B=C	5 A>B>C, A<(B+C)	6 A>B>C, A>(B+C)
Caplow	any	BC	AB or AC	none	AC or BC	none
Strict rationality[a]	any	any	any	none	any	none
Gamson	any	BC	AB or AC	none	BC	none
Actual						
AB	33	13	24	11	9	13
AC	17	12	40	10	20	13
BC	30	64	15	7	59	8
Total	80	89	79	28	88	30
No coalition	10	1	11	62	2	60
Probability[b]	NS	.01	.01	NS	.01	NS

[a] These are also the predictions made by Caplow for the "episodic" situation.
[b] From Vinacke and Arkoff: Chi Square with two degrees of freedom.

In situations one, four, and six, where there are no differences between theories, each is supported. Coalitions do not usually occur in the latter two situations, and in situation one, they seem to occur approximately at random.

In situations two and three, the results provide negative evidence for the strict rationality predictions and positive evidence for the other two theories. Apparently, the ability to perceive the necessity for a coalition in these situations is more difficult from certain positions than from others. "It is harder," Vinacke and Arkoff write, "for an initially stronger member to reach the conclusion that the relative strengths are irrelevant than for the other one or two to arrive at this interpretation. In effect, the weaker members can immediately understand the necessity for forming a coalition, whereas the stronger member must go through more complex reasoning to do so."

Situation five is perhaps the most crucial since each theory makes a different prediction for the outcome. While Caplow predicts that either of the coalitions AC or BC are equally likely, the cheapest coalition BC actually takes place three times as frequently as the alternative!

This confirmation is interpreted by Vinacke and Arkoff in a manner which echoes the general hypothesis of our theory: ". . . the weakest member was found to be most often a member of the winning coalition; furthermore, his share of the winnings was larger than his strength might seem to warrant mainly because there was competition for him, *because the other players saw him as weaker, hence more readily to be induced into partnership.*"[14]

Willerman draws similar conclusions from his study of coalitions in a fraternity

---

[14] *Ibid.*, emphasis mine.

council.[15] "... Distribution of control within the coalition was isomorphic with the relative status and resources of the members outside of the coalition. However, there seem to be occasions when the strategic position of a member gives him power out of proportion to his rank order of status or resources."

There is apparently some basis for the assumption that the size of the demands which a participant will make reflects the proportion of resources which he controls —or, at least, will affect what others will *expect* him to demand. In a situation where participants meet with each other sequentially rather than simultaneously, these expectations of others' bargaining demands become even more crucial.

In short, the small group studies of coalitions in the triad uniformly support the theory presented here. While Caplow's predictions are in most cases consistent with the predictions from our theory under the special case where payoffs and non-utilitarian strategy preferences are held constant, in one crucial difference, the results of Vinacke and Arkoff support the prediction made here.

MATHEMATICAL LITERATURE

The mathematical theory of games of strategy as it presently exists is a rich source of ideas, but it can only provide orientations in situations of the type with which we are concerned here. This is true

for several reasons. The most powerful mathematical developments of the theory are in the area of two-person, zero-sum games. The theory of games involving many players is, to quote Abraham Kaplan, "in a very unsatisfactory state."[16]

We do not object to the theory of games on the grounds that its assumptions are "unrealistic." They are, at least, clearly stated and we may substitute more plausible ones if we can find some which are workable. Luce and Raiffa write: "... it is crucial that social scientists recognize that game theory is not *descriptive* but rather (conditionally) *normative*. It states neither how people do behave nor how they should behave in an absolute sense, but how they should behave if they wish to achieve certain ends."[17] Our own object is descriptive but a normative theory often provides a useful starting point for a descriptive theory.

One attempt to handle the problem of the n-person game is the von Neumann-Morgenstern "solution" theory.[18] A *solution* generally consists of a *set of imputations* (an imputation is an n-tuple giving the payoff to each player and satisfying certain conditions) having the following two properties: (1) no imputa-

---

[15] B. Willerman, *A Final Report: Research on Cohesive and Disruptive Tendencies in Coalition Type Groups*, University of Minnesota, Mimeographed, 1957.

---

[16] In M. Shubik, *Readings in Game Theory and Political Behavior*, Garden City, New York: Doubleday, 1954.

[17] Luce and Raiffa, *op. cit.*

[18] This is discussed in relatively non-technical fashion in Luce and Raiffa, *op. cit.* In a sense, we are proposing in this paper a new definition of solution for certain classes of n-person essential games, but because of the specific meaning of "solution" in the von Neumann-Morgenstern sense, we have refrained from using the word.

tion in the set *dominates* any other imputation, and (2) every imputation not in the set is dominated by one in the set.[19]

I shall illustrate this with a solution to the three-man game: (1/2, 1/2, 0), (1/2, 0, 1/2), (0, 1/2, 1/2). No imputation among the three dominates another since only one player could improve his position by switching from one to another. Any particular imputation in the solution such as (0, 1/2, 1/2) is dominated by imputations outside of the set—for example, (1/6, 2/3, 1/6), but this and in fact any imputation outside of the solution set, is dominated by member of the solution (in this case by 1/2, 0, 1/2).

Luce and Raiffa argue that a "solution must be interpreted as a description of a set of possible payments, any of which might arise if the players chose strategies and form collusive arrangements as they 'should.' " This would seem to offer some promise for our purposes in spite of the fact that the emphasis is on distribution of payoffs. An imputation where some values are positive and others are zero defines an implicit coalition between the positive entries.

Unfortunately, we are not given a single imputation as a solution but rather a set of these, and furthermore, a set in which all possible coalitions are allowed. As if this difficulty were not sufficient, the solution to the three-man game given above is not the only solution; in fact, there is an infinity of solutions. "In their theory," write Luce and Raiffa, ". . . freedom to cooperate leads to vast numbers of 'solutions' with no

criteria to select among them. They are forced . . . to the *ad hoc* assumption that in practice there exist social standards which determine *the* solution which actually occurs, but no attempt is made to exihibit a theory of these standards."

There has been attempt by Vickrey[20] to narrow down the number of solutions to be considered. "Roughly, a solution is called *strong* if the sequence—(1) an imputation in the solution, (2) a change to a non-conforming imputation, and (3) a return to an imputation in the solution— *always* means that at least one of the players participating in the original deviation ultimately suffers a net loss. Thus, a strong solution has an inherent stability not possessed by other solutions, and so it might be expected to occur rather than one of the weaker solutions."

It turns out, encouragingly, that the *only* strong solution for the three-person game is the symmetric one given earlier: (1/2, 1/2, 0), (1/2, 0, 1/2), (0, 1/2, 1/2). Since none of these imputations dominates any other, again extra-theoretical reasons will determine which imputation in the set is chosen.

Vinacke and Arkoff[21] present data on the division of spoils made by their subjects which allow us to examine the frequency with which the strong solution did occur. In the Type One situation where all players had an equal share of the resources originally, the final imputation was a member of the solution set 60 per cent of the time, but in the Type Three situation (A < B, B = C) only 39 per cent of the time. Many of these may have occur-

---

[19] For a formal definition of imputation and domination, see Luce and Raiffa, *op. cit.*, p. 193 and p. 201.

[20] *Ibid.*, p. 213.

[21] Vinacke and Arkoff, *op. cit.*

red on those occasions (19 per cent) in which the two strong, equally powerful members joined.

We may tentatively conclude that where the initial distribution of resources *differs* among the three members of the triad, not only are the various imputations in a solution set *not* equally probable, but the tendency to divide the rewards symmetrically is considerably less than when participants have equal power.

A second mathematical concept, that of psi-stability, would seem to be more appropriate for our purposes since here a game is described by both an imputation and a coalition structure. The basis of this notion, which has been developed by Luce,[22] is that a pair—an imputation and a given coalition structure—is stable when no admissable change in the coalition structure is immediately profitable.

An important addition here is the recognition that from any given coalition structure, every possible coalition is not admissable. The concept of non-utilitarian strategy preferences developed earlier is, in part, an attempt to define the admissible changes between any two stages of the process of coalition formation.

The implications of psi-stability for the theory presented here are less important than one might hope. First, we are concerned primarily with the process of coalition formation rather than coalition stability. Although problems of stability can frequently be translated into the terms of the theory, essentially the game is over when a winning coalitions has been formed

for a particular decision, and the next decision involves a new game.[23] Secondly, psi-stable pairs, like solutions, are not generally unique and the problem of how to select just one still exists.

A full-fledged coalition situation is a strictly essential game and it is not difficult to see that any losing coalition will be psi-unstable. However, in the full-fledged triadic situation, any two-man coalition will meet the conditions of psi-stability regardless of the initial distribution of resources. If our aim is uniqueness, we are no better off here than under solution theory. Attempts by Milnor[24] to describe n-person games in terms of "reasonable outcomes" involve the same type of difficulties ascribed to solution and psi-stability theory.

Shapley[25] gives a method for evaluating the worth of an n-person game for any player that should help us to determine the relative bargaining positions of the several players in a game. He lists three *apparently* weak conditions and then shows that these uniquely determine an evaluation function. Ultimately, he arrives at an explicit formula for calculating the value for a player, i. "It amounts," to quote Luce and Raiffa, "to a weighted sum of the incremental additions made by i to all the coalitions of which he is a member." In the full-fledged triadic situation,

---

[22] R. D. Luce, "A Definition of Stability for N-Person Games," *Annals of Mathematics*, 59 (May, 1954), pp. 357–366.

---

[23] This is not a criticism of Luce since coalition stability is obviously an important problem in its own right. Eventually, a satisfactory theory of coalitions should be able to handle both coalition formation and stability.

[24] Described in Luce and Raiffa, *op. cit.*

[25] L. S. Shapley, "A Value for N-Person Games," *Annals of Mathematics Studies*, 28 (1953), pp. 307–317.

the values are 1/3 for each player. This suggests the symmetric solution.

In an article by Shapley and Shubik,[26] the authors attempt to apply the Shapley value to certain "simple" games (in a *simple* game, every coalition has as its payoff either one or zero, i.e. it is either winning or losing). They argue that the value gives an *a priori* estimation of relative power in many committee or parliamentary situations. An individual's power is given by the index, P/N, where N is the total number of permutations among the players and P is the number of permutations in which his resources are *pivotal* in turning a losing coalition into a winning one. Luce and Rogow[27] applied this to an analysis of coalitions between the President and the parties in the two houses of Congress.

The calculations involved in the Shapley-Shubik power index are relatively simple to make, especially when the N is small. In the triad, there are 31 or six permutations, and in the full-fledged coalition situation each person will be pivotal twice, giving rise to the earlier figure of 1/3.

Suppose, however, we did not assume that resources are used as a bloc. Instead of asking which person is pivotal in the permutation, we might ask which resource unit is pivotal. Referring back to Table 3, we can see that for the Type One situation, the Shapley value remains as 1/3. However, for Type Two, there are 71 permutations instead of 31. Any given resource unit will be pivotal in 61 ways since the other six units can be permuted

that many ways while it remains fixed in the pivotal spot. It follows that A's three resource units will be pivotal 3 x 61 times while B and C will have the pivotal unit in 2 x 61 ways each. The resultant Shapley values are 3/7, 2/7, 2/7 respectively or exactly proportional to the share of resources.

Finally, suppose we make the assumption that within any coalition, a player can expect to share in the payoff proportionally to his Shapley value. It then follows that one will maximize his share in a simple game if he can maximize his power relative to the other members of his winning coalition. In short, we are led to predict that the cheapest coalition will form!

It is certainly possible to question the assumptions by which we used the Shapley value to yield the predictions of our theory. Why should the resource rather than the player be considered the unit and why should the Shapley value determine the proportion of payoff within a coalition? Certainly these are not Shapley's assumptions and his analysis strongly suggests the symmetric solution to the triadic situation, but it is interesting to note that we can reach the same theoretical predictions by this slightly different pathway.

Summary

We have presented a theory of coalition formation to apply to a full-fledged coalition situation defined by four conditions. It is intended to apply where several parties are competitively attempting to determine a decision and in which no participant has either dictatorial or veto powers. The theory requires information

---

[26] Shapley and Shubik, *op. cit.*

[27] Luce and Rogow, *op. cit.*

on the initial distribution of resources, the payoff for each coalition, the non-utilitarian strategy preferences, and the effective decision point. Three additional assumptions further defined the situation to which the model applies.

Our general hypothesis stated that participants will expect others to demand from a coalition a share of the payoff which is proportional to the amount of resources which they are contributing to it. Each participant will estimate the value of any coalition strategy as the total payoff to a coalition multiplied by his share. He estimates this latter figure by the ratio of his resources to the total resources of the coalition. Every player will pursue strategies in the highest payoff class, but among alternative strategies in the same class, he will choose that one which maximizes his non-utilitarian strategy preference.

A coalition will form between two players if and only if these are reciprocal choices of coalition strategy between them. Thus, the model envisions the process of coalition formation as a step-by-step process until by successive pairing, the decision point has been reached.

The theory was compared with Caplow's predictions for coalitions in the triad and we found that in the special case where payoffs and non-utilitarian strategy preferences are constant, the two theories make identical predictions with one exception. In an experimental test by Vinacke and Arkoff, the results supported Caplow's and our own theory where they were opposed to the predictions of a strict rationality theory. At the one point where Caplow's theory differed from the one presented here, Vinacke and Arkoff's evidence supported the latter.

In examining the mathematical literature, we found that the von Neumann-Morgenstern solution theory was inadequate for our purposes because of its profusion of solutions for many games. An attempt by Vickrey to limit these somewhat by defining a *strong* solution still left the crucial difficulty of determining which member of a set of imputations would actually occur. The concept of psi-stability also left the unique specification of a coalition to extra-theoretical determination.

Finally, we explored the Shapley value and showed that it still suggests the equal probability of coalitions despite initial difference in resources. However, by the addition of two not unreasonable assumptions, it will lead to the same predictions as the theory presented here.

AN EXPERIMENTAL TEST
OF A THEORY OF COALITION FORMATION*

William A. Gamson

Coalition formation is comparatively rare among sociological phenomena in its susceptibility to experimental study. A number of such studies have already explored coalitions in the three-person group.[1] In an earlier paper,[2] a theory was

---

* William A. Gamson, "An Experimental Test of a Theory of Coalition Formation," *American Sociological Review*, 26 (1961), 565–73. Reprinted by permission.

[1] See especially, W. E. Vinacke and A. Arkoff, "An Experimental Study of Coalitions in the Triad," *American Sociological Review*, 22 (August, 1957), pp. 406–415; T. M. Mills, "Coalition Pattern in Three-Person Groups," *American Sociological Review*, 19 (December, 1954), pp. 657–667; J. R. Rond and W. E. Vinacke, "Coalitions in Mixed-Sex Triads," *Sociometry*, 24 (March, 1961), pp. 61–75; W. E. Vinacke, "Sex Roles in a Three-Person Game," *Sociometry*, 22 (December, 1959), pp. 343–360; S. Stryker and G. Psathas, "Research on Coalitions in the Triad: Findings, Problems, and Strategy," *Sociometry*, 23 (September, 1960), pp. 217–230; and H. H. Kelley and A. J. Arrowhead, "Coalitions in the Triad: Critique and Experiment," *Sociometry*, 23 (September, 1960), pp. 231–244.

[2] William A. Gamson, "A Theory of Coalition Formation," *American Sociological Review*, 26 (June, 1961), pp. 373–382. See this paper for a fuller description of the theory and its relation to the sociological and mathematical literature.

presented which attempted to generalize coalition formation beyond the triad while still handling existing results. Earlier results provided a post-hoc "test." This paper describes the results of an experiment designed to test the theory more directly.

The theory applies to situations which meet the following conditions: (1) There is a decision to be made and there are more than two social units attempting to maximize their share of the payoff; (2) No single alternative will maximize the payoff to all participants; (3) No participant has dictatorial powers, i.e., no one has initial resources sufficient to control the decision by himself; (4) No participant has veto power, i.e, no member *must* be included in every winning coalition.

To predict who will join with whom in any specific instance, information is needed on the following:

1. The initial distribution of resources. We must know what the relevant resources are for any given decision and, at some starting point, how much of these resources each participant controls.
2. The payoff for each coalition. The theory specifies that only one coalition wins and the payoff to all non-members is zero. Therefore, we need know only the payoff

associated with each possible winning coalition.

3. Non-utilitarian strategy preferences. We must have a rank ordering (with ties allowed) of each participant's inclination to join with every other player *exclusive of that player's control of the resources.*

4. The effective decision point. We must know the amount of resources necessary to determine the decision.

A minimal winning coalition is a winning coalition such that the defection of any member will make the coalition no longer winning. The cheapest winning coalition is that minimal winning coalition with total resources closest to the decision point. The general hypothesis of the theory states that *any participant will expect others to demand from a coalition a share of the payoff proportional to the amount of resources that they contribute to a coalition.*

Any participant, A, estimates the *payoff to himself* from a prospective coalition as a product of the *total payoff* to the coalition and A's expected share of that total. The total payoff is known to A and the general hypothesis specifies the share that A will expect to give to others. Thus, A can assign to any prospective coalition a personal payoff value—his proportion of the resources in the coalition multiplied by the total payoff for that coalition.

When a player must choose among alternative coalition strategies where the total payoff to a winning coalition is constant, he will maximize his payoff by maximizing his *share*. The theory states that he will do this by maximizing the ratio of his resources to the total resources of the coalition. Since his resources will be the same regardless of which coalition he joins, the lower the total resources, the greater will be his share. Thus, where the total payoff

is held constant, he will favor the *cheapest winning coalition.*

Finally, a coalition will form if and only if there are *reciprocal strategy choices* between two participants. To illustrate, let us assume the X's desired coalition in some three-person game is XY, that Y's is XY, or YZ, and that Z's favored coalition is XZ. Only X and Y have *reciprocal strategy choices,* i.e., require the other in their preferred coalition, and, thus, the coalition XY is predicted by the theory. The model envisions the process of coalition formation as a step-by-step process where the participants join two at a time. Once a coalition has been formed, the situation becomes a new one—that is, there is a fresh distribution of resources—and, in the new coalition situation, the original strategies may or may not be appropriate.

Experimental Design

A total of 120 subjects were recruited from social fraternities at the University of Michigan. They were told that they would be participating in an experimental study of "how political conventions operate" and that each of them would be playing the role of delegation chairman at a series of political conventions. At the beginning of every convention, each subject was given a sheet with the number of votes he and each of the other delegation chairmen controlled. The experiment consisted of 24 five-man groups composed of three men from one fraternity house and two from another.

The object of the game, for each subject, was to "win" political patronage or "jobs." To do this, he had to put together a majority of the votes by combining with

Table 1

INITIAL DISTRIBUTION OF RESOURCES AND PAYOFF FOR THREE
EXPERIMENTAL SITUATIONS

Convention		Player				
		Red	Yellow	Blue	Green	White
One:	Votes	20	20	20	20	20
	Jobs	100	100	100	100	100
Two:	Votes	17	25	17	25	17
	Jobs	100	100	100	100	100
Three:	Votes	15	35	35	6	10
	Jobs	90	100	0	90	0

other chairmen in a prescribed fashion. To form a coalition, he had to decide with the other chairman or chairmen how to divide up the jobs to which their coalition was entitled.

The operationalizations of the variables of the theory are:

1. *Initial distribution of resources.* The number of votes or delegates controlled by each subject were the resources of the convention; the total number of votes was 101.

2. *The payoff.* A certain number of jobs were associated with every winning coalition and the subjects were told to try to acquire as many of these jobs as possible over all the conventions.

3. *Non-utilitarian strategy preference.* The use of fraternity members as subjects was dictated by this variable. We assumed that every subject had a positive preference for the other subject or subjects who were members of the same fraternity as himself and that he was neutral between members within any one house.

Positions in the conventions were labeled by color and these colors were assigned in two different ways to vary non-utilitarian strategy preferences. In Condition RBW, the three-man contingent received the colors red, blue, and white randomly distributed among them while the two-man contingent received yellow and green. In

Condition YGW, the three-man contingent received yellow, green, and white and the two-man group received red and blue. Assignments were made alternately, resulting in 12 groups under each condition of non-utilitarian strategy preference. An effort made to keep the social status of the members the same *within* any house, i.e., active or senior fraternity members were not placed with new initiates or "pledges."

4. *Decision point.* A simple majority of the 101 votes was necessary for a coalition to be awarded the designated number of jobs and thus end the convention.

Specific Procedures

For each convention,[3] the subjects had a list giving the initial distribution in votes and information from which they could calculate the payoff to any coalition. Table 1 reproduces these figures with the positions identified by color.

The subjects were seated behind parti-

---

[3] Each group participated in four conventions altogether, with each convention adding an additional complexity. The final convention, while it had some interesting developments, was inconclusive as a test of the theory and will not be reported here.

tions so that they were not visible to each other although they could all be seen by the experimenter. Each had a set of five invitation cards which had the color of each chairman including the subject's own color. At a given signal, the subjects held up the single card of the person with whom they wished to bargain or, if they did not wish to bargain at that time, their own card. The experimenter then announced whether or not reciprocal choices had occurred.

If and only if such reciprocal choices occurred, the two subjects left their partitions and entered the "smoke filled room" where they were allowed to discuss terms of a deal for a period of three minutes. In order to form a coalition, they had to reach an agreement on some *division of the jobs* which would be their portion if they ended up in a winning coalition. They were not committed to reach an agreement simply because they had entered the bargaining room and they could meet again later by the procedure of reciprocal invitations.

At the end of each bargaining session, the experimenter announced to the rest of the group whether or not an agreement had been reached although he did not reveal the terms. If an agreement was reached and the chairmen involved possessed a majority of the votes, the convention was over and the experimenter distributed the job tokens in the manner specified by their agreement. If, as in most cases, their agreement left them short of a majority, they then returned to the "convention floor," where they were allowed to sit behind the same partition and communicate freely. For the duration of the convention, they played as a unit; the coalition acted in every way as if it were a single player with the combined resources of its members. Together the two members of a coalition held up only one card and any other player invited the whole coalition or other unattached players.

Subsequent bargaining sessions might involve three or even four people but they were essentially two-man sessions with one side of the table being represented by a two-member delegation in which one person acted as spokesman. These bargaining sessions were recorded on tape. Each convention continued by the procedure described until an agreement had been reached between chairmen who controlled a majority of the votes. The convention was then complete and the jobs were distributed.

To avoid the necessity of listing all coalitions, subjects were given the following rule by which they could calculate the payoff for any coalition: A winning coalition receives the highest number of jobs associated with any member; a losing coalition receives nothing. Thus, in Convention Three (see Table 1) a coalition between Red, Yellow, and Green would receive 100 jobs while one between Blue, Green, and White received 90 jobs.

A cash prize was given to the person with the highest job total at each position over all 24 groups. The experimenter pointed out to the subjects that this manner of awarding the prize meant that there was nothing to gain by "punishing" someone in the present group during the later conventions in the series because of his high total on earlier ones. We hoped by this means to forestall one possible interdependence between conventions. The results of each convention were not announced until the conclusion of all conventions and the subjects were prohibited from looking ahead or making any commitments beyond the duration of one convention.

An illustrative example from Convention Two might provide some feeling for the action of the experiment. On round one of the invitations, Red (with 17 votes) and Yellow (with 25 votes) hold up each other's cards and there is no reciprocity among the others. Red and Yellow enter the bargaining room and agree to divide their share, 40 per cent for Red and 60 per cent for Yellow. They return to the convention floor and there are no reciprocal invitations for a few rounds. Finally, on the fifth round, Red-Yellow and Blue hold up each other's cards.

They are unable to reach an agreement, and on round six, Red-Yellow and White hold up each other's cards and Blue and Green also choose each other. Red-Yellow and White meet in one room and Blue and Green also bargain in another. The former group reaches an agreement in which White receives 30 per cent and Red-Yellow get 70 per cent. This coalition is now winning and is entitled to 100 jobs under the formula given earlier of which White receives 30, Red receives 28 (40 per cent of 70 jobs) and Yellow gets 42 (60 per cent of 70 jobs).

EXPERIMENTAL RESULTS

The assumption that subjects would prefer members of their own fraternity to those from a different group was simpler than the actual case. Occasionally, exactly the opposite effect was true. Some players preferred to take their chances with a stranger rather than to bargain with a "difficult" fraternity brother. In short, non-utilitarian strategy preferences were somewhat uncontrolled, with fraternity affiliation as perhaps the most important but still only one of several determinants.

Convention One (see Table 1) actually tests the validity of the fraternity distinc-

tion rather than the theory. It indicates the extent to which individuals choose to join with their fraternity brothers where the "rational" parameters of the theory are held constant.

In Table 2 we can see that while there is a tendency present it is somewhat less than universal. The chance frequencies of choosing one's fraternity brothers are given in parentheses next to the actual frequencies. The choices are tabulated separately for those who had only one fraternity brother in the group and those who had two. Only when all rounds in which there were no reciprocal invitations previously are taken together is the tendency for subjects to choose their fraternity brother statistically significant; the magnitude remains slight.[4]

We must conclude that there is very little validity to fraternity membership as a measure of non-utilitarian strategy preference. Few of the results in the remainder of the experiment differed between the two methods of assigning colors. Consequently, the results for the two conditions will be combined with a few exceptions where the differences are still of interest.

The theory actually makes two kinds of predictions. One type concerns the individual invitations in each convention ("choice" hypotheses), while the other concerns the formation of coalitions through reciprocal choices ("combinatorial" hypotheses).

There is one genuine test of the theory

---

[4] The null hypothesis in this and subsequent cases is calculated on the assumption that players are choosing at random. To test the significance of departures from chance frequencies, the binomial distribution was used with a small N (under 25) and Chi Square was used with a larger N.

contained in Convention One. When two coalitions have formed without a majority being reached, the situation is a Caplow Type 3 triad[5] in which two "players" have 40 votes and a third has 20 votes. This occurred in seven of the groups. The choice hypothesis in this situation is that the players with 40 votes will choose the player with 20 votes rather than each other.

This hypothesis is tested twice, independently, every time the situation occurs, and of the 14 independent tests, 13 were predicted correctly ($P < .001$). The combinatorial hypothesis would predict that the final coalition will *not* be between the two groups with 40 votes each. This was confirmed in six of the seven cases and the one exception occurred only after three earlier bargaining sessions had failed to produce a coalition which would have confirmed the hypothesis.

Convention Two. In this convention, the theory predicts that Red, Blue, and White will choose each other and that the cheapest coalition, Red-Blue-White, will be the final coalition.

The case of Yellow and Green in Convention Two is an interesting one and raises a problem which is frequently encountered by "rational" theories. How much credit for foresight is assumed? The cheapest winning coalition for either Yellow or Green would be formed by joining with two of the players with 17 votes. Shouldn't Yellow and Green, therefore, choose among Red, Blue, and White according to the theory presented here?

Yellow and Green may reason that while *their* best interest lies with these

players; Red, Blue, and White have no incentive to choose them. Therefore, the most "rational" strategy in the circumstnaces may be to play in a manner which will disrupt the game or, in other words, to play for an "error." If Yellow and Green combine quickly, for example, they may be able to woo one of the others before they can combine. Yet, there is no reason to expect that playing for an error in this way is preferable to playing for a "direct" error by assuming that Red, Blue, or White will fail to see their proper strategy from the outset. If all errors are equally possible, Yellow and Green should still estimate their expected payoff from a coalition in the manner predicated by the theory. Accordingly, we predicted that in Convention Two, Yellow and Green will choose either Red, Blue, or White.

Table 3 shows that Red, Blue, and White do have some tendency to choose each other as predicted. Under condition YGW where Red and Blue are from one fraternity and Yellow, Green, and White are from the other, White is in a position where he *must* choose a member of a rival fraternity if he is to choose Red or Blue as the theory predicts. Therefore, we have provided in Table 3 a revised initial choice tally which excludes those cases in which *all* of the predicted choices were in a different fraternity from the chooser. With the removal of these eleven cases, the significance level goes up sharply and the hypothesis is more substantially confirmed.

More striking than the confirmation of the hypothesis concerning Red, Blue, and White is the significant *reversal* of the hypothesis concerning Yellow and Green. Not only might Yellow and Green feel that the predicted choices would not reciprocate, but they are also from the same fraternity house in both conditions.

---

[5] See Theodore Caplow, "A Theory of Coalitions in the Triad," *American Sociological Review*, 21 (August, 1956), pp. 489–493.

Table 2

FREQUENCY OF CHOOSING FRATERNITY BROTHERS IN CONVENTION ONE

		Brother	Other	N[b]	P
First Round:	3-man group	57% (50%)	43% (50%)	63	NS
	2-man group	36% (25%)	64% (75%)	45	≐.10
Other Rounds:[a]	3-man group	60% (50%)	40% (50%)	63	≐.10
	2-man group	28% (25%)	72% (75%)	46	NS
Total:	3-man group	59% (50%)	41% (50%)	131	<.05
	2-man group	32% (25%)	68% (75%)	91	NS

[a] Where no reciprocal choices occurred on earlier rounds.
[b] The total number of first round choices is only 113 since seven subjects held up their own color on the first round.

Table 3

INITIAL CHOICES FOR CONVENTION TWO

	Percentage Correctly Predicted	N	P
Red, Blue, White	61%(50%)[a]	67	<.10
Red, Blue, White (revised)[b]	66%(50%)	56	<.02
Yellow, Green	33%(75%)	48	(<.01)[c]

[a] The expected chance percentages are included next to the actual percentages in this and in subsequent tables.
[b] Excluding choices by White in Condition YGW.
[c] In opposite direction.

Where they were the only members from that house, in condition RBW, the tendency to pick each other is considerably greater. In this case, they pick each other 79 per cent of the time with a chance expectancy of 25 per cent, while in condition YGW, they choose each other only 54 per cent of the time (.10 > p > .05). Apparently, Yellow and Green are eschewing the "lost cause" of inviting Red, White, or Blue and are instead turning to each other.

As we can see in Table 4, they are sometimes successful in luring one of the players with 17 votes into the coalition and for considerably less than 1/8 of the jobs. While the predicted coalition Red-Blue-White takes place significantly more often than chance, there are numerous "errors." Occasionally, Red, Blue, and White reached the bargaining room as the theory predicted but could not reach an agreement. Subsequently, they may have

Table 4

FINAL COALITIONS AND FIRST POTENTIALLY WINNING SESSION FOR CONVENTION TWO

	Final Coalition	First Potentially Winning Session
RBW (predicted)	8 (p<.002)	10 (p<.001)
RYB	2	1
RBG	2	2
RGW	3	3
YBW	1	1
RYW	0	0
BGW	0	0
RYG	2	3
YBG	1	1
YGW	5	3
Total	24	24

joined or some other winning coalition may have formed. To be able to predict who will reach the bargaining room in this situation is at least partial support for the theory, so we have examined this criterion as well. It reveals more impressive confirmation for the theory despite the fact that where Red, Blue, and White *finally* joined they were not always the first potentially winning group to meet.

Since the theory frequently favors the initially weak against the initially strong, it is interesting to examine the following four-man situation which occurs fairly frequently in Convention Two:[6]

Red-Blue:	34 votes
Green:	25 votes
Yellow:	25 votes
White:	17 votes

Here, the cheapest winning coalition is between the strongest player, Red-Blue, and the weakest, White; those who are in between in resources are in the strategically weakest position according to the theory. This hypothesis is supported in 10 out of 12 instances (p < .001).

Many other situations develop in the step-by-step process of coalition formation that are in effect new situations. These, as in the four-man situation described above, confirm the theory, frequently with high levels of significance.[7]

Convention Three. This convention has two new elements. First, there are now

different payoffs depending on the composition of the winning coalition and, second, it is possible for two players (Yellow and Blue) to form a winning coalition in a *single* round. There are seven minimal winning coalitions, but because of the sequential nature of the coalition formation process, non-minimal coalitions can, and occasionally do, occur. Nevertheless, a "null hypothesis" of one-seventh is the most conservative estimate we can use in evaluating the results.

Differences in the number of steps necessary to form a winning coalition add a new variable not considered in the theory. It was implicitly assumed that the formation of alternative coalitions would offer the *same* practical difficulties and involve equal risk. In the experimental design, getting into the bargaining room was not always easily accomplished and the "bird in hand" philosophy frequently prevailed. Subjects would accept an offer here and now despite a belief that a better deal was possible through additional bargaining sessions.

The result was an advantage in the final division of the jobs for those who had already formed a coalition as long as the other players were divided. In Conventions One and Two, the spokesman for a coalition frequently used the argument, with considerable effectiveness, that the coalition's alternatives were immediate while the other player's single alternative depended on himself and the remaining two players joining in a process which necessarily took two steps.

A similar effect was apparently working in Convention Three. Yellow and Blue could avoid the risks and additional bargaining by *immediately* agreeing in spite of the fact that their coalition was the

---

[6] For convenience, the coalition is called Red-Blue and the player with 17 votes, White.

[7] In one particularly noteworthy triadic situation where one party has 34 votes, one has 50, and one has 17, the predicted choices are made in 29 out of 32 cases (p<.001).

least cheap of the minimal winning coalitions.

In this game, Yellow-Green-White is the cheapest coalition with the highest payoff. For Blue, the coalition Blue-Green-White is most desirable, but Green and White will prefer to join with Yellow where the coalition receives 100 instead of 90 jobs to divide. Similarly, Red-Yellow-Green will be Red's choice but not the first choice of the others. It is interesting to note that the "weakest" player, Green, is included in every player's preferred coalition strategy according to the theory.

Tables 5 and 6 indicate, as in Convention Two, a somewhat complicated pattern of support and rejection. Green and White follow the coalition strategy predicted but Yellow sharply deviates. More than 70 per cent of Yellow's "incorrect" choices are his choice of Blue. Yellow apparently prefers to try the less risky and quicker coalition with Blue than the cheaper coalition with Green and White. Similarly, the reversal of correct predictions for Blue is accounted for by his choice of Yellow on 12 occasions. In fact, the theory leads to a rather impractical

Table 5

INITIAL CHOICES FOR CONVENTION THREE

Chooser	Percentage Correctly Predicted	N	P
Green	59% (50%)	22	<.02
White	74% (50%)	23	
Yellow	25% (50%)	24	(<.02)a
Red	43% (50%)	23	NS
Blue	33% (50%)	24	(<.10)a

a In wrong direction.

Table 6

FINAL COALITIONS AND FIRST POTENTIALLY WINNING SESSION FOR CONVENTION THREE

	Final Coalition	First Potentially Winning Session
YGW (predicted)	5 (NS)	6 (NS)
RYG	4	2
BGW	1	4
RYW	2	2
RGB	3	2
RBW	1	1
YB	6 (NS)	7 (=.07)
YBG	1	0
RYB	1	0
Total	24	24

strategy for Blue since, as we shall see in discussing the final division of jobs, he can rarely do better than join with Yellow although this is *not* true of Yellow's joining with Blue.

Table 6 indicates that the distribution of final coalitions does not significantly support the theory. Yellow-Green-White, while it occurs more than average, is less frequent than Blue-Yellow. However, if we limit our attention to the 6 three-man minimal winning coalitions where *the number of steps necessary to form the coalition is held constant*, the results appear a little more favorable. The three most likely coalitions according to the theory occurred 10 out of 18 times (NS). However, using the criterion of the first potentially winning bargaining session, the three predicted coalitions met 12 out of 17 times (p = .07).

As in Convention Two, intermediate four-man and three-man situations allow for additional tests of the theory. With virtually any start other than a coalition between Yellow and Blue, the action of Convention Three gives supporting evidence.

Test of the General Hypothesis

The experimental results *indirectly* test the general hypothesis of the theory since the specific predictions of choices and coalitions are largely based upon it. However, data on the actual division of the jobs shed further light on the process.

What is the relationship between the initial distribution of resources (votes) which a player has and his share of the payoff (jobs)? In Table 7, we consider the average number of jobs per winning coalition for each color. In Convention One, where all have equal votes, there are few differences. In Convention Two, although the two strong players are included in the winning coalition less frequently than the others, on those occasions in which they are included, they are able to demand a larger share of the jobs than the others. Yellow and Green together

average 37.8 jobs against 31.1 jobs for Red, Blue, and White ($p < .001$). Similarly, job share follows resources in Convention Three. Yellow is able to fare better than Blue in Convention Three because his presence in a coalition will mean a higher total payoff.

It is interesting to compare Yellow's success with various coalition strategies in Convention Three. He is most successful when he follows the predicted strategy of joining with White and Green where he averages 55.4 jobs in five such coalitions. He does virtually as well by joining with Blue on six occasions for a 54.3 job average. However, when he is involved in any other coalition, as he was on eight occasions, he averages only 45.0 jobs. Blue, on the other hand, averages 45.7 jobs when joining with Yellow but only 38.5 when following any other strategy.

In general, the main hypothesis of the theory is supported. There are few equal divisions where the participants have unequal votes *despite equalities of strategic position*. Players are able to get more than their proportional share in some situations, but they are rarely able to achieve

Table 7

AVERAGE JOBS PER COALITION FOR EACH COLOR

Convention		R	Y	B	G	W
One:	Votes	20	20	20	20	20
	j/c[a]	33.9	33.7	33.4	30.7	32.6
	N	19	15	13	16	10
Two:	Votes	17	25	17	25	17
	j/c	27.9	38.8	32.4	37.0	33.1
	N	17	11	14	13	17
Three:	Votes	15	35	35	6	10
	j/c	27.8	50.6	41.8	22.1	24.7
	N	11	19	13	14	9

[a] Average number of jobs received when a member of the winning coalition.

what they might hope to get if differences in resources were ignored.

To illustrate this, where two non-winning coalitions have formed, the fifth player might be expected to get up to 50 per cent of the total jobs since the alternative to his inclusion is for the two coalitions to join. In practice, players in this situation rarely received anything close to 50 per cent and, in fact, *rarely demanded that much*. Some subjects settled for as little as 1/3 or less and those who received as much as 40 per cent were highly pleased. Despite the nature of their strategic position, subjects seemed to feel that any amount which they received above their proportional share was, as it were, sheer profit.

The Bargaining Process

The verbatim transcriptions of the bargaining sessions of the "smoke filled room" are a rich source of insight into the thinking processes of the subjects as they plotted and planned their future strategies and discussed the reasons for their past actions. There is much informal evidence in these dialogues for the validity of the general hypothesis. Space limitations unfortunately prevent the reproduction of verbatim excerpts.

When a two-man coalition was formed, the players generally used their additional time to discuss whom they would invite to join on the next round. Arguments which amounted to informal statements of the general hpothesis of the theory were given explicitly again and again and could be inferred from many other statements.

The argument that initial resources are irrelevant because any combination considered will be winning is also used, although less frequently, and it is used invariably by players with few resources. However, those who use it rarely demand what its logic would dictate. In fact, they appear to act as if there existed a "just price" described by their share of the votes even when they are demanding more. They are willing to benefit from the favorable position in which they find themselves, but the very words "benefit" and "favorable" imply a comparison with some standard or expectation.

Conclusions

To summarize the results, the theory was generally successful in predicting the *initial choices* of those players who were members of the predicted winning coalition. Thus, Red, Blue, and White's choices in Convention Two and Green and White's choices in Convention Three corroborated the hypotheses. However, Yellow, in Convention Three, chooses in direct opposition to the prediction.

The theory was not successful in predicting the initial choices of those players who were *not* members of the predicted winning coalition. Thus, we failed to predict successfully Yellow and Green's choices in Convention Two or Red and Blue's in Convention Three.

We were successful in predicting the final coalitions in Convention Two but not so in Convention Three. However, we were able to predict which among the three-man winning coalitions would occur in Convention Three and to predict choices and coalitions in later stages. In other words, the predictions were generally correct in those groups in which Yellow and Blue did not join initially.

Thus, the theory is genrally supported

with two important exceptions. First, there is an important variable involved which the theory neglects—the risk or difficulty involved in alternative coalition strategies. Subjects frequently preferred a strategy which took only one step for successful completion to one which required two steps.

A single player bargaining with a coalition realized that, if he failed to reach an agreement, a successful alternative strategy would require two steps. If the other players had a coalition as well, his alternative required only one step and his previous disadvantage in bargaining vanished. Similarly, Yellow and Blue in Convention Three frequently joined in the only winning coalition which could be completed in a single step. One might speculate that this occurred *only* 25 per cent of the time because it was the least *cheap* of the minimal winning coalitions.

The second exception to the general support of the theory was the failure to predict the choices of those whom the theory predicted would not be included in the final coalition. These people had an interesting duality of strategy, for if they followed the predicted strategy *and everyone else did also*, they would be excluded from the winning coalition. They might benefit the most by an error if they followed the predicted strategy. Still, by joining quickly themselves, they might hope to gain the advantage of the earlier coalition.

One method of formulating the regularities in a process as complex as coalition formation is to add variables to an incomplete formulation and, thus, successively to approximate a completely adequate theory. It is possible to include both of the exceptions mentioned in a more general variable which can be incorporated into the theory. Instead of assuming that all coalition strategies are equally difficult, it might be possible to assign probabilities of success to each alternative.

While considerable care would be required in the assignment of definitive probabilities of success for alternative strategies, an example might indicate the direction of such an attempt in this particular situation. Every bargaining session has a certain probability of success. While this is to some degree variable, for practical purposes it could be treated as a constant. Then, if this figure were, for example, 3/4, a two step strategy would have only 9/16 probability of success instead of the 3/4 probability of a one step strategy.

Similarly, those not included in the predicted winning coalition might not assume that all other players are equally likely to choose them. It may be more reasonable to assume that the reciprocity of choice necessary for entrance into the bargaining room is more likely to come from others who are excluded from the predicted coalition. The assignment of precise probabilities offers difficulties but even rough approximations would help to explain the major deviations from the present theoretical predictions.

The estimated payoff to an individual from any prospective coalition would then be a product of three factors instead of two. The share and the total payoff would be considered as before, but now the probability of the prospective strategy being successfully executed would also be part of the product.

CHOICE BEHAVIOR IN COALITION GAMES*

Richard Ofshe and S. Lynne Ofshe

Two experimental situations that are widely utilized in the study of decision making and have been the context for a multitude of research efforts are the light-guessing experiment and the coalition game. The results of researches in these settings are quite different. Investigations in the context of the former situation have shown decision-making behavior to be extremely stable, and a plethora of very precise models of behavior has resulted (Luce and Suppes, 1965). Unfortunately, research in the context of the second setting has seemed to result in confusion rather than clarification (Gamson, 1964). In this paper, we will take advantage of certain similarities between these two situations and show that a decision-making theory originally developed for the light-guessing situation can be fruitfully applied to behavior in the more complex coalition game.

The Light-Guessing Experiment

In the Humphreys' light-guessing experiment (1939), a subject is seated before two light bulbs and is instructed to predict which bulb will illuminate on each of a series of trials. After he makes his prediction, the subject is able to see whether or not he is correct by simply observing which light subsequently illuminates. If the subject is correct he receives some sort of reward. The probability that a given bulb illuminates is fixed in advance and is typically figured for a block of trials. If, for example, the probabilities were .80 and .20 and figured over blocks of twenty trials, one light would come on sixteen times and the other four times in each block.

At the start of the experiment, subjects typically distribute their choices equally between the two lights. As the experiment continues, they tend to increase their choices of the more frequently reinforced light. After one to two hundred trials, the behavior of subjects generally stabilizes, and they choose each light with about the same probability with which it illuminates; this is generally called a "matching strategy."[1] For example, in the case in which the right-hand light illuminates on 80

* Reprinted from *Behavioral Science*, Volume 15, No. 4, by permission of James G. Miller, M.D., Ph.D., Editor.

[1] The game-theoretic term, strategy, refers to the distribution of choices for the possible alternatives. The term implies that a plan has been adopted and that subjects can be treated as having selected a probability distribution for their behaviors which will be adhered to for a substantial period of time.

percent of the trials and the left light on 20 percent, the subject will, when he reaches stable-state, distribute his choices with a probability of approximately .80 for the right light and .20 for the left-hand light.

Siegel (Siegel, Siegel, and Andrews, 1964) developed a theory based on the idea that individuals act so as to maximize expected utility in their decision making. He proposed that in the context of the light-guessing experiment there were two sources of utility. The first was the utility of a correct choice deriving from both the monetary and nonmonetary payoffs associated with alternatives. Siegel identified a second source of utility. He proposed that there existed a utility for choice variability due to the intrinsic boredom of the pure strategy (choosing one light consistently), as well as from the greater satisfaction connected with being able to correctly predict the less frequent event. In post-experiment interviews with subjects, Siegel and Goldstein (1959) found that many subjects periodically predicted the less frequent event for one or the other of the reasons mentioned above. Subjects behaved in this fashion even though they reported that they were aware that the "best" strategy was to choose the more frequent event with certainty. Goodnow (1955) has also reported that subjects were able to follow a pure strategy only by inventing games which served to decrease the monotony inherent in repeatedly choosing the same alternative. Subjects in Goodnow's experiments devised games such as varying the hand used to operate

the response key or varying the pressure applied to the key.[2]

Siegel constructed a formal model which was intended to predict stable-state choice strategies.[3] The model was subjected to several experimental tests and found to be quite accurate. Over the series of experiments Siegel conducted, the mean absolute discrepancy between the predicted probabilities with which subjects chose the lights and the observed probabilities was .019. The development of the decision theory, formal model and detailed reports of the experimental program designed to test the model are reported in Siegel, Siegel, and Andrews.

The Coalition Game

A typical coalition game employs three players, each of whom is assigned a certain weight or resource on each trial. The players are instructed that on each trial a payoff, usually monetary, will be given to the individual, or coalition, controlling the majority of resources. The assignment of resources is usually designed to structure the situation such that if any two players combine, they control a majority of the resources.

Much of the current focus in coalition studies is on the effect of the distribution of resources on the selection of partners

---

[2] The results of an experiment conducted by Siegel which clearly demonstrated the existence of this source of utility can be found in Siegel.

[3] Stable-state choice strategy refers to an individual's decision strategy after he has "adjusted" to the situation. In choice experiments of the type discussed in this paper, it is typically observed that subjects adopt a stable choice strategy after a learning period of variable length. The model was designed to predict only the subjects' stable-state strategies. It was not intended to account for the learning process prior to stabilization.

and the subsequent division of rewards.[4] It has, however, been argued (Ofshe and Ofshe, in press) that the notable lack of progress in explaining behavior in the game is due to the attempt to treat both the choice process (selection of a potential coalition partner) and the bargaining aspects of the game (division of payoffs between coalition partners) at the same time and without the aid of powerful theories of either of the separate processes. In any concrete situation there is obviously an interaction effect between the two processes. Since most explanations consider only factors of resources and rewards, while the data reflect many additional variables, the relationship between the variables of primary interest is frequently obscured.

It is possible to consider the two processes separately, that is, to decompose the complex game and attempt to develop theories of its constituent general processes prior to attempting to predict their interaction. The empirical counterpart of the decomposition can readily be accomplished by fixing the payoffs for forming alternative coalitions. This permits the separate study of the choice process. Given this decomposition, the game may be viewed as an individual decision-making problem, in which each of the players is faced with a series of binary choices; that is, he can choose either of the other two players on each trial. This approach permits an analysis of the bulk of the coalition game literature in terms of three variables: the probability that a player's choice will be reciprocated; the payoff for

forming alternative coalitions; and the player's desire that the outcome of the game be equitable to all the participants. These factors are assumed to operate in the same manner as the three factors affecting behavior in the light-guessing experiment: the probability of a correct choice; the payoff associated with each alternative; and the basic monotony of the situation.

In a coalition game, an individual can win a reward only if his choice is reciprocated. This directly corresponds to a correct choice in the light-guessing experiment; an individual receives a payoff only if the light which he has chosen subsequently illuminates. Thus, it is obvious that a reciprocated choice in the coalition game is strictly analogous to a correct choice in the light-guessing experiment.

The second utility considered in the light-guessing situation, the utility of choice variability, may not seem to apply in this situation, for it can be argued that the game itself destroys boredom as well as any desire to choose the less frequently reinforced choice. However, there is a factor in this situation which is not operating in the light-guessing experiment. A player's choices have consequences not only for himself, but also for the other two players. That is, the rewards of the other players are to some extent dependent upon his choices. There is some evidence that individuals are concerned with giving everyone in the game a fair chance. Lieberman (1962) points out that the results of one of his experiments "describe the behavior of three individuals in a situation where two have a clear incentive to unite forces to the detriment of the third. In a majority of choices (70 percent) the two did just that. However, in a sizeable minority of choices (30 per-

---

[4] For an excellent review and critique of the traditional approach to coalition game research, see Gamson.

cent) this prescribed behavior did not occur. Some subjects felt it was not fair to do this." Since the equity norm results in a subjective utility for varying choices, it is directly comparable to the utility of choice variability in the light-guessing experiment.

The Model

Since the coalition choice problem is analogous to the problem confronting subjects in light-guessing situations, Siegel's model can be derived for decision making in the coalition game. It should be noted that this model will apply in cases in which the probabilities with which the events occur sum to more, or less, than one; that is, it can be applied when neither or both players choose the subject on some trials.

In deriving the model the following notation will be used:

π_i = the probability that the player is chosen by participant i, $i = 1, 2$

a_i = the marginal utility of a reciprocated choice with participant i, $i = 1, 2$

b = the marginal utility of choice variability

α_i = the ratio of the marginal utility of a reciprocated choice to the marginal utility of choice variability (a_i/b)

P_i = the stable-state probability that the subject chooses participant i, $i = 1, 2$

The purpose of this model is to enable predictions to be made for the subject's stable-state strategy, P_1 and P_2, from the values of the other variables. Employing the concept of mathematical expectation and the above definitions, it is obvious that the expectation that the subject's choice will be reciprocated is the sum of the probabilities that he has a reciprocated choice with each of the other players, or

$P_1\pi_1 + P_2\pi_2$, and the expected utility of a reciprocated choice is the sum of the expected utilities for all alternatives, or $a_1P_1\pi_1 + a_2P_2\pi_2$. Given the assumption that the utility of choice variability is proportional to the variance of the subject's choice, the interpretation of the utility or choice variability function is quite simple in the case of two alternatives. Assuming that with probability P_1 the subject chooses the first alternative and with probability $P_2 = 1 - P_1$ he chooses the second alternative, it is clear that the model of his choices is that of a sequence of Bernouli trials with parameter P_1. Thus the variance of each choice is $P_1(1 - P_1)$, and it is assumed in the model that an individual's utility of choice variability is proportional to the variance of his (random) choice, that is $2bP_1(1 - P_1)$.

The expected utility, U, of P_1, the stable strategy of choosing alternative one with probability P_1, is assumed to be the sum of these two utility functions:

$$\text{(1)} \quad \begin{aligned} U &= \alpha_1 P_1\pi_1 + \alpha_2 P_2\pi_2 + 2bP_1(1-P_1) \\ &= -2bP_1^2 + (\alpha_1\pi_1 - \alpha_2\pi_2 + 2b)P_1 \\ &\quad + \alpha_2\pi_2 \end{aligned}$$

It was assumed that the individual is maximizing his expected utility U, by his choice of a strategy, that is, by his choice of P_1. The problem is to find the value of P_1 which will maximize U in the above equation. Since U is concave downwards when graphed as a function of P_1, the maximum of U with respect to P_1 occurs when $\partial U/\partial P_1 = 0$:

$$\text{(2)} \quad 0 = \frac{\partial U}{\partial P_1} = -4bP_1 + \alpha_1\pi_1 \\ - \alpha_2\pi_2 + 2b.$$

This equation can be solved for P_1; therefore, the maximum of U occurs when

$$P_1=\left(\frac{\alpha_1\pi_1-\alpha_2\pi_2+2b}{4b}\right)$$

(3)

$$=\left(\frac{1}{4}\right)\left(\frac{\alpha_1}{b}\pi_1-\frac{\alpha_2}{b}\pi_2\right)+\frac{1}{2},$$

and substituting α_i for a_i/b:

(4)
$$P_1=(1/4)(\alpha_1\pi_1-\alpha_2\pi_2)+1/2$$
$$P_2=1-P_1.$$

This can be simplified in the case in which the utilities of the two alternatives are equal, that is, $\alpha_1=\alpha_2(\alpha_1=\alpha_2=\alpha)$:

(5)
$$P_1=(1/4)\alpha(\pi_1-\pi_2)=1/2$$
$$P_2=1-P_1.$$

These two sets of equations will predict the stable-state behavior of an individual given the probabilities of feedback and the values of the utilities.[5] The general choice model being used here is identical to the one employed for the non-social situation; the only changes are in the substantive interpretations of certain variables.

The program of experiments designed to test the applicability of the choice model to social decision making paralleled the series of researches carried out by Siegel in the nonsocial setting. The or-

dinal effects of each of the three independent variables (π_i, a_i, and b) were tested and found to follow the model's prediction.[6] The precise numeric predictions of the formal model were subjected to two tests. The first test was in a situation in which the ratio of the utility for forming a coalition to the utility for equity was the same for all alternatives. In the second test, the experiments were structured such that these ratios were unequal for alternative coalitions.

PROCEDURES

The research was conducted at a computer-controlled laboratory facility operated by the Center for Research in Management Science at the University of California at Berkeley. The major hardware of the laboratory was a *PDP 5/8* computer with a timesharing system that operated up to ten teletype stations around the laboratory. Utilization of the laboratory facility permitted nine subjects to be run simultaneously with computer control of the experiment and automatic data recording.

Subjects were scheduled in groups of nine. If some subjects did not appear at the appointed time, confederates were used to fill in during the instruction period in order to bring the total number of apparent players to six, or nine. After all the subjects (and confederates) had been seated in the large room, the following instructions were read by the experimenter:

In today's session, we are studying an aspect of group interaction. You will be

[5] It should be noted that with certain combinations of feedback probabilities utility values, the model can yield predictions for P_i greater than one or less than zero. Since P_i refers to a probability, it is meaningful only between the values of zero and one; consequently, it is necessary to impose a limiting condition on the model (*i.e.*, $0\leqq P_i\leqq 1$) and solve for the maximizing choice strategy within the range of possible values. Since the utility function is monotonically increasing, whenever the model yields a P_i greater than one it can be shown that the maximizing behavioral strategy is to choose the ith alternative with a probability of one. Analogously, when P_i is less than zero the maximizing strategy is to choose the ith alternative with a probability of zero.

[6] Tests of the ordinal predictions are reported in Ofshe and Ofshe.

taking part in what is called a coalition game. This game is played by groups of three individuals. Since there are nine (six) of you here today, there will be three (two) separate games, with three of you participating in each game. A game consists of a series of plays; on each play, every participant is asked to choose one of the other players as a coalition partner. If two persons select each other as partners, they have formed a coalition and each of them receives a reward in the form of money; the third person receives nothing. You can win only by forming a coalition. It is possible that on some plays, no one will win. This occurs when no player's choice has been reciprocated. Consequently, on each play, at most two persons can win a reward, and at least one person must lose. Your object is to win as much money as you can.

From a single player's viewpoint, the game is very simple. On each play, you must choose one of the other two participants as a partner. If the person you have selected has also chosen you, you have formed a coalition and consequently win a reward. From your viewpoint, there are four possible outcomes to a play. Assume that you are player one. You may form a coalition with either player two or player three. In both cases, you would win a reward. Players two and three may choose one another; in this case, because you are not in a coalition, you would win nothing regardless of whom you had chosen. Finally, no coalition may form; this occurs when no player's choice is reciprocated and in this situation, none of the players will win anything. Since you can win a reward only if the person whom you have chosen has also selected you, you should try to predict which of the other players are going to choose you on each trial.

In this game you and the other two players will not communicate verbally but through teletypes which are connected together. The teletypes are set up so that you will *not* necessarily be playing with the persons in the immediately adjoining rooms. For example, the player in this room (experimenter points) might be connected with a player in the room down there (experimenter points) and another player over here (experimenter points). When we have completed the instructions you will each be taken to a smaller room in which you will find a teletype. Posted on the teletype will be your player number and information about the reward that you will receive from each of your two possible coalitions.

(The next three paragraphs discussed the use of the teletype equipment.)

Before you begin playing, let's summarize the main points. You'll be playing a coalition game with two other players. On each play, each of you will choose one of the other two players for a coalition partner. After all of you have made your choices, you will be able to see which of the others has chosen you. If the person whom you have chosen has also chosen you, you will win a monetary reward. Remember that your object is to win as much as you can. You can win a reward only if the person whom you have chosen has also selected you, so you should try to predict which of the others are going to choose you on each play. You should be concerned only *with winning as much as you possibly can.*

The above instructions were used in all conditions discussed in this paper.

After the instructions were finished, the subjects were taken individually to the smaller rooms. Each subject was shown where certain keys were located on the teletype. Posted on his teletype was a sheet which informed him of the payoffs for entering each of his two possible coalitions. The subject was given a demonstration of the equipment. The game then began and was played for 100 trials.

Subjects were led to believe that they were playing against two human decision makers. In order to attain the degree of control necessary to apply the model, however, it was required that the probabilities with which each of the other players chose the subject be predetermined and blocked over sets of trials. This precluded letting subjects actually interact. Therefore, each subject in the experiment participated in a game in which the behavior of the other two players was simulated and could be precisely determined.

Post-experiment questionnaires and interviews revealed no instance in which a subject became supicious of the situation. On the contrary, subjects reported that they believed that their decisions affected the behavior of the two robots.

Although the situation was structurally analogous to the light-guessing situation, and from the point of view of the choice theory it was isomorphic to the non-social decision situation, from the point of view of subjects it was a vastly different situation. From a subject's perspective perhaps the two most important differences between the settings were the facts that (1) in the coalition game the probabilistically-determined events were believed to be the behaviors of other humans, while in the light-guessing situation they were simply states of nature; and (2) in the coalition game it was believed that the future behavior of the other players could be affected by the subject's current decision, while in the light-guessing experiment it was *impressed* upon subjects that the behavior of the lights was determined prior to the start of the experiment.

A Test of the Equal Alpha Model

For the tests of the equal alpha[7] version of the model a pair of experiments were

conducted with male subjects and then replicated with small samples of female subjects. In these experiments, the payoffs for forming coalitions were held constant for all treatment conditions; subjects were paid five cents each time they were able to enter either possible coalition. The only aspects of the experiments that were varied between conditions were the probabilities with which the subject was chosen by the other players. Table 1 summarizes the formal characteristics of the experiments and replications.

Since the model treats the utilities for choice variability and for the payoff for predicting an event rather than the monetary value of the payoff or the objective characteristics of the experiment, it is necessary to measure the utilities of these factors in order to test the model's predictive power. The procedure for testing the model under equal alpha conditions requires a pair of observations, one for measurement and one for testing predictions.

The purpose of the first observation (experiment) is to provide an estimate of the ratio of the utility of the monetary payoff associated with a reciprocated choice to the utility of response variation induced by a specified set of experimental procedures. Given all the information from one experiment it is possible to solve the choice equations for the ratio of these utilities. That is, the choice equations are structured such that given knowledge of (1) the probabilities with which each of the events occurs; and (2) the subject's

---

[7] Conceptually, the equal alpha model is similar to the Bush-Mosteller (1955) model. That is, equal payoffs or reinforcements are

associated with all alternatives. The Bush-Mosteller model is, however, primarily concerned with the learning process prior to stabilization while the model presented here predicts stable-state behavior.

Table 1

FORMAL CHARACTERISTICS OF DECISION-MAKING EXPERIMENTS IN THE
COALITION GAME (EQUAL ALPHA MODEL)

Condition	Sex of Subjects	Probabilities of Selection by Players 1 and 2		Payoffs for Formation of Coalitions with Players 1 and 2		Number of Subjects
		π_1	π_2	α_1	α_2	
A	Male	.70*	.30	5¢	5¢	22
B	Male	.60	.40	5¢	5¢	21
A'	Female	.70	.30	5¢	5¢	6
B'	Female	.60	.40	5¢	5¢	9

* In the experiments, all subjects thought themselves player number three. Half the subjects found that player number one chose them more frequently, and half discovered that it was player two who was choosing them more frequently. For reasons of clarity in presentation of data, the player who chose the subject more frequently will be identified as player one in all tables.

observed stable-state choice strategy, it is possible to solve for the ratio of a subject's utility for the payoff for prediction of an event to his utility for response variation. In arriving at this estimate of the subject's utilities, the operating assumption is that he acts so as to maximize expected utility in his decision making.

In the second, prediction, experiment only one aspect of the treatment is changed. Both the equity aspects of the situation and the monetary payoffs for predicting events remain the same as in the measurement experiment, while the probabilities with which the events occur are altered. Theoretically, changing these probabilities has the effect of changing the stable-state strategy which maximizes a subject's expected utility. The test of the formal model is its ability to predict the *precise numeric value* of the stable-state strategy adopted by subjects in the second experiment. It should be clearly understood that the procedure for testing the model leads to non-tautological predictions. Note that no information from the

test condition is used to generate predictions; although it is not strictly necessary, different subjects are used in the measurement and prediction conditions, and changes in the π values lead to substantially different maximizing strategies in the measurement and prediction experiments.

The test procedure can be summarized as follows: An estimate of the α value is obtained from a measurement experiment. This is accomplished by using all the data from one experimental treatment and solving an equation constructed on the assumption that individuals act so as to maximize expected utility in their decision making. The alpha estimate is then employed in a set of equations designed to predict the behavior of a second sample of subjects in an experiment in which the α-determining factors are unchanged and the event parameters $(\pi_1 \ldots \pi_N)$ are varied. Changing these parameters changes the strategy that subjects should adopt if they wish to maximize their expected utility and the formal theory is correct.

The accuracy with which the model's predictions match observed behavior in the test experiment is an index of the power of the model.

The experiments and replications permit two completely independent tests of the model and four different applications. Although using one condition as the measurement experiment and the other as the prediction condition and then reversing the order permits two applications of the model, each pair of applications can be considered to constitute only one independent test (carried out in two different directions as a consistency check).

Table 2 summarizes the results of the four applications of the choice model. When Condition *A* is used as the measurement experiment and predictions are made for the stable-state choice strategies of subjects in Condition *B*, the model yields a prediction which is discrepant from the observed behavior by only .0008. When the direction of the prediction is reversed, *B* used for measurement and *A*

for prediction, the model's predictions are discrepant from the observed behavior by .0017. Note that the difference in the strategy adopted by subjects in the two conditions is substantial; for example, in Condition *A* the mean stable-state probability of a player one choice is .8636, and in Condition *B* the probability of a choice of player one is .6810. The difference between the two conditions is on the order of eighteen points.

The data generated by female subjects in the replication permit a second independent test of the model. The number of subjects in these two experiments (A' = 6; B' = 9) is exceedingly small for the type of prediction attempted by the model. The data reported in Table 2 indicate, however, that the model proves to be a reasonably accurate predictor of behavior. When A' is the measurement experiment, the choice strategy adopted by subjects in B' is different from the predictions by only .0111. In the reverse application of the model the discrepancy is .0222.

Table 2

RESULTS OF APPLICATIONS OF THE EQUAL ALPHA MODEL TO DECISION MAKING IN THE COALITION GAME

Measurement Condition	Prediction Condition	π_1 π_2	Observed P_1 and P_2*	Predicted P_1 and P_2	Discrepancy
A	*B*	.60	.6810	.6818	.0008
		.40	.3190	.3182	
B	*A*	.70	.8636	.8619	.0017
		.30	.1364	.1381	
A'	B'	.60	.7056	.7167	.0111
		.40	.2944	.2833	
B'	A'	.70	.9333	.9111	.0222
		.30	.0667	.0889	

* The calculation of the subjects' stable-state choice strategy was based on the data from the last twenty trials of the experiments.

Table 3

Results of Applications of the Equal Alpha Model Using All Available Data

Experimental Conditions	π_1	π_2	Observed		Predicted		Discrepancy
			P_1	P_2*	P_1	P_2	
B	.60	.40	.6810	.3190	.6814	.3186	.0004
A	.70	.30	.8636	.1364	.8628	.1372	.0008
B'	.60	.40	.7056	.2944	.7111	.2889	.0055
A'	.70	.30	.9333	.0667	.9222	.0778	.0111

* The calculation of the subjects' stable-state choice strategy was based on the data from the last twenty trials of the experiments.

In the technique used above, none of the data from the test condition is used in generating the predictions. Since each set of subjects is a sample from the same population, it has been assumed that the value of alpha for each set will reflect the true mean alpha for the population. Obviously, because of sampling error, the alpha values for each set of subjects will reflect some difference from the true alpha value of the parent population. In order to minimize this error, all of the data could be used to arrive at the alpha estimate and this value could be used in making the predictions. Siegel devised a method (similar to a least squares solution) of obtaining the alpha value from more than minimum data.[8] The predictions generated using this technique are shown in Table 3. Note that in this case, the data used for the measurement of alpha is not independent of the data for which predictions are made.

[8] This method is described in Appendix I of Siegel, *et al.* This technique minimizes the orthogonal distance from a point to the hyperplane; the least-squares method minimizes the oblique distance.

A Test of the Unequal Alpha Model

A second set of experiments was designed to test the unequal alpha form of the model. In these experiments, the ratio of the marginal utility of the payoff for formation of a coalition to the marginal utility for maintenance of equity was different for each of the alternative coalitions. In this set of experiments, the payoff for forming a coalition with player one was five cents, while the payoff for a coalition with player two was ten cents. In all of the experiments, the robot who chose the subject more frequently is identified as player one. A subject was therefore faced with a decision situation in which he could obtain a small payoff for forming a coalition with a player who was "anxious" to unite with him, or a relatively large payoff for forming a coalition with the player who chose him less frequently. Table 4 summarizes the formal characteristics of the three experimental conditions.

In order to apply the model it is necessary to use the data from two measurement conditions in order to estimate the values of α_1 and α_2. Since there are three treatment conditions and any two can be

Table 4

FORMAL CHARACTERISTICS OF DECISION-MAKING EXPERIMENTS IN THE
COALITION GAME (UNEQUAL ALPHA MODEL)

Condition	Sex of Subjects	Probabilities of Selection by- Players 1 and 2		Payoffs for For- mation of Coalitions with Players 1 and 2		Number of Subjects
		π_1	π_2	α_1	α_2	
C	Male	.80	.20	5¢	10¢	9
D	Male	.70	.30	5¢	10¢	14
E	Male	.60	.40	5¢	10¢	13

used for measurement, with the third serving as the test condition, it is possible to make three different applications of the model. In the first application, the data from Conditions C and D were used to estimate the α's, and Condition E was employed as the test condition. In this case, the model predicted that in stable-state the probability of a player one choice would be .4070 and the probability of a player two choice would be .5930. The observed, stable-state choice strategy of subjects in Condition E was to select player one with a probability of .4397 and

player two with a probability of .5603. The absolute discrepancy between the predicted and observed behaviors of subjects in Condition E was .0327. When Conditions C and E were used to predict the choice strategies of subjects in Condition D, the discrepancy between predicted and observed strategies was .0164. Finally, when Conditions D and E served as the measurement experiment and C was the prediction condition, the discrepancy was .0382. The results of the three applications of the model are summarized in Table 5.

Table 5

RESULTS OF APPLICATIONS OF THE UNEQUAL ALPHA MODEL TO
DECISION MAKING IN THE COALITION GAME

Measure- ment Conditions	Prediction Conditions	π_1 π_2	Observed P_1 and P_2*	Predicted P_1 and P_2	Discrepancy
C and D	E	.60	.4397	.4070	.0327
		.40	.5603	.5930	
C and E	D	.70	.5393	.5557	.0164
		.30	.4607	.4443	
D and E	C	.80	.6716	.6388	.0328
		.20	.3284	.3612	

* Calculations of subjects' stable-state choice strategies were based on the last ninety trials of Condition C and on the last sixty trials of Conditions D and E.

Table 6

RESULTS OF APPLICATIONS OF THE UNEQUAL ALPHA MODEL USING ALL AVAILABLE DATA

Experimental Conditions	π_1	π_2	Observed		Predicted		Discrepancy
			P_1	P_2*	P_1	P_2	
E	.60	.40	.4397	.5603	.4340	.5651	.0048
D	.70	.30	.5393	.4607	.5501	.4499	.0108
C	.80	.20	.6716	.3284	.6653	.3347	.0063

* Calculations of subjects' stable-state choice strategies were based on the last ninety trials of Condition C and on the last sixty trials of Conditions D and E.

As in the case of the equal alpha experiments, a certain amount of sampling error occurs. Again all of the conditions can be used to generate the alpha estimates. Table 6 reports the results of the application using this method of obtaining the alpha value.

DISCUSSION OF RESULTS

The general decision-making theory was applied to a social situation, and the formal model of the theory was subjected to three independent tests. In each case the model proved to be as powerful a predictor of choice behavior in the coalition game as it was in the light-guessing experiment. The coalition game setting provided a research situation which was considerably "richer" than the light-guessing experiment. Subjects in the coalition game considered the effects of their behaviors on future relations with the other players in the game, considered the welfare of the other players, and believed that the behavior of the other players would be affected by their actions. The greater "noise" in the coalition game did not reduce the predictive power of the model.

With regard to certain gross aspects of behavior in the two situations, subjects in the light-guessing experiment and the coalition game behave in quite dissimilar fashions. The most important difference is the length of time it takes, to adapt to the probability structure of the experiments. The difference is most apparent in cases in which the probabilities of the two events are greatly divergent from .50 for each event. In the light-guessing experiment, Siegel observed that choice behavior stabilized after about 200 trials. For example, in one of Siegel's experiments the probabilities with which the events occurred were $\pi_1 = .75$ and $\pi_2 = .25$, and the payoffs, a_1 and a_2, were both five cents. In this experiment, subjects moved from a probability of prediction of event one of .475 in the first twenty-trial block to a probability of making this prediction of .850 in the tenth twenty-trial block. Over the course of 200 trials the shift in the probability of predicting event one was .375. The most similar coalition game experiment was one in which $\pi_1 = .70$, $\pi_2 = .30$, and a_1 and a_2 were both five cents. In this experiment, subjects moved from a probability of selecting player one in the first five-trial block of .391 to a probability of making this decision of .791

in the *third* five-trial block. In a situation in which the probabilitistic events were believed to be the behaviors of other individuals, subjects evidence a probability shift in their behavior of .400 over *fifteen trials*. Apart from the negligible difference in the parameters under which the experiments were run, the only possible source for an explanation of the marked differences in behavior in the two situations rests with the effects of believing that one is in interaction with other individuals rather than trying to predict a series of probabilistically determined events.

This model is designed to predict general decision strategies in a repetitive choice situation. As it is currently formulated, it does not consider the learning, or adaptation, of subjects nor the effect of the sequences of choices of the other players. However such additional considerations can easily, at least theoretically, be integrated into this approach.

In its present form, the model uses the actual probabilities of feedback for the value of π. It could equally well use the subject's perception of this probability; after the subject has reached stable-state behavior, his subjective estimates of event parameters should be the same as the actual probabilities with which events occur. However, before the subject reaches stable-state, the subjective probabilities are apt to be different. If it were possible to estimate subjective probability on each trial, this value could be used in the model and a process formulation would be the result; that is, behavior could be predicted in the adaptive phase as well as in stable-state.

This formulation would have a second advantage. In its current form, the model cannot account for the effect of the choices seen by the subject. If subjective

rather than objective probabilities were used, this effect could be taken into consideration, since the subjective probability would be influenced by the sequences.[9]

An Extension of the Model

Siegel originally developed this model for the light-guessing situation; we have applied the model to choice behavior in the coalition game and obtained results comparable to those obtained in the nonsocial situation. The theory can be applied to decision situations other than those considered above. In this section we will report on its application to the prisoner's dilemma conflict situation.

Perhaps the classic two-person game situation is that of the prisoner's dilemma. The structure of the decision problem is built on the lines of the following situation:

> Two suspects are taken into custody and separated. The district attorney is certain that they are guilty of a specific crime, but he does not have adequate evidence to convict them at a trial. He points out to each prisoner that each has two alternatives: to confess to the crime the police are sure they have done, or not to confess. If they both do not confess, then the district attorney states that he will book them on some very minor trumped-up charge, such as petty larceny and illegal possession of a weapon, and they both will receive minor punishment; if they both confess, they will be prosecuted, but he will recommend less than the most severe sentence; but if one confesses and the other does not, then the

---

[9] We are currently working on a dynamic decision making model by attempting to develop a formulation that takes into account changes in subjective probability as a function of inputs from the environment.

confessor will receive lenient treatment for turning state's evidence, whereas the latter will get "the book" slapped at him. (Luce and Raiffa, 1957)

The basic elements of the situation are that each individual is confronted with making a decision which is conditioned by his beliefs about how the other actor will choose, and by the fact that the best outcome for the pair (each not confessing) results in a less favorable outcome than does turning state's evidence (providing that the other individual is foolish enough to trust his partner). The payoff matrix for the situation described above can be represented as follows:

Prisoner X

		Not confess	Confess
	Not Confess	1 year each	Y gets 10 years X gets 3 months
Prisoner Y			
	Confess	Y gets 3 mos. X gets 10 yrs.	8 years each

In research on interpersonal conflict, the basic elements of the situation are preserved, although the prison sentences are replaced with monetary payoffs and the criminals with college students. The dilemma faced by the two decision-makers is analogous to the problem faced by the prisoners since the payoffs are arranged such that a cooperative choice (no confession) carries a smaller payoff than a competitive choice (confession) if the other individual trusts his partner.

In this situation, a player's safest strategy is to choose alternative two under all circumstances, while the best strategy to maximize gain for both players in the

game is to always choose alternative one. Luce and Raiffa have argued that for games with only a single play, there is nothing "irrational or perverse about the choice of α_2 and β_2 [each player's alternative 2], and we must admit that if we were actually in this position we would make these choices" (Luce and Raiffa, p. 96). When there are several iterations of the game, the situation is somewhat altered. Under this condition, it is proposed that "an unarticulated collusion between players will develop" (p. 101). The difference between expected behavior in single-play games and games with multiple iterations is accounted for by the fact that with repeated plays, it is possible for the two opponents to establish a pattern of behavior that results in greater benefit for each than would be achieved if both chose the uncooperative alternative (Alternative 2).

It is the case, however, that even given the possibility of establishing a form of communication by signaling intent through consistent action, players do not "lock into" the cooperative, jointly and usually individually maximizing strategy. Nor do they establish any type of complex alternation pattern which, with perfect coordination and under certain combinations of payoffs, would result in a greater joint gain than could be obtained through simple cooperation. The problem which confronts researchers is to account for the display of a choice-strategy which does not maximize the monetary payoffs available to players in the game.

Given the structure of the decision theory considered in this paper, it is obvious that the formulation should be applicable to decision making in the prisoner's dilemma game. An analysis of the game situation in terms of the concepts of the theory is as follows.

A player in a prisoner's dilemma type game is faced with a series of binary decisions; he can choose either the cooperative alternative (choice 1) or the competitive alternative (choice 2). It is assumed that in his decision making an individual will act so as to maximize expected utility and that there are two sources of utility in the situation. The first is the marginal utility of the payoffs for each of the possible outcomes, and the second is the individual's marginal utility for "relative gain."[10]

The first source of utility is analogous to the utility of a correct choice in the light-guessing situation. It is proposed that the second source of utility in the situation stems from the individual's desire to demonstrate superior ability at the strategic aspects of the game situation. This is denoted as the individual's marginal utility for "relative gain." With regard to the issue of rationality, the problematic aspect of behavior in multiple iteration games is that individuals fail to achieve a stable, permanent alternative-1 response pattern. Although an individual's maximum long-run gain is realized through establishment of an alliance with the other player, subjects usually display some propensity to attempt to "one-up" their opponents. We suggest that this result comes about because subjects recognize the competitive nature of the game and desire to out-perform the other players.

Participants in a prisoner's dilemma game are confronted with a choice situation in which they are conceived as attempting to maximize the combination of utilities from payoffs associated with outcomes of choices and utilities stemming from desires to out-perform their opponents. The formal model for decision making in the game is as follows. Letting

$\pi_i =$ the probability that the opponent chooses alternative i, $i = 1, 2$

$a_i =$ the marginal, utility of the payoff for choice i, $i = 1, 2$

$b =$ the marginal utility of relative gain

$\alpha_i =$ the ratio a_i/b, $i = 1, 2$

$P_i =$ the stable-state probability that the player chooses alternative i, $i = 1, 2$

Following the derivation presented earlier, the final equations of the model are:

$$P_1 - (1/4)(\alpha_1 \pi_1 - \alpha_2 \pi_2) + 1/2$$
$$P_2 = 1 - P_1$$

The model has not yet been empirically tested in a research program specifically designed for the evaluation of this formulation.[11] There does, however, exist in the literature a set of three experiments in which the same payoff matrix was used, the behavior of one of the players was simulated, and the π parameters were varied in a manner which permits application of the model.

Application of the model to this data is not strictly appropriate since certain necessary experimental conditions for its application are not achieved in the researches. For example, the published data report only the mean probabilities of alternative 1 and 2 choices for thirty trials

---

[10] A detailed analysis that organizes the prisoner's dilemma literature in terms of these three factors appears in Ofshe and Ofshe (in press).

[11] A program of experimentation designed specifically to test the power of the theory in prisoner's dilemma type conflict situations is in progress at the Laboratory for Research in Management Science, University of California (Berkeley).

in two experiments and for fifty trials in the third experiment. It is impossible, from this data, to judge the point at which a stable-state choice strategy is attained. Therefore, it is necessary to apply the model to the entire length of the experiments.

A second consideration is that the data were gathered by two different teams of researchers, and the procedures under which the experiments were run differed between experiments. In light of the assumption that the magnitude of utility assigned to relative gain varies with the set of instructions employed by the researcher, this is an important problem.

The third point to note is that the researches were carried out at two different universities, and therefore subjects for the three treatment conditions did not come from the same population. Since the testing procedure for the model employs estimation of α ratios from the data generated by one set of subjects and comparison of predictions against the behavior of a second set, it is necessary to make the assumption that the distribution of α ratios will be the same in both populations. Students at different institutions could differ substantially in their assignments of utility to the monetary payoffs and to relative gain.

Application of the model to this data should be regarded as constituting a preliminary test, since many of the necessary conditions for its application have clearly been violated. The data to which the model will be applied are reported in Minas, Marlowe, and Rawson, 1960 and Bixenstine, Potash, and Wilson, 1963. The research reported in the first paper was conducted at Ohio State University, while the data reported in the second paper were obtained at Kent State University. The results reported below are for male subjects.

Subjects in three different treatment conditions participated in a prisoner's dilemma game against a simulated opponent. The probabilities with which the robot chose the two alternatives were varied across conditions. The payoff matrix was fixed for all treatment conditions, with the values of the payoffs (in cents) as shown below.

		Robot	
		1	2
Subject	1	(3, 3)	(0, 5)
	2	(5, 0)	(1, 1)

The formal characteristics of the treatment conditions are presented in Table 7. Conditions *F* and *G* were run by Bixenstine, et al., and Condition H by Minas, et al. Table 8 shows the predictions generated by the model when all of the data is used to obtain the alpha estimate.

Given the experimental conditions under which the model was applied, its predictive power is quite impressive. The results indicate that, at minimum, the general decision-making formulation gives reasonably accurate predictions for choice behavior in a two-person competitive social situation. Despite rather gross violations of crucial experimental conditions, the model's predictions reflect the effects of changes in the values of the π parameter and in two of the three conditions are as accurate as predictions tested under better controlled conditions. There is currently in progress a series of experiments specifically designed to test the general formulation. The results of these experi-

Table 7

FORMAL CHARACTERISTICS OF DECISION-MAKING EXPERIMENTS
IN THE PRISONER'S DILEMMA GAME

Condition	Probabilities of Robot Selections of Alternatives 1 and 2		Payoffs for Alternatives 1 and 2		Number of Subjects	Number of Trials
	π_1	π_2	α_1	α_2		
F	.17	.83	(3, 0)	(5, 1)	12	30
G	.83	.17	(3, 0)	(5, 1)	12	30
H	1.	0	(3, 0)	(5, 1)	26	50

Table 8

RESULTS OF APPLICATION OF THE UNEQUAL ALPHA MODEL
TO THE PRISONER'S DILEMMA GAME

Prediction Condition	π_1 π_2	Observed P_1 and P_2	Predicted P and P_2	Discrepancy
H	1.	.385	.365	.020
	0	.615	.635	
G	.83	.333	.351	.018
	.17	.667	.649	
F	.17	.303	.299	.004
	.83	.697	.701	

ments will, of course, be more informative.

REFERENCES

BIXENSTINE, V., POTASH, H., and WILSON, K. "Effects of Level of Cooperative Choice by the Other Player on Choices in a Prisoner's Dilemma Game." Part I. *J. Abnor. Soc. Psychol.* 66, 1963.

BUSH, R., and F. MOSTELLER. Stochastic *Models for Learning.* New York: Wiley, 1955.

GAMSON, W. A. "Experimental Studies of Coalition Formation." In L. Berkowitz (Ed.), *Advances in Experimental Social Psychology*, Vol. I. New York: Academic Press, 1964.

GOODNOW, J. J. "Determinants of Choice-Distribution in Two-Choice Situations." *Amer. Psychol.* 68, 1955, 106–116.

HUMPHREYS, L. G. "Acquisition and Extinction of Verbal Expectations in a Situation Analogous to Conditioning." *J. Exper. Psychol.*, 25, 1939, 294–301.

LUCE, R. D., and RAIFFA, H. *Games and Decisions.* New York: Wiley 1957.

LUCE, R. D., and SUPPES, P. "Preference, Utility and Subjective Probability." In R. D. Luce, R. R. Bush, and E. Galanter (Eds.), *Handbook of Mathematical Psychology*, Vol. III. New York: Wiley, 1965.

LIEBERMAN, B. "Experimental Studies of Conflict in Some Two-Person Games." In J. Criswell, H. Solomon, and P. Suppes (Eds.), *Mathematical Methods in Small Group Processes.* Stanford: Stanford Univ. Press, 1962.

MINAS, J., SCODEL, A., MARLOWE, D., and RAWSON, H. "Some Descriptive Aspects of 2-Person, Non-Zero-Sum Games." Part II. *J. Conflict Resol.*, 4, 1960, 193–197.

OFSHE, L., and OFSHE, R. *Utility and Choice in Social Interaction.* Englewood-Cliffs, N.J.: Prentice-Hall, in press.

SIEGEL, S., and GOLDSTEIN, D. A. "Decision-Making Behavior in a Two-Choice Uncertain Outcome Situation." *J. Exper. Psychol.*, 57, 1959, 37–41.

SIEGEL, S., SIEGEL, A. E., and ANDREWS, J. M. *Choice Strategy and Utility*, New York: McGraw-Hill, 1964.

DATE DUE

LTY